# THE WORLD IS A TEXT

## Writing, Reading, and Thinking About Culture and Its Contexts

SECOND EDITION

Jonathan Silverman

Pace University

Dean Rader

University of San Francisco

PEARSON

Prentice Hall

Upper Saddle River, New Jersey 07458

**Library of Congress Cataloging-in-Publication Data**

Silverman, Jonathan.
  The world is a text : writing, reading, and thinking about culture and its
    contexts / Jonathan Silverman, Dean Rader.-- 2nd ed.
    p. cm.
  Includes bibliographical references and index.
  ISBN 0-13-193198-9 (pbk.)
   1. English language--Rhetoric.   2. Culture--Problems, exercises, etc.
  3. Readers--Culture.   4. Critical thinking.   5. College readers.
  6. Report writing.   7. Semiotics.   I. Rader, Dean.   II. Title.

    PE1408.S48785 2006
    808'.0427--dc22

                                                    2005013269

Senior Acquisitions Editor: Brad Potthoff
Editorial Director: Leah Jewell
VP/Director of Production and Manufacturing:
  Barbara Kittle
Assistant Editor: Jennifer Conklin
Editorial Assistant: Tara Culliney
Director of Marketing: Brandy Dawson
Marketing Manager: Emily Cleary
Marketing Assistant: Kara Pottle
Assistant Marketing Manager: Andrea Messineo
Production Liaison: Shelly Kupperman
Production Assistant: Marlene Gassler
Permissions Researcher: Lisa Black
Manufacturing Buyer: Mary Ann Gloriande
Manufacturing Manager: Nick Sklitsis
Creative Design Director: Leslie Osher

Interior and Cover Designer: Kathy Mrozek
Director, Image Resource Center: Melinda Reo
Manager, Rights and Permissions: Zina Arabia
Manager, Visual Research: Beth Brenzel
Manager, Cover Visual Research & Permissions:
  Karen Sanatar
Image Permission Coordinator: Frances Toepfer
Photo Researcher: Melinda Alexander
Web/Media Production Manager: Lynn Pearlman
Composition/Full-Service Project Management:
  Patty Donovan, Pine Tree Composition
Printer/Binder: R.R. Donnelley & Sons, Inc.
Cover Art: David Butow/Saba/Corbis (front);
  Corbis Royalty Free (back)
Cover Printer: Phoenix Color Corp.
Text Typeface: 10/12 Minion

Credits and acknowledgments borrowed from other sources and reproduced, with permission, in this textbook
appear on page 728.

Pearson Education LTD.
Pearson Education Singapore, Pte. Ltd
Pearson Education, Canada, Ltd
Pearson Education—Japan
Pearson Education Australia PTY, Limited

Pearson Education North Asia Ltd
Pearson Educación de Mexico, S.A. de C.V.
Pearson Education Malaysia, Pte. Ltd
Pearson Education, Upper Saddle River, NJ

10  9  8  7  6  5  4  3  2
ISBN 0-13-193198-9

# CONTENTS

## The World Is a Text: READING    62

### 1    Reading and Writing About Poetry    62

WORKSHEET    68

# ALTERNATIVE TABLE OF CONTENTS

Below are the readings in *The World Is a Text* grouped according to subject matter, genre, or style of writing. They offer cross-chapter ways of reading individual works.

## African-American Issues ▪▪▪

## Arab-American Issues ▪▪▪

## Asian-American Issues ▪▪▪

## Argumentative/Persuasive Essays ▪■▪

## Social and Economic Class ■▪■

# Comparison/Contrast ▪▪▪

# Definitional Essays ▪▪▪

# Fun! ▪▪▪

## Games (Sports and Other) ▪■▪

# Gay & Lesbian Issues ▪■▪

# Gender/Sexuality ▪■▪

## Images & Non-Traditional Texts ▪▪

## International/Global Readings ▪▪

## Latino/Latina Issues ▪▪▪

## Literature (Fiction, Literary Non-Fiction, and Poetry) ▪▪▪

## Native American Issues ▪▪▪

## Personal (Uses First Person) ▪▪

# Race/Ethnicity ▪■■

# Researched Essays (Works with Citations) ■■■

## Young Adults/Teenagers/Children ▪■▪

# PREFACE

## The World, This Text, and Thou

What you have before you is version two of our book (or as computer manufacturers would say, *The World Is a Text* version 2.0). What you also have is a compromise of sorts. Instead of the literal preface you have before you, we had grand ambitions of creating a more symbolic preface. Our plan was to turn the typically prosaic preface into something resembling a restaurant menu, with ideas and concepts about writing and reading listed where a turkey sandwich or a bowl of chili might be. We also considered making the preface a record cover, with an explanation of its contents on the back very much like the first album from the 70s band, *Boston*, or perhaps a screenplay titled, *The World Is a Text: The Movie*. Unfortunately, for a number of reasons, we could not undertake any of these visions for this edition, though it was fun thinking about them. We liked the idea of a visual preface rather than purely a written one in order to more fully connect the preface with the book's aim, which is to make non-traditional texts like menus, screenplays, and record covers part of your conscious reading material. In a very real sense they already are; indeed, from an early age, we are readers, both of so-called traditional texts—fiction, poetry, and drama—and nontraditional texts—movies, television, and especially people. While the schooling process focuses on the former, our everyday living focuses on the latter.

As a human being, this type of reading is crucial for being an active participant in the world. But too often this informal reading is given short shrift in the classroom. While we agree that training in reading traditional texts such as novels, short stories, poetry, and plays is a crucial aspect of an education, (perhaps *the* crucial aspect) we also believe that the methods used in learning to read traditional texts can be applied to nontraditional ones as well, with the overall goal of understanding the world around us and reducing the distance between the classroom and the real world.

Our first edition came out of these ideas, combined with a fruitless search for a textbook that did the work we wanted it to do. While there are many popular culture readers out there, good ones in fact, we never quite found the book we wanted; one that focused on the classroom experience and the writing situation. We think the classroom should be a dynamic place, and we think writing and discussion are crucial to learning how to think. *The World Is a Text* is as much a book for teachers as it is for students in that regard. We hope that our questions, introductions, and exercises give teachers the tools they need to teach students how to write with clarity and intelligence, to read more actively and astutely, and finally to engage the world more actively. While all three missions are crucial, the first two are clearly more aimed at academic achievement. The last we think is critical in our missions as teachers. We believe students who read their worlds more actively are not only better students but better citizens of the world.

In this edition, as in the last, *The World Is a Text* relies on a modified semiotic approach as its pedagogical theory; it is based on the assumption that reading occurs at all times and places. It also relies on traditional critical skills employed by literary scholars and the generally contextual approach employed by cultural studies scholars. The book also features a sophisticated way of thinking about texts, writing, and the rhetorical moment. Taking as its major theoretical framework I.A. Richards' claim that rhetoric is a philosophic inquiry into how words work in discourse, *The World Is a Text* considers how various texts enact rhetorical strategies and how students might begin not only to recognize these strategies but write their own. Textual analysis (reading) and textual formation (writing) jointly contribute to the larger process of knowledge making. Thus, *The World Is a Text* is interested in helping students to ask not simply *what* something means but *how* something means.

And because knowledge making requires knowledge of how we make arguments and sentences and theses and assertions, this book goes one step further than similar readers in that, in our experience, writing remains a secondary concern for most anthologies. One of our goals is to make the writing experience a vital part of the entire book from the introduction, to the section on writing, to each individual reading. For instance, Section I, *The World Is a Text: Writing* takes a comprehensive approach to the various stages of the writing process. We walk students through selecting a topic, brainstorming, outlining, developing a thesis, and revising. We offer help with research and citation. We even provide a unique chapter on making the transition from high school to college writing. One of our goals is to help students make these connections between reading and writing, thinking and writing, revising and revisioning. In this edition, we responded to instructors who wanted a more complete section on writing. We added additional material on process writing and research writing and offered more strategies for approaching writing assignments, particularly those involving non-traditional texts. In addition, we have added more student essays; each chapter has one or more examples of student responses to non-traditional texts. Additionally, a new and improved website also reinforces the emphasis on *writing*, not just reading.

*The World Is a Text* also has its focus in encountering media and texts in general; each chapter has questions that encourage students not only to respond to readings, but the texts and media themselves. Every chapter has an introduction that focuses on reading media and individual texts (not the readings themselves). In the readings that follow, each piece features questions geared toward both reading and writing. And its general apparatus in the form of worksheets and classroom exercises encourages students to use the readings as a starting point for their own explorations of television, race, movies, art, and the other media and texts we include here.

On a more theoretical level, we show how language in text and context functions to produce meaning. And we talk about how writing is fundamentally linked to other aspects of critical inquiry like reading, listening, thinking, and speaking. Ultimately, part of our approach comes from Kenneth Burke. Just as he argues that all literature is a piece of rhetoric, we suggest that all texts are rhetoric, and that every moment is a potential moment for reading and therefore for writing.

## Features of *The World Is a Text* Version 2.0

While our basic goals remain the same as the first edition, we have changed quite a few things both as a response to instructor and student suggestions, and because we are always thinking about ways to make this book better. For instance, we have added one chapter, Reading and Writing About Relationships, in which we examine relationships as a text full of all the codes, trappings, and intentions of any other kind of text. This chapter focuses on the way we encounter, and might read, relationships of all kinds. As college students, this project is often quite intense as students make the journey from dependent to independent. Accordingly, our suite focuses on the multiplicity of college relationships. For instructors, we also were conscious that in many composition courses, you want to focus on the personal when teaching writing; we hope this chapter provides some additional material for your classes and also helps students think more intentionally about their college lives.

There was one other major structural change. We altered the focus of our literature chapter from literature generally to poetry specifically because of its status as a hybrid text. The visual nature of poetry often coincides (or vies) with its literary content. We began the last edition with a chapter on literature as a way to help students and teachers make a transition between what is familiar as a writing subject to subjects less familiar; we think poetry does this work more effectively. However, you still will find short stories and poems in other chapters, as we believe they often provide excellent reads of non-traditional texts.

Finally, because popular culture changes so quickly, we changed many of the readings and suites. While we like all of our changes, we are especially excited about adding material from Lisa Mahair's *American Signs,* a wonderful examination of the signage on Route 66 and what we hope is an engaging and politically exciting suite on censorship and the arts.

Overall, our goals for this edition remain consonant with the last edition. We hope *The World Is a Text* will help students bridge culture and text. However, we present material in a way that provides context, direction, and structure. In that sense, the book is traditional; however, the expanded nature of what a text is makes our approach innovative. We hope that, in turn, this will allow students to expand their idea of reading and therefore expand their critical relationship to the world. In an academic setting, where accountability and practicality are watchwords, giving students a more interpretative way of looking at and writing about the world seems especially appropriate.

# ACKNOWLEDGMENTS

The authors need to acknowledge more people than can comfortably fit, but here's a start. First of all, we want to express our gratitude to everyone at Prentice Hall, especially our new editor, Brad Potthoff, and his helpful assistant, Tara Culliney. We also want to thank Leah Jewell, Brandy Dawson, Corey Good (our first editor on this project), and Carrie Brandon. We also thank Patty Donovan and everyone at Pine Tree Composition, as well as Lisa Black for copyright help. Thanks go out to the various authors who wrote original pieces for the book, gave us the rights to reprint things at a reduced rate, and made helpful suggestions. We also appreciate the feedback from professors and students who used the book. We really aren't joking; please email us if you have questions or suggestions.

We are also grateful for the advice, critiques, and suggestions from the people who graciously agreed to review and comment on *The World Is a Text* in manuscript: Lauren Ingraham, University of Tennessee; Steven Bidlake, Central Oregon Community College; Kelly Sassi, University of Michigan; Greg Barnhisel, Duquesne University; Pat Tyrer, West Texas A&M University; Adrienne Bliss, Ball State University.

We are also appreciative of the many other people who read and commented on the first version of the book but who are not mentioned here. We also want to thank all of the people who used or posted *The World Is a Text* bumper stickers that were floating around the CCCC convention in San Antonio. For the 2/E, we're hoping for bowling shirts. We also thank Johnny Cash, Beck, Nirvana, Radiohead, Cat Power, Aimee Mann, Lyle Lovett, The Fountains of Wayne, De La Soul, and Cornershop who, unknowingly, provided the soundtrack for the writing process of this new edition. Of course, we thank our students at VCU, USF, and Pace for giving us feedback and for providing constant inspiration.

For their valuable assistance in manuscript preparation, we want to thank Jennifer Bede, Danielle Atwood, and Erin Schietinger. For their help with the reading gender chapter, we'd like to thank Rachel Crawford, Nicole Raeburn, and Jill Ramsey; for the reading race and ethnicity chapter, Katherine Clay Bassard; for reading the technology chapter, Michael Keller; and for the introduction, Patty Strong. We also want to thank Miles McCrimmon for reading an early version of the proposal and for his work on the instructor's manuals.

A big thank you goes to Alexander Shaia of the Blue Door Retreat in Santa Fe, where we stayed while working on this new edition. We highly recommend Alexander's scenic and restive retreat. We also thank various coffee shops around Santa Fe, including the Santa Fe Baking Company, and the St. John's College Library, where we did most of our writing. We also thank the good folks at Geronimo for free wine and desserts.

Lisa Mahar, author of *American Signs,* was of great help, as was Svetlana Mintcheva, Director of the Arts Program of the National Coalition against Censorship. We're still grateful to Rigo of San Francisco for his murals.

In areas of institutional and collegial support, the following were of especial help: Catherine Ingrassia, Marcel Cornis-Pope, Richard Fine, Margret Vopel Schluer, Sharon Call Laslie, Ginny Schmitz, Bill Tester, Tom De Haven, Laura Browder, David Latane, Nick Sharp, Elizabeth Savage, Randy Lewis, Emily Roderer, Pat Perry, Elizabeth Cooper, Elizabeth

Hodges, Bill Griffin, James Kinney, Marguerite Harkness, Michael Keller, Leslie Shiel, Nick Frankel, Faye Prichard, Angier Brock Caudle, Traci Wood, Walter Srebnick, Carol Dollison, Geoff Brackett, Jeannie Chiu, Kristin di Gennaro, Martha Driver, Steven Goldleaf, Tom Henthorne, Todd Heyden, Eugene Richie, Mark Hussey, Karla Jay, Helane Levine-Keating, Amy Martin, Sid Ray, Walter Raubicheck, William Sievert, Michael Roberts, Nira Herrmann, Katie Henninger, Kathie Tovo, Frank Goodyear, Anne Collins, Jan Lisiak, Teresa Genaro, Suzanne Forgarty, Michael Tanner, Dan Marano, Elisabeth Piedmont-Marton, Jeffrey Meikle, Mark Smith, Greg Barnhisel, Fouzia Baber, Anne Darby, Matt Compton, Matt King, Carlease Briggs, Virginia Colwell, Rita Botts, Sarah Hawkins, Whitney Black, Tracy Seeley, Eileen Chia-Ching Fung, Alan Heinemann, Patricia Hill, Carolyn Brown, Carolyn Webber, Sean Michaelson, John Pinelli, Robert Bednar, Wendy McCredie, Leonard Schulze, Jean-Pierre Metereau, Steven Vrooman, Beth Barry, Amy Randolph, T. Paul Hernandez, Chris Haven, Brian Clements, George McCoy, Michael Strysick, Brian Brennan, Mike Henry, LeAnne Howe, Cary Cordova, Monica Chiu, Andrew Macalister, Aranzazu Borrachero, Cecilia Santos, Vamsee Juluri, Jeff Paris, Christopher Kamrath, Susan Steinberg, Susan Paik, Peter Novak, Heather Barkley, Colleen Stevens, Freddie Wiant, Mark Merrit, Brian Dempster, Zachary White, Marika Brussel, Loren Barroca, Michael Bloch, T-Bone Needham, Jonathan Hunt, and Brandon Brown.

Additionally, we thank the English Department at Pace University, the Henry Birnbaum Library at Pace University, English Department at Virginia Commonwealth University, the VCU James Branch Cabell Library, the Andover Summer Session, and the Department of English and the Dean's Office of the University of San Francisco, particularly Dean Jennifer Turpin and the excellent staff of the Dean s Office in the College of Arts and Sciences. A special nod goes out to John Pinelli and his staff.

Finally, we thank Melvin Silverman, Beverly Silverman, Joel Silverman, Alba Estanoz, Jason Silverman, Christian Leahy, Ginger Rader, Gary Rader, Barbara Glenn, Amy Rader Kice, and Adam Kice.

We are most grateful to all of you who have adopted this book for your classes and a particularly hearty thank you to all of the students who have made, for better or worse, this text a part of your world.

Jonathan Silverman
*Pace University*

Dean Rader
*University of San Francisco*
Email us at: World.Text@Gmail.com

# INTRODUCTION

We are born readers. From an early age, we make sense of everything by drawing conclusions based on our experiences—similar to the process we undertake when we now read a book for school or pleasure. We read for the first time when we as babies express recognition of our parents. This continues throughout childhood, adolescence, and adulthood. We become better at reading traditional texts such as short stories, novels, and poems (formal reading) through our schooling and nontraditional texts such as television, architecture, and people through our experience (informal reading), often a parallel and intersecting process. In both forms of reading, we learn how to understand what symbols mean and figure out what the author is "saying" as we try to understand our complicated relationships with other people and places; we learn what a "nice" neighborhood looks like or how to determine when a potential mate "likes" us.

■ ■ ■ The World *Really* Is a Text at the Unisphere, Queens, New York.

Over the course of our lives, we determine, question, and revise thousands of different beliefs based on our own readings, our own acts of interpretation (of which there are dozens every day). We perform these acts of informal reading when encountering popular culture and the media. When we attempt to make sense of a movie or television or news report, to put it in perspective with our experiences, we are reading and interpreting. Of course, this kind of reading may not be exactly the same type of interpretation we do with the short stories and poems we receive in English classes, but making sense of people, images, ideas, and places remains a significant form of interpretation nonetheless. Because this reading is so important, and because we do so much of it, we should think of our entire world as something that can and should be read. In short, we can think of the world as a text.

How and what we read in this text that is our world is important—we make decisions about with whom we spend time, where we live, and other important considerations based on informal reading. We also construct a worldview based on our informal readings and the readings of other people. We influence other people's readings, and they influence ours. A comment or even a physical reaction from a parent, teacher, or friend can guide our responses to a text. Sometimes these influences are harmless—not liking a particular band or television show because a friend does not is no big deal. But often these influences can have consequences that go beyond simple dislike or like; we can learn to read the world in limiting, prejudicial ways that affect not only our lives but also the lives of our fellow citizens. If we imitate our parents' (or friend's or neighbor's or teacher's) negative reaction to people of particular ethnicities or accept abusive behavior by friends or family toward a certain gender, we have incorporated someone else's negative reading into our own worldview, much like we might accept a *Cliff's Notes* view of *The Great Gatsby* as our own. But for better or worse, our readings are not permanent. As we grow older and become more adept at reading our world, we constantly rewrite our worldview. That's where this book comes in.

Our goal is to help you take texts (movies, pieces of art, experiences, people, places, ideas, traditions, advertisements) both familiar and unfamiliar to you and *read* them. Many of these texts will be visual or have visual elements, and you "see" them rather than "read" them as reading is traditionally defined. In this book, however, instead of looking through them by not actively interpreting, we will ask you to look *at* them—to slow down and look at them in ways you may not have previously. Additionally, we want you to try formalizing this reading process. What we mean by formal here is the process we undertake when analyzing literature (or depending on your training, art, music, or movies). One of the primary elements of formal reading is the breaking down of a text into smaller elements and interpreting them. Analyzing a short story for themes, character development, and figurative language (symbols, metaphors, etc.) is formal reading, as is explicating a poem. Looking at a poem's rhyme, meter, symbolism, tone, structure, and design is a formal process that involves posing questions about what the poem is trying to do and how it does it. While it may feel natural to think of reading or "decoding" poems in this way, approaching an advertisement or a television show or a gender may feel a bit foreign at first. Over the course of reading this book, we hope that this process will cease to feel alien and begin to seem natural, especially as you become more familiar with analyzing the elements associated with these texts.

In other words, the traditional analytical "work" you have done in English classes is something we want to imitate here. We believe that texts, including those that are nontraditional such as public spaces, songs, and advertisements, have meanings that can be uncovered through the exploration of their elements. You may know a public space seems ugly—but we want you to understand why. You may already sense that advertisements use sex to sell products, but we want you to understand how. The idea is not only to slow the interpretive process down but also to make more conscious your meaning-making, a process you undertake all the time—whether you intend to or not.

## Semiotics: The Study of Signs (and Texts)  ▪■▪

All reading we do, perhaps anything we do, is backed up by various ideas or theories—from the simple idea that the acts we undertake have consequences both good and bad to the more complex theories about relativity and gravity. In this book, we rely on a theory that the world itself is open to interpretation, that we can make meaning out of just about anything. The idea that the world is a text open to interpretation is itself a theory, which has a strong connection to semiotics, the study of signs. In this part of the introduction, we are going to elaborate on the idea of semiotics as a way of having you understand some of the assumptions we've made when writing this textbook. You can use the rest of the book without focusing too much on the theory.

In semiotics, the main idea is that everything is a sign of sorts. You already know what signs are, as you encounter them everywhere. There are traffic signs, signs telling whether something is open or closed, signs in your classroom telling you not to smoke, or cheat, or where the exit is. You do very little work in trying to understand these signs, which seemingly need no interpretation. Once you understand what "stop" means, or that red in fact means "stop," or that green means "go," or that yellow means "slow down" or "caution," there is little need to actively interpret these signs each time you see them. Of course, you did not always know what these signs meant; at some point in your childhood, you picked up the ideas behind these signs and now take them for granted.

We have a broader idea of signs (or texts) in this book. A sign is an object or idea or combination of the two that refers to something besides itself, and it depends on others to recognize that it's a sign. The red octagon, plus the letters "S" "T" "O" "P," mean "stop" to most of us through the combination of the shape, color, and letters; a blue diamond with "HALT" on it would catch our attention, but we would not treat it in the same way, though halt and stop are synonyms, and a blue diamond is a perfectly fine combination of color and shape. The stop sign as we now know it carries a meaning beyond a simple combination of word, color, and shape.

Another example: we know an "open" sign at a store means the store is transacting business. But "open" itself is an arbitrary sign, unique to English-speaking cultures. In Spanish, for example, "abierto" means "open." And in some places, a sign will contain both abierto and open to indicate that it's signifying to two different sets of clientele. "Open" and "abierto" can both be signs, but so can their presence together be a sign. If we saw an abierto and an open sign in one place, we might draw conclusions about where we were (a neighborhood where English and Spanish are spoken), who owned the restaurant or store (bilingual owners?), and who their audience was (primarily speakers of Spanish and English). In other words, the presence of both signs is itself a sign—taken together they create meaning.

Semioticians ("sign-studiers") have a more formal way of referring to signs. Ferdinand de Saussure, a Swiss linguist working in the nineteenth and twentieth centuries, believed that signs contained two elements: the *signifier* and the *signified,* which, taken together, often

create meaning. The signifier is the object that exists and the signified is what it means. In other words, the letters o-p-e-n are the signifier, and the message that a place is open for business is the signified, and the external reality is that the store or restaurant is open for business. Similarly, using our stop sign example, the actual red sign with the STOP written in white letters is the signifier. The signified is the message that you must bring your car to a complete halt when you approach this sign.

## Systems of Reading: Making Sense of Cultural Texts

Sometimes the same signifiers (physical signs) can have different signifieds (meanings). For instance, what do you think of when you see the word "pan"? Most of you probably imagine an item for cooking. Or, you might think of a critic "panning" or critiquing a bad movie. However, a Spanish speaker who saw the word pan in our bilingual store would most likely imagine bread. The signifier "pan" in Spanish cultures refers not to an item for cooking but to what English speakers think of when they see the signifier "bread." Thus, people from both cultures would experience the same signifier, but what is signified would be entirely different.

However, we don't even need other languages for there to be various signified meanings for the same signifier. Photographers may think of a pan or wide-angle shot. Scholars of Greek mythology may think of the Greek god who is half goat and half man. The letters "p," "a," and "n" remain the same, but the meanings change; the sign—the word—"pan" has different meanings. We also can have the same signified but with different signifiers. For example, "soda," "pop," or "Coke" are all different signifiers that different people from different parts of the country use to refer to a flavored carbonated drink.

So when we talk about signs, we are not only talking about physical signs but also a system of reading. In this system, we can interpret images, words whose letters are arbitrarily assigned meaning, and experiences really just about anything. Sometimes we make these interpretations with little or no effort and sometimes with a lot of work. Many semioticians believe that everything is a sign, including the way we are writing this introduction. The words are signs, and so is the way you are reading them (it's simply a more complex way of saying that everything is a text).

And more complex signs of course do not reveal themselves so easily. For example, let's consider a very famous sign (or text)—the *Mona Lisa*. Its power in some part comes from its simplicity and its *unreadability*. We don't know why she is smiling, we only have a vague idea of who she is, and we will likely never know. That smile, or half-smile, has become so famous that its life as a sign has transcended even its power as an image. The painting is a signifier, but its signified is ambiguous and difficult to determine. If we look at the various images of the *Mona Lisa* on shirts, mousepads, posters, even variations of the original (we like the version where Mona Lisa has a big black moustache) we can agree that the *Mona Lisa* has become a symbol of something 1) traditional, 2) artistic, 3) commercial, and yet 4) universal, and perhaps 5) modern. We can agree that something about its power has not diminished despite or because of its age. But our signified—our mental concept of what "Mona Lisa-ness" is—depends on what perspective we bring to the reality of this artwork. Does it signify our definition of a masterpiece? A commodity? A self-portrait by the artist?

We don't know exactly (but people guess all the time). And that's why sometimes sign reading is so frustrating. Some signs are easier to read and understand, so easy that we don't even know that we are reading. Others, like paintings—and more importantly, human relationships—are more difficult. One of the most complex components of reading texts is suspending judgments about a text's values. In your initial semiotic analysis—your initial reading of a text—try to consider all aspects of a text before applying a label like "good" or "bad" (or "interesting" or "boring"). Such labels can only come after a thorough reading of the text

*Source:* Leonardo da Vinci (1452–1519) *Mona Lisa,* oil on canvas, 77 × 53 cm. Inv. 779. Photo: R.G. Ojeda. Louvre, Paris. Reunion des Muses Nationaux/Art Resource, NY.

under question. Later, if you want to argue if a text has problems, then you would use the details, the information you gleaned from your reading, to support these assertions in your papers. In attacking the *Mona Lisa,* for example, it would be acceptable to most professors for you to guess about what you thought da Vinci meant in painting her if you can defend your guess. Reading visually, in fact, often means such guessing is a natural part of doing any sort of paper.

Overall, the basic idea behind semiotics should not be foreign to you—on a fundamental level, it simply means reading and interpreting nontraditional objects like you would a short story or a poem.

## The "Semiotic Situation" (or the "Moving Text") ▪■▪

As you may have guessed, you do this type of work all the time. You read people and relationships every day, having developed this skill over your years of reading the world. For instance, let's say you are walking down Wall Street in New York City. You see a man dressed in a suit, talking on a cell phone, carrying a copy of the *Wall Street Journal,* and yelling "Sell Microsoft at 42! Sell! Sell! Sell!" What would you assume his profession is? He could be a lawyer. He could be a banker. But given the context (where you are, which is Wall Street), what he's talking about (stocks) and how he's dressed (a suit), the best interpretation of this text might be that he is a stockbroker. You could be wrong, but based on the clues of the text, that's a pretty good reading.

We perform this work constantly. For example, on first dates we try to read the other person for cues of attraction and enjoyment; quarterbacks read a defense before every play and every pass; we read a classroom when we enter it; we read a friend's house and especially his or her room. These moments are what we call "semiotic situations." They are moments in which we try to make sense of our surroundings or interpret one aspect of our surroundings based on the signs or texts of our situation. The copy of the *Wall Street Journal,* the cell phone, the man's comments—all are signs which represent a text that can be read. But when we read these signs together they help us make sense of the larger text (the man) and the larger text than that (Wall Street) and an even larger text than that (America). As you may have guessed by now, this act of reading can even help you make sense of the largest text of all—the world—in both literal and mythical ways.

Because we are always trying to make sense of the world, because we are always reading, we often find ourselves in semiotic situations. This book builds on your own methods of reading and tries to sharpen them so that you will become more critical and thoughtful readers of the complex text that is our world. We keep returning to the reading metaphor because it aptly describes the process of making sense of our surroundings. When we read a poem or a short story, we pay attention to detail: we look for symbols, metaphors, and hidden themes. We "read between the lines." To read between the lines means to read not only what's there, but also what's *not* there. We do this frequently as well; we "read into things." Beer commercials never come right out and suggest that attractive, straight, single women will immediately become attracted to straight men if the men drink a certain kind of beer, but that is implied in almost every ad. People we are interested in dating may not tell us what kind of people they are, where they come from, what kind of music they like or what their political leanings are, but by paying attention to the clothes they wear or the comments they make, we may be able to begin to piece together a better interpretation of the text that is this person. In other words, we already know how to read books and poems, and we also know how to read the world itself. This book will help you bring together your ideas from formal and informal, conscious and unconscious reading.

## Texts, the World, You, and Your Papers ▪■▪

Hopefully, by now you understand what we mean by reading the world as a text, and this approach seems both comfortable and interesting to you. However, you are probably wondering how any of this figures into your writing course. As you have probably figured out by this time in your academic career, writing is fundamentally connected to reading and to thinking. In fact, the great British novelist E.M. Forster (*A Room with a View* and *Howard's End*) once wrote, "How can I tell what I think till I see what I've said?" To our knowledge, there has never been a great writer who was not also a great thinker. What's more, to be a great thinker and a great writer, we must also be great readers. Writing is so intimately tied to thinking and thinking so intimately tied to the act of *reading* the world and one's surroundings, that the three form a kind of trinity of articulation and expression:

Of course, by "reading" we mean not only reading books and newspapers and magazines but also the semiotic situation or the nontraditional text, the practice of reading the world. Writing, thinking, and reading are a symbiotic process, a cycle in which they feed off and influence each other. Thus, if we are reading and thinking, then the chances are we will be better prepared to do good writing.

Good writing is also grounded on solid *rhetorical* principles, as is good reading (as we have broadly defined it so far). Rhetoric comes from the Greek word *rhetorik,* which, in English means the art of speaking or writing effectively. We like thinking of rhetoric as an art, though Plato was not convinced. He objected to labelling rhetoric (which in Greek means "speech"), but Aristotle argued that rhetoric was one of the great arts and that its subject was all things. Today, when we think of something as being rhetorical, it usually includes elements of argumentation or persuasion, and this is also, in part Aristotle's legacy, who defined rhetoric as "the faculty of observing in any given case the available means of persuasion." We hope this book improves your faculty for observing how texts use persuasion, just as your writing course will help you write persuasive essays. We like I.A. Richards's claim that rhetoric is a philosophic inquiry into how words work in discourse or public discussion. That means that as a reader and a writer, you are figuring out the relationship between words, signs, and culture.

Our goal is to help you learn to see the rhetorical strategies of various texts and also to get you started writing your own. We are firm believers that textual analysis (reading) and textual formation (writing) jointly contribute to the larger process of knowledge making. Thus, we are interested in helping you to ask not simply *what* something means but *how* something means. This is why reading will help your writing: it teaches you how to be savvy consumers and producers of texts. You'll get to know texts from the inside out.

Part of that process will necessarily include writing. Writers and thinkers have long seen writing as a means of helping us think. When we think abstractly, we tend to gloss over ideas so fast that we don't slow down and articulate them. They are more sensations than thought. To put them down on paper, to compose them into sentences, ideas, reasons, is harder than thinking. Indeed, if you have done freewriting exercises, you may have had no idea what you thought about something until you wrote it down. It's no surprise that journaling or keeping a diary is vitally important to writers. The act of writing can often be an act of unlocking: the door opens and ideas, reactions, fears, and hopes walk right out of your head and on to the page and say "Here I am!" Sometimes, we wish they had stayed inside, but this is where the interesting work happens, and here is where learning to read the world as a text can help you as you learn to write on a college level. Learning to write well allows us to move outside of the box and out into the world of ideas, interaction, and exchange. And learning to read outside our traditional ideas of what it means to read will expand your mind even further.

Writing about the world as a text may not only facilitate writing and thinking but also writing and feeling. While we certainly do not want to diminish the logical aspect of writing, we want to pay attention to a component of writing that is often overlooked, and that is the emotional component. Franz Kafka, Emily Dickinson, Pablo Neruda and dozens of other writers turned and continue to turn to writing because it helps them get a handle on the world and relieves anxiety. Writing is or can be rewarding, refreshing, rejuvenating. In part, writing means sharing, participating in a community of language and ideas. We learn about others and ourselves through writing because writing is simultaneously self-exploration and self-examination. We see ourselves in a larger context. Of course, we may not always like what we discover (perhaps traces of sexism or racism or classism), but uncovering those elements of our personality and understanding them is an extremely rewarding experience. Writing that is honest, candid, and reflective attracts us because those are traits we value.

At the same time, we do not want to neglect the idea that writing is a difficult process to master. Between them, the authors have written thousands of papers, articles, handouts, tests, reports, and now this book. In almost every case, they went through multiple drafts, stared at the computer screen, cursed whatever picture was on the wall for its interference, and struggled at various points along the way. In fact, this very introduction went through between fifteen and twenty drafts. In some ways, writing is very much like exercising: it doesn't always feel great when you are doing it, but when you are finished it is both rewarding and good for you. Both the authors are *drafters* by nature—we believe that while writing is a form of thinking, several drafts are often needed to make that thinking into something worth showing the public.

By now, you should be beginning to see some direct connections between writing and reading. Only by reading well can you write well. A good essay is an essay that makes sense of a topic using detail, insight and purpose—the same traits one uses to read. We believe that the readings and questions in this book will be a good springboard for that writing process. Some of the essays may anger you, but that's okay. Some will make you laugh, some will confuse you, and some will make you see a movie or a place or a gender in ways you never have before. We hope that these readings and images will not only show you what writing can do but also that the texts in this book will spark your imagination and push you toward the writing process so that your own work will be as vigorous and as provocative as the texts presented here.

## Learning to Read the World as a Text: Three Case Studies ▪■▪

In this section, we want to walk you through the act of interpretation, of reading semiotically; that is, we want to help you read certain texts in ways that you may find unfamiliar. However, as articulated earlier, we feel that living critically in the world means living as an informed, questioning, engaged person. Learning to read the world as a text is a good way to begin.

### Reading Public Space: Starbucks

One of the most familiar places in our modern world is the coffee shop, and in particular, Starbucks. As a ubiquitous presence, it could make for an interesting "read"—many ideas about the world could come from reading a Starbucks. With this in mind, we sat down one morning in a Starbucks and did a reading. We began with note taking, just writing down what we saw and thought. This is a transcribed version.

> **Note taking:** brown, green, red, brown patterned carpet.
>
> Green
>
> Lighting non-fluorescent
>
> Curves
>
> Wood—metal
>
> Tables different types
>
> Products art—decoration
>
> Logo "coffee-related art" photos
>
> Baby chairs, modern garbage cans
>
> Advertisements, baskets, games, "Cranium" wood
>
> Handicapped bathrooms—*The New York Times,* windows, mahogany, metal door handles, pull to get in, push
>
> Music: "cool," varied

With this information we can begin to construct a series of observations that could develop into ideas:

> Starbucks relies on moderate earth tones for decoration.
>
> Their seating places are made of durable materials.
>
> Their artwork is a mix of coffee photographs and advertisements.
>
> There is lots of light. The lighting they use is bright but not harsh, avoiding fluorescent light.
>
> Their advertisements are prominent within the store. Their products are geared to the middle and upper classes both by design and content. (Oops—an argument slipped in!)

As you can see by the last statement, in the process of writing down observations, arguments about the text itself may slip in, which is what we were hoping for. In this case, the idea that Starbucks is geared toward a particular target audience is an argument and potentially one that you might pursue in a paper. How could you make this a paper? You could expand the idea of a target audience into multiple paragraphs: one about products, another about décor, maybe one about music, and perhaps another about the location of the particular Starbucks you are in.

If we were going to construct a thesis statement, it might sound like this: Starbucks appeals to the middle and upper classes through a combination of its décor, music, products and location. Well, that thesis statement is okay and would work to organize a paper, but it is still pretty vague. We could ask why Starbucks wants to sell its wares to a particular demographic through its design—well, we know this already, they are a commercial venture. But the question of "how" still raises itself—we can see the target audience and the tools, but how they are using them is a different story. Maybe another question is this: What is Starbucks trying to sell *besides* coffee? What experience can someone hope to get by entering Starbucks? We would argue that Starbucks is trying to sell an idea of "cool" or "hip" to its customers. And for its target audience of middle and upper class people—cool is something these people may feel they need to buy. So a new thesis could be: "Starbucks tries to sell its idea of cool to the middle and upper classes through its hip music, sturdy, smooth décor, and its sleek and streamlined products."

This could still improve, but notice that this thesis gives you an automatic organization of paragraphs about décor, music, merchandise, and location. From here, one could work incorporating the details of your observations as evidence for the points you are making. For example, you could describe in some detail the nature of the furnishings, the various songs that play over the loudspeaker, and the general location of this particular Starbucks. If you wanted to, you might research how companies use these elements to make their businesses more profitable.

Hopefully, through this example, you can see how this sort of thing might work. We began with a trip to Starbucks, and ended up talking about demographics and public space. Not all such experiences could end up as papers, but you would be suprised how many can.

## Reading a Poem: "The Red Wheelbarrow"

It's likely that your professor will ask you to write a paper on one of the literary texts in this book. While you may have had some practice writing basic literary papers in high school, you may not have much experience thinking and writing about poetry on a sophisticated level. Let's say your instructor wants you to write an analytical paper on a poem. We know that many of you become very nervous in the presence of poetry, but we want to calm your fears a bit. Poems are nothing more than words placed strategically to create an enhanced reading experience. To make sense of a poem, all you need to do is slow down and look at the individual components. Much of poetry is instinctual, so trust your reactions, and trust your observations. Write things down. We would encourage you to make notes in the margins of your book or handout.

To help you in learning how better to read a poem, we will walk you through a reading process for a short but puzzling poem. We've chosen William Carlos Williams' famous (or infamous) poem "The Red Wheelbarrow":

THE RED WHEELBARROW

so much depends
upon

a red wheel
barrow

glazed with rain
water

beside the white
chickens.

Before we try to figure out what this poem might "mean," let's take a couple of steps back and look *at* the poem before looking *through* it. If, as we suggest, the world is a constructed text that can be read semiotically, then so can a poem. If you look at the poem's design, its shape, what do you see? First of all, the poem is very short and has extremely compact lines. In fact, the second line of each stanza only has one word. You may also see that the poem is very symmetrical. As you noticed, the second line of each stanza has one word, while the first line of every stanza has three words. So there are four words per stanza and four stanzas in the poem. Also, as students have noted, each of the four stanzas look like little square wheelbarrows. Additionally, you may have seized on the kinds of words Williams places in the second lines—"upon," "barrow," "water," and "chickens." All have two syllables and, except for "upon," all are concrete nouns. Very interesting, you may be thinking, but how can reading the poem this way help me understand what the poem *means*?

In poetry, form usually contributes to content, which is to say that how a poem looks and sounds and feels probably has a lot to do with the message it's trying to send. In any poem, look at what words are stressed, where lines end and the next line (or stanza) begins. Like a cinematographer, the poet controls where your eye goes both as a reader and as a viewer. As one of our students jotted in her reading journal, "the sound stops on the nouns and so does your eye." Indeed, it is as though Williams is creating visually what he accomplishes through language. So, if we transfer this observation over to what he might be trying to do thematically, we see that the form of the poem (how it looks and sounds) resembles its theme (what it says or means). It seems as though the meaning of the poem lies in these concrete words "barrow," "water," and "chickens." What kind of words are these? One student noted that "all three words are basic things—a tool, an animal, and a mineral." That is an excellent observation, and it tells us a great deal. But the poem is not simply a picture of chickens, water, and wheelbarrows. There is something more: namely, the first stanza. The first line of every novel, short story, and poem is often profoundly important, as it sets the stage for the entire text. Here, the first line does a great deal of work. How would the text be different if the poem began without the "So much depends / upon"?

We are left to wonder *what* depends upon these things. What type of person does depend upon chickens, water, and a wheelbarrow? A lawyer? A textbook author? A student? A farmer? Perhaps one reading of the poem is that for a farmer or a rancher, his or her entire life depends upon rain, animals, and equipment. But would Williams construct such a visual text merely to make a comment about what a farmer needs? Remember, the poem is also a visual text, and as such, demands to be looked at in a certain way. As we have already noted, you may find that each of the four stanzas looks like a little wheelbarrow, effectively creating a picture of four square wheelbarrows. Perhaps a literal reading only gives us partial understanding of the poem. A larger meaning might come from the visuals of the poem—how we *see* the poem and the world. If we can look at a poem and see wheelbarrows, perhaps we can look at wheelbarrows and see poetry. A fuller reading of the poem would take the form and the content into account and suggest that so much depends upon how we see the everyday objects of the world. Of course, this is but one reading of the poem, but we think it's a good one given the connections we made between how the poem looked and the words in it. We will talk later about putting a paper together in more detail, but you can see here that organizing a paper about "The Red Wheelbarrow" in terms of the form of the poem, perhaps including paragraphs about its visual construction, its use of concrete nouns, and the more abstract notions of how those things relate to what depends on the wheelbarrow could form the beginnings of a paper.

This leads to a larger point. When reading a poem or a short story, it's very important to pay close attention to the details of the text. Instead of making the poem bigger than it is (thinking a poem is about God or death or the devil or birth), try to see the poem as something *smaller* than you think it is. Look at its individual components. See how they come together.

## Reading an Advertisement: Tommy Girls, Tommy Boys, and America

Though you may only read poetry now and then, you probably read advertisements on a daily basis. On television, on the radio, in magazines, on the Web and now even at the movies, we confront advertisements in almost every aspect of our lives. Researchers suggest we see between 100 and 300 advertisements per day, whereas it would probably be unusual if you were to read 100 poems in an entire year. What's more, most experts agree that the American public believes or is open to at least one advertisement out of every eight that it sees. That may not sound like much, but if you see 100 ads per day for 365 days, that's 36,500 ads per year. If researchers are correct, then you probably believe or consider at least 4,562 per year. Think that's a lot? Consider this. The average nineteen-year-old has probably been paying attention to advertisements for about thirteen years. So, if these estimates are correct, most nineteen-year-old Americans have taken into their consciousness and devoted some aspect of their reasoning ability to over 59,000 ads over the course of their lifetime. If you are 19, then you have likely seen over 450,000 ads. By the time you are thirty, it's probable that over one million ads will have made their way into your brain.

By now, it is a cliché to claim that ads sell an image but . . . ads sell an image. They not only sell images of us and their products but also of a culture. In advertiser's lingo, this is called the "promise." Ads make promises to people all the time, but they tend to be implied or suggested promises. When you read an advertisement, ask yourself what kind of promise the ad is making to you. In addition, ads also work to cultivate another image—their own. This is why so many companies are very protective of their names, trademarks, and product usage. For instance, you may be familiar with the recent court case in which Mattel toys sued the rock band Aqua over a critical song about "Barbie." And, in an example closer to home, we were denied permission from Tommy Hilfiger to reprint the advertisement we describe below. So, keep in mind that while ads may be funny and informative and persuasive, they help promote the company's image.

Thus, reading the image that a company tries to cultivate is all part of the larger experience of reading an advertising text. And now that you've had some background on advertising and some practice reading public space and poetry, we're going to walk you through the process of reading an ad. Unfortunately, advertisers can be tricky. Every ad we requested permission to use in this section was rejected by the advertiser—even after personal letters from the co-authors. It would appear that many advertisers worry about how we might *use* their ads. Understandably, they are concerned about how their ad, their products, their image might look out of context. So, because so much of advertising is about branding, where an ad appears is as important as the ad itself. Sadly, that means we have to *describe* the ad, rather than provide it. At press time, the ad appeared as the first image on the following website: http://lime.mediacorppublishing.com/2000-07/win.htm.

We have chosen a popular Tommy Hilfiger ad that features six young, handsome/beautiful, smiley people (two white men, two black men, a white woman, and a black woman) lounging around in red, white, and blue Hilfiger clothes on the expansive front lawn of a country home. The large house stands in the right corner of the photo, and in the upper left-hand corner of the photo, a big American flag waves just over the left shoulder of one of the models. Advertising Tommy cologne, the ad's tag line reads in large white letters along the bottom, "tommy: the real american fragrance."

When we began to read this ad so that we could write about it (the same process you will engage in), we asked ourselves, what textual cues are in the ad? Here is what we saw: In this ad for Tommy Hilfiger cologne, all the people in the photograph are young, well scrubbed, and attractive. And they are happy! Now, what about the setting of the photograph? Where does it take place? It appears to be a rural area, perhaps a country club or a farmhouse in New England. What other textual cues or signs do you see? In this ad, we see a large American flag waving in the upper left-hand corner of the ad. The text, "tommy: the real american fragrance," runs along the bottom fourth of the image, while a picture of the featured cologne balances the flag in the bottom right-hand corner. Smaller than the American flag but similar to it, the Tommy Hilfiger logo hovers above the writing, but seems to be affixed to the white woman's body.

Then we asked ourselves, how do we describe the appearance of the people in the ad? How are they dressed? Well, for one thing, they are all wearing Tommy Hilfiger clothes. This tells us a lot. What is the demographic for Tommy Hilfiger clothes? Who buys them? Who hangs out in large, well-kept farmhouses in New England, who spends time at a country club? The answer to all of these questions seems to be middle-class or upper middle-class white Americans, though the ad suggests that Tommy Hilfiger clothes and cologne appeal to a plurality of people—perhaps even that Tommy clothes and cologne promise racial harmony, an upper middle-class lifestyle, *and* a good time.

But is this so? We decided to make a list of who or what is missing—what is *not* in this picture. Off the top of our heads, we came up with quite a list: people who look poor, anyone over 30, any sign of work (a briefcase, a shovel, a computer, a uniform), anyone who is even remotely overweight, a Mexican flag, a tenement building, any sign of anger, Native Americans, anything having to do with a city, any reference to a blue collar or working class situation, clothes other than Tommy Hilfiger clothes, people who are unattractive, reading material such as books or a newspaper, and finally, any clue as to what these people are doing dressed in Tommy Hilfiger clothes out in the country. What message does the absence of these things send? Is this ad suggesting something about the role of these things in the "real

America"? We don't know exactly, but by asking these questions we might come closer to understanding not only the ad but also the culture from which it comes and the culture it tries to sell. Advertisers use various techniques to get us to respond to their ads, most of which involve making the viewer feel desired, accepted, important, or exclusive. What individual techniques does this ad use to make us feel these things? The flag? The pretty, happy people sitting close together? The sense of affluence suggested by the large house out in the country? The sense of racial harmony evoked by the people of various ethnicities laughing together? Now, when you combine all of these cues, what is the overall argument or promise of the ad? Take this one step further: What does this text suggest about how Tommy Hilfiger, the company, sees itself? And, what does this text suggest about how Tommy Hilfiger, the company, sees America? Does this version of America mesh with your own? Does this version of America reflect mainstream American values?

Though we ended up with more questions than answers here, finding what questions to ask helps us understand the text we're looking at. In more general terms, learning how to read advertisements will not only make you more aware about companies and how they market their products and themselves but also how mainstream advertising and media outlets create a vision or even a myth of our culture. What's more (and perhaps at this moment, most important to you), learning how to read advertisements, poems, and public spaces will help you write better papers, as the reading process is fundamentally linked to the writing process.

While preparing the manuscript for this new edition, we were tempted to take out the previous reading of the Tommy ad, but we like the ad so much—we still don't know why we were denied permission—we thought we'd keep it and augment this section with a shorter semiotic reading of an ad that we could actually get permission to print. But we were denied permission here, too. The ad is part of the Soft-N-Dri "Strong and Beautiful" campaign.

Chances are, you would have noticed the same things we did. An attractive white woman (blonde), dressed in skimpy tight pink clothes, work gloves and a pink gimme cap stands rather defiantly in front of a big black (and rather menacing) semi truck. Over the windshield, again in pink are the words, "PRINCESS OF THE OPEN ROAD," and lower, in the middle of the page, where her legs would begin to show, her body is cut off by the black page. Over the line separating the text from the image are the words "STRONG & BEAUTIFUL," with the "strong" in white and the "beautiful" in pink.

Rather than walk you through this ad, we'll give you the questions we asked:

- Why did the ad folks put the model in pink? What does pink suggest?
- Why a semi truck?
- Why a black semi truck?
- Why is she wearing work gloves (leather) and a hat? Why aren't the gloves pink?
- Look closely at the model's body. What is different about her body from the body of a woman or girl you might see in a Calvin Klein or Victoria's Secret ad?
- Also, what do you notice about her features? Her facial expression?
- Given the fact that this deodorant features a "power stripe," why are her gloves and the truck important?
- Is it *clear* which is strong and which is beautiful—the truck or the model?

- How about the text copy at the bottom—what do you make of the use of the phrase "long haul"?
- This is a more delicate question, but how would the ad be different with an Asian model? An African American model? A man dressed in pink?
- Do you think there is any relation between the whiteness of the model and the fact that the word "strong" is also in white? Why wouldn't it be the same color as the truck?
- Is this an effective ad? Is is sexist? What makes it effective or sexist? Could it be both?

Now its time to read an ad yourself. Open any magazine and see how advertisers try to "sell" anything.

## Reading This Text as a Text ▪▪▪

As you can see, the process of writing a paper involves posing a number of questions about the text you are writing, looking closely at your paper, and trying to organize and arrange an argument. Of course, this process is the same for *reading* a text; both involve thinking and in particular, explorative thinking. We hope that you see the necessary connections between reading and writing, writing and reading and that you understand how the processes of both facilitate the other. Learning to read with care, insight, knowledge, and openness will help you write with those same qualities.

We hope that our book is written with insight, knowledge, and openness, just as we hope that you will read it with such. To augment this, we are going to give you a brief overview of the rest of the book, so that you can become a particularly good reader of the text that is *The World Is a Text*. To that end, we have arranged the book to help you with the writing and the reading processes. We'll begin with an overview of the writing section.

### The World Is a Text: Writing

Let us be clear at the outset that we have designed our section on writing as an *introduction* to the writing process. By no means should you consider this section a comprehensive guide to constructing papers. Our section here is merely an overture to the symphony that is your paper. Virtually no other books of this kind discuss the difficult process of transitioning from high school writing to college writing. *The World Is a Text* is unique in this regard, as we begin our section on writing with a short explanation of how college essays differ from high school essays. The segment entitled "How Do I Write a Text for College? Making the Transition from High School Writing" by guest author Patty Strong is not so much a nuts and bolts essay as it is a description of how your thinking (and therefore your writing) process will need to change to do college level writing. We think you'll find this segment very helpful, and we recommend that you read it first.

One of the most difficult challenges facing beginning college writers is figuring out what they want to say in their papers. Actually settling on a thesis can be frustrating. Sadly, there is no guaranteed remedy for the malady of the elusive thesis; however, we have provided some steps that should make the thesis process slightly less anxiety provoking in the next segment. Our considerably expanded "How Do I Write About Popular Culture Texts?: A Tour Through the Writing Process" walks you through the entire paper-writing process from understanding the assignment to freewriting to outlining to building your opening paragraph.

We have also added information on constructing a good thesis and on making and building arguments. Lastly, we include an annotated student paper in which we walk you through what a student writer does well in an actual undergraduate writing assignment.

We say this throughout *The World Is a Text,* but we will restate it here—always listen to your professors in regard to your assignments. Their patterns and requirements may differ from our recommendations. While you should feel free to use this book, you should first and foremost follow your professor's advice—even if it is different from ours.

It is quite common for instructors to assign a personal essay as the first major assignment in a first-year writing class. To help you with this assignment, we have provided an overview of the personal essay. "How Am I a Text? On Writing Personal Essays" suggests the ways in which you are a text, worthy and ready to be read. You have a wealth of experiences and a mind full of ideas. This segment offers some very solid advice that should facilitate the move from private topic to public writing.

Finally, we end this segment with some information on researching popular culture texts. If you have to write a research paper in your course, pay very close attention to this segment. The simple act of going to the library and figuring out how and where to look can be intimidating, but we have broken it down into a manageable process.

Even though we think this section will provide a good entrée into the book as a whole, there is a wealth of information out there. Online writing labs like those at Purdue University and the University of Texas are accessible on the World Wide Web and have more detailed information than we can provide here. For more complete descriptions of writing, rhetoric and the construction of papers, consult our sister publication *Strategies for Successful Writing: A Rhetoric, Research Guide, Reader, and Handbook,* edited by James A. Reinking, Andrew W. Hart, and Robert von der Osten (also published by Prentice Hall).

## The World Is a Text: Reading

Of course, this is the most important section of the book—the section where you will spend most of your time. To make navigation of these chapters easy for you, we have designed each chapter the same way, so you should have no trouble navigating the readings, the worksheets, or the questions. You will find the following in each chapter:

   I. Introduction
  II. Worksheet
 III. Readings
     a. Chapter Readings
        Questions (This Text: Reading/Your Text: Writing)
     b. Suite of readings
        Questions (This Text: Reading/Your Text: Writing)
  IV. Reading Outside the Lines
     a. Classroom exercises
     b. Essay ideas

In the book, we have several goals. We want to help you become a better reader of the world generally and a better reader of texts like television and movies specifically. We also want to make you a better reader of essays about those topics. We remain confident that your increased abilities as a reader will translate into better writing.

To help with these missions, the book focuses both on the texts like public space and art, and readings about these texts. Our introductions orient you to the text being read and to some basic questions and issues surrounding these areas of study. Following the introduction in each chapter is a worksheet which focuses on both the readings in the chapter and interpretation of the general text (like gender or public space). Read these worksheets closely *before* you read the rest of the chapter.

Each chapter contains essays that focus on different aspects of texts like television and race and then a group of texts about a particular topic—called "suites"—such as reality television (television) or censorship (visual arts). These grouped essays are to show the different ways you might approach a topic, with the hope that you can use some of these ideas in approaching your own interpretation of television shows or paintings. In analyzing these essays, you will develop a better sense of how writers write.

As you read, your primary objective will be to identify the author's main points, the argument or arguments she or he tries to make. This is called the author's "rhetorical strategy," and deciphering a rhetorical strategy is just like reading any other kind of text. You will want to pay attention to the evidence that the author uses to make his or her point. Does she use statistics, personal experience, research, rumor, or the experiences of others? Read each entry at least twice. On the first reading, make notes. If there is a word you don't recognize or an idea that puzzles you, underline or highlight it. Try to find the author's thesis, and mark that. Underline other important points throughout the piece. On your second read, take your level of analysis one step further by asking questions about the passages you underlined. This process will help your transition into writing.

After each entry, you will find two sets of questions. The first set, called "This Text: Reading," is designed to help you understand the text you have just read. The second set, entitled "Your Text: Writing," will help get you started writing about the text (public space, music, race, etc.) or the article itself.

Following the texts are some supplemental items that should help with class discussion and will assist you in thinking about a paper topic. In many of the chapters, we've also included a sample student paper (or two). These are papers actually written by our students on the same topics and texts as you, so that you can see how someone in a similar semiotic situation might turn a text to read into a text to be written. We are not suggesting that you mimic these papers: we want to give you an idea of how such a paper might look. Not all are examples of stellar writing, but if you and your instructors go over them in class, they will help you visualize your own papers.

Finally, since you have worked your way through this rather long introduction to *reading* texts, we thought it might be useful for you if we read our own text. We like this book a lot; in fact, we feel very strongly about its premise: that you can become a better writer, a better student, that you can *be* in the world more fully if you are a critical, thoughtful, insightful reader of the world around you.

Our book relies on the premise that we are always reading and interpreting consciously or not. *The World Is a Text*'s goals are to 1) help you understand the relationship between reading traditional texts such as novels, short stories, and poems and other less traditional texts such as movies, the Internet, art works, and television. Equally important, 2) we want you to discover that perhaps the most valuable way of learning about the world is through writing about it. Last, and perhaps most important, 3) we want you to learn to read your surroundings actively. The first two premises are geared more toward academic achievement; the third is oriented toward helping you become a better citizen of the world, a more active participant in the world in which you live.

Some of you may take exception to specific aspects of this book. Particular images, individual essays, or even parts of our introductions may make you mad, they may upset you, and they may challenge some of your most secure assumptions. We think that is good. We believe critical inquiry is part of the college experience. Another kind of problem that you or your instructor may have with our book is what is *not* in it. We understand that there are many texts we could have included in these chapters. It pains us to think of all the great stories, essays, poems, and art works that we had to leave out. But such is the nature of textbooks. There are also many different texts we could have read, such as sports, video games, cars, business, and families. But we wanted to leave some things out there for you to explore on your own.

## So, the World Is a Text: What Can You Do With It?  ▪▪

Though digesting the book's contents is a lifetime project, a project the authors still regularly undertake and refine, our hope is that after reading this book and writing your papers that you will engage the world more actively. Doing so will make you more of an actor in your own show and enable you to understand your role in the world.

We are not saying the book will have immediate measurable effects, but the more you engage the world as a text, the more you will see subtleties as well as potential forms of manipulation. You may notice the beauty of a public courtyard or the ugliness of a building. You may find yourself arguing with film directors, questioning the structure of a sitcom, and raising objections about a political ad. But engaging the world need not be a grim, political task. You may also find that you are able to see the subtle beauty in a house in your neighborhood or the amusing effectiveness of an ad or the cleverness of a lyric. Developing higher critical faculties also allows you more control of them. Students sometimes complain that English teachers "read too much" into things or that "we're taking the fun out of watching television." If we do these things, it has to do with our ability to turn our critical abilities on and off; thinking almost becomes a new toy once you realize you can understand the world better and in different ways. Don't get us wrong—we watch dumb movies just as you do. However, if we want to engage that dumb movie—to better examine its particular dumbness—we can do that too.

We want you to have the same abilities; more than the particular skill of watching movies, we want you to engage the world more actively. In doing so, you may enhance, in all sorts of ways, the text that is your life.

**A note on format:** This book is formatted in Modern Language Association style, known by most scholars and teachers as "MLA style." Throughout the book, however, you will see several other styles of formatting including American Psychological Association (APA), Chicago or Turabian, and AP style. Each discipline such as English or history or psychology has its own preferred form. Because the book covers so many different types of texts and crosses disciplines, and our readers will come from many disciplines, we have decided to keep to the original style of the article or book portion we are reprinting whenever possible.

# The World Is a Text: WRITING

## A Short Guide to *The World Is a Text*: Writing ▪■▪

This next section provides a number of resources specifically designed to help you with the actual paper-writing process. If you have been in any large bookstore, you have probably seen the dozens, even hundreds, of books devoted to writing, which suggests that there are many different approaches to writing. Not surprisingly, these approaches have changed over time, and it is possible that in the future our suggestions here will seem outdated. That said, you should feel reassured that there is a lot of overlap among those who both teach and write about writing about the most effective ways to teach writing. And while every professor is different and every assignment has its own quirks, we are confident that the information here will be of use to you in many ways.

- **Part I** of the writing section, **"How Do I Write a Text for College? Making the Transition from High School Writing,"** by guest contributor Patty Strong, guides the new college-level writer through some basic transitional steps so that the adjustment from high school writing to college writing will not be so difficult. Just as you make an intellectual leap in math classes from high school to college, so does your writing make a big leap. This section will aid you in that transition.

- **Part II** of this section is the largest, and perhaps, the most important. **"How Do I Write about Popular Culture Texts?: A Tour Through the Writing Process"** walks you through the actual writing process, beginning with how to understand the assignment and working through brainstorming, outlining, drafting, editing and revising. We have also added a section that looks closely at the opening paragraph of student essays. This section features some good strategies for developing that important first paragraph.

- **"How Do I Argue About Popular Culture Texts?: A Guide for Building Good Arguments"** (**Part III**) focuses on the argumentation process. Also expanded, this section explains concepts like logos, pathos, and ethos, and it offers some guidance not simply on how to make good arguments but also how *not* to fall into faulty arguments and argumentative fallacies.

- **Part IV, "How Do I Get Info on Songs?: Researching Popular Culture Texts,"** offers advice on how to research non-traditional texts, such as building, cars, movies, television shows and public space. Many of your classes—regardless of topic—will require some kind of researched paper. This segment will help you get started with your research.

- **Part V** should prove one of the most useful for you. **"How Do I Know What a Good Paper Looks Like?: An Annotated Student Essay"** features an actual student paper that we have annotated. If you are a freshman, you may have no idea what a good college-level essay looks like. Here is an example of one with explanations as to what this author does well.

- **Part VI, "How Do I Cite This Car?: Guidelines for Citing Popular Culture Texts,"** will show you how to cite all of that good research you've just done. Putting together a bibliography or a Works Cited page is an important component of any research project. This section provides examples for citing unusual texts.

- Many instructors ask their students to write personal essays, especially in the first semester of composition courses, so, in the final section we have included a short guide to this process in Part VII's cleverly entitled "How Am I a Text?: Writing Personal Essays." You should always adhere to the guidelines your professor provides, but this short section should supplement what you discuss in class.

While this section might not be as compelling as essays on *The Simpsons* or *Seinfeld,* it is important nonetheless. Reading and writing feed each other in complex ways, so try to give both your attention.

## PART I. How Do I Write a Text for College? Making the Transition from High School Writing ▪▪▪

### by Patty Strong

Writing is thinking. This is what we teachers of college writing believe. Hidden inside that tiny suitcase of a phrase is my whole response to the topic assigned me by my colleague, Jonathan Silverman, one of the authors of the textbook you are currently reading. Knowing my background as a former teacher of high school English, Dr. Silverman asked me to write a piece for students on the differences between writing in high school and writing in college. I have had some time to ponder my answer, and it is this: Writing is thinking. Now that's not very satisfactory, is it? I must unpack that suitcase of a phrase. I will open it up for you, pull out a few well traveled and wearable ideas, ideas that you may want to try on yourself as you journey through your college writing assignments.

Writing is thinking. I suggest that this idea encompasses the differences between high school writing and the writing expected from students on a college level, not because high school teachers don't expect their students to think, but rather that most students themselves do not approach the writing as an *opportunity to think.* Students might construct many other kinds of sentences with writing as subject: Writing is hard. Writing is a duty. Writing is something I do to prove that I know something.

When I taught high school English, I certainly assigned writing in order to find out what my students knew. Did they, for example, know what I had taught them about the light and dark symbolism in chapter 18 of *The Scarlet Letter?* Did they know precisely what Huck Finn said after he reconsidered his letter to Miss Watson ("All right, then, I'll *go* to hell!") and did they know what I, their teacher, had told them those words meant in terms of Huck's moral development? Could my students spit this information back at me in neat, tidy sentences? That's not to say I didn't encourage originality and creativity in my students' writing, but those were a sort of bonus to the bottom line knowledge I was expecting them to be able to reproduce.

College writing is different precisely because it moves beyond the limited conception that writing is writing what we already know. In college, students write to discover what they don't know, to uncover what they didn't know they knew. Students in college should not worry about not having anything to write, because it is the physical and intellectual act of writing, of moving that pen across the page (or tapping the keyboard) that produces the thoughts that become what you have to write. The act of writing will produce the thinking.

This thinking need not produce ideas you already know to be true, but should explore meanings and attitude and questions, which are the things that we all wonder and care about.

My discussion of these matters has so far been fairly abstract, caught up in the wind of ideas. Practical matters are of importance here, too, so I will address some points that as a college student you should know. First, your professors are not responsible for your education—you are. While your teachers may in fact care very much that you learn and do well in your coursework, it is not their responsibility to see that you are successful. Your college teacher may not do things you took for granted like reminding you of assignments and tests and paper deadlines. They probably won't accept your illness or the illness of a loved one or a fight with a girlfriend as legitimate excuses for late work. Sloppy work, late work, thoughtless work, tardiness, absences from class—these things are the student's problems. Successful college students accept responsibility for their problems. They expect that consequences will be meted out. Successful students do not offer excuses, lame or otherwise, although they may offer appropriate resolutions. Successful students understand that their education is something they are privileged to own, and as with a dear possession, they must be responsible for managing it. If you wrecked your beloved car, would you find fault with the person who taught you how to drive?

On to the writing task at hand. You will want to write well in college. You probably want to write better and more maturely than you have in the past. To do this, you must be willing to take thinking risks, which are writing risks. I read an interesting quote the other day that I shared with my writing students because I believed it to be true and pretty profound. The American writer Alvin Toffler wrote that "The illiterate of the twenty-first century will not be those who cannot read and write, but those who cannot learn, unlearn, and relearn." And so it's true that when you come to the university for your "higher education" you must be willing to unlearn some old things and relearn them in new ways. That's probably true for just about every academic subject you will explore during your university career, and it is certainly true about the writing courses you will take.

Writing is thinking. Writing will lead you toward thought. Your college writing teachers will expect more of your thinking, thinking you have come to through the process of writing and rewriting. In order to get where you need to be, you must relearn what writing is. You must see that writing is not duty, obligation, and regurgitation, but opportunity, exploration, and discovery. The realization that writing is thinking and that thinking *leads* to writing is the main idea behind this book—the simple notion that the world is a text to be thought and written about. The successful college writer understands that he or she writes not just for the teacher, not just to prove something to the teacher in order to get a grade, but to uncover unarticulated pathways to knowledge and understanding.

## PART II. How Do I Write About Popular Culture Texts? A Tour through the Writing Process ▪■▪

**by Dean Rader and Jonathan Silverman**

We'd like to begin by underscoring how important being a good reader is for the writing process. Both processes are about discovery, insight, ordering, and argument. The process of writing, however, differs from the product of writing. When we say "product," we mean the produced or finished version—the completed paper that you will submit to your instructor.

The writing "process" is the always complex, sometimes arduous, often frustrating, and frequently rushed series of events that eventually lead you to the finished product. There are a lot of theories about writing, so we will not bore you with an overview of all of them. Chances are, your instructor or your institution's writing center has a series of handouts or guidelines that will help you along the way, but we thought we would take you on a quick tour of what we see as the highlights of the writing process, with an added emphasis on building a good first paragraph and building sound arguments.

But first, you need to understand the assignment . . .

## Understanding the Assignment

This is usually the easiest part of the writing process, but it, too, is important. And because you are learning how to be savvy readers of various texts, this task should be easy for you. First of all, you should read the assignment for the paper as you would read a poem or an advertisement. Look for textual clues that seem particularly important. In fact, we recommend making a list of questions about the assignment itself:

- What questions do I have to answer in order to complete or answer the assignment? Do I have a research or writing question that my paper must answer?
- Does my assignment contain any code words, such as "compare," "analyze," "research," "unpack," or "explore"? If so, what do these terms mean?
- What text or texts am I supposed to write about? Do I understand these texts?
- What is my audience? For whom am I writing?
- What are the parameters of the assignment? What can I do? What can I not do? Is there anything I don't understand before beginning?

One of the biggest mistakes students make is paying too little attention to the assignment. Like any text, it will contain textual cues to help you understand it.

## Freewriting and Brainstorming

Freewriting and brainstorming are crucial to the writing process because they generally produce your topic. While both freewriting and brainstorming are similar, there are some differences. Though there are no hard and fast rules here, we tend to think of freewriting as helping you land on a topic and brainstorming as helping you discover what you want to say about that topic. Freewriting involves the random and uncensored act of writing down anything that comes into your mind on a particular topic. There are any number of ways to freewrite; some teachers and students like visually-oriented methods, while others prefer a straightforward "write all you can down in five minutes" approach. Some of our students set a stopwatch at two minutes, and within that two minutes, write down anything and everything that pops into their heads. When the two minutes are up, they review the list to see if any pattern or ideas emerge. From this list of random stuff, you can generally narrow down a topic. Let's say your assignment is to analyze the film *The Return of the King,* and you see that you jotted down several things that have to do with the way the movie looks. From that, you could decide that you want to write on the innovative "look" of the movie.

At this point, you can move on to brainstorming. Here, you take a blank piece of paper, or sit down in front of a blank computer screen, and write the topic of your paper across the top: The "look" of *The Return of the King*. Now, write down everything that pops into your head about the look of *The Return of the King*. See if you can come up with 10 to 20 ideas, observations or questions. When you are done, look closely at your list. Does a pattern emerge? Are there certain questions or ideas that seem to fit together? Let's say you've written "cool effects," "lots of action," "scary creatures," "mythical overtones," "religious symbols," "good vs. evil," "darkness vs. light," beautiful scenery" "the camera angles were very unique," "very serious," "it felt like fantasy" and "good wins, evil loses." Based on these observations, it looks like you could write a paper about good versus evil or perhaps certain symbols in the film, like light and dark or white and black. Or, you could take things in a different direction and talk about how the "look" of the movie (camera angles, the setting, the colors, and the effects) make a certain argument or contribute to the theme in some way. Yet another possibility would be to combine these observations into a paper that looks at the theme *and* the form.

The goal here is to try to hone in on your topic—the overall subject of your paper. At this point, your topic does not have to be perfectly formulated, but you should be getting an idea of how you might narrow your topic down to something that you can feasibly write a paper about. It's possible—even likely—that as you start plotting an outline, a more defined topic will emerge.

## Outlining

Once you have your topic, you need to organize your paper. Outlines are helpful because they provide a visual map of your paper so that you can see where you're going and where you've been. An outline is also useful in enabling you to see if your ideas fit together, if the paper coheres, and if the paper is equally distributed among your various points. If you find yourself getting stuck or suffering from writer's block, an outline might help push you along. Additionally, an outline presents your ideas in a logical format, and it shows the relationship among the various components of your paper.

The truth is that *deciding upon* these various components is a process of trial and error. We change our minds all the time. So, as authors of this text, we are reluctant to say that one approach is better than another. Writing is always an *organic* process—that is, it grows at its own pace in its own way, and as a writer, you will likely need to adjust to accommodate where your ideas want to go.

No doubt, your instructor will talk a great deal about developing a thesis (which is the main argument or focus of your essay—what you *argue* about your topic), and he or she may encourage you to make this thesis part of your outline. This is a common strategy. The only problem is that you may make an outline with an idea of a thesis, finish the outline, and decide you need to change your thesis. At that point, you should make yet another outline. During the writing process, you may hone your thesis yet again, at which point, you will probably want to draft another outline so that you stay on course given your new thesis. Our point here is that there is no clear-cut process when you are talking about the very fuzzy beginning stages of writing a paper. You should do whatever works for you, whatever leads to the most organized product.

Unlike most other books, we have decided to combine a section on outlining and thesis-making because for us, the two go hand in hand. Most books will suggest that writers figure out a thesis *before* doing an outline. Our experience, however, tells us that arriving at a thesis is often hard, and we don't always know *exactly* what we want to say about our topic until we get a visual map of the paper. Just remember that the first outline you make doesn't have to be the *last* outline—you can and should change it as you see fit.

Now, to that visual map. Traditionally, an outline will state your topic (maybe state your thesis), enumerate your main points and supporting arguments in Roman numerals and beneath the Roman numerals list your evidence in letters. For an essay with two main points, an outline might look something like this:

**THE TITLE OF MY ESSAY**

I. Introduction (1–2 paragraphs)

    thesis: this is my thesis statement, if I have one at this point

II. My first point (2–4 paragraphs)

    a. my supporting evidence

    b. my supporting evidence

III. My second point (2–6 paragraphs)

    a. my supporting evidence

        1. further evidence, graphs, statistics, perhaps

    b. my supporting evidence

        1. further evidence

IV. My smart conclusion (1–2 paragraphs)

Notice how the outline helps flesh out an organizing idea, even if it is in the most general way. The final outline almost never matches up with the first version, but an outline can help you see the strengths and weaknesses of your organization, and it can help you think in an organized way.

Still, outlining in this matter may not suit everyone. Some students (and professors) do not like outlining, because they do not refer to the outline when writing, and they feel like the whole process is a waste of time. Others like to outline at various stages of writing; some outline *after* they have written a draft to make sure they have covered everything they wanted to cover. Those approaches are okay as well; so is writing an outline that is less formal in nature. At various times, the authors have written outlines that are barely outlines—just a mere list of points. Other times, they have written outlines with topic sentences of every one of their paragraphs. The approach you take will depend not only on class requirements, but also on the topic of your paper, your knowledge of the topic, and the amount of research required.

The reason we are committed to outlining is that it separates to some degree the thinking and composing stages of writing; if you know to some degree what you want to say before you start the actual putting words on paper, the more likely you are to write a clear and thoughtful draft, one that will need less extensive revision. The thinking aspect of outlining is why it is at once so difficult and eventually rewarding.

## Constructing a Good Thesis

Now that you have an idea of the work an outline can do, we'll move on to helping you construct a thesis. As we say above, a thesis is the *argument that you are making* about your topic. It is the main point, the *assertion,* you set forth in your essay.

We should say at the outset that the term "thesis" is only one possible term for the paper's argument. Some instructors like the term "claim," some like "focus," still others like "controlling idea." Regardless of what term you use, the concept is the same. The thesis is the idea you propose in your paper—it is *not a statement of fact* but rather a claim, an assertion.

The most important first step is to distinguish among a topic, a thesis, and a thesis statement. One of the great mistakes students make is that they assume a topic is a thesis. A topic is merely the avenue to the freeway that is the thesis, the appetizer to the main course. Let's say you are writing a paper about Affirmative Action. The topic is what you are writing about, which is Affirmative Action. Your thesis is the argument you are *making about* Affirmative Action. Your thesis statement is the actual articulation, the statement or statements in which you unpack or explain your thesis. Now, a thesis statement does not have to be (nor should it be) one simplified sentence; in fact, it could and probably should be two or three sentences, or even a full paragraph. (A book can have a thesis statement that goes on for page*s.*)

We might break down these three components as follows:

*Topic:* what you are writing about (Affirmative Action)

*Thesis:* what you argue *about* your topic (Affirmative Action is a necessary law)

*Thesis statement:* the reason or explanation of your overall thesis—this usually appears in the first or second paragraph of your essay (Affirmative Action is a necessary law because it prevents discriminatory hiring practices. Minorities, women, people with disabilities and gay and lesbian workers have suffered discrimination for decades. Affirmative Action not only redresses past wrongs but sets a level playing field for all job applicants. In short, it ensures democracy.)

Generally, the topic causes you the least anxiety. Your instructor will help you with your topic and may even provide one for you. In any case, you cannot start a paper without a topic.

The real task is figuring out your thesis. Many students worry about not having a thesis when they begin the writing process, but that's normal, and in a way preferable in the quest to find a thesis that is truly an argument. Sometimes it's enough to have what we might refer to as a "thesis question"—a question that when answered through writing and research will actually reveal to you your thesis. Often you will have to write a first draft of your essay before a thesis finally emerges. Remember that writing is exploration and discovery. So it may take some freewriting, brainstorming, outlining, and drafting before you land on a thesis. But stay with the process—you will eventually find an argument.

Perhaps the most confusing aspect of the thesis for students is the realization that a good thesis means you might be wrong. In fact, you will know you are on the road to a good thesis, if you think someone might be able to argue *against* your point. Writing is grounded in rhetoric, which is the art of persuasion. Your goal in your papers is not necessarily to change your audience's mind but to get them to *consider* your ideas. Thus, your thesis needs to be something manageable, something reasonable that you can argue about with confidence and clarity.

The most effective strategy we've found with helping our students understand a thesis is to use the example of the hypo*thesis.* As most of you know, a hypothesis is an educated guess. A thesis is the same thing. In the Greek, "thesis" means a proposition, an idea. "Hypo" is Greek for "under" or "beneath." So, literally, a hypothesis is a "proposition laid down." Your thesis is the same thing. It is not a fact; it is not a statement. It is an *idea,* a proposition that you lay down on paper and then set out to support. You are not absolutely sure that Affirmative Action is a necessary law, but you believe it is. You are pretty confident in your stance, but you also know that someone could write an essay arguing why Affirmative Action should be abolished. This possibility of disagreement is how you know you have a good thesis because you will have to provide sound reasons and convincing examples to support your assertion about the necessity for Affirmative Action.

Why does a thesis need to be an educated guess? Because if a thesis is a statement of fact, there is literally nothing to argue. If your thesis is "Affirmative Action is a law that was designed to prevent discrimination," you have simply stated a fact. There is nothing at stake, nothing to debate. Even a thesis like "Affirmative Action is an important law" is rather weak. Virtually no one would suggest that Affirmative Action is not important. It has been extraordinarily important in American culture. So, again, that is not the best thesis you could come up with, though it remains better than our first example. However, arguing that it is a *necessary* law makes your thesis more provocative, more risky. Therefore, it is likely to draw interest and get people excited. Readers will want to see your reasons and think about the examples you provide.

We'll break it down even further, using an example from this book. Let's say you are writing on the essays in Chapter 7. Your topic is censorship and the *Sensation* exhibit.

**Weak thesis:** The *Sensation* exhibit in New York raised a lot of questions about censorship and public money.

This is a weak thesis statement because it is a statement of fact. No one would debate this point.

**Better thesis:** The *Sensation* exhibit in New York deserved to run its course despite public opinion.

This is a better thesis statement because it proposes something a bit controversial. Many people, including the mayor of New York at the time, would argue against this thesis. That tells you that you are on the right track.

**Even better thesis:** It is important that the *Sensation* exhibit in New York was allowed to happen without being censored, despite political opposition to the conent of some of the pieces Freedom of speech and freedom of expression are critical parts of American ideas of liberty, and silencing works of art meant for public consumption is in violation of our most basic rights.

This thesis statement is even better because it provides a bit more precision, and it gives a reason for the author's stance. It will be easier, then, for this writer to prove the thesis because the reason is already articulated. Honing in on a good thesis is the foundation for building a good paragraph—which, in turn, is the foundation for building a good essay.

## Building an Opening Paragraph: A Case Study

The opening paragraph for your essay does a great deal of work, both for your essay and for your audience. For your audience it sets up your argument, and it informs them what is going to happen in the remaining pages. In the paper, it functions as the road map, pointing readers down certain avenues and telling them to avoid others. If your reader is confused after the first paragraph, she may remain confused for a good bit of your essay, and that's never what you want.

An opening paragraph should do a number of things—it should engage the reader's interest with an entertaining or provocative opening sentence, and it should provide the road map for the rest of the paper. Additionally, your opening paragraph will typically be the home for your thesis statement (though some professors will have different preferences on whether your thesis needs to go in the first paragraph). It is also the face for your paper, so it should be extremely well organized, moving from a general observation to the more specific thesis statement (think of an up-side down pyramid—broad going down to narrow). For the writer, the opening paragraph is critical because it provides the formula for working through the issues of the essay itself. A vague opener will provide too little direction; a paragraph that tries to argue three or four different topics will never get on the right track; and one that does not make an argument, has a tendency to go nowhere because it will keep restating facts instead of staking out a position and making an argument.

The purpose of this section is to avoid these pitfalls. Here, we give you some models of opening paragraphs before and after revision to show you how a thorough revising process can improve your opening paragraph, strengthen your thesis, and provide a good entrée into your essay.

Let's say you are writing about the movie *Office Space.* You know that you like the movie. You think it's funny, and all of your friends think it's funny. During parties and over lunch, you trade lines with each other. You all agree that the movie speaks to your generation in some odd way, but you are having trouble figuring out *exactly* what you want to say about it. You decide (wisely) to make a list of all possible arguments and some questions about those arguments:

- *Office Space* speaks to people of my generation (why is this important?)
- *Office Space* is funny (but that's not an argument). Office Space is the funniest movie of the last 5 years. (but how would I prove that?)
- *Office Space* makes a connection with college students like no other movie (is this true? What about Lord of the Rings or Caddyshack?)
- *Office Space* was not a huge box office hit, but it is wildly popular among college students (maybe it's biggest audience is college students??)
- We like *Office Space* because it's funny
- We like *Office Space* because it's about rebellion
- It's anti-establishment, anti-corporate.
- We identify. Maybe it's also anti-institution, like school or college.
- *Office Space* appeals to college students because they can identify with the anti-institutional theme. (but, we are all part of institutions—school, jobs)
- We like *Office Space* because it's anti-institutional and yet not. (it's kind of subversive, but not *really.* The people in it are kind of lazy.)

This is a pretty good list. We can likely get some kind of argument from it.

The trick is finding something that is truly an argument. Saying that *Office Space* is funny is not much of an argument. Most would agree with this, and really, who cares if it's funny or not? That doesn't help us understand the movie any better. Also, arguing that college students like it is also overstating the obvious. The key is to explain *why* this particular movie appeals to college students at this particular time. Of course, one could talk about the fantasy of stealing a million dollars or getting a date with Jennifer Anniston or the bigger fantasy of enjoying working construction over being in a cubicle, but those kinds of ideas occur in other movies. What sets this movie apart is the idea of being subversive (sort of) in an institutional setting. You want your paper to be unique, and you want it to tell your readers something they might actually find compelling. Readers can usually tell after an opening paragraph if there is anything in there for them or not, so as you craft your essay, ask yourself—am I giving pertinent information? Is my argument interesting? Will people *like* this?

So, the first try at an opening paragraph might look like this:

> *Office Space,* directed by Mike Judge, has become a classic movie for college students. It's funny plot, it's witty dialogue and stance on corporate life appeals to students across disciplines and states. One might wonder why a movie that was not a box-office sensation has become a cult sensation among college students, but it's clear that *Office Space* appeals to students in a number of ways. Perhaps the biggest way is the movie's theme of rebellion. Students can identify with the movie's anti-corporate message.

Okay, so what do we see here? On a micro level, there are some problems with the prose: the rogue apostrophe in *it's* (second sentence) has to go; the phrase "across disciplines and states" is vague and not really helpful; "box-office sensation" is a cliché and also vague; "number of ways" also doesn't do much work. Still, there is also a great deal of information here to work with. The beginnings of our thesis probably rest in the last two sentences—it's there that we make our argument. On closer examination, though, it would appear that the last sentence isn't *really* an argument. Almost no one would disagree with that statement, so *proving* would be easy but ultimately pointless. Essays that merely sum up what everyone agrees with do little to further our understanding of the issue or topic at hand. From an entertainment perspective, a good opening paragraph needs to give us reasons to keep reading, so the next version should incorporate some reasons why the movie appeals to students. It should also be a bit more sophisticated and precise. So, in the next version, list some reasons the movie appeals, and give the date of the film for starters. Also do a bit of research and see what you can come up with.

Draft two might come out like this:

> *Office Space* (1999), directed by Mike Judge of *Beavis and Butthead* fame, has become an underground classic among American college students. It is not uncommon to overhear students quoting entire passages from the movie, and there is even an *Office Space* drinking game. Though the movie features a couple of funny subplots involving dating and stealing a million dollars, the real draw of the movie lies in the fact that it is rather anti-establishment. The main character of the film doesn't simply quit his job—he actually stops working. What's more, he gets rewarded for it through a promotion. Thus, *Office Space* sends a message to college students that when they enter the same corporate environment, they too can be rewarded for rebelling against the corporate mindset.

Wow, what happened here? On one hand, the paragraph is much stronger. Notice the increased specificity: *American* college students, examples of how students enjoy the movie, more active verbs instead of being verbs (is, are); even some details from the movie itself. But, beyond all that, the thesis has gone off in a different direction! Our argument was that students relate to the movie's theme of rebellion; now, it would appear that we are arguing that students like the movie because they will get rewarded for rebelling. Is that what we want to argue? Is that the reason students like the movie? Does the appeal of the movie lie in the fact that students relate to it or that it gives them hope? What if it's both? Is there a way to work both into the thesis? Generally, the more precise and the more thorough, yours has gone off in a different direction! Our argument was that students relate to the movie's theme of rebellion; now, it would appear that we are arguing that students like the movie because they will get rewarded for rebelling. Is that what we want to argue? Is that the reason students like the movie? Does the appeal of the movie lie in the fact that students relate or that it gives them hope? What if it's both? Is there a way to work both into the thesis? Generally, the more precise and the more thorough your thesis is, the better. In truth, probably both things appeal to students, so why not strengthen the thesis and the essay by making arguments about both?

The resulting third draft:

> Mike Judge took slacking to new heights with his hilarious cartoon *Beavis and Butthead*, which chronicled the lives of two under-achieving teen-age boys who had a great deal of fun doing a great deal of nothing. Judge's first movie involving real humans is also about doing nothing, but this time it's recent college graduates who find themselves working in cubicles for a mind-numbing corporation. Despite the fact that *Office Space* (1999) was not a huge hit at the box office, it has become an underground classic across university campuses. Students quote entire scenes to each other from memory, *Office Space* t-shirts abound, and there is even an *Office Space* drinking game. One might wonder why a movie with no real stars except for Jennifer Anniston has made such an impact on this generation of students. Though there are some funny subplots involving dating and stealing a million dollars from a corporation, the main action of the movie comes when the main character, Peter, decides to stop working, but winds up getting a promotion. Thus, the movie appeals to students not simply because it champions rebelling against the man, but it suggests one might get rewarded for doing so. On one hand, students identify with the desire to completely stop working, and they like the idea that things might turn out better for them if they do. Ultimately, students are drawn to *Office Space* because it tells them they can be anti-establishment and successful at the same time.

This version is better not because it is longer, but because it provides detail, it is precise, and it features a thorough three-sentence thesis statement. Readers know from this opening paragraph that we are going to read an essay that 1) makes an argument and 2) makes an argument about the two ways/reasons the movie appeals to college students.

Because we have a focused thesis, we can now go into a lot of detail in the rest of our paper about how and why students related to *specific* scenes and concepts, and we can also make some interesting observations about "safe rebellion" and rewards. From here on out the writing process will involve "proving" and elaborating on the thesis.

A note here on opening paragraphs: one of the authors believes that writing the opening paragraph should come closer to the end of the composing process rather than the beginning. While getting a thesis early is important, writing an opening paragraph *before* you know what you want to say might mean you must extensively revise the paragraph or scrap it altogether. Some writers, however, need to "begin with beginning"—they can't go on until they know exactly what their argument is going to be. Ultimately, your preference regarding the writing *process* is less important that the finished product.

Lastly, avoid writing a clichéd introduction. Do not use phrases like "since the beginning of time," which is much too general and tells us little. Also, resist using a dictionary definition of an important word. These two strategies should almost never be used in college writing. If you want to use a time construction, confine it to specific knowable time, such as "the recent past" or "in the 1990s." If you find yourself drifting toward a dictionary definition, try defining it yourself, looking in a more specialized source such as a book about the subject (but be careful to cite), or engaging the definition you find by arguing with it or refining it. *Never* write: "The dictionary defines xxxx as"—there are many different dictionaries, all of which will define words differently.

If you take your opening paragraph seriously, use it as a method of organization, and make it interesting, you will be off to a good start with your paper.

## Building Good Paragraphs

Building a good paper is relatively simple, once you understand the formula. By formula, we do *not* necessarily mean a standard five-paragraph essay. Instead of thinking of your paper in terms numbers of paragraphs, think in terms of *points* or *reasons.* By points, we mean ideas, concepts, observations or reasons that support the argument you are making in your thesis. The units that will help you organize these points are the paragraphs themselves. This section will help you get a handle on how to structure your paragraphs so that you make the most of your supporting points.

For a typical undergraduate paper, you do not want too many or too few points. If you are arguing about Affirmative Action, how many reasons do you want to include in your paper to support your thesis? Do you want seven? No, that's too many. One? That's too few. Generally, we suggest two to four points or reasons for a standard three- to six-page paper. For a longer paper, like a research paper, you may want four or five points to drive home your argument. But the danger of including too many points in your paper is that, unless you can supply ample evidence for *each* point, an overabundance of points winds up having the opposite of the intended effect. Rather than bolstering your argument by the sheer number of reasons, you tend to weaken your argument because you dilute your points through an overabundance of reasons and a lack of evidence. In other words, it's better to write three or four paragraphs for one or two points than to write five paragraphs for five points. Write *more about less* as opposed to less about more.

The key to making and supporting your assertions is the paragraph. Paragraphs are the infrastructure of your essay; they frame and support the arguments you make. Every paragraph is like a mini-essay. Just as your essay has a thesis statement, so does your paragraph have a topic sentence—a sentence in which you lay out the main idea for that paragraph. Once you write your topic sentence, then you have to provide evidence to support the claim you've made in your topic sentence. Each paragraph has its own topic and its own mini-assertion, and when taken together, all of these paragraphs work together to support the overall thesis of the entire essay.

For instance, let's say your topic sentence is: "The *Sensation* exhibit was an important test for American culture because First Amendment rights were at stake." What might be your next move? You should probably quote the First Amendment, or at least part of it. Then, explain how the *Sensation* exhibit was protected by the First Amendment. Give examples of specific pieces from the show that are pertinent to this discussion. This is also the right time to bring in quotes from other people that support your assertions. If you quote from another source, or if you quote from a primary text, be sure you *explain how the passage you've quoted supports your thesis.* (And of course cite the quote's origin.) The quote cannot explain itself—you have to tell your audience why that quote is important, why and how the statistics you have included are evidence the reader should pay attention to.

Finally, and this is very important, end your paragraphs well. The most common mistake students make when writing paragraphs is that they tend to trail off. Make that last sentence a kind of connector—make it tie everything in the paragraph back to the topic sentence. Also, when possible, reinforce the fact that your paragraphs are working together by writing transition sentences from one paragraph to the next. For example, a good transition in the essay on the *Sensation* exhibit would acknowledge the topic of the paragraph preceding it and lead into the topic for the paragraph at hand. Such a sentence might look like this: "Not only did the *Sensation* exhibit reinforce first amendment rights of the artists, it underscored the right of viewers and museum-goers to enjoy art their tax dollars helped support." Note how this sentence refers to the subject of the previous paragraph (artistic freedom) and also how it informs us of the topic we are about to engage (publicly funded art).

Start on your next paragraph with the same model. Keep doing this until you have built yourself a paper. Then go back and revise and edit, revise and edit, revise and edit. The key to building good paragraphs is using them to make arguments. The following section walks you through that process.

## Drafting the Whole Essay

While we have spent a great deal of energy explaining various strategies for composing a paper, it still comes down to the actual work of thinking about a topic, doing your own method of pre-writing (outlining, brainstorming, etc.), and putting the words on paper. In other words, you still have to write that first draft.

Sentence by sentence, and paragraph by paragraph, you should start building your paper. Remember to give as much detail as possible. Include examples from the text you are writing about, and try to avoid plot summary or unnecessary description. Remember: *Analyze, don't summarize.* In other words, do not simply provide information—make sense of information for us.

Once you've finished your first draft, you may discover that buried somewhere in your closing paragraph is the very good articulation of the thesis you've been trying to prove for several pages. This happens because, as we've said, writing is a discovery process. So by working through your ideas, your arguments, your textual examples, you will start to focus on what you've been trying to say all along.

Now that you have a better idea of what you want to say, it's time for the real work—editing and revising.

## Editing and Revising, Editing and Revising, Editing and Revising

The single biggest mistake student writers make is turning in their first draft. The first draft is often little more than a blueprint—it's merely an experiment. In the editing and revising stage, you convert the process of writing into the written product. Here, you turn a bad paper into a decent one or a good paper into a great one. You can clear up confusing sentences, focus your argument, correct bad grammar, and, most importantly, make your paper clearer and more thorough. Students think that they are good writers if papers come easily. This is the *biggest* myth in writing. A good paper happens through several stabs at editing and revising. For instance, this very introduction has gone through somewhere between fifteen and twenty revisions.

There are a number of strategies for editing and revising, so we'll give you a couple of our favorites. First of all, when you are ready to edit and revise, read your paper through *backwards.* Start at the very end, and read it backwards, one sentence at a time. This forces you to slow down and see the sentence as its own entity. It's probably the most useful strategy for correcting your own writing. Even more helpful is getting a peer to read your paper. Another person can point out errors, inconsistencies, or vague statements that you may miss because you are too close to the process. An often painful but very effective way of editing is reading your paper out loud. The authors often do this, especially when presenting their work to other people.

Finally, we also recommend that while you may write hot, you should edit cold. What we mean by this is that you need to step back from your paper when you edit. Look at it objectively. Try not to get caught up in your prose or in your argument. Work on being succinct and clear. Practically, this means not working on your paper for a period of time, even if that period is hours, not days. As professors, we are well aware that you may wait until the last minute to write a paper. While we are not endorsing this way of composing, you still need to find a way to step away from the paper and come back to it to get some perspective on what you have written.

This is also the time go to back over the arguments you've made (here we introduce some terms that you will see again in the upcoming "A Guide for Building Arguments" section). Look at your logos and pathos—are they appropriate? Have you made argumentative errors? Are you guilty of using fallacies? Do you supply enough good evidence to support your assertions? Do you end your paragraphs well?

It may take several drafts (in fact it should) before you feel comfortable with your paper. So, we recommend at least *three* different passes at editing and revising before turning in your paper. We advocate going back over and looking at your language one last time. Do not use words that are not part of your vocabulary; try to avoid stating the obvious. Be original, be honest, and be engaged. We urge you above all else to think complexly but write simply.

Finally, we want to reiterate here that writing is not easy or simple for *anyone.* While you may think that you are not a strong writer, and that others write more easily and naturally, the truth is that all "good" writers spend a significant amount of time revising their work. In fact, these writers *enjoy* this part of the composing process, because it is the time when they see their writing actually turn into something worth sharing with someone else.

## Turning in the Finished Product

The most enjoyable part of the process! Doublecheck spelling and grammatical issues. Check your citations if you did a research paper, and go over your bibliography. Confirm you did *not* plagiarize.

Turn in the paper and go celebrate!

**SOME FINAL TIPS—A RECAP**

- Distinguish between a topic and a thesis.
- Your thesis doesn't have to be one concise sentence; it can be several sentences, perhaps even an entire paragraph. It might even be helpful to think of your thesis as your focus, your idea that you are trying to support.
- "Thesis" comes from "hypothesis." A hypothesis is an educated guess. So is your thesis. It's an educated guess, an idea that you are trying to support. You don't have to develop an over-the-top airtight argument; you simply want your reader to consider your point of view.
- Writing is conversation; it is dialogue. Keep asking questions of yourself, your writing and your topic. Ask yourself, "Why is this so?" Make sure you answer. *Be specific; be thorough.*
- Consider your audience. You should never assume they have read the text you are writing about, so don't toss around names or scenes without explaining them a little. It's called giving context. There is a big difference between giving context (valuable information) and summarizing the plot (regurgitation).
- Make good arguments. Use logos, pathos, and ethos appropriately. Try to avoid fallacies.

**FIVE STEPS TO WRITING A GOOD PAPER**

1. Formulate a good, supportable thesis.
2. Then, set out to explain or prove your thesis in well-constructed paragraphs using your own interpretation and details from the text to support your points.
3. Build sound, solid arguments that support your thesis.
4. Quote from other sources or provide details from the primary text, and explain *why* the passage you've quoted is important to your overall thesis.
5. Keep working through your paper in the same way.

# PART III. How Do I Argue About Popular Culture Texts? A Guide for Building Good Arguments ▪■▫

## Knowing Your Arguments

As we suggest in the previous section, building a good paper is dependent upon making good arguments and supporting them with solid evidence. In contemporary American culture, "argument" tends to carry negative connotations. Few like getting into arguments, and no one wants to be seen as an argumentative person. However, in writing, *argument* has a slightly different meaning. When we talk about arguments or argumentation, what we mean is staking out a position or taking a stance. In writing and rhetoric, to argue means to put forth an assertion, a proposition and to support that position with evidence. If you are using this book, then most of the writing you will do in your class will involve making an argument and backing it up. So, in your regular, non-writing life, feel free to go on avoiding arguments, but in your writing life, we urge you to think positively about the prospect of making a compelling argument.

Before we go into specific kinds of arguments, it might be useful to think about *why* we make arguments. In academic settings, it is important to be able to argue a specific point because almost all information is debatable, particularly in the arts, humanities and social sciences. Should welfare be abolished? Is capital punishment moral? Is Picasso's *Guernica* transgressive? Is there a relationship between Christianity and Buddhism? Should we discount the poetry of Ezra Pound, T. S. Eliot and e. e. Cummings because of some anti-Semitic passages? These are important questions with no clear answers. Accordingly, you need to be able to justify or explain your opinions on these issues. Holding an opinion and backing up that opinion is argument, and we engage in this kind of argumentation all the time. What is the best album of the 90s? What is the best horror movie? What five books would you take to a desert island and why? These are fun arguments, and perhaps mostly intellectual exercises, but down the road, being able to argue persuasively might be important in a job ("Here is why we should choose Bob's marketing strategy"), a relationship ("Honey, I know you think I should get an MBA, but let me tell you why an MFA in creative writing is better for me and the kids"), to making purchases ("Let me give you seven reasons why we don't need an SUV"). In fact, in putting this book together the co-authors had daily (but friendly and funny) arguments over what readings to publish, the tone of this very chapter, and what should go on the cover. Finally, knowing how arguments work will also help you discover more fully your own stance on a particular issue. Often, understanding how you feel about a topic is difficult if you do not write or talk about it.

The question is, *how* does one make an effective argument? There are two ways to look at this question. The first is to approach it from the perspective of the argument; the other is to approach it from the perspective of the audience. When we think of arguments, we tend to break them down into two types—logical and emotional. Arguments that appeal to our sense of logic are arguments of *logos* (Greek for "word" or "reason"); those that cater to our emotions are arguments of *pathos* (Greek for "suffering" and "feeling"). Both are effective forms of persuasion, but they function in different ways and sometimes serve different purposes. Though you should employ both in your essays, your main focus should be on building an argument based on *logos*.

Arguments of logos appeal to our sense of reason and logic. They tend to rely on facts, statistics, specific examples, and authoritative statements. Your supporting evidence for these kinds of arguments is critical. It must be accurate, valid, truthful, and specific. For instance, while looking over essays we thought might be useful for the new chapter on relationships, we came across a study arguing that long distance romantic relationships among college students generally didn't last very long. Based on this description, what kinds of evidence do you think the authors of the study relied on? Rumor and innuendo? A survey of people who graduated from college in 1979? A close examination of TV shows about college students? A review of the film *Animal House*? Of course not. The authors were sociologists who surveyed hundreds of college students who were or had been involved in long distance relationships. They provided almost six pages of statistics; they allowed for differences in age, race, gender and geographic location; and they did their survey over a respectable amount of time. In short, they relied on objective data, scientific reasoning, and sound survey practices to help make their argument that long distance relationships in college tend not to work out.

Think about what kinds of information would persuade you in certain situations. What would make you buy an iPod over some other MP3 player? Or, more importantly, what would convince you to buy a Volvo over a Hyundai for driving around your newborn twins? If you were going to write a paper on fire safety, would you rely on the expertise of a fire marshal or a medical doctor? If you were writing an essay on water pollution, would you consult scientific journals and EPA studies, or would you rely on the Web pages of chemical corporations? Readers are more likely to be moved by the soundness of your argument if your supporting evidence seems logical, objective, verifiable and reasonable.

Having said that, it would be a mistake to dismiss arguments of pathos outright. In fact, we believe that many teachers and writers have too easily separated intellect and emotion when talking about arguments. Arguments of pathos can be unusually powerful and convincing because they appeal to our needs, desires, fears, values and emotions. The statement, "You should get an iPod because they are just plain *cooler* than anything else out there" is an appeal to pathos. Notice how this claim ignores any information about warranties, durability, price, or functionality. Rather, the statement plays on our desire to be cool—a most powerful appeal. If you are truthful with yourself, you might be surprised just how often such arguments actually work.

Most television commercials and advertisements in popular magazines play on our sense of pathos. If you have found yourself moved by those Michelin tire commercials in which nothing much happens except a cute little baby plays around in an empty Michelin tire, then the good folks in the marketing department at Michelin have been successful. If you have fought back a tear at an image of an elderly couple holding hands, or believed (if even for an instant) that drinking a certain light beer might get you more dates, then you have been moved by an appeal to your sense of pathos. Now, appeals to pathos are not necessarily bad or manipulative; on the contrary, they can be effective when statistics or logic feels cold and inhuman.

The authors believe that the most effective arguments are those that combine logos and pathos, and, as we discuss next, ethos. Emotional appeals without facts will feel sleazy, and scientific data without human appeal will feel cold. We still maintain that your essays should make appeals to logos over pathos, but we encourage you to build arguments in which emotion supports or enhances logic. Arguments that feature good combinations of logos and pathos will make you and your essay appear both smart and human—a good mix.

Not only will you need to create an appropriate mix of logos and pathos for your intended audience, but you must also create an appropriate *ethos.* Greek for "character" or "disposition," a writer's ethos is her sense of credibility. For most conservative Republicans, Michael Moore has little credibility, so for them, he would have a low ethos. On the other hand, someone like Colin Powell enjoys the respect of many Republicans and Democrats. Most Americans trust him; they find him credible. Therefore, Powell's ethos is high. The ethos of public figures like Powell and Moore are easier to talk about than relatively unknown personalities, so as a beginning writer, you should be mindful of how you want to establish credibility and authority. If you are going to argue that the Vietnam Veterans memorial is the ideal example of public art, it might undermine your argument if your best friend is the architect (or if you *conceal* that your best friend is the architect). Alternatively, if you argue that the Washington Redskins should *not* change their mascot from the potentially offensive epithet "redskin" but fail to mention that you own stock in the Redskins, then your credibility might be in jeopardy, and people might not take your argument seriously. Ethos, pathos, and logos comprise what we call the "rhetorical triangle," and most arguments are made up of some combination of the three. Based on your audience, you will need to adjust your own rhetorical triangle so that your argument contains the right mixture of reason, emotion, and credibility.

A reading aside: it's also helpful in reading to understand whether or how a writer is effective by analyzing their argument on whether they are writing from logos, pathos or ethos. For example, if Colin Powell writes about the need for international diplomacy in the Middle East, it would automatically carry more weight than one made by your local city councilwoman, even if she had her master's in international relations.

## Knowing Your Audience

An outspoken advocate of the Internet's capacity to share vast amounts of information has been invited to speak at a gathering of music company executives, who are nervous about the thousands of people downloading free music. What kind of tone should she take when addressing this potentially hostile audience? Next, that person is going to speak to a gathering of college students, who are among the most avid downloaders of music. How would her presentation differ? Would she give the same presentation to both audiences? What strategies would she employ with the hostile audience that she would not need for the sympathetic one? Keeping the assumptions, education, political leanings and culture of your audience in mind will help you write a more appropriate essay than if you ignored these issues altogether.

As we write this section, Michael Moore's controversial movie *Fahrenheit 9/11* has just been released nationwide. A scathing indictment of the presidency of George W. Bush, Moore's film has polarized the nation. There is no doubt that the film makes a powerful argument, but one might ask who the audience of the movie is. Is Moore making the movie for Republicans, Democrats, or those in the middle? Many believe that because the movie is so one-sided it will change few people's minds, while others contend that it could move people on the fence to oppose the President. We would argue that Moore's audience is not right-wing Republicans but rather those voters who are undecided, or perhaps Democrats who feel apathetic about supporting their presumed nominee, John Kerry. Moore knows that his movie will probably be seen by those on the right as fabrication, but his persistent arguments in the movie seem aimed at Americans who are looking for reasons to vote Democratic. If Moore was interested in a broader audience, there are any number of ways he might have kept his message, but changed his method of delivering it—including interviewing sympathetic and thoughtful defenders of the President, toning down some of his own antics, and most importantly, editing the film differently, choosing to emphasize sympathetic portraits of the President. By the time this book is published, the election will already have happened, so the jury is out on whether Moore's film succeeded or not, but the heated discussions surrounding it underscore the importance of knowing your audience.

The examples above reflect the three types of audiences you should consider when writing your papers—a sympathetic audience, an undecided audience, and an antagonistic audience. You would likely not write the same paper for the three kinds of audiences; you would tailor your arguments based on who would be reading your essay. We do this kind of tailoring all the time. For instance, when you tell the story of a fabulous date you had the previous night to your mother, your best friend, and your ex, you will probably tell three radically different stories. The potentially hostile audience (the ex) will get one version, the undecided version (mother) will get another, and the sympathetic audience (roommate) will get yet another. All your stories might be accurate but shaded differently and delivered differently based on what you know about each of them.

When writing for a sympathetic audience, you already have them on your side, so you do not need to try to win them over. In this case, an argument grounded in pathos may be the most effective. Chances are, they already know the information that might make them think a certain way, so giving them facts, statistics, and details they are familiar with will not be effective because it could come across as overstating the obvious or simply appearing repetitive. However, an emotionally powerful appeal, supported by a strong ethos could be incredibly successful. Let's say you are going to write an essay on Kurt Cobain's contribution to American music for *Rolling Stone* or *Spin.* Most readers of these magazines will be predisposed to agree with the facts you may present, so you will not need to list the number of records Nirvana sold or the awards they won. Instead, you may want to focus on how the music has affected you and your friends.

Alternatively, if you have been asked to write an article on Cobain for *Country Music Today,* the audience will be less sympathetic to your topic. In this instance, you will need to adjust your ethos and your approach. First, you could establish credibility by informing your readers that you are a fan of country music, perhaps even mention the important contributions of various artists you know these readers will appreciate. When addressing a potentially antagonistic or skeptical audience, it is best to avoid an overly pathos-driven argument. You may come across as ill informed and even irrational. Instead, you might want to point to specific songs or chords that resemble country songs. A good strategy might be to make connections thematically, arguing that even though the music is different, Cobain, Willie Nelson, Lyle Lovett, Merle Haggard, and Waylon Jennings all write smart, catchy songs about disaffected, blue collar Americans. Look for instances of overlap. If you have time to research, you might find out that Cobain listened to country music or that the people in the area he grew up in have a strong affinity for country music. With these kinds of audiences, the best way to establish credibility is to let your audience know that you have done your homework, and that you know *their* world as well as you know your own.

In some ways, writing for an antagonistic audience is easier than writing for an uncertain one because you know what you are getting into. Writing for the vast middle can be truly challenging. When writing for an undecided audience, the best strategy will be to establish strong ethos and logos. How much you rely on ethos or logos will depend on you and your topic. If you are arguing that advertisements featuring skinny near-naked female models are empowering to women, you might need to adjust your argument based on your gender or age. If you want to argue that the "Names" quilt should be taken seriously as art, focus not simply on the formal or artistic qualities of the quilt but mention how the quilt affected you, that it fostered an interest in folk art and a love for art that inspires social change. Your audience will respond more favorably to your claims if they trust you and your evidence. Be honest. Do not try to manipulate. Write in your own voice.

## How to Make Arguments: Some Helpful Tips

Some students think that if they acknowledge any aspect of the other side of their argument that they poke a hole in their own. Actually, just the opposite is the case. Letting your readers know that you are well informed goes a long way toward establishing your credibility. What's more, if you are able not only to identify a differing opinion and then refute it or discount it, your argument could carry even more weight. For instance, if you want to argue that Mel Gibson's film *The Passion of the Christ* succeeds as a work of art, you would do well to acknowledge near the beginning of your essay that some critics have problems with the film.

In fact, you may decide to use their complaints and their weaknesses to help you make your own assertions.

## Do not be afraid to acknowledge differing opinions.

Honesty and trust come into play when you actually make your arguments. You do not want to mislead your potential audiences, you do not want to alienate them, and you do not want to manipulate them in an unethical way. Making up facts, inventing sources, leaving out important details are not merely bad argumentation, they are often unethical acts. More positively, writing is all about engagement. We write to make connections with others; we read to learn more about the world and our place in it. Below we provide some basic tips for making solid, convincing, ethical arguments.

## Use credible, detailed information and sources to help support your arguments.

This is perhaps the most important tip we can provide. Think about what kind of information convinces you to do anything. Are you persuaded by vagueness or specificity? If we wanted to convince you to meet us for dinner at a specific restaurant, which of the following would be the most persuasive?

- We heard from someone that it's really good.
- A restaurant critic we respect said this is some of the best food in town.
- A restaurant critic, two chefs and a group of our friends all recommend this place.
- We've been there a number of times, and the food is great, the service is fantastic, the scene is relaxed but cool, and the prices are reasonable.
- The restaurant's Web site claims it is the city's favorite restaurant.
- Your grandparents raved about it.

In general, we are persuaded by thorough, objective data. While we trust people who have the same taste we do, we tend not to trust people we do not know or who might have a stake in a certain argument. The best kinds of evidence are expert opinions, statistics from a reliable source (like a scientific study), facts from an objective source (like a newspaper or peer-reviewed journal), personal experience, and the testimony of others. On the other hand, if your grandparents have previously recommended good restaurants, their ethos could match the so-called experts who have recommended the place. But, then again, their tastes may be *much* different than yours. Understanding the criteria that one uses in judging restaurants, movies, and television shows is crucial. For example, Roger Ebert, the well-known critic, admits before every Adam Sandler movie review that he is no fan of Adam Sandler, giving his readers a warning that his criteria may not match their own.

## Establish your own credibility and authority, but try not to overdo it.

There are two different ways to establish authority—explicitly and implicitly. In the explicit method, you say up front that you are a specialist in a certain area. For instance, if you are going to write about the influence of Tejano music in South Texas, you might say in the opening paragraph that you are a Latina from Texas who grew up listening to your dad play in Tejano bands around San Antonio. The audience then knows your background and is likely to give your arguments more weight than if a white guy from Boston was making the same argument. Establishing authority implicitly may have less to do with you and more to do with the research you have done. Implicit authority is revealed to the reader slowly, in pieces, so that you carefully fill in gaps over the course of your essay.

There are, of course, many ways to establish authority—by being an expert, by quoting experts, and by building a knowledge base as a result of research—but however you establish authority, do so within reason. If the essay begins to become more about how much you know and less about your topic, you will alienate your reader. You want to keep your reader engaged.

## Use inductive and/or deductive reasoning when appropriate.

As you write your paper, as you make your arguments and present your evidence, your reader will have to think through your arguments. However, before that happens, you also have to think through your arguments so that you can develop them in the most cogent way. The two types of argument organization are inductive and deductive. Deductive reasoning begins big and moves to small. Or, in other terms, deductive reasoning starts with the macro and moves to the micro. In classic rhetoric, this is called a syllogism. A classic syllogism might go something like this: Most Hollywood movies have a happy ending. *Forrest Gump* is a Hollywood movie. Therefore, it is likely that *Forrest Gump* has a happy ending. A typical syllogism begins with two broad statements and arrives at a narrower proposition based on those statements.

Inductive reasoning resembles detective work. You start with many small observations or bits of evidence, and then based on that conglomeration, you make a generalization. For instance, let's say you noticed that Parker Posey starred in *Party Girl, Best in Show, The House of Yes, Short Cuts,* and *A Mighty Wind.* You also then realize that all of these movies are independent films. Therefore, based on all of this information, you make an argument about Parker Posey's contribution to independent film. Both approaches are valid, but each has its own pitfalls. Be sure you do not make big leaps in logic (see hasty generalization below) that you cannot support.

Papers that have deductive reasoning almost always begin with a thesis or main argument. Most professors prefer this type of reasoning because it indicates that the author has thought about his or her argument in advance. However, the inductive approach can also be effective in certain situations, particularly those where the writer has established her credibility. Typically, essays that follow the inductive model build an argument over the course of the essay and position the thesis near the end. While this strategy is valid, it can be more difficult for beginning writers to execute. Writing instructors tend to favor essays written in the deductive model because the formula is simpler—the writer places the thesis near the beginning of the essay and spends the rest of the paper unpacking, proving, and supporting that thesis.

## Consider thinking like a lawyer when building an argument— make a case and prove it.

One of the best ways of making and proving an assertion with insight, clarity and thoroughness is through what rhetoricians have come to call the Toulmin system. This term was derived from Stephen Toulmin, a British philosopher, who argued that the best way to win an argument is by making a *strong case*. This may sound like stating the obvious, but it really isn't. Rather than relying on airtight data to make an argument, Toulmin argued that in real-life situations, you can never be 100 percent certain of something. Someone will *always* have a comeback or an opposing view to counter yours. So, for Toulmin (and many writing teachers), you make an argument by building a case, like a lawyer would in a trial. And, in essence, Toulmin's system resembles legal reasoning in that it makes a case and lays down evidence rather than pretending you have achieved complete certainty. Toumlin's system is useful because it does not insist on absolutes, which is important when writing about texts as subjective as those in popular culture. It is next to impossible to be "right" about what a movie like *Office Space* means, but it is possible to be convincing about your particular interpretation. You can't say with complete certainty why everyone who did liked *Office Space*, but it is possible to make a strong case about why students like *Office Space*.

According to Toulmin, one makes a convincing case by first making a "claim," then by citing a "datum," or evidence, that would prompt someone to make a claim in the first place, then, one offers support for that datum via what he calls a "warrant." A warrant is a statement that underscores the logical connection between the claim and evidence. For instance, if you park your car outside a store, go inside, and return and it is gone, and say, "My car has been stolen," you are relying on the warrant that a car that is missing from a place one has left it must be stolen. Your claim: "My car has been stolen." Your datum: The car is missing. The warrant: Cars that are missing must have been stolen. But of course, another warrant could be argued—"a car that is missing might have been towed." The warrant is legitimized by what Toulmin calls "backing" or additional evidence.

How would this system work when arguing about popular culture? We'll use another film example. Say that you have noticed something about recent gangster movies. You have observed that since *Reservoir Dogs* and *Pulp Fiction* were released, the gangster genre has become increasingly popular. Based on these this observation, one could make an argument that Quentin Tarantino, the director for both movies, has had a rather significant impact on gangster films. In doing some research, we discovered that a number of recent directors cited either *Reservoir Dogs* or *Pulp Fiction* when asked about their films. In the car example, the backing might be that you have parked in a high-crime era or in a tow-away zone, depending on the warrant you use. According to Toulmin, we have here all the necessary information to make a convincing case:

> *Claim:* Quentin Tarantino has had a significant impact on the gangster movie genre.
>
> *Datum:* Two popular gangster movies, *Reservoir Dogs* and *Pulp Fiction,* were directed by Tarantino.
>
> *Warrant:* Several directors cite either *Reservoir Dogs* or *Pulp Fiction* when talking about their own movies.
>
> *Backing:* These comments appeared in respectable, reviewed publications.

Of course, if one were to build a paper out of this system, you would need one to two more pieces of data (what we have called "points" or "reasons" earlier) and additional warrants, in this case, perhaps discussing how recent movies or television shows resemble specific scenes from the Tarantino movies.

The Toulmin system is not foolproof, but it does provide a model for argumentation, and it is particularly useful for making claims about popular culture texts or any text for which there is no clear "right" or "wrong" answer.

## Try to avoid fallacies.

Fallacies are, literally, falsities, gaps, and errors in judgment. Sometimes called "logical fallacies," these missteps are mistakes of logic, and they have been around for centuries. We are all guilty of falling into the fallacy trap now and then, but avoid that trap if possible. Here are a few of the most common:

- *The Straw Man fallacy:* when the writer sets up a fake argument or a "straw man" (an argument that doesn't really exist), only to refute it later.
- *The* ad hominem *fallacy:* Latin for "to the man," this fallacy occurs when a writer attacks a person and not an argument. When a politician accuses his detractors of personal attacks in an attempt to avoid the real issues, he is claiming that his opponents are making *ad hominem* assertions.
- *The hasty generalization:* when a writer jumps to a quick and easy conclusion without thinking through the leap logically. Using an earlier example, a hasty generalization would occur if one made an argument that Parker Posey appeared in *every* independent movie in the 1990s.
- *The* post hoc ergo propter hoc *fallacy:* Latin for "after the fact therefore because of the fact," this fallacy is a favorite among beginning writers. Literally, it means that because X comes after Y, Y must have caused X. In other words, it is a faulty cause and effect relationship. Let's say someone observes that teen violence seems to be on the rise. This person also is beginning to notice more and more video games at the local video store. The *post hoc* fallacy would occur when this person concluded that the rise in teen violence was *because* of the increased video games.
- *The vague generality:* Also a favorite among college students, the fallacy of generalization takes place when a writer makes sweeping claims about a group but provides no specific detail or evidence to back up his claim. This can happen on a micro level with an overuse of the passive voice ("it is agreed that . . ." or "it is assumed that . . .") that does not attribute responsibility. It happens on a macro level when a writer makes a broad generalization about a group of people, like immigrants, lesbians, Republicans, Jews, professors, or students. In some ways, this fallacy is the cause of racism as it assumes that behavior (or imagined behavior) of one person is shared or mimicked by an entire group. This is a dangerous strategy.
- *The* non sequitur *fallacy:* This is not a particularly common fallacy, but it is still useful to know. Latin for "it does not follow," a non sequitur is a fallacy of conclusion, like a faulty assumption. An example would be, "No woman I know talks about wanting a baby, therefore, there can't be very many women in the world who want babies."

## Use common sense.

You know what arguments are likely to persuade you. You have examples of documents in this book and elsewhere of compelling, sound, reasonable arguments. Use them as your models. The best argument is one that comes from a position of reasonableness.

Overall, making an argument is a key element of writing successful papers, perhaps more important than any other. For one, knowing what you are arguing often leads to clearer writing; it allows you to separate to some degree the processes of thinking and actually putting those thoughts onto paper. In addition, while students sometimes focus on grammatical errors or sounding smart by using sophisticated vocabulary, making clear, nuanced arguments has the best chance of making the ultimate argument—that your paper is worth reading and deserves a grade that reflects such an effort.

## PART IV. How Do I Get Info on Songs?
## Researching Popular Culture Texts ▪■▪

Thus far we have focused on the process of making arguments largely from processing and elaborating on one's observations. However, non-traditional texts can also fruitful entering points for researching questions, both large and small, about culture.

For one, non-traditional texts often raise questions about the medium from which they come. When you watch a sitcom, it might make you think about other sitcoms. When you see a painting, it might make you think of other paintings. When you walk through another university's student union, you might think about how the two student unions are related—maybe a similar type of student goes to each university, or perhaps the student unions were built in different times. You might also notice that your student union has university-owned food and drink places, but your friend's union has chain restaurants. Researching the history of student unions would produce one type of paper, probably one more historical in nature, while researching the presence of corporations on campus would produce a paper that explored more explicitly political issues (the presence of corporations on campus is a highly sensitive issues for many associated with higher education). In either case, your walk through a public space might suggest to you some avenues for research.

Non-traditional texts also can raises issues about gender, race, and class, among other things. When observing stereotyped behavior on sitcoms, as Archana Mehta does when watching *Will & Grace,* it can make you think about how other television shows present the same behavior, and perhaps how other creative genres do as well. In her essay, "Society's Need for a *Queer* Solution: The Media's Reinforcement of Homophobia Through Traditional Gender Roles," in the television chapter, Mehta researched this very question in order to put her viewing into a larger context.

Non-traditional texts can also be places where one might explore how abstract concepts play out in practice, through portrayals of popular culture, as Katherine Gantz does with *Seinfeld* and the lens of queer theory. Gantz uses the concept of queerness (which is different than homosexuality) to demonstrate how *Seinfeld*'s characters have complicated relationships that test traditional definitions of masculinity. Queerness does not have to be the only lens—one could certainly use *Seinfeld* to explore issues of feminism, racism, and regionalism in current society. *Seinfeld* is ideal for this task because 1) it was for a number of years the most popular show in the country, and 2) it remains an active presence on television through syndication (reruns). That said, exploring such concepts in other, less popular media also has its value.

There are other ways of using non-traditional texts to engage research, but these methods are worth talking about further, because they offer relatively straightforward ways of using research to enhance understanding of both the texts at hand and the culture at large. In the first way of researching popular culture, the one employed in student unions, the text is a *window* to further exploration of issues such as the corporatization of universities or the function of the environment in student lives.

In the second approach (Mehta's), examining the text and stereotypes in it, the text itself is the focus, using research to undercut the notion that *Will & Grace* is an enlightened show when it comes to its portrayal of gay characters. In the third approach, the lens one looks at the non-traditional text through is the focus; the non-traditional text is more a means to further discussion and elaboration of the concepts. In other words, *queerness* is the focus of Gantz's essay more than *Seinfeld*. All three approaches share the idea that these texts matter— that they reflect larger concerns in society.

There are other reasons why researching non-traditional texts might seem daunting. You may ask yourself who could have possibly written about Barbie dolls or *The Matrix*. Or you may not have written a paper that engages popular culture as a research topic. After all, isn't research about "serious" topics? Traditionally, you have probably written research papers about historical events or movements, or about the author of a literary work, or perhaps literary movements. Although research of non-traditional texts may seem more difficult, students writing research papers about popular culture have a lot of resources at their disposal. There is a large and ever-increasing amount of work written on popular culture, such as music, the movies, technology, art, found objects, television, etc. There's even more work done on the more political elements of this textbook such as gender and media.

Because researching popular culture topics seems daunting, you might be tempted to amass as much information as possible before beginning your writing. However, we believe that one of the best ways of researching a paper about popular culture is to make sure you have a take on whatever text you are analyzing before researching. That way, you have your ideas to use as a sounding board for others that might come your way. Finding out what you think about the text will also allow you to research more effectively and probably more efficiently.

Generally, the trick to researching papers about popular culture is not only to find work that engages your specific topic, but something general or *contextual* about your topic. In the case of *The Matrix* (2000) a film popular with both viewers and critics, science fiction movies would be a good general subject to look up, but so would "computers and culture." Broadly defined, *The Matrix* is a science fiction movie, but it's also a movie "about" the roles of computers in society. One of the movie's primary arguments is that our culture is quickly moving toward one that is run by computers with decreasing human control. That's the subject of more than a few movies, including *2001: A Space Odyssey* and *I, Robot,* but its message is even more crucial given the remarkable growth of the Internet over the last decade. One could research the philosophical argument the movie is making, that man and computers are somewhat at odds. One could research how other movies or books have treated this subject both within the science fiction genre and outside it. The movie also has a political bent, about the nature of not only computers but corporations, who seem to run Neo's life before he realizes what the Matrix is. It's also about the culture of computers, which Neo is immersed in before his transformation. It's also about the future as well as the present, a temporal argument (about time). All these contexts—philosophical, genre-based, cultural, political, temporal—have strong research possibilities. You could write compelling papers on each of these topics, and each would be very different from the others. You can also see why understanding what you are arguing will affect how you research a topic.

Another possibility for research is music CDs. Instead of thinking of particular contexts right away, you might begin by asking some questions of the text. For example, take as a text Johnny Cash's album *Solitary Man: American Recordings III,* which came out in 1999. Johnny Cash was a musician who recorded music for almost 50 years; he received his start about the same time and in the same place as Elvis Presley but had the same record producer as the Beastie Boys, a popular rap group. Such biographical constructions may shape your paper's direction, or they may not. In either case, in writing this paper, you might listen to the album and note some of the themes, symbols, and ideas. You might ask yourself: Was Johnny Cash writing about issues he had written about before? You could find this out by listening to other albums or seeking research materials about his recording career. You could also ask: What is it about the life of Cash that made him write songs like this? Material contained either in biographies of Cash himself or general histories of country music would help this paper. Another question: Is Johnny Cash part of the recognizable genre of country music or a different genre altogether? Again, a general work about country music will enable you to answer this question. Any of these questions can be the beginning of a good research paper. If you decided to focus only on the album, you could also read other reviews, and after you have staked out your own position, argue against other readings of this album.

Movies and music are good choices for research because they are texts that in some ways mirror traditional texts—movies have narratives like novels, and songs have lyrics that resemble poetry. But even found objects have strong possibilities for research. Objects like cars or dolls are not only easily described but have long traditions of scholarship, especially within cultural contexts. In the case of dolls, histories of dolls in American culture or the role of toys would provide historical contexts for your arguments; the same would be true for cars. As you get closer to the present, your methods of research may change. In the case of cars, current writers may not be writing about the context of a new model, but they certainly review them, and examining the criteria of car reviews may give you insight into the cultural context of a car. So might advertisements. Researching popular culture can include placing different primary sources (the source itself like *Solitary Man* or *The Matrix* or advertisements for either of these texts) in context with one another, or using secondary sources—sources about the primary text, such as reviews, or scholarly articles, ones that are peer reviewed, reviewed by experts, and often have footnotes.

The most difficult thing about doing this research, somewhat ironically, is its flexibility; once you decide on researching popular culture, many different avenues, sometimes an overwhelming number, open to you. The authors have encountered students who enjoy this type of work but are overwhelmed by the possibilities in approaching popular culture texts as researchable topics. Most students eventually come away with not only a better understanding of their particular text but of researching generally.

## Researching Non-Traditional Texts: One Method

There are any number of ways to undertake the research process with non-traditional texts, given the complexities of the intersections between texts, issues, and culture. At Virginia Commonwealth University, where Dr. Silverman once taught, the department used the same approach in the university's required sophomore researched-writing class. Each student focused on what instructors called a "cultural text," which for their purposes meant non-literary texts.

For the class, students were required in a four-step process to 1) identify and explore a particular cultural text and write about it; 2) choose research angles or avenues and write about the arguments between sources they encountered; 3) reread and write about the text through the research; and 4) merge the first three assignments. The approach mimics to some extent the way many academics work, with a focus on text and context. Archana Mehta's piece is an example on the process at work. She first chose a text she found interesting *(Will & Grace)*, explored questions the text raised (what is the nature of homosexual stereotypes?), then wrote about the show, doing a "close reading," using her newfound knowledge. A close reading examines the details of a text, but this close reading used the details combined with a better understanding of the show to write about it more comprehensively. Peter Parisi's piece also does similar work; he uses as his text the "Black Bart" t-shirt, examines the concept of audience, than examines the phenomenon of the t-shirt using the concepts he describes earlier in the piece.

The advantages of this approach are many. For one, you get a sense of how to do in-depth research that's not done for its own end but to provide better understanding of a particular topic. It also makes you as a writer learn how to incorporate others' ideas into your essay—which is what you have to do in school and long after you leave, when you have to complete market research and prepare reports.

From a purely academic perspective, this approach also demonstrates the diversity and depth of research being done on non-traditional texts and the even deeper well of information for issues of cultural significance (such as race, gender, and class). When faced with the prospect of doing in-depth college research, not to mention research on popular culture topics, students often believe there will not be enough information for their topic. Sometimes this is true, but most times the process requires some cleverness and ingenuity.

## Nuts and Bolts Research

Clearly, your university library is the place to start. Books have a much more comprehensive perspective on any possible text than most websites. Think broadly when approaching what books you might look at; think about what category the books you are looking for might fall into. One of the best ways of doing this is through a keyword search involving "the perfect book." For a book about Johnny Cash, a simple keyword search on Johnny Cash might yield some useful sources. If not, a keyword search with "history," "country," and "music" might provide some results. If it does, write down a call number, the physical address of the book in the library, and head for the stacks; most libraries have separate floors or sections for their collection of books. When you get there, find the book you have written down, but also be careful to look around on the shelves for other possibilities. Both authors have found that some of their best sources have come from browsing on the shelves of libraries.

Then it is on to periodicals. The *Reader's Guide to Periodicals* is a complete non-electronic guide to periodicals such as newspapers and major magazines. You may be tempted to skip anything not on line, but electronic sources only generally go back a decade, so for any type of historical research, you should probably hit the *Reader's Guide.*

If you do resort to the computer, try to use an electronic database your university subscribes to; search engines like Google or Yahoo! are limited in what they will come up with and may lead users to sources that are not reliable. The authors both like electronic databases like Infotrac (or Academic Search Premier) and LexisNexis, which many universities subscribe to. The overall difference between Infotrac and LexisNexis and standard Internet searching is that Infotrac and LexisNexis for the most part have articles that appear in print form, generally, though not always, making them more reliable sources. Infotrac is an index to periodicals which tend to be scholarly, with footnotes, though some more popular magazines are there as well. Some of the articles on Infotrac are full text articles, which means the full version will appear on the screen; some you will have to head to the library to find. LexisNexis contains full-text articles from most large American and European newspapers as well as many magazines. It has a database which is geared toward general news and opinion and other databases geared toward sports, arts, science, and law. If you are working with popular culture sources, the arts index, which contains reviews, may be helpful. Speaking of computers, you may also find the Library of Congress Web site, http://www.loc.gov, or WorldCat helpful to find if there are any books on the subject; you can then use your library's interlibrary loan to request a needed book. Be aware, however, that some books may take some time to arrive from another library to yours. The Library of Congress site also has an excellent collection of images. Overall, in doing research, be creative and thorough.

## Guerilla Research

Okay, if you've exhausted your library options, and you *still* can't find what you need, try a bookstore like Borders or Barnes & Noble. Bring some index cards and a notebook, and take notes on the books you want. And if you want an alternative, look at Amazon.com, where you can research books, movies, and albums; sometimes you can see what you need, especially bibliographic information, in Amazon's "look inside the book" feature.

# PART V. How Do I Know What a Good Paper Looks Like? An Annotated Student Essay ▪ ▪

Sometimes, students have the ability to write good papers; they just can't visualize them. They simply don't know what a good paper *looks* like, what its components are.

An annotated student paper appears on the following pages. You will see that we have highlighted the positive aspects of the essay and also some elements that need work. (Careful readers might notice additional stylistic and formatting inconsistencies.) One thing we like about this piece is a good move from general information to specific. The best papers are those with a clear, narrow focus. This student's thesis is also clear and well developed.

An unannotated version of this essay appears later in Chapter 10 if you want to consult it again. Sample student papers appear throughout *The World Is a Text.*

Compton 1

Matt Compton

Professor Silverman

English 101

9 December 2001

"Smells Like Teen Spirit"

In 1991 a song burst forth onto the music scene that articulated so perfectly the emotions of America's youth that the song's writer was later labeled the voice of a generation (Moon). That song was Nirvana's "Smells Like Teen Spirit," and the writer was Kurt Cobain; one of the most common complaints of the song's critics was that the lyrics were unintelligible (Rawlins). But while some considered the song to be unintelligible, to many youth in the early 90s, it was exactly what they needed to hear. Had the song been presented differently, then the raw emotions that it presented would have been tamed. If the lyrics had been perfectly articulated, then the feelings that the lyrics express would have been less articulate, because the feelings that he was getting across were not clear in themselves. One would know exactly what Kurt Cobain was saying, but not exactly what he was feeling. The perfect articulation of those raw emotions, shared by so many of America's youth, was conveyed with perfect inarticulation.

1991 was a year when the music scene had become a dilute, lukewarm concoction being spoon-fed to the masses by corporations (Cohen). The charts and the radio were being dominated by "hair bands" and pop ballads; popular music at the time was making a lot of noise without saying anything (Cohen). Behind the scenes "underground" music had been thriving since the early eighties. Much of this underground music was making a meaningful statement, but these musicians shied away from the public eye. The general public knew little about them, because they had adopted the ideology that going public was selling out (Dettmar). Nirvana was a part of this "underground" music scene.

In 1991 Nirvana broke the credo, signing with a major label, DGC, under which they released the chart-smashing *Nevermind*. "Smells Like

---

*Marginal notes:*

The title appears in quotes because it represents a song title.

Good beginning—the "burst forth" is passive but here it seems to work.

Good clarification, although he almost moves too quickly into unintelligibility.

This is a strong explanation, although it probably could have been condensed a bit.

The thesis is great—it's argumentative and clever. We know here what the rest of the paper is about. However, the passive "was conveyed" could be turned into the active "Cobain conveyed."

The writer gives a good background of the atmosphere before the song. Those more familiar with the era might raise objections to the definitiveness of the conclusion—but he uses a source to back up his opinion. We may not agree but have to respect this research.

Compton 2

Teen Spirit" was the first single from the record, and it became a huge hit quickly (Cohen). Nirvana stepped up and spoke for the twenty something generation, which wasn't exactly sure what it wanted to say (Azerrad 223–233). A huge part of America's youth felt exactly what Cobain was able to convey through not just "Smells Like Teen Spirit" but all of his music. Nirvana shot into superstar status and paved the way for an entire "grunge" movement (Moon). No one complained that they could not hear Cobain, but many did complain that they could not understand what he was saying.

The topic sentence is weak here—there's a lot going on in this paragraph and the first sentence and even the second don't adequately prepare the reader for the information.

Kurt Cobain did not want his music to just be heard and appreciated; he wanted it to be "felt" (Moon). His music often showed a contrast of emotions; it would change from a soft lull, to a screaming rage suddenly. And few could scream with rage as could Cobain (Cohen). There is a Gaelic word, "yarrrrragh," which ". . . refers to that rare quality that some voices have, an edge, an ability to say something about the human condition that goes far beyond merely singing the right lyrics and hitting the right notes." This word was once used to describe Cobain's voice by Ralph J. Gleason, *Rolling Stone* critic (Azerrad 231). It was that voice, that uncanny ability to show emotions that Cobain demonstrated in "Smells Like Teen Spirit."

The information itself is good—he's revisiting the ideas he talked about in his thesis, which in some ways makes up for the lack of organization in this paragraph.

Good move to the songwriter, Kurt Cobain, though the transition might have been stronger. Good topic sentence.

Cool Gaelic reference. Excellent research (though he could have cited a little more elegantly).

Cobain's raging performance spoke to young Americans in a way that no one had in a long while (Moon). Michael Azerrad wrote in his 1993 book, *Come as You Are: The Story of Nirvana,* "Ultimately it wasn't so much that Nirvana was saying anything new about growing up in America; it was the way they said it" (Azerrad 226). Cobain's music was conveying a feeling through the way that he performed. It was a feeling shared by many of America's youth, but it was also a feeling that could not have been articulated any other way than the way that Cobain did it (Cohen).

Another good topic sentence.

Again a good use of research, though the repetition of Azerrad is unnecessary in parentheses.

The strong final sentence supports not only the topic sentence of the paragraph but also the thesis of the paper.

"Smells Like Teen Spirit" starts out with one of the most well-known guitar riffs of the 90s. The four chord progression was certainly nothing new, nothing uncommon. The chords are played with a single guitar with no distortion, and then suddenly the bass and drums come

This topic sentence is a bit on the narrative side and does not connect well with the previous paragraph.

Compton 3

in. When the drums and bass come in the guitar is suddenly distorted, and the pace and sound of the song changes. The song's introduction, with its sudden change, forms a rhythmic "poppy" chord progression to a raging, thrashing of the band's instruments (Moon), sets the pace for the rest of the song.

The chaos from the introduction fades, and it leads in to the first verse, which gives the listener a confused feeling (Azerrad 213). In the first verse the tune of the song is carried by the drums and bass alone, and a seemingly lonely two-note guitar part that fades in and out of the song. The bass, drums and eerie guitar give the listener a "hazy" feeling. Here Cobain's lack of articulation aids in the confused feeling, because as he sings, one can catch articulate phrases here and there. The words that the listener can discern allow them to draw their own connections. Cobain's lyrics do in fact carry a confused message, "It's fun to lose, and to pretend" (Azerrad 213).

The pre-chorus offers up clear articulation of a single word, but this articulation is the perfect precursor to the coming chorus. As the first verse ends, the pre-chorus comes in; Cobain repeats the word "Hello" fifteen times. The repetition of the word Hello draws the confusion that he implicates in the first verse to a close, and in a way reflects on it. As the tone and inflection of his voice changes each time he quotes "Hello," one is not sure whether he is asking a question or making a statement, or both. It is like he is saying, "Hello? Is anybody at home?" while at the same time he exclaims, "Wake up and answer the door!"

The reflection that he implicates in the pre-chorus builds to the raw raging emotions that he expresses in the chorus, as the guitar suddenly becomes distorted, and he begins to scream (Azerrad 214, 226). In the chorus he screams, but somehow the words in the chorus are actually more articulate than those in the verse. As Cobain sings, "I feel stupid, and contagious," anyone who has ever felt like a social outcast understands exactly what Cobain is saying (Cohen), and they understand exactly why he must scream it.

I remember the first time that I heard that line and thinking about it; I was about thirteen, and I thought that there was no better word than

---

*The description does an excellent job of describing how the song sounds. It's a very difficult task to do this well.*

*This is a very good topic sentence—it not only leads us from the last paragraph but also sums up the current one.*

*Good quote from the song. (He might have cited the song itself, but wanted to include Azerrad's ideas.)*

*Another good topic sentence. And here the transition is much better implied than in those earlier mentioned.*

*An insightful analysis of what seems to be a pretty simple lyric. This is excellent work—complicating the simple is a staple of good work in reading culture. The writer also makes a good analogy here.*

*Omit unnecessary "actually."*

*Again, good reading of the song. So far the writer has done a lot of strong work in (1) contextualizing the song, (2) studying its music, and (3) analyzing its lyrics. It's almost a formula for doing this type of work.*

Compton 4

"*contagious*" to describe the way it feels being in a social situation and not being accepted. Because no one wants to be around that person, they will look at the person with disgust, as if they have some highly *contagious* disease. There is certainly a lot of anger and confusion surrounding those feelings. People needed to hear Cobain scream; they knew how he felt, because they knew how they felt.

This personal aside adds to the paper in our opinion—but you should check with your teacher before including it.

People who were experiencing what Cobain was expressing understood what he was saying, because they understood how he felt. In much the same way when someone hits their hand with a hammer that person does not lay down the hammer and calmly say, "Ouch, man that really hurt." They throw the hammer down, and simultaneously yell an obscenity, or make an inarticulate roar, and one knows that they are going to lose a fingernail. Anyone who has smashed their finger with a hammer understands why that person is yelling; in the same way anyone who has felt "contagious" or confused about society knows why Cobain is screaming about feeling "stupid and contagious." Cobain is not examining society. He is experiencing the same things as his audience (Moon); he is "going to lose a fingernail." As the chorus draws to a close, the music still rages, but it changes tempo and rhythm slightly.

Another analogy— comparison, done in reasonable doses, is an effective technique in doing analysis, particularly if one does it thoughtfully.

The move back to narrative is jarring.

The chorus is the most moving part of the song; it is a display of pure emotion. In the chorus Cobain demonstrates what it was that connected with so many; his lyrics said what he meant (Moon). But what he said had been said before, and whether he was articulate or not, people felt what he meant. It was the articulation of that feeling that gained the song such high praise (Moon).

Good topic sentence, though it could be condensed into one sentence.

The chorus ends with the phrase, "A mulatto, an albino, a mosquito, my libido"; this line is a reference to social conformity. Cobain is referring to things, or the ideas associated with them that are "outside" of social conformity, and then relating those things back to himself with the phrase "my libido" (Azerrad 210–215). This end to the chorus again goes back to reflect on the feelings expressed in the chorus, and ties them together with a return to the confusion expressed in the verses.

See above—the topic sentence is doing excellent work but not doing it as "writerly" as it could be done.

Compton 5

The articulation of the lyrics in the second verse gives the confusion more focus than in the first verse. He begins the second verse with the lyric, "I'm worse at what I do best, and for this gift I feel blessed." Although the lyrics are more articulate in the second verse, the feelings of confusion are still there, due to the tempo and rhythm of the music. After Cobain has sung the second verse he returns to the prechorus, the repetition of the word Hello. The cycle begins anew.

*We like the way the writer connects ideas, music, and lyrics together again.*

"Smells Like Teen Spirit" in its entirety gives the listener a complete feeling after listening to it, especially if that listener is feeling confused and frustrated. The song carries one through an entire cycle of emotions, from confusion, to reflection, to frustration. Tom Moon, a Knight-Ridder Newspaper writer, described Nirvana's music as having moments of "tension and release." Being carried through those emotions allows the listener to "vent" their own feelings of confusion and frustration, and at the same time know that someone else feels the same way (Azerrad 226–227). Despite the connection that Cobain made with many there were still many who did not "get" the song; these people often complained about the inarticulation of the lyrics (Azerrad 210).

*Good summary of the song's meaning/content. The writer does a good job of making sure the reader is following his argument.*

Weird Al Yankovic utilized the common criticism of the song in his parody "Smells Like Nirvana"; Yankovic parodied "Smells Like Teen Spirit," based entirely on Cobain's obscure articulation. Yankovic is known for parodying popular music, and with lines such as, "And I'm yellin' and I'm screamin', but I don't know what I'm saying," Yankovic stated exactly what so many of the song's critiques had, though he did it with a genuine respect for the song, and its impact (Rawlins).

*Now, he switches to other voices. Because the choice is both surprising and apt, the use of Weird Al is a good choice for a source/comparison.*

Weird Al Yankovic's version struck a note with many who liked Cobain's music but could not understand his lyrics (Rawlins). There were many people who did not understand the feelings of confusion, frustration, and apathy that Cobain was getting across. In 1991 when "Smells Like Teen Spirit" first came out I was only 9, and I did not like that kind of music at all. I remember my brother, who is nine years older than me, and who listened to a lot of "heavy metal," bought Yankovic's *Off the Deep End,* with his parody "Smells Like Nirvana" on it. He

*Again, we like the personal reference. It's not as relevant as the other one, but it somehow gives the argument more weight if we know where the writer is "coming from."*

Compton 6

thought it was funny because he did not like Nirvana. He never really connected with Cobain's message; even though he did not get what Cobain was saying, he could still enjoy the music. When I became older I did connect with Cobain's music, and Nirvana was one of my favorite bands. My brother never did understand, like many people who never did understand what it was that Cobain was saying (Azerrad 210).

Nirvana made the generation gap clear. It was Nirvana that spoke for a large part of that generation (Moon), where no one else had ever really addressed the confusion and frustration about growing up in America at that time, or at least no one had expressed it in the same way that Nirvana did. They were not the first to vocalize a problem with corporate America, but they were the first *popular* band to convey the feelings that many were feeling *because* of growing up in corporate America, in the way that they did. Cobain did not just show that he has experienced those feelings, but that he was still *experiencing* them, and many young people connected with that (Moon).

In 1992 singer-songwriter Tori Amos illustrated why Cobain's "Smells Like Teen Spirit" had connected with so many by making a cover of the song that was a clear contrast to the original. She rendered the song with a piano, and a clear articulate voice. Her cover of the song became fairly popular, because it was different, and because many people could now understand the lyrics that Cobain had already popularized (Rawlins). The cover was interesting, to say the least; however, it would have been impossible for her version ever to have had the same impact as Cobain's (Rawlins). The lyrics to the song have meaning, and depth, but the emotions that the song conveyed were in and of themselves abstract.

Amos's version of the song articulated each word clearly, her clear voice hit each note on key; her song was comparable to a ballad. Cobain's "Smells Like Teen Spirit" could be described as "sloppy," his guitar distorted through much of the song; he either screamed or mumbled most of the song (Azerrad 214). The two versions of the song illustrate a clear contrast: it is as if Cobain is "angry about being confused" (Azerrad 213), while Amos sings the song to lament Cobain's feelings.

---

The transition isn't strong here, but the topic sentence is good . . . it again summarizes—this time the band, not the song.

The corporate America reference is not clear here. As readers, we vaguely know what he is talking about, but he doesn't use sources in the same way he has when making similar points.

Again, the writer puts comparison to good use. Some writers make the mistake of doing multiple comparisons which all make the same point. Here the writer uses Tori Amos, whose work is very different from that of both Nirvana and Weird Al, to useful effect—reinforcing his argument.

Compton 7

Amos's version of the song became popular for the same reason that it could never have paved the way as Cobain's version did. It was like a ballad, and after everyone heard what Cobain was saying, about society, about America, about growing up, there is one clear emotion that follows the confusion and frustration: sadness. Her "ballad-like" cover of "Smells Like Teen Spirit" exemplified that sadness. But at the same time, people had written ballads about being confused or frustrated, and performed them as Amos performed "Smells Like Teen Spirit"; that was nothing new. However, no one had yet demonstrated such clear and yet abstract confused, frustrated emotions as Cobain did, and at that moment in time that was exactly what America needed to hear (Azerrad 224–225).

> The writer does a good job of extending the comparison as a way of bringing his own argument to a close.

Cobain had written and performed a song about his own confusion, and in the process he had connected with young people all over the United States (Moon). He had helped those people to understand their own confusion better. The problem with "Smells Like Teen Spirit" was not that Cobain was not articulate; he could not have articulated his point more clearly than he did. The problem was that not everyone knew what he was talking about, just like not everyone knows what it is like to strike their finger with a hammer. And in the same way, if someone doesn't know what it is like they might say something foolish like, "That couldn't *hurt* that bad," or "What's *his* problem?" when someone else hits their finger with a hammer, and they make an inarticulate roar. That roar expresses exactly what that person is feeling, but only those who know that feeling, can really understand it. As Michael Azerrad, author of *Come as You Are: The Story of Nirvana*, put it, "you either get it, or you don't" (Azerrad 227). Thus was the case with Cobain's music. "Smells Like Teen Spirit" was his inarticulate roar; it was articulate in that it expressed exactly what he was trying to point out; however, not everyone could grasp what that was.

> The conclusion approaches, with the writer putting the work into final context.

> The conclusion could be a little stronger—the writer might have taken this argument beyond Nirvana or put it in a little greater context. He chose instead to close the work by restating the thesis, which is an acceptable way to end the paper. Overall, the work this paper does is outstanding—it approaches a "cultural text"—a famous song and brings the reader multiple perspectives on it, using comparison, literary and sound analysis, and analogy. It's a good model for doing this type of work.

Compton 8

Works Cited

Azerrad, Michael. *Come as You Are.* New York: Doubleday, 1993.

Cohen, Howard, and Leonard Pitts. "Kurt Cobain Made Rock for Everyone
 but Kurt Cobain." *Knight Ridder/Tribune* 8 Apr. 1994. Infotrac.

Dettmar, Kevin. "Uneasy Listening, Uneasy Commerce." *The Chronicle of
 Higher Education.* 14 Sept. 2001: 18. LexisNexis.

Moon, Tom. "Reluctant Spokesman for Generation Became the Rock Star
 He Abhorred." *Knight Ridder/Tribune* 9 Apr. 1994. Infotrac.

Nirvana. *Nevermind.* David Geffen Company, 1991.

Rawlins, Melissa. "From Bad to Verse." *Entertainment Weekly* 5 June 1992: 57.
 Infotrac.

## PART VI. How Do I Cite This Car?
## Guidelines for Citing Popular Culture Texts ▪■▪

As you probably know, you must cite or acknowledge any kind of text (written or otherwise) that you use in an academic or professional essay. Most students think that citing work
has mostly to do with avoiding plagiarism—and that's certainly an important part of it—
but there are other reasons why citing work is important.

As a researcher, your job is often to make sense of a particular phenomenon and in
doing so, make sense of the work done before you on the same subject. When you do that,
you perform a valuable service for your reader, who now not only has your perspective on
this phenomenon but also has an entry into the subject through the sources you cite. For this
very reason, professional researchers and academics often find the works cited pages and
footnotes as interesting as the text itself.

As writers in the humanities, you will typically use MLA (Modern Language Association) formatting in your papers. There are two other major forms of citing—APA (American Psychological Association), often used in the social sciences and science, and "Chicago"
or "Turabian," often used in history and political science.

All three ways of citing are part of a *system* of citation. How you cite (say where information comes from) is directly related to the bibliography or, in the case of MLA, the works cited
page. You indicate in the text who wrote the article or book, and at the end of the paper, the
sources are listed in alphabetical order, so the reader can see the whole work, but without the
intrusion of listing that whole work within the text; seeing (Alvarez 99) is much easier than seeing (Alvarez, Julia. *How the Garcia Girls Lost Their Accents.* New York: Plume, 1992) in an essay.

### Using Parenthetical References

In MLA, you cite using parenthetical references within the body of your essay. The format for the
parenthetical reference is easy. If you know the author's name, you include the author's last name
and the page number(s) in parentheses *before* the punctuation mark. For instance, if you are
quoting from LeAnne Howe's novel *Shell Shaker,* your parenthetical reference would look like this:

The novel *Shell Shaker* does a great job of conveying Choctaw pride: "I decide that as a final gesture I will show the people my true self. After all, I am a descendent of two powerful ancestors, Grandmother of Birds and Tuscalusa" (Howe 15).

If the author's name has already been used in the text in a particular reference (not earlier in the essay), then you simply need to provide the page number (15). If there are two or three authors, then list the authors' last names and the page number (Silverman and Rader 23). For more than three authors, use et al. (Baym et al. 234).

The same holds true for citing an article. Simply list the last name of the author of the article or story or poem, followed by the page number (Wright 7). You don't need to list the title of the book or magazine.

If you use works from the Internet, the system of citing is the same, except you sometimes do not have page numbers, and you often cannot find authors (though you should look hard—sometimes the authorship appears at the end of the text, rather than the beginning). In citing an article from the Internet, use if you can the page's title, rather than the home page. For example, if you are looking at admissions policies at Virginia Commonwealth University, you come to the page and it says "Admissions" at the top. You would then in the text, after your information, type: ("Admissions")—not "Virginia Commonwealth University" and *definitely not* the webpage address: http://www.vcu.edu/admissions. This form of citing also applies to non-Internet articles without authors. Some of your professors may ask you to tell them from which paragraph the information comes. If that is the case, your in-text citation might look like this: ("Admissions" par. 2).

## Building the Works Cited Page

A works cited page consists of an alphabetized list of the texts that you cite in your paper. This list goes at the end of an essay in MLA format. This list tells your readers all of the pertinent publication information for each source. It is alphabetized by the last name of the author or, if there is no author, by the title or name of the text. Generally, works cited pages start on a new page and bear the heading "Works Cited." For books, you will use the following format, not indenting the first line but indenting the remaining lines.

Clements, Brian. *Essays against Ruin.* Huntsville: Texas Review Press, 1997.

Notice the crucial aspects in this citation—the author's name, the title of the work, the date it was published, and who was responsible for publishing it. The general rule of citing work is to find all four of these elements in order to help a fellow researcher (or your teacher) find the source and to give appropriate credit to both those who wrote the book and who brought the book to the attention of the general public. Of course, citing a magazine requires a different format but with the same idea, as does citing a Web page or a song or a movie. We have provided examples of many different sources below.

## Plagiarism

Citing your work is critical. If you quote from a text in your paper, or if you use information in any way but do not cite this source, the use of this material is plagiarism. At most institutions, plagiarism is grounds for failing the assignment and even the class. At many universities and colleges, students can be dismissed from the institution entirely if plagiarism can be proven.

A student can commit plagiarism in several different ways. One is the deliberate misrepresentation of someone else's work as your own—if you buy a paper off the Internet, get a friend's paper and turn it is as your own, or pay someone to write the paper, you are committing the most serious form of plagiarism.

Then there is the above example of using someone's work in your text but without citing it, which is also a serious offense. Some students do this inadvertently—they forget where their ideas came from, or mean to find out where the information came from later but do not. Still others want their teacher to think they are intelligent and think that using someone else's work may help. The irony of the last way of thinking is that teachers will often be more impressed by the student who has taken the time to do research and thoughtfully incorporate those ideas into a paper—that's what real researchers do.

It is also possible to commit plagiarism without such intent. If you do not paraphrase a source's work completely—even if you cite the source—that is also plagiarism.

Besides the general ethical problem using someone else's work as your own, the more practical issue with plagiarizing is that you are likely to get caught. As teachers, we become so familiar with the student voice in writing, and a particular student's voice, that it is often not very difficult to catch a cheating student.

## Works Cited Examples

The examples below cover most citation contingencies; however, if you have trouble deciding how to cite a source, there are a number of options. The best option will be to consult the *MLA Handbook for Writers of Research Papers,* which your library will own, if you do not. Otherwise, you can find any number of World Wide Web pages that provide examples of MLA documentation. We recommend the Purdue Writing Center site (http://owl.english.purdue.edu/) and the award-winning "Guide for Writing Research Papers" site at Capitol Community College (http://webster.commnet.edu/mla.htm).

### Citing Books

Book entries include the following information: Author's last name, Author's first name. *Title.* City of publication: Publisher, year of publication.

### A Book by a Single Author

Clements, Brian. *Essays Against Ruin.* Huntsville: Texas Review Press, 1997.

**A Book by Two or Three Authors.** After the first author, list subsequent authors' names in published (*not* alphabetical) order.

Clements, Brian and Joe Ahearn, eds. *Best Texas Writing.* Dallas: Rancho Loco Press, 1997.

**Two or More Books by the Same Author.** Arrange entries alphabetically by title. After the first entry, use three hyphens instead of the author's name.

Garber, Frederick. *Thoreau's Fable of Inscribing.* Princeton: Princeton UP, 1991.
---.    *Thoreau's Redemptive Imagination.* New York: NYU Press, 1977.

### An Anthology or Compilation

Silverman, Jonathan and Dean Rader, eds. *The World Is a Text: Writing, Reading, and Thinking about Culture and Its Contexts.* New York: Prentice Hall, 2003.

## A Book by a Corporate Author

Bay Area AIDS Foundation. *Report on Diversity: 2001.* San Francisco: City Lights Books, 2001.

## A Book with No Author

*A History of Weatherford, Oklahoma.* Hinton: Southwest Publishers, 1998.

**A Government Publication.** If no author is known, begin with the government's name, and then add the department or agency and any subdivision. For the U.S. government, the Government Printing Office (GPO) is usually the publisher.

United States. Forest Service. Alaska Region. *Skipping Cow Timber Sale, Tongass National Forest: Final EIS Environmental Impact Statement and Record of Decision.* Wrangell: USDA Forest Service, 2000.

## The Published Proceedings of a Conference

Ward, Scott, Tom Robertson, and Ray Brown, eds. *Commercial Television and European Children: an International Research Digest. Proceedings of the Research Conference, "International Perspectives on Television Advertising and Children: The Role of Research for Policy Issues in Europe," Held in Provence, France, July 1st–3rd 1984.* Brookfield: Gower, 1986.

## An Edition Other Than the First

Gibaldi, Joseph. *MLA Handbook for Writers of Research Papers.* 5th ed. New York: Modern Language Association, 1999.

## Citing Articles

Articles use a similar format as books; however, you will need to include information for the article and the source of its publication. They follow the following format:

Author(s). "Title of Article." *Title of source* day month year: pages.

For newspapers and magazines, the month or the day and the month appear before the year, and no parentheses are used. When quoting from a scholarly journal, the year of publication is in parentheses. When citing articles from periodicals, the month (except May, June, and July) is abbreviated.

## An Article from a Reference Book

Deignan, Hebert G. "Dodo." *Collier's Encyclopedia.* 1997 ed.
Voigt, David G. "America's Game: A Brief History of Baseball." *Encyclopedia of Baseball.* 9th ed. New York: MacMillan, 1993. 3–13.

## An Article in a Scholarly Journal

Crawford, Rachel. "English Georgic and British Nationhood." *ELH* 65.1 (1998): 23–59.
Ingrassia, Catherine. "Writing the West: Iconic and Literal Truth in *Unforgiven*." *Literature—Film Quarterly* 26.1 (1998): 53–60.

**A Work in an Anthology.** Begin with the author of the poem, article, or story. That title will go in quotation marks. Then, cite the anthology as above. Include the page numbers of the text you use at the end of the citation.

Haven, Chris. "Assisted Living." *The World Is a Text: Writing, Reading, and Thinking about Culture and Its Contexts.* Ed. Jonathan Silverman and Dean Rader. New York: Prentice Hall, 2003. 89–99.

### An Article in a Monthly Magazine

Sweany, Brian D. "Mark Cuban is Not Just a Rich Jerk." *Texas Monthly* March 2002: 74–77.

### An Article in a Weekly Magazine.
If the article does not continue on consecutive pages, denote this with a plus sign (+).

Gladwell, Malcolm. "The Coolhunt." *The New Yorker* 17 Mar. 1997: 78+.

### An Article in a Newspaper

Hax, Carolyn. "Tell Me About It." *The Washington Post* 29 Mar. 2002: C8.

### An Article with No Author

"Yankees Net Bosox." *The Richmond Times-Dispatch* 1 September 2001: D5.

### A Letter to the Editor

McCrimmon, Miles. "Let Community Colleges Do Their Jobs." *The Richmond Times-Dispatch* 9 Mar. 1999: F7.

Silverman, Melvin J. "We Must Restore Higher Tax on Top Incomes." *The New York Times* 8 Mar. 1992: E14.

### A Review

Smith, Mark C. Rev. of *America First! Its History, Culture, and Politics,* by Bill Kauffman. *Journal of Church and State* 39 (1997): 374–375.

### A Cartoon

Jim. Cartoon. *I Went to College and It Was Okay.* Kansas City: Andrews and McNeel, 1991. N. pag.

### Electronic Sources

### A Book Published Online.
If known, the author's name goes first, followed by the title of the document or page in quotation marks. If the document/page is part of a larger work, like a book or a journal, then that title is underlined. Include the date of publication, the date of access if known, and the address or URL (uniform resource locator) in angle brackets.

Savage, Elizabeth. "Art Comes on Laundry Day." *Housekeeping—A Chapbook. The Pittsburgh Quarterly Online.* Ed. Michael Simms. Dec. 1997. 20 Mar. 2002 <http://trfn.clpgh.org/tpq/hkeep.html>.

### An Article from a Website

Silverman, Jason. "*2001:* A Re-Release Odyssey." *Wired News* 13 Oct. 2001. 20 Mar. 2002 <http://www.wired.com/news/digiwood/0,1412,47432,00.html>.

### A Review

Svalina, Mathias. Rev. of *I Won't Tell a Soul Except the World,* by Ran Away to Sea. *Lost at Sea* July 2001. 2 Mar. 2002 <http://lostatsea.net/LAS/archives/reviews/records/ranawaytosea.htm>.

**A Mailing List, Newsgroup, or E-Mail Citation.** If known, the author's name goes first, followed by the subject line in quotations, the date of the posting, the name of the forum, the date of access and, in angle brackets, the online address of the list's Internet site. If no Internet site is known, provide the e-mail address of the list's moderator or supervisor.

### An E-Mail to You

Brennan, Brian. "GLTCs." E-mail to the author. 21 Mar. 2002.

### An Electronic Encyclopedia

"Alcatraz Island." *Encyclopedia Britannica.* 3 Apr. 2002 On-line. <http:// www.eb.com>.

### An Article from a Periodically Published Database on Infotrac

Gordon, Meryl. "Seeds of Hope." *Ladies Home Journal* Sept. 1999. 2 Apr. 2002. *Infotrac.*
     (Some of your professors will ask for a more complete version of this, which includes
the place you found it and the original page number.)
Gordon, Meryl. "Seeds of Hope." *Ladies Home Journal*: 52. Sept. 1999. 2 Apr. 2002. On-
     Line *Infotrac.* Ellis Library, University of Missouri.

## Other Sources

**A Television or Radio Program.** List the title of the episode or segment, followed by the title of the program italicized. Then identify the network, followed by the local station, city and the broadcast date.

"Stirred." *The West Wing.* NBC. WWBT, Richmond, VA. 3 Apr. 2002.

### A Published Interview

Schnappell, Elissa. "Toni Morrison." *Women Writers at Work:* The Paris Review *Interviews.*
     Ed. George Plimpton. New York: Modern Library, 1998: 338–375.

### A Personal Interview

Heinemann, Alan. Personal interview. 14 Feb. 2001.

### A Film

Byington, Bob, dir. *Olympia.* With Jason Andrews, Carmen Nogales, and Damien Young.
     King Pictures, 1998.

### A Sound Recording from a Compact Disc, Tape or Record

The Asylum Street Spankers. *Spanks for the Memories.* Spanks-a-Lot Records, 1996.

### A Performance

R.E.M. Walnut Creek Auditorium, Raleigh, N.C. 27 Aug. 1999.

### A Work of Art in a Museum

Klee, Paul. *A Page from the Golden Book.* Kunstmuseum, Bern.

### A Photograph by You

United States Post Office. Bedford, NY. Personal photograph by author. 15 Aug. 2001.

**An Advertisement**

Absolut. Advertisement. *Time* 17 Dec. 2002: 12.

**Cars, Buildings, Outdoor Sculptures and Other Odd Texts.** While many of your teachers would not require you to cite a primary text like a car or a building, if you have to do so (or want to), we suggest you follow the guidelines for a text like a movie, which has a flexible citing format, but always includes the title and the date, and hopefully an author of some kind. For example, if you were going to cite something like a Frank Lloyd Wright building, you might do something like this:

Wright, Lloyd Frank, arch. *Robert P. Parker House.* Oak Park, IL: 1892. (Arch. stands for architect like dir. stands for director.)

If for some reason, you were to cite a car, you might do something like this:

Toyota Motor Company. *Camry.* 1992.

or

Toyota Motor Company. *Camry.* Georgetown, KY: 1992. (if you knew where the car was built)

But if you knew the designer of the car, you could use that person as an author, similar to the way you can use a screenwriter or a director or an actor for the "author" of a movie.

## PART VII. How Am I a Text? On Writing Personal Essays  ▪■▪

We think the best papers come from one's own viewpoint—after all, writing is thinking, and for the most part, the thinking you do is your own. The texts you have been writing about, however, were texts you read from a more general perspective.

But say your professor wants a personal essay, as many freshman composition instructors do. Is it possible to write one using the ideas and techniques of reading texts? Of course. You are a text, and so are your experiences, feelings, ideas, friends, and relatives. What's more, your experiences and emotions are not culture neutral—they have in some ways been influenced by the expectations living in our culture has generated. Take, for example, one of four ideas often used as personal essay topics in freshmen classes: the prom, the class trip to the beach, the loss of a loved one, or coming to college.

Just so you know, these are the topics we instructors often brace ourselves for, because students often have so little new to say about them. The essays are often laden with description of familiar landscapes, emotions, and events at the expense of any real reflection—they do not tell us anything new about the prom or grief.

Yet, in some way, even going to the beach should be a rich textual experience. Here's why: not only are you going to the beach, but going to the beach with ideas of the beach in mind, with cultural expectations of what beaches are like, what people do at beaches, etc. For example, how do we know to wear bathing suits, wear sunscreen, and play volleyball at the beach? Not only because we have done it before, but because we have seen others do it before and have incorporated their ideas about beachgoing into our beachgoing.

So if you write about the prom or a loved one getting ill or dying, try to focus not only on the emotions attached to such an event but your emotional expectations. Did you "not know how to feel"? Why? Was it because you had expected to feel a certain way? How did you know how to act? Were there cultural clues? Did you see a movie about a prom or about death? Proms are a particularly American phenomenon, and have been featured in any number of movies, usually teen romances (see David Denby's piece in Chapter 5 about that). Use that knowledge about the prom (or any other subject) in your own writing.

Take another common example. Dying in America has any number of traditions attached to it, depending on what American subculture you belong to. Foreign cultures have very different ways of looking at death. How you view death or illness also may have to do with religious beliefs, the closeness of your family, etc. But even these ideas about illness and death come from somewhere, and you owe your reader your best guess at how you came to them. So do ideas about what brothers, mothers, fathers, and grandmothers should be if you choose to write about them.

What we are talking about here is what personal essayists often call reflection—the idea that we are not only describing our lives but contemplating them. Entering college is a particularly ripe time for contemplation; at a minimum, you will have a new learning environment, but for most of you, there will be a change in friendships and social environments as well. For some of you, it will be time for even more upheaval—you may change your career path or your worldview. You probably won't know all this if you decide to write about entering college, but you will have some ideas about what your expectations for college are and where you received them. The university setting is a rich cultural text; reading it may provide you additional insight into your own experiences there.

There are more subjects that are worthy of personal reflection than we can count here (the ones we have already named are some of the hardest). The idea is to take an experience or event, put it in your own perspective, and reflect on how your perspective may fit in with others. Anything from a trip to the grocery store to a road trip to a phone call to a visit can be the subject of a reflective essay; so can relationships with other people. But what you have to do in these essays is to make sure they matter not only to you but to others as well—that's why focusing on putting your experiences in a cultural perspective can make your writing worth reading (not just worth writing).

Some of you might object to this sort of self-analysis and wonder why you can't just simply describe your experiences in a paper. For some papers and some teachers, that might be acceptable. But if writing is thinking and writing about oneself is thinking and self-discovery, you owe your reader—and yourself—your best shot at unearthing cultural expectations.

One last note about personal essays. Students often misunderstand their purpose. Though the topic of the personal essay might be your experience, the personal essay is not written for you but for your audience. The story that you tell about the beach or the prom or the death of a loved one is not as important as what you learned from the event. Simply recounting your trip to the beach is not nearly as interesting as what you saw, observed, and learned from your trip to the beach. Even more important is to consider what your audience can learn from what you learned. How can your experiences help the reader? The two great advantages you have as a personal essayist are recognition and discovery. In the best personal essay about a prom, the reader will recognize something familiar (an awkward moment, a romantic dance, the smell of hairspray), but will also discover something new about the text that is a prom because of your essay. So, as you sit down to draft a personal essay, think about how you might use this opportunity to help your reader learn something new about a topic they think they already know.

# The World Is a Text: READING

# Reading and Writing About Poetry

■ ■ ■  Competitors at a poetry slam.

In the first edition of this book, we began the *Reading* section with a chapter on literature. However, in this second edition, we narrowed the focus to poetry because we felt that poetry offers a more appropriate link from traditional literary texts to the type of texts we are going to ask you to read, such as movies, television, and public space. Whatever our motivations, we suspect that many of you, upon reading the previous sentence, issued an audible groan. Few students like reading poetry, though many like reading fiction. Why then, devote an entire chapter to a genre few students like? For one thing, professors believe that if students understand how to read poetry, their lives might be a bit richer and more nuanced. We agree, and we also believe that knowing how to read poetry makes you better readers of texts generally.

We are interested in reading poetry not simply as a literary form but as a constructed *text* for a number of reasons. By constructed text, we mean a text that has clearly been put together with a great deal of care; one that contains many elements both hidden and obvious that help readers or viewers understand it. A poem is never random; it is a made, crafted object. Because it has a visual and a meaningful physical presence on the page, it differs from short stories or novels, whose physical presence can take many forms, none of which is as important as the visual presence of the poem. This physicality merges many written and visual elements—what we call codes—to help create a unique effect. A poem relies on many cues such as typography (the way a text is printed on the page), rhyme, rhythm and sound to communicate to its reader "I am a poem!" or in the case of some poems, "I am an interesting and complex poem that will challenge you on many levels, but you will be rewarded if you read me closely!"

We also like looking at poems because poetry carries with it so many connections to culture. For example, we do not describe Michael Jordan as prose in motion, and we often rely on poetry for quotations during speeches, weddings, funerals and toasts. Whether it's spoken or written, poetry is a heightened, more intense, form of communication and in an increasingly informal society, poetry may feel unusually unfamiliar and even too fancy. Students also complain that reading traditional poetry makes them feel "stupid" or "illiterate," which often gets in the way of understanding poetry even on a surface level. And when a student feels like his or her grade may hinge on "understanding" a poem, then the process of reading said poem suddenly becomes even more anxiety provoking. However, as the German philosopher Friedrich Nietzsche remarked, all readings are misreadings. By this he meant that we always misinterpret any text to some degree. We can never get something *totally* right; who is to say that there are right answers in interpreting poetry or any other text? For us, the point of interpreting is the process of putting your intellect to work; only by exercising your mind does it get stronger. So, at this point, don't worry about the possibility that you are missing something; concentrate instead on what you are seeing, thinking, and feeling. Sometimes, students think that emotional responses to poems are improper, but in poetry, the emotions and the intellect are a happy couple—no need to break them up.

Hopefully, this chapter will help you in that reading process, and to that end, we have some goals. The first is to arm you with the tools to make sense of a poem as a constructed text. In other words, we want to help you identify all of the elements that make a poem *poetic*. Secondly, with these tools, we hope you will be able to answer one of the great questions plaguing any discussion of recent or innovative or "bad" poetic texts—is this a *poem*? Lastly, we hope upon completing this chapter and this book that you become interested in the cultural importance of whether something is or is not a poem. That is, why should we care if a text is a poem?

Some of what makes these questions important is the place poetry has in helping define what culture means. Walt Whitman claimed that the United States was the greatest poem, and Wallace Stevens once wrote that the theory of poetry is the theory of life. These two statements underscore the idea that poems can be metaphors for life; Whitman's statement appeals to the literal physical world, while Stevens speaks more about the way we view life. Here are some things to consider as you read the poetry in this chapter (and beyond).

### Poetry demands active reading because it is infused with many poetic elements that we do not normally rely on in everyday speech.

What if we all walked around greeting each other in poetry? What if ordering food, talking to parents, dealing with credit card companies was all done in rhymed verse? How would communication be different? Our interactions would seem odd at best, pretentious at worst. But the same conventions that would seem bizarre in everyday speech are more natural when writing and reading poetry. Such aspects of poetry sometimes intimidate students, justifiably, in our view. As any professor will tell you, there are many, perhaps an overwhelming number of, literary terms attached to the study of literature, and more specifically, poetry. Metaphors, symbols, rhyme, meter, alliteration, allusion, assonance, iambs, dactyls, anapests, enjambments, metonyms, tercets, couplets, quatrains, apostrophes are just a short list of the many techniques, tools, and structures that poets employ when writing poetry. Because we don't intentionally use or hear these techniques in normal speech, certain poems can feel as though they are part of some other world or even written in another language.

Rather than thinking of these techniques as roadblocks or tricks, it is useful to think of them as just the opposite—ways to help you decode the text of the poem. A rhymed poem that appears in organized four line stanzas is asking to be read through a more traditional lens than, say, an E. E. Cummings poem that uses no capital letters, no punctuation and is scattered across the page. Being an active reader means looking for these cues. If you do not know what the cues mean, you have a few options—use a literary handbook, which defines these terms, or take other avenues in your interpretation. It is fair to say that most poets expect readings on different levels and from different angles; if you do not know the literary terms, focus on other aspects of the poem that appeal to you, that you can get a handle on.

Active reading also means engaging the poem on a deeper level than we normally read. We have all had the frustrating experience of skimming over a few pages of a chemistry textbook only to find that we remember next to nothing. Worse is the realization that, after reading a couple of pages of a book, you have absolutely no memory of what your eyes have been scanning for the past several minutes. Too often we read but we don't really *read*. This introduction, and this book as a whole, will try to help you become an active as opposed to a passive reader. To read passively is to read a text solely for the information it provides. This kind of reading is fine for say, a recipe, or the sports page or a set of instructions, but poetry is not written merely to inform. Poetry is a complex text, perhaps the most complex of texts, and so, you must read actively. To read actively is to read critically. Reading critically means paying attention to both the words and what the words evoke in you. Poetry often relies on generating ideas or feelings when read; some students admit that when a poem does this, they think they are not experiencing a poem properly, that they should trying to figure out its rhyme scheme or symbols. While those elements are certainly a part of reading poetry, so is the "gut" response you feel. So reading critically means being a willing and active participant in the reading process but not one that relies on only one method of interpretation.

On a more practical level, this type of reading requires re-reading (just like formal writing requires re-writing (revising). Accordingly, we recommend reading each text twice. Read it the first time for plot or narrative or emotional response; read it the second time to better appreciate sounds, rhythms, and word play. Read with a pencil or pen in hand. Circle words that annoy you or that you don't know. Write yourself questions in the margins. Make notes in your book—make your book an interactive space.

## Poetry is a narrowed window into the living of life, often reflecting the ideas and emotions that people experience.

Poems condense large experiences into smaller packages that carry emotional and intellectual weight. The great American poet William Carlos Williams wrote in his poem "Asphodel That Greeny Flower"

> It is difficult
> to get the news from poems
> yet men die miserably every day
>     for lack
> of what is found there

Real life in real time unfolds rather slowly. Relationships, traveling, acquiring a system of belief, maturing, even graduating from college can take years. Poems only take a minute to read, but you can spend a good deal more time trying to unpack everything that went into them. Just as your relationships with your parents or your experiences in high school now seem to take on different shades of meaning, so do poems upon each reading. Poetry is as complicated and layered as your own life. If you wonder why some poems are hard to understand, think about how hard your *own* life is to understand.

For us, poetry is the discourse that most resembles life itself because, like life, poetry can always be re-read, re-examined, and re-considered in a new light. Many of us will puzzle over an event that happened to us until we can understand it. We can—and should—do the same with poetry; we should try to find the same type of understanding we seek in interpreting our own life events, as well as break down a poem into more manageable parts for interpretation In addition, other media do not always stand up well to re-reading. We love comic strips, but rarely do we re-read *Garfield* or *Blondie*. We also like crime novels and novels of suspense, but your typical Patricia Cornwell or John Grisham novel does not always fare well on a second read because we know the ending. Most comics and popular fiction are plot based, and our lives are more than plot—they are full of mystery and uncertainty and confusion—and we have no idea how they will end or what will happen next week or next month.

So, as you read these poems, slow down a bit. Think about all of the sounds and images and ideas that the poet has *compressed* into this one text.

### Issues of class, taste, culture—even politics—influence how we define poetry and the role poetry plays in our lives.

For both positive and negative reasons, poetry carries all sorts of connotations about class and sophistication. Let's say you wanted to impress a professor or a parent or even a date. Would you be most likely to make a reference to a certain poet or to a sit-com? Or, how about this question—which of the following texts is more important? A Shakespeare poem or an episode of *Who Wants to Marry a Millionaire?* Or, more to the point, let's say you are looking for a poem to give to someone special during a particularly emotional time, would you rely on a verse in a greeting card or a poem in a book or literature anthology? (We might use the anthology, but we understand the impulse to use greeting cards.)

We pose these questions here (and complicate them in the book) because they raise important questions about the cultural work we *assume* poems do and the importance in American culture poetry often carries. For example, what would you say if we asked you who comes from the wealthier family—a person with 30 books of comics or 30 books of poems? Or who is likely better educated—a writer for *Maxim* or the poetry editor of *The New Yorker?* With poetry comes a number of assumptions about class, race, and taste. The Western intellectual tradition has argued for centuries that you are a better-educated person, and really a better person in general, if you know and are comfortable with poetry. For better or worse, knowing poetry is a marker of sophistication, learning, even of "good breeding." Accordingly, there is a certain investment among some more conservative writers, teachers, and cultural critics in keeping poetry exclusive.

Our goal in this chapter is to de-mystify poetry. We print a number of different poems, but we refuse to label them or make arguments for why some are "better" than others. Rather, we want you to learn to pay attention to those internal sensors that respond to some texts but not to others. If you don't like one of the poems, ask yourself why that may be. Perhaps it is because you *expect* poetry to look and sound and feel a certain way. Or there might be other reasons you do not like the poem; that's okay—as long as you can understand why.

The great Mexican poet Octavio Paz claims that the poem is not a literary form but the meeting place between poetry and humanity. He did not say that the poem is a symbol of how cool or rich or sophisticated you are, or that the poem is a mechanism to confuse and frustrate undergraduates. As we have discussed, poetry has many functions, but its most important is the ways in which its brings about reflection in the reader. After the attacks of 9/11, poetry entered mainstream American culture like no time in recent history. People emailed copies of W. H. Auden's "September 1, 1939" to each other; colleges and universities held poetry readings; people established websites to oppose American military intervention in Iraq and Afghanistan; people posted poems in honor of those who died in the attacks and the rescue efforts. Though poetry may not be an important part of our everyday lives, it occupies a strangely important spot in our cultural memory. We turn to poetry because of its ability to elicit reflection; we pull it out when we want to signify something important or meaningful.

### Poetry is a combination of both visual and written cues.

How a poem looks on the page is as important as what it says. Poems are visual, and at times we are drawn to them simply by how they look. Based on the use of stanzas, typography, and margins, a poet can convey order or chaos, tradition or innovation. For instance, Dante's use of his invented poetic technique *tezra rima,* a three-lined inter-rhyming stanza, was meant to symbolize the Holy Trinity of God, Jesus, and the Holy Spirit. In the middle of one of his books, *The Moving Target,* the American poet W. S. Merwin simply *stops* using punctuation. Nikki Giovanni, a popular African-American poet, will not use the capital "I." What these specific codes mean is certainly a topic for discussion, but regardless of what they mean for each poet, they send messages to their readers, helping them understand what the poem is trying to do.

Elsewhere in *The World Is a Text,* we ask you to pay close attention to signs in advertising, television, movies and fashion. You already pay close attention to signs when you walk into someone's dorm room. For instance, if your new friend has posters of swastikas on the wall or your new boyfriend has stacks of pornographic magazines near his bed, these might be red flags. There are subtler cues we pick up on as well, such as if a person is wearing a cross necklace, a cap with a Confederate flag, earrings in the shape of Texas, or a "Re-defeat Bush" t-shirt. A poem's codes may be even subtler, but they are there. We urge you to use what you already use to unpack poetic texts. In other words, how you read poetry can serve as a bridge to how you read other kinds of coded and constructed texts.

## ▨ A SHORT GLOSSARY OF TERMS

**Allusion:** The reference to an historical event, idea, person or literary text, as when Billy Collins references lines from an Emily Dickinson poem.

**Assonance:** When repeated vowel sounds resemble each other, such as in "Oregano grows slowly over the orchard."

**Couplet:** A poetic stanza of two lines. A heroic couplet is a rhyming two-line stanza.

**Foot:** A patterned unit of poetic rhythm that measures accented words and syllables, the most famous of which is the "iamb" (as in iambic). Anapest, trochee, dactyl, spondee and pyrrhic are the other poetic feet.

**Form:** Like structure, form is the way the poem looks on the page.

**Free verse:** Poetry that does not adhere to a strict rhythm, meter or rhyme scheme.

**Iambic:** The most common poetic foot. An iamb is a two-syllable unit featuring a stressed and unstressed syllable. For instance, in the following line, the word in bold is the stressed syllable: Whose **woods** these **are** I **think** I **know.**

**Metaphor:** A comparison between two unlike objects or ideas that creates an enhanced image or meaning, such as the line from Pablo Neruda's "Ode to My Socks": "My feet were two fish made of wool." Clearly, Neruda's feet are neither fish nor made of wool, but the combined metaphors here create a fantastic and unforgettable image and meaning.

**Meter:** The rhythmic pattern of the poem—such as iambic, anapestic and so on. If a foot is the individual unit, then the poem's meter is the consistent use of that foot throughout the entire poem.

**Quatrain:** A four-line stanza.

**Rhyme:** The similarity in sounds at the end of a poetic line. A rhyme scheme is the pattern of rhyming. For instance, if the first two lines of a poem make one rhyme, and the second two lines make another rhyme, the rhyme scheme would be aa bb.

**Sonnet:** One of the most popular poetic forms. A sonnet has 14 lines and usually comprises two parts. The first eight lines is the "octet" or "octave" and typically asks a question or puts forth an argument or observation. The second six lines is the "sestet" and typically answers the question or resolves the observation or argument. A more traditional sonnet will have a rhyme scheme, but a sonnet does not have to rhyme to be a sonnet.

**Stanza:** A group of poetic lines or verses, such as a couplet, a tercet and a quatrain.

**Structure:** The architecture of the poem. Does it rhyme? Does it have a consistent meter or rhythm? Does it have fixed stanzas? In almost every case, a poem's structure will support or enhance the poem's theme.

**Tercet:** A three-line stanza.

**Tone:** The voice, mood, or emotion of the poem. Often, poems rely on evocation; that is, they evoke or elicit reactions or emotions through their tone. Is it serious? Funny? Playful? Somber?

**Sound:** Read poems aloud. Several times. Pay attention to alliteration, assonance, and rhyme. How does a poem become art through its sound?

**Speaker:** The "narrator" of the poem, the voice doing the talking, the speaking. Be sure not to confuse the "speaker" with the "author."

**Symbol:** A word or concept that stands in for or suggests something much larger than the word itself. A cross is a symbol for Christianity; rain can be a poetic symbol for dreariness, green for renewal and growth. Fire can be a symbol for passion, pain, or energy.

**Theme:** What the poem "means" or "suggests." Like prose, poems have themes, though often they are more open-ended. Still, a poem will suggest something. Avoid asking what a poem *means;* instead, ask what it *does* and what it *suggests.*

## ▪▪▪ WORKSHEET ▪▪▪

Because this is the first chapter and because we want you to transfer how you think about poetic texts to other kinds of texts, we are going to provide you with a slightly more detailed worksheet here than you will find in the rest of the book. So, if you find yourself stuck in a chapter, feel free to turn back to this worksheet and ask yourself these very questions, paying attention to these same concepts throughout the book.

### This Text: Reading

Who is the *speaker* in this poem?

To whom is he speaking? In other words, describe the speaker's *audience.*

What is the purpose of this poem?

State the poem's *central idea* or *theme* in a single sentence.

Indicate and explain (if you can) any *allusions.* Do the allusions share a common idea?

Describe the *structure* of the poem. What is its *meter* and *form?*

How do the structure of the poem and its content relate?

Is there a rhyme scheme? What is its effect?

What is the *tone* of the poem? How is it achieved?

Are there any predominant *images* in the poem?

Note *metaphors* and discuss their effect.

Try to identify any *symbols.*

Is there any significance to *sound repetition* (*alliteration,* etc.)?

**Cultural work:** The literary critic Jane Tompkins argues that we should value literature not so much for its structure or tone or plot but for how it affects and reflects culture—the cultural work it performs. Think about what kind of cultural work your text does.

**Emotional and intellectual impact:** Literature affects us on a number of levels. How does a text make us feel and think? How are the two linked?

---

### ODE TO MY SOCKS (1954)

■ **Pablo Neruda** ■

*We love this poem. Like William Carlos Williams (author of "The Red Wheelbarrow," which is in your introduction), Chilean poet Pablo Neruda is famous for finding the poetic in the everyday. In this poem, he locates magic and poetry in a pair of socks. In what way are the socks a text?*

Maru Mori brought me
a pair
of socks
which she knitted herself
with her sheepherder's hands,
two socks as soft
as rabbits.
I slipped my feet into them
as though into
two cases
knitted
with threads of
twilight
and goatskin.
Violent socks,
my feet were two fish made
of wool,
two long sharks
sea-blue, shot
through by one golden thread,
two immense blackbirds,
two cannons
my feet
were honored
in this way
by these
heavenly
socks.

They were
so handsome
for the first time
my feet seemed to me
unacceptable
like two decrepit
firemen, firemen
unworthy
of that woven
fire,
of those glowing
socks.
Nevertheless
I resisted
the sharp temptation
to save them somewhere
as schoolboys
keep
fireflies,
as learned men
collect
sacred texts,
I resisted
the mad impulse
to put them
into a golden
cage and each day give them
birdseed
and pieces of melon.
Like explorers
in the jungle who hand
over the very rare
green deer
to the spit
and eat it
with remorse,
I stretched out
my feet
and pulled on the magnificent
socks
and then my shoes.
The moral
of my Ode is this:
beauty is twice
beauty
and what is good is doubly

good
when it is a matter of two
socks
made of wool
in Winter.

 READING WRITING

## THIS TEXT: READING

1. This poem is one of Neruda's "Odas Elementales" ("Elemental Odes"—what is an ode?), in which he praises basic, everyday things. Why do good socks deserve such praise?
2. How does the form of Neruda's poem augment its theme and its tone? Would reading the poem be different if it were rhymed and were written in long, horizontal lines?
3. In celebrating something as mundane as socks, what else is Neruda celebrating?

## YOUR TEXT: WRITING

1. Write a paper comparing Neruda's ode with the famous "Ode on a Grecian Urn" by John Keats. How are the poems similar? How do they differ? What is the purpose of an ode?
2. Write a comparison/contrast paper in which you explore "Ode to My Socks" and another of Neruda's many odes, like "Ode to Salt." What does Neruda want his odes to do here?
3. Write a paper comparing "Ode to My Socks" with "The Red Wheelbarrow." Thematically and formally, they share a great deal. What? Why?

---

### BLOOD (2003)

**■ Naomi Shihab Nye ■**

*"Blood" is the most recent poem in this section, and we think, one of the most powerful. An important poetic voice for years, Naomi Shihab Nye and her work has moved more into the forefront since 9/11 and the wars in the Middle East. Nye was born in St. Louis, Missouri in 1952 to a Palestinian father and American mother. She currently lives in San Antonio, Texas. As you read, pay attention to the way Nye weaves the personal and the political.*

"A true Arab knows how to catch a fly in his hands,"
my father would say. And he'd prove it,
cupping the buzzer instantly
while the host with the swatter stared.

In the spring our palms peeled like snakes.
True Arabs believed watermelon could heal fifty ways.
I changed these to fit the occasion.

Years before, a girl knocked,
wanted to see the Arab.

I said we didn't have one.
After that, my father told me who he was,
"Shihab"—"shooting star"—
a good name, borrowed from the sky.
Once I said, "When we die, we give it back?"
He said that's what a true Arab would say.

Today the headlines clot in my blood.
A little Palestinian dangles a truck on the front page.
Homeless fig, this tragedy with a terrible root
is too big for us. What flag can we wave?
I wave the flag of stone and seed,
table mat stitched in blue.

I call my father, we talk around the news.
It is too much for him,
neither of his two languages can reach it.
I drive into the country to find sheep, cows,
to plead with the air:
Who calls anyone civilized?
Where can the crying heart graze?
What does a true Arab do now?

## READING  WRITING

### THIS TEXT: READING

1.  What is Nye trying to complicate by the repeated use of the word "true" in the poem?
2.  After a few stanzas of straightforward language, Nye slips in to a language of image and metaphor in the next-to-last stanza. What is the effect of this shft? What do these images connote?

### YOUR TEXT: WRITING

1.  Write an essay in which you read Coleman's "American Sonnet" and Nye's "Blood" through a political lens. How does writing about politics through poetry alter how we see political realities?
2.  Write and essay in which you compare the tone of this poem with the tone of Silverstein's "Bear in There."
3.  The second-to-the-last line, "Where can a crying heart graze?" seems to come out of nowhere. It is powerful, metaphorical, and, perhaps, unanswerable. Write a paper in which you use this line as a springboard for making sense of the entire poem.
4.  Do some research on Arabic realities after the American occupation. What kind of cultural work does this poem do in that regard?

---

**GOODTIME JESUS (1979)**

■ **James Tate** ■

*Perhaps the funniest American poem of the last thirty years, "Goodtime Jesus" continues to surprise, anger, and please students twenty years after its original publication. Tate's reading of the text that is Jesus offers a humorous but human perspective on a figure not often portrayed as an actual human. Do you find Tate's reading of Jesus sympathetic?*

Jesus got up one day a little later than usual. He had been dreaming so deep there was nothing left in his head. What was it? A nightmare, dead bodies walking all around him, eyes rolled back, skin falling off. But he wasn't afraid of that. It was a beautiful day. How 'bout some coffee? Don't mind if I do. Take a little ride on my donkey, I love that donkey. Hell, I love everybody.

---

## READING WRITING

### THIS TEXT: READING

1. If you are a Christian, you may find Tate's representation of Jesus offensive. Yet you may also find it liberating, funny, and humanizing. How do you account for such contradictions?
2. Like "The Colonel," which appears later in the chapter, "Goodtime Jesus" does not look like a typical poem. What makes this text a poem?
3. Read Gerard Manley Hopkins' stunning poem "The Windhover" and compare his vision of Jesus to Tate's. Which is more accurate? Which text is more innovative?

### YOUR TEXT: WRITING

1. Write a paper comparing "Goodtime Jesus" with Gerard Manley Hopkins' poem "The Windhover." Both are poems about Jesus and both "see" Jesus through a culturally appropriate lens. Does one reveal a different Jesus than the other? How? Why?
2. Write a paper comparing "Goodtime Jesus" and "Slapstick." What do these poems suggest about the matrix between heaven and earth?
3. Based on Tate's representation of Jesus, write a character sketch of Jesus. What is this Jesus like? What does he do for fun? How does this view of Jesus differ from views in the Gospels?

---

**MY MISTRESS' EYES ARE NOTHING LIKE THE SUN (SONNET 130) (1609)**

■ **William Shakespeare** ■

*We have gone against the grain and decided to publish a poem by a little known author named William Shakespeare. You may have heard of him. Renowned for plays like* Romeo and Juliet *and* Hamlet, *he is also a pretty good poet. Here, Shakespeare offers a unique perspective on Renaissance notions of beauty.*

My mistress' eyes are nothing like the sun,
Coral is far more red, than her lips red,
If snow be white, why then her breasts are dun:
If hairs be wires, black wires grow on her head:
I have seen roses damasked, red and white,
But no such roses see I in her cheeks,
And in some perfumes is there more delight,
Than in the breath that from my mistress reeks.
I love to hear her speak, yet well I know,
That music hath a far more pleasing sound:
I grant I never saw a goddess go,
My mistress when she walks treads on the ground.
And yet by heaven I think my love as rare,
As any she belied with false compare.

**READING** **WRITING**

## THIS TEXT: READING
1. This is a funny and often imitated poem. What is the source of the poem's humor?
2. As you know, the poem is a sonnet, a particular form of poetry. How does the poem work within the sonnet form?
3. In what way is the poem both an insult and a compliment?

## YOUR TEXT: WRITING
1. Write an analytical paper focusing on the language of flattery. Of course, you can compare this poem to other Renaissance love poems. How does this poem fit into the tradition of love poetry?
2. Write a comparison/contrast paper on this sonnet and Neruda's "Ode to My Socks." How are they similar? In what ways, other than the obvious, do they differ?
3. Write a personal essay on your experience of reading this poem. What was your reaction? How did it make you feel? Is it a good poem? Why? What is your favorite line? Would you like to have such a poem written about you?

## AMERICAN SONNET (1994)

### ■ Wanda Coleman ■

*Wanda Coleman is the unofficial poet laureate of Los Angeles. Coleman has published numerous books of her poems and made recordings of her readings. Concerned with issues of class and race among African American communities, Coleman is known for her honesty and her humor. Here, Coleman takes the most storied poetic form, the sonnet, and explodes it, making it a site of political commentary. How does Coleman politicize poetry and poeticize the political? This poem comes from an entire book of inventive sonnets, called* American Sonnets.

the lurid confessions of an ex-cake junky: "i blew it
all. blimped. i was really stupid. i waited
until i was forty to get hooked on white flour
and powdered sugar"

$$\frac{\text{white greed}}{\text{socio-eco dominance}} \times \frac{\text{black anger}}{\text{socio-eco disparity}} =$$

a) increased racial tension/polarization
b) increased criminal activity
c) sporadic eruptions manifest as mass killings
d) collapses of longstanding social institutions
e) the niggerization of the middle class

the blow to his head cracks his skull
he bleeds eighth notes & treble clefs

(sometimes i feel like i'm almost going)

to Chicago, baby do you want to go?

 **READING  WRITING**

## THIS TEXT: READING
1.  How is Coleman's sonnet similar and different to the Shakespeare sonnet?
2.  In what way is this poem an "American" sonnet?
3.  What makes this text "poetic"?

## YOUR TEXT: WRITING
1.  Write a comparison/contrast essay on these two sonnets.
2.  Discuss the way in which Coleman uses, ignores and manipulates poetic form. How is this manipulation, this refusal to adhere to conventions American?
3.  Reformat the poem to look like a conventional poetic text. Write a paper on how the meaning and impact of the poems changes when the form changes.

### BEAR IN THERE (1985)

**■ Shel Silverstein ■**

*The lines "He's nibbling the noodles, / He's munching the rice, / He's slurping the soda, / He's licking the ice" make the authors of this book laugh out loud. Known for his children's poems and his randy country and western songs, Shel Silverstein is a beloved figure in American writing. Perhaps surprising to some, he is listed with a website on the official Academy of American Poets website. Why is this story about a bear funnier in verse than it would be in prose?*

There's a Polar Bear
In our Frigidaire—
He likes it 'cause it's cold in there.
With his seat in the meat
And his face in the fish
And his big hairy paws
In the buttery dish,
He's nibbling the noodles,
He's munching the rice,
He's slurping the soda,
He's licking the ice.
And he lets out a roar
If you open the door.
And it gives me a scare
To know he's in there—
That Polary Bear
In our Fridgitydaire.

## READING WRITING

### THIS TEXT: READING
1. What is the rhyme scheme of this poem?
2. Is this a *good* poem? Why? Why not?
3. Even better, do you *like* this poem? Why? Why not?

### YOUR TEXT: WRITING
1. Write an essay in which you compare and contrast this poem with Coleman's "American Sonnet." Which of the two is the most "poetic?"
2. Write an essay on this poem and the "poem" by Donald Rumsfeld from the perspective of what we expect from poetry. Which of the two would Emily Dickinson and William Shakespeare prefer?
3. Read this poem out loud to ten people, noting their reactions. Write a paper on the experience of reading this poem to different people. What do you learn about others, yourself and this poem?

---

### THE COLONEL (1978)

■ **Carolyn Forché** ■

*Originally published as part of a small section of poems called "The El Salvador Poems" that appeared in Forché's book* The Country Between Us, *"The Colonel" has emerged as perhaps the most famous contemporary American poem. Its journalistic language and disturbing subject matter raise questions about what we consider "poetic." Do you think this text is, in fact, a poem?*

What you have heard is true. I was in his house. His wife carried a tray of coffee and sugar. His daughter filed her nails, his son went out for the night. There were daily papers, pet dogs, a pistol on the cushion beside him. The moon swung bare on its black cord over the house. On the television was a cop show. It was in English. Broken bottles were embedded in the walls around the house to scoop the kneecaps from a man's legs or cut his hands to lace. On the windows there were gratings like those in liquor stores. We had dinner, rack of lamb, good wine, a gold bell was on the table for calling the maid. The maid brought green mangoes, salt, a type of bread. I was asked how I enjoyed the country. There was a brief commercial in Spanish. His wife took everything away. There was some talk of how difficult it had become to govern. The parrot said hello on the terrace. The colonel told it to shut up, and pushed himself from the table. My friend said to me with his eyes: say nothing. The colonel returned with a sack used to bring groceries home. He spilled many human ears on the table. They were like dried peach halves. There is no other way to say this. He took one of them in his hands, shook it in our faces, dropped it into a water glass. It came alive there. I am tired of fooling around he said. As for the rights of anyone, tell your people they can go fuck themselves. He swept the ears to the floor with his arm and held the last of his wine in the air. Something for your poetry, no? he said. Some of the ears on the floor caught this scrap of his voice. Some of the ears on the floor were pressed to the ground.

## READING WRITING

## THIS TEXT: READING

1. Is this text a poem? Why or why not?
2. "The Colonel" is an excellent example of form and content mirroring each other. How would you describe the tone of this poem? What kind of language and vocabulary does the poet employ? How and why does this poem remind students of journalism?
3. Students generally love this poem because it seems utterly unpoetic. What are your expectations of poetry? How does this poem explode those expectations?

## YOUR TEXT: WRITING

1. Write a comparison/contrast paper on "The Colonel" and "Goodtime Jesus." How are they similar? Different? How do their forms contribute to the meaning of the poems?
2. Write an essay on the relationship between art and politics. Look at other texts that are artistic representations of terrible events—movies like *Schindler's List, Life Is Beautiful,* and *Boys Don't Cry;* literary texts like Walt Whitman's "When Lilacs Last in the Dooryard Bloom'd." Can art accurately represent horrible events?
3. Find a copy of Forché's book *The Country Between Us,* and write a paper on the El Salvador poems, from which "The Colonel" comes. What are some similarities among the poems?

### HARLEM (1951)

■ Langston Hughes ■

What happens to a dream deferred?
Does it dry up
like a raisin in the sun?
Or fester like a sore—
And then run?
Does it stink like rotten meat?
Or crust and sugar over—
like a syrupy sweet?
Maybe it just sags
like a heavy load.

*Or does it explode?*

READING WRITING

## THIS TEXT: READING

1. Hughes' poem is a scathing indictment of mainstream American culture. Why is the speaker so upset? Is his/her anger justified?
2. Who is the speaker of the poem? Hughes? Someone else?

## YOUR TEXT: WRITING

1. How would you describe the rhyme and rhythm of this poem?
2. Write a comparison/contrast paper on this poem and "Bear in There." Though they are different in terms of theme, they look and sound quite similar. Why do you think Hughes chooses a simplistic form for his poem?
3. The entire poem is a series of questions. Write an essay in which you look at the questions in this poem and those at the end of Nye's "Blood."

### THE UNKNOWN (2003)

■ Donald Rumsfeld (and Hart Seely) ■

*Originally published in* Slate, *this "poem" is a collaboration between the Secretary of Defense, Donald Rumsfeld and Hart Seely, who writes for the* Syracuse Post-Standard *newspaper. Seely took excerpts of Rumsfeld's statements during presentations and press conferences and put them into poetic form. The words in the poem quote verbatim those on the Department of Defense website. In his article, Seely notes how Secretary Rumsfeld uses poetic techniques like evasion and indirection, prompting more questions than answering them. Our question to you is, is this* poetry?

As we know,
There are known knowns.
There are things we know we know.

We also know
There are known unknowns.
That is to say
We know there are some things
We do not know.
But there are also unknown unknowns,
The ones we don't know
We don't know.

*—Feb. 12, 2002, Department of Defense news briefing*

READING WRITING

## THIS TEXT: READING

1. We ask again. Is this text a poem? If so, why? If not, then why not?
2. This poem may remind you of the final lines of the Wallace Stevens great poem "The Snow Man." What distinguishes the Stevens text from this one?

## YOUR TEXT: WRITING

1. Write an essay in which you define poetry. Use this poem in your essay if you can. In truth, it could be used as both a positive or negative example of what poetry is or is not.
2. Go to the *Slate.com* site in which this article and other poems appear (http://slate.msn.com/id/2081042) and read more poems by Rumsfeld. Write a paper in which you *read* him and his rhetorical strategies. Or, compare some of these poems with some of the actual transcripts of him speaking. What do we learn about him?
3. Write a comparison/contrast paper using this poem and one of the famous poems by baseball announcer Phil Rizutto, also "co-written" by Hart Seely. How are these unintended texts poetic?

## CAPITALIST POEM #5 (1991)

### ■ Campbell McGrath ■

*Campbell McGrath is a refreshing voice in contemporary American poetry, and his book* Capitalism, *from which this poem comes, is one of our favorites. Students are never quite sure if this particular text is a poem or not, but they like it nonetheless. Part of what makes this text a poem—or at least an interesting poem—is its context with the other poems in* Capitalism. *But we are also interested in the context here, sandwiched between Donald Rumsfeld and Emily Dickinson. McGrath, who would probably not object to this placement, teaches at Florida International University. He is the author of three other collections of poems.*

I was at the 7–11.
I ate a burrito.

I drank a Slurpee.
I was tired.
It was late, after work washing dishes.
The burrito was good.
I had another.

I did it every day for a week.
I did it every day for a month.

To cook a burrito you tear off the plastic wrapper.
You push button #3 on the microwave.
Burritos are large, small, or medium.
Red or green chili peppers.
Beef or bean or both.
There are 7–11's all across the nation.

On the way out I bought a quart of beer for $1.39.
I was aware of social injustice
In only the vaguest possible way.

**READING** WRITING

## THIS TEXT: READING

1.  What do you make of the first line of this poem? Are you prepared for poetry to begin with such a simple, unpoetic statement? Why not?
2.  If you turned in this poem to your professor, do you think s/he would think that it was a good poem? Is this a good poem? Is it a good poem because it's in this book?
3.  What do you make of the final stanza? How is this a poem about social injustice?

## YOUR TEXT: WRITING

1.  Write a paper in which you argue why this text is or is not poetry. Be sure and offer a definition of what poetry is and why it matters if a text is or is not poetry.
2.  Write a comparison/contrast essay on this poem and "The Colonel." Both poems are about (or suggest they are about) social injustice. How do they address this issue differently? What traits to they share?
3.  In what way is 7–11 a text? Is McGrath reading 7–11? America? How is 7–11 a metaphor for the United States?

---

### BECAUSE I COULD NOT STOP FOR DEATH — POEM 712 (1863)

■ **Emily Dickinson** ■

*One of the most famous American literary texts, poem 712 by Emily Dickinson, has inspired confusion, debate, admiration and imitation for decades. While some claim Dickinson romanticizes death by equating it with marriage, others argue that by coupling images of weddings and cemeteries, Dickinson suggests that marriage is a kind of death. Regardless of the poem's "meaning," it is remarkable for its brevity, rhythms, sounds and images. It remains, almost 150 years after its composition, a truly complex text.*

Because I could not stop for Death—
He kindly stopped for me—
The Carriage held but just Ourselves—
And Immortality.

We slowly drove—He knew no haste
And I had put away
My labor and my leisure too,
For His Civility—

We passed the School, where Children strove
At Recess—in the Ring—
We passed the Fields of Gazing Grain—
We passed the Setting Sun—

Or rather—He passed us—
The Dews drew quivering and chill—
For only Gossamer, my Gown—
My Tippet—only Tulle—

We paused before a House that seemed
A Swelling of the Ground—
The Roof was scarcely visible—
The Cornice—in the Ground—

Since then—'tis Centuries—and yet
Feels shorter than the Day
I first surmised the Horses' Heads
Were toward Eternity—

---

**READING** WRITING

## THIS TEXT: READING

1. Based on all of the textual clues, what do you think this poem is trying to *do?* Rather than worrying about what it *means,* what kinds of ideas or emotions does it evoke?

2. How would you describe the rhyme scheme and rhythm of this poem? How do these factors contribute to your reading experience?

3. Words like "tippet," "tulle," "gossamer," and "gown" evoke images of femininity, weddings, and formality. Does the poem feel typically "feminine" to you?

4. How do the dashes and short lines contribute to the pace and emphasis of the poem?

## YOUR TEXT: WRITING

1.  Explicate this poem. Break it down stanza by stanza, examining its sounds, images, symbols, and rhyme scheme. How does it work on a textual level?
2.  Write a comparison/contrast paper on this poem and the Shakespeare sonnet. How is the language similar? Whose is more "difficult"? Both are about love in a way, but which is the more conventional?
3.  Do some outside research on this poem. Is there an interpretation of the poem that you agree with? Write a paper in which you summarize some of the more intriguing readings of the poem, and offer one of your own.

---

| **TAKING OFF EMILY DICKINSON'S CLOTHES (1998)** |
| :---: |
| ■ **Billy Collins** ■ |

*This poem by contemporary American poet Billy Collins incorporates the text of Emily Dickinson's poems (and Dickinson herself) into his own. One of the most popular living American poets, Billy Collins was the Poet Laureate of the United States in 2001. Famous for his smart but humorous and accessible poems, Collins is a master of understatement and precision. Typically, Emily Dickinson is not considered a sex object, but Collins offers a reading of Dickinson and her sexuality that is truly unique.*

First, her tippet made of tulle,
easily lifted off her shoulders and laid
on the back of a wooden chair.

And her bonnet,
the bow undone with a light forward pull.

Then the long white dress, a more
complicated matter with mother-of-pearl
buttons down the back,
so tiny and numerous that it takes forever
before my hands can part the fabric,
like a swimmer's dividing water,
and slip inside.

You will want to know
that she was standing
by an open window in an upstairs bedroom,
motionless, a little wide-eyed,
looking out at the orchard below,
the white dress puddled at her feet
on the wide-board, hardwood floor.

The complexity of women's undergarments
in nineteenth-century America
is not to be waved off,
and I proceeded like a polar explorer
through clips, clasps, and moorings,
catches, straps, and whalebone stays,
sailing toward the iceberg of her nakedness.

Later, I wrote in a notebook
it was like riding a swan into the night,
but, of course, I cannot tell you everything
the way she closed her eyes to the orchard,
how her hair tumbled free of its pins,
how there were sudden dashes
whenever we spoke.

What I can tell you is
it was terribly quiet in Amherst
that Sabbath afternoon,
nothing but a carriage passing the house,
a fly buzzing in a windowpane.

So I could plainly hear her inhale
when I undid the very top
hook-and-eye fastener of her corset

and I could hear her sigh when finally it was unloosed,
the way some readers sigh when they realize
that Hope has feathers,
that reason is a plank,
that life is a loaded gun
that looks right at you with a yellow eye.

## READING WRITING

### THIS TEXT: READING

1. How does Collins weave Dickinson's poem into his own? His use of allusion here is quite good. Does he do justice to Dickinson and her work?
2. Read Collins's poem through a feminist lens. Is this a problematic text? What does it mean to sexualize Dickinson this way? Does Collins objectify her?
3. Does this poem make you see Dickinson and her work differently? If so, how and why?

### YOUR TEXT: WRITING

1. Write a paper in which you read these two poems alongside each other. The easy connection is to read Collins' poem through the lens of Dickinson, but if we read backwards, does Collins's poem illuminate Dickinson's?

2.  Read "My Life Had Stood—A Loaded Gun" and "I Heard a Fly Buzz" and write a paper in which you demonstrate how Collins pulls from these poems for his own. Why *these* three poems? What "Dickinson" emerges from these poems?
3.  Write a paper in which you examine this poem and the Donald Rumsfeld poem in terms of assembling new texts from previous material.

---

| **HOW TO READ A POEM** |
| :--- |
| ■ **Edward Hirsch** ■ |

*This piece comes from the opening chapter of Edward Hirsch's popular 1999 book* How to Read a Poem and Fall in Love with Poetry. *In it, Hirsch talks about how we read poems, how poets write them, and why paying close attention to poems is good for all parties involved.*

## Message in a Bottle

### Heartland

Read these poems to yourself in the middle of the night. Turn on a single lamp and read them while you're alone in an otherwise dark room or while someone else sleeps next to you. Read them when you're wide awake in the early morning, fully alert. Say them over to yourself in a place where silence reigns and the din of the culture—the constant buzzing noise that surrounds us—has momentarily stopped. These poems have come from a great distance to find you. I think of Male-branche's maxim, "Attentiveness is the natural prayer of the soul." This maxim, beloved by Simone Weil and Paul Celan, quoted by Walter Benjamin in his magisterial essay on Franz Kafka, can stand as a writer's credo. It also serves for readers. Paul Celan said:

> A poem, as a manifestation of language and thus essentially dialogue, can be a message in a bottle, sent out in the—not always greatly hopeful—belief that somewhere and sometime it could wash up on land, on heartland perhaps. Poems in this sense, too, are under way: they are making toward something.

Imagine you have gone down to the shore and there, amidst the other debris—the seaweed and rotten wood, the crushed cans and dead fish—you find an unlikely looking bottle from the past. You bring it home and discover a message inside. This letter, so strange and disturbing, seems to have been making its way toward someone for a long time, and now that someone turns out to be you. The great Russian poet Osip Mandelstam, destroyed in a Stalinist camp, identified this experience. "Why shouldn't the poet turn to his friends, to those who are naturally close to him?" he asked in "On the Addressee." But of course those friends aren't necessarily the people around him in daily life. They may be the friends he only hopes exist, or will exist, the ones his words are seeking. Mandelstam wrote:

> At a critical moment, a seafarer tosses a sealed bottle into the ocean waves, containing his name and a message detailing his fate. Wandering along the dunes many years later, I happen upon it in the sand. I read the message, note the date, the last will and testament of one who has passed on: I have the right to do so. I have not opened someone else's mail. The message in the bottle was addressed to its finder. I found it. That means, I have become its secret addressee.

Thus it is for all of us who read poems, who become the secret addressees of literary texts. I am at home in the middle of the night and suddenly hear myself being called, as if by name. I go over and take down the book—the message in the bottle—because tonight I am its recipient, its posterity, its heartland.

## To the Reader Setting Out

The reader of poetry is a kind of pilgrim setting out, setting forth. The reader is what Wallace Stevens calls "the scholar of one candle." Reading poetry is an adventure in renewal, a creative act, a perpetual beginning, a rebirth of wonder. "Beginning is not only a kind of action," Edward Said writes in *Beginnings,* "it is also a frame of mind, a kind of work, an attitude, a consciousness." I love the frame of mind, the playful work and working playfulness, the form of consciousness—the dreamy attentiveness—that come with the reading of poetry.

Reading is a point of departure, an inaugural, an initiation. Open the Deathbed Edition of *Leaves of Grass* (1891–1892) and you immediately encounter a series of "Inscriptions," twenty-six poems that Walt Whitman wrote over a period of three decades to inscribe a beginning, to introduce and inaugurate his major work, the one book he had been writing all his life. Beginning my own book on the risks and thralls, the particular enchantments, of reading poetry, I keep thinking of Whitman's six-line poem "Beginning My Studies."

> Beginning my studies the first step pleas'd me so much,
> The mere fact consciousness, these forms, the power of motion,
> The least insect or animal, the senses, eyesight, love,
> The first step I say awed me and pleas'd me so much,
> I have hardly gone and hardly wish'd to go any farther,
> But stop and loiter all the time to sing it in ecstatic songs.

I relish the way that Whitman lingers in this one-sentence poem over the very first step of studying, the mere fact—the miracle—of consciousness itself, the joy of encountering "these forms," the empowering sense of expectation and renewal, the whole world blooming at hand, the awakened mental state that takes us through our senses from the least insect to the highest power of love. We can scarcely turn the page, so much do we linger with pleasure over the ecstatic beginning. We are instructed by Whitman in the joy of starting out that the deepest spirit of poetry is awe.

Poetry is a way of inscribing that feeling of awe. I don't think we should underestimate the capacity for tenderness that poetry opens within us. Another one of the "Inscriptions" is a two-line poem that Whitman wrote in 1860. Called simply "To You," it consists in its entirety of two rhetorical questions:

> Stranger, if you passing meet me and desire to speak to me,
> why should you not speak to me?
> And why should I not speak to you?

It seems entirely self-evident to Whitman that two strangers who pass each other on the road ought to be able to loiter and speak, to connect. Strangers who communicate might well become friends. Whitman refuses to be bound, to be circumscribed, by any hierarchical or class distinctions. One notices how naturally he addresses the poem not to the people around him, whom he already knows, but to the "stranger," to the future reader, to you and me, to each of us who would pause with him in the open air. Let there be an easy flow—an affectionate commerce—between us.

Here is one last "Inscription," the very next poem in *Leaves of Grass*. It's called "Thou Reader" and was written twenty-one years after "To You."

> Thou reader throbbest life and pride and love the same as I,
> Therefore for thee the following chants.

I am completely taken by the way that Whitman always addresses the reader as an equal, as one who has the same strange throb of life he has, the same pulsing emotions. There's a desperate American friendliness to the way he repeatedly dedicates his poems to strangers, to readers and poets to come, to outsiders everywhere. Whoever you are, he would embrace you. I love the deep affection and even need with which Whitman dedicates and sends forth his poems to the individual reader. He leaves each of us a gift. *To you,* he says, *the following chants.*

## In the Beginning Is the Relation

The message in the bottle is a lyric poem and thus a special kind of communiqué. It speaks out of a solitude to a solitude; it begins and ends in silence. We are not in truth conversing by the side of the road. Rather, something has been written; something is being read. Language has become strange in this urgent and oddly self-conscious way of speaking across time. The poem has been (silently) en route—sometimes for centuries—and now it has signaled me precisely because I am willing to call upon and listen to it. Reading poetry is an act of reciprocity, and one of the great tasks of the lyric is to bring us into right relationship to each other. The relationship between writer and reader is by definition removed and mediated through a text, a body of words. It is a particular kind of exchange between two people not physically present to each other. The lyric poem is a highly concentrated and passionate form of communication between strangers—an immediate, intense, and unsettling form of literary discourse. Reading poetry is a way of connecting—through the medium of language—more deeply with yourself even as you connect more deeply with another. The poem delivers on our spiritual lives precisely because it simultaneously gives us the gift of intimacy and interiority, privacy and participation.

Poetry is a voicing, a calling forth, and the lyric poem exists somewhere in the region—the register—between speech and song. The words are waiting to be vocalized. The greatest poets have always recognized the oral dimensions of their medium. For most of human history poetry has been an oral art. It retains vestiges of that orality always. Writing is not speech. It is graphic inscription, it is visual emblem, it is a chain of signs on the page. Nonetheless: "I made it out of a mouthful of air," W. B. Yeats boasted in an early poem. As, indeed, he did. As every poet does. So, too, does the reader make, or remake, the poem out of a mouthful of air, out of breath. When I recite a poem I reinhabit it, I bring the words off the page into my own mouth, my own body. I become its speaker and let its verbal music move through me as if the poem is a score and I am its instrumentalist, its performer. I let its heartbeat pulse through me as embodied experience, as experience embedded in the sensuality of sounds. The poem implies mutual participation in language, and for me, that participation mystique is at the heart of the lyric exchange.

Many poets have embraced the New Testament idea that "In the beginning was the Word," but I prefer Martin Buber's notion in *I and Thou* that "In the beginning is the relation." The relation precedes the Word because it is authored by the human. The lyric poem may seek the divine but it does so through the medium of a certain kind of human interaction. The secular can be made sacred through the body of the poem. I understand the relationship between the poet, the poem, and the reader not as a static entity but as a dynamic unfolding. An emerging sacramental event. A relation between an I and a You. A relational process.

## Stored Magic

What kind of exchange are we dealing with? The lyric poem seeks to mesmerize time. It crosses frontiers and outwits the temporal. It seeks to defy death, coming to disturb and console you. ("These Songs are not meant to be understood, you understand," John Berryman wrote in one of his last Dream Songs: "They are only meant to terrify & comfort.") The poet is incited to create a work that can outdistance time and surmount distance, that can bridge the gulf—the chasm—between people otherwise unknown to each other. It can survive changes of language and in language, changes in social norms and customs, the ravages of history. Here is Robert Graves in *The White Goddess*:

> True poetic practice implies a mind so miraculously attuned and illuminated that it can form words, by a chain of more-than-coincidences, into a living entity—a poem that goes about on its own (for centuries after the author's death, perhaps) affecting readers with its stored magic.

I believe such stored magic can author in the reader an equivalent capacity for creative wonder, creative response to a living entity. (Graves means his statement literally.) The reader completes the poem, in the process bringing to it his or her own past experiences. You are reading poetry—I mean really reading it—when you feel encountered and changed by a poem, when you feel its seismic vibrations, the sounding of your depths. "There is no place that does not see you," Rainer Maria Rilke writes at the earth-shattering conclusion of his poem "Archaic Torso of Apollo": "You must change your life."

## The Immense Intimacy, the Intimate Immensity

The profound intimacy of lyric poetry makes it perilous because it gets so far under the skin, into the skin. "For poems are not, as people think, simply emotions (one has emotions early enough)—they are experiences," Rilke wrote in a famous passage from *The Notebooks of Malte Laurids Brigge*. I am convinced the kind of experience—the kind of knowledge—one gets from poetry cannot be duplicated elsewhere. The spiritual life wants articulation—it wants embodiment in language. The physical life wants the spirit. I know this because I hear it in the words, because when I liberate the message in the bottle a physical—a spiritual—urgency pulses through the arranged text. It is as if the spirit grows in my hands. Or the words rise in the air. "Roots and wings," the Spanish poet Juan Ramón Jiménez writes, "But let the wings take root and the roots fly."

There are people who defend themselves against being "carried away" by poetry, thus depriving themselves of an essential aspect of the experience. But there are others who welcome the transport poetry provides. They welcome it repeatedly. They desire it so much they start to crave it daily, nightly, nearly abject in their desire, seeking it out the way hungry people seek food. It is spiritual sustenance to them. Bread and wine. A way of transformative thinking. A method of transfiguration. There are those who honor the reality of roots and wings in words, but also want the wings to take root, to grow into the earth, and the roots to take flight, to ascend. They need such falling and rising, such metaphoric thinking. They are so taken by the ecstatic experience—the over-whelming intensity—of reading poems they have to respond in kind. And these people become poets.

Emily Dickinson is one of my models of a poet who responded completely to what she read. Here is her compelling test of poetry:

> If I read a book [and] it makes my whole body so cold no fire can ever warm me I know *that* is poetry. If I feel physically as if the top of my head were taken off, I know *that* is poetry. These are the only way I know. Is there any other way.

Dickinson recognizes true poetry by the extremity—the actual physical intensity—of her response to it. It's striking that she doesn't say she knows poetry because of any intrinsic qualities of poetry itself. Rather, she recognizes it by contact; she knows it by what it does to her, and she trusts her own response. Of course, only the strongest poetry could effect such a response. Her aesthetic is clear: always she wants to be surprised, to be stunned, by what one of her poems calls "Bolts of Melody."

Dickinson had a voracious appetite for reading poetry. She read it with tremendous hunger and thirst—poetry was sustenance to her. Much has been made of her reclusion, but, as her biographer Richard Sewall suggests, "She saw herself as a poet in the company of the Poets—and, functioning as she did mostly on her own, read them (among other reasons) for company." He also points to Dickinson's various metaphors for the poets she read. She called them "the dearest ones of time, the strongest friends of the soul," her "Kinsmen of the Shelf," her "enthralling friends, the immortalities." She spoke of the poet's "venerable Hand" that warmed her own. Dickinson was a model of poetic responsiveness because she read with her whole being.

One of the books Emily Dickinson marked up, Ik Marvel's *Reveries of a Bachelor* (1850), recommends that people read for "soul-culture." I like that dated nineteenth-century phrase because it points to the depth that can be shared by the community of solitaries who read poetry. I, too, read for soul-culture—the culture of the soul. That's why the intensity of engagement I have with certain poems, certain poets, is so extreme. Reading poetry is for me an act of the most immense intimacy, of intimate immensity. I am shocked by what I see in the poem but also by what the poem finds in me. It activates my secret world, commands my inner life. I cannot get access to that inner life any other way than through the power of the words themselves. The words pressure me into a response, and the rhythm of the poem carries me to another plane of time, outside of time.

Rhythm can hypnotize and alliteration can be almost hypnotic. A few lines from Tennyson's *The Princess* can still send me into a kind of trance:

> The moan of doves in immemorial elms
> And murmurings of innumerable bees.

And I can still get lost when Hart Crane links the motion of a boat with an address to his lover in part 2 of "Voyages":

> And onward, as bells off San Salvador
> Salute the crocus lustres of the stars,
> In these poinsettia meadows of her tides,—

Adagios of islands, O my Prodigal,
Complete the dark confessions her veins spell.

The words move ahead of the thought in poetry. The imagination loves reverie, the day-dreaming capacity of the mind set in motion by words, by images.

As a reader, the hold of the poem over me can be almost embarrassing because it is so childlike, because I need it so much to give me access to my own interior realms. It plunges me into the depths (and poetry is the literature of depths) and gives a tremendous sense of another world growing within. ("There is another world and it is in this one," Paul Éluard wrote.) I need the poem to enchant me, to shock me awake, to shift my waking conscious-ness and open the world to me, to open me up to the world—to the word—in a new way. I am pried open. The spiritual desire for poetry can be overwhelming, so much do I need it to experience and name my own perilous depths and vast spaces, my own well-being. And yet the work of art is beyond existential embarrassment. It is mute and plaintive in its call-ing out, its need for renewal. It needs a reader to possess it, to be possessed by it. Its very life depends upon it.

## Mere Air, These Words, but Delicious to Hear

I remember once walking through a museum in Athens and coming across a tall-stemmed cup from ancient Greece that has Sappho saying, "Mere air, these words, but delicious to hear." The phrase inscribed into the cup, translated onto a museum label, stopped me cold. I paused for a long time to drink in the strange truth that all the sublimity of poetry comes down in the end to mere air and nothing more, to the sound of these words and no others, which are nonetheless delicious and enchanting to hear. Sappho's lines (or the lines attributed to her) also have a lapidary quality. The phrase has an elegance suitable for writing, for inscription on a cup or in stone. Writing fixes the evanescence of sound. It holds it against death.

The sound of the words is the first primitive pleasure in poetry. "In poetry," Wallace Stevens asserted, "you must love the words, the ideas and images and rhythms with all your capacity to love anything at all" ("Adagia"). Stevens lists the love of the words as the first condition of a capacity to love anything in poetry at all because it is the words that make things happen. There are times when I read a poem and can feel the syllables coming alive in my mouth, the letters enunciated in the syllables, the syllables coming together as words, the words forming into a phrase, the phrase finding a rhythm in the line, in the lines, in the shape of the words crossing the lines into a sentence, into sentences. I feel the words creat-ing a rhythm, a music, a spell, a mood, a shape, a form. I hear the words coming off the page into my own mouth—in transit, in action. I generate—I re-create—the words incantatory, the words liberated and self-reflexive. Words rising from the body, out of the body. An act of language paying attention to itself. An act of the mind.

"*Mere air, these words, but delicious to heat.*" In poetry the words enact—they make manifest—what they describe. This is what Gerard Manley Hopkins calls "the roll, the rise, the carol, the creation." Indeed, one hears in Hopkins's very phrase the trills or rolled con-sonants of the letter *r* reverberating through all four words, the voiced vowels, the *r-o-l* of "roll" echoing in the back of "*carol,*" the alliterative *c*s building a cadence, hammering it in, even as the one-syllable words create a rolling, rising effect that is slowed down by the rhythm of the multisyllabic words, the caroling creation. The pleasure all this creates in the mouth is intense. "The world is charged with the grandeur of God." I read Hopkins's poems and feel the deep joy of the sounds creating themselves ("What is all this juice and all this joy?"), the nearly buckling strain of so much drenched spirit, "the achieve of, the mastery of the thing!"

The poem is an act beyond paraphrase because what is being said is always inseparable from the way it is being said. Osip Mandelstam suggested that if a poem can be paraphrased, then the sheets haven't been rumpled, poetry hasn't spent the night. The words are an (erotic) visitation, a means to an end, but also an end in and of themselves. The poet is first of all a language worker. A maker. A shaper of language. With Heinrich Heine, the linguist Edward Sapir affirmed in his book *Language,* "one is under the illusion that the universe speaks German." With Shakespeare, one is under the impression that it speaks English. This is at the heart of the Orphic calling of the poet: to make it seem as if the very universe speaks and reveals itself through the mother tongue.

## READING WRITING

### THIS TEXT: READING
1. In what way is a reader of poetry like a "pilgrim setting out, setting forth?" Explain what Hirsch means?
2. How is a poem like other kinds of constructed texts?
3. Why does Hirsch place so much emphsis on reading a poem closely? In what ways are we rewarded by reading a poem with care?

### YOUR TEXT: WRITING
1. Hirsch talks a great deal about poetry as a relationship. Pick one of the poems in this chapter and write an essay in which you explain how it facilitates a relationship between the author and you.
2. Hirsch claims that poems open up "tenderness" in us. What else do poems open up in us? Fear? Anxiety? Beauty? Write a paper in which you identify three different emotions that a poem opens in you.

### THE RESISTANCE TO POETRY
#### ■ James Longenbach ■

*James Longenbach is one of those rare beings in the contemporary United States. Like Edward Hirsch, Longenbach is a true man of letters. Known primarily for his books and essays on twentieth century poetry, he is also himself a poet, having published two collections of poems. In this essay, Longenbach discusses the dual support for and resistance to poetry in the United States. This piece comes from Longenbach's book* The Resistance to Poetry *(2004).*

IMAGINE A COUNTRY in which poetry matters because by definition poems are relevant to daily life. It would not be a large, flat country that nobody wants to visit; it would be a small island brimming with natural beauty but lacking natural resources. The inhabitants of the island would feel at every second that they are not in control of their own destiny; the language they speak is not their own. At the same time, their sense of what might constitute an indigenous culture is unmanageably complex, obscured by centuries of internal strife.

"Do not be elected to the Senate of your country," said the Irish poet William Butler Yeats to the American poet Ezra Pound. It was one of the sweetest remarks Yeats ever made, for while an Irish poet was appointed to the Senate of the newly constituted Irish state in 1922, no poet would ever be elected to the Senate of the United States. Many American poets have coveted the relevance Yeats could take for granted, and some have berated themselves for writing as if history happened somewhere else; others have addressed the most pressing issues and events of their time. But the marginality of poetry is in many ways the source of its power, a power contingent on poetry's capacity to resist itself more strenuously than it is resisted by the culture at large.

Poets have been on the defensive at least since the time of Plato, and rightly so, since philosophers and literary critics have distrusted poetry. But poems do not necessarily ask to be trusted. Their language revels in duplicity and disjunction, making it difficult for us to assume that any particular poetic gesture is inevitably responsible or irresponsible to the culture that gives the language meaning: a poem's obfuscation of the established terms of accountability might be the poem's most accountable act—or it might not. Distrust of poetry (its potential for inconsequence, its pretension to consequence) is the stuff of poetry. And the problem with many defenses of poetry is the refusal to recognize that the enemy lies within.

It has lain there for a long time. In the third century B.C.E. the Greek poet Callimachus refused the Homeric challenge of writing an epic narrative, preferring to write small poems about love rather than poems aspiring to a great deal of cultural weight. "Not I but Zeus owns the thunder," said Callimachus to critics who complained that he was ignoring his civic duties.

> When I first put a tablet on my knees, the Wolf-God
>     Apollo appeared and said:
> "Fatten your animal for sacrifice, poet,
>     but keep your muse slender."

Apollo's reprimand was extremely influential. The story echoed in the pastoral landscape of Virgil's sixth eclogue ("A Shepherd / Should feed fat sheep and sing a slender song"), and it echoed again in Propertius, whose elegies were updated by Ezra Pound. "You idiot," says Apollo to the poet, "What are you doing with that water: / Who has ordered a book about heroes?"

By the time Pound adapted these lines in 1917, justifying his antipathy toward poets who were eager to take up the epic challenge of the Great War, Apollo's reprimand had become a venerable topos, one invoked even by poets whose more programmatic defenses of poetry might seem to belie it. Yeats had recently made the Callimachian refusal in "On Being Asked for a War Poem," and W. H. Auden would make it even more bluntly in his elegy for Yeats: "poetry makes nothing happen." More recently, Callimachus's call for a "slender muse" has appeared as the epigraph to Harryette Mullen's *Muse & Drudge,* a book that advertises the possibility that its playful, punladen poems may not be performing the heavy-lifting cultural work associated with the epic. "Blurred rubble slew of vowels / stutter war no more," says Mullen, who makes us wonder if she stutters to a purpose: are her disturbances of "the natural order of things" merely the "ruses of a lunatic muse"? An unequivocal answer to this question won't be found. The point is that poets tend to be suspicious of their own designs, forcing their best discoveries against the wall of their limitations.

Of course poets have not done this consistently, and some poets have mustered the effort rarely if at all. Upbraiding Shelley, Pound once said that poets ought to be acknowledged legislators. And Yeats certainly aspired to set statesmen right when his attention was turned toward Ireland rather than toward what he perceived as England's war. What's more, as the notoriety of Auden's elegy for Yeats suggests, there can be a romance to the refusal of romance, a weightiness to the spurning of unearned weight. "The best I had done seem'd to me blank and suspicious," admitted Whitman; but rather than thwarting the desire to contain multitudes, doubt fuels the drama of ambition. If poetry is the resistance to poetry, what prevents poetry from assuming the mantle of its own greatness by virtue of its long-practiced ambition to drop it? Does dropping the mantle in Belfast mean the same thing as dropping the mantle in Brooklyn?

Imagine a country where great political leaders not only expect but regularly receive poems celebrating their achievements as well. Poems that are read immediately for their relevance but also cherished for centuries thereafter. A place where poetic achievement is so highly valued, poetic skill so desirable, that some leaders even write their own celebratory poems. This place was Augustan Rome: this pressure was what made an Augustan poet's invocation of Callimachus weighty, no matter how ritualized the gesture became. "Now everyone / Is seized with the desire to write a poem," said Horace in his epistle to Augustus, whom he advises to "know exactly / Whom you're choosing to tend the temple of / Your deeds of peace and war." Horace takes pains to recuse himself. "I'd much prefer to be able to be the teller / Of tales of heroic deeds," he admits,

> But the grandeur of your deeds is out of scale
> For such poetry as mine; and my self-knowledge
> Keeps me from trying for more than I have the strength for.

Horace did celebrate the achievements of his emperor within the smaller compass of the odes; his humility is belied by skill. But his skill is pointedly Callimachian, his true subject the epic encounters between young lovers rather than the epic as such.

If the assumption of poetry's relevance can be oppressive to poets, the assumption of its irrelevance can be liberating, especially when a culture threatens either to foreclose or to exaggerate a poem's potential for subversiveness. When Thomas Hardy grew weary of writing novels that aroused distracting controversy, he turned to poems because he knew that their revelations would be accorded less attention: "If Galileo had and in verse that the would moved, he said, "the Inquisition might have let him alone." The implications of Hardy's poems are at least as threatening as those of his novels, just as Horace's praise of Augustus is no less elaborate for being tucked away in the fourth book of the odes. But by writing poems, Hardy was released from the pressure of notoriety to be more resolutely idiosyncratic. He embraced a medium that succeeds by exploiting rather than suppressing the inevitable tendency of language to resist its own utility. To harness the cultural marginality of poetry was the next step, and a wide variety of poets, living in placed more like Brooklyn than Rome, have taken it.

"I do not appear," wrote Marianne Moore to Pound when he asked where her poems were being published. Like Pound, Moore made Callimachian gestures when other poets were eager to celebrate the Great War, but her gestures seem less compromised: can there be an arrogance to the act of dropping the mantle of poetry's greatness if nobody sees you do it? Moore neglected no opportunity to make her poems seem easily underestimable. She diminished the bravura of her intricately designed syllabic stanzas, calling them "an arrangement of lines and rhymes that I liked." Eventually the syllabics seemed to her unaccountably showy, and from 1921 until 1925, when she stopped writing poetry for several years, Moore adopted a plain-spoken, mostly end-stopped free verse. She described "Marriage," her most astonishing free-verse poem, as nothing but "statements that took my fancy which I tried to arrange plausibly."

> The blue panther with black eyes,
> the basalt panther with blue eyes,
> entirely graceful—
> one must give them the path—
> the black obsidian Diana
> who "darkeneth her countenance
> as a bear doth."
> the spiked hand
> that has an affection for one
> and proves it to the bone,
> impatient to assure you
> that impatience is the mark of independence,
> not of bondage.
> "Married people often took that way."

In this passage from "Marriage," Moore quotes from a 1609 translation of Ecclesiasticus ("The wickedness of woman changeth her face: and she darkeneth her countenance as a bear, and sheweth it like sackcloth"), but she adjusts the context, making Diana's ursine face reflect not her essential wickedness but the threat of the institution of marriage. Does this fervor enter the poem in spite of Moore's effort to diminish the poem's purchase on our attention or because of it? Is her inconsequence of manner due to a failure of nerve or to a strategic appraisal of the unpredictable ways in which the language of poetry may (or may not) discover its relevance over time?

Indisputable answers to these questions would depend on whether the poem were read in Rome or Brooklyn—in a place where poetry is by and large respected or dismissed. "In choosing his manner of death," said Nadezhda Mandelstam of her husband's decision to write a poem mocking Stalin, "M. was counting on one remarkable feature of our leaders: their boundless, almost superstitious respect for poetry." Mandelstam's own respect for poetry was more fruitfully equivocal, but he did not have the freedom to indulge in poetry's penchant for equivocation; unlike Hardy's Galileo, he lived in a country where respect for poetry helped to erode the liberties a poet might otherwise hope to preserve. Nadezhda Mandelstam's clear sense that her husband *chose* his manner of death, counting on his culture's respect for poetry, is all the more unsettling when we remember that Mandelstam's poem about the "Kremlin mountaineer" is, like many poems, a little collection of fanciful metaphors: "the ten thick worms of his fingers," "the huge laughing cockroaches on his top lip."

Imagine a country in which poetry is respected as never before. A country that supports almost 300,000 Web sites devoted to poetry. A country in which the eighth most popular term plugged into Internet search engines is poetry (edging out football, Beanie Babies, and the Bible). A country in which a poet appears on the front page of its most prestigious newspaper because of the unprecedented size of the advance against royalties he received from his publisher. A country in which another poet's dismay over the gift of one hundred million dollars to a monthly literary magazine is said to betray a patronizing attitude toward the art.

This country is of course the United States in the twenty-first century. It's difficult to complain about poetry's expanding audience, but it's more difficult to ask what a culture that wants poetry to be popular wants poetry to be. The audience has by and large been purchased at the cost of poetry's inwardness: its strangeness, its propensity to defeat its own expectations, its freedom to explore new (or old) linguistic avenues without necessarily needing to worry about economic success. The crucial events in the history of poetry make millions of dollars seem beside the point, but it is difficult to celebrate such events, even if we're able to recognize their importance while they're happening. Nor do they necessarily need to be celebrated. "If we are to save poetry," said Richard Howard in an excoriation of National Poetry Month, ". . . we must restore poetry to that status of seclusion and even secrecy that characterizes only our authentic pleasures." "Poetry is part of our shared, communal life," responded Robert Pinsky. That is certainly the case, but the force of Howard's point lingers because we can never quite be sure what constitutes our communal life, especially as it changes over time. The fact that football, Beanie Babies, or even novels are part of that life does not mean that poetry will preoccupy us in similarly meaningful ways.

Howard's point also lingers because it has been made as long as there have been poets to make it—as long, that is, as a culture has expected poems to fulfill prescribed functions rather than discover their relevance. It is "foreign to my thought, as Firmament to Fin," said Emily Dickinson when Thomas Higginson suggested that she delay publishing her poems until they were rid of their unruly rhythms and rhymes. In ways less obviously imbricated in communal life, however, Dickinson did publish her poems. She included hundreds of them in letters; she bound many more of them together with string to make the booklets we've come to call fascicles. Were these the strategies of a poet defeated by the literary culture of her time or of a poet unwilling to bend to its prescriptions?

At times Dickinson's isolation seems aggressively chosen, but at other times the dilemma seems more interestingly ambiguous. If "Best Things dwell out of Sight," as one poem begins, then how may best things be described?

> Most shun the Public Air
> Legitimate, and Rare—
>
> The Capsule of the Wind
> The Capsule of the Mind
>
> Exhibit here, as doth a Burr—
> Germ's Germ be where?

We are able to conceive of what is hidden in these lines because we are able to perceive what is visible. The capsule of the mind (the body) is as plainly apprehendable as the burr, and we assume the existence of the germ just as we assume the existence of the mind. The more exquisite "Germ's Germ" is conceivable because we may split the burr to see the germ, and even the daringly intangible metaphor of the "Capsule of the Wind" is explicable because it is followed by the more readily imagined "Capsule of the Mind." Yet the poem is thrilling because the point of these metaphors remains partially occluded: the metaphors oscillate between allowing us to picture an image (the body) and tempting us with the unpicturable (the wind's container).

"In the artist of all kinds," said the psychoanalyst D. W. Winnicott, "one can detect an inherent dilemma, which belongs to the co-existence of two trends, the urgent need to communicate and the still more urgent need not to be found." The artist merely makes this tension manifest, since for Winnicott the human psyche is divided between a need to be known and the need to remain forever occluded. It is "a sophisticated game of hide-and-seek," and a game impossible to win. For if "it is a joy to be hidden," says Winnicott with a gnomic confidence worthy of Dickinson, it is "disaster not to be found." Concealed in the concluding question of "Best Things dwell out of Sight" is a possibility that feels both threatening and enticing: if we could picture the "Capsule of the Wind," then the "Germ's Germ" ought to *beware*.

A poet's desire to sequester herself could seem alternately arrogant and precious, but it could also be liberating—the creation of a space in which a poem may be pushed to extremes the culture wouldn't know how to purchase or ignore. The literary culture of Dickinson's day could not accommodate her unruly rhythms and idiosyncratic punctuation, which were regularized by her first editors. Her equally expressive lineation continues to be regularized today, though the nature of its importance is often debated. As Dickinson set them down, the final lines of "Best Things dwell out of Sight" looked like this.

> Most shun the
> Public Air
> Legitimate, and Rare—
>
> The Capsule of the
> Wind
> The Capsule of the
> Mind
>
> Exhibit here, as
> doth a burr—
> Germ's Germ be where?

For ears educated by Milton or Williams, Dickinson's line endings function aurally: the poet who employs punctuation with no grammatical function in order to create pauses and stresses that run against meter ("You almost pitied—it—you—it worked so—") also harnesses the tension between syntax, meter, and line to control the rhythmic life of her poems: "The Capsule of the / Wind / The Capsule of the / Mind." But some readers will always maintain that Dickinson's line endings are simply produced by the collision of handwriting and margin, just as earlier readers maintained that her punctuation would have been corrected had she published her poems in conventional ways. Rather than diminishing the power of Dickinson's achievement, however, such doubts are essential to it: her poems are so strange, so shockingly themselves, that no fully programmatic account of them could ever be mustered.

Comments on Dickinson's relationship to the literary culture of her time are inevitably speculative, but inasmuch as all poets render themselves simultaneously hidden and found, Dickinson engineered highly idiosyncratic versions of familiar methods. Her poems became part of shared, communal life because she preserved a status of seclusion and even of secrecy. To ignore the nagging possibility that Dickinson may not have been in complete control of this dialectic is to ignore the tenuousness of any poem's claim on our attention. To ignore the tenuousness is to undermine the claim's power, to forget that we enjoy what we find because it was hidden. A literary culture that celebrates poetry's availability at the expense of its inwardness would ultimately become a place in which poetry finds no place to hide, no home.

Imagine having no place to hide. You are carrying a heavy burden, and you have a long way to go. But the hills around you are furred in green, and in the distance the snow-capped tips of the Carpathian mountains emerge from the clouds. Lines from a poem drift into your consciousness—lines that speak intimately of your burden. Something comes, then nothing. Just before you reach your destination, the poem's final lines appear as if by magic in your mouth. "For a moment," you say to your companion, "I forget who I am and where I am."

Primo Levi tells this story in *If This Is a Man,* his account of the ten months he endured at Auschwitz. Having spent the morning scraping the inside of an underground gas tank, Levi is selected to walk half a mile to retrieve the heavy soup pot for his Kommando; the poem he tries to remember is the Ulysses canto of the *Inferno.* "Consider well your seed," says Ulysses to his men: "You were not born to live as a mere brute does, // But for the pursuit of knowledge and the good." These lines induce in Levi a feeling of self-forgetfulness, yet their wisdom is far from consoling. For inasmuch as Ulysses's desire to transcend his brutish existence recalls Levi's desire, the parallel is darkened by the spectacular failure of Ulysses's quest: he sees the mountain of Purgatory looming before him but drowns with all his men before reaching the destination. Similarly, Levi's journey ends when he returns to his Kommando with the soup pot, and a language of terminal reality replaces a language of possibility.

*"Kraut und Rüben? Kraut und Rüben."* The official announcement is made that the soup today is of cabbages and turnips: "Choux et navels. Kaposzta és répak."

*"And over our heads the hollow seas closed up."*

Levi ends his own story with the final line of the Ulysses canto: the two journeys end in oblivion, and the inability of the poem to do anything about human suffering is poignantly clear. How did Dante's poem matter to Levi?

Levi initially recalls the Ulysses canto in order to teach his companion, a young Frenchman, a few words of Italian. He remembers several lines, then stops; he recalls a later line and tries to connect one passage to the other by reconstructing the rhyme scheme. He realizes with satisfaction that the Italian *misi me* (I set forth) does not match precisely the French *je me mis*—"it is much stronger and more audacious, it is a chain that has been broken, it is a throwing oneself on the other side of a barrier." This process, one word leading to another, qualifying another, is what consoles Levi. For a moment, he is rescued from the narratives of utility that structure every second of his life: the poem's language creates an interior space where for a moment he may hide. But at the end of the journey, Levi is plummeted back into a world in which utility is all, a world in which words cannot resist themselves because the German, French, and Polish words for "cabbages and turnips" refer perfectly and interchangeably to things. "For a moment I forget who I am and where I am," says Levi, and the phrase is powerful because it acknowledges that a poem's consolation is neither permanent nor complete.

A poem can't help but to be meaningful; it may speak as easily to one person as to a thousand. But especially when it has something urgent to say, a poem's power inheres less in its conclusions than in its propensity to resist them, demonstrating their inadequacy while moving inevitably toward them. At the same time, however, a poetry content with limitation would be merely as alluring as a poetry content with grandeur. Dickinson, Dante, Horace— these are not poets who shied away from their own strangeness, making poems that are easily consumed. Their poems are nourishing because of the fervor with which they confront themselves, harnessing the inevitable tendency of language to mean one thing because it threatens to mean another.

Poets fear wisdom. This is why great poems threaten to feel beside the point precisely when we want them to reflect our importance: language returns our attention not to confirm what we know but to suggest that we might be different from ourselves. We have only to write one poem to feel the possibility of never writing another. We have only to write the next poem to discover its inadequacy. To employ figurative language is to hear its implications slip away from us. To write in lines is to feel their control of intonation and stress beginning to waver. To discover one's true wildness is to feel the ghost of Callimachus bearing down. Still, these mechanisms of self-resistance are a gift, for without them we could not feel the wonder of poetry more than once. Nor could we rediscover our pleasure in the unintelligibility of the world. Imagine forgetting from second to second what we are for. Imagine a sense of vocation contingent on our need to remain unknown to ourselves. Rather than asking to be justified, poems ask us to exist.

**READING WRITING**

## THIS TEXT: READING

1. Why do you think Americans have such a resistance to poetry? What would Longenbach say?
2. What do you think America wants poetry to be?
3. It might come as a surprise to you, but like Longenbach, we think poetry is about wildness. How is poetry *wild*?

## YOUR TEXT: WRITING

1. Write a paper in which you talk about, in great detail, a poem you feel particular resistance to. Why do you resist it?
2. Write an essay in which you put forth an argument about what poetry should do. What should poetry's role be? What can we ask of it?
3. Compare Hirsch's and Longenbach's essays. How are they similar? Different?

*Student Essay*

**THE SOCKS OF LIFE**

■ **Ginny Zeppa** ■

*Ginny Zeppa wrote the following short essay for an introductory literature class at the University of San Francisco. The assignment was to write a 500–700-word essay on one specific part of a poem. Here, Zeppa focuses on one aspect of the poem, what socks might stand for. Note her good topic sentences and her specific examples.*

Pablo Neruda's "Ode to My Socks" epitomizes appreciation for the small things in life. He takes a pair of woolen socks, overlooked by most, and reminds us that the comfort of anything is priceless.

Neruda sees the pair of woolen socks as something more than a possession. His feet are "honored" to have a simple pair of socks. The socks mean warmth and protection from winter's cold. Neruda writes, "beauty is twice / beauty / and what is good is doubly / good / when it is a matter of two socks / made of wool / in winter." Two socks not only make feet warm, but they make life more beautiful. In any life, there is good and bad. However, the beauty and goodness are easier to see when your basic necessities are taken care of. Things like socks could even give hope. When a person doesn't have much, it is important to see all that one does have. Like the blind and deaf Helen Keller's statement, "I am one, but still I am one," socks are just socks, but still they are socks.

Though the socks don't really symbolize any one thing, they do represent a number of possibilities, one of which is the concept of something that we treasure. In the poem, they represent those small, sentimental things that we all value. They stand for how people save things and stow them away instead of using them *only* for their intended purpose. Neruda states, "I resisted / the mad impulse / to put them / into a golden / cage / and each day give them / birdseed / and pieces of pink melon." Birds, says Neruda, are like socks. Birds are meant to be free and fly and fulfill their purpose in life. Socks also have a purpose, which is to warm one's feet. But they have a purpose beyond utility—they signify possibility, magic, beauty.

This is also shown when he writes, "I resisted / the sharp temptation / to save them somewhere / as schoolboys / keep / fireflies." Like fireflies are kept in a glass jar to be admired, Neruda loves his socks so much, he would like to keep them stowed away to hold onto. But even though they play such a valuable role in his life, socks are meant to be worn. And when worn, socks can make a cold day warmer, a sad heart not so sad. For Neruda, the simple act of wearing these two magnificent socks makes everything—his feet, the ocean, his day, the entire world that much more magnificent.

In fact, the socks come to stand for the elemental but magical properties of poetry. From his book called *Odas Elementales* [Elemental Odes], these poems celebrate everyday things. For Neruda, poetry lives in the everyday, in how we see the world, in how we look at socks, salt, watermelon. Like poems, socks are made by people. Poems and socks have a function, but they can mean so much more than their designed function. Like socks, poems keep us warm, comfort us, remind us of other things, help take us where we want to go.

The socks that Neruda describes are his tools in talking about the comfort which simple things bring us. Through "Ode to My Socks," Neruda challenges the status quo and shows us how "magnificent" a simple pair of woolen socks truly can be "in Winter." Socks are a personal choice of Neruda's, but anything small yet comforting could be substituted. The idea is to appreciate that which is easily overlooked that makes life better—physically or emotionally. Because life is like a painful winter, and it is important to recognize the socks in life.

 **READING  WRITING**

THIS TEXT: READING

1.  What is Zeppa's thesis? Can you identify it? Does she do a good job of supporting her assertions?
2.  Does she like the poem? How can you tell? Is she convincing?

3.  We don't really edit the student papers much before publishing them. Aside from its length, does this paper have any weaknesses? What are they? What should she concentrate on during the revision process?

## YOUR TEXT: WRITING

1.  Write an explication of "Ode to My Socks." Take it apart line by line, image by image. How does the poem *work?*
2.  Write a comparison/contrast paper in which you contextualize your own reading of Neruda's poem against Zeppa's.

## The "Is It Poetry?" Suite

The authors have a poetry experiment they like to perform on their students. No humans or animals are harmed in this experiment, so in that sense, it causes little harm. Ours is a modified version of a classic experiment performed by the noted critic and scholar I. A. Richards in the 1920s at Cambridge University in England. At the beginning of the week, Richards would distribute to his students at Cambridge a small collection of poems that had been typed up in the same font, with the author and title removed. Essentially, the students were given around four anonymous poems—some "good" poems, some "bad" poems—and told to respond freely to them. Richards was shocked by the large percentage of his students—English honors students at Cambridge—who simply did not understand the poems on a basic level, as a simple string of words in English put together in sentences. He was also astonished by how many readers failed to note or appreciate the language and technique of poetry—its sounds, its rhythms, its many pleasures. Professors and students who are reading this section at this moment are likely nodding in agreement—things have not changed much since the 1920s. Our goal in this chapter and in this suite is to (on a very small level) take some steps toward remedying that.

The authors of this book perform a similar experiment with their students, and we have decided to replicate it here. Like Richards, we type up a number of different "texts" in the same font, with no author and no title. However, unlike Richards, we provide a series of questions that we print at the end of the section. Richards's intent was to uncover a means of better teaching poetry and poetry criticism to students. He was primarily interested in how the students interpreted the poems and why they misread them. While we share those goals, we are more interested in the assumptions about poetry that students bring to the reading process, assumptions that they may or may not bring to the process of reading gender, movies, advertisements, and so on. In the vernacular of this book, we want to know how students have constructed the very big text that is "Poetry" with a capital P. We want to know what obstacles, expectations, and preconceptions help and inhibit students when reading poetic texts.

For this suite, we have decided to replicate a fused version of our experiment. Following are seven "poems" with the titles and authors removed. Taking poetry out of its cultural and authorial context is useful only in an experiment like this. It is important to understand that we are not advocating the removal of the author from the poetic process, but as an entrée into the *reading* process. If you think that the text in front of you is just a poem and not a "SHAKESPEARE POEM," you might read it with more openness and less anxiety.

As you read, forget for a moment that you are reading "poetry," and imagine you are looking at a movie or an advertisement. Look *at* the poem, not through it. Look at how it is laid out on the page, how it sounds when you (and you should) read it out loud, and most importantly, try to pay attention to the images, emotions and ideas that the words evoke. When you are done, answer the questions above. You might be surprised to learn what your own definition of "poetic" is, and you might also learn a bit about how poems make meaning.

1.
Alcohol on my hands
I got plans
to ditch myself and get outside
dancing woman
throwing plates

decapitating their laughing dates
swirling chickens caught in flight
out of focus
much too bright
coming down
shiny teeth
game show suckers trying to bleed
but I got a drug and I got the bug
and I got something better than love.


2.
Her breast is fit for pearls
But I was not a "Diver"—
Her brow is fit for thrones
But I have not a crest
Her heart is fit for *home*—
I—a Sparrow—build there
Sweet of twigs and twine
My perennial nest.


3.
Let me be a little kinder,
Let me be a little blinder
To the faults of those about me,
Let me praise a little more.

Let me be, when I am weary,
Just a little bit more cheery . . .
Let me be a little meeker
With the brother who is weaker;
Let me strive a little harder
To be all that I should be.

Let me be more understanding,
And a little less demanding,
Let me be the sort of friend
That you have always been to me.


4.
Just off the highway to Rochester, Minnesota,
Twilight bounds softly forth on the grass.
And the eyes of those two Indian ponies
Darken with kindness.
They have come gladly out of the willows
To welcome my friend and me.

We step over the barbed wire into the pasture
Where they have been grazing all day, alone.
They ripple tensely, they can hardly contain their happiness
That we have come.
They bow shyly as wet swans. They love each other.
There is no loneliness like theirs.
At home once more, they begin munching the young tufts of spring in the darkness.
I would like to hold the slenderer one in my arms,
For she has walked over to me
And nuzzled my left hand.
She is black and white,
Her mane falls wild on her forehead,
And the light breeze moves me to caress her long ear
That is delicate as the skin over a girl's wrist.
Suddenly I realize
That if I stepped out of my body I would break
Into blossom.


5.
When the sky is a shade
Of forget-me-not blue
And the breeze
Is soft as a feather.

I think of favorite people
Like you
And the good times
We shared together.


6.
To A Poor Old Woman
munching a plum on
the street a paper bag
of them in her hand

They taste good to her
They taste good
to her. They taste
good to her

You can see it by
the way she gives herself
to the one half
sucked out in her hand

Comforted
a solace of ripe plums
seeming to fill the air
They taste good to her

7.

An external observer believes that a number of particles moving through space have purpose, because their orbits widen and contract in predictable ellipses for years.

There are rumors that other, darker particles are hidden behind the quanta of these known, and that they have a different purpose, which is not the purpose the observer observes, and not the purpose that ciphers the skies.

So the particles drive home, and go to work, and do not leap off into higher or lower orbits for risk of losing sleep over all that energy. If they are right, they fill each open episode precisely long enough to keep their own space from collapsing on the observer external to the external observer, which observes and keeps the particles fixed in a corner of its one dark eye.

READING  WRITING

## THIS TEXT: READING

1.  Which of the following is the most "poetic?"
2.  Which is the least "poetic"?
3.  Which do you *like* the best?
4.  Which do you *like* the least?
5.  Which is the most "literary"?
6.  Which are you most likely to enjoy when you are 30?
7.  Which is likely the most "famous"?
8.  Are any of these *not* a poem?
9.  Do you want to know the title and author of these poems? Ask your professor. They are in the Instructor's Edition.

## YOUR TEXT: WRITING

1.  Write a definitional essay in which you define "poetry." How will your definition differ from all of the others that are out there? What will make your definition the most compelling?
2.  Conduct your own poetry experiment on your friends and write about the results.
3.  Read the introduction and a chapter or two of I. A. Richard's book *Practical Criticism,* in which he talks about his experiment and provides numerous examples of student responses to the poems. Then write about the differences between his experiment and this one.
4.  Write a personal essay on your relationship with a particular poem. How and why is this poem important to you?
5.  Write a semiotic analysis of one of the poems above. What techniques does the writer use to make this text work like a poem?

READING *Outside the Lines*

## CLASSROOM ACTIVITIES

1. On the blackboard, write out "The Red Wheelbarrow" (from the Introduction) as one sentence. How does that alter how you see the poem? Now take a sentence from a newspaper article and write it in poetic form. How does that change your view of the sentence? How much is a poem's visible structure a part of the way we understand it?

2. Read "Because I Could Not Stop for Death" out loud in class two or three times. How does the sound of the poem mimic the rhythm of a ceremony? A horse and buggy? Can you think of other examples of this phenomenon?

3. Form a group of four to six people. One person begins by writing a four-line stanza about class. Pass the poem around, each person writing his or her own four-line stanza about class, until everyone has completed a stanza. Read your poem to the class. What does it suggest about class? How does it differ from the version that you would have written if you got to finish it yourself?

4. Talk about the word "poetry." Can you define poetry as a class?

5. In class, talk about the race, gender, and background of each of the authors in this chapter. How might their background influence their texts?

6. Compare "American Sonnet" to the the Sherman Alexie poem, "My Heroes Have Never Been Cowboys," which appears in Chapter 5. What role should literature take in exposing societal injustice? Does the Campbell McGrath poem take a similar stand?

7. Select one of the texts from this chapter that you like the best. Identify what you think is the most important passage or line or stanza and write a paper in which you argue why the poem or story turns on this individual portion of text.

8. Traditionally, critics and philosophers argued that art should celebrate the beautiful, what Matthew Arnold called "sweetness and light." But, in the last 100 years, literature has taken a turn toward realism. Does literature have a responsibility to expose or reveal societal ills? Write an essay in which you explore this idea, using two texts from this chapter to illustrate.

9. The great American poet Wallace Stevens writes in his poem "An Ordinary Evening in New Haven" that "the theory of poetry is the theory of life." Write an essay in which you analyze two poems from this chapter using Stevens' claim as your starting point. Be sure to explain what you think Stevens means by this statement.

## ESSAY IDEAS

1. Write a comparison/contrast essay on Neruda's "Ode to My Socks" and another more traditional ode, like John Keats' "Ode on a Grecian Urn." What do they have in common? Other good comparison/contrast papers include gender issues in Dickinson and Coleman; questions about America in Hughes and McGrath; questions of violence in Forché and Nye; racial inequality in Coleman and Hughes.

2. Compare differing but overlapping perspectives on America in two or three of these poems.

3. Write an argumentative paper in which you demonstrate how and why Williams' "The Red Wheelbarrow" is a poem. Be sure to articulate the criteria by which you define a poem. Or do a paper that argues the opposite, but be sure to define the criteria as well.

4.  Both Wanda Coleman and Langston Hughes are African American. Can you read their poems through an African-American lens?

5.  William Carlos Williams writes in his poem "Asphodel That Greeny Flower" that "it is difficult to get the news from poems, yet men die miserably every day for lack of what is found there." Write an essay in which you explain what Williams means and demonstrate what, exactly, one does get from poems. What does "The Red Wheelbarrow" give us that the news does not?

6.  Write an essay in which you consider "The Colonel" and "Blood" not as literary documents but as political documents. What kind of political statement do they make?

7.  On the blackboard, list, as a class, various characteristics of individual characters within a particular story. How does a story make meaning through its characters? How do characters carry and evoke values that they never actually talk about within the story itself?

8.  Pass out song lyrics to the class. In what ways do songs resemble poems? Is there any appreciable difference besides the addition of music?

# Reading and Writing About Television

■■■ A family TV moment, pre-21st century.

Y ou may be surprised by how much you already know about *reading* television as opposed to *watching* television. For example, you undoubtedly know the structure of sitcoms, talk shows, and sporting events. You know about the probable audiences of these particular shows, and you probably know something about plot devices and laugh tracks, and the way television networks spread out and time commercials.

The fact that you are familiar with television shows is more help than hindrance in writing about them. But watching television is different than reading television. Watching is passive; reading is active. Take, for example, the act of reading a traditional text such as a poem or a short story. When reading these texts, they force us to confront and unlock their meanings. We read passages over and over and think about the way writers arrange words as well as more general concerns such as theme and plot. And we are taught to think about what short stories mean. Yet when we watch television, we rarely attend to these concerns. We have been watching television since we were small children, with little guidance on how to watch; our parents, our friends, and newspapers and magazines may tell us what we can and should watch, but once we get in front of the television we tend to let the show dictate our response without our interaction. To understand television, we have to learn to question the structure and content of television shows as well as the presence and absence of ideas, people, and places. And so when watching television, we should consider a number of things.

## The structure of television encourages passive viewing.

When we read a book or magazine or newspaper, the text is in our hands. We can start and stop reading whenever we want to; we can re-read at our convenience. We can underline these texts and make notes on them. We can, of course, take this particular text with us on the bus, to the bathroom, or to the coffee shop. However, when we watch television, we are already physically disconnected from the text. Unless we have a Watchman or some small, portable television, we cannot pick it up, and worse, we cannot mark it up. Only recently have we been able to control its flow with a remote control. But even when we watch with the remote control, there is a laugh track telling us not only when but how to laugh, commercial interruptions telling us to wait, and familiar plot conventions telling us to respond in predictable ways.

Furthermore, various aspects of modern life contribute to a consumption of television that is not particularly critical. For instance, it's likely that your home lends itself to passive television watching. Most people arrange their dens so that the TV is the center of the room and focal point when we sit down. And, after a long day of work, there is often something comforting about settling down in front of the television for an episode of *Friends,* a baseball game, or a movie. Our architecture, our work, and our home lives facilitate thinking of the act of watching television as an act of disengagement.

Are networks and television producers conspiring to have us watch this way? Some of television's harsher critics, like Neil Postman, would say yes, but others would not be so bold. To some extent, the way television has evolved has led to seeing television as a kind of remedy for the ills of modern life. We have to work around this perception by watching a show with critical engagement, taking notes, and if possible, replaying the show before sitting down to write about it.

## Unlike literature, with television, there is not a recognizable author.

When we pick up a book, we know who has written it—the name of the author is usually displayed as prominently as the title. Once we know who has authored a book, we can use this information accordingly. Traditionally, when scholars study written texts, they often focus on the words on the page, the symbols, the themes, and the plot contained within, but many also use the life of the author, and the author's other texts, to gain a deeper understanding of a particular text. Though modern scholars have diminished the power of authorial reputation, the author, even if less important to scholars, still exists and may exist most profoundly for readers.

Who authors less traditional texts is not always clear. In movies, for example, we have two, and sometimes three people, to whom to attach authorship: the screenwriter, the director, and sometimes either the producer or cinematographer; in architecture, sometimes an entire firm serves as the author of a building.

In television, even more so than movies, there is no discernable author. We might consider the show's writers the authors, but as you well know, writing is only a small part of a visual text. There are the various settings, the clothing the actors wear, and the angles cameras use. In addition, we never know quite who has composed a particular show. There are writers listed, but we also hear stories about actors writing their own lines, as well as the presence of ad-libbed material. In addition, unlike authors of their own works who are responsible for virtually all of the production of the text (except of course for the book itself), the producers of a television show do not have the same direct connection to the texts they construct. They often play defining roles in shaping elements of the text that we can also make use of—the casting, the setting, the themes, even who technically writes the show— but do not do the writing, the set construction or the casting themselves.

So the question is, how do we or can we refer to a show's author? One way is to refer to the show's *authors,* and use as a possibility for discussion what the presence of group authorship means to a particular text as opposed to discussing a single author. In any case, the question of authorship is one large difference between television and more traditional texts.

## Television shows are character driven, genre based, and plot oriented.

Television shows are much more genre driven than the traditional texts we read. Where we tend to gravitate toward literary texts that "transcend" genre, television shows operate almost exclusively within genres. A genre is a type of a medium with established and expected formulas and devices. Romances and Westerns are prime examples of novel genres. Most works of fiction that critics consider as literary do not fit into a particular category of novel such as romances, Westerns, and science fiction; it's rare that a literature class will discuss works from these categories. Literary critics often consider them to be formulaic, with easily predicted plots. In recent years, critics have begun to study these works more carefully, but their interest in these texts has probably not often made it into your classroom.

Television, on the other hand, is all about genre. Dramas, comedies, action shows, reality shows, or various hybrids like "dramedies," all have recognizable components. Traditional texts have these components as well, but in television shows, they are often omnipresent. We know what to expect from sitcoms, gritty police dramas, and shows about families. The fact that shows about hospitals, lawyers, and the police comprise almost 80 percent of the hour-long dramas on prime-time network television speaks to the ubiquity of genre. One reason innovative programs like *The Days and Nights of Molly Dodd*, *Northern Exposure*, *Twin Peaks*, *Freaks and Geeks* and *Wonderfalls* had short lives on television was because they could not be placed in any particular genre. Viewers didn't know how to watch them because they didn't know what to expect from them. One of the reasons television shows are neglected as a field of study in the college classroom is because they are genre oriented; if television shows were novels, we never would study them.

So in writing about television, we have to understand that in large part shows fall into a particular category, and ask whether an individual show "transcends" the normal fare of that genre, as well as what conventions of that genre a particular show follows. Once we start thinking about genre, we might also think about how this might affect the audience's viewing experience.

## The audience pays for its free television.

On its surface, network television would appear to be free; however, upon closer scrutiny, it turns out that we do pay for TV in a number of ways. First of all, we buy (and keep buying) more and more expensive television sets. Secondly, most Americans get their programming through monthly cable or satellite subscriptions that add up to between $300 and $800 per year. More and more people are subscribing to services like TIVO, which costs additional money. Contrast the price of a TV set and cable with the fee of a library card, which is free, and TV may not seem like such a bargain.

These are direct costs that we remain aware of for the most part. What we may not consider, though, are the indirect ways we pay for television. Instead of charging viewers to watch, television networks present commercials, paid for by advertisers. Advertisers, in turn, choose shows in which to advertise. Then, the price for those ads likely gets passed onto you in the purchase price of the items you buy.

But we pay for television in another way as well, and that is with our time and attention. If you watch a commercial, then you are essentially paying for that program with your time. Advertisers know this and plan accordingly. You can often tell what audience an advertiser thinks it is getting by watching its commercials. Because they in part are responsible for paying for a show, advertisers do play a role in what makes it to television, although the networks play a much larger role. If a show's content is considered controversial, advertisers may shy away, with the idea that it may lose potential customers who attach the advertisers to the show's content. If advertisers do not want to advertise with a show, the show may not survive.

The size of an audience may also play a factor in how we view the show. We might think about how a show geared toward appealing to millions differs from a novel, which often has (and can have) a more limited appeal. Television is entertainment for the masses, and its direct connection to commerce is another factor we have to look at when writing about it.

## What is not there is often as important as what is.

What is not in a show is often as important as what is in it. For example, as Oprah Winfrey pointed out when the cast of *Friends* came on her show, there is no black "friend." Winfrey's observation raises another: what does the absence of minorities of any kind in a city of incredible diversity say about the creators of a show? (We can make the same comments about any number of sitcoms: see *Everyone Loves Raymond, Will and Grace, Frasier,* and *Seinfeld* [although *Seinfeld* is smart enough to talk about its relative whiteness].) The ethnicity of the casts may send a message about the target audience for the show but also what kind of family, relationship, or group is considered "normal" or "cool." Unlike 30 years ago, there are now a number of programs that feature people of color that are, in fact, written and perhaps even directed by people of color, which was usually *not* the case even 20 years ago. Despite this notable improvement, many American groups get little or no representation on TV. For instance, as this book goes to press, there is no show that looks at Asian-American, Arab-American, or Native-American families, relationships, or culture on prime-time television. Whether it is people of a certain age, particular areas of the country or world, or specific jobs, many aspects of modern life do not appear on television.

When looking at sitcoms or other television shows, also note the presence or absence of traditional gender roles, realistic dialogue, and typical, real-time events. Looking for absence rather than presence is difficult but rewarding; trying to understand what is missing often helps us understand the flaws of a show (or any text for that matter).

## Visual media have specific concerns.

Television is a decidedly more visual medium than traditional texts such as short stories and poems. Thus, we have to take into account how a show looks as well as sounds. The visual presence comes most obviously in its setting. In some shows, the setting is crucial. In *Seinfeld,* for example, New York City drives a great deal of the plot. In *The Simpsons,* the midwestern averageness of Springfield often determines the issues the show addresses, sometimes explaining a character's actions. *Friends* is set in New York, but how much really is New York a "character" in the show (as opposed to in *Seinfeld* for example)? We also might look at three other settings—the coffee shop, Rachel and Monica's apartment, and Joey and Chandler's apartment. Are they appropriate for people of their age and wealth? Are they particularly male or female? What does the coffee shop represent to these characters and the audience? And how come that sofa is *never* occupied by anyone else?

You might also ask how the clothing of each cast member contributes to the audience member's idea of who and what the character is supposed to represent. On shows like *The King of Queens, The Bernie Mac Show, The Sopranos, Seinfeld, Friends, NYPD Blue,* and even *Oprah,* clothing plays a crucial role in what the audience is supposed to understand about the show's characters, or in the case of *Oprah,* the host. Finally, you might ask how cameras are used and the colors that dominate the broadcast. A show like *NYPD Blue* uses hand-held cameras, ostensibly for a more realistic look. A soap opera uses close-ups held for a number of seconds before cutting away to another scene or commercial. What do these techniques say about the shows in which they used? Overall, the visual elements are crucial to understanding some of the show's intended and unintended messages, and its distinction from more traditional texts.

## Finding themes is easy, but finding meaningful ones is difficult.

Themes are the intended meanings that authors give their works. For example, a theme of Harper Lee's *To Kill a Mockingbird* would be that racism can interfere with justice, and this interference is highly destructive to a society's fabric. Every text has a theme, and whether we know it or not, we pick up on a text's thematics.

Of all the elements involved with watching television, the theme is the most easily discerned and often the least interesting. Most often, any television theme revolves around tolerance and patience and above all, the problematic nature of jumping to conclusions. Although many critics sometimes justifiably complain about the violence of television shows, most shows favor right over wrong, happiness over sadness, lessons learned over lessons forgotten. Shows like *The Sopranos* and even *Seinfeld* play with these traditions, which is one reason critics tend to praise them. All in all, looking for a theme is often the easiest task a television reader has.

What's more difficult is trying to understand whether the television author(s) handled these lessons too simplistically or offensively, or at the expense of the quality of the show. In other words, does the theme take away from the show's other elements? In watching sitcoms, finding the theme is easy, but one must be careful. *The Simpsons*, for example, has a traditional television sitcom theme in many of its shows but often brutally satirizes American culture. So which message is more important? Clearly, what happens during the show matters more than what happens at its end, which the authors of *The Simpsons* often use to criticize the conventions of television itself.

Overall, the medium of television has a number of general concerns that play into our enjoyment as well as our critical stance. As a writer, you do not have to take into account all of the above, but thinking about them is a good way of breaking free of your traditional relationship to television. There are also more specific ways of analyzing a television show. Following this introduction we give a list of questions you can ask of a television show.

## ▄▄▄ WORKSHEET ▄▄▄

### This Text

1. How does the background of the authors influence their ideas about television?
2. Do the authors have different ideas about class, race, and gender and their place in television? In what ways?
3. While it will be impossible for you to know this fully, try to figure out the writing situation of each author. Who is the audience? What does the author have at stake?
4. What is his or her agenda? *Why* is she or he writing this piece?
5. What social, political, and cultural forces affect the author's text? What is going on in the world as he or she is writing?
6. What are the main points of the essay? Can you find a thesis statement anywhere?
7. How does the author support his or her argument? What evidence does he or she use to back up any claims he or she might make?
8. Is the author's argument valid and/or reasonable?
9. Do you find yourself in agreement with the author? Why or why not?
10. Does the author help you *read* television better (or differently) than you did before reading the essay? If so, why?
11. How is the reading process different if you are reading an essay as opposed to a short story or poem?
12. What is the agenda of the author? Why does she or he want us to think a certain way?
13. Did you like this? Why or why not?
14. Do you think the author likes television?

*(cont.)*

Beyond This Text: Reading Television

**Genre:** What genre are we watching? How do the writers let us know this? (Visually, orally, etc.)

**Characters:** Who are the characters? Do they represent something beyond actors in a plot? How do the writers want us to perceive them, and why? How would changing the characters change the show?

**Setting:** What are the settings? What do they say about the show? What do the writers want us to think about the setting? Could the show take place somewhere else and remain the same?

**Plot:** What happens? Is the plot important to understanding/enjoying the show?

**Themes:** What do the show's writers think about the issues/ideas/subjects they present? (Themes are what writers believe about issues, ideas, and subjects, *not* the ideas and issues themselves.)

**Figurative language:** What symbols, metaphors, and motifs present themselves in the show? What effect does their repetition have?

**Visual constructions:** How do the writers make us see (or hear) the show?

**Absences:** What is missing? What real-world notions are not represented in the show?

**Conventional/nonconventional:** In what ways is the show typical of its genre? Atypical?

**Race/ethnicity/gender/class:** How do the writers talk (or not talk about) these issues? How do these issues show up in other categories we have mentioned, such as character, setting, plot, and theme?

---

### TV CAN BE A GOOD PARENT

#### ■ Ariel Gore ■

*In this persuasive 1998 piece, Ariel Gore, the author of* The Hip Mama Survival Guide, *takes to task a report that decries the influence of television on children.*

LET ME GET this straight.

The corporations have shipped all the living-wage jobs off to the developing world, the federal government has "ended welfare" and sent poor women into sub-minimum wage "training programs" while offering virtually no child-care assistance, the rent on my one-bedroom apartment just went up to $850 a month, the newspapers have convinced us that our kids can't play outside by themselves until they're 21 and now the American Academy of Pediatrics wants my television?

I don't think so.

Earlier this month, the AAP released new guidelines for parents recommending that kids under the age of 2 not watch TV. They say the box is bad for babies' brains and not much better for older kids. Well, no duh.

When I was a young mom on welfare, sometimes I needed a break. I needed time to myself. I needed to mellow out to avoid killing my daughter for pouring bleach on the Salvation Army couch. And when I was at my wits' end, Barney the Dinosaur and Big Bird were better parents than I was. My daughter knows that I went to college when she was a baby and preschooler. She knows that I work. And, truth be told, our television set has been a helpful co-parent on rainy days when I've been on deadline. Because I'm the mother of a fourth-grader, Nickelodeon is my trusted friend.

There was no TV in our house when I was a kid. My mother called them "boob tubes." But that was in the 1970s. My mother and all of her friends were poor—they were artists—but the rent she paid for our house on the Monterey (Calif.) Peninsula was $175 a month and my mother and her friends helped each other with the kids. The child care was communal. So they could afford to be poor, to stay home, to kill their televisions. I, on the other hand, cannot.

Now the AAP is saying I'm doing my daughter an injustice every time I let her watch TV. The official policy states that "Although certain television programs may be promoted [to young children], research on early brain development shows that babies and toddlers have a critical need for direct interactions with parents and other significant caregivers for healthy brain growth and the development of appropriate social, emotional, and cognitive skills. Therefore, exposing such young children to television programs should be discouraged."

Maybe my brain has been warped by all my post-childhood TV watching, but I'm having a little trouble getting from point A to point B here. Babies and toddlers have a critical need for direct interactions with actual people. I'm with them on this. "Therefore, exposing such young children to television programs should be discouraged." This is where they lose me. I can see "Therefore, sticking them in front of the TV all day and all night should be discouraged." But the assumption that TV-watching kids don't interact with their parents or caregivers is silly. Watching TV and having one-on-one interactions with our kids aren't mutually exclusive.

I've been careful to teach my daughter critical thinking in my one-woman "mind over media" campaign. It started with fairytales: "What's make-believe?" and "How would you like to stay home and cook for all those dwarves?" Later we moved on to the news: "Why was it presented in this way?" and "What's a stereotype?" But if you think I was reading "Winnie the Pooh" to my toddler when I thought up these questions, think again. I was relaxing with a cup of coffee and a book on feminist theory while Maia was riveted to PBS.

I read to my daughter when she was little. We still read together. But even a thoughtful mama needs an electronic baby sitter now and again. Maybe especially a thoughtful mama.

Not surprisingly, the television executives feel there's plenty of innocuous programming on television to entertain young kids without frying their brains. "It's a bunch of malarkey," said Kenn Viselman, president of the itsy bitsy Entertainment Co., about the new policy. Itsy bitsy distributes the British show "Teletubbies," which is broadcast on PBS. While I prefer Big Bird to Tinky Winky, I have to agree with him when he says, "Instead of attacking shows that try to help children, the pediatricians should warn parents that they shouldn't watch the Jerry Springer show when kids are in the room."

The AAP's policy refers to all television, of course, but it's hard not to feel like they're picking on PBS. "Teletubbies" is the only program currently shown on non-cable television marketed toward babies and toddlers. Just two weeks ago, the station announced a $40 million investment to develop six animated programs for preschoolers. The timing of the AAP's report is unfortunate.

Cable stations offer a wider variety of kid programming. Take for example Nick Jr., an offshoot of the popular Nickelodeon channel. On weekdays from 9 a.m. to 2 p.m., the programming is geared specifically toward the preschool set. "Our slogan for Nick Jr. is 'Play to Learn,'" Nickelodeon's New York publicity manager, Karen Reynolds, told me. "A child is using cognitive skills in a fun setting. It's interactive. With something like 'Blues Clues,' kids are talking back to the TV. They are not just sitting there."

Still, the station has no beef with the new AAP policy on toddlers. "Nick Jr. programs to preschool children ages 2 to 5, but we are aware that children younger than 2 may be watching television," said Brown Johnson, senior vice president of Nick Jr. "We welcome a study of this kind because it encourages parents to spend more time bonding and playing with their children."

In addition to telling parents that young children shouldn't watch television at all and that older kids shouldn't have sets in their bedrooms, the AAP is recommending that pediatricians ask questions about media consumption at annual checkups. The difference between recommending less TV-watching and actually mandating that it be monitored by the medical community is where this could become a game of hardball with parents. What would this "media file" compiled by our doctors be used for? Maybe television placement in the home will become grounds for deciding child custody. ("I'm sorry, your honor, I'll move the set into the bathroom immediately.") Or maybe two decades from now Harvard will add TV abstention to their ideal candidate profile. ("Teletubbies' viewers need not apply.") Better yet, Kaiser could just imprint "Poor White Trash" directly onto my family's medical ID cards. Not that those cards work at the moment. I'm a little behind on my bill.

I called around, but I was hard-pressed to find a pediatrician who disagreed with the academy's new policy. Instead, doctors seemed to want their kids to watch less TV, and they're glad to have the AAP's perhaps over-the-top guidelines behind them. "If all your kids did was an hour of Barney and 'Sesame Street' a day, I don't think that the academy would have come out with that statement," said a pediatrician at La Clinica de la Raza in Oakland, Calif., who asked not to be named. "It's not the best learning tool." And he scoffs at the notion of "interactive" TV. "It's not a real human interaction. When you're dealing with babies and toddlers, this screen is an integral part of their reality. You want kids to be able to understand interaction as an interaction. It's like the Internet. We're getting to a place where all of your relationships are virtual relationships."

Fair enough.

I'm not going to say that TV is the greatest thing in the world for little kids—or for anyone. I'm not especially proud of the hours I spend watching "Xena: Warrior Princess," "The Awful Truth" and "Ally McBeal." Mostly I think American television is a string of insipid shows aired for the sole purpose of rounding up an audience to buy tennis shoes made in Indonesian sweatshops.

But it seems that there is a heavy middle-class assumption at work in the AAP's new policy—that all of us can be stay-at-home moms, or at least that we all have partners or other supportive people who will come in and nurture our kids when we can't.

I say that before we need a policy like this one, we need more—and better—educational programming on TV. We need to end the culture of war and the media's glorification of violence. We need living-wage jobs. We need government salaries for stay-at-home moms so that all women have a real career choice. We do not need "media files" in our pediatricians' offices or more guilt about being bad parents. Give me a $175 a month house on the Monterey Peninsula and a commune of artists to share parenting responsibilities, and I'll kill my

TV without any provocation from the AAP at all. Until then, long live Big Bird, "The Brady Bunch" and all their very special friends!

## READING WRITING

### THIS TEXT: READING

1. What are Gore's main arguments against the American Academy of Pediatrics recommendation? In what ways does she agree with the report?
2. How does Gore suggest parents and children watch television?
3. What do you think about the relationship between children and television?

### YOUR TEXT: WRITING

1. Write about your own experience watching television growing up. Do you find your own experiences match Gore's?
2. Find the report that Gore is talking about either on line or in the library. Does she read the report accurately? Write your own reaction to the report.
3. Watch a television show aimed for kids. Notice what values the show embraces. Now notice the advertising. Is it age appropriate? Are the values at odds with the television show? Write a short paper about your viewing experience.
4. If you have a younger sister or brother or know a child, watch a kid's show with them. Ask them questions as they watch, and after. Write a short paper about your experience.

## LIFE ACCORDING TO TV

### ■ Harry F. Waters ■

*Harry Waters wrote this piece about television demographics for* Newsweek *in 1982. Though the article is mostly reportage, it does relay some of the assumptions about the world television viewers are exposed to.*

You people sit there, night after night. You're beginning to believe this illusion we're spinning here. You're beginning to think the tube is reality and your own lives are unreal. This is mass madness!

—*Anchorman Howard Beale in the film* Network

If you can write a nation's stories, you needn't worry about who makes its laws. Today television tells most of the stories to most of the people most of the time.

—*George Gerbner, Ph.D.*

THE LATE PADDY CHAYEFSKY, who created Howard Beale, would have loved George Gerbner. In *Network,* Chayefsky marshaled a scathing, fictional assault on the values and methods of the people who control the world's most potent communications instrument. In real life, Gerbner, perhaps the nation's foremost authority on the social impact of television, is quietly using the disciplines of behavioral research to construct an equally devastating indictment of the medium's images and messages. More than any spokesman for a pressure group, Gerbner has become the man that television watches. From his cramped, book-lined office at the University of Pennsylvania springs a steady flow of studies that are raising executive blood pressures at the networks' sleek Manhattan command posts. George Gerbner's work is uniquely important because it transports the scientific examination of television far beyond familiar children-and-violence arguments. Rather than simply studying the link between violence on the tube and crime in the streets, Gerbner is exploring wider and deeper terrain. He has turned his lens on TV's hidden victims—women, the elderly, blacks, blue-collar workers and other groups—to document the ways in which video-entertainment portrayals subliminally condition how we perceive ourselves and how we view those around us. Gerbner's subjects are not merely the impressionable young; they include all the rest of us. And it is his ominous conclusion that heavy watchers of the prime-time mirror are receiving a grossly distorted picture of the real world that they tend to accept more readily than reality itself.

The 63-year-old Gerbner, who is dean of Penn's Annenberg School of Communications, employs a methodology that meshes scholarly observation with mundane legwork. Over the past 15 years, he and a tireless trio of assistants (Larry Gross, Nancy Signorielli and Michael Morgan) videotaped and exhaustively analyzed 1,600 prime-time programs involving more than 15,000 characters. They then drew up multiple-choice questionnaries that offered correct answers about the world at large along with answers that reflected what Gerbner perceived to be the misrepresentations and biases of the world according to TV. Finally, these questions were posed to large samples of citizens from all socio-economic strata. In every survey, the Annenberg team discovered that heavy viewers of television (those watching more than four hours a day), who account for more than 30 percent of the population, almost invariably chose the TV-influenced answers, while light viewers (less than two hours a day), selected the answers corresponding more closely to actual life. Some of the dimensions of television's reality warp:

- *Sex:* Male prime-time characters outnumber females by 3 to 1 and, with a few star-turn exceptions, women are portrayed as weak, passive satellites to powerful, effective men. TV's male population also plays a vast variety of roles, while females generally get typecast as either lovers or mothers. Less than 20 percent of TV's married women with children work outside the home—as compared with more than 50 percent in real life. The tube's distorted depictions of women, concludes Gerbner, reinforce stereotypical attitudes and increase sexism. In one Annenberg survey, heavy viewers were far more likely than light ones to agree with the proposition: "Women should take care of running their homes and leave running the country to men."

- *Age:* People over 65, too, are grossly underrepresented on television. Correspondingly, heavy-viewing Annenberg respondents believe that the elderly are a vanishing breed, that they make up a smaller proportion of the population today than they did 20 years ago. In fact, they form the nation's most rapidly expanding age group. Heavy viewers also believe that old people are less healthy today than they were two decades ago, when quite the opposite is true. As with women, the portrayals of old people transmit negative impressions. In general, they are cast as silly, stubborn, sexually inactive and eccentric. "They're often shown as feeble grandparents bearing cookies," says Gerbner. "You never see the power that real old people often have. The best and possibly only time to learn about growing old with decency and grace is in youth. And young people are the most susceptible to TV's messages."

- *Race:* The problem with the medium's treatment of blacks is more one of image than of visibility. Though a tiny percentage of black characters come across as "unrealistically romanticized," reports Gerbner, the overwhelming majority of them are employed in subservient, supporting roles—such as the white hero's comic sidekick. "When a black child looks at prime time," he says, "most of the people he sees doing interesting and important things are white." That imbalance, he goes on, tends to teach young blacks to accept minority status as naturally inevitable and even deserved. To assess the impact of such portrayals on the general audience, the Annenberg survey forms included questions like "Should white people have the right to keep blacks out of their neighborhoods?" and "Should there be laws against marriages between blacks and whites?" The more that viewers watched, the more they answered "Yes" to each question.

- *Work:* Heavy viewers greatly overestimated the proportion of Americans employed as physicians, lawyers, athletes and entertainers, all of whom inhabit prime-time in hordes. A mere 6 to 10 percent of television characters hold blue-collar or service jobs vs. about 60 percent in the real work force. Gerbner sees two dangers in TV's skewed division of labor. On the one hand, the tube so overrepresents and glamorizes the elite occupations that it sets up unrealistic expectations among those who must deal with them in actuality. At the same time, TV largely neglects portraying the occupations that most youngsters will have to enter. "You almost never see the farmer, the factory worker or the small businessman," he notes. "Thus not only do lawyers and other professionals find they cannot measure up to the image TV projects of them, but children's occupational aspirations are channeled in unrealistic directions." The Gerbner team feels this emphasis on high-powered jobs poses problems for adolescent girls, who are also presented with views of women as homebodies. The two conflicting views, Gerbner says, add to the frustration over choices they have to make as adults.

- *Health:* Although video characters exist almost entirely on junk food and quaff alcohol 15 times more often than water, they manage to remain slim, healthy and beautiful. Frequent TV watchers, the Annenberg investigators found, eat more, drink more, exercise less and possess an almost mystical faith in the curative powers of medical science. Concludes Gerbner: "Television may well be the single most pervasive source of health information. And its overidealized images of medical people, coupled with its complacency about unhealthy life-styles, leaves both patients and doctors vulnerable to disappointment, frustration and even litigation."

- *Crime:* On the small screen, crime rages about 10 times more often than in real life. But while other researchers concentrate on the propensity of TV mayhem to incite aggression, the Annenberg team has studied the hidden side of its imprint: fear of victimization. On television, 55 percent of prime-time characters are involved in violent confrontations once a week; in reality, the figure is less than 1 percent. In all demographic groups in every class of neighborhood, heavy viewers overestimated the statistical chance of violence in their own lives and harbored an exaggerated mistrust of strangers—creating what Gerbner calls a "mean-world syndrome." Forty-six percent of heavy viewers who live in cities rated their fear of crime "very serious" as opposed to 26 percent for light viewers. Such paranoia is especially acute among TV entertainment's most common victims: women, the elderly, non-whites, foreigners and lower-class citizens.

Video violence, proposes Gerbner, is primarily responsible for imparting lessons in social power: it demonstrates who can *do* what to whom and get away with it. "Television is saying that those at the bottom of the power scale cannot get away with the same things that a white, middle-class American male can," he says. "It potentially conditions people to think of themselves as victims."

At a quick glance, Gerbner's findings seem to contain a cause-and-effect, chicken-or-the-egg question. Does television make heavy viewers view the world the way they do or do heavy viewers come from the poorer, less experienced segment of the populace that regards the world that way to begin with? In other words, does the tube create or simply confirm the un-enlightened attitudes of its most loyal audience? Gerbner, however, was savvy enough to construct a methodology largely immune to such criticism. His samples of heavy viewers cut across all ages, incomes, education levels and ethnic backgrounds—and every category displayed the same tube-induced misconceptions of the world outside.

Needless to say, the networks accept all this as enthusiastically as they would a list of news-coverage complaints from the Ayatollah Khomeini. Even so, their responses tend to be tinged with a singular respect for Gerbner's personal and professional credentials. The man is no ivory-tower recluse. During World War II, the Budapest-born Gerbner parachuted into the mountains of Yugoslavia to join the partisans fighting the Germans. After the war, he hunted down and personally arrested scores of high Nazi officials. Nor is Gerbner some videophobic vigilante. A Ph.D. in communications, he readily acknowledges TV's beneficial effects, noting that it has abolished parochialism, reduced isolation and loneliness and provided the poorest members of society with cheap, plug-in exposure to experiences they otherwise would not have. Funding for his research is supplied by such prestigious bodies as the National Institute of Mental Health, the surgeon general's office and the American Medical Association, and he is called to testify before congressional committees nearly as often as David Stockman.

## Mass Entertainment

When challenging Gerbner, network officials focus less on his findings and methods than on what they regard as his own misconceptions of their industry's function. "He's looking at television from the perspective of a social scientist rather than considering what is mass entertainment," says Alfred Schneider, vice president of standards' and practices at ABC. "We strive to balance TV's social effects with what will capture an audience's interests. If you showed strong men being victimized as much as women or the elderly, what would comprise the dramatic conflict? If you did a show truly representative of society's total reality, and nobody watched because it wasn't interesting, what have you achieved?"

CBS senior vice president Gene Mater also believes that Gerbner is implicitly asking for the theoretically impossible. "TV is unique in its problems," says Mater. "Everyone wants a piece of the action. Everyone feels that their racial or ethnic group is underrepresented or should be portrayed as they would like the world to perceive them. No popular entertainment form, including this one, can or should be an accurate reflection of society." On that point, at least, Gerbner is first to agree; he hardly expects television entertainment to serve as a mirror image of absolute truth. But what fascinates him about this communications medium is its marked difference from all others. In other media, customers carefully choose what they want to hear or read: a movie, a magazine, a best seller. In television, notes Gerbner, viewers rarely tune in for a particular program. Instead, most just habitually turn on the set—and watch by the clock rather than for a specific show. "Television viewing fulfills the criteria of a ritual," he says. "It is the only medium that can bring to people things they otherwise would not select." With such unique power, believes Gerbner, comes unique responsibility: "No other medium reaches into every home or has a comparable, cradle-to-grave influence over what a society learns about itself."

## Match

In Gerbner's view, virtually all of TV's distortions of reality can be attributed to its obsession with demographics. The viewers that prime-time sponsors most want to reach are white, middle-class, female and between 18 and 49—in short, the audience that purchases most of the consumer products advertised on the tube. Accordingly, notes Gerbner, the demographic portrait of TV's fictional characters largely matches that of its prime commercial targets and largely ignores everyone else. "Television," he concludes, "reproduces a world for its own best customers."

Among TV's more candid executives, that theory draws considerable support. Yet by pointing a finger at the power of demographics, Gerbner appears to contradict one of his major findings. If female viewers are so dear to the hearts of sponsors, why are female characters cast in such unflattering light? "In a basically male-oriented power structure," replies Gerbner, "you can't alienate the male viewer. But you can get away with offending women because most women are pretty well brainwashed to accept it." The Annenberg dean has an equally tidy explanation for another curious fact. Since the corporate world provides network television with all of its financial support, one would expect businessmen on TV to be portrayed primarily as good guys. Quite the contrary. As any fan of "Dallas," "Dynasty" or "Falcon Crest" well knows, the image of the company man is usually that of a mendacious, dirty-dealing rapscallion. Why would TV snap at the hand that feeds it? "Credibility is the way to ratings," proposes Gerbner. "This country has a populist tradition of bias against anything big, including big business. So to retain credibility, TV entertainment shows businessmen in relatively derogatory ways."

In the medium's Hollywood-based creative community, the gospel of Gerbner finds some passionate adherents. Rarely have TV's best and brightest talents viewed their industry with so much frustration and anger. The most sweeping indictment emanates from David Rintels, a two-time Emmy-winning writer and former president of the Writers Guild of America, West. "Gerbner is absolutely correct and it is the people who run the networks who are to blame," says Rintels. "The networks get bombarded with thoughtful, reality-oriented scripts. They simply won't do them. They slam the door on them. They believe that the only way to get ratings is to feed viewers what conforms to their biases or what has limited resemblance to reality. From 8 to 11 o'clock each night, television is one long lie."

Innovative thinkers such as Norman Lear, whose work has been practically driven off the tube, don't fault the networks so much as the climate in which they operate. Says Lear: "All of this country's institutions have become totally fixated on short-term bottom-line thinking. Everyone grabs for what might succeed today and the hell with tomorrow. Television just catches more of the heat because it's more visible." Perhaps the most perceptive assessment of Gerbner's conclusions is offered by one who has worked both sides of the industry street. Deanne Barkley, a former NBC vice president who now helps run an independent production house, reports that the negative depictions of women on TV have made it "nerve-racking" to function as a woman within TV. "No one takes responsibility for the social impact of their shows," says Barkley. "But then how do you decide where it all begins? Do the networks give viewers what they want? Or are the networks conditioning them to think that way?"

Gerbner himself has no simple answer to that conundrum. Neither a McLuhanesque shaman nor a Naderesque crusader, he hesitates to suggest solutions until pressed. Then out pops a pair of provocative notions. Commercial television will never democratize its treatments of daily life, he believes, until it finds a way to broaden its financial base. Coincidentally, Federal Communications Commission chairman Mark Fowler seems to have arrived at much the same conclusion. In exchange for lifting such government restrictions on TV as the fairness doctrine and the equal-time rule, Fowler would impose a modest levy on station owners called a spectrum-use fee. Funds from the fees would be set aside to finance programs aimed at specialized tastes rather than the mass appetite. Gerbner enthusiastically endorses that proposal: "Let the ratings system dominate most of prime time but not every hour of every day. Let some programs carry advisories that warn: 'This is not for all of you. This is for nonwhites, or for religious people or for the aged and the handicapped. Turn it off unless you'd like to eavesdrop.' That would be a very refreshing thing."

## Role

In addition, Gerbner would like to see viewers given an active role in steering the overall direction of television instead of being obliged to passively accept whatever the networks offer. In Britain, he points out, political candidates debate the problems of TV as routinely as the issue of crime. In this country, proposes Gerbner, "every political campaign should put television on the public agenda. Candidates talk about schools, they talk about jobs, they talk about social welfare. They're going to have to start discussing this all-pervasive force."

There are no outright villains in this docudrama. Even Gerbner recognizes that network potentates don't set out to proselytize a point of view; they are simply businessmen selling a mass-market product. At the same time, their 90 million nightly customers deserve to know the side effects of the ingredients. By the time the typical American child reaches the age of reason, calculates Gerbner, he or she will have absorbed more than 30,000 electronic "stories." These stories, he suggests, have replaced the socializing role of the preindustrial church: they create a "cultural mythology" that establishes the norms of approved behavior and belief. And all Gerbner's research indicates that this new mythological world, with its warped picture of a sizable portion of society, may soon become the one most of us think we live in.

Who else is telling us that? Howard Beale and his eloquent alarms have faded into off-network reruns. At the very least, it is comforting to know that a real-life Beale is very much with us . . . and *really* watching.

## READING WRITING

### THIS TEXT: READING

1. What is Waters's point in describing the world according to television? Do you agree or disagree—why or why not?
2. What is Waters assuming about television's audience when describing this "world"? Do you think these assumptions are appropriate? Do they apply to you?
3. This piece is now twenty years old—what do you think has changed since he wrote it? Are the ideas Gerbner wrote still valid today?

### YOUR TEXT: WRITING

1. Pick a night of television and a network and do your own demographic study. Who makes up the casts of the shows? What values do the shows display? Imply?
2. One of the techniques for watching popular culture the authors employ is to follow the implications of character action. For example, if a character is portrayed as strong or weak, smart or dumb, greedy or kind, what happens to them can be an indication of how the authors feel about that general type of character.
3. Imagine yourself in "television world"—what would it look like? How would people act in it? How would it sound? How would this world be different from the world you live in now? Write a short essay on your experiences in television world.

---

### HOW SOAPS ARE INTEGRATING AMERICA: COLOR TV

■ **Michelle Cottle** ■

*Michelle Cottle writes about how the mixing of cultures is changing the way soap operas are produced—and watched. Though the piece (2001) is mostly reportage, pay attention to the argument Cottle is making.*

LOVEBIRDS MIGUEL AND CHARITY (who happens to be a witch) watch in horror as the smoke from a burning boat begins to suffocate Tabitha (also a witch) and Timmy (her enchanted doll), trapped inside. In the shadows nearby, the deranged arsonist, Norma, babbles to herself about her triumph but frets that someone will try to save the imperiled duo. Meanwhile, at a posh resort in Bermuda, the filthy-rich and utterly wicked Julian Crane is attempting to seduce the beautiful, naive, and thoroughly inebriated Theresa, unbeknownst to Theresa's older brother Luis, who, as fate would have it, is in the adjacent suite sharing a romantic evening with his true love, Sheridan, who is also Julian's sister (and whom Julian and his father, Alistair, are plotting to kill in order to end her relationship with Luis). Julian is supposed to be using his Bermuda trip to divorce Ivy, who at that very moment is back in (the fictional New England town of) Harmony, eavesdropping on Sam (the object of her affections), Grace (Sam's wife), and David, who claims that Grace has long been his wife.

Viewers got all this—and much, much more—in last Thursday's episode of "Passions," NBC's newest, hippest, weirdest daytime drama. Just over two years old and geared toward younger viewers, "Passions" is a bit more campy than its elder brethren but still delivers pretty much what you'd expect from a soap opera: poor production values, absurd plotlines, gorgeous cast members, and wretched acting. With all the scheming, screwing, and attempted killing that go on, soaps could be Exhibit A in Bill Bennett's case that television is turning America into a modern-day Sodom.

Except that when it comes to race, the soaps are a shining model of what America claims it wants to be: diverse, integrated, and more or less equal. While activists continue to grumble about the bland whiteness of prime-time television, the big-three networks—in a bid to pump up sagging ratings—have begun a major push to lure minority viewers, particularly Latinos, to their daytime dramas. The result is Spanish simulcasts and subtitles, story lines that deal with Hispanic culture, and more Latino faces on-screen. Moreover, unlike prime time, when blacks and Latinos tend to appear in segregated shows (think Damon Wayans) or stereotypical roles (think Latina maids), the minorities in soaps are folded into integrated, middle-class (not to mention upper-class) story lines. On "daytime," African Americans, Hispanics, Caucasians, and enchanted dolls all live, love, lie, and forgive together in a melodramatic melting pot. It's enough to make you put down your vacuum cleaner, buy a box of Kleenex, and stand up and cheer.

Make no mistake: The integration of daytime television is primarily about the pursuit of green. Over the past decade, with more women working outside the home, soap operas have suffered a ratings slump. (Industry execs also blame the O.J. trial for preempting the soaps and breaking fans' viewing habits.) Even the most popular show, "The Young and the Restless," has suffered a 28 percent ratings slide since 1994. To make matters worse, the average age of soap viewers is on the rise, up nine years since 1991, which bodes ill for ad revenues. (Younger viewers tend to be freer with their spending.) All of which has sent daytime TV execs scrambling.

For a variety of reasons, Latinos are a prime target. For starters, the raw numbers are mouthwatering: According to the 2000 census, there are some 35 million Hispanics living in the United States—and market research shows that young Latinos tend to spend more of their disposable income than their non-Latino counterparts. Best of all, many Latinos (or, more often, Latinas) already have a taste for the genre. Telenovelas, Spanish-language soap operas, are a staple of Spanish-language television and are extraordinarily popular among Hispanics in the United States. Soap producers are praying that, with a little strategic tweaking, they can get telenovela fans hooked.

Most basically, much daytime programming now offers Spanish subtitles or optional Spanish audio. In addition, many soaps' websites include show summaries and star bios en español. More significantly, some shows are mimicking the format of telenovelas, which feature faster-paced story lines that wrap up after several weeks or months, instead of dragging on for years like traditional soaps. CBS executives hold regular meetings on how to use elements from the telenovelas to draw Latino audiences to "The Bold and the Beautiful," says publicist Kevin McDonald. ABC has already adopted the telenovela format on "Port Charles" and, earlier this summer, brought in a Latino consulting company to help develop plotlines and characters that appeal to Hispanic viewers. An added bonus, notes Felicia Behr, the network's senior vice president for daytime programming, is that the telenovela's faster pace appeals to young people, who like to "get conclusions" after a few weeks. Over the past few weeks, says Behr, numbers for "Port Charles" among women in the key 18-to-49 age range rose 36 percent, while its numbers among teens tripled.

The most obvious change, however, is in front of the camera: more Latino faces, particularly in central roles. Behr reports that ABC recently introduced another Hispanic character on "All My Children" and expanded the Hispanic family on "One Life to Live," keeping them "at the forefront of the story for a long time." In May, CBS added an Argentinean and a Colombian cast member to star, respectively, as a fashion model and a fashion designer—no blue-collar laborers here—on "The Bold and the Beautiful" (or, if you prefer, "Belleza y Poder"). But leading the multicultural charge is NBC's "Passions": Of its four core families, two are white, one is black, and one is Hispanic. (Hispanic-Irish, to be more precise. Intermarriage—while still rare on prime time—is becoming de rigueur in soap land.) The yummy Lopez-Fitzgerald brothers have developed quite a fan club, with young Miguel (Jesse Metcalfe) named AOL's Teen Celebrity of the Month in August. And when two older members of the Lopez-Fitzgerald clan were planning for a double wedding in July, the writers recruited the hottest talk-show host on Spanish-language television to guest star as a visiting aunt; her husband was played by a veteran telenovela actor.

A few Latino faces here and there may not sound like much, until you consider their stark absence during prime time. Although the census shows that Hispanics now make up 12.5 percent of the U.S. population, they represent only 2 percent of characters in prime time, according to the California-based advocacy group Children Now. African Americans fare somewhat better, in part because of a high-profile boycott threat last year by the NAACP. Nonetheless, of the 22 shows premiering this season, only two had minority leads.

Worse, unlike the assimilationist soaps, prime-time programming frequently pursues segregation as a marketing strategy. The vast majority of sitcoms boast either all-white or all-black casts—and leave Latinos completely out of the picture. (Weekly dramas do a better job—think Detective Ed Green on "Law and Order" or Dr. Peter Benton on "ER"—but mainly after ten o'clock in the evening. As Children Now points out, during the earlier hours, when most kids are watching, the world looks like a very segregated place.) Soaps, by contrast, try not to ghettoize minority characters in marginal or stereotypical roles. For the most part, they manage to acknowledge their characters' Latino heritage without treating them differently from other characters, says Felix Sanchez, CEO of the P.R. firm TerraCom and a founder of the National Hispanic Foundation for the Arts. "Daytime at least identifies characters as Latinos and allows them to fall into the same classic soap opera character traps."

It's true, of course, that the TV culture into which Latinos are being assimilated is a culture of schlock. But soap opera role models are better than no televised role models at all. Moreover, the soaps—which have long served as a farm system for prime time—also give young Latino actors, writers, and directors a foot in the network door. The list of soap actors turned megastars is long and distinguished, including Meg Ryan, Demi Moore, Tommy Lee Jones, Alec Baldwin, Dustin Hoffman, Christopher Reeve, and Puerto Rican pop-music phenom Ricky Martin. Seven years ago, Martin was hamming it up on "General Hospital" as singing bartender Miguel Morez. Today, he's living la . . . Well, you get the picture. Viva la revolución.

**READING** WRITING

## THIS TEXT: READING

1. What effect do you think seeing integration on television has on changing people's attitudes?
2. If you answered that you thought it had positive effects, what does that say about the impact of television in our lives? If you answered no effects or negative ones, what elements do you think can change the way we look at race and ethnicity?
3. Along the same lines, television commercials rarely feature actors of only one race. Do you think integrating commercials could have positive effects? Why or why not?

4. Why might soap operas be good vehicles for social change? Why might they not be effective for social change?

## YOUR TEXT: WRITING

1. Watch a soap opera and watch how the show handles race and ethnicity. Now watch a nighttime drama and watch how it handles these ideas. Do they address them directly or indirectly? Write a short paper comparing the two types of show.
2. Write a short paper about the effect you think television shows have on the way we view a particular social issue.
3. Write a short paper about what is realistic in a soap opera and why that realism is important.

---

**"NOT THAT THERE'S ANYTHING WRONG WITH THAT": READING THE QUEER IN *SEINFELD***

■ **Katherine Gantz** ■

*Katherine Gantz uses the lens of "queer theory" in her 2000 discussion of* Seinfeld. *Notice how Gantz strictly defines not only the term "queer" but the particular questions she intends to ask of her text using "queer."*

THE WORLD OF MASS CULTURE, especially that which includes American television, remains overwhelmingly homophobic. Queer theory offers a useful perspective from which to examine the heterosexism at the core of contemporary television and also provides a powerful tool of subversion. The aim of this article is twofold: first, it will outline and explain the notion of a queer reading; second, it will apply a queer reading to the narrative texts that comprise the situation comedy *Seinfeld*. The concept of the queer reading, currently en vogue in literary analysis, has evolved from a handful of distinct but connected sources, beginning with the popularization of the term "queer." In 1989, the AIDS activist group ACT UP created Queer Nation, an offshoot organization comprised of lesbians and gays dedicated to the political reclaiming of gay identity under the positively recoded term "queer."[1] The group was initially formed as a New York City street patrol organized to help counteract escalating hate crimes against gays. As Queer Nation gained visibility in the public eye, the use of "queer," historically a derogatory slur for homosexuals, entered into standard parlance in the gay and lesbian press.[2] Eve Kosofsky Sedgwick's *Epistemology of the Closet*[3] appropriated the term with a broadened interpretation of "queer," suggesting not that literature be read with the author's possible homosexuality in mind but instead with an openness to the queer (homoerotic and/or homosexual) contexts, nuances, connections, and potential already available within the text. The concept of "queerness" was elaborated once more in 1991, with the publication of *Inside/Out: Lesbian Theories, Gay Theories;*[4] within this assemblage of political, pedagogical, and literary essays, the term was collectively applied to a larger category of sexual non-straightness, as will be further explained.

As the political construction of "queer" became increasingly disciplinized in academia, the emerging body of "queer theory" lost its specifically homosexual connotation and was replaced by a diffuse set of diverse sexual identities. Like the path of feminism, the concept of queerness had been largely stripped of its political roots and transformed into a methodological approach accessible to manipulation by the world of predominantly heterosexual, white, middle-class intellectuals. It is with this problematic universalization of queer theory in mind that I undertake an application of queer reading.

In what could be deemed a reinsertion of the subversive into a "straightened" discipline, Alexander Doty's book *Making Things Perfectly Queer: Reading Mass Culture*[5] has taken the queer reading out of the realm of the purely literary and applied it to analyses of film and television texts. From this ever-transforming history of the queer reading, the popular situation comedy *Seinfeld* lends itself well to a contemporary application.

In the summer of 1989, NBC debuted a tepidly received pilot entitled *The Seinfeld Chronicles,* a situation comedy revolving around the mundane, urbane Manhattan existence of stand-up comic Jerry Seinfeld. Despite its initially unimpressive ratings, the show evolved into the five-episode series *Seinfeld* and established its regular cast of Jerry's three fictional friends: George Costanza (Jason Alexander), ex-girlfriend Elaine Benes (Julia Louis-Dreyfus), and the enigmatic neighbor Kramer (Michael Richards). By its return in January 1991, *Seinfeld* had established a following among Wednesday-night television viewers; over the next two years, the show became a cultural phenomenon, claiming both a faithful viewership and a confident position in the Nielsen ratings' top ten. The premise was to write a show about the details, minor disturbances, and nonevents of Jerry's life as they occurred before becoming fodder for the stand-up monologues that bookend each episode. From the start, *Seinfeld*'s audience has been comprised of a devoted group of "TV-literate, demographically desirable urbanites, for the most part—who look forward to each weekly episode in the Life of Jerry with a baby-boomer generation's self-involved eagerness," notes Bruce Fretts, author of *The "Entertainment Weekly" "Seinfeld" Companion.*[6] Such obsessive identification and self-reflexive fascination seems to be thematic in both the inter- and extradiegetic worlds of *Seinfeld.* The show's characters are modeled on real-life acquaintances: George is based on Seinfeld's best friend (and series cocreator) Larry David; Elaine is an exaggeration of Seinfeld's ex-girlfriend, writer Carol Leifer; Kramer's prototype lived across the hall from one of David's first Manhattan apartments.[7] To further complicate this narcissistic mirroring, in the 1993 season premiere entitled "The Pilot" (see videography for episodic citations), Jerry and George finally launch their new NBC sitcom *Jerry* by casting four actors to portray themselves, Kramer, and Elaine. This multilayered Möbius strip of person/actor/character relationships seems to be part of the show's complex appeal. Whereas situation comedies often dilute their cast, adding and removing characters in search of new plot possibilities, *Seinfeld* instead interiorizes; the narrative creates new configurations of the same limited cast to keep the viewer and the characters intimately linked. In fact, it is precisely this concentration on the nuclear set of four personalities that creates the *Seinfeld* community.

If it seems hyperbolic to suggest that the participants in the *Seinfeld* phenomenon (both spectators and characters included) have entered into a certain delineated "lifestyle," consider the significant lexicon of Seinfeldian code words and recurring phrases that go unnoticed and unappreciated by the infrequent or "unknowing" viewer. Catch phrases such as Snapple, the Bubble Boy, Cuban cigars, Master of My Domain, Junior Mints, Mulva, Crazy Joe Davola, Pez, and Vandelay Industries all serve as parts of the group-specific language that a family shares; these are the kinds of self-referential in-jokes that help one *Seinfeld* watcher identify another.[8] This sort of tightly conscribed universe of meaning is reflected not only by the decidedly small cast but also by the narrative's consistent efforts to maintain its intimacy. As this article will discuss, much of *Seinfeld*'s plot and humor (and, consequently, the viewer's pleasure) hinge on outside personalities threatening—and ultimately failing—to invade the foursome. Especially where Jerry and George are concerned, episodes are mostly resolved by expelling the intruder and restoring the exclusive nature of their relationship. The show's camera work, which at times takes awkward measures to ensure that Jerry and George remain grouped together within a scene, reinforces the privileged dynamic of their relationship within the narrative.

Superficially speaking, *Seinfeld* appears to be a testament to heterosexuality: in its nine-year run, Jerry sported a new girlfriend in almost every episode; his friendship with Elaine is predicated on their previous sexual relationship; and all four characters share in the discussion and navigation of the (straight) dating scene. However, with a viewership united by a common coded discourse and an interest in the cohesive (and indeed almost claustrophobic) exclusivity of its predominantly male cast, clearly *Seinfeld* is rife with possibilities for homoerotic interpretation. As will be demonstrated, the construction, the coding, and the framing of the show readily conform to a queer reading of the *Seinfeld* text.

Here I wish to develop and define my meanings of the word "queer" as a set of signifying practices and a category distinct from that of gay literature. Inspired by Doty's work, I will use "queer"—as its current literary usages suggest—as relating to a wide-ranging spectrum of "nonnormative" sexual notions, including not only constructions of gayness and lesbianism but also of transsexualism, transvestism, same-sex affinity, and other ambisexual behaviors and sensibilities. Queerness at times may act merely as a space in which heterosexual personalities interact, in the same ways that a queer personality may operate within an otherwise heterosexual sphere. In this system, "queer" does not stand in opposition to "heterosexual" but instead to "straight," a term that by contrast, suggests all that is restrictive about "normative" sexuality, a category that excludes what is deemed undesirable, deviant, dangerous, unnatural, unproductive. "Queer," then, should be understood not so much as an intrinsic property but more as the outcome of both productive and receptive behaviors—a pluralized, inclusive term that may be employed by and applied to both gay and nongay characters and spectators.[9]

The second point I wish to clarify about the use of the term "queer" as it relates to my own textual analysis of a mass culture text is the indirect, nonexplicit nature of the queer relationships represented in *Seinfeld*. Explicit references to homosexuality subvert the possibility of a queer reading; by identifying a character as "gay," such overt difference serves to mark the other characters as "not gay." Sexual perimeters become limited, fixed, rooted in traditional definitions and connotations that work contrary to the fluidity and subtle ambiguity of a queer interpretation. It is precisely the unspokenness ("the love that dare not speak its name") of homoeroticism between seemingly straight men that allows the insinuation of a queer reading. As Doty rightly notes, queer positionings are generated more often through the same-sex tensions evident in "straight films" than in gay ones:

> Traditional narrative films [such as *Gentlemen Prefer Blondes* and *Thelma and Louise*], which are ostensibly addressed to straight audiences, often have greater potential for encouraging a wider range of queer responses than [such] clearly lesbian- and gay-addressed films [as *Women I Love* and *Scorpio Rising*]. The intense tensions and pleasures generated by the woman-woman and man-man aspects within the narratives of the former group of films create a space of sexual instability that already queerly positioned viewers can connect in various ways, and within which straights might be likely to recognize and express their queer impulses. (8)

Of course, there is a multitude of possibilities for the perception and reception of queer pleasures, but, to generalize from Doty's argument, the implications in the case of the *Seinfeld* phenomenon suggest that while queer-identified viewers may recognize the domesticity between Jerry and George as that of a gay couple, straight viewers may simply take pleasure in the characters' intimate bond left unbroken by outside (heterosexual) romantic interruptions.

This is not to say that *Seinfeld* ignores the explicit category of homosexuality; on the contrary, the show is laden with references and plot twists involving gay characters and themes. In separate episodes, Elaine is selected as the "best man" in a lesbian wedding ("The Subway"); George accidentally causes the exposure of his girlfriend Susan's father's affair with novelist John Cheever ("The Cheever Letters"); and, after their breakup, George runs into Susan with her new lesbian lover ("The Smelly Car"). At its most playful, *Seinfeld* smugly calls attention to its own homosexual undercurrents in an episode in which Jerry and George are falsely identified as a gay couple by a female journalist ("The Outing").[10] Due to the direct nature of such references to homosexuality, these are episodes that slyly deflect queer reading, serving as a sort of lightning rod by displacing homoerotic undercurrents onto a more obvious target.

Such smoke-screen tactics seem to be in conflict with the multitude of queer-identified semiotics and gay icons and symbols at play within the *Seinfeld* text. Most notably, no "queer-receptive" viewer can look at the *Seinfeld* graphic logo (at the episode's beginning and before commercials) without noticing the inverted triangle—hot pink during the earliest seasons—dotting the "i" in "Seinfeld."[11] Although the symbol dates back to the Holocaust (used to mark homosexuals for persecution), the pink triangle has recently been recuperated by gay activists during ACT UP's widely publicized AIDS education campaign, "Silence Equals Death," and has consequently become a broadly recognized symbol of gayness.

Even if the pink triangle's proactive gay recoding remains obscure to the "unknowing" viewership (i.e., unfamiliar with or resistant to queerness), *Seinfeld* also offers a multitude of discursive referents chosen from a popular lexicon of more common gay signifiers that are often slurs in use by a homophobic public. In an episode revolving around Jerry and Kramer's discussion of where to find *fruit*—longstanding slang for a gay men—Jerry makes a very rare break from his standard wardrobe of well-froned button-up oxfords, instead sporting a T-shirt with the word "QUEENS" across it. Although outwardly in reference to Queens College, the word's semiotic juxtaposition with the theme of fruit evokes its slang connotation for effeminate gay men.

Narrative space is also queerly coded. Positioned as Jerry and George's "place" (or "male space"), the restaurant where they most often meet is "Monk's," a name that conjures up images of an exclusively male religious society, a "brotherhood" predicated on the maintenance of masculine presence/feminine absence, in both spiritual and physical terms.

Recurring plot twists also reveal a persistent interest in the theme of hidden or falsified identities. As early as *Seinfeld*'s second episode ("The Stakeout"), George insists on creating an imaginary biography for himself as a successful architect before meeting Jerry's new girlfriend. Throughout the *Seinfeld* texts, the foursome adopts a number of different names and careers in hopes of persuading outsiders (most often potential romantic interests) that they lead a more interesting, more superficially acceptable, or more immediately favorable existence than what their real lives have to offer: George has assumed the identity of neo-Nazi organizer Colin O'Brian ("The Limo"); Elaine has recruited both Jerry and Kramer as substitute boyfriends to dissuade unwanted suitors ("The Junior Mint" and "The Watch"); Kramer has posed as a policeman ("The Statue") and has even auditioned under a pseudonym to play himself in the pilot of *Jerry* ("The Pilot"). Pretense and fabrication often occur among the foursome as well. In "The Apartment," Jerry is troubled by Elaine's imminent move into the apartment above him. Worried that her presence will "cramp his style," he schemes to convince her that she will be financially unable to take the apartment. In private, Jerry warns George that he will be witness to some "heavy acting" to persuade Elaine that he is genuinely sympathetic. Unshaken, George answers: "Are you kidding? I lie every second of the day; my whole life is a sham." This deliberate "closeting" of one's lifestyle has obvious connections to the gay theme of "passing,"[12] the politically discouraged practice of hiding one's homosexuality behind a façade of straight respectability. One might argue that *Seinfeld* is simply a text about passing—socially as well as sexually—in a repressive and judgmental society. It must be noted, however, that George and Jerry are the only two characters who do not lie to each other; they are in fact engaged in maintaining each other's secrets and duplicities by "covering" for one another, thus distancing themselves somewhat from Kramer and Elaine from within an even more exclusive rapport.[13]

Another thematic site of queerness is the mystification of and resulting detachment from female culture and discourse. While Jerry glorifies such male-identified personalities as Superman, the Three Stooges, and Mickey Mantle, he prides himself in never having seen a single episode of *I Love Lucy* ("The Phone Message"). Even Elaine is often presented as incomprehensible to her familiar male counterparts. In "The Shoes," Jerry and George have no problem creating a story line for their situation comedy, *Jerry,* around male characters; however, when they try to "write in" Elaine's character, they find themselves stumped:

> JERRY: [In the process of writing the script.] "Elaine enters." . . . What does she say . . . ?
> GEORGE: [Pause.] What *do* they [women] say?
> JERRY: [Mystified.] I *don't know.*

After a brief deliberation, they opt to omit the female character completely. As Jerry explains with a queerly loaded rationale: "You, me, Kramer, the butler. . . . Elaine is too much." Later, at Monk's, Elaine complains about her exclusion from the pilot. Jerry confesses: "We couldn't write for a woman." "You have *no idea?*" asks Elaine, disgusted. Jerry looks at George for substantiation and replies: "None." Clearly, the privileged bond between men excludes room for an understanding of and an interest in women; like Elaine in the pilot, the feminine presence is often simply deleted for the sake of maintaining a stronger, more coherent male narrative.

Jerry seems especially ill at ease with notions of female sexuality, perhaps suggesting that they impinge on his own. In "The Red Dot," Jerry convinces the resistant George that he should buy Elaine a thank-you gift after she procures him a job at her office. Despite George's tightfisted unwillingness to invest money in such social graces as gift giving, he acquiesces. The duo go to a department store in search of an appropriate gift for Elaine. Jerry confesses: "I never feel comfortable in the women's department; I feel like I'm just a *little* too close to trying on a dress." While browsing through the women's clothing, George describes his erotic attraction to the cleaning woman in his new office:

> GEORGE: . . . she was swaying back and forth, back and forth, her hips swiveling and
>     her breasts—uh . . .
> JERRY: . . . convulsing?

George reacts with disdain at the odd word choice, recognizing that Jerry's depiction of female physicality and eroticism is both inappropriate and unappealing. (It should be noted that the ensuing sexual encounter between George and the cleaning woman ultimately results in the loss of both their jobs; true to the pattern, George's foray into heterosex creates chaos.)

Although sites of queerness occur extensively throughout the *Seinfeld* oeuvre, the most useful elucidation of its queer potential comes from a closer, more methodical textual analysis. To provide a contextualized view of the many overlapping sites of queerness—symbolic, discursive, thematic, and visual—the following is a critique of three episodes especially conducive to a queer reading of *Seinfeld*'s male homoerotic relationships.

"The Boyfriend" explores the ambiguous valences of male friendships. Celebrated baseball player Keith Hernandez stars as himself (as does Jerry Seinfeld among the cast of otherwise fictional characters), becoming the focal point of both Jerry's and, later, Elaine's attentions. Despite Elaine's brief romantic involvement with Keith, the central narrative concerns Jerry's interactions with the baseball player. Although never explicitly discussed, Jerry's attachment to Keith is represented as romantic in nature.

The episode begins in a men's locker room, prefiguring the homoerotic overtones of the coming plot. The locker room is clearly delineated as "male space"; its connection to the athletic field posits it as a locale of physicality, where men gather to prepare for or to disengage from the privileged (and predominantly homophobic) world of male sports. The locker room, as a site of potential heterosexual vulnerability as men expose their bodies to other men, is socially safe only when established as sexually neutral—or, better still, heterosexually charged with the machismo of athleticism. This "safe" coding occurs almost immediately in this setting, accomplished through a postgame comparison of Jerry's, George's, and Kramer's basketball prowess. As they finish dressing together after their game, it is the voracious, ambisexual Kramer who immediately upsets the precarious sexual neutrality, violating the unspoken code of locker-room decorum:

> KRAMER: Hey, you know this is the first time we've ever seen each other naked?
> JERRY: Believe me, *I* didn't see anything.
> KRAMER: [With disbelief.] Oh, you didn't sneak a peek?
> JERRY: No—did you?
> KRAMER: Yeah, I snuck a peek.
> JERRY: Why?
> KRAMER: Why not? What about you, George?
> GEORGE: [Hesitating] Yeah, I—snuck a peek. But it was so fast that I didn't see anything; it was just a blur.
> JERRY: I made a conscious effort *not* to look; there's certain information I just don't want to have.

Jerry displays his usual disdain for all things corporeal or carnal. Such unwillingness to participate in Kramer's curiosity about men's bodies also secures Jerry firmly on heterosexual ground, a necessary pretext to make his intense feelings for Keith "safe." The humor of these building circumstances depends on the assumption that Jerry is straight; although this episode showcases *Seinfeld*s characteristic playfulness with queer subject matter, great pains are taken to prevent the viewer from ever believing (or realizing) that Jerry is gay.

After Kramer leaves, Jerry and George spot Hernandez stretching out in the locker room. With Kramer no longer threatening to introduce direct discussion of overtly homoerotic matters, the queer is permitted to enter into the narrative space between Jerry and George. Both baseball aficionados, they are bordering on giddy, immediately starstruck by Hernandez. Possessing prior knowledge of Keith's personal life, Jerry remarks that Hernandez is not only a talented athlete but intelligent as well, being an American Civil War buff. "I wish *I* were a Civil War buff," George replies longingly. Chronically socially inept, George is left to appropriate the interests of a man he admires without being able to relate to him more directly.[14]

Keith introduces himself to Jerry as a big fan of his comedy; Jerry is instantly flattered and returns the compliment. As the jealous and excluded George looks on (one of the rare times that Jerry and George break rank and appear distinctly physically separated within a scene), Keith and Jerry exchange phone numbers and plan to meet for coffee in the future. Thus, in the strictly homosocial, theoretically nonromantic masculine world of the locker room, two men have initiated an interaction that becomes transformed into a relationship, consistently mirroring traditional television representations of heterosexual dating rituals. The homoerotic stage is set.

Later, at Monk's, Jerry complains to Elaine that three days have passed without a call from Keith. When Elaine asks why Jerry doesn't initiate the first call, he responds that he doesn't want to seem overanxious: "If he wants to see me, he has my number; he should call. I can't stand these guys—you give your number to them, and then they don't call."

Here, in his attempts not to seem overly aggressive, Jerry identifies with the traditionally receptive and passive role posited as appropriate female behavior. By employing such categorization as "these guys," Jerry brackets himself off from the rest of the heterosexual, male dating population, reinforcing his identification with Elaine not as Same (i.e., straight male) but as Other (Elaine as Not Male, Jerry as Not Straight). Elaine responds sympathetically:

ELAINE: I'm sorry, honey.
JERRY: I mean, I thought he liked me, I really thought he liked me—we were getting along. He came over to *me*, I didn't go over to *him*.
ELAINE: [Commiserating.] I know.
JERRY: Here I meet this guy, this *great* guy, ballplayer, best guy I ever met in my life . . . well, that's it. I'm *never* giving my number out to another guy again.

Jerry is clearly expressing romantic disillusionment in reaction to Keith's withdrawal from their social economy. Elaine further links her identity—as sexually experienced with men—to Jerry's own situation:

ELAINE: Sometimes I give my number out to a guy, and it takes him a *month* to call me.
JERRY: [Outraged.] A *month?* Ha! Have him call *me* after a month—let's see if *he* has a prayer!

Thus, Jerry's construction of his relationship with Keith is one bound by the rules of heterosexual dating protocol and appropriate exchange; the intensity of his feelings and expectations for his relationship with Keith have long surpassed normative (that is, conventional, expected, tolerable), straight male friendship. By stating that Keith's violation of protocol will result in Jerry's withdrawal, it is clear that Jerry is only willing to consider any interactions with Keith in terms of a romantic model—one that, as suggested by Keith's relative indifference, is based in fantasy.

Elaine suggests that he simply put an end to the waiting and call Keith to arrange an evening out. Jerry ponders the possibility of dinner but then has doubts:

JERRY: But don't you think that dinner might be coming on too strong? Kind of a turnoff?
ELAINE: [Incredulous.] Jerry, it's a *guy.*
JERRY: [Covering his eyes.] It's all very confusing.

Throughout the episode, Jerry is content to succumb to the excitement of his newfound relationship, until the moment when someone inevitably refers to its homoerotic nature (terms such as "gay" and "homosexual" are certainly implied but never explicitly invoked). Elaine's reminder that Jerry's fears about a "turnoff" are addressed to a man quickly ends his swooning; he covers his eyes as if to suggest a groggy return from a dream-like state.

To interrupt and divert the narrative attention away from Jerry's increasingly queer leanings, the scene abruptly changes to George at the unemployment office, where he is hoping to maneuver a thirteen-week extension on his unemployment benefits.[15] There, George evades the questions of his no-nonsense interviewer Mrs. Sokol until she forces him to provide one name of a company with which he had recently sought employment. Having in truth interviewed nowhere, he quickly concocts "Vandelay Industries," a company, he assures her, he had thoroughly pursued to no avail. Further pressed, he tells Mrs. Sokol that they are "makers of latex products." His blurting-out of the word "latex" must not be overlooked here as a queer signifier directly associated with the gay safe-sex campaigns throughout the last decade. Whereas "condoms" as a signifier would have perhaps been a more mainstream (straight) sexual symbol, latex evokes a larger category of products—condoms, gloves, dental dams—linked closely with the eroticization of gay safe-sex practices. When Mrs. Sokol insists on information to verify his claim, it is telling that George provides Jerry's address and phone number as the home of Vandelay latex. George's lie necessitates a race back to Jerry's to warn him of the impending phone call; once again, he will depend on Jerry's willingness to maintain a duplicity and to adopt a false identity as the head of Vandelay Industries.

As if to await the panicked arrival of George, the scene changes to Jerry's apartment, where he is himself anxiety ridden over his impending night out with Keith. In a noticeable departure from his usual range of conservative color and style, he steps out of his bedroom, modeling a bright orange and red shirt, colors so shocking that they might best be described as "flaming." Pivoting slightly with arms outstretched in a style suggesting a fashion model, he asks Elaine's opinion. Again, she reminds him: "Jerry, he's a guy." Agitated (but never denying her implication of homoerotic attraction), he drops his arms, attempting to hide his nervous discomfort.

Jerry's actual evening out with Keith remains unseen (closeted) until the end of the "date"; the men sit alone in the front seat of Keith's car outside of Jerry's apartment. In the setup that prefigures the close of Elaine's date with Keith later in the episode, Jerry sits in the passenger seat next to him; a familiar heterosexual power dynamic is at play. Keith, as both the car owner and driver, acts and reacts in his appropriate masculine role. Jerry, within the increasingly queer context of an intimate social interaction with another man, is left to identify with what we recognize as the woman's position in the car. As the passenger and not the driver, he has relinquished both the mechanical and social control that defines the dominance of the male role. In a symbolic interpretation of power relations, Jerry's jump into the feminized gender role is characterized by the absence of the steering wheel:

JERRY: [Aloud to Keith.] Well, thanks a lot, that was really fun. [Thinking to himself.] Should I shake his hand?

This anxiety and expectation over appropriate and mutually appealing physical contact expresses the same kind of desire—that is, sexual—that Keith will express with Elaine later on; whereas Keith will long for a kiss, Jerry's desires have been translated into a more acceptable form of physical contact between men. It would seem that part of Jerry's frustration in this situation comes from the multiplicity of gender roles that he plays. Whereas in his interactions with George, Jerry occupies the dominant role (controlling the discourse and the action), he is suddenly relegated to a more passive (feminine) position in his relationship with the hypermasculine Keith Hernandez. Part of the tension that comprises the handshake scene stems not only from Jerry's desire to interact physically *and* appropriately but also from wanting to initiate such an action from the disadvantaged, less powerful position of the (feminine) passenger's seat. I would suggest that the confusion arising out of his relationship with Keith is not strictly due to its potentially homosexual valences but is also the result of the unclear position (passive/dominant, feminine/masculine, nelly/butch) that Jerry holds within the homoerotic/homosexual coupling.

Once again, the humor of this scene is based on the presupposition that Jerry is straight and that this very familiar scene is not a homosexual recreation of heterosexual dating etiquette but simply a parody of it. Nonetheless, Jerry's discomfort over initiating a handshake betrays the nature of his desire for Keith. From behind the steering wheel (the seat of masculine power), Keith invites Jerry to a movie over the coming weekend. Jerry is elated, and they shake hands: a consummation of their successful social interaction. However, Keith follows up by telling Jerry that he would like to call Elaine for a date; the spell broken, Jerry responds with reluctance and thinly veiled disappointment.

Back in Jerry's apartment, George jealously asks for a recounting of Jerry's evening with Keith. Again, the handshake is reinforced as the symbol of a successful male-to-male social encounter:

GEORGE: Did you shake his hand?
JERRY: Yeah.
GEORGE: What kind of a handshake does he have?
JERRY: Good shake, perfect shake. Single pump, not too hard. He didn't have to prove anything, but firm enough to know he's there.

George and Jerry share a discourse, laden with masturbatory overtones, in which quantifying and qualifying the description of a handshake expresses information about the nature of men's relationships. This implicit connection between male intimacy and the presence and quality of physical contact clearly transcends the interpretation of the handshake in a heterosexual context. Upon hearing that Jerry had in fact shaken hands with Keith, George follows with the highly charged question: "You gonna see him again?" Here, the use of the verb "to see," implying organized social interaction between two people, is typically in reference to romantic situations; George has thus come to accept Jerry in a dating relationship with Keith.

Elaine enters and immediately teases Jerry: "So, how was your date?" Not only has she invaded Jerry and George's male habitat, but she has once again made explicit the romantic nature of Jerry's connection to Keith that he can only enjoy when unspoken. Jerry is forced to respond (with obvious agitation): "He's a guy." Elaine quickly reveals that she and Keith have made a date for the coming Friday, perhaps expressing an implicit understanding of a rivalry with Jerry. Realizing that such plans will interfere with his own "date" with Keith, Jerry protests with disappointment and resentment. Elaine mistakes his anger as being in response to some lingering romantic attachment to her:

ELAINE: I've never seen you jealous.
JERRY: You weren't even *at* Game Six—you're not even a fan!
ELAINE: Wait a second . . . are you jealous of *him* or are you jealous of *me?*

Flustered and confused, Jerry walks away without responding, allowing the insinuation of a queer interpretation to be implied by his silence.

Jerry steps outside of the apartment just as Kramer enters; he sits alone with Elaine as George disappears into the bathroom. Predictably, it is just as Kramer finds himself next to the phone that the call from the unemployment bureau arrives; Kramer, the only one uninformed about George's scheme, answers the phone and responds with confusion, assuring the caller that she has reached a residential number, not Vandelay Industries. Having overheard, George bursts from the bathroom in a panic, his pants around his ankles. Despite his frantic pleading with Kramer to pass him the phone, Kramer is already hanging up; the defeated George collapses on the floor. Precisely at this moment, Jerry reenters the apartment. In a highly unusual aerial shot, the camera shows us Jerry's perspective of George, face down, boxer shorts exposed, and prone, lying before him on the floor in an obvious position of sexual receptivity. Jerry quips: "And you want to be my latex salesman." Once again, Jerry's reinvocation of latex has powerful queer connotations in response to seeing George seminude before him.

The next scenes juxtapose Elaine and Keith's date with Jerry's alternate Friday night activity, a visit to see his friends' new baby. Elaine, the focal point of a crowded sports bar discussing Game Six of the World Series with Keith, has occupied the very place (physically and romantically) that Jerry had longed for. In the accompanying parallel scene of Jerry, he seems both out of place and uncomfortable amid the domestic and overwhelmingly heterosexual atmosphere of the baby's nursery. The misery over losing his night on the town to Elaine is amplified by his obvious distaste for the nuclear family, the ultimate signifier of "straightness."

The scene again changes to Keith and Elaine alone in his car, this time with Elaine in the passenger seat that Jerry had previously occupied. Elaine, comfortable in her familiar and appropriate role as passive/feminine, waits patiently as Keith (in the privileged masculine driver's seat) silently wonders whether or not he should kiss her, mirroring Jerry's earlier internal debate over suitable intimate physical contact. Although they kiss, Elaine is unimpressed. Later, just as George had done, Jerry pumps Elaine for information about her date. When Elaine admits that she and Keith had kissed, Jerry pushes further: "What *kind* of kiss was it?" Incredulous at Jerry's tactlessness, Elaine does not respond. Jerry at last answers her standing question: "I'm jealous of everybody."

Keith calls, interrupting one of the few moments in the episode when Jerry and George share the scene alone. After hanging up, he explains with discomfort that he has agreed to help Keith in his move to a new apartment. George seems to recognize and identify with Jerry's apprehension over this sudden escalation in their rapport. "This is a big step in the male relationship," Jerry observes, "the biggest. That's like going all the way." Never has Jerry made such a direct reference to the potential for sexual contact with Keith. Of course, Keith has by no means propositioned Jerry, which makes the queer desire on Jerry's part all the more obvious in contrast with the seemingly asexual nature of Keith's request. However, Jerry has made clear his own willingness to homoeroticize his friendship with another man. By likening "going all the way" to moving furniture, Jerry is able to fantasize that Keith shares Jerry's homosexual desire. Ingeniously, he has crafted an imaginary set of circumstances that allow him to ignore Keith's preference for Elaine as a sexual object while tidily completing his fantasy: Keith has expressed desire for Jerry, but now Jerry has the luxury of refusing his advance on the moral ground that he will not rush sexual intimacy. Once Keith arrives, Jerry tells him that he cannot help him move, explaining that it is still too soon in their relationship. Again, by positing Keith in the masculine role of sexual aggressor, Jerry in turn occupies the stereotypically feminine role of sexual regulator/withholder.

Kramer and Newman arrive just as Jerry declines Keith's request; not surprisingly, Kramer jumps at the opportunity to take Jerry's place. As he and Newman disappear out the door to help Keith move his furniture, Jerry commiserates with Elaine over the phone: "You broke up with him? Me too!" Even as Jerry's homoerotic adventure has drawn to a close, Kramer's last-minute appearance lends an air of sexual unpredictability to end the episode on a resoundingly queer note.

In contrast to "The Boyfriend," in which the queer subtext is exploited as the source of the humor, "The Virgin" and its companion episode "The Contest" present an equally queer narrative expressed in subtler and more indirect ways. Within these interwoven episodes, the "knowing" spectator—one familiar with gay culture and receptive to potentially homoerotic situations—is essentially bombarded by queer catchphrases and code words, gay themes, and gay male behavior, while the "unknowing" spectator would most likely only recognize a traditionally "straight" plot about heterosexual dating frustrations. "The Virgin" drops its first "hair-pins" almost immediately;[16] Jerry and George are drinking together in a bar when Jerry spots Marla, a beautiful woman whom he recognizes across the room. "She's in the closet business—reorganizes your closet and shows you how to maximize your closet space. She's looked into my closet." In the same instant that we are introduced to a potential female love object for Jerry, she is immediately identified with the closet, a widely recognized metaphor referring to a gay person's secret sexual identity. Queerly read, Marla could be interpreted as (and will in fact become) a nonthreatening, nonsexual female object. Having "looked into his closet," Marla functions as a woman who is aware of Jerry's homosexuality and will be willing to interact with him in ways that will permit him to pass while still maintaining the homoerotic connections to the men around him. By allowing him this duplicity, she will indeed maximize Jerry's "closet space."

While at the bar, George bemoans the fact that he is miserable in his relationship with television executive Susan, his first girlfriend in some time. He is instead more interested in the new partnership that he has developed with Jerry, writing his new situation comedy pilot for NBC. The ostensibly platonic nature of such privileged male—male relations becomes further queered by Jerry's insistence that George "maintain appearances" with Susan until she has persuaded the network to pick up their pilot. The Seinfeldian recurring theme of hidden identities and guarded appearances puts into place the knowing viewer's suspicions about the homosexual potential between George and Jerry.

In the following scene, the spectator is given a rare view of Jerry's bedroom, made even more rare by the presence of a woman with him. Although the scene employs the standard formula for a possible sexual encounter (a man and woman alone in his bedroom), the couple remains perpetually framed inside Jerry's open closet; Jerry's coded homosexuality, symbolically surrounding the couple as they speak, prevents the sex scene from occurring.

To further complicate Jerry's interaction with Marla, his friends start to invade the apartment, interrupting the potential for intimacy. First, Kramer intrudes, taking over the television in the living room. (He is desperate to see *The Bold and the Beautiful,* a show whose soap opera genre is largely identified with a female viewership.) Jerry kicks Kramer out only to have Elaine buzz over the intercom a moment later. In the few private moments left, Marla confesses that the reason for her breakup with her ex-boyfriend was his impatience with her virginity. Elaine arrives before they can discuss it.

Marla and Elaine, Jerry's current and past romantic interests, stand in stark contrast to one another. The timid, traditional, and virginal Marla is further desexualized in the presence of the heterosexually active Elaine; this contrast is intensified by Elaine's crass description of her embarrassment at a recent party when she accidentally let her diaphragm slip out of her purse. As she laughs knowingly, Jerry winces, sensing Marla's shock at Elaine's casual remark: "You never know when you might need it." This exaggerated reference to female sexuality makes Marla's virginity even more pronounced; she is unable to hide her discomfort any longer and excuses herself in haste. It seems that Jerry, socially and romantically attached to a woman horrified by even the discussion of sex, could himself not be further from heterosexual activity.

Upon hearing that her indiscretion has lost Jerry a potential girlfriend, Elaine chases after Marla in hopes of repairing the damage. Over coffee at Monk's (clearly a female invasion of Jerry and George's male space), Elaine tries to dissuade Marla from her horror of sex with men. However, her lecture quickly dissolves into a listing of male failings: their thoughtlessness, manipulations, and fear of emotional attachment after sex. Despite Elaine's outward intentions to reunite Jerry and Marla, she has instead instilled an intensified mistrust of men. Once again, Jerry's friends have been the cause of his distancing from women; he remains insulated in the homoerotic network of his male friends and is ushered through acceptable straight society by his platonic female friend.

In a strange reversal of roles, George is still engaged in a romantic relationship with a woman (even if he is unwillingly "maintaining appearances" with Susan). At the crucial meeting with the NBC executives, George greets Susan with a kiss, an appropriate and public gesture of straightness. However, by exposing Susan as his girlfriend, George compromises her professional standing with the network. Not only is she fired, but she also breaks off her relationship with George (and consequently later "becomes" a lesbian).[17] Despite George's delight at having inadvertently rid himself of Susan, the overall message is clear: straying out of his queer context sparks destructive results in the straight world.

Juxtaposed with George's ultimately disastrous straight kiss is one of Jerry's own; he and Marla, back in his bedroom, are finally embracing passionately. The (hetero)sexual potential suggested in this scene is diffused, however, by the viewer's instant recognition that the couple is not only framed by Jerry's closet but in fact that they are embracing inside of it. Marla, as a nonsexualized female object with knowledge and access to Jerry's closet(ed-ness), poses no threat of engaging in "real" sexual intimacy with Jerry. Their embrace is made comically awkward by the clutter of Jerry's hanging clothes around them; the encounter is again cut short as Marla recalls Elaine's unflattering depiction of typical male behavior after sex. Even in absentia, Jerry's friends precipitate the woman's departure and his own separation from the possibility of (hetero)sex.

"The Contest" follows up on this storyline; Jerry is still patiently dating the virginal Marla while, as usual, spending the bulk of his social time with George, Kramer, and Elaine. As George arrives to join them for lunch at Monk's, he announces sheepishly (yet voluntarily) that he had been "caught" by his mother. Although never explicitly mentioned, George is clearly making reference to masturbation. Believing himself to be alone in his mother's house, he was using her copy of *Glamour* magazine[18] as erotic material when his mother entered and discovered him masturbating. In her shock, Mrs. Costanza had fainted, hurt herself in the fall, and ultimately wound up in traction. It is essential to note the homosexual underpinnings of masturbation as a sexual act; the fetishization of one's (and in this case, George's) own genitalia is often closely linked in psychoanalytic theory to the narcissism and reflexive fixation associated with same-sex desire. Mrs. Costanza was not reacting so much to her recognition of her son as sexual but instead to his inappropriate sexual object choice, the (his) penis. George has paid dearly for being exposed to straight eyes while practicing queer pleasure.

Traumatized by his experience, George announces that he is swearing off such activity for good. Jerry and Kramer are skeptical of the claim, and the three men find themselves in a contest—regulated by the "honor system"—to see which of them can abstain the longest from masturbating. The wager is steeped in homoerotic potential; in fact, the three *Seinfeld* men have entered into a kind of sanitized "circle jerk" in which they monitor (and consequently augment) each other's sexual tension, voyeuristically waiting to see who will be the first to "relieve" himself. When Elaine, who has been listening to their conversation from the periphery of their queer circle, wants to enter the contest as well, the men protest that she would have an unfair advantage. As Kramer explains: "It's easier for women—it's part of *our lifestyle.*" By creating a stiff binary opposition between women and "our lifestyle," he not only employs a phrase closely associated with the "alternative lifestyle" of homosexuality, but he also demonstrates an obvious ignorance and detachment from female sexuality, perpetuating myths about the limited appetite and imagination of the female sexual drive. Despite her protests, Elaine is forced to stake fifty dollars extra to even the odds before entering into the contest.

In the next scene, the foursome returns to Jerry's apartment, where Kramer immediately spots a naked woman in the window across the street.[19] The sexually ravenous Kramer is unable to control himself; he excuses himself immediately and returns to announce what we had been led to predict: "I'm out." Of the three male characters, Kramer takes on the most ambisexual valence, moving freely from the homoerotic circle shared with Jerry and George to the distinctly heterosexual desire he expressed for the naked woman. While highly sexualized, neither Kramer's intimate and often seductive relationship with Jerry and George nor his frequent erotic encounters with women serve to posit him in clear homo- or heterosexual territory. Functioning as a sort of sexual fulcrum depending on the social context, Kramer may well be acting as *Seinfeld*'s embodiment of queerness.

The three remaining contestants are left to their own frustrations. In her aerobics class, Elaine finds herself positioned behind John F. Kennedy Jr., the popular object of white,

privileged heterosexual female desire. George is disturbed and aroused by his discovery that the privacy curtain separating his mother's hospital bed from her beautiful roommate's creates an erotic silhouette of the stranger's nightly sponge bath.[20] Locked in a passionate embrace in the front seat of Jerry's car, Marla pulls back and asks Jerry to "slow down"; he politely acquiesces, assuring Marla that her virginity is not hindering his enjoyment of their relationship.

On the surface, Marla's virginity is posited as an intensifying factor of her attractiveness; the withholding of not only sex but also of her sexuality seems to make the possibility of physical intimacy even more inaccessible—and thus desirable. In fact, Marla's virginity is a crucial element to balance (and perhaps camouflage) the more important discussions and representations of masturbation. Marla's introduction to the periphery of Jerry's bet with Kramer, George, and Elaine serves a twofold purpose. First, her virginity becomes both a presence and an obstacle between Jerry and Marla, impeding any progress toward a heterosexual encounter. Second, without Marla as Jerry's ostensible love object, the "masturbation episode" would take on a glaringly homosexual tone. Marla's presence serves to divert attention away from what is more or less a circle jerk among homosexualized men: a collective and voyeuristic study of each other's (auto)erotic activity, focusing—if we may momentarily exclude Elaine's participation—on the male orgasm brought on reflexively by the male participants. As a virgin, Marla serves to deflect the queerness of the contest away from Jerry while never threatening the homoerotic trinity of Jerry, George, and Kramer.

Elaine, by comparison, is indeed a heterosexually active female. Why is Elaine allowed to participate in the otherwise queerly coded masturbatory abstinence contest? In effect, she never truly is cast as an equal participant. Throughout the episode, she is consistently figured as the "odd man out"; at the restaurant table where the triangulated male bodies of Jerry, George, and Kramer construct the terms of the bet, Elaine is seated in the corner of the booth. Within the frames, she appears either alone or with her back partially turned to the camera, surrounded by the men who look toward her, clearly separated from the intimate boy talk of the others who share the booth with her. As mentioned before, the men's misconception that women are naturally predisposed to such masturbatory abstinence works to further distance female sexuality—and thus females—from their own collective experience of (same-sex) desire. Perhaps most importantly, Elaine's strongest connection to the trio is through her relationship with Jerry, a friendship that is predicated on their previous failure as (hetero)sexual partners. Her potentially menacing role as Straight Female is mitigated by her position as Not Love Object. Elaine may participate in the contest from the sidelines without truly interrupting its homosexual valence.

Despite the remaining contestants' boasts of being "queen of the castle" and "master of my domain," their sexual frustrations are evident in the four juxtaposed scenes of their private bedrooms: Jerry appears restless in his bed of white linens; George thrashes beneath his sheets printed with cartoon dinosaurs;[21] Elaine is sleepless in her darkened room; Kramer, however, long having satisfied his desire, snores peacefully.

Grumpy from his sleepless night, Jerry tells Kramer that he can no longer tolerate the view of the naked neighbor across the street. As he prepares to go over and ask the woman to draw her shades, the infuriated Kramer tries to stop him, doubting Jerry's sanity for wanting to block their view of a beautiful nude woman. Kramer has called into question Jerry's priorities, which seem to be clear: Jerry privileges his participation in the queerly coded contest over the visual pleasure Kramer experiences from the nude woman.

In the next series of juxtaposed bedroom shots, the viewer discovers from Elaine's restful sleep that she has given in. The next morning, as she sheepishly relinquishes her money, she explains that rumors of JFK Jr.'s interest in her had prompted her moment of weakness. Jerry marvels that "the queen is dead," thereby leaving only himself and George to compete for the pot.

In the following scene, two embracing figures are stretched out on the couch in Jerry's dark apartment. In the close-up shot, we see that Marla is on top of Jerry; not only does this physicality suggest a heightened potential for sexual intimacy between the ordinarily distant couple, but Jerry's positioning on the bottom of the embrace casts him in the stereotypically feminine, passive role of a woman in a straight couple (a role evocative of the one he occupied in his relationship with Keith Hernandez). In keeping with the episode's (and indeed the show's) pattern, such menacing circumstances should surely create chaotic results.

Taking her cue from Jerry's receptive position, the previously hesitant Marla becomes the aggressor, initiating a (masculine) invitation to have sex: "Let's go in the bedroom." From beneath her, Jerry's somewhat timid voice sounds unsure: "*Really?*" Now too close for comfort, Jerry must find a way to disengage from the heterosexual situation in which he is now entangled; Marla's virginity is no longer a sufficient buffer. When Marla asks why he looks so tense, he thoughtlessly (or so it would appear) recounts the details of the contest to explain his (ostensible) relief at the chance to have sex with her. Marla reacts with horror and disgust and quickly exits, leaving Jerry alone.

On the street, Marla bumps into Elaine, who is eagerly awaiting the arrival of JFK Jr. for their first arranged meeting. Marla pulls away from Elaine in revulsion: "I don't want to have anything to do with you or your perverted friends. Get away from me, you're horrible!" Having clearly identified Jerry, George, and Kramer as sexually deviant (i.e., not "straight"), Marla leaves, removing the safe, female heterosexual anchor that her presence provided to the otherwise transparently queer contest.

Believing that JFK Jr. stood her up, Elaine complains to Jerry only to hear from George that Kennedy had just driven away with Marla. As they look out the window, Jerry spots Kramer in the arms of the beautiful woman across the street.

In the final series of four bedroom shots, Jerry and George are at last also enjoying a restful sleep; Kramer snores next to his new lover, and Marla compliments "John" on his sexual prowess. Whereas the two latter scenes depict the postorgasmic satisfaction of the two heterosexual partners that share it, the two former scenes are ambiguous by contrast: no explanation is provided for how or why Jerry and George relieved their pent-up sexual energies at the same time. With no female love object available (no recent viewings of the erotic sponge bath for George, and Jerry's potential lover has left him) to dehomosexualize Jerry and George's two-member circle jerk, the viewer is left with the suggestion that they have satisfied their sexual frustrations together. Intensified by the "success" of the hypervirile JFK Jr. in the face of Jerry's sexual failure with Marla, the narrative closes with individual shots of George and Jerry—alone and yet paired off. Quite apart from the strong homoerotic sensibility of "The Contest"'s construction, the simple and familiar plot resolution—the duo's inability to sustain a romantic relationship with a woman leaves them again alone with each other—marks the episode as incontrovertibly queer.

*Seinfeld*'s narrative design would, at first glance, seem to lack the depth necessary in character and plot to facilitate a discussion of the complexities of homoerotic male rela-

tionships. The sort of nonspecific, scattered quality of the *Seinfeld* text, however, makes it well suited to the fluid nature of a queer reading, whose project is more concerned with context than fixity, more with potential than evidence. Nonetheless, *Seinfeld* is full of both context and evidence that lead the text's critics toward a well-developed queer reading. *Seinfeld* enjoys a kind of subculture defined by a discursive code that unites its members in a common lexicon of meaning. The narrative restricts its focus to the foursome, containing and maintaining the intimate bonds between the show's three men and its one woman (the latter being clearly positioned as sexually incompatible and socially separate from the others). Directly related to this intense interconnection, the foursome often causes each member's inability to foster outside heterosexual romantic interests.

Jerry and George share the most intimate relationship of them all; they aid each other in perpetuating duplicities while remaining truthful only with one another. They are the two characters who most frequently share a frame and who create and occupy male-coded narrative spaces, whether in the domestic sphere of Jerry's apartment or in the public sphere at Monk's.

All of these relationships are in motion amid a steady stream of other discursive and iconic gay referents. Their visibility admits the "knowing" viewer into a queerly constructed *Seinfeld* universe while never being so explicit as to cause the "unknowing" viewer to suspect the outwardly "normal" appearance of the show.

Reading the queer in *Seinfeld* sheds a revealing light on the show's "not that there's anything wrong with that" approach to representations of male homoeroticism. While sustaining a steadfast denial of its gay under-currents, the text playfully takes advantage of provocative semiotic juxtapositions that not only allow but also encourage the "knowing" spectator to ignore the show's heterosexual exterior and instead to explore the queerness of *Seinfeld*.

## Selected *Seinfeld* Videography
### (*Seinfeld*. Created by Jerry Seinfeld and Larry David. NBC-TV, 1989–98.)

"The Apartment." Writ. Peter Mehlman. 4 Apr. 1991.
"The Boyfriend." Writ. Larry David and Larry Levin. 12 Feb. 1992.
"The Café." Writ. Tom Leopold. 6 Nov. 1991.
"The Cheever Letters." Writ. Larry David. 28 Oct. 1992.
"The Contest." Writ. Larry David. 13 Nov. 1992.
"The Dog." Writ. Larry David. 9 Oct. 1991.
"The Junior Mint." Writ. Andy Robin. 18 Mar. 1993.
"The Limo." Writ. Larry Charles. 26 Feb. 1992.
"The Outing." Writ. Larry Charles. 11 Feb. 1993.
"The Phone Message." Writ. Larry David and Jerry Seinfeld. 13 Feb. 1991.
"The Pllot." Writ. Larry David. 20 May 1993.
"The Red Dot." Writ. Larry David. 11 Dec. 1991.
"The Shoes." Writ. Larry David and Jerry Seinfeld. 4 Feb. 1993.
"The Smelly Car." Writ. Larry David and Peter Mehlman. 15 Apr. 1993.
"The Stakeout." Writ. Larry David and Jerry Seinfeld. 31 May 1990.
"The Statue." Writ. Larry Charles. 11 Apr. 1991.
"The Subway." Writ. Larry Charles. 8 Jan. 1992.
"The Virgin." Writ. Larry David. 11 Nov. 1992.
"The Watch." Writ. Larry David. 30 Sept. 1992.

Notes

All dialogue quoted in this essay, unless otherwise indicated, comes from my own transcriptions of the television programs in question.

1. Dave Walter, "Does Civil Disobedience Still Work?" *Advocate,* 20 Nov. 1990, 34–38.
2. For further discussion of the political and semiotic history of the word "queer," see Ernesto Laclau, *New Reflections on the Revolution of Our Time* (London: Verso, 1990); Teresa de Lauretis, "Queer Theory: Lesbian and Gay Sexualities," *differences* 3:2 (1991): iii–xviii; Michelangelo Signorile, "Absolutely Queer: Reading, Writing, and Rioting," *Advocate,* 6 Oct. 1992, 17.
3. Eve Kosofsky Sedgwick, *Epistemology of the Closet* (Berkeley: University of California Press, 1990).
4. Diana Fuss, ed. *Inside/Out: Lesbian Theories, Gay Theories* (New York: Routledge, 1991).
5. Alexander Doty, *Making Things Perfectly Queer: Reading Mass Culture* (Minnesota: University of Minnesota Press, 1993).
6. Bruce Fretts, *The Entertainment Weekly "Seinfeld" Companian* (New York: Warner Books, 1993), 12.
7. Bill Zehme, "Jerry and George and Kramer and Elaine: Exposing the Secrets of *Seinfeld*'s Success," *Rolling Stone* 660–61 (6–22 July 1993): 40–45, 130–31.
8. As evidence of this Seinfeldian shared vocabulary, I offer one of my primary resources for this paper, *The Entertainment Weekly "Seinfeld" Companion.* Author Bruce Fretts creates a partial glossary of these terms, situating them in their episodic contexts, cross-referencing them with the episodes in which the term recurs, and finally providing a chronological plot synopsis of episodes 1–61, ending with the 1993 season premiere, "The Pilot."
9. Doty outlines the political and semiotic complexities of the term "queer" in his insightful introduction to *Making Things Perfectly Queer.*
10. My essay takes its title from this episode; while combating the rumor of their homosexuality, the phrase "not that there's anything wrong with that" serves as Jerry and George's knee-jerk addendum to their denials. The catchphrase becomes a running joke through the episode, being echoed in turn by Jerry's and George's mothers and, later, by Kramer as well.
11. During the 1994 season, the *Seinfeld* triangle suddenly switched to blue. Might this suggest that the show's creators wished to distance themselves from an overly gay-identified icon, or does a queer interpretation suggest that Jerry is simply attempting to be more butch during that period? The 1995 season was marked with an ambiguous green triangle; the icon continued to change in each following season. One can only speculate that the shift away from the pink triangle is meant to mirror the shift away from the queerness of the early seasons—as evidenced by Susan's abrupt renunciation of lesbianism and subsequent return to George (my thanks to colleagues Melinda Kanner and Steve Bishop for their insightful ideas on this subject).
12. A particularly useful example of this theme occurs in "The Café," in which George, terrified of his girlfriend Monica's request that he take an IQ test, fears that he will not be able to pass. Out of desperation, he arranges for the more intelligent Elaine to take the test for him by passing it out to her through an open window. Jerry too has approved their secret plan to pass George off as an intelligent, appropriate partner for Monica: "Hey, I love a good caper!" Despite their best efforts to dupe Monica by presenting George in a false light, she discovers their duplicity and breaks up with him.
13. When questioned, Jerry makes no secret about the intensity of his "friendship" with George; in "The Dog," he confesses that they talk on the phone six times a day—coincidentally, the same number of times a day that he gargles.
14. A queer reading of the social differences between Jerry and George reveals a substratum of conflict: within the homoerotic dynamic that groups them together as a couple, George is constantly portrayed as crude, unrefined, and in need of direction. When George is paired with Jerry in the intimate, caretaking relationship they share, their connection suggests a domestic partnership in which Jerry, the more successful and refined of the duo, acts as their public voice, correcting

George's social missteps allowing them to "pass" less noticeably through acceptable, urban, upper-middle-class society.

15.  It should be noted that George's presentation as both unemployed and desperate accentuate the clear class differences between him and Jerry, the successful stand-up comic being courted by a celebrity athlete.

16.  In *Gay Talk* (New York: Paragon Books, 1972). Bruce Rodgers defines the expression "drop hair-pins" (also "drop beads" or "drop pearls") as "to let out broad hints of one's sexuality" (69). Historically rooted in gay male culture, this expression is useful here to express the texts' many links to gay icons and lexicon. It should be noted, however, that the intentionality suggested by the phrase "drop hairpins" is problematic in the context of this paper, as I am not entering into an analysis of whether or not the creators of *Seinfeld* have knowingly or inadvertently produced a heavily queer text.

17.  In "The Smelly Car," George runs into Susan for the first time since their breakup and is shocked to see her with Mona, her new lover. Although Susan alludes to her longstanding attraction to women. George makes multiple references to how he "drove her" to lesbianism. After Mona is inexplicably seduced by Kramer's mystique, Susan makes a new romantic contact in Allison, another of George's ex-girlfriends. The implication is not only that George is a failure as a heterosexual but also that, even in his attempts to connect romantically with women, he is attracted to inappropriate (or equally conflicted) female object choices.

18.  George's use of *Glamour*, a women's fashion magazine, is a notably odd choice for visual sexual stimulation. In contrast to such heterosexual pornography as *Playboy*, in which nude women are presented in ways to elicit sexual responses from men. George has instead found sexual pleasure from a magazine whose focus is women's beauty culture—fashion, health, cosmetics—and not women themselves. It is essential to recognize that George's masturbatory activity was not in response to heterosexual desire for women's bodies but instead connected to something only indirectly related to their appearances.

19.  In contrast to George's interest in *Glamour*, Kramer provides us with a more familiar example of an "appropriate" erotic stimulus for the heterosexual male; the sight of a nude woman directly and immediately enacts Kramer's sexual response.

20.  This visual joke is revived in "The Outing": having been falsely identified in the newspaper as Jerry's lover. George attempts to set his shocked and still-hospitalized mother "straight." However, the tempting silhouette of the beautiful patient and her nurse has been replaced by the erotic shapes of a muscular male attendant sponge-bathing a brawny male patient.

21.  Again, the spectator is privy to a subtle material reference to the class distinctions apparent within the coupling of Jerry and George; the contrast in their choices of bed linens—Jerry's tasteful white and George's childish, colorful pattern—provide a point of reference from which to understand the power dynamic between them as middle- to upper-middle-class (Jerry) and lower-middle- to working-class (George) gay men.

**READING WRITING**

## THIS TEXT: READING

1.  Gantz indicates to an extent her writing situation when she labels American television as "homophobic." How does this play out in her essay?

2.  Gantz focuses on "queer theory" in this essay, which she essentially uses as a lens to view her text. Are there other lenses we might use in discussing popular culture? Using another lens such as gender, race, or class, examine *Seinfeld* or some other popular text.

3.  What other works might yield the same type of results with examination by queer theory?

4.  Why might *Seinfeld* be a particularly good show to examine? Does Gantz indicate this in her essay?
5.  In what ways might queer theory apply in your daily experiences of reading?
6.  What is the difference between "queer" and "homosexual"? Does Gantz make the distinction clear?

## YOUR TEXT: WRITING

1.  Using the same lens of queer theory as Gantz, examine another popular television show.
2.  Using another lens (such as race, gender, class), examine *Seinfeld* or another popular show. How does reading through a particular theory affect the writing process?
3.  Write a short response paper to the essay itself. What did you like about it? What if anything disturbed you about it?

## *Student Essay*

### SOCIETY'S NEED FOR A *QUEER* SOLUTION: THE MEDIA'S REINFORCEMENT OF HOMOPHOBIA THROUGH TRADITIONAL GENDER ROLES

### ■ Archana Mehta ■

*Archana Mehta wrote this paper in a sophomore-level writing and research class at Virginia Commonwealth University in spring 2001. The class was asked to find a "cultural text"—a text with cultural implications or importance—and research the connections it makes to academic and personal contexts. Here Mehta writes about the popular television show* Will and Grace *and comes up with some surprising conclusions about the place of gays and lesbians on the show.*

"HEY, DO YOU have a minute? I need to tell you something really important and I do not know who else to turn to."

"Sure," I replied, oblivious to what my friend was going to tell me. By the seriousness of his tone and the lifeless expression on his face, I could tell that the next couple of sentences that would pass through his mouth would be serious, but I could not determine or predict the magnitude of what he was going to discuss with me.

"Okay, I don't know exactly how to tell you this, but . . ." his voice faded out and his eyes looked down to the floor as if he was terribly embarrassed and withdrawn from any emotion. Slowly he handed me his leather journal with the page to be read already open. Dead silence followed. I began to read the writing silently to myself.

> . . . And I now gradually began to realize, on an intellectual level, what I was. Why did that take so long? I think because when one grows up and hears words like "gay" or "homosexual," one thinks of rather horrid people, who are disgusting, ugly, and immoral. Many times I would think of some of the many images that people have about gay men and would try to convince myself that their actions were revolting. I thought: I cannot be one of them! And yet, deep down, I knew I was. What I began to understand was that the term "homosexual" really did not denote anything but a description of a male person who is emotionally and sexually attracted to another male. It did not represent anything, in itself, regarding the looks, behavior or values of anyone. I know that gay people are like everyone else—some

are nice, some are rude, some are beautiful, some are ugly, some are young, some are old, etc.—this is how I convince myself that the person I am and the actions that I carry out are okay . . .

To this day, I still do not remember clearly how I initially reacted because homosexuality was a foreign concept to me. Now that I know someone who is indeed gay, my perceptions have changed a great deal. For the first time I realize how hard it is to deal with homosexuality in our society. I see the struggles that my friend encounters and the identity crises he faces, such as where he stands in his group of friends, how he is expected to behave, whether he should be open about it or not, etc. Why should anyone have to deal with these emotions because of who he is and what he believes? Why did his sexuality have to determine his identity and how his family, friends and society perceive him? Why does something so private as one's sexuality have to be discriminated against and looked down upon?

Before that day, I admit that I joked about the subject, participated in the typical gay comments and believed in many of the stereotypes that existed about homosexuals. I differentiated homosexuality and considered it a different form of identification just like a great deal of people do in our society. I ask myself why we, as a society, encourage differentiating individuals who do not follow heterosexuality and why they are deemed abnormal. My conclusion to this question was plain and simple: homosexuals act differently than what is expected in society. They do not follow the "normal" behavior that traditional gender roles outline for individuals. Some clear examples are that homosexuals lead promiscuous lifestyles, carry the AIDS virus, attend lavish parties and lead disorderly lives, enjoy shopping, and speak and walk a certain way and most obviously, they have sex with individuals of the same sex. In other words, they appear not to carry out the specific roles that are molded and expected for people in society.

Learning about my friend's homosexuality for the first time gave me an opportunity to analyze the existence of homosexuality in our culture as a form of identity. The emergence of a distinct homosexual population, the formation of their culture and their quest for acceptance and assimilation of their identity within mainstream culture is one of the most interesting and dynamic social transformations in American history. Homosexuality has gone from being an unspoken subject to a common topic of debate that appears in universities, politics and especially in mass media such as television. In fact, television conveys the traditional ideas, beliefs and generalizations that already exist about homosexuality in society. It is an excellent tool that is used to understand the status of homosexuality in our culture because, like a mirror, it reflects some very important beliefs and values permeating our society. When analyzing different sitcoms, cartoons and news broadcasts shown on television, one can say a great deal about the social and societal organization in the public, and it is especially apparent with the topic of homosexuality. Even though homosexuality is increasingly shown on television still does not imply that it is accepted. In fact, these television shows are "denormalizing" homosexuality even more by incorporating the idea of traditional gender roles even further.

Briefly observing the wide array of television shows that involve homosexuality, a great deal can be said about the status of homosexuality and how society perceives this form of sexual orientation. In the show *Ellen*, which was a very popular show for several years, the main character, played by Ellen Degeneres, decided to take a positive turn in her show by "coming out" to the public that she was gay in 1997. After her announcement, she incorporated the lifestyle of a gay person in her show very realistically, and to no surprise, the ratings plummeted. Furthermore, she was mocked on other shows such as *The Late Night Show, The Conan O'Brien Show* and even *Saturday Night* because of her sexual orientation and disparaged for her decision to go public.

On the other hand, when the NBC show *Friends* decided to show two lesbian women, Carol and Susan, raising a child together, the ratings did not alter at all because the portrayal was not realistic and was in fact very comedic. For example, the two women buy a shirt for their child that says, "I love my mommies" and both of them are mocked by the other characters because they breastfeed their child together. Not once does the show actually give a positive view on homosexual parenting. Susan and Carol are depicted as incapable of raising a child due to the lack of male influence in the child's life. Furthermore, the jokes made against Susan and Carol revolve around their "sexual practices" rather than making any positive comments about their personalities. Since Susan and Carol are not following the traditional gender roles, they are laughed at and looked down upon by other heterosexual characters on the show. Consequently, the lesbian couple on *Friends* is portrayed on television through a heterosexual view, as opposed to Ellen's realistic homosexual view, and this form of entertainment indicates the status of homosexuality in society. Why is the comedic version of homosexuality more popular than the realistic version of homosexuality on television? It shows us that homosexuality is not taken seriously. This indicates that the shows shown on primetime television are heterosexualized, meaning they are made to satisfy a heterosexual audience. In the cases of *Ellen* and *Friends,* the homosexual characters do not follow traditional gender roles and more importantly in *Friends,* the show's divergence from traditional gender roles is designed specifically to entertain rather than educate. What does this suggest about the audience? The audience, or society, does not really care to learn or understand the realistic homosexual subculture; rather they prefer it as a form of entertainment. Not wanting to understand and learn about true homosexuality suggests that there is a homophobia in our society that results from the traditional gender roles that we are taught and raised with.

Perhaps the epitome of all television shows that openly and comically portrays the lifestyles and the interactions between homosexuals and heterosexuals, and distinctly differentiates these two groups of people on primetime television, is *Will and Grace.* In fact this television show conveys a great deal about society's expectations. The show includes three main characters, Will, Grace, and Jack, who are very fascinating because they each have contrasting personalities and they demonstrate different sexual orientations. The portrayal of homosexuality on this show is represented in stark contrast to the heterosexual characters, suggesting that homosexuality is a deviant form of sexuality due to its straying from traditional gender roles. Consequently, it is apparent that the television is one of the many tools used in society to promote and preserve traditional gender roles, which generates a homophobia in the majority heterosexual population.

Grace, as a preserver of the traditional female gender role, represents the "straight heterosexual." Working for a decorating firm, Grace is perky, loud, vivacious, and fashionable. She plays the role of the typical woman, chasing after love and trying to find the "perfect" man, thus ensuring her happiness. Grace also lives with her roommate/best friend Will, an extremely educated, intellectual lawyer. Additionally, Will is known for his subtle gayness. Occasionally, he shops with Grace and together they gossip about cute men. In fact, together they discuss how there is a "drought of good looking men in their lives." Interestingly, Will is the "tolerated" homosexual. Since he gives the impression that he is straight based on his looks and behavior, he seems to be more socially accepted. Outwardly, to an objective on-looker, Will appears to preserve the traditional male gender role. Thus, it is not easy to dis-criminate his sexual orientation, as it is apparent in the third major character Jack who is spunky, well dressed, clumsy, emotional and very overtly gay. He is the complete antithesis of Will and Grace, demonstrating the typical images that are tagged onto gay men. When-ever he speaks, he moves his hands in grandiose ways, acts overly expressive when discussing his emotions, speaks with a slight lisp and wears tight pants and collared shirts from ex-pensive stores like Banana Republic. In addition to dressing well, he is loud, energetic, and very vocal about being gay. He openly flirts with other men at malls and clubs as well as loves to dance to "girly" songs by Brittany Spears and Ricky Martin. Jack appears to follow the non-traditional male gender role. He is "girly" and an embarrassing person to be seen with because of his idiosyncrasies, from which the show derives much of its humor. Most im-portantly, both Will and Jack, although to different degrees, represent the stereotypical ho-mosexual, and Grace represents the typical heterosexual.

Even though the sitcom is very comical, the portrayal of the characters on *Will and Grace* definitely represents how television serves as a mirror reflecting reality by showing the contents, values and beliefs of homosexuality in our society. In addition, the show ex-emplifies how television reinforces reality for viewing audiences by shaping their attitudes and strengthening traditional gender roles and how any deviation is considered abnormal. Moreover, the broadcasting of this show definitely expresses a great deal about how society has progressed from keeping certain issues taboo to becoming more open. However, the mere presentation of this sitcom to the entire population of the United States does not nec-essarily indicate that homosexuality is accepted. Hence, an interpretation of several theories on the topic of homosexuality may help one to understand the status of homosexuals in so-ciety as well as what the cultural implications of a show such as *Will and Grace* mean to the common person.

Before understanding the perceptions and status of homosexuality in our society, it is important to interpret the different theories explaining the evolution of the term homosex-ual and how it eventually relates to traditional gender roles. (Due to the broadness of ho-mosexuality, which can include bisexuals, transsexuals and lesbians, the topic of this paper will discuss homosexuality among men only.) The essentialists are a group of people who be-lieve that identity is natural and fixed. They therefore strongly ascertain that people who are homosexual are this way due to biological reasons (McCormick 450). Consequently, they hold that there are two distinct types of people: people who are homosexual and people who are heterosexual. Leading essentialist scientists in the area of psychoneuroendocrinology be-lieve that erotic/romantic attraction and desire for same-sex in both men and women are due to biological variables, such as genes, hormones, and brain neuroanatomy (McCormick 459). Similarly, Paul Robinson, in his essay "Freud and Homosexuality" discusses how Sigmund Freud held an important essentialist view because he believed that the essence of homosex-uality was in the mind and recognized its causes to be a result of the variation of a child's up-bringing (92). According to Freud, the child is homosexual because he/she fixates at an early stage of development or psychological growth (Robinson 92). Robinson also brings to at-tention that Freud "repeatedly, almost compulsively, refers to heterosexuality as the 'normal' result . . . of psychological maturity" (92). Since essentialists view homosexuality as a scientific anomaly, they strongly reason that this form of sexual orientation is a sickness like Parkinson's disease. Hence, essentialists try to cure homosexuality. It is evident from the essentialist view that as science advanced, social scientists explicated variation in populations. Hence, homosexual people, who were the observed minority in society, became a sort of experimental group. Consequently, they became even more differentiated in society and were considered anti-normative.

Contrary to this, the constructionist position, which opposes the essentialist, believes that identity is changeable and culture-dependent. Michel Foucault, a prominent French historian and constructionist, provides an interesting argument in his book *The History of Sexuality* that the term "homosexual" never existed before the year 1870 (43). According to him, same-sex sex acts have existed since the beginning of time, and even though religious and political leaders condemned them, everyone knew that they could fall to such temptations (43). Since anyone could submit to this sin, the population as a whole is susceptible to such activity. No one is born to behave in this manner. According to Foucault, it was not until after 1870 that the concept of the homosexual came into an identifiable type of person (43). The homosexual began to be identified in terms of his sexual activities. Rather than existing as only a behavior, it became solidified into a label. Foucault states, The sodomite had been a temporary aberration; the homosexual was now a species (43).

In fact, Annamarie Jagose, a senior lecturer at Melbourne University supports the idea that homosexuality became differentiated due to society's expectations. She states that homosexuality [became] a social role (13). This invention of the term homosexuality parallels the ideas of Foucault, who feels that sexuality became an identity due to society as well. Foucault theorizes the reason for sexuality becoming an identity. He strongly believes that Western society during the 1800s preoccupied themselves with discussing the nature of sex for two reasons. One reason was the necessity to confess all sexual practices in the Christian culture to pastors in order to monitor each person's sexual encounters, behaviors and desires in order to trace for sin (Foucault 17–35). In general, sex was a sin of flesh; hence it was important to incorporate all details. Foucault states further that there was a task of telling . . . oneself . . . as often as possible, everything that might concern the interplay of innumerable pleasures, sensations, and thoughts which, through the body and the soul, had some affinity with sex (20). The second reason was that society fixated on discovering the truth about sex and regulating it (17–35). Hence, sexuality became an even more reinforced and essential aspect in society. People believed that sex could be controlled through massive discussions or public discourse (Foucault 15). This need to converse became an obsession in order to research, analyze and understand the nature of sexuality. However, during the nineteenth century, the need to discuss sexuality in order to monitor the population gradually transformed into a need to understand sexuality in a scientific manner in order to satisfy the desire to understand such behaviors (Foucault 53–73). These scientific doctrines began to identify and postulate several unnatural sexual behaviors. Before, discourse regulated behaviors, but now it was observed and explained by logical reason; hence, homosexuality and other forms of sexual behaviors were distinguished into their own groups (Foucault 55). Homosexual relations had been seen as a sin that could be committed from time to time, but now a group of homosexuals emerged (Foucault 43). The idea of sexuality became fundamental part of the person. Most importantly, Foucault continues his claim that sexuality was not instinctive; on the contrary, it was a social construction that can exist in one society, but not in other societies (Foucault 53–73).

Now that the emergence of the term homosexual as a societal construction is well understood, the term can be further linked to the theories of gender. Annamarie Jagose, author of *Introduction to Queer Theory*, states, "there is a crucial distinction between homosexual behavior which is ubiquitous and homosexual identity, which evolves under specific . . . conditions" (15). This statement supports that homosexual behavior is considered deviant because those who actively and openly participate in same-sex activities are categorized and ostracized due to societal conditions and restraints such as gender. Moreover, Judith Lorber, a current writer of feminist theory discusses the meaning of gender in our culture in her essay "The Social Construction of Gender." Lorber writes, "Gender is so much the routine ground of everyday activities that questioning it is taken for granted" (20). Many people do not even recognize that many of the activities, thoughts and behaviors that we possess are shaped by gender. Hence, Lorber creates a very important point in that much of the generalizations that people have about homosexuality are the result of gender. The information regarding the concept of gender is vast as in how the formation of the word affects and sculpts our society. However, in this research paper, the effects of gender on homosexuality and heterosexuality will be the main focus.

The idea of gender, originally created on the basis of genitalia, also involves the "assignment of sex" to each individual, mainly the perceptions of masculine and feminine characteristics (Lorber 20). Essentially, gender generates roles for the masculine and feminine identity such as the female as the child bearer whereas the male is the provider of the family. Gender is habitual and limits what females and males can do (Lorber 21). In fact, gender binds and forces us to be what others want us to be. For example, from my observations, when a child is born, depending on the sex, the child is raised completely differently. If the child is a girl, then she wears pink clothes and plays with dolls, teddy bears and kitchen sets. However, if a child is a boy, he is given athletic equipment, trucks and cars to play with and is taught to be strong both physically and emotionally. Thus, society molds children into behaving and thinking in certain ways from the very beginning, especially in the way they are expected to participate in activities. More importantly, a girl is taught to express her feelings, whereas the boy is guided into being a tough and aggressive person, not showing his feelings as much. Maasik and Solomon, two leading gender theorists, articulately define that gender is "a culturally constructed belief system that dictates the appropriate roles and behavior for men and women in society" (438).

These observations on gender in society are summarized further by Chrys Ingraham, author of the essay "The Heterosexual Imaginary," who believes that "femininity and masculinity are achieved characteristics . . . [and that] maleness and femaleness are 'ascribed traits' " (185). It is important to realize that from this statement that maleness and femaleness can have variations in the extent of how masculine or feminine a person can be; however, a distinction in society between the two sexes and how they should behave exists. Consequently, society does not maintain the flexibility to carry out behaviors from the two sexes. Instead, Ingraham writes that gender is a form of "organizing relations between the [two] sexes" (186). According to Judith Lorber, a professor of women's studies, as a result of gender, society began to perceive heterosexuality as the way relationships should be solidified (Lorber 23). It is assumed that attraction for the opposite sex is the natural way. In the essay "Heterosexuality and Social Policy," Jean Carabine theorizes about existence of heterosexuality. She maintains that society continues to make heterosexuality the natural form of sexual relationship, creating a general perception that to be a homosexual is unnatural (61). It became the norm to have sex between the male and the female, since the function of sex was for reproduction (Lorber 23). The existence of gender molds such specific roles for partners in sexual relationships that any sort of deviance from the dominant culture signifies a rejection of culture itself. Thus, individuals in society who are "rejecting culture" by not following gender-created heterosexuality are punished and looked down upon. Consequently, gender not only creates such distinctions in sexuality such as determining what is normal and what is not, but it also creates a homophobia for those who do not follow the norm. Holly Devor validates this assumption by saying, "society demands [specific] gender performances [and relationships] from us and rewards, tolerates, or punishes us differently for conformity to, or digression from, social norms" (414).

Since gender creates distinctions between male and female and organizes the "normal" sexual relations between these two groups, it is evident that the presence of homosexuality creates a homophobia in our culture. Several examples can be seen in a single episode of *Will and Grace*. The actions of each of the characters reproduce, reaffirm and reflect the dominant ideologies of traditional gender roles and how homosexuality is deviant from these roles in our culture. For example, as previously established, Will, Grace and Jack all depict the stereotypical roles of homosexuals and heterosexuals. When a cute male tenant moves into an apartment on Will and Grace's floor, both Will and Grace attempt to get the newcomer's attention and they do so by demonstrating typical methods of approach to get a date with this guy. Grace, dressed in a tight miniskirt and a flamboyant shirt, draws attention to her breasts and legs in order to grab his attention; however, Will, who is also wearing tight jeans, converses with him and reveals his gayness with hints of gay remarks. Both characters are reaffirming and reflecting society's homosexual and heterosexual roles as well as their assigned gender roles. Grace behaves as a typical woman by wearing showy clothes and using her body to seduce men. Will remains confused between the "normal" male and female roles; wearing tight jeans and tight shirts, he tries to be flirtatious in a masculine, but "gay" way. Yet, when does an individual choose to conform to a specific type of gender role? It is the mass media that subconsciously reinforce such ways of thinking in the American public.

Similarly, both Will and Grace exemplify the roles expected of their gender when they shop with Grace's heterosexual boyfriend, Nathan, at Barney's in New York City. The juxtaposition of the three characters is very interesting. Will and Grace eagerly shop and look for the sexiest and most fashionable clothes and Nathan sits on the ledge complaining about how shopping is boring and can "drive people crazy." While Nathan talks about how he is missing the World Series on television, Will is trying on tight jeans from Paris and staring at himself in the mirror. Grace comments on how the jeans are too "girly," but despite her comment, Will still tries them on and buys them. The interesting part of this scene is that all the humorous parts have to do with Will trying on the jeans and having the same enthusiasm to shop as Grace. Furthermore, when all three return to the apartment, Nathan heads straight to the television set while Will and Grace go through piles of clothes and agree that they make great "shopping buddies." This scene says a great deal about how society perceives homosexuals and stereotypes them as having feminine characteristics such as loving to shop. In addition, the fact that Nathan, the heterosexual man, goes straight to the television to watch a baseball game again shows the expected male gender role.

Similarly, Jack's role in the show also sparks a lively debate about homosexuality. In the beginning of the show, Jack wakes up wearing a short, tight pink bathrobe and talks about how he needs to get one of Brittany Spears's souvenirs from E-bay. When Jack takes off his bathrobe, he is wearing a fitted short t-shirt that has a picture of the Eiffel Tower. The focus is on Nathan laughing at and mocking Jack, while Jack frolics around the room trying to get his tea ready. In addition, Nathan is wearing sweatpants and a sports jersey. In one aspect, the television show implies homosexuals are not taken seriously, and it also reflects and reinforces the general belief that they tend to have feminine characteristics. Once again, the "normal" structure for gender is emphasized: that males are supposed to have masculine characteristics and females are supposed to have feminine characteristics and any person who shows a mixture is considered abnormal, which can be seen through Jack and Will.

It is apparent from the juxtaposition between heterosexual and homosexual characters that a very conservative, underlying theme continues to permeate the show's storyline: traditional gender roles are preserved. The heterosexual male watches his sports, dresses casually, acting tough while the heterosexual female shops, puts on make-up and uses her body as a means to gain male attention. This contrasts with the two homosexual characters who do not fit into the conventional gender roles at all and appear to be "deviants" according to society's standards. Inevitably, people continue to think that homosexuals are abnormal and find humor in such portrayals. This representation of nontraditional gender roles contributes to a great deal of homophobia in our society.

At first, when watching a show such as *Will and Grace,* one thinks that television openly discusses controversial issues. In fact, it was initially believed that addressing such issues was a jump forward for American society. Looking back several years ago, television shows avoided homosexual issues or, at best, alluded to jokes pertaining to homosexuality. Even *Beverly Hills 90210,* a popular prime-time drama known to be a pioneer dealing with teenage issues, rarely touched upon the topic of homosexuality. One could almost conclude that American society is in the midst of a sexual revolution; perhaps society is finally accepting this form of sexual identity. However, watching shows such as *Dawson's Creek, Road Rules, Friends* and *The Real World* in addition to *Will and Grace* in detail reveals that television is not as liberal as many believe. In fact, it carries out society's preconceived notions about homosexuality. Television persists to please the major, dominating heterosexual audience by reiterating their belief that homosexuals are confused and do not follow the traditional gender roles, and so are labeled "abnormal." Television can be described as having a pendulum effect, shifting between society shaping television and vice versa. The dominating, heterosexual audience's beliefs and myths shape the portrayal of homosexuality on television. As a result, these labels for homosexuals mold the way people act and think toward homosexuals even further.

More importantly, deviating from socially normal gender roles, *Will and Grace* presents a negative image of homosexuals by exaggerating Will and Jack's behavior. Although they represent different extremes on the spectrum of homosexuality with Will being the "straighter" gay and Jack being the very overt and vocal gay, their characters are embellished to such a degree that encourages generalizations that they do not adhere to gender roles. Not only do viewers mock both characters, but even Will, the "straighter" gay, mocks his friend Jack just for being more gay than himself. This post-modern form of portrayal is a type of camp which undermines the category of homosexuality through parody and mimicry. Camp weakens the model of identity because homosexuality is unnecessarily exaggerated for the sake of comedy and hence, forms an inaccurate truth. *Will and Grace* supports an oppressive homosexual identity, which the public inherits, and exercises the belief that homosexuals are the subordinate and the inferior form of identity due to nontraditional gender roles they seem to exhibit. Hence, the portrayal of Will and Jack is indeed a form of entertainment for the heteronormative population.

The preservation of gender roles and heterosexuality through this subtle form of entertainment shows that the larger population still remains homophobic in both behavior and thought. The term "coming out" is an excellent example of vocabulary that is used by the typical homophobe. The idea implies that to tell one of his sexual preference requires an announcement. Even a person "coming out of the closet" still remains equally oppressed because this visible form of identity only leads to discrimination and stereotypes. In fact this can be seen in *Will and Grace* when Jack decides to go to his mother's home to tell her about his homosexuality. At first he is apprehensive, but when he finally gets the courage to tell her, his mother's immediate reaction is that "there were many clues when [he was] a child." She mentions that as child he loved the nursery rhyme "rub-a-dub-dub, three men in a tub" (which by the way, was a very funny remark because everyone watching the show began to laugh) and caught him wearing her high-heeled shoes, dressing in her clothes and trying on lipstick a few times. Jack's mother mentions his past in such a humorous manner that once again he feels restrained. Whether Jack did or did not "come out of the closet," he still feels the pressure of society's standards. Furthermore, Jack's mother continually mentions his confused gender when he was a child, once again showing how he was viewed as abnormal because he did not play with a football or with video games. In short, he did not display the expected male gender role. Society excels at eliminating and discriminating against deviances from heterosexuality by maintaining the limited cultural gender roles. Any person varying from this becomes an outcast, separated from society and looked down upon. Both Will and Jack go to gay bars and clubs during their free time. Therefore, they only feel normal meeting other homosexuals in an environment that eliminates ideas of restricted gender roles. By creating shows such as *Will and Grace* for a largely heterosexual population, the ideology of homophobia works to reinforce the power of heterosexism in our society.

The magnitude of homophobia is subtle, but it is apparent because a distinct and separated culture of homosexuality exists as a result of discrimination and ostracism by the majority heterosexual population. Rachel Kranz, a firm supporter of gay rights, defines homophobia as "the irrational fear of homosexuals and . . . the hatred for gay men . . . and the view that they are somehow inferior to heterosexuals" (Kranz 155). This fear of homosexuality brought about by gender roles has created a distinct homosexual culture. For example, Alan Bray, author of *Homosexuality in Renaissance England,* expresses that after the emergence of the term homosexual in the mid 1800s there came the formation of a very well established community for homosexuals called Molly houses (84). Bray states that the Molly houses were a place where men could gather and "sex was the root of the matter . . . it was as likely to be expressed in drinking together, in flirting and gossip and in a circle of friends as in actual liaisons" (84). In addition, Bray comments that the formation of a distinct culture was evident in the "ways of dressing, of talking, distinctive gestures and distinctive acts with an understood meaning, its own jargon" (86). The Molly houses were very important to the history of homosexuality because the definition of homosexuality as a distinct and different culture was put into use in society. There was a separate community with its own identity within the larger community.

In fact, Nancy Achilles addresses the two concerns of how and why a separate culture of homosexuality occurred and ties it in with the idea of homophobia. She states, in her essay "The Development of the Homosexual Bar as an Institution," that "an institution must arise from a particular social situation. . . . When an individual experiences strain in the social system, he may become motivated toward deviance . . . the choice [being] . . . to alienate himself from his environment altogether and attempt to chart his own life course" (3). Achilles justifies such actions because she believes that it is important for the "deviant form" to find a support group who may understand his social wants and needs (4). Not only does it allow for homosexuals to meet and socialize, but the individual remains comfortable within his own "type." Achilles states that the most important function of the bar is "to permit . . . the formation of sexual relationships. Sexual contacts may be made on the street, in the park, or on the bench, [but] the bar is the only place where these contacts . . . can be made with a reasonable degree of safety and respectability" (5). This statement reveals that the larger society disparages the formation of a same-sex intimate relationship, and that it must be done in a location where the "normal" heterosexual is not around. Furthermore, the existence of institutions such as gay bars and gay clubs are not only for homosexuals, but for all types of "sexual deviants" such as transvestites and lesbians. This form of gathering caused by separation of heterosexuality and homosexuality implies that in a bar, interaction between "deviants" is easier and appropriate because there are no traditional gender roles present. Achilles' observation underscores that homophobia exists in our society.

The raiding of the Stonewall Inn, a private club in New York City consisting of a predominantly gay clientele, on June 28th, 1969, is the most notorious symbol of the extreme homophobia that exists in the American culture. In the early morning hours, several police raided the bar, claiming that the charge was for illegal sale of alcohol (Kranz 23). Police raids on bars in New York City were not uncommon (Kranz 23). However, the existing trend of the raids that summer was very obvious in that they were geared toward bars consisting of homosexual, transsexual and lesbian individuals (Kranz 24). It was the second time in a week that the police targeted the bar; fourteen other gay bars had also been raided that week (Kranz 36). During the raid, police officers checked the identifications of all the patrons, but most were free to leave, with the exception of the staff and a few homosexuals (Kranz 37). Later on that day, crowds of people, especially young, gay men, gathered in front of the bar, and they did so by handholding, kissing, and forming a chorus line, overtly defying traditional gender roles, for three days (Kranz 24). The Stonewall riot represented not only a fight against police, but a fight against the American heterosexist society. In fact, the Stonewall Riot can be considered a turning point for homosexuals because it gave birth to the Gay Liberation movement for homosexuals and other "sexual deviants." It was from this riot that Americans realized the growing need and desire for homosexuals to have a rightful position in society. In fact, many commentators have described Stonewall as the "shot heard round the homosexual world" (Jagose 30). Consequently, during this Gay Liberation movement numerous organizations emerged around the country in order to bring about change for homosexuals (Kranz 25).

The events of Stonewall indicate the obvious segregation between the two forms of sexuality, and because heterosexuality is considered the "natural" and stable construction due to gender, homosexuality appears to be the inferior form, always being compared to the natural heterosexual form. Annamarie Jagose validates this when she states "heterosexuality is equally the construction whose meaning is dependent on the changing cultural models"

(35). This means that heterosexuality is a derivation from the gender roles made by society, just as much as homosexuality. So the important question is why should homosexuality gain the reputation that it has? This is a major concern for a group of people called Queer Theorists, a prominent group who gained popularity during the Gay Liberation movement (Jagose 73).

Queer Theorists believe that the reason why the American society is homophobic and gives homosexuality an inferior and negative reputation is because of traditional gender roles. Consequently, they believe that in order to eliminate the existence of homophobia, the only solution is to eradicate traditional gender roles. In order to eliminate traditional gender roles, they have introduced the very abstract term "queer." Queer Theorists believe that the term homosexual was invented by a group of people who did not understand the difference between heterosexual and homosexual (Jagose 95). According to queer theorists, homosexuality and heterosexuality is not as black and white as it appears. There is a mix of gray in this form of identification, and so the term queer was invented. Queer destroys and eliminates the traditional meaning of gay and lesbian, and homosexual. According to Jagose, these are homophobic normative definitions (88).

The goal of queer theorists is to denaturalize the categories into a broader definition (Jagose 72–100). Hence, the definition of queer is non-specificity. The term is meant to include all types of sexual practices and eradicate the distinction between homosexual and heterosexual, because theoretically speaking, queer encompasses those terms and includes all individuals. This invention of the term queer basically intends to remove traditional gender roles. The fact that traditional gender roles are not included indicates that the ideas of femininity and masculinity do not have to be so clear cut as gender roles create. Instead, an individual can exercise any form of attitude, behavior and thought, which includes sexual practice. For example, a male can behave, dress and act as feminine as he wants and vice versa.

Thus, one of the most important functions of the advent of the word queer is that it includes all forms of sexual deviants such as homosexuals, bisexuals and transvestites into the same category as heterosexuals (Jagose 72–100). Together they are grouped under the same heading, essentially eliminating distinctions such as gender labels, generalizations and stereotypes, which creates heterosexual normativity (Jagose 96). This goal of eliminating all forms of differences is a major theme of Gay Liberation, so that all people can gain equal rights and representation in society. Unlike *Will and Grace,* which purposefully differentiates the homosexuals, Will and Jack, from the heterosexual characters, Grace and Nathan, Queer Theorists hope to eliminate such distinctions. For example, in one episode Jack and Will are at the studios of the NBC *Today Show* and in order to gain Al Roker's attention, Will leans over and French-kisses Jack. The people surrounding Will and Jack all gasp and in the background of the show, you can hear the audience laughing hysterically. However, when Grace and Nathan kiss on the show, no big deal is made. Queer Theorists would see the different reactions from the audience to the kisses on *Will and Grace* as a form distinction between homosexuality and heterosexuality in our society that should not exist. Jagose brilliantly points out that since queer is suggestive of a whole range of sexual possibilities . . . normal and pathological, straight, and gay, masculine men and feminine women, all sexual behaviors grouped under one broad category are considered normal (98).

Since Queer Theorists believe that queer encompasses all individuals in one category, Calvin Thomas, in his essay Straight with a Twist, states that there is . . . a straight affiliation with the term queer (84). In fact, Thomas takes the word queer to a whole new level by describing how any individual can be called queer. He believes that every individual exhibits queer tendencies in their gender roles and sexual behaviors. He states, ". . . straights, who would be barred definitionally from the terms 'gay,' 'lesbian,' or 'bisexual,' could not be excluded from the domain of the queer" (Thomas 86). Thus, Queer Theory expands the scope of its analysis to all kinds of behaviors, including those who are gender-conforming, gender-bending and those who practice "non-normative" forms of sexuality. A person's sexuality is molded by a complex array of social codes and forces, constantly pressured by individual beliefs and institutional powers. At all times, an individual tries to conform to the ideas of what is normal and to avoid what is deviant. Consequently, the invention of the term "queer" ideally hopes to eliminate the complexity of social construction on sexuality caused by gender so that every individual is no longer ostracized, discriminated against and even laughed at because of his/her sexuality.

Imagine the ideals of Queer Theorists actually succeeding in eliminating traditional gender roles and creating the term "queer" to encompass all existent categories of sexuality under one umbrella. How would society respond to such changes? How would people act and behave? Since television acts like a mirror and reflects the social organization in our society, perhaps observing an episode of *Will and Grace* through the eyes of a Queer Theorist would guide us. First of all, the four characters—Will, Grace, Jack and Nathan—would not be referred to as the "homosexual characters and the heterosexual characters" because they would no longer be identified through such words. In fact, each of the four characters are all queer in their own unique way. Will and Jack will no longer be mocked for being "too feminine" because gender roles do not exist. Consequently, when Will is frightened by an old high-school bully who works with him and feels threatened and cannot defend himself, or when he decides to go shopping with Grace in order to look for tight jeans, Will will not be mocked because he is acting too "girly." He will be admired for his individuality. In addition, Jack frolicking around in a pink bathrobe and singing and dancing to Ricky Martin will not be seen as abnormal. Grace chasing after her men will be seen in the same light as Will chasing after men. Nathan watching his sports on television and dressed in a sports jersey will no longer be compared to Jack dressed in tight Banana Republic clothes because traditional gender roles would no longer be followed. Will and Jack French kissing will be at an equal level to Grace and Nathan kissing. In other words, everyone is equal. Everyone is different. Everyone is individual. No one is being laughed at because of their sexual identity, rather everyone is being laughed at because of their queerness. In addition, since queer includes all sexualities, why not include bisexuals, transvestites, lesbians and drag queens as well, in order to get a larger representation of the population? After all, this is a *queer* show. Moreover, rather than having all Caucasian queers, the addition of Asian, Hispanic, African American, European, Native American and Eskimo queers would be included as well since the mainstream American audience that network TV tries so hard to reach is composed of many persons from different backgrounds, different sexualities, and different queerness.

A portrayal as the one described accurately and realistically represents the queer life in America. Consequently, all people exhibiting sexual deviance will eventually be accepted and no longer be subjected to the bigotry and intolerance of the larger homophobic population. The invention of the term queer in a whole new light may actually succeed in eliminating conventional beliefs on sexuality in which society can eliminate the idea of sexuality as an identity. In fact, the innovation of Queer Theory in society will not only eliminate differences, but would offer a wider range of comedy so that instead of laughing at a certain type of people, everyone can just laugh together. Consequently, by eliminating sexual distinctions, Queer Theorists hope to "open [a] mesh of possibilities, gaps, overlaps, dissonances and resonances, lapses and excesses of meaning [so that] the constituent elements of anyone's gender, of anyone's sexuality aren't made or can't be made" (Thomas 86). The idea of queer is a term that potentially can eliminate all forms of contradictions and bigotry in our nation's social structure. Perhaps the utilization of this word will finally bring to end a history of heterosexuality in our society and triumph in creating equality for all.

Works Cited

Achilles, Nancy. "The Development of the Homosexual Bar as an Institution." *Sociology of Homosexuality.* Eds. Wayne R. Dynes and Stephen Donaldson. New York: Garland Publishing, Inc., 1992. 2–18.

Bray, Alan. *Homosexuality in Renaissance England.* London: Gay Men's Press, 1982.

Carabine, Jean. "Heterosexuality and Social Policy." *Theorizing Heterosexuality.* Ed. Diane Richardson. Philadelphia: Open University Press, 1996. 55–74.

Devor, Holly. "Becoming Members of Society: Learning the Social Meanings of Gender." *Gender Blending: Confronting the Limits of Duality.* English 200 packet.

Foucault, Michel. *The History of Sexuality.* Trans. Robert Hurley. New York: Pantheon Books, 1978.

Ingraham, Chrys. "The Heterosexual Imaginary: Feminist Sociology and Theories of Gender." *Queer Theory/Sociology.* Ed. Steven Seidman. Massachusetts: Blackwell Publishers Ltd., 1996. 168–193.

Jagose, Annamarie. *An Introduction to Queer Theory.* New York: New York University Press, 1996.

Kranz, Rachel and Tim Cusick. *Gay Rights.* New York: Facts on File Inc., 2000.

Lorber, Judith. "The Social Construction of Gender." *Women's Lives: Multicultural Perspectives.* Eds. Gwyn Kirk and Margo Okazawa-Rey. California: Mayfield Publishing Company, 2001. 20–24.

Maasik, Sonia, and Jack Solomon. "We've Come a Long Way, Maybe." *Signs of Life in the U.S.A.: Readings on Popular Culture for Writers.* 3rd ed. Boston: Bedford/St. Martin's, 2000. 437–446.

McCormick, C.M. and Witelson, S.F. "A Cognitive Profile of Homosexual Men Compared to Heterosexual Men and Women." *Psychoneuroendocrinology.* Chicago: University of Chicago Press, 1991. 459–473.

Robinson, Paul. "Freud and Homosexuality." *Homosexuality and Psychology.* Eds. Tim Dean and Christopher Lane. Chicago: University of Chicago Press, 2001. 91–97.

Thomas, Calvin. "Straight with a Twist: Queer Theory and the Subject of Heterosexuality." *The Gay 90s: Disciplinary and Interdisciplinary Formations in Queer Studies.* Eds. Thomas Foster, Carol Siegel, and Ellen E. Berry. New York: New York University Press, 1997.

**READING** WRITING

## THIS TEXT: READING

1. Notice the way Mehta mixes the personal with the observational with the analytical while researching. What about this approach makes this a successful paper? Is it an approach you think you can imitate in your own work?

2. Compare this article to Katherine Gantz's piece on *Seinfeld*. What differences do you notice between the two works? How does each work discuss what it means to be gay or lesbian? What differences in the piece have to do with the authors of the pieces or the shows themselves?

3. What other shows might benefit from the approach that Mehta takes? What "lenses" (queer theory, race theory, gender theory, etc.) might you put on in order to write about television or other popular culture media?

4. Why does this piece in itself make a case for television's importance as a text to be studied?

## YOUR TEXT: WRITING

1.  Find a television show that you feel has social issues attached to it—even if those issues are not immediately apparent. Watch the show, take notes, and then do an analysis of the work.
2.  Do a compare and contrast of two shows that engage similar issues (examples could be *NYPD Blue* and *Law and Order* or *Third Watch* or *Seinfeld* and *Will and Grace* or *Friends*).
3.  Write a paper which ties your own experience to a show you are fond of.

---

**"BLACK BART" SIMPSON: APPROPRIATION AND REVITALIZATION IN COMMODITY CULTURE**[1]

■ **Peter Parisi** ■

*In this (1993) piece, Peter Parisi, examines the phenomen of the omnipresent cultural artifact: the T-shirt. Parisi uses the phenomen as a window into the relationship artifacts audience.*

DURING THE SUMMER OF 1990, the streets of cities across the country witnessed a striking and unusual gesture in popular culture: the appropriation and re-interpretation of a mass media figure by minority group members. That summer, *The Simpsons*, a crudely drawn television cartoon that itself portrayed the cultural impact of mass media upon ideals of family and small-town life, had completed a hit season. A merchandising blitz followed up on the success, flooding stores and streets with T-shirts depicting Matt Groening's highly publicized characters: the militant under-achiever Bart Simpson; his feckless and juvenile father Homer; patient, long-suffering mother Marge; and two sisters, bright, sensitive Lisa and, wide-eyed baby Maggie who perpetually and noisily sucks a pacifier.

The summer was not far advanced, however, before innumerable blacks, men and women, young and middle-aged, appeared in cities nationwide, wearing T-shirts adorned with the bootlegged image of Bart but now dark-skinned and posed in a variety of black identities.[2] Fusing Air Jordan and MC Hammer, "Air Bart" slam dunks a basketball and says, "you can't touch this." Home Boy Bart inquires pugnaciously, "Yo, homeboy, what the hell are you looking at?" "Rastabert, Master of Respect" sprouts dreadlocks, sports a red, green and gold headband and growls, "Watch it, Mon. 'Irie'," or, in a variation on the Rastafarian theme, becomes "Rasta-Dude Bart Marley" or "RastaBart." On other shirts, Black Bart and white Bart shake hands; Black Bart appears alongside Nelson Mandela, saying "Apartheid. No!" or "My Hero!" and Black Bart insists, "I didn't do it." "Asiatic Bart" wears the robes and skull cap of a Black Muslim and, borrowing the group's rhetoric, declares himself "Cream of the Planet Earth, Dude!" Bedecked with gold chain and snazzy sneakers, Black Bart glares from another shirt that reads, "You should understand," playing on another Afrocentric T-shirt motto: "It's a Black thing. You wouldn't understand." Still another shirt mixes a pacific message with a glaring Bart, joined by sister Lisa and a graphic of the African continent. The message read, "It's cool being black" and in a box beneath, "We are all brothers and sisters so live in unity, love and peace" (118).

One striking, scatological variant suggests how pungently these graphic figures could embody and play with social meanings. Across its top, the shirt carries the legend, "Crack Kills" and across the bottom "Black Power." Pictured between is a discomfited "white" Bart clenched between the buttocks of a sizable black woman with wavy hair and purple toenails. The shirt was striking in its irreverent treatment of phrases and terms—Crack Kills, Black Power—usually regarded as too solemn for parody.

Prices for the bootlegs in the summer of 1990 ranged from six to ten dollars, and dropped to five the following summer as the craze faded and authorities clamped down on copyright violations in the fashion industry. The total number of shirts sold is virtually impossible to determine. Obviously, no industry figures were kept. Nor would it be easy to enumerate all the designs. Unlicensed as they were, the bootleggers could freely crib, modify or invent ideas. At least two versions of the "Air Bart/'You Can't Touch This'" shirt circulated and another variant featured "BartHammer." There were apparent local variations. In Washington, Mills described shirts in which Bart utters lines from rap songs, a form that was uncommon in New York City.

Black Bart was not the first popular icon appropriated and modified to reflect African-American culture. *The New York Times* article about Black Bart noted that "there have been occasional blackened Betty Boops and a few attempts last year to recast Bat Man as 'Black Man' . . ." (Marriot C1). Also in 1988, New York street vendors sold sweatshirts depicting Mickey Mouse in a warm-up suit and gold chains, saying, "Yo Baby, Yo Baby, Yo! Let's get busy!" (i.e., let's make love). And a cartoonist and graphic artist, J.T. Liehr, who worked in a Philadelphia screen printing shop used by T-shirt designers, said his shop produced not only black versions of Bart Simpson, but also of Charlie Brown and Budweiser mascot Spuds Mackenzie, who was transmuted to a spliff-smoking Rastafarian, "Buds MacSensie" (a reference to high-grade, "sinsemilla" marijuana). "Whatever was popular at the time was modified to be black," Lichr said.

If not the first, the Black Bart T-shirt was yet the most popular Afrocentric appropriation of mass culture iconography. As illicit or anarchic as it may have been, the underground fashion industry that spawned the shirts managed to distribute them "coast to coast" ("When Life Imitates Bart" 61). The *Washington Post* (Mills), *New York Times* (Marriot) and *Newsweek* ("When Life Imitates Bart") found the phenomenon worthy of notice, with *The New York Times* calling Black Bart "one of the most enduring T-shirt images of the summer" (Marriot C1).

## African Americans and the Active Audience

The consumption and display of Black Bart T-shirts represents a noteworthy case study within the growing scholarly interest in the creative activity of the mass audience, or, as Janice A. Radway puts it consumers' "power as individuals to resist or alter the ways in which . . . objects mean or can be used" (221). In *Reading the Popular,* John Fiske says popular culture "is always a culture of conflict, . . . involv[ing] the struggle to make social meanings that are in the interest of the subordinate and that are not those preferred by the dominant ideology" (2). "In the practices of consumption," he adds, "the commodity system is exposed to the power of the consumer, for the power of the system is not just top-down, or center-outward, but always two-way, always a flux of conflicting powers and resistances" (31).

Recent work on audience activity—see, for instance, David Eason and Fred Fogo's review (3–5)—has not much reflected on the contemporary culture-making activity of African-Americans. This is unfortunate not only because the influence of African-American culture on American popular culture is pervasive and under-estimated, but because "audience activity," in the sense of reaction to and upon dominant cultural products, has necessarily been essential to culture-making within the African diaspora. Both the frequently opposed views of E. Franklin Frazier—that African heritage was virtually erased during slavery—or of Melville Herskovits—that African-American culture takes shape around specific survivals of African civilization—imply vigorous interaction with Euro-American culture (see Holloway ix and Philips 225–226). Moreover, an essential feature of African-American culture is precisely the responsiveness of audience—consider the "call and response" pattern (Levine 218), the "second line" of musicians in jazz, or the dialectical interaction between improvising performer and inspired-and-inspiring audience that Charies Keil finds central to "the dialectics or mechanics of soul" (174–175).

Lawrence Levine in *Black Culture and Black Consciousness* and Charles Keil in *Urban Blues* have usefully studied both aspects of African-American popular culture. Keil describes a relationship of "appropriation and revitalization" (43) between African-American and Euro-American culture. This conception, developed in a discussion of LeRoi Jones' *Blues People,* envisions an essentially compensatory relationship in which dominant culture appropriates, largely through mass media "covers" of African-American work, and African-Americans respond by "reexpressing American Negro identity and attitudes in a new revitalized way" (45). However, if we focus too deeply on black culture as expropriated victim and reactor, we risk under-valuing its vitality and effectiveness. In culture-making it is often difficult to distinguish action from reaction, defense from offense. As Albert Murray has said:

> Much is forever being made of the deleterious effects of slavery on the generations of Black Americans that followed. But for some curious reason, nothing at all is ever made of the possibility that the legacy left by the enslaved ancestors of blues-oriented contemporary U.S. Negroes includes a disposition to confront the most unpromising circumstances and make the most of what little there is to go on, regardless of the odds—and not without finding delight in the process . . . (69–70)

Consequently, Levine's description of the appropriation–revitalization process proves somewhat more helpful in assessing the ongoing vitality of African-American popular culture. He describes the cultural interplay between African- and Euro-American culture as a "complex and multi-dimensional" relationship, "a pattern of *simultaneous* acculturation and revitalization" (italics added, 444). Cultural diffusion between whites and blacks was by no means a one-way street with blacks the invariable beneficiaries, he writes. Afro-American impact upon wide areas of American expressive culture has become increasingly obvious, though it has not yet been adequately assessed.

And in fact examples employed by Keil, Levine and others describe many instances in which black culture clearly acts upon dominant culture, not defensively or reactively, but actively, perspicaciously, and with satirical penetration. For instance, Keil acutely observes how a distinctively Negro style animates established white American entertainment forms, such as sports. He points to the nothing ball and sucker ball as pitched by Satchel Paige, the base as stolen by Maury Wills, the basket catches of Willie Mays, the antics of the Harlem Globetrotters, the beautiful ritualization of an ugly sport by Sonny Liston and Muhammed Ali (15). Similarly, George Nelson in *Elevating the Game* has described the growth in recent years of air-borne, slam-dunking basketball technique. These symbolic transformations, as

Keil calls them, represent not a return to roots, but a genuine invigoration of the possibilities of popular cultural forms.

African-American culture by definition and necessity works in relation to dominant culture products. But the result is often distinct cultural invention. Speaking of black music, for instance, Schafer and Riedel note a basic force behind all genres and modes of black music in the ability to absorb, rework, and develop every musical material and influence, to be protean, taking on any shape yet remaining substantially the same in feeling or spirit (22). Maultsby describes how the black spiritual developed as slaves . . . frequently fashioned Protestant psalms, hymns, and spiritual songs into new compositions by altering the structure, text, melody, and rhythm. They thus created an essentially autonomous art form, a body of religious music created or adapted by slaves and performed in a distinctly African style (198).

Nor does African-American culture s ability to actively absorb, rework and develop operate solely in melodic spheres. As John W. Roberts says in *From Trickster to Badman*, the lyrics of the spiritual were not simple adoptions of Biblical texts but careful selections of figures and episodes significant to black historical and social experience. Roberts quotes Sterling Brown:

> Paul . . . is generally bound in jail with Silas, to the exclusion of the rest of his busy career. Favored heroes are Noah, chosen of God to ride down the flood; Joshua, who caused the wall of Jericho to fall . . . ; Jonah, symbol of hard luck changed at last; and Job, the man of tribulation who still would not curse his God. (110)

Roberts continues, quoting Levine, in "the world of the spirituals, it was not the masters or the mistresses but God and Jesus and the entire pantheon of Old Testament figures who set the standards, established the precedents, and defined the values. . . ." It was a black world in which no reference was ever made to any white contemporary (110). A similar creative adaptation occurs in the Rastafarian re-interpretation of the Bible as a critique of dominant society ("Babylon") and manifesto of revolution and apocalypse, as Hebdige has described (33–35). A similar perspicacious and satiric adaptation is evident in dance: the cakewalk, John Storm Roberts notes in *Black Music of Two Worlds*, "began as a slaves' parody of white 'society' ways" (199).

The point of this survey is not simply and comfortably to assimilate the Black Bart T-shirt to this honorable tradition. But if, as Frederick Perls, Ralph Hefferline and Paul Goodman have pervasively argued (227–235), the process of creative adjustment is fundamental in all human conduct, we might expect it to persist even in the purchase and display of mass-produced commodities. The point is not that buying and wearing a T-shirt is as creative as singing the blues, or even dancing to them. But the deployment of such a commodity can constitute a cultural maneuver parallel to those we have just surveyed in the tradition of appropriation and revitalization as enacted in culture-making that employs the purchase of commodities. And the maneuver may engender group affirmations of some cultural significance.

Still, a variety of curiosities enter the picture when creative adjustment or appropriation and revitalization operate within the culture of mass media and commodities. As we shall see, the creators of Black Bart T-shirts may not be black, and some may question the cultural value of images of a self-declared dropout and mischief maker. Yet in the end, I will argue, the Black Bart T-shirt makes a significant comment upon the culture of mass media and enhances African-American identity. It also makes us aware of other instances of potential cultural power through the deployment of commodities.

## Complications of Commodity Culture

T-shirts, however ephemeral or "commodified," are not entirely unlikely means of social communication. Since the mid-1970s when they emerged as outerwear embellished with product images and slogans, they have functioned as literal "fashion statements," a kind of personalized advertising. The commodities displayed on them are heavy with "lifestyle" connotations—not a jar of mayonnaise, say, but a brand of beer, a soft drink, a travel destination, a rock group—entities that presumably evoke occasions and emotions significant of the wearer's personality, taste and allegiances. Correspondingly, Behling's classification of T-shirt types for an empirical study (1988)—cynical, advertising, environmental, health and exercise, political, feminism, prestige, and off-color humor—suggests the association between the T-shirt and causes, issues and activities close to the wearer's central values. The affirmation involved can have tangible social significance. When stutterers, in a study by Silverman, wore a T-shirt saying, "I stutter. So what?" store clerks were found to perceive them more positively. The apparent personal transformations negotiated by the shirt occur on a more informal level too. A mother overhearing a discussion of Black Bart T-shirts, said, "Oh yes, my son wanted one of those, but I wouldn't get him one. He has enough attitude already." Merely to don the shirt is to be taken over by an "attitude."

The Black Bart T-shirt arguably furthers group identification and cohesion and makes as well a lively implicit commentary on contemporary media. The fact that the shirt appropriates figures from an ongoing television show carries a special impact. Although television, as separate studies by Richard Allen, Fred Bales, and Carolyn Stroman ("Mass Media Effects and Black Americans") have found, is a medium highly popular and credible with African-Americans, its origins and production are largely impervious to popular modification. To be sure, in the last 20 years African-Americans have been portrayed more frequently and more positively on television, as Stroman notes ("Twenty Years Later"). But other scholars have pointed out that this gain brings a reduction of significant dimensions of black culture. Sherry Bryant-Johnson remarks on the loss of significant expressive features of black ethnic background; Ilona Holland notes that the non-standard dialect employed by blacks on television is not true to black English as actually spoken, and Todd Gitlin and Martin Bayles contend that televised representations of African-Americans back away from the presentation of realistic characters in realistic backgrounds. Without overestimating the cultural impact of a mere T-shirt, we may yet suggest that sporting the blazonry of Black Bart "broadcasts" an unsanctioned commentary on *The Simpsons* show that reverses this tendency. As we will discuss in more detail below, the Black Bart T-shirt extends the social rules portrayed on the show to include raffish, urban personae—Rastafarians, "homeboys," rappers, and Black Muslims—all of whom may seem vaguely threatening and who find scant representation in the mass media.

But at the same time, an environment of commodities and post-modern "intertextuality" complicate this affirmative culture-making picture. Appropriation and revitalization in commodity culture turn and return upon each other. Matt Groening, creator of *The Simpsons,* has recognized both the economic expropriation and artistic creativity of the Black Bart phenomenon. "You have to have mixed feelings when you're getting ripped off," he said (qtd. in Mills). But his ambivalence did not prevent him from making the "rip-off" into material for further cartooning. In "Life in Hell," another of his strips, Groening depicts Akbar and Jeff, identical figures who inexplicably wear fezzes and may be brothers or lovers, and who

Wearing Black Bart Simpson shirt (Harlem), 125 St., NY, NY.

bootleg themselves. Working from "Akbar & Jeff's Bootleg Akbar & Jeff T-shirt Hut," they vend "Blakbar and Jeff" T-shirts, including "Air Akbar" and "Akbar and Jeff go funky reggae." Dreadlocks sprouting from under his fez, one says, "Irie, Mon." The other responds, "What?" Groening thus plays with the very cultural gaps that engender the Black Bart T-shirt. A warning label on the cartoon intones: "we will prosecute bootleggers of our bootlegs and don't you forget it."

Fox Television itself briefly adapted the possible connection between a white Bart and a black Bart to its own purposes. A black-oriented show, *True Colors,* was for a time programmed to follow *The Simpsons* presumably to compete more successfully with the top-10 *Bill Cosby Show.* Advertisements for the new pairing played upon the identity of Bart and the young black hero of *True Colors,* placing their images side by side, comparing the two dancing, and having Bart say of the young black star, "He's my idol!"

More fundamental matters arise when we ask, who are the creators of Black Bart Simpson T-shirts? It is not easy to offer a definitive answer. One might ask vendors and producers of the T-shirts, but given the illegality of their operations, they could easily suspect that a scholar's interest was but a clever ruse to hunt copyright violators. Nonetheless, in T-shirt screen printing shops some aspects of the production process comes into public view. And according to some testimony from this source, the designers and producers of Black Bart and other black-oriented T-shirts emerge from a group hardly associated with empathy for African-American culture—the "middleman minority" of immigrant Korean business people in the United States.

Korean merchants in general display a strong presence in "low-end retailing" of inexpensive items such as wigs, handbags, martial arts supplies, jewelry and casual apparel, including T-shirts, much of which makes an appeal to the cultural interests of low-income groups. J.T. Liehr, the graphic artist and cartoonist quoted earlier, said that about half a dozen Korean merchants regularly used his shop to order silk screens for black-oriented shirts that were vended in Center City and west Philadelphia. "Of all the shirts aimed at blacks, I rarely saw black people involved in making them," Liehr said. (White "progressives," he added, typically produced anti-apartheid and Nelson Mandela T-shirts.) Nor did the Korean producers of Afrocentric material with their shoestring budgets seem likely to employ much help of any sort, to say nothing of black artists or collaborators, Liehr said.

Origins exert a powerful conceptual spell. The cultural and economic conflicts between Koreans and African-Americans have received so much publicity that many observers are likely to aver that if Koreans designed Black Bart T-shirts, their cultural value cannot be high. Korean–black antipathies figure prominently in such recent African-American films as Spike Lee's *Do the Right Thing* and Frederick Singleton's *Boyz in the 'Hood.* Blacks cite such grievances as the failure of Korean merchants to live in the communities where they work, firing black workers, refusing credit to black customers, treating them as potential shoplifters, and failing to contribute to black charities.[3] The possible Korean production of Black Bart T-shirts can echo too closely the old story of the financial exploitation of black cultural interests and creations for the profit of other groups. Certainly too, the likely Korean origins of the Black Bart products sit oddly in the tradition of African-American cultural creativity sketched above. And in fact it might be suspected that the casual relation to value terms that we noted in the "Crack Kills/Black Power" T-shirt implies the detached and distant perspective of a culture alien to African-American concerns.[4]

Disapproval of the possible Korean production of the shirts links with a more general disapproval of the Bart figure, black or white, by authority figures of both races. A *People Weekly* article called "Eat My Shirts!" described how principals in California and Ohio banned Bart Simpson T-shirts bearing the label "Underachiever" or Bart's rude query, "Who the hell are you?" Bart's underachieving can be viewed as particularly dangerous when the school dropout rate among many young people, including African-Americans, stands at worrisome rates. T-shirt vendor Id-Deen said she had heard a Black Muslim imam criticize Bart's disrespect for his parents. In a *Jet* magazine article headlined "Black Bart T-shirt raises concern among blacks," a black man chastises wearers at a black fraternity picnic: "With all the Black heroes in the world—Mandela and Malcolm and Martin—and that's what you are showing our children?" (In fairness, Black Bart on one shirt himself declares Mandela his "hero.") But the very effort to dismiss the Black Bart T-shirt in the name of more "positive" African-American values can contradict itself. The *Jet* article approvingly quotes an African-American vendor from Baltimore who invokes the very negative stereotypes the article seems to protest: "We are the only people in the world that let somebody take a White cartoon character, paint it Black and then sell it to us for 10 bucks."

Condemning Black Bart on the basis of his possible origins may offer a comfortable sense of superiority to the buyers' presumed foolishness but it does nothing to explain his popularity. Thousands of urban blacks proudly donned and displayed the image of Black Bart Simpson. Many even sported the "Crack Kills" variant. They did not do it to make Koreans rich or increase school dropout rates. The financial economy of popular culture wherein Korean entrepreneurs produce Black Bart T-shirts and the cultural economy wherein African-Americans eagerly buy and display them are "parallel" and "semi-autonomous," as Fiske notes in *Understanding Popular Culture* (26). "Every act of consumption is an act of cultural production, for consumption is always the production of meaning," he says (35).

For its wearers, the Black Bart T-shirt must possess an active, affirmative meaning. And as we examine this popularity the idea reasserts itself that the phenomenon, for all the curiosities surrounding it, stands in discernible continuity with more traditional, creative acts of African-American adaptation of materials from dominant culture: Koreans and African-Americans do, after all, share minority status. Spike Lee acknowledges as much in *Do the Right Thing* when the film's hero Mookie, recognizing the bond, sees to it that a family of Korean greengrocers are spared the racial conflagration that closes the film. Furthermore, there is, as Simon Bronner has pointed out, ample precedent in American culture for a group apparently detached from the African-American community to nonetheless take a central role in circulating African-American culture more widely. Although these cultural brokers may be viewed with hostility by African-Americans (witness Spike Lee's treatment of Jewish nightclub owners in *Mo' Better Blues*), in many cases the broker evinces genuine aesthetic appreciation—consider, Alan Freed's promotion of rock 'n' roll music or John Hammond's of jazz and blues. If an anonymous Korean entrepreneur understands how a black Betty Boop or Bart Simpson will appeal to African-American cultural interests, so be it. Cross-cultural understanding is not beyond the capacities of any ethnic or racial group.

Moreover, it is not as if the Black Bart figure is without its own positive vitality. Bart Simpson and Black Bart may hate school but they are at least "street smart." Black Bart's bold social assertiveness and multiplication of social roles is more imaginative than mindless. If Bart Simpson infuriates principals by calling himself an "underachiever—and proud of it," he must at least comprehend the schoolmaster's jargon. On the show Bart is certainly no scholar but is not without intellectual interest. He shows a near Jesuitical expertise with questions that torture his Sunday school teacher, like whether heaven will admit "a robot with a human brain." In other words, those concerned about the "model" set by the Bart figures might give more weight to the intelligence and penetration implicit in ironic play.

## How Does a T-Shirt Mean?

What then is the social meaning of Black Bart and how is it engendered? Young wearers of Black Bart T-shirts formulate the pleasure and meaning of this imagery with full understanding of the cultural dissonance that circulates around the Bart figure. In interviews, 11 Black and Hispanic public school students at first vigorously condemned the show, charging that Bart uses bad language, even the "S-word" and "the F-word" (which of course are not heard on television). They acknowledged solemnly that Bart does not do his homework. A seven-year-old Hispanic boy showed best how the condemnation was "in the air." He could provide no specifics about the show, but nonetheless opined heatedly that it was unnecessarily obscene and violent. "You can't learn anything from that! You don't learn your A-B-C's!" he said. It is hardly likely that on their own children gather at recess to murmur this sort of disapproval of *The Simpsons*. This lad's opinions were adapted from the children's precocious presumptions about adult views of cartoons. A six-year-old boy described the essence of the process: "The parents, they don't like Bart Simpson because they don't want us to turn out cussing when we grow up because they don't want us turning out in jail."[5]

If they piously intoned the "dangers" of Bart, the children nonetheless all but universally could produce details about the show, and in many cases said they owned Simpsons T-shirts or other products. And their more active pleasure in its meanings soon surfaced. A nine-year-old girl, who solemnly called the show "a bad influence," also vividly described an incident in which Lisa comforted baby Maggie, her tone clearly indicating she found it touching. Two girls, aged 10 and 11, who were also best friends, spontaneously said of a "Bart Marley" T-shirt, "It's nice . . . It's colorful and stuff." With her friend's agreement, one stated explicitly that she recognized the show's "bad examples" to serve a larger function:

> I don't think Bart Simpson was made to offend anyone but to show how the kids act. And some kids . . . do act like that. But Bart Simpson, I don't think he was made to do bad things. Bart Simpson . . . is taking the children's offense and Homer and Maggie [Marge] are taking the parents' offense and it's showing how we all act together.

Allowing for a fourth-grader's vocabulary, this is the perceptive observation that the show portrays family dynamics rather than glorifying bad behavior. Of Black Bart, one of the pair said, "what's nice is that there is a black person in here, his name is Bart too and they have colorful colors too." Her friend seconded the political aspect:

> On the commercials they don't show that many black people and in the magazines they hardly show any black people. All you see is white. And I don't understand why white people are scared of us because there's nothing wrong with our color.

Youngsters construct the figure of Black Bart from an active, perceptive reinterpretation of materials on the show. They select particular features of Bart Simpson's style that resonate with African-American culture, particularly his hair and dress. Krebs quoted a 14-year-old boy holding that Bart Simpson himself seemed black: "You never see white people with spiked hair like that—that's the way blacks look." Another commented, "I think Bart acts more like a black kid than a white one, especially the way he wears clothing and styles his hair." Larger elements of Bart's Simpson's character undergird Black Bart's appeal. Bart Simpson offends authority figures in part because he focuses on his own goals and pleasures, responding with singular detachment to the lures and values of adult society. One boy approved the way Bart "doesn't give a damn about anything" (qtd. in "When Life Imitates Bart"). Bart's "rowdiness" and "unvarnished chutzpah . . . speak particularly well to many black youngsters who are growing up in a society that often alienates them," said Russell Adams, chair of the Afro-American Studies Department at Howard University (qtd. in Marriott C3).

As noted earlier, the Black Bart T-shirts mobilize an implicit critique of the range of black roles on the show. The show's characterizations commendably include more than a token number of people of color. The show also plays with the sociology of racial and ethnic identity. For instance, the local convenience store is owned and operated by a regular character, Apu, who is Indian or Pakistani. African-Americans are numerous and presented in positive roles. Several of Bart's friends and schoolmates and Clarence, the mayor of Springfield City, along with the Simpson's family physician, are black. The physician, Dr. Hibbert, is an "intertextual" reference, the show's Bill Cosby. Hibbert relaxes at home in the multicolored sweaters favored by Cosby as Dr. Cliff Huxtable (*The Cosby Show* aired at the same time as *The Simpsons*). Bart knows plenty about alternative identities. He avidly collects "Radioactive Man" comics and pretends variously he is "Bart-Man," "The Caped Avenger," a ninja, and other characters. The Black Bart T-shirt builds on Bart's mischief and imagination along with the show's sociological realism to expand its spectrum of roles.

The T-shirts further domesticate these identities by steeping them in the show's acceptance and popularity. Correspondingly, many of the shirts feature a double gesture of pugnacious self-assertion and openness. "Rastabart" warns, "Watch it, Mon" but adds "Irie" ("everything's fine"). Black Bart glares and says, "It's cool being black," but a box on the T-shirt notes, "We are all brothers and sisters so live in unity, love and peace." Another changes the saying, "It's a black thing. You wouldn't understand" to "It's a black thing. You should understand"—a statement that at least opens the possibility that someone not black *could* potentially "understand." Even the "Crack Kills/Black Power" design considered from a wearer's perspective embodies a raw humor, assimilating "black power" to a carnivalesque, scatological tradition of "funky butt" humor.

Though he lives in and as a commodity, Black Bart's energetic transformations and evocations of multiple identities arguably connect with longer traditions from folk culture, recalling for instance the African-American trickster figure, whose transformations *From Trickster to Badman* Roberts has described. He also appears to draw upon the dynamic surrounding the figure of the entertainer in black culture. As Keil has described him, the African-American entertainer is not simply a charming personality skilled in some single area of public amusement. He is rather an "identity expert," whose mastery of stances and poses possesses ritual power to construct identity and social cohesion, in the process defining "a special domain of Negro culture wherein black men have proved and preserved their humanity" (15). Without effacing the difference between a T-shirt cartoon and actual, personal performance, it would nonetheless seem that Black Bart's tricky signifying evokes cultural identity and cohesion. Worn in the streets, the Black Bart figure makes a cultural assertion, a species of enacted rhetoric, commenting upon the arena of television and making it a forum for African-American values and images. As T-shirt vendor Deborah Id-Deen said, the Black Bart T-shirt "gives black people a sense that they're famous."

## Conclusion

The possible political value of this sense of "fame" is easy to underestimate. As Levine points out,

> There has been an unfortunate if understandable tendency in our political age to conceive of protest in almost exclusively political and institutional terms. Thus group consciousness and a firm sense of the self have been confused with political consciousness and organization, "manhood" has been equated with armed rebellion, and resistance with the building of a revolutionary tradition.

Levine further explains how black song serves a constructive social function that may be extended even to the public display and deployment of commodities such as the Black Bart T-shirt:

> To state that black song constituted a form of black protest and resistance does not mean that it necessarily led to or even called for any tangible and specific actions, but rather that it served as a mechanism by which Negroes could be relatively candid in a society that rarely accorded them that privilege, could communicate this candor to others whom they would in no other way be able to reach, and, in the face of the sanctions of the white majority, could assert their own individuality, aspirations, and sense of being (240).

The Black Bart T-shirt too arguably mediates a communicative candor and assertion of self and group identification.

The Black Bart T-shirt is not alone as an expressive use of a commodity to support personal and social identity and convey resistant social messages. Consider, for instance, the insouciant rejection of school deportment expressed in the gracefully untied laces of urban high tops and super sneakers. The gesture rejects that fundamental school rule—"tie your shoelaces!"—yet the shoes stay on and in fact imply spirited, gymnastic agility. "Boom boxes" or "ghetto blasters" and cars fitted with elaborate sound systems blaring rap or salsa create mobile, auditory cultural environments that are expansive—and instantly collapsible. Dance party DJs, MCs and rappers enact an even more creative relation to the commodity. They treat the completed tape or record as itself artistic material. The DJs select, reorder, "sample" and "scratch" these existing commodities into a new composition or "mix," which "priest-like" they offer up for the dancing communion of "everybody in the house."

But as the appropriation—revitalization process works in the post-modernist era with pastiche and quotation of completed, existing texts, the cultural conflict Fiske describes also manifests itself in palpable cultural and legal controversy. The racial apocalypse that concludes Spike Lee's *Do the Right Thing* begins over the use of a boom box. Sound control ordinances are passed to quell the sound-system cars (but allow exceptions for political sound trucks). Poaching on the territory of copyrighted mass media commodities, whether by T-shirt manufacturers or DJ samplers, meets prosecution for copyright violation.

But however contentiously or even illegally they go about it, these practices accomplish something significant for group life in commodity culture. They serve a social-psychological function akin to the "soul strategy" of the blues as Keil describes it: to "increase feelings of solidarity, boost morale, strengthen the consensus" (164–5). The Black Bart T-shirt and similar appropriated and revitalized commodities suggest the significant creative precisely, in the midst of commodity culture and post-modernism.

## Notes

1. This paper was originally delivered at the 1991 annual meeting of the Popular Culture Association. For their helpful comments on versions of this essay, the author wishes to thank Simon Bronner, Gary Daily, Clemmie Gilpin, Charles Keil, Suren Lalvani and William Mahar. Craig Smith provided valuable information on T-shirt production.

2. This paper will not concern itself with the many other appropriations of the ubiquitous Bart Simpson. Suffice it to say that his mischievous image was used for a variety of causes and by no means did they all represent marginalized groups. Bart was swiftly enlisted in the Gulf War: Windbreakers in Tijuana cast him as Rambo, strangling Saddam Hussein and saying, "I am your worst nightmare." On a T-shirt he urinated on a map of Iraq. Editors of the conservative *Campus Review* at the University of Iowa put a slingshot in Bart's hands and had him threaten, "Back off Faggot!" sparking a lawsuit and complaints to local human rights organizations (see "Suits and debate follow display of cartoon poster"). In California, Republican campaign strategists used Bart's visage to accuse gubernatorial candidate Diane Feinstein of "cheating" in a debate ("The Rehabilitation of Bart Simpson"). A cartoon circulated within Xerox culture incorporated Bart as well. With obscene logic it fused two key traits in characters of the show—Bart's physicality and Baby Maggie's perpetual plying of her pacifier. The photocopied drawing, circulated in south central Pennsylvania and reported printed on a T-shirt in New Orleans, finds Bart, his pants about his knees, with baby Maggie, and Mother Marge screaming in the background. Bart says, "But Mom, she lost her pacifier!" We leave to the reader's imagination what means Bart found to replace it.

3. See Light and Bonacich 322. Kim in "The Big Apple Goes Bananas Over Korean Fruit Stands" and *New Urban Immigrants: The Korean Community in New York* and McKinley describe the relations of Blacks and Koreans in New York City. In general, as Light and Bonacich note, Korean merchants in low-end retailing gain valuable entry to the American market and in the process provide American corporate interests with a variety of indirect benefits. Koreans pioneer in and distribute corporate goods in low-productivity sectors of the market, help keep labor cheap and unorganized, and promote the idea that the United States is a land where hard work is rewarded (though most entrepreneurs in fact will spend generations working long hours for low pay) (354–400). The increased economic connections between Korea and the United States is also reflected in the fact that, as Basler reports, "The Simpsons" animation is produced at Akom Studio in Seoul.

4. In fact the shirt was more offensive than other Black Bart T-shirts. T-shirt vendor Deborah Id-Deen described it *sotto voce,* asserting solemnly that she may have sold Black Bart T-shirts but she would never sell the "Crack Kills" T-shirt. Yet it was also worn and distributed at least from New York City to Washington D.C., where Mills described it.

5. The students were members of a "student activities committee" representing grades from kindergarten through fifth at the Benjamin Franklin Academic Prep School, Harrisburg, PA. They spoke to me on the understanding they would not be identified. The author wishes to thank the children for their help, Norma Gotwalt, director of the Harrisburg Division of Elementary Education, and Joann Griffin, principal of the Benjamin Franklin Academic Prep School.

## Works Cited

Allen, Richard L. "Communication Research on Black Americans." Paper presented at the Symposium on Minority Audiences and Programming Research. Lenox, MA, Oct. 1980. ERIC ED.

Bales, Fred. "Television Use and Confidence in Television by Blacks and Whites in Four Selected Years." *Journal of Black Studies* 16.3 (1986).

Basler, Barbara. "Peter Pan, Garfield and Bart—All Have Asian Roots." *The New York Times* 2 Dec. 1990.

Bayles, Martha. "Blacks on TV: Adjusting the Image." *New Perspectives* 17.3 (1985).

Behling, Dorothy U. "T-Shirts as Communicators of Attitudes." *Perceptual and Motor Skills* 66 (1988).

"Black Bart Simpson T-Shirt Raises Concern Among Blacks." *Jet* 27 Aug. 1990, 37.

Bronner, Simon. Personal Communication. 18 Sept. 1991.

Bryant-Johnson, Sherry. "Blacks on TV Soaps: Visible but Neutralized." *Perspectives: The Civil Rights Quarterly* 15.3 (1983).

de Certeau, Michel. *The Practice of Everyday Life.* Trans. Steven F. Rendall. Berkeley: U of California P, 1984.

Eason, David, and Fred Fogo. "The Cultural Turn in Media Studies." *Mass Comm Review* 15.1 (1988).

"Eat My Shirts! Pesky Bart Simpson Tees Off a California Principal—and Gets Kicked Out of School for Swearing." *People Weekly* 21 May 1990: 130.

Fiske, John. *Reading the Popular.* Boston: Unwin, 1989.

——. *Understanding Popular Culture.* Boston: Unwin, 1989.

Frazier, E. Franklin. *The Negro Church in America.* Boston, 1963.

Gitlin, Todd. "Prime-Time Whitewash." *American Film* 9.2 (Nov. 1983).

Groening, Matt. "Life in Hell." Cartoon. *Village Voice* 7 Aug. 1990: 8.

Hebdige, Dick. *Subculture: The Meaning of Style.* London: Methuen, 1979.

Herskovits, Melville J. *The Myth of the Negro Past,* 1941. Boston: Beacon, 1958.

Holland, Ilona E. "Nonstandard English on Television: A Content Analysis." Paper presented at the Annual Meeting of the International Communication Association. Chicago, 22–26 May 1986. ERIC ED.

Id-Deen, Deborah. Personal Interview. 10 Nov. 1990.

Keil, Charles. *Urban Blues.* Chicago: The U of Chicago P, 1966.

Kim, Illsoo. "The Big Apple Goes Bananas Over Korean Fruit Stands." *Asia* 4 (1981).

——. *New Urban Immigrants: The Korean Community in New York.* Princeton: Princeton UP, 1981.

Krebs, Jeanette. "Black Bart: T-Shirts Depict TV Kid with Dark Skin." *Patriot-News* [Harrisburg, PA] 29 July 1990.

Levine, Lawrence W. *Black Culture and Black Consciousness: Afro-American Folk Thought from Slavery to Freedom.* New York: Oxford UP, 1977.

Liehr, J.T. Telephone Interview. 20 Dec. 1990.

Light, Ivan, and Edna Bonacich. *Immigrant Entrepreneurs: Koreans in Los Angeles, 1965–1982.* Berkeley: U of California P. 1988.

Marriott, Michel. "I'm Bart, I'm Black and What About It?" *New York Times* 19 Sept. 1990.

Maultsby, Portia K. "Africanisms in African-American Music." *Africanisms in American Culture.* Ed. Joseph E. Holloway. Bloomington: Indiana UP, 1990.

Mills, David. "Bootleg Black Bart Simpson, the Hip-Hop T-Shirt Star." *Washington Post.* 28 June 1990: D1.

Murray, Albert. *Stomping the Blues.* New York: McGraw Hill, 1976.

Nelson, George. *Elevating the Game: Black Men and Basketball.* New York: Harper Collins, 1992.

Perls, Frederick, Ralph F. Hefferline and Paul Goodman. *Gestalt Therapy: Excitement and Growth in the Human Personality.* New York: Dell, 1951.

Philips, John Edward. "The African Heritage of White America." Ed. Joseph E. Holloway, *Africanisms in American Culture.* Bloomington: Indiana UP, 1990.

Radway, Janice A. *Reading the Romance: Women, Patriarchy, and Popular Literature.* Chapel Hill: U of North Carolina P, 1984.

"The Rehabilitation of Bart Simpson." *Mother Jones* Jan.-Feb. 1991.

Roberts, John Storm. *Black Music of Two Worlds.* New York: Praeger, 1972.

Roberts, John W. *From Trickster to Badman: The Black Folk Hero in Slavery and Freedom.* Philadelphia: U of Pennsylvania P, 1989.

Schafer, William J. & Johannes Riedel. *The Art of Ragtime.* Baton Rouge: Louisiana State University, 1973.

Silverman, Franklin H., Michele Gazzolo, & Yvonne Peterson. "Impact of a T-shirt Message on Stutterer Stereotypes: A Systematic Replication." *Journal of Fluency Disorders* 15.1 (1990).

Stroman, Carolyn A. "Mass Media Effects and Black Americans." *Urban Research Review* 9.4 (1984).

—— et al. "Twenty Years Later: The Portrayal of Blacks on Prime-Time Television." Paper presented at the Annual Meeting of the Association for Education in Journalism and Mass Communication. Portland, OR, 2–5 July 1988.

"Suits and Debate Follow Display of Cartoon Poster." *New York Times* 25 Nov. 1990.
"When Life Imitates Bart." *Newsweek* 23 July 1990.
Yoo, Woong Nyol. "Business Owners in New York's Harlem Struggle Against Anti-Korean Prejudice."
     *Koreatown* 19 Oct. 1981.

**READING** WRITING

## THIS TEXT: READING

1.  What scholarly contexts does Parisi use in the article. How might these be useful for other phenomena?
2.  Can you think of another phenomena that audiences have altered to make them reflect their interests?

## YOUR TEXT: WRITING

1.  Find another t-shirt that's commonly worn and read it as a cultural text.
2.  Go to a toystore and look at the toys related to TV shows or movies. What relationship between audience and show or movie does the related toy assume? In what ways does the toy reinterpret the show or movie?

## The Reality TV Suite

The authors of this book live on opposite coasts; so they agreed to meet in the desert Southwest do work on the new edition of this book, and in particular, to write this new suite on Reality TV. In a bizarre coincidence, as one of the authors was about to fly back to the West Coast, he found himself in an airport restaurant with the cast of *The Real World.* Cameras were everywhere; MTV handlers circled the restaurant and were staged at various places in the airport. Dozens of travelers peeked over into where the cast (and the author) were eating. It is entirely possible that one of the authors will be in the background of an episode of *The Real World* that will have already aired by the time this book reaches you. The entire scene was profoundly unreal, and yet . . . not.

This suite explores the phenomenon of reality television. Reality TV first hit American airwaves in 1992, when MTV broadcast *The Real World,* a surprise hit. However, Reality TV truly became a phenomenon in 2000, when *Survivor* appeared on CBS and completely entranced the American public. Since then, a plethora of reality shows have reached American viewers. While the fact that so many shows are successful (and so many are given chances to be successful) indicates that the American public loves them, many are critical of a genre that promises "reality" but delivers something else.

In this set of pieces originally printed in *Entertainment Weekly* (2004), Ken Tucker, a television critic for the magazine, and Henry Goldblatt face off on the nature of reality television—Goldblatt is for, and Tucker is against. Francine Prose, a novelist and journalist, draws a parallel between reality television and Republican values, while not explicitly condemning the genre. Justin T.P. Ryan comments on the unrealistic and often downright unpleasant aspects of reality television and asks whether they will translate to Real-life dating.

For the most part, media critics and conservative commentators lambaste Reality TV as bad entertainment that has no basis in reality. Others contend that it is going to become the new soap opera and that it makes celebrities out of ordinary people. Television studios love Reality TV because the shows are cheap to produce but bring in a great deal of money, suggesting the fad is not going away any time soon.

Consider, as you work your way through these essays, how Reality TV has changed television, your own ideas about the world, and how we see the entire concept of "entertainment." Also, for those of you who have become hooked on *Survivor,* or like one of the authors, the first *Bachelor* series, think about where your overt interest in these shows comes from. Why is it we watch these shows? What do they give us that the everyday world does not?

---

### REALITY TV BITES—OR DOES IT? THE NEW SOAP OPERA OR THE END OF CIVILIZATION: A POINT-COUNTERPOINT

■ **Henry Goldblatt and Ken Tucker** ■

### Love It

Wasn't it jarring to hear that Jerri from *Survivor* stormed off the live reunion special last week? How could she do that? Rachel wouldn't be allowed to leave the last episode of *Friends* in a huff. Oh, wait a minute—Rachel's not real, but Jerri is: "She was a great 'character.' It's easy to forget she's a real person," said host Jeff Probst.

We need the reminder. It's easy to treat reality contestants as fiction because they're the types of characters we had been accustomed to seeing on TV before all those detectives without personal lives showed up. We're on a first-name basis with so many reality players—Rupert, Troy, Clay, and Shandi—because their emotions are so accessible. Apologies to *The O.C.*, but for fans of character-driven television, these series are the best prime-time soaps in years.

As Albert Camus said: "An intellectual is someone whose mind watches itself." Reality characters and the dramas encasing them are so compelling because they represent our dreams and lives. Look beyond the slick and (often) crass packaging of *American Idol*'s Kelly and Clay and reach into the deepest pit of your shame. Now admit it: They are your shower-singing, pop-star fantasies come true. Watching *The Apprentice*'s Omarosa, haven't you thought: *She's like that crazy #%!@ I work with?*

What puzzles me about the hate part of critics' love-hate relationship with reality is that no other genre of entertainment is maligned so harshly. In pop music, Usher is as commercial as any Idol and performs lightweight R&B (sample lyric: "yeah yeah yeah yeah yeah yeah")—but he's called infectious. (Before anyone writes letters, I'm a fan.) The film *Van Helsing* cost $148 million and bites, yet critics are barely fazed, since it'll be out of theaters soon enough. But when critics hear *Idol*'s Jasmine hit a few wrong notes on Barry Manilow night? Quick, duck for cover—it's a sign of the apocalypse.

Speaking of the apocalypse, there's even redeeming value in the very worst of reality TV: (1) *The Swan* makes us feel good about ourselves in comparison (at least we have enough self-esteem not to enter a beauty pageant for former ugly people); and (2) *Are You Hot?* reminded us that under no circumstances does Lorenzo Lamas deserve a comeback. —*Henry Goldblatt*

## Hate It

As someone who originally got into this racket to explore what's vital, fun, and troublesome about popular culture. I'm glad I work at a magazine that doesn't accept or condemn any phenomenon at face value. Unlike a lot of my TV-critic colleagues, I don't go to bed hoping reality TV will vanish when I wake up in the morning simply because the decades-old sitcom/drama configuration was easier to deal with. There are reality shows—some editions of *Survivor, Big Brother, The Amazing Race,* and, delving into the netherworld of syndication for a moment, *Cheaters*—that are full of fascinating sociological details and, of course, laughs.

But ultimately, I find the majority of reality TV really depressing. For instance, I cannot muster enthusiasm for what's supposed to be the central conceit of *American Idol*—finding a first-rate young singer—when every piece of music the vocalists perform is the kind of schlock I datested in my previous incarnation as a rock critic. (That's the reason I love Fantasia—like Aretha Franklin and Ray Charles, she bursts the flimsy bonds of cheap ballads with agile gospel and soul inflections.)

Nearly all of the young-folks-on-the-make shows, from *The Bachelor* to *Average Joe* to *The Real World*, strike me as a vast condemnation of the education system (no one on these shows speaks with any eloquence or wit, or makes cultural references beyond sports or pop music) and the failure of upbringing (these studs and babes hold their eating utensils like monkeys and get drunk at every opportunity). The fact that parents let their kids watch swill like *Fear Factor*—which celebrates swill, as long as a contestant can keep from barfing it up—fills me with dread for the future.

Two reality television participants on *Fear Factor* (top) and *American Idol* (bottom).

I'm not foolish enough to expect civilian non-performers to be profoundly self-analytical about their motives or to crack jokes as sharp-witted as a pro like, say, Larry David (though aren't his comments unscripted too? Gee, y'think it's because he has a frame of reference beyond just getting loaded or laid?). But is it asking too much for entertainment to be entertaining, and not a constant parade of people who, if I met them in real life, I'd dash across the room to avoid? —*Ken Tucker*

---

### REALITY DATING

■ **Justin T. P. Ryan** ■

In case you thought *Survivor* and *Big Brother* offered the entirety of TV's "reality" show craze, you probably haven't been up late enough to watch *Elimidate* or *The 5th Wheel*. Feeding off a trend of such shows pioneered by MTV's Real World series which debuted 10 years ago, the scope of these programs has gone beyond just a bunch of 20 somethings from different backgrounds and beliefs perilously trying to get along in some lavish big city apartment. Now, the same age group tries to date and date not only successfully but competitively. However, these new shows do not represent simply an ignorance of traditional values, they represent an assault on such values. Whatever happened to starting off with a cup of coffee and conversation?

In a sick new rendering of *The Dating Game*, the show *Blind Date* bids two seemingly incompatible people on an expenses-paid date with a camera in tow, capturing their every romantic miscue. To embarrass the contestants further, producers have inserted pop-up thought bubbles and animations in response to the couple's verbal misfires, uncomfortable body language, and awkward silences. At different times, each participant talks on camera alone lambasting the other for usually the less important things like bodily proportions or perceived sexual mediocrity or worse yet, their finer virtues.

Shows like *Elimidate* and *5th Wheel* are no politeness parade either. Instead of just two guinea pigs, *Elimidate* pits one woman and four men (or the opposite) to go on a date all at once in backstabbing, lowest common denominator competition for the affections of the one woman or man. In the tradition of *Survivor*, contestants are voted off. They react to their elimination, of course, as if it is the defining tragedy of their lives. As contestants are weeded out, the pursuit for the sole young man or woman's favor by those still standing becomes all the more loathsome: closer dancing than the others pursuers dared try, kissing earlier on (in front of the others), simple transparent flattery laced with sexual innuendo. A few bathing suits and a jaunt into a hot tub later, you're teetering on debauchery with people who have essentially just met.

Most viewers are college students and young professionals who enjoy the simple novelty of viewing a blind date, particularly one with three or four people rather than just one. Also, the people chosen for the shows are (or at least appear) so ludicrously stupid and shallow that the viewer can easily have a laugh at their expense. Yet what most viewers of the program miss is that watching such programs merely makes them feel justified in their seemingly more minor transgressions and they do not promote any kind of respect or chivalry in courting and romantic relationships. If Randy and Crystal seem to expect so little from each other, what keeps them from settling for so little?

The passive premise of the show is that dating in any kind of traditional sense is all but dead, passe or unworkable. The prevailing wisdom is that you simply can't find good, compatible people in the workplace, through friends, at your church, temple or place of worship or in any civic activities. After having grown tired of the bar and club scene, these singles look to a TV show which is designed to make them look foolish for an audience in the hopes of just maybe finding that needle in the haystack special someone or worst yet, some disingenuous fun. Unfortunately, these all-expenses-paid shenanigans seem to offer few romantic dividends.

Of course, the show clearly and unabashedly relies on raw sexuality. But when will it wear off that your date's body is to die for when you cannot even carry on a decent conversation with them?

The programming's glamour merely sinks young people's expectations for possible mates even lower, not higher. It legitimizes objectifying of the opposite sex, encourages uncommitted unethical sexual practices outside the confines of marriage, and gives no help to those men who do not know even so much as to pick up the bill at a restaurant or open the door for a lady.

Clearly, for some, being on these programs is a novelty, not to be taken too seriously. Fair enough. However, with ABC's new The Bachelor and Fox's *Bachelorettes in Alaska,* the stakes are considerably higher. The hope amongst the participants is that they will in fact meet and fall in love with the man or woman of their dreams and do so in these exotic locations all while being the entertainment of a prime time audience.

If any antidote is in the works at all to alleviate this on television, NBC has countered with the premiere this week of *Meet My Folks,* where potential suitors have to spend an entire weekend with the family of their date, being grilled and assessed in the parents' own home. Time will tell whether the show will be a hit, but more importantly will getting the parents' blessing be as elusive as it once was?

This so-called "reality television" is nothing of the kind. Few will remember a time when they were given the opportunity to go on a date with someone for free, in a location they could never afford if it weren't free, with a person they do not even know. Perhaps the truly sinister element here is that the dream like conditions for these potential mates offers relaxed opportunities to ignore chivalry, respect, and good common sense for the young of this generation.

## VOTING DEMOCRACY OFF THE ISLAND: REALITY TV AND THE REPUBLICAN ETHOS

### ■ Francine Prose ■

Not even Melana can believe it's real. As the "former NFL cheerleader and beauty queen looking to fall in love with the perfect guy" swans a bit dazedly through the Palm Springs mansion in which she will soon undertake the task of selecting Mr. Right from among sixteen eligible bachelors, she coos about the thrill of living a "dream come true."

It's the premiere episode of NBC's *Average Joe,* one of the extremely popular and profitable "reality-based" television shows that, in recent years, have proliferated to claim a significant share of major-network prime time. Featuring ordinary people who have agreed to be filmed in dangerous, challenging, or embarrassing situations in return for the promise of money, romance, or fame, these offerings range from *Who Wants to Marry a Millionaire?* to *Who Wants to Marry My Dad?,* from long-run hits such as *Survivor* and *The Real World* to the short-lived *Are You Hot?* and *Boy Meets Boy.*

The title *Average Joe* has evidently alerted Melana to the possibility that her bachelor pool may not be stocked with the same species of dazzling hunks, those walking miracles of body sculpting, cosmetic dentistry, and hair-gel expertise who courted "The Bachelorette." Clearly, she's expecting to meet the more routinely, unself-consciously attractive sort of guy one might spot on the street or at the water cooler.

But, as frequently happens, the audience is privy to an essential truth—or, in the argot of reality programming, a "reveal"—concealed from the hapless participants. Now, as the cameras whisk us to the bachelors' quarters, we instantly get the visual joke that is, even by the standards of reality TV, sadistic.

The men about to compete for Melana's affections are not merely Joe Well Below Average but Joe Out of the Question. Several are obese; others have tics, dermatological or dental problems, or are short, bespectacled, balding, stooped. Racial and cultural diversity is provided by a diminutive "university professor" from Zimbabwe with a penchant for intellectual boasting and grave fashion miscalculations.

Although the sight of Melana's suitors is intended to amuse and titillate rather than to touch us, it would (to paraphrase Dickens amid this Dickensian crowd) take a heart of stone not to be moved by the moment when the men take a look at one another and realize that their inclusion in this confraternity of nerds is probably not a mistake.

Meanwhile, night has fallen on the desert, and the lovely Melana, all dressed up and as starry-eyed as a kid on Christmas morning, comes out to meet the guys. A white limousine pulls up. A male model emerges, and Melana's face brightens, only to darken seconds later when he announces that, sadly, he is not one of her bachelors.

The white limo carries the tease away. Presently a bus arrives.

The bus doors open. They send the fat guys out first. And by the time a half-dozen sorry specimens are lined up, grinning their hearts out, even Melana gets it. Her shock and dismay are genuine. The men cannot help but notice. "This is *bad*," she whispers, and we can read her lips. "Someone's messing with my head."

What lends the scene its special poignancy is that Melana knows, as do we, that what has befallen her is not some cruel accident of fate. Rather, she has brought misfortune on herself. In filling out the questionnaire that led to her being selected as the heroine of *Average Joe,* she indicated that "a good personality" mattered more to her than did appearance. And in doing so, she violated one of the cardinal rules, a basic article of faith, one of the values that this new version of reality pumps out, hour after hour, night after night, into the culture. Had Melana watched more reality-based TV, she would have learned that surface beauty (preferably in concert with a strong manipulative instinct, a cunning ability to play the game, and vast quantities of money) is all that counts. Melana has transgressed. And now, as we sit back and watch, she is about to be punished.

If this—a dash of casual brutality, a soupçon of voyeurism—is your recipe for entertainment, it's a taste you can satisfy, in the privacy of your living room, nearly every evening. In fact, unless you own one of those televisions that allow you to watch two programs at once, you may be forced to make some hard choices.

On a typical night—Thanksgiving Eve, November 26, 2003—you could, at eight, watch a contestant on CBS's *Survivor Pearl Islands* secure himself some sympathy by misleading his fellow tribe members into thinking that his grandmother has just died. But witnessing the "biggest lie ever told on *Survivor*" would mean missing the episode of NBC's *Queer Eye for*

*the Straight Guy* in which a quintet of homosexual fashion and lifestyle advisers convince a balding lawyer to lose his unflattering hairpiece. At nine, you could shop along with ABC's Trista for *Trista & Ryan's Wedding,* an account of the big-ticket ceremony that would solemnize the love affair spawned, as America watched, on *The Bachelorette.* And at ten, on *Extreme Makeover,* the most literally invasive series so far, two lucky souls (chosen from more than 10,000 applicants) have their lives transformed by plastic surgery. On this night a man whose 200-pound weight loss has left him looking like a shar-pei, and a rather pretty grade-school teacher—who believes that she is only a rhinoplasty and a chin implant away from rivaling her beautiful sisters—will go under the knife.

In the event that three hours of watching your fellow humans suffer and squirm and endure surgical procedures has left you feeling uneasy about how you have spent your time, or what you have found amusing, you can be reassured—as are the network executives, it would seem—by the fact that you are not alone. In January 2003 the premiere of Fox Network's *Joe Millionaire,* in which a construction worker courted women tricked into believing that he possessed a vast personal fortune, attracted 18.6 million viewers; 40 million tuned in for its conclusion. *American Idol,* the talent show that asks fans to vote for their favorite contestants by telephone, received 110 million calls in its first season and 15.5 million calls during the final show alone. By contrast, the most popular national news program—NBC's *Nightly News*—averages around 11 million viewers per night.

Like Melana, network accountants were quick to see reality shows as a dream come true. For although production values and costs have risen, reality-based programs are still relatively cheap to produce, mostly because they avoid the expense of hiring actors whose salary demands can rise astronomically if the show becomes a hit. One consequence is that television actors have seen a radical reduction in the number and range of available roles.

Despite the fact that journalists periodically hail the death of reality TV, it has proved remarkably long-lived. MTV's, *The Real World,* which sends seven attractive young strangers to spend six months turning their luxury housing into a Petri dish of sexual, racial, and interpersonal tension, has been running since 1992. Now in its eighth season, *Survivor* has airlifted a succession of warring "tribes" from the Amazon to the jungles of Thailand. During the week of November 17–23, 2003, the only shows more popular than *Survivor Pearl Islands* (which drew 19.9 million viewers) were *CSI, ER,* and *Friends.*

On aesthetic grounds alone, it's arguable that reality-based shows are no better or worse than *CSI; ER,* and *Friends.* But the most obvious difference is the most crucial one. Fans of *Friends* understand that they are watching a sitcom, cast with celebrity actors. Watching *Survivor* and *The Real World,* they believe that they are observing *real* men and women.

Viewers do, of course, realize that some of what they're seeing has been instigated or exacerbated by the show's producers. Yet the fact is that viewers *are* watching people who, regardless of their career ambitions or masochistic exhibitionism, are amateurs who may have been chosen *for* their fragility and instability. Many of the "Average Joes" could never get hired as character actors. And observing their response to stress and humiliation generates a gladiatorial, bread-and-circus atmosphere that simply does not exist when we see movie stars in scrubs sail a gurney down the halls of *ER.*

Reality-based TV, then, is not a scripted fiction but an improvisation, an apparently instructive improvisation that doles out consistent and frequently reinforced lessons about human nature and, yes, reality. These programs also generate a jittery, adrenalized buzz that produces a paradoxically tranquilized numbness in which our defenses relax and leave us more receptive to the "information" we are receiving. For this reason alone, even those who take pride in never looking at TV, except for the occasional peek at PBS, might want to tune in and see what reality their fellow citizens have been witnessing.

What might future anthropologists (or, for that matter, contemporary TV-addicted children and adults) conclude about our world if these programs constituted their primary source of information? The most obvious lesson to be drawn from reality TV, the single philosophical pole around which everything else revolves, is that the laws of natural selection are even more brutal, inflexible, and *sensible* than one might suppose from reading *Origin of Species.* Reality is a Darwinian battle-field on which only the fittest survive, and it's not merely logical but admirable to marshal all our skills and resources to succeed in a struggle that only one person can win.

Compelling its testy, frequently neurotic castaways to operate as if they were several rungs down the evolutionary ladder, grubbing roots and berries and forced to earn such basic necessities as blankets by performing acrobatic stunts, *Survivor* is the prototype. The show urges its participants to labor for their tribe but always, ultimately, for themselves. Because at the end of the day—in this case, the final episode—only one person will walk away with a million dollars. And in case we lose sight of first principles, the show's motto, which appears in its logo, is "Outwit. Outplay. Outlast."

*Survivor* is the younger American cousin of the 1997 Swedish *Expedition Robinson,* a title judged too literary for the U.S. market. It's probably just as well that the series wasn't called *Expedition Robinson. Robinson Crusoe* and *Swiss Family Robinson* extol the virtues and advantages of fellowship and cooperation, whereas on *Survivor* such considerations are useful only to a point. *Survivor* could be Defoe's masterpiece rewritten by Ayn Rand. And for all its Darwinian trappings, the series offers a skewed view of the *purpose* of the struggle for dominance. Propagating the species is the last thing on these people's minds.

And so the steps that lead toward that goal aren't determined by physical combat or brilliant displays of plumage. Rather, contestants are eliminated by a democratic process; every few days, tribe members vote on which of their fellows will be forced to leave the island. As we watch, the loser trudges across a rope bridge or rock ledge and off to a dismal future without a million dollars.

Observant readers may already have noted that the guiding principles to which I've alluded—flinty individualism, the vision of a zero-sum society in which no one can win unless someone else loses, the conviction that altruism and compassion are signs of folly and weakness, the exaltation of solitary striving above the illusory benefits of cooperative mutual aid, the belief that certain circumstances justify secrecy and deception, the invocation of a reviled common enemy to solidify group loyalty—are the exact same themes that underlie the rhetoric we have been hearing and continue to hear from the Republican Congress and our current administration.

Of course, no sensible person would imagine that Donald Rumsfeld is sitting down with the producers of reality-based TV to discuss the possibility that watching the contestants sweat and strain to bring civilization to the jungle will help us accept the sacrifices we have been and are still being asked to make in Iraq. On the other hand, there is the unsettling precedent set by *Profiles from the Front Line,* a series that aired around the time of the war in Iraq and was produced for ABC Entertainment by Jerry Bruckheimer, whose credits include *Black Hawk Down.*

According to an advance release from the network,

> the Pentagon and the Department of Defense lent their full support and cooperation to this unique production. . . . As America prepares for a possible war with Iraq, the country continues to wage a perilous war on terrorism. ABC will transport viewers to actual battlefields in Central Asia with a six-episode series that will feature actual footage of the elite U.S. Special Operations forces apprehending possible terrorists, as well as compelling, personal stories of the U.S. military men and women who bear the burden and risks of this fighting.

Indeed, ABC News complained that—in order to film the soldiers arresting a "big-time" Taliban leader, disarming rockets, providing medical care to Afghan civilians, capturing fuel-truck hijackers, and accepting the love and gratitude of the Afghan people—the show's producers were being granted a level of access to the troops that Pentagon officials denied the network's actual reporters.

But even when the collaboration between the military, the government, and the entertainment industry is not nearly so overt, these shows continue to transmit a perpetual, low-frequency hum of agitprop. The ethics (if one can call them that) and the ideals that permeate these programs at once reflect and reinforce the basest, most mindless and ruthless aspects of the current political zeitgeist. If the interests of the corporate culture that controls our television stations are at heart the same as those that fund and support lobbyists and politicians, it stands to reason that—when network executives do meet to determine what is appropriate, entertaining, profitable, what people want and need to see—they are unlikely to flinch at portraying stylized versions of the same behavior we read about in the press, or can observe on the Senate floor.

Among the notions of reality that the designers of these shows appear to hold in common with the participants in the corporate strategy session—or, one presumes, the Pentagon or Cabinet meeting—is the vision of the world as a vast human-behavior laboratory. Its population of lab rats can be coolly observed by the research scientists (the market analyst, the politician, the TV viewer), who can then draw profitable lessons from their subjects' responses. Let's see how the castaways behave when they are ordered to abandon their humble camp and exiled to a new locale. Let's watch how the homely bachelors compete for the hand of the beauty, how quickly the public embraces the next revolution in junk food, and how the citizens of the Middle East deal with their altered circumstances when we change their regimes and encourage them to adopt Western values. Meanwhile, this objective, experimental mode dispels any qualms we might feel about the fact that the research subjects are humans who may have their own ideas and opinions about how they want to live.

Presumably, many of these shows' creators would be unnerved to hear that the harmless amusements they are concocting actually reflect, reinforce, and codify a specific political agenda. But it might come as less of a surprise to, say, Mark Burnett, the executive producer of *Survivor*.

At seventeen, the London-born Burnett joined the British army and became a paratrooper, a decorated member of the elite Parachute Regiment, with which he saw combat in the Falkland Islands and in Northern Ireland. In 1982 he set out for Central America, then in the throes of widespread guerrilla warfare and counterinsurgency terrorism. En route to work there as a military adviser with the British Special Air Service, he decided instead to get off the plane in Los Angeles and seek his fortune in Hollywood.

After brief stints as a nanny and a T-shirt salesman, his military background and media ambitions inspired him to enter the Raid Gauloises, an annual French race that sent teams on rugged courses through the Oman desert and the jungles of Borneo. In 1995, Burnett started his own version of the French competition, the Eco-Challenge, which (over the objections of environmentalists) took place in Utah and was filmed for the Discovery Channel. When the 1998 Eco-Challenge, staged in Morocco, received an Emmy Award, Burnett was in an ideal position to market the American rights to *Survivor,* which he had presciently acquired.

Reading Mark Burnett's résumé cannot help but make *Survivor* seem even more like a weekly dispatch from the Central American terrorist training camp to which he may have been headed when he was lured off course by the siren song of Hollywood. And our unease about the cozy relationship between the broadcasting industry and its advertisers is hardly soothed when we learn that Burnett has given "motivational, leadership and team-building speeches" for such clients as IBM, Citibank, Sony, USA Networks, Discovery Channel, and Ad-Week Asia. Knowing all this can only make us doubly aware, and wary, of the nuggets of motivational and guerrilla training we are receiving along with the seemingly innocent pleasure of picking sides and favorites, deciding which bachelor or bachelorette we'd choose.

The merciless individualism and bloodthirsty competition turn out to represent the noblest, most heroic aspect of this new reality. The darker, more cynical message—the lesson beneath the lesson, so to speak—is that every human being can and will do *anything* for money. Like those consciousness-altering substances that hurtled the Hashishins and certain indigenous tribes into battle, the smell of $50,000 intoxicates the contestants on *Fear Factor* enough to achieve a protracted out-of-body experience. How else to explain their ability to so suppress both instinct and free will that they don't gag over goblets of liquefied night-crawler guts, don't recoil from a helmet of rats, don't rebel when they are instructed to crawl into a pitch-black cave tunnel and retrieve as many ripe skunk carcasses as possible in a limited time?

Pragmatism is the main concern, whereas morality is a luxury or, worse, an impediment, an albatross. And given the limitlessness of what our fellow humans will do for cash, considering the folly of acting according to ethical scruples, it's only logical that everyone lies all the time. In some shows—*Joe Millionaire* had twenty-five women convinced that its protagonist was rich, and the gay hero of *Boy Meets Boy* had not been informed that several of his suitors were actually straight—the lying is institutionalized; elsewhere deception is a more spontaneous, situational response. When that *Survivor* contestant cons the privilege of going off alone with a friend from home because the friend allegedly brings news of the contestant's supposedly dead grandma, it truly does take you aback. Doesn't the guy have enough common sense to be superstitious?

The notion that everyone is, at heart, mendacious is reinforced in the parallel meta-reality outside the programs themselves—in the media coverage of the scandals that regularly erupt when contestants are exposed for not being what they appear. But why should that surprise us? We've seen the lies told on the show. One assumes that the audience was less astonished than Darva Conger, the lucky winner of *Who Wants to Marry a Millionaire?*, to learn that the finances of her rich new husband were shakier than he'd let on. Nor are we amazed to hear that an eligible bachelor is a former underwear model, or that the "university professor" on *Average Joe* has his own website advertising his skill as an actor. And why was that talented contestant kicked off *American Idol* just because of her involvement in Internet porn? The problem, apparently, is not the act of lying but rather the need to maintain strict control over who is permitted to lie, and under what circumstances.

The segment of TV broadcasting that is not merely "reality-based" but claims to report "reality"—the evening news and so-called news magazines such as 20/20 and *Dateline NBC*—are learning, along with the rest of us, the lessons of *Fear Factor* and *Survivor*. Having observed the public's comfort with the notion of people's willingness to do anything for money, these quasi-journalistic shows no longer hesitate to air programs such as the one, last fall, in which kidnap victim Elizabeth Smart and her family relived her horrific ordeal and, incidentally, plugged her parents' new book. Having noted how unquestioningly all the world loves a winner, the producers of the nightly news can cease worrying about their instinct to shape their coverage in support of whichever party or idea is currently leading in the polls.

If the truth is a millstone around one's neck, civility is likewise a hobble guaranteed to slow us down. And why should we be polite when rudeness is so amusing, and when we all secretly know that the spectacle of exclusion and humiliation is the highest form of entertainment? Pity the unfortunate parent trying to instruct a school-age child in the importance of kindness and empathy when that child has been watching *American Idol* and has observed that producer Simon Cowell's star rises each time he destroys—in a hiss of clipped, Brit venom—one of the poor souls guilty of singing badly while auditioning for the show's judges.

It is almost a relief to retreat to the candlelit, soft-focus world of the mating reality shows. That is, until we realize that these too are death matches of a sort, that the competing bachelors and bachelorettes will blithely mislead and betray one another in pursuit of the man or woman of their dreams. Still, part of what sets these shows apart from the rest is that, unlike the castaways and delusional music hopefuls, the suitors and love objects are meant to be not only "real" but "nice" people. One way we know this is that they continually espouse a set of fantasies, hopes, and ideals that (although the finalists are often shown making out in the Jacuzzi and shutting the bedroom door on the film crew at the culmination of decisive "private dates") would gladden the hearts of right-wing Christian proponents of old-fashioned Family Values.

You might think we lived in a society in which divorce were not an option as the bachelors and bachelorettes burble on—in show after show, series after series—about finding "the soul mate I want to spend the rest of my life with" and about the "tremendous feelings" they are developing for whichever contestant they feel capable of loving "with all my heart and soul." Contestants remind themselves and one another to "follow your heart," to "listen to your heart," as if (and despite the observable evidence to the contrary) neither the eyes, the brain, nor the genitals deserve to be consulted. Just as the purpose of *Survivor* is to outwit, outplay, and outlast, the aim of the mating shows is to get the guy or girl and *get married*. It's sexual competition as spectator sport, true, but with an earnest, conservative face. There are deeply hurt feelings (the men scowl and shake their heads, the women weep) when suitors are rejected.

Even the families get involved. *Meet My Folks* invites competitors to live in the same house with the love object's parents. The show is partly based on a popular film, starring Robert De Niro as a paranoid, snooping, ex-CIA future father-in-law from hell. But by the time the plot reached TV, it had deftly made the leap from Hollywood high comedy to Main Street reality, to the homes of suspicious couples who subject their grown children's suitors to humiliating polygraph tests and spy on them, via hidden cameras, at play with their sons or daughters in the hot tub. In fact, the producers of these shows have gotten precisely the sort of go-ahead for which John Ashcroft has long campaigned. Plenty of eavesdropping and surveillance transpires; one Average Joe was eliminated after being secretly videotaped insulting the 400-pound "Cousin" Danielle, who was actually Melana in a fat suit. The mechanisms of surveillance—the cameras, listening devices, and polygraph tests—have been seamlessly integrated into everyday life.

Indeed, on several of these series, the last remaining suitors are taken home to meet Mom and Dad, the siblings, and best friends. And the loved ones get to weigh in on which prospective mate will fit into the family. Because what's at stake here is *marriage*. Only rarely does anyone—usually a concerned parent or friend—inquire if this is really love or something manufactured by the producers.

In case we, too, have doubts about where all this is heading, the miniseries *Trista & Ryan's Wedding* celebrates the union between a good-looking fireman and the former Miami Heat cheerleader who was a runner-up on *The Bachelor* and who was brought back as *The Bachelorette* so that this time, just to make things more equal, *she* could choose. Carrying us across the commercial breaks with hints of prenuptial jitters ("Will the wedding go on as planned?"), it's a consumer blowout, a catalogue of lavish table settings, flower arrangements, wedding gowns, and the platinum- and diamond-encrusted "most expensive bridal shoe in the history of the world." It's fitting that consumerism should be the theme of this theme wedding, not only because television is, obviously, a vehicle for advertising, or because the show's concept facilitates the product placement that's so much a part of reality programming, but also because the entire courtship has been a shopping event. A purchasing decision has been made among twenty-five suitable, competing products who labored long and hard to commodify and sell themselves.

In a nod to today's "reality," the array of suitors often includes a few non-white candidates, but although the contestants-of-color are rarely eliminated in the first round, no program so far has meant true love for an interracial couple. In fact, the gene pool is a shallow one. Ryan is a fireman, but he, like most male contestants, looks like a model. The women either resemble cheerleaders or *are* cheerleaders, perky blondes with cute bodies, pert noses, and slightly strangulated Tweetie Bird voices. Reality TV is not where you go to have your stereotypes undermined and subverted. The gay guys on *Queer Eye for the Straight Guy* tend toward the nellie hysteric with the ability to out-shop Trista and a gift for initiating the nominally heterosexual male into the taboo joys of consumer culture.

Always gently testing the limit of what the culture will put up with, careful to give the bachelorette, as well as the bachelor, a chance to choose a mate, the networks are unlikely to take a chance on an *Average Jane* in which the genders are reversed, the male model obliged to pick from twenty-six ugly bachelorettes. Perhaps it's assumed that few viewers could accept the basic premise of the male beauty falling in love with the beast, regardless of her many good qualities. And perhaps it would be rightly feared that opinion might turn against a series that evoked the old-fashioned fraternity dogfight, those contests held to see which brother could bring the ugliest date to the party. It's worth noting that in the final episode of *Average Joe*, Melana rejected the ordinary-looking guy (who turned out to be a millionaire) in favor of one of the handsome contestants who, in a typical reality-TV plot twist, had been introduced into the game near the end of the series. Opting out of the game if one fails to find a suitable soul mate is simply not a possibility, for in the Republican corporatocracy there are always enough goods in the display case so that no sane shopper could refuse to make a purchase.

If these shows observe a sort of mass-market correctness, even as they reinforce gender stereotype and cliché, they also toe a fairly traditional line when it comes to class. The producers cast these scenarios from a solidly middle-class population. The well-off families in *Meet My Folks* have the sort of houses Americans are supposed to have: houses large enough to host the team of applicants competing to take their offspring on a romantic vacation. And the very wealthiest segment of the population is shown to have a heart of gold, just as we've always been led to believe. *The Simple Life* dispatches Lionel Richie's daughter (and Michael Jackson's goddaughter) Nicole and socialite Paris Hilton to slouch around an Arkansas farm, get grossed out in the cow barn, pretend not to know what Wal-Mart is, and reveal an underlying, insouciant sweetness.

In theory, *The Real World* should get credit for at least addressing the issue of race. But it's demoralizing to watch the new housemates move into their luxury digs and to be able to predict, from the start, that the one who's not going to get along with the others (especially not the racist provocateur who often shows up in the group) is the angry or militant black guy. One of these, the loose cannon David, was ultimately thrown out of the house and off the show in *The Real World: Los Angeles.* When the black guy in the Seattle series, Stephen, hit a female cast member in the face, he was permitted to remain only after agreeing to take an anger-management course. And so the cautionary, conservative message is clear: If these happen to be the only African Americans you've observed at close range, you might think twice before seeking one out as a roommate or a neighbor.

The ways in which *The Real World* has evolved over its eleven-year history provides a window onto the pressures that its producers must face to keep the show's young demographic tuning in. The most recent round, *The Real World: Paris,* focused on a group of American kids, installed in a suburban château, who spent more time in strip clubs than at the Louvre. Assigned to write an article on Versailles, two housemates downloaded the information from the Internet rather than bothering to go there. Rarely has the American public's notorious lack of interest in the world beyond our borders been made to seem cuter or more inconsequential: xenophobia as a harmless symptom of youthful ennui.

But it's the penultimate series, *The Real World: Las Vegas,* that became one of the most talked-about so far and may be a more reliable index of where reality TV is going. In their sybaritic penthouse at the Palms Casino Hotel, the Las Vegas suitemates far outdistanced their predecessors in their lack of inhibition about on-camera nudity, sex, bisexual threesomes in the hot tub, and round-the-clock debauchery. This fall, a cast member on *The Real World: San Diego* filed charges alleging that she was given a date-rape drug and assaulted by the friend of a housemate. Reportedly, the producers have been less than cooperative with the police investigation, and one wonders what role this incident will play in the show, whether it will be mined to inject the aging series with a revivifying shot of drama.

If television in general and reality TV in particular are indeed drugs, the principles of pharmacology would suggest that viewers will need an increasingly powerful fix just to maintain the same high. The producers of *The Real World* are currently launching *Starting Over,* a daytime series in which six women, lodged in a group home and aided by "life coaches," are put through the equivalent of rehab and forced to confront their problems with overeating, substance abuse, and social isolation. Unlike *The Real World,* which usually includes at least a few mentally healthy housemates, the women in *Starting Over* will presumably be selected to create a veritable zoo of conflicting personality disorders. On cable pay-per-view channels, contestants on *Can You Be a Porn Star?* will compete for $100,000 and a contract with an "adult video distributor." And O.J. Simpson has reputedly been approached to star in his own reality series.

Most recently, *Survivor* producer Mark Burnett has turned his attentions from the actual jungle to the corporate jungle ("where staying alive means using both street smarts and book smarts") to create *The Apprentice,* which sends contestants to work in Donald Trump's office and be entertainingly bullied by the Manhattan real-estate tycoon. Divided into teams, the participants (the mix of "Ivy League MBA graduates and street entrepreneurs with no college education" promises to add a frisson of class war) are assigned tasks that involve "sales, marketing, promotions, charities, real estate deals, finance, advertising pitches and facilities management." Instead of being voted off the island, losers will be fired by Trump, and the winner will be given a $250,000 job with The Trump Organization.

By the time the competitors have run this high-stakes gauntlet, skinning and cooking rodents on a tropical island will presumably seem like a day at the beach. But even if reality TV continues to explore the far frontiers of cruelty and competition, it's unnecessary for these programs to get much more sadistic or grotesque. They merely need to stay the same, and to last long enough to produce an entire generation that has grown up watching them and may consequently have some trouble distinguishing between reality TV and reality. Because what matters is not what's on television but the ghostly afterimage that lingers in our minds and clouds our vision after we turn off the television.

It's all too easy to envision a time when the White House will no longer feel compelled to sell a projected war to the American people but can merely pitch it to Jerry Bruckheimer, whose new series will show us why we need to spread our influence—preferably by force, since diplomacy is less apt to translate into compelling TV—throughout the Middle East. And it's nearly as frightening to conjure up the specter of the singles bar haunted by baffled bachelors and bachelorettes who have spent years watching cheer-leaders mate with male models and are struggling to comparison-shop cool-headedly for the best available match while simultaneously following the daunting imperative to "follow your heart" and find "the soul mate" with whom you are destined to spend the rest of your life.

As a way of reaching the American public, and inculcating audiences with a highly particular and politicized system of values, reality TV has already proved far more effective than more literal-minded representations of the governmental agenda. On the night of December 18, the stylishly dressed Paris Hilton, working in the kissing booth in a rural fair, drew 800,000 more viewers than did President George W. Bush, who was being interviewed by Diane Sawyer after the capture of Saddam Hussein. Were the President and his advisers frustrated, or surprised, or were their tender feelings hurt, by their inability to compete with the skinny socialite whose sex tape had made the rounds of the Internet? More likely they were reassured. With the public's attention so firmly focused on Paris baking pies, the administration can rest assured that it may pretty much do what it wants.

If reality TV does turn out to be not only the present but also the future of prime-time television, it seems more than likely that a steady, high-intake, long-term diet of *Survivor* and *The Bachelorette* will subtly, or not so subtly, affect the views and values of the audiences that tune in week after week. Watching a nightly Darwinian free-for-all cannot help but have a desensitizing effect. Once you've absorbed and assimilated the idea that civility is, at best, a frill, you may find yourself less inclined to suppress an eruption of road rage or the urge to ridicule the homely Average Joe who dares to approach a pretty girl. If the lesson of reality TV is that anyone will do anything for money, that every human interaction necessarily involves the swift, calculated formation and dissolution of dishonest, amoral alliances, it seems naive to be appalled by the fact that our government has been robbing us to pay off its supporters in the pharmaceutical industry and among the corporations profiting from the rebuilding of Iraq. After you've seen a "real person" lie about his grandmother's death, you may be slightly less shocked to learn that our leaders failed to come clean about the weapons of mass destruction.

After all, it's the way the world works; it's how people behave. We can't have witnessed all that reality without having figured that out by now. How foolish it would be to object to the billing practices of companies such as Halliburton, or to the evidence that our government has been working behind the scenes to dismantle the social security system and to increase (in the guise of reducing) what the elderly will have to pay for health care. *Everybody* acts like that, given half the chance. And we all admire a winner, regardless of how the game was won.

Which is the message we get, and are meant to be getting, every time a bachelor outsmarts his rivals, every time the castaways vote a contender off the island and inch one rung up the ladder. Indeed, those weekly tribal councils at which the voting occurs, held in a cavern or cave decorated to evoke the palm-fringed exotica of the tiki lounge or the Bugs Bunny cartoon, are arguably the most disturbing and pernicious moments in the reality-TV lineup. They're a travesty of democracy so painfully familiar, so much like what our political reality is actually becoming, that it's far more unnerving than watching Donald Trump brutally fire each week's losers, or ugly single guys made to feel even more unattractive than they are.

The castaways vote, as we do, but it's a democracy that might have been conceived if the spirit of Machiavelli had briefly possessed the mind of Thomas Jefferson; indeed, the reasons behind the survivors' ballots might puzzle our Founding Fathers. Because this fun-house version of the electoral process seeks to dismantle civilization rather than to improve it; the goal is neither a common good nor the furthering of life, liberty, or the pursuit of happiness. It's a parody of democracy, robbed of its heart and soul, a democracy in which everyone always votes, for himself.

READING  WRITING

## THIS TEXT: READING

1. What do you make of the *Entertainment Weekly* articles? Which one is the most convincing? Does one use better, more compelling arguments than the other?
2. The Francine Prose piece is longer and more complex than many of the readings in the book. What is her thesis? Can you identify it?
3. Prose links Republican values with the values of reality TV. Can you identify her evidence for this connection? Are her observations valid?
4. Do what degree do relationships on reality TV shows mirror *actual* dating? Have these shows changed how we date?
5. What is Justin T. P. Ryan's thesis? Is he writing from an identifiable bias?

## YOUR TEXT: WRITING

1. Write a comparison/contrast essay in which you examine the pro/con arguments regarding reality TV.
2. Track down some of the old episodes of *TV Nation.* Is this show reality TV? How about Sunday morning political talk shows? *Queer Eye?* Are these reality TV? Write a paper in which you define reality TV and give examples of what is and is not reality TV.
3. Write an essay in which you read American culture and tastes through the popularity (and unpopularity) of certain reality TV programs.
4. Write an essay in which you explain exactly why and how reality TV programs are *not* "real."
5. Write an essay in which you explain why reality TV is so popular in the United States and Europe. Why has it caught on *now?* If it does die, what will be the cause of its death?

## *Student Essay*

| |
|---|
| **MEDIA JOURNAL:** |
| **THE ROSIE O'DONNELL SHOW** |
| ■ Hillary West ■ |

**Week of February 14, 1999**

Rosie just might be a control freak. She controls her audience. She controls her guests and she controls her production.

The very young Olympic gold medalist, Tara Lapinski appeared as Rosie's first guest on Wednesday February 17. Rosie fired questions and comments at her left and right. Tara seemed to be ok with it. What else was she to do? She was trying to plug her special that was to air that night. Maybe Rosie knew ahead that Tara would need a lot of prodding. After the interview I noticed that I was standing in the middle of my kitchen staring at the television.

There was nothing relaxing or restful about watching that bit. Now that I think about it I am always standing up when I watch the show. Rosie is quick witted and clever. It is part of her charm. But, maybe it is a little intense as well.

Rosie's next guest was fellow talk show host, Matt Lauer. Her demeanor was dramatically different. She immediately opens with the statement, "Matt, you threatened me." Evidently, earlier that morning Matt was hosting "Good Morning America" and two young ladies appeared at his outside gate where the crowds gather for the show and on the air expressed their concern that they could not get on the Rosie show for that afternoon. Matt, on live TV, gave Rosie an ultimatum, put the girls on the show or he would not come on as a guest that afternoon. That afternoon Rosie accused Matt of threatening her. He agreed. Perhaps he realized he had stepped over a line. He had stepped over Rosie's line. It is Rosie's show and she is definitely in control. But, we should never underestimate the innate goodness of Rosie. Not only did the girls get into the Rosie show, they were invited on stage to sit with Matt Lauer during his interview. Rosie played it very cool. Was she kidding or was she genuinely irritated that she had been pushed into an awkward position? Throughout the interview with Matt, Rosie was very subdued, so unlike her encounter with Tara. But, by inviting the girls to come on stage, it certainly made Rosie look like the hero, even though she may not have appreciated having been manipulated. Or, the entire episode could have been a joke.

Rosie may feel a great need to control all that she can because she extends herself so much to others. We are always learning of how she is helping someone, family, friends, neighbors, or just fans who want to meet her or one of her guests. She is very friendly with her audience. It is as if they have all come over for a drink and she is the hostess. But, she has control over the audience. She is in the limelight and they are under the darker lights. She decides if members of the audience will be mentioned or not. It can be very spontaneous and at random. This Wednesday, while in the middle of a conversation with her band leader, John, she calls out, "Oh, I just realized it is Ash Wednesday!" Several people in the audience still had their ashes on their foreheads and she was trying to make out what it was that made them look so different from the others. She was friendly, amusing and made everyone feel at ease. But, Rosie was the one in charge. The cameras then shot to those in the audience to whom Rosie was referring.

Maybe this brief encounter with Matt Lauer has revealed a different Rosie. Or, it could be that she has a weakness: the need to control. She can control whether or not she wants to be overweight, funny, successful, or a good mom. It is interesting that there is no man in her life to share with the raising of her children. Maybe she doesn't want to share the opportunity because she will have to relinquish some of her control. To be as successful as Rosie has become, she must have some drive that pushes her along. If it is the need to control all that surrounds her, then fine. As long as she doesn't hurt anyone.

## Week of March 15, 1999

It might be fake, but I don't think it is. Rosie is an honest, real life role model. She probably has some idea of the impact she makes, but maybe not. Everyone loves her and she seems to appear to be genuinely grateful when people are kind to her. As a role model she is generous, sincere, sensitive and moral.

Barbara Walters was a guest this week on Rosie. Rosie has mentioned many times that she would not and did not watch the Monica Lewinsky interview. Yet, Rosie is all too happy to have Barbara on her show and they are obviously very close. Rosie speaks her mind, though. She immediately reminds Barbara that she did not watch the interview and she doesn't want to talk about it because it upsets her so. Then Rosie launches into a two to three minute discourse about the fate of Hillary Clinton. Seldom does Rosie give a candid opinion about an issue. Perhaps it is because she is so adamant about things. Whatever the reason, the world listened and Rosie's opinion was duly noted. Tens of thousands of middle class moms heard her and have been influenced by what she had to say.

Rosie is believable because she is one of them. She cheats on her exercise and diet regime because she has had "a stressful week." What woman, what person could not relate to that? We crave her words, her thoughts, her opinions because she makes a difference and she is like us so maybe we could make a difference too even with all our faults. Rosie's stressful week began at an event, in her honor, whereby a celebrity friend was singing a song as a tribute to her and fell off the stage. The friend was alright but Rosie was not. She cried uncontrollably and all week she couldn't stop thinking about her friend. Each time she would mention the incident tears would well up in her eyes. Rosie was definitely not herself this week.

Her sensitivity makes her an emotional wreck and by some that may be perceived as a weakness. But her general audience relates to her sympathetic nature because they see themselves in the same light. For Rosie it means another session in therapy. For her viewers it probably means three more donuts and more exercise in the famous Rosie Chub Club.

What you don't want to do with Rosie is get on her list! Once the word is down, this stubborn Irish woman is not budging. If she doesn't like you, she doesn't like you. She has been very vocal about how she feels about Monica Lewinsky and consequently Bill Clinton. Although she loves the actors on *Party of Five,* her favorite TV show, she is very critical of their moral behavior. She is the last of the do gooders and does not allow R rated language on the show as she once again reminded Barbara Walters. Barbara, in mentioning the film *When Harry Met Sally* refrained, at Rosie's request from using the word orgasm. It's not even a swear word! Her strict Catholic upbringing must be the basis for her high moral fiber.

Every day members of the audience receive gifts. They are sponsor promotional pieces and the audience loves them. But Rosie's generosity stems far beyond that. She always pumps her celebrity guests for donations to E-bay to be auctioned off so that the proceeds will help needy children. And because she interacts so much with her audience, she learns quickly of a need. One visiting family lost their home and pets to a devasting fire. Rosie, sympathetic to the sorrow of the children, made arrangements for the family to receive a new cat and dog. Another elderly woman had not seen her sister in nine years and Rosie gifted her with a plane trip, car and driver and hotel room to visit her sister. Rosie confesses that giving things away makes her feel better and after all, she has had a "stressful week."

She isn't perfect, we all know that. But she is a positive role model for a sea of viewers who probably don't feel very good about themselves and spend too much time watching television and yelling at their kids. Rosie helps viewers see the good in themselves despite their faults because she is open about her own weaknesses. It is easy to look up to someone who is honest about who she is. I hope I don't discover one day that Rosie is a total hoax and I have been tricked into thinking she is a decent human being.

READING *Outside the Lines*

## CLASSROOM ACTIVITIES

### Realistic?

Watch a show in class taking notes on what is realistic about the show. Do you find its setting realistic? Its dialogue? The characters—both in the way they act and their gender, ethnic, and class make-up? In what ways do the show's creators try to be realistic? In what ways are they admitting that television shows are not realistic? Do you think whether a show is realistic an important consideration in whether you watch it? What are the differences between television shows and "real life"?

### Advertising

Watch the commercials in a particular television show. Can you tell from them who its target audience is? Do you think advertisers are reaching their intended audience?

### Is this a good show?

What are your criteria for saying a show is "good"? Are they similar or different than the ones you might use for literature and/or movies?

### Casting

Who would play you in a sitcom about your life? Why would you make this choice?

### Genre

What is your favorite type of television show? Why? Do you feel you have something in common with others who like these types of shows?

### Show Loss

Talk about a show that went off the air that you miss. What emotions did you feel when this show ended its run? Do you think the run ended too early? What do you think makes a successful television show?

## ESSAY IDEAS

### The General Television Assignment

In this paper, you will read an episode of a television show and write a paper analyzing some aspect of it. What do we mean by "read" and "analyze"? You might start by describing the text at hand, performing an inventory of sorts. Then think about what these elements say about the text; what conclusions can you draw about the work from the observations you have made? A television show has traditional elements of texts such as a narrative and symbolic language of one sort or another, as well as visual elements which contribute to the show's meaning.

### Look at the Fashion

For this paper, notice the way the characters dress on a particular television show. From what you know about fashion, what are the creators of the show trying to convey with their choices of fashion for their characters? Are they hoping to tie into prevailing opinions about the way certain groups (those of color, class, gender, and age) dress in providing clues on how we're supposed to understand these characters? Taken together, what conclusions can we draw from the fashion choices of the creators?

### Analyze the Theme

In most sitcoms and many dramas, there is an explicit "moral of the story" that those who script the episode attach to the ending. Taking one such show, a night of shows on a particular network, or an accumulation of the same shows, what sorts of morals are presented to the audience? Do you think the creators think these morals are important? If so, do they present an honest attempt to educate the audience, or are they a vehicle for laughs? Do you know any shows that do not have "a moral of the story"? How would you compare them to the shows that do have morals?

### The Unintended vs. the Intended

Sometimes television shows are explicit about what they are trying to convey. Sometimes, however, what is not present in a show says as much about the show as what is there. Taking for a cue a comment Oprah Winfrey made to the cast of *Friends* on her show "Why isn't there a black 'friend' on their show?", look at a popular sitcom and try to determine what may or may not be missing on a show. You might focus on the racial make-up of the characters or their gender, class, and/or age.

### Real vs. Unreal

Many people would say that they watch television "to escape reality." In what ways do the producers of shows try to be "real"? In what ways do they ignore reality? You may have already noticed that we tend to watch characters in action with other characters, and that basic human functions like bathing, eating, sleeping, and going to the bathroom are ignored. On a more philosophical level, you may also notice that the problems these characters face are resolved relatively quickly, and the communication between characters is highly evolved. For this paper, you might discuss what overall effect the inclusion of "reality" might have on the audience.

### Understand the Audience

Creators of television shows often target their shows to particular audiences—or their advertisers do, in order to see a greater return on their investment. Watch a television show, or several, and see if you can determine what demographic they are appealing to or what show their advertisers feel they are. Are the two audiences different? Is one more broad than the next? What do you think are some of the problems inherent in targeting a particular demographic?

### Race and Ethnicity

For the longest time, race and ethnicity has been an issue on television. Watch a show and see what they say and do not say about questions of race and ethnicity. Do members of a particular race play a particular role on the show? Do these roles embrace or reject previous stereotypes?

### Honor the Show

Write an essay on why you feel a show is "good." Your first step, of course, is defining what you mean by "good." Does good mean writing that is funny, realistic, philosophical, or a combination of these factors or others? Is defined by the quality of the actors? Can you define what a good television show is without constructing the criteria from the show you like? What other shows fit into the definition you constructed?

—or—

## Disparage the Show

Write an essay on why you feel a show is "bad," going through the same process as you did when you defined what "good" meant. A useful exercise is to write both positive and negative reviews.

## Follow the Character

What single character on a television show do you most identify with? Why? Does this identification make you at all uncomfortable? What does this identification say about you and the television character?

## MEDIA JOURNAL

Using the worksheet at the front of the book as a guide, we want you to follow a phenomenon for the length of the course. It could be a television show, a continuing story in the newspaper (make sure you choose one that will continue), or a continuing event (such as a sport). Each journal entry should provide some sort of commentary on the phenomenon, moving beyond general plot concerns. A brief (two- or three-sentence) summary is fine but should not dominate the entry. See "Media Journal, *The Rosie O'Donnell Show*," by Hillary West, for an example.

# Reading and Writing About Public and Private Space

■ ■ ■   REAL OR FAKE?: New York, New York Casino, Las Vegas.

To a large degree, we exist in relation to our surroundings. Whether we are in our bedrooms, bathrooms, coffeehouses, classrooms, stadiums, or record stores, we are always someplace, and understanding our relationship to these places and spaces gives us a better understanding of the world. How? By providing us tools to understand the way the physical world influences our inner world, the way those constructing spaces influence us—or attempt to.

In this introduction, we will talk about public and private space, architecture, and design as constructed texts. What we mean by "space" is the environment created by human-made activities, including built areas, such as classrooms, stadiums, shopping malls, and dorm rooms. Architecture and design are forces that help construct these places and spaces and give them their particular personality.

In a sense, architects and designers are the authors of buildings and public spaces; they construct these texts through a series of decisions. And if you look around you, not only will you see patterns of decisions made by architects and designers but you will also see the influence of those who pay the designers and the people who use or live in that particular space.

For example, architects may have had some leeway in designing your classroom, but their decisions about certain aspects of design or comfort might have been affected by their cost. The kind of institution you attend, whether it's a private or public university or college, probably had some impact on these decisions. The designers or architects were limited by function—putting a fireplace or a wet bar in a classroom would be inappropriate. And the designers were undoubtedly influenced by the period in which they lived; if you think about it, you can pinpoint the date within 20 years of construction based on colors, materials, and lighting. For instance, square or rectangular buildings built with brick or cinder blocks reflect the architectural style of the '60s and '70s, whereas a wooden Victorian house was probably built as much as 100 years earlier.

Such decisions also exist in corporate or retail venues. If you walk into a Starbucks, for example, you will see the results of a series of carefully made judgments: the color scheme, the décor and the lighting, the font type of the signs that describe coffee products, and where all of this is placed. It's not hard to gather from these aspects of design that Starbucks is going for both "cool" and familiar in its space. They want customers to feel they are not only purchasing coffee, but that they are having some unexpressed secondary experience as well.

Is it one element that gives us this idea? No—it's a series of details taken together. Drawing conclusions from architectural decisions and public space is not much different than making these conclusions from reading literature; each has its own "grammar," symbols, and themes that we interpret to get a picture of the work as a whole. Here are some other things to think about when considering public space and architecture.

## Colors and shapes often have symbolic value.

Part of the grammar we wrote about in the last paragraph (color and shape) help architects and designers speak to the public in a language they understand, either consciously or subconsciously. Psychologists have shown that particular shapes and colors have psychological effects on their viewers. Designers and architects also draw upon traditional uses of color and shape, again, as a sort of grammar of construction. Of course, homeowners may think they choose certain shapes or shades because they look "pretty," or "nice," but what they mean by pretty is of course arbitrary as well. Still, it is very unlikely that the walls in your classrooms are red or black. They are probably also not adobe, wood, or steel. We venture that they are not painted in a checkerboard style or with stripes. Rather, they are probably white or off white, neutral in some way so as not to distract you from the process of listening and learning.

Combinations of these colors and shapes often form recognizable designs that are imitated repeatedly, especially in regard to public structures that want to suggest something beyond mere functionality For example, arches, columns, and white picket fences often symbolize ideas that transcend their simple presence—arches and columns have often stood for power and tradition, and the white picket fence stands for tradition as well, but perhaps a different kind of tradition; the Washington Monument, for instance, on the National Mall in Washington, D. C., is, from a functional perspective, a poor use of space. You can't do anything in there. Its significance is symbolic; thus, a great deal of thought went in to selecting a design that would signify the values the government wanted. As important as the structures themselves are the spaces surrounding the structures. A house with a white picket fence around it is a much different text than a house with a high metal security gate enclosing it.

We associate certain kinds of structures with economic and social class—brick versus mobile homes, skyscrapers versus corrugated tin buildings, strip malls versus warehouses. Buildings and spaces are rarely *just* buildings and spaces. When it comes to public space, almost nothing is random.

## Cost and community preferences often contribute to the design of a public or private space.

While most designers seek to make buildings and spaces both beautiful and useful, there are other factors that often interfere with stated goals. Cost is always an issue—people can only build what they can afford, and some materials are prohibitively expensive for a given function. Design help can also cost money, as does land, construction and so on.

The surrounding community also plays a role in design. Community standards, often in the form of zoning laws, will have an effect on what something looks like. Zoning regulations determine the use of a particular piece of property and, depending on the locale, can also determine the size and function of what's built on that property. Even politics can help determine how something is designed. For example, at the University of Texas at Austin in the 1970s, a prominent student meeting-place was significantly altered when the administration built large planters to restrict student gatherings protesting administration policies. Similarly, at the State University of New York at Binghamton, a beloved and locally famous open space in the center of campus called the "Peace Quad," where students gathered to read, protest, talk, eat, and listen to music, was paved over so that a large new building could be erected in its place. Issues of class and race can also affect public and private spaces. For example, there are very few upper class communities near industrial plants, nor does one often find a poor neighborhood that has easy access to the attractive elements of a city.

In some cases entire communities determine how a city can look. Santa Fe, New Mexico has a city ordinance that requires new buildings to have an adobe look. Hilton Head, South Carolina prohibits certain kinds of signs. San Francisco, California has some prohibitions on large chains and franchises. These communities are particularly aware that how a space looks can affect how we feel in that space.

## Space can be manipulative and/or comforting.

Designers have conscious ideas about the world they construct, and they often think about how and where they want people involved with their work. If you have ever found yourself frustrated in a poorly designed building, you may have wondered what idiots designed the building. The design of casinos, for instance, is most interesting. Casinos have no windows, usually only one or two exits, and almost always you have to walk through the slot machines to get to either of them. Why might this be the case?

In your life, how do these elements of design work? Think about sidewalks. Do they always take you where you want to go? What about doorways? Are they always at the most convenient place? In your own room, think about where you put your desk, your chairs, and your bed: What is your main concern in placing them—your convenience or someone else's? All of those decisions influence those who enter your room. Think too about most classrooms at your institution. What do they resemble? Do they create a certain mood? For example, is talking about a movie or a story different in a large classroom than in a café? Why or why not? Sometimes places are friendly to their visitors or inhabitants; others are less so, either through oversight by designers, or more deliberately as in the case of the Peace Quad or student protest space at the universities mentioned before.

What is important to know is that your emotional reaction to certain spaces is *intended*. If you have been to a court, then you know that the heightened judicial bench inspires a bit of trepidation; if you have walked in a particularly beautiful cathedral, the sense of awe you feel is not arbitrary; if you enter the library of an old or prestigious university, you probably experienced a hushed sense of tradition that was designed to be elicited in you when it was still in blueprints.

## Users have ways of altering landscapes that can have personal and political implications.

One of these ways is through decoration. Humans love to personalize their spaces, whether it's a cubicle, an office, a dorm room, their computer desktop, or their cars. How we inhabit space is a means of establishing identity; space is a text we are always making and re-making. Think about your own spaces. Posters lining a room, particularly in the dorm rooms and bedrooms of your contemporaries, are usually there to send a message—that the inhabitant is a man or a woman, or someone concerned with music, art, beer, and/or cars. Some rooms scream that the inhabitants are trying to be cool, while others ooze sophistication.

When one gets older, it is usually time to say goodbye to the rock posters, M.C. Escher prints, and the beer ads, but what to replace them with becomes a question all of us grapple with for the rest of our lives. Some people decide they have a style they feel comfortable with and make their decisions based on that; others feel their way through the process; still others delegate their design choices to someone else. However, there are effects from these decisions, whether they are intended or unintended. The space you live in—how you decorate it, your traces within it—is a kind of text that people can (and do) read to understand something about you.

Entities as large as cities can try to influence the way its inhabitants and visitors feel. If you have visited Santa Fe, for example, you know that art is everywhere—in front of the state capitol, in parks, outside buildings, in restaurants, in courtyards, in and outside of tary is cautioned to hide shorthand notes, remove partially typed letters from the typewriter, lock files, and personally deliver interoffice memos to prevent unauthorized persons from gaining confidential information from the boss's office (Belker 1981, 66).

The executive secretary has access to substantial information about the company, but the highest compliment that can be paid her is that she does not divulge it to anyone or use it for personal gain. Comparing the importance of confidentiality to the seal of the confessional, Belker counsels secretaries that "the importance of confidentiality can't be overemphasized. Your company can be involved in some delicate business matters or negotiations, and the wrong thing leaked to the wrong person could have an adverse effect on the result. . . . Years ago, executive secretaries were sometimes referred to as confidential secretaries. It's a shame that title fell out of popular usage, because it's an accurate description of the job" (Belker 1981, 73–74).

## Typical Men's Work: "Closed-Door Jobs"

The largest occupational category for men is that of manager. In 1990, 8.9 million men were classified as "executive, administrative, and managerial." This group constituted 14 percent of all employed men (U.S. Department of Labor 1991, 163, 183). Thus, more than one in ten men works in a supervisory position.

Spatial arrangements in the workplace reinforce these status distinctions, partially by providing more "closed door" potential to managers than to those they supervise. Although sales and production supervisors may circulate among their employees, their higher status within the organization is reflected by the private offices to which they can withdraw. The expectation is that privacy is required for making decisions that affect the organization. Rather than sharing this privacy, the secretary is often in charge of "gate-keeping"—protecting the boss from interruptions.

Just as there are professional manuals for the successful secretary, there are also numerous guidelines for the aspiring manager. Harry Levinson's widely read *Executive* (1981) (a revision of his 1968 *The Exceptional Executive*) stresses the importance of managerial knowledge of the entire organization. A survey of large American companies asking presidents about suitable qualities in their successors revealed the following profile: "A desirable successor is a person with a general knowledge and an understanding of the whole organization, capable of fitting specialized contributions into profitable patterns. . . . The person needs a wide range of liberal arts knowledge together with a fundamental knowledge of business. . . . A leader will be able to view the business in global historical and technical perspective. Such a perspective is itself the basis for the most important requisite, what one might call 'feel'—a certain intuitive sensitivity for the right action and for handling relationships with people" (Levinson 1981, 136).

The importance of knowledge is stressed repeatedly in this description. The successful manager needs knowledge of the organization, of liberal arts, and of business in general. But equally important is the intuitive ability to carry out actions. This "feel" is not truly intuitive, of course, but is developed through observation and emulation of successful executives. Levinson identifies managerial leadership as "an art to be cultivated and developed," which is why it cannot be learned by the book; rather, "it must be learned in a relationship, through identification with a teacher" (Levinson 1981, 145).

Because the transfer of knowledge and the ability to use it are so crucial to leadership, Levinson devotes a chapter to "The Executive as Teacher." He advises that there is no pre-

## Space can be manipulative and/or comforting.

Designers have conscious ideas about the world they construct, and they often think about how and where they want people involved with their work. If you have ever found yourself frustrated in a poorly designed building, you may have wondered what idiots designed the building. The design of casinos, for instance, is most interesting. Casinos have no windows, usually only one or two exits, and almost always you have to walk through the slot machines to get to either of them. Why might this be the case?

In your life, how do these elements of design work? Think about sidewalks. Do they always take you where you want to go? What about doorways? Are they always at the most convenient place? In your own room, think about where you put your desk, your chairs, and your bed: What is your main concern in placing them—your convenience or someone else's? All of those decisions influence those who enter your room. Think too about most classrooms at your institution. What do they resemble? Do they create a certain mood? For example, is talking about a movie or a story different in a large classroom than in a café? Why or why not? Sometimes places are friendly to their visitors or inhabitants; others are less so, either through oversight by designers, or more deliberately as in the case of the Peace Quad or student protest space at the universities mentioned before.

What is important to know is that your emotional reaction to certain spaces is *intended*. If you have been to a court, then you know that the heightened judicial bench inspires a bit of trepidation; if you have walked in a particularly beautiful cathedral, the sense of awe you feel is not arbitrary; if you enter the library of an old or prestigious university, you probably experienced a hushed sense of tradition that was designed to be elicited in you when it was still in blueprints.

## Users have ways of altering landscapes that can have personal and political implications.

One of these ways is through decoration. Humans love to personalize their spaces, whether it's a cubicle, an office, a dorm room, their computer desktop, or their cars. How we inhabit space is a means of establishing identity; space is a text we are always making and re-making. Think about your own spaces. Posters lining a room, particularly in the dorm rooms and bedrooms of your contemporaries, are usually there to send a message—that the inhabitant is a man or a woman, or someone concerned with music, art, beer, and/or cars. Some rooms scream that the inhabitants are trying to be cool, while others ooze sophistication.

When one gets older, it is usually time to say goodbye to the rock posters, M.C. Escher prints, and the beer ads, but what to replace them with becomes a question all of us grapple with for the rest of our lives. Some people decide they have a style they feel comfortable with and make their decisions based on that; others feel their way through the process; still others delegate their design choices to someone else. However, there are effects from these decisions, whether they are intended or unintended. The space you live in—how you decorate it, your traces within it—is a kind of text that people can (and do) read to understand something about you.

Entities as large as cities can try to influence the way its inhabitants and visitors feel. If you have visited Santa Fe, for example, you know that art is everywhere—in front of the state capitol, in parks, outside buildings, in restaurants, in courtyards, in and outside of private homes. The message this sends is not simply that Santa Fe and its residents like to decorate their landscape but that it is a place that values art, how things look, and how art makes you feel. The abundance of art sends a message of sophistication, worldliness, and a progressiveness that is welcoming. You may not always be conscious of it, but spaces that pay close attention to design and beauty probably make you feel quite good.

Of course, there can also be a gap between what the occupant of the space wants to suggest and what is actually suggested—in this way, spaces can be revealing texts. Knowing about space will help you not only be better readers of someone else's space, but may also help you avoid pitfalls of constructing unwelcoming space yourself. You may think that posters of near-naked women reclining on cars are cool, or you may think black mammy figurines are quaint, but there will be a sizeable audience out there who might wonder about you and your values based on how you arrange and decorate your space.

## Other elements can change the landscape in ways not imagined by designers.

Graffiti alters the public landscape, and so does public art. Neglect can change public space, as well as new construction surrounding a previous design. How we use and design space gives some indication of our personality, among other things. Walking into someone's dorm room, office, or living room gives us a clue of who they are (and who they think they are). When you walk into a business, you also receive some indication of how they view themselves. For example, compare the interior at McDonalds to a fancy restaurant, or to a TGI Fridays, Applebee's, or Chili's; the interiors and exteriors are littered with clues about what these places think they are about. Similarly, how do Mexican restaurants tell us that they serve Mexican food? How do Chinese restaurants create a "Chinese" setting? Think too about the way movies and television shows set scenes; often the settings of movies give us an indication of how we're supposed to view the characters. In *Frasier* or *Friends,* for example, we see the presence of couches, bright lighting, the expensive, clean apartments (in the case of *Friends,* far too expensive for New Yorkers their age) as clues to how we are supposed to relate to them.

Public spaces are especially curious in this way. Dams completely alter natural environments, flooding entire valleys. Roads paved through forests bring cars and tourists and pollution. In urban areas, for example, some public parks have become centers for both drug use and needle exchange programs—no doubt a *very* different use of public space than was intended. The authors live in New York City and San Francisco, and the two great parks in both cities—Golden Gate Park and Central Park—get used in ways the designers never could have imagined. We leave our imprint everywhere. And, just as we make our rooms or cubicles our own, so, too, do we make public space our own—for better or worse.

Ultimately, the space that surrounds us says a number of things about that particular location—who inhabits that space, what the space is used for, and how we are to read that space. Additionally, we can discern a great deal about what kinds of spaces or buildings are important given the amount and kind of space devoted to them. As you read this chapter, think about how certain spaces force you to interpret the world in a certain way.

# ...  WORKSHEET  ...

This Text

1. How does the background of the authors influence their ideas about public space?
2. Do they define public space differently? In what ways?
3. Do the authors have different ideas about class, race, and gender? In what ways?
4. Try to figure out the writing situation of each author. Who is the audience? What does the author have at stake? What is the agenda of the author? Why does she or he want me to think a certain way?
5. What is his or her agenda? Why is she or he writing this piece?
6. What social, political, and cultural forces affect the author's text? What is going on in the world as he or she is writing?
7. What are the main points of the essay? Is there a specific thesis statement? Remember that it doesn't have to be one sentence—it could be several sentences or a whole paragraph.
8. What type of evidence does the author use to back up any claims she might make?
9. Is the author's argument reasonable?
10. Do you find yourself in agreement with the author? Why or why not?
11. Does the author help you *read* public space better than you did before reading the essay? If so, how?
12. How is the reading process different if you are reading an essay as opposed to a short story or poem?
13. Did I like this? Why or why not?

Beyond This Text: Reading Public Space

**Shapes:** What are some of the dominant shapes you see in a public space or building? Do they symbolize anything to you? Are they supposed to? Do they remind you of other shapes in other spaces? How do the shapes relate to the space's use?

**Colors:** What are the dominant colors? What emotions do they evoke? Why? How would the space or architecture change if the color changed? How does the color relate to the space's use?

**Size:** How big is this place? How does this affect the way you view it, and the feelings it inspires? Is there a way to change the size to evoke different feelings? In what ways do the space's or architecture's size relate to its use?

**Use:** What is the use of this particular space or architecture? How do we know from the elements you see? Do you see unintended uses that might result from this construction? Do you see an emphasis on practicality or ornament in this space?

**Interaction between architecture and space:** How do the two work together? What elements in the architecture affect the way the space is constructed? Are there ways of changing this interaction?

**Overall beauty:** What is your general view of the place's beauty? What standards or criteria do you find yourself relying on?

*(cont.)*

**Emotional response:** What is your overall emotional response to this place? Why? What elements contribute to this response? What elements could you change that might provoke a different response?

**Overall statement:** What do you think this space or architecture says? What is it trying to say? How might this gap between what it says and is trying to say be changed?

---

| SPATIAL SEGREGATION AND GENDER STRATIFICATION IN THE WORKPLACE<br><br>■ **Daphne Spain** ■ |
|---|

*Daphne Spain wrote this essay as part of a larger work,* Gendered Spaces *(1992). In this work, she writes about the way a specific type of public space—the workplace—and gender interact, an argument that you might find has implications beyond the workplace.*

TO WHAT EXTENT do women and men who work in different occupations also work in different spaces? Baran and Teegarden (1987, 206) propose that occupational segregation in the insurance industry is "tantamount to spatial segregation by gender" since managers are overwhelmingly male and clerical staff are predominantly female. This essay examines the spatial conditions of women's work and men's work and proposes that working women and men come into daily contact with one another very infrequently. Further, women's jobs can be classified as "open floor," but men's jobs are more likely to be "closed door." That is, women work in a more public environment with less control of their space than men. This lack of spatial control both reflects and contributes to women's lower occupational status by limiting opportunities for the transfer of knowledge from men to women.

It bears repeating that my argument concerning space and status deals with structural workplace arrangements of women as a group and men as a group, *not* with occupational mobility for individual men and women. Extraordinary people always escape the statistical norm and experience upward mobility under a variety of circumstances. The emphasis here is on the ways in which workplaces are structured to provide different spatial arrangements for the typical working woman and the typical working man and how those arrangements contribute to gender stratification. . . .

## Typical Women's Work: "Open-Floor Jobs"

A significant proportion of women are employed in just three occupations: teaching, nursing, and secretarial work. In 1990 these three categories alone accounted for 16.5 million women, or 31 percent of all women in the labor force (U.S. Department of Labor 1991, 163, 183). Aside from being concentrated in occupations that bring them primarily into contact with other women, women are also concentrated spatially in jobs that limit their access to knowledge. The work of elementary schoolteachers, for example, brings them into daily contact with children, but with few other adults. When not dealing with patients, nurses spend their time in a lounge separate from the doctors' lounge. Nursing and teaching share common spatial characteristics with the third major "women's job"—that of secretary.

Secretarial/clerical work is the single largest job category for American women. In 1990, 14.9 million women, or more than one of every four employed women, were classified as "administrative support, including clerical"; 98 percent of all secretaries are female (U.S. Department of Labor 1991, 163, 183). Secretarial and clerical occupations account for over three-quarters of this category and epitomize the typical "woman's job." It is similar to teaching and nursing in terms of the spatial context in which it occurs.

Two spatial aspects of secretarial work operate to reduce women's status. One is the concentration of many women together in one place (the secretarial "pool") that removes them from observation of and/or input into the decision-making processes of the organization. Those decisions occur behind the "closed doors" of the managers' offices. Second, paradoxically, is the very public nature of the space in which secretaries work. The lack of privacy, repeated interruptions, and potential for surveillance contribute to an inability to turn valuable knowledge into human capital that might advance careers or improve women's salaries relative to men's.

Like teachers and nurses, secretaries process knowledge, but seldom in a way beneficial to their own status. In fact, secretaries may wield considerable informal power in an organization, because they control the information flow. Management, however, has very clear expectations about how secretaries are to handle office information. Drawing from their successful experience with grid theory, business consultants Robert Blake, Jane Mouton, and Artie Stockton have outlined the ideal boss-secretary relationship for effective office teamwork. In the first chapter of *The Secretary Grid,* an American Management Association publication, the following advice is offered:

> The secretary's position at the center of the information network raises the issue of privileged communications and how best to handle it. Privileged communication is information the secretary is not free to divulge, no matter how helpful it might be to others. And the key to handling it is the answer to the question. "Who owns the information"? The answer is, "The boss does." . . . The secretary's position with regard to this information is that of the hotel desk clerk to the contents of the safety deposit box that stores the guest's valuables. She doesn't own it, but she knows what it is and what is in it. The root of the word *secretary* is, after all, *secret:* something kept from the knowledge of others. (Blake, Mouton, and Stockton 1983, 4–5; emphasis in original)

In other words, secretaries are paid *not* to use their knowledge for personal gain, but only for their employers' gain. The workplace arrangements that separate secretaries from managers within the same office reinforce status differences by exposing the secretary mainly to other secretaries bound by the same rules of confidentiality. Lack of access to and interaction with managers inherently limits the status women can achieve within the organization.

The executive secretary is an exception to the rule of gendered spatial segregation in the workplace. The executive secretary may have her own office, and she has access to more aspects of the managerial process than other secretaries. According to another American Management Association publication titled *The Successful Secretary:* "Probably no person gets to observe and see management principles in operation on a more practical basis than an executive secretary. She is privy to nearly every decision the executive makes. She has the opportunity to witness the gathering of information and the elements that are considered before major decisions are made and implemented" (Belker 1981, 191).

Yet instructions to the successful executive secretary suggest that those with the closest access to power are subject to the strictest guidelines regarding confidentiality. When physical barriers are breached and secretaries spend a great deal of time with the managers, rules governing the secretary's use of information become more important. The executive secretary is cautioned to hide shorthand notes, remove partially typed letters from the typewriter, lock files, and personally deliver interoffice memos to prevent unauthorized persons from gaining confidential information from the boss's office (Belker 1981, 66).

The executive secretary has access to substantial information about the company, but the highest compliment that can be paid her is that she does not divulge it to anyone or use it for personal gain. Comparing the importance of confidentiality to the seal of the confessional, Belker counsels secretaries that "the importance of confidentiality can't be overemphasized. Your company can be involved in some delicate business matters or negotiations, and the wrong thing leaked to the wrong person could have an adverse effect on the result. . . . Years ago, executive secretaries were sometimes referred to as confidential secretaries. It's a shame that title fell out of popular usage, because it's an accurate description of the job" (Belker 1981, 73–74).

## Typical Men's Work: "Closed-Door Jobs"

The largest occupational category for men is that of manager. In 1990, 8.9 million men were classified as "executive, administrative, and managerial." This group constituted 14 percent of all employed men (U.S. Department of Labor 1991, 163, 183). Thus, more than one in ten men works in a supervisory position.

Spatial arrangements in the workplace reinforce these status distinctions, partially by providing more "closed door" potential to managers than to those they supervise. Although sales and production supervisors may circulate among their employees, their higher status within the organization is reflected by the private offices to which they can withdraw. The expectation is that privacy is required for making decisions that affect the organization. Rather than sharing this privacy, the secretary is often in charge of "gate-keeping"—protecting the boss from interruptions.

Just as there are professional manuals for the successful secretary, there are also numerous guidelines for the aspiring manager. Harry Levinson's widely read *Executive* (1981) (a revision of his 1968 *The Exceptional Executive*) stresses the importance of managerial knowledge of the entire organization. A survey of large American companies asking presidents about suitable qualities in their successors revealed the following profile: "A desirable successor is a person with a general knowledge and an understanding of the whole organization, capable of fitting specialized contributions into profitable patterns. . . . The person needs a wide range of liberal arts knowledge together with a fundamental knowledge of business. . . . A leader will be able to view the business in global historical and technical perspective. Such a perspective is itself the basis for the most important requisite, what one might call 'feel'—a certain intuitive sensitivity for the right action and for handling relationships with people" (Levinson 1981, 136).

The importance of knowledge is stressed repeatedly in this description. The successful manager needs knowledge of the organization, of liberal arts, and of business in general. But equally important is the intuitive ability to carry out actions. This "feel" is not truly intuitive, of course, but is developed through observation and emulation of successful executives. Levinson identifies managerial leadership as "an art to be cultivated and developed," which is why it cannot be learned by the book; rather, "it must be learned in a relationship, through identification with a teacher" (Levinson 1981, 145).

Because the transfer of knowledge and the ability to use it are so crucial to leadership, Levinson devotes a chapter to "The Executive as Teacher." He advises that there is no pre-

Sundstrom, Eric, Robert Burt, and Douglas Kemp. 1980. "Privacy at Work: Architectural Correlates of Job Satisfaction and Job Performance." *Academy of Management Journal* 23 (March): 101–17.

U.S. Department of Labor. 1991. *Employment and Earnings* 38 (January). Washington, D.C.: Bureau of Labor Statistics.

READING WRITING

## THIS TEXT: READING

1. Do think such constructions of public space matter? Are symbolic values of space crucial in our world?
2. Do you think genders have different ways of looking at public space? If so, where does this difference come from? Why does it persist?
3. What do you think Spain's "writing situation" is? Is she writing from experience or observation? Can you tell by reading her essay? Why does this distinction matter?

## YOUR TEXT: WRITING

1. Find another environment where gender and space interact. What about the space you describe makes it connect to the particular gender?
2. Think about other public spaces or buildings where separation of people into genders, races, or classes is built into the design (*Hint:* Think of places where people spend more or less money to sit in different places). Are those spaces considered problematic in the same way Spain thinks about the workplace? Write a paper that addresses this question.
3. Look at several dorm rooms or apartments of friends both male and female. Write a short paper that discusses which elements in particular define these spaces as particularly male or female.
4. Look at other things that are "gendered," such as advertisements, clothing, and cars. How do these gendered texts compare to the gendered spaces you described earlier? What elements do designers of any text use to designate gender? Write a paper that ties gendered space to another gendered text.

---

### SHOPPING IN A MALL WHILE BLACK: A COACH'S STORY

■ **Kenneth Meeks** ■

*Kenneth Meeks wrote this essay as part of* Driving While Black *(2000), a book about racial profiling. This story talks about the division between public and private spaces in a powerful and immediate way.*

HOWIE EVANS WAS the basketball coach for the University of Maryland at Eastern Shore in 1985. That year he and his team were on a three-game exhibition tour in South Carolina. When they arrived in Columbia on Thanksgiving Day for their second game, the team unpacked their bags, put on their warm-up uniforms, and stretched their legs. They were hungry from their travels. The National Urban League's local chapter had a planned Thanksgiving Day dinner for the basketball team, but until then they needed something to eat.

Normally, the coach wouldn't allow his players to roam around the city. It takes away the strength in their legs. But on this particular day he bent the rules. It was an exhibition game, so he let his team out. They picked a mall about a quarter of a mile from the hotel.

Evans immediately spotted trouble when the team stepped into the shopping mall. Two security guards who had been sitting nearby went into action. Evans didn't say anything to his team about the guards behind them, but he remained mindful. As the team meandered into the center of the mall, they split into little cliques. A few disappeared into clothing stores, another went into a music store, and a few more just window-shopped. Evans himself went into a Radio Shack to buy some batteries. He never expected to see the two guards placing six of his players against the wall.

"What's going on?" Evans asked as he walked up on the scene.

The taller guard, who had sergeant stripes sewn into his uniform, answered. "They stole something from one of the stores."

"What did you see them take?"

The sergeant paused to eyeball Evans. "Who are you?"

"I'm their coach," Evans answered. He pulled out his identification. "Did you see them take anything?"

"No," the sergeant answered, "but somebody told us they did."

"Show me who told you they saw my team steal something. I want to know what he saw."

"We can't do that. He's not here."

Antennas went up. "What? You're going to search these young men based on something somebody told you, and—by your own admission—he's not even here in the mall?"

"I'm doing my job."

Evans took a deep breath and chose his words carefully.

"You know, I watched you guys when we first came in here. You were sitting by the door, and when we got about fifty feet away from you, you got up and started following us. We've only been in here twenty minutes, and already you've accused us of stealing something. Why were you following us in the first place?"

The sergeant fumbled for an answer.

"I'm not going to let you search these kids out here in public," Evans continued confidently. "If you want to search them, you're going to have to take us down to the police station."

"I'll have to call them," the sergeant explained, almost as if he hoped the idea would make Evans stand down.

"So call them. If you don't, I will."

The sergeant detained the six players against the wall while Evans huddled with the rest of his team. Spectators watched from the wings.

"Look at these guys. What are they doing now?" a black woman whispered.

It broke Evans's heart that black people were walking away shaking their heads in embarrassment because they assumed that these young black men had done something wrong. The team promised him that no one had stolen anything and that it was all a setup. In fact, a black security guard was called to the scene—Evans now believes to justify that no one was being a racist—but after a few minutes of sizing up the situation, he threw his hands in the air in disgust.

"You guys are harassing them," the black guard said and walked away.

"We need you to stay here," the sergeant commanded.

"Give me a break."

But the sergeant wasn't hearing it.

While everyone waited for the police to arrive, Evans found a pay phone and called the local chapter of the NAACP. He explained his situation and asked them to send an attorney down to the scene. His second phone call was to the local black newspaper. He informed one of the editors of what was happening to his players. It was mere coincidence that a reporter for a local mainstream newspaper was in the mall at the time. Evans and the young reporter discussed everything.

In the meantime the sergeant let the six kids relax with the rest of the team, but he wanted everyone in a group.

"Don't panic," Evans told his team.

Evans suddenly saw the situation escalate into a potentially dangerous one. He had reasons to keep his team calm. Most of his players were young freshmen and sophomores who had never been on a collegiate road trip before. And for most of them this was their first time away from home on Thanksgiving.

On the other hand, the team was up against an out-and-out Southern racist with a gun. The sergeant stood about six feet and two hundred pounds, walking among the posse of the basketball players with an overbearing attitude and his hand continuously touching his gun. As Evans saw it, the sergeant was trying to impress the other guard by showing that he could take on these young black athletes, that he was someone who was used to grabbing black kids and throwing them up against the wall on a regular basis.

Evans kept a level head and remained very professional. He never raised his voice, just maintained a dignified degree of intelligence and poise. "Are you trying to intimidate us by walking around us with your hand on your gun? Don't you think that's dangerous?"

"I have the safety catch on," he answered.

"I would hope so," Evans said. "But doesn't that present a very intimidating presence, you walking around with your hand on your gun? These kids aren't going anywhere. They will move only if I tell them to move. If I told these kids to get up and run out, they would. But then you'd probably shoot one of them in the back. Right?"

A call blared over the walkie-talkie. The police were here. The sergeant met with the police and the manager of the mall, a man in his late twenties or early thirties, separately while Evans waited with his team.

Finally the manager walked over to Evans. "My guy said that they stole something."

"You know the only reason your guys stopped these kids was because they're black. Look at all these other kids in the mall; no one stopped them. These kids are college kids, and they're wearing identifying uniforms, so why would they go into a store and steal something with all this ID on? They don't even have pockets."

But the manager wasn't convinced.

"Your guy also didn't tell you that the person who told him these kids stole something isn't in the mall either. And your guy didn't see them steal anything."

The manager listened carefully, then walked away to confer with his team. "Stay here."

They took a long time.

"So what are you guys going to do?" Evans finally asked as he approached them. "You are accusing these guys of something simply based on who they are. As soon as my lawyer comes—I have an attorney on the way—we're willing to go to the police station, where you can search these kids. But if you search them here, I'm going to bring a lawsuit against you."

"You have a lawyer?" Everyone was surprised. "Just wait for us over there. We'll be there when we're done."

Evans remembers overhearing one of them calling him a wise guy and saying, "They always bring up this we-stopped-them-because-they-were-black stuff."

From a distance Evans could see that the police officers, who were also white, were concerned. "You guys had better handle this. We're leaving."

The policemen left before the NAACP attorney arrived. And as Evans filled in the details for the attorney, the sergeant's case seemed to crumble. Close to two hours after the team walked into the mall, the manager finally had little choice but to let them go.

"Perhaps you wouldn't have a problem, Coach, if you didn't have all these kids coming into the mall at the same time."

"What are you talking about? What am I supposed to do? Bring them in two at a time, go back and bring in two more? This is a team. Would you say that to anybody else? I think you owe us an apology."

"Don't get stressed, Coach," said the attorney from the NAACP. "They're always stopping our kids at this mall."

Neither Howie Evans nor his team ever received a formal apology from the city of Columbia, South Carolina, the manager of the mall, or the security agency hired to patrol it.

## Arrest People of Color First, Then Ask Questions

Professor Charles Ogletree remembers the story of an artist who went to shop in a department store with an American Express card. He spent a couple of thousands of dollars in a very short time. He bought suits, clothes, a whole bunch of other items, and he signed his name. After he completed his shopping, one of the clerks who accepted his purchase got nervous and phoned the police. The police jumped the young man outside the store as he got into his car. They arrested him, brought him back into the store—brutalizing him in the process—and only after a few minutes of investigation discovered that he was the person whose name was on the credit card. When the clerk was asked by newspaper reporters the next day, after consulting with her bosses, why she had called the police, she answered, "Oh, it wasn't because he was black. That had nothing to do with it. It was because he was making some bad decisions in the things he was purchasing."

Ogletree is a professor at the Harvard School of Law and directs its Criminal Justice Institute. As the author of *Beyond the Rodney King Story,* a book relating to the NAACP's vision for policing the police, Ogletree is considered a leading authority in the world of legal issues regarding the police and its relationship to the minority community. He says "driving while black" was only the tip of the iceberg. Police misconduct goes deeper than racial profiling.

"As much as we talk about the drivers, there is also a crime called 'riding while black.' And for those of you who walk through the cities of New York, Washington, D.C., Los Angeles, Chicago, and Houston, there is a crime called 'walking while black.' And we don't see the books as much, but those of you who jog through Central Park, or Lincoln Park in Washington, D.C., or any park in Anywhere, USA, there is a crime called 'jogging while black.' There is also a nondiscriminatory crime that crosses gender lines called 'shopping while black.' You get all the tension in the world in department stores, so we all really have the phenomenon called 'living while black.' It's inevitable."

The sad element of the story above is that the police grabbed the young man without first checking to see if he really was the person who was signing the American Express transactions.

## Can Security Guards Stop People?

One New York City police officer I spoke with concerning the power of a security guard said a security guard has the power of a peace officer; a guard isn't allowed to carry a firearm, but as a part of his duties, if he sees someone shoplifting, he can stop and hold that person until a police officer arrives. Police officers call this a 1011, where security is holding someone in a commercial place. But let's take this a step further. The clerk who works the cash register, or the salesperson who is helping a customer, or even another customer who is just browsing has the same right to detain an individual as does a security guard. In cases where other citizens witness a crime in progress, any of those citizens can make a "civilian arrest" and detain the wrongdoer until a police officer arrives on the scene. In a civilian arrest, the good citizen has the right to physically restrain the bad citizen until an officer arrives. (But don't hurt anyone; the law gets tricky when someone is physically injured.)

So yes, security guards have the right to detain individuals, and they have the right to profile. Howard Amos, Jr., a part-time security guard who works various stadium security details like the Louisville Gardens in downtown Louisville, Kentucky, explained, "If there is an opera and everyone is dressed in formal clothing and all of a sudden someone walks in wearing overalls with a lit cigarette in his mouth, as a security guard I have the right to profile him, though it's not necessarily racial. And, as a security guard, I have the right to hold him or keep him from entering the opera. It's a security guard's job to watch the door to see who is coming and going into a show or a mall or whatever is being guarded. If a guard believes a particular individual is coming into a particular guarded area to commit a crime or to do someone harm, the security guard has the right to hold a person in the name of security. That's how the police do it.

"Probable cause also applies to security guards. They are considered policemen without guns. Security guards are considered the 'judge on the scene.' However, if a guard asks someone to leave and the person challenges the guard's authority, then a police officer has to be called to the scene."

Take this hypothetical situation: Say a photographer sneaks his camera equipment into a Janet Jackson concert, and it's clearly posted that taking photographs during the show is not permitted. If a guard confronts the photographer, he might use the tone of his voice to assert his authority, but the guard cannot by law confiscate the photographer's equipment or film. If a challenge erupts, it is a wise idea for the photographer to request the presence of a police officer immediately. Again, a security guard does not have the right to confiscate personal property.

 **READING WRITING**

## THIS TEXT: READING

1. What does this particular story say about public space and race?
2. Is a mall public or private space? Is this distinction important in this case or any other?
3. What is Meeks' writing situation? Do you think he came to this situation through experience or study? Does the writing situation matter in this particular case—why or why not?
4. Are there people who are also "reverse profiled"—given special treatment in public or private space based on their looks?

## YOUR TEXT: WRITING

1. Although not everyone has been a victim of racial profiling or even prejudice, we all have witnessed such acts either through our own experience or through media stories. One can certainly think of this as a public space issue—what authorities of any sort are doing when they racially profile is essentially identifying someone's use of space as problematic. Write about the assumptions people in power make when profiling.
2. Write a short paper assessing "reverse profiling," the preferential use of public and private space.
3. Do some research on how public space has been used for prejudicial purposes in the past.

---

**CAUGHT LOOKING: PROBLEMS WITH TAKING PICTURES OF PEOPLE TAKING PICTURES AT AN EXHIBITION**

■ **Robert Bednar** ■

*Here Robert Bednar writes about the odd relationship we have with nature and public space, using his experience with photography and tourism as a way of talking about the national park. This piece, part of his dissertation (1997), is part of a larger manuscript about public spaces and national parks.*

THE STORY BEGINS in the Black Hills of South Dakota where, as clichéd as it may sound, I had a sort of epiphany one gray August day in 1991. The epiphany occurred on day five of what would be a fourteen-day, 7,000-mile caffeine-paced reconnaissance trip through ten states in the West that started and ended in Salt Lake City, Utah. I decided to go on the trip while I was working in a fish fossil quarry in southwestern Wyoming for the summer. I thought I should take advantage of the proximity of Wyoming to many other western states I had not visited before. I also wanted to experience travelling "Out West" on the same time scale as the "typical tourists" I was beginning to become interested in academically.

For days I sped through Utah, Colorado, Wyoming, and Nebraska. I rarely stopped for anything but periodic photo opportunities and gas and food fill-ups, and rarely slowed down the pace except in my nightly searches for National Forest campsites. But as I approached the South Dakota border from the sand hills of Nebraska, I started to notice that the roads were becoming more and more crowded and the driving pace was becoming more and more frenetic. A rainstorm was also moving in, darkening the sky and giving an ominous feel to the

whole experience. For the rest of the way, the rainy highways leading into the Black Hills were packed with vehicles that displayed cultural allegiance to the myth of the west. Caravans of RVs with names like "Frontiersman," "Caribou," "Wanderer II," and "Tioga" were travelling alongside automobiles called "Pathfinder," "Wrangler Renegade," "Cherokee," and "Explorer." Both were intermixed with bands of bikers in black leather chaps and shirts and jackets with images of eagles and cow skulls on them. I saw license plates from states as far away as Vermont, Florida, and California, and as near as Montana and Minnesota.

The parking lot at the National Monument was full, so I parked my truck next to the other vehicles parked in the impromptu overflow parking on the lawn beside the parking lot. I slipped on my raincoat and prepared to face the rain. As I grabbed my camera off the seat beside me and got out of the truck, I noticed that some bikers next to me were also grabbing their still cameras and video cameras out of their saddle bags. I decided that instead of going directly to the viewing deck I would wait out the rain inside the Visitor Center directly behind it. I wandered around the Visitor Center looking at the displays, books, and postcards, surrounded by other jostling bodies doing the same. After nearly a week of solitary travel, it felt good to commune with other tourists involved in a common endeavor. I joined the people crowding around a TV screen that was playing a video about the heroic feats involved in the production of the sculpture. Because I came in in the middle of the video, I stayed on to watch the first half when the last half was over. Before long, I noticed that the rain outside had turned to a fine mist, so I wandered out onto the designated scenic overlook (which in this case was actually a scenic underlook). I took several photos of the stone faces with my camera—photos framed the same way as the post cards I had seen earlier in the Visitor Center. The only difference was that in my pictures the sky was gray, not blue. I noticed that many of the other visitors were taking similar pictures.

Soon, however, huge drops began pelting those of us standing on the one hundred square foot landing just below the Monument. I fled to the Visitor Center, but I noticed that few of my companions were joining me. Despite the rain, the pilgrims were still drawn magnetically to the wall at the edge of the viewing platform where they alternately gazed at and photographed the stone faces, and took pictures of each other standing in front of the Monument. I crept outside again and found a spot next to the few other wimps standing under the building's awning, and watched what became for me something "photographable" as a dramatic spectacle that overshadowed the intended drama of the patriotic faces carved into the side of the granite outcropping. Perhaps it was because the rain obscured the distant view, or perhaps it was because I was traveling alone and thus had no one to pose with, but, either way, the foreground of the vista became much more interesting to me than the presented vista. The gray Monument off in the distance started to look like a huge unreal hologram or backdrop prop compared to the physicality of the people there at the underlook performing their elaborately choreographed (though apparently authorless) stageplay. As I started thinking about how all of these people had learned how to act their part in this cultural drama, I pulled out my camera again, and began taking pictures of the context surrounding what I was supposed to see instead of the thing itself.

As I stood there now taking pictures and thinking about the implications of what I was seeing, I noticed that a young Japanese-American boy had become bored with his family's posing ritual and had begun looking at me as I took pictures of people on the viewing deck. I guess I had been making more of a spectacle of myself than I had intended. Soon, the boy raised his little automatic camera and took my picture, drawing me into the scene I had been

observing from afar and implicating me in the action. I was no longer an invisible passive observer, a detached post tourist. Now, as the result of a single momentary action, I had become—like the people having their pictures taken in front of the Monument and the Monument itself—something photographable according to a tourist aesthetic.

Even now I am surprised that in the rush of the "decisive moment" I had the presence of mind to quickly snap a picture of the boy as the boy "took" my picture as I "took" his picture taking my picture taking his picture, etc. The spiraling of images was dizzying to me then and still is now as I recall it and try to construct a sentence that will do it justice. The photograph I took is not very well focused and didn't really "catch" the boy in the action of taking my picture, but I have put it here because the image continues to speak to me. The boy had already started to put his camera down when I snapped my picture, but he was still looking at me. Moreover, in the picture his parents are also looking at me, wondering perhaps why their son had wasted his film, how I felt about what he had done, and whether my photographing them was hostile. I still wonder what the boy's family did with his picture of me. Did they incorporate the picture into their own family album (do they have one?) and narrate my actions as "another roadside attraction," or did they edit the picture out as an irrelevant "kid picture"? I wonder similar things about the other pictures I have taken of people looking into my camera trying to figure out what I was doing—where did they locate me?

I have told so many people this story that it has started off its own set of new meanings as my friends and students have incorporated it into their own sets of representations of touristic encounters with Mount Rushmore and with touristic landscapes in general. I began to see my experience of being implicated in the field of action as a lesson I had learned from reading Mark Klett's article, "A View of the Grand Canyon in Homage to William Bell," just before I took my trip. It would be an understatement to say that Klett's article was on my mind as I traveled. Indeed, the article was so central for me that I have titled my Mount Rushmore picture "A View of Mount Rushmore in Homage to Mark Klett."

I mention this not only to acknowledge my debts to Klett, but also to further illustrate how the process of landscape tourism works in the field for me as well as the tourists I have studied. As I began to explore the phenomenon further, I found that my experience at Mount Rushmore could serve as a case study in the ways that portions of a landscape are made both visible and meaningful for the people encountering them. Every place I visited I carried with me a set of complex legacies that I had inherited from my particular upbringing and my academic training. Learning how this worked for me as well as my "subjects" helped me understand that whether we consciously apprehend it at the site or not, all photographs of places pay homage to previous acts of inhabitation and image-making.

As I argued in the Snapshot Semiotics Overview, when we visit a landscape that has been designated a tourist landscape, we inhabit not only a landscape but also an imagescape. Just as William Bell's photographs were part of the imagescape Klett inhabited as he photographed Taroweap Point, Klett's words and images were part of the imagescape I temporarily inhabited at Mount Rushmore. They helped me notice the context that foregrounded the site, and they helped me think about ways of representing it. They helped me see my own reflection in the people I was studying as well. They did not "cause" or "determine" my epiphany in any simplistic sense, but they did highlight things that I had not yet learned to articulate. My role in doing the present study is to further that process of highlighting. I hope to add my modest input to the imagescape that my readers will inhabit if they visit one of the sites under discussion after temporarily inhabiting my text, or even if they do not.

But, more important, my picture of the boy at Mount Rushmore has served as a constant reminder to me that while I was "studying" this phenomenon as an academic, I was also thoroughly implicated in it. I started this project bewitched by Baudrillardian explanations for the role of images in postmodern culture. As a self-consciously ironic post-tourist, I reveled in the idea that the landscapes tourists who were visiting had been rendered hyperreal by their long history of representations. Like DeLillo's Murray, I gained power from that knowledge, and congratulated myself for being detached enough from those unfortunates who were mistaking a presented nature for nature itself. The obverse of the satisfaction I felt when I "understood" tourism this way was the solace I took in knowing of and seeking out places off the beaten trail where I could find authentic nature in its raw unmediated form. When I went to tourist sites I thought of myself as a disembodied tourist of tourism, but when I went camping, backpacking, or hiking off the beaten trail I thought of myself as an entirely embodied wilderness adventurer. The longer I inhabited this discourse and the more time I spent at tourist sites, however, the more I began to understand the limitations of nihilistic postmodernism as a strategy for both being-in-the-world and for studying the ways that others do the same. And as I started looking around me I found more people like myself who were trying to teach themselves and others the same lessons I was trying to teach myself every time I looked at that Mount Rushmore picture hanging on my wall.

READING WRITING

## THIS TEXT: READING

1.   What is your experience with tourist places? What had you noticed about them before reading this essay?
2.   What type of relationship do you have with public or private spaces generally? Do you notice or have you noticed when those who have constructed a space try to guide your actions?
3.   What type of tourist places do you prefer—amusement parks, national parks, museums, etc.? Why? If you go to a national park do you prefer to follow well marked trails or your own? Why?
4.   Bednar writes about this issue from a personal standpoint; in what ways does this aid the point he's making? In what ways does it detract from it?

## YOUR TEXT: WRITING

1.   Document your own experience in trying to navigate public space either familiar or unfamiliar to you. In what ways does your environment control your actions? Is this a necessity?
2.   Write a short paper talking about your experience in a national or state park. Think back about the way you were guided—or not guided—in your experience. What effect does reading Bednar's piece and reflection have on your memories?

---

## THE VISUAL CHARACTER OF CHINATOWNS

### ■ David Chuenyann Lai ■

*This short essay (1997) reads Chinatowns as a complex text that combines issues of culture, race, class and architecture. Lai also acknowledges that Chinatowns mean a number of different things to a number of different people, making them particularly slippery texts to define. Pay close attention to Lai's attention to detail as he describes the architectural character of specific buildings and communities.*

"Chinatown" means different things to different people at different times and in different cities. Chinatown can be conceived of as a social community, an inner-city neighborhood, a suburban shopping plaza, a skid row district, a historic district, a tourist attraction, a place of mysterious evil, or a cultural hearth. Although our perception of Chinatown may be shaped by our knowledge of it as a social entity, our perception is also influenced by the act of seeing.

It is the facades of the buildings in Chinatown that constitute the most striking visual component of place character. Western architects or contractors built most of the old Chinatown buildings, but they tried to create "chinoiserie" or exotica by modifying or manipulating standard Western architectural forms. In the Chinatowns of Victoria and Vancouver in British Columbia, for example, buildings exhibit both Chinese decorative details and Western facades constructed in the prevailing commercial Italianate and Queen Anne fashions of the day.[1] Other Chinatowns, such as those in San Francisco, Seattle, Vancouver, and

Decorative features such as green or yellow tiled roofs, moon-shaped entrances, and Chinese inscriptions transform these three buildings in Chicago into typical Chinatown structures. (Photo by David Chuenyan Lai.)

Montreal, still have cohesive groupings of similar nineteenth-century buildings. These blend features of both Chinese and Western architectural styles.

Although a homogenous style of Chinatown architecture has never developed, Chinatown structures usually contain several architectural features rarely found on other downtown buildings. The most common elements are recessed or projecting balconies, upturned eaves and roof corners, extended eaves covering the main balconies, sloping tiled roofs, smooth or carved columns topped with cantilevered clusters of beams, flagpoles, and parapet walls bearing Chinese inscriptions.[2]

Recessed balconies dominate the upper stories of many Chinatown buildings. This element may be a duplication of practices in Hong Kong, Macao, Canton, and other cities in south China, where the facade of a building is set back at each level and the facade plane is met by a wrought iron balcony. Recessed balconies are common in south China because they help keep building interiors cool in the summer and warm in the winter. On rainy days, residents dry their clothes on bamboo poles hung in the recessed balcony.

A recessed balcony also provides an open space for children to play and for households to worship the heavens during the Chinese New Year and other festivals. In Chinatowns, most Chinese association buildings have recessed balconies, which are useful when the interior assembly hall is too crowded during a festival celebration or when there is a street parade.

I have not come across any building with a recessed balcony outside Chinatown except one in Portland: The Waldo Block, a three-story building at the corner of Washington Street and S.W. Second Avenue, has a recessed balcony, but it is four city blocks south of Portland's Chinatown. Even so, a search of the history of the block reveals that it was owned by the

Gee How Oak Tin (Zhi Xiao Du Qin) Association during the late 1880s, when Chinatown included that block.[3]

The facades of Chinatown buildings are usually covered with Chinese decorative details.[4] The major decorative elements include schemes of gold, red, green, yellow, and other brilliant colors; animal motifs, including dragons, phoenixes, or lions; plant motifs, including pine, bamboo, plum, and chrysanthemum; other motifs, including pagodas, lanterns, bowls, and chopsticks; inscriptions of stylish Chinese characters such as *fu* (happiness or blessings) and *shou* (longevity); signboards inscribed in Chinese characters; hanging lanterns; doors, windows, or archways that are circular, moon-shaped, and overlaid with ornate lattice work; and decorative balustrades adorned with frets.

In traditional Chinese architecture, the colors and animal motifs are believed to influence the fortune and destiny of a building's occupants. Red signifies happiness, gold is linked with prosperity, yellow is the imperial color, blue is associated with peace, and green is associated with fertility. Certain mystic animals such as dragons and phoenixes are believed to be auspicious and are commonly carved or painted on walls, columns, and shop signs.

The On Leong Chinese Merchants Association Building in Washington, D.C., is a good example of a Chinatown building with many decorative and structural components. (Photo by David Chuenyan Lai.)

Chinatown also is visibly different from other city neighborhoods because of structures such as the Chinese pavilion in Seattle, the Chinese pagoda in Montreal, and the Chinese gardens in Vancouver and Winnipeg. There are also Chinese decorative features, such as telephone booths and bilingual street signs in Chinese characters and English letters. Chinese fittings such as pagodas and lanterns are used as decorative features on many restaurants and gift shops in Chinatown.

Lavishly decorated Chinese arches or gateways are prominent landmarks of many Chinatowns across North America.[5] For example, Chinese arches serve as a symbolic entrance to Chinatowns in Boston, Chicago, Edmonton, and Winnipeg. Two Chinese arches in Los Angeles function as entrances to a shopping plaza. A Chinese arch is a symbolic entrance to the Chinese Cultural Center in Vancouver. In Victoria, the Gate of Harmonious Interest was built to commemorate cooperation of the Chinese and non-Chinese citizens of the city in the rehabilitation of Chinatown, as well as the harmony of the city's multicultural society.

The way our serial views of Chinatown are linked may cause our minds to mold the chaotic images of Chinatown into a perceived coherent precinct. In Victoria, for example, intricate networks of picturesque arcades, narrow alleys, and enclosed courtyards are still found behind the commercial facades of the old buildings. The architectural components relate harmoniously to the scale of people passing through the street: We see a large, impressive gateway, then details of its design, then facades of the three-story buildings, then the street, sidewalks, people, and vehicles, and finally the alleys and courtyards. The scales of the various parts of Chinatown integrate hierarchically, giving us a sense of complexity, coherence, and satisfaction.

We are keenly conscious of objects and the intervals between them—signboards, merchandise, telephone booths, sidewalk benches, and street lamps. Closely spaced, they make us visually aware of the densely populated and over-crowded streetscape—and community—of Chinatown.

 READING WRITING

## THIS TEXT: READING
1. What is Lai's thesis? What is he arguing exactly?
2. Does he define "Chinatown?"

## YOUR TEXT: WRITING
1. For those of you who have never been to a Chinatown in person, write an essay about an imagined Chinatown. What do you imagine it to look like? Smell like? What sorts of texts are informing how you envision this mythical Chinatown?
2. If you live near a Chinatown, visit it. Take notes and pictures. Write a definitional essay in which you *define* Chinatown, but use your own experiences and observations to help make your points.
3. Compare a Chinatown with another ethnic neighborhood in your city. If you have a Little Italy, or a little Czech town or some kind of Mexican or Latino-influenced neighborhood, read that neighborhood against a Chinatown. How are they different? What do they have in common?

*Student Essay*

| READING THE NAUTICAL STAR | |
| --- | --- |
| ■ **Matthew King** ■ | *Matthew King was a student in English 101 at Virginia Commonwealth University when he wrote this piece.* |

Human beings are extremely susceptible to becoming creatures of habit. We go about our day without taking much notice of the people around us. We follow the beaten path on a kind of auto-pilot. One of the most traveled pathways near us is Schafer Court, and especially the newly installed Nautical Star (I have determined this title, for that is what it appears to be). Sitting and watching how people use the Star is a study in human behavior and habit. After a few hours of unintentionally voyeuristic "people-watching" I have found that the populace has turned an intended pathway into a place of congregation.

The Nautical Star is located directly in front of Virginia Commonwealth University's Branch-Cabell Library, a hub of student activity. Constructed out of tan and slate grey brick and bronze metal, it is inlaid into the burnt orange brick of the surrounding pathways. Four points around the Star illustrate the directions orientating the star, with North being slightly to the right of the library. The Star is surrounded also by the Hibbs Building, Schafer Court, and a pathway to VCU's Life Sciences Building. Given the immense traffic these respective locations draw, the Nautical Star becomes a hub for students and faculty who pass through it on the way to classes or meetings.

The first trend I noticed while studying the diurnal flux of VCU's student body was that the Nautical Star, seemingly intended as a centerpiece for Schafer Court, had succeeded in that regard. The heaviest flow of traffic was always on or around the star, given that it has four main entrances and exits leading to some of VCU's busiest buildings. Viewing the people milling about the circular brick decoration reminded me of looking down at the flow of people going through New York's Grand Central Station. The determined, tight-lipped looks seen in New York were the same I saw at the Star, as well. These looks were evidence to me that most people used the Star as a pathway, focused only on their respective destinations and not on the newly built brickwork that they were treading upon.

Despite the mass amounts of people going their various ways, there is a sense of calm amidst the chaos. There are no collisions between human and bike, no traffic flow issues, and no heated run-ins. There seems to be a pervasive flow or path that all participants in the journey seem to subconsciously follow. In fact, it appears as if this circular star fed by four outlets of traffic maintains a strange, unexplainable sense of efficiency, upholding the Star's intent as a way to move people through a complex courtyard to the buildings and classrooms where they need to be.

And yet, despite the seeming success of the Star's purpose (moving people and providing direction), I noticed that the people have quietly, perhaps unintentionally, changed the use of the star. While the majority of the people follow the motion flow and move through the Star to their destination, a small faction have decided to buck the trend and instead use the Star as a meeting place, a destination as opposed to a gateway to a destination.

Given this fact, it is ironic that the designers of the star saw no need to install seating anywhere near the star. They did not think to allow a structure in which to facilitate people's lollygagging. The Star remains a directional guide, pushing the people through it, around it, anywhere but onto it. That said, the desire for people to congregate there and remain there seems at once unnatural and yet completely logical, despite the obvious irony of a directional device being used as a destination in itself.

Perhaps the explanation for the student body's decision to remain on the star can be found in the layout and flow of the rest of the university. Being an extremely far-flung university, there are few main areas where mass amounts of the students congregate. In addition to the Schafer Court area, only the Student Commons (located approximately 3/4 of a block away) serves as a communal "meet market" and congregational area. That being said, however, the various designers that have toiled away at the university over the years have usually included ample seating around the veins of transportation. Benches, tables, unusually wide stairs and the like have been included to make student R&R an easily afforded benefit of campus life. Even walls near walkways have historically been constructed so as to facilitate easy seating and gathering, as evidenced by the Schafer Court/ Cabell Library shared spaces. So it seems odd that VCU's latest addition to its conduit system would lack simple elements such as seating and gathering space. And yet, the students have created these things in a non-material way, simply seating when the mood strikes and consistently meeting with friends at the Star's center or edges.

In a way, the whole system is reminiscent of Fiske's comment in "Shopping for Pleasure" of the weak unseating the powerful. The intent of the designers was for the Star to be a place for mobility and information-giving, not a place to meet fellow students or friends. So why has the star turned into something seemingly not intended when it was built? Perhaps the designers were too successful in constructing an attractive yet functional centerpiece for Schafer Court.

One main purpose of the star, besides the ones mentioned above, was for it to be an attractive centerpiece for the university. Perhaps it was just that—an attractive centerpiece that people found so magnetic that they congregated there, drawn by the uniqueness and symmetry. Numerous groups of people gather on all points of the star, engaging in conversation and gossip, scanning the hordes of passing students for friends and acquaintances. Meanwhile, solitary students dot points on the outside perimeter of the star, waiting to meet friends and significant others for shared classes or a quick bite to eat at Hibbs. Some talk on cell phones, giving directions to the star or encouraging the other party to hurry up. Whatever reason has drawn these people here, their behavior has turned the Nautical Star on its ear, so to speak. They have made a decision, though not necessarily a conscious one, to mold the Star to fit their needs and to make its seeming unfaithfulness to previous university constructs a seemingly meaningless issue in regards to seating and gathering.

Surprisingly, what I learned from this experiment was that taking a small slice of a person's day (their passage through Schafer Court and the Star) can actually tell one a tremendous amount about human behavior in general. People are often so set in their routine (or so tired or hung over) that they seem to blur out everything but their destination. In fact the zombie-like look of some members of the student body are almost frightening in their one-dimensionality. People seem bound to a sense of flow, almost unable to break free of a pre-determined path. However unconscious these movements may be, a few of them tend to shatter the paradigm with outright force, neglecting the intent or focus of architects and work-a-day construction workers in favor of simple convenience. All of these observations prove that habit is a powerful force in our lives, and even if we don't realize it, we can sub-consciously shift the intent of the powerful.

## The Suburban Suite

Suburbia has dominated the American living landscape for almost half a century, and although its not an American invention, the suburb and all that's attached to it has become a prototypically American living arrangement. But the suburbs have never been without their critics, who have criticized the reliance on cars, the social and often racial and ethnic isolation, and conformity attached to the suburbs. Here William Hamilton (1999) writes about the impact of suburbs on teenagers, while William Booth (1998) examines the reverse migration of whites from cities to the suburbs in South Florida.

In response to the continued sprawl of suburbs, architects and town planners have proposed the idea of making newer suburbs more like small towns of old. New Urbanism, most prominently displayed in *The Truman Show*'s (1998) real-life setting of Seaside, Florida, has become increasingly popular in the last decade. The architectural and public space movement encourages a return to small-town living, which revolves around common spaces and a layout that encourages walking and more social interaction. Here Sarah Boxer (1998) and Whitney Gould (1999) examine the idea of New Urbanism.

### HOW SUBURBAN DESIGN IS FAILING TEEN-AGERS
### ■ William L. Hamilton ■

AS QUICKLY AS THE WORD "alienation" can be attached to the idea of youth, the image of isolation can be attached to a picture of the suburbs. Is there an unexplored relationship between them? It is a question parents and urban planners alike are raising in the aftermath of the Columbine High School shootings in Littleton, Colo.

At a time when the renegade sprawl of suburbs themselves is being intensely scrutinized, the troubling vision of a nation re-pioneered in vast tracts of disconnected communities has produced uneasy discussion about the psychological disorientation they might house. Created as safe havens from the sociological ills of cities, suburbs now stand accused of creating their own environmental diseases: lack of character and the grounding principles of identity, lack of diversity or the tolerance it engenders, lack of attachment to shared, civic ideals. Increasingly, the newest, largest suburbs are being criticized as landscapes scorched by unthoughtful, repetitive building, where, it has been suggested, the isolations of larger lots and a car-based culture may lead to disassociation from the reality of contact with other people.

Designers of the newest American suburbs say they have largely ignored or avoided one volatile segment of the population—teen-agers. In recent conversations, three dozen urban planners, architects, environmental psychologists and sociologists, and experts on adolescent development agreed that specific community planning and places for teen-agers to make their own are missing.

"They're basically an unseen population until they pierce their noses," said William Morrish, a professor of architecture and the director of the Design Center for American Urban Landscape at the University of Minnesota. "They have access to computers and weaponry. The sense of alienation that might come from isolation or neglect will have a much larger impact than it might have before. And there are no questions coming from the design community about what we can be doing about this. We don't invite them in."

Virtually every other special interest has been addressed by enlightened suburban designers—the elderly, the disabled, families with young children. But, said Andres Duany, a planner who is a leading proponent of the "new urbanism," a model of suburban design based on principles of traditional towns, "it's the teen-agers I always bring up as a question mark." Mr. Duany said that he had only once or twice included teen-agers in the public process of planning a suburban development.

"It's a good point," he said, as though it were an unlikely idea. "I should talk to the kids."

Though teen-agers tend to resist advice and choose their own turf as a territorial issue of establishing self-identity, most experts interviewed say that design could constructively anticipate and accommodate anxieties of adolescence. They agreed that teen-agers need a place to congregate in and to call their own; it is a critical aspect of relieving the awkward loneliness of adolescence. Between home and school—spheres compromised by the presence of parents or the pressure of performance—places for teen-agers in the suburbs are as uncommon as sidewalks.

"It's a paradoxical situation," said Ray Suarez, host of "Talk of the Nation" on National Public Radio and author of *The Old Neighborhood* (The Free Press, 1999), a study of suburban migration. "Parents move there for their children; their children are dying to get out." Like much of the Western United States, Denver is experiencing vertiginous suburban growth. From 1990 to 1996, the metropolitan area expanded by two-thirds, to its current size of 535 square miles.

"Typical of the Denver metro area are the new suburbs, where 'downtown' is a four-way intersection with three shopping centers and a condo development," said Charles Blosten, community services director for Littleton's city planning division. Highlands Ranch, Denver's largest suburban development, has its own ZIP code, "nothing but rooftops and miles and miles of nothing," he said of the numbing vista of houses. "It's got to affect people."

The idea that place has an impact on adolescent development and socialization is accepted by most experts on the suburbs but is only now beginning to be studied. "A culture of impersonality has developed in the suburbs by the way they're laid out," said Jonathan Barnett, a professor of regional planning at the University of Pennsylvania and author of *The Fractured Metropolis* (HarperCollins, 1996). In the newer suburbs, "the standard of houses is high, but the standard of community isn't," he continued, adding, "It's most people's impression of modern life."

And the people it stands to impress the most are children. "They are the most vulnerable people growing up there," said Dr. Jose Szapocznik, a professor of psychiatry and behavioral sciences and director of the Center for Family Studies at the University of Miami. "As a child you're disabled by not being able to walk anywhere. Nothing is nearby."

Mr. Morrish said he thought that public transportation to metropolitan downtowns was crucial for high school students. He said that the ability to access "the system"—the world adults create—was a vital form of empowerment.

"What to do after school, how to get to the city, to see other people and how to negotiate this without parents," he said, posing the issues. "Teen-agers have to have better access to the public realm and public activity." He recalled a conversation with a group of high school students who met with the Design Center, which invites teen-agers to group meetings when it is commissioned to study neighborhoods.

"One girl said, 'All I've got is the Pizza Hut,'" Mr. Morrish said. "'You go there a lot or you go to somebody's house—we're tired of both.'"

Between home and school, in a landscape drawn by cars and the adults who drive them, is there even a particular place that teen-agers can call their own? Peter Lang, a professor of architecture at the New Jersey Institute of Technology and an editor of *Suburban Discipline* (Princeton Architectural Press, 1997), a collection of essays, said: "In most suburbs, there's not even a decent park, because everyone has a backyard. But older kids never play in the backyard. They'll find even the crummiest piece of park."

Typically, the students at Columbine High School went to Southwest Plaza, a two-level mall that has video arcades, food courts and stores, supervised by security guards and closed by 9 P.M. "Like any suburban community, there's not a lot of places to go and hang out," Mr. Blosten said of Littleton. "I tell you this because that's where my daughter goes—the mall."

Mr. Lang said he thought that places like malls were not adequate gathering spaces for teen-agers, calling them, like many public suburban venues, commercially and environmentally "controlled space." He added, "They are not places for free expression or hanging out."

Disagreeing that suburbs create greater alienation is Dr. Laurence Steinberg, a professor of psychology at Temple University and director of the MacArthur Foundation Research Network on Adolescent Development and Juvenile Justice. But he said that he thought recent tragedies like the incident in Littleton do "wake people up to the notion that there is parental disengagement in affluent suburbs." He added: "We did a study on latchkey kids. The kids most likely to be left unattended for long periods were middle class, in sprawling professional suburbs. Isolated for long periods of time, there's no counterbalancing force to fantasy."

The desire for more and cheaper land that has pushed suburbs to rural exurbia may result in teen-agers who are alone for large parts of the day. Mr. Morrish pointed out that in communities like Modesto, in the San Joaquin Valley in central California, people commute to jobs in the San Francisco area, where they enroll their children in schools.

"Some people in California are taking their kids with them," he said, "making the kids commute."

The planners who have been most vocally and visibly at work on restructuring the suburban model have been "new urbanists" like Mr. Duany. Their solutions to the wheeling nebulae of tract development are based on tighter concentrations of houses, businesses and public spaces connected by townlike elements—porches, sidewalks and parks—that have largely disappeared from the new residential landscape.

If teen-agers find their place there, in new towns like Columbia and Kentlands in Maryland or Celebration, the Disney-built town in Florida, it is not because of any bravery on the planners' part. They often foster nostalgic views of families with young children. But like conventional suburbs, they overlook the inevitability of teen-agers in their design.

Peter Katz, who with Vincent Scully wrote *The New Urbanism: Toward an Architecture of Community* (McGraw-Hill, 1993), spoke of the importance to teen-agers of a place that existed only for them, neither hidden and ignored nor exposed and supervised—in effect, a secret place in full view.

On a visit, Mr. Katz discovered that for Celebration's teen-agers, it was a narrow bridge, "with low railings, that goes from downtown to the health club." He continued: "They find each other. They sit on the railing. It's on the route to daily life—not a back alley, but not the town square." Mr. Katz suggested that such a structure could become a conscious part of a community design for teen-agers.

For Diane Dorney, a mother with two teen-age children who lives in Kentlands, Md., a 10-year-old "new urban" suburb of some 1,800 people, the hallmarks of town life work well for both parents and children. Ms. Dorney and her husband, Mark, moved their family from a typical town-house development.

"We wanted to raise our kids in a place that provided more than just a house," she said. "It's a diverse community, of age and income," with older people, young couples, families. Ms. Dorney said that she thought the gaze of the town created a sense of extended family and moral weight that were its most important success.

"Someone sneaking down the street to have a cigarette—they don't get away with it," she said. "I don't think teen-agers should be left on their own until they're caught at the small things." She continued, "When they go into the big things, they know how big they are." She added: "And we have another way of knowing these kids, other than the bad things. They're your neighbors, too. You're always seeing them. You give them another chance."

## A WHITE MIGRATION NORTH FROM MIAMI

### ■ William Booth ■

EVERYTHING HERE IS NICE AND NEAT, just the way Joanne Smith likes it. The developers call their new city on the edge of the Everglades "Our Home Town," and Smith agrees. "It's more like America," she says.

Like thousands of others, Smith moved to this planned community 40 miles north of Miami just a few years ago, searching for a safe and secure neighborhood like this one, where both modest homes and rambling mansions sit against the manicured landscape of palm and hibiscus, and gated streets called Wagon Way and Windmill Ranch gently curve around the shallow lagoons and golf links.

Weston is a boomtown filling with refugees. But the migrants pouring into this part of Broward County are rarely those from the Caribbean, Central and South America—the immigrants to the south who have transformed Miami and surrounding Dade County into a metropolis proudly called by its business and political leaders "The Gateway to Latin America." Instead, the refugees here are mostly native-born and white, young and old, and they have been streaming up from Miami for years now, creating a new version of the traditional "white flight" in reaction not to black inner cities, but to immigration.

While Miami is unique in many respects, because of both geography and politics, the out-migration of whites is occurring in other high-immigration cities. New York and Los Angeles, for example, each lost a million U.S.-born residents in the last decade, as they gained a million immigrants.

According to an analysis of the most recent census data, for almost every immigrant who came to Miami-Dade County in recent years, a white non-Hispanic left.

"I loved Miami, but it's a mad scene down there now," said Smith, who is semi-retired and asked that her occupation not be given. Before her move to Weston, Smith lived in Miami for two decades, "in a nice neighborhood gone bad. People say things, 'Oh that's change and that's progress,' but I like it clean and green—and everybody speaking English," Smith says.

In discussions about the historic demographic transformations occurring in the United States, which is absorbing almost 1 million immigrants a year, most of the attention focuses quite naturally on the newcomers: Who are they and where are they from and how do they make their way in America?

But immigration is a two-way street—and the welcome the immigrants receive from the native-born is crucial for the continued idea of America as a fabled "melting pot." Of course, there are many whites—and blacks, too—who have remained in Miami-Dade County, to either continue their lives as before or accept, even embrace the Latin tempo of Miami, who have learned how to pronounce masas de puerco at lunchtime and to fake a respectable merengue dance step, who enjoy the culture, the business opportunities and caffeinated hustle of a metropolis dominated by immigrants. No one could call Miami dull.

But it is almost as if there are two kinds of native whites—those who can deal with multiculturalism that has transformed Miami over the past several decades and those who choose not to. Either way, if the country is to successfully transform itself into a completely multicultural industrialized nation, what these internal migrants say and there are millions of them around the country needs to be heard and understood.

Those transplants interviewed by *The Washington Post,* including those who asked that their names not be used, take pains to explain that, for the most part, the people like them who are moving out of Miami-Dade to Broward are not anti-immigrant xenophobes.

In several dozen interviews with a cross-section of these domestic migrants, a picture emerges of a segment of the non-Hispanic white population in Miami-Dade County that feels marginalized, exasperated and sometimes bitter, and who move from Dade to Broward with a mix of emotions.

Migrants to Broward give many reasons for the move north: Their money buys a bigger, newer house in Broward; they are tired of the traffic and congestion; they worry about crime; they complain about the overcrowded schools; those with young families often say they are looking for a place where their children can play ball in the front yard and ride their bikes down the block.

But all these things, the good and bad, can also be found in booming Broward County. Sooner or later, many of the refugees moving north mention immigration and the sense that they are no longer, as many transplants describe it, comfortable.

Phil Phillips was born and raised near what is today downtown Miami, where his father worked for the Immigration and Naturalization Service during the postwar years, at a time when the immigrants to Florida were mostly from Europe. Phillips served in the Navy, taught vocational classes at Miami High School, and made a living running a small air conditioning and refrigeration business.

Until the rise of Fidel Castro in Cuba, Phillips described the Miami of yesteryear as a more sleepy, more southern town. It had its glitz in the fanciful playground of Jackie Gleason a city of Miami Beach, but the county was still filled with open land and farms.

Miami was a very happy place, Phillips remembers with nostalgia. We had our demarcations, don't get me wrong. But we didn't have the animosity. When pressed, Phillips does remember that the beaches, restaurants and nightclubs were often segregated, not only for African Americans. Jews had their own country clubs.

The Miami of black-and-white all began to change with the arrival of the Cubans in the early 1960s. The vast majority of the Cubans came here and worked two and three jobs, said Phillips, who is retired and living in Weston. A man who worked with his hands all his life, Phillips respects that. I saw them do it. And in time, they took over, and some people resent that. But that's the way it is.

There's this myth out there that a Cuban will screw an American in a deal, Phillips says. I don't think that is so, but that's the feeling the whites have, and it's because the two sides don't communicate, sometimes they can't communicate, and so they don't understand the other guy.

Phillips has seen decades of change, as the demographics of his home town kept skewing toward Hispanics, in fits and starts. After the first big influx of Cubans in the 1960s, there was Cuba's Mariel boatlift in 1980. Then all through the proxy wars and upheavals in Central America and the Caribbean through the 1980s and 1990s, refugees from Nicaragua, Honduras, El Salvador and Haiti kept coming to Miami.

"We're great in America at blaming somebody else for our problems," Phillips said. "But I will tell that for a lot of the people who leave Miami, they might not tell you, but they're leaving because of the ethnics."

Phillips offered his opinions as he sat sipping soup at the counter of a new restaurant here in Weston opened by Tim Robbie, whose family owned the Miami Dolphins for years, before they sold out to Wayne Huizenga, who is "The Man" in Broward County, as much as Jorge Mas Canosa, the power behind the Cuban American National Foundation, was "The Man" in Miami before his death last year.

Robbie was raised in Miami. His family, lead by his father Joe, was a civic institution. But Robbie himself recently moved to Weston, too.

"I know a lot of our friends down in Miami were disappointed with us," Robbie said. "They asked: How can you do this to us?"

Robbie agreed that something akin to "the tipping point" phenomenon might be at work, whereby one or two families in a social or business network can leave a community and nothing much changes. But at some point, if enough people leave, the balance suddenly tips, and large groups start selling their homes, and over a period of several years, they create mass demographic shifts.

Robbie himself said he was comfortable down south in Miami, but concedes that many are not. "Anglos are accustomed to being in the majority, and down in Dade, they're not. And that puts some people outside of their comfort zone. People tend to like to stick together."

Robbie's business partner is Bob Green, who also moved from Miami to Broward. A longtime denizen of funky and fun Coconut Grove, Green describes himself as one of those who never would have thought about moving north to Broward.

But then he saw the new business opportunities, and also found himself liking a place like Weston. "It has this midwestern feeling," Green said. "More downhome and friendly."

This mass internal migration is the latest version of a classic "push–pull" model of residential segregation, whereby many whites in Miami feel lured north by the offerings of a development like Weston, but also feel pushed out of Miami—not only by their fatigue with crime or congestion, but the cultural and demographic upheavals caused by three decades of immigration.

Peter Schott is a tourism official who is changing jobs and, reluctantly, moving with his wife, who works for a cruise ship line, to Broward. The couple, both in their thirties and expecting their first child, are looking for a bigger home. Schott says he will miss the exotic, foreign feel of Miami. Miami, Schott says, is a media noche, the name for a Cuban sandwich, while Broward he fears is "white bread and baloney." While he will miss Miami, Schott knows that many of those moving north to Broward may not.

"Some people are real frank," he said. "They say they want to be with more people more like us. If they're white Americans, they want white Americans around them."

For non-Hispanic, non-Spanish-speaking whites to survive in Miami, there is no choice but to move, or to adapt. "It is our city now," many Cuban Americans say, and the numbers tell part of the story.

In the 1990s, some 95,000 white non-Hispanics left Miami-Dade County, decreasing that group's presence by 16 percent, to around 492,000, or about one-fifth of the county population.

They either moved away or, in the case of elderly residents, particularly in the Jewish community, died. (The Jewish population in Miami-Dade County has decreased from about 250,000 to 100,000 in the last two decades. The new destination for Jewish retirees and younger migrants is Broward and Palm Beach counties.)

As whites left Miami, they poured into Broward. Between 1990 and 1997, the white non-Hispanic population here increased by about 82,000, or 8 percent, to more than a million residents.

These dramatic numbers follow an equally large out-migration of whites during the 1980s. So many non-Hispanic whites left Miami-Dade in the previous decade that Marvin Dunn, a sociologist at Florida International University, who has followed the trend, said in 1991, "You get down to the point below which those who are going to leave have left and the others are committed to stay. I think we're close to that with whites."

But Dunn was wrong. The whites keep leaving.

"White migration to Miami-Dade has essentially stopped," said William Frey, a demographer at the University of Michigan, who coined the phrase "demographic balkanization" to describe the ongoing trend of ethnic and racial groups to self-segregate—not only within a city, but from city to city, and from state to state.

"The two appear almost like mirror images of each other," Frey said of Broward and Miami-Dade counties. "There is definitely something going on here and we can only guess what it is. But this 'One America' that Clinton talks about is clearly not in the numbers. Segregation and non-assimilation continue."

Many times, native whites on the move explain that Miami now feels to them like "a foreign country," that they feel "overwhelmed" by the presence not just of some Spanish-speakers, but so many.

"You order a Coke without ice," said an executive and mother of three who moved to Broward from Miami in 1996 and asked that her name not be used. "And you get ice. You say no starch and you get starch. You call government offices, and they can't take a decent message in English. You spell your name letter by letter and they get it wrong. They keep saying 'Que? Que? Que?' (Spanish for 'What?') You go to the mall, and you watch as the clerks wait on the Spanish speakers before you. It's like reverse racism. You realize, my God, this is what it is like to be the minority."

"The white population feels increasingly beleaguered," said George Wilson, a sociologist at the University of Miami who is studying the phenomenon.

"Their whole domain is changing at the micro-level," Wilson continued. "At the malls, in the schools. A lot of the whites I talk to say they feel challenged by the rapid ethnic and cultural change. A whole population of whites has gone from a clear majority to a clear minority in a very short time . . . and a lot of them simply say, 'To hell with this,' and move up the road."

This feeling of being the beleaguered minority is creating among some a new consciousness of "white ethnicity," and for those who see America's future as a relatively harmonious multicultural state based on shared ideas of capitalism and freedom, this may not bode well.

For if whites do not want to share power and place, or if they feel increasingly shoved aside or overwhelmed in the cities and states with high immigration, they will continue to vote with their feet, by moving away, creating not a rainbow of citizens, but a more balkanized nation, with jobs, university enrollments, public spending, schools all seen through ethnic or racial prisms, including among whites.

Several of those interviewed complain that the politics of Miami-Dade are dominated by the issues of the newcomers, particularly the Cuban Americans, who wait for the fall of Fidel Castro; they see in the city hall, where a number of officials were recently indicted and convicted of taking kickbacks after it was discovered that the city was broke, a "banana republic" of ethnic cronyism; they dislike being referred to in Spanish media as "the Americans" by Miami's Hispanic residents and politicians, as if they were the foreigners.

And many balk at the dominance of Spanish—on television, in official news conferences, on the radio, in schools and meetings and in their day-to-day lives. The movement of so many whites from Miami-Dade to Broward is viewed by many Hispanics as understandable, even natural, though hardly something to be encouraged.

"We had a tremendous exodus of Anglos, especially Anglos who did not feel comfortable with the new demographics of Miami, who were intimidated by the Spanish language and the influx of different people," said Eduardo Padron, a Cuban American and president of the Miami-Dade Community College. "It is a natural trend for them to move out. Many of them kept working in Miami, but they found refuge in Broward."

Padron believes the rapidity of demographic changes, and the creation of a Hispanic majority, was "intimidating" for many whites, particularly those who did not speak any Spanish.

Some whites interviewed say they know they may seem like "whiners," as one woman put it, but they feel they are not being met halfway by the newcomers, and this is an especially acute feeling in Miami, where Cuban Americans and other immigrants from Latin America now dominate the political landscape, serving as city and county mayors and council members. Both of Miami's representatives to Congress are Cuban Americans.

Recent elections reveal that voters in Miami-Dade select candidates along stark racial and ethnic lines in classic bloc voting. The 1995 county mayor's race, pitting Cuban American Alex Penelas against African American Arthur Teele, Jr., turned almost entirely on demographic lines, with exit polls showing that the overwhelming majority of Cuban Americans voted for Penelas, as most blacks voted for Teele. What did whites do? A lot of them did not vote at all.

Over the years, there has been sporadic, organized resistance by whites in Miami to hold back the changes. One group, calling itself Citizens of Dade United, was successful in passing a referendum in 1980 that declared English the "official language" of county government. But it was overturned in 1993. Enos Schera, who is a co-founder of the group and who is now 71, is still filled with vinegar, and says he refuses to move from Miami—though he says he and his group have received death threats.

"I'm staying to fight this crazy thing," Schera said. "I'm not a bad guy, but I don't want to be overrun. They come here and get all the advantages of being in America and then they insult you right on top of it." He is writing a book about the changes. "That will tell all," he promises.

But it seems as if Schera is fighting in retreat. He, and his group, have largely been relegated to the role of stubborn whites whose time is over.

Many of the others, like Weston resident Joanne Smith, have already left. "There's no room for us in the discussion," said Smith. "It's like we were the oppressors."

Smith says she likes to eat at Cuban restaurants, has Hispanic neighbors in Weston and admires the strength and striving of the newcomers. She herself is the granddaughter of immigrants, from Europe. But Smith feels the immigrants should try harder to understand the feelings of native Americans. "If they can survive coming here on a raft," she says, "they can learn to speak English."

Here at Weston, almost all of the communities are closed with security gates, requiring a visitor to punch a code or be cleared by a guard before entering the enclaves. In addition to the gates, a private security firm patrols the neighborhoods.

One researcher on the topic, Edward Blakely of the University of Southern California in Los Angeles, says that gated communities like Weston's are the fastest growing new developments around the country. Blakely deplores the trend, claiming it creates "fortress neighborhoods," dividing citizens, creating walls between "us" and "them."

But obviously, many home buyers like the concept, and many of the residents of Weston say one of the things they like most about the neighborhood is its sense of community, of safety and the ability of their children to ride their bicycles on the streets.

Yet the gates cannot keep demographic change at bay. Though two of every three residents in Weston is white, most of them in their thirties, about one in four are Hispanic. But these are the most assimilated, often second-generation, solidly middle-class Cuban Americans who come north for the same new schools and golf courses as the white migrants, allowing almost everyone to continue to live within their comfort zone.

But not all. As one three-year resident, who declined to give her name, observed, "I keep hearing more and more Spanish in the grocery store. I don't know if they live here or are just working here. But I started to see some Spanish magazines for sale. Maybe I didn't move far enough north."

---

## A REMEDY FOR THE ROOTLESSNESS OF MODERN SUBURBAN LIFE?

### ■ Sarah Boxer ■

ATTACKS ON SUBURBIA are as old as cul-de-sacs. Suburbs have always been derided as bourgeois, consumerist and conformist. But now they have become the enemy of family values, too. That's right. Karl Zinsmeister, the editor of the conservative magazine *The American Enterprise,* has written that "suburbia is actually a fairly radical social experiment," one that can be linked to "the disappearance of family time, the weakening of generational links . . . the anonymity of community life, the rise of radical feminism, the decline of civic action, the tyrannical dominance of TV and pop culture over leisure time."

What is to be done? A group of architects and planners who have named themselves the Congress for the New Urbanism have vowed to halt the spread of faceless, car-centered suburbs by promoting friendly, people-centered towns with corner stores and public greens.

They call for some old-fashioned things: walkable neighborhoods with a mix of residences, businesses and public places; straight and narrow streets; wide sidewalks, and no cul de sacs. They believe houses should be built close enough together and close enough to the sidewalks to define streets and public squares. Above all, they want strong town centers and clear town boundaries. No one, they believe, should live more than a five-minute walk from most of their errands. (Otherwise, what's to stop people from getting in their cars and driving?) And like their British counterpart, the Urban Villages Group, the architects favored by the Prince of Wales, they want to preserve old towns and cities through "infill," building on unused urban lots.

"No one can be opposed to those principles," said Alex Krieger, a professor of urban design at Harvard University. They are like "mom and apple pie," he said. Yet many new-urban towns have been scorned as cutesy, regressive and un-urban. The new urbanists—or neo-traditionalists—should instead be called the "new suburbanists," some say, because they are less interested in planning principles than in porches, picket fences and gabled roofs.

Seaside, designed in the early 1980's by Elizabeth Plater-Zyberk and Andres Duany, two of the founders of new urbanism, is the oldest new-urban town. Built on a stretch of the Florida panhandle, Seaside was meant to foster community life and beach access. The houses, a pastiche of historical styles in pastel colors, are set close to one another and connected by straight brick streets and a network of sand walkways cutting through the middle of each block. When the town is finished, it is supposed to have 350 houses and 300 apartments, a school, an open-air market, a town hall, a tennis club, an amphitheater, a post office, and a number of shops, offices and beach pavillions.

If you're having trouble picturing it, think of the idyllic town in the movie *The Truman Show.* That was no movie set. That was Seaside.

Since Seaside was built, new urbanism has won a lot of fans and building contracts. There are dozens of new-urban towns and projects built or under construction, including Celebration in Florida, Laguna West in California and Kentlands in Maryland. The Department of Housing and Urban Development is renovating some of its public housing according to new urbanist principles: more porches, more fences, lower buildings, narrower streets. Jane Jacobs, the author of *The Death and Life of Great American Cities,* has praised the movement as "sound" and "promising." And publications from *The Sierra Club Yodeler* to *The American Enterprise* have smiled on the new urbanists.

"But is their particular vision of urbanization an innovative model appropriate to the 21st century," Michelle Thompson-Fawcett asked in the journal *Urban Design International,* "or is it regressive nostalgia?"

New urbanism is, by definition, nostalgic. Towns built on a human scale, with strong centers and clear edges, have been around for 5,000 years, said Robert Davis, the developer of Seaside and the chairman of the new-urban Congress. It is only in the last 50 years, with the rise of modernism, he said, that Americans have forgotten how to build them.

The new urbanists want to induce neighborliness with architecture. In this sense they are utopian. Like the modernist master planners of the 1930's, they believe social change can be brought about through architecture and planning. The difference is that most of them hate modernism.

While the modernists "tried to get to the future by destroying the past," Robert Fishman, the author of *Bourgeois Utopias,* said, the new urbanists "are reviving the past in order to change" the present. That, the new urbanists think, is why many architecture schools view them with contempt.

Most schools of architecture are "so in the grips of the modernist ideology and so defensive of the avant-garde that they see the Congress for the New Urbanism as fundamentally conservative," said Daniel Solomon, a founder of the movement. Peter Katz, the author of *The New Urbanism: Toward an Architecture of Community,* said that the nation's most powerful architects, particularly those in New York, "laugh at the poor souls who live in suburbia."

Kenneth Frampton, an architecture professor at Columbia University, agrees that many architecture schools (though he excludes Columbia) have ignored some questions about land settlement. But what bothers most professors about the new urbanists, he said, is not their critique of suburbia or land settlement. It is their design ideas.

The new-urbanist charter says nothing explicit about what styles are acceptable. Yet because many new urbanists believe that modernism ruined American cities, nearly all of their designs rely heavily on building styles from the past. Kentlands in Maryland is full of Georgian houses. Celebration, Disney's village in Florida, is full of brand new Victorians and Colonials.

"What's upsetting" about new urbanism, said Mr. Frampton, "is that the imagery is so retrograde." It is based on a "sentimental iconography" as if there were something inherently good about Victorians, Georgians and Colonials and something inherently bad about modernism. To be fair, there were a lot of modernists in the 1930's who advocated low-rise, high density housing, he said. Besides, the kind of modernism that the new urbanists see as their enemy is a straw man. No one is advocating tearing down whole cities to make way for skyscrapers.

"If you want to look for the demon that destroyed Main Street in America," Mr. Frampton said, "it is not the modern movement but the American bureaucracy that opened the way for freeways and suburbanization." The railroads were deliberately undermined by the automobile industry, he said, adding, "That was an economic, a capitalist, operation," not an architectural one.

New urbanism has not attacked the root of the problem sufficiently, suggested Alex Marshall, who has often written about new urbanism for *Metropolis* magazine. "What new urbanism tries to do is imitate older communities that existed before the automobile" without getting rid of the automobile. But if you want to return to these older forms of life, he said, you "have to bring back the transportation system." If you simply change the way houses are built, "it's like changing hemlines."

New urbanists like to see themselves as radicals, said Mr. Krieger, who was once a supporter of the movement and is now a critic. But, he added, they are "no longer the radical fringe but conventional wisdom." Developers have begun using the term new urbanism to sell their projects.

That's not to say the movement hasn't had a good effect, Mr. Krieger said. The Department of Housing and Urban Development has dedicated $2.6 billion to "Hope Six," a nationwide plan to rebuild mid-century public housing according to new urbanist principles. From Boston to Cleveland to Helena, Mont., high-rise projects are being replaced by town houses with porches and fences. "That is the part of the movement that most impresses me," said Mr. Krieger.

The problem, Mr. Marshall noted, is that most new-urban developments are not urban at all. They are rich developments on the town's edge. "They are sprawl under another name," he said, and they are as restrictive as any suburban development. Most are privately run by homeowners' associations that give developers extraordinary control.

For example, in Celebration, Disney's new-urban town, the deed restrictions specify what kind of drapery, roofing tiles and political signs are allowed. "Disney has a history of making warm and fuzzy dog movies," said Evan McKenzie, the author of *Privatopia,* a book on housing associations, but "they can take your dog if it makes too much noise."

"It's as if the people are saying: 'Who needs democracy? It's utopia already!'" said Mr. McKenzie.

People are looking for homeyness and safety, and they don't mind giving up some freedoms for it. In Kentlands, there is a gate in front of each entry into the development, Mr. Krieger said. "It's a decorative gate but it evokes the same associations as a real gate. It's a subtle form of 'Keep Out.'"

If decorative gates can evoke the same response as real gates, then maybe the look of neighborliness—porches, wide sidewalks and village greens—can evoke real neighborliness. Or can it?

The one big criticism about new-urban towns is that they are fake towns. Given that, it's curious that the developer of Seaside agreed to let *The Truman Show,* a movie about a real man in a false world, be filmed in Seaside. The movie all but said, "This is not really a town but the shell of a town, an image of a town," Mr. Krieger said.

After the filming was over, the painted plywood storefronts that had been put up for the movie stayed up for months because the developer liked the way they looked, Mr. Krieger said. After all, looking like a real town is the next best thing to being one.

## NEW URBANISM NEEDS TO KEEP RACIAL ISSUES IN MIND

### ■ Whitney Gould ■

IN THE STRUGGLE TO BUILD new towns and rebuild old ones, there's one issue no one wants to talk about much: race. And when it does come up, people tend to dance around it or dress it in euphemisms.

At a recent meeting here of the Congress for the New Urbanism, though, race had just about everyone buzzing—and the guy who started the buzz, writer James Howard Kunstler, wasn't even on the program. Kunstler, author of an anti-sprawl polemic titled *The Geography of Nowhere,* popped up from the mostly white audience at a panel on gentrification issues and said blacks should stop blaming their problems on whites. The real challenge? "Tell your kids to be nicer to white people," he exhorted. "Turn your baseball hats around, get interested in reading and quit trying to scare everyone."

A shouting match ensued. And no wonder. Could Kunstler, a middle-aged white guy and well-known provocateur, not have known how offensive his racial stereotyping would be? Did he really think that if every black person in America behaved like a well-read ambassador from *Gentleman's Quarterly* or *Vogue,* lily-white enclaves would suddenly become rainbow communities? And, as my colleague Eugene Kane observed [on these pages last week], weren't those shooters at Columbine High in Colorado a couple of white kids?

In fairness to the New Urbanists, Kunstler was not representative of the four-day gathering, which was earnest and thoughtful. But whatever his intentions, the bull-in-a-china-shop author in a very crude way did do one useful thing: He brought race front and center among a group of city-builders who have preferred to keep the spotlight more on the physical aspects of urban revitalization than on the social and economic integration that is crucial to the enduring health of communities.

The physical stuff is important, to be sure. Street-friendly architecture, slower streets and a mix of housing, businesses and public spaces all within walking distance: These are the sensible underpinnings of New Urbanism (and Old Urbanism, as well). That approach to development can make communities more neighborly, more humanly scaled and less dependent on the car. Milwaukee's new master plan for the downtown grows out of those principles. Two fledgling New Urbanist communities that I profiled recently, Middleton Hills west of Madison and CityHomes in Milwaukee, show how attractive such subdivisions can be.

But Middleton Hills is virtually all white, and CityHomes is overwhelmingly black. And there's little evidence that other New Urbanist communities are appreciably more integrated. In turn, most of the new housing being built in downtown Milwaukee is upscale, leaving working-class folks and/or minorities pretty much out of the picture. Indeed, census statistics show that 98% of the African-American population in the entire metro area lives in the City of Milwaukee, making this the most segregated of 50 large urban areas in the country.

You can argue, I suppose, that some of this segregation is voluntary: people choosing to live among folks like themselves. (Never mind that there are whites and people of color who prefer diversity.) You can argue, too, that this is just the market talking: developers going where the money is. (Never mind, too, that there is plenty of money to be made in mixed-use development.)

In fact, as experts at a University of Wisconsin–Milwaukee conference noted recently, federal highway and housing subsidies for years promoted sprawl, with all of its inevitable racial isolation and social inequity.

And today, as builders' and realtors' groups push to build smaller, more affordable houses in the suburbs, they run up against zoning rules that mandate huge minimum lot sizes and large houses. Even if the intent is not racist, the effect of such rules is both racially and economically discriminatory, shutting out working-class minorities and whites alike—and this at a time when retail and service jobs in the suburbs are going begging.

To wrap such exclusionary zoning in the mantle of environmentalism and the fight against sprawl strains credulity. After all, developers who can't build in one place will just move farther into the hinterlands. How does that promote smarter land use?

We could change all of this if we had the political will to do so. Reforming those onerous zoning rules would be a good place to start. Improving transit links to the suburbs would also help. And we could create new incentives for builders to include more modestly priced homes within new developments, whether in the city or the suburbs. Let's be clear: This doesn't mean concentrations of prison-like public housing, just some attractive single-family homes and townhouses that ordinary folks—black and white, young and old—could afford.

None of this would come easily. Such changes inevitably bring up the issue that no one wants to talk about: race. While it may be too much to expect planners and developers to solve the problems of social inequity, can we not at least hope they won't make those problems worse? How sad if New Urbanism, the most progressive planning tool in decades, were to become merely an excuse for creating beautifully designed communities as racially alienated as the old ones.

READING WRITING

## THIS TEXT: READING

1. What is your opinion of suburbs? Is this based on your own experience or what you have seen displayed in popular culture?
2. What are the advantages and disadvantages of living in the suburbs?
3. Are there ways of changing the suburbs to eliminate some of the disadvantages?
4. Do you think the behavior of teenagers is affected by the construction of public space?
5. What assumptions about suburbs are the practitioners of the New Urbanism making? Are those assumptions accurate?
6. Why is the idea of Main Street so attractive to us? Is it built on false assumptions?
7. What ages like living in suburbs the best? The least?
8. In what ways do gender, ethnicity, and race play into our ideas about the suburbs?

## YOUR TEXT: WRITING

1. Write a short piece about your experience in the suburbs.
2. What would you say the philosophy of suburban life is? Write a paper articulating what you think this philosophy is.
3. What are the defining architectural ideas behind living in the suburbs? How do these ideas affect the way people live?
4. Drive through a suburban community—both old and new. What do you notice about the public spaces and the way houses look? What do those aspects of the suburbs suggest about life there?
5. Write a short piece about the positive nature of the suburbs. Are there any cultural texts that would aid in your examination?
6. If you have grown up in the suburbs, think about your relationship to the suburbs at different times in your life. Is there a point at which you remember changing your ideas about where you live?
7. If you do not live in the suburbs, think about when you realized that there were places different from where you lived. Think about what you thought about these places growing up and what you think about them now.

READING *Outside the Lines*

## CLASSROOM ACTIVITIES

1. Look around your classroom. How do you know it's a classroom? Of course, there are the chalkboard and the desks, but what other qualities does this room have that makes it a classroom? How is it designed? Does it facilitate learning, alertness, and discussion?
2. Walk outside the classroom. What elements identify the walk as a college campus? What emotions does the walk evoke? Could it be improved?
3. What does the public space outside the classroom building say? Does it identify the campus as any particular type of school—private, public, urban, rural, suburban? What would a potential student read into this particular space? Would they be inclined to come to school or not because of this reading? Why or why not?

4.   What particular place makes you feel the most comfortable? Least? Frightened? What is it about the spaces themselves that evoke these emotions? Are they human driven or architecturally or design driven? Can you think of a space that has bad or good memories driven mostly by the space itself?
5.   Design the perfect classroom. What would it look like? What would it have in it? Where would everyone sit? What tools would everyone have? How would being in this classroom change your learning experience?
6.   Design the perfect building at college. What would it look like? What would it have in it?

## ESSAY IDEAS
### Building as analogy
Find a building you want to write about. Does it remind you of something besides a building in 1) its physical construction; 2) the emotional response it encourages; 3) its purpose; or 4) its structure? In what way are these disparate elements alike? Different? What does the analogy in general say about commonalties of texts generally?

### Emotional response
Walk around a building or a public area such as a mall or your school's common area. What do you "feel"? What about the place makes you feel such an emotion? Are these effects intended or unintended?

### Commercial versus artistic
What dominates this particular building or space—its artistic aspects or commercial ones? Or do the two work together?

### My favorite place
If possible, analyze a place you feel close to and figure out why you feel that way. Is there a theme attached to this place? How would you describe the décor? The architecture? Do you feel your attachment to this place—or places like it—is unique?

### Does this building or space "work"?
Find a place—do you think it succeeds on its own terms? What are its "terms"—what criteria is it trying to fulfill? Does is succeed? Why or why not?

### The person from the space
Go to an office or a dorm room or car, or some place that "belongs" to someone. What can you tell about this person from the space? How did you arrive at your judgments? Are there other ways to interpret the information?

## THE COMMON ELEMENT
Compare similar spaces. What makes them similar? What are their differences? What do their differences or similarities say about this type of space?

# Reading and Writing About Race and Ethnicity

■ ■ ■  An interracial romance is the subject of Spike Lee's *Jungle Fever* (1991).

O f all the introductions we have written, this one made us feel the most uncomfortable. Writing about people, the way they appear, and the relationship between their appearance and attributed behavior is a minefield for any prospective author. We wanted to put our anxiety on the table right away because we believe that this anxiety mirrors the way you might feel when you are talking about race and ethnicity whether you are Hispanic, African American, Asian American, American Indian, white, or some combination of ethnicities.

As you will notice in reading this introduction, we are constantly hedging—saying "to a degree" or "to some extent." And there is a reason for this hesitation. When it comes to race or ethnicity, there are few if any absolutes. For one, individuals do not have group experiences—and yet they do. Group experiences happen to individuals when a series of individuals have similar experiences. For example, if several people from a particular ethnic group have a similar but discrete experience because of how someone perceives them, they have had a group experience of prejudice. Anyone who has had racial epithets uttered at them has had this experience; those words are directed at someone not because of who they are inside, but because of how they look.

When these experiences occur because of perceived common characteristics—both people are of the same race, ethnicity, or gender—an individual experience becomes a group one. At the same time, individuals themselves have experiences imposed on them because they are perceived to be a member of a group. Prejudice, then, projects perceived or assumed group characteristics on a single person or groups of people. Again, saying a group of people is not qualified to do particular work because of how they look or the ethnicity they belong to is a clear example of prejudice.

To an overwhelming degree, these experiences are socially constructed. Indeed, most scientists believe that race is a social, not a biological, construction. In other words, race as it was commonly perceived in the past—as a way of attributing characteristics (usually negative, if they were not white) to individuals of a common group—is not scientifically or biologically defensible. Scientists believe that perceived traits of races are a product of social experiences, despite the way we often visually identify someone of a particular race. In other words, one's skin color does *not* determine race; factors contributing to one's race are far more complex.

We are *not* saying that biology does not determine the color of one's skin; clearly, biology determines skin color, as it does the color of our eyes. What we are saying (and what most scientists also argue) is that the idea that biological traits are associated with a particular skin color is false. As humans of different shades of color, we are much more alike biologically than we are different. Even if some groups do have higher incidents of disease (African Americans with sickle cell anemia, Jews with Tay-Sachs disease), environmental factors largely shape their existence. For example, Americans are much more likely to have heart conditions compared to the French; the characteristics of Americans are more alike than characteristics of people from Tibet, which is to say that our biology and our cultural community connect us in more ways than our perceptions of race might suggest.

Self-perception is even more of a factor in racial or ethnic identity, as people often "switch" ethnicities or at least change how they see themselves as belonging to a certain group. For instance, a study cited in one of our readings shows that over one-third of respondents in a census identified themselves as a different ethnicity than when they had taken the same census only two years later. This is not to say that race is not important—it is. Race and ethnicity, even if socially constructed, guide so much of our public life. By putting the burden on social constructions of race, we have to think about the way we construct race more completely rather than accept that race and ethnicity are the way things are.

In the past, people from various groups had a tendency to impose a set of values onto certain groups of people based simply on skin color, a tendency that has certainly diminished in the last 50 years (though we would be the last people to claim that this type of behavior is gone, and the first to acknowledge that prejudice is still very much a part of too many people's lives). Our goal in this chapter is to help you become more sensitive readers of race and ethnicity by becoming more aware of the social forces that construct the text of race and racism.

### The determination that race, ethnicity, and class are socially constructed has led to new ways of thinking about our identity that have political and social implications.

Not too long ago, and for most of the history of the Western world, people made assumptions about other people based on their appearance, most notably their skin color. White people wrongly and often tragically assumed blacks were less intelligent or that American Indians were "savages." For centuries, groups have enslaved people from other groups based on that group's race or ethnicity. In the last few decades, we have gone from the biological construction of race, one based on parentage, to one based more on social groups and associations. Hispanic means less than it did twenty years ago, as does Native American; we tend to view Native Americans by tribe or nation, and those from Central and South America, the Caribbean, and Mexico by country of origin, by nationality, rather than the catchall of ethnicity. These linguistic markers more accurately get at a more true measure of someone's identity, as anyone familiar with Native American, Latin American or Asian or African history can tell you.

To a degree, race and ethnicity are visually constructed, but those visual constructions are hardly without controversy.

We tend to categorize people by their appearance, not by their biological background, for the most obvious reason: we have no other way of reading people. We do construct race, ethnicity, and gender, and its multiplicity of meanings and ideas visually, not only through a person's skin, but also through what they wear, how they walk, how tall or short they are. We are not trying to demonize this process as much as we are trying to draw attention to it. Like other visual constructions, it has to be slowed down and digested more actively. Thus, every time we see someone and register that person's skin color, we are doing a reading of his or her ethnicity. We pick up on external codes that we think cue us into that person's racial background, but what, really do those cues tell us? For one, even if we can determine if someone is Chinese or Russian or Kenyan or Navajo, that tells us very little about who she is as a person, what he likes to eat, what she is good at, how smart he is, what sports she plays, or what his values are.

### To some extent, reading the "otherness" in someone's appearance makes us uncomfortable because of reasons both political and personal.

We want to be—and are explicitly trained to be—democratic in the way we view others, by the way they act toward us, not the way they look. "Don't judge a book by its cover," we say, but we are always judging books by their covers and people by their appearance, and this makes many of us feel uncomfortable. This discomfort is magnified when it comes to race, ethnicity, gender, and class because we know our constructions have political, cultural, social, and personal consequences for us and for the people we are trying to read. Our democratic nature wants us to read neutrally and our other less controllable side does not because we have been conditioned through decades and even centuries of reading values into otherness. Perhaps you have noticed or even commented on someone's ethnicity, then felt strange about it. This is because we want things that may seem to be mutually exclusive—to acknowledge someone's difference, but not be affected by it. Yet, how can we *not* be affected by something we notice and then think about?

The simple act of noticing that someone's ethnicity is different from your own creates an immediate otherness for both of you. Moreover, with this perception of otherness comes, perhaps, assumptions about that person and about yourself—that you are scarier or smarter or wealthier or poorer. In fact, in the history of America, the fact that we can and do see otherness in our fellow Americans has caused more hardship, violence and death than we can even imagine.

## Definitions of race are always changing.

In the late nineteenth and early twentieth centuries and to some extent afterwards, groups we now think of as ethnic groups were considered racial groups. For instance, at the turn of the century, Jews and Italians were considered racial groups (not ethnic groups). Similarly, fewer than fifty years ago, many places in the South considered anyone to be African American if they had an African-American ancestor; this was called the "one-drop" rule. Because the vast majority of Americans do not think this way now, it may seem difficult to believe that this past existed, but understanding it is crucial in understanding the way things are now.

As casinos bring more money, power and prestige to American Indian reservations and communities, Indian identity has become an increasingly sensitive issue. For some tribes, one must have a certain "blood quantum" level and/or be an enrolled member of a tribe. A hundred years ago, someone with any amount of Indian blood could be imprisoned or killed, but now the same level of "Indianness" that could have gotten you killed in the 1800s might not be enough to enable you to become a member of a tribe.

Race, like gender and class, are fluid texts, so it is important *not* to assume too much about individuals or groups based on what they appear to be.

## Although we claim to be nondiscriminatory now, discriminatory practices in the past have influenced the present social, political, economic, and cultural structure of our country.

This may seem like a highly political statement, and it is. However, the authors believe that discrimination in the past gave the white male majority a head start in this generation; race theorists call this phenomenon "white privilege." As you know, Blacks, Asians, Hispanics and Native Americans were frequently, if not regularly, denied admission to colleges, job interviews, loans, and access to restaurants and hotels and even basic medial service. Affirmative action, the idea that employers and schools should actively seek historically underrepresented individuals to fill their slots, is a response to this phenomenon by ensuring that minorities get fair consideration by employers and admission offices (for the most part, affirmative action does *not* involve a quota system despite misconceptions popularly artic-ulated). But the theory behind affirmative action, looking for ways to engage the past while living in the future in making decisions about schools and employment, is not only a gov-ernment program but a factor in admitting legacies to colleges, incorporating one's progeny into a family business, etc. While preferential treatment may be decried as un-American in some quarters—after all, the Bill of Rights says all men are created equal—the fact is the past has always shaped how people are treated in the present.

What's more, generations of broken promises, abuses of power, and institutional dis-crimination and oppression have left some members of minority communities bitter to-ward institutions of power and law. People are smart. They know that history repeats itself; they know that the past is always present in some form or another. Thus, the reality of slav-ery, the history of American Indian genocide and removal, and the memory of Asian in-ternment, constitute a legacy that still affects how members of these groups see America and its institutions, and it is a legacy that contemporary America must take seriously.

## Race, ethnicity, and gender are political constructions as well as social ones.

We now think of members of so-called races as political groups as well as social ones. If you read about politics, you will notice commentators talking about how a candidate was trying to "appeal to African Americans" or "appeal to women" (or more specific groupings like "soccer moms" or "the Catholic Latino vote"). The recognition that these groups have po-litical power in one sense has empowered members of these groups and given them politi-cal power in ways they may not have had. However, of course, some people within these groups do not want to be identified as group members; it too easily reminds them of the way society constructs their identity negatively. For example, Toni Morrison, the Nobel Prize winning author, has said that she does not want to be thought of as an African American writer but merely as a writer. The tendency, the need, in America to preface any such state-ment with the racial descriptor, goes to show how completely we see race and, perhaps, how often we cannot see past it.

Even more important, the goals of an ethnicity as a whole may not be those of the in-dividual. In fact, it may be impossible to state, with any certainty, what the goals of any one ethnicity may be, as all people are complex and in the process of change. Supreme Court Judge Clarence Thomas will have very different ideas about what African Americans need than will the Reverend Jesse Jackson or Minister Louis Farrakhan, even though all are intelligent, upper class African American men. Which of the three best represents black Americans? That may depend on what group of black Americans you poll.

## Stereotyping occurs as a result of our perceived view of racial or ethnic characteristics.

Unless you are the rare completely neutral human being, someone the authors feel does not exist, you attach stereotypes to groups—even if they seem like stereotypes that are positive, such as all professors are smart, nuns are nice, etc. You may also, without knowing it, hold negative stereotypes. The problem, of course, with all stereotypes is their propensity to attribute group characteristics to individuals. Believing all Jews are smart or all African Americans are athletic can have subsequent negative effects that balance out any positives.

How do we acquire our stereotypes? Some believe stereotypes are based on a grain of truth. That sort of thought makes the authors and others nervous, because the next logical step is thinking that traits or behaviors are inherent or natural. Researchers believe we pick up stereotypes in a variety of ways, including through popular culture and our upbringing. That is why we have stressed throughout this book the importance of looking for treatments of race and ethnicity as they appear—or do not appear—in texts.

There is also disturbing evidence that people mirror stereotyped expectations. As we discuss in the chapter on gender, mainstream American society has a tendency to punish those individuals who operate outside of the perceived norms of a certain group. Thus, stereotypes keep getting reinforced generation after generation, despite efforts from all groups to eradicate them. As the suite in this chapter suggests, many American Indian groups are frustrated by their inability to do much about the sanctioned stereotyping of Native Americans through sports mascots and nicknames. One wonders and worries about what messages these stereotypes send to both Native and non-Native communities—especially children.

## Your view of these issues probably depends on your personal relationships as well as political affiliation.

When surveying the landscape of these issues, we are likely to take our personal experiences and make them universal. If we are white and have African American friends or relatives, not only are we more likely to be more sympathetic to black causes, we are probably going to take the part of the whole for better or worse. If we have no friends of color, and our only exposure is through popular culture and our political affiliations, that too will shape the way we look at race and ethnicity. It is an overgeneralization to be sure, but the authors believe that proximity brings understanding in ways that reading about race and ethnicity can never bring. So does, we believe, actively thinking about the ways we construct race and ethnicity.

Sadly, in the United States, views on race are often influenced by financial concerns. We wonder about the number of people who are critical of immigrants from Latin American countries but whose standard of living relies on illegal immigrant labor. Similarly, in the 1800s, Asians suffered horrible forms of racism, but investors were eager to have them build railroads for almost no money.

## Class is a more crucial element in American life than many people think.

Class also has similar connections to both self-identity and outside reality. Studies show most Americans believe they are middle class. And because there is no set way of determining what someone's class is, a person making $100,000 a year can call himself middle class; so can someone earning $20,000 a year. Are their lives different? Absolutely. However, they may not see that. Of course, class issues run through issues of race and ethnicity, in ways both simple and complex. Some researchers believe that race and ethnicity are mostly a class problem; with the members of ethnic groups disproportionately represented among the nation's poor, there probably is some validity to this claim. However, since the nation has had a long bloody history of clashes between ethnicities of the same class, it is hard to see class as the primary issue in racial or ethnic discrimination.

On the other hand, perceptions of reality can be as strong or stronger than reality itself, and in a capitalist country that tends to link economic prosperity with personal worth, the prevailing perceptions of what groups have more can shape how we see certain people. Thus, while class may not be the primary factor in racial discrimination, it is difficult when talking about race to separate it from issues of class.

The complicated nature of race and ethnicity is reflected here in the selections, which include a variety of perspectives and methodologies to consider.

## ▪▪▪ WORKSHEET ▪▪▪

### This Text

1. While it will be impossible for you to know this fully, try to figure out the writing situation of each author. Who is the audience? What does the author have at stake? What is his or her agenda? *Why* is she or he writing this piece?
2. What social, political, and cultural forces affect the author's text? What is going on in the world as he or she is writing?
3. How does the author define race and ethnicity? Is the definition stated or unstated?
4. When taken as a whole, what do these texts tell you about how we construct race and ethnicity?
5. How do stories and essays differ in their arguments about race and ethnicity?
6. Is the author's argument valid and reasonable?
7. Ideas and beliefs about race and ethnicity tend to be very sensitive, deeply held convictions. Do you find yourself in agreement with the author? Why or why not? Do you agree with the editors' introduction?
8. Does the author help you *read* race and ethnicity better than you did before reading the essay? If so, why? How do we learn to read race and ethnicity?
9. Did you like this? Why or why not?
10. What role does science play in the essay?

### Beyond This Text: Reading Race and Ethnicity

**Media:** How are different ethnicities portrayed in the news or magazine articles? Is the author taking the "part for the whole" (talking to one member of a group as representative of all members of the group)?

**Advertising:** How are different ethnicities portrayed in the print or broadcast ad? Is there anything that "signals" their ethnicity—is clothing used as a "sign" of their color or identity? Is the advertiser using a "rainbow effect" in the ad, appearing to be inclusive by including multiple ethnicities? Does this effect seemed forced or genuine?

**Television:** How are different ethnicities portrayed in a particular television show? Do they conform to predictable stereotypes? Are the people of color more than merely representative? Is there a lone African American or Hispanic American on a mostly white show? One white person on an African-American dominated show? Are the members of different races allowed to date? Does their dating engage the idea of intergroup dating or ignore it?

**Movies:** How are different ethnicities portrayed in the movie? Do they conform to predictable stereotypes? Are the people of color the first to be targeted for death (if it's an action movie)? Are the people of color more than merely representative? Is there a lone African American or Hispanic American in a mostly white movie? One white person in an African-American dominated movie? Are the members of different races allowed to date? Does their dating engage the idea of intergroup dating or ignore it?

## GROWING UP, GROWING APART

■ **Tamar Lewin** ■

*Tamar Lewin wrote this story as part of* The New York Times *series (2000) on "How Race Is Lived in America." It focuses on the experiences of a group of friends of different backgrounds who are facing social pressure to split apart now that they are teenagers.*

BACK IN EIGHTH GRADE, Kelly Regan, Aqeelah Mateen and Johanna Perez-Fox spent New Year's Eve at Johanna's house, swing-dancing until they fell down laughing, banging pots and pans, watching the midnight fireworks beyond the trees in the park at the center of town.

They had been a tight threesome all through Maplewood Middle School—Kelly, a tall, coltish Irish-Catholic girl; Aqeelah, a small, earnest African-American Muslim girl; and Johanna, a light-coffee-colored girl who is half Jewish and half Puerto Rican and famous for knowing just about everyone. It had been a great night, they agreed, a whole lot simpler than Johanna's birthday party three nights before. Johanna had invited all their friends, white and black. But the mixing did not go as she had wished.

"The black kids stayed down in the basement and danced, and the white kids went outside on the stoop and talked," Johanna said. "I went out and said, 'Why don't you guys come downstairs?' and they said they didn't want to, that they just wanted to talk out there. It was just split up, like two parties."

The same thing happened at Kelly's back-to-school party a few months earlier.

"It was so stressful," Kelly said. "There I was, the hostess, and I couldn't get everybody together."

"Oh, man, I was, like, trying to help her," Aqeelah said. "I went up and down and up and down. But it was boring outside, so finally I just gave up and went down and danced."

This year the girls started high school, and what with the difficulty of mixing their black and white friends, none took on the challenge of a birthday party.

It happens everywhere, in the confusions of adolescence and the yearning for identity, when the most important thing in life is choosing a group and fitting in: Black children and white children come apart. They move into separate worlds. Friendships ebb and end.

It happens everywhere, but what is striking is that it happens even here. In a nation of increasingly segregated schools, the South Orange—Maplewood district is extraordinarily mixed. Not only is the student body about half black and half white, but in the last census, blacks had an economic edge. This is the kind of place where people—black and white—talk a lot about the virtues of diversity and worry about white flight, where hundreds will turn out to discuss the book *Why Are All the Black Kids Sitting Together in the Cafeteria?* People here care about race.

But even here, as if pulled by internal magnets, black and white children begin to separate at sixth grade. These are children who walked to school together, learned to read together, slept over at each other's houses. But despite all the personal history, all the community good will, race divides them as they grow up. As racial consciousness develops—and the practice of grouping students by perceived ability sends them on diverging academic paths—race becomes as much a fault line in their world as in the one their parents hoped to move beyond.

As they began high school, Kelly, Johanna and Aqeelah had so far managed to be exceptions. While the world around them had increasingly divided along racial lines, they had stuck together. But where their friendship would go was hard to say. And like a Greek chorus, the voices of other young people warned of tricky currents ahead.

## Different but Inseparable

On her first day at Columbia High School, Kelly Regan took a seat in homeroom and introduced herself to the black boy at the next desk.

"I was trying to be friendly," she explained. "But he answered in like one word, and looked away. I think he just thought I was a normal white person, and that's all he saw."

She certainly looks like a normal white person, with her pale skin and straight brown hair. But in middle school, she trooped with Aqeelah and Johanna to Martin Luther King Association meetings; there were only a handful of white girls, but Kelly says she never felt out of place. "Some people say I'm ghetto," she said, shrugging. "I don't care."

She had always had a mixed group of friends, and since the middle of eighth grade had been dating a mixed-race classmate, Jared Watts. Even so, she expected that it would be harder to make black friends in the ninth grade. "It's not because of the person I am," she said, "it's just how it is."

Kelly's mother, Kathy, is fascinated by her daughter's multiracial world.

"It's so different from how I grew up," said Ms. Regan, a nurse who met Kelly's father, from whom she is divorced, at a virtually all-white Catholic school. "Sometimes, in front of the high school, I feel a little intimidated when I see all the black kids. But then so many of them know me, from my oldest daughter or now from Kelly, and they say such a nice, 'Hi, Mrs. Regan,' that the feeling goes away."

Johanna Perez-Fox is intensely sociable; her mane of long black curls can often be sighted at the center of a rushed gossip session in the last seconds before class. As she sees it, her mixed background gives her a choice of racial identity and access to everybody. "I like that I can go both ways," said Johanna, whose mother is a special-education teacher and whose father owns a car service.

Johanna has a certain otherness among her black friends. "If they say something about white people, they'll always say, 'Oh, sorry, Johanna,' " she said. "I think it's good. It makes them more aware of their stereotypes."

Still, she was put off when a new black friend asked what race she was.

"People are always asking, 'What are you?' and I don't really like it," she said. "I told him I'm half white and half Puerto Rican, and he said, 'But you act black.' I told you can't act like a race. I hate that idea. He defended it, though. He said I would have a point if he'd said African-American, because that's a race, but black is a way of acting. I've thought about it, and I think he's right."

Aqeelah Mateen's parents are divorced, and she lives in a mostly black section of Maplewood with her mother, who works for AT&T. She also sees a lot of her father, a skycap at Newark Airport, and often goes with him to the Newark mosque, where he is an imam.

Aqeelah is a girl of multiple enthusiasms, and in middle school, her gutsy good cheer kept her close to black and white friends alike. But in high school, the issue of "acting black" was starting to become a persistent irritant.

After school one day, Aqeelah and two other black girls were running down the hall when one of them accidentally knocked a corkboard off the wall. Aqeelah told her to pick it up, but the girl kept going.

"What's the matter with you?" Aqeelah asked. "You knocked it over, you pick it up."

"Why do you have to be like a white person?" her friend retorted. "Just leave it there."

But Aqeelah picked it up.

"There's stuff like that all the time, and it gets on my nerves," she said later. "Like at track, in the locker room, there's people telling a Caucasian girl she has a big butt for a white person, and I'm like, 'Who cares, shut up.'"

## On an Even Playground

Johanna and Aqeelah met in kindergarten and have been friends from Day 1; Kelly joined the group in fifth grade.

"Nobody cared about race when we were little," Johanna said. "No one thought about it."

On a winter afternoon at South Mountain Elementary School, that still seemed to be the case. There were white and black pockets, but mostly the playground was a picture postcard of racial harmony, white girls and black girls playing clapping games, black boys and white boys shooting space aliens. And when they were asked about race and friendships, there was no self-consciousness. They just said what they had to say.

"Making friends, it just depends on what you like to do, and who likes to do those things," said Carolyn Goldstein, a white third grader.

"I've known Carolyn G. since kindergarten," said a black girl named Carolyn Morton. "She lives on my block. She's in my class. We even have the same name. We have so many things the same!"

As for how they might be different, Carolyn Goldstein groped for an answer: "Well, she has a mom at home and my mom works, and she has a sister, and I don't."

They know race matters in the world, they said, but not here.

"Some people in some places still feel prejudiced, so I guess it's still a kind of an issue, because Martin Luther King was trying to save the world from slaves and bad people and there still are bad people in jail," Carolyn Morton said, finishing up grandly. "I hope by the year 3000, the world will have peace, and the guys who watch the prisoners can finally go home and spend some time with their families."

## A Shifting Sandbox

All through middle school, Johanna, Kelly and Aqeelah ate lunch together in a corner of the cafeteria where they could see everyone. The main axis of their friendship was changeable: In seventh grade, Johanna and Kelly were the closest. In eighth grade, as Kelly spent more time with Jared, Johanna and Aqeelah were the tightest.

But at the end of middle school, the three were nominated as class "best friends." And while they saw their classmates dividing along racial lines, they tried to ignore it. "In middle school, I didn't want to be aware of the separation," Kelly said. "I didn't see why it had to happen."

Most young people here seem to accept the racial split as inevitable. It's just how it is, they say. Or, it just happens. Or, it's just easier to be with your own kind.

When Sierre Monk, who is black, graduated from South Mountain, she had friends of all races. But since then, she has moved away from the whites and closer to the blacks. Now, in eighth grade, she referred to the shift, sometimes, as "my drift," as in, "After my drift, I began to notice more how the black kids talk differently from the white kids."

Sierre said her drift began after a sixth-grade argument.

"They said, 'You don't even act like you're black,'" she remembered. "I hadn't thought much about it until then, because I was too young. And I guess it was mean what they said, but it helped me. I found I wanted to behave differently after that."

Sierre (pronounced see-AIR-ah) had come from a mostly white private school in Brooklyn. She is the granddaughter of Thelonius Monk, the great jazz pianist, and more than most families, her parents—Thelonius, a drummer, and Gale, who manages her husband's career and father-in-law's estate—have an integrated social life.

For Gale Monk, it has come as something of a surprise to hear Sierre talk about her new distance from her white friends.

What about the bat mitzvah this weekend? Ms. Monk asked.

Well, that's just because we used to be friends, Sierre said.

"What do you mean? She's in and out of this house all the time. I can't remember how many times she's slept over or been in my kitchen."

"That was last year, Mom. This year's different. Things have changed."

And Sierre's mother allows that some separation may be healthy.

"I don't have any problem with the black kids hanging together," she said. "I think you need to know your own group to feel proud of yourself."

There is a consensus that the split is mostly, though hardly exclusively, a matter of blacks' pulling away.

Marian Flaxman, a white girl in Sierre's homeroom, puts it this way: "You know, you come to a new school and you're all little and scared, and everybody's looking for a way to fit in, for people to like them. At that point, I think we were just white kids, blah, and they were just black kids, blah, and we were all just kids. And then a few black kids began thinking, 'Hey, we're black kids.' I think the black kids feel like they're black and the white kids feel like they're white because the black kids feel like they're black."

And Sierre does not really disagree: "Everybody gets along, but I think the white kids are more friendly toward black or interracial kids, and the black kids aren't as interested back, just because of stupid stereotypical stuff like music and style."

What they cannot quite articulate, though, is how much the divide owes to their growing awareness of the larger society, to negative messages about race and about things like violence and academic success. They may not connect the dots, but that sensitivity makes them intensely alert to slights from friends of another race, likely to pull away at even a hint of rejection.

Sometimes it is simply a misread cue, as when a black girl, sitting with other black girls, holds up a hand to greet a white friend, and the white girl thinks her greeting means, "I see you, but don't join us." Sometimes it is an obvious, if oblivious, offense: A black boy drops a white friend after discovering that the friend has told another white boy that the black family's food is weird.

And occasionally, the breach is startlingly painful: A white seventh grader considers changing schools after her best friend tells her she can no longer afford white friends. Months later, the white girl talked uncomfortably about how unreachable her former friend seemed.

"I'm not going to go sit with her at the 'homey' table," she said, then flushed in intense embarrassment: "I'm not sure I'm supposed to say 'homey.' I'm not sure that's what they call themselves; maybe it sounds racist."

And indeed, the black girl believed that some of the things her former friend had said did fall between insensitive and racist.

For their part, both mothers, in identical tones, expressed anger and hurt about how badly their daughters had been treated. Each, again in identical tones, said her daughter had been blameless. But the mothers had never been friends, and like their daughters, never talked about what happened, never heard the other side.

Marian Flaxman went to a mostly black preschool, and several black friends from those days remain classmates. But, she said, it has been years since she visited a black friend's home.

"Sometimes I feel like I'm the only one who remembers that we used to be friends," she said. "Now we don't say hello in the halls, and the most we'd say in class is something like, 'Can I borrow your eraser?' "

Asked if she knew of any close and lasting cross-race friendships, she was stumped, paging through her yearbook and offering up a few tight friendships between white and mixed-race classmates.

Diane Hughes, a New York University psychology professor who lives in South Orange, has studied the changing friendships of children here. In the first year of middle school, she found, black children were only half as likely as they had been two years before to name a white child as a best friend. Whites had fewer black friends to start with, but their friendships changed less. But blacks and whites, on reaching middle school, were only half as likely as third graders to say they had invited a friend of a different race home recently.

By the end of middle school, the separation is profound.

At 10 p.m. on a Friday in October, 153 revved-up 13-year-olds squealed and hugged their way into the South Orange Middle School cafeteria for the Eighth Grade Sleepover. At 11 they were grouped by birthday month, each group to write what they loved about school.

They loved Skittles at lunch . . . the Eighth Grade Sleepover . . . Ms. Wright, the health teacher/basketball coach/Martin Luther King Club adviser. And at the March table, a white boy wrote "interracial friendships."

But the moment the organized activities ended, the black and white eighth graders separated. And at 2 a.m., when the girls' sleeping bags covered the library floor and the boys' the gym, they formed a map of racial boundaries. The borders were peaceful, but there was little commerce across territorial lines. After lights out, some black girls stood and started a clapping chant.

"I can't," one girl called.

"Why not?" the group called back.

"I can't."

"Why not?"

"My back's hurting and my bra's too tight."

It grew louder as other black girls threaded their way through the darkness to join in.
"I can't."

"Why not?"

"I shake my booty from left to right."

Marian, in her green parrot slippers, was in a group of white girls up front, enjoying, listening, but quiet.

"It's cool, when they start stuff like that, or in the lunchroom when they start rumbling on the table and we all pick it up," she said. "It's just louder. One time in class this year, someone was acting up, and when the teacher said sit down, the boy said, 'It's because I'm black, isn't it?' I thought, no, it's not because you're black; that's stupid. It's because you're being really noisy and obnoxious. And it made me feel really white. And then I began thinking, well, maybe it is because he's black, because being noisy may be part of that culture, and then I didn't know what to think."

## Jostling for Position

Aqeelah, Kelly and Johanna refuse to characterize behavior as black or white; they just hate it, they insist, when anyone categorizes them in racial terms.

"I think what makes Kelly and Johanna and me different is that we're what people don't expect," Aqeelah said. "I'm the only Muslim most people know, and one of two African-Americans on my softball team. There's Kelly, a white girl playing basketball, and Johanna, when people ask if she's white or Puerto Rican, saying, 'Both.'"

Most students are acutely aware of the signposts of Columbia High's coexisting cultures. The popular wisdom has it that the black kids dominate football and basketball, the white kids soccer, softball and lacrosse. Black kids throw big dancing parties in rented spaces; white parties are more often in people's homes, with a lot of drinking. Everyone wears jeans, but the white kids are more preppy, the black kids more hip-hop. Black kids listen to Hot 97, a hip-hop station, or WBLS, which plays rhythm and blues; white kids favor rock stations like Z100 or K-Rock.

"I know a lot of Caucasians listen to Hot 97, too," Aqeelah said, "but even if I had a list of 200 Caucasians who listen to it, everyone still thinks it's an African-American thing."

Even though the two cultures are in constant, casual contact—and a few students cross back and forth easily—in the end, they are quite separate.

Jason Coleman, a black graduate who just finished his freshman year at Howard University, remembers how the cultures diverged, separating him from the white boy with whom he once walked to school.

"The summer before high school, we just went different ways," he said. "We listened to different music, we played different sports, we got interested in different girls. And we didn't have much to say to each other anymore. That's the time you begin to develop your own style, and mine was a different style than his."

Jason's style included heavy gold chains, a diamond ear stud, baggy pants and hair in short twists. Asked to define that style, he hesitated, then said, "I guess what bothers me least is if you say that I follow hip-hop fashion."

At the start of high school, much of Jason's energy went toward straddling the divide between hip-hop kid and honors student. He was in frequent physical fights, though never with white students; that doesn't seem to happen. Although blacks are now a slight majority at the school, he, like many of the black students, felt an underlying jostling about who really owns the school. And he felt dismissed, intellectually and socially, by some teachers and classmates.

"African-Americans may be the majority, but I don't think they feel like the majority because they don't feel they get treated fairly," he said. "You see who gets suspended, and it's the African-American kids. I had one friend suspended for eating a bagel in homeroom because his teacher said he had an attitude. That just wouldn't happen to a Caucasian boy. It doesn't have to be a big thing to make you feel like it's not really your school. We can all hold hands and talk about how united we are, but if the next day you run into a girl from your classes at the mall with her mother and she doesn't say hello, what's that?"

To avoid these issues, Jason chose a predominantly black college, Howard, and he seemed relaxed there this year. The gold chains and diamond were gone, and he was studying hard to go to medical school, as his father and brother had.

White students at Columbia High have their own issues. Many feel intimidated by the awareness that they are becoming a minority at the school, that they tend not to share academic classes, or culturally much else, with a lot of the black students. It is striking that while there are usually a few black or multiracial children in the school's white groups, whites rarely enter the black groups. Many white students are reluctant to be quoted about the racial climate, lest they seem racist. But some recent graduates are more forthcoming.

"A lot of the black kids, it was like they had a really big chip on their shoulder, and they were mad at the world and mad at whites for running the world," said Jenn Caviness, a white graduate who attends Columbia University. "One time, in 10th grade, in the hall, this black kid shoved me and said, 'Get out of the way, white crack bitch.' I moved, because he was big, but I was thinking how if I said something racial back, I would have been attacked. It was very polarized sometimes."

She and others, however, say the cultural jockeying has an upside—a freedom from the rigid social hierarchy that plagues many affluent suburban high schools.

"If you're different here, it doesn't matter, because there's so many kinds of differences already," Johanna explained when asked to identify the cool kids, the in crowd. "There's no one best way to be."

In Johanna's commercial art class one day, there was a table of black boys, a table of white girls and a mixed table, where two black girls were humming as they worked. A white girl asked what the song was.

They told her, and she said, "It's really wack."

Yeah, one answered, "You don't know music like we know music."

"Yeah, and you don't know music like I know music."

"I know," the black girl said, smiling. "It's like two completely different tastes."

## Acting Black, Acting White

Aqeelah, Kelly and Johanna did not have many classes together this year, but they had grown up in a shared academic world. While they are not superstars, they do their work and are mostly in honors classes. But if that common ground has so far helped keep them together, the system of academic tracking more often helps pull black and white children apart.

Whenever people talk about race and school, the elephant in the room—rarely mentioned, impossible to ignore—is the racial imbalance that appears when so-called ability grouping begins. Almost all American school districts begin tracking sometime before high school. And when they do, white students are far more likely than blacks to be placed in higher-level classes, based on test scores and teacher recommendations.

Nationwide, by any measure of academic performance, be it grades, tests or graduation rates, whites on average do better than blacks. To some extent, it is a matter of differences in parents' income and education. But the gap remains even when such things are factored out, even in places like this. Experts have no simple explanation, citing a tangle of parents' attitudes, low expectations of mostly white teaching staffs and some white classmates, and negative pressure from black students who believe that doing well isn't cool, that smart is white and street is black.

It can be a vicious circle—and a powerful influence on friendships.

Inevitably, as students notice that honors classes are mostly white and lower-level ones mostly black, they develop a corrosive sense that behaving like honors students is "acting white," while "acting black" demands they emulate lower-level students. Little wonder that sixth grade, when ability grouping starts here, is also when many interracial friendships begin to come apart.

"It sometimes bothers me to see how many of my African-American friends aren't in the higher-level classes, and how they try to be cool around their friends by acting up and trying to be silly and getting in fights," said Sierre, who this year moved up to honors in everything but math. "A lot of them just aren't trying. They're my friends, but I look at them and think, 'Why can't you just be cool and do your work?' "

The district does not release racial breakdowns of its classes. But at Columbia High, which is 45 percent white, ninth-grade honors classes usually seem to be about two-thirds white, middle-level classes more than two-thirds black, and the lowest level—"basic skills"— almost entirely black. The imbalance is at least as great at Marian and Sierre's middle school.

Honors is where students mix most.

"You really see the difference when you're not in honors," said Kelly, who was in middle-level English this year. "In middle level, there aren't so many white kids, and whenever you break into groups, people stick with their own race."

The contrasts are stark. In Aqeelah's mostly white honors history class, the students argued passionately about the nature of man as they compared Hobbes, Locke, Voltaire and Rousseau. But the next period, when the all-black basic-skills class arrived, the students headed to the library to learn how to look up facts for a report on a foreign country.

"I'm still taken aback, shocked, each time I walk into a class and see the complexion," said LuElla Peniston, a black guidance counselor at the school. "It should be more balanced."

The issue has become especially delicate as the district has become progressively blacker, as more students have moved in from poorer neighboring towns with troubled schools, and as the ranking on state tests has slipped. Five years ago, a quarter of the district's children were black; now, with blacks a slight majority, many people worry that the district could tip too far. (Of course, black and white parents tend to have different ideas about how far is too far.)

The schools are still impressive. Columbia High always sends dozens of graduates, black and white, to top colleges. It produced Carla Peterman, a black Rhodes scholar, and Lauryn Hill, the hip-hop star, who still lives in town. This year Columbia had more National Achievement Scholarship semifinalists—an honor for top-scoring black seniors in the National Merit Scholarship Program—than any school in the state. And last year it had an 88 percent passing rate on the state high school proficiency test, three points above average.

Still, in a society that often associates racial minorities with stereotypes of poverty, the district has an image problem. Many parents—whites, but also some blacks—talk nervously about "those kids with the boomboxes out in front of school," and wonder if they should start checking out private schools or another district.

The district's administrators have been grappling with questions of racial balance and ability grouping for years. In middle school, for example, students can temporarily move up a level, to try more challenging work. But the program is used mostly by white families— to push a child or remove him or her from a mostly black classroom—so it has only increased the skew.

Many white parents, Ms. Peniston says, are adamant about not letting their children be anywhere below honors. "They either push very hard to get their children into the level where they want them, or they leave," she said.

It is not an issue only for whites. Many black parents worry that the schools somehow associate darker-skinned children with lower-level classes.

When Kelly's boyfriend, Jared Watts, transferred from South Orange Middle School to Maplewood Middle, he was placed in lower-level classes, something his parents discovered only on parents' night.

"There were all these African-American families, asking all these basic questions," said Jared's mother, Debby Watts. "I looked around and realized they'd put him in the wrong group. I was so upset I made my husband do the calling the next day. They moved him up right away. But you can't help but wonder if it would have happened if he'd been white."

Sierre Monk's parents are watching her grades, and thinking that unless she is put in honors classes in high school next year, they will move her to private school.

Sierre says she is comfortable with her white honors classmates, even if her best friends now are black.

"I feel friendly to a lot of the white kids, and still e-mail some of them," she said. As she sees it, she can be a good student without compromising her African-American credentials. Not everyone, she observes, has been so culturally dextrous.

"A lot of people think of the black kids in the top classes, the ones who don't hang out with a lot of African-Americans, as the 'white' black kids," she said. "I'd never say it to them, but in my head I call them the white black kids, too."

Still, she said, she was happiest in her middle-level math class, where every student but one was black.

"It's my favorite, because I can do well there without struggling," she said. "And I feel closest to that class, because I have so many friends there. Once I was waiting outside, alone, when I heard a group of white kids talking about, 'Oh, those kids in Level 3, they must be stupid.' I don't want to associate with people who think like that."

## Fissures, Chasms, Islands

It was hard for Aqeelah, Kelly and Johanna to get together this year. They had different lunch periods, different study halls. Only Johanna and Kelly had any classes together. Johanna was on the varsity swim team, Kelly was on the ninth-grade basketball team and Aqeelah ran indoor track. The three could go weeks without getting together.

But they were still close. In the fall, when Johanna had big news to share about a boy she liked, she was on two phone lines simultaneously, telling Kelly and Aqeelah the latest.

When they finally met for dinner at Arturo's Pizza in November, their pleasure in being together was visible.

Aqeelah was a little late, so Kelly chose an orange soda for her. When she arrived, they were their usual frisky selves, waving to everyone who walked by and talking about the old friends they didn't see anymore and the new people they felt friendly with but would not yet ask to the movies.

They were still in giggle mode when Aqeelah said, "I get made fun of by everybody," and Johanna broke in, "Why, because you're short?" and they collapsed into laughter.

But a second later, Aqeelah was not laughing. She had her head down and her eyes covered, and when she looked up, a tear was leaking down her cheek.

"No, it's really confusing this year," she said. "I'm too white to be black, and I'm too black to be white. If I'm talking to a white boy, a black kid walks by and says, 'Oh, there's Aqeelah, she likes white boys.' And in class, these Caucasian boys I've been friends with for years say hi, and then the next thing they say is, 'Yo, Aqeelah, what up?' as if I won't understand them unless they use that kind of slang. Or they'll tell me they really like 'Back That Thing Up' by Juvenile. I don't care if they like a rapper, but it seems like they think that's the only connection they have with me.

"Last year this stuff didn't bother me, but now it does bother me, because some of the African-American kids, joking around, say I'm an Oreo."

Johanna and Kelly were surprised by her pain; they had not heard this before. But they did sense her increasing distance from them.

"It's like she got lost or something," Kelly said. "I never see her."

Aqeelah had always been the strongest student of the three, the only one in a special math class, one rung above honors. But by winter, she was getting disappointing grades, especially in history, and beginning to worry about being moved down a level. Math was not going so well either, and so she dropped track to focus on homework. She was hoping to make the softball team, and disappointed that neither of her friends was trying out. "I'll never see you," she complained.

All three, of course, have always had other friends, and they still did.

Much of Kelly's social life was with her racially mixed lunch group. She felt herself moving further from some of her white friends, the ones who hang out only with whites. "It seems like they have their whole clique," she said, and she was not terribly interested in them. Against the grain, she was still working to make friends with blacks, particularly with a basketball teammate.

Johanna found herself hanging out more with blacks, much as her older sister had—though not her brother, a college freshman whose high school friends were mostly white.

"In middle school, there were black and white tables in the cafeteria and everything, but people talked together in the hallways," Johanna said. "Now there's so many people, you don't even say hi to everybody, and sometimes it seems like the black and white people live in such different worlds that they wouldn't know how to have fun together anymore."

The three girls celebrated separately this New Year's Eve—Kelly with Jared, Johanna at a party with her family, Aqeelah at her father's mosque for Ramadan.

Kelly still tried to bring them together. One Friday night, she called Johanna and Aqeelah on the spur of the moment, and they came over in their pajamas. And at Kelly's last basketball game, in late February, Johanna and Aqeelah sat and joked with Jared, Kelly's mother, her grandmother and little brother.

The next day Kelly and Jared broke up. Kelly said she was sad and working hard to keep up her friendship with Jared, but that's about all she was saying.

And as spring arrived, Kelly, Johanna and Aqeelah acknowledged that, at least for now, their threesome had pretty much become a twosome.

Johanna and Kelly were still very tight, and did something together almost every weekend. But these days Aqeelah talked most to a black girl, a longtime family friend. It was partly logistics: Aqeelah would run into her daily at sixth period and after school, at her locker.

"I don't know why I don't call Johanna or Kelly," she said. "They'll always have the place in my heart, but not so much physically in my life these days. It seems like I have no real friends this year. You know how you can have a lot of friends, but you have no one? Everyone seems to be settled in their cliques and I'm just searching. And the more I get to know some people, the more I want to withdraw. I'm spending a lot more time with my family this year."

It's not that Aqeelah was falling apart. She was still her solid self, with all her enthusiasms—for *Dawson's Creek,* movies, and the Friday noon service at the mosque. But increasingly, the gibes about being too white were getting to her. One day, walking to class with a black boy who is an old friend, she blew up when he told her she had "white people's hair."

"I just began screaming, 'What's wrong with these people in this school?' and everyone stared at me like I was crazy," she said. "Everyone, every single person, gets on my nerves."

## Lessons and Legacies

The story of Aqeelah, Kelly and Johanna is still unfolding. But those who have gone before know something about where they may be headed.

Aqeelah's struggle is deeply familiar to Malika Oglesby, who arrived from a mostly white school in Virginia in fifth grade and quickly found white friends. Several black boys began to follow her around, taunting her. Lowering her eyes, she recited the chant that plagued her middle-school years: "Cotton candy, sweet as gold, Malika is an Oreo."

"I don't think I knew what it meant the first time, but I figured it out pretty fast," she said.

Jenn Caviness, one of her white friends from that time, clearly remembers Malika's pain.

"Malika was in tears every other day, they just tormented her," she said. "We all felt very protective, but we didn't know how to stop it."

Malika felt powerless, too.

"I didn't tell my parents about it, I didn't tell my sister, but it was a hard time," she said. "If you'd asked me about it at the time, I would have said that there was absolutely no issue at all about my having chosen all those white friends. But that's not true. By the end of seventh grade, I was starting to be uncomfortable. Everybody was having little crushes on everybody among my friends, but of course nobody was having a crush on me. I began to feel like I was falling behind, I was just the standby."

The summer before high school, she eased into a black social group.

"I found a black boyfriend, and I kind of lost contact with everyone else," said Malika, who now attends Howard.

And yet, when Malika finished talking about her Oreo problem, when Jason recalled his fighting days, when others finished describing difficult racial experiences, a strange thing happened. They looked up, unprompted, and said how much they loved the racial mix here and the window it opened onto a different culture.

"Columbia High School was so important and useful to me," said Jenn, immediately after recounting how she had been pushed in the hall by a black boy. "It shaped a lot of parts of my personality."

She and the others remembered a newfound ease as high school was ending, when the racial divide began to fade.

"Senior year was wonderful, when the black kids and the white kids got to be friends again, and the graduation parties where everyone mixed," said Malika. "It was so much better."

Many parents say that is a common pattern.

"It is an ebb and flow," said Carol Barry-Austin, the biracial mother of three African-American children. "Middle-school kids need time to separate and feel comfortable in their racial identity, and then they can come back together. I remember when I wanted to give my oldest daughter a sweet-16 party, she said no, because she couldn't mix her black and white friends. But by the time she got to a graduation party, she could."

This year, among the seniors, there was a striking friendship between Jordan BarAm, the white student council president, and Ari Onugha, the black homecoming king.

They met in ninth grade when Jordan was running for class president and knew he needed the black vote. Ari, he had heard, was the coolest kid in school, and he went to him in such a low-key and humorous way that Ari was happy to help out. From that unlikely start, a genuine friendship began when both were in Advanced Placement physics the next year.

This year they had several Advanced Placement classes together, and they talked on the phone most nights, Jordan said, "about everything"—homework, girls, college. Ari was admitted to the University of Pennsylvania's Wharton School and Jordan to Harvard.

"No one looking at me would ever think I'm in Advanced Placement," said Ari, who wears baggy Girbaud pants, a pyramid ring and a big metal watch. "Most of the black kids in the honors classes identify with white culture. I'm more comfortable in black culture, with kids who dress like me and talk like me and listen to the same music I do."

Ari and Jordan have a real friendship, but one with limits. On weekends, Ari mostly hangs out with black friends from lower-level classes, Jordan with a mostly white group of top students. When Ari and his friends performed a wildly successful hip-hop dance routine at the Martin Luther King Association fashion show, Jordan, like most white students, did not go. And when Jordan and his friends put together a fund-raising dance for a classmate with multiple sclerosis, Ari did not show up.

"We've tried to get him to white parties, everyone wants him there, but he either doesn't come or doesn't stay long," Jordan said.

Jordan thinks a lot about race and has been active in school groups to promote better racial understanding—something he has tried unsuccessfully to draw Ari into.

And while Ari often visits Jordan's home, Jordan has only rarely, and briefly, been to Ari's. Ari laughed. "Hey, dude, you could come."

**READING** WRITING

## THIS TEXT: READING

1. How do others treat Kelly Regan, Aqeelah Mateen and Johanna Perez-Fox? From your own experience, where do you think their attitude toward their friendship comes?

2.  What is the semiotic situation here? In what ways are outsiders "reading" this group of friends, individually and as a group? In what way are the insiders doing this reading? What signs do the friends display? How do others assign readings to these groups?

3.  How would you describe the writing approach Lewin takes? Is there another way she could have told this story? Is this approach effective in approaching questions of identity? Why or why not?

4.  This article is part of a series by *The New York Times* on "How Race Is Lived in America." Why do you think the *Times* devoted time and energy to this question at this point in American history?

## YOUR TEXT: WRITING

1.  Writing from your own experience, was there a time when you let others decide who your friends were? Was this decision based on a particular reading of this person?

2.  Do you remember when you first realized that others were different from you in appearance? Who had influence in helping you determining this?

3.  Do you think this essay represents a particular reality in American today? What encourages us to be close to others who may not look like us? What discourages us?

---

| IN LIVING COLOR: RACE AND AMERICAN CULTURE<br><br>■ **Michael Omi** ■ | *Michael Omi is a scholar who often writes about race and ethnicity. In this argumentative essay (1989), he takes on the stereotypes television "speaks" in when it talks about race* |

*and ethnicity.*

IN FEBRUARY 1987, Assistant Attorney General William Bradford Reynolds, the nation's chief civil rights enforcer, declared that the recent death of a black man in Howard Beach, New York and the Ku Klux Klan attack on civil rights marchers in Forsyth County, Georgia were "isolated" racial incidences. He emphasized that the places where racial conflict could potentially flare up were "far fewer now than ever before in our history," and concluded that such a diminishment of racism stood as "a powerful testament to how far we have come in the civil rights struggle."[1]

Events in the months following his remarks raise the question as to whether we have come quite so far. They suggest that dramatic instances of racial tension and violence merely constitute the surface manifestations of a deeper racial organization of American society—a system of inequality which has shaped, and in turn been shaped by, our popular culture.

In March, the NAACP released a report on blacks in the record industry entitled "The Discordant Sound of Music." It found that despite the revenues generated by black performers, blacks remain "grossly underrepresented" in the business, marketing, and A&R (Artists and Repertoire) departments of major record labels. In addition, few blacks are

---

[1]Reynold's remarks were made at a conference on equal opportunity held by the bar association in Orlando, Florida. *The San Francisco Chronicle* (7 Februaury 1987).

employed as managers, agents, concert promoters, distributors, and retailers. The report concluded that:

> The record industry is overwhelmingly segregated and discrimination is rampant. No other industry in America so openly classifies its operations on a racial basis. At every level of the industry, beginning with the separation of black artists into a special category, barriers exist that severely limit opportunities for blacks.[2]

Decades after the passage of civil rights legislation and the affirmation of the principle of "equal opportunity," patterns of racial segregation and exclusion, it seems, continue to characterize the production of popular music.

The enduring logic of Jim Crow is also present in professional sports. In April, Al Campanis, vice president of player personnel for the Los Angeles Dodgers, explained to Ted Koppel on ABC's *Nightline* about the paucity of blacks in baseball front offices and as managers. "I truly believe," Campanis said, "that [blacks] may not have some of the necessities to be, let's say, a field manager or perhaps a general manager." When pressed for a reason, Campanis offered an explanation which had little to do with the structure of opportunity of institutional discrimination within professional sports:

> [W]hy are black men or black people not good swimmers? Because they don't have the buoyancy. . . . They are gifted with great musculature and various other things. They're fleet of foot. And this is why there are a lot of black major league ballplayers. Now as far as having the background to become club presidents, or presidents of a bank, I don't know.[3]

Black exclusion from the front office, therefore, was justified on the basis of biological "difference."

The issue of race, of course, is not confined to the institutional arrangements of popular culture production. Since popular culture deals with the symbolic realm of social life, the images which it creates, represents, and disseminates contribute to the overall racial climate. They become the subject of analysis and political scrutiny. In August, the National Ethnic Coalition of Organizations bestowed the "Golden Pit Awards" on television programs, commercials, and movies that were deemed offensive to racial and ethnic groups: *Saturday Night Live,* regarded by many media critics as a politically "progressive" show, was singled out for the "Platinum Pit Award" for its comedy skit "Ching Chang" which depicted a Chinese storeowner and his family in a derogatory manner.[4]

These examples highlight the *overt* manifestations of racism in popular culture—institutional forms of discrimination which keep racial minorities out of the production and organization of popular culture, and the crude racial caricatures by which these groups are portrayed. Yet racism in popular culture is often conveyed in a variety of implicit, and at times invisible, ways. Political theorist Stuart Hall makes an important distinction between *overt* racism, the elaboration of an explicitly racist argument, policy, or view, and *inferential* racism which refers to "those apparently naturalized representations of events and situa-

---

[2]Economic Development Department of the NAACP, "The Discordant Sound of Music (A Report on the Record Industry)," (Baltimore, Maryland: The NAACP, 1987), pp. 16–17.

[3]Campanis's remarks on *Nightline* were reprinted in *The San Francisco Chronicle* (April 9, 1987).

[4]Ellen Wulfhorst, "TV Sterotyping: It's the 'Pits,'" *The San Francisco Chronicle* (August 24, 1987).

tions relating to race, whether 'factual' or 'fictional,' which have racist premises and propositions inscribed in them as a set of *unquestioned assumptions.*" He argues that inferential racism is more widespread, common, and indeed insidious since "it is largely *invisible* even to those who formulate the world in its terms."[5]

Race itself is a slippery social concept which is paradoxically both "obvious" and "invisible." In our society, one of the first things we notice about people when we encounter them (along with their sex/gender) is their *race.* We utilize race to provide clues about *who* a person is and *how* we should relate to her/him. Our perception of race determines our "presentation of *self,*" distinctions in status, and appropriate modes of conduct in daily and institutional life. This process is often unconscious; we tend to operate off of an unexamined set of *racial beliefs.*

Racial beliefs account for and explain variations in "human nature." Differences in skin color and other obvious physical characteristics supposedly provide visible clues to more substantive differences lurking underneath. Among other qualities, temperament, sexuality, intelligence, and artistic and athletic ability are presumed to be fixed and discernible from the palpable mark of race. Such diverse questions as our confidence and trust in others (as salespeople, neighbors, media figures); our sexual preferences and romantic images; our tastes in music, film, dance, or sports; indeed our very ways of walking and talking are ineluctably shaped by notions of race.

Ideas about race, therefore, have become "common sense"—a way of comprehending, explaining, and acting in the world. This is made painfully obvious when someone disrupts our common sense understandings. An encounter with someone who is, for example, racially "mixed" or of a racial/ethnic group we are unfamiliar with becomes a source of discomfort for us, and momentarily creates a crisis of racial meaning. We also become disoriented when people do not act "black," "Latino," or indeed "white." The content of such stereotypes reveals a series of unsubstantiated beliefs about who these groups are, what they are like, and how they behave.

The existence of such racial consciousness should hardly be surprising. Even prior to the inception of the republic, the United States was a society shaped by racial conflict. The establishment of the Southern plantation economy, Western expansion, and the emergence of the labor movement, among other significant historical developments, have all involved conflicts over the definition and nature of the *color line.* The historical results have been distinct and different groups have encountered unique forms of racial oppression—Native Americans faced genocide, blacks were subjected to slavery, Mexicans were invaded and colonized, and Asians faced exclusion. What is common to the experiences of these groups is that their particular "fate" was linked to historically specific ideas about the significance and meaning of race.[6] Whites defined them as separate "species," ones inferior to Northern European cultural stocks, and thereby rationalized the conditions of their subordination in the economy, in political life, and in the realm of culture.

A crucial dimension of racial oppression in the United States is the elaboration of an ideology of difference or "otherness." This involves defining "us" (i.e., white Americans) in

---

[5]Stuart Hall, "The Whites of Their Eyes: Racist Ideologies and the Media," in George Bridges and Rosalind Brunt, eds., *Silver Linings* (London: Lawrence and Wishart, 1981), pp. 36–37.

[6]For an excellent survey of racial beliefs see Thomas F. Gossett, *Race: The History of an Idea in America* (New York: Shocken Books, 1965).

opposition to "them," an important task when distinct racial groups are first encountered, or in historically specific periods where preexisting racial boundaries are threatened or crumbling.

Political struggles over the very definition of who an "American" is illustrates this process. The Naturalization Law of 1790 declared that only free *white* immigrants could qualify, reflecting the initial desire among Congress to create and maintain a racially homogeneous society. The extension of eligibility to all racial groups has been a long and protracted process. Japanese, for example, were finally eligible to become naturalized citizens after the passage of the Walter-McCarran Act of 1952. The ideological residue of these restrictions in naturalization and citizenship laws is the equation within popular parlance of the term "American" with "white," while other "Americans" are described as black, Mexican, "Oriental," etc.

Popular culture has been an important realm within which racial ideologies have been created, reproduced, and sustained. Such ideologies provide a framework of symbols, concepts, and images through which we understand, interpret, and represent aspects of our "racial" existence.

Race has often formed the central themes of American popular culture. Historian W. L. Rose notes that it is "curious coincidence" that four of the "most popular reading-viewing events in all American history" have in some manner dealt with race, specifically black/white relations in the south.[7] Harriet Beecher Stowe's *Uncle Tom's Cabin,* Thomas Ryan Dixon's *The Clansman* (the inspiration for D. W. Griffith's *The Birth of a Nation*), Margaret Mitchell's *Gone with the Wind* (as a book and film), and Alex Haley's *Roots* (as a book and television miniseries), each appeared at a critical juncture in American race relations and helped to shape new understandings of race.

Emerging social definitions of race and the "real American" were reflected in American popular culture of the nineteenth century. Racial and ethnic stereotypes were shaped and reinforced in the newspapers, magazines, and pulp fiction of the period. But the evolution and ever-increasing sophistication of visual mass communications throughout the twentieth century provided, and continue to provide, the most dramatic means by which racial images are generated and reproduced.

Film and television have been notorious in disseminating images of racial minorities which establish for audiences what these groups look like, how they behave, and, in essence, "who they are." The power of the media lies not only in their ability to reflect the dominant racial ideology, but in their capacity to shape that ideology in the first place. D. W. Griffith's aforementioned epic *Birth of a Nation,* a sympathetic treatment of the rise of the Ku Klux Klan during Reconstruction, helped to generate, consolidate, and "nationalize" images of blacks which had been more disparate (more regionally specific, for example) prior to the film's appearance.[8]

In television and film, the necessity to define characters in the briefest and most condensed manner has led to the perpetuation of racial caricatures, as racial stereotypes serve as shorthand for scriptwriters, directors, and actors. Television's tendency to address the

---

[7]W.L. Rose, *Race and Region in American Historical Fiction: Four Episodes in Popular Culture* (Oxford: Clarendon Press, 1979).

[8]Melanie Martindale-Sikes, "Nationalizing 'Nigger' Imagery Through *Birth of a Nation,*" paper prepared for the 73rd Annual Meeting of the American Sociological Association (September 4–8, 1978) in San Francisco.

"lowest common denominator" in order to render programs "familiar" to an enormous and diverse audience leads it regularly to assign and reassign racial characteristics to particular groups, both minority and majority.

Many of the earliest American films deal with racial and ethnic "difference." The large influx of "new immigrants" at the turn of the century led to a proliferation of negative images of Jews, Italians, and Irish which were assimilated and adapted by such films as Thomas Edison's *Cohen's Advertising Scheme* (1904). Based on an old vaudeville routine, the film featured a scheming Jewish merchant, aggressively hawking his wares. Though stereotypes of these groups persist to this day,[9] by the 1940s many of the earlier ethnic stereotypes had disappeared from Hollywood. But, as historian Michael Winston observes, the outsiders of the 1890s remained: the ever-popular Indian of the Westerns; the inscrutable or sinister Oriental; the sly, but colorful Mexican; and the clowning or submissive Negro.[10]

In many respects the Western as a genre has been paradigmatic in establishing images of racial minorities in film and television. The classic scenario involves the encircled wagon train or surrounded fort from which whites bravely fight off fierce bands of Native American Indians. The point of reference and viewer identification lies with those huddled within the circle the representatives of civilization who valiantly attempt to ward off the forces of barbarism. In the classic Western, as writer Tom Engelhardt observes, the viewer is forced behind the barrel of a repeating rifle and it is from that position, through its gun sights, that he receives a picture history of Western colonialism and imperialism.[11]

Westerns have indeed become the prototype for European and American excursions throughout the Third World. The cast of characters may change, but the story remains the same. The humanity of whites is contrasted with the brutality and treachery of nonwhites; brave (i.e., white) souls are pitted against the merciless hordes in conflicts ranging from Indians against the British Lancers to Zulus against the Boers. What Stuart Hall refers to as the imperializing white eye provides the framework for these films, lurking outside the frame and yet seeing and positioning everything within; it is the unmarked position from which observations are made and from which, alone, they make sense.[12]

Our common sense assumptions about race and racial minorities in the United States are both generated and reflected in the stereotypes presented by the visual media. In the crudest sense, it could be said that such stereotypes underscore white superiority by reinforcing the traits, habits, and predispositions of nonwhites which demonstrate their inferiority. Yet a more careful assessment of racial stereotypes reveals intriguing trends and seemingly contradictory themes.

While all racial minorities have been portrayed as less than human, there are significant differences in the images of different groups. Specific racial minority groups, in spite of their often interchangeable presence in films steeped in the Western paradigm, have distinct and often unique qualities assigned to them. Latinos are portrayed as being prone toward vi-

---

[9]For a discussion of Italian, Irish, Jewish, Slavic, and German stereotypes in film, see Randall M. Miller, ed., *The Kaleidoscopic Lens: How Hollywood Views Ethnic Groups* (Englewood, N.J.: Jerome S. Ozer, 1980).

[10]Michael R. Winston, "Racial Consciousness and the Evolution of Mass Communications in the United States," *Daedalus,* vol. III, No. 4 (Fall 1982).

[11]Tom Engelhardt, "Ambush at Kamikaze Pass," in Emma Gee, ed., *Counterpoint: Perspectives on Asian America* (Los Angeles: Asian American Studies Center, UCLA, 1976), p. 270.

[12]Hall, "Whites of Their Eyes," p. 38.

olent outbursts of anger; blacks as physically strong, but dim-witted; while Asians are seen as sneaky and cunningly evil. Such differences are crucial to observe and analyze. Race in the United States is not reducible to black/white relations. These differences are significant for a broader understanding of the patterns of race in America, and the unique experience of specific racial minority groups.

It is somewhat ironic that *real* differences which exist within a racially defined minority group are minimized, distorted, or obliterated by the media. All Asians look alike, the saying goes, and indeed there has been little or no attention given to the vast differences which exist between, say, the Chinese and Japanese with respect to food, dress, language, and culture. This blurring within popular culture has given us supposedly Chinese characters who wear kimonos; it is also the reason why the fast-food restaurant McDonald's can offer Shanghai McNuggets with teriyaki sauce. Other groups suffer a similar fate. Professor Gretchen Bataille and Charles Silet find the cinematic Native American of the Northeast wearing the clothing of the Plains Indians, while living in the dwellings of Southwestern tribes:

The movie men did what thousands of years of social evolution could not do, even what the threat of the encroaching white man could not do; Hollywood produced the homogenized Native American, devoid of tribal characteristics or regional differences.[13]

The need to paint in broad racial strokes has thus rendered "internal" differences invisible. This has been exacerbated by the tendency for screenwriters to "invent" mythical Asian, Latin American, and African countries. Ostensibly done to avoid offending particular nations and peoples, such a subterfuge reinforces the notion that all the countries and cultures of a specific region are the same. European countries retain their distinctiveness, while the Third World is presented as one homogeneous mass riddled with poverty and governed by ruthless and corrupt regimes.

While rendering specific groups in a monolithic fashion, the popular cultural imagination simultaneously reveals a compelling need to distinguish and articulate "bad" and "good" variants of particular racial groups and individuals. Thus each stereotypic image is filled with contradictions: The bloodthirsty Indian is tempered with the image of the noble savage; the *bandido* exists along with the loyal sidekick; and Fu Manchu is offset by Charlie Chan. The existence of such contradictions, however, does not negate the one-dimensionality of these images, nor does it challenge the explicit subservient role of racial minorities. Even the "good" person of color usually exists as a foil in novels and films to underscore the intelligence, courage, and virility of the white male hero.

Another important, perhaps central, dimension of racial minority stereotypes is sex/gender differentiation. The connection between race and sex has traditionally been an explosive and controversial one. For most of American history, sexual and marital relations between whites and nonwhites were forbidden by social custom and by legal restrictions. It was not until 1967, for example, that the U.S. Supreme Court ruled that antimiscegenation laws were unconstitutional. Beginning in the 1920s, the notorious Hays Office, Hollywood's attempt at self-censorship, prohibited scenes and subjects which dealt with miscegenation. The prohibition, however, was not evenly applied in practice. White men could seduce racial mi-

---

[13]Gretchen Bataille and Charles Silet, "The Entertaining Anachronism: Indians in American Film," in Randall M. Miller, ed., *Kaleidoscopic Lens*, p. 40.

nority women, but white women were not to be romantically or sexually linked to racial minority men.

Women of color were sometimes treated as exotic sex objects. The sultry Latin temptress—such as Dolores Del Rio and Lupe Velez—invariably had boyfriends who were white North Americans; their Latino suitors were portrayed as being unable to keep up with the Anglo–American competition. From Mary Pickford as Cho-Cho San in *Madame Butterfly* (1915) to Nancy Kwan in *The World of Suzie Wong* (1961), Asian women have often been seen as the gracious "geisha girl" or the prostitute with a "heart of gold," willing to do anything to please her man.

By contrast, Asian men, whether cast in the role of villain, servant, sidekick, or kung fu master, are seen as asexual or, at least, romantically undesirable. As Asian American studies professor Elaine Kim notes, even a hero such as Bruce Lee played characters whose "single-minded focus on perfecting his fighting skills precludes all other interests, including an interest in women, friendship, or a social life."[14]

The shifting trajectory of black images over time reveals an interesting dynamic with respect to sex and gender. The black male characters in *The Birth of a Nation* were clearly presented as sexual threats to "white womanhood." For decades afterwards, however, Hollywood consciously avoided portraying black men as assertive or sexually aggressive in order to minimize controversy. Black men were instead cast as comic, harmless, and nonthreatening figures exemplified by such stars as Bill "Bojangles" Robinson, Stepin Fetchit, and Eddie "Rochester" Anderson. Black women, by contrast, were divided into two broad character types based on color categories. Dark black women such as Hattie McDaniel and Louise Beavers were cast as "dowdy, frumpy, dumpy, overweight mammy figures"; while those "close to the white ideal," such as Lena Horne and Dorothy Dandridge, became "Hollywood's treasured mulattoes" in roles emphasizing the tragedy of being of mixed blood.[15]

It was not until the early 1970s that tough, aggressive, sexually assertive black characters, both male and female, appeared. The "blaxploitation" films of the period provided new heroes (e.g., *Shaft, Superfly, Coffy,* and *Cleopatra Jones*) in sharp contrast to the submissive and subservient images of the past. Unfortunately, most of these films were shoddy productions which did little to create more enduring "positive" images of blacks, either male or female.

In contemporary television and film, there is a tendency to present and equate racial minority groups and individuals with specific social problems. Blacks are associated with drugs and urban crime, Latinos with "illegal" immigration, while Native Americans cope with alcoholism and tribal conflicts. Rarely do we see racial minorities "out of character," in situations removed from the stereotypic arenas in which scriptwriters have traditionally embedded them. Nearly the only time we see young Asians and Latinos of either sex, for example, is when they are members of youth gangs, as *Boulevard Nights* (1979), *Year of the Dragon* (1985), and countless TV cop shows can attest to.

Racial minority actors have continually bemoaned the fact that the roles assigned them on stage and screen are often one-dimensional and imbued with stereotypic assumptions.

---

[14]Elaine Kim, "Asian Americans and American Popular Culture" in Hyung-Chan Kim, ed., *Dictionary of Asian American History* (New York: Greenwood Press, 1986), p. 107.

[15]Donald Bogle, "A Familiar Plot (A Look at the History of Blacks in American Movies)," *The Crisis,* Vol. 90, No. 1 (January 1983), p. 15.

In theater, the movement toward "blind casting" (i.e., casting actors for roles without regard to race) is a progressive step, but it remains to be seen whether large numbers of audiences can suspend their "beliefs" and deal with a Latino King Lear or an Asian Stanley Kowalski. By contrast, white actors are allowed to play anybody. Though the use of white actors to play blacks in "black face" is clearly unacceptable in the contemporary period, white actors continue to portray Asian, Latino, and Native American characters on stage and screen.

Scores of Charlie Chan films, for example, have been made with white leads (the last one was the 1981 *Charlie Chan and the Curse of the Dragon Queen*). Roland Winters, who played Chan in six features, was once asked to explain the logic of casting a white man in the role of Charlie Chan: "The only thing I can think of is, if you want to cast a homosexual in a show, and you get a homosexual, it'll be awful. It won't be funny . . . and maybe there's something there."[16]

Such a comment reveals an interesting aspect about myth and reality in popular culture. Michael Winston argues that stereotypic images in the visual media were not originally conceived as representations of reality, nor were they initially understood to be "real" by audiences. They were, he suggests, ways of "coding and rationalizing" the racial hierarchy and interracial behavior. Over time, however, "a complex interactive relationship between myth and reality developed, so that images originally understood to be unreal, through constant repetition began to *seem* real."[17]

Such a process consolidated, among other things, our "common sense" understandings of what we think various groups should look like. Such presumptions have led to tragicomical results. Latinos auditioning for a role in a television soap opera, for example, did not fit the Hollywood image of "real Mexicans" and had their faces bronzed with powder before filming because they looked too white. Model Aurora Garza said, "I'm a real Mexican and very dark anyway. I'm even darker right now because I have a tan. But they kept wanting to make my face darker and darker."[18]

Historically in Hollywood, the fact of having "dark skin" made an actor or actress potentially adaptable for numerous "racial" roles. Actress Lupe Velez once commented that she had portrayed "Chinese, Eskimos, Japs, squaws, Hindus, Swedes, Malays, and Japanese."[19] Dorothy Dandridge, who was the first black woman teamed romantically with white actors, presented a quandary for studio executives who weren't sure what race and nationality to make her. They debated whether she should be a "foreigner," an island girl, or a West Indian.[20] Ironically, what they refused to entertain as a possibility was to present her as what she really was, a black American woman.

The importance of race in popular culture is not restricted to the visual media. In popular music, race and race consciousness has defined, and continues to define, formats, musical communities, and tastes. In the mid-1950s, the secretary of the North Alabama White Citizens Council declared that "Rock and roll is a means of pulling the white man down to

---

[16]Frank Chin, "Confessions of the Chinatown Cowboy," *Bulletin of Concerned Asian Scholars,* Vol. 4, No. 3 (Fall 1972).

[17]Winston, "Racial Consciousness," p. 176.

[18]*The San Francisco Chronicle,* September 21, 1984.

[19]Quoted in Allen L. Woll, "Bandits and Lovers: Hispanic Images in American Film," in Miller, ed., *Kaleidoscopic Lens,* p. 60.

[20]Bogle, "Familiar Plot," p. 17.

the level of the Negro."[21] While rock may no longer be popularly regarded as a racially sub-versive musical form, the very genres of contemporary popular music remain, in essence, thinly veiled racial categories. "R & B" (Rhythm and Blues) and "soul" music are clearly references to *black* music, while Country & Western or heavy metal music are viewed, in the popular imagination, as *white* music. Black performers who want to break out of this artistic ghettoization must "cross over," a contemporary form of "passing" in which their music is seen as acceptable to white audiences.

The airwaves themselves are segregated. The designation "urban contemporary" is merely radio lingo for a "black" musical format. Such categorization affects playlists, advertising ac-counts, and shares of the listening market. On cable television, black music videos rarely receive airplay on MTV, but are confined instead to the more marginal BET (Black Entertainment Television) network.

In spite of such segregation, many performing artists have been able to garner a racially diverse group of fans. And yet, racially integrated concert audiences are extremely rare. Curiously, this "perverse phenomenon" of racially homogeneous crowds takes place despite the color of the performer. Lionel Richie's concert audiences, for example, are virtually all-white, while Teena Marie's are all-black.[22]

Racial symbols and images are omnipresent in popular culture. Commonplace house-hold objects such as cookie jars, salt and pepper shakers, and ashtrays have frequently been designed and fashioned in the form of racial caricatures. Sociologist Steve Dublin in an analysis of these objects found that former tasks of domestic service were symbolically trans-ferred onto these commodities.[23] An Aunt Jemima-type character, for example, is used to hold a roll of paper towels, her outstretched hands supporting the item to be dispensed. "Sprin-kle Plenty," a sprinkle bottle in the shape of an Asian man, was used to wet clothes in prepa-ration for ironing. Simple commodities, the household implements which help us perform everyday tasks, may reveal, therefore, a deep structure of racial meaning.

A crucial dimension for discerning the meaning of particular stereotypes and images is the *situation context* for the creation and consumption of popular culture. For example, the setting in which "racist" jokes are told determines the function of humor. Jokes about blacks where the teller and audience are black constitute a form of self-awareness; they allow blacks to cope and "take the edge off" of oppressive aspects of the social order which they commonly confront. The meaning of these same jokes, however, is dramatically transformed when told across the "color line." If a white, or even black, person tells these jokes to a white audience, it will, despite its "purely" humorous intent, serve to reinforce stereotypes and rationalize the existing relations of racial inequality.

Concepts of race and racial images are both overt and implicit within popular culture—the organization of cultural production, the products themselves, and the manner in which they are consumed are deeply structured by race. Particular racial meanings, stereotypes, and myths can change, but the presence of a system of racial meanings and stereotypes, of racial ideology, seems to be an enduring aspect of American popular culture.

---

[21]Dave Marsh and Kevin Stein, *The Book of Rock Lists* (New York: Dell Publishing Co., 1981), p. 8.

[22]*Rock & Roll Confidential,* No. 44 (February 1987), p. 2.

[23]Steven C. Dublin, "Symbolic Slavery: Black Representations in Popular Culture," *Social Problems*, Vol. 34, No. 2 (April 1987).

The era of Reaganism and the overall rightward drift of American politics and culture has added a new twist to the question of racial images and meanings. Increasingly, the problem for racial minorities is not that of misportrayal, but of "invisibility." Instead of celebrating racial and cultural diversity, we are witnessing an attempt by the right to define, once again, who the "real" American is, and what "correct" American values, mores, and political beliefs are. In such a context, racial minorities are no longer the focus of sustained media attention; when they do appear, they are cast as colored versions of essentially "white" characters.

The possibilities for change—for transforming racial stereotypes and challenging institutional inequities—nonetheless exist. Historically, strategies have involved the mobilization of political pressure against an offending institution(s). In the late 1950s, for instance, "Nigger Hair" tobacco changed its name to "Bigger Hare" due to concerted NAACP pressure on the manufacturer. In the early 1970s, Asian American community groups successfully fought NBC's attempt to resurrect Charlie Chan as a television series with white actor Ross Martin. Amidst the furor generated by Al Campanis's remarks cited at the beginning of this essay, Jesse Jackson suggested that a boycott of major league games be initiated in order to push for a restructuring of hiring and promotion practices.

Partially in response to such action, Baseball Commissioner Peter Ueberroth announced plans in June 1987 to help put more racial minorities in management roles. "The challenge we have," Ueberroth said, "is to manage change without losing tradition."[24] The problem with respect to the issue of race and popular culture, however, is that the *tradition* itself may need to be thoroughly examined, its "common sense" assumptions unearthed and challenged, and its racial images contested and transformed.

## READING WRITING

### THIS TEXT: READING

1. Omi's work engages popular culture actively and takes it seriously. Why do you think Omi thinks television is important to write about?
2. From what perspective is Omi writing? Do you think the problems he identifies in 1987 are still around today?
3. Who do you think is Omi's intended audience? Do you think they watch television?

### YOUR TEXT: WRITING

1. Watch an evening of television and note the presence of race and ethnicity. Do the same issues come up? Do you think things have changed since 1987? Why or why not? Write a paper assessing the status of race and ethnicity in American television, focusing either on a particular show or evening of television.
2. What stereotypes generally remain present in American television? Are the same stereotypes present in American movies? If stereotypes in movies and television are different, what differences between the two media do you think account for the difference in portrayals?
3. Take a television show you like and note how it treats those of different ethnicities. Do these portrayals show an understanding of members of these groups or rely on previously held ideas about them?

---

[24]*The San Francisco Chronicle* (June 13, 1987).

**MOTHER TONGUE**

——————

■ **Amy Tan** ■

*Amy Tan is the well-known author of* The Joy Luck Club *and other novels. In this 1991 piece, she writes about her experiences with her mother and her mother's use of language.*

I AM NOT A SCHOLAR of English or literature. I cannot give you much more than personal opinions on the English language and its variations in this country or others.

I am a writer. And by that definition, I am someone who has always loved language. I am fascinated by language in daily life. I spend a great deal of my time thinking about the power of language—the way it can evoke an emotion, a visual image, a complex idea, or a simple truth. Language is the tool of my trade. And I use them all—all the Englishes I grew up with.

Recently, I was made keenly aware of the different Englishes I do use. I was giving a talk to a large group of people, the same talk I had already given to half a dozen other groups. The nature of the talk was about my writing, my life, and my book, *The Joy Luck Club.* The talk was going along well enough, until I remembered one major difference that made the whole talk sound wrong. My mother was in the room. And it was perhaps the first time she had heard me give a lengthy speech, using the kind of English I have never used with her. I was saying things like, "The intersection of memory upon imagination" and "There is an aspect of my fiction that relates to thus-and-thus"—a speech filled with carefully wrought grammatical phrases, burdened, it suddenly seemed to me, with nominalized forms, past perfect tenses, conditional phrases, all the forms of standard English that I had learned in school and through books, the forms of English I did not use at home with my mother.

Just last week, I was walking down the street with my mother, and I again found myself conscious of the English I was using, the English I do use with her. We were talking about the price of new and used furniture and I heard myself saying this: "Not waste money that way." My husband was with us as well, and he didn't notice any switch in my English. And then I realized why. It's because over the twenty years we've been together I've often used that same kind of English with him, and sometimes he even uses it with me. It has become our language of intimacy, a different sort of English that relates to family talk, the language I grew up with.

So you'll have some idea of what this family talk I heard sounds like, I'll quote what my mother said during a recent conversation which I videotaped and then transcribed. During this conversation, my mother was talking about a political gangster in Shanghai who had the same last name as her family's, Du, and how the gangster in his early years wanted to be adopted by her family, which was rich by comparison. Later, the gangster became more powerful, far richer than my mother's family, and one day showed up at my mother's wedding to pay his respects. Here's what she said in part: "Du Yusong having business like fruit stand. Like off the street kind. He is Du like Du Zong—but not Tsung-ming Island people. The local people call putong, the river east side, he belong to that side local people. That man want to ask Du Zong father take him in like become own family. Du Zong father wasn't look down on him, but didn't take seriously, until that man big like become a mafia. Now important person, very hard to inviting him. Chinese way, came only to show respect, don't stay for dinner. Respect for making big celebration, he shows up. Mean gives lots of respect. Chinese custom. Chinese social life that way. If too important won't have to stay too long. He come to my wedding. I didn't see, I heard it. I gone to boy's side, they have YMCA dinner. Chinese age I was nineteen."

You should know that my mother's expressive command of English belies how much she actually understands. She reads the Forbes report, listens to Wall Street Week, converses daily with her stockbroker, reads all of Shirley MacLaine's books with ease—all kinds of things I can't begin to understand. Yet some of my friends tell me they understand 50 percent of what my mother says. Some say they understand 80 to 90 percent. Some say they understand none of it, as if she were speaking pure Chinese. But to me, my mother's English is perfectly clear, perfectly natural. It's my mother tongue. Her language, as I hear it, is vivid, direct, full of observation and imagery. That was the language that helped shape the way I saw things, expressed things, made sense of the world.

Lately, I've been giving more thought to the kind of English my mother speaks. Like others, I have described it to people as "broken" or "fractured" English. But I wince when I say that. It has always bothered me that I can think of no way to describe it other than "broken," as if it were damaged and needed to be fixed, as if it lacked a certain wholeness and soundness. I've heard other terms used, "limited English," for example. But they seem just as bad, as if everything is limited, including people's perceptions of the limited English speaker.

I know this for a fact, because when I was growing up, my mother's "limited" English limited my perception of her. I was ashamed of her English. I believed that her English reflected the quality of what she had to say. That is, because she expressed them imperfectly her thoughts were imperfect. And I had plenty of empirical evidence to support me: the fact that people in department stores, at banks, and at restaurants did not take her seriously, did not give her good service, pretended not to understand her, or even acted as if they did not hear her.

My mother has long realized the limitations of her English as well. When I was fifteen, she used to have me call people on the phone to pretend I was she. In this guise, I was forced to ask for information or even to complain and yell at people who had been rude to her. One time it was a call to her stockbroker in New York. She had cashed out her small portfolio and it just so happened we were going to go to New York the next week, our very first trip outside California. I had to get on the phone and say in an adolescent voice that was not very convincing, "This is Mrs. Tan."

And my mother was standing in the back whispering loudly, "Why he don't send me check, already two weeks late. So mad he lie to me, losing me money."

And then I said in perfect English, "Yes, I'm getting rather concerned. You had agreed to send the check two weeks ago, but it hasn't arrived."

Then she began to talk more loudly. "What he want, I come to New York tell him front of his boss, you cheating me?" And I was trying to calm her down, make her be quiet, while telling the stockbroker, "I can't tolerate any more excuses. If I don't receive the check immediately, I am going to have to speak to your manager when I'm in New York next week." And sure enough, the following week there we were in front of this astonished stockbroker, and I was sitting there red-faced and quiet, and my mother, the real Mrs. Tan, was shouting at his boss in her impeccable broken English.

We used a similar routine just five days ago, for a situation that was far less humorous. My mother had gone to the hospital for an appointment, to find out about a benign brain tumor a CAT scan had revealed a month ago. She said she had spoken very good English, her best English, no mistakes. Still, she said, the hospital did not apologize when they said they had lost the CAT scan and she had come for nothing. She said they did not seem to have any sympathy when she told them she was anxious to know the exact diagnosis, since her husband and son had both died of brain tumors. She said they would not give her any more information until the next time and she would have to make another appointment for that. So she said she would not leave until the doctor called her daughter. She wouldn't budge. And when the doctor finally called her daughter, me, who spoke in perfect English—lo and be-hold—we had assurances the CAT scan would be found, promises that a conference call on Monday would be held, and apologies for any suffering my mother had gone through for a most regrettable mistake.

I think my mother's English almost had an effect on limiting my possibilities in life as well. Sociologists and linguists probably will tell you that a person's developing language skills are more influenced by peers. But I do think that the language spoken in the family, es-pecially in immigrant families which are more insular, plays a large role in shaping the lan-guage of the child. And I believe that it affected my results on achievement tests, IQ tests, and the SAT. While my English skills were never judged as poor, compared to math, English could not be considered my strong suit. In grade school I did moderately well, getting perhaps B's, sometimes B-pluses, in English and scoring perhaps in the sixtieth or seventieth percentile on achievement tests. But those scores were not good enough to override the opinion that my true abilities lay in math and science, because in those areas I achieved A's and scored in the ninetieth percentile or higher.

This was understandable. Math is precise; there is only one correct answer. Whereas, for me at least, the answers on English tests were always a judgment call, a matter of opin-ion and personal experience. Those tests were constructed around items like fill-in-the-blank sentence completion, such as, "Even though Tom was _____, Mary thought he was _____." And the correct answer always seemed to be the most bland combinations of thoughts, for example, "Even though Tom was shy, Mary thought he was charming," with the grammati-cal structure "even though" limiting the correct answer to some sort of semantic opposites, so you wouldn't get answers like, "Even though Tom was foolish, Mary thought he was ridicu-lous." Well, according to my mother, there were very few limitations as to what Tom could have been and what Mary might have thought of him. So I never did well on tests like that.

The same was true with word analogies, pairs of words in which you were supposed to find some sort of logical, semantic relationship—for example, "Sunset is to nightfall as _____ is to _____." And here you would be presented with a list of four possible pairs, one of which showed the same kind of relationship: red is to stoplight, bus is to arrival, chills is to fever, yawn is to boring. Well, I could never think that way. I knew what the tests were asking, but I could not block out of my mind the images already created by the first pair, "sunset is to nightfall"—and I would see a burst of colors against a darkening sky, the moon rising, the lowering of a curtain of stars. And all the other pairs of words—red, bus, stop-light, boring—just threw up a mass of confusing images, making it impossible for me to sort out something as logical as saying: "A sunset precedes nightfall" is the same as "a chill pre-cedes a fever." The only way I would have gotten that answer right would have been to imag-ine an associative situation, for example, my being disobedient and staying out past sunset, catching a chill at night, which turns into feverish pneumonia as punishment, which indeed did happen to me.

I have been thinking about all this lately, about my mother's English, about achieve-ment tests. Because lately I've been asked, as a writer, why there are not more Asian Ameri-cans represented in American literature. Why are there few Asian Americans enrolled in creative writing programs? Why do so many Chinese students go into engineering? Well, these are broad sociological questions I can't begin to answer. But I have noticed in sur-veys—in fact, just last week—that Asian students, as a whole, always do significantly better on math achievement tests than in English. And this makes me think that there are other

Asian-American students whose English spoken in the home might also be described as "broken" or "limited." And perhaps they also have teachers who are steering them away from writing and into math and science, which is what happened to me.

Fortunately, I happen to be rebellious in nature and enjoy the challenge of disproving assumptions made about me. I became an English major my first year in college, after being enrolled as pre-med. I started writing nonfiction as a freelancer the week after I was told by my former boss that writing was my worst skill and I should hone my talents toward account management.

But it wasn't until 1985 that I finally began to write fiction. And at first I wrote using what I thought to be wittily crafted sentences, sentences that would finally prove I had mastery over the English language. Here's an example from the first draft of a story that later made its way into *The Joy Luck Club,* but without this line: "That was my mental quandary in its nascent state." A terrible line, which I can barely pronounce.

Fortunately, for reasons I won't get into today, I later decided I should envision a reader for the stories I would write. And the reader I decided upon was my mother, because these were stories about mothers. So with this reader in mind—and in fact she did read my early drafts—I began to write stories using all the Englishes I grew up with: the English I spoke to my mother, which for lack of a better term might be described as "simple"; the English she used with me, which for lack of a better term might be described as "broken"; my translation of her Chinese, which could certainly be described as "watered down"; and what I imagined to be her translation of her Chinese if she could speak in perfect English, her internal language, and for that I sought to preserve the essence, but neither an English nor a Chinese structure. I wanted to capture what language ability tests can never reveal: her intent, her passion, her imagery, the rhythms of her speech and the nature of her thoughts.

Apart from what any critic had to say about my writing, I knew I had succeeded where it counted when my mother finished reading my book and gave me her verdict: "So easy to read."

## READING WRITING

### THIS TEXT: READING

1. Tan points out that language is a sign for others trying to read her mother. What other non-visual elements might be signs? How do we normally read them?
2. Talk about the way we discuss or react to people with accents. Why do accents mark, or set off as different, people? Is there any established non-marked way of speaking? Who speaks this way?
3. How do you think Tan feels about the situation in which she is placed by having to serve as her mother's "agent"? Is there a way around it?

### YOUR TEXT: WRITING

1. Write an essay talking about ways we mark people as different through non-visual means though popular culture. What forms of popular culture are especially guilty of this?
2. One of the things that Tan's essay brings up is the idea of Americanness. How should we define such a concept? Are there degrees of Americanness? Research and see what others say about this.
3. In what way is this piece an argument? What is Tan arguing? In your own work, use a story to argue a particular point.

# TRUE TALES OF AMERIKKKAN HISTORY PART II: THE TRUE THANKSGIVING

■ **Jim Mahfood** ■

*Jim Mahfood is a comic artist who often takes on stereotypes and race in his work. Here is his 1998 response to popular ideas about Thanksgiving.*

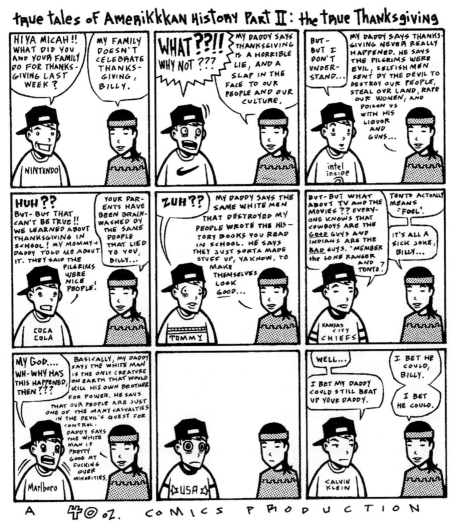

Source: *Stupid Comics* © 1998 by Jim Mahfood

READING WRITING

## THIS TEXT: READING

1. If you have read Scott McCloud's piece, what do you think he would say about this cartoon? In what ways does the reader participate in making meaning here?
2. Compare Mahfood's approach to Handsome Lake's, another piece concerned with Native American issues.
3. What other subtext does Mahfood address with the boy's t-shirt? With the girl's Native American garb? Are these relevant to the main storyline? Why or why not?
4. What perspective do you think Mahfood is writing/drawing from? What do you think is motivating his writing?
5. Who do you think is Mahfood's audience? Does your answer depend on consideration of the medium he's using?

## YOUR TEXT: WRITING

1. Find a political cartoon and analyze it in terms of signs.
2. Write a short essay discussing why visual texts can communicate ideas effectively. You might compare a visual text and written text that have similar ideas but present them differently.
3. How does your previous experience with comics affect your ability to take political cartoons seriously? Write a short essay making the case for teaching visual culture at an early age.

---

### WHY ARE ALL THE BLACK KIDS SITTING TOGETHER IN THE CAFETERIA?

#### ■ Beverly Daniel Tatum ■

*Beverly Tatum is a psychologist who writes about race and race relations in America. This essay is taken in part from her book,* Why Are All the Black Kids Sitting Together in the Cafeteria? And Other Conversations About Race *(1999). Here she argues that both teachers and students need to talk actively about race, especially in the teen-age years when identity is being formed.*

WALK INTO ANY RACIALLY MIXED high school cafeteria at lunch time and you will instantly notice an identifiable group of black students sitting together. Conversely, there are many white students sitting together, though we rarely comment about that. The question is "Why are the black kids sitting together?"

It doesn't start out that way. In racially mixed elementary schools, you often see children of diverse racial boundaries playing with one another, sitting at the snack table together, crossing racial boundaries with an ease uncommon in adolescence.

Moving from elementary school to middle school means interacting with new children from different neighborhoods than before, and a certain degree of clustering by race might therefore be expected, presuming that children who are familiar with one another would form groups. But even in schools where the same children stay together from kindergarten through eighth grade, racial grouping begins by the sixth or seventh grade. What happens?

One thing that happens is puberty. As children enter adolescence, they begin to explore the question of identity, asking "Who am I? Who can I be?" in ways they have not done before. For black youths, asking "Who am I?" includes thinking about "Who I am ethnically? What does it mean to be black?"

Why do black youths, in particular, think about themselves in terms of race? Because that is how the rest of the world thinks of them. Our self-perceptions are shaped by the messages we receive from those around us, and when young black men and women reach adolescence, the racial content of those messages intensifies.

Here is a case in point. If you were to ask my 10-year-old son, David, to describe himself, he would tell you many things: that he is smart, that he likes to play computer games, that he has an older brother. Near the top of his list, he would likely mention that he is tall for his age. He would probably not mention that he is black, though he certainly knows that he is. Why would he mention his height and not his racial group membership?

When David meets new adults, one of the first questions they ask is "How old are you?" When David states his age, the inevitable reply is, "Gee, you're tall for your age!"

It happens so frequently that I once overheard David say to someone, "Don't say it, I know. I'm tall for my age." Height is salient for David because it's salient for others.

When David meets new adults, they don't say, "Gee, you're black for your age!" Or do they?

Imagine David at 15, six-foot-two, wearing the adolescent attire of the day, passing adults he doesn't know on the sidewalk. Do the women hold their purses a little tighter, maybe even cross the street to avoid him? Does he hear the sound of automatic door locks on cars as he passes by? Is he being followed around by the security guards at the local mall? Do strangers assume he plays basketball? Each of these experiences conveys a racial message.

At 10, race is not yet salient for David, because it's not yet salient for society. But it will be.

## Understanding Racial Identity Development

Psychologist William Cross, author of *Shades of Black: Diversity in African American Identity,* has offered a theory of racial identity development that I have found to be a very useful framework for understanding what is happening with those black students in the cafeteria. In the first stage of Cross's five-stage model, the black child absorbs many of the beliefs and values of the dominant white culture, including the idea that it's better to be white.

Simply as a function of being socialized in a Eurocentric culture, some black children may begin to value the role models, lifestyles and images of beauty represented by the dominant group more highly than those of their own cultural group. But the personal and social significance of one's racial group membership has not yet been realized, and racial identity is not yet under examination.

## The Encounter Stage

Transition to the next stage, the encounter stage, is typically precipitated by an event—or series of events—that forces the young person to acknowledge the personal impact of racism.

For example, in racially mixed schools, black children are much more likely to be in a lower track than in an honors track. Such apparent sorting along racial lines sends a message about what it means to be black. One young honors student said, "It was really a very paradoxical existence, here I am in a school that's 35 percent black, you know, and I'm the only black in my class. That always struck me as odd. I guess I felt that I was different from the other blacks because of that."

There are also changes in the social dynamics outside the school. In racially mixed communities, you begin to see what I call the "birthday party effect." The parties of elementary school children may be segregated by gender, but not by race. At puberty, when the parties become sleepovers or boy–girl events, they become less and less racially diverse.

Black girls who live in predominantly white neighborhoods see their white friends start to date before they do. One young woman from a Philadelphia suburb described herself as "pursuing white guys throughout high school" to no avail. Because there were no black boys in her class, she had little choice. She would feel "really pissed off" that those same white boys would date her white friends.

Another young black woman attending a desegregated school to which she was bussed was encouraged by a teacher to attend the upcoming school dance. Most of the black students did not live in the neighborhood and seldom attended the extracurricular activities. The young woman indicated that she wasn't planning to come. Finally the well-intentioned teacher said, "Oh come on, I know you people love to dance." This young woman got the message.

## Coping with Encounter

What do these encounters have to do with the cafeteria? Do experiences with racism inevitably result in so-called self-segregation?

While a desire to protect oneself from further offense is understandable, it's not the only factor at work. Imagine the young eighth-grade girl who experienced the teacher's use of "you people" and the dancing stereotype as a racial affront. Upset and struggling with adolescent embarrassment, she bumps into a white friend who can see that something is wrong. She explains. Her white friend responds—perhaps in an effort to make her feel better—and says, "Oh, Mr. Smith is such a nice guy, I'm sure he didn't mean it like that. Don't be so sensitive."

Perhaps the white friend is right, but imagine your own response when you are upset, and your partner brushes off your complaint, attributing it to your being oversensitive. What happens to your emotional thermostat? It escalates. When feelings, rational or irrational, are invalidated, most people disengage. They not only choose to discontinue the conversation but are more likely to turn to someone who will understand their perspective.

In much the same way that the eighth-grade girl's white friend doesn't get it, the girls at the "black table" do. Not only are black adolescents encountering racism and reflecting on their identity, but their white peers—even if not racist—are unprepared to respond in supportive ways.

The black students turn to each other for the much needed support they are not likely to find anywhere else.

We need to understand that in racially mixed settings, racial grouping is a developmental process in response to an environmental stressor, racism. Joining with one's peers for support in the face of stress is a positive coping strategy. The problem is that our young people are operating with a very limited definition of what it means to be black, based largely on cultural stereotypes.

## READING WRITING

### THIS TEXT: READING

1.  Do you find yourself personally involved (or implicated) in Tatum's analysis? How do you think she would respond to your response?
2.  In what ways is Tatum performing a semiotic analysis of the idea of race? In what ways have race and ethnicity contributed to "semiotic situations" in your own life?
3.  Where does her analysis fit into what we traditionally think of as the American Dream?
4.  Why is the cafeteria such an important location for a discussion like this? What happens in a cafeteria that might not happen in a classroom?

### YOUR TEXT: WRITING

1.  Using your own experiences, write an essay about the role race and ethnicity have played—or didn't play—in your experiences growing up.
2.  Tatum's essay balances personal experience with research; do you think this method of writing is effective? Why or why not? Do you think this is important for this type of topic? Why or why not?
3.  Can you think of a personal topic that would benefit from a combined research/personal approach?

---

### THE SPORTS TABOO

■ **Malcolm Gladwell** ■

*Malcolm Gladwell is a writer for* The New Yorker *who often writes about social issues. In this essay (1997) he uses an analogy to describe the relationship between perceived race and sports achievement.*

**1.**

THE EDUCATION OF ANY ATHLETE BEGINS, in part, with an education in the racial taxonomy of his chosen sport—in the subtle, unwritten rules about what whites are supposed to be good at and what blacks are supposed to be good at. In football, whites play quarterback and blacks play running back; in baseball whites pitch and blacks play the outfield. I grew up in Canada, where my brother Geoffrey and I ran high-school track, and in Canada the rule of running was that anything under the quarter-mile belonged to the West Indians. This didn't mean that white people didn't run the sprints. But the expectation was that they would never win, and, sure enough, they rarely did. There was just a handful of West Indian immigrants in Ontario at that point—clustered in and around Toronto—but they owned Canadian sprinting, setting up under the stands at every major championship, cranking up the reggae on their boom boxes, and then humiliating everyone else on the track. My brother and I weren't from Toronto, so we weren't part of that scene. But our West Indian heritage meant that we got to share in the swagger. Geoffrey was a magnificent runner, with powerful legs and a barrel chest, and when he was warming up he used to do that exaggerated, slow-motion jog that the white guys would try to do and never quite pull off. I was a miler, which was a little outside the West Indian range. But, the way I figured it, the rules meant that no one should ever outkick me over the final two hundred metres of any race. And in the golden summer of my fourteenth year, when my running career prematurely peaked, no one ever did.

When I started running, there was a quarter-miler just a few years older than I was by the name of Arnold Stotz. He was a bulldog of a runner, hugely talented, and each year that he moved through the sprinting ranks he invariably broke the existing four-hundred-metre record in his age class. Stotz was white, though, and every time I saw the results of a big track meet I'd keep an eye out for his name, because I was convinced that he could not keep winning. It was as if I saw his whiteness as a degenerative disease, which would eventually claim and cripple him. I never asked him whether he felt the same anxiety, but I can't imagine that he didn't. There was only so long that anyone could defy the rules. One day, at the provincial championships, I looked up at the results board and Stotz was gone.

Talking openly about the racial dimension of sports in this way, of course, is considered unseemly. It's all right to say that blacks dominate sports because they lack opportunities elsewhere. That's the "Hoop Dreams" line, which says whites are allowed to acknowledge black athletic success as long as they feel guilty about it. What you're not supposed to say is what we were saying in my track days—that we were better because we were black, because of something intrinsic to being black. Nobody said anything like that publicly last month when Tiger Woods won the Masters or when, a week later, African men claimed thirteen out of the top twenty places in the Boston Marathon. Nor is it likely to come up this month, when African-Americans will make up eighty per cent of the players on the floor for the N.B.A. playoffs. When the popular television sports commentator Jimmy (the Greek) Snyder did break this taboo, in 1988—infamously ruminating on the size and significance of black thighs—one prominent N.A.A.C.P. official said that his remarks "could set race relations back a hundred years." The assumption is that the whole project of trying to get us to treat each other the same will be undermined if we don't all agree that under the skin we actually are the same.

The point of this, presumably, is to put our discussion of sports on a par with legal notions of racial equality, which would be a fine idea except that civil-rights law governs matters like housing and employment and the sports taboo covers matters like what can be said about someone's jump shot. In his much heralded new book *Darwin's Athletes,* the University of Texas scholar John Hoberman tries to argue that these two things are the same, that it's impossible to speak of black physical superiority without implying intellectual inferiority. But it isn't long before the argument starts to get ridiculous. "The spectacle of black athleticism," he writes, inevitably turns into "a highly public image of black retardation." Oh, really? What, exactly, about Tiger Woods's victory in the Masters resembled "a highly public image of black retardation"? Today's black athletes are multimillion-dollar corporate pitchmen, with talk shows and sneaker deals and publicity machines and almost daily media opportunities to share their thoughts with the world, and it's very hard to see how all this contrives to make them look stupid. Hoberman spends a lot of time trying to inflate the significance of sports, arguing that how we talk about events on the baseball diamond or the track has grave consequences for how we talk about race in general. Here he is, for example, on Jackie Robinson:

> The sheer volume of sentimental and intellectual energy that has been invested in the mythic saga of Jackie Robinson has discouraged further thinking about what his career did and did not accomplish. . . . Black America has paid a high and largely unacknowledged price for the extraordinary prominence given the black athlete rather than other black men of action (such as military pilots and astronauts), who represent modern aptitudes in ways that athletes cannot.

Please. Black America has paid a high and largely unacknowledged price for a long list of things, and having great athletes is far from the top of the list. Sometimes a baseball player is just a baseball player, and sometimes an observation about racial difference is just an observation about racial difference. Few object when medical scientists talk about the significant epidemiological differences between blacks and whites—the fact that blacks have a higher incidence of hypertension than whites and twice as many black males die of diabetes and prostate cancer as white males, that breast tumors appear to grow faster in black women than in white women, that black girls show signs of puberty sooner than white girls. So why aren't we allowed to say that there might be athletically significant differences between blacks and whites?

According to the medical evidence, African-Americans seem to have, on the average, greater bone mass than do white Americans—a difference that suggests greater muscle mass. Black men have slightly higher circulating levels of testosterone and human-growth hormone than their white counterparts, and blacks overall tend to have proportionally slimmer hips, wider shoulders, and longer legs. In one study, the Swedish physiologist Bengt Saltin compared a group of Kenyan distance runners with a group of Swedish distance runners and found interesting differences in muscle composition: Saltin reported that the Africans appeared to have more blood-carrying capillaries and more mitochondria (the body's cellular power plant) in the fibres of their quadriceps. Another study found that, while black South African distance runners ran at the same speed as white South African runners, they were able to use more oxygen—eighty-nine per cent versus eighty-one per cent—over extended periods: somehow, they were able to exert themselves more. Such evidence suggested that there were physical differences in black athletes which have a bearing on activities like running and jumping, which should hardly come as a surprise to anyone who follows competitive sports.

To use track as an example—since track is probably the purest measure of athletic ability—Africans recorded fifteen out of the twenty fastest times last year in the men's ten-thousand-metre event. In the five thousand metres, eighteen out of the twenty fastest times were recorded by Africans. In the fifteen hundred metres, thirteen out of the twenty fastest times were African, and in the sprints, in the men's hundred metres, you have to go all the way down to the twenty-third place in the world rankings—to Geir Moen, of Norway—before you find a white face. There is a point at which it becomes foolish to deny the fact of black athletic prowess, and even more foolish to banish speculation on the topic. Clearly, something is going on. The question is what.

## 2.

If we are to decide what to make of the differences between blacks and whites, we first have to decide what to make of the word "difference," which can mean any number of things. A useful case study is to compare the ability of men and women in math. If you give a large, representative sample of male and female students a standardized math test, their mean scores will come out pretty much the same. But if you look at the margins, at the very best and the very worst students, sharp differences emerge. In the math portion of an achievement test conducted by Project Talent—a nationwide survey of fifteen-year-olds—there were 1.3 boys for every girl in the top ten per cent, 1.5 boys for every girl in the top five per cent, and seven boys for every girl in the top one per cent. In the fifty-six-year history of the

Putnam Mathematical Competition, which has been described as the Olympics of college math, all but one of the winners have been male. Conversely, if you look at people with the very lowest math ability, you'll find more boys than girls there, too. In other words, although the average math ability of boys and girls is the same, the distribution isn't: there are more males than females at the bottom of the pile, more males than females at the top of the pile, and fewer males than females in the middle. Statisticians refer to this as a difference in variability.

This pattern, as it turns out, is repeated in almost every conceivable area of gender difference. Boys are more variable than girls on the College Board entrance exam and in routine elementary-school spelling tests. Male mortality patterns are more variable than female patterns; that is, many more men die in early and middle age than women, who tend to die in more of a concentrated clump toward the end of life. The problem is that variability differences are regularly confused with average differences. If men had higher average math scores than women, you could say they were better at the subject. But because they are only more variable the word "better" seems inappropriate.

The same holds true for differences between the races. A racist stereotype is the assertion of average difference—it's the claim that the typical white is superior to the typical black. It allows a white man to assume that the black man he passes on the street is stupider than he is. By contrast, if what racists believed was that black intelligence was simply more variable than white intelligence, then it would be impossible for them to construct a stereotype about black intelligence at all. They wouldn't be able to generalize. If they wanted to believe that there were a lot of blacks dumber than whites, they would also have to believe that there were a lot of blacks smarter than they were. This distinction is critical to understanding the relation between race and athletic performance. What are we seeing when we remark black domination of elite sporting events—an average difference between the races or merely a difference in variability?

This question has been explored by geneticists and physical anthropologists, and some of the most notable work has been conducted over the past few years by Kenneth Kidd, at Yale. Kidd and his colleagues have been taking DNA samples from two African Pygmy tribes in Zaire and the Central African Republic and comparing them with DNA samples taken from populations all over the world. What they have been looking for is variants—subtle differences between the DNA of one person and another—and what they have found is fascinating. "I would say, without a doubt, that in almost any single African population—a tribe or however you want to define it—there is more genetic variation than in all the rest of the world put together," Kidd told me. In a sample of fifty Pygmies, for example, you might find nine variants in one stretch of DNA. In a sample of hundreds of people from around the rest of the world, you might find only a total of six variants in that same stretch of DNA—and probably every one of those six variants would also be found in the Pygmies. If everyone in the world was wiped out except Africans, in other words, almost all the human genetic diversity would be preserved.

The likelihood is that these results reflect Africa's status as the homeland of Homo sapiens: since every human population outside Africa is essentially a subset of the original African population, it makes sense that everyone in such a population would be a genetic subset of Africans, too. So you can expect groups of Africans to be more variable in respect to almost anything that has a genetic component. If, for example, your genes control how you react to aspirin, you'd expect to see more Africans than whites for whom one aspirin stops a bad headache, more for whom no amount of aspirin works, more who are allergic to aspirin, and more who need to take, say, four aspirin at a time to get any benefit—but far fewer Africans for whom the standard two-aspirin dose would work well. And to the extent that running is influenced by genetic factors you would expect to see more really fast blacks—and more really slow blacks—than whites but far fewer Africans of merely average speed. Blacks are like boys. Whites are like girls.

There is nothing particularly scary about this fact, and certainly nothing to warrant the kind of gag order on talk of racial differences which is now in place. What it means is that comparing elite athletes of different races tells you very little about the races themselves. A few years ago, for example, a prominent scientist argued for black athletic supremacy by pointing out that there had never been a white Michael Jordan. True. But, as the Yale anthropologist Jonathan Marks has noted, until recently there was no black Michael Jordan, either. Michael Jordan, like Tiger Woods or Wayne Gretzky or Cal Ripken, is one of the best players in his sport not because he's like the other members of his own ethnic group but precisely because he's not like them—or like anyone else, for that matter. Elite athletes are elite athletes because, in some sense, they are on the fringes of genetic variability. As it happens, African populations seem to create more of these genetic outliers than white populations do, and this is what underpins the claim that blacks are better athletes than whites. But that's all the claim amounts to. It doesn't say anything at all about the rest of us, of all races, muddling around in the genetic middle.

## 3.

There is a second consideration to keep in mind when we compare blacks and whites. Take the men's hundred-metre final at the Atlanta Olympics. Every runner in that race was of either Western African or Southern African descent, as you would expect if Africans had some genetic affinity for sprinting. But suppose we forget about skin color and look just at country of origin. The eight-man final was made up of two African-Americans, two Africans (one from Namibia and one from Nigeria), a Trinidadian, a Canadian of Jamaican descent, an Englishman of Jamaican descent, and a Jamaican. The race was won by the Jamaican-Canadian, in world-record time, with the Namibian coming in second and the Trinidadian third. The sprint relay—the 4 3 100—was won by a team from Canada, consisting of the Jamaican-Canadian from the final, a Haitian-Canadian, a Trinidadian-Canadian, and another Jamaican-Canadian. Now it appears that African heritage is important as an initial determinant of sprinting ability, but also that the most important advantage of all is some kind of cultural or environmental factor associated with the Caribbean.

Or consider, in a completely different realm, the problem of hypertension. Black Americans have a higher incidence of hypertension than white Americans, even after you control for every conceivable variable, including income, diet, and weight, so it's tempting to conclude that there is something about being of African descent that makes blacks prone to hypertension. But it turns out that although some Caribbean countries have a problem with hypertension, others—Jamaica, St. Kitts, and the Bahamas—don't. It also turns out that people in Liberia and Nigeria—two countries where many New World slaves came from—have similar and perhaps even lower blood-pressure rates than white North Americans, while studies of Zulus, Indians, and whites in Durban, South Africa, showed that urban white males had the highest hypertension rates and urban white females had the lowest. So it's likely that the disease has nothing at all to do with Africanness.

The same is true for the distinctive muscle characteristic observed when Kenyans were compared with Swedes. Saltin, the Swedish physiologist, subsequently found many of the same characteristics in Nordic skiers who train at high altitudes and Nordic runners who train in very hilly regions—conditions, in other words, that resemble the mountainous regions of Kenya's Rift Valley, where so many of the country's distance runners come from. The key factor seems to be Kenya, not genes.

Lots of things that seem to be genetic in origin, then, actually aren't. Similarly, lots of things that we wouldn't normally think might affect athletic ability actually do. Once again, the social-science literature on male and female math achievement is instructive. Psychologists argue that when it comes to subjects like math, boys tend to engage in what's known as ability attribution. A boy who is doing well will attribute his success to the fact that he's good at math, and if he's doing badly he'll blame his teacher or his own lack of motivation—anything but his ability. That makes it easy for him to bounce back from failure or disappointment, and gives him a lot of confidence in the face of a tough new challenge. After all, if you think you do well in math because you're good at math, what's stopping you from being good at, say, algebra, or advanced calculus? On the other hand, if you ask a girl why she is doing well in math she will say, more often than not, that she succeeds because she works hard. If she's doing poorly, she'll say she isn't smart enough. This, as should be obvious, is a self-defeating attitude. Psychologists call it "learned helplessness"—the state in which failure is perceived as insurmountable. Girls who engage in effort attribution learn helplessness because in the face of a more difficult task like algebra or advanced calculus they can conceive of no solution. They're convinced that they can't work harder, because they think they're working as hard as they can, and that they can't rely on their intelligence, because they never thought they were that smart to begin with. In fact, one of the fascinating findings of attribution research is that the smarter girls are, the more likely they are to fall into this trap. High achievers are sometimes the most helpless. Here, surely, is part of the explanation for greater math variability among males. The female math whizzes, the ones who should be competing in the top one and two per cent with their male counterparts, are the ones most often paralyzed by a lack of confidence in their own aptitude. They think they belong only in the intellectual middle.

The striking thing about these descriptions of male and female stereotyping in math, though, is how similar they are to black and white stereotyping in athletics—to the unwritten rules holding that blacks achieve through natural ability and whites through effort. Here's how *Sports Illustrated* described, in a recent article, the white basketball player Steve Kerr, who plays alongside Michael Jordan for the Chicago Bulls. According to the magazine, Kerr is a "hard-working overachiever," distinguished by his "work ethic and heady play" and by a shooting style "born of a million practice shots." Bear in mind that Kerr is one of the best shooters in basketball today, and a key player on what is arguably one of the finest basketball teams in history. Bear in mind, too, that there is no evidence that Kerr works any harder than his teammates, least of all Jordan himself, whose work habits are legendary. But you'd never guess that from the article. It concludes, "All over America, whenever quicker, stronger gym rats see Kerr in action, they must wonder, How can that guy be out there instead of me?"

There are real consequences to this stereotyping. As the psychologists Carol Dweck and Barbara Licht write of high-achieving schoolgirls, "[They] may view themselves as so motivated and well disciplined that they cannot entertain the possibility that they did poorly on an academic task because of insufficient effort. Since blaming the teacher would also be out of character, blaming their abilities when they confront difficulty may seem like the most reasonable option." If you substitute the words "white athletes" for "girls" and "coach" for "teacher," I think you have part of the reason that so many white athletes are underrepresented at the highest levels of professional sports. Whites have been saddled with the athletic equivalent of learned helplessness—the idea that it is all but fruitless to try and compete at the highest levels, because they have only effort on their side. The causes of athletic and gender discrimination may be diverse, but its effects are not. Once again, blacks are like boys, and whites are like girls.

### 4.

When I was in college, I once met an old acquaintance from my high-school running days. Both of us had long since quit track, and we talked about a recurrent fantasy we found we'd both had for getting back into shape. It was that we would go away somewhere remote for a year and do nothing but train, so that when the year was up we might finally know how good we were. Neither of us had any intention of doing this, though, which is why it was a fantasy. In adolescence, athletic excess has a certain appeal—during high school, I happily spent Sunday afternoons running up and down snow-covered sandhills—but with most of us that obsessiveness soon begins to fade. Athletic success depends on having the right genes and on a self-reinforcing belief in one's own ability. But it also depends on a rare form of tunnel vision. To be a great athlete, you have to care, and what was obvious to us both was that neither of us cared anymore. This is the last piece of the puzzle about what we mean when we say one group is better at something than another: sometimes different groups care about different things. Of the seven hundred men who play major-league baseball, for example, eighty-six come from either the Dominican Republic or Puerto Rico, even though those two islands have a combined population of only eleven million. But then baseball is something that Dominicans and Puerto Ricans care about—and you can say the same thing about African-Americans and basketball, West Indians and sprinting, Canadians and hockey, and Russians and chess. Desire is the great intangible in performance, and unlike genes or psychological affect we can't measure it and trace its implications. This is the problem, in the end, with the question of whether blacks are better at sports than whites. It's not that it's offensive, or that it leads to discrimination. It's that, in some sense, it's not a terribly interesting question; "better" promises a tidier explanation than can ever be provided.

I quit competitive running when I was sixteen—just after the summer I had qualified for the Ontario track team in my age class. Late that August, we had travelled to St. John's, Newfoundland, for the Canadian championships. In those days, I was whippet-thin, as milers often are, five feet six and not much more than a hundred pounds, and I could skim along the ground so lightly that I barely needed to catch my breath. I had two white friends on that team, both distance runners, too, and both, improbably, even smaller and lighter than I was. Every morning, the three of us would run through the streets of St. John's, charging up the hills and flying down the other side. One of these friends went on to have a distinguished college running career, the other became a world-class miler; that summer, I myself was the Canadian record holder in the fifteen hundred metres for my age class. We were almost terrifyingly competitive, without a shred of doubt in our ability, and as we raced along we never stopped talking and joking, just to prove how absurdly easy we found running to be. I thought of us all as equals. Then, on the last day of our stay in St. John's, we ran to the bottom of Signal Hill, which is the town's principal geographical landmark—an abrupt outcrop as steep as anything in San Francisco. We stopped at the base, and the two of them turned to me and announced that we were all going to run straight up Signal Hill backward. I don't know whether I had more running ability than those two or whether my Africanness gave me any genetic advantage over their whiteness. What I do know is that such questions were irrelevant, because, as I realized, they were willing to go to far greater lengths to develop their talent. They ran up the hill backward. I ran home.

## READING WRITING

### THIS TEXT: READING

1. What do you think of the analogy that Gladwell raises? What are some objections you have or do you think others have had? How would Gladwell answer those?
2. Why is the sports question in regard to race such an important and generally sensitive one?
3. What role does Gladwell attribute to sociology in achieving sports success?
4. What are some of the signs of sports—some elements of sports that can be read as signs, items to interpret? Are there semiotic situations you can think of?
5. Who is Gladwell's audience? Why do you think he's writing about this topic?

### YOUR TEXT: WRITING

1. Gladwell uses the personal voice in the essay, but the essay's content is mostly about what research has been done on this topic. What do you think of this approach? Is this one you can imitate? Think of a social issue that you have a stake in and try your hand at this approach, using this article as a model.
2. What are some other issues that are "taboo"? Write an essay exploring another subject that is generally off limits for discussion.

---

### QALLUNAAT 101: INUITS STUDY WHITE FOLKS IN THIS NEW ACADEMIC FIELD

### ■ Zebedee Nungak ■

*A long-time Inuit activist, Zebedee Nungak is also the co-author with Eugene Arima of* InuitStories: Povungnauk-Légendes inuic Povungnituk. *(1988). In this wry piece, Nungak turns the traditional anthropologist subject-observer relationship on its head.*

Like many Inuit boys of my generation, I had a fascination with Qallunaat that bordered on awe. The few we encountered lived in warm wooden houses, while we grew up in igloos. They seemed to lack no material thing. Their food was what the word *delicious* was invented for, all their women were beautiful, and even their garbage was impressive! As a boy, I had an innocent ambition to be like them. The measure of my success would be when my garbage equaled theirs.

I lived among the Qallunaat for seven years. In my time in their land, my discoveries of their peculiarities sparked my interest in what could be called Qallunology.

Many of us who have been exposed to Qallunaat-dom through deep immersion in their world could write some credible discourses on the subject. Their social mores and standards of etiquette could fill several volumes. Their language contains all sorts of weirdness. Their sameness and distinctness can be utterly baffling. An Irishman from Northern Ireland looks exactly the same as one from the Irish Republic. A close look at Albanians and Serbs has them all looking like bona fide Qallunaat. Why such savage conflict among such same-looking civilized people?

Look, Look! See Sally Run! Oh Dick, Oh Jane! Why do your parents have no name? Are all dogs in Qallunaat-dom Spot, all cats Puff? There was absolutely no Fun with Dick and Jane as we Inuit children crashed head-on into the English language. The cultural shocks and tremors have never completely worn off those of us who were zapped with such literature.

The Qallunaat custom of abbreviating first names does not seem to follow a standard formula. Robert can be Rob, Robbie, Bob, Bobby or Bert. Joseph is Joe, James/Jim, Sidney/Sid, Arthur/Art, and Peter/Pete. Charles is Charlie but can be Chuck. What sleight of hand makes a Henry a Hank? And how does Richard become a Dick, if not a Rich or a Rick? Do you see a B in William on its way to be a Bill? Don't ever say *Seen* for Sean (sh-AWN) or *John* for Jean, if the person is a francophone male.

Qallunaat women can have very masculine names clicked feminine by ending them with an A: Roberta, Edwina, Phillippa. Shortened names are mostly chopped versions—Katherine/Kate, Deborah/Debbie—except for some ready-made like Wendy and Kay. Liz is drawn from the midsection of Elizabeth, unlike in Inuit use, where these names are entirely separate as Elisapi and Lisi. Many names can fit both sexes: Pat, Jan, Leslie, Kit.

One of the most distinctive features of life among Qallunaat, the one most markedly different from Inuit life, can be summed up in this expression of theirs: keeping up with the Joneses. Not much is communal and few essentials are shared. Life is based on competition, going to great lengths to "get ahead," and amassing what you gain for yourself. People around you may be in want, but that is their problem.

We know Qallunaat, of course, by the way they eat: with a fork and a dull knife known by Inuit as *nuvuittuq* (without point). There is a whole etiquette to eating too cumbersome to describe in detail. But, if one has the misfortune to burp, belch, or fart during the meal, one has to be civil and say "Excuse me!" in a sincere enough demeanor. Never forget to say "please" in asking for the salt or potatoes to be passed. Don't ever just up and walk away from the table.

Having visitors over (company) is mostly attached to some ritual or activity, such as a bridge game. If alcohol is served to guests, it is amazingly incidental, and not the main item of attention. Nobody gets drunk, but there is a lot of talking! Then there seems to be an obligation to talk even more at the door before leaving. Guests and hosts lingering forever at the entrance to talk about nothing in particular is one of the surest trademarks of being in Qallunaat-dom.

There is a ritual called dating, which is hard to describe in Inuit terms. It can't really be described as husband- or wife-hunting. Maturing people of opposite sexes mutually agree to "go out" to some form of enjoyable activity. Sometimes it is to test their compatibility as a possible couple, sometimes simply to genuinely enjoy each other's company. It seems to be a permanent occupation of some, whom Inuit might call *uinitsuituq* or *nulianitsuituq*, meaning "un-attachable to a husband or wife."

I don't proclaim to be an expert on Qallunaat and what makes them tick. But my commentaries on Qallunology are based on having eaten, slept, and breathed their life for some years, learning their language, and tumbling along in their tidy-square thought processes. The resulting recollections are no more superficial than those of the first Qallunaat to encounter the Inuit, who unwittingly illustrated their educated ignorance when they tried to describe us. That has changed. Today, even Qallunaat with strings of academic degrees attached to their names are more often seeking guidance from the reservoir of traditional Inuit knowledge.

Eskimology has long been a serious field of study by Qallunaat. Scores of museums and universities all over the world have great departments and sections devoted solely to the subject. Serious Qallunologists, on the other hand, are likely to sweat and toil in unrewarding anonymity until the academic currency of their field of study attains the respectability of being labeled officially with an "-ology."

Eskimologists have carted off traditional clothing, artifacts, hunting implements, tools, ancient stories and legends, and human remains for display in museums, bartering these for very little. Qallunologists will find nothing worth carting away for display. All Qallunaat stuff is for immediate use, much of it disposable, easily replaceable, and now available in mass quantities to Inuit as well. It all costs quite a lot, and one will be prosecuted for stealing any of it.

Eskimology was triggered by others' curiosity about who we are and how we live. It has flourished to the point that we Inuit have in some ways benefited from it by reclaiming some essences of our identity from various collections in others' possession. Qallunaat, meanwhile, are not in any danger of having to go to museums to pick up remnants of who they once were.

## READING WRITING

### THIS TEXT: READING

1.  Do you think this piece is funny? Why or why not?
2.  What points is Nungak making about the relationships between Inuits and whites? Have you heard these issues before? Is Nungak treating these ideas differently?
3.  Does anyone study white people as an anthropological study? If not, should they? If so, who does?

### THIS TEXT: WRITING

1.  Do your own anthropological study of a group or phenomenon that seems familiar but can still be studied (think: cafeteria, gym, supermarket, etc.).
2.  Find a traditional anthropological study and write a compare and contrast piece.

---

### RACE IS A FOUR-LETTER WORD

**■ Teja Arboleda ■**

*In this piece, taken his from his 1998 book,* In the Shadow of Race, *Arboleda explores what it means to be multiracial. A producer and peformer, Arboleda wrote and directed* Got Race, *his first feature-length movie; it premiered in October 2003.*

I'VE BEEN CALLED *nigger* and a neighbor set the dogs on us in Queens, New York.
    I've been called *spic* and was frisked in a plush neighborhood of Los Angeles.
    I've been called *Jap* and was blamed for America's weaknesses.
    I've been called *Nazi* and the neighborhood G.I. Joes had me every time.
    I've been called *Turk* and was sneered at in Germany.

I've been called *Stupid Yankee* and was threatened in Japan.

I've been called *Afghanistani* and was spit on by a Boston cab driver.

I've been called *Iraqi* and Desert Storm was America's pride.

I've been called *mulatto, criollo, mestizo, simarron, Hapahaoli, masala, exotic, alternative, mixed-up, messed-up, half-breed,* and *in between.* I've been mistaken for Moroccan, Algerian, Egyptian, Lebanese, Iranian, Turkish, Brazilian, Argentinean, Puerto Rican, Cuban, Mexican, Indonesian, Nepalese, Greek, Italian, Pakistani, Indian, Black, White, Hispanic, Asian, and being a Brooklynite. I've been mistaken for Michael Jackson and Billy Crystal on the same day.

I've been ordered to get glasses of water for neighboring restaurant patrons. I've been told to be careful mopping the floors at the television station where I was directing a show. Even with my U.S. passport, I've been escorted to the "aliens only" line at Kennedy International Airport. I've been told I'm not dark enough. I've been told I'm not White enough. I've been told I talk American real good. I've been told, "Take your humus and your pita bread and go back to Mexico!" I've been ordered to "Go back to where you belong, we don't like *your* kind here!"

I spent too much time and energy as a budding adult abbreviating my identity and rehearsing its explanation. I would practice quietly by myself, reciting what my father always told me: "Filipino-German." He never smiled when he said this.

My father's dark skin told many stories that his stern face and anger-filled tension couldn't translate. My mother's light skin could never spell empathy—even suntanning only made her turn bright red. My brother Miguel and I became curiosity factors when we appeared in public with her. During the past 34 years, my skin has lightened, somewhat, but then in the summers (even in New England where summers happen suddenly, and disappear just as quickly), I can darken several degrees in a matter of hours. This phenomenon seems a peculiar paradigm to which people's perceptions of my culture or race alter with the waning and waxing of my skin tone. I can almost design others' perceptions by counting my minutes in the sun. My years in Japan, the United States, Germany, and the numerous countries, cities, and towns through which I've traveled, have proven that my flesh is irrelevant to the language I speak, to the way I walk and talk, or the way I jog or mow my lawn or to the fact that I often use chopsticks to eat. It is irrelevant to *who* or *what* I married, my political viewpoints, my career, my hopes, desires and fears.

I don't remember being taught by my parents never to *question* skin color, yet when I compare the back of my hand to these pages, I cannot help myself—I must know. Like a sickness coursing through my veins with the very blood that makes me who I am, I ask: What color am I? And, what color was I yesterday? Tomorrow? There is also that pesky, familiar feeling I get when, in the corner of my eye, I catch passing strangers with judgments written on their brows. Maybe paranoia, maybe vanity, but the experiences and memories of too often being "different" or "undefinable" have left me with a weary sense of instant verdict on my part. And sometimes I study their thousands of faces, hoping somehow to connect. I know that they ask themselves the same questions, as they are plagued by the same epidemic, asking and reasking themselves, ourselves, "Who and what are we?"

Overadapting to new environments has become second nature to me, as my father and my mother eagerly fed me culture. As a child I felt like I was being dragged to different corners of the planet with my parents, filling their need for exploration and contact, and teaching us the value and beauty of difference. Between packing suitcases and wandering through unfamiliar territory, all I had ever wanted was to be "the same."

They were successful in some respects—I do believe I am liberal in my thinking—but inevitably there was a price to pay. With each step, each move, each landing through the thick and tenuous atmosphere of a new culture, my feet searched for solid ground, for something familiar. The concept of home, identity, and place become ethereal, like a swirl of gases circling in orbit, waiting for gravity to define their position.

In a sense, I have been relegated to ethnic benchwarmer, on a hunt for simplicity in a world of confusing words that deeply divide us all. In response, I learned to overcompensate. New places and new faces have rarely threatened me, but I have a desperate need to belong to whatever group I'm with at any particular moment. I soak in the surrounding elements to cope with what my instincts oblige, and deliver a new temporary self. I am out of bounds, transcending people and places. I carry within my blood the memories of my heritage connected in the web of my mind, the marriage of history and biology. I breathe the air of my ancestors as if it were fresh from the sunrises of their past. I am illogical, providing argument to traditional categories of race, culture, and ethnicity. I am a cultural chameleon, adapting out of necessity only to discover, yet again, a new Darwinism at the frontiers of identity.

"What are you, anyway?" sometimes demandingly curious Americans like to ask. "I'm Filipino-German," I used to say. I have never been satisfied with abbreviating my identity to the exclusion of all the other puzzle pieces that would then be lost forever in shadowy corners where no one ever looks.

Do I throw a nod at a Black brother who passes me on the street? And if I did so, would he understand why I did? Do I even call him "brother?" Does *he* call *me* "brother?" If not, should he call me a "half-brother," or throw me a half nod? In the United States do I nod or bow to Japanese nationals in a Japanese restaurant? Would they know to bow with me? In Jamaica Plain, Massachusetts, if a Hispanic male gestures hello to me, is it a simple greeting, or a gesture of camaraderie because I might be Hispanic? Do I dress up to go to a country club because, in the eyes of its rich White men, I would otherwise live up to their idea of the stereotypical minority? Should I dance well, shaking and driving my body like Papa's family afforded me, or should I remain appropriately conservative to preserve the integrity of a long-gone Puritan New England? Do I shave for the silver hallways of white-collar highrises so as not to look too "ethnic?" Do I agree to an audition for a commercial when I know the reason I'm there is just to fill in with some skin color for an industry quota?

"I know you're *something*," someone once said. "You have some Black in you," another offered. "He must be ethnic or something," I've overheard. "I've got such a boring family compared to yours," another confided. "You're messed-up," an elementary school girl decided. "Do you love your race?" her classmate wondered. "*What* did you marry?" I've been asked. "*Who* did you marry?" I've been asked. "Is she just like you?" I've been asked. "You are the quintessential American," someone decided.

■ ■ ■

America continues to struggle through its identity crisis, and the simple, lazy, bureaucratic checklist we use only serves to satisfy an outdated four-letter word—*race*. Like the basic food groups, it is overconsumed and digested, forming a hemorrhoid in the backside of the same old power struggle. I am only one of many millions of Americans, from this "League of Outsiders," demanding a change in the way we are designated, routed, cattle-called, herded, and shackled into these simplified classifications.

The United States is going through growing pains. The immigrants coming to the United States and becoming citizens are no longer primarily of European origin. But let's not fool ourselves into thinking that America is only now becoming multicultural.

In 1992, *Time* magazine produced a special issue entitled, "The New Face of America" with the subtitle, "How immigrants are shaping the world's first multicultural society." The cover featured a picture of a woman's face. Next to the face was a paragraph that suggested her image was the result of a computerized average of faces of people of several different races.

The operative words on the cover are "races," "culture," and "first." Race and culture are very different words. Race in America is predominantly determined by skin color. Culture is determined by our experiences and our interactions within a society, large or small.

Then there is this idea of being "first." Are we to say that this continent was never populated by a mix of people? Are we to say that the Lacota and Iroquois were of exactly the same culture? What about the different Europeans who settled here later on? Of course, African slaves were not all from the same tribe, and they certainly were not of the same culture as the slave traders.

In the middle of the magazine, there was a compilation, more like a chart of photographs of people from all over the world. The editor and computer artist scanned all the pictures into a computer. Then, by having the computer average the faces together, they produced a variety of facial combinations. Remember, however, they said on the cover, "People from different *races* . . . to form the world's first *multicultural* society." But in the body of the article and its accompanying pictures, many people were not identified by their *race,* but rather by their *nationalities*—such as Italian and Chinese—in other words *citizenship,* a very different word.

Through it all, *Time* was trying to educate us, but at the same time, we're miseducated. The world—not just this country—has always been and always will be a multicultural environment. So what is it about the words *multicultural* or *diversity* that is confusing or overwhelming?

In the next 20 years, the average American will no longer be technically White. This will have to be reflected in the media, in the workplace, and in the schools, not out of charitable interest, but out of necessity. More people are designating themselves as multiracial or multicultural. People continue to marry across religious, cultural, and ethnic barriers. A definition for "mainstream society" is harder to find.

■ ■ ■

My mother's father, Opa, died a year after Oma passed away. The day after the funeral in Germany, my mother's relatives told her, for the first time, that her father was not really her father (i.e., biologically). All the people who knew the true identity of her father have long since passed away. So, if my mother's biological father was, let's say, Italian or Russian, does that make her German-Italian or German-Russian? She says no. German, only German, because that's how she was raised.

My brother, Miguel, married a Brazilian. (*Pause.*) Do you have an image in your head of what she looks like? I did when he first told me about her over the phone. Well, she is Brazilian by culture and citizenship, but her parents are Japanese nationals who moved to Brazil in their early 20s to escape poverty in Japan after World War II. So she *looks stereo-*

*typically* Japanese. But she speaks Portuguese and doesn't interact socially like most Japanese do.

■ ■ ■

I offer myself as a case study in transcending the complex maze of barriers, pedestals, doors, and traps that form the boundaries that confine human beings to dominant and minority groups.

I am tired. I am exhausted. I am always looking for new and improved definitions for my identity. My very-mixed heritage, culture, and international experiences seem like a blur sometimes, and I long for a resting place. A place where I can breathe like I did in my mother's womb: without having to open my mouth.

## READING WRITING

### THIS TEXT: READING

1. In what ways does Aborleda present himself as a text? In what ways do people "misread" him?
2. The author writes in a vivid first person style; in what ways would this story be different if it were in the third person?
3. How does Aborleda describe his identity? How is his idea of identity different from the identity he finds in others' reactions to him?

### YOUR TEXT: WRITING

1. Write about a time where you are mistaken for another group, whether enthnicity, gender, class, or age. What assumptions did the people mistaking you for someone else make?
2. Do research on multi-racial identity and determine what issues are "in the air." *Hint:* Both the recent census and Tiger Woods's statements about his identity have made this issue more prominent. Then re-read this text or another one that involves this issue, such as the movie *The Human Stain.* In what ways do the text and research speak to one another?

---

### CENSORING MYSELF

■ **Betty Shamieh** ■  *Betty Shamieh, an Arab American, is a highly regarded writer and performer. Her play* Chocolate in the Heat—Growing Up Arab in America *was staged in 2001 in New York. A graduate of Harvard and the Yale School of Drama, Shamieh's essay (2003) is about being read as a certain kind of text—an Arab American—in the wake of 9/11.*

I AM A PALESTINIAN-AMERICAN PLAYWRIGHT—and I'm Christian. Significant numbers of Arabs are Christian, which is something many Americans do not know; Arab society is not by any means homogeneous.

I was born in San Francisco, so I'm a citizen of this country. I went to Harvard and Yale and what attending institutions like that provides is access to people in positions of power.

Yet, part of me is terrified to be writing these words singling myself out as an Arab-American at this stage in American history, because I don't know what the ramifications of that are or will be. Part of me wants to heed President Bush when he lets it be known on national television that he thinks citizens better "watch what they say," but part of me is extremely cognizant of the fact that over a thousand Arab- and Muslim-Americans were picked up and held for months without trials and without our government releasing their names following the attacks of Sept. 11; that it was 18 months after Pearl Harbor that Japanese-Americans were sent to internment camps; and that this country does not have a history of showing tolerance toward any racial minority whose members are easy to pick out of a crowd.

There are certainly acts of intolerance short of internment of which governments are capable. I have been censored in many ways. But I think the most overt example of censorship I have yet faced is my experience with a project called the Brave New World Festival.

The Brave New World Festival at New York City's Town Hall was—as its Web site declared—designed for artists to explore "the alternate roots of terrorism." For the most part, only very well-established playwrights were asked to participate, but I—who had just finished Yale School of Drama a year before—was invited partly because of my work at the "Imagine: Iraq" reading, which drew 900 people to Cooper Union in New York City in November 2001, to hear plays about the Middle East. I am an actress as well as a playwright, and, at the "Imagine: Iraq" reading, I performed a monologue I wrote about the sister of a suicide bomber who mourns not knowing what her brother planned to do and not being able to stop him. The piece is very clearly a plea for non-violence.

When the organizers of the Brave New World Festival asked me to perform the same monologue for them, my first thought was that I did not want to be in Town Hall on the first anniversary of Sept. 11 presenting a play that deals with such potent subject matter. Then I realized that it was especially important at that time and in that place to present precisely such work. So, despite all my fears and concerns, I agreed to their request—but asked the organizers to get Marisa Tomei (who was already involved in the project) or an actress of that caliber to play the role. I felt that if there was going to be a backlash, I didn't want to be dealing with it alone.

I got a call from an organizer a few weeks later. She told me she loved the piece and that—at my request—she had given it to Marisa Tomei. But she also said that some of her colleagues had objected to the content of my piece. She informed me that I was welcome to write something different but that they were rescinding their offer to present my monologue.

At this time, I did not know that they were also censoring people like Eduardo Machado, who is the head of the playwriting MFA program at Columbia and one of the best-known playwrights of his generation.

So, in an Uncle Tom–like manner, instead of holding my ground, I wrote another piece. I did so because I was the only Arab-American playwright in the lineup. Arab-American artists are largely faceless in this country and I felt that, by dropping out, I would be helping those who are trying to keep it that way.

The new piece I wrote for them was a very mild and humorous short play. The narrator, an Arab-American girl, tells the audience of a fantasy she has about ending up on a hijacked plane and talking the hijackers out of their plans. The people on the plane listen to the hijackers' grievances and actually refuse to get off the flight until all people have a right to live in safety and freedom. Then, in her fantasy, the narrator ends up on "Oprah," and has a movie made about her starring Julia Roberts.

Harmless, right? Especially for a forum designed to present theater that asked real questions.

But when I got into rehearsal on the day of the performance with the director, Billy Hopkins, and actresses including Rosie Perez, I realized someone had censored the text, deleting chunks of my work that deal with the main character talking to the hijackers and making them see the error of their ways.

Of course, I had my own original copy with me. I had just begun to distribute it when the stage manager stepped into the rehearsal. She announced that because the performance schedule had grown overlong, my piece, the token Arab-American playwright's play, had been cut, along with a number of others.

What made the experience particularly disturbing was that the organizers had touted this event as a venue for alternative ideas and voices. To censor voices that present exactly those perspectives made it seem as though those voices don't exist.

Many people ask me if I—as a Palestinian-American playwright living in New York in a post–Sept. 11 world—have been facing more censorship in the wake of that horrific event that changed all of our lives. The answer—which might surprise many—is no.

The reason is that there was such as astounding level of censorship in American theater when it comes to the Palestinian perspective before Sept. 11, that I really haven't felt a difference in the past two years.

Indeed, the last time there was a serious attempt to bring a play written by a Palestinian to a major New York stage was in 1989. Joe Papp, artistic director of the Joseph Papp Public Theatre, asked a Palestinian theater troupe that had toured throughout Europe to bring its highly acclaimed show, "The Story of Kufur Shamma," to his theater.

Joe Papp was a theatrical visionary. In other words, he wasn't going to stick a piece of mindless propaganda on his theater's stage. But his board objected to his decision to bring the show to New York.

Papp, arguably the most powerful man in the history of American theater, did not feel he could stand up to his board members. He rescinded his offer because, as the *Philadelphia Inquirer* reported, "he had come under a great deal of pressure and that he could not jeopardize his theater."

I'm telling this story only because I think its relationship with my work is intriguing. For the three years I was a graduate student at the Yale School of Drama, I, in effect, censored myself. I did not produce a single play about the Palestinian experience, which is an enormous part of who I am as a person and an artist.

I wanted to avoid confronting the kind of censorship anybody faces when portraying the Palestinians as human beings. I wanted to avoid that kind of controversy until I had a bit of a name for myself, a bit of a following.

Unfortunately, what happened as a result of my self-censorship was my work was eviscerated. Now, I write about the Palestinian experience not only just because it deserves—as all stories deserve—to be heard, but also because if I hope to make vital theater I can only write about what I care deeply about. And vital theater is the only kind of theater I'm interested in making.

It came down to a very clear choice for me. I either had to give up writing for the stage or decide to write about what I knew and cared about and, therefore, face what it meant to be a Palestinian-American playwright working in New York at this time. I, either wisely or unwisely, have chosen the latter.

When you think of all the ethnic minorities in this country who have had their story told multiple times in the theater, you wonder—would it do such harm to add to that mosaic one story about the Palestinian perspective?

Are the people involved in the incidents I mentioned being rational when they try so hard to keep a Palestinian perspective out of the public eye, which they unfortunately and—in my opinion—unnecessarily see as contrary to their own?

Aren't they overreacting a little bit? I mean, really. Is theater that powerful?

The answer is yes. A good play, a play that makes you feel, allows you to see its characters as fully human, if only for two hours.

If more people actually saw Palestinians as human beings, our foreign policy could not and would not be the same.

## READING  WRITING

### THIS TEXT: READING
1. What are some of the problems Shamieh has had to face as an Arab American?
2. Shamieh refers to a decision as being Uncle Tom-esque. What does she mean by this?
3. How is this essay about identity? Does Shamieh have a thesis? If so, what is it?

### YOUR TEXT: WRITING
1. Write a first-person essay, like Shamieh's, in which you talk about your own identity as a text. How have people read and misread you?
2. Write an essay in which you respond to Shamieh's. What did you learn from her piece?
3. Write a comparison/contrast paper on Shamieh's essay and Amy Tan's "Mother Tongue." How are they similar? How does gender figure in to issues of race?

## *The Native American Mascot Suite*

The very day we sat down to write the introduction to this suite, we read in the papers that Southeast Missouri State University will soon drop their Native American mascots. The board of regents voted unanimously to cease using "Indians" for its men's athletic teams and "Otahkians" for the women's and instead go by the "Redhawks." The move by SMSU is one of over 300 mascot changes that have occurred in the past thirty years. Activists first began raising questions about the ethics of Native American mascots in 1968, when the National Congress of American Indians began a campaign to address issues of stereotypes in the media. The following year, students, faculty and other interested parties protested Dartmouth College's "Indian" nickname. However, it was on April 17, 1970 that the dam burst. The University of Oklahoma retired "Little Red," its disturbing Indian mascot that it had used since the 1940s. Over the next few years, Marquette, Stanford, Dickinson State, Syracuse, St. Bonaventure, and Southern Oregon all got rid of their Indian mascots. Since then, a number of groups such as the United Methodist Church, the state of Minnesota, The Amer-

ican Jewish Committee, the State of Wisconsin Department of Public Instruction, The U. S. Patent and Trademark Office, The United States Commission on Civil Rights and even the National Collegiate Athletics Association (NCAA) have taken official, public stances against the use of American Indian stereotyping.

That said, there remains a strong enclave of support for Native American mascots. Fans of the Washington Redskins, Cleveland Indians, Chicago Blackhawks, Kansas City Chiefs, Illinois Illini, and Florida State Seminoles have repeatedly fought movements to change mascots. The issue at the University of Illinois is among the most public and the most hotly contested. Alumni, students and administrators remain divided over the use of an Indian in full headdress as the university's mascot and in particular the "chiefing" (an invented ritualistic dance) of Chief Illiniwek. Supporters of the mascot and the chief claim both honor the dignity, nobility and bravery of Native peoples, while opponents claim the mascots and the dance engender and perpetuate stereotypes, racism, and bigotry.

The following texts explore the cultural, racial, aesthetic, historical, emotional, and political issues surrounding the Native American mascot issue. Scholar and critic Ward Churchill was one of the first academics to polemicize the mascot issue, and his essay, "Let's Spread the 'Fun' Around," remains the classic document on this issue. Known for his brutally frank

observations, Churchill pulls no punches in this essay, so be forewarned—certain racial slurs appear in this piece that you may not be accustomed to seeing in an academic setting. Still, Churchill's arguments remain cogent and persuasive. C. Richard King and Charles Fruehling Springwood's piece "Imagined Indians, Social Identities, and Activism" comes from the introduction to their book *Team Spirits: Native Mascots.* King and Springwood do not simply trace the history of Native mascots and resistance to those mascots; they also make connections between the pervasive acceptance of mascots and the history of the United States' treatment of American Indians. King and Springwood also make a pitch for social activism on this front. S. L. Price's article "The Indian Wars" appeared in a recent issue of *Sports Illustrated* and stands as perhaps the most widely accessible piece on the mascot issue, even though it has been decried by some American Indian scholars and activists for allegedly inaccurate statistics regarding the stance of reservation Indians on mascots. An excellent rhetorical assignment would be to read the article closely to determine whether you find the arguments balanced or not.

The mascot issue remains a critical topic of public debate because it hones in on the conflicts between freedom of expression and civil rights. It also marks an interesting overlap between politics, sports, and visual culture. Do images carry weight? To what degree are caricatures racist? Do these comical, infantilizing, and hostile images contribute—even subconsciously—to the way in which most Americans view American Indians? Lastly, how do these images affect Native American identity?

### LET'S SPREAD THE FUN AROUND: THE ISSUE OF SPORTS TEAM NAMES AND MASCOTS

#### ■ Ward Churchill ■

*If people are genuinely interested in honoring Indians, try getting your government to live up to the more than 400 treaties it signed with our nations. Try respecting our religious freedom which has been repeatedly denied in federal courts. Try stopping the ongoing theft of Indian water and other natural resources. Try reversing your colonial process that relegates us to the most impoverished, polluted, and desperate conditions in this country. . . . Try understanding that the mascot issue is only the tip of a very huge problem of continuing racism against American Indians. Then maybe your ["honors"] will mean something. Until then, it's just so much superficial, hypocritical puffery. People should remember that an honor isn't born when it parts the honorer's lips, it is born when it is accepted in the honoree's ear.*

*—Glenn T. Morris*
*Colorado AIM*

During the past couple of seasons, there has been an increasing wave of controversy regarding the names of professional sports teams like the Atlanta "Braves," Cleveland "Indians," Washington "Redskins," and Kansas City "Chiefs." The issue extends to the names of college teams like Florida State University "Seminoles," University of Illinois "Fighting Illini," and so on, right on down to high school outfits like the Lamar (Colorado) "Savages." Also involved have been team adoption of "mascots," replete with feathers, buckskins, beads, spears, and "warpaint" (some fans have opted to adorn themselves in the same fashion), and nifty little "pep" gestures like the "Indian Chant" and "Tomahawk Chop."

A substantial number of American Indians have protested that use of native names, images, and symbols as sports team mascots and the like is, by definition, a virulently racist practice. Given the historical relationship between Indians and non-Indians during what has been called the "Conquest of America," American Indian Movement leader (and American Indian Anti-Defamation Council founder) Russell Means has compared the practice to contemporary Germans naming their soccer teams the "Jews," "Hebrews," and "Yids," while adorning their uniforms with grotesque caricatures of Jewish faces taken from the nazis' antisemitic propaganda of the 1930s. Numerous demonstrations have occurred in conjunction with games—most notably during the November 15, 1992, match-up between the Chiefs and Redskins in Kansas City—by angry Indians and their supporters.

In response, a number of players—especially African-Americans and other minority athletes—have been trotted out by professional team owners like Ted Turner, as well as university and public school officials, to announce that they mean not to insult, but instead to "honor," native people. They have been joined by the television networks and most major newspapers, all of which have editorialized that Indian discomfort with the situation is "no big deal," insisting that the whole thing is just "good, clean fun." The country needs more such fun, they've argued, and "a few disgruntled Native Americans" have no right to undermine the nation's enjoyment of its leisure time by complaining. This is especially the case, some have contended, "in hard times like these." It has even been contended that Indian outrage at being systematically degraded—rather than the degradation itself—creates "a serious barrier to the sort of intergroup communication so necessary in a multicultural society such as ours."

Okay, let's communicate. We may be frankly dubious that those advancing such positions really believe in their own rhetoric, but, just for the sake of argument, let's accept the premise that they are sincere. If what they are saying is true in any way at all, then isn't it time we spread such "inoffensiveness" and "good cheer" around among *all* groups so that *everybody* can participate *equally* in fostering the round of national laughs they call for? Sure it is—the country can't have too *much* fun or "intergroup involvement"—so the more, the merrier. Simple consistency demands that anyone who thinks the Tomahawk Chop is a swell pastime must be just as hearty in their endorsement of the following ideas, which—by the "logic" used to defend the defamation of American Indians—should help us all *really* start yukking it up.

First, as a counterpart to the Redskins, we need an NFL team called "Niggers" to "honor" Afroamerica. Halftime festivities for fans might include a simulated stewing of the opposing coach in a large pot while players and cheerleaders dance around it, garbed in leopard skins and wearing fake bones in their noses. This concept obviously goes along with the kind of gaiety attending the Chop, but also with the actions of the Kansas City Chiefs, whose team members—prominently including black team members—lately appeared on a poster looking "fierce" and "savage" by way of wearing Indian regalia. Just a bit of harmless "morale boosting," says the Chiefs' front office. You bet.

So that the newly-formed "Niggers" sports club won't end up too out of sync while expressing the "spirit" and "identity" of Afroamericans in the above fashion, a baseball franchise—let's call this one the "Sambos"—should be formed. How about a basketball team called the "Spearchuckers"? A hockey team called the "Jungle Bunnies"? Maybe the "essence" of these teams could be depicted by images of tiny black faces adorned with huge pairs of lips. The players could appear on TV every week or so gnawing on chicken legs and spitting watermelon seeds at one another. Catchy, eh? Well, there's "nothing to be upset about," according to those who love wearing "war bonnets" to the Super Bowl or having "Chief Illiniwik" dance around the sports arenas of Urbana, Illinois.

And why stop there? There are plenty of other groups to include. "Hispanics"? They can be "represented" by the Galveston "Greasers" and San Diego "Spics," at least until the Wisconsin "Wetbacks" and Baltimore "Beaners" get off the ground. Asian Americans? How about the "Slopes," "Dinks," "Gooks," and "Zipperheads"? Owners of the latter teams might get their logo ideas from editorial page cartoons printed in the nation's newspapers during World War II: slant-eyes, buck teeth, big glasses, but nothing racially insulting or derogatory, according to the editors and artists involved at the time. Indeed, this Second World War-vintage stuff can be seen as just another barrel of laughs, at least by what current editors say are their "local standards" concerning American Indians.

Let's see. Who's been left out? Teams like the Kansas City "Kikes," Hanover "Honkies," San Leandro "Shylocks," Daytona "Dagos," and Pittsburgh "Polacks" will fill a certain social void among white folk. Have a religious belief? Let's all go for the gusto and gear up the Milwaukee "Mackerel Snappers" and Hollywood "Holy Rollers." The Fighting Irish of Notre Dame can be rechristened the "Drunken Irish" or "Papist Pigs." Issues of gender and sexual preference can be addressed through creation of teams like the St. Louis "Sluts," Boston "Bimbos," Detroit "Dykes," and the Fresno "Faggots." How about the Gainesville "Gimps" and Richmond "Retards," so the physically and mentally impaired won't be excluded from our fun and games?

Now, don't go getting "overly sensitive" out there. *None* of this is demeaning or insulting, at least not when it's being done to Indians. Just ask the folks who are doing it, or their apologists like Andy Rooney in the national media. They'll tell you—as in fact they *have* been telling you—that there's been no harm done, regardless of what their victims think, feel, or say. The situation is exactly the same as when those with precisely the same mentality used to insist that Step'n'Fetchit was okay, or Rochester on the *Jack Benny Show,* or Amos and Andy, Charlie Chan, the Frito Bandito, or any of the other cutesey symbols making up the lexicon of American racism. Have we communicated yet?

Let's get just a little bit real here. The notion of "fun" embodied in rituals like the Tomahawk Chop must be understood for what it is. There's not a single non-Indian example deployed above which can be considered socially acceptable in even the most marginal sense. The reasons are obvious enough. So why is it different where American Indians are concerned? One can only conclude that, in contrast to the other groups at issue, Indians are (falsely) perceived as being too few, and therefore too weak, to defend themselves effectively against racist and otherwise offensive behavior. The sensibilities of those who take pleasure in things like the Chop are thus akin to those of schoolyard bullies and those twisted individuals who like to torture cats. At another level, their perspectives have much in common with those manifested more literally—and therefore more honestly—by groups like the nazis, aryan nations, and ku klux klan. Those who suggest this is "okay" should be treated accordingly by anyone who opposes nazism and comparable belief systems.

Fortunately, there are a few glimmers of hope that this may become the case. A few teams and their fans have gotten the message and have responded appropriately. One illustration is Stanford University, which opted to drop the name "Indians" with regard to its sports teams (and, contrary to the myth perpetrated by those who enjoy insulting Native Americans, Stanford has experienced *no* resulting drop-off in attendance at its games). Meanwhile, the local newspaper in Portland, Oregon, recently decided its long-standing editorial policy prohibiting use of racial epithets should include derogatory sports team names. The Redskins, for instance, are now simply referred to as being "the Washington team," and will continue to be described in this way until the franchise adopts an inoffensive moniker (newspaper sales in Portland have suffered no decline as a result).

Such examples are to be applauded and encouraged. They stand as figurative beacons in the night, proving beyond all doubt that it is quite possible to indulge in the pleasure of athletics without accepting blatant racism into the bargain. The extent to which they do not represent the norm of American attitudes and behavior is exactly the extent to which America remains afflicted with an ugly reality which is far different from the noble and enlightened "moral leadership" it professes to show the world. Clearly, the United States has a very long way to go before it measures up to such an image of itself.

## IMAGINED INDIANS, SOCIAL IDENTITIES, AND ACTIVISM

■ **C. Richard King and Charles Fruehling Springwood** ■

Native American mascots are a pervasive, ubiquitous feature of American culture. Dozens of professional and semi-professional sports teams have (or have had) such monikers. A quarter of a century after Stanford University, the University of Oklahoma, and Dartmouth College retired "their" Indians, according to the National Coalition on Racism in Sports and Media, more than eighty colleges and universities still use Native American mascots (Rodriguez 1998).

Innumerable high schools continue to refer to themselves and their sports teams as the Indians, the Redskins, the Braves, the Warriors, or the Red Raiders.

Euro-American individuals and institutions initially imagined themselves as Indians for a myriad of reasons. Whereas some institutions, such as Dartmouth College, had historically defined themselves through a specific relationship with Native Americans, more commonly, especially at public universities, regional histories and the traces of the Native nations that formerly occupied the state inspired students, coaches, and administrators to adopt Indian mascots, as in the University of Utah Running Utes or the University of Illinois Fighting Illini. Elsewhere, elaborations of a historical accident, coincidence, or circumstance seem to account for the beginnings of playing Indian. The students at Simpson College, in Indianola, Iowa, became the Redmen, later adopting a victory cheer known as the "Scalp Song" and using idioms of Indianness in their annual rituals such as homecoming, following remarks that they played like a bunch of red men. Similarly, St. John's University teams were known as the Redmen initially because their uniforms were all red; only later did fans and alumni transform this quirk into a tradition of playing Indian. Whatever the specific origins of these individual icons, Euro-Americans were able to fabricate Native Americans as mascots precisely because of prevailing sociohistorical conditions. That is, a set of social relations and cultural categories made it possible, pleasurable, and powerful for Euro-Americans to incorporate images of Indians in athletic contexts. First, Euro-Americans have always fashioned individual and collective identities for themselves by playing Indian. Native American mascots were an extension of this long tradition. Second, the conquest of Native America simultaneously empowered Euro-Americans to appropriate, invent, and otherwise represent Native Americans and to long for aspects of their cultures that had been destroyed by conquest. Third, with the rise of public culture, the production of Indianness in spectacles, exhibitions, and other sundry entertainments proliferated, offering templates for elaborations in sporting contexts.

Importantly, Native American mascots increasingly have become questionable, contentious, and problematic (Banks 1993; Churchill 1994; Davis 1993; Frazier 1997; Jackson and Lyons 1997; King 1998; King and Springwood forthcoming; Pewewardy 1991; Slowikowski 1993; Springwood and King forthcoming; Vanderford 1996; Wenner 1993). Across the United States and Canada, individuals and organizations, from high school students and teachers to the American Indian Movement and the National Congress of American Indians, passionately and aggressively have contested Native American mascots, forcing public debates and policy changes.

At the professional level, in April 1999, the federal Trademark Trial and Appeal Board voided the trademark rights of the Washington Redskins of the National Football League, finding that the name and logo used by the team were disparaging and hence violated the law (Kelber 1994; Likourezos 1996; Pace 1994; see also Sigelman 1998). The seven prominent Native Americans who brought the case in 1992, including contributors Vine Deloria Jr. and Susan Shown Harjo, hoped that the cancellation of trademark protection would encourage the franchise to drop its derogatory moniker. In an effort to fend off similar claims and defuse criticism, the Cleveland Indians have offered an origin myth of sorts that suggests the name and logo memorialize a past player and thus honor Native Americans more generally (Staurowsky 1998, this volume).

Arguably, collegiate mascots have evoked more debate than their professional counterparts. In the past decade, several colleges and universities have taken great strides in response to public concern. Whereas a handful of institutions, including the University of Utah and Bradley University, have *revised* their use of imagery, many others, including St. John's University, the University of Miami (Ohio), Simpson College, the University of Tennessee at Chattanooga, and Adams State College (Colorado) have *retired* their mascots. Some schools without Native American mascots, such as the University of Wisconsin and the University of Minnesota, have instituted policies prohibiting their athletic departments from scheduling games against institutions with racist icons. At the same time, countless communities and boards of education have confronted the issue. Many have deemed Native American mascots to be discriminatory, opting as the Minnesota State Board of Education and the Los Angeles and Dallas School Districts did, to require that schools change them. Of course, many other schools have retained them, often becoming the site of intense protest and controversy, such as the highly visible struggle continuing to unfold at the University of Illinois at Urbana-Champaign (see King 1998; King and Springwood forthcoming; Prochaska, this volume; Spindel 1997; Springwood and King forthcoming). Not surprisingly, media attention has increased markedly. On the one hand, the media have detailed numerous local and national struggles, while on the other hand, they have taken a leading role in modifying public perceptions of mascots, such as when the *Portland Oregonian* changed its editorial policy and refused to print derogatory team names. In both capacities, they have opened a crucial space of public debate about mascots. . . .

For all of this, Native American mascots remain understudied, too often taken for granted, and rarely questioned by scholars and citizens alike. *Team Spirits* challenges these tendencies, reinterpreting the forgotten histories of many of these "invented" Indians, unraveling their significance for players, coaches, spectators, students, and Native Americans more generally, and, finally, revealing their complicated relevance for an array of postcolonial American social relations and identities.

■ ■ ■

Native American mascots perpetuate inappropriate, inaccurate, and harmful understandings of living people, their cultures, and their histories (Banks 1993; Churchill 1994; Davis 1993; Frazier 1997; Gone 1999; Jackson and Lyons 1997; King 1998; King and Springwood forthcoming; Pewewardy 1994; Slowikowski 1993; Springwood and King forthcoming; Vanderford 1996; Wenner 1993). Through fragments thought to be Indian—a headdress, tomahawk, war paint, or buckskin—Native American mascots reduce them to a series of wellworn clichés, sideshow props, and racist stereotypes, masking, if not erasing, the complexities of Native American experiences and identities. Halftime performance, fan antics, and mass merchandizing transform somber and reverent artifacts and activities into trivial, shallow, and lifeless forms. Indeed, Native American mascots misappropriate sacred ideas and objects, such as the headdress war bonnet, relocating them in sacrilegious contexts. They misuse and misunderstand the elements of Native American cultures and their symbolic meanings. Importantly, since many Euro-Americans encounter Native Americans *only* as mascots and moving images, these unreal Indians materialize the most base images of Native Americans, presenting them as warriors battling settlers and soldiers, noble savages in touch with nature, uncivilized barbarians opposing the civilized and ultimately triumphant advance of Euro-America.

The many invented Indians used in sporting contexts reveal a nuanced system of signs comprising a broad performative space. This space, largely designed by and for a white

America, has broad historical dimensions that turn on imaginary images of Native Americans (see Berkhofer 1979; Bird 1996; Dilworth 1996; Drinnon 1980; Mihesuah 1996; Pearce 1988; Steedman 1982). These embodied "Indian" caricatures have been *tropically* produced as, variously, the warring body (Berkhofer 1979; King 1998; Springwood and King forthcoming), the drunken Native (Duran 1996), the dancing Native (Drinnon 1980; Bloom 1996; King and Springwood forthcoming), the sexual Native (van Lent 1996), the magical Native (Colin 1987; Duran 1996), and the maiden Native (Albers and James 1987; Green 1975; Sparks 1995). These Indian mascots conceptually *freeze* Native Americans, reducing them to rigid, flat renderings of their diverse cultures and histories. Moreover, these invented mascots indicate moments of writing and rewriting a Euro-American identity in terms of conquest, hierarchy, and domination. From center courts to athletic turfs, Indian mascots typically stage the historical relations between Native Americans and Euro-Americans as unmarked by violence. Indian mascots are often situated as warlike and bellicose, while others—commonly barefooted and bare-chested—imply a constellation of savagery and sexualized wildness. We suggest that these kinds of images dehumanize and demonize Native Americans, constraining the ability of the non-Indian community to relate to Indians as contemporary, significant, and real human actors. The narratives inscribed by these mascot exhibitions are punctuated by an ambivalence that includes contact, friendship, and subsequent submission. It is a sensual narrative that turns on wildness, sexuality, and savagery, and it is a nostalgic narrative mourning the loss of these once great warriors and their glorious society. To be sure the performance seeks on some level to "honor" the Indian, but it does so through unconscious forms, by allowing white America to simultaneously enact its grief for and consecrate the memory of the Indian. It is a celebration of the Indian sacrifice in the name of imperial progress according to the divine plan of Manifest Destiny. It is a celebration of imperial power then that ritually incorporates the tragic figure of the Indian into the "Imagined community," in Benedict Anderson's (1983) words, of the United States of America. It allows white America to primitively reimagine itself as a partial embodiment of Indianness and, in the process, attempts to psychically and sympathetically join with the Indian in the formation of a "shared" American consciousness. But, as the contributors to the volume demonstrate, it is not a liberating ritual, for it remains comfortably informed by oblique relations of power.

Significantly, then, Native American mascots do not merely craft disparaging images of others but facilitate the dynamic stagings of self. They permit Euro-Americans to construct an individual identity—as fans, athletes, students, citizens, and the like—while solidifying a transcendent sense of community, a unifying communitas. In essence, Native American mascots are masks, which when worn enable Euro-Americans to do and say things they cannot in everyday life, *as though by playing Indian they enter a transformative space of inversion wherein new possibilities of experience reside* (Deloria 1998; Green 1988; Huhndorf 1997; Mechling 1980). For example, on numerous occasions all-male, fraternal clubs have chosen to name and ritually adorn themselves after particular Native American tribes in ways that perhaps allow them to bond at spiritual and emotional levels that—to their non-Indian selves—may seem otherwise unattainable.

Thus, Native American mascots are one instance within a much broader complex of practices of playing Indian. We would argue that in the present moment, such mascots represent the most conspicuous, hotly contested, and broadly consumed form of playing Indian. To fully appreciate the significance of such mascots, the ideological and political economy grounding them must be examined. Playing Indian has always opened a space in which to articulate American identities, as illustrated here by a handful of examples. At the (much celebrated and so-called) Boston Tea Party of December 16, 1773, for instance, a group of locals who fashioned themselves as "Indians" by smearing their faces and shouting "war calls" relieved the British ship *Dartmouth* of its East India Company's tea (see Deloria 1998). Later, as the new republic and its citizens searched for symbols and stories through which to create themselves, they invariably poached Native American communities or at least idealized notions of their Indianness. Perhaps most important, as early as the late eighteenth century, was a proliferation across the young nation of fraternal orders—often secret "clubs" joining learned, masculine patriots—(in)vested in invented Indianness (Deloria 1998:46). The importance of these homosocial organizations intensified precisely as industrial modernity reshaped the racial and gender contour of everyday life. If sport promotes contexts in which to negotiate these crises, sporting clubs often enhanced the productivity of play by playing Indian (Davis 1993). Moreover, throughout the nineteenth century, Euro-Americans played at being Indian on stage and in literature, while encouraging Native Americans to enact notions of Indianness at fairs, in museums, and for other public performances. These stagings peaked in their popularity and sophistication in the late nineteenth and early twentieth centuries at world's fairs (Rydell 1984) and in Wild West shows (Moses 1996). Importantly, the increased use of Native American culture to (re)create self and society for fun and profit corresponded with the final stages of the Euro-American subjugation of Native America in which reformers and politicians endeavored through increasingly ambitious programs and policies to assimilate Native Americans and in the process sought to restrict their traditional practices and precepts, particularly dance, ritual, and spirituality. It was in this context of well-worn and accepted patterns of playing Indian, imperial nostalgia, and the imperial momentum to control Indian expression that Euro-Americans began to fashion Native American mascots.

Scholars and Native American activists have invested great energy in constructing a critique of Indian mascots by foregrounding their colonial legacies and deconstructing the stereotypes they embody. Efforts to challenge mascots emerged from a broader movement to reclaim sovereignty, redress historical inequities, and assert a sociopolitical identity in American public culture (Cornell 1988; Johnson, Nagel, and Champagne 1997; Nagel 1996; Smith and Warrior 1996). Fueled by the civil rights movement, anti-colonial struggles, including opposition to the Vietnam War, and using demands for self-determination in Native American communities, activists and allies demanded a voice in the representation of Native American cultures throughout popular culture. Importantly, struggles over images, although lacking the violence and spectacle of many earlier interventions, have been among the most visible and arguably the most successful examples of American Indian activism and socio-cultural resurgence. Importantly, efforts to challenge and retire Native American mascots have largely been left out of this history. . . .

■ ■ ■

Students and their allies called for the retirement of Native American mascots, rightly highlighting the hurtful images, hateful practices, and hostile learning environments associated with them. Initially, as detailed above, their struggles resulted in a measure of success, forcing the retirement of mascots at Stanford University and Dartmouth College and the alteration of practices at Oklahoma University and Marquette University. Over the next thirty years, activists and organizations have continued to struggle against mascots, using litigation, petitions, and protests. Indeed, during this period, combining sociopolitical intervention with sociohistorical education, they have raised formerly unspeakable and unremarkable issues to the forefront of current debates about public culture. Moreover, as discussed in greater detail above, they have encouraged many colleges, universities, and communities to rethink their uses and understandings of Indianness. The results of these reconsiderations have been quite impressive, as prominent schools have retired or modified "their" Indians.

For all of their success, activism against mascots has met vigorous reactionary responses. Indeed, many Euro-Americans, even well-intentioned ones, and some Native Americans do not understand such criticisms or grasp the significance of implementing such changes. The 1995 World Series clarifies some of the difficulties associated with this counter-hegemonic, anti-imperial sociopolitical movement. When members of the American Indian Movement as well as representatives from other Native American organizations demonstrated with placards and bull horns outside Atlanta's Fulton County Stadium during baseball's 1995 World Series—pitting the Atlanta Braves against the Minnesota Twins—they voiced objections to the Braves' spectators, many of whom carried large, colorful Styrofoam tomahawks to wave during the now famous "chop." These demonstrations apparently caught the attention of Jane Fonda, the one-time activist and movie star, who met with the leaders of some of these groups. After listening to Clyde and Vernon Bellecourt of AIM, she promised that she would no longer do the "tomahawk chop." Braves' fans tend to collectively stand and perform this syncopated chop to stadium organ music—a rhythmic "Indian" beat. The promise of Jane Fonda, married to the team owner, millionaire Ted Turner, was significant. And yet, a few games further into the series, with the Braves "rallying," Fonda stood, along with her husband and some 60,000 other spectators, to do the tomahawk chop. Clearly, Native American activism, for all of its success, continues to struggle against racist ideologies.

## References

Albers, Patricia C., and William R. James. 1987. "Illusion and Illumination: Visual Images of American Indian Women in the West." In *The Women's West*, ed. Susan Armitage and Elizabeth Jameson, pp. 35–50. Norman: University of Oklahoma Press.

Anderson, Benedict. 1983. *Imagined Communities.* New York: Verso.

Banks, Dennis J. 1993. "Tribal Names and Mascots in Sports." *Journal of Sport and Social Issues* 17: 5–8.

Berkhoffer, Robert F., Jr. 1979. *The White Man's Indian.* New York: Vintage Press.

Bird, S. Elizabeth, ed. 1996. *Dressing in Feathers: The Construction of the Indian in American Popular Culture.* Boulder CO: Westview Press.

Bloom, John. 1996. "There Is Madness in the Air: The 1926 Haskell Homecoming and Popular Representations of Sports in Federal Indian Boarding Schools." In *Dressing in Feathers: The Construction of the Indian in American Popular Culture*, ed. S. Elizabeth Bird. Boulder CO: Westview Press.

Brown, Bill. 1991. "The Meaning of Baseball in 1992 (with Notes on the Post-American)." *Public Culture* 4(1): 43–69.

Churchill, Ward. 1994. "Let's Spread the 'Fun' Around." In *Indians Are Us? Culture and Genocide in Native North America*, pp. 65–72. Monroe ME: Common Courage Press.

Colin, Susi. 1987. "The Wild Man and the Indian in Early 16th Century Book Illustration." In *Indians and Europe*, ed. C. F. Freest. Herodot, Netherlands: Rader Verlag.

Comoroff, John, and Jean Comoroff. 1991. *From Revolution to Revelation.* Chicago: University of Chicago Press.

Cornell, Stephen. 1988. *The Return of the Native: American Indian Political Resurgence.* Oxford: Oxford University Press.

Davis, Laurel. 1993. "Protest against the Use of Native American Mascots: A Challenge to Traditional, American Identity." *Journal of Sport and Social Issues* 17(1): 9–22.

Deloria, Philip. 1998. *Playing Indian.* New Haven: Yale University Press.

Dilworth, Leah. 1996. *Imagining Indians in the Southwest: Persistent Visions of a Primitive Past.* Washington DC: Smithsonian Institution Press.

Drinnon, Richard. 1980. *Facing West: The Metaphysics of Indian-Hating and Empire-Building.* Minneapolis: University of Minnesota Press.

Duran, Bonnie. 1996. "Indigenous versus Colonial Discourse: Alcohol and American Indian Identity." In *Dressing in Feathers: The Construction of the Indian in American Popular Culture,* ed. S. Elizabeth Bird, pp. 111–28. Boulder CO: Westview Press.

Frazier, Jane. 1997. "Tomahawkin' the Redskins: 'Indian' Images in Sports and Commerce." In *American Indian Studies: An Interdisciplinary Approach to Contemporary Issues,* ed. Dane Morrison, pp. 337–46. New York: Peter Lang.

Gone, Joseph P. 1999. "Not Enough Indians, Too Many Chiefs: Authority and Performance in the Movement to End Chief Illiniwek." Unpublished manuscript.

Green, Rayna. 1975. "The Pocahontas Perplex: The Image of Indian Women in American Culture." *Massachusetts Review* 16: 698–714.

——. 1988. "The Tribe Called Wannabee: Playing Indian in America and Europe." *Folklore* 99: 30–55.

Hall, Stuart, ed. 1997. *Representation: Cultural Representations and Signifying Practices.* Thousand Oaks CA: Sage.

Harvey, David. 1990. *The Condition of Postmodernity.* Cambridge MA: Blackwell.

Huhndorf, Shari. 1997. "Playing Indian, Past and Present." In *As We Are Now: Mixblood Essays on Race and Identity,* ed. William S. Penn, pp. 181–98. Berkeley: University of California Press.

Jackson, E. N., and Robert Lyons. 1997. "Perpetuating the Wrong Image of Native Americans." *Journal of Physical Education, Recreation, and Dance* 68(4): 4–5.

Jameson, Fredric. 1991. *Postmodernism, or, the Cultural Logic of Late Capitalism.* Durham NC: Duke University Press.

Johnson, Troy, Joane Nagel, and Duane Champagne, eds. 1997. *American Indian Activism: Alcatraz to the Longest Walk.* Urbana: University of Illinois Press.

Jordan, Glenn, and Chris Weedon. 1995. *Cultural Politics: Class, Gender, Race and the Postmodern World.* Oxford: Blackwell.

Kaplan, Amy, and Donald E. Pease, eds. 1993. *Cultures of United States Imperialism.* Durham NC: Duke University Press.

Kelber, B. C. 1994. "Scalping the Redskins': Can Trademark Law Start Athletic Teams Bearing Native American Nicknames and Images on the Road to Reform?" *Hamline Law Review* 17: 533–588.

King, C. Richard. 1998. "Spectacles, Sports, and Stereotypes: Dis/Playing Chief Illiniwek." In *Colonial Discourse, Collective Memories, and the Exhibition of Native American Cultures and Histories in the Contemporary United States,* ed. C. Richard King, pp. 41–58. New York: Garland.

King, C. Richard, ed. 2000. *Postcolonial America.* Urbana: University of Illinois Press.

King, C. Richard, and Charles Fruehling Springwood. Forthcoming. "Choreographing Colonialism: Athletic Mascots, (Dis)Embodied Indians, and EuroAmerican Subjectivities." In *Cultural Studies: A Research Volume,* vol. 5, ed. Norman Denzin. Stamford CT: JAI Press.

Likourezos, G. 1996. "A Case of First Impression: American Indians Seek Cancellation of the Trademarked Term 'Redskins.'" *Journal of the Patent and Trademark Office Society* 78: 275–90.

Mechling, Jay. 1980. " 'Playing Indian' and the Search for Authenticity in Modern White America." *Prospects* 5: 17–33.

Mihesuah, Devon A. 1996. *American Indians: Stereotypes and Realities.* Atlanta: Clarity Press.

Moses, L. G. 1996. *Wild West Shows and the Images of American Indians, 1883–1933.* Albuquerque: University of New Mexico Press.

Nagel, Joane. 1996. *American Indian Ethnic Renewal: Red Power and the Resurgence of Identity and Culture.* Oxford: Oxford University Press.

Pace, K. A. 1994. "The Washington Redskins and the Doctrine of Disparagement." *Pepperdine Law Review* 22: 7–57.

Pearce, Roy Harvey. 1988. *Savagism and Civilization: A Study of the Indian and the American Mind.* Rev. ed. Berkeley: University of California Press.

Pease, Donald E., ed. 1994. *National Identities and Post-Americanist Narratives.* Durham NC: Duke University Press.

Pewewardy, Cornel D. 1991. "Native American Mascots and Imagery: The Struggle of Unlearning Indian Stereotypes." *Journal of Navaho Education* 9(1): 19–23.

Rodriguez, Roberto. 1998. "Plotting the Assassination of Little Red Sambo." *Black Issues in Higher Education* 15(8): 20–24.

Rydell, Robert W. 1984. *All the World's a Fair: Visions of Empire at American International Expositions, 1876–1916.* Chicago: University of Chicago Press.

Sigelman, Lee. 1998. "Hail to the Redskins? Public Reactions to a Racially Insensitive Team Name." *Sociology of Sport Journal* 15: 317–25.

Slowikowski, Synthia Sydnor. 1993. "Cultural Performances and Sports Mascots." *Journal of Sport and Social Issues* 17(1): 23–33.

Smith, Paul Chaat, and Robert Allen Warrior. 1996. *Like a Hurricane: The Indian Movement from Alcatraz to Wounded Knee.* New York: New Press.

Sparks, Carol Douglas. 1995. "The Land Incarnate: Navajo Women and the Dialogue of Colonialism, 1821–1870." In *Negotiators of Change: Historical Perspectives on Native American Women,* ed. Nancy Shoemaker, pp. 135–56. New York: Routledge.

Spindel, Carol. 1997. "We Honor Your Memory: Chief Illiniwek of the Halftime Illini." *Crab Orchard Review* 3(1): 217–38.

Springwood, Charles Fruehling, and C. Richard King. Forthcoming. "Race, Ritual, and Remembrance Embodied: Manifest Destiny and the Symbolic Sacrifice of 'Chief Illiniwek.'" In *Exercising Power: The Making and Remaking of the Body,* ed. Cheryl Cole, John Loy, and Michael Messner. Albany: SUNY Press.

Staurowsky, Ellen J. 1998. "An Act of Honor or Exploitation? The Cleveland Indians' Use of the Louis Francis Sockalexis Story." *Sociology of Sport Journal* 15(4):299–316.

Steedman, Raymond William. 1982. *Shadows of the Indian: Stereotypes in American Culture.* Norman: University of Oklahoma Press.

Vanderford, Heather. 1996. "What's in a Name? Heritage or Hatred: The School Mascot Controversy." *Journal of Law and Education* 25:381–88.

van Lent, Peter. 1996. "'Her Beautiful Savage': The Current Sexual Image of the Native American Male." In *Dressing in Feathers: The Construction of the Indian in American Popular Culture,* ed. S. Elizabeth Bird, pp. 211–27. Boulder CO: Westview Press.

Wenner, L. 1993. "The Real Red Face of Sports." *Journal of Sport and Social Issues* 17:1–4.

## THE INDIAN WARS

■ S. L. Price ■

Solve this word problem: Billy Mills, the former runner who won the gold medal in the 10,000 meters at the 1964 Olympics, is on a commercial airliner hurtling somewhere over the U.S. It is August 2001. Because Mills's father and mother were three-quarters and one-quarter Native American, respectively, he grew up being called half-breed until that was no longer socially acceptable. As sensibilities shifted over the years, he heard a variety of words and phrases describing his ethnic background, from Indian to Sioux to Native American to the one with which he is most comfortable, the age-old name of his tribal nation: Lakota.

Mills is sitting in first class. A flight attendant—the words steward and stewardess are frowned upon today—checks on him every so often. The man is African-American, the preferred designation for his racial background; before that, society called him black or colored or Negro. The man is friendly, doing his job. Each time he addresses Mills, he calls him Chief. Mills doesn't know if the flight attendant realizes that he is Lakota. Maybe he calls everyone Chief. Maybe he means it as a compliment. Mills motions him over.

"I want to tell you something," Mills says. The man leans in. "I'm Native American, and you calling me Chief, it turns my stomach. It'd be very similar to somebody calling you Nigger."

The flight attendant looks at Mills. He says, "Calling you Chief doesn't bother me . . . Chief."

Who is right and who wrong? Whose feelings take precedence? Most important, who gets to decide what we call one another?

If you've figured out an answer, don't celebrate yet. The above confrontation is only a warmup for sport's thorniest word problem: the use of Native American names (and mascots that represent them) by high school, college and professional teams. For more than 30 years the debate has been raging over whether names such as Redskins, Braves, Chiefs and Indians honor or defile Native Americans, whether clownish figures like the Cleveland Indians' Chief Wahoo have any place in today's racially sensitive climate and whether the sight of thousands of non-Native Americans doing the tomahawk chop at Atlanta's Turner Field is mindless fun or mass bigotry. It's an argument that, because it mixes mere sports with the sensitivities of a people who were nearly exterminated, seems both trivial and profound—and it's further complicated by the fact that for three out of four Native Americans, even a nickname such as Redskins, which many whites consider racist, isn't objectionable.

Indeed, some Native Americans—even those who purportedly object to Indian team nicknames—wear Washington Redskins paraphernalia with pride. Two such men showed up in late January at Augustana College in Sioux Falls, S.Dak., for a conference on race relations. "They were speaking against the Indian nicknames, but they were wearing Redskins sweatshirts, and one had on a Redskins cap," says Betty Ann Gross, a member of the Sisseton-Wahpeton Sioux tribe. "No one asked them about it. They looked pretty militant."

Gross's own case illustrates how slippery the issue can be. She grew up on a reservation in South Dakota and went to Sisseton High, a public school on the reservation whose teams are called the Redmen. Gross, 49, can't recall a time when people on the reservation weren't arguing about the team name, evenly divided between those who were proud of it and those who were ashamed. Gross recently completed a study that led the South Dakota state government to change the names of 38 places and landmarks around the state, yet she has mixed feelings on the sports issue. She wants Indian mascots and the tomahawk chop discarded, but she has no problem with team names like the Fighting Sioux (University of North Dakota) or even the Redskins. "There's a lot of division," Gross says. "We're confused, and if we're confused, you guys should be really confused."

Indeed, a recent SI poll . . . suggests that although Native American activists are virtually united in opposition to the use of Indian nicknames and mascots, the Native American population sees the issue far differently. Asked if high school and college teams should stop using Indian nicknames, 81% of Native American respondents said no. As for pro sports, 83% of Native American respondents said teams should not stop using Indian nicknames, mascots, characters and symbols. Opinion is far more divided on reservations, yet a majority (67%) there said the usage by pro teams should not cease, while 32% said it should.

"I take the middle ground," says Leigh J. Kuwanwisiwma, 51, director of the Hopi Cultural Preservation Office in Kykotsmovi, Ariz., and an avid devotee of the Atlanta Braves. "I don't see anything wrong with Indian nicknames as long as they're not meant to be derogatory. Some tribal schools on Arizona reservations use Indians as a nickname themselves. The Phoenix Indian High School's newspaper is The Redskin. I don't mind the tomahawk chop. It's all in good fun. This is sports, after all. In my living room, I'll be watching a Braves game and occasionally do the chop."

Native American activists dismiss such opinion as misguided ("There are happy campers on every plantation," says Suzan Harjo, president of the Morning Star Institute, an Indian-rights organization based in Washington, D.C.) or as evidence that Native Americans' self-esteem has fallen so low that they don't even know when they're being insulted. American Indians—unlike, say, the Irish Catholics who founded Notre Dame and named its teams the Fighting Irish—had no hand in creating most of the teams that use their names; their identities were plucked from them wholesale and used for frivolous purposes, like firing up fans at ball games.

"This is no honor," says Michael Yellow Bird, an associate professor of social work at Arizona State. "We lost our land, we lost our languages, we lost our children. Proportionately speaking, indigenous peoples [in the U.S.] are incarcerated more than any other group, we have more racial violence perpetrated upon us, and we are forgotten. If people think this is how to honor us, then colonization has really taken hold."

Regardless, the campaign to erase Indian team names and symbols nationwide has been a success. Though Native American activists have made little progress at the highest level of pro sports—officials of the Atlanta Braves, Chicago Blackhawks, Cleveland Indians and Washington Redskins, for example, say they have no intention of changing their teams' names or mascots—their single-minded pursuit of the issue has literally changed the face of sports in the U.S. Since 1969, when Oklahoma disavowed its mascot Little Red (a student wearing an Indian war bonnet, buckskin costume and moccasins), more than 600 school teams and minor league professional clubs have dropped nicknames deemed offensive by Native American groups.

What's more, the movement continues. On Jan. 9 the Metropolitan Washington Council of Governments, which represents 17 local governments in D.C., southern Maryland and northern Virginia, voted 11-2 to adopt a resolution calling the Redskins name "demeaning and dehumanizing" and asking team owner Dan Snyder to change it by next season. A week earlier former Redskins fullback Dale Atkeson had been told by the California Department of Motor Vehicles to remove his vanity plates reading 1 REDSKN. The word Redskin was banned on plates by the DMV in 1999.

"We consider ourselves racially sensitive," says D.C. council member Carol Schwartz, who introduced the resolution against the Redskins, "yet in this one area we are so hypocritical. Since when is a sports team's name more important than the sensitivities of our fellow human beings? For decades we had the Washington Bullets, and [owner] Abe Pollin on his own changed the name [in 1997, because of the high murder rate in D.C.].

Guess what? The world did not stop spinning. Why we would keep this racist term is beyond me."

While those who support names such as Seminoles (Florida State) and Braves can argue that the words celebrate Native American traditions, applying that claim to the Redskins is absurd. Nevertheless, Redskins vice president Karl Swanson says the name "symbolizes courage, dignity and leadership and has always been employed in that manner"—conveniently ignoring the fact that in popular usage dating back four centuries, the word has been a slur based on skin color. Swanson trots out research that traces the term redskin to Native Americans' custom of daubing on red paint before battle. Many experts on Native American history point out that the red paint was used not for war but for burial, and that the word redskin was first used by whites who paid and received bounties for dead Indians. "If you research the origin of redskin, no one would want that associated with his team," says pro golfer Notah Begay III, who is half Navajo and half Pueblo. "Trading-post owners used to offer rewards for Indian scalps. Signs would say something like, 'Redskin scalps, worth so much.'"

However, what's most important, Swanson counters, is intent: Because the Redskins and their fans mean nothing racist by using the nickname, it isn't racist or offensive. "This has been the name of our organization for 70 years," Swanson says. "We believe it has taken on a meaning independent of the word itself—and it's positive."

Not so, says Harjo: "There's no more derogatory word that's used against us, about us, in the English language. Even if it didn't have such heinous origins, everyone knows that it has never been an honorific. It's a terrible insult."

Harjo is not alone in her thinking. A slew of dictionaries agree that redskin is contemptuous, and so do Native American academics, nearly every Native American organization and three judges on the U.S. Trademark Trial and Appeal Board. In April 1999, responding to a lawsuit brought by Harjo and six other Indian leaders, the board stripped the Washington Redskins of federal protection on their seven trademarks. If the decision stands up under appeal, the team and the NFL could lose an estimated $5 million annually on sales of licensed merchandise.

Even though no team name is under more sustained attack, there's evidence that for the Redskins, a name change would be good for business. In 1996, after much pressure from alumni threatening to withdraw their financial support, Miami (Ohio) University acceded to the Miami tribe's request that it change its team names from Redskins to Redhawks. The following year alumni gave a record $25 million to the school. "Someday it will change," Miami spokesman Richard Little says of the Washington Redskins name. "And you know what? There'll still be a football team there, and there'll still be those ugly fat guys in dresses cheering for it."

Swanson says the vast majority of Redskins fans like the name, and indeed, beyond the protests of politicians, there's no groundswell of outrage against it in D.C. In a city so racially sensitive that an aide to mayor Anthony Williams was forced to resign in 1999 for correctly using the nonracial term niggardly, there's nothing hotter than the mass pilgrimage of 80,000 fans to Landover, Md., on Sundays in autumn to sing Hail to the Redskins at FedEx Field. Williams mentioned changing the name at a press conference once, but "no one really paid attention," says his aide Tony Bullock. "It's not something that anyone is really talking about." Nevertheless, Bullock says, "the mayor believes it is time to change the name."

That the name is offensive to Native Americans is easy for non-Natives to presume. It resonates when an Olympic hero and former Marine Corps captain such as Mills, who speaks out against Indian names and mascots at schools around the country, insists that a team named Redskins in the capital of the nation that committed genocide against Native Americans is the equivalent of a soccer team in Germany being called the Berlin Kikes. Says Mills, "Our truth is, redskin is tied to the murder of indigenous people."

Somehow that message is lost on most of Mills's fellow Native Americans. Asked if they were offended by the name Redskins, 75% of Native American respondents in SI's poll said they were not, and even on reservations, where Native American culture and influence are perhaps felt most intensely, 62% said they weren't offended. Overall, 69% of Native American respondents—and 57% of those living on reservations—feel it's O.K. for the Washington Redskins to continue using the name. "I like the name Redskins," says Mark Timentwa, 50, a member of the Colville Confederated Tribes in Washington State who lives on the tribes' reservation. "A few elders find it offensive, but my mother loves the Redskins."

Only 29% of Native Americans, and 40% living on reservations, thought Snyder should change his team's name. Such indifference implies a near total disconnect between Native American activists and the general Native American population on this issue. "To a lot of the younger folks the name Redskins is tied to the football team, and it doesn't represent anything more than the team," says Roland McCook, a member of the tribal council of the Ute tribe in Fort Duchesne, Utah.

The Utes' experience with the University of Utah might serve as a model for successful resolution of conflicts over Indian nicknames. Four years ago the council met with university officials, who made it clear that they would change their teams' name, the Running Utes, if the tribe found it objectionable. (The university had retired its cartoonish Indian mascot years before.) The council was perfectly happy to have the Ute name continue to circulate in the nations' sports pages, but council members said they intended to keep a close eye on its use. "We came away with an understanding that as long as the university used the Ute name in a positive manner that preserved the integrity of the Ute tribe, we would allow the use of the name and the Ute logo [two eagle feathers and a drum]," says McCook. Florida State, likewise, uses the name Seminoles for its teams with the express approval of the Seminole nation.

Like the Ute tribe, most Native Americans have no problem with teams using names like Indians and Fighting Illini—or even imposed names like Sioux. "People get upset about the Fighting Sioux, but why?" Gross says. "We're not Sioux people, anyway. The French and the Ojibway tribe gave us that name, and they're our hereditary enemies. We're not braves, and we're not really Indians. I know the history. For me those names are not a problem." Many Native Americans are offended, however, by mascots such as Illinois's Chief Illiniwek and others that dress up in feathers and so-called war paint. "Just do away with the imagery—the dancing, the pageantry," says Gross.

Which brings us to the point at which the word problem becomes a number problem. Say you are a team owner. You kiss Chief Wahoo goodbye. Stop the chop. Dump the fake Indian garb, the turkey feathers and the war paint. Get rid of, say, the Redskins name because it's got a sullied history and just sounds wrong. Rename the team the Washington Warriors—without the Indian-head logo—and watch the new team hats and jackets hit the stores. Money is going to pour in, you see, and someone will have to count it.

## A SUITE OF CARTOONS
## THREE COMICS ON THE MASCOT ISSUE

*Source:* © 2002 Lalo Alcaraz/Universal Press Syndicate.

**READING** WRITING

## THIS TEXT: READING

1.  Which of the previous essays do you find the most compelling? What evidence does the author employ to help make his point? Why are *these* bits of evidence the most convincing?

2.  It is easy to discern the position Churchill, King and Freuling, but Price's stance is more difficult. Is he writing from a particular perspective? Elements of the essay make it feel more balanced than the others, but is it?

3.  What techniques does Price employ to make his essay feel more balanced? What objective data does he use to help make his argument sound convincing?

4.  Based on this chapter, do you think the authors of this book take a position regarding the mascot issue? What evidence is there that we make a particular argument here?

5.  How do the comics add to the arguments that Churchill makes?

6.  What do you think of Churchill's arguments? How would you characterize his tone? He uses words that many of us find offensive, so he has clearly thought about the wisdom including them. What is his strategy in employing these words? Do they hurt or help his arguments?

7.  Whose essay, Churchill's or Price's, is the most logos-based? Which is the most pathos-based?

## YOUR TEXT: WRITING

1.  Write an essay in which you take a stand on the Native American mascot issue. What evidence will you use to help support your assertions?

2.  Write an essay in which you analyze the rhetorical strategies of Churchill and Price. Look closely at the "evidence" each uses to help make their points.

3.  Write an essay in which you explore why there are still dozens of Native American mascots in the United States. Why is there resistance to changing them? Why do non-Indians have so much invested in holding on to Native American mascots?

4.  Write an essay in which you look at the mascot issue through the lens of freedom of expression.

5.  Write an essay on the mascot issue through the lens of hate speech and civil rights.

6.  Are there other arguments for or against the mascot issue that these writers and artists have not provided? What are they?

**READING** *Outside the Lines*

## CLASSROOM ACTIVITIES

1.  Although most scientists believe that race is socially constructed, that still leaves open the question of how we construct our ideas of race. In class, discuss some of the ways you see this process working in culture attributed to particular ethnic groups, and in white America as well.

2.  In his essay, "In Living Color: Race and American Culture," Michael Omi discusses the way race and ethnicity are portrayed on television. Using your own observations, discuss how popular culture treats race and ethnicity.

3. Discuss clothing and what pieces of clothing signify in general. Do you tend to characterize different groups by what clothes they wear?

4. After reading Beverly Tatum's piece, talk about the presence of race and ethnicity on campus. Do you notice patterns that can be inferred? Do you feel your campus is enlightened about race and ethnicity?

5. Some people still believe races and ethnicities have particular cultures, or cultures which are generated from groups from particular ethnicities. Discuss the phenomenon of people from different cultures participating in each other's culture.

6. Watch *Do the Right Thing* in class. What ideas about race does Spike Lee explore? What about his narrative makes you uncomfortable? What do you think his ideas about race are?

7. Watch *Mississippi Burning* with *Rosewood*. Compare how the two treat the idea of African-American participation in remedying racism. What problems do you see in the narratives? What have the filmmakers emphasized in their narratives? Is it at the expense of more "real" or important issues?

8. Watch two television shows, one with an all white or largely white cast, and one with an all African American or largely African American cast. How does each treat the idea of race and ethnicity?

9. Using the same shows, notice the commercials playing—how do these construct a view of race and/or ethnicity?

## ESSAY IDEAS

1. Trace the evolution of the portrayal of race and/or ethnicity in a particular medium—television, movies, art, public space. Has it changed in your lifetime? Why or why not?

2. Go to the library or the computer and do a keyword search on a particular ethnicity and a politician's name (example: "Cheney" and "African-American"). What comes up when you do this? Is there a trend worth writing about?

3. Do some research on the nature of prejudice. What do researchers say about its nature?

4. Get stories or novels from 75 years ago; look and see how different authors, African-American, white, Italian, Jewish, etc., portrayed people of different skin color and ethnicity. How would you characterize the treatment as a whole?

5. What are the signs that are encoded in race and ethnicity? How are they portrayed in popular culture and the media? Do a sign analysis of a particular show or media phenomenon.

6. Watch two television shows, one with a largely white cast, one with a largely African-American cast. Compare how each deals with the idea of race or ethnicity.

7. Using the same shows, notice the commercials playing—how do these construct a view of race and/or ethnicity?

8. Look at a film or films made by African-American, Hispanic, or other ethnic directors. How do these directors deal with the idea of race and ethnicity, compared to white directors dealing with similar ideas?

# Reading and Writing About Movies

■ ■ ■ Every movie set is a meticulously constructed text.
*Source:* Walt Disney Pictures/The Kobal Collection/Elliott Marks.

The contemporary American poet Louis Simpson writes in one of his poems: "Every American is a film critic." He is probably right. Just about everyone we know loves movies, and as much as we love movies, we love talking about them. And when we watch movies, we often feel qualified as critics; we freely disagree with movie reviewers and each other. Oscar Wilde once quipped, that in literature as in love, we are shocked by what others choose. That may be doubly so for movies.

Despite our familiarity with movies and our apparent willingness to serve as movie critics, we sometimes resist taking a more analytical approach to them. For many of us, movies are an escape from school or critical thinking. After a long day at school or at work, most of us want to sit in front of a big screen and veg out with *Miss Congeniality* or *Spider-Man 2* for a couple of hours. Your authors confess that we have been known to veg out too, so we aren't knocking the idea of losing oneself in front of a seemingly mindless action flick. However, we do want you to be aware of the fact that movies are never *just* mindless action flicks. They are always some kind of cultural text, loaded with ideas about a particular culture, either consciously or unintentionally expressed.

For instance, some film and cultural critics have argued that the *Star Wars* movies create a sense of nostalgia for the value systems of the 1950s; values that by today's standards may seem racist, sexist, and blindly patriotic. In fact, one of our students has written an essay along these lines, which we have included here. For others, the 90s favorite *Fatal Attraction* is more than a suspenseful movie about a crazed psycho-killer boiling a bunny. Some see the film as an allegory on AIDS, in that the film reinforces the central fear of AIDS—if you sleep around, you risk death. Still others see the film as a document that confirms the backlash against women during the conservatism of the Reagan years. In a much different vein, cultural critics and film historians have argued that genre movies like comedies, family melodramas, and gangster flicks tell stories about and reinforce mainstream American values. For instance, many have argued that Westerns like *The Searchers*, *Red River*, and *Broken Arrow* reflect an era's views on race, justice, and "American Values." You may disagree with these particular readings, but they show how movies can be a rich source for cultural exploration and debate.

However, there are obstacles when reading movies through a purely cultural lens. In some ways, our familiarity with movies becomes a liability when trying to analyze them. Because you have seen so many movies, you may believe that you already know how to read them. In some ways you do. As informal movie critics, you are already geared toward analyzing the plot of a movie or determining whether the movie is realistic or funny or appropriately sad. And if asked about music, fashion, setting, and dialogue in a movie, you would likely be able to talk about these aspects of filmmaking. But, when reading literature, you probably prepare your brain for a more intense act of *analysis* than you do when you watch *Legally Blonde 2*. You probably have not been taught to look *through* the plot and dialogue of movies to see the film as a cultural text. Though at times difficult, the process is often rewarding.

For instance, pay attention to how many Asian or American Indians you see in contemporary movies. Watch for roles for strong, confident women. Look for movies in which poor or blue collar people are treated not as a culture but as interesting individuals. See how many films are directed by women or minorities. Pay attention to product placements (that is, brand products such as soda cans, cereal, kinds of cars, or computers) in movies. Work on seeing cinematic texts as products, documents, and pieces of evidence from a culture. Rather than diminishing your enjoyment of movies, this added component of movie watching should enhance not only the actual film experience but also your understanding and appreciation of movies as produced, constructed texts.

## Like literature and music, movies are comprised of genres.

Movies, perhaps even more than literature and music, are comprised of genres, such as Westerns, science fiction, comedy, drama, adventure, horror, documentaries, and romance. You may not think about film genres that often, but you probably prepare yourself for certain movies depending on the genre of that particular film. You come to comedies prepared to laugh; you arrive at horror movies prepared to be scared; you go to "chick flicks" expecting romance, passion, and a happy ending. If you don't get these things in your movie experience, you will likely feel disappointed, as though the film didn't hold up its end of the bargain. Notice, in reading the selections here and movie reviews generally, how critics do or do not pay attention to genre. Though they should be familiar with genre, many critics insist on reviewing all movies as if they are supposed to be as earnest and dramatic as *Casablanca* or *Titanic,* when movies like *Mean Girls* or *Office Space* clearly try to do different things.

The idea of genre in movies is as old as Hollywood itself. In the early days of Hollywood, the studio system thrived on genre movies, and in fact, genre films were pretty much all that came out of Hollywood for several decades. Even today, blockbuster movies are most often genre pieces that adhere to the criteria of a particular genre. *I, Robot* is not *50 First Dates.* Different genres evoke different emotions, and they comment on (and reinforce) different values.

Being aware of genres and their conventions will help you when it comes time to write a paper on movies. When you "read" a film, think about how it fits into a particular genre. Taking into account formal, thematic, and cultural forces (the Cold War, civil rights, Vietnam, feminism, the Great Depression, the economic pressure to turn a profit) will allow you to see movie production as a dynamic process of exchange between the movie industry and its audience. You should be mindful of why we like certain genres and what these genres tell us about our culture and ourselves. The fact that some writers and critics distinguish between "movies" (cinema for popular consumption) and "films" (cinema that tries to transcend or explode popular genre formulations) suggests the degree to which genres influence how we read movie texts.

## Movies are a powerful cultural tool.

A hundred years ago, people satisfied their cravings for action, suspense, and character development by reading books and serials; today, we go to the movies, or, more and more frequently, avoid the communal experience of the theater for the private experience of renting videos and DVDs. Innovations like TIVO and Netflix have made staying at home even easier. Still, we are living in a visual age. In America, video and visual cultures have become the dominant modes of expression and communication, and learning to "read" these media with the same care, creativity, and critical acumen with which we read written texts is crucial. To better understand the phenomenon of movies, we need to contextualize the movie experience within American culture, asking in particular how thoroughly American movies affect (and reflect) American culture.

In addition, movies are not just indicators for American culture—they determine culture itself. Fashion, songs, modes of behavior, social and political views and gender and racial values are all underscored by movies. For instance, *Wayne's World* made certain songs and phrases part of everyday American life. On a more complex level, many critics claim the movie *Guess Who's Coming to Dinner,* in which a wealthy White woman brings home her Black fiancée, went a long way toward softening racial tensions in the 1960s. We even define eras, movements, and emotions by movies—the 1960s is often symbolized by *Easy Rider;* the 1970s by *Saturday Night Fever* and *Star Wars;* the 1980s by movies like *Fast Times at Ridgemont High* and *Do the Right Thing;* and the 1990s by *Titanic* and *You've Got Mail.* Because more people see movies than read books, one could argue that the best documents of American popular culture are movies. Thus, we tend to link the values and trends of certain eras with movies from those eras. Movies help us understand culture because they embody culture.

Movies also guide our behavior. In contemporary society, we often learn how to dress, how to talk, and even how to court and kiss someone, from the cinema. In fact, for many young people, their model for a date, a spouse, and a romantic moment all come from what they have seen in movies. In other words, influential models of behavior, aspects of their hopes and dreams, come not from life but from movies. So, as you read the following pieces and as you watch movies, ask yourself if the things you desire, you desire because movies have planted those seeds in your heads.

## The advertising and marketing of a movie affect how we view the movie and how the studio views itself and us.

Next time you watch previews in a theatre or on a video or DVD you have rented, pay attention to how the film being advertised is presented to you. Be aware of how movies are packaged, how they are marketed, how actors talk about them in interviews. Whether you know it or not, you are being prepped for viewing the movie by all of these texts. Even independent films have become mainstream by marketing themselves as similar to other (popular) independent movies. Marketing is selling, and studios fund, market, and release movies not so much to make the world a better place but primarily to make money (though directors and actors may have different motivations). Also, unlike a book publisher, a studio has likely paid tens of millions of dollars to make a movie, so it needs a lot of us to go see it. We might ask ourselves how these considerations affect not only the advertising but also the movie itself.

Additionally, Hollywood studios rarely have your best interest at heart. This is not to say that studios want to make you an evil person, but moviemakers have only rarely seen themselves as educators. For instance, few studios fund documentaries—and the recent controversy over Disney/Miramax refusing to distribute Michael Moore's incendiary documentary *Fahrenheit 9/11* is a testament to this fact. Few studios seem eager to make movies about poets, painters, composers, or philosophers because they know that not many people will go to see them. Movie studios began as a financial enterprise; studios and the film industry grew as America and American capitalist ideals grew. Nowadays, the topics and subjects of movies have been largely market-tested just like any other consumer product such as toys, soft drinks, and shoes.

## Movies use various techniques to manipulate audiences.

Manipulation is not necessarily a negative term, when we talk about the manipulation of everyday objects; but when we move into the realm of emotions, manipulative texts become problematic. Film is such a wonderful medium because directors have so many tools at their disposal; however, it is relatively easy to use those tools to manipulate audiences. Directors use music, lighting, special effects, and clever editing to help make their movies more powerful. Music reinforces feelings of excitement (*Lord of the Rings*), fear (*Jaws*), romance (*Titanic*), or anger (*Do the Right Thing*). Lighting and filters can make people, especially women, appear more delicate or fragile. The famous film star from the 1930s and 1940s, Marlene Dietrich, would only be shot from one side and insisted on being lit with overhead lights. The first several minutes of *Citizen Kane*, widely considered the best American film ever made, are shot largely in the dark to help drive home the sense that the reporters are "in the dark" about media mogul Charles Foster Kane. In movies like *I, Robot, The Matrix* movies and *Lord of the Rings,* special effects make the story we are watching seem less like light and shadow and more like reality. Even how a filmmaker places a camera affects how we view the film. The close-up, spookily lit shots of Anthony Hopkins's face in *Silence of the Lambs* make us feel like Hannibal Lector might eat *our* liver with "some fava beans and a nice Chianti." Similarly, in many Westerns, the camera is placed at knee level, so that we are always looking up at the cowboy, reinforcing his stature as a hero. Director Orson Welles uses similar techniques in *Citizen Kane*. Alfred Hitchcock was a master of placing the camera in manipulative places. From *Psycho* to *Rear Window* to *Rope,* we see exactly what he wants us to see and how he wants us to see it. We see nothing more than what the camera shows us.

There are other forms of manipulation as well. Many people feel Steven Spielberg's movies end with overly manipulative scenes that pluck at the heartstrings of the audience, forcing over-determined emotions because of over-the-top melodrama. Such accusations are often leveled at teen romance flicks and so-called bio-pics because they make a person's life seem more maudlin, more heart wrenching than it could possibly be.

Costumes, colors, sounds and sound effects, editing, and set design all contribute to how the movie comes to us. Sound and music are particularly effective. In *Star Wars,* for instance, each character has a specific musical profile—a kind of theme song—whose tone mirrors how you are supposed to feel about that character. You probably all remember the dark, deep foreboding music that always accompanies Darth Vader. Like music, the clothes a character wears tell us how to feel about that person. The costumes worn by Ben Affleck and Will Smith in various movies probably reinforce gender expectations, as do the clothes of Julia Roberts or Jennifer Lopez. How a space ship or a dark, scary warehouse looks puts us in the mood so that the plot and action can move us. Savvy viewers of movies will be aware of the ways in which films try to manipulate them because in so doing, they will be better able to read other forms of manipulation in their lives.

## Movies are not just about ideas and action; they are also about values.

Next time you see a Hollywood movie, consider the value system the movie supports. By value system, we mean the values, priorities, and principles a movie advocates. For instance, while we liked the first *Legally Blonde* movie, we were shocked by how traditional the movie's ending was. While the entire movie demonstrates the ways in which her character eventually gets the best of boys, law school colleagues, and professors, even her enemies in the courtroom, all of these very important successes take a back seat to the fact that she gets the guy. It is as though all of her accomplishments were important *so* that she could win the cute boy in the end. The ultimate message, then, is that what women accomplish on their own is fine, if that is of interest, but the real victory, the real triumph, is snagging the man.

Similarly, many Hollywood movies advocate the importance of social class, as Michael Parenti points out in his essay "Class and Virtue." Movies like *Maid in Manhattan* and *Jerry McGuire* and classic romantic comedies such as *Pretty Woman, Trading Places* and *My Fair Lady* spend most of their energy figuring out ways for their characters to make a jump in social class. It is worth asking how many truly popular Hollywood movies are at the same time truly radical and how many reinforce traditional, mainstream middle-class values. We are not suggesting traditional middle-class values are *bad* but rather, we are suggesting that you consider the value system advocated by the most powerful cultural machinery in the country. Our contention here is that this value system directly affects the movies you see, the stars acting in the movie, the plot structures, and the ultimate messages these movies send. Again, paying attention to these issues will make you a smarter watcher of movies and a better writer about them as well.

## ▪▪▪ WORKSHEET ▪▪▪

### This Text

1. While it will be impossible for you to know this fully, try to figure out the writing situation of each author. Who is the audience? What does the author have at stake? What is his or her agenda? Why is she or he writing this piece? For instance, would David Denby, a white male, give the same reading of *Waiting to Exhale* as bell hooks?
2. What are the main points of the essay? Can you find a thesis statement anywhere?
3. Do you think the authors "read into" movies too much? If so, why do you say this?
4. As you read the essays, pay attention to the language the critics use to read movies.
5. If you have not seen the movies the authors mention, rent and watch them—preferably with a group of people from your class.
6. Try to distinguish between a review and an argumentative or persuasive essay. Additionally, you should be aware of a distinction between a short capsule review, which is more of a summary, and a longer analytical review (like the ones printed here).

### Beyond This Text: Film Technique

**Camera angles and positioning:** How is the camera placed? Is it high, low, to the side? And how does it move? Is it a hand-held camera, or is it stationary? How does it determine how you *see* the movie?

**Lighting:** Light and shading are very important to movies. Are there shadows? Is the film shot during the day or mostly at night? How do shadows and light affect the movie and your experience of it?

**Color and framing:** Often, directors try to give certain scenes an artistic feel. Is the shot framed similar to a painting or photograph? Does the movie use color to elicit emotions? How does the movie frame or represent nature?

### Content

**Theme:** What are the themes of the movie? What point is the director or writer trying to get across?

**Ideology:** What ideas or political leanings does the movie convey? Are there particular philosophies or concepts that influence the message the movie sends?

### The Whole Package

**Celebrities:** What movie stars appear (or don't appear) in the movie? How do certain stars determine what kind of movie a film is? Do the actors ever look ugly or dirty or tired or sloppy?

**Technology:** What kind of technology is at work in the film? How do special effects or stunts or pyrotechnics affect the film viewing experience?

**Genre:** What genre does a particular movie fit into? Why? What are the expectations of that genre?

**Culture:** As a cultural document, a cultural text, what does this movie say about its culture? How does it transmit values? What kinds of ideas and values does it hold up or condemn?

**Effectiveness:** Does the movie "work" as a movie? Why? Why not? What cultural forces might be influencing your criteria of effectiveness?

---

### GREAT MOVIES AND BEING A GREAT MOVIEGOER

#### ■ Roger Ebert ■

*Roger Ebert is probably the most famous movie reviewer in the country. A Pulitzer-prize winning columnist for the* Chicago Sun-Times, *he became a household name through his participation in* Siskel and Ebert at the Movies, *a popular television show in which he and the late Gene Siskel argued (sometimes bitterly) about current movies. Ebert wrote this piece in 2000 to celebrate reaching the milestone of 100 "great movies" in his ongoing series. We like it because Ebert talks about why he likes certain movies and what it takes to be a good watcher of them. As you read, think about how movies are both public and private texts. Why do we love them, and what roles do they play in our lives? The entire Great Movies project can be found at http://www.suntimes.com/ ebert/greatmovies/.*

Every other week I visit a film classic from the past and write about it. My "Great Movies" series began in the autumn of 1996 and now reaches a landmark of 100 titles with today's review of Federico Fellini's "8 1/2," which is, appropriately, a film about a film director. I love my job, and this is the part I love the most.

We have completed the first century of film. Too many moviegoers are stuck in the present and recent past. When people tell me that "Ferris Bueller's Day Off" or "Total Recall" are their favorite films, I wonder: Have they tasted the joys of Welles, Bunuel, Ford, Murnau, Keaton, Hitchcock, Wilder or Kurosawa? If they like Ferris Bueller, what would they think of Jacques Tati's "Mr. Hulot's Holiday," also about a strange day of misadventures? If they like "Total Recall," have they seen Fritz Lang's "Metropolis," also about an artificial city ruled by fear?

I ask not because I am a film snob. I like to sit in the dark and enjoy movies. I think of old films as a resource of treasures. Movies have been made for 100 years, in color and black and white, in sound and silence, in wide-screen and the classic frame, in English and every other language. To limit yourself to popular hits and recent years is like being Ferris Bueller but staying home all day.

I believe we are born with our minds open to wonderful experiences, and only slowly learn to limit ourselves to narrow tastes. We are taught to lose our curiosity by the bludgeon-blows of mass marketing, which brainwash us to see "hits," and discourage exploration.

I know that many people dislike subtitled films, and that few people reading this article will have ever seen a film from Iran, for example. And yet a few weeks ago at my Overlooked Film Festival at the University of Illinois, the free kiddie matinee was "Children of Heaven," from Iran. It was a story about a boy who loses his sister's sneakers through no fault of his own, and is afraid to tell his parents. So he and his sister secretly share the same pair of shoes. Then he learns of a footrace where third prize is . . . a pair of sneakers.

"Anyone who can read at the third-grade level can read these subtitles," I told the audience of 1,000 kids and some parents. "If you can't, it's OK for your parents or older kids to read them aloud—just not too loudly."

The lights went down and the movie began. I expected a lot of reading aloud. There was none. Not all of the kids were old enough to read, but apparently they were picking up the story just by watching and using their intelligence. The audience was spellbound. No noise, restlessness, punching, kicking, running down the aisles. Just eyes lifted up to a fascinating story. Afterward, we asked kids up on the stage to ask questions or talk about the film. What they said indicated how involved they had become.

Kids. And yet most adults will not go to a movie from Iran, Japan, France or Brazil. They will, however, go to any movie that has been plugged with a $30 million ad campaign and sanctified as a "box-office winner." Yes, some of these big hits are good, and a few of them are great. But what happens between the time we are 8 and the time we are 20 that robs us of our curiosity? What turns movie lovers into consumers? What does it say about you if you only want to see what everybody else is seeing?

I don't know. What I do know is that if you love horror movies, your life as a filmgoer is not complete until you see "Nosferatu." I know that once you see Orson Welles appear in the doorway in "The Third Man," you will never forget his curious little smile. And that the life and death of the old man in "Ikiru" will be an inspiration every time you remember it.

I have not written any of the 100 Great Movies reviews from memory. Every film has been seen fresh, right before writing. When I'm at home, I often watch them on Sunday mornings. It's a form of prayer: The greatest films are meditations on why we are here. When I'm on the road, there's no telling where I'll see them. I saw "Written on the Wind" on a cold January night at the Everyman Cinema in Hampstead, north of London. I saw "Last Year at Marienbad" on a DVD on my PowerBook while at the Cannes Film Festival. I saw "2001: A Space Odyssey" in 70mm at Cyberfest, the celebration of HAL 9000's birthday, at the University of Illinois. I saw "Battleship Potemkin" projected on a sheet on the outside wall of the Vickers Theater in Three Oaks, Mich., while three young musicians played the score they had written for it. And Ozu's "Floating Weeds" at the Hawaii Film Festival, as part of a shot-by-shot seminar that took four days.

When people asked me where they should begin in looking at classic films, I never knew what to say. Now I can say, "Plunge into these Great Movies, and go where they lead you."

There's a next step. If you're really serious about the movies, get together with two or three friends who care as much as you do. Watch the film all the way through on video. Then start again at the top. Whenever anyone sees anything they want to comment on, freeze the frame. Talk about what you're looking at. The story, the performances, the sets, the locations. The camera movement, the lighting, the composition, the special effects. The color, the shadows, the sound, the music. The themes, the tone, the mood, the style.

There are no right answers. The questions are the point. They make you an active movie watcher, not a passive one. You should not be a witness at a movie, but a collaborator. Directors cannot make the film without you. Together, you can accomplish amazing things. The more you learn, the quicker you'll know when the director is not doing his share of the job. That's the whole key to being a great moviegoer. There's nothing else to it.

**READING** WRITING

## THIS TEXT: READING

1. What makes a "great movie" for you? Do you think it would differ from Ebert's criteria? Based on his essay, what does it take for a movie to be "great" in Ebert's eyes?
2. What does Ebert mean when, in the final paragraph, he asks you to be a "collaborator?" How is this similar to being an active reader of texts?
3. What is Ebert's thesis in this essay? Does he have a clear argument, and if so what is it? How would you describe his tone?

## YOUR TEXT: WRITING

1. Write an essay in which you argue that a certain movie is "great." This is a wonderful opportunity to write a definitional essay. Define what a great movie must be, then show how your movie is, in fact, great.
2. Take an oppositional stance to Ebert regarding one of the movies on the list. Make a compelling argument why a certain movie is *not* great. Be sure that your argument is more logos-based than pathos-based.
3. Write a paper about the entire process of labeling "great" movies. Why do we care if a movie is great or not? What is at stake in movie hierarchies like this?

---

### CLASS AND VIRTUE

■ **Michael Parenti** ■    *A long-time critic of contemporary media, Parenti suggests how and why Hollywood movies reinforce class distinctions in American society. Drawing from several types of movies, Parenti's argumentative essay (1992) claims that American movies support the virtues of the upper class.*

THE ENTERTAINMENT MEDIA present working people not only as unlettered and uncouth but also as less desirable and less moral than other people. Conversely, virtue is more likely to be ascribed to those characters whose speech and appearance are soundly middle- or upper-middle class.

Even a simple adventure story like *Treasure Island* (1934, 1950, 1972) manifests this implicit class perspective. There are two groups of acquisitive persons searching for a lost treasure. One, headed by a squire, has money enough to hire a ship and crew. The other, led by the rascal Long John Silver, has no money—so they sign up as part of the crew. The narrative implicitly assumes from the beginning that the squire has a moral claim to the treasure, while Long John Silver's gang does not. After all, it is the squire who puts up the venture capital for the ship. Having no investment in the undertaking other than their labor, Long John and his men, by definition, will be "stealing" the treasure, while the squire will be "discovering" it.

To be sure, there are other differences. Long John's men are cutthroats. The squire is not. Yet, one wonders if the difference between a bad pirate and a good squire is itself not preeminently a matter of having the right amount of disposable income. The squire is no less acquisitive than the conspirators. He just does with money what they must achieve with cutlasses. The squire and his associates dress in fine clothes, speak an educated diction, and drink brandy. Long John and his men dress slovenly, speak in guttural accents, and drink rum. From these indications alone, the viewer knows who are the good guys and who are the bad. Virtue is visually measured by one's approximation to proper class appearances.

Sometimes class contrasts are juxtaposed within one person, as in *The Three Faces of Eve* (1957), a movie about a woman who suffers from multiple personalities. When we first meet Eve (Joanne Woodward), she is a disturbed, strongly repressed, puritanically religious person, who speaks with a rural, poor-Southern accent. Her second personality is that of a wild, flirtatious woman who also speaks with a rural, poor-Southern accent. After much treatment by her psychiatrist, she is cured of these schizoid personalities and emerges with a healthy third one, the real Eve, a poised, self-possessed, pleasant woman. What is intriguing is that she now speaks with a cultivated, affluent, Smith College accent, free of any low-income regionalism or ruralism, much like Joanne Woodward herself. This transformation in class style and speech is used to indicate mental health without any awareness of the class bias thusly expressed.

Mental health is also the question in *A Woman Under the Influence* (1974), the story of a disturbed woman who is married to a hard-hat husband. He cannot handle—and inadvertently contributes to—her emotional deterioration. She is victimized by a spouse who is nothing more than an insensitive, working-class bull in a china shop. One comes away convinced that every unstable woman needs a kinder, gentler, and above all, more middle-class hubby if she wishes to avoid a mental crack-up.

Class prototypes abound in the 1980s television series *The A-Team*. In each episode, a Vietnam-era commando unit helps an underdog, be it a Latino immigrant or a disabled veteran, by vanquishing some menacing force such as organized crime, a business competitor, or corrupt government officials. As always with the make-believe media, the A-Team does good work on an individualized rather than collectively organized basis, helping particular victims by thwarting particular villains. The A-Team's leaders are two white males of privileged background. The lowest ranking members of the team, who do none of the thinking or the leading, are working-class palookas. They show they are good with their hands, both by punching out the bad guys and by doing the maintenance work on the team's flying vehicles and cars. One of them, "B.A." (bad ass), played by the African-American Mr. T., is visceral, tough, and purposely bad-mannered toward those he doesn't like. He projects an image of crudeness and ignorance and is associated with the physical side of things. In sum, the team has a brain (the intelligent white leaders) and a body with its simpler physical functions (the working-class characters), a hierarchy that corresponds to the social structure itself.[1]

Sometimes class bigotry is interwoven with gender bigotry, as in *Pretty Woman* (1990). A dreamboat millionaire corporate raider finds himself all alone for an extended stay in Hollywood (his girlfriend is unwilling to join him), so he quickly recruits a beautiful prostitute as his playmate of the month. She is paid three thousand dollars a week to wait around his superposh hotel penthouse ready to perform the usual services and accompany him to business dinners at top restaurants. As prostitution goes, it is a dream gig. But there is one cloud on the horizon. She is low-class. She doesn't know which fork to use at those CEO power feasts, and she's bothersomely fidgety, wears tacky clothes, chews gum, and, y'know, doesn't talk so good. But with some tips from the hotel manager, she proves to be a veritable Eliza Doolittle in her class metamorphosis. She dresses in proper attire, sticks the gum away forever, and starts picking the right utensils at dinner. She also figures out how to speak a little more like Joanne Woodward without the benefit of a multiple personality syndrome, and she develops the capacity to sit in a poised, wordless, empty-headed fashion, every inch the expensive female ornament.

She is still a prostitute but a classy one. It is enough of a distinction for the handsome young corporate raider. Having liked her because she was charmingly cheap, he now loves her all the more because she has real polish and is a more suitable companion. So suitable that he decides to do the right thing by her: set her up in an apartment so he can make regular visits at regular prices. But now she wants the better things in life, like marriage, a nice house, and, above all, a different occupation, one that would allow her to use less of herself. She is furious at him for treating her like, well, a prostitute. She decides to give up her profession and get a high-school diploma so that she might make a better life for herself—perhaps as a filing clerk or receptionist or some other of the entry-level jobs awaiting young women with high school diplomas.[2]

After the usual girl-breaks-off-with-boy scenes, the millionaire prince returns. It seems he can't concentrate on making money without her. He even abandons his cutthroat schemes and enters into a less lucrative but supposedly more productive, canny business venture with a struggling old-time entrepreneur. The bad capitalist is transformed into a good capitalist. He then carries off his ex-prostitute for a lifetime of bliss. The moral is a familiar one, updated for post-Reagan yuppiedom: A woman can escape from economic and gender exploitation by winning the love and career advantages offered by a rich male. Sexual allure goes only so far unless it develops a material base and becomes a class act.[3]

### Notes

1. Gina Marchetti, "Class, Ideology and Commercial Television: An Analysis of *The A-Team,*" *Journal of Film and Video*, 39, Spring 1987, pp. 19–28.
2. See the excellent review by Lydia Sargent, *Z Magazine*, April 1990, pp. 43–45.
3. *Ibid.*

## READING WRITING

## THIS TEXT: READING

1. Parenti's examples may seem a bit dated to you, though you have probably seen *Pretty Woman.* Can you think of more recent examples of classist and sexist films?

2. Find Parenti's thesis statement. *Hint:* He hits you with it right off the bat. Do you agree with his contention about Hollywood?

## YOUR TEXT: WRITING

1. *Sling Blade* is a fairly popular movie that deals with issues of class. Write an essay on *Sling Blade, The Full Monty, Titanic* or some other movie that foregrounds class tensions. How does Hollywood deal with class? Is that different than the way an independent film might approach class?

2. *Pretty Woman* bears a strong resemblance to *Cinderella,* which is also about class. Write an essay in which you explore the links between gender and class. Are issues of power involved?

3. Write a comparative essay in which you compare a film and a short story or poem in terms of what each has to say about social and economic class.

## MOCK FEMINISM: *WAITING TO EXHALE*

### ■ bell hooks ■

*Taken from her provocative book* Reel to Reel: Race, Sex, and Class at the Movies, *bell hooks' essay (1996) offers a reading of the popular movie* Waiting to Exhale. *Unlike most reviews that praised the film for its depiction of black women, hooks' review charges the film merely masks harmful stereotypes.*

IN THE PAST A BLACK FILM was usually seen as a film by a black filmmaker focusing on some aspect of black life. More recently the "idea" of a "black film" has been appropriated as a way to market films that are basically written and produced by white people as though they in act represent and offer us—"authentic" blackness. It does not matter that progressive black filmmakers and critics challenge essentialist notions of black authenticity, even going so far as to rethink and interrogate the notion of black film. These groups do not have access to the levels of marketing and publicity that can repackage authentic blackness commodified and sell it as the "real" thing. This was certainly the case with the marketing and publicity for the film *Waiting to Exhale.*

When Kevin Costner produced and starred in the film *The Bodyguard* with Whitney Houston as co-star, the film focused on a black family. No one ever thought to market it as a black film. Indeed, many black people refused to see the film because they were so disgusted by this portrayal of interracial love. No one showed much curiosity about the racial identity of the screenwriters or for that matter, anybody behind the scenes of this film. It was not seen as having any importance, for black women by the white-dominated mass media. Yet *Waiting to Exhale*'s claim to blackness, and black authenticity, is almost as dubious as any such claim being made about *The Bodyguard*. However, that claim could be easily made because a black woman writer wrote the book on which the movie was based. The hiring of a fledgling black director received no critical comment. Everyone behaved as though it was just normal Hollywood practice to offer the directorship of a major big-budget Hollywood film to someone who might not know what they are doing.

The screenplay was written by a white man, but if we are to believe everything we read in newspapers and popular magazines, Terry McMillan assisted with the writing. Of course, having her name tacked onto the writing process was a great way to protect the film from the critique that its "authentic blackness" was somehow undermined by white-male interpretation. Alice Walker had no such luck when her book *The Color Purple* was made into a movie by Steven Spielberg. No one thought this was a black film. And very few viewers were surprised that what we saw on the screen had little relationship to Alice Walker's novel.

Careful publicity and marketing ensured that *Waiting to Exhale* would not be subjected to these critiques; all acts of appropriation were carefully hidden behind the labeling of this film as authentically a black woman's story. Before anyone could become upset that a black woman was not hired to direct the film, McMillan told the world in *Movieland* magazine that those experienced black women directors in Hollywood just were not capable of doing the job. She made the same critique of the black woman writer who was initially hired to write the screenplay. From all accounts (most of them given by the diva herself) it appears that Terry McMillan is the only competent black woman on the Hollywood scene and she just recently arrived.

It's difficult to know what is more disturbing: McMillan's complicity with the various acts of white supremacist capitalist patriarchal cultural appropriation that resulted in a film as lightweight and basically bad as *Waiting to Exhale,* or the public's passive celebratory consumption of this trash as giving the real scoop about black women's lives. Some bad films are at least entertaining. This was just an utterly boring show. That masses of black women could be cajoled by mass media coverage and successful seductive marketing (the primary ploy being that this is the first film ever that four black women have been the major stars of a Hollywood film) to embrace this cultural product was a primary indication that this is not a society where moviegoers are encouraged to think critically about what they see on the screen.

When a film that's basically about the trials and tribulations of four professional heterosexual black women who are willing to do anything to get and keep a man is offered as a "feminist" narrative, it's truly a testament to the power of the mainstream to co-opt progressive social movements and strip them of all political meaning through a series of contemptuous ridiculous representations. Terry McMillan's novel *Waiting to Exhale* was not a feminist book and it was not transformed into a feminist film. It did not even become a film that made use of any of the progressive politics around race and gender that was evoked however casually in the novel itself.

The film *Waiting to Exhale* took the novelistic images of professional black women concerned with issues of racial uplift and gender equality and turned them into a progression of racist, sexist stereotypes that features happy darkies who are all singing, dancing, fucking, and having a merry old time even in the midst of sad times and tragic moments. What we saw on the screen was not black women talking about love or the meaning of partnership and marriage in their lives. We saw four incredibly glamorous women obsessed with getting a man, with status, material success and petty competition with other women (especially white women). In the book one of the women, Gloria, owns a beauty parlor; she is always, always working, which is what happens when you run a small business. In the movie, girlfriend hardly ever works because she is too busy cooking tantalizing meals for the neighbor next door. In this movie food is on her mind and she forgets all about work, except for an occasional phone call to see how everything is going. Let's not forget the truly fictive utopian moment in this film that occurs when Bernie goes to court divorcing her husband and wins tons of money. This is so in the book as well. Funny though, the novel ends with her giving the money away, highlighting her generosity and her politics. McMillan writes: "She also wouldn't have to worry about selling the house now. But Bernadine wasn't taking that fucker off the market. She'd drop the price. And she'd send a nice check to the United Negro College Fund, something she'd always wanted to do. She'd help feed some of those kids in Africa she'd seen on TV at night . . . Maybe she'd send some change to the Urban League and the NAACP and she'd definitely help out some of those programs that BWOTM [Black Women on the MOVE] had been trying to get off the ground for the last hundred years. At the rate she was going, Bernadine had already given away over a million dollars." Definitely not a "material girl." It would have taken only one less scene of pleasure fucking for audiences to have witnessed Bernie writing these checks with a nice voice-over. But, alas, such an image might have ruined the racist, sexist stereotype of black women being hard, angry, and just plain greedy. No doubt the writers of the screenplay felt these "familiar" stereotypes would guarantee the movie its crossover appeal.

Concurrently, no doubt it helps that crossover appeal to set up stereotypically racist, sexist conflicts between white women and black women (where if we are to believe the logic

Loretta Devine, Lela Roaton, Angela Bassett, and Whitney Houston in *Waiting to Exhale* (1995).
*Source:* 20th Century Fox/The Kobal Collection.

of the film, the white woman gets "her" black man in the end). Let's remember. In the novel the movie is based on, only one black man declares his love for a white woman. The man Bernie meets, the lawyer James, is thinking of divorcing his white wife, who is dying of cancer, but he loyally stays with her until her death, even though he makes it very clear that the love has long since left their marriage. Declaring his undying love for Bernie, James moves across the country to join her, sets up a law practice, and gets involved with "a coalition to stop the liquor board from allowing so many liquor stores in the black community." Well, not in this movie! The screen character James declares undying love for his sick white wife. Check out the difference between the letter he writes in the novel. Here is an excerpt: "I know you probably thought that night was just something frivolous but like I told you before I left, it meant more to me than that. Much more. I buried my wife back in August, and for her sake, I'm glad she's not suffering anymore . . . I want to see you again, Bernadine, and not for another one-nighter, either. If there's any truth to what's known as a 'soul mate,' then you're as close to it as I've ever come . . . I'm not interested in playing games, or starting something I can't finish. I play for keeps, and I'm not some dude just out to have a good time . . . I knew I was in love with you long before we ever turned the key to that hotel room." The image of black masculinity that comes through in this letter is that of a man of integrity who is compassionate, in touch with his feelings, and able to take responsibility for his actions.

In the movie version of *Waiting to Exhale*, no black man involved with a black woman possesses these qualities. In contrast to what happens in the book, in the film, James does not have a one-nighter with Bernie, because he is depicted as utterly devoted to his white wife. Here are relevant passages from the letter he writes to Bernie that audiences hear at the movie: "What I feel for you has never undercut the love I have for my wife. How is that possible? I watch her everyday. So beautiful and brave. I just want to give her everything I've got in me. Every moment. She's hanging on, fighting to be here for me. And when she sleeps, I cry. Over how amazing she is, and how lucky I've been to have her in my life." There may not have been any white women as central characters in this film, but this letter certainly places the dying white wife at the center of things. Completely rewriting the letter that appears in the novel, which only concerns James's love and devotion to Bernie, so that the white wife (dead in the book but brought back to life on-screen) is the recipient of James's love was no doubt another ploy to reach the crossover audience: the masses of white women consumers that might not have been interested in this film if it had really been about black women.

Ultimately, only white women have committed relationships with black men in the film. Not only do these screen images reinforce stereotypes, the screenplay was written in such a way as to actively perpetuate them. Catfights between women, both real and symbolic, were clearly seen by the screenwriters as likely to be more entertaining to moviegoing audiences than the portrayal of a divorced black woman unexpectedly meeting her true love—an honest, caring, responsible, mature, tender, and loving black man who delivers the goods. Black women are portrayed as so shrewish in this film that Lionel's betrayal of Bernie appears to be no more than an act of self-defense. The film suggests that Lionel is merely trying to get away from the black bitch who barges in on him at work and physically attacks his meek and loving white wife. To think that Terry McMillan was one of the screenwriters makes it all the more disheartening. Did she forget that she had written a far more emotionally complex and progressive vision of black female-male relationships in her novel?

While we may all know some over-thirty black women who are desperate to get a man by any means necessary and plenty of young black females who fear that they may never find

What values are truly driving *Waiting to Exhale?*
*Source:* 20th Century Fox/The Kobel Collection/Nicole Goode.

a man and are willing to be downright foolish in their pursuit of one, the film was so sim-plistic and denigrating in its characterization of black womanhood that everyone should be outraged to be told that it is "for us." Or worse yet, as a reporter wrote in *Newsweek,* "This is our million man march." Whether you supported the march or not (and I did not, for many of the same reasons I find this film appalling), let's get this straight: We are being told, and are telling ourselves that black men need a political march and black women need a movie. Mind you—not a political film but one where the black female "stars" spend most of their time chainsmoking themselves to death (let's not forget that Gloria did not have enough breath to blow out her birthday candle) and drowning their sorrows in alcohol. No doubt McMillan's knowledge of how many black people die from lung cancer and al-coholism influenced her decision to write useful, unpreachy critiques of these addictions in her novel. In the novel the characters who smoke are trying to stop and Black Women on the Move are fighting to close down liquor stores. None of these actions fulfill racist fantasies. It's no accident that just the opposite images appear on the screen. Smoking is so omnipresent in every scene that many of us were waiting to see a promotional credit for the tobacco industry.

Perhaps the most twisted and perverse aspect of this film is the way it was marketed as being about girlfriend bonding. How about that scene where Robin shares her real-life trauma with Savannah, who is busy looking the other way and simply does not respond? Meaning-ful girlfriend bonding is not about the codependency that is imaged in this film. At its best *Waiting to Exhale* is a film about black women helping each other to stay stuck. Do we re-ally believe that moment when Savannah rudely disses Kenneth (even though the film has in no way constructed him as a lying cheating dog) to be a moment of profound "feminist" awakening? Suddenly audiences are encouraged to believe that she realizes the dilemmas of being involved with a married man, even one who has filed for a divorce. Why not depict a little mature communication between a black man and a black woman? No doubt that too would not have been entertaining to crossover audiences. Better to give them what they are used to, stereotypical representations of black males as always and only lying, cheating dogs (that is, when they are involved with black women) and professional black women as wild, irrational, castrating bitch goddesses.

Nothing was more depressing than hearing individual black women offering personal testimony that these shallow screen images are "realistic portrayals" of their experience. If this is the world of black gender relations as they know it, no wonder black men and women are in serious crisis. Obviously, it is difficult for many straight black women to find black male partners and/or husbands. Though it is hard to believe that black women as conventionally feminine, beautiful, glamorous, and just plain dumb as the girlfriends in this film can't get men (Bernie has an MBA, helped start the business, but is clueless about everything that concerns money; Robin is willing to have unsafe sex and celebrate an unplanned pregnancy with a partner who may be a drug addict; Gloria, who would rather cook food for her man any day than go to work; Savannah has sex at the drop of a hat, even when she does not want to get involved). In the real world these are the women who have men standing in line.

However, if they and other black women internalize the messages in *Waiting to Exhale* they will come to their senses and see that, according to the film, black men are really undesirable mates for black women. Actually, lots of younger black women, and their over-thirty counterparts, go to see *Waiting to Exhale* to have their worst fears affirmed: that black men are irresponsible and uncaring; that black women, no matter how attractive, will still be hurt and abandoned, and that ultimately they will probably be alone and unloved. Perhaps it feels less like cultural genocide to have these messages of self-loathing and disempowerment brought to them by four beautiful black female "stars."

Black women seeking to learn anything about gender relationships from this film will be more empowered if we identify with the one black female character who rarely speaks. She is the graceful, attractive, brown-skinned lawyer with naturally braided hair who is a professional who knows her job and is also able to bond emotionally with her clients. Not only does she stand for gender justice (the one glimpse of empowering feminist womanhood we see in this film), she achieves that end without ever putting men down or competing with any woman. While we never see her with a male partner, she acts with confident self-esteem and shows fulfillment in a job well done.

The monetary success of a trashy film like *Waiting to Exhale,* with its heavy sentimentality and predicable melodrama shows that Hollywood recognizes that blackness as a commodity can be exploited to bring in the bucks. Dangerously, it also shows that the same old racist/sexist stereotypes can be appropriated and served up to the public in a new and more fashionable disguise. While it serves the financial interests of Hollywood and McMillan's own bank account for her to deflect away from critiques that examine the politics underlying these representations and their behind-the-scenes modes of production by ways of witty assertions that the novel and the film are "forms of entertainment, not anthropological studies," in actuality the creators of this film are as accountable for their work as their predecessors. Significantly, contemporary critiques of racial essentialism completely disrupt the notion that anything a black artist creates is inherently radical, progressive, or more likely to reflect a break with white supremacist representations. It has become most evident that as

Female bonding or female stereotyping?
*Source:* 20th Century Fox/The Kobal Collection/Nicolas, Randee St.

black artists seek a "crossover" success, the representations they create usually mirror dominant stereotypes. After a barrage of publicity and marketing that encouraged black people, and black women in particular, to see *Waiting to Exhale* as fictive ethnography, McMillan is being more than a bit disingenuous when she suggests that the film should not be seen this way. In her essay, "Who's Doin' the Twist: Notes Toward a Politics of Appropriation," cultural critic Coco Fusco reminds us that we must continually critique this genre in both its pure and impure forms. "Ethnographic cinema, in light of its historical connection to colonialist adventurism, and decades of debate about the ethics of representing documentary subjects, is a genre that demands a special degree of scrutiny." Just because writers and directors are black does not exempt them from scrutiny. The black female who wrote a letter to the *New York Times* calling attention to the way this film impedes the struggle to create new images of blackness on the screen was surely right when she insisted that had everyone involved in the production of this film been white and male, its blatantly racist and sexist standpoints would not have gone unchallenged.

 READING WRITING

## THIS TEXT: READING

1. At first, you might find hooks overly critical of *Waiting to Exhale.* But are her contentions reasonable? Why? Why not? What standards is she holding the film to?
2. What political and cultural forces are influencing her review of the film? Or, what can you glean about her political leanings from her review? What is hooks's writing situation?

3.  Do you agree with hooks that a seemingly harmless film like *Waiting to Exhale* is culturally dangerous?

## YOUR TEXT: WRITING

1.  Write your own review of *Waiting to Exhale*. Will you focus on the representations of gender, or are you more interested in plot and character development?
2.  Compare *Waiting to Exhale* with *How Stella Got Her Groove Back*. Both movies are adaptations of Terry McMillan novels. How are the films similar? How are they different? How does the film version depart from the novel?
3.  Write a personal essay in which you analyze Hollywood representations of *your* gender and ethnicity. For instance, if you are a Hispanic male, write an essay in which you analyze how Hispanic males are represented in movies. What do you notice?
4.  Write a comparative paper analyzing what hooks has to say about women in *Waiting to Exhale* with the suite in Chapter 6. How do women define representations of women?

---

### HOLY HOMOSEXUALITY BATMAN!: CAMP AND CORPORATE CAPITALISM IN *BATMAN FOREVER*

#### ■ Freya Johnson ■

*Both intellectually challenging and humorously insightful, Johnson's candid essay (1995) sheds light on the semiotics of gayness in the popular movie* Batman Forever. *Is Johnson reading too much into the film, or are American audiences not reading enough into it? Johnson's essay and our own reaction to it and the movie may allow an interesting reading of sexual orientation and American culture.*

> *Only someone ignorant of the fundamentals of psychiatry and the psychopathology of sex can fail to realize a subtle atmosphere of homoeroticism which pervades the adventure of the mature "Batman" and his young friend "Robin."*
>
> —*Frederic Wertham,* Seduction of the Innocent

SO PSYCHIATRIST FREDERIC WERTHAM warned parents and lawmakers in 1953, as he detailed the "factually proven" method by which comic books turned innocent children into homosexually and pederastically inclined "deviants and perverts." In this hilariously paranoiac document of homophobic panic, he unwittingly anticipates queer theoretical practice as he ransacks the comics for "clues" (nowadays we call them "signifiers") revealing the homoeroticism leaking from the pages of the books into impressionable pre-pubescent brains. Sure enough, his spot-the-homo routine reveals Bruce Wayne and "Dick" Grayson (Wertham supplies the snide quotation marks) enacting "the wish dream of two homosexuals living together" as Wertham presents this condemning evidence:

> Sometimes Batman ends up in bed injured and young Robin is shown sitting next to him. At home they lead an idyllic life. They are Bruce Wayne and "Dick" Grayson. Bruce is described as a "socialite" and the official relationship is that Dick is Bruce's ward. They live in sumptuous quarters, with beautiful flowers in large vases, and have a butler, Alfred. Batman is sometimes shown in a dressing gown . . .

Obviously, they *must* be fags: otherwise they'd have a butler named "Butch," live in cramped quarters littered with beer-cans, wouldn't show concern for one another's injuries or be caught dead in a dressing gown and cultivate only (what?) cactuses in small ugly metal pots?

More damning than the flowers and dressing gowns, however, is that the "muscular male supertype whose primary sex characteristics are usually well emphasized, is in the setting of certain stories the object of homoerotic sexual curiosity and stimulation." In that case, one can easily imagine a now-decrepit Wertham feverishly taking notes in the back of the theater when Dick dons his Robin costume in *Batman Forever* and the camera lovingly focuses on what looks like a glowing violet dildo showing through the codpiece of his uniform. "We're not just friends," says Dick, "we're partners"; the next shot is the dynamic duo's clasped hands. Indeed, queer signification so saturates *Batman Forever* that it would be inaccurate to call it a subtext. With his earring, haircut and leather jacket Chris O'Donnell looks like he's just come straight from an ACT UP meeting, while Val Kilmer's body is exposed and eroticized only in the scenes with O'Donnell (as he wanders out of the shower barechested in towel, is treated for injuries, or puts on the new bat-suit while the image of his butt-cleavage fills the screen). During the sterile "love-scenes" with Nicole Kidman he remains fully clothed as the camera coyly pans down only as far as the top of his chest at most: her body entirely escapes the emblematic "male gaze" of cinema and her breasts or legs never once fill the screen.

How did director Joel Schumacher get away with turning loose so many queer signifiers to float freely about in Warner Brothers' biggest asset? By turning the queer *sub*text hidden beneath the surface of many Batman representations into an overtly queer *supra*text that goes right over the head of the mainstream viewing audience. Although Batman and Robin are shrieking "queer," Jim Carrey's Riddler (who even the willfully obtuse *National Review* managed to describe as "campy") is much much queerer. Yet because he's a villain, his prancing around in a diamond tiara and skin-tight green unitard exclaiming "Spank me!" doesn't offend the sensibilities of the homophobic mainstream McAudience: in fact, it draws their attention away from the homoerotic electricity between the heroes and invites the misreading "if the bad guy's gay, the good guys must be straight," while Two-Face's troops of thugs tricked out in now universally recognizable (thanks to *Pulp Fiction*) queer S&M gear help keep queerness and villainy aligned. And significantly, it's Ed Nygma's extreme reaction to his rejection by Bruce Wayne, a rejection that mimics a straight man's rejection of homosexual advances ("We're two of kind"; "You were supposed to understand," laments Ed), that drives him to criminality.

In fact the villains mirror and exaggerate the heroes in more than just homoerotics: their *raison d'être* also originates in some traumatic event that has irrevocably altered their lives—a correlation which is certainly no accident. Schumacher reports ignoring the previous Bat-films and looking instead to the original 1939–40's DC Batman comics to inspire *Batman Forever,* comics in which it's the villains' traumas that drive them to madness, crime and a quest for world domination. As Bill Botchel points out in *The Many Lives of the Batman* (1991), these villains, who share Bruce Wayne's status as respected members of society, enact the contemporaneous anxieties about fascism suffusing the culture during Batman's early years. They are similar to Bruce Wayne, perhaps, in the same way that American society is similar to a European fascist state (similar origins), yet the differences are oh-so-crucial as Wayne turns his trauma-forged obsessions toward upholding goodness and the de-

Are the Batman movies loaded with "queer signifiers?"
*Source:* Warner Bros./The Kobal Collection/Isenberg, Robert.

mocratic ideal while his opponents strive to become nightmarish versions of the Nazi *Übermensch*. This Democracy vs. Fascism conflict is retooled for *Batman Forever* and played out as Good Corporate Capitalism vs. Bad Corporate Capitalism.

We first hear of Bruce Wayne as the camera pans over the sunlit commercial district of Gotham City while a newscaster reports "Billionaire Bruce Wayne has extended his trend-setting profit-sharing program to the employees of the highly successful electronics division of Wayne Enterprises." Swooping inside Wayne's skyscraper (which is crowned with a massive statue of muscle-bound Atlas holding up the globe), we find him in the midst of a corporate walk-through, African-American woman exec by his side, benignly smiling on his employees who are working, we are told, on such projects as "fire remediation" and "alternative fuels." After listening politely to E. Nygma's psychotically enthusiastic presentation of his "brain-wave" device, he turns down the project on ethical grounds ("it just raises too many questions"), thanks the crew of employees, tells them the factory "looks great," and departs.

This benevolent democratic corporate capitalism (Wayne even extends "full benefits" to the widow of Nygma's first victim, despite the official verdict of suicide as cause-of-death) where workers share in the profits from projects which benefit society and ethical concerns are placed above marketing potential, is in direct contrast to Nygma's version of unbridled capitalist exploitation. Literalizing predatory capitalism (with start-up capital obtained by robbery, no less) his product actually *feeds* off the consumer, invading their minds and channeling their brain waves to the Riddler. His blissed-out expression and shuddering body as he absorbs these waves leaves no doubt that the thrill is sexual as well as intellectual. That the Riddler's corporate headquarters is topped with a giant Nygma-Box (in contrast to Wayne's Atlas) underscores the masturbatory self-consumption of "Bad Capitalism," and lest we miss this elision of malignant consumption with sexual perversion the Riddler lasciviously gloats to Batman during the film's penultimate scene that his new improved mind-reading version of the device will soon spread throughout the world, feeding him "credit card numbers, bank codes and sexual fantasies." (Also echoing, perhaps, the homophobic panic surrounding queer discourse "contaminating" mainstream culture and penetrating the sanctity of the home, which has many an irate PTA member screeching about the Internet's capacity to bring queer newsgroups and chatrooms into their child's bedroom.)

Since the Riddler aligns "Bad Capitalism" with "Bad Sexuality," it's hardly surprising to find that the film's proforma heteronormative narrative manifests when Wayne is performing his role of "Good Capitalist." His ethical rejection of Nygma's design is coded as sexual rejection, while his first meeting with Dr. Meridian for a "consultation" (wherein he refers to the riddle as a "love letter" and the sender as a "he") results in her being his date to the Circus opening-night extravaganza for Gotham's wealthy elite—his public performance of the ultra-successful business tycoon bound up with his performance of heterosexuality.

She again performs the date-function for Wayne at the capitalist debutante ball where the mind-reading version of the Nygma-Box is unveiled and Nygma usurps Wayne's media-appellation of "Gotham's most eligible bachelor," while also coopting his public manifestation and sporting identical glasses, suit, and haircut—mimicking Wayne right down to the mole on his cheek and the token woman on his arm. On loan from Two-Face and overtly ogling Wayne, Nygma's date is clearly for appearances sake only as is his dance with Dr. Meridian during which he openly camps it up, saucily flirting with Wayne and making it abundantly clear that the women are entirely ancillary to the coded transactions between the men. Although Wayne's "romance" with Dr. Meridian satisfies the plot-level demand for heteronormativity, its credibility is perpetually undermined by both its stock formulaicity and by the similarity of Wayne's supposed genuineness to Nygma's obvious self-conscious falsity.

But what is the pay-off of marketing this safely contained and topically sanitized Camp suitable for mass-consumption—"Bat-Camp" if you will—to the mainstream audience? In fact, Bat-Camp appears to be central to Warner Bros.'s carefully designed campaign to woo back its wavering corporate sponsors who were disconcerted by the darkness and violence of *Batman Returns.* Following the film's release angry parents' groups lashed out at the studio, licensees and promotional partners, prompting McDonald's Corp. (the largest and most desirable promo-partner) to change its film promotional strategy; retailers howled as Batman products languished on store shelves; and the film took in a disappointing $90 million less domestically than its predecessor. Clearly the studio needed to lighten up the film in order to entice wary licensees back to the table for a third course, and began by replacing director Tim Burton with Joel Schumacher (who's come a long way since his days as a window display designer). When Warner Bros.'s marketing mavens unveiled the new Batman characters to about 200 potential corporate sponsors thereby "setting the mood for *Batman Forever,*" Schumacher was charged with convincingly presenting the transformation of the old Dark Knight into the new Bat Lite. Remarked one attendee, "It was lighthearted, particularly with Schumacher joking around. He said—and we could tell because he's very flamboyant— that it was going to be a more adventurous, entertaining Batman." Apparently this "flamboyance" paid off: Warner Bros. lined up a reported $45–$50 million worth of media money commitments from McDonald's, Kellogg's, Kenner Toys and others. Following in the tradition of the first comic books which debuted in 1933 not as commodities-in-themselves but as marketing devices—promotional giveaways and premiums for such companies as Procter and Gamble, Milk-O-Malt, and Kinney Shoe Stores—*Batman Forever* was conceived as much as a promotional vehicle for its corporate sponsors as a product in its own right.

Given the importance of the sub-teen market to the film's heavy-weight promo-partners and Schumacher's determination "not to have kids terrified" but instead to create a movie "light enough to be a living comic book," the deployment of Bat-Camp makes perfect marketing sense—theorists have long noted camp's appeal to children's sense of play, their love of exaggeration, and their consciousness of the gap between who they are and who they would like to pretend to be. And according to some, its irreverence toward gender difference and mockery of the extremes of femininity and masculinity titillates kids because it implicitly undermines the authority of parents who are seen to embody these constructions.

But Bat-Camp even goes one step further in converting what Susan Sontag once termed "a secret sensibility" into mass market symbolic currency. As well as being consciously about capitalism and consumption, *Batman Forever* self-consciously draws attention to its own status as a marketing vehicle and commodity, highlighting its own artificiality with playful irony and making reference to its position within the matrix of production and promotion surrounding the movie. With today's media-savvy audience who take the homoeconomic synergy among mega-corporations as a given, there is no need to disguise promotional relationships; instead, the film affectionately mocks these connections and flatters the audience by letting them in on the joke.

By the time the movie was released mid-June, everyone had seen the Batman McDonald's commercial (airing since May) in which Batman turns down his butler's offer of a sandwich with the line "No thanks—I'll get drive-through" before zooshing away in the Batmobile. But this was not just the standard commercial-inspired-by-feature-film: it was the actual first scene of the film, a revelation that had the audience giggling immediately. Just as camp highlights and mocks gender by exaggeration and reversal of gender-norms, "Campy Capitalism" does the same thing to its own constructions. That the movie opens with a commercial rather than the commercial spinning off from the movie draws attention to usually veiled marketing mechanisms by this reversal of the standard form in which commercial relationships are publicly represented, thereby reminding us of the film's artificiality at the moment when the viewer is traditionally called upon to exercise a willing suspension of disbelief. After this postmodern version of the invocation of the muse, even the "serious" moments in the film are given a possibly ironic valance. In other words, this nod to the viewer's knowledge of the film's status as a promotional vehicle invites the audience to participate in the movie's light-hearted irreverence toward itself.

When Nygma upbraids Two-Face for ostentatiously crashing his party without prior warning, his complaint that "We could have pre-sold the movie rights!" is as much the film's campy reference to its own well documented marketing strategies as it is Nygma's campy awareness of his strategy for marketing himself. Both the Wayne Enterprises logo that looks like Warner Bros.'s minus the "B," and the "GNN" news which replaces the generic newscasts of the previous movies, remind us of the fictional nature of the world inside the film by meta-commercial references to the world outside. Meanwhile, Dr. Meridian's sarcastic question to Batman "or do you prefer black leather and a whip?" does double discursive duty as an extratextual reference to *Batman Returns* (and the heavily hyped Michelle Pfeiffer as Catwoman) as well as an internal reference to the fictive world of the three films for the sake of some nominal consistency.

But perhaps the most telling example of this commercial performativity is what *has* to be a corporate tie-in for The Club (because when a product fills the screen for several precious seconds in a big budget film it is *never* an accident—e.g., E.T.'s Reese's Pieces) in which Batman—who has just deployed some of his emblematic Batgadgets to penetrate concrete, scale a skyscraper, secure a plummeting multi-ton metal canister and harness a helicopter—is foiled when Two-Face snaps The Club onto the helicopter's steering wheel, thereby forcing him to evacuate. Whether this is a serious commercial suggestion that The Club is unassailable, or a parody of commercials suggesting The Club is unassailable, seems impossible to determine, and is ultimately unimportant. To the marketing-conscious consumer this spot may be taken as a refusal to patronize, a sharing of an in-joke, a kind of "Outing" of itself; with the unaware viewer it does the same work as a traditional irony-free commercial.

The movie's climactic scene, then, where Batman triumphantly tells the Riddler he had to save both Dr. Meridian and Robin because he is both Bruce Wayne and Batman, while allowing for a wistfully optimistic bisexual reading, can be taken as a metaphor for the film's campy marketing and marketing of camp—replacing polymorphous perversity with polycommodified performativity, one might say. Although *Batman Forever* highlights its own commercial artifice, it carefully maintains its promotional earnestness beneath the veneer of irreverence: without the metatext we still have product tie-ins, commercial spin-offs, and a film custom designed for its corporate sponsors. The irony about promotion is, after all, for promotional purposes. And the film may be replete with queer signification, but the heteronormative narrative and over-the-top Riddler provide the homophobic viewer with just enough plausible deniability for the rumors that the Caped Crusaders are queers. So provided the queen is put safely back in his box in the end, the McAudience can tolerate him as a viable means of producing an appealing yet suitable kid's film without resorting to nauseating Care Bears variety sweetness; meanwhile their offspring clamor for a Batman Super Value Meal and limited-time-only (Collect all six!) McDonald's commemorative *Batman Forever* mug.

READING WRITING

## THIS TEXT: READING

1.  This is a complex essay on a very popular text. Can you locate Johnson's thesis? What she is trying to argue? Also, how does she support her thesis with details from the text?
2.  Johnson uses some complex terms like "heteronormative," "camp," and "performativity." Look these words up in a good dictionary. Are their definitions helpful? Ask your instructor to define "camp."
3.  What is Johnson's justification for linking capitalism and homosexuality in the movie?

## YOUR TEXT: WRITING

1.  Write a paper in which you look at gay/lesbian issues in a movie that does not *appear* to be about gay and lesbian issues.
2.  Write a response to Johnson. Do you agree with her thesis?
3.  Do you see a link between capitalism and Hollywood? Write an analytical paper in which you scrutinize the values of Hollywood and American capitalism.

## Indians and Cowboys: Two Poems That Re-Cast Hollywood Indians  ▪▪

Of the many disturbing legacies of Hollywood, perhaps the most disturbing is its history of Native American representation. Though Hollywood films have not always been friendly to women, African Americans and the poor, no group has likely gotten as much negative and potentially harmful screen time as American Indians. In fact, for some Americans their only information about Indian culture, behavior, and values comes from Western movies. The two poems below take a critical look at Westerns and their impact on the Native American community. "Dear John Wayne" (1984) by Ojibwe writer Louise Erdrich "reads" the Western icon John Wayne through a Native lens, noting the violent overtones of Western films. In "My Heroes Have Never Been Cowboys," (1993) Spokane/Coeur d'Alene writer Sherman Alexie also notes the overwhelming cultural presence of Wayne, but like Erdrich, deconstructs the iconography of Wayne and Westerns in general. Alexie even has a short story entitled "Dear John Wayne," influenced by Erdrich's poem. As you read, think about what it might be like to watch a Western from a Native American perspective.

### DEAR JOHN WAYNE

▪ Louise Erdrich ▪

August and the drive-in picture is packed.
We lounge on the hood of the Pontiac
surrounded by the slow-burning spirals they sell

John Wayne is an icon for the rugged, violent, and white West.
*Source:* Warner Bros./The Kobal Collection.

at the window, to vanquish the hordes of mosquitoes.
Nothing works. They break through the smoke screen for blood.

Always the lookout spots the Indians first,
spread north to south, barring progress.
The Sioux or some other Plains bunch
in spectacular columns, ICBM missiles,
feathers bristling in the meaningful sunset.

The drum breaks. There will be no parlance.
Only the arrows whining, a death-cloud of nerves
swarming down on the settlers
who die beautifully, tumbling like dust weeds

into the history that brought us all here
together: this wide screen beneath the sign of the bear.

The sky fills, acres of blue squint and eye
that the crowd cheers. His face moves over us,
a thick cloud of vengeance, pitted
like the land that was once flesh. Each rut,
each scar makes a promise: *It is
not over, this fight, not as long as you resist.*

*Everything we see belongs to us.*

A few laughing Indians fall over the hood
slipping in the hot spilled butter.
*The eye sees a lot, John, but the heart is so blind.*
*Death makes us owners of nothing.*
He smiles, a horizon of teeth
the credits reel over, and then the white fields

again blowing in the true-to-life dark
The dark films over everything.
We get into the car
scratching our mosquito bites, speechless and small
as people are when the movie is done.
We are back in our skins.

How can we help but keep hearing his voice,
the flip side of the sound track, still playing:
*Come on boys, we got them*
where we want them, drunk, running.
They'll give us what we want, what we need.
Even his disease was the idea of taking everything.
Those cells, burning, doubling, splitting out of their skins.

## MY HEROES HAVE NEVER BEEN COWBOYS

■ Sherman Alexie ■

1.

In the reservation textbooks, we learned Indians were invented in 1492 by a crazy mixed-blood named Columbus. Immediately after class dismissal, the Indian children traded in those American stories and songs for a pair of tribal shoes. *These boots are made for walking, babe, and that's just what they'll do. One of these days these boots are gonna walk all over you.*

2.

Did you know that in 1492 every Indian instantly became an extra in the Great American Western? But wait, I never wondered what happened to Randolph Scott or Tom Mix. The Lone Ranger was never in my vocabulary. On the reservation, when we played Indians and cowboys, all of us little Skins fought on the same side against the cowboys in our minds. We never lost.

3.

Indians never lost their West, so how come I walk into the supermarket and find a dozen cowboy books telling me *How The West Was Won?* Curious, I travel to the world's largest shopping mall, find the Lost and Found Department. "Excuse me," I say.

"I seem to have lost the West. Has anybody turned it in?" The clerk tells me I can find it in the Sears Home Entertainment Department, blasting away on fifty televisions.

**4.**

On Saturday morning television, the cowboy has fifty bullets in his six-shooter; he never needs to reload. It's just one more miracle for this country's heroes.

**5.**

My heroes have never been cowboys; my heroes carry guns in their minds.

**6.**

*Win their hearts and minds and we win the war.* Can you hear that song echo across history? If you give the Indian a cup of coffee with six cubes of sugar, he'll be your servant. If you give the Indian a cigarette and a book of matches, he'll be your friend. If you give the Indian a can of commodities, he'll be your lover. He'll hold you tight in his arms, cowboy, and two-step you outside.

**7.**

Outside it's cold and a confused snow falls in May. I'm watching some western on TBS, colorized, but the story remains the same. Three cowboys string telegraph wire across the plains until they are confronted by the entire Sioux nation. The cowboys, 19th century geniuses, talk the Indians into touching the wire, holding it in their hands and mouths. After a dozen or so have hold of the wire, the cowboys crank the portable generator and electrocute some of the Indians with a European flame and chase the rest of them away, bareback and burned. All these years later, the message tapped across my skin remains the same.

**8.**

It's the same old story whispered on the television in every HUD house on the reservation. It's 500 years of that same screaming song, translated from the American.

**9.**

Lester FallsApart found the American dream in a game of Russian Roulette: one bullet and five empty chambers. "It's Manifest Destiny," Lester said just before he pulled the trigger five times quick. "I missed," Lester said just before he reloaded the pistol: one empty chamber and five bullets. "Maybe we should call this Reservation Roulette," Lester said just before he pulled the trigger once at his temple and five more times as he pointed the pistol toward the sky.

**10.**

Looking up into the night sky, I asked my brother what he thought God looked like and he said "God probably looks like John Wayne."

**11.**

We've all killed John Wayne more than once. When we burned the ant pile in our backyard, my brother and I imagined those ants were some cavalry or another. When Brian, that insane Indian boy from across the street, suffocated neighborhood dogs and stuffed their bodies into the reservation high school basement, he must have imagined those dogs were cowboys, come back to break another treaty.

**12.**

Every frame of the black and white western is a treaty; every scene in this elaborate serial is a promise. But what about the reservation home movies? What about the reservation heroes? I remember this: Down near Bull's Pasture, Eugene stood on the pavement with a gallon of tequila under his arm. I watched in the rearview mirror as he raised his arm to wave goodbye and dropped the bottle, glass and dreams of the weekend shattered. After all these years, that moment is still the saddest of my whole life.

**13.**

Your whole life can be changed by the smallest pain.

**14.**

*Pain is never added to pain. It multiplies.* Arthur, here we are again, you and I, fancy-dancing through the geometric progression of our dreams. Twenty years ago, we never believed we'd lose. Twenty years ago, television was our way of finding heroes and spirit animals. Twenty years ago, we never knew we'd spend the rest of our lives in the reservation of our minds, never knew we'd stand outside the gates of the Spokane Indian Reservation without a key to let ourselves back inside. From a distance, that familiar song. Is it country and western? Is it the sound of hearts breaking? Every song remains the same here in America, this country of the Big Sky and Manifest Destiny, this country of John Wayne and broken treaties. Arthur, I have no words which can save our lives, no words approaching forgiveness, no words flashed across the screen at the reservation drive-in, no words promising either of us top billing. Extras, Arthur, we're all extras.

**READING** WRITING

## THIS TEXT: READING

1. What arguments do these two poems make about Indians, Westerns, America and Hollywood?
2. Consider the "form" of each poem. How does the poem's formal qualities (its typography, how it looks on the page, its language) contribute to its overall meaning? Which poem is more "poetic"?
3. bell hooks argues that a seemingly harmless movie like *Waiting to Exhale* is dangerous to African Americans. How dangerous, then, are movies like Westerns to American Indians? Is there a difference in the dangers they pose?

## YOUR TEXT: WRITING

1. Write a comparison/contrast paper on these two poems. Pay close attention to language, form, symbolism and metaphor. Be sure you make an argument in your essay.
2. Watch a famous movie starring John Wayne, like *The Searchers* or *Rio Bravo*. Write a paper in which you compare your own reading of Wayne with Erdrich's and Alexie's.
3. Talk to your parents or professor about John Wayne. Ask them how important he was during the 1950s and '60s. Write a paper in which you analyze the power certain Hollywood stars have over American culture—even American politics.

**DECIPHERING *I, ROBOT*: RANDOM THOUGHTS FROM AN EVOLVING FILM REVIEWER**

■ Jason Silverman ■

*Below are two different pieces by Jason Silverman, both written in 2004. The first is an original essay on the process of watching movies from the perspective of a movie reviewer, with specific examples from the recent movie* I, Robot. *Following the essay is Silverman's actual review of* I, Robot *that he wrote for wired.com. Silverman has been working in the film industry for over a decade. A former artistic director for the Taos Moving Pictures Festival, Silverman is active in all facets of the independent movie scene. Currently, he is a film reviewer for wired.com and other publications.*

I've spent a good chunk of the last 12 years watching and thinking about movies, and I still don't know what I'm doing. I'm not sure how to prepare or how to "watch" the movie once it starts. A kind of schizophrenia sets in when I'm in the theater, with voices in my head competing for attention: the (pseudo)-intellectual forcing me to take notes on socio-political-aesthetic issues; the eager-to-please freelance writer testing out witty phrases to use; and the little kid yanking on my sleeve, saying, "Loosen up! It's just a movie!"

It's not surprising that I'm conflicted while watching a movie. Movies are *complicated*. They rely on highly technical processes, and their mechanics remain a mystery to most viewers. Though the movies are mostly a form of amusement—a colossally expensive one—some film lovers insist that cinema is the ultimate form of art—a medium hat incorporates all other media. Then there are the watchdogs, who are concerned that the movies have a variety of negative effects on our culture. They are right to worry; movies, after all, are persuasive transmitters of information, the favored medium of both propagandists and advertising firms.

For these and other reasons, cinema is a tricky medium to write about. The more I learn, the more I realize I don't know. But I have seized upon a few concepts to help me tackle the film reviews, articles, and essays I write. Here's how these concepts helped shape a review I wrote of *I, Robot* (reprinted below) for the online magazine *Wired News* (wired.com).

**There are lots of pieces in this puzzle.**   Every second of a movie is packed with information, far too much to take in. But I try and get a sense of how the various elements—the writing, music, lighting, camera angles, performances, film stock, effects, editing—work together. Doing that helps me understand why the filmmakers made the choices they did.

- In Hollywood films, clumsy elements can jump out at me—an awkward edit, dialogue that feels staged, an especially bogus special effect. Studio films are generally supposed to be seamless. *I, Robot*'s team built a smooth-running film, and the cinematography, sets and performative, and editing style well suited to the subject matter. From a technical standpoint, at least, *I, Robot* is highly proficient.

The most impressive element of *I, Robot* was the convincing interaction between the computer-generated (CG) characters (the CG imaging work is done long after the human actors have left the set). And, while I didn't think much of the screenplay as a whole (more on that below), the writers created a good part for the star, Will Smith. Like most Hollywood scores, the *I, Robot* music was overwrought and intrusive.

Will Smith, Human, in *I, Robot* (2004). *Source:* 20th Century Fox/The Kobal Collection/Digital Domain.

**Story rules.**    Filmmakers say it again and again: good movies come from telling good stories. It's a cliché, maybe, but it's also true, especially if you expand your notion of what a story can be. Most feature films rely on conventional narratives—boy meets girl, alien attacks planet, detective hunts murderer, king grows paranoid, etc.—and unfold in specific three-act structure. Occasionally, artistic-minded filmmakers will experiment with more adventurous narrative forms. Experimental, non-narrative films (some have no characters, dialogue or plot) seek to tell stories of some kind. The form of the story is less important than its relevance—does it matter to me?—and the level of passion and ingenuity the filmmakers use in transmitting it.

- The many loose ends and nonsensical scenes in *I, Robot* left me wondering how much the filmmakers cared about the integrity of the story. Give the plot a few lingering thoughts and it begins to disintegrate. More importantly, the filmmakers chose to take a highly relevant subject—our relationship to technology—and turn it into a relative caricature (robots bad, humans good).

**It's more than entertainment.**    I think movies can influence behavior. Not that there is a one-to-one correlation—watching some dumb violent movie won't make every teen in the audience start knocking over convenience stores. But every movie, intentionally or not, can serve as a political and sociological text, transmitting information that can challenge or reinforce what we believe about ourselves and the world.

- I was initially excited at the prospect of an *I, Robot* movie—it's based on a 1950 Isaac Asimov book that explores the tension between humans and their increasingly sophisticated machines. The book feels a bit dated, but there's plenty of meaty, brainy stuff for an ambitious film to delve into. Unfortunately, this *I, Robot* movie sends simplistic, technophobic messages: Smart machines are to be feared, but human ingenuity will save the day.

On the surface, *I, Robot's* takes an anti-corporate stance (the villain is a big robotics company). Look a bit deeper, though: the film was made by 20th Century Fox—owned by the same multinational corporation that runs the business-friendly Fox News and scores of conservative newspapers—and it's filled with product placements (those mini-commercials for things like sneakers and soft drinks that Hollywood studios sneak onto the screen).

There are also interesting gender and race issues in the movie. Smith, playing the African-American policeman Del Spooner, is accused of being an anti-robot bigot, while old-fashioned, anti-Black racism never becomes an issue. Nancy Calvin, the female protagonist, is the latest in a long Hollywood line of lonely, frigid female professionals who have problems connecting with men. What does that stereotype tell us? That women who are successful in the workplace lead miserable personal lives.

**Movies are magic.**    I try not to get *too* caught up in the politics of every single movie—a good one can be a mind-altering substance, transporting me to new, weird and/or wonderful places. I'm at my best when I can tune in intellectually to a film *and* experience it on a gut level.

- With special effects becoming more spectacular every month, it's easy to take for granted how great the new breed of sci-fi/fantasy films look. Five years ago, the visuals in *I, Robot* would been groundbreaking, but the computerized, futuristic landscapes somehow don't seem quite as startling in this age of digital wizardry, when any visual is possible. I found the robots to be remarkable, and genuinely frightening in a plastic, banal way. The lead robot, Sonny, was especially convincing. Unfortunately, the magical moments weren't sustained for very long—*I, Robot's* narrative gaps shook me out of any brief reverie.

**Business rules.**    Entrepreneurs built the American film industry and, 100 years later, money still drives the movies. The average Hollywood film costs nearly $100 million to produce and market, so there's lots at stake with every release. Filmmakers are not immune to the profit motive—even Martin Scorsese and Woody Allen juggle financial considerations with artistic concerns.

- It's difficult to balance philosophical discourse and blockbuster action. When in doubt, Hollywood generally slugs it out—disposing of the brainy stuff and emphasizing fight and chase scenes. That's certainly true in *I, Robot,* which radically diverges from Asimov's edgy book. Did the producers worry that an idea-driven movie would scare off audiences? Perhaps. There are other signs of financial pressures here, including the movie's implausible happy ending, the casting of a beautiful young actress as Susan Calvin (she's something of an old bat in the book); and the inclusion of liberal amounts of product placements.

**Beware the tricks.**    The so-called "moving image" is actually a physiological fluke: flash a series of images past the human eye and the human brain will read them as seamless motion. The idea that cinema exists thanks to a trick of the eye represents one level of movie manipulation. I'm also wary of the other tricks filmmakers have developed: the schmaltzy music to try and make me cry, the shrouding of a villain in sinister shadow, an explosion so fiery that I fear for my eyebrows. I admire a good cinematic trick as much as anyone, but also am aware that these tricks too often cover up inept storytelling.

- *I, Robot,* a film about the future, enjoyed showing off futuristic machinery. That's the advantage of sci-fi and other tech-oriented stories. I liked the filmmakers' relationship with gadgetry. It wasn't fetishistic; instead, they showed enough of the robots to give me an understanding of how they worked. The CG imagery was also used to good effect. Other standard-issue tricks—the button-pushing music, the sappy ending, the film noir–inspired lighting—were restrained, at least in terms of Hollywood blockbusters.

**Don't be seduced by style.**    What passed for great filmmaking 50 years ago can today look stilted and clumsy. I've seen films made on laptops that have better effects than the original *Star Wars*. Styles that seem innovative and timeless right now will pass into obsolescence sometime soon (yes, that includes *The Matrix* and *The Lord of the Rings*). Style in itself does not qualify a film as a work of art. The stylistic choices in any good film reflect and deepen that film's intent. That's not to say I don't *ooh* and *aah* over eye-bending effects or stunning cinematography. I just try to avoid confusing them with artful filmmaking.

- *I, Robot* made some smart stylistic choices. The cinematographer shot the film, probably using filters, striving for a sci-fi/pulp fiction look, with shades of blue replacing the shades of gray familiar to fans of classic film noir. The result was relatively subtle and unified, and not especially memorable or innovative. But it was appropriate and served the story well.

**Watch old stuff, too.**    The movies are only a century old—an infant compared to other forms of expression—and they continue to evolve at a fast pace. I don't claim a comprehensive knowledge of film history (there's just too many movies out there) but the more old movies I watch, the better I understand cinema's evolutionary path. That gives me more confidence when I critique a new film.

- What makes great science fiction, and why did *I, Robot* fall short? To me, the best sci-fi films do at least one of two things: they build a complete world and live within the rules that govern that world; or they use the future as prism through which to investigate issues that affect our culture today. I love the first two *Terminator* films, both of which fulfil the first rule. You could think about them over and over and they still seemed to make sense. I remain one of the few defenders of *A.I: Artificial Intelligence,* which was as moving and troubling an examination of human-machine relationships as I've seen. Other sci-fi movies I've been impressed with: *A Clockwork Orange, Alphaville, Metropolis, Close Encounters, The Truman Show.* It's not a long list, partly because good sci-fi is hard to create. Special effects make these films expensive, and expensive movies usually don't have the luxury of exploring deep, philosophical issues. To me, that's *I, Robot's* central problem: Despite its potentially rich subject matter, it dedicated most of its resources to more conventional action sequences.

**Read some books, too.**    My favorite film writers are able to put movies into the context of art, history, sociology, literature, theory, philosophy, geography, geology, theology . . . anything and everything. Good film writers do more than just compare one film to another. They offer a context in which to understand the movies as an artistic and cultural form, and as a window into the world.

- I re-read *I, Robot,* which I last picked up as a teenager, to prepare for this film. It's amazing how sharp and relevant Asimov's thoughts on artificial intelligence remain, given that the book predates the computer age. Reading the book, far more than seeing the movie, reinforced the urgency of considering our relationship to technology. Movies like *I,*

*Robot* may not do all of the intellectual and philosophical work I want them to, but they do help push important issues into the pop-cultural slipstream.

■ ■ ■

## *I, Robot,* No Deep Thinker

Near the beginning of his classic 1950 novel *I, Robot,* Isaac Asimov laid out the three commandments governing robot behavior: Thou shalt not allow harm to come to a human, thou shalt obey humans, thou shalt protect thyself.

Hollywood blockbusters have their own set of rules, too: Drop in little commercials for products whenever you can, replace meaningful dialogue with witty repartee, build lots of fight scenes, end happily (by saving the world, if budget permits) and dilute any brainy stuff.

In the movie version of *I, Robot,* Hollywood's rules rule. Asimov fans and others who like their sci-fi on the chewy side will probably revolt—the essence of the book is gone. But the average popcorn muncher will appreciate *I, Robot*—it's a good example of why the blockbuster formula works. It's funny, has a chilly, blue visual style (the robots look like the clamshell iBooks) and moves fast.

This *I, Robot* began life as a screenplay called *Hardwired,* about a robot alleged to have killed a human. The film's producers then acquired the rights to the Asimov book and decided to combine the two stories.

It's not clear how the novel influenced the finished film (the credits describe *I, Robot* as "suggested by," rather than "adapted from," Asimov). But this movie definitely has made the book's most sensational bit—the idea that robots could follow the three laws and take over the world—central to the plot.

Of course, if any alien group is plotting a hostile global takeover, best to cast Will Smith to stop them—he's a one-man Department of Homeland Security. In *I, Robot,* Smith plays Officer Del Spooner, a guy with a grudge against robots—he's even been accused of being an anti-tech bigot. Spooner also hates United States Robotics, the world's largest "mecha" manufacturer.

USR is preparing to roll out its new Automated Domestic Assistant, the almost-human NS-5, when one of the company's founders, Alfred Lanning, jumps to his death, leaving Spooner a cryptic message.

Convinced that Lanning's death is part of a bigger plot, Spooner sets out to investigate with help from USR scientist Susan Calvin (played by Bridget Moynahan as a distant relation, at best, to the Calvin of the book) and a robot named Sonny. His opponents include some pesky mecha assassins and Lawrence Robertson, USR's hard-edged CEO. *I, Robot* displays plenty of high-tech wizardry—cars rolling on balls instead of wheels; a slow-mo, airborne robot fight and, best of all, Sonny, who is one of the best movie robots yet. The film is set in 2035, and the NS-5s are still a few generations behind the Terminators and Steven Spielberg's A.I. mechas. Sonny is much more robot than human, a plastic, nearly affectless, truly creepy creature.

I've yet to see a convincing CG replication of human movement. Sonny, however, is supposed to move like a machine—like CG itself, Sonny is mechanical but aspires to be more lifelike.

*I, Robot; You, Bored Viewer? Source:* 20th Century Fox/The Kobal Collection/Digital Domain.

Through Sonny, director Alex Proyas (*The Crow, Dark City*) takes a few stabs at exploring deeper man-machine questions. How will artificial intelligence parallel human thought processes? How can robots reconcile a complex world with their rigid rules of behavior? What happens when machines grow conflicted about the wisdom of their creators?

But Proyas' film never settles down long enough to dig deep. He's nodding in Asimov's general direction, not exploring his ideas.

Worse, Proyas' *I, Robot* stops making sense once you think about it. There are too many loose ends, too many plot-convenient moments and far from enough rigorous thought. To enjoy this *I, Robot*, you'll have to turn off your brain.

That may be what moviegoers expect to do over the summer, but it's the last thing Asimov, a master of clear, sharp logic, would have wanted.

**READING** **WRITING**

## THIS TEXT: READING

1. What connections do you see between Silverman's observations in the first essay and his actual review?
2. In what ways does Silverman read movies as "texts"?
3. What is the most interesting (or unexpected) aspect of the way in which Silverman looks at movies? How is his system similar or different than your own?
4. Find Silverman's thesis (it's pretty clear). How does he try to "prove" his thesis throughout the essay?

## YOUR TEXT: WRITING

1. Write a rebuttal to Silverman's review of *I, Robot*. What don't you like about his review?
2. Find a more positive review of *I, Robot* and write a comparison/contrast paper on the two reviews. Which review is the more convincing? Why?

*Student Essay*

| |
|---|
| **STAR WARS AND AMERICA** |
| ■ **Whitney Black** ■ |

*Whitney Black wrote this essay while a student at the University of San Francisco in 2003. In her short persuasive essay, she takes what is perhaps to most readers an unpopular stance. Black reads* Star Wars *through the lens of a classic American Western, arguing that the film essentially replicates the standard formula of Hollywood Westerns—right down to the good guys in white and the bad guys in black.*

*As you work through her essay, you might ask if Black reads too much into the film. Or, does she pick up on deep-seeded American values that many people are reluctant to question? Lastly, is it possible to identify problematic aspects of a movie but still love it?*

Though *Star Wars* takes place in the far off frontier of space, and is less concerned with recreating America's past than it is with imagining the future, the film is still a classic American Western, right down to the requisite good versus evil, us against them dualities. Like all formulaic Westerns, *Star Wars* is about opposition and the promotion of good old-fashioned American values. The environment is the unfamiliar galaxy, but the underlying message is pure Americana; *Star Wars* subverts patriotism within the rebel forces and religious "force," and establishes the rebellion's struggle against the tyrannical Empire as a pro-American ideological battle. The rebel forces, with their pared down attire and allegiance to the old "force" religiosity, are the antithesis to the techno-driven, machine heavy homogeneity of the Evil Empire; similar to how the American identity, with its commitment to traditional democratic values, differed from the oppressive threat of communism. Communism, during both the Red Scare and the Vietnam War, served as both a threat to American ideals as and a way to glorify those ideals by contrast. The un-American construct of the Empire, like the un-American Communist mentality, function as the perfect counterparts; both are outsider systems, whose differences illuminate America's "greatness," and generate a need to preserve that "greatness." The Rebellion is obligated to defend *a way of life,* a sense of individual freedom, from the Empire.

Like the Western's struggle between Cowboy and Indian, civilization and savagery, *Star Wars* simply modernizes the conflict, replacing cowboys with Jedi and Indians with evil empire affiliates. Though the characters have changed, the implicit Western message of expelling a threatening "other" remains. Both *Star Wars* and the classic Western are filmic homage to an American ideal; while the classic western re-writes the past to stabilize and reassure the present, *Star Wars* acts as a cautionary against what an absence of those ideals means for the future. The "us against them" duality is less about racial differences than it is about America's ideological system. It is glorious democracy against a "bad" countergovernment. Though *Star Wars* does not directly ally itself with America's geography, location is inconsequential; the rebels are as American as Indians killing cowboys, symbols of a filmic tradition advocating American values by setting them against an external threat.[1]

*Star Wars* succeeds at its "western-ness" because of its dependence on opposition. Nothing solidifies the righteousness of "good" as much as the presence of a contrasting evil. The Evil Empire justifies the Rebellion (obviously a *force* is necessary to confront the manifestation of evil) while divulging the danger of sacrificing the rebel cause to the empire. The Empire is the ominous threat and represents everything opposing the rebel value system, persona, and way of life. The result is audience approval of the rebel cause; audiences, whether aware of it or not, identify with the rebels as individual heroes fighting against a different, and thus threatening, authority. While the rebellion, and its association to the Imperial Senate, most certainly symbolizes the people's voice, the Empire is ignorant of the wants of the common people, and is a realization of abused power, and a warning against forces opposed to American democracy. While America, with its own structured Senate, associates its ideals with a "power to the people" mentality, the Empire is in obvious contrast, determined to exploit technology (the Death Star) and become an ultimate power and oppressive regime.

Not only does *Star Wars* link technology to tyranny and oppression, but it also creates another opposition of technology versus nature, with nature encompassing the rural American identity of honor, duty, and goodness while technology embodies the age-old fear of change. Clearly, the death star is both an example of misused power, and a warning against change. The machine, because of its relation to the Evil Empire, is a digression away from humanity; technology threatens the existence of individual power and becomes an instrument for proliferating evil. The protagonist Luke Skywalker succeeds against the Empire by relying on the power of his subconscious, turning off his computerized tracking system to respond on instinct. He uses his faith in the force, a religion of nature, and old fashioned and unquestioned belief; the outcome of his success, his ability to defeat the Empire, perpetuates yet another American notion. Believe in its value systems and justice will be restored.

The film's message is clear: Hold fast to our present way of life and the future will be saved. Like any Western, *Star Wars* is a cinematic love letter to Americana, and the country's perpetual fear of confrontation. Westerns deal in oppositions, because the rebel in space or in the west is always sacrificing their own safety to salvage a community. Community salvation mirrors American salvation, and the protagonist's determination and commitment to deep-rooted American rightness serves as the best possible form of American patriotism and duty. The Western always needs a hero willing to die for the cause, ready to save America from the threat of change. Westerns contend that America is the "best and only way," oppositions are the worst imagined evil; both feared and destroyed and ultimately never tolerated.

### Note

1. For more information on *Star Wars* and American values, see Peter Lev's *American Films of the 70s: Conflicting Visions.*

### Works Cited

Lev, Peter. *American Films of the 70s: Conflicting Visions* (Austin: University of Texas Press, 2000).

# The Passion of the Christ *Suite*

Mel Gibson's *The Passion of the Christ* is that rare movie—one that engenders strong reactions from many sides. Praised by Christian groups for its human portrayal of Jesus Christ, whom Christians believe is the son of their God, the film brought Christian viewers into theaters like no movie in recent history. However, the film also alienated many Jews, who saw in this depiction anti-Semitic stereotypes come to life; they and other mainstream Christians questioned Gibson's interpretation of the crucifixion. Rather than focusing on Christ's life, teachings and miracles (as most films on Jesus have done in the past), Gibson's film concentrates on the last few agonizing hours before Jesus was put to death by being crucified on a large wooden cross. Indeed, the film offers an unflinching and often brutal window into what death by crucifixion might have been like and highlights the literal and metaphorical suffering of Christ, whose death Christians believe was a sacrifice that would bring about their own eventual salvation.

Regardless of or perhaps because of the controversy it stirred up, passion was popular. Christian groups bought up huge blocks of tickets on the film's opening weekend so that it would post a powerful showing at the box office. For the past thirty years, conservative Christians have been somewhat critical of Hollywood movies, noting an increase in sexually explicit, violent, immoral and anti-family movies. Indeed conservative film critics like Michael Medved have decried what they see as Hollywood's anti-church, anti-Christian programming. However, even conservative Christians were flocking to large multiplexes in support of *Passion*. It is hard to think of another pop culture event that galvanized so much of the Christian community.

Mainstream film critics, though, were less moved by Gibson's project. Some claim the film is anti-Semitic, some say it is overly violent, and still others argue the movie foregrounds Christ's death, ignoring the world-altering teachings of his life. David Denby of *The New Yorker* went so far as to call the film "pornography" and "anti-Christian."

We have included four different reviews of *The Passion of the Christ,* including Denby's, Roger Ebert's, David Edelstein's, and Charity Dell's. Denby's is among the most scathing we encountered, though Ebert and Edelstein also have their problems with the movie. Dell's enthusiastic review offers a reading of *Passion* from an African-American perspective, a view that was often ignored in the media blitz surrounding the movie's reception.

Our intent in printing these reviews of the movie is to provide you with four very different readings of the same text. We urge you to pay attention to the "voice" of each review. Whose is the most formal? Whose is the most casual? Based on the tone and vocabulary of each review, can you guess who the audience or readership of the review might be? Also, are any of the reviews "unfair"? Do you get the sense that any of the reviewers were looking to dislike the movie? Lastly, do any of the reviews make an argument, and if so, what are they?

## THE PASSION OF THE CHRIST

### ■ Roger Ebert ■

If ever there was a film with the correct title, that film is Mel Gibson's "The Passion of the Christ." Although the word passion has become mixed up with romance, its Latin origins refer to suffering and pain; later Christian theology broadened that to include Christ's love for mankind, which made him willing to suffer and die for us.

The movie is 126 minutes long, and I would guess that at least 100 of those minutes, maybe more, are concerned specifically and graphically with the details of the torture and death of Jesus. This is the most violent film I have ever seen.

I prefer to evaluate a film on the basis of what it intends to do, not on what I think it should have done. It is clear that Mel Gibson wanted to make graphic and inescapable the price that Jesus paid (as Christians believe) when he died for our sins. Anyone raised as a Catholic will be familiar with the stops along the way; the screenplay is inspired not so much by the Gospels as by the 14 Stations of the Cross. As an altar boy, serving during the Stations on Friday nights in Lent, I was encouraged to meditate on Christ's suffering, and I remember the chants as the priest led the way from one station to another:

> At the Cross, her station keeping . . .
> Stood the mournful Mother weeping . . .
> Close to Jesus to the last.

For we altar boys, this was not necessarily a deep spiritual experience. Christ suffered, Christ died, Christ rose again, we were redeemed, and let's hope we can get home in time to watch the Illinois basketball game on TV. What Gibson has provided for me, for the first time in my life, is a visceral idea of what the Passion consisted of. That his film is superficial in terms of the surrounding message—that we get only a few passing references to the teachings of Jesus—is, I suppose, not the point. This is not a sermon or a homily, but a visualization of the central event in the Christian religion. Take it or leave it.

David Ansen, a critic I respect, finds in Newsweek that Gibson has gone too far. "The relentless gore is self-defeating," he writes. "Instead of being moved by Christ's suffering or awed by his sacrifice, I felt abused by a filmmaker intent on punishing an audience, for who knows what sins."

This is a completely valid response to the film, and I quote Ansen because I suspect he speaks for many audience members, who will enter the theater in a devout or spiritual mood and emerge deeply disturbed. You must be prepared for whippings, flayings, beatings, the crunch of bones, the agony of screams, the cruelty of the sadistic centurions, the rivulets of blood that crisscross every inch of Jesus' body. Some will leave before the end.

This is not a Passion like any other ever filmed. Perhaps that is the best reason for it. I grew up on those pious Hollywood biblical epics of the 1950s, which looked like holy cards brought to life. I remember my grin when Time magazine noted that Jeffrey Hunter, starring as Christ in "King of Kings" (1961), had shaved his armpits. (Not Hunter's fault; the film's Crucifixion scene had to be re-shot because preview audiences objected to Jesus' hairy chest.)

If it does nothing else, Gibson's film will break the tradition of turning Jesus and his disciples into neat, clean, well-barbered middle-class businessmen. They were poor men in a poor land. I debated Martin Scorsese's "The Last Temptation of Christ" with commentator Michael Medved before an audience from a Christian college, and was told by an audience member that the characters were filthy and needed haircuts.

The Middle East in biblical times was a Jewish community occupied against its will by the Roman Empire, and the message of Jesus was equally threatening to both sides: to the Romans, because he was a revolutionary, and to the establishment of Jewish priests, because he preached a new covenant and threatened the status quo.

In the movie's scenes showing Jesus being condemned to death, the two main players are Pontius Pilate, the Roman governor, and Caiaphas, the Jewish high priest. Both men want to keep the lid on, and while neither is especially eager to see Jesus crucified, they live in a harsh time when such a man is dangerous.

Pilate is seen going through his well-known doubts before finally washing his hands of the matter and turning Jesus over to the priests, but Caiaphas, who also had doubts, is not seen as sympathetically. The critic Steven D. Greydanus, in a useful analysis of the film, writes: "The film omits the canonical line from John's gospel in which Caiaphas argues that it is better for one man to die for the people [so] that the nation be saved.

"Had Gibson retained this line, perhaps giving Caiaphas a measure of the inner conflict he gave to Pilate, it could have underscored the similarities between Caiaphas and Pilate and helped defuse the issue of anti-Semitism."

This scene and others might justifiably be cited by anyone concerned that the movie contains anti-Semitism. My own feeling is that Gibson's film is not anti-Semitic, but reflects a range of behavior on the part of its Jewish characters, on balance favorably. The Jews who seem to desire Jesus' death are in the priesthood, and have political as well as theological reasons for acting; like today's Catholic bishops who were slow to condemn abusive priests, Protestant TV preachers who confuse religion with politics, or Muslim clerics who are silent on terrorism, they have an investment in their positions and authority. The other Jews seen in the film are viewed positively; Simon helps Jesus to carry the cross, Veronica brings a cloth to wipe his face, Jews in the crowd cry out against his torture.

A reasonable person, I believe, will reflect that in this story set in a Jewish land, there are many characters with many motives, some good, some not, each one representing himself, none representing his religion. The story involves a Jew who tried no less than to replace the established religion and set himself up as the Messiah. He was understandably greeted with a jaundiced eye by the Jewish establishment while at the same time finding his support, his disciples and the founders of his church entirely among his fellow Jews. The libel that the Jews "killed Christ" involves a willful misreading of testament and teaching: Jesus was made man and came to Earth in order to suffer and die in reparation for our sins. No race, no man, no priest, no governor, no executioner killed Jesus; he died by God's will to fulfill his purpose, and with our sins we all killed him. That some Christian churches have historically been guilty of the sin of anti-Semitism is undeniable, but in committing it they violated their own beliefs.

This discussion will seem beside the point for readers who want to know about the movie, not the theology. But "The Passion of the Christ," more than any other film I can recall, depends upon theological considerations. Gibson has not made a movie that anyone would call "commercial," and if it grosses millions, that will not be because anyone was entertained. It is a personal message movie of the most radical kind, attempting to re-create events of personal urgency to Gibson. The filmmaker has put his artistry and fortune at the service of his conviction and belief, and that doesn't happen often.

Is the film "good" or "great?" I imagine each person's reaction (visceral, theological, artistic) will differ. I was moved by the depth of feeling, by the skill of the actors and technicians, by their desire to see this project through no matter what. To discuss individual performances, such as James Caviezel's heroic depiction of the ordeal, is almost beside the point. This isn't a movie about performances, although it has powerful ones, or about technique, although it is awesome, or about cinematography (although Caleb Deschanel paints with an artist's eye), or music (although John Debney supports the content without distracting from it).

It is a film about an idea. An idea that it is necessary to fully comprehend the Passion if Christianity is to make any sense. Gibson has communicated his idea with a singleminded urgency. Many will disagree. Some will agree, but be horrified by the graphic treatment. I myself am no longer religious in the sense that a long-ago altar boy thought he should be, but I can respond to the power of belief whether I agree or not, and when I find it in a film, I must respect it.

Note: I said the film is the most violent I have ever seen. It will probably be the most violent you have ever seen. This is not a criticism but an observation; the film is unsuitable for younger viewers, but works powerfully for those who can endure it. The MPAA's R rating is definitive proof that the organization either will never give the NC-17 rating for violence alone, or was intimidated by the subject matter. If it had been anyone other than Jesus up on that cross, I have a feeling that NC-17 would have been automatic.

## NAILED

### ▪ David Denby ▪

In "The Passion of the Christ," Mel Gibson shows little interest in celebrating the electric charge of hope and redemption that Jesus Christ brought into the world. He largely ignores Jesus' heart-stopping eloquence, his startling ethical radicalism and personal radiance—Christ as a "paragon of vitality and poetic assertion," as John Updike described Jesus' character in his essay "The Gospel According to Saint Matthew." Cecil B. De Mille had his version of Jesus' life, Pier Paolo Pasolini and Martin Scorsese had theirs, and Gibson, of course, is free to skip over the incomparable glories of Jesus' temperament and to devote himself, as he does, to Jesus' pain and martyrdom in the last twelve hours of his life. As a viewer, I am equally free to say that the movie Gibson has made from his personal obsessions is a sickening death trip, a grimly unilluminating procession of treachery, beatings, blood, and agony—and to say so without indulging in "anti-Christian sentiment" (Gibson's term for what his critics are spreading). For two hours, with only an occasional pause or gentle flashback, we watch, stupefied, as a handsome, strapping, at times half-naked young man (James Caviezel) is slowly tortured to death. Gibson is so thoroughly fixated on the scourging and crushing of Christ, and so meagerly involved in the spiritual meanings of the final hours, that he falls in danger of altering Jesus' message of love into one of hate.

And against whom will the audience direct its hate? As Gibson was completing the film, some historians, theologians, and clergymen accused him of emphasizing the discredited charge that it was the ancient Jews who were primarily responsible for killing Jesus, a claim that has served as the traditional justification for the persecution of the Jews in Europe for nearly two millennia. The critics turn out to have been right. Gibson is guilty of some serious mischief in his handling of these issues. But he may have also committed an aggression against Christian believers. The movie has been hailed as a religious experience by various Catholic and Protestant groups, some of whom, with an ungodly eye to the commercial realities of film distribution, have prepurchased blocks of tickets or rented theatres to insure "The Passion" a healthy opening weekend's business. But how, I wonder, will people become better Christians if they are filled with the guilt, anguish, or loathing that this movie may create in their souls?

"The Passion" opens at night in the Garden of Gethsemane—a hushed, misty grotto bathed in a purplish disco light. Softly chanting female voices float on the soundtrack, accompanied by electronic shrieks and thuds. At first, the movie looks like a graveyard horror flick, and then, as Jewish temple guards show up bearing torches, like a faintly tedious art film. The Jews speak in Aramaic, and the Romans speak in Latin; the movie is subtitled in English. Gibson distances the dialogue from us, as if Jesus' famous words were only incidental and the visual spectacle—Gibson's work as a director—were the real point. Then the beatings begin: Jesus is punched and slapped, struck with chains, trussed, and dangled over a wall. In the middle of the night, a hasty trial gets under way before Caiaphas (Mattia Sbragia) and other Jewish priests. Caiaphas, a cynical, devious, petty dictator, interrogates Jesus, and then turns him over to the Roman prefect Pontius Pilate (Hristo Naumov Shopov), who tries again and again to spare Jesus from the crucifixion that the priests demand. From the movie, we get the impression that the priests are either merely envious of Jesus' spiritual power or inherently and inexplicably vicious. And Pilate is not the bloody governor of history (even Tiberius paused at his crimes against the Jews) but a civilized and humane leader tormented by the burdens of power—he holds a soulful discussion with his wife on the nature of truth.

Gibson and his screenwriter, Benedict Fitzgerald, selected and enhanced incidents from the four Gospels and collated them into a single, surpassingly violent narrative—the scourging, for instance, which is mentioned only in a few phrases in Matthew, Mark, and John, is drawn out to the point of excruciation and beyond. History is also treated selectively. The writer Jon Meacham, in a patient and thorough article in Newsweek, has detailed the many small ways that Gibson disregarded what historians know of the period, with the effect of assigning greater responsibility to the Jews, and less to the Romans, for Jesus' death. Meacham's central thesis, which is shared by others, is that the priests may have been willing to sacrifice Jesus—whose mass following may have posed a threat to Roman governance—in order to deter Pilate from crushing the Jewish community altogether. It's also possible that the temple élite may have wanted to get rid of the leader of a new sect, but only Pilate had the authority to order a crucifixion—a very public event that was designed to be a warning to potential rebels. Gibson ignores most of the dismaying political context, as well as the likelihood that the Gospel writers, still under Roman rule, had very practical reasons to downplay the Romans' role in the Crucifixion. It's true that when the Roman soldiers, their faces twisted in glee, go to work on Jesus, they seem even more depraved than the Jews. But, as Gibson knows, history rescued the pagans from eternal blame—eventually, they came to their senses and saw the light. The Emperor Constantine converted in the early fourth century, and Christianized the empire, and the medieval period saw the rise of the Roman Catholic Church. So the Romans' descendants triumphed, while the Jews were cast into darkness and, one might conclude from this movie, deserved what they got. "The Passion," in its confused way, confirms the old justifications for persecuting the Jews, and one somehow doubts that Gibson will make a sequel in which he reminds the audience that in later centuries the Church itself used torture and execution to punish not only Jews but heretics, non-believers, and dissidents.

I realize that the mere mention of historical research could exacerbate the awkward breach between medieval and modern minds, between literalist belief and the weighing of empirical evidence. "John was an eyewitness," Gibson has said. "Matthew was there." Well, they may have been there, but for decades it's been a commonplace of Biblical scholarship that the Gospels were written forty to seventy years after the death of Jesus, and not by the disciples but by nameless Christians using both written and oral sources. Gibson can brush aside the work of scholars and historians because he has a powerful weapon at hand—the cinema—with which he can create something greater than argument; he can create faith. As a moviemaker, Gibson is not without skill. The sets, which were built in Italy, where the movie was filmed, are far from perfect, but they convey the beauty of Jerusalem's court-yards and archways. Gibson, working with the cinematographer Caleb Deschanel, gives us the ravaged stone face of Calvary, the gray light at the time of the Crucifixion, the leaden pace of the movie's spectacular agonies. Felliniesque tormenters gambol and jeer on the sidelines, and, at times, the whirl of figures around Jesus, both hostile and friendly, seems held in place by a kind of magnetic force. The hounding and suicide of the betrayer Judas is accomplished in a few brusque strokes. Here and there, the movie has a dismal, heavy-souled power.

By contrast with the dispatching of Judas, the lashing and flaying of Jesus goes on for-ever, prolonged by Gibson's punishing use of slow motion, sometimes with Jesus' face in the foreground, so that we can see him writhe and howl. In the climb up to Calvary, Caviezel, one eye swollen shut, his mouth open in agony, collapses repeatedly in slow mo-tion under the weight of the Cross. Then comes the Crucifixion itself, dramatized with a curious fixation on the technical details—an arm pulled out of its socket, huge nails ham-mered into hands, with Caviezel jumping after each whack. At that point, I said to myself, "Mel Gibson has lost it," and I was reminded of what other writers have pointed out—that Gibson, as an actor, has been beaten, mashed, and disembowelled in many of his movies. His obsession with pain, disguised by religious feelings, has now reached a frightening apotheosis.

Mel Gibson is an extremely conservative Catholic who rejects the reforms of the Sec-ond Vatican council. He's against complacent, feel-good Christianity, and, judging from his movie, he must despise the grandiose old Hollywood kitsch of "The Robe," "The King of Kings," "The Greatest Story Ever Told," and "Ben-Hur," with their Hallmark twinkling skies, their big stars treading across sacred California sands, and their lamblike Jesus, whose simple presence overwhelms Charlton Heston. But saying that Gibson is sincere doesn't mean he isn't foolish, or worse. He can rightly claim that there's a strain of morbidity run-ning through Christian iconography—one thinks of the reliquaries in Roman churches and the bloody and ravaged Christ in Northern Renaissance and German art, culminating in such works as Matthias Grünewald's 1515 "Isenheim Altarpiece," with its thorned Christ in full torment on the Cross. But the central tradition of Italian Renaissance painting left Christ relatively unscathed; the artists emphasized not the physical suffering of the man but the sacrificial nature of his death and the astonishing mystery of his transformation into godhood—the Resurrection and the triumph over carnality. Gibson instructed De-schanel to make the movie look like the paintings of Caravaggio, but in Caravaggio's own "Flagellation of Christ" the body of Jesus is only slightly marked. Even Goya, who hardly shrank from dismemberment and pain in his work, created a "Crucifixion" with a nearly unblemished Jesus. Crucifixion, as the Romans used it, was meant to make a spectacle out of degradation and suffering—to humiliate the victim through the apparatus of torture. By embracing the Roman pageant so openly, using all the emotional resources of cinema, Gibson has cancelled out the redemptive and transfiguring power of art. And by casting James Caviezel, an actor without charisma here, and then feasting on his physical destruction, he has turned Jesus back into a mere body. The depictions in "The Passion," one of the cruellest movies in the history of the cinema, are akin to the bloody Pop representation of Jesus found in, say, a roadside shrine in Mexico, where the addition of an Aztec sacrificial flourish makes the passion a little more passionate. Such are the traps of literal-mindedness. The great modernist artists, aware of the danger of kitsch and the fascination of sado-masochism, have largely withdrawn into austerity and awed abstraction or into fervent humanism, as in Scorsese's "The Last Temptation of Christ" (1988), which features an existential Jesus sorely tried by the difficulty of the task before him. There are many ways of putting Jesus at risk and making us feel his suffering.

What is most depressing about "The Passion" is the thought that people will take their children to see it. Jesus said, "Suffer the little children to come unto me," not "Let the little children watch me suffer." How will parents deal with the pain, terror, and anger that children will doubtless feel as they watch a man flayed and pierced until dead? The despair of the movie is hard to shrug off, and Gibson's timing couldn't be more unfortunate: another dose of death-haunted religious fanaticism is the last thing we need.

## AN AFRICAN-AMERICAN CHRISTIAN'S VIEW OF *PASSION*

### ■ Charity Dell ■

*Editors' Note: In this essay, Charity Dell uses several phrases in quotation marks to indicate assumed statements—not actual facts. We do not recommend this technique or the repeated use of all capital letters for emphasis.*

Everyone viewing THE PASSION OF THE CHRIST sees this film through a unique "lens"—our gender, religious upbringing—or lack of it—our ethnocultural heritage—combined with the accumulated collection of our personal experiences, shape the "lens" through which we perceive cinematic art. As an African-American Christian viewer of Mel Gibson's film, I must share what I saw, heard and felt when I and a friend attended a matinee showing of THE PASSION OF THE CHRIST one Friday in Newark, New Jersey.

At the outset, everyone is drawn in to the movie's plot—immediately, you are "plunked down" in the Garden of Gethsemane and are "watching and praying", as it were, with Yeshua of Nazareth during His final hours. The theatre is completely quiet—except for a few muted voices here and there quoting remembered scripture—and people have neglected to bother with snack purchases and popcorn buckets.

The most riveting part of the film begins with the punishment of the young Jewish Rabbi at the hands of the Romans. Many of us literally FLINCHED in the seats when Yeshua was caned and whipped—and all around you were muffled, anguished cries of "Lord, have mercy!" and "Lord Jesus!"—the classic gut-wrenching phrases black people use to express shock, outrage and extreme horror. Men wept and attempted to stifle their sobs—one elderly black patron told me in the library in which I work that he "was not religious at all", but that, while watching this movie, he started crying and his stomach got sick, and he literally could not bear to watch the first nail driven into the hand of Jesus: "I just HAD to turn my head away!" But he stated that "the film was good", and that the movie "essentially told the truth."

Descendants of slaves FULLY UNDERSTAND why Gibson's cameras show the instruments of torture and repression—whips and chains evoke powerful collective memories of the suffering of our African foremothers and forefathers HERE in this country at the hands of so-called "Christians." It wasn't so long ago that our great-grandparents literally bore the scars of slavery in their bodies—and the infamous cat o'nine tails was ALSO used on subjugated Africans by viscious, sadistic overseers who acted just like the Roman legionnaries and lictors depicted in the film.

One of the reasons people of color are responding so positively to THE PASSION OF CHRIST is due to Gibson's frank, realistic depiction of the horrors of scourging and crucifixion. The Yeshua of Nazareth depicted in this film shows a full range of emotions—He cries, laughs with His mother, stands up to angry religious authorities who want the adulteress stoned—but most of all, THIS Jesus experiences mental anguish and physical torture, is mocked by Herod and spit upon by the Roman soldiers and bears the full brunt of human hatred manifested in unspeakable brutality. In no other commercial movie venue is there ANY comparable depiction of the Suffering Servant of Isaiah 53—the "Man of sorrows" Who "hid not His face from shame and spitting," although "we hid as it were, our faces from Him . . . His visage was marred . . . yet it pleased Yahweh to bruise Him."

It is THIS Jesus—the JEWISH, biblical "Lamb of God"—not the "Pale Pitiful Mystical Robot-Poppet" of Hollywood's imagination—that African-Americans and Latinos recognize as "OUR Jesus"—the God Who let Himself be beaten, humiliated and crushed, Who felt the sting of violence under a harsh regime, Who suffered injustice and oppression, and Whose torn, lacerated flesh bore the marks of a savage, repressive empire bent on world conquest. Black Christians identify with the God Who becomes a "slave" during Passover, the Festival of Freedom—He is bought for 30 pieces of silver, the market value of a slave in first-century Israel—in order to free humanity from its captivity to sin and death. The honest, unsparing depiction of the harsh reality of Roman punishment "hits home" and "rings true" for those whose lives are impacted daily by systemic injustice and senseless violence.

African-Americans immediately recognized the "Jesus" we've heard about in our Sunday Schools, Vacation Bible Schools and worship services, on the knees of our parents and grandparents and community elders—the "Jesus" of our prayer chants, our lined-out psalms and our spirituals and gospel anthems, Who inspired our slave ancestors with hope and gave us joy in the midst of sorrowful lives—and we have ALWAYS heard from our pulpits the message of discipleship—"NO CROSS, NO CROWN!"

Mel Gibson's artistic vision does not spare theatergoers the simply stated, awful truth of the "Apostle's Creed"—"He suffered under Pontius Pilate, was crucified, dead and buried. He descended into hell. The third day He rose again from the dead . . ." Black Christians find it easy to identify with the God Who endured unspeakable agony to redeem a sinful, evil world and reconcile humanity back to Yahweh our Father.

Hollywood is understandably "upset" with Mel Gibson for his "failure" to trivialize suffering and spare them the horrid truth of the ENORMOUS COST of humanity's redemption. For the last 25 years, the Movie Establishment was content to serve up a "saccharine slop of syrupy sweets" and sell these sentimental trifles as "biblical movies" to a jaded public. But then its collective little stomach "heaved" when scourging and crucifixion were accurately portrayed on film! We know from history that the backs of scourged victims were essentially reduced to raw hamburger meat and the internal organs, tendons, bones and muscles were frequently exposed—so Yeshua of Nazareth certainly looked far WORSE than anything imagined by the production company's make-up department!

The "Pampered Princes of Suburbia"—including "media pundits", "leading theologians" and "religious scholars"—who are all whining "Ooooooooh; it's just too bloody for meeee—I can't deal with all that mess and gore!!" ought to try seeing this movie—and the Messiah's suffering—through the eyes of those intimately acquainted with violence and degradation. Scourging and crucifixion cannot and should not be "sanitized, scrubbed clean and prettied-up" to charm the "comfortable folks" who want the movie to "prophesy unto us SMOOTH things"!

Those of us deemed "marginal" by the media elites are NOT the ones complaining "there's just too much graphic, gratuitous violence"—Hollywood and the media moguls have not bothered to sample the opinions of black or Latino audiences—who are buying literal blocks of tickets and keeping the theatres filled with busloads and carloads of theater-goers! Nor are black and Latino viewers muttering "anti-semitic slogans" or "cursing all Italians" for "what the Romans did to Jesus"—most black and Latino Christians leave the cinema THINKING and quietly discussing all we have seen and felt.

Inasmuch as Mel Gibson's picture has illustrated the suffering of the biblical Yeshua of Nazareth—and has not shied away from showing that redemption was "bought with a price"—*THE PASSION OF THE CHRIST* is destined to become a movie classic embraced by people of color who have suffered and can recognize the crushed Son of God Who was mistreated, and yet triumphed through it all.

"And let the church say, "AMEN!"

---

### JESUS H. CHRIST: *THE PASSION*, MEL GIBSON'S BLOODY MESS

■ David Edelstein ■

Ever since his star began to rise after the 1979 Australian thriller *Mad Max*, Mel Gibson hasn't seemed fully alive on screen unless he's being tortured and mutilated. In the *Road Warrior* and *Lethal Weapon* films, as well as such one-shots as *Conspiracy Theory* (1997) and *The Patriot* (2000), Gibson courted martyrdom, and he achieved it. He won an Oscar for his labors in *Braveheart* (1995), which ends with its hero managing to scream "FREEEEE-DOM!!" as he's drawn and quartered. Gibson snatched the pulp movie *Payback* (1999) away from its writer-director, Brian Helgeland, to make the torture of his character even more gruelingly explicit: He added shots of his toes being smashed by an iron hammer. Payback: That's what almost all of Gibson's movies are about (including his 1990 Hamlet). Even if he begins as a man of peace, Mad Mel ends as a savage revenger.

A devout Catholic—albeit one who believes that Vatican II, which formally absolved the Jews of responsibility for the death of Jesus, is illegitimate—Gibson has said that what moves him most about the Christ story is that Jesus was whipped, scourged, mocked, spat on, had spikes driven through his hands and feet, and was left to die on the cross—and that he didn't think of payback; he thought of forgiveness. But by wallowing in his torture and death for two hours, the director of *The Passion of the Christ* (Newmarket) suggests that he's thinking of anything but.

Gibson had an ingenious idea for promoting his Passion: as the film that the Jews don't want you to see. Now watch those lines form! Bad reviews won't matter, either, since Gibson has called his critics "the forces of Satan" or, more charitably, the "dupes of Satan." After Gibson's pre-emptive blasts, an attack on his Passion will be interpreted by some as an attack on their religious beliefs instead of on filmmaking that is theologically, morally, and—by the way—artistically suspect.

As you probably know, *The Passion of the Christ* recounts the last 12 hours of the life of Jesus of Nazareth (played by the lean, high-cheekboned Jim Caviezel), with flashbacks to the Last Supper and a few shots of the little-boy Jesus being hugged by his mother, Mary. (The latter are cross-cut with spikes being hammered through his hands.) The lashes of the soldiers (dispatched by the Jewish priesthood) begin about 15 minutes into the film; by the time Jesus is dragged into the presence of the Roman governor Pontius Pilate (the Bulgarian actor Hristo Naumov Shopov), his face has already been smashed to a pulp.

Pilate, whom historians identify as a surpassingly cruel ruler responsible for crucifying many thousands to maintain his authority, is portrayed as a sorrowful, even-tempered man whose wife (Claudia Gerini) shows acts of loving kindness toward Mary (Maia Morgenstern) and Mary Magdalene (Monica Bellucci). Pilate is shocked by the Jews' brutality and by the determination of the priest Caiphas (Mattia Sbragia) to see this so-called blasphemer executed. While Pilate wrinkles his forehead, searching his tender conscience, sundry Jews lean into the camera and hiss or keen through rotted teeth.

I know, it sounds like a Monty Python movie. You're thinking there must be something to *The Passion of the Christ* besides watching a man tortured to death, right? Actually, no: This is a two-hour-and-six-minute snuff movie—The Jesus Chainsaw Massacre—that thinks it's an act of faith. For Gibson, Jesus is defined not by his teachings in life—by his message of mercy, social justice, and self-abnegation, some of it rooted in the Jewish Torah, much of it defiantly personal—but by the manner of his execution.

That doesn't exactly put him outside the mainstream: The idea that Jesus died for the sins of mankind is one of the central tenets of Christian faith. But Gibson has chosen those sections of the Gospels (especially the Gospel of Matthew) that reflect the tension between Jews and Christians 50 years after the crucifixion, when the new religion's proselytizers were trying to convert, rather than incite, the Roman authorities. This is the sort of passion play that makes people mad.

Gibson uses every weapon in his cinematic arsenal to drive home the agony of those last dozen hours. While his mother and Mary Magdalene watch, Jesus is lashed until his entire body is covered in bloody crisscrossing canals. When he rises, amazing the Roman soldiers with his stamina, they go for the scourges, which rip and puncture his flesh in slow motion—all while the Romans and the Jews cackle wildly. Carrying his cross, he falls again and again in slow motion on his swollen, battered body while the soundtrack reverberates with heavy, Dolby-ized thuds. It is almost a relief when the spikes are driven into his hands and feet—at least it means that his pain is almost over.

What does this protracted exercise in sadomasochism have to do with Christian faith? I'm asking; I don't know. Gibson's revenge movies end with payback—or, in *Braveheart,* the promise of payback to come. When Jesus is resurrected, his expression is hard, and, as he moves toward the entrance to his tomb, the camera lingers on a round hole in his hand that goes all the way through. Gibson's Jesus reminded me of the Terminator—he could be the Christianator—heading out into the world to spread the bloody news. Next stop: the Crusades.

## READING WRITING

### THIS TEXT: READING

1. As you have no doubt discerned, the four reviews above read the same movie *very* differently, though each notices the same kinds of objective details. How do you account for the varying interpretations?

2. Which of the reviews makes the most compelling argument? What makes this argument the most convincing?

3. Read again the Dell and Denby reviews. What external forces might account for two such varying reviews?

4. In the previous version of this book, our movie suite focused on film violence, which has become a rather heated topic over the past few years. Roger Ebert claims this is the most violent movie he has ever seen. Why do you think the violence in *Passion* did not draw the ire of conservative groups like other films?

5. Is there a delicate line between criticizing a movie about Jesus Christ and criticizing Jesus Christ?

6. Elsewhere David Denby calls *Passion* "pornography." What do you make of this claim? Is Denby's assertion valid?

### YOUR TEXT: WRITING

1. Write your own review of *The Passion of the Christ.* Feel free to agree or disagree with any of the reviews above. What factors influence your own "reading" of the film?

2. Write a comparison/contrast essay using the Denby/Dell reviews. Whose review do you agree with more? Who makes the most compelling argument? More importantly, *how* do Denby and Dell make and support their arguments? Is one more logos-based than the other? More ethos-based?

3. Write a paper on *Passion* and *The Last Temptation of Jesus Christ,* another controversial movie about Jesus. How are the films similar? Different?

4. Write a comparison/contrast paper on *Passion* and *Monty Python's The Life of Brian.* Which film is more engaging? What argument does each film make?

5. Write a paper on the film from a purely aesthetic perspective—that is, focusing solely on the way the movie looks, the quality of the acting, the quality of the direction, the music, the editing and so on. How is the movie *constructed?* How does its design and composition contribute to the argument it wants to make?

6. Write a definitional essay in which you argue that the *Passion* is or is not pornography. How you define pornography will greatly influence your essay, so choose your sources wisely.

## READING *Outside the Lines*

### CLASSROOM ACTIVITIES

1. As a class, watch one of the movies under review in this section. Write your own review of the movie without talking to anyone else in class about the movie. Then, after a class discussion, write yet another review of the movie. How does your own reading of the movie change after class discussion?

2.  Watch a movie in class and write a group review. What are the major points of disagreement? On what was it easy to agree?

3.  View any of the movies that you have read about in the previous texts. Do you agree with the writers? Why or why not?

4.  Is watching a movie in class different than watching one at home or in a theater? Why? Have a class discussion on the space of watching movies.

5.  Write a poem about the *experience* of watching a particular film (like Erdrich's "Dear John Wayne"). How does writing a poem about a movie differ from writing a journal entry or a formal paper? Is there a relationship between poems and film?

6.  Bring advertisements or commercials about particular movies to class. Discuss the demographic the studio is targeting. Do the commercials and ads *tell* you how to read the movie?

7.  As you watch a movie in class, write down every form of manipulation you notice (such as music, close-ups, special effects, camera angles, unusual editing, intense colors).

8.  Watch a recent movie that was praised by critics but was seemingly ignored by the general public (these might include: *Tully, The Fast Runner,* Three *Kings, Red, Simple Men, Vanya on 42nd Street, The Straight Story, Rushmore, Secrets and Lies, You Can Count on Me, Boys Don't Cry, American Movie, The Winslow Boy, Ghost World*). Why do you think not many people saw these films? Why do you think critics loved these particular movies? Is there tension between critical and popular taste?

9.  Talk about the criteria and expectations of different genres in class. What characteristics must a romantic comedy have? What is the purpose of a Western? What does an action–adventure movie need to do? What makes a good scary movie?

10. Find a copy of the American Film Institute's top 100 American movies. Talk about the list in class. Why did these movies make the list? What movies are missing? Why?

## ESSAY IDEAS

1.  What is the "greatest" movie you've seen? Write an essay in which you argue why your choice is the greatest.

2.  Chances are, you have seen *The Passion of the Christ* or *Waiting to Exhale.* Write your own analytical review of one of these films. Feel free to reference one of the reviews you have read. Perhaps you will agree or disagree with one (or many) of the reviewers. Be sure to analyze the film; don't simply write a plot summary.

3.  bell hooks's review of *Waiting to Exhale* is a provocative text. Track down a positive review of the film and write a comparison/contrast paper in which you not only identify but also explore the variant readings of the films.

4.  Write an essay on a director's body of work. People like Steven Spielberg, Woody Allen, Quentin Tarantino, Penny Marshall, Stanley Kubric, John Sayles, Spike Lee, Michael Bay, Paul Verhoven, or Howard Hawkes, who have directed a number of different movies, will make your essay more interesting. Is there an overarching theme to their movies? How have they contributed to film history? To American culture?

5.  Write an essay in which you explore issues of gender in one or two recent movies. Perhaps you can pick a movie directed by a woman and one directed by a man. How are women represented? How are women's bodies presented or framed? Male bodies? Do

the women have strong roles, or are they limited, stereotypical roles? Do the women date or love men their own age, or are the men much older? Do the women have good jobs and healthy lifestyles?

6. Write an essay in which you explore issues of race. As in gender, how are issues of race and power represented in the film? What kind of music runs through the film? Are minority characters filmed or framed differently than Anglo characters? There is an old joke that the one black character in a horror film is one of the first to die. Is this still the case? While there are a number of wonderful movies by people of color (*Do the Right Thing, Smoke Signals, The Joy Luck Club, Mississippi Masala, El Mariachi*), you might also consider how minorities are represented in movies made by Anglos.

7. Explore notions of class in American cinema. How often are poor people in movies? While there may be women and people of color in Hollywood and in the studio system, how well does Hollywood understand low-income America? Are there realistic film portrayals of working-class or low-income families? Some would say that America is more classist than racist: Is this theory proven or refuted by Hollywood?

8. Write an essay in which you offer a reading of a film based solely on the film techniques: sound, lighting, camera angles, music, framing, and editing. How can technique determine meaning?

9. *Star Wars* is beloved by millions. Do you agree with Whitney Black's critical reading of the film?

# INTERCHAPTER
# Reading and Writing
# About Images

With the proliferation of television, movies, video games, computers, and advertising, we have become a culture that tends to define itself through visual images. Even the act of reading these words on this page remains a visual activity. As we explain in the introduction, reading is nothing more than visual decoding of images so familiar that we do not even think of them as images. We don't imagine of text on the page as pictures, but each word is a small picture of curved, slanted and dotted marks that we call "letters." When we put certain combinations of these letters together, they conjure up a particular idea or image in our heads. While words are images themselves and reflect other images, we're more concerned here with the way we constantly decode, often with little conscious effort, the multiple images that we encounter each day—from people's faces to television shows to book covers to signs to architecture. One of this book's main ideas, in fact, is slowing down the reading process of visual images. As you may have noticed, almost all of the chapters in this book involve visual decoding of some sort.

Our book's insistence on this type of reading stands behind our idea to present some images here as a way of focusing our attention on the visual. The kinds of images we offer in this chapter need little introduction, but we will provide a brief entrée into our thinking behind this chapter. First of all, we present pairs of images. We remain interested in how images speak (both directly and indirectly) to each other and how details of specific images become highlighted or accentuated when placed in context with another picture. For instance, a small, older wooden house in a working class neighborhood may appear quite different depending on its context. Next to the white house, it may seem tiny and almost shabby, but next to a grass hut from a poor country, it could appear downright spacious and luxurious. In this chapter, you will be given several combinations of images. Our hope is that you will engage a semiotic reading not only of the individual images but also that you will do a semiotic analysis of the pair of images.

To this end, we've identified and reiterated a few points about reading visual images:

## Images are texts that can and should be read.

Again, as we point out in our discussion of semiotics in the introduction to this text, we ask that you apply the vocabulary and attention you devote to reading written texts to reading visual texts. When we open a book or look at directions or scan a newspaper, we are conscious of the act of reading. We know that our eyes move across a page and process information, and most important, we are conscious of the information that this process of looking produces. That is, we know we are reading for information, for content—we know that there is a message to most written texts.

However, the title and the thesis of this book is that the world is a text; that means that all images are texts, and as such, demand to be read as thoroughly as a poem or textbook. In fact, we would argue that visual images such as advertisements, television and movies, photographs, album covers, movie posters, and t-shirts should be read with particular care because images transmit so many values and assumptions but are transmitted quietly and subconsciously. Because images do not come in the language of analysis (words), we tend not to analyze them as closely, if at all. We urge you to analyze all images.

## Reading images is usually an informal rather than a formal process.

As we note above, reading images tends to be an informal process—that is, we are not aware of the process of reading images. We take them in and move on, giving very little thought to the thousands of visual cues we see every few seconds. To formalize the process of reading images, all we need to do is become conscious readers of images as constructed texts. For instance, this morning if you combed your hair, washed, shaved, put on make-up—if you thought about what to wear at all—then you did some work in constructing yourself as a text. You knew that today, like every other day, you were going to be read, on some level, and you wanted to send certain cues. Perhaps you wanted to suggest that you are alternative, conservative, athletic, bookish, or sophisticated. Depending on the image you wanted to project, you would don the appropriate signifiers.

When the other students look at you as you walk into class or as patrons in the coffee shop regard you as you order a latte, they do an informal reading of you—even if it is very brief and even if they don't know they are doing it at all. They might notice something has changed about you, but they would likely acquire even this information informally—virtually no one would actively ask the question, "how has x changed her appearance today? Let me take a thorough inventory of hairstyle, clothing, grooming." The same kind of quick informal reading usually goes into our appraisal of images. How often do we really stop to consider everything, all the details, that contribute to the overall message of the image? Here is where reading images mirrors reading visual arts—we must be aware of issues of composition, how the image is put together. As soon as you begin asking questions about what message a certain image is supposed to send, as soon as you read the image on your own terms—that is, when you begin to read the image not as the image wants to be read but as something to analyze—then you will formalize the reading process and begin to see the world in a more complex way.

## The reader/viewer always participates in the construction and significance of the image.

The Confederate flag, the "Stars and Bars," has become one of the most controversial American images in the last 50 years. Perhaps more than any other American icon, the Stars and Bars reveals how deeply our own backgrounds, culture, and political beliefs determine how we "read" images. For some white Southerners, the flag stands as a symbol of rebellion and independence. For white Northerners or those not from the South, the stars and bars may reinforce negative stereotypes about southern culture. For yet another population, African Americans, the stars and bars stand as a salient and prominent symbol of slavery and racism. Why do each of these groups have such different interpretations of a simple red rectangle, crossed by two blue bars and some white stripes? The answer is simple. We cannot "see" the flag (or any image) outside of our own ideas.

Whether the image under debate is a photo of Osama bin Laden, Bill Clinton talking with Monica Lewinsky, a topless supermodel, a multiracial couple, an electric chair, a fetus, a church, or a chemistry textbook, we each bring to the image our own set of assumptions and prejudices. This realization is important because it underscores the gap between intention and reception. By intention or intent, we mean the motivation behind producing or displaying the text, whereas reception is the reaction to the text—how the text is received. In many instances, intention and reception have nothing to do with each other. Not long ago, the chief justice of the Alabama Supreme Court, Roy Moore, was removed from office for placing a monument of the Ten Commandments in the rotunda of the courtroom. A number of people were outraged, claiming that hanging up the Ten Commandments was publicly stating that the judge would rule from a position that is sympathetic to an Old Testament Judeo-Christian perspective, thereby admitting de facto discrimination against non-Christians. Was the judge intending to send this message? Maybe, maybe not. Is this message a valid reception of the text? Probably.

In addition, the American flag means something different in Afghanistan than it does in Ireland. The logo for the Atlanta Braves sends one message to folks in Georgia and another to folks on the Rosebud Indian Reservation in South Dakota. The photograph of incoming first lady Hillary Rodham Clinton holding hands with outgoing first lady Barbara Bush incites very different reactions depending on your political leanings. Our point is that no reading of an image is ever value free. We are active participants in the construction and reception of an image, and by extension, the world.

▪ America, Cowboys, The West, & Race ▪

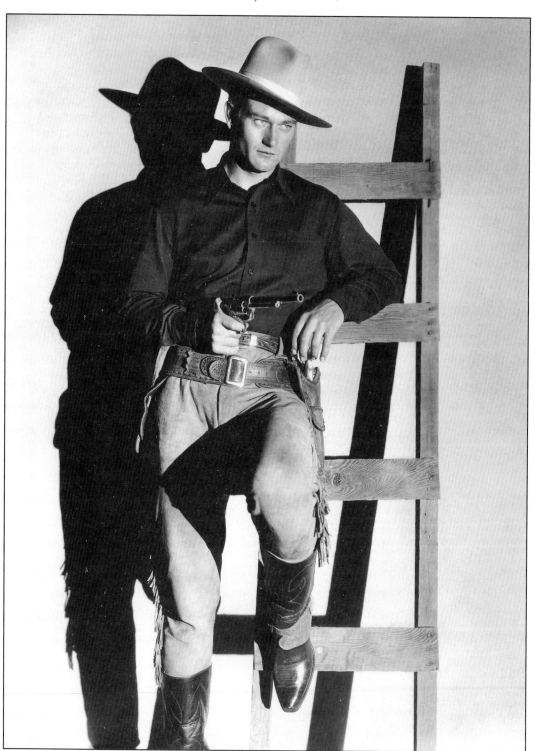

■ America, Cowboys, The West, & Race ■

■ Two Images of Gender ■

*Source:* Leonardo da Vinci (1452–1519), *Mona Lisa,* oil on canvas, 77 × 53 cm. Inv. 779. Photo: R.G. Ojeda. Louvre, Paris. Reunion des Musees Nationaux/Art Resource, NY.

## Two Images of Gender

## The Semiotics of Architecture

## ▪ Flags ▪

■ Laundry ■

◼ Laundry ◼

# ▪ Neighborhoods ▪

## ◾ Cars ◾

▪ Signs ▪

## ◦ Signs ◦

## ▪ Two Photos by Diane Arbus ▪

A young Brooklyn family going for a Sunday outing, N.Y.C. 1966.
*Source:* Diane Arbus/Digital Images. © The Museum of Modern Art/Licensed by Scala-Art Resource, NY.

## ▪ Two Photos by Diane Arbus ▪

A Jewish giant at home with his parents in the Bronx, N.Y. 1970.
*Source:* The Museum of Modern Art/Licensed by Scala-Art Resource, NY.

## Private Symbol/Public Space: The Virgin of Guadalupe

## Two Murals by Rigo

■ Diners ■

## Postcards from Texas

READING WRITING

## THIS TEXT: READING

1. The photograph of John Wayne contains a number of signifiers. How many icons or symbols do you see in the photograph?
2. Does the photo of Jackie Chan seem out of place next to John Wayne? Why? If the shot of Chan included all of the icons in the photo of Wayne, would it seem even more odd?
3. What are the similarities between the Mona Lisa and Britney Spears?
4. How do a photograph and painting differ in terms of their signifiers? Does one allow more input from the viewer?
5. Greek revival houses in the United States often have unsavory connotations, namely as fraternity houses and plantations. Why do you think this is the case?
6. How do the two "laundry" photographs represent different notions of what laundry does and is?
7. Can you gauge your physical reaction when looking at the American flag versus the Mexican flag? Do the colors symbolize different things for you in each flag?
8. Which flag do you find more aesthetically pleasing?
9. What do you make of the Diane Arbus photographs? Both are about families/friends, yet both are a bit discomfiting. Why?
10. What is your immediate reaction to the neighborhood photos?
11. Are you surprised the two bizarre postcards are from Texas? Why? Why not? What symbols (racist or otherwise) are at work in the El Jardin hotel postcard?
12. Which of the two cars would you like? What would you assume about the owner of each based on the "text" of each car?

## YOUR TEXT: WRITING

1. Write a comparison/contrast essay on the cowboy images. How does race figure into the myth of the American west?
2. Give a semiotic reading of the images of the Mona Lisa and Britney Spears. Identify at least three signifiers in each image.
3. Why do you think the white house and many other official buildings are modeled on the Parthenon and Greek architecture in general? What kind of message does such a structure send?
4. Write a descriptive paper on the place where you do your laundry. How is the act of doing or hanging laundry in a public place an intimate act?
5. Compare or contrast the laundry photos. How are they similar? What is missing from each?
6. Write down the first five things that pop into your head when you see the Mexican flag. Do the same for the American flag. Write an essay in which you explore the different values you assign to each.
7. Write a paper in which you unpack the two Diane Arbus photographs. What is going on in them? Are they exploitive?
8. Write a comparison/contrast paper looking at the murals by Rigo and the murals of the Virgin de Guadalupe. All four are public art and versions of public "texts." How are they similar? different?

9.  Do a semiotic reading of the neighborhoods. What assumptions do you make about each neighborhood based on the photographs?

10. Write a paper in which you give a semiotic reading of the two cars. What messages does each send?

11. Give a semiotic reading of the diners. What does each evoke?

## The American Signs on Route 66 Suite

In reading through dozens and dozens of books for the new edition of this text, we came across what both of the authors think is one of the coolest books we have seen in years—*American Signs: Form and Meaning on Route 66*, by Lisa Mahar. One of the authors grew up in a small town in which Route 66 was the town's main street, and he is familiar with many of the signs featured, but even without that personal connection, the book is simply amazing.

Mahar begins with the premise that the roadside sign is not simply a symbol of the open road but a marker of economic, social and cultural trends. Signs are larger-than-life clues to the values, images, icons, and traditions of the areas in which they exist. Examining motel signs on both a micro and macro level, Mahar traces their influences, shows their arguments, unpacks their conceptual framework, and explains their appeal.

We have reprinted here (with the gracious help of Mahar herself) the opening pages of chapter three. What we like about these images is not simply how Mahar notes the influences of popular signs, but the care and detail with which she reads them. The book is also a model of document design—it is itself a text as rich and provocative as the motel signs it features.

PLASTIC: USED AS A UNIFORM LIGHT SOURCE TO ACCURATELY PORTRAY ILLUSTRATIONS AND TRADEMARKS

BULBS: USED FOR VARIETY AND DYNAMIC FLASHING EFFECTS

NEON: USED FOR ILLUMINATING AND OUTLINING LETTERS AND FOR ANIMATION

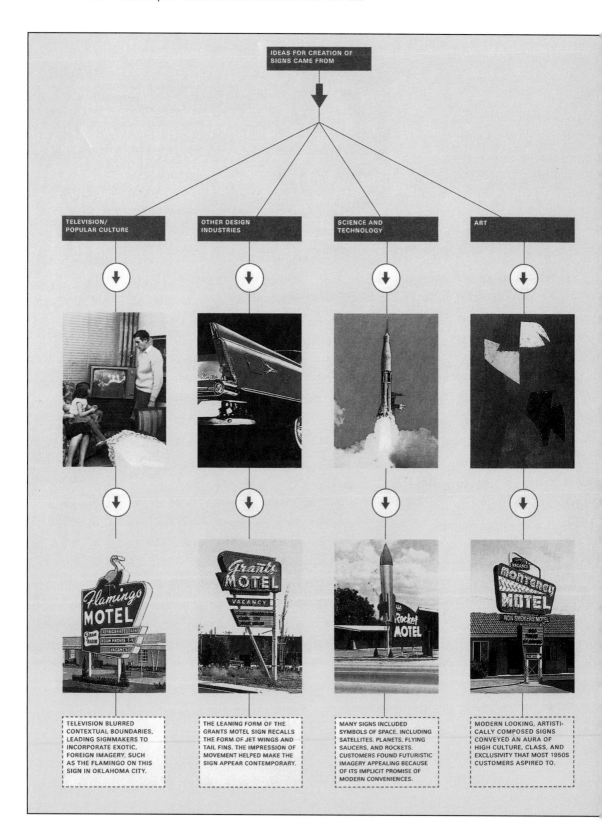

**IDEAS FOR CREATION OF SIGNS CAME FROM**

**TELEVISION/ POPULAR CULTURE**

**OTHER DESIGN INDUSTRIES**

**SCIENCE AND TECHNOLOGY**

**ART**

TELEVISION BLURRED CONTEXTUAL BOUNDARIES, LEADING SIGNMAKERS TO INCORPORATE EXOTIC, FOREIGN IMAGERY, SUCH AS THE FLAMINGO ON THIS SIGN IN OKLAHOMA CITY.

THE LEANING FORM OF THE GRANTS MOTEL SIGN RECALLS THE FORM OF JET WINGS AND TAIL FINS. THE IMPRESSION OF MOVEMENT HELPED MAKE THE SIGN APPEAR CONTEMPORARY.

MANY SIGNS INCLUDED SYMBOLS OF SPACE, INCLUDING SATELLITES, PLANETS, FLYING SAUCERS, AND ROCKETS. CUSTOMERS FOUND FUTURISTIC IMAGERY APPEALING BECAUSE OF ITS IMPLICIT PROMISE OF MODERN CONVENIENCES.

MODERN LOOKING, ARTISTI-CALLY COMPOSED SIGNS CONVEYED AN AURA OF HIGH CULTURE, CLASS, AND EXCLUSIVITY THAT MOST 1950S CUSTOMERS ASPIRED TO.

### 3.2 > FORMAL ETYMOLOGY

The Hacienda Holiday Motel sign in Oklahoma City is an example of how far signmakers went to create original compositions for their clients. Fearing that they might lose control over the design process to an emerging class of professional designers, signmakers looked for inspiration in other disciplines, especially art and science.

he use of abstract symbols common in art
the period, such as this detail from Joan
liro's *Woman in Front of the Sun* (1950),
ade signs appear up-to-date.

cript lettering was used to convey unique-
ess and add visual drama to the sign.

Forms and structures were often angled to
create more dynamic, and therefore noticeable, compositions, as seen in this late
1950s building.

Bold, stylized arrows were common additions
to signs during this period. Artists such as
Paul Klee also found them enticing.

bstracted figurative elements
vere also found in the design world, as
een in this mid-1950s engraved bowl
esigned by Ingeborg Lundin.

Irregular shapes were non-traditional
and therefore appropriate forms for
signmakers looking to create original
signs. Artists also made use of them,
as in this 1959 mobile, "Big Red," by
Alexander Calder.

Asymmetrical compositions, as in this plate
design by Florence Wainwright, conveyed
individuality and uniqueness.

## 3.4 > FORM

Nowhere was the break from tradition seen more dramatically than in a sign's form. Signmakers chose irregular, asymmetrical shapes over traditional ones, whether or not the business the sign identified was new. By the mid-1950s, many signmakers had begun creating their signs as fragmented compositions, a final abandonment of traditional form.

In the mid-1950s, the Wishing Well Motel in Springfield, Missouri, replaced its traditional sign, which was based on a 1:2 rectangular sign box, with an L-shaped composition of four elements. Though the L shape recalls earlier Main Street signs, the shape of the Wishing Well's sign box is irregular, more dramatic, and includes decorative elements. The words "Wishing Well" and "motel" are treated as separate elements through the use of different colors and type styles.

The asymmetrical form, large wrapping arrow, script type, and advertising panels of the Rest Haven Court's mid-1950s sign are characteristic features of motel signs from the period.

The only elements that remained the same on these two signs from the mid-1940s and the early 1950s were the name (although depersonalized with the removal of "Clark's") and the square, sans serif letters. The newer sign has no formal relationship to its context. The angled structure, palette-shaped sign box, and bright red paint all help to separate it from nearby buildings and natural elements.

The updated Tower Motel sign in Santa Rosa, New Mexico, formally distances itself from the traditional inverted T form of the mid-1940s sign. Each element on the new sign is perceived as a distinct component: the name "Tower" is spatially segregated from "motel," and the letters are treated as individually articulated elements.

The simple, symmetrical sign for the Skyline Motel in Flagstaff, Arizona, was replaced with a larger and bolder asymmetrical arrangement.

Early signs, like the one for the Conway Motel in El Reno, Oklahoma, were often composed of geometrically pure shapes. In this example, the form also reflected the circular motel office. The late-1950s replacement was designed with only contemporary stylistic trends in mind—it was no longer important to maintain a formal connection to the motel's architecture.

**3.4 > FORM**

Although motel chains did not gain widespread popularity until the late 1950s, Holiday Inn had begun to expand nationwide much earlier. The most visible aspect of the first major chain's growth was the "great sign," as it was referred to. And like the older signs it took its aesthetic cues from, the Holiday Inn sign garnered recognition that attested to the skill with which independent motel owners and signmakers were able to define their businesses' identity. A sign functioned as the motel's logo; it appeared on stationery, ads, and other materials. While independent motel signs influenced the first Holiday Inn sign, as the chain expanded it was the Holiday Inn sign that began to influence the vernacular.

BEFORE 1952

**STAR**

The star, a traditional symbol used in vernacular signs, denoted quality of service.

**WRAPPING ARROW**

Early arrows were generally thin and functioned more as a border than as a primary visual element.

**LEANING FORM**

By the late 1940s, a "slant" form was used to add visual interest and to attract the attention of passing motorists.

**COLOR**

**NAME**

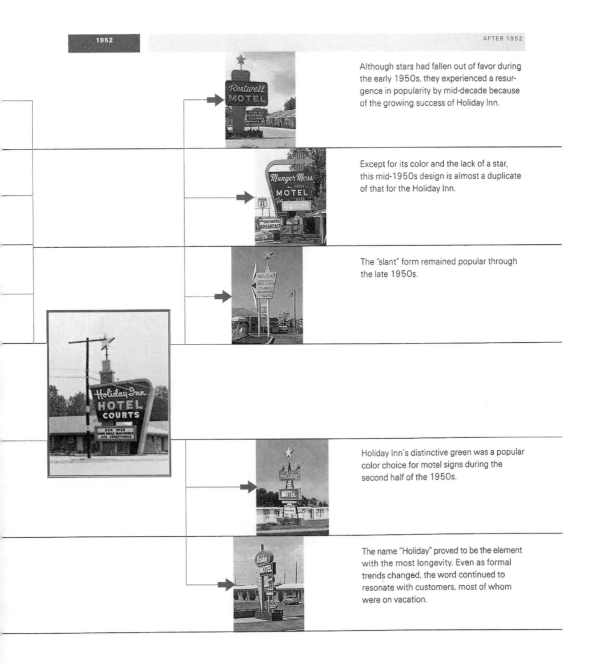

**1952**

Although stars had fallen out of favor during the early 1950s, they experienced a resurgence in popularity by mid-decade because of the growing success of Holiday Inn.

Except for its color and the lack of a star, this mid-1950s design is almost a duplicate of that for the Holiday Inn.

The "slant" form remained popular through the late 1950s.

Holiday Inn's distinctive green was a popular color choice for motel signs during the second half of the 1950s.

The name "Holiday" proved to be the element with the most longevity. Even as formal trends changed, the word continued to resonate with customers, most of whom were on vacation.

> STRUCTURE

As compositions became more complex, structure became an increasingly important element of the sign. Structure was used either as an abstract framework for organizing the sign's varied elements or as a conceptual and visual connection to a motel's architecture. Only rarely was it used as an overtly thematic component of the sign, as it had been during the late 1940s and early 1950s.

Early attempts to make structure an important aesthetic component were focused on creating a solid, relatively permanent visual barrier that contrasted with the natural context and related to the man-made one. This early-1950s structure for the Pine Tree Lodge in Gallup, New Mexico, was massive and therefore more noticeable. It was built from the same materials as the motel building, thus creating a visual connection between the sign and the architecture.

The sign box for the Tower Motel sign in Oklahoma City conveyed the visual weight of earlier, architectural structures like the Pine Tree Lodge's, but the structure consisted of easy-to-install metal poles. Unlike traditional pole structures, however, their placement was determined as much by aesthetic reasons as by functional ones. The gradual return to pole-based structures also made it possible to build taller signs—those constructed from architectural building materials had to remain relatively small.

Poles made it easy to arrange separate, irregular components such as those on the Flamingo Motel sign in Elk City, Oklahoma. They were readily available and did not require specialized labor, as did architectural materials like brick.

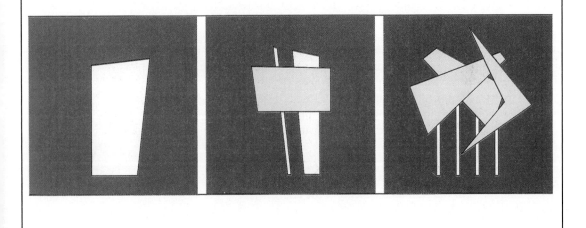

READING  WRITING

## THIS TEXT: READING

1. What do you make of Mahar's connection between motel signs and rockets, cars, Miro paintings and fish? Are her arguments solid?
2. Mahar argues that in the 1950s signs entered a kind of revolution, becoming irregular, asymmetrical and original. What cultural and artistic forces might account for this shift in signs and sign making?
3. Look at the various arguments about art (e.g., Chricton's and Diana Mack's) in Chapter 7: Reading and Writing about Art. Based on their criteria, are these signs art? Why or why not?
4. Why do you think Mahar chose motel signs? Why motel and not restaurant signs?

## YOUR TEXT: WRITING

1. Find some classic motel or restaurant signs in your town. Write a paper in which you read them in the same way as Mahar.
2. Write a paper in which you break down the logo of your college. What kind of symbolism is at work?
3. Many of these signs appear in Oklahoma, New Mexico and Arizona. Is there something about the Southwest that lends itself to these kinds of irregular images? Write a paper in which you examine the cultural influences on these signs.
4. Write a comparison/contrast paper in which you read the sign of a popular local chain hotel (Wyndham, Hyatt, Marriott, Hampton Inn, La Quinta) against one of the classic signs in the book. What "work" does each sign do? How does it do that work?

## ▪▪▪ WORKSHEET ▪▪▪

### This text

1. What is the semiotic situation of the image? What are its signifiers?
2. What social, political, and cultural forces affect the image?
3. What visual cues appear in the text?
4. What kinds of details, symbols, and codes send messages in the image?
5. What is the composition of the image?
6. Do you think there might be any tension between the image's intention and reception?
7. What kind of story does the image tell? How does it tell that story?
8. Does the image rely on patriotic or sentimental associations to manipulate the viewer?
9. Can you sum up the theme of the image?

### Beyond this text

**Media:** How do news programs, magazines, and newspapers use images to tell stories or convey ideas?

**Advertising:** Advertising is perhaps the most notorious user of loaded images. How do magazine ads and billboards use images to help sell products? What values do we tend to see in ads? What kind of associations, people, and cultures tend to reappear over and over?

**Television:** To what degree does television rely on images? Would you sit in front of a TV if there were only words and no picture? How are characters in shows carefully constructed texts? And, what about commercials? How do commercials use images to manipulate viewers?

**Movies:** Do movies use images differently than television? If so, how?

**Icons:** The swastika. The peace symbol. The bald eagle. A cactus. A white cowboy hat. The McDonald golden arches. The American flag. The Mexican flag. High heels. All of these are icons. How do icons rely on strong values associated with visual images? How are icons constructed texts?

**Public space:** How do public and private areas rely on images to get us to feel a certain way? More specifically, what roles do billboards and murals play in public life? What about things like posters or framed art in a dorm room, bedroom, or house?

**Music:** How does what a band looks like, or what an album looks like, influence the way we look at a band?

# Reading and Writing About Gender

■ ■ ■ Various gender signifiers transform RuPaul Andre Charles into "RuPaul!"

*Source:* © Mitchell Gerber/Corbis/Getty Images Entertainment, Inc.

"How in the world does someone *read* gender? Isn't gender obvious?" If you are looking at this introduction for the first time, we suspect this is what a lot of you are thinking right now. For many of you, details of gender are cut and dried, black and white, male and female. This book deals with gender as a text, and, as you will soon see, there are many other reasons why one might be interested in reading gender in a sophisticated way.

Without question, gender has become one of the most hotly contested subjects in recent American culture, but this debate is not new. On the contrary, it's been at the forefront of public debate for centuries. Ancient poets like Sappho, and Greek plays like Aristophanes' *Lysistrata* explored issues of inequality between the genders long before Gloria Steinem, (perhaps the most public feminist of the past three decades). More recently than Sappho or Aristophanes, an amazing Mexican nun named Sor Juana de la Cruz wrote poems and letters extolling the virtues of education for women, citing Biblical passages as examples for equality. And over 200 years before Susan Faludi's *Backlash* (a controversial book appearing in 1992 that posited a backlash against American women), Mary Wollstonecraft wrote an important and influential essay entitled "Vindication on the Rights of Women" in which she called for a recognition of women as "rational creatures" capable of the same intellectual and emotional proficiency as men. So while certain aspects of this chapter may feel new to you, in truth, people have been reading (and writing about) gender for centuries.

Still, perhaps it would be beneficial to talk about what we mean by the term "gender." When we use "gender" we refer to socially constructed behaviors and identity tags, such as "feminine" and "masculine." Gender should not be confused with "sex," which speaks only to biological differences between males and females. "Sex" then refers to biology, "gender" to culture and society.

If you've read the chapters on movies or television, then you know that having experience reading a certain text is not the same as reading it well. Similarly, many of you have significant experience reading genders, but you may not be very *probing* readers of gender. This chapter in particular (and college in general) is designed to remedy that. On one hand, reading gender implies a kind of superficial determination of another person's sex. In some cultures, that used to be easier than it is now; in fact, it can be somewhat difficult to tell if a person is a man, a woman, or neither. Those of you with a soft spot for classic rock may remember a similar line from the long-haired Bob Seeger, who, in his song "On the Road Again," adopts the persona of someone making a critical remark about his long hair: "same old cliché / Is it a woman or a man?" This statement and the simple fact that we assume that we can tell if a person is male or female suggests that there are traits or cues that might tip us off about gender. Using or reading these codes or behaviors is called "doing gender," and we all do gender at some point. "Doing gender" means participating in any behavior associated with a certain gender such as painting your nails, growing a beard, and wearing high heels, earrings, make-up, neckties, and sports jerseys. In each of the previous examples, every one of you associated a certain trait with a certain gender. Did you link painting nails with men or wearing neckties with women? Probably not, but it is likely that most of you have seen a man sport painted nails or a woman wear a necktie. These people are playing with typical expectations of gender, and to some degree, we all do that a little bit. In fact, if, like us, you've lived in New York or San Francisco where gender diversity is more common and more accepted, then you've likely encountered women sporting facial hair and men donning heels.

If there are external traits in a culture, then it's probable that there are assumed internal gender traits in a culture as well. Though these external indicators may seem minor, ultimately, as you have probably noticed by now, doing gender often translates into men doing dominance and women doing submission. For instance, in America, most people tend to associate nurturing behavior with women and aggressive behavior with men. Similarly, women are "dainty" while men are "rough;" women are "refined," whereas men are "brutish." But is this always the case? As you read this, you are probably thinking of some dainty guys you know and some brutish women. What's more, you should be able to identify specific moments in your own lives and in the lives of your parents, siblings and close friends when they have, even for an instant, done something that reminded you of another gender. The point is that we carry so many assumptions—many of them dangerous—about genders that we may discover that we have already *interpreted* gender before we have read and thought deeply about gender and genders.

Our goal in this chapter is to encourage you to rethink any preconceptions about gender and expectations of gender. Why do we expect women to be "emotional"? Why do we expect men to be "responsible"? Why is there societal pressure on women to be thin? Why aren't men expected to wear make-up and shave their legs? Why is there no male equivalent for "slut"? Why aren't women taught to see marriage as the end of a certain kind of independence the same way men are? Why don't boys get dressed up and play groom? Why are all of our presidents men? Why are most kindergarten teachers women? These are puzzling phenomena that raise more questions than answers; however, what we do know is that learning to read gender as a text will help you make sense of the world as roles become less black and white, less right and wrong, less male and female.

Social scientists remind us that gender is socially constructed, and therefore, in a way, we are recruited to gender. Consequently, society tends to punish those who don't conform to its gender roles. The goal of this chapter is to help you read the various means of recruitment; we want you to become savvy readers of the texts that encourage you to *do* gender.

## While one's sex may be determined by biology, gender is constructed.

What we mean by "constructed" is that gender is built, invented, created. Of course, while some gender traits might seem to be related to one's biological make-up, gender can still be constructed or "performed." We can think of these traits in both external and internal terms. For instance, our culture assigns certain behaviors or characteristics to maleness. These may include strength, rationality, virility, affluence, and stability. To send out cues that he possesses all these things, a man may bulk up, he may wear designer clothes and drive a sports car, he may watch and play a lot of sports, he may date a lot of women or men. However, what if the values our culture assigned to maleness were grace, daintiness, refinement, monogamy, and nurturing? What if *these* traits were the most male traits? Would men still bulk up, watch football, go hunting, watch *Rambo* movies, and drive pickups? Some might, but most would not. Why? Because they would be ostracized and stigmatized, not seen as "real" men, according to society's expectations of masculine behavior. Men who adhere to socially constructed codes of gender behavior have read the texts of maleness and America well—they know how to fit in.

Just as external elements connote gender, so do internal elements. For instance, what if mainstream heterosexual female behavior were characterized by aggression, dominance, sexual assertiveness and independence? Would women still wait for men to make the first move? Would women still link their sense of identity with men? Would women think of marriage

in the same way? Would women feel differently about their bodies? Would women be afraid to beat their dates in bowling or fear appearing smarter than their male partners? So, without even knowing it, you are probably performing or doing gender in various aspects of your lives. There is not necessarily anything wrong with this; however, you should be aware that there can be negative implications, and we would encourage you to read your own gender and the genders of others with increased care and sensitivity.

Though we've talked mostly about gender in heterosexual terms, doing gender is not reserved for straight folks. Chances are, you are familiar with terms like "butch," "femme," and "queen." That these terms exist suggests how important gender constructs are to our identities, and they reveal how, even in same-sex relationships, we do gender. What's more, as many gay and lesbians will confirm, gender has nothing to do with biology. Most gays and lesbians would argue that genders are, in fact, fluid. For many, having a penis does not prohibit someone from being or living as a woman, just as having breasts and a vagina does not prohibit many people from living or passing as a man. Here, the distinction between "sex" and "gender" is critical. You may have your own assumptions about how gay men and women do gender, just as you have expectations about how straight men and women do gender.

## Our perceptions of gender can be influenced by a number of factors, including stereotypes, tradition, popular culture, and family.

We are all aware of stereotypes surrounding gender: Women are better communicators, men are stronger; men like power tools, women like chick flicks. Without realizing it, you may make gendered assumptions about traits of women all the time. For instance, if you are in a grocery store, and you want to know the ingredients for a cake, who are you most likely to ask: a woman or a man? If someone tells you they have a wonderful new doctor, are you more likely to assume it s a man or a woman? If you hear that someone went on a shooting spree in a school, are you most likely to assume that person was male or female? Stereotypes are amazingly powerful, and we may not realize the degree to which our thoughts, beliefs, and actions are shaped by them.

Similarly, cultural and family traditions continue to affect how we see ourselves and other genders. We have a number of female and male friends who complain about how, after every holiday dinner, the men adjourn to the living room to watch sports, while the women clear the tables and do the dishes. At that same dinner, it is likely that the father or grandfather carves the turkey or ham and even says the prayer. One might say that these are roles that both genders silently agree to, yet others might say that these behaviors reflect and inscribe a pattern suggesting that the important duties are reserved for men, while the menial tasks remain women s work. Thus, we grow up not merely ascribing values to genders but linking the importance of specific genders to the importance our society places on the kind of duties we think of as female and male.

Equally persuasive is popular culture. How many of our preconceptions about gender come from billboards, television shows, advertisements, movies, and commercials? Research indicates quite a bit. For instance, psychologists and advertisers suggest that the average viewer believes about one in eight commercials she or he watches. That may not seem like a great deal, but over the course of eighteen or nineteen years, you have seen (and probably internalized) a number of commercials, many of which have, no doubt, influenced your own views of gender. From rock and country music lyrics to commercials for cleaning products

to NFL pregame shows to advertisements for jeans and tequila to television sitcoms to the infamous beer commercials, images of men and women doing gender flood us from all sides. Because of this, pop culture can fuse into stereotype, and tradition can meld into popular culture at times we may not know which comes from which. So many people conform to the expectations of gender roles, that gender roles appear natural or innate. We urge you to stop and think for a moment before assuming anything about gender.

Oddly, perhaps the most influential source for our gender roles comes from our own families. Before we are even aware of it, we see our mothers *be* women, and we see our fathers enact maleness. In fact, most agree that our early caretakers whether it is our mothers, grandmothers, nannies, fathers, uncles or siblings provide for us the foundations of gender roles. What we see our fathers do, we think is what most men do, and more importantly, what men are supposed to do. As you get older, you will be shocked at how easily you slip into the same gender roles and gendered duties you observed your family engaging in for eighteen years. What's more, over time, these behaviors get coded, recoded and coded again. Every time you see your father turn on the TV and not help clear the table, it sends messages about what men and women do and don't do. Similarly, every time you do see your father change a diaper or your mom fix a car, it sends other messages about what men and women can do. Most importantly, these behaviors can send subtle but powerful messages about what *you* can do. So, as you think about gender roles in your own life, consider how gender in your family is a complex but powerful text.

## Feminism (or feminisms) can and should be supported by both men and women.

Often we ask our students if they believe that women should be paid the same as men. They say yes. We ask them if they think men are inherently smarter than women. They say no— usually an emphatic no. We ask them if they believe that women should be afforded the same opportunities for employment as men. They all say yes. We ask them if they think that there should be equality between men and women. All claim there should. Yet, when we ask how many are feminists, virtually none raise their hands. This reality continues to be perplexing and frustrating. The authors of this book are straight men, and both identify as feminists—so why the resistance among students?

One reason may be the text "feminism." There are any number of definitions of feminism, ranging from very open definitions (if you think men and women should be treated equally then you are a feminist) to more forceful definitions, such as Barbara Smith's ("Feminism is the political theory and practice that struggles to free *all* women: women of color, working class women, poor women, Jewish women, disabled women, lesbians, old women— as well as white, economically privileged, heterosexual women"). Some people think that a definition of feminism must be religiously conceived, since much discrimination has ties to religious conservatism (a feminist is a person who supports the theory that God the Mother is equal to God the Father). Though neither of the authors are women, both lean toward a definition of feminism that is broad enough to take in all interested parties. For us, feminism is the understanding that there has been an imbalance between how men and women have been treated and that balance among genders must be restored. We also tend to believe that feminism implies more than a passing interest in bringing about this change; feminists must, on some level, act in a way that helps facilitate a more equitable balance. These actions might

be as small as refraining from using sexist language or as large as protesting in front of the Capitol. Thus, we prefer the term "feminisms" because it acknowledges the fact that feminism is as individual as each individual.

For some reason, many students associate feminism with hating men, refusing to shave legs, being bitchy, being militant, being strident and in general, being unlikable. None of these traits has ever been part of the mission of feminism. Rather, feminism as an idea, as an ideology, has always been about equality. In fact, there remains no single feminism but, as we've suggested, inclusive and intriguing "feminisms." Instead of thinking of feminisms as exclusionary, it is more helpful and more accurate to think of feminisms as inclusive. And, like any text, feminism is always open to revision.

## There is a double standard in America regarding men and women.

You really don't need a textbook to tell you this—most of you already know it. Many women would acknowledge that they feel a palpable pressure to be thin, virginal, and refined, whereas American culture not only allows but encourages males to be physically comfortable, sexually adventurous, and crass. Similarly, women who work in the corporate world have argued for decades that female behavior characterized as bitchy, cold, and calculating when enacted by women is praised and considered commanding, rational, and strategic when carried out by men. On the other hand, both men and women have suggested recently that cultural pressure on men to be in control, in charge, and emotionally cool, leaves little room for personal growth and fulfillment.

Even though America has grown immensely in terms of gender equity, there remain dozens of unwritten or even unspoken codes that both men and women feel compelled to adhere to. Thus, how people of different genders act in the world has everything to do with cultural expectations placed on their genders. Moreover, when men and women do gender properly—that is, as society dictates they should—they make gender seem invariable and inevitable, which then seems to justify structural inequalities such as the pay gap, the lack of elected female politicians, or even good roles for women in theater, film, and television.

In short, issues of gender involve more than leaving the toilet seat up; they arise out of personal, public, private, and cultural worlds. We hope that this chapter will make you a more engaged reader of how gender gets enacted in each of these worlds.

## ■■■ WORKSHEET ■■■

This Text

1. While it will be impossible for you to know this fully, try to figure out the writing situation of each author. Who is the audience? What does the author have at stake? What is his or her agenda? Why is she or he writing this piece?
2. What social, political, and cultural forces affect the author's text? What is going on in the world as he or she is writing?
3. This is a chapter about gender, so, obviously, you should be aware of the gender of the author.
4. How does the author define gender? Does s/he confuse "gender" and "sex"?
5. When taken as a whole, what do these texts tell you about how we construct gender?

6.  How do stories and essays differ in their arguments about gender?

7.  Is the author's argument valid? Is it reasonable?

8.  Ideas and beliefs about gender tend to be very sensitive, deeply held convictions. Do you find yourself in agreement with the author? Why or why not? Do you agree with the editors' introduction?

9.  Does the author help you read gender better than you did before reading the essay? If so, why? How do we learn to read gender?

10. If you are reading a short story or poem, then where does the text take place? When is it set?

11. What are the main conflicts in the text? What issues are at stake?

12. What kinds of issues of identity is the author working with in the text?

13. Is there tension between the self and society in the text? How? Why?

14. How do gender codes and expectations differ among cultures?

15. Did I like this? Why or why not?

## Beyond This Text

**Media:** How are men and women portrayed in television shows, movies, video games, and music videos? Do the media try to set the criteria for what is "male" and what is "female?" How do they do this?

**Advertising:** How are women and men portrayed in magazine ads? Do advertisers tend to associate certain products or tasks with a specific gender? How do ads influence how we read gender roles?

**Television:** Is there much variance in how men are portrayed on television? What kinds of shows are geared toward men? What about women? What kinds of activities do we see women engage in on television? Are gender roles related to stereotypes about race, class, and geography?

**Movies:** Many actors and actresses bemoan the lack of good movie roles for women. Why is this the case? Can you think of many movies in which a younger man falls for an older woman? How often do women rescue men in movies? Why is male nudity so rare and female nudity so coveted?

**Public space:** How do we know that a place is geared toward men or women? What visual clues do we see?

---

## MARKED WOMEN, UNMARKED MEN

### ■ Deborah Tannen ■

*Linguist Deborah Tannen uses a conference as a semiotic setting to read three other women. Based on textual cues (or signs) of the women's hair, clothes, and mannerisms, this 1993 essay gives a reading of each of these "texts," suggesting that women, more than men, are marked by cultural expectations.*

SOME YEARS AGO I was at a small working conference of four women and eight men. Instead of concentrating on the discussion I found myself looking at the three other women at the table, thinking how each had a different style and how each style was coherent.

One woman had dark brown hair in a classic style, a cross between Cleopatra and Plain Jane. The severity of her straight hair was softened by wavy bangs and ends that turned under. Because she was beautiful, the effect was more Cleopatra than plain.

The second woman was older, full of dignity and composure. Her hair was cut in a fashionable style that left her with only one eye, thanks to a side part that let a curtain of hair fall across half her face. As she looked down to read her prepared paper, the hair robbed her of bifocal vision and created a barrier between her and the listeners.

The third woman's hair was wild, a frosted blond avalanche falling over and beyond her shoulders. When she spoke she frequently tossed her head, calling attention to her hair and away from her lecture.

Then there was makeup. The first woman wore facial cover that made her skin smooth and pale, a black line under each eye and mascara that darkened already dark lashes. The second wore only a light gloss on her lips and a hint of shadow on her eyes. The third had blue bands under her eyes, dark blue shadow, mascara, bright red lipstick and rouge; her fingernails flashed red.

I considered the clothes each woman had worn during the three days of the conference: In the first case, man-tailored suits in primary colors with solid-color blouses. In the second, casual but stylish black T-shirts, a floppy collarless jacket and baggy slacks or a skirt in neutral colors. The third wore a sexy jump suit; tight sleeveless jersey and tight yellow slacks; a dress with gaping armholes and an indulged tendency to fall off one shoulder.

Shoes? No. 1 wore string sandals with medium heels; No. 2, sensible, comfortable walking shoes; No. 3, pumps with spike heels. You can fill in the jewelry, scarves, shawls, sweaters—or lack of them.

As I amused myself finding coherence in these styles, I suddenly wondered why I was scrutinizing only the women. I scanned the eight men at the table. And then I knew why I wasn't studying them. The men's styles were unmarked.

The term "marked" is a staple of linguistic theory. It refers to the way language alters the base meaning of a word by adding a linguistic particle that has no meaning on its own. The unmarked form of a word carries the meaning that goes without saying—what you think of when you're not thinking anything special.

The unmarked tense of verbs in English is the present—for example, visit. To indicate past, you mark the verb by adding ed to yield visited. For future, you add a word: will visit. Nouns are presumed to be singular until marked for plural, typically by adding s or es, so visit becomes visits and dish becomes dishes.

The unmarked forms of most English words also convey "male." Being male is the unmarked case. Endings like ess and ette mark words as "female." Unfortunately, they also tend to mark them for frivolousness. Would you feel safe entrusting your life to a doctorette? Alfre Woodard, who was an Oscar nominee for best supporting actress, says she identifies herself as an actor because "actresses worry about eyelashes and cellulite, and women who are actors worry about the characters we are playing." Gender markers pick up extra meanings that reflect common associations with the female gender: not quite serious, often sexual.

Each of the women at the conference had to make decisions about hair, clothing, makeup and accessories, and each decision carried meaning. Every style available to us was marked. The men in our group had made decisions, too, but the range from which they chose was incomparably narrower. Men can choose styles that are marked, but they don't have to, and in this group none did. Unlike the women, they had the option of being unmarked.

Take the men's hair styles. There was no marine crew cut or oily longish hair falling into eyes, no asymmetrical, two-tiered construction to swirl over a bald top. One man was unabashedly bald; the others had hair of standard length, parted on one side, in natural shades of brown or gray or graying. Their hair obstructed no views, left little to toss or push back or run fingers through and, consequently, needed and attracted no attention. A few men had beards. In a business setting, beards might be marked. In this academic gathering, they weren't.

There could have been a cowboy shirt with string tie or a three-piece suit or a necklaced hippie in jeans. But there wasn't. All eight men wore brown or blue slacks and nondescript shirts of light colors. No man wore sandals or boots; their shoes were dark, closed, comfortable and flat. In short, unmarked.

Although no man wore makeup, you couldn't say the men didn't wear makeup in the sense that you could say a woman didn't wear makeup. For men, no makeup is unmarked.

I asked myself what style we women could have adopted that would have been unmarked, like the men's. The answer was none. There is no unmarked woman.

There is no woman's hair style that can be called standard, that says nothing about her. The range of women's hair styles is staggering, but a woman whose hair has no particular style is perceived as not caring about how she looks, which can disqualify her for many positions, and will subtly diminish her as a person in the eyes of some.

Women must choose between attractive shoes and comfortable shoes. When our group made an unexpected trek, the woman who wore flat, laced shoes arrived first. Last to arrive was the woman in spike heels, shoes in hand and a handful of men around her.

If a woman's clothing is tight or revealing (in other words, sexy), it sends a message—an intended one of wanting to be attractive, but also a possibly unintended one of availability. If her clothes are not sexy, that too sends a message, lent meaning by the knowledge that they could have been. There are thousands of cosmetic products from which women can choose and myriad ways of applying them. Yet no makeup at all is anything but unmarked. Some men see it as a hostile refusal to please them.

Women can't even fill out a form without telling stories about themselves. Most forms give four titles to choose from. "Mr." carries no meaning other than that the respondent is male. But a woman who checks "Mrs." or "Miss" communicates not only whether she has been married but also whether she has conservative tastes in forms of address—and probably other conservative values as well. Checking "Ms." declines to let on about marriage (checking "Mr." declines nothing since nothing was asked), but it also marks her as either liberated or rebellious, depending on the observer's attitudes and assumptions.

I sometimes try to duck these variously marked choices by giving my title as "Dr."—and in so doing risk marking myself as either uppity (hence sarcastic responses like "Excuse me!") or an overachiever (hence reactions of congratulatory surprise like "Good for you!").

All married women's surnames are marked. If a woman takes her husband's name, she announces to the world that she is married and has traditional values. To some it will indicate that she is less herself, more identified by her husband's identity. If she does not take her husband's name, this too is marked, seen as worthy of comment: she has done something; she has "kept her own name." A man is never said to have "kept his own name" because it never occurs to anyone that he might have given it up. For him using his own name is unmarked.

A married woman who wants to have her cake and eat it too may use her surname plus his, with or without a hyphen. But this too announces her marital status and often results in a tongue-tying string. In a list (Harvey O'Donovan, Jonathan Feldman, Stephanie Woodbury McGillicutty), the woman's multiple name stands out. It is marked.

I have never been inclined toward biological explanations of gender differences in language, but I was intrigued to see Ralph Fasold bring biological phenomena to bear on the question of linguistic marking in his book *The Sociolinguistics of Language.* Fasold stresses that language and culture are particularly unfair in treating women as the marked case because biologically it is the male that is marked. While two X chromosomes make a female, two Y chromosomes make nothing. Like the linguistic markers s, es or ess, the Y chromosome doesn't "mean" anything unless it is attached to a root form—an X chromosome.

Developing this idea elsewhere, Fasold points out that girls are born with fully female bodies, while boys are born with modified female bodies. He invites men who doubt this to lift up their shirts and contemplate why they have nipples.

In his book, Fasold notes "a wide range of facts which demonstrates that female is the unmarked sex." For example, he observes that there are a few species that produce only females, like the whiptail lizard. Thanks to parthenogenesis, they have no trouble having as many daughters as they like. There are no species, however, that produce only males. This is no surprise, since any such species would become extinct in its first generation.

Fasold is also intrigued by species that produce individuals not involved in reproduction, like honeybees and leaf-cutter ants. Reproduction is handled by the queen and a relatively few males; the workers are sterile females. "Since they do not reproduce," Fasold says, "there is no reason for them to be one sex or the other, so they default, so to speak, to female."

Fasold ends his discussion of these matters by pointing out that if language reflected biology, grammar books would direct us to use "she" to include males and females and "he" only for specifically male referents. But they don't. They tell us that "he" means "he or she," and that "she" is used only if the referent is specifically female. This use of "he" as the sex-indefinite pronoun is an innovation introduced into English by grammarians in the 18th and 19th centuries, according to Peter Muhlhausler and Rom Harre in "Pronouns and People." From at least about 1500, the correct sex-indefinite pronoun was "they," as it still is in casual spoken English. In other words, the female was declared by grammarians to be the marked case.

Writing this article may mark me not as a writer, not as a linguist, not as an analyst of human behavior, but as a feminist—which will have positive or negative, but in any case powerful, connotations for readers. Yet I doubt that anyone reading Ralph Fasold's book would put that label on him.

I discovered the markedness inherent in the very topic of gender after writing a book on differences in conversational style based on geographical region, ethnicity, class, age and gender. When I was interviewed, the vast majority of journalists wanted to talk about the differences between women and men. While I thought I was simply describing what I observed—something I had learned to do as a researcher—merely mentioning women and men marked me as a feminist for some.

When I wrote a book devoted to gender differences in ways of speaking, I sent the manuscript to five male colleagues, asking them to alert me to any interpretation, phrasing or wording that might seem unfairly negative toward men. Even so, when the book came out,

I encountered responses like that of the television talk show host who, after interviewing me, turned to the audience and asked if they thought I was male-bashing.

Leaping upon a poor fellow who affably nodded in agreement, she made him stand and asked, "Did what she said accurately describe you?" "Oh, yes," he answered. "That's me exactly." "And what she said about women—does that sound like your wife?" "Oh yes," he responded. "That's her exactly." "Then why do you think she's male-bashing?" He answered, with disarming honesty, "Because she's a woman and she's saying things about men."

To say anything about women and men without marking oneself as either feminist or anti-feminist, male-basher or apologist for men seems as impossible for a woman as trying to get dressed in the morning without inviting interpretations of her character. Sitting at the conference table musing on these matters, I felt sad to think that we women didn't have the freedom to be unmarked that the men sitting next to us had. Some days you just want to get dressed and go about your business. But if you're a woman, you can't, because there is no unmarked woman.

## READING WRITING

### THIS TEXT: READING

1. What do you make of Tannen's claim that women are "marked"? Is that an appropriate word?
2. Would you agree with her that men are not marked?
3. What is Tannen's evidence for her claims? Is it solid evidence? Do Tannen's arguments follow a logical progression?

### YOUR TEXT: WRITING

1. Go to a coffee shop or a restaurant and read a group of women sitting together. Are they marked? How? Then write an essay, similar to Tannen's, on your reading of the women. How do contemporary cultural expectations of women influence how you read other women?
2. Write an essay on how men are marked.
3. Are there other female markings that Tannen does not mention? Write an essay in which you give a reading of other kinds of female markings.
4. Read Maxine Hong Kingston's "No Name Woman," and write an essay in which you demonstrate how the aunt was marked.

---

### GENDER ROLE BEHAVIORS AND ATTITUDES

### ■ Holly Devor ■

*Taken from her 1989 book* Gender Blending: Confronting the Limits of Duality, *Holly Devor argues that terms like "masculinity" and "femininity" are problematic because they tend to signify "natural" roles of men and women. However, Devor suggests that these terms are little more than social constructions. Devor has a sophisticated argument, so, as you read, pay attention to how she makes and supports her assertions about gender roles; also, if you are writing a research paper, note how Devor works her research into her prose and into her arguments.*

THE CLUSTERS OF SOCIAL DEFINITIONS used to identify persons by gender are collectively known as femininity and masculinity. Masculine characteristics are used to identify persons as males, while feminine ones are used as signifiers for femaleness. People use femininity or masculinity to claim and communicate their membership in their assigned, or chosen, sex or gender. Others recognize our sex or gender more on the basis of these characteristics than on the basis of sex characteristics, which are usually largely covered by clothing in daily life.

These two clusters of attributes are most commonly seen as mirror images of one another, with masculinity usually characterized by dominance and aggression, and femininity by passivity and submission. A more evenhanded description of the social qualities subsumed by femininity and masculinity might be to label masculinity as generally concerned with egoistic dominance and femininity as striving for cooperation or communion.[1] Characterizing femininity and masculinity in such a way does not portray the two clusters of characteristics as being in a hierarchical relationship to one another but rather as being two different approaches to the same question, that question being centrally concerned with the goals, means, and use of power. Such an alternative conception of gender roles captures the hierarchical and competitive masculine thirst for power, which can, but need not, lead to aggression, and the feminine quest for harmony and communal well-being, which can, but need not, result in passivity and dependence.

Many activities and modes of expression are recognized by most members of society as feminine. Any of these can be, and often are, displayed by persons of either gender. In some cases, cross gender behaviors are ignored by observers, and therefore do not compromise the integrity of a person's gender display. In other cases, they are labeled as inappropriate gender role behaviors. Although these behaviors are closely linked to sexual status in the minds and experiences of most people, research shows that dominant persons of either gender tend to use influence tactics and verbal styles usually associated with men and masculinity, while subordinate persons, of either gender, tend to use those considered to be the province of women.[2] Thus it seems likely that many aspects of masculinity and femininity are the result, rather than the cause, of status inequalities.

Popular conceptions of femininity and masculinity instead revolve around hierarchical appraisals of the "natural" roles of males and females. Members of both genders are believed to share many of the same human characteristics, although in different relative proportions; both males and females are popularly thought to be able to do many of the same things, but most activities are divided into suitable and unsuitable categories for each gender class. Persons who perform the activities considered appropriate for another gender will be expected to perform them poorly; if they succeed adequately, or even well, at their endeavors, they may be rewarded with ridicule or scorn for blurring the gender dividing line.

The patriarchal gender schema currently in use in mainstream North American society reserves highly valued attributes for males and actively supports the high evaluation of any characteristics which might inadvertently become associated with maleness. The ideology which the schema grows out of postulates that the cultural superiority of males is a natural outgrowth of the innate predisposition of males toward aggression and dominance, which is assumed to flow inevitably from evolutionary and biological sources. Female attributes are likewise postulated to find their source in innate predispositions acquired in the evolution of the species. Feminine characteristics are thought to be intrinsic to the female facility for childbirth and breastfeeding. Hence, it is popularly believed that the social position of females is biologically mandated to be intertwined with the care of children and a "natural" dependency on men for the maintenance of mother-child units. Thus the goals of femininity and, by implication, of all biological females are presumed to revolve around heterosexuality and maternity.[3]

Femininity, according to this traditional formulation, "would result in warm and continued relationships with men, a sense of maternity, interest in caring for children, and the capacity to work productively and continuously in female occupations."[4] This recipe translates into a vast number of proscriptions and prescriptions. Warm and continued relations with men and an interest in maternity require that females be heterosexually oriented. A heterosexual orientation requires women to dress, move, speak, and act in ways that men will find attractive. As patriarchy has reserved active expressions of power as a masculine attribute, femininity must be expressed through modes of dress, movement, speech, and action which communicate weakness, dependency, ineffectualness, availability for sexual or emotional service, and sensitivity to the needs of others.

Some, but not all, of these modes of interrelation also serve the demands of maternity and many female job ghettos. In many cases, though, femininity is not particularly useful in maternity or employment. Both mothers and workers often need to be strong, independent, and effectual in order to do their jobs well. Thus femininity, as a role, is best suited to satisfying a masculine vision of heterosexual attractiveness.

Body postures and demeanors which communicate subordinate status and vulnerability to trespass through a message of "no threat" make people appear to be feminine. They demonstrate subordination through a minimizing of spatial use: people appear feminine when they keep their arms closer to their bodies, their legs closer together, and their torsos and heads less vertical than do masculine-looking individuals. People also look feminine when they point their toes inward and use their hands in small or childlike gestures. Other people also tend to stand closer to people they see as feminine, often invading their personal space, while people who make frequent appeasement gestures, such as smiling, also give the appearance of femininity. Perhaps as an outgrowth of a subordinate status and the need to avoid conflict with more socially powerful people, women tend to excel over men at the ability to correctly interpret, and effectively display, nonverbal communication cues.[5]

Speech characterized by inflections, intonations, and phrases that convey nonaggression and subordinate status also make a speaker appear more feminine. Subordinate speakers who use more polite expressions and ask more questions in conversation seem more feminine. Speech characterized by sounds of higher frequencies are often interpreted by listeners as feminine, childlike, and ineffectual.[6] Feminine styles of dress likewise display subordinate status through greater restriction of the free movement of the body, greater exposure of the bare skin, and an emphasis on sexual characteristics. The more gender distinct the dress, the more this is the case.

Masculinity, like femininity, can be demonstrated through a wide variety of cues. Pleck has argued that it is commonly expressed in North American society through the attainment of some level of proficiency at some, or all, of the following four main attitudes of masculinity. Persons who display success and high status in their social group, who exhibit "a manly air of toughness, confidence, and self-reliance" and "the aura of aggression, violence, and daring," and who conscientiously avoid anything associated with femininity are seen as exuding masculinity.[7] These requirements reflect the patriarchal ideology that masculinity results from an excess of testosterone, the assumption being that androgens supply a natural impetus toward aggression, which in turn impels males toward achievement and success.

This vision of masculinity also reflects the ideological stance that ideal maleness (masculinity) must remain untainted by female (feminine) pollutants.

Masculinity, then, requires of its actors that they organize themselves and their society in a hierarchical manner so as to be able to explicitly quantify the achievement of success. The achievement of high status in one's social group requires competitive and aggressive behavior from those who wish to obtain it. Competition which is motivated by a goal of individual achievement, or egoistic dominance, also requires of its participants a degree of emotional insensitivity to feelings of hurt and loss in defeated others, and a measure of emotional insularity to protect oneself from becoming vulnerable to manipulation by others. Such values lead those who subscribe to them to view feminine persons as "born losers" and to strive to eliminate any similarities to feminine people from their own personalities. In patriarchally organized societies, masculine values become the ideological structure of the society as a whole. Masculinity thus becomes "innately" valuable and femininity serves a contrapuntal function to delineate and magnify the hierarchical dominance of masculinity.

Body postures, speech patterns, and styles of dress which demonstrate and support the assumption of dominance and authority convey an impression of masculinity. Typical masculine body postures tend to be expansive and aggressive. People who hold their arms and hands in positions away from their bodies, and who stand, sit, or lie with their legs apart—thus maximizing the amount of space that they physically occupy—appear most physically masculine. Persons who communicate an air of authority or a readiness for aggression by standing erect and moving forcefully also tend to appear more masculine. Movements that are abrupt and stiff, communicating force and threat rather than flexibility and cooperation, make an actor look masculine. Masculinity can also be conveyed by stern or serious facial expressions that suggest minimal receptivity to the influence of others, a characteristic which is an important element in the attainment and maintenance of egoistic dominance.[8]

Speech and dress which likewise demonstrate or claim superior status are also seen as characteristically masculine behavior patterns. Masculine speech patterns display a tendency toward expansiveness similar to that found in masculine body postures. People who attempt to control the direction of conversations seem more masculine.[9] Those who tend to speak more loudly, use less polite and more assertive forms, and tend to interrupt the conversations of others more often also communicate masculinity to others. Styles of dress which emphasize the size of upper body musculature, allow freedom of movement, and encourage an illusion of physical power and a look of easy physicality all suggest masculinity. Such appearances of strength and readiness to action serve to create or enhance an aura of aggressiveness and intimidation central to an appearance of masculinity. Expansive postures and gestures combine with these qualities to insinuate that a position of secure dominance is a masculine one.

Gender role characteristics reflect the ideological contentions underlying the dominant gender schema in North American society. That schema leads us to believe that female and male behaviors are the result of socially directed hormonal instructions which specify that females will want to have children and will therefore find themselves relatively helpless and dependent on males for support and protection. The schema claims that males are innately aggressive and competitive and therefore will dominate over females. The social hegemony of this ideology ensures that we are all raised to practice gender roles which will confirm this vision of the nature of the sexes. Fortunately, our training to gender roles is neither complete nor uniform. As a result, it is possible to point to multitudinous exceptions to, and variations on, these themes. Biological evidence is equivocal about the source of gender roles; psychological androgyny is a widely accepted concept. It seems most likely that gender roles are the result of systematic power imbalances based on gender discrimination.[10]

### Notes

1. Egoistic dominance is a striving for superior rewards for oneself or a competitive striving to reduce the rewards for one's competitors even if such action will not increase one's own rewards. Persons who are motivated by desires for egoistic dominance not only wish the best for themselves but also wish to diminish the advantages of others whom they may perceive as competing with them. See Maccoby, p. 217.
2. Judith Howard, Philip Blumstein, and Pepper Schwartz, "Sex, Power, and Influence Tactics in Intimate Relationships," *Journal of Personality and Social Psychology* 51 (1986), pp. 102–09; Peter Kollock, Philip Blumstein, and Pepper Schwartz, "Sex and Power in Interaction: Conversational Privileges and Duties," *American Sociological Review* 50 (1985), pp. 34–46.
3. Chodorow, p. 134.
4. Jon K. Meyer and John E. Hoopes, "The Gender Dysphoria Syndromes: A Position Statement on So-Called 'Transsexualism,'" *Plastic and Reconstructive Surgery* 54 (Oct. Devor444-5.1 Gender Role Behaviors *Gender Advertisements* (New York: Harper Colophon Books, 1976); Judith A. Hall, *Non-Verbal Sex Differences: Communication Accuracy and Expressive Style* (Baltimore: Johns Hopkins University Press, 1984); Nancy M. Henley, *Body Politics: Power, Sex and Non-Verbal Communication* (Englewood Cliffs, New Jersey: Prentice Hall, 1979); Marianne Wex, *"Let's Take Back Our Space": "Female" and "Male" Body Language as a Result of Patriarchal Structures* (Berlin: Frauenliteraturverlag Hermine Fees, 1979).
6. Karen L. Adams, "Sexism and the English Language: The Linguistic Implications of Being a Woman," in *Women: A Feminist Perspective*, 3rd edition, ed. Jo Freeman (Palo Alto, Calif.: Mayfield, 1984), pp. 478–91; Hall, pp. 37, 130–37.
7. Elizabeth Hafkin Pleck, *Domestic Tyranny: The Making of Social Policy Against Family Violence from Colonial Times to the Present* (Cambridge: Oxford University Press, 1989), p. 139.
8. Goffman, *Gender Advertisements*: Hall; Henley; Wex.
9. Adams; Hall, p. 37, Baul Theroux Being a Man
10. Howard, Blumstein, and Schwartz; Kollock, Blumstein, and Schwartz.

## READING WRITING

### THIS TEXT: READING

1. Many of Devor's claims resemble the claims in the introduction to this chapter. Make a list of "masculine" and "feminine" traits. Based on your list, what do you make of Devor's assumptions? Are any changing? What political or cultural movements or concerns might be affecting Devor's readings of gender?
2. According to Devor, how do children acquire gender roles? Do you agree? What evidence does Devor use to support her assertions that gender is constructed?

### YOUR TEXT: WRITING

1. Write an essay on your own history of doing gender. What gender roles do you engage in? Which ones do you avoid?
2. Make a list of various gender roles of a different gender than yourself. What is the basis for this list? If you showed it to someone of that gender, would he or she agree with you?
3. Write a paper in which you talk about your own gender assumptions.

4.  Think of gender roles as film roles. Write an essay in which you explore how men and women are represented differently in film or on television. Use specific examples to support your points.

---

**BEING A MAN**

■ **Paul Theroux** ■

*In this 1985 essay, Theroux offers a reading of masculinity from the perspective of someone who "always disliked being a man." Much like Devor, Theroux is troubled by the expectations of masculine behavior and finds writing at variance with many of them.*

THERE IS A PATHETIC SENTENCE in the chapter "Fetishism" in Dr. Norman Cameron's book *Personality Development and Psychopathology*. It goes, "Fetishists are nearly always men; and their commonest fetish is a woman's shoe." I cannot read that sentence without thinking that it is just one more awful thing about being a man—and perhaps it is an important thing to know about us.

I have always disliked being a man. The whole idea of manhood in America is pitiful, in my opinion. This version of masculinity is a little like having to wear an ill-fitting coat for one's entire life (by contrast, I imagine femininity to be an oppressive sense of nakedness). Even the expression "Be a man!" strikes me as insulting and abusive. It means: Be stupid, be unfeeling, obedient, soldierly, and stop thinking. Man means "manly"—how can one think about men without considering the terrible ambition of manliness? And yet it is part of every man's life. It is a hideous and crippling lie; it not only insists on difference and connives at superiority, it is also by its very nature destructive—emotionally damaging and socially harmful.

The youth who is subverted, as most are, into believing in the masculine ideal is effectively separated from women and he spends the rest of his life finding women a riddle and a nuisance. Of course, there is a female version of this male affliction. It begins with mothers encouraging little girls to say (to other adults) "Do you like my new dress?" In a sense, little girls are traditionally urged to please adults with a kind of coquettishness, while boys are enjoined to behave like monkeys towards each other. The nine-year-old coquette proceeds to become womanish in a subtle power game in which she learns to be sexually indispensable, socially decorative, and always alert to a man's sense of inadequacy.

Femininity—being ladylike—implies needing a man as witness and seducer; but masculinity celebrates the exclusive company of men. That is why it is so grotesque; and that is also why there is no manliness without inadequacy—because it denies men the natural friendship of women.

It is very hard to imagine any concept of manliness that does not belittle women, and it begins very early. At an age when I wanted to meet girls—let's say the treacherous years of thirteen to sixteen—I was told to take up a sport, get more fresh air, join the Boy Scouts, and I was urged not to read so much. It was the 1950s and if you asked too many questions about sex you were sent to camp—boy's camp, of course: the nightmare. Nothing is more unnatural or prisonlike than a boy's camp, but if it were not for them we would have no Elks' Lodges, no pool rooms, no boxing matches, no Marines.

And perhaps no sports as we know them. Everyone is aware of how few in number are the athletes who behave like gentlemen. Just as high school basketball teaches you how to be a poor loser, the manly attitude towards sports seems to be little more than a recipe for creating bad marriages, social misfits, moral degenerates, sadists, latent rapists, and just plain louts. I regard high school sports as a drug far worse than marijuana, and it is the reason that the average tennis champion, say, is a pathetic oaf.

Any objective study would find the quest for manliness essentially right-wing, puritanical, cowardly, neurotic, and fueled largely by a fear of women. It is also certainly philistine. There is no book-hater like a Little League coach. But indeed all the creative arts are obnoxious to the manly ideal, because at their best the arts are pursued by uncompetitive and essentially solitary people. It makes it very hard for a creative youngster, for any boy who expresses the desire to be alone seems to be saying that there is something wrong with him.

It ought to be clear by now that I have something of an objection to the way we turn boys into men. It does not surprise me that when the President of the United States has his customary weekend off he dresses like a cowboy—it is both a measure of his insecurity and his willingness to please. In many ways, American culture does little more for a man than prepare him for modeling clothes in the L.L. Bean catalogue. I take this as a personal insult because for many years I found it impossible to admit to myself that I wanted to be a writer. It was my guilty secret, because being a writer was incompatible with being a man.

There are people who might deny this, but that is because the American writer, typically, has been so at pains to prove his manliness that we have come to see literariness and manliness as mingled qualities. But first there was a fear that writing was not a manly profession—indeed, not a profession at all. (The paradox in American letters is that it has always been easier for a woman to write and for a man to be published.) Growing up, I had thought of sports as wasteful and humiliating and the idea of manliness was a bore. My wanting to become a writer was not a flight from that oppressive role-playing but I quickly saw that it was at odds with it. Everything in stereotyped manliness goes against the life of the mind. The Hemingway personality is too tedious to go into here, and in any case his exertions are well known, but certainly it was not until this aberrant behavior was examined by feminists in the 1960s that any male writer dared question the pugnacity in Hemingway's fiction. All the bullfighting and arm wrestling and elephant shooting diminished Hemingway as a writer, but it is consistent with a prevailing attitude in American writing one cannot be a male writer without first proving that one is a man.

It is normal in America for a man to be dismissive or even somewhat apologetic about being a writer. Various factors make it easier. There is a heartiness about journalism that makes it acceptable—journalism is the manliest form of American writing and, therefore, the profession the most independent-minded women seek (yes, it is an illusion, but that is my point). Fiction-writing is equated with a kind of dispirited failure and is only manly when it produces wealth—money is masculinity. So is drinking. Being a drunkard is another assertion, if misplaced, of manliness. The American male writer is traditionally proud of his heavy drinking. But we are also a very literal-minded people. A man proves his manhood in America in old-fashioned ways. He kills lions, like Hemingway; or he hunts ducks, like Nathanael West, or he makes pronouncements like, "A man should carry enough knife to defend himself with," as James Jones once said to a *Life* interviewer. Or he says he can drink you under the table. But even tiny drunken William Faulkner loved to mount a horse and go fox hunting, and Jack Kerouac roistered up and down Manhattan in a lumberjack shirt (and spent every night of *The Subterraneans* with his mother in Queens). And we are familiar with the lengths to which Norman Mailer is prepared, in his endearing way, to prove that he is just as much a monster as the next man.

When the novelist John Irving was revealed as a wrestler, people took him to be a very serious writer, and even a bubble reputation like Eric (*Love Story*) Segal's was enhanced by the news that he ran the marathon in a respectable time. How surprised we would be if Joyce Carol Oates were revealed as a sumo wrestler or Joan Didion active in pumping iron. "Lives in New York City with her three children" is the typical woman writer's biographical note, for just as the male writer must prove he has achieved a sort of muscular manhood, the woman writer—or rather her publicists—must prove her motherhood.

There would be no point in saying any of this if it were not generally accepted that to be a man is somehow—even now in feminist-influenced America—a privilege. It is on the contrary an unmerciful and punishing burden. Being a man is bad enough; being manly is appalling (in this sense, women's lib has done much more for men than for women). It is the sinister silliness of men's fashions and a clubby attitude in the arts. It is the subversion of good students. It is the so-called Dress Code of the Ritz-Carlton Hotel in Boston, and it is the institutionalized cheating in college sports. It is the most primitive insecurity.

And this is also why men often object to feminism, but are afraid to explain why: of course women have a justified grievance, but most men believe—and with reason—that their lives are just as bad.

---

## READING WRITING

### THIS TEXT: READING

1. Why does Theroux not like being a man? Are his reasons valid? Is his argument and progression well reasoned?
2. Can you think of "any concept of manliness that does not belittle women"? What do you make of the way Theroux claims we turn boys into men? Do you agree with him? Do you share his distaste?
3. Do Theroux's claims about manliness and writing still hold true? Why? Why not? His piece seems a bit dated—how can you tell it was written in a previous era?

### YOUR TEXT: WRITING

1. Write an essay entitled "On Being a Woman." How will yours differ from Theroux's?
2. Write an essay about being the opposite gender. What would be good about being the other gender? What would not be so good?
3. This is the only text in this section written by a man. Write an essay on the fact that there is only one piece by a man in a chapter about gender. Should it be evenly balanced? Is the rest of *The World Is a Text* balanced in terms of gender? Should there be a female co-author?

---

### YOU WOULD HAVE ME WHITE

■ **Alfonsina Storni** ■

*One of South America's most important poets, Alfonsina Storni spent most of her life in Argentina until her death in 1938. "Tu me quieres blanca" was published in 1918 and remains her most famous poem and a significant text for North and South American women. Edgy and poetic, angry and beautiful, her poem is a strong statement on the universal stereotyping of women. As a side note, you should know that in Spanish, "white" is* blanca. *However,* blanca *also means "empty" and "blank."*

| | |
|---|---|
| Tú me quieres alba, | You want me white, |
| me quieres de espumas, | you want me foam, |
| me quieres de nácar. | you want me pearl. |
| Que sea azucena | That I would be white lily, |
| sobre todas, casta. | above all the others, chaste. |
| De perfume tenue. | Of tenuous perfume. |
| Corola cerrada. | Closed corolla. |
| | |
| Ni un rayo de luna | That not even a ray of filtered |
| filtrado me haya. | moonlight have me. |
| Ni una margarita | Nor a daisy |
| se diga mi hermana. | call itself my sister. |
| Tú me quieres nívea, | You want me snowy, |
| tú me quieres blanca, | you want me white, |
| tú me quieres alba. | you want me dawn. |
| | |
| Tú que hubiste todas | You who had all |
| las copas a mano, | the cups in hand, |
| de frutos y mieles | Your lips purple |
| los labios morados. | with fruits and honey. |
| Tú que en el banquete | You who at the banquet |
| cubierto de pámpanos | covered with ferns |
| dejaste las carnes | relinquished your flesh |
| festejando a Baco. | celebrating Bacchus. |
| Tú que en los jardines | You who in black |
| negros del engaño | gardens of deceit |
| vestido de rojo | dressed in red |
| corriste al estrago. | ran yourself to ruin. |
| Tú que el esqueleto | You whose skeleton |
| conservas intacto | is still intact |
| no sé todavía | by what miracles |
| por cuáles milagros, | I'll never know, |
| me pretendes blanca | you want me to be white |
| (Dios te lo perdone), | (God forgive you), |
| me pretendes casta | you want me to be chaste |
| (Dios te lo perdone), | (God forgive you), |
| ¡me pretendes alba! | you want me to be dawn! |
| | |
| Huye hacia los bosques; | Go to the woods; |
| vete a la montaña; | go to the mountains; |
| límpiate la boca; | wash out your mouth; |
| vive en las cabañas; | live in a hut; |
| toca con las manos | touch the damp earth |

| la tierra mojada; | with your hands; |
|---|---|
| alimenta el cuerpo | nourish your body |
| con raíz amarga; | with bitter roots; |
| bebe de las rocas; | drink from stones; |
| duerme sobre escarcha; | sleep on frost; |
| renueva tejidos | restore your body |
| con salitre y agua; | with saltpeter and water; |

| Habla con los pájaros | Speak with birds |
|---|---|
| y lévate al alba. | and get up at dawn. |
| Y cuando las carnes | And when your flesh |
| te sean tornadas, | is restored to you, |
| y cuando hayas puesto | and when you've put the |
| en ellas el alma | back into the flesh |
| que por las alcobas | which was entrapped |
| se quedó enredada, | in bedrooms, |
| entonces, buen hombre, | then, good man, |
| preténdeme blanca, | pretend I'm white, |
| preténdeme nívea, | pretend I'm snowy, |
| preténdeme casta. | pretend I'm chaste. |

## READING WRITING

## THIS TEXT: READING

1. How do the connotations of *blanca* in Spanish alter your reading of the poem?
2. Why does Storni want her man to "go to the mountains," "wash out his mouth" and "live in a hut"? Why must he restore his flesh? Why will returning to nature accomplish this?
3. How is Storni using the various symbolisms surrounding "white"?
4. Why does Storni think the man in question needs God's forgiveness?

## YOUR TEXT: WRITING

1. Who is Storni addressing here? Write an essay in which you explore issues of male and female gender in the poem.
2. Give a feminist reading of the poem. What kind of statement is Storni making about how men see women?
3. Write an essay in which you explore the various connotations of whiteness in Storni's poem and *Snow White*.

---

### WHY CHICKS DIG VAMPIRES: SEX, BLOOD, AND BUFFY

■ Alice Rutkowski ■

*In her engaging and insightful 2002 essay, Alice Rutkowski takes a critical look at* Buffy the Vampire Slayer *and the ways in which the main character, Buffy, is "one of the first in a long line champions of this new breed of girl power." Rutkowski argues that* Buffy *is liberating not only because Buffy herself is a strong female character but be-*

*cause the show places a female lead in the context of vampires, which have always been associated with power and eroticism. Rutkowski claims that* Buffy *helps reclaim these traits for girls. We like this essay because Rutkowski sees the role of girls in the horror genre as a "text" that can be (and is being) rewritten by shows like* Buffy.

Nowadays, powerful girls are everywhere on television and in the movies, even in genres previously populated only by men, especially action, science-fiction, and fantasy. Buffy Summers, the protagonist of television's *Buffy the Vampire Slayer* (1997–present) (1), was one of the first in a long line of champions of this new breed of girl power. For example, both Max, from the sci-fi post-apocalyptic *Dark Angel,* and the good-witch sisters of *Charmed* probably owe more than they'd like to admit to the power and influence of Buffy. It is, of course, important to acknowledge Buffy's foremothers, the kick-ass women who preceded her. Yet the most iconic examples, Sigourney Weaver's Ripley in *Aliens* (1986) and Linda Hamilton's Sarah Conner in *Terminator 2* (1991) (both films directed by James Cameron) are motivated to heroic action explicitly by their maternal instincts. In other words, for these characters, anger and active resistance are acceptable and understandable only in the context of motherhood, woman's "natural" role. (2)

For a change in this model to occur, it seems we needed to look to women from a different generation—emphatically not mothers. (3) When *Buffy* began (in 1997), its heroine was a sophomore in high school in Southern California—not a girl, not yet a woman (to borrow from Britney). But she's also the Chosen One: in the mythology of the series, from every generation a girl is chosen to stand alone against the forces of evil, the protector of all of humanity. And the creation of Buffy was literally a response to the fate of a certain kind of girl who inhabited the horror genre. In an interview in *Rolling Stone,* Joss Whedon, the creator of the series, described his original idea for Buffy:

> It was pretty much the blond girl in the alley in the horror movie who keeps getting killed.
> I felt bad for her, but she was always more interesting to me than the other girls. She was fun,
> she had sex, she was vivacious. But then she would get punished for it. Literally, I just had
> that image, that scene, in my mind, like the trailer for a movie, what if the girl goes into the
> dark alley. And the monster follows her. And she destroys him. (62)

This genesis story is rather remarkable—it turns a horror-movie cliche into an ambush, where the perennially-preyed-upon not only fights back but is the aggressor.

Certainly girls who look like Buffy aren't a new sight on prime-time television: blond, blue-eyed, and strikingly pretty she certainly wouldn't look out of place on, say, Beverly Hills, 90210.(4) But Buffy has the speed and strength of a superhero as well as some jaw-droppingly-cool martial arts moves. But these abilities are not evident solely from her appearance—a fact that some badly-informed vampire discovers in just about every episode. Because Buffy looks more like someone in need of protection than the protector of all humanity, people—and monsters—who don't know her consistently underestimate her abilities.

The show itself echoes this principle—it is much more than it seems. Buffy offers that rare combination of critical and commercial success, adored by both teen-aged girls and academics. (5) But because of its mix of comedy and drama, reality and horror, it's been consistently snubbed by the Emmys. Just as its older brother, *The X-Files,* it is often described as a "genre" series, industry-speak for science-fiction or fantasy (as if somehow cop shows, lawyer shows, and doctor shows don't qualify as genres). But it goes a step beyond the science fiction of Mulder and Scully—"I Want to Believe"—to unquestioned belief. Buffy and

The very feminine Buffy with a very masculine weapon.

her friends live in a world where the existence of a plethora of evil, bloodsucking monsters is a given.

As *The X-Files* did before it, Buffy often uses monsters as metaphors, which allows the show both to work in hyperbole and still root its stories in a kind of realism. As Mim Udovitch writes in *Rolling Stone*, "when it comes to dealing with what's inside you that you can't control, Buffy is the most realistic show on the air" (66). For example, the cool (and brutally mean) kids from high school literally turn into a pack of vicious hyenas and Buffy's freshman roommate turns out actually to be a demon from a hell dimension (the Celine Dion poster clearly should have tipped her off).

But the primary interest of *The X-Files* was in aliens from outer space. Mulder and Scully dealt with the occasional vampire or demon; Buffy specializes in them. I think it is precisely this reason that Buffy is so compelling to vastly different audiences: the power of this figure—the vampire. Although it seems as if Bram Stoker's *Count Dracula* has always been with us, *Dracula* was first published in 1897, making it only a little more than a hundred years old. Although Stoker drew on folklore and myths which had been in existence for centuries, his Dracula became the definitive vampire story. Now every film, book, or TV show about vampires owes its existence to this text, whether it makes use of its terms and imagery or consciously re-writes them. In his article, "Metaphor into Metonymy: The Vampire Next Door," Jules Zanger, a scholar of vampire lore and literariness, describes the divide between what he sees as the "old" and "new" figure of the vampire. The "old" vampire is Stoker's: a damned soul that embodies metaphysical evil. He is a solitary figure with a single purpose—to pollute and destroy humanity (most often figured as the pure, virginal woman). Zanger argues that the power and mystery of this compelling figure has been lost in modern retellings. Recent films and fiction have domesticated the vampire: "new" vampires tend to be communal rather than solitary and have lost their religious significance and many of their folkloric attributes—in short, they have become more human than monster. As evidence he cites films such as *The Lost Boys* (1987), which features California teenagers as vampires, and Anne Rice's slew of vampiric anti-heroes.

Generally speaking, the evidence supports Zanger's argument. One of my favorite *X-Files* episodes, "Bad Blood," self-consciously dramatizes just this conundrum—that evil monsters have become terrifyingly banal. In this episode, vampires have lost not only their mythical characteristics—their ability to seduce their prey into submission, for example—but even their sharp incisors. In a trailer-park town, the villainous vampire is a teenaged pizza delivery boy who must drug the pizza he delivers to incapacitate his victims and then use prosthetic incisors to access their blood.

This "diminished" vampire is also, in Zanger's view, somewhat disturbing in its moral implications. Zanger believes this humanization of the vampire echoes the trajectory of the figure of the Mafia don in popular culture.

Whereas the gangster movies that proliferated in the 1930s figured the don as an evil villain, by the 1960s, ". . . the Mafia emerged to dominate the popular imagination, replacing those older, individualistic [figures] . . . with a new, corporate, communal, familial image of the criminal" (24). Although Zanger's article was written before the appearance of Tony Soprano, HBO's *The Sopranos* furnishes a perfect example of the phenomenon Zanger describes. Critics claim that by putting criminals at the center and making them the focus, the victims of the violence perpetrated by these (anti)heroes are marginalized. Our sympathy and identification rightly belong with the victim, one might argue, not the murderer.

Zanger is worried less about the moral implications of the "new" vampire than he is about the loss of the mystical power of the figure itself:

Dracula . . . [existed] in a context of clear moral certainties that has in our time become increasingly muddled. . . . Our new secularized . . . vampires must content themselves with bloodier and bloodier slasher killings, and lose, with each additional murder, some of their original mythic integrity, so that finally they threaten to merge indistinguishably with all the other nightmare monsters and murderers haunting and splattering our popular culture. (26)

The modern (or postmodern) vampire, according to Zanger, has become little more than a glorified serial killer, a Jeffrey Dahmer with fangs.

This may be true for many of the films and television shows that make use of vampire lore, but Buffy manages to stay smart and vital by playing with exactly this contradiction. On Buffy, vampires can certainly be boring, stupid, and banal: the mean hipster girl who humiliates new college freshmen or the smarmy guy at the bar in the shiny shirt that's so five-years-ago. But Buffy also remains committed to the power of the original archetypal vampire. This is best seen in the episode "Buffy vs. Dracula" where the prince of darkness himself makes a guest appearance (although looking less like Bela Lugosi and more like a Backstreet Boy). By having the characters respond to Dracula like a celebrity, the episode moves between an irreverent, self-conscious critique and a reminder of his original, darker significance—death, evil, and ruin.

In the context of our current culture of celebrity worship, the first few scenes of the Dracula episode make for some highly allusive humor. When Buffy first encounters him, she doesn't believe he is who he says he is: "So let me get this straight. You're—Dracula. The guy, the count . . . And you're sure this isn't just some fanboy thing? Cause I've fought more than a couple of pimply overweight vamps that called themselves Lestat," refering directly to Anne Rice's most well-known anti-hero. Xander, a friend of Buffy's, assuming he's seeing a vampire with "a bad case of dark prince envy," mocks Dracula's accent by talking like the Count from Sesame Street. These exchanges acknowledge that the figure of the vampire— and Dracula in particular—is relentlessly over-determined, overused, and even over-parodied ("I wonder if he knows Frankenstein," Xander muses later) but at the same time insists on the truth and power of the original myth.

Dracula has traveled to Sunnydale specifically to seek our Buffy. ("Why else would I come here? For the sun?" he asks.) His approach to conquering her is the same as with Lucy, the virginal victim in Stoker's novel: he drains her blood gradually as he visits the victim nightly in her bedroom. The modus operandi differs from the garden-variety vampire, but, as another character on Buffy notes: "though he goes through the motions of an intimate seduction, the end result is the same. He turns them into a vampire." In the final confrontation, Dracula suggests to Buffy they are kindred spirits: "All those years fighting us. Your power is so near our own. And you've never wanted to know what it is that we fight for?" For a moment it seems as if she will succumb to his offer; she tastes the blood he offers and is immediately barraged by a flashing series of images, of pulsing blood cells, Slayers from long ago, and her own violent encounters with past vampires. This implies Dracula's claim of affinity has some truth—their powers are both rooted in darkness—a disconcerting admission about a story's hero(ine). But at the moment when Dracula believes she will consent, she stakes him in the heart (although being the Dracula, he is shown to be able to reconstitute himself, to return perhaps in a future episode). Stoker's novel betrayed a deep anxiety about women's sexuality, but Buffy rewrites that by having its heroine forcefully refuse the fate of Lucy.

According to Rutkowski, Buffy plays on the erotics of vampirism.

In addition to giving access to over a century of vampire stories, the other striking consequence of putting vampires at the center of the series is it opens up all sorts of sexual
configurations, pairings and practices nor available—or at least not permissible—on a more
"realistic" show. Vampires already embody multiple contradictions in their bodies and beings: dead yet somehow alive; murderous, impulse-driven animals and yet suave, nattily-
dressed seducers—and so on. And the act of drinking a victim's blood can't help but be read
as sexual, although this sexuality confounds any attempt to equate it with simple male-female
intercourse: there is penetration, yet certainly not in a conventional manner; there is a release
of a bodily fluid, but the victim's rather than the penetrator's; the act often results in the death
of the victim, but the process is often depicted as a seduction rather than an outright assault
(so issues of consent get terribly murky, to the point that even the word "victim" is problematic). And nearly all vampire narratives represent the method of reproducing new vampires,
which although perhaps sexy—depending on your tastes—is distinctly asexual, in which the
victim, once drained of blood by the vampire, is then offered the vampire's blood to drink.
Vampires can be male or female, as can victims, so the matrix of available partners expands
infinitely. In human sexual practice, then, vampires might represent queer acts and identities, as well as sadomasochism, deliberate submission, and other "unconventional" practices.

Buffy is certainly not the first to recognize the erotic alternatives which vampires open
up. Many of Anne Rice's novels, for example, are filled with intense, homoerotic relationships
between male vampires. But Buffy uses the metaphor to its fullest extent: the vampire is an
ever-changing signifier which opens up multiple avenues of characterization and storytelling. For instance, one addition that Buffy offers to existing vampire mythology is the ap-

Rutkowski also claims that the vampire's face stands in for "sexual organs."

pearance of its monsters. Most of the vampires on *Buffy* initially show no outward signs of their monstrousness—if careful, they can even pass for mortal. But, in addition to showing their fangs, when they become excited their faces become swollen, bumpy, and grotesque. Hunger (of course), but also pain and sexual arousal, can draw this hidden self to the surface. So the face stands in for the sexual organs, becoming engorged with desire and/or hunger. Simultaneously, the animal in them literally becomes written on their face, so their outer appearance now matches their inner self.

*Buffy* offers a vast array of specific examples that illustrate the erotic possibilities suggested by featuring vampires as main characters, but I'll offer just two. The first involves Willow, Buffy's best friend. A high-achieving computer nerd in high school, she is predictably shy and introverted. In the episode "Doppelgangland," a maverick spell releases Willow's counterpart from another dimension—an evil vampire Willow. Bad Willow is strong, assertive, and aggressively sexual. (Bad Willow, on being pulled out of her home dimension: "This is a dumb world. In my world there are people in chains, and we can ride them like ponies.") She's especially lecherous with pretty girls (in an interesting twist that deserves further analysis, even with "herself," good Willow). So basically, Bad Willow is everything that (good) Willow from this dimension is not. Towards the end of the episode, as they lock up her evil doppelganger, Willow talks to Buffy and Angel (a good vampire), about the experience of encountering her evil counterpart:

> WILLOW: It's horrible! That's me as a vampire? I'm so evil and skanky. And I think I'm kinda gay.
> BUFFY: Willow, just remember, a vampire's personality has nothing to do with the person it was.
> ANGEL: Well, actually . . . (Buffy shoots him a look of warning.) That's a good point.

It's unclear exactly what insight Angel, a vampire himself, was about to provide—maybe that our vampire selves enact our hidden desires, or that they're simply amplified versions of what we as mortals—but Angel turns out to be right. At this point on the show, Willow is dating a man, but a year later in college, Willow becomes romantically involved with a woman, Tara, and comes out as a lesbian. This earlier moment foreshadows her shifting sexual identity in a dramatic way.

The existence of vampire Willow offers some perhaps disconcerting insights into mortal Willow's character, but ultimately some liberating ones as well. Buffy has also used vampire sexuality to deal with troubled relationships: Buffy's college boyfriend (in seasons three and four), Riley, is part of a secret government paramilitary anti-demon unit and fights vampires by her side. He comes to realize that Buffy, although she cares for him, does not love and need him as deeply as he does her; her calling as the Slayer is always her first priority. Despairing and sure he will lose Buffy, he begins secretly visiting a vampire "whorehouse" of sorts, where he pays a pretty female vampire to suck his—blood. As a metaphor this works marvelously on a number of levels: there's the obvious pun on "suck" for vampire feeding and oral sex; also, the vampire prostitute needs Riley in a way Buffy does not—his blood literally sustains her, she hungers for him, devouring the blood from his arm; lastly, the choice of his arm as a site for extraction also conjures images of intravenous drug use—secret, illicit, dangerous, addictive. But it's also a terrible, intimate betrayal and is one of the factors which lead Riley and Buffy to break up.

*Buffy* certainly accomplishes its goal of rethinking and rewriting the role of girls in the horror genre; and it isn't interested in merely exchanging the values in the standard mascu-

Both Buffy and Willow frustrate traditional assumptions about gender.

line/feminine, aggressive/passive dichotomy, but rather in something more complicated. Unlike the girls who preceded her in the genre, Buffy need not fear the monster will punish her for having sex; the figure of the monster instead works to open up the choice of partners and acts, and in this way provides a window into adolescent girl sexuality. Finally, Buffy's accumulation of references not only to popular culture but to its literary and cinematic ancestors rewards both the fan and the close reader. Nowadays, when the "girl power" mantle is claimed by anyone and everyone, *Buffy the Vampire Slayer* thoughtfully offers a powerful heroine whose power has real consequences, good and bad.

### Notes

1. It's important to note that Buffy was originally a 1992 film, also written by Joss Whedon, the creator of the television series; but the film version bore little resemblance to his original vision (and is, in fact, quite bad). For an account of how things went terribly wrong with the film, see the interview with Whedon in *The Onion* (September 5, 2001) at http://www.theonionavdub.com/avclub3731/avfeature_3731.html
2. One might argue the exception to this rule comes in *Alien: Resurrection,* possibly the most disturbing *Alien* film to date, with its deeply macabre meditations on motherhood and reproduction. Significantly, *Resurrection* was written by Buffy creator Joss Whedon.
3. And perhaps a different culture as well: Buffy's debt to Chinese kung-fu practice, culture and film—in which women have played prominent roles throughout history—is significant.
4. Buffy's core cast is composed almost entirely of attractive, white, twenty-something actors (excepting the attractive, white, forty-something man who plays the mentor/Either figure). The show has been criticized for its lack of racial diversity, a critique which has some basis.
5. For example, in October of 2002, the University of East Anglia (in Norwich, England) is sponsoring a scholarly conference, "Blood, Text and Fears: Reading around Buffy the Vampire Slayer."

### Works Cited

Udovitch, Mim. "What Makes Buffy Slay?" *Rolling Stone* (May 11, 2000) 62–66.

Zanger, J. "Metaphor into Metonymy: The Vampire Next Door." *Blood Red: Vampires in Contemporary Culture,* ed. Gordon and Hollinger. Philadelphia: U. Penn Press, 1997. 17–26.

READING WRITING

## THIS TEXT: READING

1. See if you can identify Rutkowski's thesis statement. What is her argument exactly? What kind of supporting evidence does she provide? Is her argument convincing?
2. How does your own reading of *Buffy the Vampire Slayer* compare with Rutkowski's? Does she "read too much" into the show?
3. In our mind, Rutkowski's argument is a pretty good blend of logos and pathos. How would you describe her ethos? Do you trust her? Is she a reliable source? Do you feel manipulated?

## YOUR TEXT: WRITING

1. Write an essay in which you read *Buffy* through the lens of feminism. How is the show a feminist text?
2. Write a comparison/contrast essay in which you read *Buffy* alongside another popular television show that features a young woman, like, *Sister, Sister* or *The Sopranos*

(Meadow). How are the shows' representations of young women different? Which show does the best cultural work?

3. Write an essay comparing *Buffy* the television show with *Buffy* the movie—both of which were created by Joss Whedon. What changes? What stays the same? Is Sarah Michelle Gellar a good Buffy?

*Student Essay*

## UNREAL CITY: GENDER AND WAR

### ■ Elizabeth Greenwood ■

*Elizabeth Greenwood, a student at the University of San Francisco, wrote this paper for a Women's Literature class in 2003. Greenwood's paper is a good example of using a lens to read a text. Here, she argues that the gender of Virginia Woolf and T. S. Eliot shape how both write about war. In essence, then, she reads not only Woolf's and Eliot's texts, but she reads gender and war as texts as well.*

*Under a brown fog of a winter dawn,*
*A crowd flowed under London Bridge, so many*
*I had not thought death had undone so many*[1]

World War I brought death and destruction to the people of Europe in apocalyptic proportions never before imaginable. Having lost an entire generation of men in the Great War, Europeans were forced to reevaluate their culture, which appeared to be dissipating like the smoke from the fire-bombed countryside. While wives, daughters and mothers mourned the loss of their men, artists set out to reveal the far-reaching effects of the violence and ruin the returning war veterans encountered. Virginia Woolf's groundbreaking novel *Mrs. Dalloway* and T.S. Eliot's epic poem *The Waste Land* explore, in quite distinct manners, the unsuspected casualties of war in London.

Both writers frequented the same Bloomsbury circle of writers. They were not only colleagues but also friends. Woolf commented on *The Waste Land* in her diary on June 23, 1922, saying, "Eliot dined last Sunday & read his poem. He sung it & chanted it & rhythmed it. It has great beauty & force of phrase: symmetry; & tensity. What connects it together, I'm not so sure. One was left, however, with some strong emotion."[2] They engaged in discourse and criticism of each others' work, and the first edition of *The Waste Land* was published on Leonard and Virginia Woolf's Hogarth Press in 1923.[3] However, the approaches Eliot and Woolf employed and perspective each wrote from are quite distinct. Is it possible that their respective genders influenced their perception of war-ravaged London? I maintain that gender played a key role in the writings by Eliot and Woolf on life after war. Gender manifests itself in *Mrs. Dalloway* and *The Waste Land* through the structures of time, symbolism, characterization, and tone.

One of the most notable and experimental features of each work is the frame of time. While each work is a journey—a virtual odyssey—for all characters involved, the parameters of time Woolf and Eliot chose to work within are quite divergent. In *The Waste Land*, time

---

[1]T.S. Eliot, *The Waste Land* (New York, 1998), p. 35.
[2]Virginia Woolf (Anne Oliver Bell, Ed.) *The Diary of Virginia Woolf, Volume II* (New York, 1978), p. 178.
[3]Jan Goldman, *The Feminist Aesthetics of Virginia Woolf* (Cambridge, 1998), p. 154.

ranges infinite. Eliot's vision of a hell without beginning or end is not a prescribed literary formula. It is certainly stream of consciousness in light of how thoughts ebb and flow. But the spectrum of linear time spans from prehistoric to present to abstract. Eliot employs seasonal cycles as a unifying element throughout the poem, but history is absent of pattern. From Dante to Christian and Buddhist allusions to medieval folklore to Shakespeare, Eliot's century-jumping references add to the texture of time in *The Waste Land*. He remarked on the significance of omitting a more structured version of time, saying, "The one thing time is ever sure to bring about is the loss: gain or compensation is almost always conceivable but never certain.[4] Loss was by all means the most visible effect of World War I. While Eliot demonstrates that death is timeless and boundary-less, he employs a parallel structure of fluid time. Like Woolf, time flashes forward and backward (seen in the memories of Marie and "the Hyacinth Girl" in "The Burial of the Dead"), but time in our traditional perception is arbitrary.

To demonstrate his vision of eternal hell, Eliot made time limitless. To demonstrate her conception of post-War London, Woolf chose to focus on a solitary day in *Mrs. Dalloway*. In this basic, structural difference, the reader witnesses the gender divide. Similarly, however, time is a periscope to examine choice, regret, and personal hell. Woolf's stream of consciousness form presents a mosaic of characters that evolve not only over the course of a day, but through their entire lives. *Mrs. Dalloway* is full of tensions of past and present that manifest themselves in Clarissa's ruminations on her girlhood at Bourton and past loves Peter and Sally. Yet the main antagonists in the story are life and death. The illumination of past events and the future struggle over the course of a few hours versus Eliot's employment of infinite time point directly to male and female differences. In *Mrs. Dalloway*, men and women are portrayed traditionally, as polar opposites. Women cultivate and nurture sentiments, while men think abstractly.[5] This theory can be applied in some ways to Eliot's abstract universe of time and space in *The Waste Land* and Woolf's more coherent, concrete world in *Mrs. Dalloway*. The fact that Woolf formulated the action of her novel within the course of a day instead of over the course of infinity speaks to the creative borders that female artists faced. The stream of consciousness style Woolf employed was risky and daring enough on its own. If Woolf, as a woman, had been as audacious as Eliot to attempt to hurdle time and make it insignificant, she most likely would have received a much colder reception.

Symbolism in *Mrs. Dalloway* and *The Waste Land* is also quite gendered. "Mrs. Dalloway said she would buy the flowers herself"[6] is a recognized phrase that has become part of the literary landscape. Flowers traditionally represent innocence and purity, but also femininity and fertility. By declaring that she, herself, would buy the flowers, Clarissa is abandoning patriarchy and masculine protection. Similarly, she shades herself from patriarchy, represented by the Freudian symbol of masculinity—the sun.[7] The parasol with which she shades herself is described as ". . . a sacred weapon which a Goddess, having acquitted herself hon-

---

[4]Nancy K. Gish *Time in the Poetry of T.S. Eliot* (Totowa, New Jersey, 1981) p. 57.

[5]Ellen Bayuk Rosenman, *A Room of One's Own: Women Writers and the Politics of Creativity* (New York, 1955) p. 36.

[6]Virginia Woolf, *Mrs. Dalloway* (New York, 1925), p. 3.

[7]Goldman p. 15.

orably in the field of battle, sheds, and places . . . in the umbrella stand, Fear no more, said Clarissa. Fear no more the heat o' the sun."[8]

Conversely, the state car that passes through the crowd on that June morning is a masculine symbol. It emits a funeral-like presence through the crowd, and is the first uniting moment between Clarissa and Septimus. Woolf writes,

> People must notice, people must see. People, she thought, looking at the crowd staring at the motor car; the English people, with their children and their horses and their clothes, which she admired in a way; but they were "people" now, because Septimus had said "I will kill myself'; what an awful thing to say.[9]

The state car is a symbol for nationalism—a male impulse. Clarissa, who becomes a symbol for empathy—a female impulse—sentimentalizes the war. She admires the stoicism of the soldiers, and as to Britain, she says, "This late age of the world's experience had bred in them all, all men and women, a well of tears."[10] In the new, war-torn world Clarissa needs to find comfort in the familiar. Woolf realized that the war gave women new legal advantages, but the horror of the war made many women retreat back under the wing of what men they had left. Clarissa says that perhaps in another life she "would be interested in politics like a man."[11] But as an aged woman in this brave, new world, interest in politics or any gesture away from being just Mrs. Richard Dalloway is a movement into dangerous, uncharted territory.

Interestingly, women become symbols themselves in *The Waste Land*. It is known that Eliot was not the most liberated man of his time, and more than seeing women as less equal than men, he held a bitter repulsion for them. He referred to women as "the enemy of the absolute."[12] Throughout *The Waste Land*, there are four female characters—Marie, the Hyacinth Girl, Lil, and Madame Sosotris. All of them represent weakness, deceit, and greed. Like the nymphs who have departed, these women are presented as fallen, or in the process of becoming so. Madame Sosotris practices black magic, Lil has had five abortions, and Marie and the Hyacinth Girl live in a constant state of fear. In Part II, "A Game of Chess," the female speaker, Lil, is portrayed as neurotic and demanding, while the male speaker answers her prophetically:

> "Speak to me. Why do you never speak. Speak.
> "What are you thinking of? What thinking? What?
> "I never know what you are thinking. Think."
> I think we are in rats' alley
> Where the dead men lost their bones.[13]

Women in *The Waste Land* are used almost explicitly to juxtapose the male voice. According to literary critic Carol Christ, "Images of women are intimately connected with gender and voice."[14]

---

[8]Wool p. 43.

[9]Ibid., p. 22.

[10]Ibid., p. 28.

[11]Ibid., p. 26.

[12]Lyndall Gordon, *T.S. Eliot* (Cambridge, 1991), p. 11.

[13]Eliot, p. 37.

[14]Gordon, p. 36.

Gender and voice meet nowhere more clearly than in the character (or "spectator,"[15] as Eliot explained) of Tiresias. This mythological figure from Ovid is an old man with female breasts of whom Eliot said, ". . . so all women are one woman, and the two sexes meet. What Tiresias *sees* is, in fact, the substance of the poem."[16] What Tiresias sees is a sexual encounter between a typist and a clerk at tea time. The person the typist is waiting for is a pompous young man, "One for whom assurance sits / As a silk hat on a Bradford millionaire." While he attempts to seduce the young woman, he encounters only indifference from her. Tiresias says he has lived the same interaction, stating prophetically, "(And I Tiresias have foresuffered all / Enacted on this same divan or bed; I who have sat by Thebes below the wall / And walked among the lowest of the dead.)" At the end of the interaction, after her lover has departed, the typist says, "Well now that's done: and I'm glad it's over."

The cryptic characterization of Tiresias is significant on a number of levels. First, Tiresias is symbolic of England after the ruin of World War I. Eliot writes that Tiresias, "though blind, throbbing between two lives" is the great allegory of the poem. "Blind" refers to Britain's short-sightedness at the damages of the war. "Throbbing between two lives" is Europe, and the limbo its culture rests in. The gender issues in Tiresias are profound and multi-faceted. Tiresias, the true "seer" of the truth in the aftermath of World War I, is neither male more female, but an unproportional combination of the two. Is Eliot suggesting that women are auxiliary to men, and can only be the seers of truth and vision when attached to a male counterpart? The character is more male than female—he has only female breasts. Obviously there are sexual undertones in this section. Eliot could arguably be sexualizing the war, or using sex as a symbol for the passions of war. Sexualizing an extreme situation such as war is a definitively a male reaction. Although sexualization may be a temporary escape for the man or the artist, Eliot knows the true ramifications of war that left his beloved London changed forever.

The character of Septimus is the most parallel figure in *Mrs. Dalloway* to Tiresias. He is a periscope through which to see the truth of war. Septimus experiences flashbacks, or "shell-shock," as a result of the horrific suffering he witnessed during the war. He saw his close friend Evans killed in the trenches. While he was awarded for bravery, he still feels like a failure, and his shell-shock is wholly misunderstood by Sir William Bradshaw. Woolf wrote of Septimus:

> Gulled by the feverish rhetoric of nationalism, Septimus congested to sacrifice individual liberty to collective aggression. As a soldier in battle, he became a cog in the machinery of death and tacitly condoned the insanity of war. He returned from the inferno, like Lazarus, only to create his own private hell.[17]

Through Septimus, Woolf demonstrates how patriarchal society victimizes its subjects through false values. Prior to the War, Septimus was fighting the deeply embedded Victorian code of male gender roles. He was born a lover of Shakespeare, not a warrior. But upon his return from the trenches five years later, it was still impossible to return to normalcy. Woolf writes, "The War had taught him. It was sublime. He had gone through the whole show, friendship, European War, death, had won promotion . . . He was right there. The last shells met him. He watched them explode with indifference."[18] But life would never be the

---

[15]Eliot, p. 54.
[16]Ibid., p. 55.
[17]Suzette A. Henke, *New Feminist Essays on Virginia Woolf* (Lincoln, Nebraska, 1981), p. 139.
[18]Woolf, pp. 130–131.

same. Septimus cannot enjoy Shakespeare the way he used to because the war discredited all the beauty that gave his life meaning before. "Fire and flame" is the world Septimus now lives in—a vision of hell similar to Eliot's—and his only way of escaping is by throwing himself through a fifth floor window. Woolf communicates Septimus' suicide with the utmost respect and empathy. Clarissa understands his death as ". . . defiance. Death was an attempt to communicate."[19]

Woolf is just as empathetic to the female victims of war as she is to Septimus and the thousands of veterans like him. Her illumination of the sacrifices females made and what they lost in post-War society is unique and ahead of her time. Septimus' war-bride wife, Lucrezia, is an example of one way in which women, too, suffered from war. She leaves Italy and comes to a foreign land as a symbol of British conquest and victory. Septimus brought her home out of desperation. Woolf says he ". . . had married his wife without loving her; had lied to her; seduced her."[20] Lucrezia is lonely and unhappy, but Septimus is too saturated by his own issues to deal with hers. With the double whammy of being both a foreigner and a woman, Lucrezia has no one to turn to outside of her husband. Woolf's sensitivity to the other victims of war—those outside society's mainstream—proves her to have a rich, complex understanding to the exponential corollaries of war.[21]

Perhaps the most distinct difference between Woolf and Eliot's works is the tone each employs. While both demonstrate the cruelties of post-War Britain, Woolf's tone is more optimistic, empathetic, and softer than Eliot's. This is not to suggest that Woolf is less critical of the causes and effects of war than Eliot. But she shines her definitive, typical sense of life's irony and value through her words. Eliot is also compassionate, but he chooses to accentuate the culture clash and loss of innocence in London ("the nymphs are departed") and Europe at large rather than the individual lives of strangers. This divide between the two writers is a testimony to the impact of gender in perception.

Eliot is almost accusatory in his tone at times. He writes, for example, "What are the roots that clutch, what branches grow / Out of this stony rubbish? Son of man, / You cannot say, or guess, for you know only."[22] Eliot suggests that the truth is transcendental of humanity—it is somewhere out in the ether, just within reach but never realized. Woolf, oppositely, believes truth and goodness live within each person. At the end of the novel, most of the characters, Septimus and Clarissa included, reach peace with the day and with their lives. But in *The Waste Land,* there is no space for such redemption, even in the embrace of death Clarissa reveres. Eliot says, "He who has living is now dead / We who were living are now dying / With a little patience."[23]

Images of prisons resonate at the end of both pieces, but ironically add to the distinct tone each carries. In *Mrs. Dalloway,* Sally Seton comments:

> . . . for what can one know even of the lives with everyday? Are we not all prisoners? She had read a wonderful play about a man who scratched on the wall of his cell, and she felt that was true of life—one scratched on a wall. Despairing of human relationships (people were

---

[19]Ibid., pp. 280–281.

[20]Ibid., p. 137.

[21]Masami Usui, *Virginia Woolf and War: Fiction, Reality and Myth* (Syracuse, New York, 1991), pp. 156–157.

[22]Eliot, p. 33.

[23]Ibid., p. 47.

so difficult), she often went into her garden and got from her flowers a peace which men and women never gave her.[24]

To Woolf, prison is subjective and escapable. Truly, we are all prisoners, but freedom comes in precious, simple moments, daily. To Eliot, our human cells are tightly locked. He says, "I have heard the key / Turn in the door once and turn once only / We think of the key, each in his prison / Thinking of the key, each confirms a prison."[25] His tone suggests that our suffering is existential and unavoidable. Whereas Woolf writes with just as much optimism as realism, realism for Eliot is deeply ingrained in hardship. *The Waste Land* is much more esoteric and less humane than *Mrs. Dalloway.* As a marginalized person in society, Woolf ironically exudes more charisma and sanguinity than Eliot, one who lead a more advantaged life unconsciously.

In these two celebrated, groundbreaking pieces of literature, the connection between sorrow and the proliferation of gender is fascinating. Post-World War I London produced an arena for writers to make art both therapeutic and critical. Woolf and Eliot's works have left significant marks in all literary circles, and their language as become a part of the literary landscape. But Woolf's brilliant, prismatic insight into human experience could never be superseded. For those who have suffered understand the suffering of others. As a woman who lived in the cell of Victorianism and dodged the apparition of "the Angel in the House," Woolf's work transcends time and cultural shifts. She speaks not only to women but to all oppressed people. Through Clarissa, we find hope, and through Woolf we hear the key turn not once only but with every turn of the page.

---

[24]Woolf, pp. 293–294.

[25]Eliot, p. 50.

## *The Myths of Gender Suite*

In her essay "Cinderella: Saturday Afternoon at the Movies," Louise Bernikow writes about how, for her, watching Cinderella was like watching a woman in peril: "The girl onscreen, as I squirm in my seat, needs to be saved. A man will come and save her. Some day my prince will come. Women will not save her. They will thwart her." Bernikow goes on to argue that *Cinderella* teaches two bad lessons: that women are each other's enemies and that women need a man to save them.

■ ■ ■ Milton Berle as Cinderella.

Many writers agree with Bernikow. Indeed, scholars have argued that women's sense of men, other women, and themselves are shaped by powerful cultural myths that get replayed over and over in fairy tales and folktales. What's more, it is just as likely that men's notions of gender roles are influenced by these stories. Thus, reading (or being read) *Cinderella* and *Snow White* over and over again will probably make women feel as though they need to be saved. Additionally, it will probably also make men feel women need to be saved, and that may not be good for either gender.

In this suite, we have selected three different texts that explore myths and gender. The first two focus on cultural myths retold by the Disney Studios. "Construction of the Female Self: Feminist Readings of the Disney Heroine" is a traditional academic paper that traces the representation of women across five different Disney films and several decades. Jane Yolen's piece examines *Cinderella* in particular because she claims that Cinderella comes to represent *the* ideal American woman, that the film links female behavior and expectations with larger American values. There is no doubt, for instance, that the popularity of *Pretty Woman* among women is directly tied to the cultural power of *Cinderella* and similar myths.

Though each of these readings focuses on how myths have influenced women, we would like to urge you to think about how these myths alter how men see the world as well. This is especially the case in the piece by Maxine Hong Kingston. In her "talk story," Kingston uncovers the hidden rules governing female behavior in China. Through a mixture of literature, folklore and autobiography, Kingston tells a story about the relationship between gender and culture.

Ultimately, we are in control of how we see the world, but we should also understand that we are not always in control of the messages encoded in cultural texts. Our goal is that we all can become better readers of gender, regardless of the setting.

---

## CONSTRUCTION OF THE FEMALE SELF: FEMINIST READINGS OF THE DISNEY HEROINE

■ **Jill Birnie Henke, Diane Zimmerman Umble, Nancy J. Smith** ■

THIS ESSAY EXAMINES THE WAY in which the female self is constructed in five Disney films: *Cinderella, Sleeping Beauty, The Little Mermaid, Beauty and the Beast,* and *Pocahontas.* Standpoint feminist theory and feminist scholarship on the psychological development of the perfect girl are used to form questions about selfhood, relationships, power, and voice. Although heroines have expressed voice and selfhood in some of the later films, Disney's interpretations of children's literature and history remain those of a white, middle-class, patriarchal society.

Americans swim in a sea of Disney images and merchandise. Children can watch Disney videos before they brush their teeth with Disney character toothbrushes, go to sleep in *Beauty and the Beast* pajamas, rest their heads on *The Little Mermaid* pillow cases, check the time on *Pocahontas* watches, and drift off to sleep listening to Cinderella sing, "No matter how your heart is grieving, if you keep on believing, the dream that you wish will come true" on their tape recorders. American children and their families watch Disney stories over and over again courtesy of their home video recorders. The Disney corporation produces myriad texts that form part of the cultural experience of American children and adults. Not only does Disney create a "wonderful world" of images, but the corporation also makes money in the process.

Disney re-releases its animated features to theaters on a seven-year rotation as a marketing strategy to attract a following in each new generation (Landis, "Hibernation," p. 5D). Following theatrical showings, video cassettes are sold for a limited time. *Aladdin* earned $200 million in theaters in 1993, while its predecessor *Beauty and the Beast* grossed $20 million from the sale of videotapes alone (Landis, "Princely," p. 1D). This home video library provides families with opportunities for repeated viewing of such Disney films as *The Little Mermaid, Sleeping Beauty, Cinderella,* and *Pocahontas.*

This essay focuses on five animated features that span over fifty years of Disney storytelling and that portray a heroine as central to the story line: *Cinderella* (1950), *Sleeping Beauty* (1959), *The Little Mermaid* (1989), *Beauty and the Beast* (1991), and *Pocahontas* (1995).[1] In light of the ubiquity of Disney's images, sounds, and stories, we examine the kind of world the Disney corporation constructs through its animated feature films, specifically what it means to be young and female.

This project grew out of our own experiences as media consumers, teachers, scholars, and mothers of daughters. We began with the assumption that mass media articulates cultural values about gender by portraying women, men, and their relationships in particular ways. In addition, Julia Wood (1994) argues that the media also reproduces cultural definitions of gender by defining what is to be taken for granted. Disney stories, then, have become part of a cultural repertoire of ongoing performances and reproductions of gender roles by children and adults; moreover, these stories present powerful and sustained messages about gender and social relations. Because our analysis is shaped by conversations with our daughters and our students as they began to adopt a critical stance toward Disney texts, the analytical framework we apply to these films is based on a synthesis of two streams of feminist thought: the psychological development of females, and standpoint feminist theory. Together, the perspectives illuminate the meaning and implications of Disney's filmic portrayal of girls.

## The Oxymoron of Power and the Perfect Girl

Research by Carol Gilligan and her colleagues chronicles the psychological development of women's conceptualizations of the self. Gilligan (1982) argues that women learn to value connections with others and at least in part define themselves through their relationships with others. Orenstein (1994), who examines the related concern of how gender is constructed in the classroom, describes the hidden curriculum that teaches girls to view silence and compliance as virtues. Those values present a dilemma for bright girls who must simultaneously be "selfless and selfish, silent and outspoken, cooperative and competitive" (pp. 36–37). After studying white middle-class girls at all-girls schools, Brown and Gilligan (1992) suggest that the solution to this dilemma rests with females' invention of a self: the "perfect girl." The perfect girl, in white middle-class America, is "the girl who has no bad thoughts or feelings, the kind of person everyone wants to be with, the girl who, in her perfection, is worthy of praise and attention, worthy of inclusion and love. . . . [She is the] girl who speaks quietly, calmly, who is always nice and kind, never mean or bossy" (p. 59). Yet, these same girls know from their own experiences that people do get angry, wish to speak, and want to be heard. The consequence of these contradictory gender/social messages is that a girl is "caught between speaking what she knows from experience about relationships and increased pressure to negate this knowledge for an idealized and fraudulent view of herself and her relationships" (p. 61). Hence, Brown and Gilligan (1992) conclude that on the way to womanhood a girl experiences a loss of voice and loss of a sense of self as she silences herself.

During the process of this intellectual and emotional silencing, girls also are developing physically in new ways. According to Brown and Gilligan (1992), changes in girls' bodies "visually disconnect them from the world of childhood and identify them in the eyes of others with women" (p. 164). Girls conflate standards of beauty and standards of goodness by learning to pay attention to their "looks" and by listening to what others say about them. They learn to see themselves through the gaze of others, hear about themselves in ways that suggest they can be perfect, and believe that relationships can be free of conflict. These girls "struggle between knowing what they know through experience and what others want them to know, to feel and think" (p. 64). As a result, girls learn that speaking up can be disruptive and dangerous because it might put relationships at risk. The cruel irony is that by withholding their voices, girls also risk losing relationships that are genuine and authentic. In effect, girls struggle daily with the "seduction of the unattainable, to be all things to all people, to be perfect girls and model women" (p. 180).

Julia Wood's (1992) critique of Gilligan's line of research expands our application of Gilligan's work on the construction of the female self to Disney films. Wood explores the tension between Gilligan's apparently essentializing stance and a post-structural stance which emphasizes the structural effects of cultural life on individuals. The result is what Wood calls "standpoint epistemology."

"Standpoint theory prompts study of conditions that shape lives and the ways individuals construct those conditions and their experiences within them" (Wood, 1992, p. 15). For women, this theory helps explain how a female's position within a culture shapes her experiences. Because cultures define people by gender, race, and class, they often impose limits on women's experiences and women's ability to appreciate the experiences of others. Standpoint feminism argues that women have been and still are treated as "others" and "outsiders" in patriarchal societies. Although women's experiences are diverse to be sure, Wood (1992) argues that scholars should look for conditions among women that unify them. Oppression, for example, is one condition that seems universal among women: "Survival for those with subordinate status often depends quite literally on being able to read others, respond in ways that please others, and assume responsibility for others' comfort" (p. 16).

Yet, differences among women, as individuals and as members of identifiable categories within broadly shared social conditions, should not be overlooked. Our analysis of Disney characters responds to this call by articulating their similarities and their differences. Indeed, our analysis suggests that one value of standpoint feminist epistemology lies in unveiling which differences are conspicuously absent. For example, the heterosexist assumption underlying all five Disney films is not only the dominant social construct influencing relationships, it is the only social construct. None of the female figures questions that assumption. Standpoint theory, then, provides the means to understand how women's voices are muted and how women can regain their voices and become empowered (Wood, 1991).

Mary Parker Follett, an American intellectual whose ideas were touted by the business community in the 1940s, wrote about the construction and use of power in society in *Creative Experience* (1924). "Coercive power," Parker Follett wrote, "is the curse of the universe; coactive power, the enrichment of every human soul" (p. xii). In later works she defined two types of power—"power-over" and "power-with": "It seems to me that whereas power usually means power-over, the power of some person or group over some other person or group, it is possible to develop the conception of power-with, a jointly developed power, a co-active, not a coercive power" (1944, p. 101). While Parker Follett did not explicitly use the expression "power from within," this understanding is embedded in her discussion of the need for social constructs which preserve the integrity of the individual. She argues that a society can only progress if individuals' internal needs are met in the processes adopted by the group.

Parker Follett's conceptualization of power, in conjunction with the principles contained in standpoint feminist theory and Gilligan's perspective on the psychological development of girls, forms the foundation for a series of questions that the following analysis of Disney's animated films hopes to answer: How do the worlds of Disney films construct the heroine's sense of self? To what degree is her self-knowledge related to or in response to her relationships with others? Do Disney heroines model the "perfect girl"? On the way to womanhood, what does the Disney heroine give up? What are the ways in which the female characters experience their lives as "others" and themselves as strangers in their relationship to self and others? And what are the power dynamics of those relationships?

Until the recent publication of *From Mouse to Mermaid: The Politics of Film, Gender, and Culture* (Bell, Haas, & Sells, 1995), few scholarly analyses addressed the foregoing questions about gender constructions in the worlds of Disney animated films.[2] However, with the Bell, Haas, and Sells' edition, critical analyses of Disney discourses entered a new phase. This edited collection maps "the ideological contours of economics, politics, and pedagogy by drawing Disney films as vehicles of cultural production" (p. 7). Within this ideological map, the cultural reproduction of gender is examined by several authors.

For example, Jack Zipes (1995) argues that characterizations of Disney heroines remain one-dimensional and stereotypical, "arranged according to a credo of domestication of the imagination" (p. 40). The values imparted in Disney fairy tales are not those of original folk tellers, nor of the original writers such as Perrault or Andersen; instead, they are the values of Disney's male writers. Thus, even when the fairy tale is supposed to focus on the heroine (Snow White, Cinderella, Sleeping Beauty, Beauty, or the Little Mermaid), "these figures are pale and pathetic compared to the more active and demonic characters in the film" (p. 37). These alleged heroines are "helpless ornaments in need of protection, and when it comes to the action of the film, they are omitted" (p. 37). In contrast, while Laura Sells' (1995) Marxist feminist analysis of *The Little Mermaid* sees the story's resolution as a "dangerous message about appropriation" (p. 185), Sells remains hopeful nevertheless because "Ariel enters the white male system with her voice—a stolen, flying voice that erupted amidst patriarchal language, a voice no longer innocent because it resided for a time in the dark continent that is the Medusa's home" (p. 185).

Our analysis elaborates upon the two themes that Zipes and Sells introduce: the relative power or powerlessness of the Disney heroine, and the discovery or loss of that heroine's voice. Thus, our exploration of the construction of the female self and the interaction of that self with other film characters corroborates and extends the work of Bell, Haas, and Sells. We utilize standpoint feminist theory, Follett's theories of power, and Gilligan and Brown's theories of female psychological development to chronicle the nature and evolution of Disney's construction of the female self.

## Construction of the Female Self

Disney's early heroines, Cinderella and Aurora, are portrayed as helpless, passive victims who need protection. Indeed, Cinderella is the quintessential "perfect girl," always gentle, kind, and lovely. Their weaknesses are contrasted with the awesome and awful power of the evil women with whom they struggle. However, later Disney films shift from simple stories of passive, young virgins in conflict with evil, mature women to more complex narratives about rebellion, exploration, and danger. Heroines Ariel, Belle, and Pocahontas display an increasingly stronger sense of self, of choice, and of voice.

This growing empowerment of Disney heroines is reflected in shifting depictions of their intimate relationships. While early heroines fall in love at first sight and easily marry to live happily ever after, love relationships for the later heroines come at a cost. Ariel temporarily gives up her voice and ultimately relinquishes her cultural identity. Belle discovers love only through trials, sacrifice, and learning to look beneath the surface. Ultimately, though, her love releases the Beast from the bonds of his own selfishness so they, too, are "empowered" to live happily ever after together.

Of all of Disney's characters, Pocahontas seems to break new ground. The narrative begins with her as a young woman in possession of a strong, well-developed sense of self, and a conviction that her destiny only remains to be discovered. Unlike other Disney heroines, she resists losing her identity to another for the sake of a marriage relationship. Her position and value in her community, her relationships with other females, and her understanding of her interdependence with the earth provide the most holistic picture yet of a co-actively empowered character in Disney animated films.

In her classic essay, "The Solitude of Self," Elizabeth Cady Stanton (1892) advanced a feminist vision in which women experience the sovereignty of the self, and women and girls are empowered from within. Stanton indicted patriarchy for systematically denying women the skills and rights to exist as sovereign selves. Over a century later, feminists still envision a diversity of female figures acting on the world from knowledge of their own worth and dreams. Are traces of these visions contained in Disney's filmic heroines?

The five films we examine situate the central female character—who is portrayed as gentle, kind, beautiful, and virginal—in an oppressive social milieu where mothers or other sources of female guidance and wisdom are largely absent. Until *Pocahontas*, in fact, these young heroines faced the challenges of their lives without the benefit of other women's support, nurturance, or guidance.

Cinderella, Aurora, Ariel, Belle, and Pocahontas also share another quality: they all have dreams. Each differs, however, in her power to make that dream come true. The conventional Disney tale introduces the heroine near the film's beginning through a song in which she expresses these dreams. For example, viewers first meet Cinderella when she awakens from a dream and sings, "No matter how your heart is grieving, if you keep on believing, the dream that you wish will come true." Minutes later, viewers discover that her daily reality is anything but dreamy. Supported by an army of mice and barnyard animals who come to her aid, Cinderella is continuously reminded by humans in the household that she is unworthy of their "refined" company. Cinderella's stepmother and stepsisters control Cinderella, keeping her locked away from both society and opportunity. Cinderella is portrayed as powerless to act on her own behalf. Hence, she can only dream.

Perhaps Cinderella best illustrates the Disney pattern of subjugating and stifling heroines' voices and selfhood. Her gentleness and goodness are defined by her lack of resistance to abuse by her stepfamily in the film's world. She never disobeys an order, never defends her rights, and never challenges their authority over her. She rarely eats, seldom sleeps, and receives not even the simplest of courtesies, except from her animal friends. Her father's fortune is squandered for the benefit of her stepsisters. She is powerless to control her own fate in her own home. Unable to control her own time, she also is unable to control her own destiny. Cinderella does not act, she only reacts to those around her, a sure sign of both external and internalized oppression. In the face of all this abuse, she somehow remains gentle, kind and beautiful—the perfect girl.

Similarly, *Sleeping Beauty*'s Aurora is a playful teenager whose friends are forest animals, and whose dream is expressed in the song "Some day my prince will come." Aurora is on the verge of celebrating her sixteenth birthday—the day her identity will be revealed to her. At this point she has no knowledge that she really is a princess who was betrothed at birth. Her parents' choices for her define Aurora's destiny and she has no voice in shaping that destiny.

Like Cinderella, Aurora is obedient, beautiful, acquiescent to authority, and essentially powerless in matters regarding her own fate. Furthermore, there is no one Aurora can trust. Although the fairies "protect" her from the truth about her identity and the curse on her future "for her own good," Aurora can take no action on her own behalf. Passively, she is brought back to the castle where she falls under the spell of Maleficent, touches the spinning wheel, and sleeps through most of the film while others battle to decide her future. When she awakens, she finds her "dream come true," a tall, handsome prince who rescues her from an evil female's curse.

Beginning with *The Little Mermaid*, however, the female protagonist shows signs of selfhood. Near the beginning of the film, Ariel sings of her dream to explore and her feelings of being misunderstood. She also expresses frustration and resistance: "Betcha on land they understand. Bet they don't reprimand their daughters. Bright young women, sick of swimmin', ready to stand." She asks, "When's it my turn?"

In contrast to the two previous demure female protagonists, Ariel is characterized as willful and disobedient. She follows her dreams even though she knows her actions run counter to the wishes of her father, King Triton. As a result, Triton charges the crab, Sebastian, with chaperoning his daughter "to protect her from herself." One might also read his actions as patriarchy's efforts to prevent her from achieving an independent identity. However, despite Triton's efforts to control Ariel, she explores, she asks questions, she makes choices, and she acts. For example, she rescues the human, Prince Eric, from the sea. She strikes a bargain with the sea witch, Ursula, to trade her voice for legs. Additionally, she prevents Eric's marriage to Ursula and protects him from Ursula's attack in the film's final battle. Nevertheless, it is Eric who finally kills the sea witch and it is Triton whose power enables Ariel to return to the human world by transforming her permanently into a human. Thus, while Ariel chooses to leave her own people for a life with Eric, it is still not her power but her father's power which enables her dreams to come to fruition.

Articulating one's own dreams and wishes—possessing an autonomous voice—is a strong indicator of the development of selfhood. Little wonder, then, that alarms sound for feminists concerned with the psychological development of girls and women's sense of self when Ariel literally sacrifices her voice and mermaid body to win Eric's love. What is gained by females who silence themselves in a masculinist society? What are the costs to their psychic selves for not doing so? Scholars in feminist psychological development describe the seductiveness of external rewards by denying one's selfhood (Brown & Gilligan, 1992). Having a voice, a sense of selfhood, is risky because it is inconsistent with images of the "perfect girl" or the true woman. When one's loyalty is not to the "masculinist system," one can end up on the margins at best and at worst socially "dead." Ultimately, Ariel's voice is silenced and she sacrifices her curiosity to gain the love of a man.

Reality for Belle in *Beauty and the Beast* means being female and wanting to experience adventure in the "great wide somewhere." Like the earlier Disney heroines, Belle dreams of having "so much more than they've got planned." Belle is the first of the Disney heroines to read, but her reading also alienates her from others in the community. She experiences herself as an "other." Townspeople call her peculiar and say that "she doesn't quite fit in." While Belle is aware of their opinions of her, and understands that she is supposed to marry a villager, raise a family, and conform, she also knows that she *is* different and *wants* something different—something "grand." Although Belle is unsure about how to attain her dreams, she does refuse to marry Gaston, the community "hunk" and its most eligible bachelor. She reads rather than socialize with the villagers, and she accepts that she can be nothing other than different from them. Belle likes herself and trusts her own judgment. Nevertheless, Belle is marginalized by the community for her uniqueness, for her sense of self.

Unlike her counterparts in *Cinderella* and *Sleeping Beauty*, Belle is no damsel in distress. Neither is she a helpless witness to the film's action nor removed from it. Belle occupies double the screen time of any other character in the film (Thomas, 1991), and Belle acts for herself. She dreams of more than a "provincial life"; she wants adventure and, as she sings, "for once it might be grand, to have someone understand, I want so much more than they've got planned." The line might have continued, "for a girl!"

Gaston, the village brute, is attracted to Belle because of her appearance not her brain. He sings that she's "the most beautiful, so that makes her the best." He offers her a place in the community with his marriage proposal. While other women swoon for his attention, Belle rejects him: "His little wife. No, sir. Not me!" Belle's sense of self is strong enough that she refuses to settle for less than a relationship which acknowledges and values her mind, in essence, her self. However, when her father is captured by the Beast, Belle comes to his rescue and offers herself in his place. By trading her life for her father's, she seems to have relinquished her selfhood. Once a prisoner in the Beast's castle, she laments to Mrs. Potts, a kind teapot, that she has lost her father, her dreams, "everything." However, this lament suggests that she still has dreams of her own and a sense of identity apart from that of a dutiful daughter.

Belle's dilemma occurs in part because she has a caring, co-active power relationship with her father (Parker Follett, 1944). Decision making undertaken by women who attempt to maintain selfhood but also exist in a power-with relation to others becomes much more complex, as Gilligan (1977) notes. This complexity is further illustrated by the choices that Belle subsequently makes in her relationship with the Beast. Belle negotiates the conflict she feels between freedom from the Beast and her growing affection for him. She decides not to leave him in the woods after he rescues her from wolves. Although she could escape, she chooses to help him instead. Later in the film, she again chooses to return to the Beast's castle to warn him of the impending mob, even though the Beast has released her from her promise to stay in his castle.

Like Ariel, Belle has freedom to make choices and to act on her own behalf as well as on the behalf of others; and she exercises that freedom. However, whereas Ariel at least initially seems to act out of a sense of rebellion, Belle's motivation appears to come from a craving for intellectual engagement. A simple masculinist interpretation might be that Belle acts out of a sense of personal honor or duty (to sacrifice her freedom first to help her father and later to keep the Beast). A more feminist interpretation based on Gilligan's psychoanalytic developmental work and standpoint theory might be that Belle acts as a result of the tension from seeking selfhood and relationships with others simultaneously. Thus, Belle's actions can be read as a series of complex decisions about when to act, and when to care for someone, how to administer comfort, when to take matters into her own hands, when to risk her personal safety. She is concerned not only with others but with herself as well, and her actions speak to both needs.

No victim, Belle sets the terms for the bargains she makes. In this sense, she exercises more power on her own behalf than previous Disney heroines. For Cinderella, Aurora, and Ariel, someone in power established the conditions within which their dreams could be realized. For example, Cinderella's fairy godmother gave her only until midnight to make her dream come true. At Aurora's christening, the good fairy Merryweather saved Aurora from Maleficent's death curse by decreeing that Aurora would sleep until awakened by a prince's kiss. And when Ariel gave her voice to Ursula in return for the sea witch's magical ability to transform Ariel into a human, Ursula placed a three day time limit on Ariel's pursuit to win Eric's love. Unlike Belle, these females have limited and tenuous opportunities to achieve their dreams. In contrast, Belle exercises substantial control over setting the terms of her own fate. She preserves her own options—by refusing Gaston's overtures and brushing off the villagers' criticisms, and she gives others options—by freeing her father from the Beast's prison, becoming a prisoner herself, and saving the Beast from the wolves. *She* holds *their* futures in her hands. Yet, ironically, one reading of the narrative conclusion is that Belle's liberation of the Beast from his spell ends with her becoming yet another "perfect girl" who marries the prince and lives happily ever after.

Another theme introduced in *Beauty and the Beast*—heroine as teacher—is expanded in *Pocahontas*. Just as Belle teaches the Beast how to be civil, gentle, and caring, Pocahontas teaches John Smith, her tribe, and the Englishmen about nature, power, and peace. Like Belle, Pocahontas exercises power over her future. Viewers first are introduced to Pocahontas going where the wind (the spirit of her mother) leads her; as the chief's daughter, however, she knows that she must take "her place" among her people. Her father tells her, "Even the wild mountain stream must someday join the big river." She sings, "We must all pay a price. To be safe, we lose our chance of ever knowing what's around the river bend. . . . Why do all my dreams stand just around the river bend. . . . Is all my dreaming at an end?"

Like Ariel, Pocahontas defies her father in exploring her world. Like Belle, she is an active doer, not a passive victim. She also has a savage to tame in the form of an Englishman. Pocahontas introduces John Smith to the colors of the wind and to the mysteries of the world of nature. She takes political stances such as advocating alternatives to violence, and she makes choices about her life. For example, Pocahontas' decision to reject both her father's wish that she marry Kocoum, the Powhatan warrior, and John Smith's plea to go with him back to England signify that the power to control her actions is in her hands. Pocahontas' choices reflect a sense of selfhood that is a bold stroke for a Disney heroine. A feminist psychological reading might see in her decision to embrace her cultural roots an alternative to Disney's typical

It is little wonder, then, that Cinderella should be a perennial favorite in the American folktale pantheon.

Yet how ironic that this formula should be the terms on which "Cinderella" is acceptable to most Americans. "Cinderella" is *not* a story of rags to riches, but rather riches recovered; *not* poor girl into princess but rather rich girl (or princess) rescued from improper or wicked enslavement; *not* suffering Griselda enduring but shrewd and practical girl persevering and winning a share of the power. It is really a story that is about "the stripping away of the disguise that conceals the soul from the eyes of others. . . ."[1]

We Americans have it wrong. "Rumpelstiltskin," in which a miller tells a whopping lie and his docile daughter acquiesces in it to become queen, would be more to the point.

But we have been initially seduced by the Perrault cinder-girl, who was, after all, the transfigured folk creature of a French literary courtier. Perrault's "Cendrillon" demonstrated the well-bred seventeenth-century female traits of gentility, grace, and selflessness, even to the point of graciously forgiving her wicked stepsisters and finding them noble husbands.

The American "Cinderella" is partially Perrault's. The rest is a spun-sugar caricature of her hardier European and Oriental forbears, who made their own way in the world, tricking the stepsisters with double-talk, artfully disguising themselves, or figuring out a way to win the king's son. The final bit of icing on the American Cinderella was concocted by that master candy-maker, Walt Disney, in the 1950s. Since then, America's Cinderella has been a coy, helpless dreamer, a "nice" girl who awaits her rescue with patience and a song. This Cinderella of the mass market books finds her way into a majority of American homes while the classic heroines sit unread in old volumes on library shelves.

Poor Cinderella. She has been unjustly distorted by storytellers, misunderstood by educators, and wrongly accused by feminists. Even as late as 1975, in the well-received volume *Womenfolk and Fairy Tales,* Rosemary Minard writes that Cinderella "would still be scrubbing floors if it were not for her fairy godmother." And Ms. Minard includes her in a sweeping condemnation of folk heroines as "insipid beauties waiting passively for Prince Charming."[2]

Like many dialecticians, Ms. Minard reads the fairy tales incorrectly. Believing—rightly—that the fairy tales, as all stories for children, acculturate young readers and listeners, she has nevertheless gotten her target wrong. Cinderella is not to blame. Not the real, the true Cinderella. Ms. Minard should focus her sights on the mass-market Cinderella. She does not recognize the old Ash-girl[3] for the tough, resilient heroine. The wrong Cinderella has gone to the American ball.

The story of Cinderella has endured for over a thousand years, surfacing in a literary source first in ninth-century China.[4] It has been found from the Orient to the interior of South America and over five hundred variants have been located by folklorists in Europe alone. This best-beloved tale has been brought to life over and over and no one can say for sure where the oral tradition began. The European story was included by Charles Perrault in his 1697 collection *Histoires ou Contes du temps passé* as "Cendrillon." But even before that, the Italian Straparola had a similar story in a collection. Since there had been twelve editions of the Straparola book printed in French before 1694, the chances are strong that Perrault had read the tale "*Peau d'Ane*" (Donkey Skin).[5]

Joseph Jacobs, the indefatigable Victorian collector, once said of a Cinderella story he printed that it was "an English version of an Italian adaption of a Spanish translation of a Latin version of a Hebrew translation of an Arabic translation of an Indian original."[6]

It is little wonder, then, that Cinderella should be a perennial favorite in the American folktale pantheon.

Yet how ironic that this formula should be the terms on which "Cinderella" is acceptable to most Americans. "Cinderella" is *not* a story of rags to riches, but rather riches recovered; *not* poor girl into princess but rather rich girl (or princess) rescued from improper or wicked enslavement; *not* suffering Griselda enduring but shrewd and practical girl persevering and winning a share of the power. It is really a story that is about "the stripping away of the disguise that conceals the soul from the eyes of others. . . ."[1]

We Americans have it wrong. "Rumpelstiltskin," in which a miller tells a whopping lie and his docile daughter acquiesces in it to become queen, would be more to the point.

But we have been initially seduced by the Perrault cinder-girl, who was, after all, the transfigured folk creature of a French literary courtier. Perrault's "Cendrillon" demonstrated the well-bred seventeenth-century female traits of gentility, grace, and selflessness, even to the point of graciously forgiving her wicked stepsisters and finding them noble husbands.

The American "Cinderella" is partially Perrault's. The rest is a spun-sugar caricature of her hardier European and Oriental forbears, who made their own way in the world, tricking the stepsisters with double-talk, artfully disguising themselves, or figuring out a way to win the king's son. The final bit of icing on the American Cinderella was concocted by that master candy-maker, Walt Disney, in the 1950s. Since then, America's Cinderella has been a coy, helpless dreamer, a "nice" girl who awaits her rescue with patience and a song. This Cinderella of the mass market books finds her way into a majority of American homes while the classic heroines sit unread in old volumes on library shelves.

Poor Cinderella. She has been unjustly distorted by storytellers, misunderstood by educators, and wrongly accused by feminists. Even as late as 1975, in the well-received volume *Womenfolk and Fairy Tales,* Rosemary Minard writes that Cinderella "would still be scrubbing floors if it were not for her fairy godmother." And Ms. Minard includes her in a sweeping condemnation of folk heroines as "insipid beauties waiting passively for Prince Charming."[2]

Like many dialecticians, Ms. Minard reads the fairy tales incorrectly. Believing—rightly—that the fairy tales, as all stories for children, acculturate young readers and listeners, she has nevertheless gotten her target wrong. Cinderella is not to blame. Not the real, the true Cinderella. Ms. Minard should focus her sights on the mass-market Cinderella. She does not recognize the old Ash-girl[3] for the tough, resilient heroine. The wrong Cinderella has gone to the American ball.

The story of Cinderella has endured for over a thousand years, surfacing in a literary source first in ninth-century China.[4] It has been found from the Orient to the interior of South America and over five hundred variants have been located by folklorists in Europe alone. This best-beloved tale has been brought to life over and over and no one can say for sure where the oral tradition began. The European story was included by Charles Perrault in his 1697 collection *Histories ou Contes du temps passé* as "Cendrillon." But even before that, the Italian Straparola had a similar story in a collection. Since there had been twelve editions of the Straparola book printed in French before 1694, the chances are strong that Perrault had read the tale "*Peau d'Ane*" (Donkey Skin).[5]

Joseph Jacobs, the indefatigable Victorian collector, once said of a Cinderella story he printed that it was "an English version of an Italian adaption of a Spanish translation of a Latin version of a Hebrew translation of an Arabic translation of an Indian original."[6]

Brody, M. (1976). The wonderful world of Disney—Its psychological appeal. *American Image, 33,* 350–360.

Brown, L., & Gilligan, G. (1992). *Meeting at the crossroads: Women's psychology and girl's development.* Cambridge, MA: Harvard University Press.

Collins, P. (1986). Learning from the outsider within. *Social Problems, 33,* 514–532.

Follett, M. (1924). *Creative experience.* New York: Longmans, Green.

Follett, M., Metcalf, H., & Urwick, L. (Eds.). (1944). *Dynamic administration: The collected papers of Mary Parker Follett.* New York: Harper.

Gilligan, C. (1982). *In a different voice: Psychological theory and women's development.* Cambridge, MA: Harvard University Press.

Gilligan, C. (1977). In a different voice: Women's conceptions of self and of morality. *Harvard Educational Review, 47,* 481–517.

Harding, S. (1991). *Whose science? Whose knowledge? Thinking from women's lives.* Ithaca, NY: Cornell University Press.

Holmlund, C. (Summer, 1979). Tots to tanks: Walt Disney presents feminism for the family. *Social Text,* 122–132.

Landis, D. (9 February 1993). Disney classics go into hibernation. *USA Today,* p. 5D.

Landis, D. (28 September 1993). Princely predictions for "Aladdin" video. *USA Today,* p. 1D.

Levinson, R. (1975). From Olive Oyl to Sweet Polly Purebread: Sex role stereotypes and televised cartoons. *Journal of Popular Culture, 9,* 561–572.

May, J. (1981). Walt Disney's interpretation of children's literature. *Language Arts, 4,* 463–472.

Morrow, J. (1978). In defense of Disney. *Media and Methods, 14,* 28–34.

Murphy, P. (1995). The whole wide world was scrubbed clean: The androcentric animation of denatured Disney. In E. Bell, L. Haas, & L. Sells (Eds.), *From mouse to mermaid: The politics of film, gender, and culture* (pp. 125–136). Indianapolis, IN: Indiana University Press.

Orenstein, P. (1994). *School girls.* New York: Anchor Books, Doubleday.

Rich, A. (1986). *Of woman born: Motherhood as experience and institution.* New York: W.W. Norton & Co.

Sells, L. (1995). Where do the mermaids stand?: Voice and body in "The Little Mermaid." In E. Bell, L. Haas, & L. Sells (Eds.), *From mouse to mermaid: The politics of film, gender, and culture* (pp. 175–192). Indianapolis, IN: Indiana University Press.

Stanton, E. (1892). Solitude of self. Convention of National American Suffrage Association. Washington, D.C.

Stone, K. (1975). Things Walt Disney never told us. *Journal of American Folklore, 88,* 42–50.

Thomas, B. (1991). *Art of animation: From Mickey Mouse to Beauty and the Beast.* New York: Hyperion.

Trites, R. (1991). Disney's sub/version of Andersen's "The Little Mermaid." *Journal of Popular Film and Television, 18,* 145–152.

Wood, J. (1992). Gender and moral voice: Moving from women's nature to standpoint epistemology. *Women's Studies in Communication, 16,* 1–24.

Wood, J. (1994). *Gendered lives: Communication, gender, and culture.* Belmont, CA: Wadsworth.

Zipes, J. (1995). Breaking the Disney spell. In E. Bell, L. Haas, & L. Sells (Eds.), *From mouse to mermaid: The politics of film, gender, and culture* (pp. 21–42). Indianapolis, IN: Indiana University Press.

## AMERICA'S CINDERELLA

■ Jane Yolen ■

IT IS PART OF THE AMERICAN CREED, recited subvocally along with the pledge of allegiance in each classroom, that even a poor boy can grow up to become president. The unliberated corollary is that even a poor girl can grow up and become the president's wife. This rags-to-riches formula was immortalized in American children's fiction by the Horatio Alger stories of the 1860s and by the Pluck and Luck nickel novels of the 1920s.

heterosexual narratives in which the "perfect girl's" destiny is a monogamous relationship with a (white) man. Indeed, far more than Belle, Pocahontas finds power within to express a self which is separate from that defined through relationships to a father or love interest.

Our reading of Pocahontas implies that she is clearly the most elaborate and complex character in this group of heroines. Her dreams direct her choices. She weighs the risks of choosing a smooth course versus seeking the unknown course to see what awaits her just around the river bend. With counsel from female mentors, Grandmother Willow and the spirit of the wind that symbolizes her mother, Pocahontas finds the strength to listen to her own inner voice, and to choose the less safe, uncharted course of autonomous womanhood. When confronted with the option of leaving her community in order to accompany her love interest, John Smith, she rejects his offer and instead takes her place as an unattached female leader of her people.

Pocahontas brings to the forefront the absence of diversity among Disney's previous female characters. From Cinderella through Belle, Disney's female protagonists easily could be the same characters with only slight variations in hair color. Pocahontas, too, varies only slightly in skin color, but she is the first non-Anglo heroine who is the subject of a Disney animated film. Furthermore, although some of the women may not have difficult family circumstances (e.g., Cinderella), as Caucasians, they all belong to the privileged class in their societies, as daughters of kings, Indian chiefs, and educated inventors.

As this examination of Cinderella, Aurora, Ariel, Belle, and Pocahontas demonstrates, over time Disney's female protagonists have begun to look beyond home, to practice resistance to coercion, and to find their own unique female voices. Indeed, in Pocahontas Disney offers an adventurous female who develops a sense of self in a culture other than the dominant Anglo culture, and who chooses a destiny other than that of heterosexual romantic fulfillment.

### Notes

1. When we first began our study of the Disney animated heroines, *Snow White* had not been released on video nor re-released in the theaters, so it was not included among the films we analyzed. However, the themes introduced in the two earliest films, *Cinderella* and *Sleeping Beauty*, were also present in *Snow White*. We did not include *Aladdin* because the story really centers around the boy, Aladdin, whereas Princess Jasmine is cast in a secondary role and commands little screen time. Princess Jasmine is important, however, in that she is Disney's first non-Caucasian princess.

2. Brody (1976) describes the success of Disney fairy tales from a psychoanalytic perspective. Trites (1991) contrasts Disney's version of *The Little Mermaid* with the original Hans Christian Andersen tale from a Freudian perspective. Other analysts (May, 1981; Stone, 1975) critique the way in which Disney selectively appropriates classics of children's literature. Sex role stereotyping is the focus of work by Levinson (1975) and Holmlund (1979). They extend concerns about stereotyping using a Marxist feminist approach to the sexual politics of Disney films. Some work has celebrated the Disney tradition for its connections with the oral tradition (Allan, 1988) and its artistic accomplishments (Morrow, 1978).

### References

Allen, R. (1988). Fifty years of Snow White. *Journal of Popular Film and Television, 15,* 156–163.

Bell, E., Haas, L., & Sells, L. (Eds.). (1995). *From mouse to mermaid: The politics of film, gender, and culture.* Bloomington, IN: Indiana University Press.

Like Ariel, Belle has freedom to make choices and to act on her own behalf as well as on the behalf of others; and she exercises that freedom. However, whereas Ariel at least initially seems to act out of a sense of rebellion, Belle's motivation appears to come from a craving for intellectual engagement. A simple masculinist interpretation might be that Belle acts out of a sense of personal honor or duty (to sacrifice her freedom first to help her father and later to keep the Beast). A more feminist interpretation based on Gilligan's psychoanalytic developmental work and standpoint theory might be that Belle acts as a result of the tension from seeking selfhood and relationships with others simultaneously. Thus, Belle's actions can be read as a series of complex decisions about when to act, and when to care for someone, how to administer comfort, when to take matters into her own hands, when to risk her personal safety. She is concerned not only with others but with herself as well, and her actions speak to both needs.

No victim, Belle sets the terms for the bargains she makes. In this sense, she exercises more power on her own behalf than previous Disney heroines. For Cinderella, Aurora, and Ariel, someone in power established the conditions within which their dreams could be realized. For example, Cinderella's fairy godmother gave her only until midnight to make her dream come true. At Aurora's christening, the good fairy Merryweather saved Aurora from Maleficent's death curse by decreeing that Aurora would sleep until awakened by a prince's kiss. And when Ariel gave her voice to Ursula in return for the sea witch's magical ability to transform Ariel into a human, Ursula placed a three day time limit on Ariel's pursuit to win Eric's love. Unlike Belle, these females have limited and tenuous opportunities to achieve their dreams. In contrast, Belle exercises substantial control over setting the terms of her own fate. She preserves her own options—by refusing Gaston's overtures and brushing off the villagers' criticisms, and she gives others options—by freeing her father from the Beast's prison, becoming a prisoner herself, and saving the Beast from the wolves. *She* holds *their* futures in her hands. Yet, ironically, one reading of the narrative conclusion is that Belle's liberation of the Beast from his spell ends with her becoming yet another "perfect girl" who marries the prince and lives happily ever after.

Another theme introduced in *Beauty and the Beast*—heroine as teacher—is expanded in *Pocahontas.* Just as Belle teaches the Beast how to be civil, gentle, and caring, Pocahontas teaches John Smith, her tribe, and the Englishmen about nature, power, and peace. Like Belle, Pocahontas exercises power over her future. Viewers first are introduced to Pocahontas going where the wind (the spirit of her mother) leads her; as the chief's daughter, however, she knows that she must take "her place" among her people. Her father tells her, "Even the wild mountain stream must someday join the big river." She sings, "We must all pay a price. To be safe, we lose our chance of ever knowing what's around the river bend. . . . Why do all my dreams stand just around the river bend. . . . Is all my dreaming at an end?"

Like Ariel, Pocahontas defies her father in exploring her world. Like Belle, she is an active doer, not a passive victim. She also has a savage to tame in the form of an Englishman. Pocahontas introduces John Smith to the colors of the wind and to the mysteries of the world of nature. She takes political stances such as advocating alternatives to violence, and she makes choices about her life. For example, Pocahontas' decision to reject both her father's wish that she marry Kocoum, the Powhatan warrior, and John Smith's plea to go with him back to England signify that the power to control her actions is in her hands. Pocahontas' choices reflect a sense of selfhood that is a bold stroke for a Disney heroine. A feminist psychological reading might see in her decision to embrace her cultural roots an alternative to Disney's typical room to room. The immigrants I know have loud voices, unmodulated to American tones even after years away from the village where they called their friendships out across the fields. I have not been able to stop my mother's screams in public libraries or over telephones. Walking erect (knees straight, toes pointed forward, not pigeon-toed, which is Chinese-feminine) and speaking in an inaudible voice, I have tried to turn myself American-feminine. Chinese communication was loud, public. Only sick people had to whisper. But at the dinner table, where the family members came nearest one another, no one could talk, not the outcasts nor any eaters. Every word that falls from the mouth is a coin lost. Silently they gave and accepted food with both hands. A preoccupied child who took his bowl with one hand got a sideways glare. A complete moment of total attention is due everyone alike. Children and lovers have no singularity here, but my aunt used a secret voice, a separate attentiveness.

She kept the man's name to herself throughout her labor and dying; she did not accuse him that he be punished with her. To save her inseminator's name she gave silent birth.

He may have been somebody in her own household, but intercourse with a man outside the family would have been no less abhorrent. All the village were kinsmen, and the titles shouted in loud country voices never let kinship be forgotten. Any man within visiting distance would have been neutralized as a lover—"brother," "younger brother," "older brother"—one hundred and fifteen relationship titles. Parents researched birth charts probably not so much to assure good fortune as to circumvent incest in a population that has but one hundred surnames. Everybody has eight million relatives. How useless then sexual mannerisms, how dangerous.

As if it came from an atavism deeper than fear, I used to add "brother" silently to boys' names. It hexed the boys, who would or would not ask me to dance, and made them less scary and as familiar and deserving of benevolence as girls.

But, of course, I hexed myself also—no dates. I should have stood up, both arms waving, and shouted out across libraries, "Hey, you! Love me back." I had no idea, though, how to make attraction selective, how to control its direction and magnitude. If I made myself American-pretty so that the five or six Chinese boys in the class fell in love with me, everyone else—the Caucasian, Negro, and Japanese boys—would too. Sisterliness, dignified and honorable, made much more sense.

Attraction eludes control so stubbornly that whole societies designed to organize relationships among people cannot keep order, not even when they bind people to one another from childhood and raise them together. Among the very poor and the wealthy, brothers married their adopted sisters, like doves. Our family allowed some romance, paying adult brides' prices and providing dowries so that their sons and daughters could marry strangers. Marriage promises to turn strangers into friendly relatives—a nation of siblings.

In the village structure, spirits shimmered among the live creatures, balanced and held in equilibrium by time and land. But one human being flaring up into violence could open up a black hole, a maelstrom that pulled in the sky. The frightened villagers, who depended on one another to maintain the real, went to my aunt to show her a personal, physical representation of the break she had made in the "roundness." Misallying couples snapped off the future, which was to be embodied in true offspring. The villagers punished her for acting as if she could have a private life, secret and apart from them.

If my aunt had betrayed the family at a time of large grain yields and peace, when many boys were born, and wings were being built on many houses, perhaps she might have escaped such severe punishment. But the men—hungry, greedy, tired of planting in dry soil—

had been forced to leave the village in order to send food-money home. There were ghost plagues, bandit plagues, wars with the Japanese, floods. My Chinese brother and sister had died of an unknown sickness. Adultery, perhaps only a mistake during good times, became a crime when the village needed food.

The round moon cakes and round doorways, the round tables of graduated sizes that fit one roundness inside another, round windows and rice bowls—these talismans had lost their power to warn this family of the law: a family must be whole, faithfully keeping the descent line by having sons to feed the old and the dead, who in turn look after the family. The villagers came to show my aunt and her lover-in-hiding a broken house. The villagers were speeding up the circling of events because she was too shortsighted to see that her infidelity had already harmed the village, that waves of consequences would return unpredictably, sometimes in disguise, as now, to hurt her. This roundness had to be made coin-sized so that she would see its circumference: punish her at the birth of her baby. Awaken her to the inexorable. People who refused fatalism because they could invent small resources insisted on culpability. Deny accidents and wrest fault from the stars.

After the villagers left, their lanterns now scattering in various directions toward home, the family broke their silence and cursed her. "Aiaa, we're going to die. Death is coming. Death is coming. Look what you've done. You've killed us. Ghost! Dead ghost! Ghost! You've never been born." She ran out into the fields, far enough from the house so that she could no longer hear their voices, and pressed herself against the earth, her own land no more. When she felt the birth coming, she thought that she had been hurt. Her body seized together. "They've hurt me too much," she thought. "This is gall, and it will kill me." With forehead and knees against the earth, her body convulsed and then relaxed. She turned on her back, lay on the ground. The black well of sky and stars went out and out and out forever; her body and her complexity seemed to disappear. She was one of the stars, a bright dot in blackness, without home, without a companion, in eternal cold and silence. An agoraphobia rose in her, speeding higher and higher, bigger and bigger; she would not be able to contain it; there would be no end to fear.

Flayed, unprotected against space, she felt pain return, focusing her body. This pain chilled her—a cold, steady kind of surface pain. Inside, spasmodically, the other pain, the pain of the child, heated her. For hours she lay on the ground, alternately body and space. Sometimes a vision of normal comfort obliterated reality: she saw the family in the evening gambling at the dinner table, the young people massaging their elders' backs. She saw them congratulating one another, high joy on the mornings the rice shoots came up. When these pictures burst, the stars drew yet further apart. Black space opened.

She got to her feet to fight better and remembered that old-fashioned women gave birth in their pigsties to fool the jealous, pain-dealing gods, who do not snatch piglets. Before the next spasms could stop her, she ran to the pigsty, each step a rushing out into emptiness. She climbed over the fence and knelt in the dirt. It was good to have a fence enclosing her, a tribal person alone.

Laboring, this woman who had carried her child as a foreign growth that sickened her every day, expelled it at last. She reached down to touch the hot, wet, moving mass, surely smaller than anything human, and could feel that it was human after all—fingers, toes, nails, nose. She pulled it up on to her belly, and it lay curled there, butt in the air, feet precisely tucked one under the other. She opened her loose shirt and buttoned the child inside. After resting, it squirmed and thrashed and she pushed it up to her breast. It turned its head this way and that until it found her nipple. There, it made little snuffling noises. She clenched her teeth at its preciousness, lovely as a young calf, a piglet, a little dog.

She may have gone to the pigsty as a last act of responsibility: she would protect this child as she had protected its father. It would look after her soul, leaving supplies on her grave. But how would this tiny child without family find her grave when there would be no marker for her anywhere, neither in the earth nor the family hall? No one would give her a family hall name. She had taken the child with her into the wastes. At its birth the two of them had felt the same raw pain of separation, a wound that only the family pressing tight could close. A child with no descent line would not soften her life but only trail after her, ghostlike, begging her to give it purpose. At dawn the villagers on their way to the fields would stand around the fence and look.

Full of milk, the little ghost slept. When it awoke, she hardened her breasts against the milk that crying loosens. Toward morning she picked up the baby and walked to the well.

Carrying the baby to the well shows loving. Otherwise abandon it. Turn its face into the mud. Mothers who love their children take them along. It was probably a girl; there is some hope of forgiveness for boys.

"Don't tell anyone you had an aunt. Your father does not want to hear her name. She has never been born." I have believed that sex was unspeakable and words so strong and fathers so frail that "aunt" would do my father mysterious harm. I have thought that my family, having settled among immigrants who had also been their neighbors in the ancestral land, needed to clean their name, and a wrong word would incite the kinspeople even here. But there is more to this silence: they want me to participate in her punishment. And I have.

In the twenty years since I heard this story I have not asked for details nor said my aunt's name; I do not know it. People who can comfort the dead can also chase after them to hurt them further—a reverse ancestor worship. The real punishment was not the raid swiftly inflicted by the villagers, but the family's deliberately forgetting her. Her betrayal so maddened them, they saw to it that she would suffer forever, even after death. Always hungry, always needing, she would have to beg food from other ghosts, snatch and steal it from those whose living descendants give them gifts. She would have to fight the ghosts massed at crossroads for the buns a few thoughtful citizens leave to decoy her away from village and home so that the ancestral spirits could feast unharassed. At peace, they could act like gods, not ghosts, their descent lines providing them with paper suits and dresses, spirit money, paper houses, paper automobiles, chicken, meat, and rice into eternity—essences delivered up in smoke and flames, steam and incense rising from each rice bowl. In an attempt to make the Chinese care for people outside the family, Chairman Mao encourages us now to give our paper replicas to the spirits of outstanding soldiers and workers, no matter whose ancestors they may be. My aunt remains forever hungry. Goods are not distributed evenly among the dead.

My aunt haunts me—her ghost drawn to me because now, after fifty years of neglect, I alone devote pages of paper to her, though not origamied into houses and clothes. I do not think she always means me well. I am telling on her, and she was a spite suicide, drowning herself in the drinking water. The Chinese are always very frightened of the drowned one, whose weeping ghost, wet hair hanging and skin bloated, waits silently by the water to pull down a substitute.

READING  WRITING

## THIS TEXT: READING

1. What do you make of how Henke, Umble, and Smith trace the female heroine in Disney? Is their reading fair? What cultural contexts prompted their investigation?
2. What cultural contexts may account for the transformation of Disney female heroines?
3. According to Yolen, what are the reasons for the dramatic change in how Americans *read* Cinderella? What does Cinderella symbolize for Yolen?
4. How is the Henke/Umble/Smith reading of Cinderella similar to and different from Yolen's reading of Cinderella? What accounts for the differences?
5. How is Cinderella similar to Kingston's "No Name Woman"?
6. What is the effect of transforming ethnic folktales about gender into contemporary short stories?

## YOUR TEXT: WRITING

1. Pick a myth or a folktale or a fairytale that has a female as the main character. Give a semiotic reading of the text in which you examine what messages the text sends about gender and gender roles.
2. Write a personal essay on how myths and fairy tales have shaped your ideas of gender and gender roles. What text was particularly influential in your life?
3. Based on Yolen's model, write an analytical paper in which you analyze a character from a Disney movie in terms of American values and cultures. What character seems to embody American ideals of beauty, innocence, submission, and virtue?
4. Using a myth one of the authors has mentioned, write an essay examining male gender and gender roles. What do these myths say about men? Are men as affected by myths as women? More so?
5. If women and girls tend to get their visions of female behavior from fairy tales, where do men get theirs? Write an argumentative essay in which you demonstrate which texts influence male behavior.
6. Write an essay on the links between gender and ethnicity. How do the codes and mores of a certain ethnic culture play into gender roles?

READING  *Outside the Lines*

## CLASSROOM ACTIVITIES

1. Send all of the males to another room to discuss a specific text. Now that all the guys are absent, hold a discussion for 20 minutes on one or two texts in this section. How is your classroom experience different without males around? Why is it different?
2. In class, watch a television show from the '50s or '60s like *Leave it to Beaver* or *Father Knows Best* or *Bonanza*. Compare the gender roles to those in a show like *Will and Grace*, *Frasier*, or *Ally McBeal*. What has changed? What hasn't? How do cultural norms and mores affect how gender gets represented?
3. Go around the room, and ask students to identify how they are themselves "marked," or ask them to provide one example of how they "do gender."

4. As a class, identify five famous women. How do they do gender? Or, using Devor's essay, how do they adhere to feminine expectations?

5. Do the same with five famous men.

6. As a class, discuss why words like slut, whore, bitch, easy, loose, cold, frigid and manipulative are generally reserved for females. Why are similar words used to describe males, like stud, player, gigolo, pimp, shrewd and rational, so different from those used to describe women?

7. As a class, write a companion poem to Storni's "You Would Have Me White," but from a male perspective. What would the male's claim be? "You Would Have Me _____"

8. Is America more racist or sexist? Do you think we will have a black male or a white woman president first? What's your reasoning here?

9. Have everyone in the class bring in a magazine ad that has to do with gender or gender roles. When taken together, what emerges?

10. Break up into groups and discuss the contradictions of gender we see in television, movies, music and magazines. Compare your answers.

11. Listen to some rap, country, pop and folk songs in class. How are issues of gender reinforced by song lyrics, album covers and videos?

## ESSAY IDEAS

1. Write a paper in which you examine and debunk three stereotypes about gender.

2. Most of the essays here have dealt with gender issues and women. Write an essay in which you examine how music, sports, business, movies and even pornography determines what admirable "masculine" traits are.

3. Write a personal essay in which you examine three ways in which you do gender. What do your means of doing gender say about you?

4. Write an argumentative essay about certain texts that you think are harmful in terms of how they perpetuate gender stereotypes.

5. Read a magazine that is aimed at another gender. If you are a woman, read *Maxim, Sports Illustrated, GQ, Details, Men's Health* or *Field and Stream;* if you are a man, read *Cosmopolitan, Shape, Redbook, Ladies Home Journal, Martha Stewart Living, Ms.,* or *Working Woman.* Write a paper in which you give a semiotic analysis of the magazine.

6. Write a paper on daytime television. What messages do the commercials and the programming send to women (and men) about women (and men)?

7. As this book goes to press, there is a proliferation of pro-anorexia sites on the World Wide Web. Write a paper that is a reading of anorexia and/or bulimia. Why does this disease affect mostly middle-class white women? Why don't men suffer from these ailments?

8. Give a semiotic reading of male/female dating. What roles are men and women supposed to play early in the dating process? What behavior is okay? What is forbidden? How do we know these rules?

9. Go to the room or the apartment of a friend of yours of a different gender. Give a semiotic reading of that person's room. How is it different from yours? How does your friend's room reflect his or her gender?

10. Give a reading of the gender dynamics in your household. What gender roles do your parents or stepparents fall into? Your siblings?

# Reading and Writing About Art

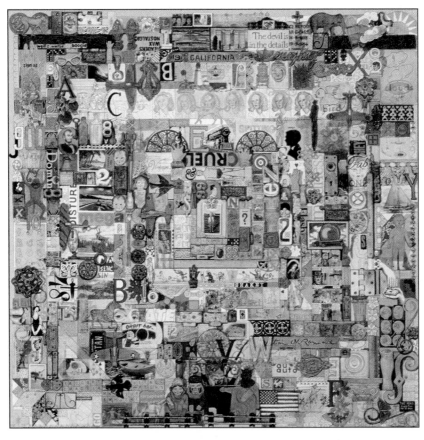

■ ■ ■  Marnie Spencer, *Between the Devil and the Deep Blue Sea*.
*Source:* Courtesy of the artist and Julie Baker, Fine Art, Grass Valley, California.

For many of us, art is intimidating. When confronted with a piece of artwork, particularly if it is abstract (made more from shapes rather than recognizable figures), we do not often know how we should look at it. We want to appreciate art because we know "people" think it's important, but how to do so can be a mystery. We agree both with the fact that learning how to read art is important and that it seems a daunting task at times. That's where this chapter comes in—we hope to make it easier for you to approach what can be a rewarding and even enjoyable process. In fact, it could turn out to be one of the most rewarding skills in your repertoire as a human being.

Let's begin with a quick overview of what we mean by visual art. Though visual art has undergone transformations with technological innovations, we generally mean paintings, sculpture, and photographs, though items like artistic installations (large works of art often taking up entire rooms) or collages are often considered visual arts. Traditionally, these arts are texts that make meaning through visual signs—colors, shapes, shadings, and lines—as opposed to texts that make meaning with words or music, though modern art has sought to bring both of these into its world. In this chapter, we will confine our comments to paintings, sculpture, images, installations, and photographs, as these are the most common forms of visual art that you are likely to encounter in your everyday lives. Like everything else we talk about in this book, works of visual art are complex texts that you are encouraged and invited not simply to look at but to *read*.

In helping you make sense of art as a medium, one of the most important aspects to recognize about art is its universality and longevity. Long before there were written languages, there were visual ones. Since human beings could hold sticks and dab them in mud, there has been art. In caves in France, on cliffs in Utah, on tablets in the Middle East, on paper in the Orient, and on tombs in Egypt, men and women have been drawing pictures. If you have visited any of these places and seen these texts, you get a sense of the artist's overwhelming urge to represent the world—that is to re-present or remake the world. That is really all art of any kind is—an individual's way of presenting the world in a new way. Van Gogh's sunflowers, Monet's water lilies, Picasso's musicians, El Greco's Jesus, even Jackson Pollock's splatterings are attempts to make us experience some aspect of the world in a way we had not before.

For a variety of reasons, art resonates with us in ways other media don't and perhaps can't. For one, we are visual creatures. We see millions of things every day and in so doing rely heavily on our sight. Visual artists take our enormous practice of seeing the world and use it to make us see something new. So, in some regard, there is very little to learn. Artists use what you already use. All you have to do is get an idea of the very few tools they use to make their art do what they want it to.

Now, on to some hints for reading and writing about art:

## Test your first reactions, both emotionally and intellectually.

Painting and photography often have definite advantages over poetry and fiction in that when you look at a painting, you don't immediately ask yourself what a certain tree symbolizes or what the rain is a metaphor for, though in abstract art, some of the same questions come up. Instead of trying to figure out what the painting "means," try to pay attention to what the painting or photo "evokes." What sort of reaction or response does the piece elicit? Is there a mood or tone? Does the painting or its colors create any particular emotion? You might also ask yourself how the artist works with notions of beauty. Is the picture or sculpture conventional in its use of beauty, or does s/he challenge typical ideas of beauty? If Hieronymus Bosch's *Garden of Earthly Delights* makes you uncomfortable, then the painting has succeeded as a rhetorical and semiotic text. If Monet's paintings of waterlillies give you a sense of calmed, pastoral elegance, then Monet has probably achieved his goal. If you find Georgia O'Keeffe's paintings of flowers, pistils, and stamens strangely erotic, then you are probably experiencing the kind of reaction that she intended. Works like Picasso's *Guernica* might affect you emotionally first, then begin to move you on an intellectual level—or vice versa. Either way, artists use shapes, colors, scale, and tone to make you feel a certain way. Thus, you may be reading the text of the painting on a subconscious level and not even know it.

In many ways, poetry resembles painting more than prose, so, like poetry, paintings may take a while to work on you. But that's okay; be patient. Let yourself be drawn into the painting.

### Pay attention to the grammar or syntax of visual art.

Like written language, visual art enjoys its own set of rules and structures. You don't have to know all or many of these terms or ideas to enjoy or understand art, but knowing these ideas and terms does help to decode individual artistic texts. For instance, let's look at the notion of composition. Chances are that you are in a composition course right now, and while artistic composition is slightly different, it is also quite similar. To compose is to "put together" or "assemble." It comes from two Latin words: *com* which means "together" and *poser* which means to "place or to put down." Accordingly, composition means to place together. In this way, the composition of a painting resembles the composition of your essays: both are texts that have been assembled from various "components" (a word with the same origin). So then the composition of a work of art is the plan or placement of the various elements of the piece. Most of the time, a painting's composition is related to the principles of design, such as balance, color, rhythm, texture, emphasis and proportion.

Let's say you are looking at Leonardo da Vinci's masterpiece, *The Last Supper*. You might notice the symmetry or balance of the painting, how the table and the men are perfectly framed by the walls of the building and how Jesus is framed in the very center of the piece by the open doorway. Placing Jesus in this position, lighting him from the back, gives him a certain emphasis the disciples lack. His red robe and his blue sash add to his stature, as does his posture. He looks as though he is offering a blessing, a gesture that underscores da Vinci's interpretation of Christ as a giver and a healer. Thus how the artist places his subject (at the center) and how he depicts him (as offering both thanks and blessing) and how his subject is contrasted against the rest of the painting (in red and almost radiating light, power and glory) is a kind of argument or thesis to the painting, just as you will create an argument or thesis for your own composition.

Taken all together, then, the various components of a painting or a photograph contribute to the piece's effect.

### How we see, evaluate, and interpret "art" is influenced by a number of forces.

The visual arts extend beyond paintings we find in museums—they include digital images, installations, LED texts, performances, collages, comics, and a host of other media. For a long time, a rift has existed between so-called "high" and "low" art. Artists like Picasso,

C.M. Coolidge, *A Friend in Need.*
*Source:* Getty Images, Inc.

Monet, Manet, van Gogh, da Vinci, Michelangelo, Goya, Degas, and the like are considered high art, where say, Nagel prints, photos of cars, most outdoor murals, much folk or "primitive" art, digital images, cartoons, Hummel figurines, Precious Moments statuettes, and any mass-produced or popular design is probably seen by some as "low" or "populist" art. For instance, we love the Dogs Playing Poker pictures, but you are unlikely to see any of these paintings (despite how funny they are) in the Louvre, the Metropolitan Museum of Modern Art or the Chicago Art Institute because they are considered "blue collar" or "pedestrian" or "unsophisticated." That said, William Wegman's photos of dogs *are* considered art. You can find calendars and postcards in the gift shops of most museums.

It's unclear from the content why one is "art" and one is "tacky." Both are color images of dogs at tables. What makes the Wegman piece art? (One reason might be that the Wegman dogs in a way are mocking the dogs playing poker. Of course, the dogs playing poker might be themselves mocking something.) These kinds of questions are at the heart of the art world and continue to serve as cultural markers of education, sophistication, social class and good taste. There are many, many people who would judge your sense of taste depending on which of these two images you think is the best "art." Now, if you "like" the poker dogs better than the eating dogs, that's one thing; but if you argue that the poker dogs are better *art,* that is another matter altogether.

William Wegman, *Jack Sprat.*

## Art reflects not only the artists themselves but also their culture.

Like music, literature, and film, the visual arts are products not only of artists but also of the culture in which the artist lives and works. It should come as no surprise that during the Middle Ages and the Renaissance, when the Catholic Church dominated the religious and political landscape of Europe, that most of the paintings reflected Biblical themes. Similarly, during the Romantic period, large, dark, brooding, tumultuous paintings tended to mimic "romantic" characteristics that worked their way into both architecture and fiction. Even the earliest cave paintings and rock art focuses on themes important to the artists of the time—hunting, fishing, keeping warm, and invoking the gods. The belief that art reflects the world in which it exists is called *mimesis*. Some people would argue that artistic movements such as Surrealism and Cubism were movements away from mimetic art because people like Marcel Duchamp, Georges Braque, Picasso, and Man Ray distorted reality in their work. However, if we consider that, at this time, most artists, writers, and thinkers found the early twentieth century to be a time of chaos, disorder, violence, alienation, and fragmentation, then one can make a compelling argument that Picasso's and Braque's fissured pictoral landscapes reflected a fissured cultural and political landscape.

Currently, as our culture becomes more politically conscious, so too does our art. Andres Serrano has become famous for his photographs of guns, murdered corpses and Ku Klux Klan members; Native American artist Jaune Quick-to-See Smith assembles journalism articles about violence toward American Indians, sports mascots from teams whose mascots are Indians, and stereotypes of "natives" such as toy tomahawks and moccasins to make comments on contemporary American Indian life; photographer Cindy Sherman did a series of disturbing photographs of mutilated female mannequins as a commentary on the violence toward and objectification of women; and Michael Ray Charles, an African. American painter, has made a career out of augmenting representations of "Sambo," a disturbing stereotype used to mock African Americans. In each of these situations, art crosses over from the aesthetic world and into the world of ethics. Although the ties between Abstract Expressionism and the Cold War may not be as obvious as the ones tying religious art to Catholicism, they are strong nonetheless.

## Often, there is a gap between the artist and the public.

It's somewhat of a cliché by now, but what an artist finds appealing is not always what the public finds appealing. The furor over the *Sensation* exhibition in 1999 is only the most recent in a long line of controversial artistic moments. In 1989, Jesse Helms (a Republican senator from North Carolina), conservative politician and commentator Patrick Buchanan, and art critic Hilton Kramer launched an all-out attack on "The Perfect Moment," a traveling exhibit of photographs by Robert Mapplethorpe that was funded by the National Endowment for the Arts, which gets some of its money from tax dollars. Some of Mapplethorpe's photographs crossed the line of decency, according to some, because of their explicit homoerotic themes and because two photographs were of naked children. What resulted was a long legal and cultural battle over pornography, public funding for the arts, morality, and artistic freedom. Similarly, Andres Serrano's wildly controversial photograph *Piss Christ* nearly got the NEA shut down for good. This 1987 photograph of a crucifix dropped in urine angered so many people that it brought about the most thorough scrutiny of public financial support for the arts in American history. But America is not the only battleground for art and culture. To this day, if you visit Picasso's famous painting *Guernica* in Madrid, you will likely be accosted by locals who will want to give you a revisionist reading of the painting, which still remains behind glass to protect it from vandalism.

Photography tends to draw more fire than other art forms because people do not always see photographs as texts but as the actual world. Also, art tends to be publicly displayed. We encourage our children to go to museums to get "enlightened." If what parents find at the museum disturbs them, then the public role of art gets called into question. Even though some fringe groups have burned books and banned records, literature, music, and even painting seems to escape the level of scrutiny of film and photography. As readers of the world, be aware of the various forces that determine how we see art and how we see art's role in forging a vision of contemporary culture.

Additionally, art is not just social and economical, it is also political. Some of the images in the Censorship Suite have caused a lot of people a lot of grief. Since, for centuries, certain values and ideals have been associated with the term "art," when certain texts that challenge those ideas are marketed or displayed as "art," some aspects of American society get pretty worked up. In other words, for some, "art" is more than aesthetics, more than how something looks. Content also comes into play.

## Works of modern and contemporary art deserve your attention because they are often important texts about the contemporary world.

Chances are, if you are like most people, you are totally confused by modern art, which often seems like an endless series of nonsensical images: people with square heads, splatters of paint, chaos. What's important to recognize about modern art is the audience's role in constructing the painting. While modern artists do create work that may reflect their perspective and their culture, they also rely on the viewer to bring to their work an idea about what art is and how art functions. Frequently, viewers of modern art complain that they could have done the work themselves; they focus on the craftsmanship of modern art. But the modern artist might argue that the conception of art and the discussion of what art is and what it means is what makes modern art so compelling, and being a good reader of modern and contemporary art can give you valuable insights into recent social, political, and artistic moments.

Modern art saw the rise of the most recognizable schools: cubism, expressionism, fauvism, futurism, abstract expressionism, pop art, and collage. Figures like Pablo Picasso, Paul Klee, Wassily Kandinsky, Joan Miro, Gustav Klimt, Georges Braque, Edvard Munch, Henri Rousseau, Henri Matisse, Jackson Pollock, Robert Motherwell, Andy Warhol and a host of others ushered in an entirely new way of looking at art. Most modern art is abstract or non-representational, which means that the subjects of the paintings may not be nature or people but ideas, politics, or art itself (but they might just look like shapes). It's no coincidence that art took such a radical turn in the twentieth century: The innovations in technology, literature, film, psychology, and communication found commensurate innovations in the art world. Modern artists believe that if you change the way you see the world, you change the world. So you have artists playing with reality: Paul Klee said he wanted to make the non-visible, visible; Kandinsky claimed that form was the outer expression of inner content; Picasso once wrote that if he wanted to express the roundness of a glass, he might have to make it square. Thus the changes in the world, the growths in perspective and innovation, get reflected and chronicled in modern art.

## Reading art helps you see the world in new ways.

Again, look at the perspective of the picture or the sculpture. Has the artist made you see the world or nature or a person or an object differently? If so, how? Ask yourself how the artist has represented the world, that is, how has s/he re-presented the world? Why might an artist be interested in altering your perception of something? Perhaps because if you learn to see the world in a new way fairly often, then looking at the world will be a way of creating your own art.

## ■■■ WORKSHEET ■■■

### This Text

1. While it will be impossible for you to know this fully, try to figure out the writing situation of each author. Who is the audience? What does the author have at stake? What is his or her agenda? Why is she or he writing this piece?
2. What are the main points of the essay? Can you find a thesis statement anywhere? Remember, it doesn't have to be one sentence—it can be several sentences or a whole paragraph.
3. What textual cues does the author use to help get his or her point across?
4. How does the author support her argument? What evidence does he use to back up any claims he might make?
5. Is the author's argument valid? Is it reasonable?
6. Do you find yourself in agreement with the author? Why or why not?
7. Does the author help you read the visual arts better than you did before reading the essay? If so, why?
8. What issues about race, ethnicity, class, and gender does the writer raise? Do you think the writer has an agenda of sorts?
9. Did you like the piece? Why or why not?

### Beyond This Text

1. What are the major themes of the work? What is the artist trying to suggest?
2. What techniques does the artist use to get his or her message across? Why *these* techniques?
3. What are we to make of the characters in the painting or photograph? What is their function? What is their race? Their social class? Are they like you? How?
4. Where does the text take place? When is it set?
5. What are the main conflicts of the text? What issues are at stake?
6. What kinds of issues of identity is the artist working on in the text?
7. Is there tension between the self and society in the text? How? Why?
8. What is the agenda of the artist? Why does she or he want me to think a certain way?
9. How is the text put together? What is its composition? How does it make meaning?
10. What techniques is the author using? How does it adhere to issues of artistic design?
11. Did you like this artwork? Why or why not?

---

### WAYS OF SEEING

■ **John Berger** ■

*John Berger's semiotic approach toward looking at and thinking about art and images mirrors the stance this book takes in encouraging you to think of the world as a text. For Berger, sight and perception are crucial to making sense of the world. As you read, you might think about what art you have seen in person and reproduced. Also, how do cultural and political forces affect how we see art and the world? This photo essay is the first chapter from his groundbreaking book* Ways of Seeing *(1972), which we recommend.*

*Seeing comes before words. The child looks and recognizes before it can speak.*

But there is also another sense in which seeing comes before words. It is seeing which establishes our place in the surrounding world; we explain that world with words, but words can never undo the fact that we are surrounded by it. The relation between what we see and what we know is never settled. Each evening we *see* the sun set. We *know* that the earth is turning away from it. Yet the knowledge, the explanation, never quite fits the sight. The Surrealist painter Magritte commented on this always-present gap between words and seeing in a painting called *The Key of Dreams.*

*The Key of Dreams* by Magritte 1898–1967.

*Source:* © 2005 C. Herscovici, Brussels/ Artists Rights Society (ARS), New York/Art Resource, NY.

The way we see things is affected by what we know or what we believe. In the Middle Ages when men believed in the physical existence of Hell the sight of fire must have meant something different from what it means today. Nevertheless their idea of Hell owed a lot to the sight of fire consuming and the ashes remaining—as well as to their experience of the pain of burns.

When in love, the sight of the beloved has a completeness which no words and no embrace can match: a completeness which only the act of making love can temporarily accommodate.

Yet this seeing which comes before words, and can never be quite covered by them, is not a question of mechanically reacting to stimuli. (It can only be thought of in this way if one isolates the small part of the process which concerns the eye's retina.) We only see what we look at. To look is an act of choice. As a result of this act, what we see is brought within our reach—though not necessarily within arm's reach. To touch something is to situate oneself in relation to it. (Close your eyes, move round the room and notice how the faculty of touch is like a static, limited form of sight.) We never look at just one thing; we are always looking at the relation between things and ourselves. Our vision is continually active, continually moving, continually holding things in a circle around itself, constituting what is present to us as we are.

Soon after we can see, we are aware that we can also be seen. The eye of the other combines with our own eye to make it fully credible that we are part of the visible world.

If we accept that we can see that hill over there, we propose that from that hill we can be seen. The reciprocal nature of vision is more fundamental than that of spoken dialogue. And often dialogue is an attempt to verbalize this—an attempt to explain how, either metaphorically or literally, 'you see things', and an attempt to discover how 'he sees things'.

In the sense in which we use the word in this book, all images are man-made.

An image is a sight which has been recreated or reproduced. It is an appearance, or a set of appearances, which has been detached from the place and time in which it first made its appearance and preserved—for a few moments or a few centuries. Every image embodies a way of seeing. Even a photograph. For photographs are not, as is often assumed, a mechanical record. Every time we look at a photograph, we are aware, however slightly, of the photographer selecting that sight from an infinity of other possible sights. This is true even in the most casual family snapshot. The photographer's way of seeing is reflected in his choice of subject. The painter's way of seeing is reconstituted by the marks he makes on the canvas or paper. Yet, although every image embodies a way of seeing, our perception or appreciation of an image depends also upon our own way of seeing. (It may be, for example, that Sheila is one figure among twenty; but for our own reasons she is the one we have eyes for.)

Images were first made to conjure up the appearances of something that was absent. Gradually it became evident that an image could outlast what it represented; it then showed how something or somebody had once looked—and thus by implication how the subject had once been seen by other people. Later still the specific vision of the image-maker was also recognized as part of the record. An image became a record of how X had seen Y. This was the result of an increasing consciousness of individuality, accompanying an increasing awareness of history. It would be rash to try to date this last development precisely. But certainly in Europe such consciousness has existed since the beginning of the Renaissance.

No other kind of relic or text from the past can offer such a direct testimony about the world which surrounded other people at other times. In this respect images are more precise and richer than literature. To say this is not to deny the expressive or imaginative quality of art, treating it as mere documentary evidence; the more imaginative the work, the more profoundly it allows us to share the artist's experience of the visible.

Yet when an image is presented as a work of art, the way people look at it is affected by a whole series of learnt assumptions about art. Assumptions concerning:

Beauty

Truth

Genius

Civilization

Form

Status

Taste, etc.

Many of these assumptions no longer accord with the world as it is. (The world-as-it-is is more than pure objective fact, it includes consciousness.) Out of true with the present, these assumptions obscure the past. They mystify rather than clarify. The past is never there waiting to be discovered, to be recognized for exactly what it is. History always constitutes the relation between a present and its past. Consequently fear of the present leads to mystification of the past. The past is not for living in; it is a well of conclusions from which we draw in order to act. Cultural mystification of the past entails a double loss. Works of art are made unnecessarily remote. And the past offers us fewer conclusions to complete in action.

When we 'see' a landscape, we situate ourselves in it. If we 'saw' the art of the past, we would situate ourselves in history. When we are prevented from seeing it, we are being deprived of the history which belongs to us. Who benefits from this deprivation? In the end, the art of the past is being mystified because a privileged minority is striving to invent a history which can retrospectively justify the role of the ruling classes, and such a justification can no longer make sense in modern terms. And so, inevitably, it mystifies.

Let us consider a typical example of such mystification. A two-volume study was recently published on Frans Hals. It is the authoritative work to date on this painter. As a book of specialized art history it is no better and no worse than the average.

*Regentesses of the Old Men's Alms House* by Hals 1580–1666.
*Source:* Museum Franz Hals, Haarlan, Holland/Superstock.

The last two great paintings by Frans Hals portray the Governors and the Governesses of an Alms House for old paupers in the Dutch seventeenth-century city of Haarlem. They were officially commissioned portraits. Hals, an old man of over eighty, was destitute. Most of his life he had been in debt. During the winter of 1664, the year he began painting these pictures, he obtained three loads of peat on public charity, otherwise he would have frozen to death. Those who now sat for him were administrators of such public charity.

The author records these facts and then explicitly says that it would be incorrect to read into the paintings any criticism of the sitters. There is no evidence, he says, that Hals painted them in a spirit of bitterness. The author considers them, however, remarkable works of art and explains why. Here he writes of the Regentesses:

> Each woman speaks to us of the human condition with equal importance. Each woman stands out with equal clarity against the *enormous* dark surface, yet they are linked by a firm rhythmical arrangement and the subdued diagonal pattern formed by their heads and hands. Subtle modulations of the *deep,* glowing blacks contribute to the *harmonious fusion* of the whole and form an *unforgettable contrast* with the *powerful* whites and vivid flesh tones where the detached strokes reach *a peak of breadth and strength.* (our italics)

The compositional unity of a painting contributes fundamentally to the power of its image. It is reasonable to consider a painting's composition. But here the composition is written about as though it were in itself the emotional charge of the painting. Terms like harmonious fusion, unforgettable contrast, reaching a peak of breadth and strength transfer the emotion provoked by the image from the plane of lived experience, to that of disinterested 'art appreciation'. All conflict disappears. One is left with the unchanging 'human condition', and the painting considered as a marvellously made object.

Very little is known about Hals or the Regents who commissioned him. It is not possible to produce circumstantial evidence to establish what their relations were. But there is the evidence of the paintings themselves: the evidence of a group of men and a group of women as seen by another man, the painter. Study this evidence and judge for yourself.

*Source:* Museum Franz Hals, Haarlan, Holland/Superstock.

The art historian fears such direct judgement:

> As in so many other pictures by Hals, the penetrating characterizations almost seduce us into believing that we know the personality traits and even the habits of the men and women portrayed.

What is this 'seduction' he writes of? It is nothing less than the paintings working upon us. They work upon us because we accept the way Hals saw his sitters. We do not accept this innocently. We accept it in so far as it corresponds to our own observation of people, gestures, faces, institutions. This is possible because we still live in a society of comparable social relations and moral values. And it is precisely this which gives the paintings their psychological and social urgency. It is this—not the painter's skill as a 'seducer'—which convinces us that we *can* know the people portrayed.

The author continues:

> In the case of some critics the seduction has been a total success. It has, for example, been asserted that the Regent in the tipped slouch hat, which hardly covers any of his long, lank hair, and whose curiously set eyes do not focus, was shown in a drunken state.

This, he suggests, is a libel. He argues that it was a fashion at that time to wear hats on the side of the head. He cites medical opinion to prove that the Regent's expression could well be the result of a facial paralysis. He insists that the painting would have been unacceptable to the Regents if one of them had been portrayed drunk. One might go on discussing each of these points for pages. (Men in seventeenth-century Holland wore their hats on the side of their heads in order to be thought of as adventurous and pleasure-loving. Heavy drinking was an approved practice. Etcetera.) But such a discussion would take us even farther away from the only confrontation which matters and which the author is determined to evade.

In this confrontation the Regents and Regentesses stare at Hals, a destitute old painter who has lost his reputation and lives off public charity; he examines them through the eyes of a pauper who must nevertheless try to be objective, i.e., must try to surmount the way he sees as a pauper. This is the drama of these paintings. A drama of an 'unforgettable contrast'.

Mystification has little to do with the vocabulary used. Mystification is the process of explaining away what might otherwise be evident. Hals was the first portraitist to paint the new characters and expressions created by capitalism. He did in pictorial terms what Balzac did two centuries later in literature. Yet the author of the authoritative work on these paintings sums up the artist's achievement by referring to

> Hals's unwavering commitment to his personal vision, which enriches our consciousness of our fellow men and heightens our awe for the ever-increasing power of the mighty impulses that enabled him to give us a close view of life's vital forces.

That is mystification.

In order to avoid mystifying the past (which can equally well suffer pseudo-Marxist mystification) let us now examine the particular relation which now exists, so far as pictorial images are concerned, between the present and the past. If we can see the present clearly enough, we shall ask the right questions of the past.

Today we see the art of the past as nobody saw it before. We actually perceive it in a different way.

This difference can be illustrated in terms of what was thought of as perspective. The convention of perspective, which is unique to European art and which was first established in the early Renaissance, centres everything on the eye of the beholder. It is like a beam from a lighthouse—only instead of light travelling outwards, appearances travel in. The conventions called those appearances *reality*. Perspective makes the single eye the centre of the visible world. Everything converges on to the eye as to the vanishing point of infinity. The visible world is arranged for the spectator as the universe was once thought to be arranged for God.

According to the convention of perspective there is no visual reciprocity. There is no need for God to situate himself in relation to others: he is himself the situation. The inherent contradiction in perspective was that it structured all images of reality to address a single spectator who, unlike God, could only be in one place at a time.

After the invention of the camera this contradiction gradually became apparent.

> I'm an eye. A mechanical eye. I, the machine, show you a world the way only I can see it. I free myself for today and forever from human immobility. I'm in constant movement. I approach and pull away from objects. I creep under them. I move alongside a running horse's mouth. I fall and rise with the falling and rising bodies. This is I, the machine, manoeuvring in the chaotic movements, recording one movement after another in the most complex combinations.

Still from *Man with Movie Camera* by Vertov.

Freed from the boundaries of time and space, I co-ordinate any and all points of the universe, wherever I want them to be. My way leads towards the creation of a fresh perception of the world. Thus I explain in a new way the world unknown to you.*

The camera isolated momentary appearances and in so doing destroyed the idea that images were timeless. Or, to put it another way, the camera showed that the notion of time passing was inseparable from the experience of the visual (except in paintings). What you saw depended upon where you were when. What you saw was relative to your position in time and space. It was no longer possible to imagine everything converging on the human eye as on the vanishing point of infinity.

This is not to say that before the invention of the camera men believed that everyone could see everything. But perspective organized the visual field as though that were indeed the ideal. Every drawing or painting that used perspective proposed to the spectator that he was the unique centre of the world. The camera—and more particularly the movie camera—demonstrated that there was no centre.

The invention of the camera changed the way men saw. The visible came to mean something different to them. This was immediately reflected in painting.

For the Impressionists the visible no longer presented itself to man in order to be seen. On the contrary, the visible, in continual flux, became fugitive. For the Cubists the visible was no longer what confronted the single eye, but the totality of possible views taken from points all round the object (or person) being depicted.

*Still Life with Wicker Chair* by Picasso, 1881–1973.

<hr>

*This quotation is from an article written in 1923 by Dziga Vertov, the revolutionary Soviet film director.

Church of St. Francis at Assisi.

The invention of the camera also changed the way in which men saw paintings painted long before the camera was invented. Originally paintings were an integral part of the building for which they were designed. Sometimes in an early Renaissance church or chapel one has the feeling that the images on the wall are records of the building's interior life, that together they make up the building's memory—so much are they part of the particularity of the building.

The uniqueness of every painting was once part of the uniqueness of the place where it resided. Sometimes the painting was transportable. But it could never be seen in two places at the same time. When the camera reproduces a painting, it destroys the uniqueness of its image. As a result its meaning changes. Or, more exactly, its meaning multiplies and fragments into many meanings.

This is vividly illustrated by what happens when a painting is shown on a television screen. The painting enters each viewer's house. There it is surrounded by his wallpaper, his furniture,

*Source: Mona Lisa* by Dennis Wiemer © Layne Kennedy/Corbis.

his mementoes. It enters the atmosphere of his family. It becomes their talking point. It lends its meaning to their meaning. At the same time it enters a million other houses and, in each of them, is seen in a different context. Because of the camera, the painting now travels to the spectator rather than the spectator to the painting. In its travels, its meaning is diversified.

One might argue that all reproductions more or less distort, and that therefore the original painting is still in a sense unique. Here is a reproduction of the *Virgin of the Rocks* by Leonardo da Vinci.

*Virgin of the Rocks* by Leonardo da Vinci 1452–1519. National Gallery.

*Source:* By kind permission of the Trustees of the National Gallery, London/Corbis. Leonardo da Vinci, ca. 1485.

Having seen this reproduction, one can go to the National Gallery to look at the original and there discover what the reproduction lacks. Alternatively one can forget about the quality of the reproduction and simply be reminded, when one sees the original, that it is a famous painting of which somewhere one has already seen a reproduction. But in either case the uniqueness of the original now lies in it being *the original of a reproduction.* It is no longer what its image shows that strikes one as unique; its first meaning is no longer to be found in what it says, but in what it is.

This new status of the original work is the perfectly rational consequence of the new means of reproduction. But it is at this point that a process of mystification again enters. The meaning of the original work no longer lies in what it uniquely says but in what it uniquely is. How is its unique existence evaluated and defined in our present culture? It is defined as an object whose value depends upon its rarity. This value is affirmed and gauged by the price it fetches on the market. But because it is nevertheless 'a work of art'—and art is thought to be greater than commerce—its market price is said to be a reflection of its spiritual value. Yet the spiritual value of an object, as distinct from a message or an example, can only be explained in terms of magic or religion. And since in modern society neither of these is a living force, the art object, the 'work of art', is enveloped in an atmosphere of entirely bogus religiosity. Works of art are discussed and presented as though they were holy relics: relics which are first and foremost evidence of their own survival. The past in which they originated is studied in order to prove their survival genuine. They are declared art when their line of descent can be certified.

Before the *Virgin of the Rocks* the visitor to the National Gallery would be encouraged by nearly everything he might have heard and read about the painting to feel something like this: 'I am in front of it. I can see it. This painting by Leonardo is unlike any other in the world. The National Gallery has the real one. If I look at this painting hard enough, I should some-

*Virgin of the Rocks* by Leonardo da Vinci 1452–1519. Louvre.

how be able to feel its authenticity. The *Virgin of the Rocks* by Leonardo da Vinci: it is authentic and therefore it is beautiful.'

To dismiss such feelings as naive would be quite wrong. They accord perfectly with the sophisticated culture of art experts for whom the National Gallery catalogue is written. The entry on the *Virgin of the Rocks* is one of the longest entries. It consists of fourteen closely printed pages. They do not deal with the meaning of the image. They deal with who commissioned the painting, legal squabbles, who owned it, its likely date, the families of its owners. Behind this information lie years of research. The aim of the research is to prove beyond any shadow of doubt that the painting is a genuine Leonardo. The secondary aim is to prove that an almost identical painting in the Louvre is a replica of the National Gallery version.

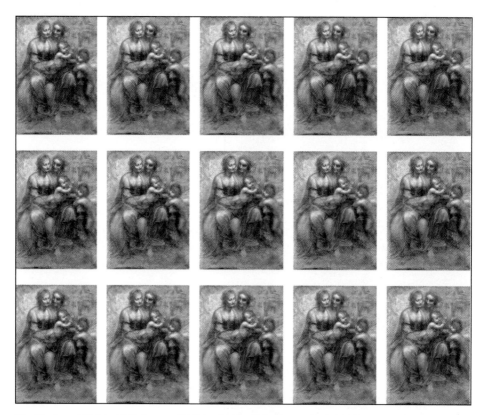

*The Virgin and Child with St Anne and St John the Baptist* by Leonardo da Vinci 1452–1519.

The National Gallery sells more reproductions of Leonardo's cartoon of *The Virgin and Child with St Anne and St John the Baptist* than any other picture in their collection. A few years ago it was known only to scholars. It became famous because an American wanted to buy it for two and a half million pounds.

Now it hangs in a room by itself. The room is like a chapel. The drawing is behind bullet-proof perspex. It has acquired a new kind of impressiveness. Not because of what it shows—not because of the meaning of its image. It has become impressive, mysterious, because of its market value.

The bogus religiosity which now surrounds original works of art, and which is ultimately dependent upon their market value, has become the substitute for what paintings lost when the camera made them reproducible. Its function is nostalgic. It is the final empty claim for the continuing values of an oligarchic, undemocratic culture. If the image is no longer unique and exclusive, the art object, the thing, must be made mysteriously so.

The majority of the population do not visit art museums. The following table shows how closely an interest in art is related to privileged education.

National proportion of art museum visitors according to level of education: Percentage of each educational category who visit art museums

|  | Greece | Poland | France | Holland |
|---|---|---|---|---|
| With no educational qualification | 0.02 | 0.12 | 0.15 | — |
| Only primary education | 0.30 | 1.50 | 0.45 | 0.50 |
| Only secondary education | 10.5 | 10.4 | 10 | 20 |
| Further and higher education | 11.5 | 11.7 | 12.5 | 17.3 |

Source: Pierre Bourdieu and Alain Darbel, *L'Amour de l'Art,* Editions de Minuit, Paris 1969, Appendix 5, table 4

The majority take it as axiomatic that the museums are full of holy relics which refer to a mystery which excludes them: the mystery of unaccountable wealth. Or, to put this another way, they believe that original masterpieces belong to the preserve (both materially and spiritually) of the rich. Another table indicates what the idea of an art gallery suggests to each social class.

Of the places listed below which does a museum remind you of most?

| | Manual workers | Skilled and white collar workers | Professional and upper managerial |
|---|---|---|---|
| | % | % | % |
| Church | 66 | 45 | 30.5 |
| Library | 9 | 34 | 28 |
| Lecture hall | – | 4 | 4.5 |
| Department store or entrance hall in public building | – | 7 | 2 |
| Church and library | 9 | 2 | 4.5 |
| Church and lecture hall | 4 | 2 | – |
| Library and lecture hall | – | – | 2 |
| None of these | 4 | 2 | 19.5 |
| No reply | 8 | 4 | 9 |
| | 100 (n = 53) | 100 (n = 98) | 100 (n = 99) |

*Source:* as above, appendix 4, table 8

In the age of pictorial reproduction the meaning of paintings is no longer attached to them; their meaning becomes transmittable: that is to say it becomes information of a sort, and, like all information, it is either put to use or ignored; information carries no special authority within itself. When a painting is put to use, its meaning is either modified or totally changed. One should be quite clear about what this involves. It is not a question of reproduction failing to reproduce certain aspects of an image faithfully; it is a question of reproduction making it possible, even inevitable, that an image will be used for many different purposes and that the reproduced image, unlike an original work, can lend itself to them all. Let us examine some of the ways in which the reproduced image lends itself to such usage.

*Venus and Mars* by Botticelli 1445–1510. *Source:* Art Resource, NY.

Reproduction isolates a detail of a painting from the whole. The detail is transformed. An allegorical figure becomes a portrait of a girl.

When a painting is reproduced by a film camera it inevitably becomes material for the film-maker's argument.

A film which reproduces images of a painting leads the spectator, through the painting, to the film-maker's own conclusions. The painting lends authority to the film-maker.

This is because a film unfolds in time and a painting does not.

In a film the way one image follows another, their succession, constructs an argument which becomes irreversible.

In a painting all its elements are there to be seen simultaneously. The spectator may need time to examine each element of the painting but whenever he reaches a conclusion, the simultaneity of the whole painting is there to reverse or qualify his conclusion. The painting maintains its own authority.

*Procession to Cavalry* by Breughel 1525–1569.

Paintings are often reproduced with words around them.

This is a landscape of a cornfield with birds flying out of it. Look at it for a moment. Then turn the page.

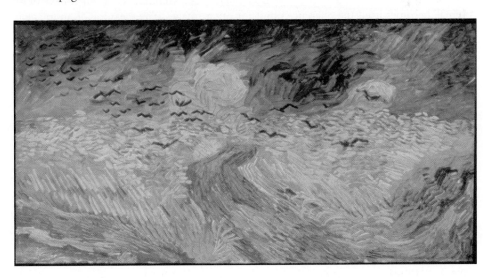

*Wheatfield with Crows* by Vincent van Gogh 1853–1890.

*Source:* Van Gogh Museum, Amsterdam, The Netherlands. Art Resource, NY.

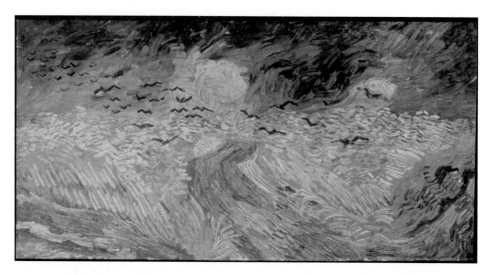

This is the last picture that Vincent van Gogh painted before he killed himself.

It is hard to define exactly how the words have changed the image but undoubtedly they have. The image now illustrates the sentence.

In this essay each image reproduced has become part of an argument which has little or nothing to do with the painting's original independent meaning. The words have quoted the paintings to confirm their own verbal authority. (The essays without words in this book may make that distinction clearer.)

Reproduced paintings, like all information, have to hold their own against all the other information being continually transmitted.

Consequently a reproduction, as well as making its own references to the image of its original, becomes itself the reference point for other images. The meaning of an image is changed according to what one sees immediately beside it or what comes immediately after it. Such authority as it retains, is distributed over the whole context in which it appears.

Because works of art are reproducible, they can, theoretically, be used by anybody. Yet mostly—in art books, magazines, films or within gilt frames in living-rooms—reproductions are still used to bolster the illusion that nothing has changed, that art, with its unique undiminished authority, justifies most other forms of authority, that art makes inequality seem noble and hierarchies seem thrilling. For example, the whole concept of the National Cultural Heritage exploits the authority of art to glorify the present social system and its priorities.

The means of reproduction are used politically and commercially to disguise or deny what their existence makes possible. But sometimes individuals use them differently.

Adults and children sometimes have boards in their bedrooms or living-rooms on which they pin pieces of paper: letters, snapshots, reproductions of paintings, newspaper cuttings, original drawings, postcards. On each board all the images belong to the same language and all are more or less equal within it, because they have been chosen in a highly personal way to match and express the experience of the room's inhabitant. Logically, these boards should replace museums.

What are we saying by that? Let us first be sure about what we are not saying.

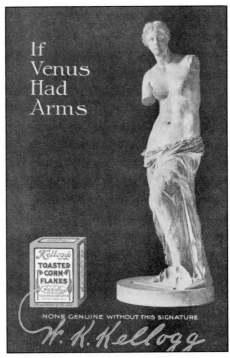

We are not saying that there is nothing left to experience before original works of art except a sense of awe because they have survived. The way original works of art are usually approached—through museum catalogues, guides, hired cassettes, etc.—is not the only way they might be approached. When the art of the past ceases to be viewed nostalgically, the works will cease to be holy relics—although they will never re-become what they were before the age of reproduction. We are not saying original works of art are now useless.

*Woman Pouring Milk* by Vermeer 1632–1675.

Original paintings are silent and still in a sense that information never is. Even a reproduction hung on a wall is not comparable in this respect for in the original the silence and stillness permeate the actual material, the paint, in which one follows the traces of the painter's immediate gestures. This has the effect of closing the distance in time between the painting of the picture and one's own act of looking at it. In this special sense all paintings are contemporary. Hence the immediacy of their testimony. Their historical moment is literally there before our eyes. Cézanne made a similar observation from the painter's point of view. 'A minute in the world's life passes! To paint it in its reality, and forget everything for that! To become that minute, to be the sensitive plate . . . give the image of what we see, forgetting everything that has appeared before our time . . .' What we make of that painted moment when it is before our eyes depends upon what we expect of art, and that in turn depends today upon how we have already experienced the meaning of paintings through reproductions.

Nor are we saying that all art can be understood spontaneously. We are not claiming that to cut out a magazine reproduction of an archaic Greek head, because it is reminiscen of some personal experience, and to pin it on to a board beside other disparate images, is to come to terms with the full meaning of that head.

The idea of innocence faces two ways. By refusing to enter a conspiracy, one remains innocent of that conspiracy But to remain innocent may also be to remain ignorant. The issue is not between innocence and knowledge (or between the natural and the cultural) but between a total approach to art which attempts to relate it to every aspect of experience and the esoteric approach of a few specialized experts who are the clerks of the nostalgia of a ruling class in decline. (In decline, not before the proletariat, but before the new power of the corporation and the state.) The real question is: to whom does the meaning of the art of the past properly belong? To those who can apply it to their own lives, or to a cultural hierarchy of relic specialists?

The visual arts have always existed within a certain preserve; originally this preserve was magical or sacred. But it was also physical: it was the place, the cave, the building, in which, or for which, the work was made. The experience of art, which at first was the experience of ritual, was set apart from the rest of life—precisely in order to be able to exercise power over it. Later the preserve of art became a social one. It entered the culture of the ruling class, whilst physically it was set apart and isolated in their palaces and houses. During all this history the authority of art was inseparable from the particular authority of the preserve.

What the modern means of reproduction have done is to destroy the authority of art and to remove it—or, rather, to remove its images which they reproduce—from any preserve. For the first time ever, images of art have become ephemeral, ubiquitous, insubstantial, available, valueless, free. They surround us in the same way as a language surrounds us. They have entered the mainstream of life over which they no longer, in themselves, have power.

Yet very few people are aware of what has happened because the means of reproduction are used nearly all the time to promote the illusion that nothing has changed except that the masses, thanks to reproductions, can now begin to appreciate art as the cultured minority once did. Understandably, the masses remain uninterested and sceptical.

If the new language of images were used differently, it would, through its use, confer a new kind of power. Within it we could begin to define our experiences more precisely in areas where words are inadequate. (Seeing comes before words.) Not only personal experience, but also the essential historical experience of our relation to the past: that is to say the experience of seeking to give meaning to our lives, of trying to understand the history of which we can become the active agents.

The art of the past no longer exists as it once did. Its authority is lost. In its place there is a language of images. What matters now is who uses that language for what purpose. This touches upon questions of copyright for reproduction, the ownership of art presses and publishers, the total policy of public art galleries and museums. As usually presented, these are narrow professional matters. One of the aims of this essay has been to show that what is really at stake is much larger. A people or a class which is cut off from its own past is far less free to choose and to act as a people or class than one that has been able to situate itself in history. This is why—and this is the only reason why—the entire art of the past has now become a political issue.

*Many of the ideas in the preceding essay have been taken from another, written over forty years ago by the German critic and philosopher Walter Benjamin.*

His essay was entitled *The Work of Art in the Age of Mechanical Reproduction.* This essay is available in English in a collection called *Illuminations* (Cape, London 1970).

READING WRITING

THIS TEXT: READING

1.  In what way is how we see the world affected by what we believe or what we know?
2.  Why does Berger argue, "today we see the art of the past as nobody ever saw it before"?
3.  According to Berger, how does actual written text around a painting change the text of the painting itself?
4.  Do you think mechanical reproduction has changed how we see art? How? Why?

YOUR TEXT: WRITING

1.  Find a reproduction of a famous painting that places that painting in an unusual context, or, go hang up a print of a painting you like in an odd place (the bathroom, a locker room). Write a paper on how that context changes how you see that painting.

2. Find an advertisement that features a famous work of art. Write an essay in which you explore how the advertisement uses the value of the work of art to enhance the value of the product being advertised.

3. Berger suggests, "images are more precise and richer than literature." Do you agree? Write an essay in which you compare a poem or short story on a certain place or idea with a painting or photograph on that same place or idea.

4. How do the reproductions of art in this book affect how you see that art? Write an essay in which you explore how this textbook affects how you *read* the art in it.

---

## ANDY WARHOL: THE MOST CONTROVERSIAL ARTIST OF THE TWENTIETH CENTURY?

### ■ Alan Pratt ■

*In this piece, Alan Pratt gives a semiotic and a cultural reading of Andy Warhol's art and critical reception (2000). Pratt suggests that because Warhol divided critics and audience alike, he is perhaps the most controversial artist of the century. What makes Pratt's approach intriguing is that he explores the major hot button issues surrounding art and artists—their persona as artists and their "originality."*

WHEN ANDY WARHOL HIT HIS STRIDE in the early sixties by appropriating images from advertising design and serializing them with a hands-off austerity, he became a lightning rod for criticism.

Studying the public perception of the artist in 1966, critic Lucy Lippard noticed that "Warhol's films and his art mean either nothing or a great deal. The choice is the viewer's. . . ." In retrospect, Lippard's early, tentative appraisal is revealing. While the images Warhol stumbled across have a deep resonance with the public, the problem of interpreting them is, depending one's point of view, simple or complex.

In the current polemic, Warhol's reputation still depends on the reviewer's ideological or art-historical preoccupations. If, as has been suggested, Warhol succeeded in redefining the art experience, then the critical response required redefinition as well. In retrospect, it appears that one problem that confronted critics and journalists was that established critical approaches simply didn't lend themselves to an art which they perceived as "artless, styleless, and anonymous."

While the debate still hasn't resolved itself, three interconnected issues figure prominently in the disagreements about Warhol's reputation: his persona, his originality, and his antecedents.

### Warhol's Persona

The problematic nature of Warhol's critical reputation is attributable, in part, to the evasive, equivocal persona he cultivated—the calculated indifference, the monosyllabic rejoinder, the flat, vacuous affect of the I-think-everybody-should-be-a-machine Warhol. And while it's true that he suffered from a debilitating shyness, he nevertheless delighted in baffling his critics.

In reviewing Warhol's life it's often impossible to distinguish the authentic Warhol from the act. As a result, a significant portion of the critical response, if only anecdotally, is to Warhol's personality. And with little that's reliable to go on, critics have wide latitude in extrapolating or inventing motives for him. Currently, psychological interpretations of Warhol's work are the fashion.

## Warhol's Originality

Like the problems of personality which have intrigued critics for years, the issue of Warhol's artistic legitimacy has also been the basis of ongoing debate. The subjects of some of his most famous works—the soup cans, Coke bottles, dollar bills, flowers, and cows—were apparently recommendations.

That Warhol borrowed his images from others, from photographs, advertisements, and food labels and developed a technique by which they were serially mass-produced by anonymous Factory hands remains one of the most contentious issues in the criticism.

By erasing himself from his creations, minimizing the artist's responsibility, the significance of talent, and the value of originality, Warhol challenged presumptions about what art is supposed to be and how one is to experience it. This abnegation of responsibility was deemed unethical, if not subversive, by the critical audience, further fueling the controversy about whether or not his work should even be regarded as art.

## Warhol's Antecedents

From the beginning, critics have addressed the connections between what Warhol was doing and what Marcel Duchamp had done. It was Duchamp who in 1914 broke the rules and outraged the art world when he began exhibiting his objets trouvés, the coat-stands, bottle racks, and bicycle wheels. Duchamp, critics suggested, had shown Warhol that appropriating common consumer items could be art.

Warhol was a particularly culpable pioneer of cultural nihilism because the silkscreened readymades—soup cans, bottles, and such—were perceived to be the apotheoses of the objets trouvés.

So why is Warhol the most controversial artist of the century? Read on:

## Warhol's Place in Modernism

As a study of the criticism makes clear, Warhol appalled the art establishment because he represented a complete transvaluation of the aesthetic principles that had dominated for several generations. What for years modernists had deliberately ignored or contemptuously spurned, Warhol embraced. As appropriated mass-culture images—such as his *Turquoise Marilyn* (1962)—his "art" was indistinguishable from advertising—meaning it was crass and pedestrian—and thus lampooned the modern emphasis on noble sentiment and good taste. No doubt Warhol's comments about art, that it should be effortless, that it's a business having nothing to do with transcendence, truth, or sentiment, also infuriated detractors.

Both Warhol's subject matter and his flippant attitudes toward the conventions of the art world were the antithesis of the high-seriousness of modernism. And the rub of it was that his celebrations of the inconsequential were being taken seriously. It was a nasty slap in the face for those seeped in the myths of modernism.

Warhol's aesthetic contributed to the breakdown of the hierarchial conventions of modernism, dissolving distinctions between commercial design and serious art and the boundaries between popular taste and high culture—or, as some would have it, between trash and excellence.

## Warhol and Postmodernism

As many observers now agree, the early 1960s mark the beginnings of a postmodern sensibility, where the modernist desire for closure and aesthetic autonomy has been rapidly replaced with indeterminacy and eclecticism.

If that's true, Warhol's art forecast and then highlighted the changes that were occurring. And it has been argued that his art anticipated many ploys of this aesthetic new world, including the emphasis on irony, appropriation, and commonism, as well as promoting intellectual engagement through negation.

## So What's Warhol's Place in the Criticism?

*"Criticism is so old fashioned. Why don't you just put in a lot of gossip?"*

—Warhol to Bob Colacello, longtime editor of Warhol's magazine Interview

In reviewing the critical record, one can conclude that Warhol's role in art history is as a transitional figure. Stylistically his work is a bellwether, and the critical issues raised about

*Source: Marilyn Monroe,* Andy Warhol, 1962. Oil on canvas. 81" × 66 ¾".™ 2002 Marilyn Monroe LLC by CMG Worldwide Inc. www.MarilynMonroe.com. © 2003 Andy Warhol Foundation for the Visual Arts/ARS, New York.

*Source:* Andy Warhol (1928–1987), *One Hundred Cans,* 1962, synthetic polymer paint on canvas, 72 × 52 in. © 2003. The Andy Warhol Foundation for the Visual Arts/ARS, New York. Albright Knox Art Gallery, Buffalo, New York. The Andy Warhol Foundation, Inc.

him often converge with those at the center of the modern/postmodern debate. As a "mirror of the times," Warhol criticism reflects the trepidation and enthusiasm in response to shifting paradigms. Lucy Lippard's proposition is still valid—Warhol's images are ambiguous. It's this ambiguity that gives his work its edge. His images function as a sort of cultural Rorschach blot allowing for the projection of personalities, theoretical orientations, and ideological biases.

Why put fifty Cambell's soup cans on canvas? So far, there are scores of explanations. And the debate rages on . . .

**READING** WRITING

## THIS TEXT: READING

1. What are the three areas that Pratt cites as being important to Warhol's success and controversy? Are these important areas?

2. What criteria does Pratt establish for being "most controversial"?

3. How does Pratt place Warhol within the context of contemporary art history?

## YOUR TEXT: WRITING

1. Pick an artist and write a similar essay on that artist's work and reputation.

2. Look at some of Warhol's art. Is he an important artist? Is his art important? Is there a distinction between being an important artist and making important art?

3. What social and political events might have influenced Warhol's unique art?

> **WHICH ART WILL TOP THE CHARTES? FOUR CURATORS SHARE THEIR TOP 10 PICKS AND REASONING BEHIND THE MOST INFLUENTIAL VISUAL ARTWORKS OF THE PAST 1,000 YEARS**

*When asked to name the most influential 10 works of art (2000), Kimberly Davenport, Director of the Rice University Art Gallery in Houston, said "This will be fun." We agree—this piece is fun. We have included it not so much as a model for your own writing but as a prompt to help you begin to think about art and influence. Notice how each of these prominent art curators differs over which works of art have been the most influential. Equally interesting is the rationale behind the choices. You may be surprised at what objects get considered "visual artworks."*

### "This will be fun"

—Kimberly Davenport, Director,
Rice University Art Gallery, Houston

When approached with the idea of coming up with a list of the 10 most influential works of the past 1,000 years, I thought, "This will be fun!" Beloved, familiar images—the Mona Lisa, a still life by Cézanne—flowed across my mind. As I sat down to write, however, the task seemed more daunting. Where in such a "Top 10" list, for instance, would fall African tribal sculpture, Indian miniatures, Amish quilts, and the sublime raked-sand gardens of Kyoto, Japan? I approached my list, finally, based on personal encounters with works that have inspired me, as well as many of the living artists with whom I have worked. Artists do not see the art of the past as frozen in time, but as a kind of living library of ideas, solutions, and inspiration. They look at works that offer insights about ways to convey space, color, light, and movement, or that redefine the nature of art itself.

1. **Giotto—*Arena Chapel frescoes* (1305–06).** Three narratives depicting the life of the Virgin, the life of Christ, and the Passion, Crucifixion, and Resurrection span the walls of Arena Chapel in Padua, Italy. The figures are remarkable for their humanity, not only as real bodies having bulk and weight, but for their extraordinary psychological connections to one another. Expressive, "knowing" glances between figures are zones of silent communication detached from the cacophony of events taking place.

2. **Jan Vermeer—*Woman Holding a Balance* (1664),** oil on canvas. Vermeer takes a simple, everyday act and through the use of light and composition transforms it into a sanctified moment of private reflection. The light flooding through the window permeates the scene and infuses it with a sense of the mystery present in the familiar.

3. **Eadweard Muybridge**—*Head-spring, a Flying Pigeon Interfering* (1885). Muybridge's photographic studies of motion broke down the stages of movement to reveal the components of a single action. Using the camera to demonstrate what the eye could not see, Muybridge contributed significantly to the ability of both artists and scientists to understand and portray the world around them.

4. **Marcel Duchamp**—*Fountain* (1917), Porcelain urinal, 23-5/8 in. tall. Duchamp changed the definition of art when he turned a detached urinal on its side, signed it with the pseudonym R. Mott, and submitted it to the exhibition of the Society of Independent Artists. By removing an everyday object from its normal context and calling it art, Duchamp empowered the artist to determine the definition of art.

5. **Kazimir Malevich**—*White on White* (1918), oil on canvas. Malevich was the first artist to use pure geometric abstraction as the subject of his work. "White on White" abandons any reference to the outside world in favor of the artist's depiction of pure feeling. Malevich intended this type of expression as a kind of universal language, accessible and familiar to all people.

6. **Georgia O'Keeffe**—*The Lawrence Tree* (1929), oil on canvas. O'Keeffe opened our eyes to the natural world in a unique way. We experience the tree not from the "superior" point of view—observing it on our own horizontal plane—but from beneath it, rooted in the earth and gazing heavenward.

7. **Pablo Picasso**—*Guernica* (1937), oil on canvas, 11 ft., 6 in. by 25 ft., 8 in. Picasso painted Guernica in response to the bombing of the ancient Basque city during the Spanish Civil War. The painting has become an internationally recognizable image of pacifism that testifies to the power of art to serve as an active forum for social critique and as an instrument for change.

8. **Jackson Pollock**—*Alchemy* (1947), oil, aluminum paint, and string on canvas. Pollock brought physicality and intuition to the forefront of artistic consciousness. By putting the canvas on the floor and physically moving around it to fling paint onto it, Pollock created paintings significant both as objects in and of themselves and as evidence of the process of their creation.

9. **Andy Warhol**—*Marilyn Diptych* (1962), acrylic and silkscreen on canvas. The first work in his celebrity series exemplifies Warhol's (and our) fascination with pop culture, the creation and consequences of fame, and the influence of mass media. His deadpan approach to the world is still common in contemporary life and art.

10. **Sol LeWitt**—*Wall Drawing No. 652* (1990), color ink washes superimposed. LeWitt's view of the idea as the machine that makes the art took the relationship between concept and art object to an unprecedented extreme. Drawn directly on a gallery wall, LeWitt's wall drawings are significant for their intrinsic impermanence and for their ability to be constantly renewed and re-created in different locations.

### *"Difficult and frustrating"*

—Erica E. Hirshler, Croll Senior Curator of Paintings,
Art of the Americas, Museum of Fine Arts, Boston

I accepted this assignment thinking it would be fun, and have found instead that it has been a difficult and frustrating task. So I begin with a disclaimer: For every object I have selected, others easily could have been chosen with equally compelling arguments.

1. **Chartres Cathedral (1145–1220)**, Chartres, France. For me, Chartres epitomizes spiritual power and the unity of the arts. Every aspect of its architecture, sculpture, and stained glass reflects the devotion of its makers, each individual working to create a harmonious design that expresses profound faith.

2. **Michelangelo—Sistine Ceiling (1508–1512)**, frescoes, Sistine Chapel in Rome. Leonardo, Raphael, or Michelangelo? Painting or sculpture? I have changed my list countless times, and have selected the Sistine Ceiling to stand for the many accomplishments of the Italian Renaissance. A painting of compelling beauty, it celebrates both the spiritual and physical worlds.

3. **Rogier van der Weyden—*The Deposition from the Cross* (1435)**, oil on wood. This is one of the most beautiful and moving paintings I have ever seen. Artists of the northern Renaissance are admired for their ability to render even the smallest details of the physical world. In addition to that technical prowess, van der Weyden expressed deep psychological insight in his "Deposition," communicating great sorrow through pose, gesture, and expression.

4. **Rembrandt van Rijn—*The Artist in His Studio* (1627–28)**, oil on panel. I have selected one image to represent Rembrandt's self portraits. In it, I see the mystery of the artist's relationship with his own work—he stands dwarfed by a canvas that only he can see, in a shadowy and obscure space. It also marks a secular, not a religious, experience; such subjects begin their steady increase in popularity during the Baroque period.

5. **Louis-Jacques-Mandé Daguerre—portrait photographs (1839 to 1840s)**. The development of photographs by Daguerre and others in 1839 started a revolution in visual culture that continues today. At first regarded as mechanical representations of the physical world, and as a cheap method of creating portraits, photographs are now valued for their artistic qualities.

6. **Joseph Mallord William Turner—*The Slave Ship: Slavers Throwing Overboard the Dead and Dying, Typhoon Coming On* (1840)**, oil on canvas. Turner devoted himself to landscape painting, which he transformed to convey not only natural effects, but also emotion and perception. In this example, his interpretation of an actual event had political impact, particularly in the United States, where it became a powerful symbol for the abolitionist movement when it entered a Boston collection.

7. **Édouard Manet—*Olympia* (1863)**, oil on canvas. I had first thought to include on my list a nude by Titian, whose Venus of Urbino (1538) established a tradition of sensual images of women that was carried forward by many painters. Then I decided on Manet's nude, which shocked Paris by its bold representation of a naked prostitute, unembellished by the trappings of mythology, which by its very realism provoked a discussion of the nature of art.

8. **Claude Monet—*Impression: Sunrise* (1873)**, oil on canvas. It marks the beginning of Impressionism, an artistic style that has proven to be one of the most long-lasting and popular. For Monet, the artist's perception of the visual world was paramount, and on his canvases design is as important as representation and one sees the transformation of three-dimensional worlds into two-dimensional surfaces.

9. **Pablo Picasso—*Les Demoiselles d'Avignon* (1907)**, oil on canvas. Picasso and his colleagues believed that an artist need not be confined by a single vantage point, and invented a new method of representation that incorporated different points of view

into a single image. This move toward abstraction had an enormous impact on 20th-century art.

10. **Jackson Pollock**—*Autumn Rhythm: Number 30, 1950,* oil on canvas. The center of the art world moved to the U.S. after World War II. Pollock's abstract, emotional celebration of the unconscious, free from any confinement or convention, was among its most influential products, and like Manet's "Olympia," provoked new discussions about the nature of art.

### *"A very humbling experience"*

—Suzanne Folds McCullagh, Curator of Earlier Prints and Drawings,
The Art Institute of Chicago

It has been a very humbling experience trying to define the 10 greatest works of art of the past millennium. A scholar of the 18th century, I have not included a single work from that era (although Jean-Antoine Watteau's "Sign of Gersaint in Berlin" is perhaps my single favorite painting).

I have favored instead the most ambitious and successful of the vast painted decorations, architectural jewels, and sculptural schemes through the Baroque era, and masterpieces that show the depth, breadth, conceptual, and emotional power of the greatest masters of the art of painting from that point on. These are works that have shaped our civilization, and without them, we would be immeasurably spiritually bereft.

1. **Chartres Cathedral**—*Northwest Tower* (1140); the Rose Windows (1217–25). The only existing Gothic cathedral fully glazed with a unified program of stained glass to create a saturated, electric atmosphere. Both the tower and the stained glass make the spirit soar and serve as a landmark of architectural ensembles.

2. **Jan and Hubert Van Eyck**—*Ghent Altarpiece* (1423–32), oil on panel. These brothers introduced the art of oil painting at a level that it would seldom achieve. Their technical accomplishment is surpassed only by the complexity and reverence of their conception in this extraordinary altarpiece, moving in its vastness as well as its details.

3. **Masaccio**—*Brancacci Chapel* (1427), frescoes. The founder of Italian Renaissance painting not only introduced linear perspective but brought his figures a convincing sense of weight and volume, and a compellingly powerful, emotional tenor.

4. **Michelangelo**—*Sistine Chapel* (1508–12 and 1535), frescoes, Rome. Although Michelangelo considered himself a sculptor, his painted decoration of the Sistine Chapel ceiling and altar wall is simply the most comprehensive and spiritually charged ensemble of all time. Its force is so great that its impact can be read in the work of artists who have experienced it.

5. **Raphael**—*Vatican Stanze* (1508–20), frescoes. The papal apartments that Raphael decorated dominated the mature years of his brief life. The wide-ranging subjects of these elegant works include some of the most beautifully painted figures and the most inspirational concepts of civilization.

6. **Gianlorenzo Bernini**—*The Ecstasy of St. Theresa* (1645–52), marble statue, life size, Cornaro Chapel, Rome. This piece not only reveals the overwhelming emotive power of sculpture, but does so in a carefully conceived situation that takes advantage of the architectural environment. Wrapped in swirling draperies, her passionate gaze directed

to heaven, Bernini's saint epitomizes the age of the Baroque, and is among the first to break traditional boundaries of media and meaning.

7. **Diego Velázquez**—*Las Meniñas* (1656), oil on canvas. Called by Neapolitan artist Luca Giordano the "theology of painting," this enigmatic and sublimely crafted canvas is notable for its fresh, persuasive immediacy and the seemingly disparate challenge of its mysterious psychological and political interconnections. It is a single large canvas that invites yet defies interpretation by its viewers.

8. **Rembrandt van Rijn**—*The Return of the Prodigal Son* (1665), oil on canvas. No Top 10 list would be complete without this giant of the Dutch school, whose humanity is expressed in Rembrandt's equally wondrous paintings, prints, and drawings. Like the late work of Titian, it is particularly in his last great paintings, especially of biblical subjects, that his narrative insight and tremendous stature as an artist is revealed.

9. **Georges Pierre Seurat**—*A Sunday Afternoon on the Island of La Grande Jatte* (1884–86), oil on canvas. Painting in France in the 19th century reached a height and subsequent popularity that has rarely been equaled. Few artists brought as much genius, scientific thought, theoretical insight, innovative technique, and conceptual ambition to a canvas as did Seurat in this complex masterwork.

10. **Pablo Picasso**—*Guernica* (1937), oil on canvas. Certainly the most talented, versatile, and productive artist of the past century, Picasso stretched his art in form and content when he created this immense and powerful diatribe against war that also eerily foretold horrors to come. Produced in an intense and volatile period, it represents the culmination of his art up to that time and speaks for modernism in general.

### *"I could not resist"*

—Stephan F. Jost, Director, Mills College Art Museum

My first reaction to making a list of the 10 most influential works of the past 1,000 years was to exempt myself completely and simply say "no." In the end, I could not resist.

Are the criteria aesthetic or are influential works of art simply a product of dominant cultures? Is influence about later imitation or the number of people who seek to see the work of art today?

I tried to select objects from a broad range of cultures and media.

1. *Chartres* Cathedral—*the Rose Windows* (1217–1225), stained glass, Chartres, France. As part of one of the most complete medieval buildings, the Rose Windows at Chartres transform light into stunning colors and depict the teachings of the Christian faith.

2. **Huang Kung-Wang**—*Dwelling in the Fu-ch'un Mountains* (1347–1350), handscroll, ink on paper. Huang Kung-wang was one of several great masters of the late Yüan period, and this magnum opus is one of the most influential works of the long history of Chinese landscape painting.

3. **Michelangelo**—*Sistine Ceiling* (1508–1512), frescoes. This work is a tour de force of painting, illusion, and design. It is also one of the most copied (and parodied) works of art.

4. **Albrecht Dürer**—*Melencolia I* (1514), engraving. As one of Dürer's master engravings, Melencolia I is both a stunning display of technical ability and a complex meditation on philosophy and theology.

5. **Matthias Grünewald—***Isenheim Altarpiece* (1510–1515), oil on panel. Perhaps more than any other work of art, the "Isenheim Altarpiece" was the work I had the most difficult time including. While the altarpiece has inspired many artists, including Jaspar Johns, Grünewald enjoyed limited fame until the 20th century. I included this work because it inspired me to become a curator.

6. **The Koranic inscriptions on Taj Mahal (completed in 1647),** glazed tiles, Agra, India. In the Islamic world, calligraphy has long been the preeminent art form. Many of these texts begin with an invocation of the name of God and represent a particularly long, rich tradition.

7. **Benin ancestral Altarpiece of Oba Akenzua I, Brass (18th century),** Berlin, Museum für Völkerkunde. The art of Benin has been recognized as being technically and intellectually sophisticated and extraordinarily beautiful. This brass altar depicts the Oba, a Benin king, and was part of an ancestral altar.

8. **Vincent van Gogh—***The Church at Auvers* (1890), oil on canvas. The vibrant colors, the humility of the subject, and the inspired handling of paint led me to select this work. Van Gogh radically represented painting as a dynamic and modern form of expression.

9. **Dorothea Lange—***Migrant Mother, Nipomo, California* (1936), gelatin silver print. This photograph of a woman and her three children captures the spirit of humanity and motherhood while recognizing the harsh reality of poverty. There is also embedded in this selection the acknowledgement of the influence of American society, women artists, and photography on 20th-century culture.

10. **Various artists—***AIDS Memorial Quilt* (mid-1980s), various media. I couldn't think of a more appropriate work that captures the democratic ideals of the late 20th century. With more than 41,000 panels, listing more than 80,000 names, the AIDS Memorial Quilt covers more than 17 football fields and is a monument to the common person, expressing heartfelt emotions.

---

 **READING** WRITING

### THIS TEXT: READING

1. What was your experience reading these lists? Did a pattern emerge? Did the various reasonings help you arrive at a definition of art?
2. Is there a piece of art you know of that you would like to see on the list? What? Why?
3. What were some of the criteria for influential art?

### YOUR TEXT: WRITING

1. Write an essay in which you list and justify the three most influential works of visual art over the past 2000 years.
2. Write an essay in which you explain how impossible it is to make such a list. How can one narrow down *all* visual art?
3. Define visual art. Here, a church and a quilt make the list. Are these things art?
4. What do you think the authors of the article mean by "influential"? Have *you* been influenced by any of these pieces of art? Who has? How do these art objects influence us?

## IS THE NAMES QUILT ART?

### ■ E. G. Chrichton ■

*E. G. Chrichton asks the same question many of you have probably asked at some point: "Is it art?" In this provocative essay (1988), Chrichton asks important questions about so-called "high art" and the role art should play in contemporary society. As you read, you might ask if Acton's ideas of composition apply to the NAMES quilt and also if Chrichton's claims about art mesh with your own. A good example of a definitional essay, note how Chrichton defines what he thinks art is, then demonstrates how the NAMES quilt meets those criteria.*

IT IS BEAUTIFUL, POWERFUL, and inspirational. But is it art? The NAMES Project Quilt started in San Francisco with one cloth panel to commemorate one AIDS victim. In a little more than a year it has grown to over 5000 panels from every region in the country. For each person who has taken up needle and thread, paint, and mixed media to create a piece of the Quilt, there are many more who have walked among its connected grids, often in tears. No one with this experience would deny its force and magic as a national symbol of the AIDS tragedy. But from where does this power derive? Why has the NAMES Project Quilt captured our hearts and minds like no other project to come out of the gay community? One answer lies in the Quilt's power as art: art that lives and grows outside established art channels.

The NAMES Project organizers promote the Quilt as the "largest community arts project in the nation." They are aided by a national media that is surprisingly willing to report on events surrounding its display. The art world, however—that ivory tower that is reported to us via a handful of glossy national art magazines—has overlooked the Quilt. The art critics who write in these magazines are not rushing to interpret the Quilt's significance in the history of art.

Art is important, most people agree, but the reasons why are sometimes elusive. There is nothing elusive, though, about the NAMES Project Quilt; it is extremely concrete as visual communication. This accessibility is exactly what throws the Quilt's status as "real art" into question. Unlike much of what we find in galleries and museums, the Quilt has a connection to our daily lives that seems unrelated to the remote world of "high art," or "fine art"— art that is promoted by critics, museum curators, and art historians. To understand the source of discrepancies about how our culture defines art, it helps to look at some of the assumptions made about art and who makes them.

Art, in Western culture, is first and foremost made by the artist—that individual genius whose work and life we come to recognize through a network of museums, media, dealers, and historians. Despite the fact that a myriad of people make art, a very select few are promoted in a way that grabs our attention. This process works like any good marketing strategy: we are told which art is hot, and why, by those who seem to know best. As a result, our taste is inevitably influenced by what appears to be an objective window on aesthetics. It is very hard to regard art found outside these institutional channels as serious. We don't go to the local craft fair to find serious art. It is not the needlepoint your grandmother did, nor the sketches you do in your spare time. And it's not a project like the NAMES Quilt that thrives entirely outside the art world. "Real art" is a luxury item for sale in an elite marketplace that takes it away from the artist's hands, and any community connection we might relate to.

Critics argue a bit about art, trying to maintain the illusion of democratic options, but they essentially define "good art" around a fairly narrow set of assumptions. It is virtually im-

possible to understand most modern mainstream art without the translation of these in-
termediaries. They generally promote obscurity as a desirable feature, and cast accessibility
in an untrustworthy light; art we can too easily understand is more like entertainment. And,
if you want to include a social message, make it vague at best.

Given this milieu, it is no wonder that potential art fans often feel suspicious of famous
artists, seeing them as con-artists instead who try to fool us into thinking their enigmatic puzzles are great art. In contrast, the Quilt seems trustworthy partly because we are the artists.
Although not for sale on the art market, it generates important funding for local AIDS services networks. It is not the offspring of a famous artist, yet its scale is monumental and attention grabbing. And it isn't found where most important art is found; the "museums"
where we view the Quilt are convention centers, pavilions, gymnasiums, and the Capitol
Mall—hardly the retreats of high art. Yet one thing is clear: the Quilt has succeeded in creating a visual metaphor for the tragedy of AIDS that transcends individual grieving to communicate beauty and hope. What more could be expected of a great work of art?

If the establishment art world places the NAMES Quilt outside the holy realm of high art,
other art traditions do not. In the early seventies, feminist artists working within the art
world successfully revived an interest in the folk art of quilting and sewing bees—"low art"
historically associated with women. New materials explored during this period gained acceptance as legitimate fine art ingredients: cloth, clay, and rope, for example. Many artists,
both male and female, started to inject more personal and autobiographical content into
their work. In general, the division between high and low art melted a little.

Several large-scale projects were also organized that introduced the idea of bringing together many people's labor into one artistic vision. Judy Chicago attracted hundreds of crafts-
people to her "Dinner Party" project. The end result was a huge and complex installation
illustrating the lives of specific women throughout history with china place settings around
a huge table. In a very different project, the artist Christo engaged the help of hundreds of
people to set up a "Running Fence" of fabric that wound for miles through northern California countryside, focusing attention on the land and its natural contours. In both cases, people skeptical about the initial vision were drawn in and became enthusiastic through
participation. Chicago and Christo are the rare mainstream artists whose work and vision
have crossed out of the exclusive art world to be accessible. The Vietnam War Memorial, designed by an architectural student named Maya Ying Lin, set a precedent for the simple naming of victims of a tragic war instead of merely immortalizing the warmonger leaders.

Tribal art from all ages has influenced Western artists interested in introducing ritual to
their work. The holistic integration of art with the spiritual and survival needs of a community, characteristic of tribal art, appeals to many of us brought up on the doctrine of "art for
art sake." Many artists have also been influenced by ancient art like the prehistoric Stone-
henge. Monuments like this reveal a very different set of assumptions about art and the artist.
No one knows exactly who created them—their massive scale obviously required the labor and
creativity of many people, over many life spans. It seems as though the individual artistic ego
was not important here, and that art had a function in society beyond visual aesthetics.

The contemporary art that is perhaps most similar to the NAMES Project Quilt are the
*arpilleras* created by anonymous Chilean women resisting the fascist junta ruling their country. Pieced together from scavenged factory remnants, these patchwork pictures use decorative imagery to protest specific government policies or to commemorate "disappeared"

political prisoners, often relatives of the artists. They are smuggled out of the country to communicate the conditions in Chile to the rest of the world. The *arpilleras* are also the only surviving indigenous Chilean visual art, now that murals have been destroyed and artists of all kinds murdered and imprisoned.

What the NAMES Project Quilt has in common with feminist, environmental, ancient, tribal, and Chilean art is a tradition of collaboration, a mixing of media, and an emphasis on process that makes the reason for the art just as important as the finished product. In art like this, the individual artist's identity is less important than the purpose of the art in the life of a community or people. This purpose might be the need to remember a part of history in a visual way, a means of marking time, or a tribute to the dead created not by a government, but by those who mourn. The NAMES Project Quilt started as one panel, one person's need to commemorate a dead friend. It soon expanded to a collaborative vision with a plan for how the Quilt could grow: panels approximately the size of a human body or a casket; panels to remember people who are most often cremated and leave no grave plot to visit; panels sewn together into grids—individual lost lives stitched together, woven into an enormous picture of the effect of AIDS.

This vision is dependent on the contributions of a growing number of individual artists who work alone or with others to stitch and paint a memory of someone they loved. They do this in the best tradition of quilting, using pieces from the person's life, articles of clothing, teddy bears, photographs, messages to the dead from the living who mourn them. People who have never before felt confident about making art testify about the healing nature of this participation in a larger artwork—one that also allows them to "come out" around AIDS. Instead of mourning alone, they link their grief to others both visually and organizationally. Finally, in keeping with the unifying principle of the whole Quilt, they stitch or paint the person's name who died, committing that name to an historical document that physically shows real people, not mere statistics.

Art needs an audience. The NAMES Project Quilt has an unusually large one: hundreds of thousands of us across the nation who have walked amidst the panels, stood in the sea of colorful memories, cried, found panels of people we've known, hugged strangers—in general been awed, moved, and inspired by the power of the total vision. We, the audience, have received much of the healing communicated by the artists through the ritual reading of names and physical beauty of the Quilt. It is a rare work of art that can transcend its material components to communicate this kind of collective power. A political demonstration could not have done the same. Neither could a single memorial service nor a walk through a graveyard.

■ ■ ■

There are other reasons the Quilt is effective art. The quilt form itself feels very American. It is almost apple pie in its connotations, and when used to communicate thoughts and feelings about AIDS with all the stigma, a powerful dialectic occurs. Tangible evidence of individuals who lie outside of society's favored status gets woven into a domestic metaphor. The Quilt reveals that these people had domestic lives of one kind or another—family, friends, lovers who banded together to make the panels. The quilt form historically is a feminist metaphor for integration, inclusiveness, the breaking down of barriers, the pieces of someone's life sewn together. It is not surprising that women and gay men would pick up on this traditional women's art. Sewing and weaving have been metaphors for life, death, creation, and transformation in many cultures. Just as the spider weaves from material that is pulled from inside, women have woven their ideas and emotions into cloth decorated with the symbols of their culture. The NAMES Quilt picks up on all these traditions.

The grid pattern is another important part of the Quilt's effect as art. Formed by a huge (and growing) number of individually made panels, the pattern signifies inclusiveness and equality. Unlike a cemetery where class differences are obvious, this grid unites the dead regardless of who they were. It is as though the dead are woven together, visually mirroring the networks the living form to create the quilt. Within this grid pattern there is an amazing and unplanned repetition of imagery. Items of clothing dominate—remnants of someone's wardrobe, T-shirts, jeans, jewelry, glittery gowns, and sashes. Teddy bears are common, too, a kind of cuddly accompaniment to the dead, a lively symbol of rest and sleep. The dates that show up so often are shocking because of the abbreviated life spans they illustrate. Some of the most powerful panels contain messages written directly to the dead, stitched or painted: "Sweet dreams," "I miss you every day."

The NAMES Quilt bridges the gap between art and social consciousness. Art is too often peripheral to our society, seen as superfluous fluff. Political activism, on the other hand, is often perceived as uncreative and separate from culture. The Quilt is a rare successful integration of these two worlds so separate in Western culture. We should be proud of an art form that originated in the gay community and that is able to communicate beyond to other communities. What is communicated is as complex as any art would strive for, something that will have historical significance beyond all of our lives. Developed outside established art channels, shown mostly in non-art environments, the Quilt could nevertheless teach the art world a great deal about organization, collaboration on a grand scale, and the communication of an aesthetic that crosses many boundaries. Very few artists or art projects are able to reach so many people in such a way.

The *NAMES Project AIDS Memorial Quilt,* October 1989.

Volunteers and others walk on the 21,000 panel *NAMES Project AIDS Memorial Quilt* in Washington.

Parts of the art world have started to hear about the Quilt. At least two or three well-known artists have created panels. In Baltimore, the Quilt will not be hung in one of the pavilions, gymnasiums, and civic centers that house the Quilt elsewhere on its national tour—it will be hung on the walls of the Baltimore Art Museum. Organizers are excited by these developments, viewing them as evidence of the far-reaching effects of the Quilt. But what will happen to the present spirit of the Quilt? Will focus turn to "famous" panels more than others? Will museums become a more targeted locale for the Quilt, changing the vantage point from ground to wall? These are important questions because so much of the Quilt's power lies in its existence outside the official art world. It would be unfortunate if the category of "non-artist" became accentuated by more of a focus on "real" artists, and intimidated wider participation. I would hate to see the Quilt swallowed up in the land of institutional art and co-opted from its community roots.

We should be proud of the Quilt, but we should also stand back and reflect on its process as often as necessary. The NAMES Project is growing at an overwhelming pace, one that demands a look at how centralized the vision can remain. The power of the Quilt is fully communicated when people walk among the squares, physically becoming part of the vast grid, feeling tiny in scale compared to the whole. Its power also lies in its capacity to educate about AIDS in the universal language of quilting. I am concerned that continuing centralization will make the Quilt unwieldy, both in organization and in size. Will continuous expansion make it impossible to display in one location? Will people have to see it only in pictures, or only in its home resting place of San Francisco?

*AIDS Quilt*—overhead shot.

What about communities deeply affected by AIDS but not yet familiar with the NAMES Project Quilt? In New York City, for instance, women of color and their children form a growing percentage of victims, yet I wonder how many panels reflect this. A continued centralization of the Quilt could stand in the way of the outreach that makes the Quilt's vision so powerful. One possible solution would be regional quilts that are more accessible to people. Smaller cities have already created their own quilts and displayed them locally before sending them to join the larger work. This link to something larger is an important part of the Quilt process, and it could easily continue with local areas concentrating on new outreach before joining together regionally. Stores in areas where there are many AIDS deaths could be organized to hang quilt grids in their windows. People could get involved who would never travel to Phoenix, or Baltimore, or other places on the tour, people who would never hear about the Quilt through existing channels.

It must be hard to think about giving up control of a project that has been so successful so quickly—especially in an age of media co-optation of art and social movements. But one of the most important roles the Quilt has played is as a tool for organization: individuals networking to make panels, groups networking to form local quilt tour organizations. A central vision has been important and may be for some time to come. But AIDS is unfortunately with us for longer than that, and the vision could become stronger by branching out. The ritual unfolding of the panels and reading of names might change from region to region. New cultural influences would add new dimensions. The Northeast's Quilt might take on a very different character from the Southwest's. These differences would be exciting and would expand the Quilt's dimensions as art. It would reach more people. And the inevitable difficulties of large organizations would be strengthened by more autonomy at the local level. People could still feel part of a larger-than-life whole, yet not be subsumed by an abstraction out of reach. If four football fields of panels are overwhelming, are ten necessarily better?

These are questions and reactions I have amidst my own emotions about the power of the Quilt and its significance as art in an age when the institutions of art can be so devoid of spirit. Art and artists survive regardless of art market trends, and most art will never be seen in a museum or gallery. It is the art made by your neighbor or your lover, the art that someone is compelled to make for reasons other than money. I hope the Quilt will never be a commodity on the art market, never owned by an individual or corporation, never laid to rest in one museum. The NAMES Project Quilt is a living, breathing, changing work of art, one that was inspired by grief and grew to communicate hope. Let it continue to live in good health.

## READING WRITING

### THIS TEXT: READING
1. According to Chrichton, is the *NAMES Quilt* art?
2. How does Chrichton distinguish between "real" or "high" art and the *NAMES Quilt*? Do you agree with this distinction?
3. What does the NAMES project share with feminist, environmental, and native art?
4. What is the audience for the NAMES quilt? How is it different than the audience for, say, the *Sensation* exhibition or a Picasso exhibit?

### YOUR TEXT: WRITING
1. Write an essay in which you define art. Then look at two or three different texts and explain why they either are or are not art, according to your definition.
2. If you can see the *NAMES Quilt*, do so. If not, try to watch a video about it or find pictures of it. Write an essay on the experience of seeing the *NAMES Quilt*. What kind of text is it?
3. Write an essay exploring the idea of artistry and authorship. Who is the artist of the *NAMES Quilt*? How does the quilt change how we think of art as the product of an "individual genius"? What is the role of the community in the creation of an art object?
4. Write an essay in which you explore the cultural climate in which the *NAMES Quilt* was made. What prompted the makers of the quilt? What is the artistic situation?

## SEQUENTIAL ART: "CLOSURE" AND "ART"

### ■ Scott McCloud ■

*These "essays" come from Scott McCloud's* Understanding Comics *(1994), a comic about the importance—and semiotics—of comics and comic books. McCloud forces us to think about what art is and how we see it. He also raises interesting questions about the intersection of comics and art.*

CLOSURE CAN TAKE *MANY FORMS*. SOME *SIMPLE*, SOME *COMPLEX*.

SOMETIMES, A MERE *SHAPE* OR *OUTLINE* IS ENOUGH TO TRIGGER CLOSURE.

THE MENTAL PROCESS DESCRIBED IN *CHAPTER TWO* WHEREBY THESE LINES BECOME A *FACE* COULD BE CONSIDERED CLOSURE.

EVERY TIME WE SEE A *PHOTOGRAPH* REPRODUCED IN A *NEWSPAPER* OR *MAGAZINE*, WE COMMIT CLOSURE.

OUR *EYES* TAKE IN THE *FRAGMENTED, BLACK-AND-WHITE IMAGE* OF THE "HALF-TONE" PATTERNS--

--AND OUR MINDS TRANSFORM IT INTO THE "REALITY"--

--OF THE *PHOTOGRAPH!*

IN *ELECTRONIC MEDIA,* CLOSURE IS *CONSTANT,* EVEN *OVER-POWERING!*

IN *FILM,* CLOSURE TAKES PLACE *CONTINUOUSLY--* TWENTY-FOUR TIMES PER *SECOND,* IN FACT-- AS OUR MINDS, AIDED BY THE *PERSISTENCE OF VISION,* TRANSFORM A SERIES OF *STILL PICTURES* INTO A STORY OF *CONTINUOUS MOTION.*

A MEDIUM REQUIRING EVEN *MORE* CLOSURE IS *TELEVISION,* WHICH, IN REALITY, IS JUST A *SINGLE POINT OF LIGHT,* RACING *ACROSS* THE SCREEN SO *FAST* THAT IT'S DESCRIBED MY FACE *HUNDREDS OF TIMES* BEFORE *YOU* CAN EVEN SWALLOW THAT *CORN CHIP!!* *

BETWEEN SUCH *AUTOMATIC ELECTRONIC* CLOSURE AND THE SIMPLER CLOSURE OF *EVERYDAY LIFE--*

--THERE LIES A MEDIUM OF COMMUNICATION AND EXPRESSION WHICH USES CLOSURE LIKE *NO OTHER...*

...A MEDIUM WHERE THE AUDIENCE IS A WILLING AND CONSCIOUS *COLLABORATOR* AND CLOSURE IS THE AGENT OF *CHANGE, TIME* AND *MOTION.*

* MEDIA GURU TONY SCHWARTZ DESCRIBES THIS AT LENGTH IN HIS BOOK *MEDIA, THE SECOND GOD,* ANCHOR BOOKS, 1983.

THE CLOSURE OF *ELECTRONIC* MEDIA IS *CONTINUOUS,* LARGELY *INVOLUNTARY* AND *VIRTUALLY IMPERCEPTIBLE.*

BUT CLOSURE IN **COMICS** IS *FAR* FROM CONTINUOUS AND *ANYTHING* BUT *INVOLUNTARY!*

*NOW YOU DIE!!*

*NO! NO!*

*EEYAA!!*

EVERY ACT COMMITTED TO PAPER BY THE COMICS ARTIST IS *AIDED* AND *ABETTED* BY A *SILENT ACCOMPLICE.*

AN *EQUAL PARTNER IN CRIME* KNOWN AS *THE READER.*

I MAY HAVE DRAWN AN *AXE* BEING *RAISED* IN THIS EXAMPLE, BUT I'M NOT THE ONE WHO LET IT *DROP* OR DECIDED HOW *HARD* THE BLOW, OR *WHO* SCREAMED, OR *WHY.*

*NOW YOU DIE!!* *NO! NO!* *EEYAA!!*

*THAT,* DEAR READER, WAS *YOUR SPECIAL CRIME,* EACH OF YOU COMMITTING IT IN YOUR OWN *STYLE.*

ALL OF YOU *PARTICIPATED* IN THE MURDER. ALL OF YOU *HELD THE AXE* AND *CHOSE YOUR SPOT.*

TO KILL A MAN BETWEEN PANELS IS TO CONDEMN HIM TO A THOUSAND DEATHS.

*PARTICIPATION* IS A *POWERFUL FORCE* IN *ANY* MEDIUM. FILMMAKERS *LONG AGO* REALIZED THE IMPORTANCE OF ALLOWING VIEWERS TO USE THEIR *IMAGINATIONS.*

BUT WHILE *FILM* MAKES USE OF AUDIENCES' IMAGINATIONS FOR *OCCASIONAL EFFECTS,* *COMICS* MUST USE IT FAR MORE *OFTEN!*

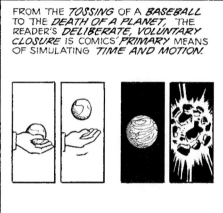

FROM THE *TOSSING* OF A *BASEBALL* TO THE *DEATH OF A PLANET,* THE READER'S *DELIBERATE, VOLUNTARY CLOSURE* IS COMICS' *PRIMARY* MEANS OF SIMULATING *TIME AND MOTION.*

CLOSURE IN COMICS FOSTERS AN INTIMACY SURPASSED ONLY BY THE *WRITTEN WORD,* A *SILENT, SECRET CONTRACT* BETWEEN *CREATOR* AND *AUDIENCE.*

HOW THE CREATOR *HONORS* THAT CONTRACT IS A MATTER OF BOTH *ART* AND *CRAFT.*

LET'S TAKE A LOOK AT THE *CRAFT.*

ART, AS I SEE IT, IS ANY HUMAN ACTIVITY WHICH *DOESN'T* GROW OUT OF *EITHER* OF OUR SPECIES' TWO BASIC INSTINCTS: *SURVIVAL* AND *REPRODUCTION!*

GRAAH!

EEEK!!

*EXAMPLE:* HERE'S A *PREHISTORIC MALE* CHASING A *PREHISTORIC FEMALE.* WITH ONLY ONE THING ON HIS MIND-- *REPRODUCTION!*

SO *STRONG* IS THIS INSTINCT THAT IT GOVERNS HIS *EVERY MOVE!* NOT ONE STEP IS WASTED IN THE *PURSUIT OF* HIS *GOAL!*

THE *FEMALE*--AFRAID FOR HER *SURVIVAL* -- MANAGES TO *HIDE.* NOW, *DEPRIVED* OF HIS GOAL, THE MALE STANDS *INDECISIVE.*

?  ?

*SUDDENLY--!*

ROAR!!!

*NOW* ALL OF HIS THOUGHTS AND ACTIONS ARE FOCUSED ON THAT *OTHER* VITAL HUMAN INSTINCT-- *SURVIVAL!*

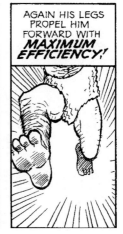

AGAIN HIS LEGS PROPEL HIM FORWARD WITH *MAXIMUM EFFICIENCY!*

WHAT MAY LOOK LIKE A TRIBE OF *BORED, INACTIVE CAVE-DWELLERS* BELOW US IS, IN FACT, A *THRIVING ART COLONY!*

SEE THAT OLD WOMAN WITH THE *STICK?* NOTICE THE *LINES* SHE'S MAKING IN THE *DIRT?*

TODAY SHE HAS A *STOMACHACHE* AND HER LINES ARE *TIGHT* AND *ANGULAR.* YESTERDAY SHE FELT *BETTER* AND HER LINES WERE *OPEN* AND *CURVED.*

AND *OVER THERE* A MAN BEATS A *SIMPLE RHYTHM* WITH A *PAIR OF STONES.* HE DOESN'T KNOW WHY, BUT THE SOUND *PLEASES* HIM.

TAP! TAP! TAP! TAP! TAP! TAP!

NEARBY, A BOY *KICKS UP PEBBLES AND DIRT* AND *PUMMELS THE AIR* WITH HIS *FIST.*

TODAY HE LOST A FIGHT WITH HIS BROTHER. NOW ALL HE CAN DO IS *DANCE AWAY* HIS FRUSTRATION.

WHILE OVER *HERE,* A LITTLE GIRL *SINGS HER SONG OF YOUTH!*

Dooooo°RRooooo° YB-BIP-BIP-BIP! GREEEGAH! WUK! WUK!

BECAUSE OF ITS INDEPENDENCE FROM OUR EVOLUTION-BRED INSTINCTS, ART IS THE WAY WE *ASSERT OUR IDENTITIES* AS *INDIVIDUALS* AND *BREAK OUT* OF THE *NARROW ROLES* NATURE CAST US IN.

OF COURSE, THE *GENIUS* OF *"MOTHER NATURE"* IS SUCH THAT EVEN *THESE* THINGS DO HAVE THEIR USES FROM AN *EVOLUTIONARY STANDPOINT.*

*THREE,* IN FACT.

FIRST, THEY PROVIDE EXERCISE FOR MINDS AND BODIES NOT RECEIVING OUTSIDE STIMULUS.

SECOND, THEY PROVIDE AN OUTLET FOR EMOTIONAL IMBALANCES, AIDING IN THE RACE'S MENTAL SURVIVAL.

THIRD AND PERHAPS MOST IMPORTANTLY TO OUR SURVIVAL AS A RACE, SUCH RANDOM ACTIVITIES OFTEN LEAD--

--TO USEFUL DISCOVERIES!

AAH!!!

FUMF!

THIS FUNCTION WOULD ALSO BE PERFORMED IN LATER CENTURIES BY SPORTS AND GAMES.

ART AS SELF EXPRESSION, THE ARTIST AS HERO; FOR MANY, ITS HIGHEST PURPOSE.

ART AS DISCOVERY, AS THE PURSUIT OF TRUTH, AS EXPLORATION; THE SOUL OF MUCH MODERN ART AND THE FOUNDATIONS OF LANGUAGE, SCIENCE AND PHILOSOPHY.

A LOT HAS CHANGED IN HALF A MILLION YEARS, BUT SOME THINGS NEVER CHANGE.

OH NO! I'M GONNA BE LATE FOR THAT JOB INTERVIEW!

THE PROCESSES ARE MORE COMPLEX NOW, BUT THE INSTINCTS *REMAIN THE SAME. SURVIVAL AND REPRODUCTION STILL HOLD THE UPPER HAND.

YET IN ALMOST EVERYTHING WE DO THERE IS AT LEAST AN *ELEMENT* OF ART.

PERHAPS A LITTLE *UNNECESSARY CHOREOGRAPHY* ON THE *ASSEMBLY LINE.*

OOOH, *BEHBEE!*

OR THE *PERSONAL STYLE* OF A *BICYCLE MESSENGER.*

HONK! HONK!

OR JUST THE WAY WE *SIGN OUR NAMES!*

...do herein pleag...

IN *SOME* OCCUPATIONS, THE LATITUDE FOR SELF-EXPRESSION IS *GREATER.* *SURVIVAL*--MAKING A LIVING--GOES HAND IN HAND WITH *CREATIVE DESIRE.*

I THINK IT'S FAIR TO SAY THAT SOME ACTIVITIES HAVE MORE ART *IN* THEM THAN OTHERS.

LIFE IS A SERIES OF *MINUTE DECISIONS,* SOME MOTIVATED BY *SURVIVAL,* SOME *NOT,* AND PROPORTIONS DO *VARY.*

*BUT* TO PROCLAIM, AS SO MANY SO OFTEN *DO,* THAT--

*THAT'S NOT ART!*

--PRESUMES THAT ART IS AN *EITHER/OR* PROPOSITION. I DON'T THINK IT IS.

RARE IS THE PERSON IN *ANY* OCCUPATION WHO EXPRESSES *NOTHING...*

...AND RARE IS THE *ARTIST* WHO CARES NOTHING FOR *SUCCESS,* I.E., *SURVIVAL!*

BUT THE *IDEAL* OF THE LATTER IS ALIVE IN THE HEARTS OF MANY ARTISTS WHO MAY *HOPE* FOR SUCCESS, BUT WON'T ALTER THEIR WORK TO *OBTAIN* IT.

THE *"FINE ARTIST"*--THE *PURE ARTIST*-- SAYS TO THE WORLD: "I DIDN'T DO THIS FOR *MONEY!* I DIDN'T DO THIS TO MATCH THE COLOR OF YOUR *COUCHES!*

"I DIDN'T DO THIS TO GET *LAID!* I DIDN'T DO THIS FOR *FAME* OR *POWER* OR *GREED* OR *ANYTHING ELSE!* I DID THIS FOR *ART!*"

IN *OTHER* WORDS: *"MY ART HAS NO PRACTICAL VALUE WHATSOEVER!"*

"BUT IT'S *IMPORTANT!*"

AND SOMETIMES IT *IS*, THOUGH IT MIGHT TAKE A *CENTURY* OR TWO FOR THE *REST* OF THE WORLD TO FIND OUT!

*"PURE"* ART IS ESSENTIALLY TIED TO THE QUESTION OF *PURPOSE*-- OF DECIDING WHAT YOU *WANT* OUT OF ART.

THIS IS AS TRUE IN *COMICS* AS IT IS IN *PAINTING, WRITING, THEATRE, FILM, SCULPTURE,* OR *ANY OTHER FORM*...

...BECAUSE THE CREATION OF *ANY* WORK IN *ANY* MEDIUM WILL ALWAYS FOLLOW A CERTAIN *PATH.*

## READING WRITING

### THIS TEXT: READING

1. What do you think McCloud's aims are in these pieces?
2. Do you agree with his idea about what art is? Why? If not, what is he leaving out?
3. Do you agree with McCloud's idea about the role of the audience in determining meaning? Do you feel you have such a role in what you watch? When do you perform such a role?
4. How does presenting this information in comic form change the way you view the information? Is it appropriate to present "serious" information in comic form? What might prevent us from receiving this information in the way the author might have intended it?
5. What is McCloud's writing situation—what is he writing against?

### YOUR TEXT: WRITING

1. In a short essay, make a case for nontraditional presentation of informational material.
2. Write about the way the text itself influences the reader. Can you think of other texts whose format invokes a reaction from the reader?
3. Write your own definition of art based on your own experience as a reader.
4. Write about your own experience as a reader in participating in making meaning.
5. How would you draw your paper? Who would narrate it? What would it look like? Just for fun, draw out your paper.

## IT ISN'T PRETTY . . . BUT IS IT ART?

### ■ Diana Mack ■

*In this essay (1999), Diana Mack argues that questions surrounding "good" art have resonances beyond the art world. She wonders who can and should define the standards for good or even acceptable public art. In a classic definitional essay manner, Mack lays out three principle for evaluating art. As you read, pay attention to how she makes her argument.*

FEW AMERICANS WAKE UP MORNINGS contemplating the question of what makes a good work of art. But surprisingly enough, three belligerent public disputes have recently centered on this very question.

New York Mayor Rudolph Giuliani made headlines last month when he vowed to withhold municipal funding if the Brooklyn Museum of Art went through with its controversial British art exhibition, *Sensation.* The major object of contention: an image of the Virgin Mary, her breast rendered in elephant dung. (See page 530).

Then, a few weeks later, parents in South Carolina, Georgia, and Minnesota protested the presence in public school classrooms of J.K. Rowling's bestselling Harry Potter series, one mother claiming this fantasy literature carried "a serious tone of death, hate . . . and . . . evil."

Finally, there was the public uproar in Seattle over the heavily bosomed and pregnant *Picardo Venus,* a community garden statue many find too suggestive.

In each case, those objecting to the disbursement of public funds for the display of art they find offensive insist they are not for censorship. They claim they merely want publicly funded and publicly presented artwork to reflect community standards of taste, decency, and respect for religious faith. All well and good; but who is to define those standards? Chris Ofili, painter of the *Sensation* exhibition's much maligned *Holy Virgin Mary,* claims that Mr. Giuliani falsely assigned deprecatory motives to his work. He is not out to desecrate the image of the Virgin Mary, he says.

Rather, he's a Roman Catholic earnestly coming to terms with his faith, his African heritage, and a long Western tradition of representing the Madonna.

Similarly, J.K. Rowling might claim that the Harry Potter books also stand in a long "pre-apologetic" literary tradition: Yes, they deal with magic and witchcraft. Their tone is dark. But no less a devout Christian than C.S. Lewis understood the power of pagan imagery in preparing the young imagination for the moral rigors and spiritual comforts of biblical religion. Indeed, if there is something wrong with a "tone of death" in children's literature, then we might as well jettison all our volumes of fairy tales. For these distilled popular narratives exert their charm and power precisely, as Bruno Bettelheim pointed out, because they allow children a reality-removed way to confront the "existential predicament."

And what of the *Picardo Venus?* Must she be rejected, as one citizen-critic contended, because she "glorifies fertility a little too much for kids," or because, as another said, "no normal woman looks like that"?

Do "normal" women look like Picasso painted them? Or Rubens? Did not Botticelli's immortal *The Birth of Venus* also glorify fertility? The point is that almost all the arguments we bring against public support of controversial new works are at best specious, at worst manifestly wrongheaded. Informed aesthetic judgments seem to elude us.

Faced with creative works that seem to us alien and unappealing, we are forced to fall back on that proverbial disclaimer, "I don't know much about it . . . I only know what I like."

Just because an artwork doesn't make us feel warm and fuzzy doesn't mean it's worthless. The Seattle man who protests against the *Picardo Venus* on the basis that "art is supposed to evoke all these good feelings" is wrong. Good art is not necessarily pleasing. It is, however, disciplined. It is about mastery of medium, form, and style. And good art must communicate something comprehensibly worthwhile, something worthy of contemplation. And here we get closer to the aesthetic problem facing the American public today. More and more so-called artists today call attention to themselves by shocking and agitating rather than by promoting reflection. In reaction to these salvos, the public has come to anticipate offense.

How do we move past the disturbing impasse of public contention over art and toward a healthier, more vital cultural life? One answer is to be guided in our aesthetic judgments by three important principles:

1. Art doesn't do. It says. Art is not action; it is speculation. It is looking, listening, digesting, speaking. Art can make a controversial statement; but it cannot do controversial things. If the primary effect of a so-called artwork is physical repulsion or titillation, if it acts on us rather than speaks to us, it is simply not up to the standards of art. If it makes us think, however, we should take up the challenge.

2. Art is about content, not context. Art is the schematic arrangement of forms and symbols through specific, culturally recognized mediums. If we exhibit, say, a cow's embryo in an art museum, it does not suddenly become a work of visual art simply by virtue of its surroundings.

3. Similarly, if we hung a print of Titian's *Woman on a Couch* in a biology lab, it would scarcely transform that painting into a science display. We need to be open to the possibilities of the creative process; yet, we must recognize that not everything offered up in the artistic arena is art.

The greater the knowledge, the sounder the judgment. When we venture onto the battlefield of the culture wars, we owe it to our artists and ourselves to come armed with knowledge. In a multicultural society such as America's, that means making the attempt to familiarize ourselves with the major artistic traditions of Europe, Asia, and Africa. Before we criticize, we need first to understand. Indeed, there is nothing more inspiring to good artists than a public that can be communicated with on the highest and most subtle levels of creativity and skill.

## READING WRITING

### THIS TEXT: READING
1. Do you agree with Mack's three principles for evaluating art?
2. Would you add another principle? If so, what?
3. What is Mack's thesis statement?
4. Does she rely on ethos, pathos, or logos for her argument?

### YOUR TEXT: WRITING
1. Write your own essay on art. Give 2–3 criteria for what makes good art. Be sure to explain and support your assertions.
2. Take a look at some the of images from the *Sensation* exhibit. Are the pieces from this exhibit good art? The Chris Ofilii painting in the Censorship Suite was a lightning rod at the exhibit. Is *it* good art? Why or why not?
3. Write an essay on a piece of public art in your city. Find a sculpture or a mural and talk about its relationship to its environs. What makes good *public* art?

*Student Essay*

### #27: READING CINDY SHERMAN AND GENDER

■ **Anne Darby** ■

*Among the most well known of Cindy Sherman's work is her* Untitled Film Stills *in which, using herself as a model, she creates staged scenes that could have been derived from black and white movies from the 1950s. None of these photographs were based on any specific film; they were meant to portray stereotypical female roles as created by or perpetuated by these movies in particular. To me, the most striking image in this series is* Untitled Film Still #27, *which depicts a woman dressed as if for a party with tears streaking her face. Though the aesthetic aspect of the photo-graph is simple, it appeals directly to the viewer, specifically women, via her own personal experience. The power of the image is in the viewer's projection and her empathy for the subject.*

The woman is seated, and the photograph is cropped from the middle of her forehead to the table on which her hands are resting. In her right hand she holds a half-smoked cigarette, and her left hand is curled distractedly around some indistinguishable object. In front of her right hand are a glass of champagne and a decorative ashtray. Before her left hand lies a pack of wooden matches, and on the ring finger of that hand there is a ring with a dark stone. It is impossible to discern whether it is merely a piece of jewelry or an indication of engage-ment, but either way it is enough to make the viewer speculate about her future marital sta-tus and, by association, her future in general.

The table is strewn with cigarette ash, which alludes to her preoccupation. She is wear-ing a low cut dress with a faux leopard fur collar that spans almost the width of her shoul-ders. The most noticeable aspect of the photograph is the emotion displayed on her face. Her heavy eye makeup is smeared by the tears which have run down her face in dark lines. Tears have caught on her eyelashes, held there by the heavy mascara. Light glints off of the exces-sive liquid, distorting and accentuating her eyes. Her mouth is partially open and her col-larbones protrude, which indicate that she is in mid-gasp.

We are all familiar with that moment, near the end of a heavy cry, when we begin to try to compose ourselves and regain the oxygen we have lost. It is my assumption that the mo-ment portrayed will be more poignant and powerful to female viewers, though it is possi-ble male viewers would be able to relate on some level. The photograph stands for me as a symbol of the struggle between a person's façade and their soul. The symbols shown can be divided into those that stand as signifiers of façade and those that portray the true self com-ing through.

The dress, specifically the low neckline, suggests that this woman has dressed for some-one other than herself. The idea that a woman, seen as a sexual object, lets (whether passively or actively, consciously or not) other parts of her character and psyche suffer is a predomi-nant theme in Sherman's early work. For example, her *Centerfolds* series acts as commentary on pornographic images of women, and many of those images depict women in what could be sensual poses, were it not for the emotion or in some cases fear or sickness, that pervades the scene.

It has been my experience that the great majority of women to some extent project an image of who they think they are expected to be. (I know that this is also an issue with men, but that is a whole different topic, about which I am not qualified to write.) We *want* to be all of these things: beautiful, collected, intelligent, happy, witty (yet demure!) and success-ful. Furthermore the presence of the alcohol and the cigarette, as well as the subject's outfit, lead me to believe that she is involved in a certain lifestyle in which a woman plays a slightly different role than she does in the home or the workplace.

In a bar, at a party, or at any sort of gathering which is meant on the surface to be celebratory, most of us switch gears, and attempt to maintain a pleasant front. At a party one drinks, smokes, and talks about nothing. One is attractive and easy to get along with, never tired or moody, never undergoing stressful situations or tragedy. For a little while, that is amusing, even positive, but any length of time spent in that world causes detriment to the body and the soul. Again, this is more applicable to women than to men, and especially in the movies on which this photograph was based, but certainly not specific to those.

Alcohol and cigarettes are crutches on which one may rely to numb pain, pass time, or ignore real issues. Drinking makes one dull, and in the long term, stunts emotional growth. It causes one to lose touch with one's self. The juxtaposition of the tears with the traditional meanings associated with champagne is what makes the photograph so real. In fact, the champagne works more effectively to make this comparison than any other form of alcohol would.

The theme of a woman's misery threatening her façade has found its way many times into art and literature. I am automatically reminded of Justine, a character in Lawrence Durell's *Alexandria Quartet.* Succinctly, Justine is a beautiful woman, married to a wealthy banker, who is haunted by events of her past, most of which she is not at liberty to talk about. She had a child that was stolen from her, and she was constantly reminded of the presence of a man who had taken advantage of her in her youth, to name just a few of her woes. On the surface, she was highly visible socially, and in a position to be envied; she was untouchably beautiful, was the wealthiest woman in the city, had a husband who loved her, but inside she was ravaged by her regrets and neuroses. In a similar vein, Neil Jordan wrote a short story about a woman making idle conversation at a party while in the back of her mind wondering where it was that her soul had gone. Granted, all of the stories here have very different elements, but that particular theme ties them all together.

For me, and possibly for many other women, the smeared makeup is the most powerful single signifier of this woman's self breaking through her projected persona. When a woman prepares herself to face the world, she puts on a mask. It is a defense mechanism, as well as a beauty aid. Some women rely on this more than others, some are more conscious of it than others, but the effect is essentially the same. The activities that smear eye makeup are the activities that threaten our façade of coolness. Sleeping, crying, or a mistake in application all reveal our real human qualities. If the photograph were to be narrowed down to just the eyes and the streaks of stained tears, it would still be a loaded visual text; the rest of the photograph only elaborates on what the eyes have already said.

This photo is of Sherman herself, but because she uses herself in every image she creates, through repetition she herself is phased out of significance, giving the spotlight to each specific persona. Sherman becomes a non-element in each photograph. The significance is placed on the aspects that are different from picture to picture, which create the person, or the stereotype. Of course, if the viewer sees only one of Sherman's photographs, this is not an issue. The image is so strikingly genuine that it is difficult, even with knowledge of the subject, to imagine its staging. Also, the woman's failure to acknowledge the camera makes us believe that we really are glimpsing straight into the scene, uninvited and unnoticed.

Through staged photographs Sherman is able to solidify this nebulous concept. The success of the photograph is in the fact that it has pinpointed the perfect image to display such a moment, and such an emotion. Its delivery relies on the viewer to make it anything other than thoughtless voyeurism, but it is unlikely that an image this powerful will miss its mark.

Works Cited

Durrell, Lawrence. The Alexandria Quartet. 4 vols. New York: Dutton, 1957.

Jordan, Neil. The Collected Fiction of Neil Jordan. London: Vintage, 1997.

Krauss, Rosalind. Cindy Sherman, 1975–1993. New York: Rizzoli Internation, 1993.

Photography Exhibitions: Videocassette #No. 11. Writ. Mark Miller. Art/New York, 1982.

Sherman, Cindy. Centerfolds. New York: Skarstedt Fine Art, 2003.

---. Untitled Film Stills. New York: Rizzoli, 1990.

Krauss, Rosalind. *Cindy Sherman, 1975–1993.* New York: Rizzoli International. 1993.

*Photography Exhibitions,* videocassette #11. Text and Interviews by Mark Miller. Art/New York. 1982.

Sherman, Cindy. *Untitled Film Stills.* Essay by Arthur C. Danto. New York: Rizzoli. 1990.

Jordan, Neil. "Her Soul," from *The Collected Fiction of Neil Jordan.* London: Vintage. 1997.

Durrell, Lawrence. *The Alexandria Quartet.* 4 vols. New York: E.P.Dutton & Co., Inc. 1957.

## READING WRITING

## THIS TEXT: READING

1. What method does Darby use to examine the photograph? Do you think this method would be effective for other photographs or texts?
2. What role does gender play in our ability to understand both Darby's essay and the photograph? In what ways does Darby address these concerns within the text?

## YOUR TEXT: WRITING

1. Write a short paper that examines the role a piece of popular culture played in your life, or a way a popular culture text you think reflects your own life.
2. Find a popular culture text you think reflects a particular attitude toward gender and do a reading of it through the lens of gender.

# The Censorship Suite

"Every work of art is an uncommitted crime," according to the German philosopher Theodore Adorno. Similarly, Pablo Picasso, a painter whose name probably rings a bell, said in 1935 that for him, "a picture is a sum of destructions." Those of you who think of art as primarily "pretty" or "uplifting," might find both of these statements rather shocking. We tend not to think of art as either dangerous or criminal, yet for many, that is what it has become.

In the last twenty years, a number of artists, museums, and granting agencies have lost funding, incurred fines, been shut down and in some cases arrested for supporting, producing and exhibiting art that some have found indecent. Indeed, one of the great clashes of American democracy occurs when freedom of expression bumps up against laws and civil codes prohibiting pornography and hate speech. Fundamental American values clash with questions about morality, standards, and public funding. For example, who decides what is pornography and what is art? Is art that employs racist images and ideas itself racist? Who gets to censor art? What are the criteria for art censorship? Should art that is funded by tax dollars be subject to public approval?

These questions came to the fore in 1987 with the appearance of two separate art events. The first was a photograph by Andres Serrano, who was awarded a $15,000 grant by the Southeastern Center for Contemporary Art in Winston-Salem, North Carolina, a program funded by the National Endowment for the Arts (NEA). The photograph in question featured a crucifix in a golden, bubbly haze, a photograph that according to *The New York Times,* "appears reverential, and it is only after reading the provocative and explicit label that one realizes the object has been immersed in urine." Of course, the artwork in question is the now infamous *Piss Christ.* That same year, the Philadelphia Institute of Contemporary Art (ICA) received an NEA grant to host a retrospective of Robert Mapplethorpe's photographs, entitled "The Perfect Moment." The show included some homoerotic photographs and a couple of portraits of naked children (commissioned by their parents). The exhibit ran in Philadelphia and Chicago without incident. However, enraged by federal funding for *Piss Christ,* some conservative congressmen such as Jesse Helms (R–N.C.), Alphonse D'Amato (R–N.Y.) and Dick Armey (R–Tex.) got wind of the NEA-funded Mapplethorpe exhibit, slated to arrive at the Corcoran Gallery in Washington, D. C. In June of 1989, 108 congressmen filed a formal complaint against the NEA charging it supported indecent art with public funds. Two days previously, the director of the Corcoran had cancelled the Mapplethorpe exhibit out of fear of negative publicity, but it did no good. The war over art, decency, and public monies was ratcheted to a new level, and public art and the public funding for visual art has never been the same in the United States.

Not only does this debate raise questions about funding for art, but it also brings the role of visual art into the spotlight as a particularly vulnerable and powerful text. Why is it that visual texts remain a lightning rod for censorship over written ones? Granted, on occasion novels like *Catcher in the Rye* or *The Adventures of Huckleberry Finn* find themselves in a touchy case with a local schoolboard, but we rarely hear of people banning essays or poetry. On the contrary, paintings, sculptures, movies, and especially photographs worry watchdog groups a great deal and are the examples most commonly used to decry the immorality of American art. On the other hand, artists, professors and critics have hailed this debate as proof that art *matters,* that it is powerful, and that people must take it seriously.

All of the images in this suite have incurred some kind of censorship or controversy. We reprint them here not to add to that controversy but to foreground the symbolic importance of visual texts. This entire book makes the argument that texts, signs and symbols carry enormous social and cultural weight—that these images engender such strong reactions is proof that the world is a text full of complicated texts. We also believe that it is important to engage any text that elicits powerful responses; in fact, almost nothing makes for better writing. Forcing yourself to articulate why a painting moves you (either positively or negatively) is one of the most effective strategies for vigorous writing and compelling argument.

As a side note, we got the idea for this suite from two sources—a free public information pamphlet from the National Coalition against Censorship (NCAC) and a photo-timeline based on this pamphlet that appeared in a wonderful book by the National Arts Journalism Program (NAJP) entitled *The New Gatekeepers: Emerging Challenges to Free Expression in the Arts.* We wish to thank Svetlana Mintcheva, Director of the Arts Advocacy Project at the NCAC for her help with this suite.

Andres Serrano, *Piss Christ*

Dread Scott, *What Is the Proper Way to Display a US Flag?*

Avalus, Hock and Sisco, *Welcome to America's Finest Tourist Plantation*

Andres Serrano, *Klanswoman*

Gran Fury, *Kissing Doesn't Kill*

Andres Andy Cox, *CityBank Posters*

Chris Ofili, *The Holy Virgin Mary*

Alma Lopez, *Our Lady*

Renee Cox, *Yo Mama's Last Supper*

*A Boondocks Cartoon*

  READING  WRITING

## THIS TEXT: READING

1. Some might argue that some of these images are not, in fact, "art." Would you agree? Which ones are "art" and which ones are not? How do you make your determination?
2. Does the artistry or aesthetics of a visual text affect how you perceive it? That is, if its form is beautiful but its content is disturbing, can it still be art? Does its content diminish (or enhance) its artistry?
3. Which of the images is the most disturbing? Why?
4. If you could own any of these pieces, which would you want? Why?
5. If *Piss Christ* had a different title would it have caused such an uproar? What if it had been titled *Golden Christ* or *What the Modern World Has Done to Religion*? How does the title affect how we see the photograph?
6. In 1997, author Anthony Julius wrote a paper called "Art Crimes," in which he argues for "the creative complicity of art with crime—what he calls "crimes of art that are also crimes *against* art." He favors these kinds of art crimes because they challenge the boundaries of what is art and what is law. Are any of these texts crimes against art?

7.  Do you think these works of art mirror American values and culture or ignore them?

8.  In his engaging book *Arresting Images: Impolitic Art and Uncivil Actions,* Steven C. Dubin argues that "a combination of two critical elements is required for art controversies to erupt: there must be a sense that values have been threatened, and power must be mobilized in response to do something about it." In what ways do these art works *threaten* American values? In what ways do they uphold American values?

## YOUR TEXT: WRITING

1.  Write an argumentative paper in which you claim that these works should or should not be censored. Be sure to supply reasonable information to support your assertions.

2.  Write a definitional paper on art and show why and how these pieces are (or are not) art.

3.  Write an essay comparing one of the works here with a classic work of art. For instance, you might compare *Piss Christ* with a more revered painting of a crucifixion from the middle ages or even more recently, such as Eugene Carriere's 1897 *Crucifixion.* Or, perhaps *Yo Mama's Last Supper* with da Vinci's; Mapplethorpe's photographs of nude men with Michaelangelo's *David.*

4.  Write a personal essay about looking at these images in your classroom. Is it odd to be confronted with disturbing images in a college classroom? Is it appropriate?

5.  Write an argumentative essay in which you take a stance on public funding for art. Should tax-payer dollars go to fund controversial exhibits? What is the difference between funding art and funding wars? Paintings vs. missiles? Sculptures over monuments?

6.  Write an essay on the placement of this suite in this book. Do the authors make an argument about censorship and art with this suite? Are they objective?

7.  Do a semiotic analysis of one of the works in this suite. Talk about the various signs, symbols and codes the artist uses to achieve an effect.

READING   *Outside the Lines*

## CLASSROOM ACTIVITIES

1.  Bring in a slide or a photograph of a famous work of art. As a class, read the artistic text. How does reading it as a group change how you see it?

2.  As a class, select an image from the book. Then, spend 15 minutes trying to redraw or reproduce the image. How does that change the image? How does it change how you see the image?

3.  Bring a painting by Elsworth Kelley or Barnett Newman or Morris Louis to class. Or, look at a sculpture by Claes Oldenburg or Jeff Koonz. Have a discussion on whether these pieces are art. Why? Why not?

4.  Look at a particularly incendiary artistic text in class, like Andres Serrano's *Piss Christ* or a Robert Mapplethorpe photograph or the Chris Ofili painting from the *Sensation* exhibit. What is the role of art, decency, and public opinion? Where and how do aesthetics and ethics meet? What cultural forces might prompt this kind of art?

5.  Look at some photographs by Diane Arbus. What sort of comment is Arbus making about the world? As a class, discuss the ethics of Arbus's photos. Bring some of your own photos to class. How do your portraits of people differ from Arbus's? What do Arbus's photographs tell us about how she sees the world? (See pp. 374–375)

6.  Look at some Warhol prints in class. Are his pieces art? Why or why not?

7.  Talk about the differences between painting and photography. What can one do that the other cannot?

8.  Take a field trip to look at some pieces of sculpture near or on your campus. How does sculpture adhere to the principles of artistic design?

9.  Talk about the role of art in American culture. Compare how you think about art to how you think about television, film, and literature.

## ESSAY IDEAS

1.  Write a paper in which you define art, then show why three paintings, photographs, or sculptures meet your definition of art.

2.  Compare one of the images in this chapter to one of the poems in Chapter 1. How are painting and poetry similar? How are they different?

3.  Write a poem about one of the images in this chapter, and then write an essay about the process of writing a poem about the image.

4.  What is the relationship between gender and art? Many of the most famous paintings, photographs, and sculptures are of nude women. How has art altered how men and women see the female body?

5.  In what way is how we see the world affected by what we believe or what we know? How does our background, our beliefs, our interests, and our personality affect how we see art? How does the political climate of our society affect how we see art?

6.  Compare a Diane Arbus photograph with a classic painting. Are both art? Compare what della Francesca or da Vinci or Vermeer tries to do in his art with what Arbus tries to accomplish in hers. How might their respective cultures influence their ideas of what art should do?

7.  Write an essay comparing Chrichton's questions about art and the NAMES quilt with Mack's questions about art and the *Sensation* exhibit. How do both pieces rise out of social or political unrest?

8.  Look at some of the advertisements in this book. Using Acton's notion of composition, argue how advertisements adhere to notions of artistic design.

9.  Write an essay in which you demonstrate and explain how a work of art makes a political statement.

10. Do you believe that public funding for the arts should be cut if the public finds the art objectionable? Can the public, if it supports an exhibit with its tax dollars, censor a work of art?

11. Write an essay on the artistic situation for one of the texts. What cultural or societal forces may influence what or how an artist creates?

# Reading and Writing About Advertising, Journalism, and the Media

■ ■ ■  Jon Stewart is the anchor of *The Daily Show*.

In the last twenty years, the word "media" has become almost an obscenity, particularly to those who are caught in its gaze. Such a sticky word demands a definition.

While anything from books to magazines to news programs to radio shows to films is technically a medium—media is the plural of medium. For the purposes of this chapter, we will define the media as organizations or companies that seek to cover any kind of news in whatever form. Probably the most technically correct way to refer to news organizations would be just that—news organizations—but because "media" has itself become a hot text, we want to engage it here. We include advertising in this chapter as well, because although it does not cover anything, often it helps pay for the coverage we see. "The media" has become a symbol of a world whose happenings are broadcast 24 hours a day, where no subject seems too trivial to be covered. Everyone seems to think the media are too intrusive. And yet . . . we watch, and we watch, and we read, and we watch. If we did not watch or read, the media would change because the media are not one entity but many, which are always changing. For instance, there was no cable television when the authors of this book were born, and thus no CNN. Moreover, when many of you were born, the Internet was only a military communications system, hardly the consuming force it is today. So, whatever we write and think about the media now is destined to change for better or worse as our world changes.

Though the media are diverse in nature, they share a number of concerns that connect them. Almost all forms of media struggle to balance various concerns: public interest versus profit, fairness and objectivity versus bias, national coverage versus local, depth of coverage versus breadth of coverage, as well as some other more temporal concerns. The first conflict, balancing the public interest and the need to have the public watch, read, or listen, is often the one that gets the media into the most trouble; it leads to the charge that the media are shallow, intent on sensationalizing news. Nevertheless, all the conflicts lead to our sense that there is something "wrong" with the media, that something is not quite working right in the system. Yet, while the media are far from perfect (what is, after all?), they do perform a crucial role in American life and American culture. This introduction will begin to explain some of the difficulties and misconceptions attached to the media before going into articles that explore the media in more depth.

Separate but related elements of the media are advertisers and marketers who have a crucial financial relationship with newspapers, magazines, web pages, television news, and television shows. In essence, advertising pays for our free television and subsidizes our purchase of magazines and newspapers—without ads, we would pay for broadcast television (it's why cable television generally and premium channels like HBO cost money) and pay a lot more for newspapers and magazines. What do advertisers get in return for their ads? The simple answer is public exposure for their products or services. The more complicated (and perhaps unintended) one is an influence in public life. Although some critics object to the very existence of advertising in public life, most everyone acknowledges that advertising is the price we pay for living in a capitalist society. What is most criticized about advertising is the way advertising seeks to sell us products through manipulation and base appeals—its use of implicit and often inflated promises of various forms of happiness (sexual gratification, satiation of hunger, thinness, coolness) with the purchase of advertised items. When we consider these issues plus the sheer proximity of where and how ads and other media appear, it makes sense to think of these two entities as two sides of the same coin. While advertisers are not what people automatically think of as the media, their influence and importance in American society and their impact on various media outlets cannot be denied.

This introduction may seem one of our more political ones, but there is a reason for that: everyone, from liberals to conservatives, from the rich to the poor, from young to old, seems to criticize what the media do. Our purpose in asking you to "read" media and advertising in a complex way is to help you broaden and complicate your view of them. Some things to consider about the media:

## The media are businesses not a public service.

While they cover the news, the media are in the business of selling newspapers or garnering ratings points. But as accepted protectors of the public interest, they also have obligations to the public—their connection to public interest is part of their business credibility. Some argue that because of the advantages given to television and radio networks by the government—exclusive use of broadcast frequencies for radio stations and various broadcast advantages to the big three television networks (NBC, CBS, and ABC)—that media outlets have further obligations to the public interest.

And yet, at the heart, the media are business organizations. As a way of trying to maintain some distance between the business side and the editorial (news) side, media organizations often try to separate the two divisions: the editorial side covers the news; the business side gets advertising and does accounting work. But these two elements often meet anyway. Special sections in magazines and in newspapers in which coverage is devoted to a particular event or phenomenon are the most obvious examples, but when we watch television some decisions seem motivated by the business component; local coverage of a business opening or prominently mentioning sponsorship of local events is an example of this interchange.

Nevertheless, in a media outlet with split organizations, keeping the business and editorial sides completely separate is impossible. Even the editorial side of large newspapers like *The New York Times* and *The Washington Post* may have unconscious motivations toward the business end; a newspaper is generally designed toward highlighting the most important stories, a tactic which will "sell" the newspaper to the patron. However, the editorial side does not solicit ads directly and makes few of those types of decisions. On the other hand, small town papers may make even less of a distinction between the editorial and business side. In smaller communities, the publisher, who either represents the owner or is the owner, *will* often influence editorial decisions, especially in the editorials of a paper.

So, what are we to do with such information? Again, given the fact that the basic structures of media organizations are unlikely to change, the most important thing to do is to watch or read news with an active, sometimes skeptical eye, looking for links between business interests and media outlets. Even more importantly, read news widely. Look at "alternative" papers or read media criticism. Taking such steps will help you become a better reader of the media.

## The media are made up of a variety of people.

Do you think Tom Brokaw and the local weekly's columnist have similar roles in the media? Of course not—but the latter is as much a media member as the former. The large differences between members of the media (some of whom claim not to be) demonstrate what the media mean and do is complicated rather than simple. When columnists, politicians, or sport figures refer to the media, whom, specifically, do they mean? Miss Manners? National Public Radio? The folks at the History Channel? The obituary writer of your hometown newspaper? Probably they are thinking of the very few, very public media outlets like the major television networks, the overly aggressive talk radio personalities and perhaps some writers for national newspapers and magazines. However, most members of "the media" are regular, virtually anonymous people who try to bring you interesting, important stories.

Although many members of the media have similar aims, their format and their audience shape their content. Radio news can only read a few paragraphs of a traditional newspaper story in its allotted time and has to rely on taped interviews to enhance it. A television news report has to focus on visual material, and national newspapers have different expectations attached to them than does the local weekly. To an extent, the format and mission of a news organization will dictate how it covers an event and sometimes even whether it will cover that event.

Additionally, different media do different things well, and the variety is what gives our media wonderful breadth and scope. Newspapers analyze long-term events better than television does, and magazines do it even better. But in covering house fires and the weather, and showing sports highlights, television is significantly better. Overall, the media have different elements that make various organizations better suited to do one job rather than another. There are very few absolutes when it comes to the media. Some newspapers and television stations are civic-minded organizations dedicated to upholding the public trust. Sometimes newspapers seem motivated more by financial concerns. Some ads are very entertaining. Some are offensive. Some media outlets try to present the news in the most balanced, most objective way they can. Other sources make no bones about being biased. The crucial thing is to be able to view the media generally, and advertising and the news specifically, with a critical eye.

### Despite what your favorite conservative radio or television talk show host says, the media are not particularly liberal.

You may not be familiar with the ongoing controversy of the supposed "liberal bias" of the media, but if you spend any time watching or reading columnists—both from the left (liberal) and right (conservative)—you will encounter claims of a liberal media. Actually the fact that someone points out that there is a liberal bias itself undermines the idea of one. If there is such a liberal bias, then how have we heard about it? Through the conservative media.

You may think we exhibit a so-called liberal bias in taking this stance, but the business element that often shapes editorial content, especially in small communities and perhaps the networks as well, tends to be more sympathetic to conservative political ideals. In addition, the fact that most media outlets recognize many conservative commentators probably shows how baseless this idea of a liberal media really is. Additionally, most publications do not foreground information that is of concern to liberals or liberal organizations. For instance, do you know of any major news publication with a "Labor" section? How about a section entitled "Feminism"? Or, for that matter, "Racial Equality"? Does your local radio station give an environmental awareness update? Probably not. However, every major paper devotes a great deal of time to its business section, and just about every radio station gives some kind of market news or stock report. Sports never get the short shrift, yet many sportswriters, owners of sports franchises, and many athletes themselves tend to be both politically and socially conservative. Lastly, simple coverage of events can reflect bias. In the September 2002 issue of *Harper's Magazine,* for example, the *Harper's* index lists the number of appearances made by corporate representatives on U.S. nightly newscasts in 2001 at 995, while the number of appearances of labor representatives was 31.

On the other hand, it may be unfair to accuse the media of leaning too far to the right. Most actors, filmmakers, and singers find affinity with left-leaning causes and, as you know, entertainment always makes the news. Both liberal and conservative groups assail the media for bias, which probably indicates that the media's bias falls somewhere in the middle. The media's political bias may or may not be of concern to you now, but it is one aspect of the media you will continually hear about as they play a larger and larger role in public discourse.

## The media are not objective, but its members try to be fair.

Reporters and editors are human beings with political, social, and cultural preferences that they hope to acknowledge and put away when reporting. Reporters quickly learn they have to ask both (or many) sides questions when it comes to an issue. News stories often have this "she said, he said" quality. Does that mean the media always do a good job of being objective or fair? Definitely not, but they generally aim to do so. Those outlets with a specific political agenda are usually responsible enough to make that orientation clear in their editorial page or early in the publication or program. It is also worth noting that editorial writers and columnists are absolutely under no obligation to be fair or objective; their object is to deliver their opinion for better or worse. Calls for their objectivity miss the point of what an editorial is supposed to do—deliver opinions.

Questions of objectivity and fairness are not only important when talking about the media but in your own work. As writers and researchers, we hope we are being objective when we undertake a subject, but we naturally come to any subject with a viewpoint that is shaped by our experiences and the ideas that come from them. That is why we may disagree with each other over whether we liked a movie or a book, or over which candidate we support in an election (or even who we find attractive or not).

Though reporters come to the news with biases, they generally do understand their obligations to report fairly and generally serve the public interest, just as editorial writers and columnists understand their *mission* to seek to influence public opinion. The bigger point here is that critics who claim a lack of objectivity from the media are uninformed about the reality of the media (sometimes deliberately so). The media often deserve the criticism they get from both liberals and conservatives, but an imperfect media is destined in any system— in particular, one whose primary focus is business. Understanding these concerns will help you to understand the media in a more inclusive and a more informed way.

## Advertisers reflect consumers' desires as well as business's desire to sell to them.

There is a long-standing belief that advertising is manipulative and somehow unsavory. While we won't argue fully with those ideas, we believe it is important to think about what exactly advertising does. For one, we do think that advertising generally tries to sell us things we want (even if we "shouldn't" want them). Advertising items that consumers do not want is not a particularly effective use of advertiser's dollars. If you look at the majority of what advertisers sell, they consist of consumer items such as food, cars, clothing, electronics, and services—things that people want, though again the issue of how many of these things we should have or want is another question. Advertising can only influence a consumer so much—if a new snack food tastes like soap or broccoli, endorsements by every celebrity will still fail to sell it. Accordingly, some advertising experts believe that the greatest influence happens in choosing a brand at the point of sale, not in actually choosing to buy the product itself. Most of the marketing research that businesses do is *not* geared toward learning how to manipulate but learning what consumers will buy.

Yet the question of how far advertisers go in changing our attitudes about our world and what we should want is an open question that researchers continue to try to answer. We think that blaming advertisers for the perceived shallowness of human desire oversimplifies the role advertisers and consumers play in deciding what they want.

In addition, both authors have been confronted in the classroom with the idea that the public is not very smart compared to the students themselves. This kind of thinking on the part of students probably underestimates the intelligence of the public. If you assume the public is as savvy as you are, you will avoid many pitfalls both now and in the future.

## Advertising and graphic design can be considered artistic.

Artistic components abound in advertising. Advertisers and directors of commercials compose their ads so that they are both aesthetically pleasing and effective at getting us to buy. Advertisers often use the same principles as artists by seeking tension, drama, comedy, and beauty in their work. And sometimes directors and artists do both commercial and more "artistic" work. For instance, film directors such as David Lynch and the Coen brothers have all done television commercials, and many artists do graphic design (including those involved in the Absolut Vodka campaign). What complicates graphic design and television commercials as art is their associations with commercial interests. Americans like to separate art from commerce; we would rather have our artists make their money from selling their art to the community not to companies. However, increasingly, the two worlds are merging.

What do we do when we see a funny or clever commercial or a piece of advertising that is particularly striking? Perhaps we feel at war with ourselves in trying to place within a context what is clearly artistic expression and yet is trying to sell us something. Can we enjoy the art of advertising while decrying its influence? It is a difficult question. There are a lot of clever advertisements and interesting graphic design out there; to make a false distinction between high art and commercialism is to ignore how the texts of advertising and the texts of art actually work.

## Advertisers appeal to us through common images, whose meaning we have already learned.

Advertisers appeal to us through images that are iconic—standing directly in for something—or symbolic. Diamond manufacturers do not have to tell us that diamonds serve as an icon for sophistication and wealth—we already know that. Thus, the diamond ring has become an icon for luxury, as has a spacious car with a leather interior and adjustable seats.

We have learned what manicured lawns, Bermuda shorts, and gold jewelry mean by association. We know what it means to see a beach, golf clubs, a city, or any number of things or settings in a commercial. Because advertisers communicate through images as much as they do words, and these images seem to convey what they want without too much effort, looking at the visual language they use can tell us more about the role these images play in American culture.

## Researchers disagree about advertising's effects on consumers.

Many researchers, including some of the writers included here, believe there is a connection between advertisements and harmful behavior. Jean Kilbourne (not included here), for example, suggests that ads influence our children in harmful ways, particularly young women. William Lutz argues that the way in which advertisers alter the meaning of words can have a harmful effect on language and how we use it. Others are not so sure. Malcolm Gladwell's piece on "The Coolhunt" details advertisers' search for what is cool, so that can be advertised toward a sale.

The authors are not convinced in one particular way, with this caveat. We believe the relationship between humans and any form of culture is complicated. We are not denying that there is a relationship between advertising and behavior—we are just not convinced about how direct it is. Similarly, we are not making any specific claims about the relationship between the media and advertising except to say that the two are increasingly intimately related and that we urge you to continue to be literate readers of both.

### ■■■ WORKSHEET ■■■

News Media

**Medium:** What form of media are you watching or reading? How does form contribute to coverage?

**Bias:** What point of view does the story seem to have? Are there some key words that indicate this? Do all the same stories seem to have the same viewpoint? If there is a bias, is the story still "fair"—does the reporter seek multiple perspectives?

**Signs:** When watching a newscast, how does the program communicate in image (video, photograph, graphic)? What symbols does it use? Are there any unintended meanings? How does the clothing of the reporters and anchors contribute to what we take from the newscast?

**Audience:** To what audience does the news article or news report appeal? How can you tell? Will others outside the target audience feel alienated by the report or article? What are news organizations assuming about their audience in a particular piece or the newscast, magazine, Web site, or newspaper as a whole?

**Reality:** Do the images and ideas match your idea of reality? Are they supposed to? Do they (the people reporting and presenting the news) see the world the way you do?

**Race, ethnicity, gender, class:** How are images of any or all of these groups presented? Can you tell the bias of the reporter or news organization from their presentation?

Advertising

**Signs:** How does the advertisement speak to you through images? What do the images symbolize? Are there unintended meanings attached to the symbols? Can you classify the symbols into types? What do advertisers assume about the connections you will make between the signs presented and what researchers call "the point of purchase"?

**Audience:** What is the target audience of this advertisement? How do you know? What assumptions are advertisers making about their audience?

**Race, ethnicity, gender, class:** How are images of any or all of these groups presented? Can you tell what advertisers think of these groups through their portrayal? Or their absence?

---

| **THE COOLHUNT** |
| --- |
| ■ **Malcolm Gladwell** ■ |

*Malcolm Gladwell is the author of* The Tipping Point, *and a frequent writer about culture for* The New Yorker, *a national magazine about the arts and politics. Here he explores the idea of cool and how advertisers try to find it (1997). In what way does Gladwell give a semiotic reading of "cool"?*

> ### Who decides what's cool? Certain kids in certain places—and only the coolhunters know who they are.

## 1.

Baysie Wightman met DeeDee Gordon, appropriately enough, on a coolhunt. It was 1992. Baysie was a big shot for Converse, and DeeDee, who was barely twenty-one, was running a very cool boutique called Placid Planet, on Newbury Street in Boston. Baysie came in with a camera crew—one she often used when she was coolhunting—and said, "I've been watching your store, I've seen you, I've heard you know what's up," because it was Baysie's job at Converse to find people who knew what was up and she thought DeeDee was one of those people. DeeDee says that she responded with reserve—that "I was like, 'Whatever'"— but Baysie said that if DeeDee ever wanted to come and work at Converse she should just call, and nine months later DeeDee called. This was about the time the cool kids had decided they didn't want the hundred-and-twenty-five-dollar basketball sneaker with seventeen different kinds of high-technology materials and colors and air-cushioned heels anymore. They wanted simplicity and authenticity, and Baysie picked up on that. She brought back the Converse One Star, which was a vulcanized, suede, low-top classic old-school sneaker from the nineteen-seventies, and, sure enough, the One Star quickly became the signature shoe of the retro era. Remember what Kurt Cobain was wearing in the famous picture of him lying dead on the ground after committing suicide? Black Converse One Stars. DeeDee's big score was calling the sandal craze. She had been out in Los Angeles and had kept seeing the white teen-age girls dressing up like cholos, Mexican gangsters, in tight white tank tops known as "wife beaters," with a bra strap hanging out, and long shorts and tube socks and shower sandals. DeeDee recalls, "I'm like, 'I'm telling you, Baysie, this is going to hit. There are just too many people wearing it. We have to make a shower sandal.'" So Baysie, DeeDee, and a designer came up with the idea of making a retro sneaker-sandal, cutting the back off the One Star and putting a thick outsole on it. It was huge, and, amazingly, it's still huge.

Today, Baysie works for Reebok as general-merchandise manager—part of the team trying to return Reebok to the position it enjoyed in the mid-nineteen-eighties as the country's hottest sneaker company. DeeDee works for an advertising agency in Del Mar called Lambesis, where she puts out a quarterly tip sheet called the L Report on what the cool kids in major American cities are thinking and doing and buying. Baysie and DeeDee are best friends. They talk on the phone all the time.

They get together whenever Baysie is in L.A. (DeeDee: "It's, like, how many times can you drive past O.J. Simpson's house?"), and between them they can talk for hours about the art of the coolhunt. They're the Lewis and Clark of cool.

What they have is what everybody seems to want these days, which is a window on the world of the street. Once, when fashion trends were set by the big couture houses—when cool was trickle-down—that wasn't important. But sometime in the past few decades things got turned over, and fashion became trickle-up. It's now about chase and flight—designers and retailers and the mass consumer giving chase to the elusive prey of street cool—and the rise of coolhunting as a profession shows how serious the chase has become. The sneakers of Nike and Reebok used to come out yearly. Now a new style comes out every season. Apparel designers used to have an eighteen-month lead time between concept and sale. Now they're reducing that to a year, or even six months, in order to react faster to new ideas from the street. The paradox, of course, is that the better coolhunters become at bringing the mainstream close to the cutting edge, the more elusive the cutting edge becomes. This is the first rule of the cool: The quicker the chase, the quicker the flight. The act of discovering what's cool is what causes cool to move on, which explains the triumphant circularity of coolhunting: because we have coolhunters like DeeDee and Baysie, cool changes more quickly, and because cool changes more quickly, we need coolhunters like DeeDee and Baysie.

DeeDee is tall and glamorous, with short hair she has dyed so often that she claims to have forgotten her real color. She drives a yellow 1977 Trans Am with a burgundy stripe down the center and a 1973 Mercedes 450 SL, and lives in a spare, Japanese-style cabin in Laurel Canyon. She uses words like "rad" and "totally," and offers non-stop, deadpan pronouncements on pop culture, as in "It's all about Pee-wee Herman." She sounds at first like a teen, like the same teens who, at Lambesis, it is her job to follow. But teen speech—particularly girl-teen speech, with its fixation on reported speech ("so she goes," "and I'm like," "and he goes") and its stock vocabulary of accompanying grimaces and gestures—is about using language less to communicate than to fit in. DeeDee uses teen speech to set herself apart, and the result is, for lack of a better word, really cool. She doesn't do the teen thing of climbing half an octave at the end of every sentence. Instead, she drags out her vowels for emphasis, so that if she mildly disagreed with something I'd said she would say "Maalcolm" and if she strongly disagreed with what I'd said she would say "Maaalcolm."

Baysie is older, just past forty (although you would never guess that), and went to Exeter and Middlebury and had two grandfathers who went to Harvard (although you wouldn't guess that, either). She has curly brown hair and big green eyes and long legs and so much energy that it is hard to imagine her asleep, or resting, or even standing still for longer than thirty seconds. The hunt for cool is an obsession with her, and DeeDee is the same way.

DeeDee used to sit on the corner of West Broadway and Prince in SoHo—back when SoHo was cool—and take pictures of everyone who walked by for an entire hour. Baysie can tell you precisely where she goes on her Reebok coolhunts to find the really cool alternative white kids ("I'd maybe go to Portland and hang out where the skateboarders hang out near that bridge") or which snowboarding mountain has cooler kids—Stratton, in Vermont, or Summit County, in Colorado. (Summit, definitely.) DeeDee can tell you on the basis of the L Report's research exactly how far Dallas is behind New York in coolness (from six to eight months). Baysie is convinced that Los Angeles is not happening right now: "In the early nineteen-nineties a lot more was coming from L.A. They had a big trend with the whole Melrose Avenue look—the stupid goatees, the shorter hair. It was cleaned-up aftergrunge. There were a lot of places you could go to buy vinyl records. It was a strong place to go for looks. Then it went back to being horrible." DeeDee is convinced that Japan is happening: "I linked onto this future-technology thing two years ago. Now look at it, it's huge. It's the whole resurgence of Nike—Nike being larger than life. I went to Japan and saw the kids just bailing the most technologically advanced Nikes with their little dresses and little outfits and I'm like, 'Whoa, this is trippy!' It's performance mixed with fashion. It's really superheavy." Baysie has a theory that Liverpool is cool right now because it's the birthplace of the whole "lad" look, which involves soccer blokes in the pubs going superdressy and wearing Dolce & Gabbana and Polo Sport and Reebok Classics on their feet. But when I asked DeeDee about that, she just rolled her eyes: "Sometimes Baysie goes off on these tangents. Man, I love that woman!"

I used to think that if I talked to Baysie and DeeDee long enough I could write a coolhunting manual, an encyclopedia of cool. But then I realized that the manual would have so many footnotes and caveats that it would be unreadable. Coolhunting is not about the articulation of a coherent philosophy of cool. It's just a collection of spontaneous observations and predictions that differ from one moment to the next and from one coolhunter to the next. Ask a coolhunter where the baggy-jeans look came from, for example, and you might get any number of answers: urban black kids mimicking the jailhouse look, skateboarders looking for room to move, snowboarders trying not to look like skiers, or, alternatively, all three at once, in some grand concordance.

Or take the question of exactly how Tommy Hilfiger—a forty-five-year-old white guy from Greenwich, Connecticut, doing all-American preppy clothes—came to be the designer of choice for urban black America. Some say it was all about the early and visible endorsement given Hilfiger by the hip-hop auteur Grand Puba, who wore a dark-green-and-blue Tommy jacket over a white Tommy T-shirt as he leaned on his black Lamborghini on the cover of the hugely influential "Grand Puba 2000" CD, and whose love for Hilfiger soon spread to other rappers. (Who could forget the rhymes of Mobb Deep? "Tommy was my nigga / And couldn't figure / How me and Hilfiger / used to move through with vigor.") Then I had lunch with one of Hilfiger's designers, a twenty-six-year-old named Ulrich (Ubi) Simpson, who has a Puerto Rican mother and a Dutch-Venezuelan father, plays lacrosse, snowboards, surfs the long board, goes to hip-hop concerts, listens to Jungle, Edith Piaf, opera, rap, and Metallica, and has working with him on his design team a twenty-seven-year-old black guy from Montclair with dreadlocks, a twenty-two-year-old Asian-American who lives on the Lower East Side, a twenty-five-year-old South Asian guy from Fiji, and a twenty-one-year-old white graffiti artist from Queens. That's when it occurred to me that maybe the reason Tommy Hilfiger can make white culture cool to black culture is that he has people working for him who are cool in both cultures simultaneously. Then again, maybe it was all Grand Puba. Who knows?

One day last month, Baysie took me on a coolhunt to the Bronx and Harlem, lugging a big black canvas bag with twenty-four different shoes that Reebok is about to bring out, and as we drove down Fordham Road, she had her head out the window like a little kid, checking out what everyone on the street was wearing. We went to Dr. Jay's, which is the cool place to buy sneakers in the Bronx, and Baysie crouched down on the floor and started pulling the shoes out of her bag one by one, soliciting opinions from customers who gathered around and asking one question after another, in rapid sequence. One guy she listened closely to was maybe eighteen or nineteen, with a diamond stud in his ear and a thin beard. He was wearing a Polo baseball cap, a brown leather jacket, and the big, oversized leather boots that are everywhere uptown right now. Baysie would hand him a shoe and he would hold it, look at the top, and move it up and down and flip it over. The first one he didn't like: "Oh-kay." The second one he hated: he made a growling sound in his throat even before Baysie could give it to him, as if to say, "Put it back in the bag—now!" But when she handed him a new DMX RXT—a low-cut run/walk shoe in white and blue and mesh with a translucent "ice" sole, which retails for a hundred and ten dollars—he looked at it long and hard and shook his head in pure admiration and just said two words, dragging each of them out: "No doubt."

Baysie was interested in what he was saying, because the DMX RXT she had was a girls' shoe that actually hadn't been doing all that well. Later, she explained to me that the fact that the boys loved the shoe was critical news, because it suggested that Reebok had a potential hit if it just switched the shoe to the men's section. How she managed to distill this piece of information from the crowd of teenagers around her, how she made any sense of the two dozen shoes in her bag, most of which (to my eyes, anyway) looked pretty much the same, and how she knew which of the teens to really focus on was a mystery. Baysie is a Wasp from New England, and she crouched on the floor in Dr. Jay's for almost an hour, talking and joking with the homeboys without a trace of condescension or self-consciousness.

Near the end of her visit, a young boy walked up and sat down on the bench next to her. He was wearing a black woolen cap with white stripes pulled low, a blue North Face pleated down jacket, a pair of baggy Guess jeans, and, on his feet, Nike Air Jordans. He couldn't have been more than thirteen. But when he started talking you could see Baysie's eyes light up, because somehow she knew the kid was the real thing.

"How many pairs of shoes do you buy a month?" Baysie asked.

"Two," the kid answered. "And if at the end I find one more I like I get to buy that, too." Baysie was onto him. "Does your mother spoil you?"

The kid blushed, but a friend next to him was laughing. "Whatever he wants, he gets."

Baysie laughed, too. She had the DMX RXT in his size. He tried them on. He rocked back and forth, testing them. He looked back at Baysie. He was dead serious now: "Make sure these come out."

Baysie handed him the new "Rush" Emmitt Smith shoe due out in the fall. One of the boys had already pronounced it "phat," and another had looked through the marbleized-foam cradle in the heel and cried out in delight, "This is bug!" But this kid was the acid test, because this kid knew cool. He paused. He looked at it hard. "Reebok," he said, soberly and carefully, "is trying to get butter."

In the car on the way back to Manhattan, Baysie repeated it twice. "Not better. Butter! That kid could totally tell you what he thinks." Baysie had spent an hour coolhunting in a shoe store and found out that Reebok's efforts were winning the highest of hip-hop praise. "He was so fucking smart."

## 2.

If you want to understand how trends work, and why coolhunters like Baysie and DeeDee have become so important, a good place to start is with what's known as diffusion research, which is the study of how ideas and innovations spread. Diffusion researchers do things like spending five years studying the adoption of irrigation techniques in a Colombian mountain village, or developing complex matrices to map the spread of new math in the Pittsburgh school system. What they do may seem like a far cry from, say, how the Tommy Hilfiger thing spread from Harlem to every suburban mall in the country, but it really isn't: both are about how new ideas spread from one person to the next.

One of the most famous diffusion studies is Bruce Ryan and Neal Gross's analysis of the spread of hybrid seed corn in Greene County, Iowa, in the nineteen-thirties. The new seed corn was introduced there in about 1928, and it was superior in every respect to the seed that had been used by farmers for decades. But it wasn't adopted all at once. Of two hundred and fifty-nine farmers studied by Ryan and Gross, only a handful had started planting the new seed by 1933. In 1934, sixteen took the plunge. In 1935, twenty-one more followed; the next year, there were thirty-six, and the year after that a whopping sixty-one. The succeeding figures were then forty-six, thirty-six, fourteen, and three, until, by 1941, all but two of the two hundred and fifty-nine farmers studied were using the new seed. In the language of diffusion research, the handful of farmers who started trying hybrid seed corn at the very beginning of the thirties were the "innovators," the adventurous ones. The slightly larger group that followed them was the "early adopters." They were the opinion leaders in the community, the respected, thoughtful people who watched and analyzed what those wild innovators were doing and then did it themselves. Then came the big bulge of farmers in 1936, 1937, and 1938—the "early majority" and the "late majority," which is to say the deliberate and the skeptical masses, who would never try anything until the most respected farmers had tried it. Only after they had been converted did the "laggards," the most traditional of all, follow suit. The critical thing about this sequence is that it is almost entirely interpersonal. According to Ryan and Gross, only the innovators relied to any great extent on radio advertising and farm journals and seed salesmen in making their decision to switch to the hybrid. Everyone else made his decision overwhelmingly because of the example and the opinions of his neighbors and peers.

Isn't this just how fashion works? A few years ago, the classic brushed-suede Hush Puppies with the lightweight crepe sole—the moc-toe oxford known as the Duke and the slip-on with the golden buckle known as the Columbia—were selling barely sixty-five thousand pairs a year. The company was trying to walk away from the whole suede casual look entirely. It wanted to do "aspirational" shoes: "active casuals" in smooth leather, like the Mall Walker, with a Comfort Curve technology outsole and a heel stabilizer—the kind of shoes you see in Kinney's for $39.95. But then something strange started happening. Two Hush Puppies executives—Owen Baxter and Jeff Lewis—were doing a fashion shoot for their Mall Walkers and ran into a creative consultant from Manhattan named Jeffrey Miller, who informed them that the Dukes and the Columbias weren't dead, they were dead chic. "We were being told," Baxter recalls, "that there were areas in the Village, in SoHo, where the shoes were selling—in resale shops—and that people were wearing the old Hush Puppies. They were going to the ma-and-pa stores, the little stores that still carried them, and there was this authenticity of being able to say, 'I am wearing an original pair of Hush Puppies.'"

Baxter and Lewis—tall, solid, fair-haired Midwestern guys with thick, shiny wedding bands—are shoe men, first and foremost. Baxter was working the cash register at his father's shoe store in Mount Prospect, Illinois, at the age of thirteen. Lewis was doing inventory in his father's shoe store in Pontiac, Michigan, at the age of seven. Baxter was in the National Guard during the 1968 Democratic Convention, in Chicago, and was stationed across the street from the Conrad Hilton downtown, right in the middle of things. Today, the two men work out of Rockford, Michigan (population thirty-eight hundred), where Hush Puppies has been making the Dukes and the Columbias in an old factory down by the Rogue River for almost forty years. They took me to the plant when I was in Rockford. In a crowded, noisy, low-slung building, factory workers stand in long rows, gluing, stapling, and sewing together shoes in dozens of bright colors, and the two executives stopped at each production station and described it in detail. Lewis and Baxter know shoes. But they would be the first to admit that they don't know cool. "Miller was saying that there is something going on with the shoes—that Isaac Mizrahi was wearing the shoes for his personal use," Lewis told me. We were seated around the conference table in the Hush Puppies headquarters in Rockford, with the snow and the trees outside and a big water tower behind us. "I think it's fair to say that at the time we had no idea who Isaac Mizrahi was."

By late 1994, things had begun to happen in a rush. First, the designer John Bartlett called. He wanted to use Hush Puppies as accessories in his spring collection. Then Anna Sui called. Miller, the man from Manhattan, flew out to Michigan to give advice on a new line ("Of course, packing my own food and thinking about 'Fargo' in the corner of my mind"). A few months later, in Los Angeles, the designer Joel Fitzpatrick put a twenty-five-foot inflatable basset hound on the roof of his store on La Brea Avenue and gutted his adjoining art gallery to turn it into a Hush Puppies department, and even before he opened—while he was still painting and putting up shelves—Pee-wee Herman walked in and asked for a couple of pairs. Pee-wee Herman! "It was total word of mouth. I didn't even have a sign back then," Fitzpatrick recalls. In 1995, the company sold four hundred and thirty thousand pairs of the classic Hush Puppies. In 1996, it sold a million six hundred thousand, and that was only scratching the surface, because in Europe and the rest of the world, where Hush Puppies have a huge following—where they might outsell the American market four to one—the revival was just beginning.

The cool kids who started wearing old Dukes and Columbias from thrift shops were the innovators. Pee-wee Herman, wandering in off the street, was an early adopter. The million six hundred thousand people who bought Hush Puppies last year are the early majority, jumping in because the really cool people have already blazed the trail. Hush Puppies are moving through the country just the way hybrid seed corn moved through Greene County—all of which illustrates what coolhunters can and cannot do. If Jeffrey Miller had been wrong—if cool people hadn't been digging through the thrift shops for Hush Puppies—and he had arbitrarily decided that Baxter and Lewis should try to convince non-cool people that the shoes were cool, it wouldn't have worked. You can't convince the late majority that Hush Puppies are cool, because the late majority makes its coolness decisions on the basis of what the early majority is doing, and you can't convince the early majority, because the early majority is looking at the early adopters, and you can't convince the early adopters, because they take their cues from the innovators. The innovators do get their cool ideas from people other than their peers, but the fact is that they are the last people who can be convinced by a marketing campaign that a pair of suede shoes is cool. These are, after all, the people who spent hours sifting through thrift-store bins. And why did they do that? Because their definition of cool is doing something that nobody else is doing. A company can intervene in the cool cycle. It can put its shoes on really cool celebrities and on fashion runways and on MTV. It can accelerate the transition from the innovator to the early adopter and on to the early majority. But it can't just manufacture cool out of thin air, and that's the second rule of cool.

At the peak of the Hush Puppies craziness last year, Hush Puppies won the prize for best accessory at the Council of Fashion Designers' awards dinner, at Lincoln Center. The award was accepted by the Hush Puppies president, Louis Dubrow, who came out wearing a pair of custom-made black patent-leather Hush Puppies and stood there blinking and looking at the assembled crowd as if it were the last scene of "Close Encounters of the Third Kind." It was a strange moment. There was the president of the Hush Puppies company, of Rockford, Michigan, population thirty-eight hundred, sharing a stage with Calvin Klein and Donna Karan and Isaac Mizrahi—and all because some kids in the East Village began combing through thrift shops for old Dukes. Fashion was at the mercy of those kids, whoever they were, and it was a wonderful thing if the kids picked you, but a scary thing, too, because it meant that cool was something you could not control. You needed someone to find cool and tell you what it was.

## 3.

When Baysie Wightman went to Dr. Jay's, she was looking for customer response to the new shoes Reebok had planned for the fourth quarter of 1997 and the first quarter of 1998. This kind of customer testing is critical at Reebok, because the last decade has not been kind to the company. In 1987, it had a third of the American athletic-shoe market, well ahead of Nike. Last year, it had sixteen per cent. "The kid in the store would say, 'I'd like this shoe if your logo wasn't on it,'" E. Scott Morris, who's a senior designer for Reebok, told me. "That's kind of a punch in the mouth. But we've all seen it. You go into a shoe store. The kid picks up the shoe and says, 'Ah, man, this is nice.' He turns the shoe around and around. He looks at it underneath. He looks at the side and he goes, 'Ah, this is Reebok,' and says, 'I ain't buying this,' and puts the shoe down and walks out. And you go, 'You was just digging it a minute ago. What happened?'" Somewhere along the way, the company lost its cool, and Reebok now faces the task not only of rebuilding its image but of making the shoes so cool that the kids in the store can't put them down.

Every few months, then, the company's coolhunters go out into the field with prototypes of the upcoming shoes to find out what kids really like, and come back to recommend the necessary changes. The prototype of one recent Emmitt Smith shoe, for example, had a piece of molded rubber on the end of the tongue as a design element; it was supposed to give the shoe a certain "richness," but the kids said they thought it looked overbuilt. Then Reebok gave the shoes to the Boston College football team for wear-testing, and when they got the shoes back they found out that all the football players had cut out the rubber component with scissors. As messages go, this was hard to miss. The tongue piece wasn't cool, and on the final version of the shoe it was gone. The rule of thumb at Reebok is that if the kids in Chicago, New York, and Detroit all like a shoe, it's a guaranteed hit. More than likely, though, the coolhunt is going to turn up subtle differences from city to city, so that once the cool-hunters come back the designers have to find out some way to synthesize what was heard, and pick out just those things that all the kids seemed to agree on. In New York, for example, kids in Harlem are more sophisticated and fashion-forward than kids in the Bronx, who like things a little more colorful and glitzy. Brooklyn, meanwhile, is conservative and preppy, more like Washington, D.C. For reasons no one really knows, Reeboks are coolest in Philadelphia. In Philly, in fact, the Reebok Classics are so huge they are known simply as National Anthems, as in "I'll have a pair of blue Anthems in nine and a half." Philadelphia is Reebok's innovator town. From there trends move along the East Coast, trickling all the way to Charlotte, North Carolina.

Reebok has its headquarters in Stoughton, Massachusetts, outside Boston—in a modern corporate park right off Route 24. There are basketball and tennis courts next to the building, and a health club on the ground floor that you can look directly into from the parking lot. The front lobby is adorned with shrines for all of Reebok's most prominent athletes—shrines complete with dramatic action photographs, their sports jerseys, and a pair of their signature shoes—and the halls are filled with so many young, determinedly athletic people that when I visited Reebok headquarters I suddenly wished I'd packed my gym clothes in case someone challenged me to wind sprints. At Stoughton, I met with a handful of the company's top designers and marketing executives in a long conference room on the third floor. In the course of two hours, they put one pair of shoes after another on the table in front of me, talking excitedly about each sneaker's prospects, because the feeling at Reebok is that things are finally turning around. The basketball shoe that Reebok brought out last winter for Allen Iverson, the star rookie guard for the Philadelphia 76ers, for example, is one of the hottest shoes in the country. Dr. Jay's sold out of Iversons in two days, compared with the week it took the store to sell out of Nike's new Air Jordans. Iverson himself is brash and charismatic and faster from foul line to foul line than anyone else in the league. He's the equivalent of those kids in the East Village who began wearing Hush Puppies way back when. He's an innovator, and the hope at Reebok is that if he gets big enough the whole company can ride back to coolness on his coattails, the way Nike rode to coolness on the coattails of Michael Jordan. That's why Baysie was so excited when the kid said Reebok was trying to get butter when he looked at the Rush and the DMX RXT: it was a sign, albeit a small one, that the indefinable, abstract thing called cool was coming back.

When Baysie comes back from a coolhunt, she sits down with marketing experts and sales representatives and designers, and reconnects them to the street, making sure they have the right shoes going to the right places at the right price. When she got back from the Bronx, for example, the first thing she did was tell all these people they had to get a new men's DMX RXT out, fast, because the kids on the street loved the women's version. "It's hotter than we realized," she told them. The coolhunter's job in this instance is very specific. What DeeDee does, on the other hand, is a little more ambitious. With the L Report, she tries to construct a kind of grand matrix of cool, comprising not just shoes but everything kids like, and not just kids of certain East Coast urban markets but kids all over. DeeDee and her staff put it out four times a year, in six different versions—for New York, Los Angeles, San Francisco, Austin–Dallas, Seattle, and Chicago—and then sell it to manufacturers, retailers, and ad agencies (among others) for twenty thousand dollars a year. They go to each city and find the coolest bars and clubs, and ask the coolest kids to fill out questionnaires. The information is then divided into six categories—You Saw It Here First, Entertainment and Leisure,

Clothing and Accessories, Personal and Individual, Aspirations, and Food and Beverages—which are, in turn, broken up into dozens of subcategories, so that Personal and Individual, for example, includes Cool Date, Cool Evening, Free Time, Favorite Possession, and on and on. The information in those subcategories is subdivided again by sex and by age bracket (14–18, 19–24, 25–30), and then, as a control, the L Report gives you the corresponding set of preferences for "mainstream" kids.

Few coolhunters bother to analyze trends with this degree of specificity. DeeDee's biggest competitor, for example, is something called the Hot Sheet, out of Manhattan. It uses a panel of three thousand kids a year from across the country and divides up their answers by sex and age, but it doesn't distinguish between regions, or between trendsetting and mainstream respondents. So what you're really getting is what all kids think is cool—not what cool kids think is cool, which is a considerably different piece of information. Janine Misdom and Joanne DeLuca, who run the Sputnik coolhunting group out of the garment district in Manhattan, meanwhile, favor an entirely impressionistic approach, sending out coolhunters with video cameras to talk to kids on the ground that it's too difficult to get cool kids to fill out questionnaires. Once, when I was visiting the Sputnik girls—as Misdom and DeLuca are known on the street, because they look alike and their first names are so similar and both have the same awesome New York accents—they showed me a video of the girl they believe was the patient zero of the whole eighties revival going on right now. It was back in September of 1993. Joanne and Janine were on Seventh Avenue, outside the Fashion Institute of Technology, doing random street interviews for a major jeans company, and, quite by accident, they ran into this nineteen-year-old raver. She had close-cropped hair, which was green at the top, and at the temples was shaved even closer and dyed pink. She had rings and studs all over her face, and a thick collection of silver tribal jewelry around her neck, and vintage jeans. She looked into the camera and said, "The sixties came in and then the seventies came in and I think it's ready to come back to the eighties. It's totally eighties: the eye makeup, the clothes. It's totally going back to that." Immediately, Joanne and Janine started asking around. "We talked to a few kids on the Lower East Side who said they were feeling the need to start breaking out their old Michael Jackson jackets," Joanne said. "They were joking about it. They weren't doing it yet. But they were going to, you know? They were saying, 'We're getting the urge to break out our Members Only jackets.'" That was right when Joanne and Janine were just starting up; calling the eighties revival was their first big break, and now they put out a full-blown videotaped report twice a year which is a collection of clips of interviews with extremely progressive people.

What DeeDee argues, though, is that cool is too subtle and too variegated to be captured with these kind of broad strokes. Cool is a set of dialects, not a language. The L Report can tell you, for example, that nineteen-to-twenty-four-year-old male trendsetters in Seattle would most like to meet, among others, King Solomon and Dr. Seuss, and that nineteen-to-twenty-four-year-old female trendsetters in San Francisco have turned their backs on Calvin Klein, Nintendo Gameboy, and sex. What's cool right now? Among male New York trendsetters: North Face jackets, rubber and latex, khakis, and the rock band Kiss. Among female trendsetters: ska music, old-lady clothing, and cyber tech. In Chicago, snowboarding is huge among trendsetters of both sexes and all ages. Women over nineteen are into short hair, while those in their teens have embraced mod culture, rock climbing, tag watches, and bootleg pants. In Austin–Dallas, meanwhile, twenty-five-to-thirty-year-old women trendsetters are into hats, heroin, computers, cigars, Adidas, and velvet, while men in their twenties are into video games and hemp. In all, the typical L Report runs over one hundred pages. But with that flood of data comes an obsolescence disclaimer: "The fluctuating nature of the trendsetting market makes keeping up with trends a difficult task." By the spring, in other words, everything may have changed.

The key to coolhunting, then, is to look for cool people first and cool things later, and not the other way around. Since cool things are always changing, you can't look for them, because the very fact they are cool means you have no idea what to look for. What you would be doing is thinking back on what was cool before and extrapolating, which is about as useful as presuming that because the Dow rose ten points yesterday it will rise another ten points today. Cool people, on the other hand, are a constant.

When I was in California, I met Salvador Barbier, who had been described to me by a coolhunter as "the Michael Jordan of skateboarding." He was tall and lean and languid, with a cowboy's insouciance, and we drove through the streets of Long Beach at fifteen miles an hour in a white late-model Ford Mustang, a car he had bought as a kind of ironic status gesture ("It would look good if I had a Polo jacket or maybe Nautica," he said) to go with his '62 Econoline van and his '64 T-bird. Sal told me that he and his friends, who are all in their mid-twenties, recently took to dressing up as if they were in eighth grade again and gathering together—having a "rally"—on old BMX bicycles in front of their local 7-Eleven. "I'd wear muscle shirts, like Def Leppard or Foghat or some old heavy-metal band, and tight, tight tapered Levi's, and Vans on my feet—big, like, checkered Vans or striped Vans or camouflage Vans—and then wristbands and gloves with the fingers cut off. It was total eighties fashion. You had to look like that to participate in the rally. We had those denim jackets with patches on the back and combs that hung out the back pocket. We went without I.D.s, because we'd have to have someone else buy us beers." At this point, Sal laughed. He was driving really slowly and staring straight ahead and talking in a low drawl—the coolhunter's dream. "We'd ride to this bar and I'd have to carry my bike inside, because we have really expensive bikes, and when we got inside people would freak out. They'd say, 'Omigod,' and I was asking them if they wanted to go for a ride on the handlebars. They were like, 'What is wrong with you. My boyfriend used to dress like that in the eighth grade!' And I was like, 'He was probably a lot cooler then, too.'"

This is just the kind of person DeeDee wants. "I'm looking for somebody who is an individual, who has definitely set himself apart from everybody else, who doesn't look like his peers. I've run into trendsetters who look completely Joe Regular Guy. I can see Joe Regular Guy at a club listening to some totally hardcore band playing, and I say to myself 'Omigod, what's that guy doing here?' and that totally intrigues me, and I have to walk up to him and say, 'Hey, you're really into this band. What's up?' You know what I mean? I look at everything. If I see Joe Regular Guy sitting in a coffee shop and everyone around him has blue hair, I'm going to gravitate toward him, because, hey, what's Joe Regular Guy doing in a coffee shop with people with blue hair?"

We were sitting outside the Fred Segal store in West Hollywood. I was wearing a very conservative white Brooks Brothers button-down and a pair of Levi's, and DeeDee looked first at my shirt and then my pants and dissolved into laughter: "I mean, I might even go up to you in a cool place."

Picking the right person is harder than it sounds, though. Piney Kahn, who works for DeeDee, says, "There are a lot of people in the gray area. You've got these kids who dress ultra funky and have their own style. Then you realize they're just running after their friends."

The trick is not just to be able to tell who is different but to be able to tell when that difference represents something truly cool. It's a gut thing. You have to somehow just know. DeeDee hired Piney because Piney clearly knows: she is twenty-four and used to work with the Beastie Boys and has the formidable self-possession of someone who is not only cool herself but whose parents were cool. "I mean," she says, "they named me after a tree."

Piney and DeeDee said that they once tried to hire someone as a coolhunter who was not, himself, cool, and it was a disaster.

"You can give them the boundaries," Piney explained. "You can say that if people shop at Banana Republic and listen to Alanis Morissette they're probably not trendsetters. But then they might go out and assume that everyone who does that is not a trendsetter, and not look at the other things."

"I mean, I myself might go into Banana Republic and buy a T-shirt," DeeDee chimed in.

Their non-cool coolhunter just didn't have that certain instinct, that sense that told him when it was O.K. to deviate from the manual. Because he wasn't cool, he didn't know cool, and that's the essence of the third rule of cool: you have to be one to know one. That's why Baysie is still on top of this business at forty-one. "It's easier for me to tell you what kid is cool than to tell you what things are cool," she says. But that's all she needs to know. In this sense, the third rule of cool fits perfectly into the second: the second rule says that cool cannot be manufactured, only observed, and the third says that it can only be observed by those who are themselves cool. And, of course, the first rule says that it cannot accurately be observed at all, because the act of discovering cool causes cool to take flight, so if you add all three together they describe a closed loop, the hermeneutic circle of coolhunting, a phenomenon whereby not only can the uncool not see cool but cool cannot even be adequately described to them. Baysie says that she can see a coat on one of her friends and think it's not cool but then see the same coat on DeeDee and think that it is cool. It is not possible to be cool, in other words, unless you are—in some larger sense—already cool, and so the phenomenon that the uncool cannot see and cannot have described to them is also something that they cannot ever attain, because if they did it would no longer be cool. Coolhunting represents the ascendancy, in the marketplace, of high school.

Once, I was visiting DeeDee at her house in Laurel Canyon when one of her L Report assistants, Jonas Vail, walked in. He'd just come back from Niketown on Wilshire Boulevard, where he'd bought seven hundred dollars' worth of the latest sneakers to go with the three hundred dollars' worth of skateboard shoes he'd bought earlier in the afternoon. Jonas is tall and expressionless, with a peacoat, dark jeans, and short-cropped black hair. "Jonas is good," DeeDee says. "He works with me on everything. That guy knows more pop culture. You know: What was the name of the store Mrs. Garrett owned on 'The Facts of Life'? He knows all the names of the extras from eighties sitcoms. I can't believe someone like him exists. He's fucking unbelievable. Jonas can spot a cool person a mile away."

Jonas takes the boxes of shoes and starts unpacking them on the couch next to DeeDee. He picks up a pair of the new Nike ACG hiking boots, and says, "All the Japanese in Niketown were really into these." He hands the shoes to DeeDee.

"Of *course* they were!" she says. "The Japanese are all into the tech-looking shit. Look how exaggerated it is, how bulbous." DeeDee has very ambivalent feelings about Nike, because she thinks its marketing has got out of hand. When she was in the New York Niketown with a girlfriend recently, she says, she started getting light-headed and freaked out. "It's cult, cult, cult. It was like, 'Hello, are we all drinking the Kool-Aid here?'" But this shoe she loves. It's

Dr. Jay's in the Bronx all over again. DeeDee turns the shoe around and around in the air, tapping the big clear-blue plastic bubble on the side—the visible Air-Sole unit—with one finger. "It's so fucking rad. It looks like a platypus!" In front of me, there is a pair of Nike's new shoes for the basketball player Jason Kidd.

I pick it up. "This looks . . . cool," I venture uncertainly.

DeeDee is on the couch, where she's surrounded by shoeboxes and sneakers and white tissue paper, and she looks up reprovingly because, of course, I don't get it. I can't get it. "Beyoooond cool, Maalcolm. Beyoooond cool."

**READING  WRITING**

## THIS TEXT: READING

1.  What do you think Gladwell's opinion about advertising generally is? How about the people he writes about? What words or phrases in the essay contribute to this idea?
2.  Do you know anyone who would be a good candidate for a "coolhunter"? What qualities does that person have? Are those qualities you want?
3.  How do you define cool? What's the difference between the qualities advertisers and video makers think are cool and the ones you think are cool?
4.  From what perspective is Gladwell writing? What audience do you think he's appealing to?
5.  What do you think Gladwell's opinion of advertising is? What reveals this in the article?

## YOUR TEXT: WRITING

1.  Spend an afternoon in a public space and do your own cool hunt. What do you notice as being cool? What are the semiotics involved—what signs do you interpret as cool? Do you think your coolhunt would be the same as someone else's? Write a short essay on your idea of cool and how it's reflected in society.
2.  Cool is a term that's been around for ages, at least since the 1930s, when it was associated with jazz music. And yet it means something different to different people in every era and is constantly undergoing change. Can you think of other words or ideas which have undergone such changes in your own life or in the culture around you? Write a short essay.
3.  Do you think that once something is proclaimed as cool, it loses some or all of its "coolness"? Trace the cool factor of a particular item, like a piece of clothing or a toy.

---

### ADVERTISING AND PEOPLE OF COLOR

■ **Clint C. Wilson and Felix Gutierrez** ■    *By giving semiotic readings of some disturbing advertisements, Wilson and Gutierrez demonstrate how people of color and stereotypes about ethnicities have been exploited to sell various items (1995). As you read, pay attention to how the authors blend research and their own interpretation of visual texts.*

*Also, as we mention in "Reading an Advertisement" in our introduction, it is often difficult to obtain permission to reprint advertisements. As it turns out, we were denied permission to print all three ads that appear in the original version of this essay—most likely because companies have become more sensitive to the personal and legal ramifications of racial stereotyping. In one ad for Cream of Wheat, Rastus, a black servant in a chef's cap, holds a blackboard containing information about Cream of Wheat written in African-American dialect. The other, an ad for Crown Royal aimed at Hispanic audiences, shows five clearly wealthy well-dressed Latinos and Latinas drinking Crown Royal at what appears to be a fancy birthday party. The text for the ad, "Comparta sus riquezas" ("Share the Wealth") is in Spanish. Finally, though AT&T did deny us permission to print the original ad, they did agree to let us run an updated one. The original shows a young Chinese girl holding a phone. Appearing in Chinese newspapers in the United States, the ad ran only in Chinese.*

GIVEN THE SOCIAL AND LEGAL RESTRICTIONS on the participation of racial minorities in the society of the United States during much of this country's history, it is not hard to see how the desire to cater to the perceived views of the mass audience desired by advertisers resulted in entertainment and news content that largely ignored people of color, treated them stereotypically when they were recognized, and largely avoided grappling with such issues as segregation, discriminatory immigration laws, land rights, and other controversial issues that affected certain minority groups more than they did the White majority. Although the entertainment and editorial portrayal of non-Whites is amply analyzed in other chapters of this book, it is important to recognize that those portrayals were, to a large extent, supported by a system of advertising that required the media to cater to the perceived attitudes and prejudices of the White majority and that also reinforced such images in its own commercial messages. For years advertisers in the United States reflected the place of non-Whites in the social fabric of the nation either by ignoring them or, when they were included in advertisements for the mass audience, processing and presenting them in a way that would make them palatable salespersons for the products being advertised. These processed portrayals largely mirrored the stereotypic images of minorities in the entertainment media that, in turn, were designed to reflect the perceived values and norms of the White majority. In this way, non-White portrayals in advertising paralleled and reinforced their entertainment and journalistic images in the media.

The history of advertising in the United States is replete with characterizations that, like the Frito Bandito, responded to and reinforced the preconceived image that many White Americans apparently had of Blacks, Latinos, Asians, and Native Americans. Over the years advertisers have employed Latin spitfires like Chiquita Banana, Black mammies like Aunt Jemima, and noble savages like the Santa Fe Railroad's Super Chief to pitch their products to a predominately White mass audience of consumers. In 1984 the Balch Institute for Ethnic Studies in Philadelphia sponsored an exhibit of more than 300 examples of racial and ethnic images used by corporations in magazines, posters, trade cards, and storyboards. In an interview with the advertising trade magazine *Advertising Age,* institute director Mark Stolarik quoted the catalog for the exhibit, which capsulized the evolution of images of people of color and how they have changed.

"Some of these advertisements were based on stereotypes of various ethnic groups. In the early years, they were usually crude and condescending images that appealed to largely Anglo-American audiences who found it difficult to reconcile their own visions of beauty, order and behavior with that of non-Anglo-Americans," said Stolarik. "Later, these images were softened because of complaints from the ethnic groups involved and the growing so-phistication of the advertising industry."[1]

> The advertising examples in the exhibit include positive White ethnic stereotypes, such as the wholesome and pure image of Quakers in an early Quaker Oats advertisement and the clean-liness of the Dutch in a turn-of-the century advertisement for Colgate soaps. But they also featured a late 19th century advertisement showing an Irish matron threatening to hit her husband over the head with a rolling pin because he didn't smoke the right brand of to-bacco. Like Quaker Oats, some products even incorporated a stereotypical image on the package or product line being advertised.

"Lawsee! Folks sho' whoops with joy over AUNT JEMIMA PANCAKES," shouted a bandanna-wearing Black mammy in a magazine advertisement for Aunt Jemima pancake mix, which featured a plump Aunt Jemima on the box. Over the years, Aunt Jemima has lost some weight, but the stereotyped face of the Black servant continues to be featured on the box. Earlier advertisements for Cream of Wheat featured Rastus, the Black servant on the box, in a series of magazine cartoons with a group of cute but ill-dressed Black children. Some of the advertisements played on stereotypes ridiculing Blacks, such as an advertisement in which a Black school teacher standing behind a makeshift lectern made out of a boldly let-tered Cream of Wheat box, asks the class "How do you spell Cream of Wheat?" Others ap-peared to promote racial integration, such as a magazine advertisement captioned "Putting it down in Black and White," which showed Rastus serving bowls of the breakfast cereal to Black and White youngsters sitting at the same table.

Racial imagery was also integrated into the naming of trains by the Santa Fe railroad, which named one of its passenger lines the Super Chief and featured highly detailed portraits of the noble Indian in promoting its service through the Southwestern United States. In an-other series of advertisements, the railroad used cartoons of Native American children to show the service and sights passengers could expect when they traveled the Santa Fe line.

These and other portrayals catered to the mass audience mentality by either neutraliz-ing or making humor of the negative perceptions that many Whites may have had of racial minorities. The advertising images, rather than showing people of color as they really were, portrayed them as filtered through Anglo eyes. This presented an out-of-focus image of racial minorities, but one that was palatable, and even persuasive, to the White majority to which it was directed. In the mid-1960s Black civil rights groups targeted the advertising in-dustry for special attention, protesting both the lack of integrated advertisements including Blacks and the stereotyped images that the advertisers continued to use. The effort, accom-panied by support from federal officials, resulted in the overnight inclusion of Blacks as models in television advertising in 1967 and a downplaying of the images that many Blacks found objectionable.

"Black America is becoming visible in America's biggest national advertising medium," reported the *New York Times* in 1968. "Not in a big way yet, but it is a beginning and men in high places give assurances that there will be a lot more visibility."[2]

But the advertising industry did not generalize the concerns of Blacks, or the conces-sions made in response to them, to other groups. At the same time that some Black concerns were being addressed with integrated advertising, other groups were being ignored or sin-gled out for continued stereotyped treatment in such commercials as those featuring the Frito Bandito.

Among the Latino advertising stereotypes cited in a 1969 article[3] by sociologist Tomás Martínez were commercials for Granny Goose chips featuring fat gun-toting Mexicans, an advertisement for Arrid underarm deodorant showing a dusty Mexican bandito spraying his underarms after a hard ride as the announcer intones, "If it works for him it will work for you," and a magazine advertisement featuring a stereotypical Mexican sleeping under his sombrero as he leans against a Philco television set. Especially offensive to Martínez was a Liggett & Meyers commercial for L&M cigarettes that featured Paco, a lazy Latino who never "feenishes" anything, not even the revolution he is supposed to be fighting. In response to a letter complaining about the commercial, the director of public relations for the tobacco firm defended the commercial's use of Latino stereotypes.

"'Paco' is a warm, sympathetic and lovable character with whom most of us can identify because he has a little of all of us in him, that is, our tendency to procrastinate at times," wrote the Liggett & Meyers executive. "He seeks to escape the violence of war and to enjoy the pleasure of the moment, in this case, the good flavor of an L&M cigarette."[4] Although the company spokesman claimed that the character had been tested without negative reactions from Latinos (a similar claim was made by Frito-Lay regarding the Frito Bandito), Martínez roundly criticized the advertising images and contrasted them to what he saw as the gains Blacks were then making in the advertising field.

"Today, no major advertiser would attempt to display a black man or woman over the media in a prejudiced, stereotyped fashion," Martínez wrote.

> Complaints would be forthcoming from black associations and perhaps the FCC. Yet, these same advertisers, who dare not show "step'n fetch it" characters, uninhibitedly depict a Mexican counterpart, with additional traits of stinking and stealing. Perhaps the white hatred for blacks, which cannot find adequate expression in today's ads, is being transferred upon their brown brothers.[5]

In 1970 a Brown Position Paper prepared by Latino media activists Armando Rendón and Domingo Nick Reyes charged that the media had transferred the negative stereotypes it once reserved for Blacks to Latinos, who had become "the media's new nigger."[6] The protests of Latinos soon made the nation's advertisers more conscious of the portrayals that Latinos found offensive. But, as in the case of the Blacks, the advertising industry failed to apply the lessons learned from one group to other racial minorities.

Although national advertisers withdrew much of the advertising that negatively stereotyped Blacks and Latinos, sometimes replacing them with affluent, successful images that were as far removed from reality as the negative portrayals of the past, the advances made by those groups were not shared with Native Americans and Asians. Native Americans' names and images, no longer depicted either as the noble savage or as cute cartoon characters, have all but disappeared from broadcast commercials and print advertising. The major exceptions are advertising for automobiles and trucks that bear names such as Pontiac, Dakota, and Navajo and sports teams with racial nicknames such as the Kansas City Chiefs, Washington Redskins, Florida State University Seminoles, Atlanta Braves, and Cleveland Indians. Native Americans and others have protested these racial team names and images, as well as the pseudo-Native American pageantry and souvenirs that accompany many of them but with no success in getting them changed.

Asians, particularly Japanese, continue to be dealt more than their share of commercials depicting them in stereotypes that cater to the fears and stereotypes of White America. As was the case with Blacks and Latinos, it took organized protests from Asian American groups to get the message across to the corporations and their advertising agencies. In the mid-1970s, a Southern California supermarket chain agreed to remove a television campaign in which a young Asian karate-chopped his way down the store's aisles cutting prices. Nationally, several firms whose industries have been hard-hit by Japanese imports fought back through commercials, if not in the quality or prices of their products. One automobile company featured an Asian family carefully looking over a new car and commenting on its attributes in heavily accented English. Only after they bought it did they learn it was made in the United States, not Japan. Another automobile company that markets cars manufactured in Japan under an English-language name showed a parking lot attendant opening the doors of the car, only to find the car speaking to him in Japanese. For several years Sylvania television ran a commercial boasting that its television picture had repeatedly been selected over competing brands as an off-screen voice with a Japanese accent repeatedly asked, "What about Sony?" When the announcer responded that the Sylvania picture had also been selected over Sony's, the off-screen voice ran off shouting what sounded like a string of Japanese expletives. A 1982 *Newsweek* article observed that "attacking Japan has become something of a fashion in corporate ads" because of resentment over Japanese trade policies and sales of Japanese products in the United States, but quoted Motorola's advertising manager as saying, "We've been as careful as we can be" not to be racially offensive.[7]

But many of the television and print advertisements featuring Asians featured images that were racially insensitive, if not offensive. A commercial for a laundry product featured a Chinese family that used an "ancient Chinese laundry secret" to get their customer's clothes clean. Naturally, the Chinese secret turned out to be the packaged product paying for the advertisement. Companies pitching everything from pantyhose to airlines featured Asian women coiffed and costumed as seductive China dolls or exotic Polynesian natives to pitch and promote their products, some of them cast in Asian settings and others attentively caring for the needs of the Anglo men in the advertisement. One airline boasted that those who flew with it would be under the care of the Singapore Girl.

Asian women appearing in commercials were often featured as China dolls with the small, darkened eyes, straight hair with bangs, and a narrow, slit skirt. Another common portrayal featured the exotic, tropical Pacific Islands look, complete with flowers in the hair, a sarong or grass skirt, and shell ornament. Asian women hoping to become models sometimes found that they must conform to these stereotypes or lose assignments. Leslie Kawai, the 1981 Tournament of Roses Queen, was told to cut her hair with bangs by hairstylists when she auditioned for a beer advertisement. When she refused, the beer company decided to hire another model with shorter hair cut in bangs.[8]

The lack of a sizable Asian community, or market, in the United States was earlier cited as the reason that Asians are still stereotyped in advertising and, except for children's advertising, are rarely presented in integrated settings. The growth rate and income of Asians living in the United States in the 1980s and 1990s, however, reinforced the economic potential of Asian Americans to overcome the stereotyping and lack of visibility that Blacks and Latinos challenged with some success. By the mid-1980s there were a few signs that advertising was beginning to integrate Asian Americans into crossover advertisements that, like the Tostitos campaign, were designed to have a broad appeal. In one commercial, television actor Robert Ito was featured telling how he loves to call his relatives in Japan because the calls make them think that he is rich, as well as successful, in the United States. Of course, he adds, it is only because the rates of his long distance carrier were so low that he was able to call Japan so often.

In the 1970s mass audience advertising in the United States became more racially integrated than at any time in the nation's history. Blacks, and to a much lesser extent Latinos and Asians, could be seen in television commercials spread across the broadcast week and in major magazines. In fact, the advertisements on network television often appeared to be more fully integrated than the television programs they supported. Like television, general circulation magazines also experienced an increase in the use of Blacks, although studies of both media showed that most of the percentage increase had come by the early 1970s. By the early 1970s the percentage of prime-time television commercials featuring Blacks had apparently leveled off at about 10%. Blacks were featured in between only 2% and 3% of magazine advertisements as late as 1978. That percentage, however small, was a sharp increase from the 0.06% of news magazine advertisements reported in 1960.[9]

The gains were also socially significant, because they demonstrated that Blacks could be integrated into advertisements without triggering a White backlash among potential customers in the White majority. Both sales figures and research conducted since the late 1960s have shown that the integration of Black models into television and print advertising does not adversely affect sales or the image of the product. Instead, a study by the American Newspaper Publishers Association showed, the most important influences on sales were the merchandise and the advertisement itself. In fact, while triggering no adverse affect among the majority of Whites, integrated advertisements were found to be useful in swaying Black consumers, who responded favorably to positive Black role models in print advertisements.[10] Studies conducted in the early 1970s also showed that White consumers did not respond negatively to advertising featuring Black models, although their response was more often neutral than positive.[11] One 1972 study examining White backlash, however, did show that an advertisement prominently featuring darker-skinned Blacks was less acceptable to Whites than those featuring lighter-skinned Blacks as background models.[12] Perhaps such findings help explain why research conducted later in the 1970s revealed that, for the most part, Blacks appearing in magazine and television advertisements were often featured as part of an integrated group.[13]

Although research findings have shown that integrated advertisements do not adversely affect sales, the percentage of Blacks and other minorities in general audience advertising did not increase significantly after the numerical gains made through the mid-1970s. Those minorities who did appear in advertisements were often depicted in upscale or integrated settings, an image that the Balch Institute's Stolarik criticized as taking advertising "too far in the other direction and created stereotypes of 'successful' ethnic group members that are as unrealistic as those of the past."[14] Equally unwise, from a business sense, was the low numbers of Blacks appearing in advertisements.

Advertisers and their ad agencies must evaluate the direct economic consequences of alternative strategies on the firm. If it is believed that the presence of Black models in advertisements decreases the effectiveness of advertising messages, only token numbers of Black models will be used, wrote marketing professor Lawrence Soley at the conclusion of a 1983 study.

Previous studies have found that advertisements portraying Black models do not elicit negative affective or conative responses from consumers. . . . Given the consistency of the research findings, more Blacks should be portrayed in advertisements. If Blacks continue to be under-represented in advertising portrayals, it can be said that this is an indication of prejudice on the part of the advertising industry, not consumers.[15]

Notes

1. "Using Ethnic Images," p. 9.
2. Cited in Philip H. Dougherty, "Frequency of Blacks in TV Ads," *New York Times,* May 27, 1982, p. D19.
3. Martínez, "How Advertisers Promote," p. 10.
4. Martínez, "How Advertisers Promote," p. 11.
5. Martínez, "How Advertisers Promote," pp. 9–10.
6. Domingo Nick Reyes and Armando Rendón, *Chicanos and the Mass Media* (Washington, DC: The National Mexican American Anti-Defamation Committee, 1971).
7. Joseph Treen, "Madison Ave. vs. Japan, Inc.,"*Newsweek* (April 12, 1982), p. 69.
8. Ada Kan, *Asian Models in the Media,* Unpublished term paper, Journalism 466: Minority and the Media, University of Southern California, December 14, 1983, p. 5.
9. Studies on increase of Blacks in magazine and television commercials cited in James D. Culley and Rex Bennett, "Selling Blacks, Selling Women," *Journal of Communication* (Autumn 1976, Vol. 26, No. 4), pp. 160–174; Lawrence Soley, "The Effect of Black Models on Magazine Ad Readership," *Journalism Quarterly* (Winter 1983, Vol. 60, No. 4), p. 686; and Leonard N. Reid and Bruce G. Vanden Bergh, "Blacks in Introductory Ads," *Journalism Quarterly* (Autumn 1980, Vol. 57, No. 3), pp. 485–486.
10. Cited in D. Parke Gibson, *$70 Billion in the Black* (New York: Macmillan, 1979), pp. 83–84.
11. Laboratory studies on White reactions to Blacks in advertising cited in Soley, "The Effect of Black Models," pp. 585–587.
12. Carl E. Block, "White Backlash to Negro Ads: Fact or Fantasy?" *Journalism Quarterly* (Autumn 1980, Vol. 49, No. 2), pp. 258–262.
13. James D. Culley and Rex Bennett, "Selling Blacks, Selling Women."
14. "Using Ethnic Images," p. 9.
15. Soley, *The Effect of Black Models,* p. 690.

---

**READING  WRITING**

## THIS TEXT: READING

1. It's likely that you found the descriptions of some of these ads shocking. What do these advertisements tell you about how America and Americans used to see people of color?
2. This is one of the few essays that examine how all people of color have been represented. Were you surprised to read about images of Hispanics and American Indians? If so, why?
3. What is the argument of the essay?

## YOUR TEXT: WRITING

1. With some research, you should be able to track down some images of a similarly disturbing nature. What is the semiotic setting of these ads? Write a paper in which you analyze the ads from today's perspective but are mindful of the ad as being a cultural document.
2. Write an essay on advertising and white people. Based on ads, what assumptions can we make about Anglos?
3. Write a comparative paper examining what Wilson and Guiterrez say about race with a similar essay from the Race chapter.

THE AMERICA THE MEDIA
DON'T WANT YOU TO SEE
──────────
■ David McGowan ■

*Taken from his controversial book* Derailing Democracy:
The America the Media Don't Want You to See *(2000),
this excerpt attempts to justify why Americans must look for
news from alternative sources. You will notice that McGowan makes reference to documents the reader will encounter later—these are references to stories from his book that
we have not reprinted here.*

> ### *I know of no country in which there is so little independence of mind
> and real freedom of discussion as in America.*
>
> —Alexis de Tocqueville (1805–1859)

IT HAS BEEN ALMOST 40 YEARS since President Eisenhower, in his final address to the nation before leaving office in 1961, issued a rather extraordinary warning to the American people that
the country "must guard against unwarranted influence, whether sought or unsought, by
the military-industrial complex. The potential for the disastrous rise of misplaced power
exists and will persist." Tragically, Eisenhower's warning was not heeded, and the beast has
been allowed not only to grow, but to mutate into something that should more accurately
be referred to as the military-industrial-media complex.

Following the same course that virtually every other major industry has in the last two
decades, a relentless series of mergers and corporate takeovers has consolidated control of
the media into the hands of a few corporate behemoths. The result has been that an increasingly authoritarian agenda has been sold to the American people by a massive, multi-
tentacled media machine that has become, for all intents and purposes, a propaganda organ
of the state.

It is precisely because most readers get their news filtered through that same organ that
many will readily disagree with this assessment. The American free press is the envy of the
world, they will argue, and this unprecedented ability that we as Americans have to enjoy un-
restricted access to unfiltered news is one of the unique freedoms that makes America the
icon of democratic ideals that we all know it to be. And it is certainly true that by all outward
appearances the United States does appear to have the very epitome of a free press.

After all, do not CNN and a handful of would-be contenders broadcast a continuous
stream of news to America's millions of cable subscribers? Are Tom Brokaw, Peter Jennings,
Dan Rather and Ted Koppel, as well as countless lesser-knowns, not welcomed into our
homes nightly, bearing the day's news—both good and bad? Would not our morning rituals seem woefully lacking without the comfort of the morning paper on the breakfast table?
And don't the radio waves crackle incessantly with the political musings of Rush Limbaugh
and his legions of ideological clones, while a bustling "alternative" press brings the "progressive" version of news and events to those of a slightly different political persuasion? Miss
something during the week? Not to worry: *Time, Newsweek* or *U.S. News and World Report*
are there with a handy weekly round-up of the big stories. Don't have time to read? No problem: *60 Minutes, 20/20, 48 Hours* and *Dateline NBC* have already read them for you—just sit
back and mainline the week's events.

Yet behind this picture of plurality there are clear warning signs that an increasingly in-
cestuous relationship exists between the media titans and the corporate military powers that

Eisenhower so feared. For example, the number-one purveyor of broadcast news in this country—NBC, with both MSNBC and CNBC under its wing, as well as NBC news and a variety of "newsmagazines"—is now owned and controlled by General Electric, one of the nation's largest defense contractors. Is it not significant that as GE's various media subsidiaries predictably lined up to cheerlead the use of U.S. military force in Kosovo, it was at the same time posting substantial profits from the sale of the high tech tools of modern warfare it so shamelessly glorifies?

Would we not loudly condemn such a press arrangement were it to occur in a nation such as Russia or China? Equally alarming is that those viewers choosing to change channels to CNN, the reigning king of the cable news titans, were treated to the surreal daily spectacle of watching Christiane Amanpour, who is the wife of State Department mouthpiece James Rubin, analyze her husband's daily press briefings, as though she could objectively respond to the mounds of disinformation spewing forth from the man with whom she shares her morning coffee. Were it to occur elsewhere, would this not be denounced as symptomatic of a state-run press?

Maybe. Yet it can still be argued that corporate media ownership, despite the ominous implications, does not necessarily preclude the notion of a free press in that ownership has little to do with the day-to-day functioning of the news media. After all, one could reasonably argue, the press operates on the principle of competition to break the big story, and if one news outlet is reticent to report unfavorably on its owners or the government, surely it risks being beaten by competitors. We all know that ambitious reporters are driven by an obsessive desire to get "the scoop." Does not the mere existence of literally thousands of print and broadcast news sources, all keeping their eyes on the Pulitzer Prize, provide *ipso facto* proof of a free press? Does it not guarantee that all the news that merits reporting will arrive on our doorstep each morning in a relatively objective form?

This is a perfectly logical argument, yet there is substantial evidence that suggests that competition does not in itself overcome the interests of the corporate media. For example, while saturation coverage is given to such non-news events as the premier of a new *Star Wars* movie, there has not been a single American media source reporting the fact that the first successful human clones have been created, despite the staggering implications of such a scientific milestone. Surely a press motivated by competition to break the big story would have stumbled upon this one by now, especially considering that as of this writing, more than a year has passed since the world was blessed with the first human clone, courtesy of an American biotechnology firm.

Of course, this could be due not to media suppression, but to the simple fact that the press failed to uncover this story. However, this interpretation fails to account for the fact that this is far from being the only newsworthy event that the American media have failed to take note of, as evidenced throughout this book. It also fails to explain why the British press seem to have had little trouble unearthing this particular story, or why the U.S. news media continued to ignore the issue even after it had appeared in print in the U.K. Had this story been aired by our own press corps, it surely would have received an overwhelmingly negative response. This is, no doubt, the very reason that this story, as well as countless others, has failed to make its American debut.

Yet the illusion of a free and competitive press persists and has become ingrained to the point that it is nearly universally accepted as a truism. And with it comes the illusion that

America's people are among the world's best informed. If not, then it is surely our own fault for being too lazy or otherwise preoccupied to avail ourselves of the media barrage. *Politically Incorrect*'s Bill Maher can be heard regularly haranguing guests for failing to utilize these readily-available resources to gain an informed knowledge of the issues, occasionally even offering up the opinion that anyone who has failed to do so should be stripped of the right to vote. Maher is only stating outright what is implied in the message of the media in general: the truth is right here before your eyes—you have only to partake to become an informed citizen.

But the "truth" offered by the media is a systematic and deliberate distortion of reality. In some cases, such as the previously cited example of human cloning, this distortion takes the form of outright suppression. In many other cases, it takes the form of distraction, never more prominently on display than during the O.J. Simpson media circus. The coverage afforded this case, and others such as the JonBenet Ramsey case, while creating the illusion that the press is examining the seamy underbelly of American society, does little to shed light on the very real problems facing the average American. These stories, as well as the countless tales of individual human failing that spring forth from the media fascination with the cult of celebrity, are clearly not meant to inform, but to distract and entertain.

Sometimes something far more insidious is at play than mere distraction, however. By far the most dangerous form of distortion, and one that has become increasingly prominent, involves the willful misrepresentation of issues in such a way that the "debate" on the issue then begs solutions that actually exacerbate the real problem that was being masked. In this way, problems that are themselves borne of the increasingly reactionary agenda being pursued are perceived to be solved by resorting to yet further erosion of democratic and civil rights.

One example where this phenomenon can be seen at work is in the media coverage of school shootings. Following each such incident, a pseudo debate is conducted in which the blame is variously placed on guns, rock/rap music, or video games as the cause in the rise in "youth violence." The debate is restricted to these now familiar parameters. But behind the sensational headlines, the media fail to note that youth violence has actually declined, and that these incidents are not a uniquely adolescent phenomenon, but are in fact patterned after the acts of adults, with the high school serving as the teenage equivalent of the post office or the day trading center.

The problem, viewed in a larger context, is not with the current generation of kids, but with society as a whole. The fact that Americans of all ages choose to strike out violently against society and its institutions, however infrequently, is a clear warning sign of a pronounced decay in America's social fabric. Why does the current social system, purportedly the very model of freedom and justice, breed such extreme levels of anger, frustration and despair, as well as the willingness to express these feelings in such explosive outbursts? This question is outside the media's scope.

Neither is it questioned why all of society, including our youth, is bombarded from literally all directions with the message that the use of force is an effective, and even desirable, means of achieving one's goals, and that pity and compassion for others is a sign of weakness. This message is certainly not confined to pop culture and the entertainment media.

Virtually the same message is conveyed by America's increasing reliance on brute force as an instrument of foreign policy and by the shameless glorification of U.S. military prowess.

It is conveyed as well by the increasingly militarized tactics of the nation's police, most recently visible in the heavy-handed approach of the Seattle police towards the tens of thousands of overwhelmingly peaceful protestors at the December 1999 conference of the World Trade Organization. It is further reinforced by Congress each time it drafts a new round of "law and order" legislation, and by the increasingly free rein given the nation's police and correctional officers to enforce those laws.

Rather than acknowledge any of this, each school shooting will be propagandized for its fear-inducing value, with the same script being played out, leading to the same preordained solution: while repeating the mantra that "we will never be able to fully understand why these things occur" (which is certainly true if we don't ask the right questions), yet another round of reactionary sentencing legislation will be passed with additional laws designed to criminalize our children. Far from solving the underlying problems and social tensions, all such legislation will ultimately serve only to foster increased feelings of anger, resentment and hopelessness.

This is but one example of how a handful of key media players determine what the "issues" are and what the parameters of public debate on those issues will be by controlling both the flow and the shape of the news. When a problem is identified, it is defined in the narrowest of contexts so as to preempt any discussion outside of the pre-defined boundaries—any argument put forth outside of those boundaries can then be mocked or ignored. In this way, anything remotely resembling an informed public debate on the serious issues facing this country is effectively cut off.

Instead, what we have is artificially truncated debate, usually by a relentless procession of allegedly politically informed pundits clustering into various formations to populate the cable news talk shows, where the rapid fire verbiage can almost obscure the fact that nothing of relevance is actually being said. These programs, and the broadcast media in general, are not meant to enlighten; they are intended to provide a pre-packaged debate, presenting the acceptable arguments for both sides. At the same time, they are meant to entertain and distract attention away from whatever essential information is being withheld from the discussion.

An informed populace is a critical component of any truly democratic system, and a nation that has only the illusion of public debate has no more than the illusion of democracy as well. That is why it is absolutely crucial that the people of America have full access to all the information that affects their lives as citizens of this country, and of the world community. As an effort towards achieving that goal, presented here you will find some of the news that wasn't quite fit to print.

A brief discussion on sources, credibility and context is warranted here. The source material for this book falls into one of five general categories:

- U.S. government documents and statements by U.S. officials
- Documents and reports issued by Non-Governmental Organizations (NGOs), such as Amnesty International and the Justice Policy Institute
- "Mainstream" media sources, e.g. the *Los Angeles Times* and the *New York Times*
- "Alternative" media sources, including *The Nation* and *The Mojo Wire* (the electronic version of *Mother Jones*)
- The foreign press, such as the *London Times* and Australia's *The Age*

Of these five, official government documents were considered the most credible, and were therefore the most sought after. This is certainly not to suggest that the various branches of the U.S. government are noted for their honesty. On the contrary, lying is an integral element of the business of government, not only in America but around the world. However, government disinformation tends to follow a fairly steady pattern, namely casting the purveyor of the propaganda in the best possible light.

Given that the documents excerpted here tend, to the contrary, to damage America's carefully crafted public image, they were deemed to be the most credible and therefore the most difficult to refute. The other primary source of documents was from NGOs, which were considered to be somewhat less credible due to the obvious fact that all such organizations have a political agenda, leaving them open to charges of bias. It is notable, however, that the media generally finds the information released by these entities quite credible when it casts America in a positive light, carefully sidestepping the more unsavory facts, issues and trends.

The balance of the material presented here was culled from the various newsmedia sources listed above. Whenever possible, what are generally considered to be mainstream sources were consulted first, beginning with the largest and most influential of the major daily newspapers. In those cases where the mainstream media failed to yield the desired information, the alternative media was next utilized. As a last resort, the foreign press was turned to on those issues which drop completely off the American media's radar screen.

And why, given that a central argument thus far has been that the function of the media is to obscure rather than to inform, should any credence be given to these sources? For the simple reason that occasionally bits and pieces of the truth manage to filter through, and by assembling all these fragments together, it is possible to begin to construct a more accurate representation of the socio-political conditions within the United States today.

It is notable that the typical reaction when information of this sort does appear in print is to deride it as yet further proof of the supposed "liberal" bias of the press. The notion that the American media has a liberal bias has never been remotely grounded in reality, but has rather been kept alive as a myth precisely so that embarrassing press coverage could be more easily discredited. As no less a conservative than Pat Buchanan has stated with uncharacteristic candor: "For heaven sakes, we kid about the liberal media, but every Republican on Earth does that."[1]

Another area of concern on the subject of sources is that of context. It will inevitably be charged that all of the excerpts and quotations contained in this book have been taken out of context. In a literal sense, this is of course quite true. Quoting material from another source requires, by definition, removing it from its original context. To do otherwise would require reproducing all of the source materials used in this book in their entirety.

This being an obviously unworkable proposition, the real question to be asked is: has this material been excerpted in such a way as to not fundamentally change its meaning in the original context in which it appeared. I think that I can, in good conscience, state that this is indeed the case here. Of course, every writer brings his own personal bias to his work, and it is entirely possible that this writer's bias has affected this work. To claim otherwise would reek of hypocrisy.

What do all these facts, taken together as a whole, add up to? The answer, which I believe will become increasingly apparent to the reader, is an ominous trend towards a more controlled, more authoritarian form of rule in the United States, leaving increasingly more democratic rights and freedoms lying in the wake of the reactionary agenda being sold to the American people.

### Notes

1. *Los Angeles Times*, March 14, 1996.

### READING WRITING

## THIS TEXT: READING

1. What is McGowan's argument here? Would you agree with his assessment of America's media? Why? Why not? How does he support his assertions?
2. McGowan employs a classic rhetorical strategy in this piece. He offers a logical rebuttal to his argument, and then rebuts the rebuttal. Is this effective? Why?
3. Based on his arguments, what are McGowan's political leanings? Does it change how you read his text? Based on the arguments of *The World Is a Text*, what are the political leanings of the authors? The publishers?

## YOUR TEXT: WRITING

1. Track down a copy of *Derailing Democracy*. Write an essay on one of the chapters in the book. How do McGowan's figures and facts undermine notions of the "free press"?
2. What is the writing situation for McGowan? What changes are going on in the world as he writes his book? How is technology affecting how information gets dispersed?

## *Student Essay*

### HANES HER WAY

**■ Brittany Gray ■**

*Brittany Gray was a freshman at Virginia Commonwealth University in Richmond when she wrote this analysis of a "Hanes Her Way" ad in 2001. In her analysis of an ad piece, Gray reads her ad through the lens of the familiar vs. fantasy.*

IT KNOWS WHO YOU ARE. It knows what you want. It gets into your psyche, and then—onto your television, your computer screen, your newspapers and your magazines. It is an advertisement, folks, and it's studying every little move you make, be it in the grocery store or the outlet mall. These advertisement executives know just what the consumer needs to hear to convince him or her to buy the product. Grocery stores even consult such advertisement firms on matters such as just how to set up the store in order to maximize consumer purchase. It has been watching, and it knows just what mood to set to get into the head of the consumer, and just how to set the scene.

This particular scene is a mild, relaxed morning. The sun streams in through the windows. The lighting is a tranquil yellow, and the background music is "Fade Into You" by Mazzy Star, a soft and haunting ballad which perfectly complements the temperate setting.

Through a doorway a man watches a woman who is wearing a white t-shirt and white cotton underwear as she makes a bed, snapping a sheet into the air and watching it drift back down onto the bed in slow motion. Then a voiceover begins. The man talks over the music about how when they were dating, his girlfriend used to wear such tiny, sexy underwear. Then he says that now that they are married she just wears old worn cotton underwear by Hanes. He goes on to say that there is something comforting about the cotton underwear. He says he loves when he opens the laundry hamper and sees the worn out underwear in there waiting to go into the wash, because it reminds him of his mother and his childhood. The commercial then fades out on the Hanes trademark.

The ethical appeal in this commercial is particularly strong. For starters, the brand name of Hanes goes back a long way and has been trusted for years. There is nothing more comforting about buying a product than knowing that millions of people aside from oneself also trust the product. Also, the people in the ad seem to trust the product. It seems that trust and stability are the qualities that Hanes wants the customer to attribute to their underwear.

The pathos in this commercial was the strongest of all the appeals. The fact that, first of all, the couple is married, and also that the man seems to love and accept his wife so openly plays a part in the emotional appeal. It is not often that couples on television are married anymore, and when they are, their lives and marital stress are often the topic of comedy. This couple is not only happily married, but obviously has been married for a while as well, given the fact that the wife has had time to change her style of underwear *and* the fact that her Hanes Her Way cotton briefs are well worn.

Another aspect of the pathos is the setting of the scene. The tranquility of the lighting, the airy atmosphere consisting of so much white cotton and linen, and the relaxing background music all play a role in the manipulation of emotion. The way the man stands there with such a nostalgic look on his face, watching his wife and speaking about her so wistfully is meant to really touch something inside—and it does. Not only that, but the man still finds his wife beautiful, even after so many years, and even after the underwear that he initially found so attractive is gone. The entire ad evokes a sense of tranquility and comfort, seeming to say, "our product will fulfill you just the way these people are fulfilled."

The appeal to logic in this ad was for the most part absent, aside from one thing. After all, there is no real logic to a man liking his wife's underwear, nor is there any rhyme or reason behind the comfort that seeing the underwear lying in the hamper brings him, reminding him of his childhood and his mother. Hanes underwear does not make the sun come out in the morning, and it certainly won't find someone a spouse. The logic of the commercial, as well as the fact of the matter, is that Hanes underwear is comfortable—especially Hanes Her Way white cotton briefs.

The audience targeted in this commercial was without question middle-class women, probably aged 12 and up. Most men do not get misty-eyed hearing pretty music, and they are not particularly struck watching a man speak so fondly of his wife. However, women thrive on such things. Every woman loves to see a man talk about his wife as though she were the only woman on the earth, because it is such a rare occurrence.

That is not the only aspect of the ad directed at women, however. The lighting in the commercial, paired with the beautiful sunny morning, as well as the crisp white linens shown throughout the commercial, are all aimed at women in middle-class families. Women love to see that level of comfort and cleanliness within a home, as it all touches on a woman's romantic, idealistic side. Also, the fact that the couple and their home is so completely average shows that Hanes is for average, normal people. Everyone wants to feel that what they do is normal and accepted, especially women trying to run a home. It is one less thing to worry about, one less thing that can be criticized when it comes to a woman's running of her home. It also shows that the happiness of the couple is not out of reach—they are just like every other working class American couple.

These audience clinchers are not entirely in opposition to the ones used in men's underwear commercials. Many men's underwear commercials portray scenes containing rumpled beds in the morning, and fresh white linen. Underwear commercials in general seem to abound in their portrayal of morning sunrises and beautiful people making beds. In men's commercials, though, it seems that there is always that bittersweet touch of masculinity. There is constantly some muscular role model, doing the types of things that strong, ideal men should do. The man in the commercial always seems to do the same stereotyped things. He gives the dog a bath, he plays with the kids. He does the dishes with a smile, pausing to toss a handful of bubbles at his adoring wife. He goes jogging in the morning before his coffee. He shows his son how to throw a baseball just right, and of course he doesn't neglect his daughter—he tosses her into the air, and playfully dodges her blows during a pillow fight. And of course, he feels perfectly comfortable sitting around in nothing but his white cotton briefs.

Women on the other hand don't need examples of femininity. They know how to be women, and showing what the typical woman does in a day would be cheesy and clichéd. Just show a woman a good old fashioned love scene and most likely she's sold.

This commercial probably shouldn't appeal to me so strongly. It is exactly like most other commercials for women's underwear I have seen. They all have the same basic elements: white linen, sunny mornings, happy families, and beautiful, smiling people. I'm not sure if I can place my finger on exactly what made this commercial stand out for me. I think it was the combination of the music and the couple. I've never heard music like that in an underwear commercial. The music used is normally that sunny, get-up-and-go type of music, but this commercial utilized the softer sound of Mazzy Star. The voiceover and the utilization of romance really struck me too. Though the ad was not particularly original, I still felt that it was a beautifully done commercial.

The ethos of this commercial was definitely strong. The name of Hanes is one of the most trusted in underwear, and the advertisers used the stability of the marital relationship to illustrate this. However, the pathos was the most outstanding of the appeals in this ad. The fact that the underwear was made by Hanes was made known, as well as the reasons why Hanes should be trusted. However, the vivid sensory imagery in this commercial which made it so pleasing to the eye and such a joy to watch rules over the ethical appeal. A sunny morning means much more to me personally than the comfort of knowing that I'm wearing sturdy underwear, which is a comfort that is forgotten soon after putting the underwear on. A morning as beautiful as the one on TV is not commonly seen, nor is a couple more obviously in love. It is simple joys such as these that the commercial strikes at, and the joys seem to overpower the main ethical and logical appeal—that Hanes makes good underwear.

READING  WRITING

## THIS TEXT: READING

1. What qualities of the advertising does Gray identify as worthy of discussion? If you have seen the ad, do you agree with her emphasis?
2. Have you purchased underwear based on commercials? Where do you think your influences to purchase come from?
3. In what ways do the home generally and bedroom specifically serve as a sign? What products are most appropriate for this approach? Can you think of other places that serve similar purposes?

## YOUR TEXT: WRITING

1. Perform a similar sign analysis using an advertisement that uses another familiar place (a front lawn, an office, sports field, etc.). What about the place's familiarity is part of the appeal?
2. Write a paper discussing the presence of fantasy and familiarity in a typical advertisement. What types of ads rely more on fantasy? Which on familiarity?
3. Examine the types of intimate relationships portrayed in advertisements. Write a paper examining how advertisers use those relationships to appeal to their target audience.

## WEASEL WORDS

■ **William Lutz** ■

*In his essay taken from his book,* Doublespeak *(1989), on words in advertising, William Lutz, a professor of English at Rutgers University, points out code words that advertisers use to make false claims about their products.*

ONE PROBLEM ADVERTISERS HAVE when they try to convince you that the product they are pushing is really different from other, similar products is that their claims are subject to some laws. Not a lot of laws, but there are some designed to prevent fraudulent or untruthful claims in advertising. Even during the happy years of nonregulation under President Ronald Reagan, the FTC did crack down on the more blatant abuses in advertising claims. Generally speaking, advertisers have to be careful in what they say in their ads, in the claims they make for the products they advertise. Parity claims are safe because they are legal and supported by a number of court decisions. But beyond parity claims there are weasel words.

Advertisers use weasel words to appear to be making a claim for a product when in fact they are making no claim at all. Weasel words get their name from the way weasels eat the eggs they find in the nests of other animals. A weasel will make a small hole in the egg, suck out the insides, then place the egg back in the nest. Only when the egg is examined closely is it found to be hollow. That's the way it is with weasel words in advertising: Examine weasel words closely and you'll find that they're as hollow as any egg sucked by a weasel. Weasel words appear to say one thing when in fact they say the opposite, or nothing at all.

Just what do these words mean? The use of the word "new" is restricted by regulations, so an advertiser can't just use the word on a product or in an ad without meeting certain requirements. For example, a product is considered new for about six months during a national advertising campaign. If the product is being advertised only in a limited test market area, the word can be used longer, and in some instances has been used for as long as two years.

What makes a product "new"? Some products have been around for a long time, yet every once in a while you discover that they are being advertised as "new." Well, an advertiser can call a product new if there has been "a material functional change" in the product. What is "a material functional change," you ask? Good question. In fact it's such a good question it's being asked all the time. It's up to the manufacturer to prove that the product has undergone such a change. And if the manufacturer isn't challenged on the claim, then there's no one to stop it. Moreover, the change does not have to be an improvement in the product. One manufacturer added an artificial lemon scent to a cleaning product and called it "new and improved," even though the product did not clean any better than without the lemon scent. The manufacturer defended the use of the word "new" on the grounds that the artificial scent changed the chemical formula of the product and therefore constituted "a material functional change."

Which brings up the word "improved." When used in advertising, "improved" does not mean "made better." It only means "changed" or "different from before." So, if the detergent maker puts a plastic pour spout on the box of detergent, the product has been "improved," and away we go with a whole new advertising campaign. Or, if the cereal maker adds more fruit or a different kind of fruit to the cereal, there's an improved product. Now you know why manufacturers are constantly making little changes in their products. Whole new advertising campaigns, designed to convince you that the product has been changed for the better, are based on small changes in superficial aspects of a product. The next time you see an ad for an "improved" product, ask yourself what was wrong with the old one. Ask yourself just how "improved" the product is. Finally, you might check to see whether the "improved" version costs more than the unimproved one. After all, someone has to pay for the millions of dollars spent advertising the improved product.

Of course, advertisers really like to run ads that claim a product is "new and improved." While what constitutes a "new" product may be subject to some regulation, "improved" is a subjective judgment. A manufacturer changes the shape of its stick deodorant, but the shape doesn't improve the function of the deodorant. That is, changing the shape doesn't affect the deodorizing ability of the deodorant, so the manufacturer calls it "improved." Another manufacturer adds ammonia to its liquid cleaner and calls it "new and improved." Since adding ammonia does affect the cleaning ability of the product, there has been a "material functional change" in the product, and the manufacturer can now call its cleaner "new," and "improved" as well. Now the weasel words "new and improved" are plastered all over the package and are the basis for a multimillion-dollar ad campaign. But after six months the word "new" will have to go, until someone can dream up another change in the product. Perhaps it will be adding color to the liquid, or changing the shape of the package, or maybe adding a new dripless pour spout, or perhaps a _____. The "improvements" are endless, and so are the new advertising claims and campaigns.

"New" is just too useful and powerful a word in advertising for advertisers to pass it up easily. So they use weasel words that say "new" without really saying it. One of their favorites is "introducing," as in, "Introducing improved Tide," or "Introducing the stain remover." The

Just what do these words mean? The use of the word "new" is restricted by regulations, so an advertiser can't just use the word on a product or in an ad without meeting certain requirements. For example, a product is considered new for about six months during a national advertising campaign. If the product is being advertised only in a limited test market area, the word can be used longer, and in some instances has been used for as long as two years.

What makes a product "new"? Some products have been around for a long time, yet every once in a while you discover that they are being advertised as "new." Well, an advertiser can call a product new if there has been "a material functional change" in the product. What is "a material functional change," you ask? Good question. In fact it's such a good question it's being asked all the time. It's up to the manufacturer to prove that the product has undergone such a change. And if the manufacturer isn't challenged on the claim, then there's no one to stop it. Moreover, the change does not have to be an improvement in the product. One manufacturer added an artificial lemon scent to a cleaning product and called it "new and improved," even though the product did not clean any better than without the lemon scent. The manufacturer defended the use of the word "new" on the grounds that the artificial scent changed the chemical formula of the product and therefore constituted "a material functional change."

Which brings up the word "improved." When used in advertising, "improved" does not mean "made better." It only means "changed" or "different from before." So, if the detergent maker puts a plastic pour spout on the box of detergent, the product has been "improved," and away we go with a whole new advertising campaign. Or, if the cereal maker adds more fruit or a different kind of fruit to the cereal, there's an improved product. Now you know why manufacturers are constantly making little changes in their products. Whole new advertising campaigns, designed to convince you that the product has been changed for the better, are based on small changes in superficial aspects of a product. The next time you see an ad for an "improved" product, ask yourself what was wrong with the old one. Ask yourself just how "improved" the product is. Finally, you might check to see whether the "improved" version costs more than the unimproved one. After all, someone has to pay for the millions of dollars spent advertising the improved product.

Of course, advertisers really like to run ads that claim a product is "new and improved." While what constitutes a "new" product may be subject to some regulation, "improved" is a subjective judgment. A manufacturer changes the shape of its stick deodorant, but the shape doesn't improve the function of the deodorant. That is, changing the shape doesn't affect the deodorizing ability of the deodorant, so the manufacturer calls it "improved." Another manufacturer adds ammonia to its liquid cleaner and calls it "new and improved." Since adding ammonia does affect the cleaning ability of the product, there has been a "material functional change" in the product, and the manufacturer can now call its cleaner "new," and "improved" as well. Now the weasel words "new and improved" are plastered all over the package and are the basis for a multimillion-dollar ad campaign. But after six months the word "new" will have to go, until someone can dream up another change in the product. Perhaps it will be adding color to the liquid, or changing the shape of the package, or maybe adding a new dripless pour spout, or perhaps a _____. The "improvements" are endless, and so are the new advertising claims and campaigns.

"New" is just too useful and powerful a word in advertising for advertisers to pass it up easily. So they use weasel words that say "new" without really saying it. One of their favorites is "introducing," as in, "Introducing improved Tide," or "Introducing the stain remover." The be amazed at how often it occurs. Analyze the claims in the ads using "help," and you will discover that these ads are really saying nothing.

There are plenty of other weasel words used in advertising. In fact, there are so many that to list them all would fill the rest of this book. But, in order to identify the doublespeak of advertising and understand the real meaning of an ad, you have to be aware of the most popular weasel words in advertising today.

## Virtually Spotless

One of the most powerful weasel word is "virtually," a word so innocent that most people don't pay any attention to it when it is used in an advertising claim. But watch out. "Virtually" is used in advertising claims that appear to make specific, definite promises when there is no promise. After all, what does "virtually" mean? It means "in essence of effect, although not in fact." Look at that definition again. "Virtually" means *not in fact*. It does *not* mean "almost" or "just about the same as," or anything else. And before you dismiss all this concern over such a small word, remember that small words can have big consequences.

In 1971 a federal court rendered its decision on a case brought by a woman who became pregnant while taking birth control pills. She sued the manufacturer, Eli Lilly and Company, for breach of warranty. The woman lost her case. Basing its ruling on a statement in the pamphlet accompanying the pills, which stated that, "When taken as directed, the tablets offer virtually 100 percent protection," the court ruled that there was no warranty, expressed or implied, that the pills were absolutely effective. In its ruling, the court pointed out that, according to the *Webster's Third New International Dictionary,* "virtually" means "almost entirely" and clearly does not mean "absolute" (*Whittington* v. *Eli Lilly and Company,* 333 F. Supp. 98). In other words, the Eli Lilly company was really saying that its birth control pill, even when taken as directed, *did not in fact* provide 100 percent protection against pregnancy. But Eli Lilly didn't want to put it that way because then many women might not have bought Lilly's birth control pills.

The next time you see the ad that says that this dishwasher detergent "leaves dishes virtually spotless," just remember how advertisers twist the meaning of the weasel word "virtually." You can have lots of spots on your dishes after using this detergent and the ad claim will still be true, because what this claim really means is that this detergent does not *in fact* leave your dishes spotless. Whenever you see or hear an ad claim that uses the word "virtually," just translate that claim into its real meaning. So the television set that is "virtually trouble free" becomes the television set that is not in fact trouble free, the "virtually foolproof operation" of any appliance becomes an operation that is in fact not foolproof, and the product that "virtually never needs service" becomes the product that is not in fact service free.

## New and Improved

If "new" is the most frequently used word on a product package, "improved" is the second most frequent. In fact, the two words are almost always used together. It seems just about everything sold these days is "new and improved." The next time you're in the supermarket, try counting the number of times you see these words on products. But you'd better do it while you're walking down just one aisle, otherwise you'll need a calculator to keep track of your counting.

### "Help"—The Number One Weasel Word

The biggest weasel word used in advertising doublespeak is "help." Now "help" only means to aid or assist, nothing more. It does not mean to conquer, stop, eliminate, solve, heal, cure, or anything else. But once the ad says "help," it can say just about anything after that because "help" qualifies everything coming after it. The trick is that the claim that comes after the weasel word is usually so strong and so dramatic that you forget the word "help" and concentrate only on the dramatic claim. You read into the ad a message that the ad does not contain. More importantly, the advertiser is not responsible for the claim that you read into the ad, even though the advertiser wrote the ad so you would read that claim into it.

The next time you see an ad for a cold medicine that promises that it "helps relieve cold symptoms fast," don't rush out to buy it. Ask yourself what this claim is really saying. Remember, "helps" means only that the medicine will aid or assist. What will it aid or assist in doing? Why, "relieve" your cold "symptoms." "Relieve" only means to ease, alleviate, or mitigate, not to stop, end, or cure. Nor does the claim say how much relieving this medicine will do. Nowhere does this ad claim it will cure anything. In fact, the ad doesn't even claim it will *do* anything at all. The ad only claims that it will aid in relieving (not curing) your cold symptoms, which are probably a runny nose, watery eyes, and a headache. In other words, this medicine probably contains a standard decongestant and some aspirin. By the way, what does "fast" mean? Ten minutes, one hour, one day? What is fast to one person can be very slow to another. Fast is another weasel word.

Ad claims using "help" are among the most popular ads. One says, "Helps keep you young looking," but then a lot of things will help keep you young looking, including exercise, rest, good nutrition, and a facelift. More importantly, this ad doesn't say the product will keep you young, only "young *looking*." Someone may look young to one person and old to another.

A toothpaste ad says, "Helps prevent cavities," but it doesn't say it will actually prevent cavities. Brushing your teeth regularly, avoiding sugars in foods, and flossing daily will also help prevent cavities. A liquid cleaner ad says, "Helps keep your home germ free," but it doesn't say it actually kills germs, nor does it even specify which germs it might kill.

"Help" is such a useful weasel word that it is often combined with other action-verb weasel words such as "fight" and "control." Consider the claim, "Helps control dandruff symptoms with regular use." What does it really say? It will assist in controlling (not eliminating, stopping, ending, or curing) the *symptoms* of dandruff, not the cause of dandruff nor the dandruff itself. What are the symptoms of dandruff? The ad deliberately leaves that undefined, but assume that the symptoms referred to in the ad are the flaking and itching commonly associated with dandruff. But just shampooing with *any* shampoo will temporarily eliminate these symptoms, so this shampoo isn't any different from any other. Finally, in order to benefit from this product, you must use it regularly. What is "regular use"—daily, weekly, hourly? Using another shampoo "regularly" will have the same effect. Nowhere does this advertising claim say this particular shampoo stops, eliminates, or cures dandruff. In fact, this claim says nothing at all, thanks to all the weasel words.

Look at ads in magazines and newspapers, listen to ads on radio and television, and you'll find the word "help" in ads for all kinds of products. How often do you read or hear such phrases as "helps stop . . . ," "helps overcome . . . ," "helps eliminate . . . ," "helps you feel . . . ," or "helps you look . . ."? If you start looking for this weasel word in advertising, you'll

READING WRITING

## THIS TEXT: READING

1. What qualities of the advertising does Gray identify as worthy of discussion? If you have seen the ad, do you agree with her emphasis?
2. Have you purchased underwear based on commercials? Where do you think your influences to purchase come from?
3. In what ways do the home generally and bedroom specifically serve as a sign? What products are most appropriate for this approach? Can you think of other places that serve similar purposes?

## YOUR TEXT: WRITING

1. Perform a similar sign analysis using an advertisement that uses another familiar place (a front lawn, an office, sports field, etc.). What about the place's familiarity is part of the appeal?
2. Write a paper discussing the presence of fantasy and familiarity in a typical advertisement. What types of ads rely more on fantasy? Which on familiarity?
3. Examine the types of intimate relationships portrayed in advertisements. Write a paper examining how advertisers use those relationships to appeal to their target audience.

## WEASEL WORDS

■ **William Lutz** ■

*In his essay taken from his book,* Doublespeak *(1989), on words in advertising, William Lutz, a professor of English at Rutgers University, points out code words that advertisers use to make false claims about their products.*

ONE PROBLEM ADVERTISERS HAVE when they try to convince you that the product they are pushing is really different from other, similar products is that their claims are subject to some laws. Not a lot of laws, but there are some designed to prevent fraudulent or untruthful claims in advertising. Even during the happy years of nonregulation under President Ronald Reagan, the FTC did crack down on the more blatant abuses in advertising claims. Generally speaking, advertisers have to be careful in what they say in their ads, in the claims they make for the products they advertise. Parity claims are safe because they are legal and supported by a number of court decisions. But beyond parity claims there are weasel words.

Advertisers use weasel words to appear to be making a claim for a product when in fact they are making no claim at all. Weasel words get their name from the way weasels eat the eggs they find in the nests of other animals. A weasel will make a small hole in the egg, suck out the insides, then place the egg back in the nest. Only when the egg is examined closely is it found to be hollow. That's the way it is with weasel words in advertising: Examine weasel words closely and you'll find that they're as hollow as any egg sucked by a weasel. Weasel words appear to say one thing when in fact they say the opposite, or nothing at all.

first is simply saying, here's our improved soap; the second, here's our new advertising campaign for our detergent. Another favorite is "now," as in, "Now there's Sinex," which simply means that Sinex is available. Then there are phrases like "Today's Chevrolet," "Presenting Dristan," and "A fresh way to start the day." The list is really endless because advertisers are always finding new ways to say "new" without really saying it. If there is a second edition of this book, I'll just call it the "new and improved" edition. Wouldn't you really rather have a "new and improved" edition of this book rather than a "second" edition?

## Acts Fast

"Acts" and "works" are two popular weasel words in advertising because they bring action to the product and to the advertising claim. When you see the ad for the cough syrup that "Acts on the cough control center," ask yourself what this cough syrup is claiming to do. Well, it's just claiming to "act," to do something, to perform an action. What is it that the cough syrup does? The ad doesn't say. It only claims to perform an action or do something on your "cough control center." By the way, what and where is your "cough control center"? I don't remember learning about that part of the body in human biology class.

Ads that use such phrases as "acts fast," "acts against," "acts to prevent," and the like are saying essentially nothing, because "act" is a word empty of any specific meaning. The ads are always careful not to specify exactly what "act" the product performs. Just because a brand of aspirin claims to "act fast" for headache relief doesn't mean this aspirin is any better than any other aspirin. What is the "act" that this aspirin performs? You're never told. Maybe it just dissolves quickly. Since aspirin is a parity product, all aspirin is the same and therefore functions the same.

## Works Like Anything Else

If you don't find the word "acts" in an ad, you will probably find the weasel word "works." In fact, the two words are almost interchangeable in advertising. Watch out for ads that say a product "works against," "works like," "works for," or "works longer." As with "acts," "works" is the same meaningless verb used to make you think that this product really does something, and maybe even something special or unique. But "works," like "acts," is basically a word empty of any specific meaning.

## Like Magic

Whenever advertisers want you to stop thinking about the product and to start thinking about something bigger, better, or more attractive than the product, they use that very popular weasel word, "like." The word "like" is the advertiser's equivalent of a magician's use of misdirection. "Like" gets you to ignore the product and concentrate on the claim the advertiser is making about it. "For skin like peaches and cream" claims the ad for a skin cream. What is this ad really claiming? It doesn't say this cream will give you peaches-and-cream skin. There is no verb in this claim, so it doesn't even mention using the product. How is skin ever like "peaches and cream"? Remember, ads must be read literally and exactly, according to the dictionary definition of words. (Remember "virtually" in the Eli Lilly case.) The ad is making absolutely no promise or claim whatsoever for this skin cream. If you think this cream will give you soft, smooth, youthful-looking skin, you are the one who has read that meaning into the ad.

The wine that claims "It's like taking a trip to France" wants you to think about a romantic evening in Paris as you walk along the boulevard after a wonderful meal in an intimate little bistro. Of course, you don't really believe that a wine can take you to France, but the goal of the ad is to get you to think pleasant, romantic thoughts about France and not about how the wine tastes or how expensive it may be. That little word "like" has taken you away from crushed grapes into a world of your own imaginative making. Who knows, maybe the next time you buy wine, you'll think those pleasant thoughts when you see this brand of wine, and you'll buy it. Or, maybe you weren't even thinking about buying wine at all, but now you just might pick up a bottle the next time you're shopping. Ah, the power of "like" in advertising.

How about the most famous "like" claim of all, "Winston tastes good like a cigarette should"? Ignoring the grammatical error here, you might want to know what this claim is saying. Whether a cigarette tastes good or bad is a subjective judgment because what tastes good to one person may well taste horrible to another. Not everyone likes fried snails, even if they are called escargot. (*De gustibus non est disputandum*, which was probably the Roman rule for advertising as well as for defending the games in the Colosseum.) There are many people who say all cigarettes taste terrible, other people who say only some cigarettes taste all right, and still others who say all cigarettes taste good. Who's right? Everyone, because taste is a matter of personal judgment.

Moreover, note the use of the conditional, "should." The complete claim is, "Winston tastes good like a cigarette should taste." But should cigarettes taste good? Again, this is a matter of personal judgment and probably depends most on one's experiences with smoking. So, the Winston ad is simply saying that Winston cigarettes are just like any other cigarette: Some people like them and some people don't. On that statement, R. J. Reynolds conducted a very successful multimillion-dollar advertising campaign that helped keep Winston the number-two-selling cigarette in the United States, close behind number one, Marlboro.

### Can't It Be Up to the Claim?

Analyzing ads for doublespeak requires that you pay attention to every word in the ad and determine what each word really means. Advertisers try to wrap their claims in language that sounds concrete, specific, and objective, when in fact the language of advertising is anything but. Your job is to read carefully and listen critically so that when the announcer says that "Crest can be of significant value . . . ," you know immediately that this claim says absolutely nothing. Where is the doublespeak in this ad? Start with the second word.

Once again, you have to look at what words really mean, not what you think they mean or what the advertiser wants you to think they mean. The ad for Crest only says that using Crest "can be" of "significant value." What really throws you off in this ad is the brilliant use of "significant." It draws your attention to the word "value" and makes you forget that the ad only claims that Crest "can be." The ad doesn't say that Crest *is* of value, only that it is "able" or "possible" to be of value, because that's all that "can" means.

It's so easy to miss the importance of those little words, "can be." Almost as easy as missing the importance of the words "up to" in an ad. These words are very popular in sales ads.

You know, the ones that say, "Up to 50 percent Off!" Now, what does that claim mean? Not much, because the store or manufacturer has to reduce the price of only a few items by 50 percent. Everything else can be reduced a lot less, or not even reduced. Moreover, don't you want to know 50 percent off of what? Is it 50 percent off the "manufacturer's suggested list price," which is the highest possible price? Was the price artificially inflated and then reduced? In other ads, "up to" expresses an ideal situation. The medicine that works "up to ten times faster," the battery that lasts "up to twice as long," and the soap that gets you "up to twice as clean" all are based on ideal situations for using those products, situations in which you can be sure you will never find yourself.

## Unfinished Words

Unfinished words are a kind of "up to" claim in advertising. The claim that a battery lasts "up to twice as long" usually doesn't finish the comparison—twice as long as what? A birthday candle? A tank of gas? A cheap battery made in a country not noted for its technological achievements? The implication is that the battery lasts twice as long as batteries made by other battery makers, or twice as long as earlier model batteries made by the advertiser, but the ad doesn't really make these claims. You read these claims into the ad, aided by the visual images the advertiser so carefully provides.

Unfinished words depend on you to finish them, to provide the words the advertisers so thoughtfully left out of the ad. Pall Mall cigarettes were once advertised as "A longer finer and milder smoke." The question is, longer, finer, and milder than what? The aspirin that claims it contains "Twice as much of the pain reliever doctors recommend most" doesn't tell you what pain reliever it contains twice as much of. (By the way, it's aspirin. That's right; it just contains twice the amount of aspirin. And how much is twice the amount? Twice of what amount?) Panadol boasts that "nobody reduces fever faster," but, since Panadol is a parity product, this claim simply means that Panadol isn't any better than any other product in its parity class. "You can be sure if it's Westinghouse," you're told, but just exactly what it is you can be sure of is never mentioned. "Magnavox gives you more" doesn't tell you what you get more of. More value? More television? More than they gave you before? It sounds nice, but it means nothing, until you fill in the claim with your own words, the words the advertisers didn't use. Since each of us fills in the claim differently, the ad and the product can become all things to all people, and not promise a single thing.

Unfinished words abound in advertising because they appear to promise so much. More importantly, they can be joined with powerful visual images on television to appear to be making significant promises about a product's effectiveness without really making any promises. In a television ad, the aspirin product that claims fast relief can show a person with a headache taking the product and then, in what appears to be a matter of minutes, claiming complete relief. This visual image is far more powerful than any claim made in unfinished words. Indeed, the visual image completes the unfinished words for you, filling in with pictures what the words leave out. And you thought that ads didn't affect you. What brand of aspirin do you use?

Some years ago, Ford's advertisements proclaimed "Ford LTD—700 percent quieter." Now, what do you think Ford was claiming with these unfinished words? What was the Ford

LTD quieter than? A Cadillac? A Mercedes Benz? A BMW? Well, when the FTC asked Ford to substantiate this unfinished claim, Ford replied that it meant that the inside of the LTD was 700 percent quieter than the outside. How did you finish those unfinished words when you first read them? Did you even come close to Ford's meaning?

## Combining Weasel Words

A lot of ads don't fall neatly into one category or another because they use a variety of different devices and words. Different weasel words are often combined to make an ad claim. The claim, "Coffee-Mate gives coffee more body, more flavor," uses Unfinished Words ("more" than what?) and also uses words that have no specific meaning ("body" and "flavor"). Along with "taste" (remember the Winston ad and its claim to taste good), "body" and "flavor" mean nothing because their meaning is entirely subjective. To you, "body" in coffee might mean thick, black, almost bitter coffee, while I might take it to mean a light brown, delicate coffee. Now, if you think you understood that last sentence, read it again, because it said nothing of objective value; it was filled with weasel words of no specific meaning: "thick," "black," "bitter," "light brown," and "delicate." Each of those words has no specific, objective meaning, because each of us can interpret them differently.

Try this slogan: "Looks, smells, tastes like ground-roast coffee." So, are you now going to buy Taster's Choice instant coffee because of this ad? "Looks," "smells," and "tastes" are all words with no specific meaning and depend on your interpretation of them for any meaning. Then there's that great weasel word "like," which simply suggests a comparison but does not make the actual connection between the product and the quality. Besides, do you know what "ground-roast" coffee is? I don't, but it sure sounds good. So, out of seven words in this ad, four are definite weasel words, two are quite meaningless, and only one has any clear meaning.

Remember the Anacin ad—"Twice as much of the pain reliever doctors recommend most"? There's a whole lot of weaseling going on in this ad. First, what's the pain reliever they're talking about in this ad? Aspirin, of course. In fact, any time you see or hear an ad using those words "pain reliever," you can automatically substitute the word "aspirin" for them. (Makers of acetaminophen and ibuprofen pain relievers are careful in their advertising to identify their products as nonaspirin products.) So, now we know that Anacin has aspirin in it. Moreover, we know that Anacin has twice as much aspirin in it, but we don't know twice as much as what. Does it have twice as much aspirin as an ordinary aspirin tablet? If so, what is an ordinary aspirin tablet, and how much aspirin does it contain? Twice as much as Excedrin or Bufferin? Twice as much as a chocolate chip cookie? Remember those Unfinished Words and how they lead you on without saying anything.

Finally, what about those doctors who are doing all that recommending? Who are they? How many of them are there? What kind of doctors are they? What are their qualifications? Who asked them about recommending pain relievers? What other pain relievers did they recommend? And there are a whole lot more questions about this "poll" of doctors to which I'd like to know the answers, but you get the point. Sometimes, when I call my doctor, she tells me to take two aspirin and call her office in the morning. Is that where Anacin got this ad?

## Read the Label, or the Brochure

> Weasel words aren't just found on television, on the radio, or in newspaper and magazine ads. Just about any language associated with a product will contain the doublespeak of advertising. Remember the Eli Lilly case and the doublespeak on the information sheet that came with the birth control pills. Here's another example.

In 1983, the Estée Lauder cosmetics company announced a new product called "Night Repair." A small brochure distributed with the product stated that "Night Repair was scientifically formulated in Estée Lauder's U.S. laboratories as part of the Swiss Age-Controlling Skincare Program. Although only nature controls the aging process, this program helps control the signs of aging and encourages skin to look and feel younger." You might want to read these two sentences again, because they sound great but say nothing.

First, note that the product was "scientifically formulated" in the company's laboratories. What does that mean? What constitutes a scientific formulation? You wouldn't expect the company to say that the product was casually, mechanically, or carelessly formulated, or just thrown together one day when the people in the white coats didn't have anything better to do. But the word "scientifically" lends an air of precision and promise that just isn't there.

It is the second sentence, however, that's really weasely, both syntactically and semantically. The only factual part of this sentence is the introductory dependent clause—"only nature controls the aging process." Thus, the only fact in the ad is relegated to a dependent clause, a clause dependent on the main clause, which contains no factual or definite information at all and indeed purports to contradict the independent clause. The new "skincare program" (notice it's not a skin cream but a "program") does not claim to stop or even retard the aging process. What, then, does Night Repair, at a price of over $35 (in 1983 dollars) for a .87-ounce bottle do? According to this brochure, nothing. It only "helps," and the brochure does not say how much it helps. Moreover, it only "helps control," and then it only helps control the "*signs* of aging," not the aging itself. Also, it "encourages" skin not to *be* younger but only to "look and feel" younger. The brochure does not say younger than what. Of the sixteen words in the main clause of this second sentence, nine are weasel words. So, before you spend all that money for Night Repair, or any other cosmetic product, read the words carefully, and then decide if you're getting what you think you're paying for.

## Other Tricks of the Trade

Advertisers' use of doublespeak is endless. The best way advertisers can make something out of nothing is through words. Although there are a lot of visual images used on television and in magazines and newspapers, every advertiser wants to create that memorable line that will stick in the public consciousness. I am sure pure joy reigned in one advertising agency when a study found that children who were asked to spell the word "relief" promptly and proudly responded "r-o-l-a-i-d-s."

The variations, combinations, and permutations of doublespeak used in advertising go and on, running from the use of rhetorical questions ("Wouldn't you really rather have a Buick?" "If you can't trust Prestone, who can you trust?") to flattering you with compliments ("The lady has taste." "We think a cigar smoker is someone special." "You've come a long way baby."). You know, of course, how you're *supposed* to answer those questions, and you know that those compliments are just leading up to the sales pitches for the products. Before you dismiss such tricks of the trade as obvious, however, just remember that all of these statements and questions were part of very successful advertising campaigns.

A more subtle approach is the ad that proclaims a supposedly unique quality for a product, a quality that really isn't unique. "If it doesn't say Goodyear, it can't be polyglas." Sounds good, doesn't it? Polyglas is available only from Goodyear because Goodyear copyrighted that trade name. Any other tire manufacturer could make exactly the same tire but could not call it "polyglas," because that would be copyright infringement. "Polyglas" is simply Goodyear's name for its fiberglass-reinforced tire.

Since we like to think of ourselves as living in a technologically advanced country, science and technology have a great appeal in selling products. Advertisers are quick to use scientific doublespeak to push their products. There are all kinds of elixirs, additives, scientific potions, and mysterious mixtures added to all kinds of products. Gasoline contains "HTA," "F–130," "Platformate," and other chemical-sounding additives, but nowhere does an advertisement give any real information about the additive.

Shampoo, deodorant, mouthwash, cold medicine, sleeping pills, and any number of other products all seem to contain some special chemical ingredient that allows them to work wonders. "Certs contains a sparkling drop of Retsyn." So what? What's "Retsyn"? What's it do? What's so special about it? When they don't have a secret ingredient in their product, advertisers still find a way to claim scientific validity. There's "Sinarest. Created by a research scientist who actually gets sinus headaches." Sounds nice, but what kind of research does this scientist do? How do you know if she is any kind of expert on sinus medicine? Besides, this ad doesn't tell you a thing about the medicine itself and what it does.

## Advertising Doublespeak Quick Quiz

Now it's time to test your awareness of advertising doublespeak. (You didn't think I would just let you read this and forget it, did you?) The following is a list of statements from some recent ads. Your job is to figure out what each of these ads really says.

**Domino's Pizza:** "Because nobody delivers better."

**Sinutab:** "It can stop the pain."

**Tums:** "The stronger acid neutralizer."

**Maximum Strength Dristan:** "Strong medicine for tough sinus colds."

**Listermint:** "Making your mouth a cleaner place."

**Cascade:** "For virtually spotless dishes nothing beats Cascade."

**Nuprin:** "Little. Yellow. Different. Better."

**Anacin:** "Better relief."

**Sudafed:** "Fast sinus relief that won't put you fast asleep."

**Advil:** "Better relief."

**Ponds Cold Cream:** "Ponds cleans like no soap can."

**Miller Lite Beer:** "Tastes great. Less filling."

**Philips Milk of Magnesia:** "Nobody treats you better than MOM (Philips Milk of Magnesia)."

**Bayer:** "The wonder drug that works wonders."

**Cracker Barrel:** "Judged to be the best."

**Knorr:** "Where taste is everything."

**Anusol:** "Anusol is the word to remember for relief."

**Dimetapp:** "It relieves kids as well as colds."

**Liquid Drano:** "The liquid strong enough to be called Drano."

**Johnson & Johnson Baby Powder:** "Like magic for your skin."

**Puritan:** "Make it your oil for life."

**Pam:** "Pam, because how you cook is as important as what you cook."

**Ivory Shampoo and Conditioner:** "Leave your hair feeling Ivory clean."

**Tylenol Gel-Caps:** "It's not a capsule. It's better."

**Alka-Seltzer Plus:** "Fast, effective relief for winter colds."

## The World of Advertising

In the world of advertising, people wear "dentures," not false teeth; they suffer from "occasional irregularity," not constipation; they need deodorants for their "nervous wetness," not for sweat; they use "bathroom tissue," not toilet paper; and they don't dye their hair, they "tint" or "rinse" it. Advertisements offer "real counterfeit diamonds" without the slightest hint of embarrassment, or boast of goods made out of "genuine imitation leather" or "virgin vinyl."

In the world of advertising, the girdle becomes a "body shaper," "form persuader," "control garment," "controller," "outerwear enhancer," "body garment," or "anti-gravity panties," and is sold with such trade names as "The Instead," "The Free Spirit," and "The Body Briefer."

A study some years ago found the following words to be among the most popular used in U.S. television advertisements: "new," "improved," "better," "extra," "fresh," "clean," "beautiful," "free," "good," "great," and "light." At the same time, the following words were found to be among the most frequent on British television: "new," "good-better-best," "free," "fresh," "delicious," "full," "sure," "clean," "wonderful," and "special." While these words may occur most frequently in ads, and while ads may be filled with weasel words, you have to watch out for all the words used in advertising, not just the words mentioned here.

Every word in an ad is there for a reason; no word is wasted. Your job is to figure out exactly what each word is doing in an ad—what each word really means, not what the advertiser wants you to think it means. Remember, the ad is trying to get you to buy a product, so it will put the product in the best possible light, using any device, trick, or means legally allowed. Your own defense against advertising (besides taking up permanent residence on the moon) is to develop and use a strong critical reading, listening, and looking ability. Always ask yourself what the ad is *really* saying. When you see ads on television, don't be misled by the pictures, the visual images. What does the ad say about the product? What does the ad *not* say? What information is missing from the ad? Only by becoming an active, critical consumer of the doublespeak of advertising will you ever be able to cut through the doublespeak and discover what the ad is really saying.

Professor Del Kehl of Arizona State University has updated the Twenty-third Psalm to reflect the power of advertising to meet our needs and solve our problems. It seems fitting that this chapter close with this new Psalm.

## The Adman's 23rd

The Adman is my shepherd;
I shall ever want.
He maketh me to walk a mile for a Camel;
He leadeth me beside Crystal Waters In the High Country of Coors;
He restoreth my soul with Perrier.

*Student Essay*

> **SISTER ACT (SÍS·TER ÁKT) N.**
> **1. A DESTRUCTIVE FORM OF WRITING**
> ─────────────────
> ■ **Arianne F. Galino** ■

*In this essay, written for Rhetoric and Composition 220 (a class similar to Composition II) at the University of San Francisco, Arianne Galino responds to Evan Wright's now well-known essay, "Sister Act," a scathing indictment of the Greek system at Ohio State that appeared in* Rolling Stone *in 1999. Galino deftly analyzes the way in which Wright makes his arguments, poking holes in his seemingly objective account of Greek life.*

Through the Constitution, upon which our great nation is solemnly grounded, and the Emancipation Proclamation of 1863 that released thousands from the two hundred year shackles of slavery, one can gain an understanding of the power of the written word. As a writer, one is often bound to certain ethical responsibilities. Such limitations ensure the protection of the reader and keep the writer up to par in conveying information that is truthful and ethically sound. Alice Walker, award-winning author of *The Color Purple,* claims, "Deliver me from writers who say the way they live doesn't matter. I'm not sure a bad person can write a good book. If art doesn't make us better, then what on earth is it for" (qtd. in BrainyMedia.Com). On the contrary, certain literary works may be lacking in this principle. Such works include Evan wright's "Sister Act," which is a destructive form of writing since it aims to entertain rather than provide solutions and uses stereotypical reasoning.

In October 1999, Evan Wright's "Sister Act" appeared in the pages of *Rolling Stone* magazine. The article takes an insider's view of the Greek system in one of the nation's largest universities, Ohio State. It takes on an interesting form as the individuals interviewed come to life and engage in a series of college activities. Through Wright's vivid descriptions, the reader is able to grasp the raw reality of the Greek system, its members, non-members, and the surrounding college atmosphere.

The technique used in "Sister Act" is most similar to that initiated by today's "reality TV" shows, such as MTV's *The Real World* and the CBS hit *Survivor.* According to Vida Zorah Gabe, the "unscripted coverage of ordinary people being themselves" gives this form of entertainment its "edge." Gabe further claims that these shows are edited to ensure that it is "real—but still entertaining" (bit 1-2). In the case of "Sister Act," the notion that "alcohol and sex sells" is used to its advantage in that it is entertaining.

The thematic and literal use of alcohol is extensive in the article. For instance, one of the first activities described in "Sister Act" is Alcohol Awareness Day, where a sorority member "throws up" between her two "wobbly-legged" sisters after the event (473). The article then closes with Jeff, a Kappa Sig member, in dire need of medical attention as a result of his drinking. Furthermore, throughout Wright's writing, the word "alcohol," along with alcohol-related terms like "beer" and "drunk," appears more than thirty times. One passage states, "Fraternities . . . are allowed to serve *beer* . . . to get *drunk*" (473, my emphasis). Such usage of the word "alcohol" in the context of the Greek system, induces the reader to create a correlation between the two. This, in turn, leads to a stereotype that all Greek members are drunks.

A similar technique of repetition is used with the term "sex" and other sex-related notions. According to an ABC News article by Joanne Ramos, "American culture is permeated with sex . . . That sex sells is nothing new" (par.1-2). In "Sister Act," the words "clit," "whore," "fuck," "porno," "ass," and "jerking off" are used time and again. Not only does this also create a correlation between sex and the Greek system, but it clearly shows Evan Wright's devious method of drawing attention to his article. Where his negligence begins, his writing goes awry. He uses such strong explicit words with no concern for how it may affect his readers and without any real guidance as to the ethics of such principles. It almost seems as though Evan Wright's primary goal is to entertain rather than find solutions.

Although Wright's guidance is generally and apparently absent in his article, he manages to speak amid the mayhem and clutter of people in "Sister Act." His description of specific people and events surrounding the Greek system serves as a passage to his condemnation of the institution. In this way, he draws on the editing technique used by reality TV shows once again. But the manner in which he presents his views through stereotypes is further evidence of his recklessness.

A rift between social classes is clearly depicted in "Sister Act." Wright begins by saying, "Some people say that the Greek system is a sort of apartheid, enabling children from predominately white, upper-middle-class enclaves to safely attend a messily diverse university . . . without having to mix with those who are different" (475). His "theory seems . . . to be affirmed" through the example of Andrea, a former cheerleader and sorority member. At first, she points to a black area and warns that it is a "total ghetto a few blocks from here" (475). Wright seems to ridicule Andrea, who points out, to her own surprise, that five of her sorority sisters were dating black guys. She now has a black boyfriend, who used to chase her around because she was "scared of the fact that he was black" (476). Thus, Andrea seems to be solely motivated by her fellow sisters to date a black guy. However, her stereotypical views remain, as she warns Wright about the ghettos and recounts her first impression of her boyfriend. In this case, the author is able to use Andrea to prove the statement he made earlier.

In the passage above, Wright emphasizes the social class requirements for Greek members. Furthermore, he describes a person who did not meet the qualifications in the system. Wright begins by describing an individual named Mary. He states, "Mary is Hispanic and on full financial aid." Mary then says, "I could never get in. A sorority is a class thing. It's a breeding ground for the next conservative America" (qtd. in Wright 476). The author, therefore, employs his description of one "on full financial aid" as a stereotype for people who cannot be a part of a sorority or fraternity.

Evan Wright continues to reveal similar stereotypes on the basis of physical appearance. Wright depicts two young women in the main pedestrian crossroads. He writes, "One has hair dyed flashbulb yellow; the other has dark purple hair braided in strands around alphabet beads. They are both first-year students, and neither would dream of joining a sorority . . . Yellow hair leads the way to a residential tower on north campus" (47–74).

Wright then switches his criticism to the Greek novice, Heather. He states, "Heather says her own sorority is cruelty-free. Even if it weren't, she has little to worry about since her teeth are straight, her body is slim and her skin is as pure as a cold glass of pure milk . . . Heather is soon to be a resident of Chi Omega's sandstone-and-brick mansion" (474). Through Wright's unique method of characterization, he is able to depict the qualities that separate a Greek member from a non-Greek. He also points out that fitting into the Greek member model certainly has its benefits. The "mansion," after all, is more appealing than the "residential tower on north campus" (474). Once again, such reasoning cannot help but lead many readers to stereotypes, according to which these superficial qualities become universal truths that apply to all people.

Lastly, the author introduces a partition of gender roles as expressed in various passages. Wright claims that fraternities "offer the only Greek parties that sorority girls can go to in order to get drunk" (473). He ends his essay with Jeff, a fraternity member, who upholds his fellow members' ideals by saying, "we learn how to treat girls like ladies" (479). After surveying the dismal turnout of the party, he declares, "Let's go fuck some sorority girls. It can be arranged. Anyone you want" (479). The fraternity men are apparently the authoritative figures in the system. First, they determine when the sorority girls can party and "get drunk." And they are very much in control of their sex lives. In this way, the author seems to uphold a clear generalization of a woman and a man's place in the Greek system with the latter dictating and the former adhering to her superior's orders.

One may argue that Evan Wright is merely revealing the stereotypes that are already present in the Greek system. In other words, he had no hand in creating them. However, by recalling Vida Zorah Gabe's essay "How Real is Real?" one can grasp Wright's usage of the same method in reality TV shows throughout his essay. Gabe writes, "Never mind that unscripted doesn't necessarily mean unedited. Never mind that *ordinary people* generally refers to a . . . diverse group of . . . men and women with strong personalities that make for much more interesting conflict or that these people themselves have sometimes been charged with . . . playing up to the camera by deliberately being provocative or stereotypical . . . Never mind, in other words, that the *reality* in *reality TV* isn't very real, after all" (bit 1). In "Sister Act," we seldom see a Greek member or non-member cross the other's definitive territory. A fusion between the two groups is revealed only in the character of Rachel Glass— a sorority member and feminist. But even Rachel claims the rarity of such an emergence. She states, "I'm probably one of the only . . . feminists in my sorority" (477). Notice the individuals that Wright uses in his essay. He describes them vividly and categorizes these descriptions as Greek or non-Greek. The emphasis on alcohol and sex in Wright's essay is almost absurd. It may have sparked the interest of more readers, but it also raises questions. For example, what ever happened to going to school, doing homework, being sober, and abstaining from sex? Wright's generalizations, usage of certain individuals, and overemphasis of certain issues are evidence enough of his role in not only generating stereotypes but also distorting the truth.

There is an old saying that goes, "the truth shall set you free." In this case, however, "Sister Act" constrains the reader's perspective on all aspects of the Greek system. The impact of the essay on my thinking, which may or may not be shared by other readers, is immense. Never again can I look at a Greek system member without associating him or her with being a white upper-middle class, sex-driven alcoholic. Perhaps it is immature for me to think in this manner, but with such an effect on thinking, Wright cannot "wash his hands clean" of generating such ideas in the minds of his readers.

Moreover, Evan Wright falls short of conveying his message on a higher level of communication. As mentioned earlier, writers have an ethical responsibility toward their readers. Yet, Wright's representation of alcohol, sex, social classes, physical appearances, and gender roles in the context of the Greek system are overtly stereotypical. His form of writing presents a series of stereotypes without a differentiation between right and wrong or the guidance of his personal opinions. He fails to unveil the destructive consequences of such thinking. Thus, he makes readers, such as myself, highly susceptible to stereotypical reasoning. The readers are not the only victims of such writing. It is also unfair to the misrepresented members and non-members of the Greek system. They should not be made to feel that by falling under one of these groups, one is predisposed to a particular manifestation. Such close-mindedness can make the world a more difficult place to live.

The destruction ensues when we are unable to live in a world in which we cannot be recognized and appreciated for who we are, and in which our daily lives are clouded by unethical, close-minded thinking. Until we can all learn to approach all aspects of life—from the words we speak to the books we read—with prudence, we will continue to be victims of and contributors to a destructive world.

Works Cited

BrainyMedia.Com. "Authors: Alice Walker." *Brainy Quote.* 2002. 8 Sep. 2002. <http://www.brainyquote.com/quotes/authors/a/a125270.html>.

Gabe, Vida Zorah. "How Real is Real?" *M/C Reviews Features* 4 May 2001. 10 Sep. 2002. <http://moby.curtin.edu.au/~ausstud/mc/reviews/features/realitytv/realitytv.html>.

Ramos, Joanne. "For Adults Only?" *ABCNews.Com Original Report* 12 June. 2002. 10 Sep. 2002. <http://abcnews.go.com/sections/business/DailyNews/Ramos_adultproducts_020612.html>.

Wright, Evan. "Sister Act." *Good Reasons with Contemporary Arguments.* Ed. Lester Faigley and Jack Selzer. Boston: Allyn and Bacon, 2000. 472–80.

## READING WRITING

### THIS TEXT: READING

1. Can you identify Galino's thesis? What is she arguing here? Is she persuasive?
2. What do you make of Galino's introductory paragraph? What effect does it have on the reader? On her overall argument?
3. Note how Galino's final paragraph moves the essay from the specific back to the general. Why is this effective?

### YOUR TEXT: WRITING

1. Track down Evan Wright's essay and write a response to it. Is it good journalism?
2. Write a comparison/contrast piece on Wright's and Galino's essays. How does each make their respective argument? Does one rely more on ethos or logos than the other?
3. Write an exposé of the Greek system at your own college. How can one be objective in this situation? Is objectivity something a writer of essays should strive for?

## *The Baylor University Journalism Suite*

In 2004, the *Baylor Lariat,* the student newspaper at Baylor University, published an editorial advocating the legalization of same-sex marriages. On its surface, the editorial wasn't radical—many mainstream news outlets wrote similar editorials, and several clergy and religious organizations came out in support of gay marriage. For example, on February 18, 2004, *The New York Times* wrote: "The Massachusetts and San Francisco events are a welcome indication that the nation is having a long-overdue discussion about the right of gay people to marry, and that the states are beginning to serve as laboratories for reform in the important area." But at Baylor, the largest Southern Baptist university in the world, the editorial prompted a negative reaction from the administration, whose president, Robert B. Sloan, Jr., publicly disagreed with both the nature of the editorial and decision to publish it in the first place. This in turn provoked reaction from some Baylor alumni, who protested the heavy-handedness of the Baylor response.

The incident for us has raised a number of issues, but most prominently—where does free speech lie in a university whose mission explicitly states adherence to Christian principles? Here we have reprinted a number of documents from the controversy—the actual editorial, the president's response on the university's website, two sections from the Baylor student handbook, a column from Jim Bryant responding, and then a student response.

Our interest in this story gets to the heart of the complicated forces surrounding journalism, morality, public information, and censorship. Those of you at religiously-affiliated institutions will recognize the complexities at work in this story. As you read, think about the power of words and arguments; what might an essay about this issue look like?

Also, given the fact that we are talking about freedom, publication and ethics, we thought we should say up front that one of the authors earned his bachelor's degree from Baylor and even wrote for the *Lariat,* though he is no longer involved with the newspaper or the program. The inclusion of the Baylor journalism controversy here is not necessarily an endorsement or a critique of any of the parties involved.

---

> **THE BAYLOR QUESTION**

### 1. from *The Baylor Lariat*

#### San Francisco Should Pursue Gay Marriage Suit (Staff Editorial)

For the past few weeks, San Francisco city workers have been working overtime, volunteering their services to help process marriage licenses for more than 3,200 gay couples who have flocked to the city after Mayor Gavin Newsom announced it would give marriage licenses to gay couples on Feb. 12.

Since then, opinions about legal gay marriage have filled newspapers, television, court rooms and city offices.

Last week, California Gov. Arnold Schwarzenegger ordered the state's Attorney General to "take immediate steps" to get a court ruling stopping the city from issuing licenses to gay couples, The Associated Press reported. Two California judges declined orders to put an immediate stop to the weddings.

Even President Bush has decided to take a stance on same-sex marriage, urging approval of a constitutional amendment banning gay marriage Tuesday. He told the AP judges and city officials were attempting to "change the most fundamental institution of civilization" by allowing the gay marriages.

Back in California, San Francisco city lawyers filed a lawsuit against the state, arguing local government officials are allowed to advance their own interpretations of state constitutions.

The city also is asking Superior Court Judge James Warren to declare unconstitutional sections of the California Family Code defining marriage as a union of a man and a woman, the AP reported. San Francisco officials believe barring gay marriages violates the equal protection and due process clauses of the state constitution.

The editorial board supports San Francisco's lawsuit against the state. Taking into account equal protection under the law, gay couples should be granted the same equal rights to legal marriage as heterosexual couples. Without such recognition, gay couples, even those who have co-habitated long enough to qualify as common law spouses under many state laws, often aren't granted the same protection when it comes to shared finances, health insurance and other employee benefits, and property or power of attorney rights.

Like many heterosexual couples, many gay couples share deep bonds of love, some so strong they've persevered years of discrimination for their choice to co-habitate with and date one another. Just as it isn't fair to discriminate against someone for their skin color, heritage or religious beliefs, it isn't fair to discriminate against someone for their sexual orientation. Shouldn't gay couples be allowed to enjoy the benefits and happiness of marriage, too?

*February 27, 2004*

## 2.  Statement from President Robert B. Sloan Jr. from the Baylor.edu website

Baylor University's student newspaper, *The Baylor Lariat,* last Friday published an editorial supporting the city of San Francisco's lawsuit against the state of California to declare sections of the California Family Code defining marriage as a union of a man and woman unconstitutional.

By a 5-2 vote, the student editorial board opined that, taking into account equal protection under the law, gay couples should be granted the same equal rights to legal marriage as heterosexual couples.

It is important for Baylor constituents to know this position held by five students does not reflect the views of the administration, faculty, staff, Baylor Board of Regents or Student Publications Board, which oversees *The Lariat.* Nor do I believe this stance on gay marriage is shared by the vast majority of Baylor's 14,000 students and 100,000 alumni.

We have already heard from a number of students, alumni and parents who are, as am I, justifiably outraged over this editorial. Espousing in a Baylor publication a view that is so out of touch with traditional Christian teachings is not only unwelcome, it comes dangerously close to violating University policy, as published in the Student Handbook, prohibiting the advocacy of any understandings of sexuality that are contrary to biblical teaching. The

Student Publications Board met with *Lariat* staff yesterday to discuss this matter. The board's conclusions are printed elsewhere in today's paper.

In the meantime, I would like to assure Baylor constituents that, while we respect the right of students to hold and express divergent viewpoints, we do not support the use of publications such as the *Lariat,* which is published by the University, to advocate positions that undermine foundational Christian principles upon which this institution was founded and currently operates.

## 3.  Statement from Baylor Student Publications Board

The Student Publications Board has determined the editorial published in the *Lariat* on Friday ("San Francisco should pursue gay marriage suit") violates university policy as defined in the Student Handbook, as well as student publications policy. The Student Publications Policy states that "since Baylor University was established and is still supported by Texas Baptists to conduct a program of higher education in a Christian context, no editorial stance of Student Publications should attack the basic tenets of Christian theology or of Christian morality." Clearly, the editorial published on Friday is inconsistent with this policy. The guidelines have been reviewed with *The Lariat* staff, so that they will be able to avoid this error in the future.

## 4.  B. General Expectations of Baylor Students
## (from *The Baylor Student Handbook*)

Baylor University is controlled by an all-Baptist board of regents, operated within the Christian-oriented aims and ideals of Baptists, and affiliated with the Baptist General Convention of Texas, a cooperative association of autonomous Texas Baptist churches. It is expected that each Baylor student will conduct himself or herself in accordance with Christian principles as commonly perceived by Texas Baptists. Personal misconduct either on or off the campus by anyone connected with Baylor detracts from the Christian witness Baylor strives to present to the world and hinders full accomplishment of the mission of the University.

While attending Baylor, a student is expected to obey the laws of the United States, the State of Texas, and municipalities, or, if studying abroad, the laws of other countries. A student is also expected to obey the rules, regulations, and policies established by Baylor University.

It is the responsibility of the student to become familiar with the Baylor University Student Disciplinary Procedure. The Division of Student Life attempts to ensure that the procedure is communicated to all students through various means. However, the student is responsible to the University for his or her conduct that violates university policies. Moreover, should a student witness a violation of university policies on the part of other students, it is his or her responsibility to report it to the appropriate university official.

## 5.  Statement on human sexuality (from *The Baylor Student Handbook*)

Baylor University welcomes all students into a safe and supportive environment in which to discuss and learn about a variety of issues, including those of human sexuality. The University affirms the biblical understanding of sexuality as a gift from God. Christian churches across the ages and around the world have affirmed purity in singleness and fidelity in marriage between a man and a woman as the biblical norm. Temptations to deviate from this norm include both homosexual and heterosexual sex outside of marriage. It is thus expected that Baylor students will not participate in advocacy groups which promote understandings of sexuality that are contrary to biblical teaching.

The University encourages students struggling with these issues to avail themselves of opportunities for serious, confidential discussion and support through University Ministries.

*November 18, 2002*

## 6. From *The Houston Chronicle*

### Closed Minds (By Censoring Students, Baylor Diminishes University)

Baylor officials' censure last week of student newspaper staff members offered a striking example of the administration's closed mind. Its intolerant reaction to an editorial on gay marriage is characteristic of policies that have dismayed so many of the university's faculty, alumni and friends.

It is not the school's Christian ideals that have unnerved many of its supporters, including the *Chronicle*. It is Baylor's increasing unwillingness to brook any challenge to its insistence that all university endeavors must be aligned with biblical precepts.

Such a stance is incompatible with the mission of a great university, which is to educate succeeding generations of critical thinkers, not serve as a training ground for the dogmatic and doctrinaire. The ability to mount a credible defense of the Baptist tenets that are Baylor's philosophical backbone requires exposing students to competing philosophies and teaching them to think for themselves.

University President Robert Sloan and members of the student publications board stood together Monday in condemning members of the student newspaper, *The Baylor Lariat,* for writing a Feb. 27 editorial supportive of San Francisco's same-sex marriage experiment.

Lariat editorial board members had voted 5 to 2 in favor of the paper's stance, which questioned how discrimination based on sexual orientation differs from discrimination based on "skin color, heritage or religious beliefs."

"Taking into account equal protection under the law, gay couples should be granted the same equal rights to legal marriage as heterosexual couples," the board opined, which is a legal argument, rather than a moral one.

Sloan said that he was outraged and declared that the editorial was "out of touch with traditional Christian teachings" and "unwelcome." Oddly, Sloan's umbrage over the students' free expression ran hotter and faster than his chagrin over last year's basketball scandal in which a former player stands accused of murder and a former coach allegedly conspired to cover up major violations of NCAA rules and tried to persuade team members to say the dead player had been involved with drugs.

Despite the browbeating, *Lariat* editor in chief Lacy Elwood issued her own statement that the newspaper's editorial board members "stand by our decision to address an issue at the forefront of national public debate."

Under the circumstances, it would be better for Baylor to disband the student newspaper than to continue to train journalists to function in a manner at odds with the First Amendment. Better yet, Sloan and other school officials inclined to banish intellectual curiosity from the university ought to resign.

## 7.  Jon Tallman

### Baylor University Scandal

Although the faculty of Baylor did have a specific charter in the student handbook, barring such a story from being printed, there is still the matter of the first amendment. Yes, they broke the school rules, but last time I checked, the constitution trumps that. If publications censored their content because of the looming threat of archaic institutions, the press would not be able to function without bias. Objectivity is the foundation of the press. Without that, journalism would cease to function properly. Unfortunately, the school does fund the publication, and has the power to stop. They can strip the paper of its finances, essentially dissolving it, and because they are a private institution, they can punish the students involved however they please. Makes you wonder what may happen next time President Caputo sees something he doesn't like at the press.

*March 11, 2004*

 **READING** WRITING _____

## THIS TEXT: READING

1.  Do you think *The Baylor Lariat* should have printed the editorial? Why or why not?
2.  Do you think the President Sloan's reaction was appropriate? Why or why not?
3.  In what ways, does the information from the handbook influence your reception of the controversy? Given this information, do you think *The Lariat* might have acted inappropriately?
4.  What principles support *The Lariat*? What principles support President Sloan?
5.  The last piece makes the argument that freedom of the press in a way trumps other concerns in this issue. Do you agree or disagree?
6.  Is it possible that all the parties—the newspaper, the president, and the outraged alum—acted appropriately?
7.  In what ways is this situation a "text" to be read? What does this text say about religion? Higher education? Student newspapers? The media?
8.  Would this situation would have been different were we talking about high school, not college? Why or why not?

## YOUR TEXT: WRITING

1.  Write a paper responding to the situation; who is right and wrong?
2.  Write a paper that defends the idea of freedom of the press.
3.  Look on the Internet and find other situations where a student newspaper was criticized or even disbanded by the university's administration. Compare and contrast the two situations.
4.  Write a paper explaining the place of student newspapers on campus—what should be their role?

READING  *Outside the Lines*

## CLASSROOM ACTIVITIES

1. Find an event or occurrence—a Supreme Court decision, a major decision or action made by the President, a law passed or not passed by Congress—and find an article from a conservative newspaper or magazine, a liberal one, and one that seems to be moderate. Compare how they evaluate the decision or action. What are their criteria? Can you tell what they value based on how they argue their point?

2. Watch and tape an episode of the local news. Do some sign-reading first. What impressions do you get from the set itself? How do you know it's a news set? What are the anchors wearing? Why is that important? What about the symbols—both in the "field" and the graphics section? How might this differ from a newspaper's coverage?

3. Share your experiences with dealing with a reporter, either from a school newspaper, a television station, or local newspapers. What are some common elements of these perceptions? Do you find yourself wishing the reporters handled themselves differently? In what way?

4. As a class, come up with a code of ethics, a set of ideas that all media should live by. Now critique it. What practical restrictions would this place on media outlets? How would it change the interpretation of the first amendment (freedom of speech)? How would it affect the way you receive news?

5. If you were a reporter, what type of reporter would you want to be? Why? What do you think the rewards of being a member of the media are?

6. Looking at some advertisements, either print or broadcast, what trends do you notice? Have these trends changed over time? What human characteristics do you think advertising appeals to? Do you think advertisers know you well enough to appeal to you? To the general public?

7. Notice the signs of advertisements. What elements do you see again and again?

8. Write a code of ethics for advertisers, advising them of the tactics they should or should not use when selling products to the public. If put into place, how would this change advertising as we know it?

## ESSAY IDEAS

1. Read a week of editorial pages from a local newspaper. What are some things you notice? How do columnists use particular words? What do they stand for?

2. See the attached handout on a rhetorical analysis.

3. Examine some of the signs of an advertisement.

4. Put yourself in the shoes of an advertiser for a particular product. Write an ad campaign for that product taking into account target audience, signs, and the medium you would use to advertise it.

5. What issues on campus could be covered better (or at all) by the local media? Why do you think they are not covered now?

## ASSIGNMENT: THE RHETORICAL ANALYSIS

One of the easiest ways of analyzing an advertisement is by using Aristotle's three appeals; the appeals provide a natural organization of the paper.

### Aristotle's Three Appeals: Ethos, Pathos, Logos

#### Ethos—The Ethical Appeal

An advertisement or other visual text uses the trustworthiness and credibility of the author to make its appeal.

The ethos many times is the brand name itself—a brand we are familiar with itself may bring credibility. Or the advertiser may use someone famous or with expertise to present the advertisement. Politicians will often use endorsements to provide credibility.

Many times the ethical appeal is the weakest in an advertisement, however.

#### Pathos—Appeal to Emotions

This appeal tries to get the reader to feel a particular emotion through the use of images or words, or both. An advertisement typically wants us to be motivated to purchase the particular item. The copywriters may do this by presenting images, colors, people, letters, or a combination of the above to evoke feelings of intrigue, happiness, or pleasure in some form. The images are often aimed at reminding us of other ideas or images.

The appeal to emotions is often the strongest in an advertisement.

#### Logos—Appeal to Reason or Logic

Advertisements will often try to present a logical appeal, using facts of one sort or another. For example, an advertisement might use claims that it is the most popular brand or has won the most awards. It might claim the time to purchase the item is sooner rather than later because of the discounts its manufacturer is providing.

### The Target Audience

When talking about visual texts, you might also talk about who its target audience is—how old or young, how rich or poor, where they are from, and so on.

### A Typical Paper

1. An introduction talking about advertising.
2. A thesis statement describing the argument you are making about the ad.
3. A paragraph providing an organized general description of the ad.
4. Three or more paragraphs about the strengths and weaknesses of the three appeals.
5. A paragraph that talks about the target audience.
6. A concluding paragraph that explains why one appeal is stronger than the other.

# Reading and Writing About Relationships

■ ■ ■  Human relationships can be complicated (but passionate) texts.

O f all the chapters in this book, you may find this one the most perplexing: what do the authors mean by "reading relationships?" We live relationships, you might say, we don't *read* them, as if they were something to be analyzed or interpreted.

But of course, we are always reading relationships, trying to make sense of why people we know, love, or observe behave the way they do. Think about it—how much time have you spent going over a conversation you had with someone, trying to interpret the actual words as well as the sentiment behind them? Your conversation, in this case, is the text; you are doing similar work that you might do with a poem or a passage in a novel (not to mention the other texts we have talked about here). Anytime you try to make sense of a relationship, you are attempting to de-code that relationship.

And though we do much of this work in romantic or close family relationships, we also do this kind of interpretation with those who may be less close, such as professors, acquaintances, sorority sisters, distant relatives, clerks in stores, and even physical objects. *Seinfeld* is essentially about the difficulty of interpretation, as the characters go through each day reading (and re-reading) their interactions with each other, strangers, potential romantic partners, and employers. There is no question that relationships are constructed texts—built by our expectations of them, our behavior in them and the power differentials behind them.

While reading the small details of a relationship is something we all do, reading the larger issues in relationships is something that intrigues the authors as well. For example, we may think about the proper roles of professors and students both inside and outside the classroom, what constitutes a committed relationship (and when to pursue one), what the rules are for interacting with family members, and the relationship we have to our country. While each of these can be an extremely powerful relationship, each one is marked by its own demands and its own unique contexts. When we take a close look at these relationships, we see that we are the authors (at least co-authors) of such texts and that we imbue them with shades, themes, tones and rhythms, like a writer, composer, or painter.

When reading relationships on a detail level or a structural level, here are some things to consider:

## Our readings of specific relationships are influenced by a number of factors.

Personal experiences and societal expectations influence the way we think about and behave in relationships. If we have good relationships with family members, we might think of the family as a positive aspect of our lives; if we have terrible relationships with our teachers, we might think negatively about the whole idea of higher education. The difficult part is separating personal experiences from what we see and read in popular culture. Whether you argue that television reflects or influences society (or both), you may unconsciously compare your own experience with those portrayed on screen. The family relationship we see in *The Brady Bunch*, for example, is a text that we might compare to the text that is our own family relationship. How we view and read relationships is based on a number of complicating factors, such as income, geography, gender, race, age, sexual orientation, and education, just to name a few. Understanding the aspects of a relationship can help us understand what it does for us and how we can be better in it.

Sometimes we feel trapped by relationships; we feel bored, confused, and even angry. If we feel this way while watching a movie, we can walk out of the theater or turn off the television. It's harder to "turn off" a relationship, but we can change the terms of those relationships. We can, in effect, revise and rewrite the texts that are our relationships.

## Relationships are fluid texts.

One of the most difficult things about reading relationships is how often they vary from day to day and even hour to hour. One reason for this is that when you talk about human relationships you are talking about complexities that often the two parties in the relationship do not understand completely. Some of the work psychologists do, in fact, is try to understand why people act the way they do, often with mixed results.

But such work is not easy because people are not fixed in their personalities over time; indeed, our personalities vary in our interactions with different people. Think about how much you have changed over the years, most notably how you have changed from junior high or high school to the person you are now, in college. Now think about all of the relationships in your life—your relationship with your parents, your boyfriend or girlfriend, your hometown, your favorite songs, your group of friends, your faith, your educators—and consider how these relationships have (or have not) changed along with you. Now imagine all of the people in your life and all of the changes *they* have gone through. It's not surprising that we move in and out of relationships so frequently.

College is a particularly volatile time for relationships. There may be no other time in your life when so many of your relationships change so drastically as they do when you begin college. Suddenly, your relationship with your parents is different, as it is with your friends from home. Most people experience their first mature romantic relationships in college, and they also have to deal with this new and somewhat bizarre phenomenon—the roommate. The nurturing, friendly presence of high school teachers and coaches gives way to a much different relationship with professors. In fact, almost every significant relationship undergoes some kind of transformation when you enter the world of the college student. So many new texts, all with their own subtexts, can make *reading* them unusually complicated.

## You cannot be objective about relationships.

No matter how hard you try to take yourself out of a discussion about relationships, it seems impossible to see a relationship from an unbiased perspective. For one, you often have a stake in the reading you do—it matters to you, and not only on an academic basis, that you do a good job of interpreting. You also have a rooting interest that your discussion puts you in a better light than someone else.

Just as you cannot be objective about your favorite movie or song, so, too, can you not read the text of a relationship objectively. William Butler Yeats once wrote that you cannot tell the dancer from the dance, and this is particularly the case for relationships. *Fahrenheit 9/11* exists in the world whether you do or not, but *your* relationship with your grandparents does *not* exist if you don't. Every relationship you have relies on your being part of that text. It should be no surprise, then, that reading certain relationships with a critical eye is difficult (and uncomfortable).

The Tracy Seeley essay printed here is a wholly subjective reading of her relationship with her mother. She can *try* to get outside of that relationship, and she may succeed to some degree, but never completely. We may also find that we do not want to read our relationships objectively. If you've ever had someone criticize your brother or sister, you can relate to the sense of subjective loyalty. Of course, *you* can criticize your sibling, but no one else can.

## What constitutes "good relationships" varies over time, place, and culture.

What we think of as good relationships here and now may not have been the case for our parents, or for people who live in other cultures or other parts of the country. For example, the authors have noticed their friends treat their children differently than they themselves were treated. Other observers have noted that the generation gap between this generation of college students and their parents is not as pronounced as in previous eras. Studying the differences between the way we look at relationships now, and how people in other times and places view them, can result in insights about gender, race, class, and cultural difference.

In addition, problems sometimes arise when we have expectations of how a relationship *should* be and find that in reality it is much different. Thus, we can experience a disturbing gap between the text we have constructed in our heads and the text that is our actual relationship. For instance, you may have found that your "good" friendships in college bear little resemblance to those from high school. Or, there is no doubt that you each had an idea of what "college" should be and were probably shocked and unsettled when your own college experience was a text for which you felt unprepared.

For instance, one of the authors has worked as a professor in Europe and India. While the role of the professor and the relationship the professor has with his or her students varies dramatically from Europe to India, both are vastly different than typical professor-student interactions in the United States. Also, both authors have taught at universities in different parts of the country, including the South, the Southwest, and the Northeast. We have also been graduate students at large, competitive universities. Though all are American colleges, each place and each dynamic was unique—as were our relationships with each place.

As you grow older, your relationships will also change. You'll author new texts and with each one, revise your sense of who you are and what you *mean* to yourself and others.

## Texts of all sorts spend much of their energy trying to explain relationships.

Of all the chapters we have put together, this one cries out most for inter-chapter connection. Many (if not all) texts either explore what relationships mean and how they work or narrate them. In fact, all of the readings in this book reveal a relationship with a certain text. That text might be race, gender, music, or film, and those relationships are themselves complicated texts that the authors try to "interpret" by writing about them. And, as you may have gathered by now, this book is about the texts we all construct. Understanding the texts that are our relationships can help us understand a world that is both familiar and confusing.

### ▪▪▪ WORKSHEET ▪▪▪

**This Text**

1. How does the background of the authors influence their ideas about relationships?
2. Do the authors have different ideas about relationships?
3. While it will be impossible for you to know this fully, try to figure out the writing situation of each author. Who is the audience? What does the author have at stake?
4. What is his or her agenda? *Why* is she or he writing this piece?
5. What social, political, and cultural forces affect the author's text? What is going on in the world as he or she is writing?
6. What are the main points of the essay? Can you find a thesis statement anywhere?
7. How does the author support his argument? What evidence does he use to back up any claims he might make?
8. Is the author's argument valid and/or reasonable?
9. Do you find yourself in agreement with the author? Why or why not?
10. Does the author help you *read* relationships better (or differently) than you did before reading the essay? If so, why?
11. How is the reading process different if you are reading an essay as opposed to a short story or poem?
12. What is the agenda of the author? Why does she or he want us to think a certain way?
13. Did you like this? Why or why not?

**Beyond This Text: Reading Relationships**

1. What are the traditional structures and roles of the relationships you are analyzing? How does the relationship coincide or disagree with these roles and structures?
2. What role do you play in the relationship you are describing? What determined your role?
3. How has the relationship you are describing changed over time? What has made it change?
4. In what ways does the "setting" of your relationship change the relationship? Have you experienced a relationship that was altered because of the place and/or time in which it was located?
5. How have your relationships been different or not because of differences in backgrounds—race, gender, sexual orientation, class, and age? (See Tamar Lewin's piece in the "Reading and Writing about Race and Ethnicity" chapter for an example.)
6. Think about how you came to your ideas about relationships. As an exercise, write down the "unwritten rules" about relationships you carry around with you.

---

| **HAPPY ENDINGS** |
| --- |
| ▪ **Margaret Atwood** ▪ |

*Margaret Atwood is one of the world's most well-known novelists, producing among her 19 novels,* The Handmaid's Tale *(1985),* The Blind Assassin *(2000) (which won the Booker Prize for literature), and her latest,* Oryx and Crake *(2003). So it's perhaps a little surprising that she wrote the following piece, which both describes and analyzes the nature of romantic relationships. One question to ask of this piece is whether she means to cri-tique fiction or fact; in other words, whether it's life that is so predictable or writing about life.*

John and Mary meet.
What happens next?
If you want a happy ending, try A.

A.   John and Mary fall in love and get married. They both have worthwhile and remuner-ative jobs which they find stimulating and challenging. They buy a charming house. Real estate values go up. Eventually, when they can afford live-in help, they have two children, to whom they are devoted. The children turn out well. John and Mary have a stimulating and challenging sex life and worthwhile friends. They go on fun vacations together. They retire. They both have hobbies which they find stimulating and chal-lenging. Eventually they die. This is the end of the story.

B.   Mary falls in love with John but John doesn't fall in love with Mary. He merely uses her body for selfish pleasure and ego gratification of a tepid kind. He comes to her apart-ment twice a week and she cooks him dinner, you'll notice that he doesn't even con-sider her worth the price of a dinner out, and after he's eaten the dinner he fucks her and after that he falls asleep, while she does the dishes so he won't think she's untidy, hav-ing all those dirty dishes lying around, and puts on fresh lipstick so she'll look good when he wakes up, but when he wakes up he doesn't even notice, he puts on his socks and his shorts and his pants and his shirt and his tie and his shoes, the reverse order from the one in which he took them off. He doesn't take off Mary's clothes, she takes them off herself, she acts as if she's dying for it every time, not because she likes sex exactly, she doesn't, but she wants John to think she does because if they do it often enough surely he'll get used to her, he'll come to depend on her and they will get married, but John goes out the door with hardly so much as a goodnight and three days later he turns up at six o'clock and they do the whole thing over again.

   Mary gets run down. Crying is bad for your face, everyone knows that and so does Mary but she can't stop. People at work notice. Her friends tell her John is a rat, a pig, a dog, he isn't good enough for her, but she can't believe it. Inside John, she thinks, is another John, who is much nicer. This other John will emerge like a butter-fly from a cocoon, a Jack from a box, a pit from a prune, if the first John is only squeezed enough.

   One evening John complains about the food. He has never complained about the food before. Mary is hurt.

   Her friends tell her they've seen him in a restaurant with another woman, whose name is Madge. It's not even Madge that finally gets to Mary; it's the restaurant. John has never taken Mary to a restaurant. Mary collects all the sleeping pills and aspirins she can find, and takes them and half a bottle of sherry. You can see what kind of a woman she is by the fact that it's not even whiskey. She leaves a note for John. She hopes he'll discover her and get her to the hospital in time and repent and then they can get mar-ried, but this fails to happen and she dies.

   John marries Madge and everything continues as in A.

C.   John, who is an older man, falls in love with Mary, and Mary, who is only twenty-two, feels sorry for him because he's worried about his hair falling out. She sleeps with him even though she's not in love with him. She met him at work. She's in love with some-one called James, who is twenty-two also and not yet ready to settle down.

John on the contrary settled down long ago: this is what is bothering him. John has a steady respectable job and is getting ahead in his field, but Mary isn't impressed by him, she's impressed by James, who has a motorcycle and a fabulous record collec-tion. But James is often away on his motorcycle, being free. Freedom isn't the same for girls, so in the meantime Mary spends Thursday evenings with John. Thursdays are the only days John can get away.

John is married to a woman called Madge and they have two children, a charming house which they bought just before the real estate values went up, and hobbies which they find stimulating and challenging, when they have the time. John tells Mary how im-portant she is to him, but of course he can't leave his wife because a commitment is a commitment. He goes on about this more than is necessary and Mary finds it boring, but older men can keep it up longer so on the whole she has a fairly good time.

One day James breezes in on his motorcycle with some top-grade California hybrid and James and Mary get higher than you'd believe possible and they climb into bed. Everything becomes very underwater, but along comes John, who has a key to Mary's apartment. He finds them stoned and entwined. He's hardly in any position to be jealous, considering Madge, but nevertheless he's overcome with despair. Finally he's middle-aged, in two years he'll be bald as an egg, and he can't stand it. He purchases a handgun, saying he needs it for target practice—this is the thin part of the plot, but it can be dealt with later—and shoots the two of them and himself.

Madge, after a suitable period of mourning, marries an understanding man called Fred and everything continues as in A, but under different names.

D.    Fred and Madge have no problems. They get along exceptionally well and are good at working out any little difficulties that may arise. But their charming house is by the seashore and one day a giant tidal wave approaches. Real estate values go down. The rest of the story is about what caused the tidal wave and how they escape from it. They do, though thousands drown. Some of the story is about how the thousands drown, but Fred and Madge are virtuous and lucky. Finally on high ground they clasp each other, wet and dripping and grateful, and continue as in A.

E.    Yes, but Fred has a bad heart. The rest of the story is about how kind and understanding they both are until Fred dies. Then Madge devotes herself to charity work until the end of A. If you like, it can be "Madge," "cancer," "guilty and confused," and "bird watching."

F.    If you think this is all too bourgeois, make John a revolutionary and Mary a counter-espionage agent and see how far that gets you. Remember, this is Canada. You'll still end up with A, though in between you may get a lustful brawling saga of passionate in-volvement, a chronicle of our times, sort of.

You'll have to face it, the endings are the same however you slice it. Don't be deluded by any other endings, they're all fake, either deliberately fake, with malicious intent to deceive, or just motivated by excessive optimism if not by downright sentimentality.

The only authentic ending is the one provided here:

*John and Mary die. John and Mary die. John and Mary die.*

So much for endings. Beginnings are always more fun. True connoisseurs, however, are known to favor the stretch in between, since it's the hardest to do anything with.

That's about all that can be said for plots, which anyway are just one thing after another, a what and a what and a what.

Now try How and Why.

## READING WRITING

### THIS TEXT: READING

1. Would you say Atwood is referring more to real life or fairy tales here? What is the difference?
2. What aspects of relationships is Atwood leaving out? Why does she do this?
3. What is a happy ending? Is there any such thing? What would Atwood say?

### THIS TEXT: WRITING

1. Watch a romantic comedy such as *We've Got Mail* or any teen movie. What "relationship texts" do these movies construct? What do they leave out?
2. Read Jane Yolen's piece on Cinderella in the gender section. In what ways does her essay comment on this one? Is this piece about gender? Write a paper analyzing this piece through the lens of gender.

## YOU CAN HAVE IT

### ■ Philip Levine ■

*Philip Levine is one of America's best and best loved poets. Known for writing poems about working-class Americans that are both lucid and poetic, "You Can Have It" (1979) is Levine at his best. The poem explores the tense relationship between brothers and their relationship to a city. It also looks at the relationship males have with work and explores how male identity is formed through work, individuality and memory.*

My brother comes home from work
and climbs the stairs to our room.
I can hear the bed groan and his shoes drop
one by one. You can have it, he says.

The moonlight streams in the window
and his unshaven face is whitened
like the face of the moon. He will sleep
long after noon and waken to find me gone.

Thirty years will pass before I remember
that moment when suddenly I knew each man
has one brother who dies when he sleeps
and sleeps when he rises to face this life,

and that together they are only one man
sharing a heart that always labours, hands
yellowed and cracked, a mouth that gasps
for breath and asks, Am I gonna make it?

All night at the ice plant he had fed
the chute its silvery blocks, and then I
stacked cases of orange soda for the children
of Kentucky, one gray boxcar at a time

with always two more waiting. We were twenty
for such a short time and always in
the wrong clothes, crusted with dirt
and sweat. I think now we were never twenty.

In 1948 the city of Detroit, founded
by de la Mothe Cadillac for the distant purposes
of Henry Ford, no one wakened or died,
no one walked the streets or stoked a furnace,

for there was no such year, and now
that year has fallen off all the old newspapers,
calendars, doctors' appointments, bonds
wedding certificates, drivers licenses.

The city slept. The snow turned to ice.
The ice to standing pools or rivers
racing in the gutters. Then the bright grass rose
between the thousands of cracked squares,

and that grass died. I give you back 1948.
I give you all the years from then
to the coming one. Give me back the moon
with its frail light falling across a face.

Give me back my young brother, hard
and furious, with wide shoulders and a curse
for God and burning eyes that look upon
all creation and say, You can have it.

**READING   WRITING**

## THIS TEXT: READING

1. Describe the relationship in this poem.
2. What kind of relationship is this? What other relationships are going on other than the obvious one?

3.  In stanzas seven and eight, Levine writes that "In 1948 . . . no one wakened or died, / no one walked the streets or stoked a furnace, / for there was no such year." What is Levine doing here? Clearly, there was a 1948 in Detroit and elsewhere.

## YOUR TEXT: WRITING

1.  Write a poem about your relationship with a sibling. Then, write a paper in which you talk about your poem and your relationship compared to how Levine talks about the relationship with his brother in the poem.
2.  Write an essay in which you discuss this poem as a constructed text—looking at its poetic technique, its theme, its sounds, the way it looks on the page. What makes this text interesting?

---

| TO MAKE A FRIEND, BE A FRIEND |
|---|
| ■ **David Sedaris** ■ |

*Over the past five years, David Sedaris has become one of America's most popular essayists. Along with Anthony Lane, Sarah Vowell, and George Saunders, he is one of America's funniest writer. This essay was originally broadcast on* This American Life *on National Public Radio and appeared in 2001 in* Esquire. *It was also published in* The Best American Nonrequired Reading 2002 *under this title. This piece looks primarily at friendships but also at other kinds of relationships, both as a teenager and as an adult.*

EVERY NIGHT before going to bed, my boyfriend, Hugh, steps outside to consider the stars. His interest is not scientific—he doesn't pinpoint the constellations or make casual references to Canopus. Rather, he just regards the mass of them, occasionally pausing to sigh. When asked if there's life on other planets, he says, "Yes, of course. Consider the odds."

It hardly seems fair we'd get the universe all to ourselves, but on a personal level I'm highly disturbed by the thought of extraterrestrial life. If there are, in fact, billions of other civilizations, where does that leave our celebrities? If worth is measured on a sliding scale of notoriety, what would it mean if we were all suddenly obscure? How would we know our place?

In trying to make sense of this, I think back to a 1968 Labor Day celebration at the Raleigh Country Club. I was at the snack bar, listening to a group of sixth graders who lived in another part of town and sat discussing significant changes in their upcoming school year. According to the girl named Janet, neither Pam Dobbins nor J. J. Jackson had been invited to the Fourth of July party hosted by the Pyle twins, who later told Kath Matthews that both Pam and J. J. were out of the picture as far as the seventh grade was concerned. "Totally, completely out," Janet said. "Poof."

I didn't know any Pam Dobbins or J. J. Jackson, but the reverential tone of Jane's voice sent me into a state of mild shock. Call me naive, but it had simply never occurred to me that other schools might have their own celebrity circles. At the age of twelve I thought the group at E. C. Brooks was, if not nationally known, then at least its own private phenomenon. Why else would our lives revolve around it so completely? I myself was not a member of my school's popular crowd, but I recall thinking that, whoever they were, Janet's popular crowd couldn't begin to compete with ours. But what if I was wrong? What if I'd wasted my entire life comparing myself with people who didn't really matter? Try as I might, I still can't wrap my mind around it.

They banded together in the third grade. Ann Carlsworth, Christie Kaymore, Deb Bevins, Mike Holliwell, Doug Middleton, Thad Pope: this was the core of the popular crowd, and for the next six years my classmates and I studied their lives the way we were supposed to study math and English. What confused us most was the absence of any specific formula. Were they funny? No. Interesting? Yawn. None owned pools or horses. They had no special talents, and their grades were unremarkable. It was their dearth of excellence that gave the rest of us hope and kept us on our toes. Every now and then they'd select a new member, and the general attitude among the student body was *Oh, pick me!* It didn't matter what you were like on your own. The group would make you special. That was its magic.

So complete was their power that I actually felt honored when one of them hit me in the mouth with a rock. He'd gotten me after school, and upon returning home I ran into my sister's bedroom, hugging my bloody Kleenex and crying, "It was Thad!!!"

Lisa was a year older, but still she understood the significance. "Did he *say* anything?" she asked. "Did you save the rock?"

My father demanded I retaliate, saying I ought to knock the guy on his ass.

"Oh, Dad."

"Aww, baloney. Clock him on the snot locker and he'll go down like a ton of bricks."

"Are you talking to *me?*" I asked. The archaic slang aside, who did my father think I was? Boys who spent their weekends making banana-nut muffins did not, as a rule, excel in the art of hand-to-hand combat.

"I mean, come on, Dad," Lisa said. "Wake *up.*"

The following afternoon I was taken to Dr. Povlitch for x-rays. The rock had damaged a tooth, and there was some question over who would pay for the subsequent root canal. I figured that since my parents had conceived me, given birth to me, and raised me as a permanent guest in their home, they should foot the bill, but my father thought differently. He decided the Popes should pay, and I screamed as he picked up the phone book.

"But you can't just . . . call Thad's house."

"Oh, yeah?" he said. "Just watch me."

There were two Thad Popes in the Raleigh phone book, a Junior and a Senior. The one in my class was what came after a Junior. He was a Third. My father called both the Junior and the Senior, beginning each conversation with the line, "Lou Sedaris here. Listen, pal, we've got a problem with your son."

He always said the name as if it meant something, as if we were known and respected. This made it all the more painful when he was asked to repeat it. Then to spell it.

A meeting was arranged for the following evening, and before leaving the house, I begged my father to change his clothes. He'd been building an addition to the carport and was wearing a pair of khaki shorts smeared with paint and spotted here and there with bits of dried concrete. Through a hole in his tattered T-shirt, it was possible to see his nipple.

"What the hell is wrong with this?" he asked. "We're not staying for dinner, so what does it matter?"

I yelled for my mother, and in the end he compromised by changing his shirt.

From the outside, Thad's house didn't look much different from anyone else's—just a standard split-level with what my father described as a totally inadequate carport. Mr. Pope answered the door in a pair of sherbet-colored golf pants and led us downstairs to what he called the "rumpus room."

"Oh," I said. "This is nice!"

The room was damp and windowless and lit with hanging Tiffany lampshades, the shards of colorful glass arranged to spell the words *Busch* and *Budweiser*. Walls were paneled in imitation walnut, and the furniture looked as though it had been hand-hewn by settlers who'd reconfigured parts of their beloved Conestoga wagon to fashion such things as easy chairs and coffee tables. Noticing the fraternity paddle hanging on the wall above the television, my father launched into his broken Greek, saying, "*Kalispera sas adelphos!*"

When Mr. Pope looked at him blankly, my father laughed and offered a translation. "I said, 'Good evening, brother.'"

"Oh . . . right," Mr. Pope said. "Fraternities are Greek."

He directed us toward a sofa and asked if we wanted something to drink. Coke? A beer? I didn't want to deplete Thad's precious cola supply, but before I could refuse, my father said sure, we'd have one of each. The orders were called up the stairs, and a few minutes later Mrs. Pope came down carrying cans and plastic tumblers.

"Well, *hello* there," my father said. This was his standard greeting to a beautiful woman, but I could tell he was just saying it as a joke. Mrs. Pope wasn't *un*attractive, just ordinary, and as she set the drinks before us I noticed that her son had inherited her blunt, slightly upturned nose, which looked good on him but caused her to appear overly suspicious and judgmental.

"So," she said. "I hear you've been to the dentist." She was trying to make small talk, but due to her nose, it came off sounding like an insult, as if I'd just had a tooth filled and was now looking for someone to pay the bill.

"*I'll* say he's been to the dentist," my father said. "Someone hits you in the mouth with a rock, and I'd say the dentist's office is pretty much the first place a reasonable person would go."

Mr. Pope held up his hands. "Whoa, now," he said. "Let's just calm things down a little." He yelled upstairs for his son, and when there was no answer he picked up the phone, telling Thad to stop running his mouth and get his butt down to the rumpus room ASAP.

A rush of footsteps on the carpeted staircase, and then Thad sprinted in, all smiles and apologies. The minister had called. The game had been rescheduled. "Hello, sir, and you are . . . ?"

He looked my father in the eye and firmly shook his hand, holding it in his own for just the right amount of time. While most handshakes mumbled, his clearly spoke, saying both *We'll get through this* and *I'm looking forward to your vote this coming November.*

I'd thought that seeing him without his group might be unsettling, like finding a single arm on the sidewalk, but Thad was fully capable of operating independently. Watching him in action, I understood that his popularity was not an accident. Unlike a normal human, he possessed an uncanny ability to please people. There was no sucking up or awkward maneuvering to fit the will of others. Rather, much like a Whitman's Sampler, he seemed to offer a little bit of everything. Pass on his athletic ability and you might partake of his excellent manners, his confidence, his coltish enthusiasm. Even his parents seemed invigorated by his presence, uncrossing their legs and sitting up just a little bit straighter as he took a seat beside them. Had the circumstances been different, my father would have been all over him, probably going so far as to call him son—but money was involved, so he steeled himself.

"All right, then," Mr. Pope said. "Now that everyone's accounted for, I'm hoping we can clear this up. Sticks and stones aside, I suspect this all comes down to a little misunderstanding between friends."

I lowered my eyes, waiting for Thad to set his father straight. "*Friends?* With *him?*" I expected laughter or the famous Thad snort, but instead he said nothing. And with his silence, he won me completely. A little misunderstanding—that's *exactly* what it was. How had I not seen it earlier?

The immediate goal was to save my friend, so I claimed to have essentially thrown myself in the path of Thad's rock.

"What the hell was he throwing rocks for?" my father asked. "What the hell was he throwing them at?"

Mrs. Pope frowned, implying that such language was not welcome in the rumpus room.

"I mean, Jesus Christ, the guy's got to be a complete idiot."

Thad swore he hadn't been aiming at anything, and I backed him up, saying it was just one of those things we all did. "Like in Vietnam or whatever. It was just friendly fire."

My father asked what the hell I knew about Vietnam, and again Thad's mother winced, saying that boys picked up a lot of this talk by watching the news.

"Aww, you don't know what you're talking about," my father said.

"What my wife meant —"

"Aww, baloney."

The trio of Popes exchanged meaningful glances, holding what amounted to a brief, telepathic powwow. "This man crazy," the smoke signals read. "Make heap big trouble for others."

I looked at my father, a man in dirty shorts who drank his beer from the can rather than pouring it into his tumbler, and I thought, You don't belong here. More precisely, I decided that he was the reason *I* didn't belong. The hokey Greek phrases, the how-to lectures on mixing your own concrete, the squabble over who would pay the stupid dentist bill—little by little, it had all seeped into my bloodstream, robbing me of my natural ability to please others. For as long as I could remember, he'd been telling us that it didn't matter what other people thought: their judgment was crap, a waste of time, baloney. But it did matter, especially when those people were *these* people.

"Well," Mr. Pope said, "I can see that this is going nowhere."

My father laughed, saying, "Yeah, you got that right." It sounded like a parting sentence, but rather than standing to leave, he leaned back in the sofa and rested his beer can upon his stomach. "We're all going nowhere."

At this point, I'm fairly sure that Thad and I were envisioning the same grim scenario. While the rest of the world moved on, in a year's time my filthy, bearded father would still be occupying the rumpus room sofa. Christmas would come, friends would visit, and the Popes would bitterly direct them toward the easy chairs. "Just ignore him," they'd say. "He'll go home sooner or later."

In the end, they agreed to pay for half the root canal, not because they thought it was fair, but because they wanted us out of their house.

Some friendships are formed by a commonality of interests and ideas: you both love judo or camping or making your own sausage. Other friendships are forged by mutual hatred of a common enemy. On leaving Thad's house, I decided that ours would probably be the latter. We'd start off grousing about my father, and then, little by little, we'd move on to the hundreds of other things and people that got on our nerves. "You hate olives?" I imagined him saying. "I hate them, *too!*"

As it turned out, the one thing we both hated was me. Rather, I hated me. Thad couldn't even work up the enthusiasm. The day after the meeting, I approached him in the lunchroom, where he sat at his regular table, surrounded by his regular friends. "Listen," I said. "I'm really sorry about that stuff with my dad." I'd worked up a whole long speech, complete with imitations, but by the time I finished my mission statement, he'd turned to resume his conversation with Doug Middleton. Our perjured testimony, my father's behavior, even the rock throwing: I was so far beneath him that it hadn't even registered.

Poof.

The socialites of E. C. Brooks shone even brighter in junior high, but come tenth grade, things began to change. Desegregation drove a lot of the popular people into private schools, and those who remained seemed silly and archaic, deposed royalty from a country the average citizen had ceased to care about.

Early in our junior year, Thad was jumped by a group of the new black kids, who yanked off his shoes and threw them in the toilet. I knew I was supposed to be happy, but part of me felt personally assaulted. True, he'd been a negligent prince, yet still I believed in the monarchy. When his name was called at graduation, it was I who clapped the longest, outlasting even his parents, who politely stopped once he'd left the stage.

I thought about Thad a lot over the years, wondering where he went to college and if he joined a fraternity. The era of the Big Man on Campus had ended, but the rowdy houses with their pool tables and fake moms continued to serve as reunion points for the once popular, who were now viewed as date rapists and budding alcoholics. While his brothers drifted toward a confused and bitter adulthood, I tell myself he stumbled into the class that changed his life. He's the poet laureate of Liechtenstein, the surgeon who cures cancer with love, the ninth-grade teacher who insists that the world is big enough for everyone. When moving to another city, I'm always hoping to find him living in the apartment next door. We'll meet in the hallway and he'll stick out his hand, saying, "Excuse me, but don't I—*shouldn't I*—know you?" It doesn't have to happen today, but it does have to happen. I've kept a space waiting for him, and if he doesn't show up, I'm going to have to forgive my father.

The root canal that was supposed to last ten years has now lasted more than thirty, though it's nothing to be proud of. Having progressively dulled and weakened, the tooth is now the brownish gray color the Conran's catalog refers to as "kabuki." While Dr. Povlitch worked out of a converted brick house beside the Colony Shopping Center, my current dentist, Docteur Guige, has an office near the Madeleine, in Paris. The receptionist calls my name and it often takes a while to realize she's referring to me.

On a recent visit, Dr. Guige gripped my dead tooth between his fingertips and gently jiggled it back and forth. I hate to exhaust his patience unnecessarily, so when he asked me what had happened, it took me a moment to think of the clearest possible answer. The past was far too complicated to put into French, so instead I envisioned a perfect future, and attributed the root canal to a misunderstanding between friends.

**READING WRITING**

## THIS TEXT: READING

1.  The essay begins by invoking celebrities. What is our relationship with celebrities? What roles do they play in our lives?
2.  How are relationships when we are teenagers different when we move into college? How do high school relationships differ from those in college?
3.  See if you can identify a thesis in Sedaris' essay. What is his argument?

## YOUR TEXT: WRITING

1.  Write a personal essay in which you *read* a particularly bizarre or unusual relationship from your past. Now that you have distance, what does this relationship tell you about yourself?
2.  Write an essay in which you define friendship. What do you *want* from a friendship? Do you have different types of friendships? Why?
3.  Write an essay in which you explain what celebrity you would most like to be friends with. Explain why *this* celebrity.

---

### MY MOTHER'S HANDS

### ■ Tracy Seeley ■

*Tracy Seeley's piece (2004) is part of a longer memoir project that looks at the intersections of geographical place and the human body. In this short essay, Seeley reads her mother via her mother's hands, making her mother's hands a kind of semiotic text that reveals a great deal about her character, her duties, the setting, the era, and Seeley's own family. As you read, you might pay attention not only to the essay's content but also to its form.*

The day before she went to hospice, she polished her nails. We found, on her dressing table, 18 shades of pink.

Afterwards, we divided the photos, the one box she kept.

Standing against the Rockies, looking into the sun, she is wearing her Aran Isle sweater, cabled to catch the light. She almost smiles in that cool way that says, no big deal. No big deal to be living in Aspen, leaving Balsam Lake, Wisconsin, behind, teaching kindergarten in the morning, schussing through powder every afternoon, and tutoring Gary Cooper's child. Her left hand drapes the wooden fence post, an unblemished row of fingers, all smooth skin and manicured nails. In her right hand, the two thin strips of her skis stand upright, their curved tips sprouting above her light fingers touch. She wears a ring, three colors of gold in a braided wreath around a dark red stone. It is 1948. She is 20.

They merge into one dark figure against the flowered drapes, his black suit and her black dress like ebony against the marble of their skin. Her face, in profile, yearns upward to kiss his mouth, the fingers of her right hand spreading gently across his back. Her other hand cups his neck, her thumb a feather against his hair line, while his hand around her waist pulls her close. The air is electric, their flesh luminous. Behind them, the wedding candles burn. Later, her exquisite fingers hold a bite of frosted cake, her wrist wrapped in pearls. It is 1953.

Leaning against the Studebaker, cream over bronze, she poses in her fitted blue print sundress. It falls just below her knees, well above her crossed ankles and high-heeled pumps. This car is headed into the future, its chrome bubble front like the prow of a ship, like a wide-open mouth, like, wow! a brand new car for this brand new marriage in a neighborhood too new for grass or trees! The sun glints off the windshield, off the chrome, off the paint. Her left hand must be burning it lies atop the blazing hood, her thumb and pinky lifted into arcs above the metal—but she holds the pose.

Glenn Miller glamour, big bands and ballrooms, she clung to those rhythms all of her life. Her real father played a big band clarinet, licorice-stick swing, and she intoned the names Ginger and Fred as though they'd been friends in school. Once, when she went out dancing with my father, draped in black taffeta and rhinestones, she bent over our beds to kiss our foreheads goodnight. Her halo cloud of Chanel Number Five lingered after she'd quietly closed the door and gone. But mostly, she danced at home. When they began the beguine on the record player, she would sway and dip and whirl across the carpet in her white Keds and Capri pants, her sun-speckled shins shining, one hand at her invisible swain's waist, the other resting lightly in his uplifted palm.

At other times, in the midst of dusting or carrying in the mail, she'd break out a few little dance steps, wagging her finger, Charleston style, in the suburban air.

That's when I knew she had once been a person, before she became a mother, like when she taught us to whistle with a blade of grass. Pluck a fat reed, stretch it tight between your pressed-together thumbs, put your lips right there and blow. Like a high wailing clarinet when the joint was really jumpin. She knew how to play.

Sometimes my mother sat still. But not her pointer finger. It wrote secret, invisible words and runes on the surface of the glass-topped table. Little circles, lines, messages, the sign of something moving through her that was not worry or work. The moving finger was always dancing. No matter what, there was joy in her hand.

She has Carol Merrill hands at Christmas and birthdays, the hands of the game show hostess. Carol, will you show our contestant what she has won? Holding up the red boots, the Play-Doh, the red dress with petticoats. Showing the presents to the camera, to the birthday girl. Delivering the Christmas boxes to our pajamaed laps, our legs stuck straight out in front on the floor.

We found an 8-mm reel in the dusty bottom of the cardboard box.

*Take One.* 1965. Her hands are on TV. We are all on TV! Faking excitement, my sisters and I jump up and down, throwing tinsel on a Christmas tree, also imitation. Cut to close-up. Her blue-veined right hand and perfect pink nails glide atop the cabinet of a brand new RCA. Carol Merrill again. See the lovely hand caress the RCA, the pale, pointed fingers reflected in the sheen of polished wood. Cut to the star on the Christmas tree, glinting in the studio lights. Cut to the RCA Logo. The Most Trusted Name in Electronics.

*Take Two.* Sitting close together on tall stools, she and Dad smile and confer over the scrolling Christmas list that unfurls in her delicate hands. I can't hear what they're saying. For some reason, the sound has disappeared. The camera glides past their shoulders to reveal the RCA's behind them. Move to close-up and pan across five new models, each one bigger than the last. Then Mom and Dad stroll into the showroom, and Mom lays a big red bow on the biggest TV.

Wearing a bonnet and looking doubtful, I sit in her lap, and she sits behind me with an unconvincing smile. It's 1959. We both look off to the left. Her hand holds me close, pressing into the small, white buttons of my coat. Her smooth girl's hands now have bones and blue veins. Her thumb and finger make a little oval, like a puppet mouth, like a long, flat 'o.

Four years later, she said that Daddy would be living somewhere else. On Saturdays, she said, she would pack us a little lunch and we would spend the day with him. She cried and I cried, and she asked if we wanted to go for a walk, but I was the only one who did, so she took my hand and we walked outside, where we stood on the burnt summer grass and my mother talked to Annie, our neighbor, in a quiet, grown-up voice. I stared at the trickle of sprinkler water creeping through the powdery dirt in the gutter, and at the sailboats on my tennis shoes. I wasn't wearing any socks. Three days later or was it a week?—my father came home and they hugged, then holding the back of his neck with her hands, she studied his face up close and cried. I didn't know what was happening. When Saturday came, Daddy wasn't living somewhere else and we didn't get little lunches. I decided that my mother was lying.

Sometime in the 60's, she started painting her nails and never stopped. Frosted Melon; Paint the Town Pink; Love Me Red.

1961. Was this the year she dragged the Christmas tree home, her hands cracked and bleeding?

In 1964, my father bought her three slim gold bands, one for each daughter, to wear next to her wedding ring. I loved to see myself wrapped around her finger.

Up and down the back of her hand, I traced the blue veins that stood up like mine, her long, thin fingers. Bony knuckles, perfect nails, Frosted Rose. She was sitting on the couch with her hand on the armrest, talking to company. It was 1967. I camped at her feet and softly pinched the translucent skin on her hand, making a little ridge. She let me. When I let go, it stayed there. And she let it.

By 1957, since the wedding in Juneau, they've moved to Colorado, Los Angeles, Des Moines, Los Angeles again, then back to Colorado, Montrose this time. Her hands have kept busy wrapping, unwrapping, boxing, unboxing, lining shelves in new closets, cleaning new windows, waxing another new house full of floors, diapering two babies, 14 months apart, the new one, me, born in April. In 55 in California, she had buried a baby, born too soon. Before she let it go, did she stroke its quiet head?

Pumping the peddles on her tricycle fast, my older sister Tara tore up the block, one neighbor kid perching on her handlebars and two riding shotgun on the platform behind. My mother was pushing the mower across the new green Colorado lawn, the motor roaring and green grass smell all around. The circus act careened around the corner and spilled on to the sidewalk, my sister's arm broke and all four kids started screaming. Shutting off the mower, my mother lifted up the wailing wounded. Two weeks later, my sister Shannon was born. That year, 1960, we moved three times. My mother had her hands full.

My grandmother sent dresses to my sister and me in our third Kansas house: skirts out to here with crisp crinolines; sailor dresses with red ties; polished yellow cotton; stripes and lavender plaid; red with bows and white collars. We wore white anklets and a different dress to school every day. My mother, who in 1962, had seen the handwriting on yet another wall, was finishing her teaching degree, even as she washed and ironed ten dresses a week then hung them up in the closet. But before she washed them, she took out the hems. And before she ironed them, she put the hems back up. Ten hems a week, down, up. So that when we grew and she lowered the hems, the old line wouldn't show.

She didn't know how to sew on a button. She said she wasn't handy.

The day she posed in Aspen with her skis and nonchalance, back in 48, that very afternoon, a man, a friend, held her hand as they talked their way home from the slopes, held her hand as they walked through town, held her hand as he pulled her into an abandoned house. Did she struggle, strike his chest, gouge his face, as the Aran Isle sweater was wrenched and torn, as the ski pants were ripped, as she bled, a virgin? She never told. Not for fifty years.

Box, unbox, box, unbox. By 1970, she had moved eighteen times since she married, one for every year. She wasn't moving again. She put her wedding band in her jewelry box and adorned her bare fingers with red stones and green, party rings and everyday. One, at least, for her pinky. Hands off marriage, she said. She wasn't going to pick up someone else's socks. Ever. Again. She never did. And she didn't move again either, not for eighteen years.

When the child support didn't come, she took a second job. Until three o'clock, she taught first grade and after school, she went to Lewin's, where she helped women with money and husbands try on every season's latest. She hauled sizes smaller, larger, longer, shorter and colors brighter, darker, more muted, more fun and options what do you think of this, have you considered something like that—to the dressing room and back. Carol Merrill again, this time a little depressed. After seven, she cooked dinner, graded papers, wrote lesson plans, folded laundry, and wrote checks, pulling the shoebox of bills down from the closet shelf, licking envelopes and stamps. On weekends, at home, she polished the windows then got down on her knees, dunking a scrub brush into the Pine-Sol suds.

In 1973, her fingers crawled up the wall like a spider, a little bit higher each day. Up the wall and down. Up the wall and down. The mastectomy excised muscle, damaged nerves, tightened tendons. Every day, her fingers moved up the wall. Stretch.

The grandchildren begin to arrive in 1978. In the photos, she holds babies in her arms, her hands holding theirs. Then toddlers in her lap, her hands around their tummies, or holding a storybook, a puzzle, a Raggedy Ann. The grandchildren multiply and begin to grow up. First communion pictures, her hands in theirs. Her arm around a teenager's waist. Fingers laying down a Scrabble tile, slapping down a queen of hearts for War or Go Fish. Rings on her fingers, polish on her toes, she plays with children wherever she goes.

Eyes smile at the camera and her hand gladly grasps my sister's arm. A few tawny spots sprinkle wrinkling flesh. Every fall, she taught 25 fidgety six-year-olds how to fold their hands quietly in their laps. Now at her retirement party, in 1989, her pinky ring shines.

When she was six, her father the clarinetist had knelt in front of her, kissed her goodbye and wept. She never saw him again, never heard him play. At 62 in Arizona, she became Ginger Rogers, finally learning to tap dance to her long-dead father's tunes. A vision in feathers and satin and bows, she glided and shuffle-ball-changed, her six-year-old heart swinging with Benny, her hands held aloft like birds.

When her retirement funds dried up in 1991, she became a Wal-Mart greeter, waving hello and shaking hands, patting the babies arms. Not exactly Carol Merrill. But she liked the babies.

She wanted to play Scrabble with her grandchildren. Besides, Arizona was getting crowded. So she retired from sunshine and tap dancing and moved to Indiana in 1997. Her finger danced above the tiles as she carefully chose her words. She didn't care if she won. While she waited her turn, her pointer finger wrote its secrets.

1999. An Indiana January. Cancer has moved in. Fresh snow, opalescent and quiet, spreads itself across the dark fields. As she dozes in her recliner, her hands folded as if in prayer, I stare at her closed eyes and parted lips, her stilled hands.

2000. June. Her grandchildren and her daughters, and our husbands and partners, carry a box of ashes into the mountains of Glacier National Park, up Avalanche Gorge, along the streambed, under the shade of summer trees. One at a time, we dip into the box, hold her powdery bones in our hands, and let them go, cinders like sand through our fingers. The ashes dance, held aloft in a watery cloud, then begin to separate and, easing toward the center of the stream, pause for a moment, suspended. Then the current catches hold and she surges away in the turbulent rush of early summer snow melt, merging with the splash and play of flashing water, racing over boulders, over ledges, over stones, down toward the valley to become soil, streambed, life. We wash our hands in the icy water.

In the grainy, jittery frames of the 8-mm print, her hands hold mine, steering my lumbering steps toward the chocolate frosting on the two-layer cake and the single burning candle.

Naked, squat, glistening with bath water, I stand in the tub and grip the edge, grinning at the camera with two sharp teeth, doing the jerky bouncy dance of the proud, standing baby. It's a Loony Tunes home movie. Two slender hands reach into the frame, lifting me just enough to plop my bottom down in the water. The hands disappear, and I stare unsmiling, saucer eyes wide. I scowl at the water around my waist. I shoot the camera a dirty look, lean forward onto one hand, grip the tub edge with the other, plant one stolid leg then the other, and haul myself, wobbling, up. With two chubby hands clutching the tub, I look into the camera, straight-faced and innocent, then break out the two-tooth grin and begin the jerky bouncy dance again. The silent, honky-tonk jug band plays for eight more beats, then the hands reappear, reach under my arms, and my bent, shining legs fly through the air.

**READING WRITING**

## THIS TEXT: READING

1. What is Seeley's argument in this essay? Does she have a thesis statement? If so, where is it?
2. Make a list of the various things Seeley's mother's hands represent. What sorts of signs does Seeley pay attention to regarding her mother's hands.

3.  How is this essay not simply about Seeley's mother's hands but about Seeley herself? What do we learn about the author by learning about the author's mother's hands?

## YOUR TEXT: WRITING

1.  Write an essay in which you *read* someone close to you by focusing on a specific physical attribute of that person. It could be that person's nose, or dialect, or height or hair color. What does this attribute reveal about this person?

2.  Write an essay in which you read someone based not on a physical attribute but a chosen obsession or hobby, such as a musical interest, a devotion to a sport, the participation in a club or activity, a beloved car or bicycle, a certain way of dressing. How is identification by object different than identification by physical attribute.

3.  Write an essay in which you read you relationship with your guardian (parent, stepparent, grandparent) through something specific. How does this specific item speak for this person?

4.  Write a comparison/contrast essay on "My Mother's Hands" and Amy Tan's "Mother Tongue."

## *The College Relationship Suite*

For many people, college is the first significant choice one makes; for many it marks the beginning of independence as students leave home and go to a place they have chosen to live for the first time. While society has conventionally described college as the best four years of one's life, it can also be a confusing time, as old ties may weaken and new ties forged. Students, faculty, and parents often have conflicting ideas about what college should represent; faculty expect students to devote their time to studies—students may seek this too but also want to experience a social life for their first time away from home; parents hope that college will lead to some sort of employment.

As we note in the introduction to this chapter, college marks the beginning not simply of new relationships but of new *kinds* of relationships. In fact, almost every relationship dynamic in college is new—you likely never had roommates before, dating is likely different in college, professors are not the same as high school teachers, you have never been in a sorority/fraternity before—even your friends are likely different. Negotiating these new contexts can be difficult. This suite looks specifically at college relationships and their unique demands and expectations.

Relationships between students can be difficult, as some want different things from one another, as Emily Littlewood (2000) describes in her essay on the types of college dating. Littlewood, a student at Virginia Commonwealth University, identifies three kinds of romantic relationships in college and reads each of them as specific texts with their own codes, rules and expectations. Libby Copeland (2004) also looks at romantic relationships, most notably the pain of the unrequited crush, which exits in high school, but seems to intensify in college, perhaps because of the ubiquitous opportunities for dating.

The other three readings in this suite take a look at another new relationship in college—the professor/student relationship. While regulations at colleges and universities govern some of the behavior of faculty and students, there exists a great deal of ambiguity, not only in the popular topic of student-teacher romantic relationships (they make it into every movie and television show about college), but how students and teachers should act with one another on a daily basis.

Both authors are professors and both value collegial, friendly relationships with students. Both also feel very strongly that professor-student dating is not a good idea. Yet, more and more colleges and universities are encouraging faculty to spend educational time with students outside of class, fostering seamless learning environments, research and publication opportunities, and service learning experience. But what kind of student-professor relationship is "proper?" Laura Kipnis (2004), author of *Against Love: A Polemic,* argues that we should alter how we think about relationships between students and professors rather than banning them altogether. Kathleen Dean More and Lani Roberts, professors of philosophy at Oregon State, take two differing stances on whether professors should hug students. In this article and the next, you might find it interesting to see how professors feel about their relationships with students—they are often as anxious as you are. Deni Elliott and Paul Martin Lester are life partners as well as professors. In their essay, published in the *Chronicle of Higher Education* in 2001, they provide questions that professors should ask before initiating non-classroom meetings with students. Are these the same questions students should ask?

The authors have had professors whose classes, writings, and ideas have changed their worlds. And we have also had students in our classes whose commitment, humor and liveliness have enriched our lives tremendously. We hope that this suite (and your college days) lead to similar experiences for you.

*Student Essay*

## CAN YOU HANDLE THE COMMITMENT?: THREE TYPES OF COLLEGE RELATIONSHIPS

### ■ Emily Littlewood ■

Everyone participates in some type of romantic relationship at some point in his or her life. On campus there are, unsurprisingly, many different types of these relationships, few with specific boundaries or limits. There is a lot of "gray area" when dealing with relationships between people who are just "coming of age," such as college students. Though there are just about as many different types of these relationships as there are people participating in them, there are three main categories in which they fall. These groupings are simply split by level of commitment, which boils down to true underlying emotions. Of these groupings, the random hook up category has the least amount of commitment, followed by the dating / friends with benefits group, with the going out grouping being the "ultimate" commitment level. The fact that there are so many different levels of commitment and intimacy just goes to show that while in this period of self-confusion, students have varied views upon how much effort and emotion should be placed into a romantic relationship.

The relationships that fall into the random hook up group contain the least amount of attachment and emotional involvement. This category is most likely the broadest because there are so many different definitions of what a hook up is, which makes explaining the exact boundaries of the category difficult. The one thing which all hook ups must have in common is their singularity. Anything from a kiss to sex can be a hook up, as long as there is no intent of forming any emotional bond with the person. A hook up is a singular occasion with that specific person, and no type of stronger relationship forms because of it. The people who are most likely to participate in these hook ups are either those who fear commitment or those who simply enjoy being single (or both).

Most hook ups occur for the sake of instant gratification, the claimed motto of our generation, the apparent reincarnate of the '60's. Hooking up is a non-committal way of satisfying sexual needs but very rarely has an impact upon an emotional level. This type of relationship seems to be most popular with college-aged students, because many do not feel comfortable with a serious commitment. Hooking up also provides the most convenient way of making physical contact with other people. Being in a situation where one meets huge amounts of new people, and in a state of change in general, a person seems to be most at ease with an interaction that needs no effort put into it.

The next level of commitment consists of the "dating" or "friends with benefits" category. This entails a semi-relationship, still without full emotional involvement. Dating requires the *repetition* of hook ups with the same person, taking hooking up to a more serious level. This type of relationship lacks any type of exclusiveness, though a slight concept of loyalty does exist. This loyalty leads to the repetitiveness. By dating the same person again and again, one is staking a claim that, yes, the sense of caring and desire to be with that other person subsists. This desire, however, lacks the amount of strength needed to invoke fidelity. Dating includes slight emotional involvement other than loyalty, requiring the two people involved to at least like each other enough to be around the other on more than one occasion.

Friends with benefits requires a bit more caring on the part of the two people. Friends take their relationship that began as a platonic one and has, over time incorporated the physicality of a sexual relationship. Most people who are in this type of situation have the mindset that they are in a relaxed form of "going out," not having to deal with the issue of fidelity but being able to have everything else, mainly sexual and some emotional support.

The plus side of these types of relationships is that the people involved get most of the perks of an exclusive relationship, without having to actually make a commitment. There is an emotional connection between the partners, a sense of caring and *liking*. These relationships are much more laid back than their exclusive counterparts, not requiring the self-control needed to be completely committed. There are a few downsides to these relationships, however. There may be underlying jealousy because either of the partners can date other people, and this jealousy cannot truly be addressed, because the relationship is not exclusive. In general, one of the people involved cares more than the other, which creates a problem because that person usually asks to "upgrade" the relationship to exclusiveness, while their partner protests their happiness with the freedom of dating many people.

The third type of relationship is the "going out" category. These relationships are mutually exclusive and are meant to satisfy all emotional needs. If one of the partners were to "hook up" with someone other than their relationship partner, he or she would be cheating. When a couple has decided to go out, it often shows that their emotional bond has become much stronger, and they want to become even closer. This type of relationship exhibits a much more powerful sense of caring than the other two types, as well as a sense of devotion. By agreeing to see only each other, the two people involved are agreeing to be devoted to one another. In a *good* relationship, the two people care deeply about each other's happiness, as well as maintaining a sense of respect for the other person.

When talking about this type of relationship, the pros and cons seem to be to the extreme. One gains a safety net, in a sense, not needing to look for random hook ups anymore. There should be a sense of extreme like, or even love, between the two people, which generally adds to one's well being. There is always someone to connect to, and trust. On the other hand, to be in a relationship like this one must make themselves vulnerable, and completely opening one's self to another is a very hard and dangerous thing to do. To be devoted to the other person, one needs to be willing to trust them, and just by doing that a world of pain can be brought about. At the college age, many people are just finding the ability to be devoted and reliable, which makes it hard to expect those qualities in another person. Many people at this age feel stifled by the exclusive nature of these relationships, because they are under the impression that college is the time to have fun, which, to them, means dating many different people.

Different people choose to be in particular types of relationships for different reasons. That decision usually includes consideration of how much physical attraction there is between the people as well as how strong of an emotional connection is present. When choosing what level of intensity to make the relationship, a person must decide how much emotional support and attachment, as well as how strong of a physical relationship, he or she wants. There must be a weighing of how devoted and committed a person can be to someone else against how much of a desire for the freedom to be with as many people as they choose. Making this choice shows character. People who are afraid to commit, or prefer to "play the field" generally stick to random hook ups, avoiding any need to becoming emotionally attached or devote themselves to another person. Those who choose to either date or begin a sexual relationship with a friend are usually craving some type of emotional support but without the desire of relying too heavily on anyone else. The people that choose to commit themselves to the status of "going out" seem to have the most maturity and will power. They exude self-control and confidence, able to, on most occasions, remain faithful to their partner and remaining emotionally steadfast. Just by choosing what type of relationship to participate in, people are telling others their secret fears of being hurt, or the stability of their being, by having someone rely upon them. By knowing this information, the world can look at teenage relationships in a new light. The choices that teenagers make regarding levels of commitment or physicality are not always careless. Changes affect teenagers as an age group in almost every aspect of life, and do play a role in what type of relationships a college aged student may want to involve themselves in. So maybe we have *reason* to not commit ourselves completely to one person, instead of the general view that we simply lack the capability to do it.

## BOY FRIEND: BETWEEN THOSE TWO WORDS, A GUY CAN GET CRUSHED

### ■ Libby Copeland ■

The worst kind of temptation, as Tantalus found out, is the sort that's closest, the fruit that's barely out of reach. This holds true for infatuation, which is why the cruelest crush is one between friends.

We call this the friend-crush, and it happens when one member of a platonic relationship secretly harbors a desire for something more. The friend-crush survives through crying jags and significant others and drunken walks home. And when it ends, it often goes out with a humiliating fizzle, accompanied by something like, "I can't date you, Jason/Bobby/Steven/Mike. I value our friendship too much."

Apparently, no one talks about the friend-crush, about the fact that it's quite common, that it usually seems to be the guy doing the crushing, and that it is endemic to high schools and college campuses. Last autumn a college kid named Matt Brochu wrote about it in his school newspaper, and it was as if he'd just translated the Rosetta Stone of adolescent longing.

When Brochu's column ran in the University of Massachusetts paper in November, a cry of recognition arose from the young people of this nation. At last, someone had given voice to their silent suffering. Through instant messaging, the column spread from Amherst, Mass., to Boston to Austin to Muncie to Berkeley. It spread to England and Belgium and to a Navy enlistee in the middle of the Pacific Ocean and to a woman in eastern Canada who "almost cried" when she read it.

The Web site for the Massachusetts Daily Collegian, where Brochu's column was posted, was flooded. A typical column gets at most 1,000 readers in one month. Brochu's got 570,000 hits from November to March.

The column was an anatomy of Brochu's real-life crush, embellished by past experiences and by a sprinkling of imagination. Brochu, now a 21-year-old senior, fell into infatuation last summer, after he became friends with a girl from his home town of East Longmeadow, Mass. She was three years younger, an incoming freshman at UMass and—the way Brochu tells it—burdened by a boyfriend who wasn't good enough for her. (They never are.) She was flirtatious and beautiful and had an air of innocence. She and Matt wound up in psychology class together, where they chatted through each seminar and Brochu's roommate took notes for both of them. Then she broke up with her boyfriend.

Brochu started writing. When he finished, the column was effusive and tragic the way love paeans usually are. It was called "What she doesn't know will kill you," and it was written in the second person and filled with references specific to his slice of generation. You met her a few months ago, and somehow she managed to seep into your subconscious like that "Suga how you get so fly" song. . . . She's gorgeous, but gorgeous is an understatement. More like you're startled every time you see her because you notice something new in a "Where's Waldo" sort of way.

It described how a crush works on memory, causing the desirer to remember everything ever told to him by the object of his desire. It talked about the guy's everyday indecisions, such as what to get the girl for her birthday and whether to instant-message her at any given moment. It talked of "that cute little scar on her shoulder," and her love for calzones, and her utter obliviousness to his ardor. It talked of her boyfriend, the "tool," who didn't appreciate her.

Collegian Web site readers are allowed to write responses to articles. Most columns get three or four. Brochu's column got over 500, nearly all in gratitude and praise. Eventually, the exhausted editor running the feedback section told readers they couldn't write in any more. But the old messages are still up there, steeped in the drama of young love.

> "Thank you for showing me that I'm not alone on this in this crazy world," wrote someone under the name "Hobbes."

> "By the time I finished it, I was speechless and light-headed from the truthfulness of it all," wrote "Abel."

> "i laughed when i saw resemblances of myself, yet inside i was really crying," wrote "Krunk."

Readers were inspired by the end of Brochu's column, a romantic call to arms that included a blank space where each reader could write the name of his beloved. The last lines are these:

> Now cut this out, fill in her name, and give it to her, coward. Just let me know how it works out.

> "Damn, I wish I could be so eloquent," wrote "P. Che." "Maybe it really is worth a shot no?"

Brochu thought so. He'd made up his mind to tell the girl.

Unlike the infatuation from afar, the friend-crush is especially powerful because the romance seems so almost possible. By its very nature, the friend-crush encourages Talmudic dissections of the beloved's psyche, hashing and rehashing of missed opportunities, optimistic interpretations of neutral behavior.

There's Brad Clark, 17, of Glen Burnie, who years ago became friends with a girl he had a crush on and tried to ask her out via a passed note. She wrote back, "I think you're really cool so we can be friends but I have a boyfriend."

For a week, Clark listened to moody Dashboard Confessional songs and analyzed the note over and over. He considered the phrase, But I have a boyfriend.

> "Have. That's not a very strong word there," he thought.

There's Carl M. Schwarzenbach, a 17-year-old high school junior in Southwick, Mass., who had a crush on a certain girl since the first moment he saw her, 2 1/2 years ago, on the first day of school. It was the beginning of fifth period, choir class, at 12:03 p.m., as he recalls. He was a freshman. She was a senior. She was blond and beautiful and wearing a black tank top and jeans. They became close. Schwarzenbach says they kissed a few times, but they stayed just friends.

> "She always had this mind-set that she was afraid of commitment and she didn't want to commit to anything 'cause she was afraid she would hurt me," Schwarzenbach says.

When Brochu's column came out, Schwarzenbach e-mailed it to the girl, with her name filled out in the blank. She's in college now, and they haven't seen each other much. She e-mailed him back, in pink, as always.

> "She just said, uh, that it was really, really sweet and it made her smile," Schwarzenbach says. "I think it might have brought us a little closer."

The friend-crush is largely a phenomenon of adolescence, when hope is more persuasive then experience. Though it happens in high school, it blossoms in college, when a new culture shakes everything up. College is when you consider important questions like: Is there such a thing as a platonic back rub? Is there such a thing as a long-distance boyfriend?

It might have to do with the coed dorm setting, where near-strangers are thrust into an intimacy previously reserved for family. (Suitemates pass by in towels.) It might be the fluidity of college dating, in which nothing is defined, and in any case, no one knows what the definitions mean. Are you friends? Are you taking it slow? One person's "seeing each other" is another person's "dating each other," which is another person's "hanging out," which is another person's "friends with benefits."

Consider the experience that countless college guys have had. At a party, a certain girl— one you thought was taken—seems to be flirting with you. She takes your arm when you walk her home. The next day, when you instant-message her with the vaguely suggestive "I had a nice time last night," she says, "Me, too," and then mentions her boyfriend. What could it possibly mean?

Brian Murphy, a freshman at Robert Morris University in Pittsburgh, met a girl from his dorm on move-in day, and they became best friends. They walked to class together, ate lunch and dinner together, went to parties together. After parties, they had a ritual where they would go back to her room and cuddle. Murphy fell for her, hard. He says it was the kind of situation where—forced to choose between going out with guy friends and staying in with her to watch a chick flick—he'd watch the chick flick.

But she had a boyfriend of three years.

Murphy and the girl shared one guilty kiss, then they went home for Christmas break. During the break, Murphy read Brochu's column, and inspired by it, resolved to tell the girl how he felt. He made a scrapbook filled with pictures of the two of them. When they came back to school, he gave her the scrapbook and confessed his feelings.

> "Get over me," she said. She said she had realized how much she loved her boyfriend.

> Murphy was crushed.

> "It's definitely the first time that I ever fell in love," he says.

Love is like wealth, or the world food supply. Some people hog it; others get nothing at all. To scroll down the feedback column below Matt Brochu's article is to realize how much love goes unrevealed, unrecognized and unrequited. If only there were some mechanism for spreading love around, everybody could get enough.

Instead, the postings sit static in cyberspace, declarations of love to people who may never read them.

> "I've seen the sun rise over the mountains of Vermont and seen it set over the Caribbean. I've swam with tropical fish and seen the view from the top of Katahdin. But none of that even begins to compare to how beautiful she is."

"Katie Norris—if you ever read this, you know how I felt about you during that first month when I was in Mexico . . . look me up sometime. . . . I'd still like to try again."

"Shandie although i only just met you it seems like u are the one . . . dang girl ur perfect"

Some female readers, impressed by Brochu's way with words, try to woo the author himself.

"As a woman that constantly prays for a man with those sensitive values and beautiful words, you definitely took the right approach with this lucky lady. And as a little side note . . . if she didn't think she was as lucky as everyone thought she was; I would love to hear back from you."

A reader incensed by the number of girls praising Brochu writes:

"Girls, stop saying you hope to find someone like the guy who wrote this . . . you already have but you call them your best friend and what you don't know is that they are In Love with you."

The feedback column is a strange sort of conversation, taking place among 500 strangers over the course of months. Readers post responses that reference other posts and debate the efficacy of Brochu's just-tell-her approach. All the theories on love present themselves. There are the cynics. They write that if romance hasn't happened yet, it isn't meant to. They suggest that women want jerks more than "nice guys," and they question whether it's even possible to move from friendship to love. They offer cautionary tales.

"I guess all good stories aren't supposed to have a happy ending and all heroes are not supposed to win," writes a fellow named "Ryan," who posts a harrowing account of running two miles in the rain to a woman's house to declare his love. The woman listened, then told him they were better off as friends. "It was a long walk home that day, the rain. . . . laughing at me in a steady and harsh flow."

But there are more romantics than cynics. A girl writes in to reconsider the "dateability" of guys who are "right under my nose." Another writes in to say she knows a guy has a crush on her and she thinks she feels the same way, but she needs to take it slow. Some confess their love to the people they like, and contacted later, two guys say it actually worked out.

Someone named "Kate" writes:

"As heard one thousand times before . . . amazing article. But, answer us all one question, because we're all dying to know . . . did you get the girl?!"

The answer is: After the story ran, Brochu sent the link over instant messaging to his crush. She wrote back, asking who the column was about. He sent her a cautious, rambling set-up, which he saved, along with her responses, so that he could analyze them later. His set-up started like this:

"First off, I'm not really obsessed with this girl, I'm just interested, and I have been since the day I met her, and she doesn't have to worry about letting me down easy, b/c I'm not the type of person to let things get awkward and let it ruin the friendship we already have, b/c she's gotta realize. . . ."

It went on like this for a while. Then: "So yeah, it's you, sorry I had to make things all weird."
She called it the "sweetest thing" she'd ever read and the "nicest thing" that had ever happened to her, and they agreed to sleep on it and talk the next day.
She called him.
"You never know whether to believe it or not, whether she was letting me down nicely," Brochu says. She talked about her long relationship with her ex-boyfriend, and how she didn't want to get into something serious, and how she felt she'd get too serious with Brochu.

"She said that she could only hang out with people in that way that she couldn't see herself getting to like," Brochu says.

It hurt, but the strange thing is, it hurt only for two days and then Brochu was over it. He says it was as if a light switch inside of him was turned off. He wonders now how much of the crush was just him enjoying the chase, the thrill of the unattainable.

"I think it goes to show that my crush was just building upon itself from me not knowing," he says. "It was completely constructed."

They're still friends, and Brochu says he's totally over her.

Anyway, he's dating someone now. Or, seeing someone. He doesn't quite know what to call it. At the very least, they're hanging out.

---

## OFF LIMITS: SHOULD STUDENTS BE ALLOWED TO HOOK UP WITH PROFESSORS?

### ■ Laura Kipnis ■

The burning academic question of the day: Should we professors be permitted to "hook up with" our students, as the kids put it? Or they with us? In the olden days when I was a student (back in the last century) hooking up with professors was more or less part of the curriculum. (OK, I went to art school.) But that was a different era, back when sex—even when not so great or someone got their feelings hurt—fell under the category of experience, rather than injury and trauma. It didn't automatically impede your education; sometimes it even facilitated it.

But such things can't be guaranteed to turn out well—what percentage of romances do?—so colleges around the country are formulating policies to regulate such interactions, to protect against the possibility of romantic adversity. In 2003, the University of California's nine campuses ruled to ban consensual relationships between professors and any students they may "reasonably expect" to have future academic responsibility for; this includes any student known to have an interest in any area within the faculty member's expertise. But while engineering students may still pair-bond with professors of Restoration drama in California, many campuses are moving to prohibit all romance between any professor and any student.

Feminism has taught us to recognize the power dynamics in these kinds of relationships, and this has evolved into a dominant paradigm, the new propriety. But where once the issue was coercion or quid pro quo sex, in institutional neo-feminism the issue is any whiff of sexuality itself—or any situation that causes a student to "experience his or her vulnerability." (Pretty much the definition of sentience, I always thought.) "The unequal institutional power inherent in this relationship heightens the vulnerability of the student and the potential for coercion," the California code warns, as if any relationship is ever absent vulnerability and coercion. But the problem in redressing romantic inequalities with institutional blunt instruments is that it just confers more power on the institutions themselves, vastly increasing their reach into people's lives.

Ironically, the vulnerability of students has hardly decreased under the new paradigm; it's increased. As opportunities for venting injury have expanded, the variety of opportunities to feel injured have correspondingly multiplied. Under the "offensive environment" guidelines, students are encouraged to regard themselves as such exquisitely sensitive creatures that an errant classroom remark impedes their education, such hothouse flowers that an unfunny joke creates a lasting trauma—and will land you, the unfunny prof, on the carpet or in the national news.

My own university is thankfully less prohibitive about student-professor couplings: You may still hook up with students, you just can't harass them into it. (How long before hiring committees at these few remaining enclaves of romantic license begin using this as a recruiting tool? "Yes the winters are bad, but the students are friendly.") But don't think of telling them jokes! Our harassment guidelines warn in two separate places that inappropriate humor violates university policy. (Inappropriateness—pretty much the definition of humor, I always thought.)

Seeking guidance, realizing I was clinging to gainful employment by my fingernails, I signed up for a university sexual-harassment workshop. (Also two e-mail communiqués from the dean advised that nonattendance would be noted.) And what an education I received—though probably not the intended one.

Things kicked off with a "Sexual Harassment Pretest," administered by David, an earnest mid-50ish psychologist, and Beth, an earnest young woman with a masters in social work. It consisted of unanswerable true-false questions like: "If I make sexual comments to someone and that person doesn't ask me to stop, then I guess that my behavior is probably welcome." Everyone seemed grimly determined to play along—probably hoping to get out by cocktail hour—until we were handed a printed list of "guidelines." No. 1: "Do not make unwanted sexual advances."

Someone demanded querulously from the back, "But how do you know they're unwanted until you try?" (OK, it was me.) David seemed oddly flummoxed by the question, and began anxiously jangling the change in his pants pocket. "Do you really want me to answer that?" he asked.

Another person said helpfully, "What about smoldering glances?" Everyone laughed. A theater professor guiltily admitted to complimenting a student on her hairstyle that very afternoon (one of the "Do Nots" on the pretest)—but wondered whether as a gay male, not to have complimented her would be grounds for offense. He started mimicking the female student, tossing her mane around in a "notice my hair" manner. People shouted suggestions for other pretest scenarios for him to perform. Rebellion was in the air. Someone who studies street gangs whispered to me, "They've lost control of the room." David was jangling his change so frantically you had to strain to hear what anyone was saying.

My attention glued to David's pocket, I recalled a long-forgotten pop psychology guide to body language that identified change-jangling as an unconscious masturbation substitute. (And isn't Captain Queeg's habit of toying with a set of steel marbles in his pants pocket diagnosed by the principal mutineer in Herman Wouk's Caine Mutiny as closet masturbation?) If the very leader of our sexual harassment workshop was engaging in potentially offensive public masturbatory-like behavior, what hope for the rest of us!

Let's face it: Other people's sexuality is often just weird and creepy. Sex is leaky and anxiety-ridden; intelligent people can be oblivious about it. Of course the gulf between desire and knowledge has long been a tragicomic staple; these campus codes do seem awfully optimistic about rectifying the condition. For a more pessimistic account, peruse some recent treatments of the student-professor hook-up theme—Coetzee's Disgrace; Francine Prose's Blue Angel; Mamet's Oleanna—in which learning has an inverse relation to self-knowledge, in which professors are emblems of sexual stupidity, and such disasters ensue that it's hard not to read these as cautionary tales, even as they send up the new sexual correctness.

Of course, societies are always reformulating the stories they tell about intergenerational desire and the catastrophes that result, from Oedipus to faculty handbooks. The details vary, also the kinds of catastrophes prophesized—once it was plagues and crop failure, these days it's trauma and injury. Even over the last half-century the narrative has drastically changed. Consider the Freudian account, yesterday's contender as big explanatory story: Children desire their parents, this desire meets up with prohibitions—namely the incest taboo—and is subject to repression. But the desire persists nevertheless, occasionally burbling to the surface in the form of symptoms: that mysterious rash, that obsessional ritual.

Today, intergenerational desire remains the dilemma; what's shifted is the direction of arrows. In the updated version, parents (and parent surrogates) do all the desiring, children are innocent victims. What's excised from the new story is the most controversial part of the previous one: childhood sexuality. Children are returned to innocence, a far less disturbing (if less complex) account of childhood.

Excising student sexuality from campus romance codes just extends the same presumption. But students aren't children. Whether or not it's smart, plenty of professors I know, male and female, have hooked up with students, for shorter and longer durations. (Female professors do it less, and rarely with undergrads.) Some act well, some are assholes, and it would definitely behoove our students to learn the identifying marks of the latter breed early on, because post-collegiate life is full of them too. (Along with all the well-established marriages that started as student-teacher things, of course—another social reality excised from the story.)

Let's imagine that knowledge rather than protectionism (or institutional power-enhancement) was the goal of higher education. Then how about workshops for the students too? Here's an idea: "10 Signs That Your Professor Is Sleeping With You To Assuage Mid-Life Depression and Will Dump You Shortly Afterward." Or, "Will Hooking Up With a Prof Really Make You Feel Smarter: Pros and Cons." No doubt we'd all benefit from more self-knowledge about sex, but until the miracle drug arrives that cures the abyss between desire and intelligence, universities might try being educational instead of regulatory on the subject.

---

## CASE STUDY: HARMFUL HUG?

■ **Kathleen Dean More and Lani Roberts** ■

*[editor's note: This case study is one of several posted on the website for the Program for Ethics, Science and the Environment within the Department of Philosophy at Oregon State University. The website provides the following disclaimer/introduction:*

*The case studies (all of which are constructed and modified from actual situations) and commentaries that constitute this issue of Reflections explore perennial issues, such as academic freedom, deception and cheating, and cooperation with perceived moral wrong. We begin, however, with two situations that pointedly raise issues of relationship and responsibility between student and professor. As academia readies itself for a new millennium, we hope that these scenarios contribute to a discussion about the ethical integrity and meaning of a university.]*

At the beginning of a course on death and dying, a philosophy professor is delighted to see a student who has taken a prior course from him enrolled in the class. As the term progresses, the student seems to be having difficulty in the course, which she attributes on one occasion to the fact that her grandmother is dying. However, upon reading her class journal, the professor realizes that the student is experiencing a lot of other things that are difficult and contributing to stress.

On the day an important assignment is due, the student misses class. She drops by the professor's office the next day to turn in the assignment. It is apparent to the professor from the student's sad countenance and tear-stained cheeks that the student is experiencing great distress, and he asks, "do you want to talk about things?" The student hesitates for a moment, then says "yes," and the professor invites her into his office. The student talks about her life situation for close to an hour and a half, often breaking into tears as she relates her story, and as she and the professor think about different courses of action. As the conversation comes to an end, and the student rises to leave, the professor is inclined to give the student a shoulder hug of reassurance. Should he?

## Commentary: Kathleen Dean More

Call me cold. Call me cautious. I just don't think any professor should hug any student. Part of my response is simply self-protective. The meaning of a hug is not only in the mind of the person giving a hug, but in the mind of the recipient as well. It follows that no matter what the professor intends, no matter what feelings of compassion or paternalism move him to embrace his troubled student, the student's response to the hug will be an important part of its meaning. She may welcome it as an offer of comfort, but she may just as well see it as a sign of aggression, or paternalism, or presumption. Again, she may welcome the embrace in the warmth of the moment, but then reconsider later. In any event, no matter what his intent, a professor who hugs a student is open to justifiable charges of making unwelcome, uninvited physical contact. And that is a very unpleasant position to be in.

But, someone might object, doesn't a professor have a moral duty to risk being unfairly accused, in order to offer comfort to a person in need? Isn't the spontaneous offer of loving beyond criticism? No, and no again. A hug is comforting, when it is comforting, just because it is an act of intimacy. It crosses the barriers between people, closes the distance. But when a hug is not comforting, it is an invasion—of personal space, surely, of privacy, perhaps—as anyone who knows who has been held in an uninvited, unwelcome embrace. So a professor who hugs his student is either inappropriately intimate or inappropriately presumptuous—an unfortunate choice.

Far better to keep a conversation from getting to the point where it would end with a hug. Professors aren't pastors. We aren't professional counselors. We aren't parents to our students. We are human beings who happen to know a lot about some sorts of things higher mathematics, or the endocrinology of chimpanzees, or the history of the Roman Empire. The professor should have helped the student find a person who could help her.

## Commentary: Lani Roberts

Are there any conditions under which it is permissible for a professor to hug a student? Although the situation that gives rise to this question involves a male professor and a female student, it could just as easily apply to a female professor and male student, or a same sex professor and student. In this broader context of professor-student relationships, the question at issue can be answered in two distinct ways: morally, and prudentially. It is entirely possible for a professor to hug a student without committing an immoral act, yet, he or she may still be well advised not to do so for very practical reasons. It would be foolish to overlook or minimize considerations and dangers of gender, sexual orientation, and race that complicate the inherent power differences between students and professors. The unfortunate facts of actual, potential, and perceived abuse involved in physical touching challenge any presuppositions that every hug is an act of consolation, empathy, and concern. Given these prudential considerations, and acknowledging that there may be opposing arguments, I nonetheless argue that we are embodied selves, needing affirmation and assurance, and therefore advocate a middle ground: proceed with caution.

Before proceeding, a caveat is in order. I am deeply concerned that my position can be misused in the service of the evil of professorial exploitation of vulnerable students. I am not providing any justification for use and abuse of power between teacher and student.

There is nothing inherently immoral in a professor hugging a student; indeed, within an area of great care, there are good reasons that professors may hug specific students and have it be the right thing to do. Students are not disembodied minds; they are persons, intelligent and embodied beings, rational and also emotional and spiritual. I conceive of myself as teaching and learning from whole dynamic beings. As such, I read body language and facial expressions in the classroom to gauge whether the students and I are communicating. I am also fully aware that students' lives are as complex and multifaceted as my own. They simply are not compartmentalized into their "student selves," somehow distinct from the whole persons they are.

Some will argue that the professor-student relationship is a professional one in which expressions of intimacy, such as a hug, are entirely out of place. However, when a student is confiding pain and confusion, as illustrated by this case, it can be argued that this crosses a boundary precluding inappropriate intimacy. Sharing personal information and concerns is often more intimate than physical expressions. Although some professors are unapproachable, most are not going to refuse to be a sounding board for a struggling, even desperate, student seeking guidance. The appropriate institutional action for the professor is, of course, to refer the student to counseling resources on campus. This, though, does not negate the value of a hug as a gesture of personal concern in such a situation.

If a hug is a gift, offered to an upset student solely for the benefit of the student, to console, affirm or encourage her or him, then I do not see it as immoral. On the rare occasions when I have hugged a student, the following common conditions were in play:

The student was tearful and confiding, seeking an anchor in a storm;

I listen and gain commitment from the student to seek counseling, sometimes calling myself to set up the appointment;

I offer a hug to the student, prefaced with a question, "Could you use a hug?", or "Would you like a hug?"

Only if the student says, "yes," only if there is no question of coercion or expectations on my part, will I then hug the student. If a hug is offered with expectations that it will be accepted, there is subtle coercion and what is offered as a gift is a gift no longer.

Some students decline; others accept. The very thought of a young person, away from home, experiencing her or his life as overwhelming and tenuous moves me to reach out to the person across an abyss created by power and professionalism, and offer a hug, subject to the conditions described above. With great care and caution, if the professor in the case offers a hug to the distraught student, with no expectations of an affirmative response, and she accepts, he may hug her without committing a moral wrong.

## WHEN IS IT OK TO INVITE A STUDENT TO DINNER?

### ■ Deni Elliott and Paul Martin Lester ■

Don't have sex with your students.

It would be hard to find faculty members who do not know that sex with their own students is taboo. But, if reciting that rule is the extent to which professors examine the boundaries of their student-teacher relationships, they ignore a whole set of norms and conventions. They may cross the line without even knowing it. Or they may avoid contact with students, out of fear of crossing the line, and deny both themselves and their students some rich educational experiences.

Boundaries are the moral and sometimes legal protective limits that help define any relationship. Some are set by explicit negotiation of those involved, but most are governed by ritual and custom. Without much effort, most people can describe the boundaries that define a marital relationship, a lawyer-client relationship, or a parent-child relationship.

The two of us think and talk constantly about boundaries, both in our lives and in our work. We are life partners as well as professional colleagues. We write a monthly column together for a national magazine, but are also deeply engrossed in separate projects and research.

One of us directs a University of Montana program, which offers a master's degree on how to teach practical ethics, and the other serves as an informal mentor in the program from time to time. The program attracts a diverse group of students who range in age from 23 to 63. Academic norms are unfamiliar to many of them and often a mystery. Because the program is intensive—with the possibility of earning the master's in a calendar year—students and professors are thrown together quite often in both academic and social settings. From our interactions with students in the program, we've learned a few things about the boundaries of the teacher-student relationship.

Taking that relationship to a more personal level is morally acceptable when it enhances the educational experience of the student. A friend of ours who is a kindergarten teacher, Leslie Black, inspired our favorite example of that. For most of her 30-plus years of teaching, Mrs. Black has invited her students—one 5-year-old at a time—to have dinner with her and her family. Decades later, former students recall how valued they felt by that attention and how receptive it made them to her teaching in the classroom.

Our variation is to invite graduate students in the program and their partners—two couples at a time—to our house for dinner. These dinners, planned for the first months of study, help set a tone of informality and clearly state our honest interest in each student. In return the students report that they have an easier time taking intellectual risks and trusting in the support and criticism that is offered.

Even in the most common of campus settings, professors can find ways to break from the conventional teacher-student relationship in an acceptable way. Most instructors, at one time or another, run into trouble attempting to coach a student one-on-one about a problem or a paper. The student is frustrated and uncomprehending. She seems to be creating obstacles to keep her from using what the instructor offers. Both teacher and student feel the tension in their guts.

Rather than abandoning the student to her own devices with phrases like, "Why don't you think about this on your own for a while," or "We don't seem to be getting anywhere on this," we look for an approach that keeps professor and student connected. "Let's go get coffee," "How about a walk around the block," or even, "Let's both stand up and stretch for a minute" are examples of how we cut the tension. The change in venue or even just the unexpected distraction opens up alternative ways for mentor and student to examine the challenge at hand.

We also begin our initial student appointments with a firm handshake and good eye contact. Few young adults are practiced in such social interchange, but the ability to greet an interviewer with poise and confidence can make the difference in a job or internship decision. As time goes on and a comfortable relationship is established, the appointments may end with a hug or a hand on a student's shoulder.

Sometimes professors face less-than-ideal situations in which they are called upon to step outside the norm of the teacher-student relationship. Our Montana community of Missoula, like many university towns, is small enough that students and professors trip over one another in a variety of settings. It is rare that a faculty member can enjoy an afternoon soak at a hot springs, take a morning yoga class, listen to music at a local bar, shop at the Saturday morning farmer's market, or attend a church service without running into students who are doing the same.

How a professor handles these unintentional, but largely unavoidable, meetings is critical. It is up to the professor to set the tone. Ignoring students in these settings can be perceived as rejection or arrogance, but neither is it necessary to invite students into the faculty member's circle of friends. As long as the student is unlikely to be harmed or made more vulnerable, a range of social interactions is acceptable. What is inappropriate is for professors to allow external settings to turn into annex offices. Physicians do not provide clinical judgments outside of their professional settings. Neither should professors.

Professors have gone too far when students are made to feel more vulnerable than the power imbalance in the faculty-student relationship already implies. That's one of the problems of sexual intimacy between instructors and students, but sex is not the only example.

The most commonplace violations occur when professors put their own agenda or egos above the educational experience of their students. It is wonderful when the lab director's research project and the student's thesis topic are naturally interwoven, but that kind of symbiosis is rarely a product of coincidence. More often, students adjust their learning goals and expectations to fit the lab that supports them. Even more often, students are expected to put aside their own studies in favor of the director's research agenda. That conflict is not confined to graduate students in labs. It is common for research and teaching assistants across campus to be pressured to put the professor's needs ahead of their own studies.

Even more depressingly common is the professor who uses the office or the lectern to demonstrate his or her brilliance and the corresponding students' ignorance. This run-of-the-mill abuse of faculty power interferes with students' education, and professors should be called on it.

Here are some questions that we ask ourselves, and that may guide you, as we examine our own relationships with students:

- If a professor extends a social invitation, is it easy for the student to decline? When we send out our e-mail messages at the beginning of the year alerting graduate students to a forthcoming dinner invitation, we include the information that some students have chosen not to come. We make it safe for them to say no.

- When students and professors gather socially, is it a model for how students can better interact with one another? Departmental parties for professors and graduate students, or faculty suggestions that a seminar group gather afterward for dinner or dessert, are accomplishing their teaching goals if those opportunities spark student study groups and independent socializing among peers.

- Are students taking inappropriate advantage of the relationship? When students start asking for special favors, it is time to re-examine what we are willing to do. We talk directly with students who make such requests about why granting the favor would be unfair.

- What about students who are left out of the social loop? Some students require more clear and formal boundaries than others do. Some may want to be included, but are shy in expressing themselves. Occasionally, we have students with whom we are nervous about extending boundaries. The trick is to be flexible enough to meet the needs of each student and still be consistent. If a student requires more formal interaction, so be it. Likewise, if a student needs repeated invitations from her peers and instructor to join the group meeting outside the formal classroom, those invitations should be forthcoming. However, we keep aware of our own comfort zone and refrain from extending invitations that make us uncomfortable.

- How willing are we to talk openly about this with colleagues and students? As with most acts that go against convention, publicity is a good test for moral permissibility. If we are willing to be direct and open about our relationships with students, it is more likely than not that these relationships are in the students' interest.

Ultimately, academics must examine their views about the ideal teaching role. Few faculty members emulate Charles W. Kingsfield Jr., the irritable and intimidating professor made famous by John Houseman in The Paper Chase or Harry Bailey, the dope-smoking, counter-culture radical graduate student played by Elliott Gould in Getting Straight. But, when we were students, most faculty members encountered both types along with teachers somewhere in the middle. We all were taught by professors who we called by their first names and by those, who even today, we would be uncomfortable addressing with such familiarity. To some extent, how most of us teach best reflects how we best learned. Considering the unique learning needs of each student, and noticing opportunities for interaction both within and outside of classrooms and offices, enhances the learning experience for all.

READING *Outside the Lines*

## CLASSROOM ACTIVITIES

### Compare and Contrast

Watch a sit-com and/or drama and see how television producers use traditional ideas of relationships in their shows. Which use relationships more traditionally—sit-coms or dramas? Why do you think that is?

## Advertising
Watch the commercials in a particular television show. How do they use traditional ideas of relationships as a point of selling?

## The "perfect" relationship
Talk about what the perfect relationship with your significant other, friend, parent, and/or professor would be. Where did you get your ideas for this? Now think about how the opposing person would feel about this relationship—would they find it perfect?

## Relationships
On the board, make a list of different kinds of relationships. How many do you come up with? Which make the best material for writing?

## Objects
Talk about our complicated relationships with objects—cars, stuffed animals, jewelry, old t-shirts, pictures, books, records. How are these relationships formed? What makes them strong?

## Places
Spend class time talking about how we have special relationships with places. How are these relationships different than those we have with objects?

## ESSAY IDEAS
1. Write a short essay examining your favorite relationship and what made it so.
2. Write an essay comparing the reality of relationships with their mythic counterparts, as often displayed in popular culture.
3. Watch a reality television show. How would you describe their relationships? What does the television camera do to change their relationships? As part of this essay, try to imagine the presence of the camera in every filmed scene. How would you act in this scenario?
4. Write an essay in which you articulate what you *expected* your relationship to be like with your college professor versus what it is *really* like. What are some unexpected benefits and drawbacks?
5. Write a personal essay chronicling the first month with your new roommate(s). What is your room like as a text? How would you describe the text that is this new relationship?
6. Write an essay in which you *read* your college as a text. How would you describe your relationship with your college?
7. *Read* your relationship with your parent(s). How has that relationship changed since you went off to college?

# Reading and Writing About Music

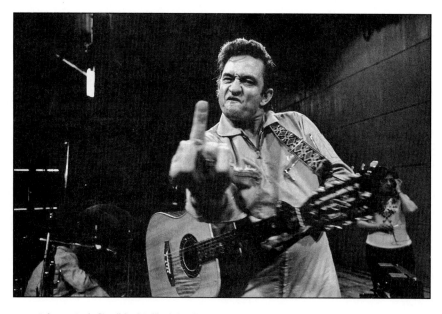

■ ■ ■ Johnny Cash flips "the bird" while playing at San Quentin prison in 1969.

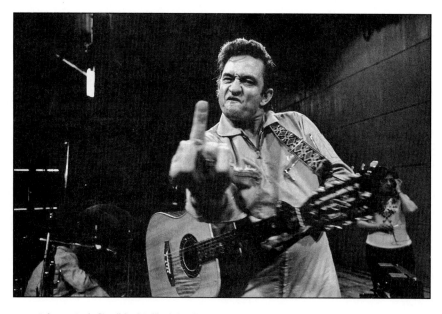

**10**
CHAPTER

We can't escape music. Almost wherever we go music is playing—in the supermarket, at the Starbucks, in the car, and on television. In fact, as we write this, we're listening to Beck's *Odelay*. Accordingly, music often serves as the soundtrack for our lives; we attach memories to particular songs, and those song–memory attachments tend to be long lasting.

Music too is one medium we are at once reading actively (by listening to lyrics) and passively as we emotionally connect to the sounds and tones—we don't think so much about the mood a song evokes as much as how it makes us feel. Accordingly, we actively read music, if we read it at all, by focusing on its lyrics—after all, the content of what's sung in a song is the easiest element to interpret. In addition, we have the tools for interpreting words already: We know how to read and make sense of language or literature. And such tools can be useful in understanding music.

Of all the texts in this book, music may be the most emotionally powerful. We can argue about books and movies and television shows, but discussions about music—favorite artists, what albums you would take to a desert island, who is better, the Beatles or the Stones—elicit the most passionate responses. We turn to music to put us in a romantic mood, to celebrate events, to announce the arrival of the bride, to begin graduation ceremonies, to initiate all sporting events. Our lives are framed by music—it may be the text we are the most unable to live without, which is why it is particularly important to be a good reader of it.

But we have any number of other considerations to decipher a song's intentional meanings, as well as some of its unintentional ones. Here are some to keep in mind when listening to and writing about music:

## Music is made up of genres.

Both professional and amateur listeners often classify a music's type in trying to understand or enjoy it. There are many genres of music—classical, rhythm and blues, rock and roll, rap, country, jazz, and "pop," as well as numerous subgenres within these groups (alternative, trip-hop, fusion, etc.). Bands often combine genres, transcend genres, or even comment on them as they play within them. Sometimes, for example in the case of rap music, the commentary is part of the music itself. Genres are especially important for some when deciding to listen to particular music—they want ways to understand what experience is ahead of them, and whether, based on past experience, they will like a particular song or band.

Of the genres we've listed, the one hardest to qualify is pop music (which is why we place it in quotes). For many, the term has negative connotations—it stands for "popular," which in some circles means unsophisticated or that it panders to a popular sensibility instead of artistic integrity. For the authors, pop music is an umbrella which often covers parts or wholes of entire genres at one time or another—classical music was the pop music of its day, as was early jazz or swing. Even much "classic rock" was once popular. Having said that, what is popular oftentimes is worth studying for the light it may shed on our contemporary world.

Yet, musical genres are not value free. We tend to associate certain traits with particular genres. If we see a number of Country and Western CDs in someone's car, we may (often incorrectly) assume something about them or their socio-economic class. Genres are themselves complex texts whose significations change over time as culture, tastes and people change.

## Music is (or isn't) a reflection of the culture that surrounds it.

Music is often of a time and place and can offer clues to the society in which it's written. For example, much of Bob Dylan's work in the turbulent '60s directly reflects the world around it; his songs are frequently about protests or are themselves protests. Gangsta rap also seemingly helps tell stories from disadvantaged areas with its focus on the dilemmas of living in such areas. These forms of music can bring a broader understanding of various social ailments to the "average" listener. By a bizarre and unfortunate coincidence, Ryan Adams's catchy tribute to New York City, "I Love New York," was gaining in popularity just as the World Trade Centers fell on September 11, 2001. The song became an unintended anthem/tribute and has, for many, come to symbolize the hope and sacrifice that New Yorkers felt after the attacks.

But making automatic leaps from music to culture and vice versa can be problematic. Songwriters sometimes have social aims that go along with their music, and sometimes they don't. Even if they do, there can be unintended messages that flow from their music; music may unintentionally reflect society as well. For example, some people believe that disco music with its programmed beats and the sexual innuendo in many of its lyrics reflected the so-called shallow values of the 1970s, though those writing the music probably did not intend their music to have this effect. Similarly, since Kurt Cobain's suicide, some critics have associated the entire grunge sound with nihilism—something Cobain would have never wanted.

On a purely musical level, we can also listen to a song and place it in a particular era because of certain musical conventions of the period—particular instruments or sounds in general will often give this away. Can you think of some conventions used today? Some used in previous eras? Think not only of songs but also of commercials. Do you remember when rap beats became a big part of commercials? It wasn't always so. . . .

Finally, sometimes musicians write songs that seem not to be of a time and place. Gillian Welch's popular album *Revival* sounds as though it is a relic from early twentieth-century Appalachia, yet Welch, a Californian with classical music training, recorded the album in 1995. Smash Mouth could fool some into believing they were around in the early '60s. What qualities do these artists convey in their songs? What do they avoid?

## The packaging of music reflects the aims of the bands, or the record companies, or both, and it has an effect on the way we view the music.

The packaging of music involves a variety of things. Consumers are presented bands not only with their music, but their record cover, their band name, the album or song name—components that sit outside of the actual music itself. As you know, how musicians present themselves can be crucial to how we perceive them and probably how we perceive their music. For example, how would we view the music of Britney Spears coming from Tupac Shukar, and vice versa? The persona of each of these artists contributes to the way we perceive them and their work.

Often we read performers not only from the packaging of an album but also visually through photographs in rock magazines, reports on entertainment shows, live concerts, and videos. In particular, the music video is a way for the handlers of the musician or the musician himself or herself to provide another way of determining how potential consumers see the artist. Web sites do similar work but may offer different portrayals of the performer if the artist, a fanatical listener, or the record company sponsors the site.

Sometimes the packaging of an artist helps us understand what musicians think they are doing; other times the package is a wall that interferes with our experiencing music honestly or directly. The listener has to recognize that packaging comes as a part of listening to the music, and one can do with that information as she will. For example, many fans of musicians assume that these musicians "sell out" when they sign a record deal with a large corporation, often looking for evidence of such behavior in the music, as did the fans of the band R.E.M. in the 1990s when they moved from the independent label I.R.S. to the mega-label Warner Brothers. Others just listen to the music with little regard to packaging, marketing, or in some instances, lyrics.

Packaging also can reflect the times—if we see an image of a band from a different time, we may understand a more complex relationship between the band and its era. But in reading packaging of bands from different eras we have to take into account the same factors we do in evaluating packaging from our own era.

## While the music we like may reflect personal taste, it may also reflect cultural tastes.

How many of you have heard of Toni Price? Kathy McCarty? The Derailers? The Gourds? The Damnations? Dale Watson? Texan students may recognize these names, as all of these performers are hugely popular in the Austin, Texas area, selling out concerts and receiving considerable air time on local radio stations. Yet, few people outside of Austin and even fewer outside of Texas know this music, despite the fact that Austin enjoys a reputation as a progressive musical city. Similarly, if you have grown up in a small town outside of Austin, rap, grunge, and trip-hop may never make it to local radio stations or to the record collections of your friends, and, therefore, by extension, it may never make its way into your life (although MTV's presence now makes that less likely). Even worse, if you are from the United States, you may never get exposure to British punk bands, fado music from Portugal, or Bulgarian *a cappella* choruses. Record stores and video music channels have gotten much better at featuring international music in the past few years, but there remain vast quantities of music we will never hear, simply because those forms of music belong to other cultures and places.

Furthermore, for many people, what they encounter on television, the Internet, and in print determines their musical tastes. If bands do not make videos or are not featured in popular magazines, we may never know they exist. Many forms of alternative music never make it onto the airwaves; thus, potential listeners never find music outside of the mainstream. American trends toward playing and replaying market-tested music like pop, rock, country, and rap tends to reinforce listening tastes and habits. In short, you may like the music you do simply because that's all you've been exposed to. Thus, our tastes may depend less on comparison shopping or eclectic listening than the demands of the marketplace.

## The music itself contains readable elements that contribute to the listener's experience.

Music creates moods as well as meaning. It's often hard to isolate the aspects of songs that make us feel a particular way. Often, performers intend the pace of a song, its intensity, or the sounds of the notes to affect listeners in specific ways. Hard-driving punk, smooth jazz, rap with samples and scratches, and string concertos with a lot of violins spark conscious and subconscious reactions. Sometimes, these reactions are strong and mysterious; other times, we know all too well why we feel what we do. Music functions much like poetry in that it evokes as much as it overtly states.

We can often tell by the pace of a song what the mood is—a fast song means something different than a slow song. The instruments in a song indicate/signify something (the presence of trumpets or violins). They are there to make the song sound better, but the way they sound better is often indicative of something else as well. Similarly, how the lyrics are sung may indicate how we are to read the song. For instance, Kurt Cobain's voice demands a kind of response that Celine Dion's does not; how we read Johnny Cash's voice will differ from how we read Aretha Franklin's.

The recent popularity of MP3 players such as the iPod have completely altered our relationship to music and public space. On the bus, the subway, while walking down the street or across campus, we see people bobbing their heads in giddy oblivion, and until we see the headphones protruding from their ears, we may think they are suffering some kind of seizure from an unknown malady. But these compact players have increased our ability to add soundtracks to our days. In fact, in the past few months, psychologists have argued that listening to music this way actually makes people happier—and if you listen in the morning, it can dramatically affect your mood for the entire day.

## The listeners create the music.

What we as listeners make of this sound, the packaging, and lyrics is largely up to us. We can choose to ignore the packaging, the lyrics, or the music, or a combination of the above, and arrive at one kind of interpretation. We can read biographies of musicians, watch their videos, or read the lyric sheets in a CD to get at a more complete reading of a musician or band. We can choose to listen to music on an expensive system that enhances the effects of a CD, listen to them on a car stereo, or a Walkman, and have that transform our understanding of the song. Or we can put our car radios on scan and find the first song that we like. . . .

### ▪▪▪ WORKSHEET ▪▪▪

This Text

1. Notice how each writer approaches the song or artist differently. Why do you think that's the case?
2. Do you think all the writers are music critics? What might distinguish a critic from a writer?
3. Do you think the writers are fans of the music they are writing about? What about their writing makes you draw that conclusion? Do you think writers should be fans of the music they write about?
4. Notice whether you can get the criteria for each writer's idea of what a good song or album would be.
5. How much do these writers think about the social impact of the music they write about? Do you think they think about it enough, or too much?
6. How are things like race and gender a part of the analysis here?
7. How does the background of the authors influence their ideas about music?

8. While it will be impossible for you to know this fully, try to figure out the writing situation of each author. Who is the audience? What does the author have at stake?

9. What social, political, economic, and cultural forces affect the author's text? What is going on in the world as he or she is writing?

10. What are the main points of the essay? Can you find a thesis statement anywhere?

11. How does the author support her argument? What evidence does he use to back up any claims he might make?

12. Is the author's argument valid and/or reasonable?

13. Do you find yourself in agreement with the author? Why or why not?

14. Does the author help you read music better than you did before reading the essay? If so, why?

15. How is the reading process different if you are reading an essay, as opposed to a short story or poem?

16. What is the agenda of the author? Why does she or he want me to think a certain way?

17. Did I like this? Why or why not?

## Beyond This Text

### Lyrics

**Theme:** What are some of the themes of the song (themes are generally what the author thinks of the subject)? Are there both intentional and unintentional themes?

**Plot:** Is there a plot to the song? Does the song tell a story or convey a narrative?

**Literary devices:** Do you notice any such devices such as the use of figurative language (metaphor, simile) or repetition or rhyme? Are there notable symbols? Are these devices effective? Do they add to your enjoyment?

**"Literariness":** Do you think the lyrics have literary quality? Would the lyrics stand alone as a poem? Why or why not?

### Music

**The instruments:** What instruments does the band use? Does it use them effectively? Does their use symbolize anything outside of normal use?

**Mood:** What is the mood of the song? How does the music reflect this—through the makeup of its instruments, its speed, its tone (minor or major), or a combination of factors?

**Technology:** Are there technological aspects in the song? What are they? What effects do they have on the song?

### The Whole Package

**Genre:** How would you classify this song by genre? Would you do so by the lyrics or music? Why? Are there ways that songs resist classification? If so, in what ways?

**Effectiveness:** Does this song "work"? Why or why not? Is there an element of the song that's stronger than the others?

**How and where it's played:** Unlike a poem, you can hear songs in the car, in a dance club, in the elevator, on a date, in the doctor's office, and at church. How does setting influence how you hear a song?

## MUSICAL CHEESE: THE APPROPRIATION OF SEVENTIES MUSIC IN NINETIES MOVIES

■ **Kevin J.H. Dettmar**
**and William Richey** ■

*In this piece (1999), Kevin Dettmar and William Richey use the term "cheese" to examine the idea of music in movies. In doing so, they acknowledge the power that directors have in shaping not only audience responses to the music but to the movies in which music appears.*

RECENTLY, WROQ, A GREENVILLE, SOUTH CAROLINA, radio station with a "classic rock" format, had a seventies weekend, featuring all the music from the 1970s that the station's moguls are trying to smuggle in under the classic rock umbrella (primarily dreck like Boston, Kansas, Aerosmith, et al.). At one point late on Saturday afternoon, the DJ came on the air at the close of a song and pleaded, with a note of some real desperation in his voice, not to have to field any more requests for the Bee Gees or Barry Manilow.

In our local battle of the FM airwaves, the other new player is a station, called "The New Q," that fashions itself as a homey, corporate alternative-rock venue (playing bands such as Pearl Jam, R.E.M., Soundgarden, Collective Soul, and Nirvana). Every Friday morning, however, they have an all-request show that features extended dance-mix versions of disco songs you haven't heard or thought about in years (but remember instantly—with a groan—when they come on). Listeners sat by helplessly the other morning as the full, unedited, and unexpurgated "Disco Duck" came on, followed in short order by Donna Summer's witty and sublime "MacArthur Park." In the few months since its inception, this retrodisco show has been successful enough that a local nightclub has installed a lighted, shamrock-shaped dance floor on which eighteen and ups can shake their boo-tays all night long: they can boogie-oogie-oogie till they just can't boogie no more. As we write this, we've now learned that they've instituted a platform-shoe night on Tuesdays. Lawsuits just waiting to happen.

So what's going on here? Just when you thought it was safe to turn the radio back on, seventies' schlock is back, in spades (and in bell-bottoms). And remember, this is South Carolina we're talking about, not L.A. or New York or Chicago. We're not a remarkably avantgarde group; this state has been sending Strom Thurmond to the U.S. Senate since before we were born.

What we would argue is that this new fondness for the disco decade is simply the South Carolina manifestation (or, to use a more regionally appropriate metaphor, infestation) of the national phenomenon that some commentators have called "cheese." Like "camp"—which Susan Sontag in the 1960s saw as so uniquely characteristic of the modern sensibility—cheese is a highly rhetorical embrace of those things that many would consider to be in bad taste. But, as a postmodern version of this mentality, cheese—we believe—differs from camp in two primary ways. First, it is somewhat more exclusive than camp, in that cheese is derived solely from the detritus of consumer culture. Thus, while Sontag can list both "The Brown Derby restaurant on Sunset Boulevard in LA" and "Bellini's operas" in her "canon of Camp," cheese is almost entirely a celebration of canceled TV shows, artless pop songs, and useless cultural artifacts like the lava lamp and the Chia Pet.[1] Second, we would argue that the attitudes encoded in cheese are even more indecipherable than those of camp. Despite camp's apparent delight in things usually considered excessive or overwrought, it never really loses sight of what good taste is. With cheese, however, the distinction between good and bad taste threatens to break down altogether, to the point that it becomes nearly impossible to tell when something is being celebrated and when it is being parodied.[2]

To explore the rather twisted metaphysics of cheese, we wish to examine how this current taste for third-rate music, to which WROQ's request line and The New Q's disco-on-demand program bear witness, has begun to assert itself in recent films, specifically how, over the past few years, movie soundtracks have started recycling some of the very worst of seventies' and eighties' pop/rock.[3] Our first example is Ben Stiller's *Reality Bites* (Universal Pictures, 1994), a film that at first glance appears to exemplify the concept of cheese perfectly. For the film's central quartet, the flotsam and jetsam of seventies' and eighties' popular culture assume an almost cultic status; they adorn their apartments with posters of Shawn Cassidy and disco-era Travolta, they pass their days watching reruns of seventies' sitcoms such as *Good Times* and *One Day at a Time,* and, of course, they delight in listening to the most mindless music from this thoroughly forgettable period in rock 'n' roll history. The most glaring instance of this adoration of cheese occurs when the Knack's "My Sharona" comes on the radio as the main characters are purchasing Pringles and diet Pepsis at an AM/PM mini-mart. After persuading the clerk to pump up the volume, the two women (Lalaina and Vicki) begin a manic but clearly choreographed dance routine to the song, much to the amazement of the forty-something clerk and the apparent distaste of their friend, Troy, the group's resident grunge philosopher.

Though the film's trailer would emphasize Lalaina and Vicki's giddy gyrations, the scene in its original context indicates that Troy's disdain is the appropriate response. Once the women have abandoned themselves to their dance, the camera cuts to a long shot in which we see them boogalooing wildly through the window of the convenience store. Seemingly, then, this moment of ironized fun soon gives way to some rather dour social commentary in which Stiller equates the music of the Knack with the disposable consumerism of contemporary society. This is junk music for a junk food culture, the film none too subtly says— or, to put it in Jamesonian terms, "post-modernism is the consumption of sheer commodification as a process."[4] The Knack, of course, provides perfect fodder for such a reading as they never pretended that they were anything more than a hit-making machine. In fact, as the *Meet the Beatles*-inspired cover of their first album suggests, the Knack's primary model was the Fab Four of the early sixties, the producers of catchy, easy-to-dance-to hits, not the Beatles' later incarnation as the prophets of universal peace and love. And "My Sharona" is essentially "I Want to Hold Your Hand" repackaged to cash in on the relaxed sexual mores of the seventies ("When you gonna give it to me, give it to me / It's just a matter of time, Sharona").[5]

A similarly ironic use of seventies' music immediately follows this scene. The film cuts directly from the convenience store back to Lalaina's apartment as she is getting ready for a date with Michael, a rising executive for a new music video network (it's "like MTV, but with an edge") whom Troy instantly deems a "yuppyhead cheeseball." Though somewhat sympathetically portrayed by Stiller himself, we soon realize that Michael is bad news, and again it is the soundtrack that provides the principal clue. As Michael and Lalaina sit in his BMW convertible drinking Big Gulps, Peter Frampton's "Baby I Love Your Way" plays in the background. When Lalaina naively asks, "Who's this again?" Michael replies incredulously, "I can't believe you don't remember *Frampton Comes Alive.* That album like totally changed my life." Frampton's music—though wildly popular in the late seventies—is no less gimmicky or vapid than the Knack's (e.g., "Ooh baby I love your way / Wanna tell you I love your way");

and so the film clearly indicates that the only fitting response to a man who claims his life was changed by such music is, "Get a life."[6] When Frampton serves as the accompaniment to Michael's seduction of Lalaina, it forcefully demonstrates how morally and aesthetically tainted she is becoming in this relationship: it's as if she's sleeping with her father's record collection. But, if Lalaina has temporarily lost her ironic distance from this seventies' dreck, Troy has not. Happening along just as Lalaina and Michael begin making love, he seems as disgusted by the Frampton as by Lalaina's taste in men. Once again, music acts as a kind of diacritical marker alerting us to the presence of irony. And the filmmakers assume that we can read the clues. While otherwise there might be some ambiguity to Michael's character, the music serves as a surefire sign that Michael is as slickly shallow as an Abba single.

Despite the film's gestures toward cheese, then, its irony ultimately takes a rather stable and traditional form: it enacts, in effect, a kind of a musical morality play. As her documentary about Gen Xer's "trying to find [their] own identity without having any real role models or heroes or anything" suggests, the character of Lalaina represents her generation's potential for optimism, and so her relationship with Michael poses the danger that her idealism might become corrupted. By contrast, Troy's problem is a deep-seated, almost crippling cynicism. During a club appearance with his band, Hey That's My Bike, he performs "I'm Nuthin'," a song that neatly sums up his sense of aimlessness and resentment. Here, he not only characterizes the nineties as a time of diminishing expectations ("I'm sick of people talkin' / About American dreams"), but he explicitly blames the previous generation, the baby boomers, for causing this situation.[7] By abandoning their youthful sixties' ideals for the greedy consumerism of the seventies and eighties, the boomers have at once destroyed their own moral credibility and sold the next generation down the river ("Before I was born / It was all gone"). In short, they pawned the future in exchange for big TVs, flashy garages, and designer drugs. The song's most potent irony, however, comes from its sly appropriation of the opening riff to the Stones' "Street Fighting Man." Whereas this sixties' rock anthem exhibits a similar sense of alienation ("'Cause in sleepy London town / There's no place for a Street Fighting Man"), the speaker's outrage seems on the verge of erupting into decisive action ("the time is right for a palace revolution").[8] For the despairing speaker of "I'm Nuthin'," this kind of action—thanks to the failed example of the boomers—has ceased to be a viable option. Sixties-style rebellion has become just another discredited cliché, a cultural myth that is no more believable than the American dream; the Beatles' "Revolution" is now just a Nike commercial. Thus, unlike the "street fighting man," who can define himself through his opposition to the status quo, this speaker has lost all sense of identity. He's "nuthin,'" as alienated by the left as by the right, by the counterculture as much as by the establishment.

Ultimately, though, Troy's jaded perspective is no more valorized than Lalaina's naïveté because something like sixties' idealism consistently threatens to rear its long-haired head from beneath the film's ironic surface. Lalaina—as we have seen—hopes that her documentary will have some impact on her g-g-g-generation and makes a promise to herself not to "unintentionally commercialize it." And even Troy says that he would like his band to "travel the country like Woody Guthrie," harking back to a time before music had become a multimillion dollar industry. As a result, much of the soundtrack has a distinctly sixties' flavor. While several selections sound like warmed-over psychedelic rock (e.g., Dinosaur Jr.'s "Turnip Farm"), others have a retro-folk (Lisa Loeb's "Stay") or sixties-revival quality (the Posies' "Going, Going, Gone") that contrasts with the slickly produced hits of contemporary Top 40. But, predictably, the film's touchstone for sincerity and commitment comes from those poster boys of socially conscious rock, U2, whose ballad "All I Want Is You" accompanies the "Dover Beach"–like efforts of Lalaina and Troy to find love and security amid the chaos of nineties' America, to blend their respective idealism and skepticism into a harmonious and productive union. Clearly, then, the film's sensibility is a long way from the irony Jameson sees as characteristic of our postmodern moment, an attitude characterized by "a new kind of flatness or depthlessness, a new kind of superficiality."[9] This is not to say that Jameson misunderstands postmodernism but rather that *Reality Bites*—for all its hipper-than-thou attitude—is just faux po-mo. Troy talks bravely about "riding his own melt," and most of the characters, for most of the film, seem happy enough with Bono's injunction to "slide down the surface of things";[10] but when the going gets really tough—when Troy's dad dies, and Troy and Lalaina's relationship seems on the verge of breaking up—the film shows its true colors. It comes through with a big, orchestrally reinforced ballad to reassure us that everything'll be all right.

By now, we hope it's clear how much the value system that *Reality Bites* promotes grows out of, or is disseminated through, its soundtrack. The Knack and Frampton, we are led to believe, are "bad" because their vacuousness is symptomatic of the commercialism of the seventies and eighties; U2 and the other usually acoustic, sixties-tinged music on the soundtrack is "good" because it symbolizes the social commitment of that decade. Still, despite the simplicity of this allegory, the film's use of music is actually more sophisticated than that of most rock soundtracks. Rather than using a sixties' song simply to evoke the decade of the sixties as *The Big Chill* or *Forrest Gump* do, *Reality Bites* uses the music and musical styles of the sixties, seventies, and eighties to frame and comment on its Generation X narrative. Moreover, unlike most soundtracks, it is not simply our response to this music that is important but that of the characters as well. Throughout *Reality Bites*, we regularly see the central characters listening to, reacting to, and talking about the songs on the soundtrack, and it is principally these reactions that enable us to assess their states of mind and values. In Bret Easton Ellis's *American Psycho*,[11] we know not to trust Patrick Bateman in part because he can narrate entire chapters about Huey Lewis and the News and (post-Peter Gabriel) Genesis; in *Reality Bites*, we know that Troy and Lalaina are OK because Bono sings at their reunion.

A purer, less processed form of cheese appears in *Wayne's World*, the 1992 Mike Myers film that we would argue began this trend toward ironically recontextualizing baby boomer music in Gen X movies. Of course, *Wayne's World* takes nothing from the previous generation seriously. The movie opens with some poor middle-aged schmuck named Ron Paxton showcasing his new invention, the Suck Kut, on Wayne and Garth's public-access cable show. Bad idea, Ron. Wayne's first comment is that Ron's brain-child "certainly does suck," and while Ron's doing a demo trim on Garth's melon, Wayne surreptitiously calls in the "Get-A-Load-Of-This-Guy Cam." Poor Paxton's sent packing as the show ends, with Wayne remarking that the Suck Kut is "a totally amazing, excellent discovery. Not!" Later in the film, of course, the hapless, terminally unhip video arcade tycoon Noah Van Der Hoff gets much the same treatment when Wayne uses his idiot cards as message boards with which to make an idiot of the founder of Noah's Arcades during his live interview on "Wayne's World," calling Van Der Hoff a "sphincter boy," suggesting that "this man has no penis," and insisting that "he blows goats. I have proof."

But like *Reality Bites*, *Wayne's World*'s most sublime irony, for our money, comes when Myers gets his hands on the boomers' music. The obvious place to start is with the film's use and abuse of Queen's "Bohemian Rhapsody." Wayne, cruising down the street in the passenger's seat of his buddy Garth's vintage AMC Pacer (a.k.a. the Mirthmobile), queries the passengers about car tunes: "I think we'll go with a little 'Bohemian Rhapsody,' gentlemen?" His pilot, Garth, answers in the affirmative ("Good call"), and Wayne pops his cassette into the tape deck (though we almost expect an 8-track player), while the whole carful—including a drunk guy in the back seat named Phil who's upright only because he's wedged between two others—sing along and begin to thrash their stringy hair (in fact, obviously cheap hairpieces, like Wayne's and Garth's) in synch with the music and one another. In the process, seventies' superstars Queen—and particularly one of their signature songs, "Bohemian Rhapsody"—get "spun" in *Wayne's World*. It seems clear to us that Myers is sending the band up; the overproduced and deadly self-important music of Queen and the torch singer role so eagerly adopted by Freddie Mercury make a great source of cheese, and Myers uses Wayne and Garth's devotion to them as a way to flesh out their characterization. But it's finally a judgment call, for there's no firm textual or contextual evidence that the boys in the Mirthmobile think the song is anything but "Excellent": Wayne maintains a steady accompaniment of air guitar and air drums throughout and has a beatific grin on his face (as does Garth) as the song fades out that looks strangely like afterglow. Indeed, the sing-along participation in the song in the tight space of Garth's Pacer represents, among other things, a socially sanctioned moment of male bonding in a youth culture that provides few such opportunities. How bad can a song be, finally, if it allows adolescent males to connect in the midst of a homophobic atmosphere that forbids absolutely any such engagement?

This is the kind of unstable, postmodern irony that Linda Hutcheon describes: suspicious of "transcendental certitudes of any kind, including the subject" (and, we might add, taste), "postmodern irony . . . denies the form of dialectic and refuses resolution of any kind in order to retain the doubleness that is its identity."[12] Try as you might, you'll find no way to establish an ironic reading of this scene. To judge it an ironic treatment of "Bohemian Rhapsody," as we are, one must assert a distance between Mike Myers as writer and Wayne Campbell as narrator. This is doubly difficult because part of the dynamic in *Wayne's World* is that Myers is himself a late boomer rather than a Generation Xer: his character, Wayne, however, is an Xer, a slacker, all dressed up in black T-shirt and blue jeans—as well as "an extensive collection of name tags and hair nets"—but no place to go. It thus seems to us that the irony of "Bohemian Rhapsody" in the Mirthmobile—Schlock Opera lip-synched in the 1970's version of the Edsel—cuts two ways. The music of Queen is shown up as cheesy through the comic stylings of Wayne, Garth, and crew; thus Myers points a condemning finger at the excesses and narcissism of the progressive seventies' art rock with which he must have grown up that contrasts so sharply with the self-consciously disposable pop of "My Sharona." At the same time, however, Wayne and Garth are indicted, for they've pulled "Bohemian Rhapsody" from the trash heap of contemporary history, dusted it off, and popped it into the tape deck; no saturation airplay has forced them to listen to, and hum along with, Queen against their will. They've brought this on themselves.

But wait: there's more. It gets weirder. After *Wayne's World*'s theatrical release, and the MTV video of the boys popping their heads to "Bohemian Rhapsody" in their Pacer got a lot of airplay, Queen actually enjoyed something of a renaissance, akin to the brief *Reality Bites*–inspired rebirth of the Knack—including a retrospective (and, in Freddie Mercury's case, posthumous) live album and live videos released and put in heavy rotation on MTV—which leads us to suspect that the irony that we think we see was missed by much of the audience. Freddie Mercury's death from AIDS in November 1991, only months before the film's release, doubtless had something to do with the revival of Queen's fortunes, and we don't wish to downplay this aspect. But an entire generation of music consumers was introduced to Queen, and "Bohemian Rhapsody," by *Wayne's World,* and they didn't see anything wrong with it: indeed, they thought it was "Excellent."

There are any number of other examples of this unstably ironic use of boomer tunes in the film. One thematic that we'd like to note briefly is the way that this avowedly cheesy music determines the structure of romantic and sexual desire in the Dynamic Duo. Garth's pure, chaste love of the Dreamwoman who works behind the counter at Stan Mikita's donut shop is figured in the soundtrack by Tchaikovsky's "Fantasy Overture" from *Romeo and Juliet,* surely a musical cliché of romantic love if ever there was one. But tellingly, when spurred on by Cassandra actually to break his silence and speak to her, Garth soundtracks his daydream/fantasy with Jimi Hendrix's "Foxy Lady." The choreography of this number is absolutely masterful; at one point in his waltz toward the counter, it appears as though Garth is being pulled toward his Dreamwoman by an invisible fishhook in the zipper of his trousers; as he gyrates toward her, he looks down in amazement at his seemingly possessed crotch. And as for the lyrics: well, most of us who listened to Hendrix before he was retro didn't listen for the lyrics, and when Garth makes little feral ears with his fingers while calling his Lady "Foxy," we're painfully reminded of *why* we ignored the lyrics. Ouch. As for Wayne and his lady, Cassandra, his theme song is—gulp—Gary Wright's eminently forgettable "Dream Weaver."

Aerosmith is the moral/aesthetic equivalent of Queen in *Wayne's World 2.* How many folks turned out to see *Wayne's World 2* simply because it contains live footage of Aerosmith? This makes for very complicated irony, of course, because Aerosmith, we think, takes itself pretty seriously even if Mike Myers doesn't. As with all interesting, postmodern irony, the use of Queen and Aerosmith in the *Wayne's World* films poses one particularly tricky question: *you* know that Mike Myers doesn't take Steve Tyler as seriously as Tyler takes himself, and *we* know it, but *how* do we know it? This irony is unstable because one can never prove with any certainty that it is even irony. Watching Aerosmith at Waynestock, the spectator is at some loss to discover precisely how s/he's to read Aerosmith's concert performance and Steve Tyler's adolescent mike humping. It's as if Wayne and Garth put Aerosmith up on the Waynestock stage and announce, "Hey, these guys are great! Not!!" But that "not" teasingly remains unvoiced.

In fact, the closest we get to a theory of irony in the *Wayne's World* films is at the end of the first movie, after the credits have been rolling for a time. Wayne and Garth are suddenly back up on the screen, to bid us adieu, and Wayne says into the camera: "Well, that's all the time we have for our movie. We hope you found it entertaining, whimsical, and yet relevant, with an underlying revisionist conceit that belied the film's emotional attachments to the subject matter." Wow! This is Wayne Campbell talking? Suddenly Wayne's become a native philosopher of postmodernism, positing in one economical sentence a theory of postmodern irony as compelling as anything written by Jameson or Hutcheon. But Wayne and Garth are a team; Wayne's brief disquisition is only half the story without Garth's rejoinder: "I just hope you didn't think it sucked." For postmodern irony can allow nothing to stand unscathed, not even Wayne's definition of postmodern irony itself.

In the soundtracks to the films of Quentin Tarantino, we also find something approaching an aesthetics of pure cheese. The director's fondness for bad pop music is unmistakable, for rather than simply mixing in an occasional rock song for period color, he constructs entire soundtracks out of successions of not-quite-forgotten pop singles. *Reservoir*

*Dogs,* for example, uses nothing but K-Billy's "Super Sounds of the Seventies" for the film's musical score, a strategy that, according to Tarantino himself, provides "somewhat of an ironic counterpoint to what you are seeing on the screen."[13] This is, for the most part, an accurate assessment: these unrelentingly superficial songs generally do help to distance us from the blood and often gut-wrenching violence of the film. Plus the cheesiness of the soundtrack constantly reminds us of the fact that this is a story about cheap hoods. Unlike its precursors in the heist movie genre—*The Asphalt Jungle, Riffifi, The Killing*—*Reservoir Dogs* does not ask us to empathize with the characters or to find tragic dignity in their plight, something that would be far more likely to happen if it had used a more conventional Miklos Rozsa/Jerry Goldsmith score. At the same time, though, we have to take the "somewhat" in Tarantino's statement seriously. Often, his specific musical choices have an unexpected aptness as in the most famous and memorable scene from the film: the torture sequence performed to Stealers Wheel's "Stuck in the Middle with You."[14] At first, the bouncy, hand-clap-accented beat of this "Dylanesque, pop, bubble-gum favorite" seems thoroughly out of keeping with the uncompromising violence of the scene. But without this accompaniment, we would miss the glee that the torturer, Mr. Blonde, takes in his task, especially when he breaks into an impromptu dance in between his assaults on the young cop tied to the chair. Moreover, as the scene continues, the nasal drone of Gerry Rafferty's vocal becomes increasingly irritating, thereby intensifying the agony of this already agonizing scene. And, finally, if we can bring ourselves to concentrate on the lyrics to the song, we notice that Tarantino himself seems to be taking an almost sadistic glee in the grim ironies of the scene. While the opening line, "I'm so scared I guess I'll fall off my chair," clearly contrasts with the condition of this thoroughly bound and gagged cop, the words of the song's title become cruelly literalized. The cop is stuck in the middle of this warehouse where his torturer is sticking him in the gut with a razor.

In *Pulp Fiction,* Tarantino's use of music is even more creative and unorthodox. With its eclectic mix of various music genres from the sixties, seventies, eighties, and nineties, the soundtrack exhibits the kind of "depthlessness" that Frederic Jameson decries in his jeremiads against postmodern art, and so—in sharp contrast to most rock soundtracks—it provides no reliable contextual clues to ground the narrative or situate the viewer. The opening credits sequence exemplifies how this kind of aesthetic and temporal destabilization works. First, we hear Dick Dale's sixties' surf guitar instrumental, "Misirlou," and then, in what may be an ironic nod at the soundtrack of *Reservoir Dogs,* the channel is changed to a new station on which Kool and the Gang's R&B hit "Jungle Boogie" is playing. Tarantino's rationale for these choices is instructive. "Misirlou" he describes as sounding like "the beginning of like *The Good, the Bad, and the Ugly* with those trumpets, that almost Spanish sound. Having 'Misirlou' as your opening credits, it just says, 'You're watching an epic, you're watching this big old movie, just sit back.'" The sudden switch to Kool and the Gang, however, works both to startle the viewer and to signal the film's "other personality": its appropriation of "this black exploitation thing."[15]

In this way, Tarantino provides his viewer with quite a bit of information. There is no whiter music on the planet than surf music, while "Jungle Boogie" is obviously very black and urban. The only common denominator is their mutual cheesiness. With the coming of the British Invasion, psychedelia, and the Summer of Love, surf music was—until its recent Dick Dale–led renaissance—rendered terminally uncool, its clean-cut, All-American image being totally out of step with the increasingly radicalized atmosphere of the sixties. Similarly, Kool and the Gang are never going to be confused with Stevie Wonder or Marvin Gaye, and this song in particular seems designed to create as insulting a stereotype of African-American culture as possible. Nonetheless, Tarantino claims to be genuinely fond of both songs. He says that he "always really dug surf music," and while he admits "if I had to choose between Al Green or 'Jungle Boogie' I would probably choose Al Green," he maintains that "the early Kool and the Gang records were great." Here, then, the irony seems to be at least as unreadable as anything in *Wayne's World*. While in that film the distinction between Wayne and Mike Myers occasionally blurs, in *Pulp Fiction* such a distinction is impossible to find because Tarantino seemingly recognizes the ironic effect that such musical choices have but refuses to pass judgment on them or to acknowledge them as bad. This is a man who truly likes surf music and who can distinguish between the early, golden age of Kool and the Gang and their later decadence—who can distinguish for us among the good, the bad, and the ugly.

This suspension of judgment—this mixture of emotional involvement and ironic detachment—is, we believe, the principle on which Tarantino's brand of postmodernism depends. To construct his narrative, he creates a pastiche of B-movie allusions (*Kiss Me Deadly, The Killers, The Set-Up*) as well as several references to more mainstream fare (*Rocky, Deliverance*), but he puts them to unfamiliar, unexpected ends; he carefully creates atmosphere and attitude but divorces them from any clearly identifiable content or message. His use of pop music works similarly. These familiar or seemingly familiar songs set our toes tapping and heads bobbing involuntarily, even as our minds ask, "What *is* this shit?" They both draw us in and draw attention to themselves. During the episode in which the hit man, Vincent Vega, takes Mia Wallace, his boss's young wife, out on a date, we see two more examples of this strategy in action. When Vincent first comes to pick her up, she is playing Dusty Springfield's "Son of a Preacher Man" on the stereo. According to Tarantino, he wrote the scene with this song in mind: "That whole sequence, I've had in my head for six or seven years. And it was always scored to 'Son of a Preacher Man.' That was the key to the sequence. I can't even imagine it without 'Son of a Preacher Man.'" But to most viewers—ourselves included—the immediate reaction would be simply, "Why?" What is it about this song that is so central to this scene? First of all, that Mia would be playing this song seems highly unlikely given the fact that it was released before she would have been born. Plus, when we consider the lyrics to the song, they seem to contradict the situation in the film flatly: this heroin-shooting hit man is unlikely to be taken for the son of a preacher man. And yet—as in Tarantino's earlier use of "Stuck in the Middle with You"—there is indeed something right about the way the song works in this scene. Much of the tension in the episode results from the fact that Mia, like the preacher's son, is off limits; it's not just that she's the wife of Vincent's boss but that her husband reportedly ordered another employee to be thrown out of a four-story building for giving Mia a foot massage. She's forbidden fruit—something that Mia herself underscores later in the episode when she says, "Besides it's more exciting when you don't have permission"—and it's this taboo aspect of the meeting that makes Mia and Vincent so desirable to one another.

Furthermore, this white man's—or in this case—white woman's soul music helps to establish the ersatz quality that will pervade the rest of the episode. Mia's choice of a restaurant is Jack Rabbit Slim's, a faux-fifties' diner, complete with Ed Sullivan, Marilyn Monroe, and Buddy Holly impersonators and tables inside Chrysler convertibles. Though this environment creates a superficial sense of wholesomeness (the soundtrack for much of this segment is by that most clean-cut of fifties' pop idols, Ricky Nelson), the seamlessness of Tarantino's pulp fiction is never far beneath the surface. For example, when Mia excuses herself—in good fifties' fashion—to go "powder my nose," Tarantino perversely literalizes this seemingly decorous euphemism by showing her snorting coke in the bathroom. Once they return to Mia's house—euphoric over their victory in the Jack Rabbit Slim's dance contest—the sexual subtext becomes overt. Now, when Vincent goes off to "take a piss," Mia puts on some mood music—which, in one further knowing anachronism, she plays on a reel-to-reel tape recorder. This time her choice is somewhat more contemporary—Urge Overkill's cover version of Neil Diamond's "Girl, You'll Be a Woman Soon"—and here, again, Tarantino seems to be constructing a largely unreadable irony. On one level, this song serves as the flip side of "Son of Preacher Man." Just as Vincent is clearly no preacher's kid, Mia—with her Cleopatraesque hairdo, her vampish makeup, and sex-kitten manner—is clearly already a woman. Still, the irony does not work through simple inversion or kitsch. Tarantino doesn't appear to be ridiculing this silly love song, and, as we might expect by now, he claims even to like the original version: "Well, I love Neil Diamond, and I have always loved Neil Diamond's version of that song, but [Urge Overkill's] version is even better." Here, however, we think Tarantino is being somewhat disingenuous as there is no way that the scene would have worked if he had used the Neil Diamond version: the irony would be overdetermined, and we would laugh out loud as we do at "My Sharona" in *Reality Bites* or "Dream Weaver" in *Wayne's World.* On the other hand, by using this bass-heavy, flamenco version, Tarantino defamiliarizes Neil Diamond's cheesy ballad so that—in spite of its pedigree—the song succeeds in heightening the intensity of the scene. In this case, rock 'n' roll really does have "the beat of sexual intercourse"[16]—and so while we may be aware that this is a Neil Diamond song, we don't let that intrude on the mounting sexual tension until the scene yields a final grim irony. Mistaking Vincent's heroin for a bag of cocaine, Mia snorts it, with the result that it seems this girl will be a corpse soon.

Perhaps, though, the best way to demonstrate what makes Tarantino's use of music so distinctive is by viewing it in direct comparison with Ben Stiller's more conventional handling of his films' soundtracks. In a key scene from Stiller's recent directorial effort, *The Cable Guy,* Jim Carey's Chip Douglas, the title character, performs a thoroughly over-the-top karaoke version of Jefferson Airplane's "Somebody to Love." Gyrating in front of a TV screen swirling with psychedelic colors and patterns, he flaps the ridiculously long fringes of his sixties' leather jacket while grotesquely exaggerating the vibrato of Grace Slick's original vocal. Clearly, the song is being ironized as we are asked to participate in this knowing send-up of Bay Area psychedelia, but, at the same time, we are also intended to recognize how revealing this character's choice of songs is. After all, the entire narrative of the film revolves around the attempts of this TV-obsessed cable guy to achieve some real human contact by befriending a customer: he truly does want someone to love. Thus Stiller's basic strategy is to make fun of the song's surface features while using its lyrical content to further the plot and provide reliable insight into his character's psyche.[17] As his use of "Son of a Preacher Man" and "Girl, You'll Be a Woman Soon" indicates, Tarantino's modus operandi is the exact opposite. Unlike Stiller, he never openly parodies the music he selects, and—rather than using the soundtrack to underscore the film's narrative line—he often creates a highly unstable, even contradictory relationship between the song lyrics of the soundtrack and the action taking place on the screen.

A second example comes from what is for us a very fortuitous coincidence. At one point, Tarantino considered using "My Sharona" for the "sodomy rape sequence" during the later

"Gold Watch" episode in *Pulp Fiction* because, as he explains, "'My Sharona' has a really good sodomy beat to it." The plan eventually fell through because the Knack objected to this appropriation of their song and decided to let Stiller use it in *Reality Bites* instead. Thinking back on his original plan, Tarantino is now pleased that he had to use "Comanche," another surf music cut: "I like using stuff for comic effect, but I don't want it to be har, har, wink, wink, nudge, nudge, you know?"[18] Once again, this kind of irony is for Tarantino too broad and easily decipherable, and so he sets up a far more complex and demanding scenario for his viewers. He expects us to recognize the songs he selects and to acknowledge their cheesiness, but, by using them in unexpected and unfamiliar contexts, he alters our experience of them. As a result, we start to hear them in something like the way Tarantino himself does, a man who boasts of liking "certain music that nobody else on the planet has an appreciation for."

From this last comment, it seems to us, a whole new problematic arises because here Tarantino appears to take a perverse pride in his sense of taste, a stance that appears to conflict with his usual self-representation as an aesthetic man of the people. In a recent *New York Times* interview, for instance, he dismissed the idea that he is a "collector" of pop culture by saying, "I don't believe in elitism. I don't think the audience is this dumb person lower than me. I am the audience."[19] But, as in the above quotation, Tarantino does on occasion appear to congratulate himself for having a more highly evolved sensibility, an aesthetic sense so acute that he can find beauty in things that most people see as having no socially redeeming value. It may be something of a Bizarro standard of taste, but it's a standard of taste nonetheless. Such a statement, then, reveals how difficult it is to maintain the kind of instability and undecidability that we see as the hallmarks of cheese and how tenuous the distinction between camp and cheese really is. Cheese may be, finally, all about self-consciousness, but, paradoxically, cheese that betrays its self-consciousness, its aesthetic investments, quickly spoils and loses its ability to delight and instruct.

Notes

1. Susan Sontag, "Notes on Camp," in *A Susan Sontag Reader* (New York: Vintage, 1983), p. 107.
2. Since cheese is of relatively recent vintage, there have been few academic or theoretical treatments of it. To our knowledge, the fullest discussion is in Michiko Kakutanti's August 7, 1992, *New York Times* article, "Having Fun by Poking Pun: A New Esthetic Called Cheese" (B1, B6). Here, Kakutani usefully compares cheese to camp, noting very accurately that cheese "willfully focuses on the vulgar, the meretricious, the bogus"; she goes on to argue that, unlike the "generous" spirit of camp, "cheese tends to be judgmental, cynical, and detached" (B6). This—as the following examples we hope will demonstrate—is a severe misrepresentation of how genuine cheese functions. No less than camp, cheese "relishes, rather than judges" (Sontag, "Notes," 119), but it takes this process one step further, effectively obliterating or at least ignoring the distinctions between good and bad art, high and popular culture that underlie most standards of aesthetic judgment.
3. For other analyses of rock music soundtracks, see Claudia Gorbham, *Unheard Music: Narrative Film Music* (London: BFI, 1987); R. Serge Denisoff, *Risky Business: Rock in Film* (New Brunswick, NJ: Transaction, 1991); Lawrence Grossberg, "The Media Economy of Rock Culture: Cinema, Post-Modernity, and Authenticity" in *Sound and Vision: The Music Video Reader,* ed. Simon Frith, Andrew Goodwin, and Lawrence Grossberg (London: Routledge, 1993), pp. 185–209.
4. Fredric Jameson, *Postmodernism: or, The Cultural Logic of Late Capitalism* (Durham, NC: Duke University Press, 1991), pp. x, 17.
5. The Knack, "My Sharona," *Reality Bites* (RCA 44364, 1994).
6. Peter Frampton, "Baby I Love Your Way," *Frampton Comes Alive* (A&M 540930, 1976; reissue, 1998).

7. Ethan Hawke, "I'm Nuthin'," *Reality Bites.*
8. The Rolling Stones, "Street Fighting Man," *Beggar's Banquet* (ABKCO 7539, 1968).
9. Jameson, *Postmodernism,* p. 9.
10. U2, "Even Better than the Real Thing," *Achtung Baby* (Island 314–510 347-2, 1991).
11. Bret Easton Ellis, *American Psycho* (New York: Vintage, 1991).
12. Linda Hutcheon, "The Power of Postmodern Irony," in *Genre, Trope, Gender: Critical Essays by Northrop Frye, Linda Hutcheon, and Shirley Neuman* (Ottawa: Carelton University Press, 1992), p. 35.
13. "Truth and Fiction," liner notes to *Pulp Fiction/Reservoir Dogs* (MCACD 11188, 1994), p. 7.
14. Stealer's Wheel's "Stuck in the Middle with You," *Reservoir Dogs* (MCA 10541, 1992).
15. "Truth and Fiction," pp. 5–7.
16. This infamous quotation is, of course, from Allan Bloom, *The Closing of the American Mind* (New York: Simon and Schuster, 1987), p. 73. Bloom continues with a comment that sheds an interesting light on the flamenco feel of Urge Overkill's cover: "That is why Ravel's *Bolero* is the one piece of classical music that is commonly known and liked by them ["young people"]."
17. As in *Reality Bites,* Stiller's use of music may not be as enigmatic as Tarantino's, but it is by no means simplistic. This scene works on an additional level as well because Carey's performance is intercut with the foreplay of Steven—the Cable Guy's would-be friend—and a young woman whom we later learn is a prostitute hired by the Cable Guy. The song thus also applies to Steven—especially when we consider that he only subscribes to cable because he has just broken up with his girlfriend. This may only be a pay-per-screw version of the Summer of Love, but Steven, too, is seeking someone to love.
18. "Truth and Fiction," p. 16.
19. Lynn Hirschberg, "The Man Who Changed Everything," *New York Times Magazine,* 16 November 1997, p. 116.

READING WRITING

## THIS TEXT: READING

1. What value does Dettmar place on the intelligent use of music in movies? How do we know this? Do you have similar values?
2. Review Dettmar's definition of cheese. Is it a positive definition or a negative one? Name something else that is "cheesy."
3. How often do you pay attention to the music in movies? Or do you try to avoid paying attention?
4. Like other forms of expression, music necessarily reflects a variety of factors, some of them beyond the control of the musician. What do you think of Quentin Tarantino's ideas about using music in movies? Do you think they are consistent with the musician's intent?

## YOUR TEXT: WRITING

1. Do your own examination of cheese in a popular text. What other popular culture form contains its share of cheese?
2. Music soundtracks are notorious for being manipulative. Watch—and listen to—a movie and document where the director uses music to indicate mood. Write a short paper examining this idea.
3. How does "seeing" a favorite song change your view of it? Write a short paper examining your response to a favorite song in a movie.

*Student Essay*

| **IS TUPAC REALLY DEAD?** |
| :---: |
| ■ **Fouzia Baber** ■ |

Even though Tupac Amaru Shakur was gunned down on the streets of Las Vegas in front of at least a hundred people, there are those who refuse to believe that he died from the wounds he suffered that hot September night. Is he "dead or alive?" Many people concerned with the 25-year-old rap artist and film star continue to raise this question. Although reported evidence of his death has been convincing to many Tupac fans, the role of the media and commercial industries have led some to believe that the gangster rap star is still alive today. New conspiracies claiming that Tupac faked his own death accumulate on the World Wide Web and in magazines, books, and television. Some people have chosen to believe that Tupac is still alive, with rumors that he is hiding somewhere in Cuba, and has been seen in Manhattan, Arizona, South America, and the Caribbean. The main question that came to my mind about Tupac's death was not whether he is "dead or alive," but how and why anyone would disavow his death. The answer is simple: money. More specifically, Death Row Records, the record label that Tupac was signed under, attracted media hype about Tupac's death in order to earn publicity and increase their sales. Facts about Tupac's life and work lead many to believe that he legitimately faked his death. The actual shooting and the autopsy, his supposed "rebirth," his lyrics and videos, and accusations on Death Row Records all distort truthful evidence of his death.

> I'm ready to die right here tonight
> And mother* they life
> That's what they screamin as they drill me
> But I'm hard to kill, so open fire.
>
> (Shakur, Ambitionz Az a Ridah)

Some people believe that Tupac is still living because of the seemingly unresolved nature of events following his death. To many, Tupac's death seemed more like a setup than an actual death. On the night of September 7, 1996, Tupac was leaving a Mike Tyson fight without his bulletproof vest (something very uncommon and unusual for Tupac to do), with Death Row Records owner, and close friend, Suge Knight, when an unknown assailant fired thirteen bullets at the BMW. Tupac was allegedly shot five times. He lived through the shooting and was taken to a nearby hospital in Las Vegas and was not pronounced dead until Friday, September 13. Much of the speculation dealing with the murder stems from the air of secretiveness surrounding the events after his death. One reason why his death could be questioned is because no one ever saw the body leave the hospital. Many people claim that no photographs were taken after the murder showing his injuries. The one autopsy photo that was taken does not show the tattoo on his neck with the word Cleopatra written on it, increasing doubt to the public of his actual death (Light 123). Lieutenant Brad Simpson, who oversaw Las Vegas Metro's criminalistics unit, which included the photo lab, said his office's photos of the Tupac Shakur investigation have been locked up. There was interest from some of the tabloids in getting some of those photos, Simpson said. The tabloids offered a lot of money, but they didn't get any photos (qtd. in Scott 171). Of all the photos taken, all were kept except one, which tabloids such as the *Globe* and the *National Enquirer* offered as much as $100,000 for (Scott 170). The press hoped readers might take to the theory that Tupac faked his own death. They pointed out the missing tattoo on his neck to the public, leading it to believe it was not Tupac after all. Another issue that Tupac-is-alive theorists cite is the fact that he was cremated instead of buried. As shown in the quote from Ambitionz az a Ridah, Tupac often rapped about his funeral and being buried, but instead Tupac was cremated one day after the autopsy in Los Angeles, where he had no family or close friends.

Mixed with the mystery conspiracies attached to Tupac's memory is grief from the fans. The night his death was confirmed, crowds began to disperse around the hospital, blaring "If I Die Tonight":

—I'll live eternal
Who shall I fear
Don't shed a tear for me nigga
I ain't happy here
I hope they bury me and send me to my rest
Headlines readin murdered to death
My last breath

—(Shakur, The Rose That Grew)–

These lyrics suggest that Tupac wanted to be out of the limelight. Threatened by East–West Coast gangsta rap, troubled with the law, and harassed by the public, it is no surprise that Tupac may not have been satisfied with his life. This assumption leads many people to believe that he wanted to die in the eyes of the world and live secretly, away from the glare of publicity, thus faking his death. Even actor Tim Roth told *Showbiz* magazine that Tupac talked about dying a lot because he knew it would happen. He knew he wasn't going to live to ripe old age. He really wanted to get away from what was expected from him, from how people had pigeonholed him, and move away from all these different things (qtd. in Dyson 89). Confused and shocked by the apparent death of their rap idol, numerous fans turned to the inspiration of Tupac's poetry and lyrics to help them cope with his death, or even deny it altogether.

Another reason some believe that Tupac faked his own death comes from Tupac's obsession with the teachings of political philosopher Niccol Machiavelli, who some believe inspired Tupac's desire to get out of the limelight. While in prison, Tupac studied his books in depth. Machiavelli was a sixteenth-century philosopher who advocated the staging of one's death in order to evade one's enemies and gain power. In one of Machiavelli's books, *Discourses Upon the First Ten Books of Titus Livy,* he says, a prince who wishes to achieve great things must learn to deceive (qtd. in Ledeen). This is Machiavelli's main idea and is the connection between him and what many believe as Tupac's own deceitful death. Only six weeks following his passing, Death Row Records released Tupac's posthumous album, *Don Killuminati: The 7 Day Theory* under the pseudonym Makaveli. Another one of Machiavelli's recognized theories seen in his book, *The Prince,* is the Seven Day Theory which refers to faking one's death. The cover of Tupac's *7 Day Theory* album depicts Tupac nailed to a cross under a crown of thorns, with a map of the country's major gang areas superimposed on it (Donno). There is a great deal of evidence that leads many people to believe that Tupac followed Machiavelli's teachings and faked his own death. There was nothing in the new album that said Tupac R.I.P. 1971–1996 or anything to pay respects to the dead artist. The only thing mentioned are the words exit Tupac, enter Makaveli leading people to believe that Tupac has died and Makaveli is born. In an interview while in jail in 1994, Tupac states that when he returns from prison he will be reborn into a new man. Perhaps this means he will be reborn into Makaveli. He claims;

When I ended up in jail, my spirit died. The addict in me knew if I went to jail, then it couldn't live. The addict, the old Tupac is dead. The excuse maker in Tupac is dead. The vengeful Tupac is dead. The Tupac that would stand by and let dishonorable things happen is dead. God let me live for me to do something more extraordinary than this (qtd. in Light 46)

The title of the album by Makaveli, *The 7 Day Theory,* has many symbolic references to Tupac's death. For instance, Tupac was shot on September 7th, and died seven days later. Tupac officially died at 4:03 PM; $4 + 3 = 7$. Also he died at age 25; $2 + 5 = 7$. Tupac's album, *All Eyes on Me* was released on February 13, 1996, and Tupac died on September 13, exactly seven months later. These references of marketing hype by Death Row and the media have brought incredible amounts of attention to Tupac's death. Death Row could even have used the seven-day strategy to attract buyers. It makes perfect sense for Death Row to indirectly lead people to think that Tupac is still alive. The album sold over three million copies, which proves that Death Row was successful in marketing Tupac's music even after his death, perhaps even because of his death. Tupac's lyrics and music videos have also led many people to believe he staged his death and may still be alive today. There are various references that Tupac makes to his own death in his songs. For example, the video "I Ain't Mad at Cha" was released only a few days after his death. The video shows Tupac as an angel in heaven. In the video, Tupac was shot after leaving a theater with a friend, which is very similar to how he was shot in real life. In the video Hail Mary, released under the name Makaveli, there is a gravestone that says Makaveli, but the gravestone is cracked and there is a hole right in the front of it, implying that Makaveli rose from the dead (Dyson 20). In rapper Richie Rich's album *Seasoned Veteran,* which was released on the same day as *The 7 Day Theory,* on the song "N*ggas Done Changed" which is a duet with Tupac, Tupac says the following: "I've been shot and murdered, can't tell you how it happened word for word/but best believe that n*ggas' gonna get what they deserve." This phrase implies that Tupac knows he will be dead when Richie Rich's album is released. In Tupac's song "Ambitionz az a Ridah" on the album *All Eyes On Me,* he says "Blast me but they didn't finish, didn't diminish my powers but I'm back reincarnated (emphasis added). This may imply that Tupac is reincarnated as Makaveli. In the song, "Hold Ya Head" on the Makaveli CD, before Tupac begins rapping, a voice says, "Can you see him?" and another voice replies, "I see him." Then Tupac softly says, "I'm alive." Clearly, Tupac's lyrics and videos showed numerous references to his murder.

Even if they didn't actively conspire against Tupac, music companies, especially Death Row Records, had and have monetary incentive to make Tupac's death seem like more of a conspiracy than an accident. One speculation is that the killing of Tupac (and to an extent, Biggie Smalls) was a by-product of top record-company executives as a way of boosting sales. The similarities in the lives and deaths of Tupac Shakur and rap artist Biggie Smalls are striking. Both rappers, who were controversially considered as enemies in the East—West Coast rivalry, were at the peak of their careers before their deaths, both were killed in drive-by shootings, and both of the murder cases remain unsolved today. While the murders of Tupac and Biggie spurred record sales, the long-term effects were not good for business. The big record companies and distributors questioned whether business should continue as usual or if they needed a new strategy. The CEO of Death Row Records Marion "Suge" Knight's state of affairs definitely took a turn for the worse after Tupac's death. Rumors were already swirling about trouble at Death Row, and now he'd lost his top moneymaker, Tupac Shakur. Some have gone as far as to say Death Row was on the brink of failure (Scott 107). Some speculation even goes as far as questioning whether Suge himself ordered Tupac's attack to sell more CDs and make a financial comeback for Death Row. Is Tupac worth more dead than alive? Kevin Powell, a writer for the *New York Times* and the music industry had this to say about Tupac's death:

Here's my theory. At first these rap artists are small-time investments. They're lucky if they make one album. When they start getting up to four albums, they're big investments. Then they become a liability. And they remain a liability as long as they're alive. But if they're dead and they've already cut their albums, their record companies are just selling their albums and not giving money to them anymore. (qtd. in Scott 159–160).

Making money off of Tupac's albums after his death was not a problem at all since he had so many songs yet to be released. Within three days after his release from prison, he had recorded seven songs. The period after his release from prison marked the beginning of about 200 songs that Tupac would record between this time until his fatal shooting a year later (Dyson 84). The trail clearly leads to money. The record companies benefit from all of Tupac's albums. Makaveli's (Tupac's) posthumous *7 Day Theory* album, released six weeks after Tupac's death, sold 664,000 units in the first week and 3 million copies by April 1997 (Donno). Death Row records sold hats, T-shirts, and sweatshirts connected with Tupac's murder. Clearly the record labels were interested in making money off of Tupac, when he was alive and when he was dead.

No matter how many times we read about it, hear about it, and learn about it, so many of us still cannot grasp the idea of Tupac being dead. We could research and study and ask questions and speculate about every aspect of the murder, but it remains a conspiracy. Perhaps Tupac's death is legendary in the same way as those of John F. Kennedy or Martin Luther King, Jr. who was responsible? Maybe we'll never know. It might be postmortem denial, along with several ironic coincidences that lead so many to believe that Tupac's death was a hoax. The only sure thing is that Death Row Records was well aware of the influence and impact that Tupac's life, work, and death had on his fans. Indeed, they played off of it very well, making money off of his work, dead, alive, or just faking dead. The bittersweet reality of the music world is that it does not really matter who owns the music. The real question is, who gets the money for releasing it or playing it? As for the fans, there are those who believe that Tupac's story is legendary, just as there are those who believe we will reunite with him and Elvis some day. However, it's not just about the special days of his death or of his birthday that we celebrate. For the real fans and the real believers, we celebrate Tupac every day, through his music, and through his words. They say that a person is never truly gone until he is forgotten. If that is the case then Tupac lives forever.

## Works Cited

Donno, Daniel. Is Tupac Alive? *Tupac Fans The #1 Resource for Tupac Shakur Fans.* 31 Dec. 1999. <http://www.tupacfans.com>.

Dyson, Eric Michael. *Holler if You Hear Me: In Search of Tupac Shakur.* New York: Civitas, 2001.

Ledeen, Michael A. "Machiavelli." *Tupac Fans The #1 Resource for Tupac Shakur Fans.* 4 Nov. 1998. <http://www.tupacfans.com>.

Light, Alan. *Tupac Shakur.* New York: Three Rivers, 1998.

Rich, Richie. *Seasoned Veteran.* Def Jam Records, 1996.

Scott, Cathy. *The Killing of Tupac Shakur.* Nevada: Huntington, 1997.

Shakur, Tupac. *Ambitionz Az a Ridah. All Eyes on Me.* Death Row Records, 1996.

—. *Don Killuminati: The 7 Day Theory.* Death Row Records, 1996.

—. *The Rose That Grew From Concrete Volume 1.* Amaru/Interscope Records, 2000.

**READING** WRITING

## THIS TEXT: READING

1. What makes this paper appropriate for a music chapter?
2. In what ways did Baber's research enhance this work? Are there other sources she might have consulted?
3. Why is this subject an important one for many people?

## YOUR TEXT: WRITING

1. Do your own investigation of a popular phenomenon in popular culture that people continue to disagree on (UFOs, other rock star deaths, etc.).
2. Do a short paper examining Tupac's legacy as a musician. How does his death play into his reputation?
3. Do a short paper examining celebrity deaths as a popular culture phenomenon. Are there patterns to how they are portrayed in American culture?

*Student Essay*

| **RIGHT ON TARGET: REVISITING ELVIS COSTELLO'S *MY AIM IS TRUE*** ■ **Sarah Hawkins** ■ |
| --- |

*Sarah Hawkins wrote this review/re-evaluation for an advanced composition class at the University of San Francisco in 2001. A persuasive piece of sorts, she tries to reintroduce an artist (with whom many of her professors are familiar) to a younger audience.*

ELVIS COSTELLO IN A NUTSHELL: a frustrated, neurotic, nonconformist who just so happens to be endlessly talented. With a song-writing capability second only to John Lennon and an Ani Difranco-esque tenacity, Elvis Costello is a pop music figure that cannot be ignored. *My Aim Is True* blends the personal with the political, shapes music to emotion, and captures moods ranging from stark depression to danceable irony. Costello writes songs on edge, displaying the sensitivity and conceit of any true elitist. Ever feel a little at odds with society? Feel left out by the mainstream? Feel simultaneously rejected and superior? Well, Elvis Costello has and he is not going to take it lying down. Successfully, he throws all of these feelings in a bag with a dry sense of humor, adds more than a pinch of cynicism, and blends them with musical accuracy. The result? A musical masterpiece that deserves attention even twenty-four years after its release.

The underdog offbeat brilliance of *My Aim Is True* has aged like fine wine, creating a modern cult following much like that of actor John Cusack. Both speak a familiar language—that of the common man experiencing failure. Costello through his lyrics, Cusack through roles such as the down-trodden record store owner Rob in the movie *High Fidelity*, or the awkward teens he plays in both *Say Anything*, and *Better Off Dead*. Part of the attraction to figures such as Costello and Cusack is that people of an ordinary nature can relate to them. Everyone wants to see pop stars that are not perfect looking, perfectly graceful, or perfectly happy. And everyone likes to see the underdog represented in a way that is unique rather than stereotypical. Both Elvis Costello and John Cusack do this and do it well.

Take for example the opening song from Costello's *My Aim Is True*. He launches into the album singing, "Welcome to the Working Week," and reaching out to any unsatisfied employee. One of the album's simplest moments, this song places the chorus "Welcome to the working week, I know it don't thrill ya I hope it don't kill ya," against a fierce yet sing-along tune, automatically winning the hearts of all those disgruntled, tired and unsure. A manifesto of the working class, this song portrays the life of pre-fame Elvis. Just an average Joe working a passionless day job as a computer operator, straining his eyes day in and day out to the point where he needs those now infamous thick-rimmed glasses reminiscent of Buddy Holly and favored among members of his current cult following.

The glasses might have helped a man born Declan McManus to see, but they framed the style and stage presence of Elvis Costello, making Declan the computer operator look every bit Elvis's intellectual/outcast/critic of society. Yes, even the stage name, taken from "the King" of popular rock 'n roll, is an attack on the music industry. In the face of an emerging, dance-happy new wave, *My Aim Is True* threw a monkey wrench in the commercialized system. While pseudo-angry, underground, punk rock bands only managed to reinforce the traditional conventions of the music industry, Elvis Costello and his band the Attractions presented a vastly talented, deliriously fresh voice for stale angst. Only an album with such sophisticated musical influences—think British Rock classics: the Beatles, the Kinks, and the Who meet Motown—could possibly be taken seriously when fronted by such a funny-looking guy. No glam rock. No gimmick. No apologies. No love songs.

Well—no love songs in the traditional sense, anyway. There is "Allison," the fifth track, and the reflective breath amidst a furious storm, the bluesy phantom that promises in its opening lines not "to get too sentimental like those other sticky Valentines." The music strikes a sorrowful chord, one any regretful lover could appreciate. Proving more elusive, the lyrics refuse the position of the heartbroken crooning for lost love. Instead, Costello once again widens the scope by reaching out for his more comfortable position as a keen observer, obscuring this obviously personal experience—so personal, in fact, that he no longer performs the song live. While affectionate and regretful, the song is also edgy and controlled. Using the encounter with a past flame to cynically portray marriage, Costello huskily vocalizes his disapproval, "Well I see you've got a husband now/did he leave your pretty fingers lying in the wedding cake/you used to hold him right in your hand/I bet it took all that he could take."

As quickly and comfortably as Elvis slipped into the introspective shoes of Allison, he ditches them for the furious funk of "Sneaky Feelings." One would get the impression that Mr. Costello must indeed have a closet full of shoes he fills quite perfectly. In "I'm Not Angry"— yeah, right—he sports a good pair of trainers. The first five seconds of fast guitar, intense keyboard and oddly timed cymbals are enough to get anyone running. No, Elvis Costello is not angry, he's irate. While some might mistake this as a chip on his embittered shoulder, the truth is that Elvis Costello's songs extend far beyond self-depreciation and personal failures. Take "Less Than Zero" for example—a song written in response to a disturbing broadcast he saw on T.V., the BBC segment on the supposed reform of Oswald Moseley, one of the British leaders of the fascist regime. Capturing what he sees as the ultimate decline of an already unraveling society, Costello creates a narrative in which Moseley is the main character, representing not only himself but consumer society at large. "Mr. Oswald has an understanding with the law/he said he heard about a couple living in the USA/they traded in their baby for a Chevrolet/let's talk about the future/we'll put the past away." This song shows that if London is welcoming the likes of Moseley back with open arms, it is no place for Elvis Costello.

Similar bitter irony is reflected in the songs "Waiting for the End of the World," "Cheap Reward," "No Dancing," and "Pay it Back." Okay, so Mr. Costello may never get the award for most happy camper. He *admits* in an interview that most of his songs are inspired by "regret and guilt." He *does* sing about failure and misunderstanding and bitterness and all the things people never want to talk about but feel all the time. He *really* used to keep a list—a blacklist—of all the record executives and industry bigwigs he saw as the root of musical evil. BUT. He managed to break the system. He got the last laugh. He made it. Unleashing his fury in the form of *My Aim Is True,* he broke musical ground. He blended jazz, funk, rock and new age with impeccable perfection. He said something that mattered at a time when no one was saying anything. He mastered language and music, introduced them, made them shake hands, then fight, then dance together and laugh about it all.

Most importantly, he didn't stop there. He went on to build a musical legacy. Not only did he record an expansive body of work showcasing his varying talents, he became a producer, guiding other brilliant bands. As a producer, Costello worked with bands as diverse as his own influences. One of these bands, the Specials, embodies the soul of two-tone ska, a musical genre emphasizing the importance of racial diversity and social consciousness. Another band that he worked with—The Clash—has been an instrumental part of the punk rock scene. Echoes of Costello can be heard in much of today's experimental indie rock. Elliot Smith, indie rock darling, cites Costello as a major influence. One of the most impressive contemporary songwriters, Smith wrote songs that while of a mellower and more melodic musical variety, echo the underdog sentiments popularized by Costello.

Perhaps his contribution to indie sensibilities of attitude and style are equal if less tangible than those he made in music. To be indie is to have a love of irony and embrace—on multiple levels—social awkwardness. In fact, indie owes much of this attitude to Costello. This "antiking" of pop was the first one to successfully bring these two elements into the spotlight. Traces of his fashion statement, namely the trademark glasses, can be seen among geek rock favorites like Weezer and on the faces of infinite "indie kids." And it all started twenty-four years ago. One little record untouchable in the eyes of major record labels. A record heralded by *Rolling Stone* as 1977's album of the year and remembered by VH1 as one of the best rock albums of all time. If the industry originally believed he had missed the mark, at least Elvis Costello knew he was right on target.

READING WRITING

## YOUR TEXT: READING
1. How would you describe the tone of this piece? Does it work for you? Why or why not? Is it appropriate for the type of writing she's doing?
2. How would you classify this piece? Is it a review? An essay? A paper? What makes you think so?

3. Why does the writer like Elvis Costello? How does she try to make others like him? Who does she think will like him? Look at specific places in the text where she does this work.

4. What other albums of a certain age deserve this type of revisiting? Name a few and talk about them in class.

## YOUR TEXT: WRITING

1. Do an assignment similar to Hawkins: Find an older album and re-introduce it to a younger crowd. What things might you have to consider about "youth" and "age" when doing this assignment?

2. Think about your criteria when choosing to listen to an album. How does that change when looking at an older album? Write a short paper about why you choose what you listen to.

3. If it's possible, go to the record collection of an older friend or relative and interview them about the experience with one of their favorite albums. Now go back and listen to it on your own and write a paper about your experience.

# Reading Music—The Song Suite

Our focus here is songs because we believe they are the basic element of music. Though we might think in albums, we feel in songs—their immediacy may engage our brain, but more often targets the heart. Albums to an extent are the extended element of an artist's vision, but a song often captures a feeling or a moment.

Here we've chosen a diverse group of pop songs and diverse approaches to them. Most if not all of these songs are familiar to you. "Johnny B. Goode" is a "classic" song from the 1950s, a song truly revolutionary for its time. So are "Coal Miner's Daughter," "Like a Rolling Stone," and "Smells Like Teen Spirit." In a paper written in 2001, student Matt Compton gives a cultural review of "Smells Like Teen Spirit," arguing that the song is the "perfect articulation" of American youth in the early 1990s. "Cop Killer" shows the machinery at work when a controversial song enters public consciousness.

---

## "JOHNNY B. GOODE"

### ■ Dave Marsh ■

BURIED DEEP IN THE COLLECTIVE UNCONSCIOUS of rock and roll there's a simple figure drawn from real life: One man, one guitar, singing the blues. But he's not any man. He's black, Southern, poor, and (this is the part that's easiest to miss) dreaming. In many ways, his story is terrible and terrifying. We're speaking after all of someone like Robert Johnson, by all the evidence every bit as sensitive and perceptive as, say, F. Scott Fitzgerald, but rather than pursuing lissome Zeldas through Alabama mansions, enduring the pitiless reality of sharecropping segregation, the threat of lynching, and all but inescapable twentieth-century serfdom in Mississippi.

Chuck Berry's genius lay in his ability to shape those gruesome facts into a story about joy and freedom. Not that he didn't have to make concessions to the reality he was subverting. He says in his autobiography that he wanted to sing "There lived a colored boy named Johnny B. Goode," rather than the "country boy" we now have, but "I thought it would seem biased to white fans." Especially, no doubt, those white listeners who programmed the radio stations that would determine whether the record became a hit or was not heard at all.

Already a star, Chuck Berry was on intimate terms with the pop game and the limits it imposed on famous men with black skin. Standing at the edge of the rules, Berry shot himself right past one crucial dilemma of American culture into the center of another. By changing "colored" to "country," he found that, instead of speaking for himself alone, he'd created a character who also symbolized the likes of Elvis Presley, another kid whose momma promised that "someday your name will be in lights." Horrible as the source of the compromise may have been, its effect was to treble the song's force. For ultimately, if you could identify with either Presley or Berry, there was a chance you could identify with both. The result is history—and not just pop music history.

But that isn't all. "Chuck Berry's gotta be the greatest thing that came along/He made the guitar beats and wrote the all-time greatest songs," the Beach Boys once sang. They knew this better than most since Brian Wilson not only converted "Sweet Little Sixteen" into "Surfin' U.S.A.," a tale oft-told because it wound up in court, but modernized "Johnny B. Goode," right down to the guitar intro, into that much less ambiguous anthem, "Fun Fun Fun."

You can't copyright guitar licks and maybe that's good, because if you could, Chuck might have hoarded them as he does his Cadillacs. Without The Chuck Berry Riff, we'd lose not just the Beach Boys, but essential elements of the Beatles, the Rolling Stones, Bob Dylan, Bob Seger, and Bruce Springsteen—to mention only the most obvious examples. In a way, what was at the center of the first wave of the British Invasion could be described as a Chuck Berry revival.

In those days, you weren't a rock guitarist if you didn't know the riveting lick that kicks off "Johnny B. Goode." Cut without echo or reverb, a basic progression that still demanded a suppleness that immediately separated the worthy from the merely aspiring, this—more than any other—is what people mean when they talk about "The Chuck Berry Riff." Throughout the record, that machine-gun burst of notes never leaves center stage, even after Chuck sprays out those indelible opening lines, each multisyllabic phrase all one word, a voice in imitation of a guitar:

> DeepdowninLouisiana'crossfromNewOrleans,
> waybackupinthewoodsamongtheevergreens.

Rattled off in just six seconds, it's the most exciting way that Berry could have found to sing the song, and he slows down only long enough to set the scene. When he hits the chorus, the guitar returns, splitting each phrase, propelling Chuck Berry toward fame, ecstasy, any old place he chooses that's gotta be better than here and now.

In the bridge, the riff—which by now seems to have its own life, separate from the guitar and whoever plays it—collaborates with Johnny Johnson's chugging piano to form the kind of solo conceived by guys who had to think on their feet in barrooms night after night, already beat from their day jobs but *hoping*. It's that hope that "Johnny B. Goode" drives home just like a-ringin' a bell.

## "LIKE A ROLLING STONE"

### ■ Robert Shelton ■

IN 1976, *NEW MUSICAL EXPRESS* CALLED IT "the top rock single of all time." It develops suspense right through its six minutes. At first, the narrator seems vindictive, as if he enjoys watching an overprotected person forced out into a cruel world. Dylan had little sympathy with those who hadn't fought easy comforts. Yet this and subsequent versions reveal a sad resignation that softens the tone of "I told you so." One night, I got Dylan to talk about this song:

"Why does everybody say of something like 'Like a Rolling Stone,' 'That Dylan . . . is that all he can do, put down people?' I've never put down anybody in a song, man. It's their idea. 'Like a Rolling Stone,' man, was very vomitific in its structure. . . . It seemed like twenty pages, but it was really six. I wrote it in six pages. You know how you get sometimes. And I did it on a piano. And when I made the record, I called the people who made the record with me, and I told them how to play on it, and if they didn't want to play it like that, well, they couldn't play with me. . . . When I wrote 'all you got to do is find a school and learn to get juiced in it,' I wasn't making this song about school. That's their idea. Their definition of school is much different than mine. My language is different than theirs. I mean REALLY TOTALLY DIFFERENT! The finest school, I mean, might just be out in the swamps. 'School' here can be anything. This song is definitely not about school."

He was probably using "school" as a symbol of a way of life. He sees horror enveloping anyone who suddenly makes a break after being closely attached to any form of life. For some, the experience is liberating; to others, it brings panic and helplessness. The "school-girl" he seems to be chastising here is probably anyone afraid to step out of his or her cocoon and into life's mainstream without guidance, parents, structure, or crutches. The words seem crueler on the page than they sound in performance. A song that seems to hail the dropout life for those who can take it segues into compassion for those who have dropped out of bourgeois surroundings. "Rolling Stone" is about the loss of innocence and the harshness of experience. Myths, props, and old beliefs fall away to reveal a very taxing reality.

Musically, the song jells beautifully; there is little feeling of prestudio rehearsal, just of a group that takes off on a splendid progression of chords. Dylan says the song was recorded in one take. The organ work—Al Kooper's strongly cohesive legato tones, the lighter filigree of runs and configurations—is brilliant. Thanks to Mike Bloomfield's guitar, even clichés are flavorful and skillfully timed. The drums swing brightly, while Dylan's voice urgently seems to anticipate the beat. The basic chord sequence is curiously familiar, suggesting "La Bamba," "Guantanamera," "Twist and Shout." Yet the massive, full sound moves away into a very complex structure. In *Backstage Passes*, Al Kooper tells how he improvised what is now a famous instrumental part to the delight of Dylan and all hands. Twenty years later, Dylan recalled recording it in a single day. Sara and he lived in a Woodstock cabin and he wrote it there. "It just came, you know," he said.

---

## "SMELLS LIKE TEEN SPIRIT"

### ■ Michael Azerrad ■

"IT WAS BASICALLY A SCAM," Kurt says of the song. "It was just an idea that I had. I felt a duty to describe what I felt about my surroundings and my generation and people my age."

One night, Kurt and Kathleen Hanna from Bikini Kill had gone out drinking and then went on a graffiti spree, spray painting Olympia with "revolutionary" and feminist slogans (including the ever-popular "GOD IS GAY"). When they got back to Kurt's apartment, they continued talking about teen revolution and writing graffitti on Kurt's walls. Hanna wrote the words "Kurt smells like Teen Spirit." "I took that as a compliment," says Kurt. "I thought that was a reaction to the conversation we were having but it really meant that I smelled like the deodorant. I didn't know that the deodorant spray existed until months after the single came out. I've never worn any cologne or underarm deodorant."

Virtually ever since he arrived, Kurt had been inundated with the Calvinists' discussions of "teen revolution" in Olympia coffee shops; after all, that's what bohemian people in their early twenties do—it's in the rule book. "I knew there was some kind of revolution," he says. "Whether it was a positive thing or not, I didn't really care or know."

The Calvinists would bridle at the comparison, but in many respects, teen revolution resembled the aims of the Woodstock Nation. It meant that young people were creating and controlling their own culture as well as their political situation, rescuing them from a cynical and corrupt older generation. The idea was to make youth culture honest, accessible, and fair in all respects—on the artistic side, on the business side, and even in the audience—making it the diametrical opposite of what corporate America had turned it into. After that, political change would be inevitable.

Kurt didn't doubt that the Calvinists were earnest and he liked their ideas, but he also was dubious about their prospects. He found their altruism naive—they didn't seem to realize it was all a pipe dream. "Everyone seems to be striving for Utopia in the underground scene but there are so many different factions and they're so segregated that it's impossible," Kurt says. "If you can't get a fucking underground movement to band together and to stop bickering about unnecessary little things, then how the fuck do you expect to have an effect on a mass level?"

Kurt even felt that pressure was being put on Nirvana to help with the revolutionary effort. "I just felt that my band was in a situation where it was expected to fight in a revolutionary sense toward the major corporate machine," says Kurt. "It was expected by a lot of people. A lot of people just flat out told me that 'You can really use this as a tool. You can use this as something that will really change the world.' I just thought, 'How dare you put that kind of fucking pressure on me. It's stupid. And I feel stupid and contagious.'"

So "Teen Spirit" is alternately a sarcastic reaction to the idea of actually having a revolution, yet it also embraces the idea. But the point that emerges isn't just the conflict of two opposing ideas, but the confusion and anger that that conflict produces in the narrator—he's angry that he's confused. "It's fun to lose and to pretend" acknowledges the thrill of altruism, even while implying that it's plainly futile. "The entire song is made up of contradictory ideas," Kurt says. "It's just making fun of the thought of having a revolution. But it's a nice thought."

Part of embracing the revolution is blasting the apathetic types who aren't part of it. Even Kurt admits that his generation is more blighted by apathy than most. "Oh, absolutely," he says. "Especially people in rock bands who aren't educated. That's also an attack on us. We were expected to shed a minimal amount of light on our ideals, where we come from, but we're not even capable of that, really. We've done a pretty good job of it, but that was never our goal in the first place. We wanted to be in a fucking band."

"Teen Spirit" sounds violent—the drums clearly take a vicious pounding, the guitars are a swarming mass of barely contained brutality, the vocals are more screamed than sung. "I don't think of the song like that," Kurt says. "It's really not that abrasive of a song at all, really. It only really screams at the end. It's so clean and it's such a perfect mixture of cleanliness and nice candy-ass production and there were soft spots in it and there was a hook that just drilled in your head throughout the entire song. It may be extreme to some people who aren't used to it, but I think it's kind of lame, myself."

Kurt's family turmoil may have had a lot to do with why Nirvana's music sounds so angry. "I'm sure it did," Kurt says, "but I have enough anger in me just toward society that I would definitely have looked for this kind of music anyhow."

Dave Grohl has a slightly different take on the song's message. "I don't think there was one, to tell you the truth," he says. "Most of it has to do with the title of the song, and that was just something that a friend had written on the wall. It was funny and clever. That, paired with the video of us at the pep rally from hell, I think that had a lot to do with it. Just seeing Kurt write the lyrics to a song five minutes before he first sings them, you just kind of find it a little bit hard to believe that the song has a lot to say about something. You need syllables to fill up this space or you need something that rhymes."

Impromptu scribblings aside, one remarkable aspect of "Teen Spirit" was that unlike many previous songs of its type, it didn't blame the older generation for anything—it laid the blame at the feet of its own audience. That implies a sense of responsibility that didn't quite fit the slacker stereotype. Although "Teen Spirit" was a bold and provocative dare, Kurt feels he crossed the line into condemnation. "I got caught up in pointing the finger at this generation," says Kurt. "The results of that aren't very positive at all. All it does is alienate people and make them feel the same feeling you get from an evil stepdad. It's like, 'You'd better do it right' or 'You'd better be more effective or I'm not going to like you anymore.' I don't mean to do that because I know that throughout the eighties, my generation was fucking helpless. There was so much right wing power that there was almost nothing we could do."

"I know that I've probably conveyed this feeling of 'Kurt Cobain hates his audience because they're apathetic,' which isn't the case at all. Within the last two years, I've noticed a consciousness that's way more positive, way more intelligent in the younger generation and the proof is in stupid things like *Sassy* magazine and MTV in general. Whether you want to admit that or not, there is a positive consciousness and people are becoming more human. I've always been optimistic, but it's the little Johnny Rotten inside me that has to be a sarcastic asshole."

"Introducing that song, in the position that we were in, I couldn't possibly say that I was making fun or being sarcastic or being judgmental toward the youth-rock movement because I would have come across as instantly negative. I wanted to fool people at first. I wanted people to think that we were no different than Guns n' Roses. Because that way they would listen to the music first, accept us, and then maybe start listening to a few things that we had to say, after the fact, after we had the recognition. It was easier to operate that way."

*Student Essay*

## "SMELLS LIKE TEEN SPIRIT"

■ **Matt Compton** ■

IN 1991 A SONG BURST FORTH onto the music scene that articulated so perfectly the emotions of America's youth that the song's writer was later labeled the voice of a generation (Moon). That song was Nirvana's "Smells Like Teen Spirit," and the writer was Kurt Cobain; one of the most common complaints of the song's critics was that the lyrics were unintelligible (Rawlins). But while some considered the song to be unintelligible, to many youth in the early 90s, it was exactly what they needed to hear. Had the song been presented differently, then the raw emotions that it presented would have been tamed. If the lyrics had been perfectly articulated, then the feelings that the lyrics express would have been less articulate, because the feelings that he was getting across were not clear in themselves. One would know exactly what Kurt Cobain was saying, but not exactly what he was feeling. The perfect articulation of those raw emotions, shared by so many of America's youth, was conveyed with perfect inarticulation.

1991 was a year when the music scene had become a dilute, lukewarm concoction being spoon-fed to the masses by corporations (Cohen). The charts and the radio were being dominated by "hair bands" and pop ballads; popular music at the time was making a lot of noise without saying anything (Cohen). Behind the scenes "underground" music had been thriving since the early eighties. Much of this underground music was making a meaningful statement, but these musicians shied away from the public eye. The general public knew little about them, because they had adopted the ideology that going public was selling out (Dettmar). Nirvana was a part of this "underground" music scene.

In 1991 Nirvana broke the credo, signing with a major label, DGC, under which they released the chart-smashing *Nevermind*. "Smells Like Teen Spirit" was the first single from the record, and it became a huge hit quickly (Cohen). Nirvana stepped up and spoke for the twenty-something generation, which wasn't exactly sure what it wanted to say (Azerrad

223–233). A huge part of America's youth felt exactly what Cobain was able to convey through not just "Smells Like Teen Spirit" but all of his music. Nirvana shot into superstar status and paved the way for an entire "grunge" movement (Moon). No one complained that they could not hear Cobain, but many did complain that they could not understand what he was saying.

Kurt Cobain did not want his music to just be heard and appreciated; he wanted it to be "felt" (Moon). His music often showed a contrast of emotions; it would change from a soft lull, to a screaming rage suddenly. And few could scream with rage as could Cobain (Cohen). There is a Gaelic word, "yarrrrragh," which ". . . refers to that rare quality that some voices have, an edge, an ability to say something about the human condition that goes far beyond merely singing the right lyrics and hitting the right notes." This word was once used to describe Cobain's voice by Ralph J. Gleason, *Rolling Stone* critic (Azerrad 231). It was that voice, that uncanny ability to show emotions that Cobain demonstrated in "Smells Like Teen Spirit."

Cobain's raging performance spoke to young Americans in a way that no one had in a long while (Moon). Michael Azerrad wrote in his 1993 book, *Come as You Are: The Story of Nirvana,* "Ultimately it wasn't so much that Nirvana was saying anything new about growing up in America; it was the way they said it" (Azerrad 226). Cobain's music was conveying a feeling through the way that he performed. It was a feeling shared by many of America's youth, but it was also a feeling that could not have been articulated any way other than the way that Cobain did it (Cohen).

"Smells Like Teen Spirit" starts out with one of the most well-known guitar riffs of the 90s. The four chord progression was certainly nothing new, nothing uncommon. The chords are played with a single guitar with no distortion, and then suddenly the bass and drums come in. When the drums and bass come in the guitar is suddenly distorted, and the pace and sound of the song changes. The song's introduction, with its sudden change, forms a rhythmic "poppy" chord progression to a raging, thrashing of the band's instruments (Moon), sets the pace for the rest of the song.

The chaos from the introduction fades, and it leads in to the first verse, which gives the listener a confused feeling (Azerrad 213). In the first verse the tune of the song is carried by the drums and bass alone, and a seemingly lonely two-note guitar part that fades in and out of the song. The bass, drums and eerie guitar give the listener a "hazy" feeling. Here Cobain's lack of articulation aids in the confused feeling, because as he sings, one can catch articulate phrases here and there. The words that the listener can discern allow them to draw their own connections. Cobain's lyrics do in fact carry a confused message, "It's fun to lose, and to pretend" (Azerrad 213).

The pre-chorus offers up clear articulation of a single word, but this articulation is the perfect precursor to the coming chorus. As the first verse ends, the pre-chorus comes in; Cobain repeats the word "Hello" fifteen times. The repetition of the word Hello draws the confusion that he implicates in the first verse to a close, and in a way reflects on it. As the tone and inflection of his voice changes each time he quotes "Hello," one is not sure whether he is asking a question or making a statement, or both. It is like he is saying, "Hello? Is anybody at home?" while at the same time he exclaims, "Wake up and answer the door!"

The reflection that he implicates in the pre-chorus builds to the raw raging emotions that he expresses in the chorus, as the guitar suddenly becomes distorted, and he begins to scream (Azerrad 214, 226). In the chorus he screams, but somehow the words in the chorus are actually more articulate than those in the verse. As Cobain sings, "I feel stupid, and contagious," anyone who has ever felt like a social outcast understands exactly what Cobain is saying (Cohen), and they understand exactly why he must scream it.

I remember the first time that I heard that line and thinking about it; I was about thirteen, and I thought that there was no better word than "contagious" to describe the way it feels being in a social situation and not being accepted. Because no one wants to be around that person, they will look at the person with disgust, as if they have some highly *contagious* disease. There is certainly a lot of anger and confusion surrounding those feelings. People needed to hear Cobain scream; they knew how he felt, because they knew how they felt.

People who were experiencing what Cobain was expressing understood what he was saying, because they understood how he felt. In much the same way when someone hits their hand with a hammer that person does not lay down the hammer and calmly say, "Ouch, man that really hurt." They throw the hammer down, and simultaneously yell an obscenity, or make an inarticulate roar, and one knows that they are going to lose a fingernail. Anyone who has smashed their finger with a hammer understands why that person is yelling; in the same way anyone who has felt "contagious" or confused about society knows why Cobain is screaming about feeling "stupid and contagious." Cobain is not examining society. He is experiencing the same things as his audience (Moon); he is "going to lose a fingernail." As the chorus draws to a close, the music still rages, but it changes tempo and rhythm slightly.

The chorus is the most moving part of the song; it is a display of pure emotion. In the chorus Cobain demonstrates what it was that connected with so many; his lyrics said what he meant (Moon). But what he said had been said before, and whether he was articulate or not, people felt what he meant. It was the articulation of that feeling that gained the song such high praise (Moon).

The chorus ends with the phrase, "A mulatto, an albino, a mosquito, my libido"; this line is a reference to social conformity. Cobain is referring to things, or the ideas associated with them that are "outside" of social conformity, and then relating those things back to himself with the phrase "my libido" (Azerrad 210–215). This end to the chorus again goes back to reflect on the feelings expressed in the chorus, and ties them together with a return to the confusion expressed in the verses.

The articulation of the lyrics in the second verse gives the confusion more focus than in the first verse. He begins the second verse with the lyric, "I'm worse at what I do best, and for this gift I feel blessed." Although the lyrics are more articulate in the second verse, the feelings of confusion are still there, due to the tempo and rhythm of the music. After Cobain has sung the second verse he returns to the pre-chorus, the repetition of the word Hello. The cycle begins anew.

"Smells Like Teen Spirit" in its entirety gives the listener a complete feeling after listening to it, especially if that listener is feeling confused and frustrated. The song carries one through an entire cycle of emotions, from confusion, to reflection, to frustration. Tom Moon, a Knight-Ridder Newspaper writer, described Nirvana's music as having moments of "tension and release." Being carried through those emotions allows the listener to "vent" their own feelings of confusion and frustration, and at the same time know that someone else feels the same way (Azerrad 226–227). Despite the connection that Cobain made with many there were still many who did not "get" the song; these people often complained about the inarticulation of the lyrics (Azerrad 210).

Weird Al Yankovic utilized the common criticism of the song in his parody "Smells Like Nirvana"; Yankovic parodied "Smells Like Teen Spirit," based entirely on Cobain's obscure articulation. Yankovic is known for parodying popular music, and with lines such as, "And I'm yellin' and I'm screamin', but I don't know what I'm saying," Yankovic stated exactly what so many of the song's critiques had, though he did it with a genuine respect for the song, and its impact (Rawlins).

Weird Al Yankovic's version struck a note with many who liked Cobain's music but could not understand his lyrics (Rawlins). There were many people who did not understand the feelings of confusion, frustration, and apathy that Cobain was getting across. In 1991 when "Smells Like Teen Spirit" first came out I was only 9, and I did not like that kind of music at all. I remember my brother, who is nine years older than me, and who listened to a lot of "heavy metal," bought Yankovic's *Off the Deep End,* with his parody "Smells Like Nirvana" on it. He thought it was funny because he did not like Nirvana. He never really connected with Cobain's message; even though he did not get what Cobain was saying, he could still enjoy the music. When I became older I did connect with Cobain's music, and Nirvana was one of my favorite bands. My brother never did understand, like many people who never did understand what it was that Cobain was saying (Azerrad 210).

Nirvana made the generation gap clear. It was Nirvana that spoke for a large part of that generation (Moon), where no one else had ever really addressed the confusion and frustration about growing up in America at that time, or at least no one had expressed it in the same way that Nirvana did. They were not the first to vocalize a problem with corporate America, but they were the first *popular* band to convey the feelings that many were feeling *because* of growing up in corporate America, in the way that they did. Cobain did not just show that he has experienced those feelings, but that he was still *experiencing* them, and many young people connected with that (Moon).

In 1992 singer-songwriter Tori Amos illustrated why Cobain's "Smells Like Teen Spirit" had connected with so many by making a cover of the song that was a clear contrast to the original. She rendered the song with a piano, and a clear articulate voice. Her cover of the song became fairly popular, because it was different, and because many people could now understand the lyrics that Cobain had already popularized (Rawlins). The cover was interesting, to say the least; however, it would have been impossible for her version ever to have had the same impact as Cobain's (Rawlins). The lyrics to the song have meaning, and depth, but the emotions that the song conveyed were in and of themselves abstract.

Amos's version of the song articulated each word clearly, her clear voice hit each note on key; her song was comparable to a ballad. Cobain's "Smells Like Teen Spirit" could be described as "sloppy," his guitar distorted through much of the song; he either screamed or mumbled most of the song (Azerrad 214). The two versions of the song illustrate a clear contrast: it is as if Cobain is "angry about being confused" (Azerrad 213), while Amos sings the song to lament Cobain's feelings.

Amos's version of the song became popular for the same reason that it could never have paved the way as Cobain's version did. It was like a ballad, and after everyone heard what Cobain was saying, about society, about America, about growing up, there is one clear emotion that follows the confusion and frustration: sadness. Her "ballad-like" cover of "Smells Like Teen Spirit" exemplified that sadness. But at the same time, people had written ballads about being confused or frustrated, and performed them as Amos performed "Smells Like Teen Spirit"; that was nothing new. However, no one had yet *demonstrated* such clear and yet abstract confused, frustrated emotions as Cobain did, and at that moment in time that was exactly what America needed to hear (Azerrad 224–225).

Cobain had written and performed a song about his own confusion, and in the process he had connected with young people all over the United States (Moon). He had helped those people to understand their own confusion better. The problem with "Smells Like Teen Spirit" was not that Cobain was not articulate; he could not have articulated his point more clearly than he did. The problem was that not everyone knew what he was talking about, just like not everyone knows what it is like to strike their finger with a hammer. And in the same way, if someone doesn't know what it is like they might say something foolish like, "That couldn't hurt *that* bad," or "What's *his* problem?" when someone else hits their finger with a hammer, and they make an inarticulate roar. That roar expresses exactly what that person is feeling, but only those who know that feeling can really understand it. As Michael Azerrad, author of *Come as You Are: The Story of Nirvana* put it, "you either get it, or you don't" (Azerrad 227). Thus was the case with Cobain's music. "Smells Like Teen Spirit" was his inarticulate roar; it was articulate in that it expressed exactly what he was trying to point out; however, not everyone could grasp what that was.

Works Cited

Azerrad, Michael. *Come as You Are.* New York: Doubleday, 1993.

Cohen, Howard and Leonard Pitts. "Kurt Cobain Made Rock for Everyone but Kurt Cobain." *Knight Ridder/Tribune* 8 April 1994: Infotrac.

Dettmar, Kevin. "Uneasy Listening, Uneasy Commerce." *The Chronicle of Higher Education.* 14 Sept. 2001: 18. Lexis-Nexis.

Moon, Tom. "Reluctant Spokesman for Generation Became the Rock Star He Abhorred." *Knight-Ridder/Tribune* 9 April 1994. Infotrac.

Nirvana. *Nevermind.* David Geffen Company, 1991.

Rawlins, Melissa. "From Bad to Verse." *Entertainment Weekly.* 5 June 1992: 57. Infotrac.

## "COAL MINER'S DAUGHTER"

### ■ Alessandro Portelli ■

*When I state myself, as the Representative of the Verse—it does not mean me—but a supposed person.*

—Emily Dickinson

## 1.

There is a scene in Robert Altman's *Nashville,* in which a singer with long wavy black hair steps on the stage at Opryland, sings a song and then, as the band starts vamping for the next number, breaks into a rambling speech, which soon turns into a loose reminiscence of childhood:

> I think there's a storm a-brewing. That's what my granddaddy used to say before he lost his hearin' and sometimes he'd say, "Oh gosh," or "Durn it," or "My word" . . . My granny, she'd go round the house clickin' her false teeth to the radio all day. She was a lot of fun, and al-

ways cooked my favorite roast beef and she was a sweetheart. She raised chickens, too. She, uh—in fact, did ya ever hear a chicken sound?[1]

This scene is a fictionalized account of the most famous crackup in country-music history: that of Loretta Lynn in the early '70s. An authorized version of the same episode appears in a later film, Michael Apted's *Coal Miner's Daughter,* based on Loretta Lynn's autobiographical book by the same title (the episode, however, is not discussed in the book). Both films concur in showing the breakdown as an eruption of private memories: a compulsive autobiographical act.

## 2.

The book takes its title, in turn, from Loretta Lynn's best and most successful song, "Coal Miner's Daughter." The song appears at first hearing as another autobiographical act, containing many features of Lynn's later descriptions of her own life: the sentimental cliché ("We were poor but we had love"), the precise description of background details, the relish in the sound of vernacular speech. In her book, Lynn says:

> I'd always wanted to write a song about growing up, but I never believed anybody would care about it. One day I was sitting around the television studio at WSIX, waiting to rehearse a show. . . I went off to the dressing room and just wrote the first words that came into my head. It started: "Well, I was borned a coal miner's daughter. . .", which was nothing but the truth.[2]

Before we go on to examine her autobiographies, let us take a quick look at Loretta Lynn's life. She was in fact born a coal miner's daughter in the mid-Thirties in Western Kentucky; she barely learned to read and write, married at thirteen, followed her husband to Washington state, worked hard, live poor, had four children by the time she was eighteen (was a grandmother at twenty-nine), and never though of a career in music until she was twenty-four. Since then, she has moved to Nashville, had two twin daughters, and worked her way up to be the most successful female country singer and one of the most successful entertainers in the history of show business.

It was more than a year before Lynn and her entourage could bring themselves to issue "Coal Miner's Daughter" as a record. The time in which the song was "kept. . . in the can" seems like a metaphor for a repressed autobiographical urge. Lynn says that she did not think that people would be interested in a song about her life; in fact, the first important decision in autobiography is always accepting that one's life is worth telling in public. Once the song hit the charts, however, all doubts were removed, and the floodgates of autobiography were thrown open. In further songs, interviews, ceremonies, and finally in a book and a film, the story of the coal miner's daughter, the Washington housewife, the Nashville Opry star was told over and over, in a variety of media but with remarkable consistency.

> I was given up when I was a baby. I came close to drowning near my ranch a few years ago. I never told anybody about that until now. And the doctors told me that my heart stopped

---

[1]*Nashville,* screenplay by Joan Tewkesbury (New York: Bantam Books, 1976), no page numbers.
[2]Loretta Lynn with George Vecsey, *Coal Miner's Daughter* (New York: Warner Books, 1980), p. 201. All further quotations will be indicated in the text with page numbers.

on the operating table when I had chest surgery in 1972. Ever since then, I've wanted to tell my life story (p. 18).

Autobiography as a response to a death threat is a standard concept not necessarily to be taken at face value. In fact, the song "Coal Miner's Daughter" was composed before Lynn's surgery. It is a fact, however, that telling her life story means more to Loretta Lynn than the public relations gesture it is for many other public figures.

In 1974, an interviewer asked her how country music had changed since she came to Nashville. Most musicians would be content to give a professional answer to this professional question. But terms like "change" and memories of coming to a new place start a whole other chain of associations in Loretta Lynn's mind:

> I didn't live in Nashville. Of course I had never been any place except I went to the state of Washington—my husband sent for me and I went on the train. I was pregnant. . . .[3]

The interviewer comes back to the original question shortly afterwards, asking "How has country music changed?"—and again Lynn digresses freely, associating autobiographical thoughts:

> It seems like everything has changed. When I was growing up. . . like for me to see a loaf of bread [. . .] There ain't many people live the way we did in Butcher Holler, and Butcher Holler has changed.

When asked about career and business, Lynn almost compulsively responds in terms of her early life, of before she became a professional musician. There is an undeniable degree of authenticity in this urge, as the episode of the breakdown confirms, an inner need. On the other hand, the autobiographical urge also sells. Within a year after "Coal Miner's Daughter," she had three more singles out with songs of an autobiographical nature, signaling both the open floodgates of autobiography and the sequels to a commercial hit—from coal mine to gold mine, as it were. "Coal Miner's Daughter" becomes a trademark, designating a song, a bestselling book, a major movie, a publishing company (Coal Miner Music), a band (Lynn's backup group changed names, from Western—Trailblazers—to Appalachian—Coal Miners).

On the other hand, some members of the band did come from coal mining families, and all were supposed to have been factory workers at one time (at least, this is the point she was making at the time her autobiography was written). The same sign, then, designates a commercial gimmick, and a factual truth: the constant tension in all of Loretta Lynn's autobiographical image-making and soul-searching. The most obvious example of this process is, of course, her name. Contrary to the practice of many stars, she did not change her name (which happens to possess the feature of alliteration, highly prized in advertising); on the other hand, her name increasingly designates objects other than her person—her voice, her image, her records, all the way to Crisco shortening and franchised western wear stores.

---

[3]Rick Broan and Sue Thrasher, "Interview with Loretta Lynn," February 25, 1974, typescript (courtesy of Sue Thrasher). The interview appeared in *The Great Speckled Bird;* Lynn refers approvingly to it in *Coal Miner's Daughter,* p. 91.

**3.**

If we look at the front and back cover of a paperback edition of *Coal Miner's Daughter* (in this case, the 1977 Warner paperback), we find there one of the most concise statements of the nature of autobiography anywhere. The two pictures—the glamorous star on the front, the bucktoothed little girl on the back—are the same person, and yet two different people. The contrast shows the distinction between past and present selves, public and private lives, which creates the inner tension in the autobiographical genre; and it also underlies that this contrast takes place within what remains, after all, one and the same person.

Structurally, this means that autobiography has much in common with metaphor. A metaphor is the discovery of similarity in a context of difference: "Achilles is a lion" makes sense as a metaphor precisely because Achilles is not a lion. Jean Starobinski has pointed out that in order for autobiography to exist, there must have been a change, a dramatic development in the subject; I would stress the fact that the change is only significant because the subject remains the same. The difference between the narrating and the narrated self is worthy of our attention because these two selves happen to belong to the same person.

This is true also at another level. Autobiography is a public performance; but the story teller is expected to reveal the private self in it. On one level, the autobiographer is supposed to abolish the difference between public and private self; on another, this act is only relevant inasmuch as the reader is constantly reminded that the two selves are logically distinct. "One does not dress for private company as for a public ball," says Benjamin Franklin, the founding father of modern autobiography; and Nathaniel Hawthorne muses that "it is scarcely decorous to speak all."

This double metaphorical structure is best expressed in the autobiographies of stars. Their success story enhances difference and change, but they always strive to prove continuity and identity insisting that success has not changed them; they build an elaborate public image, but must persuade their fans that it also coincides with their private selves. Country music as a genre claims sincerity to a very high degree, linking it closely with autobiography: "A hillbilly is more sincere than most entertainers," Hank Williams used to say, "because a hillbilly was raised rougher."

In fact, the ideal country star must be born in a cabin and live in a mansion, like Loretta Lynn; and, as she does, must travel back and forth between them, at least in imagination. Most importantly, they are expected to live in a mansion as they would in a cabin. Stars must look dazzlingly glamorous on the stage, declaring distance; but must open their homes to visiting fans and tourists, stressing familiarity. No wonder autobiography is also a thematic staple in so many country songs.

> My fans and writers—says Lynn—are always making a big deal about me acting natural, right from the country. That's because I come from Butcher Holler, Kentucky, and I ain't never forgot it. [. . .] We're country musicians; I don't think we could play our kind of music if we didn't come from little places like Butcher Holler (p. 59).

In her book, Lynn presents herself as a regular housewife (an image doubled by her Crisco commercials), who has some problems with her husband but still understands and loves him, who hangs drapes and even worries about where the money for the children's braces is coming from. "When you're lookin' at me, you're lookin' at country," she sings; "I was Loretta Lynn, a mother and a wife and a daughter, who had feelings just like other women," she says (p. 151). And yet—if she were just another housewife, mother, and daughter, who would buy her book and see her movie? But then—*who* is she? As in most autobiographies, the answer is blowing somewhere along the continuum of past and present, public and private.

### 4.

Let us begin with public and private. *Coal Miner's Daughter* opens in the bedroom; there's another bedroom scene two pages later, and early in the book Lynn describes her wedding night in detail. These, however, are not love scenes. In the opening episode, she has a nightmare and winds up bloodying her husband's nose with her wedding ring; the next thing she mentions is the gun her husband keeps on the night table. The wedding night scene, though ostensibly humorous, describes a rape: "He finally more or less had to rip off my panties. The rest of it was kind of a blur" (p. 78).

One one level, Lynn is grappling with inner dreams and deepseated fears; on another, she is casting herself in the folksy role of the country girl whose mother never told her about the facts of life and who—"just like other women"—had to find out the hard way. The autobiographical urge merges with the commercial image-making: Lynn takes her fans into her bedroom, but then resents the invasion and hides.

This is true also literally. When she was in the hospital, "the fans heard I was in bed [and] they trooped right into my room and started taking pictures" (p. 163). Every year, Loretta Lynn opens her house to thousands of fans, in a ritual of reunion between the star and her social constituency that blurs the line where the public ends and the private begins. Fans "just pop into my kitchen when we're sitting around. It sounds terrible, but I can't relax in my own home," she complains. So she winds up checking in at a motel—leaving her private residence to seek shelter in public places. The same process function in the autobiographies: the need to show and the need to hide establish a constant tension. She displays her inner self to the public, but when the public gets there she has retired somewhere else—and regrets it, and thinks "it's terrible."

A similar contradiction occurs in the relationship between past and present. Being a coal miner's daughter is both an inner identity actively sought and a mask imposed by business associates and fans. Fidelity to roots is an authentic part of herself as well as a role imposed from outside. Thus, in order to play up continuity she is forced to repress the changes that make her what she is. She speaks dialect freely and spontaneously, but a critic has noticed that "from time to time, she will repeat a word which she has pronounced correctly, only to repeat it *incorrectly* (as *born* to *borned*), almost as though she were reminding herself."[4]

Thus, the same sets of signs designate truth and fiction, spontaneity and manipulation. Loretta Lynn does artificially what comes naturally—like speaking dialect—and does naturally what comes artificially—like wearing a mask.

### 5.

All the theory and practice of autobiography revolve around the first person pronoun, "I." The question is, what does Loretta Lynn mean, to what exactly does she refer, when she uses that word?

---

[4]Dorothy A. Horstman, "Loretta Lynn," in Bill C. Malone and Judith McCulloch, eds., *Stars of Country Music* (Urbana: University of Illinois Press, 1975), p. 32.

Let us consider the songs first. When she sings "I was borned a coal miner's daughter," she is using the autobiographical first person; but when she sings "I'm a honky tonk girl," her first hit, she is using the fictional-lyrical first person of popular song. These two meanings of "I" interact intensively in her work. Because she uses autobiography so much, many songs that are not about herself have been taken for autobiography: an exchange favored by the fact that in all her repertoire Lynn consistently projects a character based very much upon herself, the spunky woman who does not question the system but won't take no nonsense from nobody—"Don't Come Home a-Drinkin' with Lovin' on Your Mind" because "Your Squaw's on the Warpath Tonight."

The interaction of autobiographical and fictional-lyrical "I" generates intermediate forms: first-person songs, written by herself, but not autobiographical; first-person songs, written by others, but based on aspects of her life. She wrote "The Pill," a song about contraceptives which was one of her most controversial hits, though she says she hardly ever used it herself (it would have been harder to write, and sell, a song about her husband's vasectomy, which she talks about in the book). On the other hand, "One's On the Way"—a vivid description of a housewife with four kids, a careless husband, maybe twins on the way, the pot boiling over, and the doorbell ringing—is based on recollections of her early married life, but was written by Shel Silverstein. There is even another Shel Silverstein song, called "Hey, Loretta," in which Lynn sings to herself as if she were somebody else.

To further confuse matters, there is the problem of performance. Singers—like all oral performers—present even the most impersonal material through their body and their voice, thus making it intrinsically personal. Even when she performs someone else's songs, Lynn steps closer to an autobiographical act, although it might not be technically described as such. On the other hand, when Emmylou Harris records Lynn's "Blue Kentucky Girl," the autobiographical overtones are lost.

In conclusion, there are at least four meanings of the word "I" as used in Lynn's repertoire and performances, going from the purely autobiographical to the purely fictional-lyrical, through at least two intermediate forms. Each of these forms shades or may turn into another through the processes of performance and reception.

Much the same can be said about the book. A capsule definition of autobiography is based on the coincidence between the hero and the narrator inside the book's covers and the author outside: they all have the same name. But if we look at the cover of *Coal Miner's Daughter,* we see that the names on the cover are split: "by Loretta Lynn with George Vecsey." *Coal Miner's Daughter* is one of those "as told to" autobiographies in which famous people delegate the writing to a professional when they are too busy or unable to take care of it themselves. Although these books are billed as autobiographies, the person who says "I" in them is not the same person that does the actual writing. Loretta Lynn makes no pretense about it: George Vecsey is frequently mentioned in the text as "my writer," in the third person. In quite a postmodern fashion, Vecsey writes about himself in the third person, about somebody else in the first, and enters his own text as a character in someone else's story: while he writes his own name, he pretends that this is Loretta Lynn talking about him. One assumes that, when the "I" character is different from the author, we are dealing with fiction; *Coal Miner's Daughter,* however, is supposed to be factually straight. The only fiction about it has to do with the uses of the first person.

With the film, we take another step. By definition, there can be no autobiographical film in the strict formal sense. When a book is turned into a film, the first consequence is the disappearance of the first-person narrator: films are always in the third person. In the movie *Coal Miner's Daughter* (whose credits are reproduced on the back cover of the paperback) the "author's" name on the cover is Michael Apted, filming a screenplay by Tom Rickman based on the book written by George Vecsey as told by Loretta Lynn. The face and voice on the screen belong to Sissy Spacek. Yet, the name is still Loretta Lynn: the film is clearly intended as a "true" statement, largely meant to "set the record straight" after *Nashville*. Many side characters in *Coal Miner's Daughter* actually play themselves, reinforcing the "documentary" overtones.

We come full circle when we turn to the paperback and discover that the film has been incorporated into the book. First of all, as we have already pointed out, the book displays the film credits, making it look as if the book was a novelization of the film: the written autobiography is somehow validated by having been the subject of a fictional movie. In the second place, the images from the film are also included in the book.

In the book, indeed, Loretta Lynn tells her story not one, but three times: with words, with photographs from her family album, with stills from the movie. The two sets of photographs are almost interchangeable: the family album's captions, however, are in the first person, while those of the movie stills are in the third. But the pictures themselves are sometimes hard to tell apart. The picture of Loretta Lynn in her first stage outfit is so similar to the one of Sissy Spacek wearing the replica of it that they perform a sort of reversal of the autobiographical process: while the pictures on the cover portray two different people who are yet the same person, those two photographs inside portray one character who is in fact two different persons. It may not be irrelevant, in the book's rhetorical structure, that the film stills come before the family album: it looks as though Loretta Lynn's photos were patterned after Sissy Spacek's. Which, of course, has been the problem all along: which of the two, the image or the person, is the real one, which one comes first.

## 6.

In a passage in *The Day of the Locust,* Nathanael West describes the main female character, Faye Greener, as she tries out one identity after another:

> She would get some music on the radio, then lie down on her bed and shut her eyes. She had a large assortment of stories to choose from. After getting herself in the right mood, she would go over them in her mind, as though they were a pack of cards, discarding one after another until she found one that suited. On some days, she would run through the whole pack without making a choice[. . .] While she admitted that her method was too mechanical for best results [. . .] she said that any dream was better than no dream.[5]

Let us compare this passage to one from *Coal Miner's Daughter,* in which Lynn describes her belief in reincarnation—a subject clearly related to the question of the mutable and multiple self.

---

[5]Nathanael West, *The Day of the Locust,* in *The Collected Works of Nathanael West* (Harmondsworth, Midds.: Penguin, 1975), p. 60–61.

I once read that you could feel your past lives if you concentrated real hard. So I tried it in my hotel room. I wasn't asleep but kind of in a trance. I lay down quiet and let my mind drift.

All of a sudden I was an Indian woman wearing moccasins and a long buckskin dress and I had my hair in pigtails. Even the sound and smell were vivid to me. All around me there was a huge field with Indians riding horseback. I was standing next to a mounted Indian. I sensed that he was about to go off into battle, and I was saying good-bye to him. Then a shot rang out, and my husband fell off his horse [. . .] In the second such experience, I saw myself dressed up in an Irish costume, doing an Irish dance down a country lane in front of a big white house (p. 98).

Loretta Lynn is part Cherokee, and almost as proud of her Indian blood as she is to be a coal miner's daughter. The rest of her ancestry is the Scots-Irish stock prevalent in Appalachia. As she thumbs through her past lives, she meets her ancestors: the idea that one's past lives are those our ancestors lived is not as flat a banality as one would expect in the autobiography of a star. Like Faye Greener's second-hand dreams, however, Loretta Lynn's earlier selves are fashioned after artificial patterns. The Indian warrior chief on horseback is more reminiscent of plains Indians, of Western movie Sioux, that of a mountain Cherokee. The "big white house" is a plantation house, and in anybody's book an Irish girl in front of a Southern plantation house is named Scarlett O'Hara. "I never picture myself after Scarlett O'Hara," says Lynn later in the book—but she makes this claim in the context of buying her new house because its "huge white columns" remind her of Tara (p. 136). The more she seeks inside to find her true self, the more she encounters someone else's fictions.

The paradox in *The Day of the Locust* is that, by having only masks and no face, Faye Greener achieves a sort of purity: she hides nothing, because there is nothing to hide. She is incapable of deceit because she lives in a world (Hollywood, which is to her what Nashville is to Loretta Lynn) in which deceit is real life and fiction is the only truth.

*The Day of the Locust* anticipates many developments which would later be labelled as "postmodern"; it concerns the relationship between mass culture, the fragmentation of the self, the erasure of distinctions between image and substance, sign and referent, truth and fiction in a universe in which image is the only substance and signs are the only referents of signs.

"In country music," Lynn complains, "we're always singing about home and family. But because I was in country music, I had to neglect my home and my family" (p. 140). Let us not be deceived by the sentimental wording: these are the only words she has, but her problem is serious. She is dealing with the disappearance of reality in a sign-dominated universe. Success in country music is based on foregrounding the autobiographical ingredient (one need only think of the early Dolly Parton and Merle Haggard); but the more an artist achieves success, the less "life" there is to talk about. In many cases, this erosion of reality turns the autobiographical urge of country music toward the writing of songs about being a country-music singer—metasongs like self-reflexive postmodern metanovels about novels, composed much for the same causes.

In Loretta Lynn, we can see the autobiographical impulse grow stronger while her career develops, as if she were groping back toward a time when she was a nobody but knew who she was (or now thinks she did). She lives through some of the basic problems with which many contemporary intellectuals are concerned, and deals with them with her limited means and ambitions, in the most direct way there is: by trying her level best, over and over again, to tell the story of her life.

<table>
<tr>
<td>

**COP OUT? THE MEDIA, "COP KILLER,"
AND THE DERACIALIZATION OF BLACK RAGE
(CONSTRUCTING [MIS]REPRESENTATIONS)**

■ **Christopher Sieving** ■

</td>
</tr>
</table>

FOR ABOUT SEVEN WEEKS in the sizzling summer of 1992, the most contentious issue in American society was not about who deserved to be elected to the presidency in the upcoming election or what should be done to rebuild the nation's second largest city after it had suffered the worst civil disturbances in the United States in a century and a half. Instead, the most hotly debated concern involved a black, thirtyish rap artist named Tracy Marrow (better known as Ice-T) and the multimedia conglomerate (Time Warner) that represented him. Specifically, at issue was a song Ice-T recorded for Sire/Warner Bros. Records with his thrash-metal band, Body Count. The sentiments evoked in the lyrics to "Cop Killer," Ice-T's detractors cried, constituted an exhortation to kill police officers. For two months, the recording industry, public officials, police groups, and civil liberties advocates squared off over the right to express and circulate these ideas in public, culminating with Ice-T's "voluntary" withdrawal of the song on July 28.

The public debate over "Cop Killer" was unique in many respects, but perhaps one of its most striking characteristics was that only a tiny minority of Americans actually heard the song at all. "Cop Killer" was not played on the radio, it was not shown on MTV, and the album on which it appeared (*Body Count*) sold fewer than 500,000 copies before the song was permanently withdrawn from distribution. For this reason, the key issues for a cultural analysis of the "Cop Killer" controversy involve how the song was put into discourse and circulated in other forms of media. If "Cop Killer" was too "hot" for direct experience, the American press was more than willing to supply its own mediated versions. This is how L.A. County Supervisor Gloria Molina, one of the many elected officials who called on Time Warner to have "Cop Killer" withdrawn, initially encountered it: "I have not listened to this song, but I am convinced by what I've read in news accounts that this is a totally inappropriate rap (sic) song" (Goldberg 1992, M2).

The willingness with which interested parties accepted versions of Ice-T's words at least once removed from the context he had intended them to appear in should remind one of Foucault's ideas on the social dimensions of discourse, as modified by John Fiske. In an age marked by a promiscuity of image and sound representations, no person may dictate the ways in which they are represented. "The way that experience, and the events that constitute it, is put into discourse," Fiske (1996, 4) writes, "is never determined by the nature of experience itself, but always by the social power to give it one set of meanings rather than another." Ice-T's experience, his black knowledge (to use another of Foucault's terms) of the policing system in Los Angeles, entered into dramatic contestation with white power. To retain its status of truth, white power had to repress Ice-T's black knowledge by seizing control of it and making it mean in very different ways. To a large extent, it succeeded.

The explosive racial dimensions of the "Cop Killer" affair also dictate a close examination of the media's part in fanning the flames of controversy. The ways in which candidates Dan Quayle, Bill Clinton, and George Bush employed the press to attack "Cop Killer," Ice-T, and black culture in general have been duly noted and are consonant with the methods by which the presidential and vice presidential candidates used race as a wedge issue in 1992. Furthermore, some critics, including Robin D.G. Kelley (1996, 131), have also noted the media's substantive role in creating and putting into discourse the notion of a black, criminalized "underclass," that shadowy, nebulous body responsible for all of America's social ills.

While accusations of the white-controlled American media's complicity in the promulgation of '90s-style institutional racism are well founded, it is also true, as Tricia Rose (1994, 101) alludes to in her study of rap and black culture, *Black Noise,* that the current-day system of mass cultural production—"mass-mediated and mass-distributed"—grants oppressed groups far greater access to popular media than previously possible. "The media" are not a homogeneous blob, devouring all potential discourses that run counter to the ideology of capitalist enterprise. Rather, they are a site of struggle, analogous to Gramsci's notion of "common sense," as explained by Stuart Hall (1980, 20–21). The conservative Right's "family values" battled Ice-T's black consciousness in the media for a place within the common sense of the American public. The fact that Ice-T's black consciousness lost the battle—his words erased from the public record—does not mean that the war is unwinnable. Through a close analysis of the strategies and countertactics used by both sides in the "Cop Killer" dispute, I hope to clarify how Ice-T's case was weakened by the misguided attempts of his defenders to deracialize "Cop Killer." Their disarticulation of lower-class black struggle from the debate mirrored, and thus empowered, the strategies employed by their detractors. In analyzing how this was accomplished, I hope to provide suggestions on how to avoid similar tactical mistakes in the racial and cultural clashes of the future.

*Body Count* was released by Sire/Warner Bros. in March 1992. The first album recorded by Ice-T's rock band, it was his first group project for the label after four gold-selling solo albums. The album's tracks, all recorded between September and December 1991, were mostly versions of songs the group had performed on tour with the previous summer's Lollapalooza festival. *Body Count* closed with "Cop Killer," a staple of the band's live show. In a spoken-word lead-in, Ice-T "dedicated" this final track to "every cop that has ever taken advantage of somebody, beat 'em down or hurt 'em" out of blind prejudice or race hatred (*Body Count* 1992b). Ice-T's lyrics (the music was written by lead guitarist Ernie C.), printed in full in the accompanying CD booklet, forcefully dramatized the vengeful intent of the song's narrator. Switching between first- and second-person address, the would-be Cop Killer describes the ritual of preparing for an ambush ("I got my black gloves on/I got my ski mask on") before serving notice to his target: "I know your family's grieving, but tonight we get even." The narrator's motivation for settling the score is, at first, purely personal ("A pig stopped me for nuthin'!"); later, a call-and-response chorus suggests a larger, more broadly social revenge: "Fuck the police, for Rodney King/Fuck the police, for my dead homies" (*Body Count* 1992a).

Such sentiments raised few eyebrows prior to the late spring of 1992—the period of L.A.'s black and Latino uprisings in the wake of the acquittals in the Rodney King trial. In early June, however, "Cop Killer" was condemned publicly for the first time: a Dallas police captain, writing in his column for the Dallas Police Association newsletter, urged his readers to "boycott any and all Time Warner products and movies until such time as they have recalled this tape" (Duffy and Orr 1992). This suggestion was immediately taken up and amplified by the Combined Law Enforcement Association of Texas (CLEAT). CLEAT's press conference on June 11 at Six Flags amusement park in Arlington broke the story nationwide. In calling for a boycott of Time Warner entertainment (including Six Flags), CLEAT director Mark Clark specified who his organization was targeting (and previewed a major discursive strategy of the anti-"Cop Killer" forces): "Our quarrel is not with Ice-T, but with the beautiful people that run Time Warner who like to present themselves as being in the business of family entertainment . . . the people who made a decision to reap huge dividends by distributing music that advocates the murder of police officers" (Philips 1992a). Within a week, the New York State Sheriff's Association joined ranks with CLEAT, and Alabama Governor Guy Hunt called for a statewide ban on selling the *Body Count* album. This initial burst of protest culminated with Dan Quayle's attack on Time Warner for "making money off a record that is suggesting it's O.K. to kill cops" at a luncheon for the National Association of Radio Talk Show Hosts ("Vice President Calls Corporation Wrong" 1992).

Why "Cop Killer"? Why did this song prove to be such an attractive target for conservative forces? Why did the formation of a strong counterdiscourse in opposition to Ice-T's ideas come to be seen by the nation's power brokers as a top national priority? The motives were many and varied. The justification most often given for opposing the distribution of "Cop Killer"—the fear that it would incite murder and mayhem—was undoubtedly a genuine one for some. But their concern does not explain why this particular work—one of countless mediated representations of violence—was singled out for special criticism.

Three major contextual factors brought about the targeting of "Cop Killer" at this time. One was the growing white hostility toward certain types of rap music. The increasingly confrontational style of several major rap artists put the genre on a collision course with white authorities by the late 1980s. The outcry over Professor Griff's (of Public Enemy) anti-Semitic remarks in a *Washington Times* interview, the NWA song "— tha Police" (which Ice-T cites in "Cop Killer"), and the 2 Live Crew album *As Nasty as They Wanna Be* influenced the increasingly negative coverage of rap in the mainstream press. As public hysteria broke out over the nation's perceived inability to contain its hyperviolent black population, rap music came to be seen as the original sin of the underclass. The equation of black crime with black culture was made explicit by pundits such as George Will (1990), who implied that the sexual violence depicted in 2 Live Crew's lyrics influenced the infamous Central Park "wilding" incident of April 1989. And Timothy White (1991), in a controversial *Billboard* editorial, condemned Ice Cube's 1991 album *Death Certificate* for advocating violence against Koreans and Jews. Although *Body Count* was not a rap group (and "Cop Killer" was not a rap song), it was drawn into this nexus by virtue of employing Ice-T (noted "gangsta" rapper, who had previously been singled out by Parents' Music Resource Center head Tipper Gore for the "vileness of his message") (Donnelly 1992, 66) as its lead singer.

The L.A. rebellion of late April and early May 1992 further helped to foreground in the minds of white Americans the link between rap artists and black insurrection. In the absence of "rational" (white) explanations for the destruction of South Central L.A., television, radio, and print coverage of the rebellion relied heavily on the contextualizing commentary of rappers, those whose music provided, in Alan Light's (1992a, 15) words, the only "source . . . available to communicate the attitudes of inner-city America to the white mainstream." Ice-T quickly emerged as one of the "hard-edged rappers" the *Washington Post* later designated as "[spokespersons] for the black lower class, delegates of America's angry youth" (Mills 1992, B1). Yet, for all the likeminded opinions expressed in the media on the premonitory power of L.A. hard-core, an equal number of dissenters felt that rap had incited, as opposed to predicted, the violence that followed the first Rodney King verdict. Ice Cube's (1991) rap "Black Korea," an attack on South Central's Korean store owners, was frequently cited by columnists for its couplet "Pay respect to the Black fist/Or we'll burn your store right down to a crisp." For some white Americans, residual hostility toward the rioters and "looters" surely fed the hostility toward those black cultural voices who claimed to represent them.

Finally, Bill Clinton's criticisms of rapper/activist Sister Souljah (Lisa Williamson), occurring just three days prior to Quayle's attack on "Cop Killer," helped to legitimate the vilification of rappers as an election year discursive strategy. Democratic candidate Clinton, following Jesse Jackson at a Rainbow Coalition convention, denounced remarks made by Souljah in a *Washington Post* interview ("I mean, if black people kill black people every day, why not have a week and kill white people?") (Mills 1992, B1). While it may have been the case (as was widely believed) that Clinton was more concerned about his appeal with conservative voters than about the impact of Souljah's words, the immediate result of his Rainbow Coalition address was to put rap on the political map. In the scramble for swing issues (à la Willie Horton) they could claim as their own, Republicans were only too receptive to the increasingly vocal cries of the upholders of law and order.

In the wake of Dan Quayle's condemnation on June 19, police organizations across the country pledged to support CLEAT's call for a Time Warner boycott; in addition, the 23,000-member National Sheriffs Association spearheaded a movement to persuade sympathetic law enforcement organizations with Time Warner investments to divest ("Quayle, Congressmen" 1992, 83). State officials began calling on Time Warner to withdraw *Body Count* from the marketplace. In Los Angeles, councilwoman (and congressional candidate) Joan Milke Flores and the Los Angeles Police Protective League—echoed later by the Los Angeles Police Commission—motioned for just such a ban in a city council meeting (Philips 1992b). A Florida sheriff petitioned the state attorney general to investigate whether Time Warner's marketing of "Cop Killer" violated sedition laws, an action also advocated by Iran-Contra figure Oliver North ("Count Rises" 1992, 74). Perhaps most significantly (and ominously), sixty congressional representatives (including three Democrats and fifty-seven Republicans) sent a letter to Time Warner vice president Jeanette Lerman stating that the conglomerate's "decision to disseminate these despicable lyrics advocating the murder of police officers is unconscionable" ("Quayle, Congressmen" 1992, 83).

As the controversy was reaching fever pitch, Time Warner held its annual shareholders' meeting on July 16 at the Regent Beverly Wilshire Hotel in Beverly Hills. As had been anticipated for weeks, the meeting was infiltrated by angry police group representatives and conservative spokespersons such as 2 Live Crew prosecuting attorney Jack Thompson (who was roundly booed) and Charlton Heston, who recited the lyrics to "Cop Killer" and "KKK Bitch" (a second *Body Count* song) to the stunned stockholders. Time Warner president and co-CEO Gerald Levin fielded hostile inquiries indoors, while outside the hotel around thirty protesters (some of whom reportedly chanted "Ice-T should be put to death") (Trent 1992) picketed the corporation (Morris 1992b, 71).

The result of this highly visible, direct confrontation was perhaps surprising, at least for the protesters: Time Warner refused to budge. In public, Levin continued to uphold the right of his artist to express himself in accordance with his First Amendment rights. In response, his opposition turned up the heat even further. Following a July 21 appearance by Ice-T on *The Arsenio Hall Show*, Hall's office received a flood of threatening phone calls from angry viewers (Shaw 1992). On July 23, *The Today Show* fanned the flames of the controversy by broadcasting excerpts from a home video of Ice-T addressing a crowd of L.A. urban dwellers on the third day of the Los Angeles rebellion; in the video, Ice-T tells the crowd that "police ain't shit to me and never will be. . . . They're a Gestapo organization in Los Angeles and until you start taking them cops down out here in the street, then y'all still fucking pissing in the wind, you know what I'm sayin'?" (Morris 1992c, 83). Most seriously, as reported in *Entertainment Weekly,* Time Warner's headquarters had received at least one bomb threat, while "one exec received a phone death threat from an anonymous bigot who called him a 'nigger-loving Jew'" (Sandow 1992).

As he would later recount in his book *The Ice Opinion,* the various threats made to Time Warner executives and to his own fifteen-year-old daughter played a pivotal part in Ice-T's decision to voluntarily pull "Cop Killer" from the *Body Count* album (Ice-T and Siegmund 1994, 176). In his press conference of July 28, Ice-T announced that Time Warner would cease the distribution of *Body Count* in its original form. Subsequent editions of the album would not contain the "Cop Killer" track.

Jon Pareles (1992b, C13), writing in *The New York Times* the day following Ice-T's press conference, was one of many who appreciated the irony of the "Cop Killer" protest, acknowledging the protesters' "part in building the album's popularity." The notoriety bestowed on the *Body Count* album clearly boosted its sales; in the month prior to Ice-T's announcement, *Body Count* had sold about 100,000 copies, despite the fact that at least a half-dozen major music retailers refused to carry it. (Barry Layne [1992], writing one month earlier in *The Hollywood Reporter,* dryly noted that "the first fruits of [CLEAT's] action . . . was a tripling of '*Body Count*' album sales in the Lone Star state.") The demand for the album immediately intensified upon news of its withdrawal; by the beginning of August, *Body Count* surged from number seventy-three to number twenty-six on *Billboard*'s pop album chart, and runs on the original version were reported in several cities ("A Run on Ice-T's Album" 1992).

So what did these police organizations and public officials gain from publicizing an album and a song that might otherwise have barely registered on the cultural imaginary? Quite a bit, in fact, and a close reading of the discursive strategies these white-dominated groups employed during the "Cop Killer" controversy throws some of these suppressed motivations into sharp relief.

"Cop Killer" posed a problem for those who wished to demonize it. It was written and performed by a black group; thus, those who called for its censoring risked appearing overtly racist. The musician who wrote the lyrics was primarily associated with rap music, a form increasingly unpopular with "middle" America; however, the song was not, strictly speaking, a rap song. Furthermore, the sentiments of "Cop Killer" were protected by the First Amendment, and the song had the backing of a gigantic, American-owned conglomerate—a powerful symbol of free market enterprise.

How, then, could "Cop Killer" be fought? What strategies could be employed, and what sentiments could be exploited? Not surprisingly, the strategies the Right eventually settled on were, for the most part, profoundly deracializing. Even though racial difference had played an undeniable role in the creation, transmission, and reception (an *Entertainment Weekly* poll found that "nearly 60 percent of nonblacks said they were angry at [Ice-T], as opposed to 34 percent of blacks") (Sandow 1992) of "Cop Killer," its critics had to recode that difference as something "beyond" race. The discursive strategy summed up by the now-familiar tenet "race had nothing to do with it" that had been deployed, with some success, just weeks earlier in the official white reaction to the L.A. rebellion. *The Source* editor James Bernard (1992) noted how the news media's riot coverage had focused almost exclusively on the "mindless" destruction of black-owned businesses as "a particularly tragic example of Black-on-Black violence, that these people wouldn't even give their own hardworking middle class a chance" (p. 41). In doing so, reporters and newscasters implied (and, at times, explicitly stated) that the rebellion was not motivated by anger over racial injustice but by sheer lawlessness, or that it was, as *Billboard*'s Chris Morris (1992a) described it, simply "beyond rational explanation." It is no surprise, then, that this discourse of deracialization was applied in the attacks on Ice-T's black rage. What is surprising is how often the defenses against these attacks were equally deracializing.

## Reaccentualization

As the U.S. market economy and its institutions have become more integrated over the past several decades, the importance of language as a way to construct one's identity, to create one's own space—in sum, to serve as a tactic of resistance—has exploded. Perhaps the most helpful theoretical explication of the defiant social uses of language is found in Russian philosopher Volosinov's (1973) *Marxism and the Philosophy of Language*—particularly in his conception of accentuality. He argues that words do not have predetermined, fixed meanings; rather, the "meaning of a word is determined entirely by its context. . . . It is precisely a word's multiaccentuality that makes it a living thing" (pp. 79, 81). Volosinov's observation that "in the alternating lines of a dialogue, the same word may figure in two mutually clashing contexts" is certainly applicable to the debate over the meaning of the "Cop Killer"'s lyrics (p. 80). These words, spoken with a black accent by Ice-T, are spoken with a white accent by Charlton Heston and thus "mean" in vastly different ways. Heston's July 16 reaccenting of "Cop Killer" verifies Volosinov's idea that accent is where the social politics of the speaker enter the linguistic system. Heston's imposition of the voice of white authority so completely changed the original black meaning of the song that, for many of the shareholders in attendance, the song now seemed to contain its own rebuttal. An L.A. resident who heard Heston's recitation over KFI radio certified the objectives of this reaccenting in her letter to the *Los Angeles Times:* "It was rather startling to listen to such words coming from the magnificent voice of Moses, Andrew Jackson, John the Baptist, but I am grateful to him for expressing this aspect of the album" (Agreda 1992).

As a counterstrategy, Heston's reaccenting method is much subtler than the explicit race baiting found in a contemporaneous piece for the *National Review,* in which James Bowman (1992, 37) doubts "that Sister Souljah or Ice-T or even the Los Angeles ghetto dwellers for whom both of them have at various times purported to speak are actually oppressed; rather, they have inherited from their ancestors, who were, a form of speech and imagery characterized by a kind of fantastical moral chiaroscuro." In the end, Heston's is clearly the more effective strategy, as it was readily taken up by the mainstream; the attempt to account for racially differentiated modes of reception is relegated to the pages of a marginal right-wing periodical.

It seems apparent, then, that one way to counter the widespread deracialization of "Cop Killer" would have been to call attention to its black accent and to the ways in which meaning is struggled over by blacks and whites. Thomas Kochman's (1981) account of "fighting words" in his influential book *Black and White Styles in Conflict* illustrates the cultural framework that governs the codes used in urban black language. Kochman's research on the use of fighting words in both black and white communities demonstrates that

> angry verbal disputes [or woofing], even those involving insults and threats, can be maintained by blacks at the verbal level without violence necessarily resulting. . . . On the streets

[woofing's] purpose is to gain, without actually having to become violent, the respect and fear from others that is often won through physical combat. (pp. 48, 49)

Ice-T himself says as much when he declares that "within my community, rap is verbal combat. We get around a lot of fights and aggression simply by talking" (Ice-T and Siegmund 1994, 103).

The failure of Ice-T's defenders to use a theoretical framework such as Kochman's to explain the verbal arrows slung throughout *Body Count* is perhaps attributable to the white community's inability to conceive of fighting words as anything but an invitation to physical aggression; according to Kochman (1981, 48), "whites tend to see the public expression of hostility as a point on a words—action continuum." The furor over "Cop Killer" illustrates the full extent of white ignorance, conscious or not, of what John Fiske (1996, 187) terms "sociocultural conventions that are clear to [their] native speakers." During the controversy, Ice-T repeatedly asserted that language is raced and expressed his frustration with having to explain his lyrics to whites. Before deciding to withdraw the *Body Count* album, Ice-T told *Time* that "[white America] shouldn't sweat us on what words we use with each other. I hate to say rap is a black thing, but sometimes it is" (Donnelly 1992, 66). Unfortunately, white America refused to listen to his admonitions.

## Decontextualization

The reaccenting of "Cop Killer" by white voices was mirrored by the selective excerpting of the song's lyrics by its opponents. By extracting certain lines (or "sound bites," to borrow a phrase) from the context of the song, the album, and Ice-T's body of work in their entirety, Ice-T's opponents more easily succeeded in making his statements fit their own discursive project, one that explained the song in terms of brutal lawlessness. Bill Clinton put the strategy of decontextualization to use in his attack on Sister Souljah; not only did Clinton ignore the meaning of Souljah's *Washington Post* comments within the larger context of the L.A. rebellion, but he ignored the whole of the quotation itself:

> I mean, if black people kill black people every day, why not have a week and kill white people? You understand what I'm saying? In other words, white people, this government and that mayor were well aware of the fact that black people were dying every day in Los Angeles under gang violence. So if you're a gang member and you would normally be killing somebody, why not kill a white person? Do you think that somebody thinks that white people are better, or above dying, when they would kill their own kind? (Mills 1992, B1)

*The Today Show* aided Clinton's efforts by broadcasting only one segment of Sister Souljah's music video, a segment in which a white police officer is shot and killed by a black woman (Leo 1992). The context for the character's action—the reimplementation of slavery in the United States—was excised from NBC's "sampling."

To my knowledge, the lyrics to "Cop Killer" were never reprinted in full in any mainstream or "general-interest" American magazine or newspaper (even though they were readily available to anyone who took a look at the album's sleeve). *The Los Angeles Times'* initial report on the boycott excerpted what would become perhaps the most reprinted verse of the song, "I got my 12 gauge sawed off/I got my headlights turned off/I'm 'bout to bust some shots off/I'm 'bout to dust some cops off" (Philips 1992a). Paul M. Walters (1992) repeated this excerpt in his *Times* op-ed piece of July 8, adding that "the verse and chorus that follow are far too vulgar to discuss." This sentiment was apparently shared by Mike Royko (1995, 175), who deleted the "obscenities" from the portion of the song he cited in his June 23 syndicated column, and by the National Rifle Association, whose full-page advertisements in the June *26 USA Today* and the June 28 *Washington Times* quoted the chorus to "Cop Killer" as "DIE PIG DIE! (expletive) the Police . . . don't be a (expletive). Have some (expletive) courage . . . I'm a (expletive) Cop Killer!" ("White Time Warner Counts Its Money" 1992).

The forced dislocation of the Cop Killer's murderous intentions from the rest of his narrative served to frame his imagined crimes as groundless. The intent of extracting, for example, only the words "'bout to dust some cops off" and "die, pigs (sic), die" from the song, as was the case in an Associated Press report of June 19, was to justify the application of just such a meaning ("Rapper Ice-T Defends Song" 1992). Thus, Michael Kinsley (1992), writing in both the *New Republic* ("Momma Dearest" 1992) and *Time*, can point to the call-and-response chorus and the line "I know your family's grievin'—f—'em" as evidence that "Cop Killer'"s message is that "premeditated acts of revenge against random cops . . . is a justified response to police brutality" (Kinsley 1992). Few media pundits agreed with Ice-T's claim ("better you than me . . . if it's gonna be me, then better you") (Ice-T and Siegmund 1994, 168) that the song's protagonist acts in self-defense; none, to my knowledge, excerpted the spoken-word track that prefaced the song on the *Body Count* CD.

Like the Rodney King and the Latasha Harlins videos, with which there are intriguing parallels, "Cop Killer" was almost never publicly "aired" in its entirety; the public knew little, even during the height of the furor, of what preceded the "fuck the police" chorus. Few of Ice-T's defenders, in fact, looked to the larger context of the album (the only way in which "Cop Killer" could be experienced, as it received no radio play and was not commercially available as a single); had they done so, they would have discovered a song titled "The Winner Loses," which puts forth an unequivocally anti-drug statement at odds with white America's conception of the narcoticized young black male. While it should be apparent why the anti- "Cop Killer" contingent felt it necessary to suppress Ice-T's larger critique of racially differentiated policing, it is less understandable why Ice-T's defenders failed to reintroduce this critique into the context of the debate.

## Articulation with Sexism and Racism

Volosinov's (1973) shifting of the social struggle paradigm from the traditional Marxists' class-versus-class model to a more heterogeneous subordinated model allows for the cultural analyst to admit that a step forward in racial politics may represent a step backward in gender politics. John Fiske's (1996, 66) notion of multiaxiality, informed by the realization that "because power is everywhere, it flows along all the axes of social difference," modifies Volosinov's and Foucault's ideas through observing that the knowledge flowing along a single axis of power often works by repressing other knowledge. Critics such as Robin D. G. Kelley (1996, 143) understand this when they qualify their endorsements of contemporary urban black culture, such as rap, with stinging critiques of the misogyny and homophobia of several leading black artists (including Ice-T). It is clear even to rap's defenders that rap's struggle over race cannot be won by repressing the gender struggle, as many male rappers have discovered.

Although "Cop Killer" makes no mention of gender issues, critics frequently articulated its message with the misogyny (alleged or otherwise) found elsewhere on *Body Count*, in

Ice-T's rap music, and in mass culture in general. The editors of the *Los Angeles Times* placed "Cop Killer . . . in the dubious tradition of a long line of exploitative commercial work, along with heavy-metal songs that bash gays, women or minorities" ("Outrage and Ice-T" 1992); Sheila James Kuehl (1992) added that "like too much of rap, the cuts before and after 'Cop Killer' are an insistent demand, a veritable how-to, of multilated women." Kuehl, a director at the California Women's Law Center, enriches the debate by bringing the question of woman-bashing to the table, but her more hyperbolic statements are far removed from the outright distortions advanced by Charlton Heston (1992), who falsely asserted that "KKK Bitch" advocated the raping of women and the sodomizing of "little girls."

More problematic than accusations of sexism, however, is the articulation of black rap with racism against whites. David Samuels's (1991, 28) assertion (voiced in a notorious 1991 *New Republic* cover story on "the black music that isn't either") that rap reduces racism to "fashion" is typical of the rhetoric that asserts that contemporary racism is the product of inflammatory black people, with whites serving as the victims. "Cop Killer" was frequently articulated (and, by implication, equated) with anti-Semitic expression, despite the fact that several Time Warner executives—those who most consistently defended Ice-T's work—were Jewish. At the July 16 Time Warner shareholders meeting, Charlton Heston asked Gerald Levin, a Jew, "[if] that line were 'Die, die, die, Kike, die,' would Time Warner defend it then?" while CLEAT president Ron DeLord compared Time Warner executives to Joseph Goebbels (Morris 1992b, 71).

Another favorite strategy of critics of Ice-T and Sister Souljah—including Bill Clinton (Philips 1992c, Calendar 6), John Leo (1992), and Barbara Ehrenreich (1992)—was to link their black adversaries with ex-Klansman and defeated Louisiana gubernatorial candidate David Duke. *The New Republic* even linked "Cop Killer" to George Bush's infamous Willie Horton ad ("Momma Dearest" 1992). These types of strategies served to disarticulate white, illegal policing methods from public discussions of racism. The qualitative difference between the racist effects of, on one hand, lynchings and the Holocaust and, on the other hand, black resistance to racially motivated police brutality in Los Angeles was never explained.

## Corporatization

Perhaps the most common deracializing strategy used by Ice-T's opponents during the "Cop Killer" controversy was one of corporatization, or the transference of blame for "Cop Killer"'s potential ill effects from its author to the company that distributed it. The idea that the kinds of messages black rap acts choose to advance are dictated by their white employers is one that had gained significant credibility within the white media by the summer of 1992; David Samuels's (1991) *New Republic* article had perhaps the most success in popularizing this theory.

A strategy such as this might seem counter to the conservative agenda. However, if one adopts Gramscian notions of "hegemony" and "common sense," it becomes easier to understand how conservative capitalists could recast the issue as a referendum on corporate ethics. Stuart Hall (1980, 16) has remarked on how Gramsci's conceptualization of hegemony "implies that the actual social or political force which becomes decisive in a moment of organic crisis . . . will have a complex social composition. . . . Its basis of unity will have to be, not an automatic one, given by its position in the mode of economic production, but rather a 'system of alliances.'" Under late capitalism, there may be (and frequently are) splits within social groups lumped together by ideology theorists under the category of "ruling class"; the alliance between corporate America and the political Right forged along the economic axis is susceptible to breakdown along the cultural, moral, or legal axes.

The "Cop Killer" case is perhaps the clearest manifestation of this principle from this decade. In Foucauldian terms, Ice-T's black knowledge entered into contestation with white knowledge; to retain its status as "troth," white knowledge found it necessary to repress that of Ice-T. However, in order for white power to operate at maximum efficacy within a hegemonic order, it has to exercise its power "invisibly." The problem, then, for these white interests lay in the fact that the censoring of an artwork, especially one created by blacks, is bound to be very visible. By recoding the debate as an issue of ethics, Quayle, Heston, and their compatriots were allowed to talk about race through nonracial discourse.

From the very beginning, those opposed to "Cop Killer" couched their opposition in terms of corporate responsibility. When Ice-T addressed his audience at the New Music Seminar in New York on June 19 and stated "if the cops got a problem, let them come after me, not Time Warner," Mark Clark of CLEAT responded in *The New York Times* that the issue "is Time Warner making a corporate decision to make a profit off of a song that advocates the murder of police officers and they are the ones we are going to attempt to hold accountable" (Rule 1992, C16). In his speech of the same day, Dan Quayle implied that the inability of the U.S. government to revoke Ice-T's free speech rights dictates that Ice-T's sponsor be targeted in his stead ("Vice President Calls Corporation Wrong" 1992). As was the case in his Murphy Brown speech one month earlier (a speech primarily comprising his observations on the causes of the L.A. rebellion), Quayle avoided charges of election year race baiting by recoding race problems into the effects of the nation's poverty of values. George Bush echoed Quayle's strategy two weeks later at an appearance at a new Drug Enforcement Administration office in Manhattan. "I stand against those who use films or records or television or video games to glorify killing law enforcement officers," Bush proclaimed. "It is wrong for any company—I don't care how noble the name of the company—it is wrong for any company to issue records that approve of killing law enforcement officers" (Rosenthal 1992). The will with which police organizations avoided assigning responsibility to Ice-T reached its height after the artist decided to pull the song, when a representative of the Los Angeles Police Protective League lauded Ice-T for showing "more intestinal fortitude than Time Warner" (Cusolito 1992).

Stuart Hall (1986, 53) conceives of articulation as the formation of linkages, "the form of the connection that can make a unity of two different elements, under certain conditions." The fluid status of any one articulation necessitates the articulation of elements that, in that particular combination, expose the artificiality of the dominant articulation. In recoding "Cop Killer" as the product of an unethical corporation, Quayle and his colleagues disarticulated what Ice-T's defenders needed, but barely attempted, to rearticulate: the links between black hostility toward police officers and the racist system of policing in the United States.

This is not to say that all of those who opposed the distribution of "Cop Killer" employed the strategies of deracialization to denigrate it before the eyes of middle America. Some critics, such as James Bowman (1992) in the *National Review*, risked accusations of racism by drawing articulations between the (presumed) black audience for *Body Count* and the white stereotype of the hyperviolent, narcoticized black criminal. Doug Elder, president of a Houston police organization, warned that "Cop Killer," when mixed "with the summer, the violence and a little drugs (sic) . . . [will] unleash a reign of terror on communities all across this country," while the head of the Fraternal Order of Police opined that "people who ride around all night and use crack cocaine and listen to rap music that talks about killing cops— it's bound to pump them up" (Donnelly 1992, 66; Philips 1992b). These articulations are relatively oblique compared with Rush Limbaugh's: On his syndicated radio show, Limbaugh labeled Ice-T's fans "savages and the people who beat up Reginald Denny" (Pollack 1992).

A more subtle form of racialization was performed by the countless number of reporters, officials, and spokespersons who referred to "Cop Killer" and *Body Count* as rap music rather than metal. Rose's (1994, 130) claim that, within white discourse, metal fans are "victims of its influence" whereas rap fans "victimize us" helps to clarify the purpose behind the shift in labeling. Ice-T is thus correct to assert that the word rap was used during the "Cop Killer" debate to "[conjure] up scary images of Black Ghetto" (Ice-T and Siegmund 1994, 170); even the widespread, less misleading use of the designation "rapper Ice-T" served a similar end.

And yet the tracks on *Body Count* are rap, in a certain sense; more specifically, *Body Count* is a "rock album with a rap mentality," as Ice-T himself has suggested (Light 1992b, 30). Sans sampling, the rap "mentality" manifests itself on *Body Count* not only in the gritty, urban scenarios carried over from Ice-T's solo projects but in Ice's clipped, decidedly nonmelodic vocal delivery. I wish to suggest that the considerable fuss raised by Ice-T and his comrades over the media's use of the term rap to categorize "Cop Killer" is misdirected and in fact serves to obscure the debate's more significant implications as explained throughout this article.

The fact that Ice-T's defenders repeatedly, if unknowingly, participated in obscuring these implications is perhaps the most revealing aspect of the media coverage of the controversy. A range of tactics was used to discredit the conservative attacks on "Cop Killer," yet for the most part these avoided assessing the efficacy of Ice-T's message as a strategy of resistance. Instead, many in the pro-Ice-T faction chided their opponents for believing a rock song could inspire its listeners to murder. "Entertainment is about fantasy and escapism," asserted ACLU chair Danny Goldberg (1992) in a *Los Angeles Times* column: "literalism has nothing to do with entertainment" (p. M2). Goldberg's thesis is founded in the timeworn axiom "it's only a representation," a justification that rings somewhat hollow in an alleged age of Baudrillardian "hyperreality."

Another common tactic used by Ice-T's supporters was to articulate *Body Count* with "legitimate" (i.e., white) art. Writers, including David Hershey-Webb (1995) and Jon Pareles (1992b), decontextualized "Cop Killer"'s black American origins and specificity by placing the song within American culture's "long-established anti-authoritarian streak that often casts the police as symbols of oppression" (Pareles 1992b, C13). Likewise, Barbara Ehrenreich (1992) and Chuck Philips (1992c) invoke rock heroes Bob Dylan, the Beatles, the Rolling Stones "and the other '60s icons who stormed the gates of the Establishment" (Philips 1992c, Calendar 6). "Look, white artists wrote anti-Establishment songs, too," these pundits seem to argue, using a kind of logic easily adaptable for those who wished to associate "Cop Killer" with more commonly denigrated white forms of entertainment. Ehrenreich (1992), Andrew Rosenthal (1992), and Ice-T himself (Philips 1992d) duly noted that neither Dan Quayle nor George Bush saw fit to condemn the cop-killing character played by Bush supporter Arnold Schwarzenegger in *The Terminator* and *Terminator 2: Judgment Day,* while Pareles (1992a) blasted police associations for failing to call for a boycott of "any of the Warner film studio's so-called 'body count' movies." While Pareles's intent may have been to simply bring about a more level playing field, his articulation of "Cop Killer" and Schwarzenegger shoot-em-ups furthers the wrenching of Ice-T's words from their social context.

The most consistent tactic used to support Ice-T's right to express the sentiments of "Cop Killer" was the invocation of his rights under the First Amendment. Employed so frequently that it served as the discursive counterpart to the opposition's corporate ethics articulation, the freedom-of-speech defense was first established by Time Warner in its initial "official" response to the CLEAT boycott: "Time Warner is committed to the free expression of ideas for all our authors, journalists, recording artists, screenwriters, actors and directors. We believe this commitment is crucial to a democratic society, where the full range of opinion and thought—whether we agree with it or not—must be able to find an outlet" (Philips 1992a). The mainstream news media immediately took the bait Time Warner had set: Peter Jennings (1992) defined the "Cop Killer" furor as a "freedom of speech" story on the June 19 telecast of *World News Tonight*. The recording industry and civil liberties groups rallied around Time Warner on these grounds. The president of Capitol Records/EMI Music informed the *Los Angeles Times* that "when you realize that this giant multibillion-dollar corporation is taking a free-speech stand on a record that barely sold a few hundred thousand copies, there can be only one reason why they're holding their ground. It's a matter of principle" (Philips 1992c, 77). The call to ban "Cop Killer" became, to some extent, a free speech issue for Ice-T as well; in the altered version of the album sold by Time Warner starting in August, the First Amendment appears in place of the printed lyrics to "Cop Killer" in the *Body Count* cassette inset and CD booklet.

The freedom-of-speech defense for "Cop Killer" is deficient in many ways, not the least of which is how its use seemed to endorse the defense of the work only on these grounds. Editorials in both *Billboard* and the *Los Angeles Times* lamented that ink had to be spilled in defense of a song "repugnant . . . to most law-abiding citizens," an "artless and mediocre effort" ("Body Count: The Issue Is Censorship" 1992; "Outrage and Ice-T" 1992); the *Times* reminded Time Warner that "while Americans highly value their strong First Amendment rights, they weary of the Constitution being trotted out to justify any hate-filled, titillating venom that hits the airwaves or bookstores" ("Outrage and Ice-T" 1992). This kind of rhetoric—used to oppose a ban on "Cop Killer"—perhaps influenced Ice-T's later thoughts on the controversy:

> I didn't need anybody to come and say I had the fight to say it. I needed people with credibility to step up and say, "Ice-T not only has the fight to say it, but also fuck the police! . . . We're not apologizing to you cops for what YOU'VE been doing. It's time for people to get angry along with the guy who wrote 'Cop Killer'." (Ice-T and Siegmund 1994, 171)

Finally, the defenders of Ice-T must share responsibility with the voices of the Right for the evacuation of considerations of hybridity, or "genre crossing" in regard to *Body Count* and "Cop Killer." The interface of cultures represented by Ice-T's thrash-metal experiment was "the unmentionable" in the debate, as neither side wished to engage the implications of the mix of frequently segregated "black" and "white" cultures.

The discourse of gangsta rap is emblematic of our historical period, one in which the power bloc (to borrow Gramsci's term) is relatively insecure and in crisis. American society in the 1990s is characterized by heterogeneity and assimilation, brought about by economic and demographic shifts. Adding to white uncertainty is the effort by subordinated peoples to force the nation to face up to its racial divisions. The racially polarized, discursive fallout from the Rodney King beating, the L.A. rebellion, and the O.J. Simpson trial have encouraged some quarters of white America to locate the problems of American society outside the (figurative and literal) borders of "whiteness."

The significance of rap within this social climate is enormous. Rap is, in Rose's (1994, 100) paraphrasing of James Scott, "a hidden transcript . . . [using] cloaked speech and disguised cultural codes to comment on and challenge aspects of current power inequalities." White anxieties over these distinctly black recodings of hostility and resentment are given expression through the deracialized attacks on rap music and artists by pundits such as David Samuels (1991). Samuels's "exposé" of rap's young white audience instead exposes the white fear of black cultural infiltration, the targets of which are white children.

Blacks justifiably fear that white audiences and manufacturers may "steal" black culture through the increasing commodification of rap. Nevertheless, Ice-T's incursion into white rock and roll should be seen, rather than a concession to white interests, as the tactical theft of white culture. There is a crucial difference: whereas whites have long appropriated black cultural forms (including rhythm and blues, the site of rock and roll's origin) for the sake of profit, *Body Count*'s counterappropriation—though it also makes money—serves to break down the barriers that help segment American culture into white and black contingents. Ice-T was very much aware of the alarms his cultural miscegenation would set off; in his *Rolling Stone* interview, he noted how *Body Count* "got inside suburbia a little deeper than a normal rap record would. . . . I think by being rock it infiltrated the homes of a lot of parents not used to having their kids play records by rappers" (Light 1992b, 30). In the same article, Ice-T estimated that "ninety-nine percent of the *Body Count* fans are white"—a hyperbolic statement, perhaps, but one that matches in spirit the press accounts of the racial breakdown of *Body Count* album sales and the nearly all-white audiences at the band's live shows (Light 1992b, 31; Muller 1992; Cusolito 1992).

Through the use of the thrash-metal format, Ice-T designed the *Body Count* album to be heard by an audience whose racial composition he understood from his band's experience on the 1991 Lollapalooza tour. This complicates our understanding of the lyrics to "Cop Killer"; Kochman's (1981) work on fighting words does not readily apply to a case in which blacks, in their own accent, speak to whites. This point is absolutely essential for a deeper appreciation of what Ice-T attempted to pull off with his rock band. In disseminating "white" music with a black accent, *Body Count*—to a greater degree than Ice-T's rap material—teaches the suburban white teenager about social conditions far outside of his or her lived experience: a project of extreme importance in an increasingly multicultural, multidiscursive age.

In nearly all of the many interviews Ice-T granted in the year of "Cop Killer," the rapper expresses his insistence that white America learn to listen to its ghettoized black counterpart. For Ice, rap's popularity with suburban white teens is not a cause for concern but a cause for hope: "They're saying: 'Hold up, these rappers are talking to me, and it's making me understand. Why did John Wayne always win? Weren't we taking that land from the Indians? Haven't we been kind of fucked-up to people?' They're starting to figure it out" (Light 1992a, 17). In *The Ice Opinion,* Ice-T writes,

> We are entering a renaissance period, an educational revolution, where people are questioning the lies. . . . Our country can't run off lies for much longer. The key to keeping the lies alive for the racists was the elimination of communication. They kept saying, "Don't let

them communicate. Don't let them talk to each other. They'll never know how much they have in common." (Ice-T and Siegmund 1994, 137)

The upshot of David Samuels's (1991) argument in the *New Republic* is that white rap fans use their interaction with "hard" black culture as a substitute for "real," meaningful social interaction with blacks (and, presumably, assistance in the alleviation of black poverty). This conclusion is used as a club by Samuels to discredit all whites who enjoy hard-core black music: that is, white fandom does nothing to address the real problem; it only exempts you from it. Rose (1994, 4) provides a useful corrective to the Samuels position in *Black Noise:* "To suggest that rap is a black idiom that prioritizes black culture and that articulates the problems of black urban life does not deny the pleasure and participation of others." Whereas Samuels's view, ironically, ridicules white "cultural tourism" without suggesting a constructive alternative, Rose's view illuminates the possibility that the mixing of black and white culture may educate America, teaching us that social struggle in the late twentieth century must be a partnership. It is a lesson embedded in the hybridity of Ice-T's music and one we should not soon forget.

## References

Agreda, Ann Latham. 1992. An artist reflects society. *Los Angeles Times,* 10 August, F4.

Bernard, James. 1992. The L.A. rebellion: Message behind the madness. *The Source,* August, 38–48.

Body Count. 1992a. Cop killer. *On* Body Count. Sire/Warner Bros. Records.

———. 1992b. Out in the parking lot. *On* Body Count. Sire/Warner Bros. Records.

Body Count: The issue is censorship. 1992. *Billboard,* 18 July, 4.

Bowman, James. 1992. Plain brown rappers. *National Review,* 20 July, 36–38, 53.

Count rises on dealer Body Count ban. 1992. *Billboard,* 18 July, 3, 74.

Cusolito, Karen. 1992. Ice-T tells WB to kill "Cop." *The Hollywood Reporter,* 29 July.

Donnelly, Sally B. 1992. The fire around the Ice. *Time,* 22 June, 66–68.

Duffy, Thom, and Charlene Orr. 1992. Texas police protest Ice-T song. *Billboard,* 20 June, 98.

Ehrenreich, Barbara. 1992. . . . Or is it creative freedom? *Time,* 20 July, 89.

Fiske, John. 1996. *Media matters.* Minneapolis: University of Minnesota Press.

Goldberg, Danny. 1992. By taking today's pop culture literally, critics miss the point of entertainment. *Los Angeles Times,* 28 June, M2, M6.

Hall, Stuart. 1980. Gramsci's relevance for the study of race and ethnicity. *Journal of Communication Inquiry* 20 (2): 5–27.

———. 1986. On postmodernism and articulation: An interview with Stuart Hall. *Journal of Communication Inquiry* 10 (2): 45–60.

Hershey-Webb, David. 1995. Number one, with a bullet: Songs of violence are part of America's folk tradition. In *Rap on rap: Straight-up talk on hip-hop culture,* edited by Adam Sexton, 100–6. New York: Delta.

Heston, Charlton. 1992. Heston speaks for women. *Los Angeles Times,* 3 August, F4.

Ice Cube. 1991. Black Korea. *On* Death Certificate. Priority Records.

Ice-T, and Heidi Siegmund. 1994. *The Ice opinion: Who gives a fuck?* New York: St. Martin's.

Jennings, Peter, anchor. 1992. *World News Tonight with Peter Jennings,* ABC, 19 June.

Kelly, Robin D. G. 1996. Kickin' reality, kickin' ballistics: Gangsta rap and postindustrial Los Angeles. In *Droppin' science: Critical essays on rap music and hip hop culture,* edited by William Eric Perkins, 117–58. Philadelphia: Temple University Press.

Kinsley, Michael. 1992. Ice-T: Is the issue social responsibility . . . *Time,* 20 July, 88.

Kochman, Thomas. 1981. *Black and white styles in conflict.* Chicago: University of Chicago Press.

Kuehl, Sheila James. 1992. Ice-T critics miss the rapper's real target. *Los Angeles Times*, 27 July, F3.

Layne, Barry. 1992. Quayle, black cops blast "Killer." *The Hollywood Reporter*, 22 June.

Leo, John. 1992. Rap music's toxic fringe. *U.S. News & World Report*, 29 June, 19.

Light, Alan. 1992a. Rappers sounded warning. *Rolling Stone*, 9–23 July, 15–17.

———. 1992b. Ice-T: The Rolling Stone interview. *Rolling Stone*, 20 August, 28–32, 60.

Mills, David. 1992. Sister Souljah's call to arms. *Washington Post*, 13 May, B1, B4.

Momma dearest. 1992. *New Republic*, 10 August, 7.

Morris, Chris. 1992a. TV a platform for rappers' reactions to riot as Ice-T, Chuck D, MC Ren, others speak out. *Billboard*, 16 May, 65.

———. 1992b. The spotlight turns to freedom in the arts: Police, Time Warner face off over "Cop Killer." *Billboard*, 25 July, 1, 71.

———. 1992c. "Cop" removal satisfies foes, to a point. *Billboard*, 8 August, 1, 83.

Muller, Judy, correspondent. 1992. *World News Tonight with Peter Jennings*, ABC, 24 July.

Outrage and Ice-T: What is the responsibility of the artist? 1992. *Los Angeles Times*, 4 August, B6.

Pareles, Jon. 1992a. Dissing the rappers is fodder for the sound bite. *The New York Times*, 28 June, sec. 2, 20.

———. 1992b. The disappearance of Ice-T's "Cop Killer." *The New York Times*, 30 July, C13, C16.

Philips, Chuck. 1992a. Texas police calls for boycott of Time Warner. *Los Angeles Times*, 12 June, F7.

———. 1992b. Police groups urge halt of record's sale. *Los Angeles Times*, 16 June, F1.

———. 1992c. The uncivil war. *Los Angeles Times*, 19 July, Calendar 6, 76, 77.

———. 1992d. A q&a with Ice-T about rock, race and the "Cop Killer" furor. *Los Angeles Times*, 19 July, Calendar 7.

Pollack, Phyllis. 1992. Uninformed media serve Ice-T bashers' aims. *Billboard*, 11 July, 4.

Quayle, congressmen, L.A. polls join "Cop Killer" posse. 1992. *Billboard*, 4 July, 1, 83.

Rapper Ice-T defends song against spreading boycott. 1992. *The New York Times*, 19 June, C24.

Rose, Tricia. 1994. *Black noise: Rap music and black culture in contemporary America.* Hanover, NH: University Press of New England/Wesleyan University Press.

Rosenthal, Andrew. 1992. Bush denounces rap recording and gives D'Amato a hand. *The New York Times*, 30 June, A21.

Royko, Mike. 1995. A different story if it were "Exec Killer." In *Rap on rap: Straight-up talk on hip-hop culture,* edited by Adam Sexton, 173–76. New York: Delta.

Rule, Sheila. 1992. Rapping Time Warner's knuckles. *The New York Times*, 8 July, C15–C16.

Run on Ice-T's album. 1992. *The New York Times*, 30 July, C16.

Samuels, David. 1991. The rap on rap. *New Republic*, November, 24–29.

Sandow, Greg. 1992. Fire and Ice. *Entertainment Weekly*, 14 August, 30.

Shaw, Bella, anchor. 1992. Ice-T appears on "Arsenio" to discuss controversy. *CNN Showbiz Today*, 22 July.

Trent, Andrea D. 1992. Cops not constructive. *Billboard*, 8 August, 6.

Vice president calls corporation wrong for selling rap song. 1992. *The New York Times*, 20 June, 9.

Volosinov, V. N. 1973. *Marxism and the philosophy of language.* New York: Seminar Press.

Walters, Paul M. 1992. Ice-T's "Cop Killer" can't be justified. *Los Angeles Times* (Orange County ed.), 8 July, B11.

While Time Warner counts its money, America may count its murdered cops (advertisement). 1992. *USA Today*, 26 June, 9A.

White, Timothy. 1991. Editorial. *Billboard*, 23 November, 8.

Will, George F. 1990. America's slide into the sewer. *Newsweek*, 30 July, 64.

*Author's note:* I would like to extend my appreciation to my colleagues from Professor John Fiske's media events seminar at the University of Wisconsin—Madison, spring 1997, for their helpful comments and suggestions regarding the first draft of this article. In particular, I wish to thank Doug Battema, John Fiske, Jennifer Fuller, Elana Levine, and Jennifer Wang.

## YOUR TEXT: READING

1. What criteria is Marsh using to qualify "Johnny B. Goode" as "great"? Do you share these criteria? If not, what are they?
2. How important is it to you that a song is "influential"? Does it enhance your enjoyment of a particular song to know the influences?
3. What role does race play in these pieces? In music generally?
4. How important is it that a group sings their own songs? In other words, what roles do composition of the song and performance play in your acceptance of a song?
5. What songs do you feel qualify as "poetry"? Does thinking about songs as poetry affect the way you experience the song?
6. How can one describe a song as an "autobiography"? Does Portelli make a good case?
7. Dylan is considered to be one of rock music's most important lyricists and performers. Do you get a sense of that in listening to this song?
8. In what ways does the music of "Smells Like Teen Spirit" reflect the lyrics?
9. What do you think of the approach of Kurt Cobain and Nirvana to songwriting? Do you get a sense of their considerations while writing? Does knowing this approach affect the way you understand the song?
10. How are the two approaches to the song different? Which piece is more analytical? More geared to getting the flavor of the song?
11. Some critics think songs like "Like a Rolling Stone" and "Smells Like Teen Spirit" are the "song of a generation"—do you agree? If so, who makes up these generations—who was Bob Dylan and Nirvana speaking to (and for)? Do you think these songwriters would think they were speaking for anyone?
12. What approach is the author taking in his examination of "Cop Killer"? Do you think it's effective—why or why not? Can you think of other songs for which this approach might be effective?

## YOUR TEXT: WRITING

1. Choose a song you think is poetic. Write about the poetic aspect of it. Now write about how music either enhances or detracts from the poetic intent.
2. Choose a song that you think symbolizes what some people in your generation (age group) believe. Examine how well this song addresses this idea.
3. Compare two songs like "Smells Like Teen Spirit" and "Like a Rolling Stone" that some critics have labeled as songs that represent a particular generation.
4. Look at a song that tells a movie story. "Hurricane" by Bob Dylan is one that comes to mind. How is the song effective at telling the story? What are the differences between the song and the movie?
5. Mirroring Matt Compton's approach, look at how the lyrics and sounds of the song work together.
6. Are there any albums you are familiar with that sound like a song with many parts? Instead of focusing on a song, look how songs work together on an album.

READING  *Outside the Lines*

## CLASSROOM ACTIVITIES

1. Compare your experiences listening to songs and reading the lyrics. First listen to a song, then read its lyrics. For a different song, reverse the procedure. What differences in understanding the song does this make?
2. If possible, listen to a song, then watch a video. What differences in understanding the song does this make?
3. Before listening to its content, read its album/CD cover. What symbols and themes does the band use in designing the cover? What do they suggest about the album's content? About the nature of the band? Now listen to some of the music. How do your preconceived ideas about the music compare to those presented by the music itself?
4. Watch a section of a movie with a soundtrack. What emotions does the soundtrack try to convey? Now watch the same movie with the sound lowered. Do you get the same ideas without the music? Does the music enhance your understanding of the movie? Detract from it?
5. Come up with some sample band names. Name genres for which the band's name would be appropriate. What does this exercise say about the way we view a band's name?

## ESSAY IDEAS

1. Pick a song. What is the mood of the music compared to its lyrics? Do they work well together? Why or why not? Are the lyrics more sophisticated than the music or vice versa? Write a paper that makes an argument about the compatibility of music and lyrics.
2. Find a CD you do not know well. Study its cover, making notes on what the cover is "saying" to a potential listener. Now listen to the songs (reading the lyrics if you wish). Does the message behind the cover reflect the music? Why or why not? You can also do similar work with the band's name.
3. Find a well-known song you like. How would you find out information about the song? What sources might be appropriate? How might you approach writing a paper if you had this information? As you think about this question, look for information on the song. When you have gathered enough information, think of arguments or ideas about the song about which you could write.
4. Take a band you like that has produced more than one album. Trace its critical history. What elements of the band's work do the critics pick up on on a consistent basis? What is their general opinion of the band? How do they classify its genre? Now sit and think about whether you agree or disagree with these critics—and why.
5. Find two songs that have similar subjects. Compare and contrast their approaches to the subject, through both their music and lyrics. What approach do you favor, and why?
6. Find a band or bands with an explicitly political approach. Do you know their politics through their music or outside of it? Does their outside behavior argee with their music? How do critics and other members of the media approach their relationship between politics and music? What do their fans think?
7. Find a movie or television show with a prominent soundtrack—does the music work well with the movie or TV series? What are your criteria? Is there a specific moment in the movie or television show that embodies the success or failure of the director's use of music?

# Reading and Writing About Technology

■ ■ ■ i-Pods are everywhere

W hat does it mean to read technology? Technology is not a traditional text like a poem, nor does it have the clearly defined elements that public space and architecture possess. It's both the idea of technology—the often-symbolic elements that we think of when we hear the word—and the concrete applications that are worth reading, that on examination yield insight into how the world works. Most of us use technology without actively considering it. We often think about technology as computers, when in reality, we use technology when we do any number of simple tasks, from washing our faces to turning on a light, listening to music, to talking on the telephone, to running errands in our car. Even the places we live are built using technologies our ancestors could not have imagined.

While the selections here often focus on computers, we want you to consider the technological components that often play an important role in our daily lives, the impact they have, and the impact their absence might have. Here are some other ideas that may help you read and write about technology in more complex ways.

## Technology has artistic components.

While technology is generally concerned more with function (how it works) than form (how it looks), we know by experience that design plays an important function in whether consumers purchase and use technology such as cars, computers, and even faucets. How technological elements look may not be a factor in *how* something works, but they may indeed be a factor in *whether* someone uses it. Indeed, the word technology comes from the Greek word *technae,* which means "art." The most practical car may not be the most beautiful—which is why not everyone owns a Volvo—and the more attractive computer may not be the most practical—not everyone owns a Macintosh. Yet technology relies on many of the same characteristics that we look for in art, such as symmetry, flow, exchange, and utility. We tend to forget that people create, design, and to some degree make tools, radios, personal digital assistants, cell phones, CD burners, can openers, pens, and scissors. Elements of design go into the shape, weight, feel, and function of each of these items.

In the case of Apple computers, art and technology merge in interesting ways, making form almost as important as function. A great deal of time and effort goes into designing the machines, the operating system, and the components—even the speakers. Many users of Macs—both authors included—would argue that the artistic design and operation of the computers *is* an element of its technology.

## Technology has both an intentional and an unintentional impact on people and environments.

When a person invents something in response to a perceived problem or void—those are technology's intentional aspects. But with almost every invention comes a consequence that its inventor may not have considered, whether it's to the environment, to society's work or play habits, or to our domestic habits. Cell phones, for example, have made it more convenient to contact people and be contacted, but perhaps with this convenience has come safety and etiquette implications. Driving behind someone who is talking on the phone can be as annoying as hearing a cell phone ring during a movie. Is the convenience of communication worth the inconvenience that accompanies it? The proliferation of the Internet and home computing has had similar, hard-to-measure effects. We get things done quicker, but we also have more to do. Cell phones, pagers, laptops, and email make it harder to get away from work. As Marshal McLuhan suggests, we are surrounded by technology—we have built it into our environment. The question persists: does increased technology mean increased freedom or more work—or both?

Technology also has a complicated relationship with the environment. Our history is littered with the negative effects technology has had on the environment, especially in its release of pollutants into the air and water, and the growing landfills that contain manmade elements that are not biodegradable. But often technology is marshaled against environmental problems as well—it was technology that helped fight technology's impact on our growing industrial world. We mention this only because it's important to recognize we often use technology against itself, whether it's solar power plants and windmills battling nuclear power plants, or ergonomic chairs battling carpal tunnel syndrome caused by overusing word processing equipment. In a sense, technology is always confronting itself—which, in a sense, means humans are doing the same.

## Technology has societal impacts, often involving race, gender, and class.

Especially in the era of the computer, technological advances tend to affect individuals directly, whether it's the invention of the cell phone, the proliferation of home computers, or PDAs. But the accumulation of individual effects forces societal impact as well, whether it is driving with cell phones (or having them ring during class) or increased access to the World Wide Web. In turn, a more tuned-in populace forces employers to crack down on email use, forces advertisers to respond to an increased use of the remote control, movie theaters to post notices about cell-phone use, etc. Then, there are the environmental effects—pollution and the filling of landfills, to name two—that of course affect society as well.

Then there are the specific effects on people. Individuals in various groups who do not have access to technological changes or are not prone to use technology are obviously affected by technological changes; they often make it harder to keep up with those who have increased access to such technology. Recent studies have shown the existence of a digital divide between rich and poor and between white Americans and members of various ethnic groups, particularly African Americans and Hispanics. Men and women often have a different and complicated relationship with technology, which may shed light on their traditional roles. On the other hand, technology can be liberating to those who find that it can level the playing field; the young and skilled, whatever their identity, often have the advantage over the old and experienced when it comes to utilizing technology.

Access to technology can also symbolize class sophistication. In many Latin American countries, for instance, cell phones have become a symbol of middle- and upper-class status. An increasingly popular item is the fake cell phone. For pennies, you can buy a very convincing replica of a cell phone—which people actually do—and walk around pretending to be many things you are not.

## Technology has changed the way we work and play.

Whether it's easier constant access to others through cell phones or email, or the ability to do work from anywhere, technology has changed our lives in ways its inventors might not have been able to anticipate. Perhaps because of technology, the lines between work and play have blurred; emails are always waiting for us, and the cell phone can make us instantly available to both friends and colleagues. Many of us prefer this lifestyle, while others find it intrusive. Technological advances often make us think about these divisions, and accordingly, how we live our lives and why we do what we do, for better or worse.

Technology has also redefined work and play; the Internet is the most prominent example. Many businesses block employees from surfing the Internet or employ web site trackers that monitor what sites workers visit. Similarly, the proliferation of videos, portable CD and DVD players, and video games has utterly changed our notions of play, relaxation, and entertainment. Contemporary Americans spend so much time intimately involved with technology, some critics have speculated about more direct connections between technology and the human body. Are we already cyborgs—beings that are part human and part machine?

For the new edition of this book, the authors have relied on cell phones, PDAs, wireless Internet, laptop computers, and in a couple of instances, connections to GPRS via Bluetooth. When we were working on the first edition, we used virtually none of these, yet it is impossible to imagine working without them now. Similarly, by the time you graduate from college, your interactions with technology will have come so far from those of your high school days, you'll hardly recognize them.

## ▪▪▪ WORKSHEET ▪▪▪

### This Text: Reading

1. How does the background of the authors influence their ideas about technology?
2. Do the authors have different ideas about class, race, and gender and their place in technology? In what ways?
3. While it will be impossible for you to know this fully, try to figure out the writing situation of each author. Who is the audience? What does the author have at stake?
4. What is his or her agenda? *Why* is she or he writing this piece?
5. What social, political, economic, and cultural forces affect the author's text? What is going on in the world as he or she is writing? Has that world changed?
6. What are the main points of the essay? What is the thesis statement?
7. How does the author support her argument? What evidence does he use to back up any claims he might make?
8. Is the author's argument reasonable?
9. Do you find yourself in agreement with the author? Why or why not?
10. Does the author help you read technology better than you did before reading the essay? If so, why?
11. How is the reading process different if you are reading an essay, as opposed to a short story or poem?
12. Did you like this? Why or why not?
13. Do you think the author likes technology overall?

### Beyond This Text: Writing

**Use:** What is this piece of technology for? What does it do? What doesn't it do that it's supposed to do? That its designers imply it should do?

**Need:** What human needs does this technology attempt to meet? Does it meet those needs?

**Design:** What are the strengths of this piece of technology's design? Its weaknesses? What is artistic about the design?

**Unintended effects:** What are some of the unintended effects of this piece of technology? Could the designer have foreseen such effects? Can improvements to its design or function change these effects?

**Societal impact:** What impact has this piece of technology had on society? What impact will it have?

**Personal impact:** What impact has this piece of technology had on you? On those who you know? Can you see any future impact it may have?

---

### INFURIATING BY DESIGN: EVERYDAY THINGS NEED NOT WREAK HAVOC ON OUR LIVES

#### ■ Donald A. Norman ■

*Though he has a Ph.D. in mathematical psychology and a master's in engineering, Donald Norman, like the rest of us, still has trouble with technology and design. Taken from his book* The Psychology of Everyday Things *(1988), this piece examines the frustrating nature of poorly designed technology. Notice the mix of both the personal and research material in this work.*

EVERDAY THINGS NEED NOT wreak havoc on our lives. "You would need an engineering degree from MIT to work this," someone once told me, shaking his head in puzzlement over his brand-new digital watch. Well, I have an engineering degree from MIT. Give me a few hours and I can figure out the watch. But why should it take hours? I've talked with many people who couldn't use all the features of their washing machines or cameras, who couldn't figure out how to work a sewing machine or a video-cassette recorder, who habitually turned on the wrong stove burner.

Why do we put up with the frustrations of everyday objects, with devices that we can't figure out how to use? After all, we already know how to design certain common items so that they may be used gracefully, the very first time, without explanation. But time and again we are stymied by products that promise to do everything but are constructed in such a way as to make it impossible to do anything.

I have gathered, from among the thousands of items with which we have daily contact, examples of good and bad design that illustrate why the interaction between people and things sometimes goes well but more often does not. With these, I offer some general principles of good design that can be used both by those who construct devices and by those who use and misuse them.

Take car door handles, for example. They come in an amazing variety of shapes and sizes. The outside door handles of most modern automobiles are excellent examples of design. They are often recessed into the door, immediately indicating what to do with them: The handles cannot be used except by inserting the fingers and pulling.

Strangely enough, the inside door handles of automobiles tell a vastly different story. Here the designers have faced another set of problems, and the appropriate solution has yet to be found. As a result, these handles are often difficult to find, hard to figure out and problematic to use.

Why should this be? After all, with doors, we need to know only two things: what to do and where to do it. But how do you best convey that to the user? One general principle is to ensure that the knowledge required for a task is available in the world or readily derivable from it. In the case of doors, physical placement of the hardware or the color and composition of the handle can offer strong signals. With car doors, a horizontal slit on the outside door readily guides the hand into a pulling position; no such clue is available for the inside door handle.

Before beginning actual construction of an everyday object, a designer needs to develop a conceptual model of it that is appropriate for those who use the object, that captures the important parts of its operation and that is readily understandable by those who use it.

Think of the standard room thermostat. How does it work? Here is a device that offers almost no evidence of its operation except in a highly roundabout manner. You enter a room and feel cold, so you set the thermostat higher. Eventually you feel warmer. But suppose you are in a hurry to get warm?

Many people reach for the thermostat dial and turn it all the way up, mistakenly believing that a maximum setting yields maximum heating. But the thermostat is actually only a simple on-off switch; it does not control the amount of heat. The heater remains on, at full power, until the temperature setting on the thermostat is reached. Setting it to maximum does not heat the room any more quickly, yet the design of the device gives people no information that would counter this belief.

Using everyday devices should be simple, requiring a minimal amount of planning or problem solving. When such tasks become unnecessarily complex, technology can be used to restructure them and simplify their operation.

However, applying technology can be tricky. A designer must avoid the temptation to add functions to a device that make it even more complicated. Telephones, for example, used to be marvelous examples of simple design. The telephone on my desk today, however, has 24 functions, some of which I have never learned how to use. This is not simply a matter of having too many functions; my car has about 110 functions, none of which puzzles me in the least. Why is the telephone so much more difficult to master?

The answer, in part, lies in the ratio of controls (knobs, dials or levers) to the number of functions. The telephone has only 15 buttons to control all 24 tasks. Each button may activate more than one function. On the other hand, the car, with rare exceptions, has only one control for each function. That is, each control is specialized. Generally, whenever the number of possible functions of a device exceeds the number of controls, as in my telephone, there is apt to be difficulty in using it.

Designers must also pay attention to the limits of memory and to the limit on how many active thoughts people may pursue at once. Long-distance telephone charge cards, for example, are notoriously difficult to use for just this reason. Each company insists upon providing a long code, with individual numbers for each account. In addition some provide codes that are so secret, they aren't even printed on the long-distance charge card. If I wish to dial a long-distance number using my credit card from a hotel, I often must dial nearly three dozen digits in a precisely regulated sequence—assuming that I am able to remember what I am dialing. No wonder my failure rate for dialing correctly the first time is so high.

Physical and motor skills also place limits on certain abilities. Tying a shoelace, for example, is one standard task that is actually quite difficult to learn. Adults may have forgotten how long it took them, but injury, age or disease may provide a quick reminder through the loss of agility in the fingers. The introduction of Velcro fasteners, however, has now made the task simpler, requiring a minimum of motor skills and, for children, a minimum of memory.

People who use everyday objects need to know what kinds of things they can do with them and how these actions should be completed. One way to accomplish this is to offer ample visual hints. These should be readily interpretable and should match most people's intentions and expectations. In other words, the possible outcome of any action should be immediately obvious to the user of a device.

When important sensory cues are missing, the result can be more than inconvenient. I once stayed in the guest apartment of a technological institute in the Netherlands. The building was newly completed and contained many interesting architectural features. All was fine until I took a shower. The bathroom seemed to have no ventilation at all, so everything became wet, and eventually cold and clammy.

I looked all over the bathroom but never did find anything that looked like a ventilation grate or opening. However, I was able to find a switch that I thought might be the control for an exhaust fan. When I pushed it, a light nearby went on. The light stayed on, but nothing seemed to happen. Further pushing seemed to have no effect. Each time I returned to the apartment, however, I noticed that the light had gone off.

Later, I learned that the button did indeed control the exhaust fan in the bathroom. It was on as long as the light remained on, and it turned itself off, automatically, after about five minutes. Too bad I never figured this out. In this case, the architect was too successful in concealing feedback from the ventilation system. A ventilation grate or a noise of some kind would have signaled that there really was a change in the air.

Not only should a device's controls be visible but the spatial relationship between a device and its controls should also be as direct as possible. The controls should either be on the device itself or arranged to have an analogical relationship with it. Similarly, the movement of the controls should be analogous to the expected operation of the device.

The seat adjustment control in a Mercedes Benz automobile is an excellent example of what I call "natural mapping." The control is in the shape of the seat itself. To move the front edge of the seat higher, the driver lifts up on the front part of the button. To make the seat-back recline, the driver simply pushes the button backward. There are no directions—none are needed. This is important, since if labels are required, this is a signal that the design for the device may be faulty. Labels are often necessary, but the appropriate use of natural mapping can minimize the need for them.

The seat control succeeds because there is a natural relationship between the switch movements and the seat motion. If it isn't possible to make the choices in using a device as obvious as this, another solution is to limit the number of possible bad choices. In other words, a device should have constraints built in so that the user feels as if there is only one thing to do—the right thing.

Good designers can anticipate almost any conceivable error that a user of an everyday object might make. In fact, a good rule of design is to assume that any possible error will be made. One clever design incorporating this consideration is the package shelf found in some public rest rooms. It is placed on the wall just behind the cubicle door, folded into a vertical position. To make it into a shelf, you have to lower it to the horizontal position, where the weight of a package keeps it there. To get out of the cubicle, you have to remove whatever is on the shelf in order to raise it out of the way of the door. This forces you to remember your package.

Not all everyday objects are so well thought out. In fact, many people have died needlessly in building fires because architects did not anticipate all the errors people could make. When fires break out, people tend to flee in panic, down the stairs, past the ground floor and into the basement, where they become trapped. The solution—which has been reinforced by fire safety laws throughout the country—is to hinder simple passage from the ground floor of most large buildings to the basement.

This safety feature is mainly a nuisance in normal use. I have never yet been in a burning building, but it often happens that I must pass from a higher floor to the basement, encountering all kinds of obstacles along the way. Yet I believe that this minor problem is worth the bother, since it undoubtedly saves many lives.

Sometimes a designer cannot provide all of the necessary information to use an everyday object or cannot fully exploit natural mapping. Then there is generally only one viable choice: Standardize the actions, outcomes, layout and displays involved in its use. The nice thing about standardization is that no matter how arbitrary, it only has to be learned once.

A case in point is the layout of the modern typewriter keyboard, which has a long and peculiar history. In the end, the keyboard was designed by an evolutionary process, but the main driving forces were mechanical. Almost all typewriters and computers today make use of the "Qwerty" keyboard, named for the first six letters appearing at the upper left-hand side. Better designs exist (the so-called "Dvorak" keyboard can increase the top speed of expert typists by at least 10 percent), but that is not enough to merit a change. Millions of people would have to learn a new style of typing and millions of typewriters would have to be replaced.

Once a satisfactory product, such as a keyboard, has been standardized, further change may be counterproductive, especially if the product is successful. Standardization is not the ideal solution, but sometimes it is the only choice and, when followed consistently, it works well.

If I were placed in the cockpit of a jet airplane, my inability to perform gracefully would neither surprise nor bother me. But I shouldn't have trouble with doors, switches, water faucets and stoves. Moreover, I know that other people have the same unnecessary troubles. Instead of causing problems, design of everyday objects should eliminate them, without any need for words or symbols and certainly without any need for trial and error.

Remember, problems with design affect all of us. Recently, a computer scientist at my university proudly showed me his new compact disc player, complete with remote control. The remote unit had a little metal loop protruding from one end. My friend told me that when he first got the set, he assumed that the loop was an antenna, and he always tried to aim it at the player. Unfortunately, the remote control barely functioned this way. Later he discovered that the loop was only a loop, meant to be used to hang up the control when it wasn't in use. He had been aiming the unit at his own body for weeks, an unknowing victim in the battle against poor design.

**READING WRITING**

## THIS TEXT: READING
1. Can you think of examples of Norman's phenomenon in your own life?
2. Though this was written more than ten years ago, does this seem dated? Why or why not?

3. Why aren't designers of technology more responsive to customer use (given the purpose of technology is to make something easier to do)?
4. In what ways is the use or misuse of technological design a culture problem? What cultures are clashing, according to Norman?

## YOUR TEXT: WRITING

1. Write about a problematic relationship you have or had with a piece of technology.
2. Write about an invention or design you find especially useful or helpful. What sets apart this design from more problematic designs?
3. Write an open letter to designers suggesting changes in the way understand the consumer. Cite specific examples of poorly designed technology.

---

### HOW THE COMPUTER CHANGED MY WRITING

#### ■ Steven Johnson ■

*Steven Johnson, a Web commentator for* Slate *and the author of three books about science and computers, including his latest,* Mind Wide Open: Your Brain and the Neuroscience of Everyday Life, *describes the way his writing changed as he used a computer. In the essay, taken from his 1997 work* Interface Culture: How New Technology Transforms the Way We Create and Communicate, *he makes a point to differentiate the way the different processes work.*

I was twelve when my parents shelled out for our first home PC—an Apple IIe souped up with an astonishing 32K of RAM—and while my recollections of the preceding years are not particularly vivid, I can still conjure up a little of the rhythm of life back then, in the dark ages before the digital revolution. Among my peers, this sometimes seems to be an unusual ability. I often hear friends wonder aloud: "How did we ever get along without e-mail and word processors?" And yet for the most part I can readily imagine how things happened in that world, the pace of that more settled and disconnected existence. It all seems rather obvious to me. We got along because we didn't know what we were missing. Folks have always griped about the postal service's sluggish performance, but the lag time only becomes intolerable once you have a taste of e-mail.

It's not life without computers that confounds me; it's life in the strange interregnum after the PC first appeared in our house. I lived within thirty feet of a fully functional computer from my twelfth to my eighteenth year, and yet the sad truth is, I used it almost exclusively as a presentation device for those six years, like a visit to Kinko's at the end of a term paper. Whatever I was writing—papers, poems, stories, plays—I dutifully etched out by hand on yellow legal pads, crossing out passages, scribbling new lines in the margins. Only when the language had reached a tolerable state did I bother typing it into the PC. The idea of composing on (and not transcribing into) the machine seemed somehow inauthentic to me. It was more like typing than writing, in Truman Capote's memorable phrase, somehow more mechanical, more mediated, a few steps removed from the whole books-on-tape phenomenon.

This continues to be a normal state of mind for the millions of people who still sense something menacing in the glare of the PC monitor, who find themselves more perplexed than enlightened by the digital revolution. But that fifteen-year-old version of me didn't belong to that demographic: I genuinely liked computers, and spent the requisite hours of my adolescence frittering away my allowance at the arcade. Like many kids of my generation, I dabbled with rudimentary programming languages (BASIC and Pascal) long enough to toss a few stray colored pixels up on the screen or scroll through the call-and-response formula of the medieval text adventures then in vogue. I wasn't even close to being what we would now call a "hacker," but I certainly felt confident enough with the PC to put a new word processor through its paces without spending much time with the manual. (In those days, you had to give the documentation at least a cursory glance before booting up the software.) I harbored no ill will toward the machine, no superstitions. But I could not bring myself to write on it.

Fast-forward a decade or two, and I can't imagine writing *without* a computer. Even jotting down a note with pen and paper feels strained, like a paraplegic suddenly granted the use of his legs. I have to *think* about writing, think about it consciously as my hand scratches out the words on the page, think about the act itself. There is none of the easy flow of the word processor, just a kind of drudgery, running against the thick grain of habit. Pen and paper feel profoundly different to me now—they have the air of an inferior technology about them, the sort of contraption well suited for jotting down a phone number, but not much beyond that. Writing an entire book by hand strikes me as being a little like filming *Citizen Kane* with a camcorder. You can make a go at it, of course, but on some fundamental level you've misjudged the appropriate scale of the technology you're using. It sounds appalling, I know, but there it is. I'm a typer, not a writer. Even my handwriting is disintegrating, becoming less and less *my* handwriting, and more the erratic, anonymous scrawl of someone learning to write for the first time.

I accept this condition gladly, and at the same time I can recall the predigital years of my childhood, writing stories by hand into loose-leaf notebooks, practicing my cursive strokes and then surveying the loops and descenders, seeing something there that looked like me, my sense of selfhood scrawled onto the page. On a certain level these two mental states are totally incompatible—bits versus atoms—but the truth is I have no trouble reconciling them. My "written" self has always fed back powerfully into my normal, walking-around-doing-more-or-less-nothing self. When I was young that circuit was completed by tools of ink and paper; today it belongs to the zeros and ones. The basic shape of the circuit is unchanged.

But what interests me now, looking back on it, is the *transition* from one to the other. That feeling of artificiality that undermined me as I typed into a word processor, the strangeness of the activity—all this is very difficult to bring back. How could I have resisted so long? Sure, the software was less powerful back then, but the basic components of word processing—the cutting and pasting, the experimentation, the speed of typing—were all very much in place. There were clear advantages to working on the computer, advantages I genuinely understood and appreciated. But they were not compelling enough to dissipate the aura of inauthenticity that surrounded the machine. My writing didn't seem real on the screen somehow. It felt like a bureaucratic parody of me, several steps removed, like a recycled Xerox image shuffled around the office one too many times.

So now I wonder: what force finally brought me over to the other side? After more than half a decade of tinkering with computers, what was it that finally allowed me to recognize myself in those bright pixels on the screen, to see those letterforms as real extensions of my thought? I wasn't totally aware of it at the time, of course, but I can now see that what drew me into the language-space on the screen was nothing less than interface design. The Mac's paper-on-desktop metaphor—the white backdrop, the typographic controls, Alan Kay's stacked windows—lured me away from real-world paper. The "user illusion" sucked me in, and I was hooked forever. I'd understood the benefits of using a word processor before I bought my Mac, but it took a fully realized graphic interface to make me feel comfortable enough to use one for honest-to-God *writing*. Everything before that twelve-point New York font first appeared on the screen, black pixels marching boldly across the whiteness—everything before that was just transcribing.

I suspect there are millions of people with similar stories to tell: the mind naturally resists the dull glare of the screen, feels ill at case with it, unnatural. And then something in the user experience changes—the "direct manipulation" of the mouse, perhaps, or the resolution of the display—and suddenly you find yourself at home in front of the machine, so acclimated to the environment that you're no longer fighting the software. Before you know it, you're composing directly into the word processor, and the artifice, that original sense of mediation, is gone.

There are two lessons here, one relatively straightforward, the other more indirect. It's clear that the graphic interface played a crucial role in creating today's colossal market for word-processing applications, a market drawn not only to the functionality of the products but also to their look-and-feel. Plenty of us labored along with word processors in the days of the command-line interface, but the ease and fluidity of today's digital writing owe a great deal to the aesthetic innovations of the desktop metaphor. It's not just that the software has accumulated more features. It's also that the software has grown more seductive, more visually appealing over that period. For the creative mind, wrestling with language on the screen, that heightened visual sensibility can be enormously comforting.

But this is more than just a story about the sales records set by WordPerfect and Microsoft Word in the past decade. It also extends beyond the long-term trend of folks becoming more comfortable with their word processors as the user interface grows increasingly sophisticated. The truly interesting thing here is that using a word processor changes how we write— not just because we're relying on new tools to get the job done, but also because the computer fundamentally transforms the way we conjure up our sentences, the thought process that runs alongside the writing process. You can see this transformation at work on a number of levels. The most basic is one of sheer volume: the speed of digital composition—not to mention the undo commands and the spell checker—makes it a great deal easier to churn out ten pages where we might once have scratched out five using pen and paper (or a Smith-Corona). The perishability of certain digital formats—e-mail being the most obvious example—has also created a more casual, almost conversational writing style, a fusion of written letter and telephone-speak.

But for me, the most intriguing side effect of the word processor lies in the changed relationship between a sentence in its conceptual form and its physical translation onto the page or the screen. In the years when I still wrote using pen and paper or a typewriter. I almost invariably worked out each sentence in my head before I began transcribing it on the page. There was a clear before and after to the process: I would work out the subject and verb, modifiers, subsidiary clauses in advance; I would tinker with the arrangement for a minute or two; and when the mix seemed right, I'd turn back to the yellow legal pad. The method made sense, given the tools I was using—changing the sequence of words after you'd scrawled them out quickly made a mess of your document. (You could swap phrases in and out with arrows and cross-outs, of course, but it made reading over the text extremely unpleasant.) All this changed after the siren song of the Mac's interface lured me into writing directly at the computer. I began with my familiar start-and-stop routine, dutifully thinking up the sentence before typing it out, but it soon became clear that the word processor eliminated the penalty that revisions normally exacted. If the phrasing wasn't quite right, you could re-arrange words with a few quick mouse gestures, and the magical "delete" key was always a split second away. After a few months, I noticed a qualitative shift in the way I worked with sentences: the thinking and the typing processes began to overlap. A phrase would come into my head—a sentence fragment, an opening clause, a parenthetical remark—and be-fore I had time to mull it over, the words would be up on the screen. Only then would I start fishing around for a verb, or a prepositional phrase to close out the sentence. Most sentences would unfold through a kind of staggered trial and error—darting back and forth between several different iterations until I arrived at something that seemed to work.

It was a subtle change, but a profound one nonetheless. The fundamental units of my writing had mutated under the spell of the word processor: I had begun by working with blocks of complete sentences, but by the end I was thinking in smaller blocks, in units of dis-crete phrases. This, of course, had an enormous effect on the types of sentences I ended up writing. The older procedure imposed a kind of upward ceiling on the sentence's complex-ity: you had to be able to hold the entire sequence of words in your head, which meant that the mind naturally gravitated to simpler, more direct syntax. Too many subsidiary clauses and you lost track. But the word processor allowed me to zoom in on smaller clusters of words and build out from there—I could always add another aside, some more descriptive frippery, because the overall shape of the sentence was never in question. If I lost track of the subject-verb agreement, I could always go back and adjust it. And so my sentences swelled out enor-mously, like a small village besieged by new immigrants. They were ringed by countless peripheral thoughts and show-off allusions, paved by endless qualifications and false starts. It didn't help matters that I happened to be under the sway of French semiotic theory at the time, but I know those sentences would have been almost impossible to execute had I been scribbling them out on my old legal pads. The computer had not only made it easier for me to write; it had also changed the very substance of what I was writing, and in that sense, I sus-pect, it had an enormous effect on my thinking as well.

 **READING** WRITING

## THIS TEXT: READING

1. How does Johnson talk about the process of writing? Why does it change with a computer?
2. Why does he tell his story from the first person? Does it mean the story to have more universal significance?
3. How do you compose your writing? In what ways does Johnson's piece make you think about your own writing?

## YOUR TEXT: WRITING

1. Write a short essay talking about the ways your writing has changed and what technol-ogy has to do with that change.

2.   Interview your parents or someone who learned to write without computers. Find out how they view the writing process compared to you.

---

## CONFESSIONS OF AN ONLINE JOURNALIST

### ■ Heidi Pollock ■

*Heidi Pollock is a writer and web designer whose work has focused mostly on technology. She has had columns for ivillage and Hotwired.com, and has written for many national publications; she has also had 'zines, and has written about those as well. In these piece (2004), she writes about the short history of online journalism.*

In the time-honored tradition of all fledging writers, I was living in New York City and totally broke. When an old friend from San Francisco asked if I'd be interested in writing something for one of Wired Magazine's online ventures, I whipped up my first paid web article faster than she could fax me the writer's contract. Although only eight years ago, this was the dawn of time for online journalism. Websites flirted with subscription-based versus ad-supported formats, print outlets fought with their unionized staff over reprint rights, money was being thrown around faster than industry buzz words and intellectuals were falling all over themselves to re-appropriate the philosophical media observations made by Marshall McLuhan during the didactic 1960s.[1] Overnight, coffee shop slackers looked up from their dog-eared copies of Baudrillard and commenced speaking in sound bites whose meanings remain as opaque today as they were back then. Content was king, the village global, the medium and the message fused to form a gleaming new gestalt.

As vapid as all the hoopla was, it proved easier for most people to migrate philosophies than to migrate mediums. Prior to my career as an online journalist, I'd had so little experience writing for print that only the lull period, a.k.a., "unemployment," following the burst bubble in 2000 allowed me time to reflect on how different the two medias really were. Having kept a website from before the Mosaic group ["Mosaic" was the precursor to Netscape, simultaneously, a browser, a consortium, and a corporation] entered the commercial market as Netscape, I realized only much later that I'd jumped into the arena with a broad understanding and intuitive feel for online journalism that, to this day, many writers seem to lack.

Although the web never proved as radical as the pundits claimed, it did prove to be more different than most journalists expected. From its inception, writing online has always seemed to invoke a far less formal, more intimate voice than writing for print. This cozy camaraderie may have been a psychological trick spawned by idyllic visions of a global "village." Or maybe it was simply that the bulk of Silicon Valley writers morphed from temp slave 'zine publishers into paid journalists at fiber-optic lightspeeds. Personally, I think the stylistic, casual tone of professional online writing is largely due to technical constraints and corporate business models.

One such technical constraints is the screen itself—the medium of a limited screen size literally constrains the message in a manner both similar to and distinct from magazine and

---

[1]Marshall McLuhan in *Understanding Media: The Extensions Of Man,* wrote in a famous quote that the medium is the message. He meant, in part, that the way information is presented us is part of meaning it creates. In other words, the Internet itself presents its own meaning outside the information it presents.

newspaper layouts. Early monitor resolutions were ridiculously cramped and while readers never liked scrolling much, the per-page-view advertising model driving the early web was entirely dependent on getting the reader to turn the page. Though the constraints have eased over the years, an online writer still has to draw those coveted eyeballs through the looking glass, counteract the cold technicality of the intangible medium and keep people clicking through to the end of an article.

Page-turning readers are desirable in all text-based media—for writers as well as for deep-pocketed, full-page advertisers. Unlike a website, magazines and newspapers can't monitor their audience's attention span. I'd like to think that I've never personally fallen victim to web statistic data mining, but I'm certain that at least one outlet I used to work for was dissolved thanks to low click counts. Online job security rests partly in knowing how to write for a publication's page length, knowing how to hook the reader with personality and enticing cliff-hangers that lull them into clicking the dreaded "read more" link.

If I sound obsessed with link clicking, you have to remember that the web is bound together by links, not cover pages. Magazines and newspapers are discrete, physical objects. You may not be able to read the *Sunday Times* in one sitting, but, technically, you could because it has a fixed number of pages to turn. There is no end to reading online. There is always another link to follow—as many a procrastinating researcher is sure to know. Fundamentally, links make the web. They are the "Hyper Text" referenced in "HTML." So, not only do online writers have to worry about being interesting enough to hold a reader's attention, the smart ones act as subtle marketing agents, utilizing as many reference links to the publishing site's other pages as is possible without seeming like a marketing hack.

As a working journalist, the How-To side of this is rife with ethical landmines. Readers are unlikely to trust reference links if they lead exclusively to other pages within the same site. Maintaining journalistic integrity and impartial accuracy weigh heavily against the marketing desires of the publisher, whose goals are to trap visitors in between their virtual pages. For this reason, many outlets still forbid linking to external sites. Aside from the obvious marketing and liability concerns, some offsite links are impossible to include because they raise contextual content dilemmas rarely encountered in a printed footnote. Simply put, a great reference link may reside on competitor's site or, worse, within a site containing questionable material. I once wanted to link to a great technical page but the parent site contained some wildly religious material which was totally inappropriate for my publisher. I chose to drop the reference rather than brave the storm of outraged reader email.

Which brings us now to a second type of web link and the clearest emblem of the profound difference between print and web: the email link. The ubiquitous author link in every byline was enough of a burden on the writer before the explosion of spam email, but the sheer quantity of reader feedback is astonishing. While all journalists labor under the double-edged sword of accountability and liability, online writers feel that edge every time they publish. Well-trained readers who readily click through links to read complete articles are all too adept at clicking those email links too. Praise and scorn arrive in equal measure, flooding inboxes and begging for response. This communication between author and reader is euphemistically referred to "community building," and, in many cases, actually is. Whether or not the actual interchange builds real communities or simply forces the journalist into an auxiliary email account, the ready access to the journalist behind the text binds an author's personality and identity to both their work and the web in a way that no level of stylistic, slang-ridden, confessional writing ever could in print.

As the web—and its writers—matures, this entire concept of personal accountability catches many journalists off-guard. All authors are accustomed to accountability in the form of factual accuracy, relevancy, liability and slander, but due to the sprawling, endless and nearly perpetual existence of web texts, only online writers are confronted with the immediacy of being accountable to themselves in the form of their persistent identities. The sheer ease of following links or launching a web search means that everything online bearing your full name is theoretically within the world's reach—personal websites, bulletin board posts, ancient online diaries, florid prose, family reunion photographs, everything.

Hardcopy magazines and newspapers do not come with search tools; the web has never been without them. Print writers can cultivate and craft their tearsheets, burying articles they are less than proud of, but thanks to the miracle of search engines, online writers exist in a world where their past is as readily available as the next set of well-constrained search terms. Practically speaking, this persistence of text can prove more inspiring to an unproductive writer than mere poverty. Because recent work is likely to rank highly in search results, a prolific author can easily flood the web with new texts, knocking old pieces out of the top hundred and into virtual obscurity.

The power of links and search engines to exhume ancient articles and other embarrassing online creations simultaneously provides writers with an unprecedented ability to manipulate their visibility and their careers. Many of the promises of the early web have finally come to fruition as technical barriers have dissipated. In the web's salad days, we online writers actually had to submit our articles in code; today, you don't even need to know how to use a telnet connection to publish a professional looking site. With simplified web log ("blog") tools and the maturity of newsfeeds, the web is finally a place where anyone can be heard.

While blogging has engendered an explosion of online writers, the community has become a lightning rod for heated debates about the nature of journalism, both online and off, the role of accountability, the influence of editorial power, and even the nature of identity online. Much of these debates hinge on our culturally driven sense of professionalism, what it means and, more importantly, what it looks like.

Unlike print publications, the professionalism and respectability of websites are more difficult to assess for the uninitiated. In the print world, price tag and circulation are ready measures of a publication's professional standing. Writing for a local free weekly is easier to do than writing for Vanity Fair, and pretty much everyone knows that. It is my experience that pay scale is a nearly useless yardstick by which to judge professional, quality writing, but as any working journalist knows, bylines in well-known publications are better for one's resume than those in more obscure sources, regardless of the respective articles' quality. Print and online publications are both judged according to esthetically-apparent production value and the quality of the contributers, but websites are additionally judged by the context they create through links.

The overwhelming importance given to context online has a concrete impact on your career; where an article is published is equally, if not more, important than what it says. When writing for yourself, for a personal website or blog, you are writing for an audience of your own creation but when you write for an edited journal, paid or no, you demonstrate an ability to identify with a previously targeted audience and adapt to the editorial needs and voice of someone else's publication—a quality most editors actually seem to value more than any native ability to write.

It all comes back to the nature of the medium. When you mail or fax clips of articles, the recipient sees merely the collection of your written words. Where they are familiar with a publication, they will weigh your words accordingly, but in general your text is judged as a body of work in its own light. It is an entirely different game online. When you send an email or post a resume with links to your published works, these articles are read in the context of the greater publication, and your words will be judged, in part, by the professionalism of the site as a whole. This bias toward professionalism can help as often as it can hurt. I have recently begun writing for a rather cheap local real estate magazine in a half-hearted attempt to add some home renovation features to my portfolio—something easier said than done for a long-time tech writer. I've devoted a disproportionate amount of energy to writing for them because their website is incredibly elegant—more so, really, than the print publication itself. For my online resume, the obscurity of the publication is eclipsed by the professionalism of the site.

As exacerbating as these intangible esthetic and visual factors can be, the medium is, once again, and perhaps always, the message.

---

## READING WRITING

### THIS TEXT: READING

1. What differences between writing online and in text do you notice when you read? Which do you prefer?
2. Have you ever sent an email you regretted? Would you have made the same mistake with a letter or phone call?
3. Have you ever emailed a writer of an article online? Written a letter to the editor? In what ways did the experience differ?
4. What are differences between reading the Internet and reading physical objects like newspapers or books? Which do you prefer and why?

### THIS TEXT: WRITING

1. Write a piece comparing reading an article in a newspaper and then online. What differences do you notice in the experience?
2. Research the McLuhan quote, "The medium is the message." Now write a short piece musing about how his quote applies in today's world, citing specific examples of media.

---

## KILL-FOR-KICKS VIDEO GAMES DESENSITIZING OUR CHILDREN

### ■ John Leo ■

*John Leo is a well-known conservative columnist who writes for a number of publications, most frequently,* U. S. News and World Report. *In this essay, published as an op-ed piece in the* Seattle Times *in 1999, Leo argues that the all-too-real technology of video games is largely responsible for teen violence, including the Columbine shootings. Pay attention to the arguments Leo makes and the data he uses to support those assertions.*

Was it real life or an acted-out video game?

Marching through a large building using various bombs and guns to pick off victims is a conventional video game scenario. In the Colorado massacre, Dylan Klebold and Eric Harris used pistol-grip shotguns, as in some video arcade games. The pools of blood, screams of agony and pleas for mercy must have been familiar; they are featured in some of the newer and more realistic kill-for-kicks games.

"With each kill," the *Los Angeles Times* reported, "the teens cackled and shouted as though playing one of the more morbid video games they loved." And they ended their spree by shooting themselves in the head, the final act in the game Postal, and in fact, the only way to end it.

Did the sensibilities created by the modern video kill games play a role in the Littleton massacre? Apparently so. Note the cool and casual cruelty, the outlandish arsenal of weapons, the cheering and laughing while hunting down victims one by one. All of this seems to reflect the style and feel of the video killing games they played so often.

No, there isn't any direct connection between most murderous games and most murders. And yes, the primary responsibility for protecting children from dangerous games lies with parents, many of whom like to blame the entertainment industry for their own failings.

But there is a larger problem here: We are now a culture in which the chief form of play for millions of youngsters is making large numbers of people die. Hurting and maiming others is the central fun activity in video games played so addictively by the young. A widely cited survey of 900 fourth- through eighth-grade students found that almost half of the children said their favorite games involve violence. Can it be that all this constant training in make-believe killing has no social effects?

The conventional argument is that this is a harmless activity among children who know the difference between fantasy and reality. But the games are often played by unstable youngsters who are unsure about the difference. Many have been maltreated or rejected and left alone most of the time (a precondition for playing the games obsessively). Adolescent feelings of resentment, powerlessness and revenge pour into the killing games. In these children, the games can become dress rehearsal for the real thing.

Psychologist David Grossman of Arkansas State University, a retired Army officer, thinks "point and shoot" video games have the same effect as military strategies used to break down a soldier's aversion to killing. During World War II, only 15 percent to 20 percent of all American soldiers fired their weapons in battle. Shooting games in which the target is a man-shaped outline, the Army found, made recruits more willing to "make killing a reflex action."

Video games are much more powerful versions of the military's primitive discovery about overcoming the reluctance to shoot. Grossman says Michael Carneal, the schoolboy shooter in West Paducah, Ky., showed the effects of video-game lessons in killing. Carneal coolly shot nine times, hitting eight people, five of them in the head or neck. Head shots pay a bonus in many video games. Now, the Marine Corps is adapting a version of Doom, the hyperviolent game played by one of the Littleton killers, for its own training purposes.

More realistic touches in video games help blur the boundary between fantasy and reality—carefully modeled real guns, accurate-looking wounds, screams and other sound effects, even the recoil of a heavy rifle.

Some newer games seem intent on erasing children's empathy and concern for others. Once, the intended victims of video slaughter were mostly gangsters or aliens. Now, some games invite players to blow away ordinary people who have done nothing wrong—pedestrians, marching bands, an elderly woman with a walker. In these games, the shooter is not a hero, just a violent sociopath. One ad for a SONY game says: "Get in touch with your gun-toting, testosterone-pumping, cold-blooded murdering side."

These killings are supposed to be taken as harmless over-the-top jokes. But the bottom line is that the young are being invited to enjoy the killing of vulnerable people picked at random. This looks like the final lesson in a course to eliminate any lingering resistance to killing.

SWAT teams and cops now turn up as the targets of some video-game killings. This has the effect of exploiting resentments toward law enforcement and making real-life shooting of cops more likely. The sensibility turns up in the hit movie *Matrix:* world-saving hero Keanu Reeves, in a mandatory Goth-style long black coat packed with countless heavy-duty guns, is forced to blow away huge numbers of uniformed law-enforcement people.

"We have to start worrying about what we are putting into the minds of our young," says Grossman. "Pilots train on flight simulators, drivers on driving simulators, and now we have our children on murder simulators." If we want to avoid more Littleton-style massacres, we will begin taking the social effects of the killing games more seriously.

**READING WRITING**

## THIS TEXT: READING

1. What is Leo's thesis in this article?
2. To what degree is technology responsible for teen violence?

## YOUR TEXT: WRITING

1. Write a rebuttal to Leo or an essay in which you agree with him. Be sure to justify your assertions with data *since* 1999.
2. The authors have friends who are video game critics for newspapers, though the authors are not themselves video game aficionados (there is no time; they have textbooks to write). What are the authors *missing* by not playing video games? Is there a specific gaming culture? Write a paper in which you explore this culture and its reliance on technology.
3. Recently, some universities have started majors in game design. Write a persuasive essay in which you argue for or against such programs.

*Student Essay*

> **HUNGRY FOR A SCAPEGOAT: A REBUTTAL TO JOHN LEO'S "KILL-FOR-KICKS VIDEO GAMES DESENSITIZING OUR CHILDREN"**
>
> ▪ **Dan Walsh** ▪

*Dan Walsh is a student at the University of San Francisco. He wrote this paper in 2003 for his Rhetoric and Composition 220 class (USF's version of Composition II). A rebuttal to the John Leo piece, Walsh responds to specific assertions in Leo's article, ultimately claiming that Leo relies on generalizations and circumstantial evidence. What does Walsh do well in this essay? Are his arguments convincing?*

I was running late for school again. It had snowed the night before, and the roads still had at least three inches of slippery snow left on them. For obvious safety reasons, I was forced to creep along in my Mitsubishi Eclipse at a measly 40 miles per hour. I tried to make up some lost time by taking a back road that should have saved me about five minutes of driving time. A glance at my watch told me my plan was working. About 100 yards from the stop sign at the end of the road, I let my foot off the gas and began to slow down. I slowly pressed my brake and realized I wasn't going to stop in time. I pressed a little harder and cringed as I felt the wheels lose traction as they came in contact with the ice that had formed on the road the night before. I started pumping my brake like I was taught to in Driver's Ed, but it wasn't helping.

"Oh well," I thought, "So I don't stop before the stop sign. At least there isn't a car coming." I looked toward the intersecting road and saw that I was wrong; there was indeed a car coming. I tried pumping my brakes again, but it still wasn't working. My wheels caught on some snow, and the car began sliding towards the left side of the road. I tried to correct the car but over-steered and began heading towards the ditch on the right side of the road. I tried to correct the car again but started sliding to the left again. I wasn't going to stop in time. I couldn't even take the ditch because I couldn't steer the car well enough. I was going to hit that car!

Just as fear began to paralyze my brain, a calm came over me. I confidently glanced at my surroundings. I cranked the emergency (E) brake with my right hand and slammed the wheel as far as it could go to the left with my other. The car entered into a full out spin. I spun with it three full rotations before coming to a stop parallel to the intersecting road and right in front of the stop sign. The green Saturn passed me no less than a second after I came to a stop, the driver wide-eyed and extremely scared. I looked him in the eyes and gave him a grand salute as I grinned from ear to ear. Crisis averted!

The rest of my trip to school was uneventful, and I really didn't think about what had happened. I was halfway through first period before the adrenaline wore off; I was suddenly perplexed. Where had I learned to do that? I was never taught that maneuver in Driver's Ed. In fact, Driver's Ed had almost gotten me killed. So how did I know to pull the E brake and crank the wheel? That's when it hit me. Video games! I learned that maneuver when I was trying to earn my rally license in Gran Turismo 3. A video game just saved my life!

John Leo published an article in *The Seattle Times* on April 27, 1999, in which he blatantly blamed video games for many of society's ills. Leo uses circumstantial evidence and very few facts to back up his extraordinary claims. Despite the negative press video games receive from people like Leo, I would like to make it clear that video games are not the root of all evil, and as my being alive today exemplifies, do indeed have many beneficial side effects. They are a safe recreational activity, an outlet for stress and anger, and they can even provide the skills necessary to avoid a collision. They do not warp the realities of those who play them, they are not responsible for lessening American youth's aversion to killing, they do not teach children to kill, they do not increase one's accuracy with a firearm, and above all, they are not responsible for the past trend of school shootings.

Contrary to Leo's belief, video games are in fact very safe and much less dangerous than other forms of childhood play. In his article, Leo states, "We are now a culture in which the chief form of play for millions of youngsters is making large numbers of people die" (467). I don't see a problem with this. We are talking about pixels and polygons on a television screen. These are not people; these are 0's and 1's on a CD. I would ask Leo what the chief form of play was before video games. I know before I got my first Nintendo I used to go out in my backyard and make booby traps for my little brother (I stopped after I gave him a concussion). I used to play war with my friends at recess, or we would have slingshot fights, or throw rocks at each other on the weekends. My god, what kind of injuries we could have sustained! It boggles my mind how many times someone was hurt outside playing touch football, one of the most accepted of childhood pastimes. Children do get hurt when they participate in these violent activities. But I've never heard of anyone sustaining an injury from playing a video game. Don't get me wrong—video games are no substitute for physical activity, but some activities are just better off experienced through a virtual medium.

I believe video games actually reduce physical violence in anyone who plays them. Leo believes that "Adolescent feelings of resentment, powerlessness and revenge pour into the killing games" (467). His statement is faulty. It should have read, "Players' feelings of resentment, powerlessness, and revenge pour into video games." I pour hatred, frustration, and yes, even resentment, powerlessness, and revenge into any and all of the games I play. Would he rather have us pour them into reality? That's what Dylan Klebold and Eric Harris did in Columbine. I don't think they should have played less Doom (the game frequently cited as "hyperviolent"); I think they should have played more Doom. I can't count the number of times I've been angry enough to hurt someone but instead decided to take my anger out on a **fake** Martial Artist in Virtua Fighter 4 or by slaying vampires in Soul Reaver 2. Video games don't cause pent-up emotions to spill over into reality. If anything, they help keep violent tendencies in check by being an incredibly safe outlet for stress and rage.

I am no longer a child, and I am still offended by Leo's comment about children not being able to tell the difference between a video game and real life. He claims "games are often played by unstable youngsters who are unsure about the difference" (467). In my opinion, if kids are even able to understand how to play a particular video game, they know the difference. I used to baby-sit a hyperactive 4-year-old who played Pokemon and Super Mario Bros. all the time, yet his sense of reality was never warped. Never once did he try to catch the family dog with a ball or jump on me, so I would squish like the goombas in Super Mario Bros. I never caught him trying to eat mushrooms or flowers in an attempt to gain superpowers. I did, however, catch him shooting at me with sticks he called guns. None of his games had guns in them. Where did he learn to shoot at me then? I know I didn't teach him. It is quite possible that he learned this behavior by watching the many war documentaries on the History Channel that his father is so fond of.

I refuse to believe video games cause anyone's, including children's, aversion to killing to be reduced. "I" have easily "killed" over 2,000 "people" in Grand Theft Auto III, many of whom never deserved being blown away with a shotgun, getting torched with a Molotov cocktail, or getting run over with their own car after I stole it from them. I didn't even bat an eye after the third time "I" "killed" someone. This may not sound like a convincing argument in favor of the innocence of video games, but it is, and for one very good reason: I felt horrible the last time I hit a bunny rabbit with my car. It wasn't even my fault, but I felt so bad. I felt empathy for a suicidal woodland creature who wanted to end it so badly that he jumped in front of my Goodyears. Try to tell me that video games erode empathy and cause one's aversion of killing to fade. I couldn't even accidentally kill a rabbit without feeling remorse, let alone kill a person.

Leo uses statistics in an attempt to prove video games are effective at teaching children to kill. It is too bad the statistics are taken out of context and prove nothing. He writes, "During World War II, only 15 percent to 20 percent of all American soldiers fired their weapons in battle" (468). He then goes on to quote psychologist David Grossman by citing an Army experiment which found that recruits who shot at man-shaped targets were "more willing to 'make killing a reflex action'" (qtd. in Leo 468). Great, so we have a well-trained army. How many students do you know who carry side arms around with them and are frequently bombarded by dangerous people jumping out at them like cardboard targets? Must I also remind Leo that video games are played mainly with a controller? It is nothing like a gun. I can get headshot after headshot while playing Counter-Strike but couldn't hit the bull's-eye on a target 50 feet away with a bb gun. Just because someone is good at an activity in video games, it doesn't make them good at that activity in real life. This brings me to another one of the fallacies perpetuated by Leo and others in the press.

Leo and his colleagues believe killing games actually increase the accuracy a player has with a real gun. According to this logic, I should be able to get my driver's license after spending a few hours playing a racing game. The game Doom has come under attack after it was found that one of the Littleton boys played it frequently. It has been attributed to improving the accuracy of both the Littleton shooters and shooters involved in other school incidents. The people who slander this game have obviously never played it before. If they had, they would know that it is a computer game that is controlled with a mouse and keyboard. The movement of the mouse is much more akin to a DJ's record scratching than it is to aiming a gun. Hell, I might even give it to them if they blamed a stabbing incident on Doom because at least that is similar to the motion used to control the character. The only skill Doom and other computer games promote are better keyboarding skills and more control over a computer's mouse.

Leo's most absurd claim is his use of circumstantial evidence to falsely liken Dylan Klebold's and Eric Harris' suicide at the end of their rampage to the ending sequence in the video game Postal. Apparently the game's main character can't take it anymore and just goes postal, killing and maiming people along the way. At the end of the game he shoots himself in the head. True, Klebold and Harris shot themselves in the head, but I'm sorry—they were already planning on suicide before they went into that school. They had guns with them; what were they going to do, hang themselves? They were not going to try and commit suicide by shooting themselves in the foot now were they? Mr. Leo doesn't even say if the boys even played Postal, so how can he compare it to them?

Yes, as you probably gleamed from my excursions in Grand Theft Auto III, video games have become steadily more realistic and increasingly more violent. As fun as they are, I do not believe young children should be exposed to violent video games any more than I believe they should be allowed to see R rated movies. What some people don't realize is video games have a rating system on them, just like movies. I applaud merchants who only sell rated M (for mature) games to those buyers who are 17 and above. This is, I believe, a giant leap in the right direction towards getting politicians and journalists off video games' back. For some reason, however, people still neglect to acknowledge that this rating system has been put into effect and is indeed very effective.

Video games are not responsible for the slew of problems that people blame on them, of which I have only scratched the surface, yet they continue to be held responsible. I can't make people stop blaming their children's and society's problems on video games; I can only hope they find a new scapegoat. Not that that is the answer either, but at least they won't be ruining perfectly good games that perfectly normal people, including myself, enjoy playing.

Society is great at finding scapegoats for the problems they refuse to claim as their own. Society's problems used to be blamed on demons and witchcraft, literature, pornography, and eventually backward masked messages in rock music during the 1970s. Not long after, movies and television were unfairly blamed, and now video games are the new target. What's next? I thought society had learned to admit their mistakes and shortcomings, but I guess it just finds something new to blame. Must video games be sacrificed so society can satiate its hunger for denial? It sure looks that way.

### Works Cited

Leo, John. "Kill-for-Kicks Video Games Desensitizing Our Children." *Writing Arguments*. Eds. John D. Ramage, John C. Bean, and June Johnson. Boston: Allyn & Bacon, 2001. 467–468.

**READING WRITING**

## THIS TEXT: READING

1. What is Walsh's thesis? Is it clear?
2. Does Walsh do a good job of poking holes in Leo's arguments? What is his most compelling assertion?
3. How does Walsh's opening contribute to the overall feeling of the essay?

## YOUR TEXT: WRITING

1. Write a rebuttal to one of the essays in this chapter. Be sure to pay attention to questions of logos, pathos and ethos when formulating your arguments.
2. Write a review of a new video game. What makes a video game *good?*
3. Write a comparison contrast paper in which you "read" a movie and then the video game of that movie. How are they similar? In what way does technology contribute to each?

---

| WHERE DO YOU WANT TO GO TODAY? CYBERNETIC TOURISM, THE INTERNET, AND TRANSNATIONALITY ■ Lisa Nakamura ■ | *Lisa Nakamura (2000) looks at the relationship between culture, technology, and advertising, taking as her thesis the idea that advertisers are using foreign culture as a way* |

*of selling technological innovation.*

*There is no race. There is no gender. There is no age. There are no infirmities. There are only minds. Utopia? No, Internet.*

—"Anthem," television commercial for MCI

THE TELEVISION COMMERCIAL "Anthem" claims that on the Internet, there are no infirmities, no gender, no age, that there are only minds. This pure, democratic, cerebral form of communication is touted as a utopia, a pure no-place where human interaction can occur, as the voice-over says, "uninfluenced by the rest of it." Yet can the "rest of it" be written out as easily as the word *race* is crossed out on the chalkboard by the hand of an Indian girl in this commercial?

It is "the rest of it," the specter of racial and ethnic difference and its visual and textual representation in print and television advertisements that appeared in 1997 by Compaq, IBM, and Origin, that I will address in this chapter. The ads I will discuss all sell networking and communications technologies that depict racial difference, the "rest of it," as a visual marker. The spectacles of race in these advertising images are designed to stabilize contemporary anxieties that networking technology and access to cyberspace may break down ethnic and racial difference. These advertisements, which promote the glories of cyberspace, cast the viewer in the position of the tourist, and sketch out a future in which difference is either elided or put in its proper place.

The ironies in "Anthem" exist on several levels. For one, the advertisement positions MCI's commodity—"the largest Internet network in the world"—as a solution to social problems. The advertisement claims to produce a radical form of democracy that refers to and extends an "American" model of social equality and equal access. This patriotic anthem, however, is a paradoxical one: the visual images of diversity (old, young, black, white, deaf, etc.) are displayed and celebrated as spectacles of difference that the narrative simultaneously attempts to erase by claiming that MCI's product will reduce the different bodies that we see to "just minds."

The ad gestures towards a democracy founded upon disembodiment and uncontaminated by physical difference, but it must also showcase a dizzying parade of difference in order to make its point. Diversity is displayed as the sign of what the product will eradicate. Its erasure and elision can only be understood in terms of its presence; like the word "race" on the chalkboard, it can only be crossed out if it is written or displayed. This ad writes race and poses it as both a beautiful spectacle and a vexing question. Its narrative describes a "postethnic America," to use David Hollinger's phrase, where these categories will be made not to count. The supposedly liberal and progressive tone of the ad camouflages its depiction of race as something to be eliminated, or made "not to count," through technology. If computers and networks can help us to communicate without "the rest of it," that residue of difference with its power to disturb, disrupt, and challenge, then we can all exist in a world "without boundaries."

Another television commercial, this one by AT&T, that aired during the 1996 Olympics asks the viewer to "imagine a world without limits—AT&T believes communication can make it happen." Like "Anthem," this narrative posits a connection between networking and a democratic ethos in which differences will be elided. In addition, it resorts to a similar visual strategy—it depicts a black man in track shorts leaping over the Grand Canyon.

Like many of the ads by high tech and communications companies that aired during the Olympics, this one has an "international" or multicultural flavor that seems to celebrate national and ethnic identities. This world without limits is represented by vivid and often sublime images of displayed ethnic and racial difference in order to bracket them off as exotic and irremediably other. Images of this other as primitive, anachronistic, and picturesque decorate the landscape of these ads.

Microsoft's recent television and print media campaign markets access to personal computing and Internet connectivity by describing these activities as a form of travel. Travel and tourism, like networking technology, are commodities that define the privileged, industrialized first-world subject, and they situate him in the position of the one who looks, the one who has access, the one who communicates. Microsoft's omnipresent slogan "Where do you want to go today?" rhetorically places this consumer in the position of the user with unlimited choice; access to Microsoft's technology and networks promises the consumer a "world without limits" where he can possess an idealized mobility. Microsoft's promise to transport the user to new (cyber)spaces where desire can be fulfilled is enticing in its very vagueness, offering a seemingly open-ended invitation for travel and new experiences. A sort of technologically enabled transnationality is evoked here, but one that directly addresses the first-world user, whose position on the network will allow him to metaphorically go wherever he likes.

This dream or fantasy of ideal travel common to networking advertisements constructs a destination that can look like an African safari, a trip to the Amazonian rain forest, or a camel caravan in the Egyptian desert. The iconography of the travelogue or tourist attraction in these ads places the viewer in the position of the tourist who, in Dean MacCannell's words, "simply collects experiences of difference (different people, different places)" and "emerges as a miniature clone of the old Western philosophical subject, thinking itself unified, central, in control, etc., mastering Otherness and profiting from it" (xv). Networking ads that promise the viewer control and mastery over technology and communications discursively and visually link this power to a vision of the other which, in contrast to the mobile and networked tourist/user, isn't going anywhere. The continued presence of stable signifiers of otherness in telecommunications advertising guarantees the Western subject that his position, wherever he may choose to go today, remains privileged.

An ad from Compaq that appeared in the *Chronicle of Higher Education* reads "Introducing a world where the words 'you can't get there from here' are never heard." It depicts a "sandstone mesa" with the inset image of a monitor from which two schoolchildren gaze curiously at the sight. The ad is selling "Compaq networked multimedia. With it, the classroom is no longer a destination, it's a starting point." Like the Microsoft and AT&T slogans, it links networks with privileged forms of travel, and reinforces the metaphor by visually depicting sights that viewers associate with tourism. The networked classroom is envisioned as a glass window from which networked users can consume the sights of travel as if they were tourists.

Another ad from the Compaq series shows the same children admiring the networked rain forest from their places inside the networked classroom, signified by the frame of the monitor. The tiny box on the upper-right-hand side of the image evokes the distinctive menu bar of a Windows product, and frames the whole ad for its viewer as a window onto an "other" world.

The sublime beauty of the mesa and the lush pastoral images of the rain forest are nostalgically quoted here in order to assuage an anxiety about the environmental effects of cybertechnology. In a world where sandstone mesas and rain forests are becoming increasingly rare, partly as a result of industrialization, these ads position networking as a benign, "green" type of product that will preserve the beauty of nature, at least as an image on the screen. As John Macgregor Wise puts it, this is part of the modernist discourse that envisioned electricity as "transcendent, pure and clean," unlike mechanical technology. The same structures of metaphor that allow this ad to dub the experience of using networked communications "travel" also enables it to equate an image of a rain forest in Nature (with a capital *N*). The enraptured American schoolchildren, with their backpacks and French braids, are framed as user-travelers. With the assistance of Compaq, they have found their way to a world that seems to be without limits, one in which the images of nature are as good as or better than reality.

The virtually real rain forest and mesa participate in a postcyberspace paradox of representation—the locution "virtual reality" suggests that the line or "limit" between the authentic sight/site and its simulation has become blurred. This discourse has become familiar, and was anticipated by Jean Baudrillard pre-Internet. Familiar as it is, the Internet and its representations in media such as advertising have refigured the discourse in different contours. The ads that I discuss attempt to stabilize the slippery relationship between the virtual and the real by insisting upon the monolithic visual differences between first- and third-world landscapes and people.

This virtual field trip frames Nature as a tourist sight and figures Compaq as the educational tour guide. In this post-Internet culture of simulation in which we live, it is increasingly necessary for stable, iconic images of Nature and the Other to be evoked in the world of technology advertising. These images guarantee and gesture toward the unthreatened and unproblematic existence of a destination for travel, a place whose beauty and exoticism will somehow remain intact and attractive. If technology will indeed make everyone, everything, and every place the same, as "Anthem" claims in its ambivalent way, then where is there left to go? What is there left to see? What is the use of being asked where you want to go today if every place is just like here? Difference, in the form of exotic places or exotic people, must be demonstrated iconographically in order to shore up the Western user's identity as himself.

This idyllic image of an Arab on his camel, with the pyramids picturesquely squatting in the background, belongs in a coffee-table book. The timeless quality of this image of an exotic other untouched by modernity is disrupted by the cartoon dialogue text, which reads "What do you say we head back and download the results of the equestrian finals?" This dissonant use of contemporary vernacular American techoslang is supposed to be read comically; the man is meant to look unlike anyone who would speak these words.

The gap between the exotic Otherness of the image and the familiarity of its American rhetoric can be read as more than an attempt at humor, however. IBM, whose slogan "solutions for a small planet" is contained in an icon button in the lower left hand side of the image, is literally putting these incongruous words into the Other's mouth, thus demonstrating the hegemonic power of its "high speed information network" to make the planet smaller by causing everyone to speak the *same* language—computer-speak. His position as the exotic Other must be emphasized and foregrounded in order for this strategy to work, for the image's appeal rests upon its evocation of the exotic. The rider's classical antique "look and feel" atop his Old Testament camel guarantee that his access to a high speed network will not rob us, the tourist/viewer, of the spectacle of his difference. In the phantasmatic world of Internet advertising, he can download all the results he likes, so long as his visual appeal to us, the viewer, reassures us that we are still in the position of the tourist, the Western subject, whose privilege it is to enjoy him in all his anachronistic glory.

These ads claim a world without boundaries for us, their consumers and target audience, and by so doing they show us exactly where and what these boundaries really are. These boundaries are ethnic and racial ones. Rather than being effaced, these dividing lines are evoked over and over again. In addition, the ads sanitize and idealize their depictions of the Other and Otherness by deleting all references that might threaten their status as timeless icons. In the camel image, the sky is an untroubled blue, the pyramids have fresh, clean, sharp outlines, and there are no signs whatsoever of pollution, roadkill, litter, or fighter jets.

Including these "real life" images in the advertisement would disrupt the picture it presents us of an Other whose "unspoiled" qualities are so highly valued by tourists. Indeed, as Trinh Minh-Ha notes, even very sophisticated tourists are quick to reject experiences that challenge their received notions of authentic Otherness. Trinh writes, "the Third World representative the modern sophisticated public ideally seeks is the *unspoiled* African, Asian, or Native American, who remains more preoccupied with his/her image as the *real* native—the *truly different*—than with the issues of hegemony, feminism, and social change." Great pains are taken in this ad to make the camel rider appear real, truly different from us, and "authentic" in order to build an idealized Other whose unspoiled nature shores up the tourist's sense that he is indeed seeing the "real" thing. In the post-Internet world of simulation, "real" things are fixed and preserved in images such as these in order to anchor the Western viewing subject's sense of himself as a privileged and mobile viewer.

Since the conflicts in Mogadishu, Sarajevo, and Zaire (images of which are found elsewhere in the magazines from which these ads came), ethnic difference in the world of Internet advertising is visually "cleansed" of its divisive, problematic, tragic connotations. The ads function as corrective texts for readers deluged with images of racial conflicts and bloodshed both at home and abroad. These advertisements put the world right; their claims for better living (and better boundaries) through technology are graphically acted out in idealized images of Others who miraculously speak like "us" but still look like "them."

The Indian man (pictured in an IBM print advertisement that appeared in *Smithsonian*, January 1996) whose iconic Indian elephant gazes sidelong at the viewer as he affectionately curls his trunk around his owner's neck, has much in common with his Egyptian counterpart in the previous ad. (The ad's text tells us that his name is Sikander, making him somewhat less generic than his counterpart, but not much. Where is the last name?) The thematics of this series produced for IBM play upon the depiction of ethnic, racial, and linguistic differences, usually all at the same time, in order to highlight the hegemonic power of IBM's technology. IBM's television ads (there were several produced and aired in this same series in 1997) were memorable because they were all subtitled vignettes of Italian nuns, Japanese surgeons, and Norwegian skiers engaged in their quaint and distinctively ethnic pursuits, but united in their use of IBM networking machines. The sounds of foreign languages being spoken in television ads had their own ability to shock and attract attention, all to the same end—the one word that was spoken in English, albeit heavily accented English, was "IBM."

Thus, the transnational language, the one designed to end all barriers between speakers, the speech that everyone can pronounce and that cannot be translated or incorporated into another tongue, turns out not to be Esperanto but rather IBM-speak, the language of American corporate technology. The foreignness of the Other is exploited here to remind the viewer—who may fear that IBM-speak will make the world smaller in undesirable ways (for example, that they might compete for our jobs, move into our neighborhoods, go to our schools)—that the Other is still picturesque. This classically Orientalized Other, such as the camel rider and Sikander, is marked as sufficiently different from us, the projected viewers, in order to encourage us to retain our positions as privileged tourists and users.

Sikander's cartoon-bubble, emblazoned across his face and his elephant's, asks, "How come I keep trashing my hardware every 9 months?!" This question can be read as a rhetorical example of what postcolonial theorist and novelist Salman Rushdie has termed "globalizing Coca-Colonization." Again, the language of technology, with its hacker-dude vernacular, is figured here as the transnational tongue, miraculously emerging from every mouth. Possible fears that the exoticism and heterogeneity of the Other will be siphoned off or eradicated by his use of homogeneous technospeak are eased by the visual impact of the elephant, whose trunk frames Sikander's face. Elephants, rain forests, and unspoiled mesas are all endangered markers of cultural difference that represent specific stereotyped ways of being Other to Western eyes. If we did not know that Sikander was a "real" Indian (as opposed to Indian-American, Indian-Canadian, or Indo-Anglian) the presence of his elephant, as well as the text's reference to "Nirvana," proves to us, through the power of familiar images, that he is. We are meant to assume that even after Sikander's hardware problems are solved by IBM's "consultants who consider where you are as well are where you're headed" he will still look as picturesque, as "Indian" as he did pre-IBM.

Two other ads, part of the same series produced by IBM, feature more ambiguously ethnic figures. The first one of these depicts a Latina girl who is asking her teacher, Mrs. Alvarez, how to telnet to a remote server. She wears a straw hat, which makes reference to the Southwest. Though she is only eight or ten years old, her speech has already acquired the distinctive sounds of technospeak—for example, she uses "telnet" as a verb. The man in the second advertisement, an antique-looking fellow with old fashioned glasses, a dark tunic, dark skin, and an untidy beard proclaims that "you're hosed when a virus sneaks into your hard drive." He, too, speaks the transnational vernacular—the diction of Wayne and Garth from *Wayne's World* has sneaked into *his* hard drive like a rhetorical virus. These images, like the preceding ones, enact a sort of cultural ventriloquism that demonstrates the hegemonic power of American technospeak. The identifiably ethnic faces, with their distinctive props and costumes, that utter these words, however, attest to the importance of Otherness as a marker of a difference that the ads strive to preserve.

This Origin ad appeared in *Wired* magazine, which, like *Time, Smithsonian,* the *New Yorker,* and *The Chronicle of Higher Education,* directs its advertising toward upper-middle-class, mainly white readers. In addition, *Wired* is read mainly by men, it has an unabashedly libertarian bias, and its stance toward technology is generally utopian. Unlike the other ads, this one directly and overtly poses ethnicity and cultural difference as part of a political and commercial dilemma that Origin networks can solve. The text reads, in part,

> [W]e believe that wiring machines is the job, but connecting people the art. Which means besides skills you also need wisdom and understanding. An understanding of how people think and communicate. And the wisdom to respect the knowledge and cultures of others. Because only then can you create systems and standards they can work with. And common goals which all involved are willing to achieve.

The image of an African boy, surrounded by his tribe, seemingly performing a *Star Trek* Vulcan mind meld with a red-haired and extremely pale boy, centrally situates the white child, whose arm is visible in an unbroken line, as the figure who is supposedly as willing to learn as he is to teach.

However, the text implies that the purpose of the white boy's encounter with an African boy and his tribe is for him to learn just enough about them to create the "systems and standards that THEY can work with." The producer of marketable knowledge, the setter of networking and software-language standards, is still defined here as the Western subject. This image, which could have come out of *National Geographic* any time in the last hundred years, participates in the familiar iconography of colonialism and its contemporary cousin, tourism. And in keeping with this association, it depicts the African as unspoiled and authentic. Its appeal to travel across national and geographical borders as a means of understanding the Other, "the art of connecting people," is defined as a commodity which this ad and others produced by networking companies sell along *with* their fiber optics and consulting services.

The notion of the computer-enabled "global village" envisioned by Marshall McLuhan also participates in this rhetoric that links exotic travel and tourism with technology. The Origin image comments on the nature of the global village by making it quite clear to the viewer that despite technology's claims to radically and instantly level cultural and racial differences (or in a more extreme statement, such as that made by "Anthem," to literally cross them out) there will always be villages full of "real" Africans, looking just as they always have.

It is part of the business of advertising to depict utopias: ideal depictions of being that correctively reenvision the world and prescribe a solution to its ills in the form of a commodity of some sort. And like tourist pamphlets, they often propose that their products will produce, in Dean MacCannell's phrase, a "utopia of difference," such as has been pictured in many Benetton and Coca-Cola advertising campaigns.

Coca-Cola's slogan from the seventies and eighties, "I'd like to teach the world to sing," both predates and prefigures these ads by IBM, Compaq, Origin, and MCI. The Coca-Cola ads picture black, white, young, old, and so on holding hands and forming a veritable Rainbow Coalition of human diversity. These singers are united by their shared song and, most important, their consumption of bottles of Coke. The viewer, meant to infer that the beverage was the direct cause of these diverse Coke drinkers overcoming their ethnic and racial differences, was given the same message then that many Internet-related advertisements give us today. The message is that cybertechnology, like Coke, will magically strip users down to "just minds," all singing the same corporate anthem.

And what of the "rest of it," the raced and ethnic body that cyberspace's "Anthem" claims to leave behind? It seems that the fantasy terrain of advertising is loath to leave out this marked body because it represents the exotic Other which both attracts us with its beauty and picturesqueness and reassures us of our own identities as "*not* Other." The "rest of it" is visually quoted in these images and then pointedly marginalized and established *as Other*. The iconography of these advertising images demonstrates that the corporate image factory *needs* images of the Other in order to depict its product: a technological utopia of difference. It is not, however, a utopia *for* the Other or one that includes it in any meaningful or progressive way. Rather, it proposes an ideal world of virtual social and cultural reality based on specific methods of "Othering," a project that I would term "the globalizing Coca-Colonization of cyberspace and the media complex within which it is embedded."

## Acknowledgments

I would like to thank the members of the Sonoma State University Faculty Writing Group: Kathy Charmaz, Richard Senghas, Dorothy Freidel, Elaine McHugh, and Virginia Lea for their encouragement and suggestions for revision. I would also like to thank my research assistant and independent study advisee at Sonoma State, Dean Klotz, for his assistance with permissions, research, and all things cyber. And a very special thanks to Amelie Hastie and Martin Burns, who continue to provide support and advice during all stages of my work on this topic.

### References

Hollinger, David. *Postethnic America: Beyond Multiculturalism.* New York: Basic Books, 1995.
McCannell, Dean. *The Tourist: A New Theory of the Leisure Class.* New York: Schocken Books, 1989.
McLuhan, Marshall. *Understanding Media: The Extensions of Man.* Cambridge: MIT Press, 1994.

Rushdie, Salman. "Damme, This Is the Oriental Scene For You!" *New Yorker,* 23 and 30 June 1997, 50–61.

Trinh Minh-ha. *Woman, Native, Other: Writing Postcoloniality and Feminism.* Bloomington: University of Indiana Press, 1989.

Wise, John Macgregor. "The Virtual Community: Politics and Affect in Cyberspace." Paper delivered at the American Studies Association Conference, Washington D.C., 1997.

**READING WRITING**

## THIS TEXT: READING

1. What about the relationship between commerce and technology is Nakamura exposing?
2. What is the logic behind the ads Nakamura talks about? Why might people be inclined to purchase these products?
3. What assumptions about technological change are the ads implying? Do you think this is general trend among manufacturers? The media?

## YOUR TEXT: WRITING

1. Nakamura looks at the world through the reflection of advertising. Write about an ad that does similar forms of advertising.
2. Is there a special need to be truthful when advertising for technology? Does Nakamura think so? Write a short piece that examines some of the ways computer makers and Internet merchants use technological advances as promises to the consumer.
3. In what ways does the United States pretend that it is similar to other countries when it comes to technology? What is the reality? Write a paper talking about the technological dominance of the United States, and why we have an ambivalent relationship with this idea.

# Technology and Communication Suite

Fifteen years ago, there were essentially three ways people communicated with one another—by mail, by phone, or in person. Maybe, but rarely, you might communicate by fax, walkie talkie, or CB radio, but only if you were a geek. Now, there are the basic three forms of communication, plus email, text messaging, picture-phone, and cell phone. One can also meet in a chat room, or receive text messages on a personal digital assistant (PDA). One can post messages to a bulletin board, or in class, type responses to a question on a system like Blackboard. The ways we are communicating are expanding, and though it might seem we have reached certain limits to the methods of communicating, we certainly could improve on their efficiency.

More important are some of the implications of this communication. We can now communicate in a multitude of ways, but do we communicate *better*? This suite's articles explore some of the implications of communicating over the Internet. Deborah Tannen explores the ways technology has improved communication, but cannot replace more traditional forms. Camille Sweeney writes about the way the Internet makes communication both liberating and concealing. Focusing on Internet mail-order brides, Virginia Colwell examines the way the Internet has become a place where "reality, identity, and fantasy" meet.

## CONNECTIONS
### ■ Deborah Tannen ■

My father never knew his father. Until he was seven, he lived with his mother and sister in his grandparents' home: a Hasidic household in Warsaw. His grandfather was the closest he ever came to having a father.

In 1920, when my father was twelve, he left Poland to emigrate with his mother and sister to the United States, and he saw his grandfather for the last time. As my father tells it, his grandfather took him on his knee to say good-bye. Tears ran down the old man's face and into his long white beard. He knew he would never see his grandchild again. Even if the Holocaust had not taken his grandfather's life, my father would not have been able to return to Poland for a visit during his grandfather's life-time. He wouldn't have been able to take the time off work to sail across the ocean, and he wouldn't have been able to afford the trip.

In 1966, I graduated from college, worked for six months, saved all the money I earned, and flew to Europe on a one-way ticket through Luxembourg on Icelandic Airlines. I ended up in Greece, where I lived for nearly two years, teaching English. I communicated with my parents by mail—but from time to time I would telephone them: I'd go to the main post office in downtown Athens, fill out a form, and wait until someone called my name and indicated in which booth my parents' voices would materialize. Sometimes I waited hours for the call to be put through—until the planned evening surprise had become a terrifying, sleep-destroying, wee-hours-of-the-morning alarm. "Do me a favor," my mother once said. "If it's after midnight, don't call." "But I've been waiting to put the call through for four hours," I said. "I didn't plan it to be after midnight." And there were not only telephones, but airplanes. During that year, my parents celebrated their thirty-fifth wedding anniversary; and they gave each of their children $1000. I used a portion of mine to fly home to New York City for their anniversary party.

In 1996, my oldest sister went to Israel for a year. Within a few weeks, she subscribed to Compuserve and hooked up her laptop computer to e-mail—and my other sister and my nieces all got on e-mail, too. Within a month, my sister was in daily communication with us all—much more frequent contact than our weekly (or biweekly or monthly) telephone calls had been when my sister was home in upstate New York.

And another surprise: my other sister, who generally is not eager to talk about her feelings, opened up on e-mail. One time I called her and we spoke on the phone; after we hung up, I checked my e-mail and found a message she had sent before we spoke, in which she revealed personal information that she hadn't mentioned on the phone. I asked her about this (on e-mail), and she explained, "The telephone is so impersonal." At first this seemed absurd: How could the actual voice of a person in conversation be more impersonal than on-screen little letters detached from the writer? But when I thought about it, it made sense: Writing e-mail is like writing in a journal; you're alone with your thoughts and your words, safe from the intrusive presence of another person.

I was the second person in my university department to get a computer. The first was my colleague Ralph. The year was 1980. Ralph got a Radio Shack TRS 80; I got a used Apple 2-Plus. He helped me get started, and before long helped me get on Bitnet, the precursor to the Internet. Though his office was next to mine, we rarely had extended conversations except about department business. Shy and soft-spoken, Ralph mumbled, so I could barely tell he was speaking. But when we were using e-mail, we started communicating daily in this (then) leisurely medium. We could send each other messages without fear of imposing, since the receiver determines when to log on and read and respond. Soon I was getting long self-revealing messages from Ralph. We moved effortlessly among discussions of department business, our work, and our lives. Through e-mail Ralph and I became friends.

Ralph recently forwarded to me a message he had received from his niece, a college freshman. "How nice," I commented, "that you have such a close relationship with your niece. Do you think you'd be in touch with her if it weren't for e-mail?" "No," he replied. "I can't imagine we'd write each other letters regularly or call on the phone. No way." E-mail makes possible connections with relatives, acquaintances, or strangers, that wouldn't otherwise exist. And it enables more frequent and different communication with people you're already close to. Parents are in daily contact with their children at college; people discover and reunite with long lost friends. One woman discovered that e-mail brought her closer to her father. He would never talk much on the phone (as her mother would), but they have become close since they both got on-line.

The Internet and the World Wide Web are creating networks of human connection unthinkable even a few years ago. But at the same time that technologically enhanced communication enable previously impossible loving contact, it also enhances hostile and distressing communication. Along with the voices of family members and friends, telephones bring into our homes the annoying voices of solicitors who want to sell something—at dinnertime. (My father-in-law startles a telephone solicitor by saying, "We're eating dinner, but I'll call you back. What's your home phone number?" To the nonplussed caller he explains, "Well, you're calling me at home; I thought I'd call you at home, too.") Even more unnerving, in the middle of the night come frightening obscene calls and stalkers.

The Internet ratchets up anonymity by homogenizing all messages into identical-appearing print and making it almost impossible to trace messages back to the computer that sent them. As the ease of using the Internet has resulted in more and more people logging on and sending messages to more and more others with whom they have a connection, it has also led to more communication with strangers, and this has led to "flaming": viluperative messages that verbally attack. Flaming results from the anonymity not only of the sender but also of the receiver. It is easier to feel and express hostility against someone far removed whom you do not know, like the rage that some drivers feel toward an anonymous car that cuts them off. If the driver to whom you've flipped the finger turns out to be someone you know, the rush of shame you feel is evidence that anonymity was essential for your expression—and experience—of rage.

Less and less of our communication is face to face, and more often with people we don't know. Technology that brings people closer also isolates us in a bubble. When I was a child, my family got the first television on our block, and the neighborhood children gathered in our dining room to watch *Howdy Doody*. Before long, every family had their own TV—just one, so that in order to watch it, families came together. Now many families have more than one television, so each family member can watch what they like—alone. The spread of radio has followed the same pattern. Early radios were like a piece of furniture around which a family had to gather in order to listen. Now radio listeners may have a radio in every room, one in the car, and another—equipped with headphones—for jogging. These technologies now exert a centrifugal force, pulling people apart—and increasing the likelihood that their encounters with each other will be anonymous and hostile.

Electronic communication is programs; it makes human relationships different. But it also makes human relationships more the same—there's more of what's good and more of what's bad. In the end, we graft the new possibilities onto what has always been there.

E-mail gave me the chance to be in touch with someone who was dying far away. College friends, Larry and I were not so close that we would make special trips to visit each other on opposite coasts, but we kept in touch through occasional notes, and we got together whenever we found ourselves in the same town. I learned from another college friend—on e-mail—that Larry was diagnosed with lung cancer. I didn't want to call Larry on the phone; that seemed too intrusive. I didn't know if he wanted to talk about his cancer with people like me; maybe he wanted to curl into his family. So I sent him an e-mail message, and he sent one in reply. Soon we were exchanging messages regularly. E-mail gave me a little path I could walk along. For two years, Larry kept me informed of how he was doing, and what the chemotherapy was doing to him—and asked me how my book was coming and whether I had managed to put up pictures in my new house yet. In April 1996 he was back to work and gaining weight. But then e-mail brought the bad news: new lesions were found, and the doctors held out no more hope.

On December 24, 1996, Larry wrote, "I will miss our e-mails, Deb. It was great being your friend, and I will always remain so." On December 27 I got messages—both on e-mail and on my telephone answering machine—telling me Larry had died the night before. I could not just sit at my desk that day and work. And e-mail was not immediate enough for the connection I wanted. I called friends who had been closer to Larry than I, to learn as much as I could about his last days. And I called friends who had been less close, to tell them. I spent much of that day talking with friends from our college circle. We told each other our memories of Larry's life, creating our own memorial to observe his passing from our lives.

My father never knew exactly when his grandfather died. When my friend Larry died, how much it meant that the telephone made it possible to spend the day talking to others who know him. How much it meant that Larry said good-bye. This is a gift he gave me, and technology made it possible. That is progress. But the way we used technology—the telephone and e-mail—that was human emotion and experience as old as time.

### IN A CHAT ROOM, YOU CAN BE NE1: CONSTRUCTING A TEEN-AGE SELF ON LINE

#### ■ Camille Sweeney ■

"Yo yo yo, what's up what's up?" The lines scroll up my screen. Different fonts, different colors, the words whiz by, everyone's screen name sounding vaguely pornographic. I'm on America Online, in a chat room for young adults. There are hundreds of such chat rooms on AOL, and it has taken a lot of Net navigating simply to find one that has room enough to let me in.

For all the crowds and clamoring, there's not much being said in this chat room, or rather, not much that's being paid attention to. A 16-year-old girl is talking about her baby due in two months. A grumpy 15-year-old guy reluctantly wishes her well. Another girl, 17, asks, "Are your parents cool with it?" The lines continue to scroll, a word here, a phrase there, live text that reads much like a flow of conversation you might overhear in a crowded high-school hallway or parking lot between classes in old-fashioned meat space (that is, anyplace not in the cyberworld).

I've been on line, off and on, for months trying to determine if there is such a thing as a cyberself and, if so, what goes into the making of this most modern of personality constructs. Teen-agers especially are fitting specimens for this experiment because they are the first generation saturated in this new medium. In any given week, according to Teenage Research Unlimited, nearly 70 percent of all 12- to 19-year-olds go on line. The Internet has shaped them—just as television shaped their parents, and radio their grandparents. Once a generation saw itself grow up on TV; now a generation is watching itself grow up on line. It would follow then that the 31 million teen-agers of Gen Y or Generation Why or Echo Boomers or Millennials, as this group is variously called, would have completely new ways of perceiving one another and themselves. I went undercover as a cyberteen to find out.

Teen-age years—at least in my memory—are reserved largely for trying out different personas. As the psychoanalyst Erik Erikson contended, adolescence is a period "during which the individual through free role experimentation may find a niche in some section of his society, a niche which is firmly defined and yet seems to be uniquely made for him."

Herein lies the thrill of the on-line self: its malleability, its plasticity, the fact that it can be made up entirely of your own imagination. You can take your old self, or don a fresh one, and hang out in a group of jocks for a postgame chat, argue the banality of Britney Spears with an international posse of pop connoisseurs, post a note to a cool-sounding guy from Detroit—all without ever having to leave your bedroom. Maybe this is the Internet's greatest asset to teendom: access, and the confidence to slip in and out of personalities, the ability to try on identities, the adolescent equivalent of playing dress-up in the attic, standing before the mirror in heels and lipstick long before you own your own.

## March 1999

I'm on line as Red720720, a cumbersome screen name that I believe, nonetheless, sounds teenage blunt and allows me gender flexibility. I've been slow to get started. In fact, I really haven't said much beyond commiserating with the pregnant girl, telling her that when my sister was pregnant she found cocoa butter helpful, that it helped her skin feel "not as stretchy." I'm trying to talk in their language, although I worry that I'm not. For all the identify shifting that occurs on line, teen-agers tend to talk in a uniform way that leaves me scrambling. Not only is it teen talk—it's 90's teen talk. I have to think to remember "girl" not "woman." I have to think to remember "cool" not "very cool."

A crew of teen-agers suddenly bursts into the room crying out to get it on: "Want 2 cyber? Want 2 cyber?" They beg for "pics" (pictures) and often stop chatters in their tracks for what amounts to an all-room booty call. "Everybody, give me age, sex and favorite position," one guy writes; "everybody" is written in capital letters, the online version of shouting. The crew is ignored, washing over the room like a tide, before heading back out to sea. I chat with a Croatian teen-ager about obscure Scandinavian death-metal bands. He says he is 18. A lot of people post their ages and sex at the outset—"18/m." I find this frankness a little startling. I write "16/f" and ask him if his screen name, Flock82, was inspired by the 80's synth-pop band A Flock of Seagulls. He writes that he has never heard of them. I struggle to remember their big hit but realize I'm dating myself in doing so. "I can't remember their biggest hit," I write, "maybe I'll ask my older brother." Perhaps sensing a fraud, Flock82 moves on. I suddenly feel out of place, as if I'm wearing a thick turtleneck at a summer rave. Someone new has just entered the room, looking for love. "Watch out," he writes, in a flashy robin's-egg-blue font, "I'm coming in. . . ."

## May 1999

The Internet has been compared to a fun house, a free-for-all, a place where you might be robbed or cheated or deceived, a place where you can be promised a rainbow but given a mouthful of ashes. I spend a lot of time cruising E-zine sites for teen-agers and connecting to the ever-multiplying number of hyperlinks a lot of the Web pages offer. The randomness makes me dizzy. But in fact, I manage my first cyber-romance with a guy I meet a series of links away from a surfing site. He calls himself Brian_the_Hawaiian. He has something like a million screen names on a million different sites. He tells me he is 16, from Honolulu, but wants to get out of there soon to come to the continental U.S. We chat a few times, about waves and about whether the volcanoes in Hawaii are cool. (I have to think to remember not "very cool.") We become pals, going as far as to search for each other in a variety of spots if a couple of days go by without contact.

Then one night, out of nowhere, he asks me if I want to cyber. (He actually sounds serious!) I say no, but agree to send him a kiss, which I do. I write something like "peck." Actually, I write "peck peck," and, yes, I'm still mortified about it. Even though this is an experiment, and even though he says he's "crazy 4 older women" (this time I've said I'm 18), it still feels weird. He tells me his favorite movie star is Austin Powers, though I don't have the heart to mention to him that Austin Powers isn't real. He also says that maybe he wants to be an actor someday, or a professional surfer. I tell him "2 go 4 it." And I don't start getting worried until he wonders exactly how far I live from the Brooklyn Bridge. (I've told him I can see the bridge from my window.)

This feels a little too real. I tell him I have a boyfriend and say, "my boyfriend n i are planning 2 b 2gether 4 ever," and after I log off I begin to wonder if "Brian" isn't actually some 11-year-old boy living two floors above me. This kind of access is new to me. Are teen-agers all over the globe meeting up with their on-line pals in real life—at concerts, in the second-class compartments of European trains? Are they surfing the waves together off Waikiki? I never hear from Brian again.

## August 1999

The measure of a successful site, an Internet entrepreneur tells me, is its "stickiness." This is the number of hits a site receives, people checking it out, multiplied by the amount of time they spend on it. Bolt.com is sticky, a cyber-friend says, definitely a place where a lot of teen-agers go to hang and mostly talk about stuff teen-agers talk about—romance being No. 1. I log on to the friendly blue-and-orange home page, with features and bulletins, a quote of the day and a daily poll: "Would you date someone of different ethnicity?" "Would you date someone your parents don't approve of?" "Where would you say you get your style from?" Unlike so many dismally designed sites for teen-agers. Bolt seems like a breezy, busy, cool community. I choose "camarules" as my screen name, ditching my letter-digit combo. Dan Pelson, cofounder of the site, is right—if being on AOL is like driving your father's Oldsmobile on the Interstate, being on Bolt.com is like riding a Day-Glo mountain bike with a beefy shock absorber and no particular place to go.

Though there are plenty of other places for teen-agers to hang out on line, I spend most of my time on Bolt's bulletin boards. There are many to choose from, with topics ranging from Activism and Jobs and Money to Style and Sex and Dating. This is where you can post a message that either attracts a response or goes completely unheeded. The success of a message depends on a lot of factors the catchiness of the subject line, the popularity of the board and, most important, the general level of boredom of those on line. If people are bored, they'll check out just about anything.

And judging from my time on line, people are bored. "I'm so bored," writes a 16-year-old guy who refers to himself as Baron Vampire. Unlike a lot of the Boltsters, but like a lot of teen-agers, Baron Vampire doesn't really follow the topic being discussed on the board; instead, he turns the conversation back to himself. And he seems to attract attention—maybe because he's a bored vampire, maybe because the icon he uses with his screen name is a tiny bat, hanging upside down, blinking. I feel a maternal tug to respond, but I hold back, letting some of the girls on the board jump in to console him—it would be like getting in the way of a tribal dance.

Before long a group of female Boltsters have virtually surrounded the wounded vampire. "Why are you bored V?" they ask, firing him note after note. Doubtless some are even using a private note system that only he can see. He responds with an emoticon —:*(— that evokes both childhood pathos and "Rebel Without a Cause." "Crying on the net strange," one girl writes without punctuation. After several messages of concern, the vampire seems to perk up. "So how is everyone else?" he writes. "I don't want to hear if you're bored." I skate away.

A girl who calls herself Cool_P2 is giving a party in an area marked Miscellaneous. It's got the feel of a younger girls' party—too much soda, no boys. I look up the personal profile Cool_P2 filled out for Bolt: it includes things like date of birth, favorite movies, music. She has written that she's 11. Unlike many adult boards on the Net where everyone claims to be a teen-ager (even when no one is), the registered members of Bolt, now approaching 1.5 million worldwide, are mostly actual teen-agers. Even if Cool_P2 is lying about her (or his) age, I think a party's a great idea. Imagine letting your kids go to a party and not having to worry what time they come home. Cool_P2 kicks off using the asterisks code, which means that anything written between asterisks is considered action as opposed to dialogue. It's like a scene from a screenplay or a little theater piece, written, starring and directed by teen-agers, each line added onto by someone else.

9:05:51    *puts on music and shakes her thang*
9:07:02    Oh, so we're going to try this party thing again? Good luck!
9:07:03    Oh god . . . *shakes her head and walks away*
9:07:14    *busts a move*
9:07:52    Yumphf humphf! You people are weiiiiiiiird!

It gets later. I go to the Sex Questions board. A 15-year-old girl wants to know if cyber-ing with a guy she met on line is cheating on her boyfriend. There's frenzy of response. One guy writes, "You're so stupid!!" I consider writing something about lust in the heart, but de-cide to let them work it out on their own and scroll to the next posting. A real problem is being discussed. A 14-year-old girl writes: "My bf doesn't like taking off his hat when we make out. I like to rub my fingers threw [sic] his hair but I can't with his hat!!?? How do I get it off??? Help." A 15-year-old girl from Australia replies, "I bet he has some nasty, nasty hat hair." A guy of the same age writes that she should start playing the national anthem so he'll be forced to take it off. "I know that wasn't funny," he writes. "I'm bored." A younger girl writes that she should just tell him that "it's hard for u 2 make out when he's got his hat on." A 16-year-old girl calling herself Lollypop writes, "Let him kiss your ears if he lets you fondle his hair." That seems fair.

A few days later. I meet Stifbizkit. His screen name's a rip of Limp Bizkit, a popular hip-hop rock band out of Florida. Stif says he is 16 and posts a message on the Girl Trouble board; "popping the question" is his subject. He wants to know the sweetest way to do it: should he play a song, give her a letter or play a song and give her a letter. He writes that he is open to suggestions. I write asking him exactly what question he wants to pop. He jets me a note saying he wants to ask her to go out with him. We have several back-and-forths over the next couple of days. I'm happy to give him "girl" advice, and he is happy to report that in the interim he has spent a non-cyber evening with her and another couple. The girl from the other couple has told him that the girl he's after likes him. "She thinks I'm really hot," he writes, but also reports that despite a long night spent on top of a mountain, in his parent's hot tub and on a beach, all they did was talk. I tell him that sounds like cool progress and to keep it up.

No sooner have we finished than the board becomes transfixed with the plight of Four-traxman, a 14-year-old whose girlfriend, he says, broke up with him two hours ago and has already got back together with her ex. He says "she's one of those girls that's hard to get over." In the short time since the breakup. Fourtraxman has solicited a lot of advice. I watch as guys and girls from all over the world weigh in with remedies, consolation and just pure commiseration.

The on-line immediacy is astounding. This is not something that has to wait until first period Monday morning. Gold_Angel, an 18-year-old girl, writes that what that girl's done to him is just plain mean. "To ditch your current man for an ex is just wrong!" she writes, adding, "write me if you need to talk more!"

Where was this when I was their age? Where was this when Wade turned me down for the junior prom? In my teenage world, to get that rapid-fire attention would have taken sev-eral phone calls and lots of jockeying for phone time with my sisters, and maybe because of it my predicament would have gone undiscussed, at least through an entire evening. It's dif-ficult to know just what has changed for teen-agers today. Much of it is a general overexpo-sure to the adult world, but the new teen-age cyberself is demanding to be acknowledged and won't go away. The new teen-ager says: Here's what I'm thinking about. Here's what's happening to me right now. What am I going to do?

Maybe this isn't all that new. After all, speaking from my own increasingly distant experience, teen-agers have never been free from self-absorption. What is different is that, like everything in this cyberworld, kids are moving through their teen-age years at a lightning pace. The songs of teen-age life remain the same, but they're being remixed, played at a faster speed and at a much higher volume.

Once on line, you can get the definitive word on the date you left an hour ago, a review of a concert that just ended, advice on the right sling-pack to carry, a report on the latest come-on line. But you also get something else, something no other generation has ever had: the ability to leave your teen-age body behind and take advantage of the almost limitless freedom to explore your personal identity. Today's teen-agers can discover themselves (or the many parts of themselves) by roaming the boards and the chat rooms, connecting, disconnecting, shooting questions out into the universe—and maybe, just maybe, receiving answers.

*Student Essay*

## MAIL-ORDER BRIDES: THE CONTENT OF INTERNET COURTSHIP

■ **Virginia Colwell** ■

Within mail-order bride websites women are arranged on the monitor in yearbook-like configuration. A suitor can select a bride by clicking on her picture which leads to her personal page and gives details such as her occupation, height, religion, and eye color while also providing a brief personal statement and several photographs. Once a suitor has become interested in a bride he can purchase her email address to begin the relationship. While mail-order bride sites illustrate new arenas for communication and courtship on the Internet, they also illuminate the ways which this technology effects our traditional cultural conventions. Aided by the insight of A.R. Stone, author of *The War of Desire and Technology at the Close of the Mechanical Age,* I became "interested in prosthetic communication for what it shows of the real' world that might otherwise go unnoticed. I am interested because of the potential of cyberspace for the emergent behavior for new social forms that arise in a circumstance in which *body, meet, place,* and even *space* mean something quite different from our accustomed understanding" (37). Though often stereotyped and blurred by taboo, mail-order bride websites provide an ample basis for analyzing how people are pioneering new transitions between meeting and interacting in virtual reality with the intention of transferring this relationship into a real life affair. Challenging traditional ideas of dating and the importance of face to face contact for developing intimacy, mail-order bride websites exemplify a contemporary sense of reality, identity, and fantasy.

To begin my analysis I shall examine communication via the Internet and how it affects our perceptions of reality. As the Internet has become more widely accessible to the public, social constructions must adapt to the ambiguous nature of the Web and thus develop new behaviors to supercede the Internet's limitations. Secondly I shall examine how the hyperreality of the Internet affects how each individual constructs an identity. The translation of one's self from reality to virtual reality is an explicit example of portraying the self that is uniquely postmodern in its fabrication. And finally, as one generates themselves on the Web in pursuit of a relationship, a contemporary sense of seduction and fantasy become apparent. Romance takes on an especially fantastical context in the electronic format as one's imagination has an unparalleled freedom within cyberspace. Through this analysis of mail-order bride websites it is evident that they provide a perplexing insight into social behaviors that straddle reality and technology as brides look to make a clean transformation from virtual reality into the real world with an intimate relationship intact.

Central to our postmodern culture is the way in which we grapple with the distinction between reality and an increasingly prominent virtual sphere. Electronic formats permit both a concrete and simulated perspective of reality, often blurring the two. Interactive communication highlights this ambiguous area as words and text become disembodied from their authors and without any tangible referents. In an interview entitled "The Work of Art in the Electronic Age," Jean Baudrillard contends that the goals of communication can be surmounted by the medium when dealing with electronic formats: "It is often said that we are within communication and we are perhaps no longer exactly within exchange. At this time, what has changed is that the means of communication, the medium, is becoming a determinant element in exchange . . . and then the strategies which revolve around the medium . . . become more essential than the strategies which concern the contents" (qtd. in Gane 145). The Internet can provide an amazing capacity for communication, yet it also involves a paradoxical connection and disconnection simultaneously. The important dialogue of gesture, touch, sound, and smell are deprived, thus editing a full range of communicative possibilities and bringing into question the reality and depth of correspondence via the Net. A complete sense of reality is further suspended because the viewer can have no personal experience in which to add a greater amount of information or verify that which is received. What results from this incomplete amount of information is a hyper-reality in which "the reality or unreality, the truth or falsity of something" can no longer be discerned (Gane 146). These difficult aspects of hyper-reality are especially disconcerting when establishing sincere relationships via the Internet. One of the tricky aspects of the web is the ability of one to play with their identity. Truth is constantly called into question online, as the possibility for deception is a reality. However, in spite of this common fear, online courtship centers flourish as people attempt to find love within the hypertext.

Online match-making places are an interesting study in trusting another's identity. However, the acknowledgment that plays of identity do happen on the Internet makes it difficult to completely trust any source of personal information. Because mail-order bride sites look to develop real life intimate relationships in virtual reality, this can be problematic. Further complicating the problem is the structure for an individual bride's personal page which gives a synopsis version of her identity. Much like a driver license with some additional personal statements, the tendency of these mail-order bride sites is to present a vague notion of a bride's identity rather than solidifying a bride's personality through many images and lengthy personal information. While the visual information and personal statistics given are specific enough to judge one's own likes and dislikes against, for example someone might be too tall or too young, they can also lead to simplified conclusions. This curtailed information through images and personal statistics allows only a simplified judgment and conclusion based on vague and flexible details. This might not be so much of a concern after all it is similar to the way dating columns or dating agencies work however, considering that the relationship will have its primary basis online, one can continue to believe their idea of an individual purely through conclusions based upon text-based information and some photos without any palpable experience to demonstrate otherwise. On the web a persona is reduced to flexible words and images that not only carry with them a questionable truth but also are inherently a simulacrum of one's true self. Yet, before entirely discounting the presentation of one's identity through the Internet, I feel that the contemporary state of identity in the real world must be examined for a more precise understanding.

The creation of an identity on the Internet exemplifies a contemporary questioning of the self and how one begins to present the self to others. In her book, *Life on the Screen*, Sherry Turkle argues that, "Internet experiences help us to develop models . . . that are in a meaningful sense postmodern: They admit a multiplicity and flexibility. They acknowledge the constructed nature of reality, self, and other" (263). Contemporary scholars on postmodern identity have argued a range of vantage points on the postmodern self, yet most generally admit that the fast pace of our culture along with a globalized and media saturated landscape have fragmented and destabilized the notion of identity. Thus, there is no longer the one true self which modernity maintained with its essentialist ideas. Also unlike modernity, an identity crisis no longer has a distinct resolution but is a forever unresolvable riddle of what constitutes the self (Kellner 141–144). From these vantage points the Internet becomes a logical and luminous ground upon which to further continue the postmodern identity play. According to Kenneth Gergen, as the sense of an authentic self recedes into the past, what emerges in its place is the pastiche of personality. "The pastiche personality is a social chameleon, constantly borrowing bits and pieces of identity from whatever sources are available and constructing them as useful or desirable in a given situation" (150). The Internet, because it is restricted to text and images, forces users to creatively manipulate these two avenues to present a synopsis of character. On brides' personal pages they aim to show a variety of complex ideas regarding their character through only a few posed photographs. Take for example Natalia Dedyukhina, a bride who has a page on the Internet. We first encounter her close up, the largest of the pictures, in which we are invited to feel an intimacy, focusing on the features of her face and warm smile. In a smaller picture Natalia poses playfully wearing blue patent leather pants and a zebra striped blouse tied at her navel. In the third photograph Natalia is dressed in a tailored white blouse looking sophisticated and easy going. And in another, Natalia appears in an evening gown, striking a forties movie star pose to convey femininity and beauty. The result of this photo collage is the impression that Natalia is not simply one definable persona, but rather various personality types which are presented and easily understood through poses and clothing that emphasize traits that she wishes to demonstrate as her own. What is especially interesting about this is that Natalia is Russian and by using the Internet's global reach, is appealing to American men. Thus, Natalia and women like her are adopting internationally understandable images and meanings to more aptly portray a more detailed sense of self to the viewer despite the constraints of the Net.

However, despite the fact that the images and words can be manipulated to express a greater sense of character, maintained throughout the Internet medium is a suspended reality that can be difficult to overcome and especially precarious for transposing relations from virtual reality to real life. As discussed earlier, the Internet adds a strange distortion to its contents because they lack direct referents. The repercussions of this are not only a blurred distinction between reality and virtual reality but also what Jean Baudrillard contends is a powerful self fulfilling prophecy. Baudrillard argues that, "Miracles never result from a surplus of reality but, on the contrary, form a sudden break in reality and the giddiness of feeling oneself fall . . . Something emerges for want of something better" (63). In the format of the Internet what emerges is an imagined array of sensations which merely compensate for a lack of reality undermined by hyper-reality. Thus, because a multitude of concrete information cannot be derived from the images and personal descriptions giving by a prospective bride, the viewer projects their imagination of these sensations onto her, filling that void. Reconsidering Natalia the viewer can understand through her photographs that she can be fun, easygoing, or sexy but it is up to the viewer to extrapolate the varying degrees to which she is these things. For the mail-order bride, her ability to electronically seduce can be attributed to how clear yet provoking her personal presentation is. To go with a sweet face one might project a sweet voice (in clear unbroken English of course), or an even temperament, or imagine a graceful gait when constructing a fuller identity for a bride. Thus, the lack of a concrete personality, the adoption of cultural images as signifiers of identity, and the hyper-reality of the Internet format all create a masterful world for this seduction that, if orchestrated well, benefits the appeal of the mail-order bride. Furthermore, because a suitor's courtship of a bride mostly rests upon emails exchanged over time, it is conceivable that he can continue to enhance the seductive image without the context of experience to verify it.

But someday swooning lovers online want to continue their pursuit of marriage and thus must meet. Their meeting will determine whether online seduction can carry over into real life. Scholarly writers on online relationships are skeptical of the possibilities and often include several stories of cyber romance disappointment, highlighting the complaint that those involved developed inaccurate interpretations of the other. Yet, there are some redeeming relationships written about where couples are able to successfully cross that difficult divide between real life and virtual reality. Nonetheless, the desire and ability to forge online relationships raises the question of whether we can ever have accurate interpretations of Internet correspondence because of its leniency toward imagination and seduction. Romance, being one of the ultimate frontiers that plays to the imagination, has an amazing adaptability to the Internet despite the restraints of the electronic format. The suitors of mail-order brides have the possibility of conversing with these women via the Internet and constructing an intimate relationship while simultaneously floating within the vast array of possibilities generated by one's own fantasy. Ultimately these sites take on an area in which one can be forever intrinsically intertwined in fantasy through the seductive nature of Internet relationships, while also conceivably believing in the possible reality for a future fiance. As flexible as one is imaginative, the initial allure of the mail-order bride is in the disjointed space of virtual reality which she occupies far removed from tangible reality. Though avant-garde in their approach to pursuing marriage, these sites provide a perplexing question to how the Internet affects our perception of reality, construction of identity, and seduces our imagination. The result of these electronic courtship havens is a creation of fantasy and romance that is fitting for our postmodern electronic age.

Works Cited

Baudrillard, Jean. *Seduction.* New York: St. Martin's, 1990.
Gane, Mike. ed. *Baudrillard Live.* London: Routledge, 1993.
Gergen, Kenneth. *The Saturated Self.* New York: Basic Books, 1991.
Kellner, Douglas. "Popular Culture and the Construction of Postmodern Identities." *Modernity and Identity. Ed.,* Jonathan *Friedman* and Scott *Lash.* Oxford: Blackwell, 1992.
Stone, A.R. *The War of Desire and Technology at the Close of the Mechanical Age.* Cambridge: MIT Press, 1995.
Turkle, Sherry. *Life on the Screen.* New York: Simon and Schuster, 1995.

**READING** WRITING

## THIS TEXT: READING

1. All three authors recognize that technology has changed the way we communicate—where do they disagree?
2. According to the authors, what role does gender play in technology and communication? Do women benefit or suffer more than men in regarding technological change in regard to communication?
3. How does one define "reality" when participating in Internet communication? How do the different authors deal with this question?
4. In her piece, Colwell uses the mail-order bride as a window into several ideas about modern communication. What are those ideas, and how does she use the Internet mail-order bride as a window into them?
5. How do the authors use research in their work? What type of research seems to work best in these pieces?

## YOUR TEXT: WRITING

1. Examine another Internet phenomenon that could be used as a window into modern ideas.
2. Write a paper comparing three conversations: one on-line, one face-to-face, and one by phone. How do they differ? How are they the same or different?
3. Research the reactions when the telephone was introduced. Are they the same reactions we have today with cell phones or the internet?
4. Watch movies or television shows and trace how they portray communication over the phone or the Internet. Specifically, you might look at *Pillow Talk* from the early 1960s and *You've Got Mail* from the 1990s.

**READING** *Outside the Lines*

## CLASSROOM ACTIVITIES

1. Take five minutes and find something in the immediate area that is designed poorly. Explain why—and talk about what could make it better.
2. What single technological advance do you think has been the most important in your lifetime? Why? In the last fifty years? In the last 200 years? Ever? Do you notice a trend in this development?
3. What technological advances do you think have been the most harmful in your lifetime? Do these advances have advantages too? How should we balance the strengths and weaknesses of technology: Through the free market? Government intervention?
4. Do you know people who resist new technology? What are their reasons for doing so? Do you find their logic convincing? Do you know people who embrace all new technology? Can you make any determinations of how they view the world from their ideas about technology?
5. How does the media portray technology—positively or negatively? Why?
6. How do movies and television portray technological advances? How about people who are fascinated with technology? Why?
7. Would you say that the United States embraces or resists technology? Why?

## ESSAY IDEAS

### Trace Technology

Find a technological advancement, modern or otherwise, and read media accounts of its invention through the present time. According to the initial invention, has the promise of this invention been fulfilled? Why or why not? What mistakes in judgment did the inventors—and reporters—make when they first communicated about this technology? Do these mistakes represent a trend of any sort?

### Read a Piece of Technology

Sit down with a piece of technology such as a computer, household appliance, your automobile, anything. First, read the piece without thinking too much about its use. What messages does the technology give you in terms of design and function? Now think about its use. Do the messages coincide? If you were using this piece of technology for the first time, would you be disappointed with the execution of the technology compared to its promise? Is this important?

### Find a Technological Hole

Can you think of something that you would like to do that a technological advance would aid? Why do you think the technology has not been invented? What might some of the implications of this particular advance be?

### Read and Evaluate an Artistic Portrayal of Technology

Find a text such as *The Matrix* or another movie or television episode that has at its center technology as a subject. What do the writers think of technology generally? How do they show this stance in their portrayal? Do you agree with their assessment? If not, what might they not be taking into account?

# CREDITS

## Text Credits ▪■▪

## Photo Credits ■■■

Bob Bednar, "Scenic View," Glen Canyon Dam Overlook, Page, Arizona, July 1994. Photo: Bob Bednar.

Bob Bednar, A View of Mount Rushmore in Homage to Mark Klett, Mount Rushmore National Monument, South Dakota, August 1991. Photo: Bob Bednar.

Chinese Merchants Association building in Washington, D.C. Courtesy of Dr. David Chuenyan Lai, C.M.

The On Leong Chinese Merchants Association building in Chicago. Courtesy of Dr. David Chuenyan Lai, C.M.

"Jungle Fever," 1991, with Annabella Sciorra and Wesley Snipes. Directed by Spike Lee. Photo: Universal/The Kobal Collection/David Lee.

*Stupid Comics* (c) 1998 by Jim Mahfood. " true tales of amerikkkan history Part II: the true Thanksgiving . . ." Stupid comics. Jim Mahfood.

Indians fan Jim Stamper shows a Chief Wahoo sign prior to game 3 of the AL Division Series at Jacobs Field in Cleveland, Oct. 1997. The series between the Indians and the New York Yankees stands at 1-1. Photo: AP Wide World Photos.

Jets vs Washington. A fan holds up a sign. Photo: Joe Rogate/AI Photo Service/Newscom.

Fans hold up Chief Wahoo logo signs as they celebrate the Cleveland Indians' opening win over the Minnesota Twins in Cleveland, Ohio, April, 2002. Photo: AP Wide World Photos.

"Which One is the Mascot?". Thomas Little Moon.

BUT I'M HONORING YOU, DUDE! (c) 2002 Lalo Alcaraz/Universal Press Syndicate.

"Pow Wow" cartoon. Richard Crowson Illustration.

*Pirates of the Caribbean,* Bloom, Orlando, 2003. Verbinski, Gore. Credit: Walt Disney Pictures/The Kobal Collection/Marks, Elliott.

*Waiting to Exhale,* Devine, Loretta/Rochon, Lela/Bassett, Angela/Houston, Whitney, 1995. Credit: 20th Century Fox/The Kobal Collection.

*Batman and Robin* (1997). Clooney, George, Schumacher, Joel. Credit: Warner Bros/The Kobal Collection/Isenberg, Robert.

*Rio Bravo.* Wayne, John, 1959. Credit: Warner Bros/The Kobal Collection.

*The Searchers,* with John Wayne and a Native American. Photo: Photofest.

*I, Robot,* Smith, Will, 2004. Credit: 20th Century Fox/The Kobal Collection/Digital Domain.

John Wayne in *The Telegraph Trail.* Photo: Photofest.

MTV Movie Awards, 1999 Ceremony. The actor Jackie Chan with his award. Photo: Corbis/Sygma.

Leonardo da Vinci (1452–1519), "Mona Lisa", oil on canvas, 77 x 53 cm. Inv. 779. Photo: R.G. Ojeda. Louvre, Paris. Reunion des Musees Nationaux/Art Resource, NY.

Britney Spears at the Super Bowl Party hosted by Britney Spears and Justin Timberlake to benefit their individual foundations. Planet Hollywood, New York, NY. Photo: Fashion Wire Daily.

Exterior of the Parthenon and surrounding ruins, Athens, Greece. Photo: PhotoEdit.

State Capitol Building designed in Greek architectural style with unfluted Ionic columns, Richmond, VA. Photo: PhotoEdit.

Mexican flag hangs on white block wall. Photo: PhotoEdit.

American flag. Photo: (c) Joseph Nettis/Photo Researchers, Inc.

Evelyn Street Laundry. Photo: Cheryl Aaron.

Teddy bears hanging on clothesline. Photo: David Graham.

A sign advertising a model home stands in a housing development of new homes. Sinking Spring, Pennsylvania on September 2004. Photo: Bradley C. Bower/Bloomberg News/Landov.

1979 Pontiac Firebird Trans Am 6.6 litre special edition. Photo: Alvey & Towers.

Lowrider truck. Photo: Ron Kimball Photography.

Pedestrian Crossing Sign. Photo: (c) Royalty-Free/CORBIS.

Student crossing sign (like they are drunk). Photo: Courtesy of bCreative, Inc.

Deer Crossing Sign. New Britain, PA. Photo: William Thomas Cain/Getty/Newscom.

Dear Crossing Sign. Photo: Eunice Harris/Index Stock/PictureQuest.

"Arbus, Diane (1923–1971). A Young Brookyn Family Going Out for a Sunday Outing, New York City. 1966. Gelatin Silver print, 15 3/8 X 14 13/16". Lily Auchincloss Fund. (322.1972). Diane Arbus/Digital Image .(c) The Museum of Modern Art/Licensed by Scala-Art Resource, NY.

"Arbus, Diane (1923–1971). A Jewish Giant at Home with His Parents in the Bronx, New York. 1970. Gelatin silver print, 15 9/16. Photo: The Museum of Modern Art/Licensed by Scala-Art Resource, NY.

Mural of Our Lady of Guadalupe. Photo: Richard Puchalsky.

Our Lady of Guadalupe on side of a building. Photo: Kim Karpeles, *Life Through The Lens*. The Museum of Modern Art/Licensed by Scala-Art Resource, NY.

*One Tree.* Rigo 1995, Indian Water, acrylic on wood and cement 80' x 7'. Courtesy of artist and Gallery Paule Anglim, San Francisco, CA.

Exterior of Denny's Classic Diner. Copyright (c) Ronald C. Saari.

Exterior of Diner called Halfway Diner in Salem. Copyright (c) 1997 Ronald C. Saari.

*Glurpo,* World's only underwater clown, Aquarena, San Marcos, Texas postcard The Greater Beaumont Chamber of Commerce.

El Jardin Hotel postcard. The Greater Beaumont Chamber of Commerce.

Pages 114, 117, 118, 119, 120, 122, 123, 126, 127, 128, & 129 from *American Signs* by Lisa Mahar Courtesy of Lisa Mahar from her book, *American Signs*.

RuPaul Poses on New York Sidewalk. Original caption: RuPaul, © Mitchell Gerber/CORBIS. (c) Mitchell Gerber/CORBIS.

RuPaul as a man at the 2000 Soul Train Lady of Soul Awards. Photo: Getty Images Entertainment, Inc.

Sarah Michelle Gellar, *Buffy the Vampire Slayer* (US TV Series). Picture Desk, Inc./Kobal Collection.

Mark Metcalf and Sarah Michelle Gellar, *Buffy the Vampire Slayer* (US TV Series). Picture Desk, Inc./Kobal Collection.

Alyson Hannigan and Sarah Michelle Gellar, *Buffy the Vampire Slayer* (US TV Series). Picture Desk, Inc./Kobal Collection.

Milton Berle, Grand Marshall of the 1981 Macy's Thanksgiving Day Parade, dressed as Cinderella. Photo: Corbis/Bettmann.

Marnie Spencer, *Between the Devil and the Deep Blue Sea,* 2003, acrylic, ink, pencil on canvas, 60 x 60 inches. Collection of Howard and Judy Tullman. Image courtesy of Julie Baker Fine Art, Grass Valley, CA. Collection of Howard and Judy Tullman. Image courtesy of Julie Baker Fine Art, Grass Valley, CA.

Cassius Marcellus Coolidge (*Dogs at Table Playing Cards*). Photo: Getty Images, Inc.

*Two Dogs Dressed Up at a Table Called Jack Sprat,* 1996. Photo: William Wegman.

Magritte, Rene (1898–1967) (c) ARS, NY. *The Key of Dreams.* 1930. Oil on canvas, 81 x 60 cm. Location: Private Collection. (c) 2005 C. Herscovici, Brussels/Artists Rights Society (ARS), New York/Art Resource, NY.

*Women Regents of the Harlem Almshouse,* 1664, Frans Hals, 1580/5-1666, Dutch. Museum Franz Hals, Haarlem, Holland/SuperStock.

Still from "Man With A Movie Camera" by Dziga Vertov 1928.

*Modern 1939 Venus* by Reginald Marsh. © Geoffrey Clements/CORBIS Photographer: Geoffrey Clements. Creator Name: Reginald Marsh. Date Created: 1939. (c) Geoffrey Clements/CORBIS.

Pablo Picasso, Spanish, 1881–1973. *Still Life with Chair Caning,* 1911–12. Collage of oil and pasted oilcloth, simulating chair caning, on canvas, oval 10 5/8 x 13 3/4". Musee Picasso, Paris; Reunion des Musees Nationaux. (c) 1998 Estate of Pablo Picasso.

Upper and lower Basilice di San Francesco (Basilicas of Saint Francis), 13th century, Assisi, Umbria, Italy. Credit: The Art Archive/Dagli Orti. Picture Desk, Inc./Kobal Collection.

Interior, Lower Basilica di San Francesco (Saint Francis), 13th century, Assisi, Umbria, Italy Dagli Orti/The Art Archive/Kobal Collection.

*Mona Lisa,* by Dennis Wiemer of Ladysmith, Wisconsin, was painted on a barn after the University of Wisconsin won the Rose Bowl in 1994. © Layne Kennedy/CORBIS. Mona Lisa by Dennis Wiemar (c) Layne Kennedy/CORBIS.

*The Virgin of the Rocks.* © National Gallery Collection. Creator Name: Leonardo da Vinci. By kind permission of the Trustees of the National Gallery, London/CORBIS Leonardo da Vinci, ca. 1485.

*The Virgin of the Rocks,* Oil on arched wood. Leonardo da Vinci (1452–1519). Photo: Gerard Blot. Louvre, Paris, France. Reunion des Musees Nationaux/Art Resource, NY.

Leonardo da Vinci (1452–1519). *Madonna and Child with Saint Anne and Infant St. John the Baptist.* Madona and Child with Saint Anne and Infant St. John the Baptist (cartoon). National Gallery, London, Great Britain/Art Resource, NY.

Botticelli, Sandro (1444–1510) *Venus and Mars.* Location: National Gallery, London, Great Britain (c) Art Resource, NY.

"Brueghel, *Pieter the Elder* (c. 1525–1569), Jesus Carrying the Cross, or The Way to Calvary, 1564. Location: Kunsthistorisches Museum, Vienna, Austria Art Resource, N.Y.

van Gogh, Vincent, *Wheatfield with Crows,* 1890. Van Gogh Museum, Amsterdam, The Netherlands. Art Resource, NY.

KOSS ad of Mona Lisa Ever Wonder Why She's Smiling? The Advertising Archives.

Kellogg's ad, If Venus had Arms. The Advertising Archives.

An employees peeks over the wall into her artist-boyfriend's cubicle at There, a company that is designing an "alternate reality" for the web. He uses the various postcards as visual inspiration in his work. Bob Sacha/IPN/Aurora.

Vermeer, Jan (Johannes) (1632–1675). *The Milkmaid,* 1658–1660. Location: Rijksmuseum, Amsterdam, The Netherlands. Photo credit: Erich Lessing/Art Resource, NY. Image Reference: ART174753. Art Resource, N.Y.

Photo of Walter Benjamin. Photo by Gisele Freund, Courtesy of Suhrkamp Verlag.

Andy Warhol, *Marilyn Monroe,* 1962. Oil on canvas. 81" x 66-3/4".™ 2002 Marilyn Monroe LLC by CMG Worldwide Inc. www.MarilynMonroe.com. (C)2003 Andy Warhol Foundation for the Visual Arts/ARS, New York.

Andy Warhol (1928–1987), *One Hundred Cans,* 1962, synthetic polymer paint on canvas, 72 x 52 in. (c) 2003. The Andy Warhol Foundation for the Visual Arts/ARS, New York. Albright Knox Art Gallery, Buffalo, New York. The Andy Warhol Foundation, Inc.

AIDS quilt—overhead shot. Photo: Photo Researchers, Inc.

Washington, DC: The AIDS memorial quilt is spread out near the White House, forming an ellipse. Agence France Presse/Corbis.

Volunteers and others walk on the 21,000 panel. Names Project AIDS Memorial Quilt in Washington. Organizers anticipated more than 300,000 people would view the quilt during the weekend. Photo: AP Wide World Photos.

Cartoon from Understanding Comics by Scott McCloud. From Understanding Comics by Scott McCloud. Copyright (c) 1993, 1994 by Scott McCloud. Reprinted by permission of HarperCollins Publishers Inc.

*Piss Christ.* Photo courtesy Paula Cooper Gallery, New York.

Art exhibit display called "What is the proper way to display the US flag?". Photo: Scott Tyler (AKA Dread Scott).

Welcome to America's finest tourist plantation. Courtesy of Louis Hock, David Avalos and Elizabeth Sisco.

Klanswoman ( Grand Klaliff II) 1990. Courtesy Paula Cooper Gallery, New York.

Kissing Doesn't Kill. Gran Fury Records, Manuscripts and Archives Division, The New York Public Library, Astor, Lenox and Tilden Foundations.

Kurt Cobain & Arnold Swarzenegger, Citybank Poster. Credit: Andy Cox.

Chris Ofili's, *The Holy Virgin Mary,* a controversial painting of the Virgin Mary embellished with a clump of elephant dung and two dozen cutouts of buttocks from pornographic magazine, is shown at the Brooklyn Museum of Art Monday, Sep. 27, 1999, in New AP Wide World Photos.

*Our Lady* (c) 1999 Alma Lopez.

*Yo Mama's Last Supper,* 1996. Courtesy Robert Miller Gallery.

Boondocks cartoon AHEM_ IN THIS TIME OF WAR AGAINST OSAMA BIN LADEN AND THE OP-PRESSIVE TALIBAN REGIME. Boondocks (c) 2001 Aaron McGruccr/Universal Press Syndicate.

The Daily Show (US TV Series) with Jon Stewart Comedy Central/Mad Cow Productions/The Kobal Collection.

Alfred Eisenstaedt, V-J Day: Sailor Kissing Girl (1945). Alfred Eisenstaedt, V-J Day: Sailor Kissing Girl (1945). Life Magazine. (c) 1945 TimePix.

Johnny Cash (1969) flipping off the photographer. Photo: Jim Marshall.

iPod in Antarctica & iPod in France with the Eiffel Tower in background. Photo courtesy of iPodlounge.com.